Children's Thinking

Cognitive Development and
Individual Differences

FOURTH EDITION

David F. Bjorklund

Florida Atlantic University

THOMSON

WADSWORTH

Australia • Canada • Mexico • Singapore • Spain
United Kingdom • United States

THOMSON

WADSWORTH

Psychology Editor: Michele Sordi
Technology Project Manager: Michelle Vardeman
Assistant Editor: Jennifer Keever
Editorial Assistant: Chelsea Junget
Marketing Manager: Chris Caldeira
Marketing Assistant: Laurel Anderson
Advertising Project Manager: Tami Strang
Project Manager, Editorial Production: Cheri Palmer
Print/Media Buyer: Doreen Suruki

Permissions Editor: Joohee Lee
Production Service: Robin Gold/Forbes Mill Press
Text Designer: Lisa Devenish
Copy Editor: Robin Gold
Cover Designer: Denise Davidson
Cover Image: © Photo Alto Photography/Veer.com
Cover Printer: The Lehigh Press, Inc.
Compositor: Linda Weidemann, Wolf Creek Press
Printer: Maple-Vail Book Manufacturing Group/Binghamton

For more information about our products,
contact us at:
Thomson Learning Academic Resource Center
1-800-423-0563

For permission to use material from this text,
contact us by:
Phone: 1-800-730-2214
Fax: 1-800-730-2215
Web: http://www.thomsonrights.com

Library of Congress Control Number: 2003110790

ISBN 0-534-62245-3

Wadsworth/Thomson Learning
10 Davis Drive
Belmont, CA 94002-3098
USA

Asia
Thomson Learning
5 Shenton Way #01-01
UIC Building
Singapore 068808

Australia/New Zealand
Thomson Learning
102 Dodds Street
Southbank, Victoria 3006
Australia

Canada
Nelson
1120 Birchmount Road
Toronto, Ontario M1K 5G4
Canada

Europe/Middle East/Africa
Thomson Learning
High Holborn House
50/51 Bedford Row
London WC1R 4LR
United Kingdom

Latin America
Thomson Learning
Seneca, 53
Colonia Polanco
11560 Mexico D.F.
Mexico

Spain/Portugal
Paraninfo
Calle/Magallanes, 25
28015 Madrid, Spain

When talking to a friend and the question "So, what's new with you" is asked, the response "I've been working on the fourth edition of my textbook," can be a real conversation stopper. You imagine your friend thinking, "Poor man. He needs to get a life." Yet, for the author, the labor on what, to almost anyone else, would seem to be the operational definition of tedium, is actually quite exciting. Once I started the revision, I found myself waking up at 5 A.M., eager to make changes on a chapter I'd been mulling over the day before. I'd get excited about a new way of looking at something that had been in front of me for years, but it wasn't until I started writing about it that I saw its importance. How could I make theory and data that I'm still grappling with comprehensible to my readers? I'd write and re-write paragraphs in my head while falling asleep, and these same ideas would wake me up in the morning. Yes, working on the fourth edition of a textbook can be an exciting thing for the author, and I hope that I have conveyed some of this excitement to the reader.

Cognitive development continues to be a dynamic field. Theories and research findings from a variety of areas combine to produce a picture of a developing child who is born prepared to make some sense of the world, but whose mind is also shaped by forces in the physical and social environment. This theme, of the continuous transaction between an embodied child embedded in a social world, continues to serve as the focus of the fourth edition. This book is still unique in that it deals with both the typical pattern of change in thinking observed over time (cognitive development), and individual differences in children's thinking in infancy and childhood. But much is new and exciting in the field of cognitive development, and much of it is presented in the pages that follow.

The fourth edition consists of 16 chapters plus an epilogue, two more chapters than was in the third edition. But the book actually contains fewer words (830 fewer by my count) than the previous edition, with chapters being shorter and more focused on a single topic. (For those who protest that they had trouble getting through 14 chapters and they can't possibly complete 16 chapters in a single semester, I urge them to apply their conservation-of-number scheme to pages in the text.) All 14 chapters that were in the third edition are in the fourth. These include a chapter introducing key concepts in the field (1), chapters presenting both the biological and sociocultural basis of cognitive development (Chapters 2 and 3), chapters providing an overview of Piaget's theory (4) and information-processing approaches (5), and chapters dealing with specific topics in cognitive development, including infant perception (7), representation (9), memory (10), language (11), problem solving (12), and social cognition (13). The last three chapters deal primarily with issues of individual differences in children's thinking, specifically schooling and cognition (14), approaches to the study of intelligence (15), and the origins, modification, and stability of intellectual differences (16). The two new chapters deal with children's strategies (Chapter 6, titled "Learning to Think on Their Own") and spatial cognition (8). Children's use of strategies has always been central to cognitive development (at least to me), and issues related to strategy development were found in many chapters of the previous edition. Given the central importance of this topic, I decided it deserved a chapter of its own, and much information that was previously found in the chapters on information processing and memory are now in the "strategies" chapter. Strategies are still discussed in many of the other chapters in this book, but I think that a chapter devoted to issues of strategy development—how children gain control over their own, purposeful problem-solving behavior—makes the story of cognitive development easier to tell and understand.

The second new chapter on spatial cognition takes information that was previously reported mainly in the chapters on perception and representation. Spatial cognition had never been a major interest of mine, in part, I'm sure, because I often have as much difficulty as the average 6-year-old in rotating a figure or locating an object embedded on a page crowded with distracting images. ("Where *is* Waldo, anyway?") But as I looked more closely, both at older and recent work on the topic, I saw it as central to children's developing intellects. Understanding how objects in the physical world relate to one another is about as basic an ability as a child must develop, equally as important as learning to talk or to remember sequences of events. It deserved a chapter of its own, and now has one in this edition.

Several themes, present in the third edition, have greater emphasis in the fourth edition, reflecting, I believe, how the science of cognitive development has changed during the last five years. First, there is a greater recognition of the dynamic nature of development. Dynamic system approaches are discussed in some detail in the introductory chapter, explaining concepts such as *self-organization, emergence,* and *dynamic systems* itself. My intention is that this more explicit treatment of dynamic systems up front will help the reader better understand

discussions based on these concepts that follow in later chapters.

This edition also extends a trend begun in the third edition of including more research from cognitive developmental neuroscience. There has been a "biologizing" of cognitive development occurring during the last decade, and this is most reflected in research looking at how the brains of infants and children respond to certain situations and how they change over time. Don't get me wrong. Our job is to develop an understanding of how children's *minds* change over time, and how such changes effect how children function in their world. But I firmly believe that mind is a state of brain, and, although knowing what's happening in the brain will not, by itself, tell us what we, as psychologists, need to know, it is an essential ingredient in understanding cognitive development.

Related to this biologizing of development is an increased interest in evolutionary psychology—how selective pressures in our ancient past may influence how children develop today. I have been a proponent of the emerging field of *evolutionary developmental psychology* and believe that such a perspective has much to offer the field of cognitive development. This perspective is outlined in Chapter 2 on the "Biological Bases of Cognitive Development," and found, where appropriate, in various chapters throughout the book.

The organization of most of the "old" chapters is similar to that of the third edition. There are some new topics, of course, such as a discussion of inhibition and ADHD in Chapter 5, the development of tool use in Chapter 12, forms of social learning in children and apes in Chapter 13, and intuitive mathematics in Chapter 14, among others. To make room for these new topics, others had to be omitted. Some were dropped because recent research had questioned the validity of some of the claims (such as the relation between music instruction and quantitative ability in children, or identifying genes for IQ), others because the focus of the field has changed (for example, children's humor), and others simply for want of space (the development of brain lateralization, for instance). It is impossible to include all the important and relevant information in a single textbook, and I hope my choice of what to keep, what to add, and what to cut has resulted in a book that represents the field fairly and presents an interesting and integrated picture of a discipline that I believe is of great theoretical and practical importance.

This edition continues a trend I began in the third of keeping the number of citations to a minimum, to make the book more readable to an undergraduate audience. One result of this is that I fail to acknowledge many authors who made important contributions to the field, and I apologize for this. But on the plus side, I believe that this makes the text more readable and prevents the reference section from getting too large. Of the approximately 1600 references, about a quarter of them are new, most of them presenting research and theory published in the new millennium.

I have done my best to make this book readable. I have attempted to present complicated theory and data in an intellectually honest way and to be comprehensible (and, I hope, exciting) to advanced undergraduate and graduate students. I have provided examples of actual children whenever possible, although I have avoided making the book a list of cute stories devoid of theoretical concepts. Continuing with the trend of the third edition, I have also made liberal use of figures and tables (165 in total, 20% new to this edition) to support the text and to foster comprehension. I have sprinkled through the book several cartoons, which I find often make a point better than a couple of pages of text, and I have included about as many photographs, mainly to illustrate some procedure or apparatus.

I have kept several pedagogical features from the second and third editions. These include the "Key Terms and Concepts" and "Suggested Readings" sections at the end of each chapter, and a glossary that includes all the key terms at the end of the book. I provide a brief paragraph about each suggested reading to explain why each particular paper or book is worth perusing.

I've enjoyed writing this fourth edition and have learned a lot in the process. I hope that this book conveys the excitement I felt in discovering some of these new findings in the field of cognitive develop-

ment. The book is not just about "what's new," however, but about the field as a whole, including classic studies from earlier decades. Although I have focused on the "new," I have attempted not to forget the "tried and true" research that still informs us about the nature of children's thinking today. And I have tried to make connections among different levels of analysis—macroprocesses and microprocesses, biology and environment, developmental function and individual differences—to provide a synthesis of the field of cognitive development. I have had great fun while doing this.

Acknowledgments

Anyone who writes a book such as this does so with much help from many people. My greatest gratitude goes to my wife Barbara who provided constructive criticism on many chapters, while working on a textbook of her own—all in addition to being a supportive and understanding spouse. I would like to thank my editor, Edith Beard Brady, my copy editor Robin Gold, and the Wadsworth staff for their support and advice through the entire process. Portions of this book were written while I was a guest at the University of Würzburg, Germany, as a recipient of an Alexander von Humboldt Research Award, and I would like to thank the Alexander von Humboldt Society and my friend, colleague, and host Professor Wolfgang Schneider for their support. I also want to thank my students and colleagues for their comments on early versions of chapters, including Carlos Hernández Blasi, Charles Brainerd, Chris Cormier, Thomas Coyle, Marc Lindberg, Justin Rosenberg, and Viviana Weekes-Shackelford. Finally, I would like to thank the conscientious professional reviewers for their consistently constructive comments:

Rhonda Douglas Brown, University of Cincinnati
Eric S. Buhs, University of Nebraska–Lincoln
Anne O. Eisbach, Quinnipiac University
Elizabeth M. Elliott, Florida Gulf Coast University
Jennifer B. Esterly, California State University, Stanislaus

Jane F. Gaultney, University of North Carolina at Charlotte

Troianne T. Grayson, California State University, Stanislaus

August John Hoffman, Compton Community College

Martha J. Hubertz, Florida Atlantic University

Elaine M. Justice, Old Dominion University

Katherine Kipp, University of Georgia

Elizabeth Pemberton, University of Delaware

Darrel Dean Richards, California State University, Northridge

Theresa A. Thorkildsen, University of Illinois at Chicago

Michelle D. Weissman, California State University, Sacramento

David F. Bjorklund
Jupiter, Florida

Teaching and Learning Supplements

An expanded array of supplements accompanies this latest edition of *Children's Thinking*. These supplements are designed to make teaching and learning more effective. Most are available free to professors or students. For more information on any of the listed resources, please call the Thomson Learning™ Academic Resource Center at 800-423-0563.

Student Support Materials

The *Children's Thinking* Companion Web Site This new book-specific Web site is a great one-stop resource. The site contains chapter outlines, electronic flashcards, Web links, simulations, demonstrations, video clips, interactive self-assessments, InfoTrac College Edition keywords, and more. To preview the site, go to http://psychology.wadsworth .com/bjorklund_4e.

InfoTrac® College Edition InfoTrac College Edition is a powerful online learning resource, consisting of thousands of full-text articles from hundreds of journals and periodicals. Students using *Children's Thinking* receive four months of free access to the InfoTrac College Edition database. By doing a simple keyword search, students can quickly generate a list of relevant articles from thousands of possibilities. Then they can select full-text articles to read, explore, and print for reference or further study. InfoTrac College Edition's continuously updated collection of articles can be useful for doing reading and writing assignments that reach beyond the pages of this text.

Essential Teaching Resources

Instructor's Manual with Test Bank The *Instructor's Manual with Test Bank* (0-534-62248-8) has been expanded from being just a Test Bank in the previous edition to a full instructor's resource. Revised by Jane Gaultney of the University of North Carolina, Charlotte, this manual contains chapter outlines, key terms, suggested readings, Web links, InfoTrac College Edition keywords, and a variety of additional activities and exercises for use both in the classroom and as homework assignments. For your testing needs, this package includes a variety of multiple-choice and essay questions, with 10 multiple-choice questions per chapter also designed for use in the online quizzes.

***ExamView*™ Computerized Testing** This software helps you create, deliver, and customize tests and study guides both in print and online. In just minutes, this easy-to-use system can generate the assessment and tutorial materials your students need. Using a database prepared by Katherine Kipp, University of Georgia, you can build tests of as many as 250 questions using 12 question types. *ExamView*'s complete word processing capabilities also allow you to enter an unlimited number of new questions or edit existing questions (ISBN: 0-534-62247-X).

1

An Introduction to Cognitive Development

Intelligence is our species' most important tool for survival. Evolution has provided other species with greater speed, coats of fur, camouflage, or antlers to help them adapt to changing environments. Human evolution is different. It has provided us with powers of discovery and invention by which we change the environment or develop techniques for coping with environments we cannot change. Although we are not the only thinkers in the animal kingdom, no other species has our powers of intellect. How we think and the technological and cultural innovations afforded by our intellect separate us from all other species.

This remarkable intelligence does not arise fully formed in the infant, however. Because human intelligence is flexible, we require substantial experience to master the cognitive feats that typify adult thinking, and we spend the better part of two decades developing an adult nervous system. Little in the way of complex thought patterns is built into the human brain, ready to go at birth, although biology obviously predisposes us to develop the ability for complex thought. Our mental prowess develops gradually over childhood, changing in quality as it does.

In this first chapter, I introduce the topic of cognitive development—how thinking changes over time. In addition to describing developmental and individual differences in cognition, scientists who study children's thinking are also concerned with the mechanisms that underlie cognition and its development. How do biological (genetic) factors interact with experiences in the physical and social world to yield a particular pattern of development? Do children develop all their intellectual skills uniformly, or do some skills develop at faster rates than others? Is development relatively continuous and gradual over childhood, or are there major disruptions in its course? These and other issues are introduced in this chapter. Before delving too deeply into these issues, however, I need to define some basic terms. (See Table 1-1.) These definitions are followed by a look at some issues that have dominated the field of cognitive development during the last century and other issues that concern the contemporary scientist.

Basic Concepts in Cognitive Development

Cognition

Cognition refers to the processes or faculties by which knowledge is acquired and manipulated. Cognition is usually thought of as being mental. That is, cognition is a reflection of a mind. It is not directly observable. We cannot see the process whereby an 8-month-old discovers that the Mickey Mouse doll hidden under the blanket continues to exist even though it is out of his sight; nor can we directly assess the steps a 7-year-old child takes to compute the answer to the problem $15 - 9 = ?$. Although we cannot see or directly measure what underlies children's performance on these and other tasks, we can infer what is going on in their heads by assessing certain aspects of their behavior. That is, cognition is never measured directly but is inferred from the behaviors we can observe.

What psychologists can observe and quantify are things such as the number of words children remember from a list of 20, the number of seconds it takes to identify well-known pictures or words, or the amount of time 6-month-olds spend looking at a picture of a familiar face relative to that of an unfamiliar one. For the most part, cognitive developmentalists are really not interested in these overt, countable behaviors; what they *are* interested in, however, are the processes or skills that underlie them. What mental operations does a 6-year-old engage in that are different from those performed by a 4-year-old or an 8-year-old? How does speed in identifying words reflect how information is stored in the minds of children of different ages? What kind of mental picture has the infant formed of the familiar face of his mother that allows him to tell her face apart from all other faces? How are such mental pictures created? How are they modified?

This is not to say that cognitive psychologists are unconcerned with socially important phenomena such as reading, adding numbers, or communicating effectively. Many are, and they have developed re-

TABLE 1-1 Some basic concepts in cognitive development

Cognition: The processes or faculties by which knowledge is acquired and manipulated. Cognition is usually thought of as being mental. That is, cognition is a reflection of a mind. It is not directly observable but must be inferred.

Development: Changes in structure or function over time. **Structure** refers to some substrate of the organism, such as nervous tissue, muscle, or limbs, or—in cognitive psychology—the mental knowledge that underlies intelligence. **Function** denotes actions related to a structure and can include actions external to the structure being studied, such as neurochemical or hormonal secretions, and other exogenous factors that can best be described as "experience"—that is, external sources of stimulation. Development is characteristic of the species and has its basis in biology. Its general course, therefore, is relatively predictable. Development progresses as a result of a **bidirectional,** or reciprocal, relationship between structure and function and can be expressed as structure ↔ function.

Developmental function: The species-typical form that cognition takes over time.

Individual differences: Differences in patterns of intellectual aptitudes among people of a given age.

search programs aimed at fostering in children these and other intellectual skills critical for success in a technological society. But, for the most part, the behaviors themselves are seen as secondary. What is important and what needs to be understood are the mechanisms that underlie performance. By discovering the mental factors that mediate intelligent behavior, we can better understand that behavior and its development, which in turn can help us better understand children.

Cognition includes not only our conscious and deliberate attempts at solving problems but also the unconscious and nondeliberate processes that are involved in routine daily tasks. We are not aware of the mental activity that occurs when we recognize a familiar tune on the radio or even when we read the

morning paper. Yet, much in the way of cognitive processing is happening. For most of us, reading has become nearly automatic. We can't drive by a billboard without reading it. It is something we just do without giving it any "thought." But the mechanisms involved in reading are complex, even in the well-practiced adult.

Cognition involves mental activity of all types, including activity that is geared toward acquiring, understanding, and modifying information. Cognition includes such activities as developing a plan for solving a problem, executing that plan, and evaluating the success of the plan, making modifications as needed. These can be thought of as higher-order processes, or *macromechanisms* of cognition, which are often available to consciousness (that is, we are aware that we're doing them). Cognition also involves the initial encoding of a stimulus (that is, deciding how to define a physical stimulus so it can be thought about) and classifying what kind of thing it is ("Is this a letter, a word, a picture of something familiar?"). These can be thought of as basic processes, or *micromechanisms* of cognition, that occur outside of consciousness (we experience the product but are unaware of the process).

Cognition, then, reflects knowledge and what one does with it, and the main point of this book is that cognition develops.

Development

Change over Time

Development refers to changes in structure or function over time. **Structure** refers to some substrate of the organism, such as nervous tissue, muscle, or limbs, or—in cognitive psychology—the mental knowledge that underlies intelligence. When speaking of cognitive development, we use *structure* to mean some hypothetical mental construct, faculty, or ability that changes with age. For example, children's knowledge of terms such as *dog, lion,* and *zebra* could be construed as existing in some sort of mental structure, with the meanings of these words changing over time. Or we could hypothesize some form of mental organization that permits children to place objects in serial arrays according to height.

In contrast to structure, **function** denotes actions related to a structure. These include actions external to the structure being studied, such as neurochemical or hormonal secretions, and other exogenous factors (that is, factors external to the individual) that can best be described as "experience"—that is, external sources of stimulation. Function can also be endogenous, or internal, to the structure itself—for example, the exercise of a muscle, the firing of a nerve cell, or the activation of a cognitive process, such as retrieving from memory the name of your first-grade teacher or computing the answer to the problem 26 + 17 = ?. With respect to cognitive development, function refers to some action by the child, such as retrieving the definition of a word from memory, making comparisons between two stimuli, or adding two numbers to arrive at a third.

Development is characteristic of the species and has its basis in biology. Its general course, therefore, is relatively predictable. By viewing development as a biological concept that is generally predictable across all members of the species, I do not mean to imply that experience and culture do not also play a role in development. During the last several decades, developmental psychologists have become increasingly aware that a child's development cannot be described or understood outside of the context in which it occurs. Several "ecological" approaches to cognitive development have emerged recently (Ceci, 1996; Rogoff, 1990; see Chapter 3), stemming, in part, from the rediscovery of the work of the Soviet psychologist Lev Vygotsky (1978). Writing in the 1920s and 1930s, Vygotsky proposed a sociocultural view, emphasizing that development was guided by adults interacting with children, with the cultural context determining largely how, where, and when these interactions would take place. There are many cultural universals, with children around the world being reared in socially structured, language-using groups, and thus some aspects of development are also universal. But many aspects of culture vary considerably among people, such as the available technology and how and when children are expected to learn the survival skills of their society (for example, formal schooling versus no formal schooling). Such differences can have considerable influence on how cognition develops.

Although not all cognitive developmental psychologists adhere to such a sociocultural perspective, nearly all recognize the importance of a child's culture in shaping his or her development. This does not contradict a belief that there are strong biological constraints on development. What it does is recognize that members of *Homo sapiens* are social animals and that it doesn't make sense to talk of human nature (or human development) independent of human culture.

Structure, Function, and Development

Development is usually conceived as a bidirectional relationship between structure and function, in which the activity of the structure itself and stimulation from the environment can contribute to changes in the structure, which in turn contribute to changes in how that structure operates. Function does more than just maintain a structure (that is, prevent atrophy); function is necessary for proper development to occur. Function is limited, of course, to the actions that structures are capable of performing. This bidirectional, or reciprocal, relationship between structure and function can be expressed as structure ↔ function.

The **bidirectionality of structure and function** can best be illustrated with work in embryology. Chick embryos, for example, display spontaneous movement before muscle and skeletal development is complete. Such movement obviously stems from the maturation of the underlying structures, in this case bones, muscle, and nervous tissue. When embryonic chicks are given a drug to temporarily paralyze them for as little as one to two days, deformations of the joints of the legs, toes, and neck develop, which in turn affect the subsequent movement of the limbs (Drachman & Coulombre, 1962). In other words, the spontaneous activity (function) of the skeletal structures is necessary for the proper development and functioning of the joints.

Let me provide an example of the bidirectional relationship between structure and function at the behavioral level. Individual differences in activity level are found in newborns and are believed to be biologically based (Phillips, King, & DuBois, 1978). A highly active toddler will make it difficult for her parents to confine her to a playpen, resulting in a child who has a greater number of experiences outside of her playpen than a less active child has. These experiences will presumably affect the child's developing intellect (structure), which in turn will affect that child's actions (function). Thus, inherent characteristics of the child (biological structures) influence her behavior, the experiences she has, and the reactions of others to her—all of which influence the development of the child's underlying cognitive/behavioral structures, and so on.

The *functioning* of mental structures promotes changes in the structures themselves. This view is most clearly reflected in the work of the Swiss psychologist Jean Piaget. He believed that the activity of the child (or of the child's cognitive structures) is a necessary condition for development to occur. That is, for structures to change, they must be active. It is the structures' making contact with the external world that is responsible, to a large extent, for their development. Such a viewpoint makes children important contributors to their own development. Intellectual growth is the result of an active interaction between thinking children and their world, rather than simply the environment shaping children's intellect or genes dictating a particular level of cognitive ability. (More will be said of Piaget's theory in Chapter 4.)

I think it is fair to say that all developmental psychologists agree there is a reciprocal, bidirectional influence between "structures" (be they physical, such as neurons, or hypothetical, such as cognitive structures) and the activity of those structures (that is, the child's behavior). There is still much room for debate concerning *how* various subsystems of the child (neuronal, behavioral, social) interact to produce development, but developmental psychologists agree that development must be viewed as a two-way street. Development is *not* simply the result of the unfolding of genetic sequences unperturbed by vari-

ations in environment (structure → function), nor the product of "experience" on an infinitely pliable child (function → structure). The concept of the bidirectionality of structure and function is central to developmental psychology and will be a theme throughout this book. A more in-depth discussion of bidirectional models of development, along with more examples, is provided in Chapter 2 in a discussion of the developmental systems approach.

Developmental Function and Individual Differences

I will examine two aspects of cognitive development in this book: **developmental function** and **individual differences.** In the present context, developmental function refers to the form that cognition takes over time—to age-related differences in thinking. What are the mental abilities of infants? What is a 2-year-old's understanding of numbers, words, and family relations? What about that of a 4- or 6-year-old? How do school-age children and adolescents conceptualize cause and effect? How do they evaluate the relative worth of two products in the grocery store? People concerned with developmental function are usually interested in universals—what is true about the course and causes of development for all members of the species. I should actually rephrase this to "what is *generally* true about the course of development for all members of the species," for clearly there is substantial variation. Assessments of developmental function, then, are typically based on averages, with individual variations among children being seen as unimportant.

But we all know that at some level this variation *is* important. Our impressive intellectual skills are not uniform among members of the species. Some people at every age make decisions more quickly, perceive relations among events more keenly, or think more deeply than others. How can these differences best be described and conceptualized? What is the nature of these differences? Once differences have been established, to what extent can they be modified? Will differences observed in infancy and early childhood remain stable, or are some intellectual differences limited to a particular time during development?

There is also substantial variability in cognitive functioning *within* any given child. A particular 4-year-old will often show a wide range of behaviors on very similar tasks, depending on the context that he or she is in. Increasingly, developmental psychologists have come to realize the significance of individual differences and variability in cognitive performance among and within people of a given age and to see these variations as providing interesting and important information about developmental outcomes.

Although the people who study individual differences in thinking have traditionally not been the same people who study developmental function (Cronbach, 1957), the picture is changing, and I will attempt, where possible, to integrate the two concepts. Individual differences, like thought itself, have developmental histories, making the relationship between developmental function and individual differences a dynamic one. That is, individual differences do not simply constitute genetic or "innate" characteristics of a child, but emerge as children develop, often showing different manifestations at different times in development. Several chapters in this book are devoted exclusively to examining individual differences. In other chapters, individual differences in intellectual abilities are discussed in conjunction with the developmental function of those same abilities. The concept of within-child variability appears throughout the book.

The Adaptive Nature of Cognitive Immaturity

We usually think of development as something progressive—going from simple to more complex structures or behaviors, with children getting "better" or more "complete" over time. This is a wholly reasonable point of view, but such a perspective can cause us to interpret early or immature forms of cognition as merely less effective and incomplete versions of the adult model. Although this might be generally true, it is not always the case. Early or immature forms of development can serve some function of their own, adapting the infant or young child to his or her particular environment (Oppenheim, 1981).

For example, young infants' relatively poor perceptual abilities might protect their nervous systems from sensory overload (Turkewitz & Kenny, 1982), preschool children's tendencies to overestimate their physical and cognitive skills might bolster their self-esteem (Bjorklund, Gaultney, & Green, 1993), and infants' slow information processing might prevent them from establishing intellectual habits early in life that will be detrimental later on when their life conditions are considerably different (Bjorklund & Green, 1992). The point I want to make here is that infants' and young children's cognitive and perceptual abilities might be well suited for their particular time in life rather than being just incomplete versions of the more sophisticated abilities they will one day possess (Bjorklund, 1997a). What we consider to be immature and ineffective styles of thought might sometimes have an adaptive value for the young child at that particular point in development and should not be viewed solely as "deficiencies."

Children's immature cognition can be seen as having an integrity and possibly a function of its own, rather than being seen only as something that must be overcome. Such a perspective can have important consequences not only for how we view development but also for education and remediation. Expecting children who are developmentally delayed or who have learning deficits to master "age-appropriate" skills might be counterproductive, even if possible. Young and delayed children's immature cognition might suit them for mastering certain skills; although attempting to "educate" them beyond their present cognitive abilities could result in advanced surface behavior, the general effectiveness of that behavior might be minimally or even detrimentally influenced, despite the considerable effort expended (Bjorklund & Schwartz, 1996; Goodman, 1992).

Some Issues in Cognitive Development

Most issues central to cognitive development are central to developmental psychology in general. For example, the nature/nurture issue, stages of development, the dynamic nature of development, and the stability of behavior over time are as significant to social and personality development as they are to cognitive development. Yet, each area of psychology has its own way of expressing these concerns and of defining the questions that stimulate research and theory. The following section introduces some of the issues key to cognitive development research.

Nature and Nurture

Perhaps the central issue of all developmental psychology is the nature/nurture issue. How do we explain how biological factors, in particular genetics, interact with environmental factors, especially learning and the broader effects of culture, to produce human beings? At the extreme are two philosophical camps: Proponents of **nativism** hold, essentially, that human intellectual abilities are innate. The opposing philosophical position is **empiricism,** which holds that nature provides only species-general learning mechanisms, with cognition arising as a result of experience. As stated, each of these two extreme positions is clearly wrong. In fact, as far as developmental psychologists are concerned, there is no nature/nurture dichotomy. Biological factors are inseparable from experiential factors, with the two continuously interacting. This makes it impossible to identify any purely biological or experiential effects. But it is often convenient to speak of "biological" and "experiential" factors, and when psychologists do, there is always the implicit assumption of the bidirectional interaction of these factors, as discussed earlier in this chapter (that is, structure ↔ function).

At one level, it is trivial to state that biology and experience interact. There is really no other alternative. It's *how* they interact to yield a particular pattern of development that is significant. For example, one currently popular view holds that children's genetic constitutions influence how they experience the environment. A sickly and lethargic child seeks less stimulation and gets less cognitively facilitating attention from adults than does a more active,

healthy child, resulting in slower or less advanced levels of cognitive development for the sickly child. A child who processes language easily might be more apt to take advantage of the reading material that surrounds him than will a child whose genetically based talents lie in other areas, such as the ability to comprehend spatial relations. Environment is thus seen as very important from this perspective, but one's biology influences which environments are most likely to be experienced and, possibly, how those experiences will be interpreted. These issues will be discussed in greater detail in the chapters devoted to individual differences, particularly in Chapter 16, where the heritability of intelligence and the role of experience in individual differences in intelligence will be explored.

What Does It Mean to Say Something Is "Innate"?

The term "innate" can be contentious, and many psychologists would prefer not to see it used at all. What exactly does it mean for something to be "innate"? If we simply mean "based in genetics," then surely just about every human behavior can be deemed innate at some level and the term is meaningless. If, however, we mean a specific type of behavior or knowledge (of grammar, for example) is determined by genetics with little or no input needed from the environment, the term has a more specific meaning, but again, it is still not very useful. For, as we'll see more clearly in our discussions in Chapter 2, all genetic effects are mediated by "environment," broadly defined.

Usually, when developmental psychologists use the term "innate," they mean that there are some genetically based *constraints* on behavior or development. By constraints, we usually mean that the brain can only process a certain type of information in a certain way. Constraints here mean that the brain is not flexible enough to make sense of any information in any possible way. (More about such constraints in Chapter 2.) But even here there are different types of constraints. Jeffrey Elman and his colleagues (1996) have specified three general types of innate constraints: *representational, architectural,* and *chronotopic,* and I will discuss each of them briefly.

Representational constraints (or **representational innateness**) refer to representations that are hardwired into the brain so that some types of "knowledge" are innate. For example, several theorists have proposed that infants come into the world (or develop very early in life) some basic ideas about the nature of objects (their solidity, for example), mathematics (simple concepts of addition and subtraction), or grammar (see Pinker, 1997; Spelke & Newport, 1998; Chapters 8, 9, and 11 of this book). This type of innateness corresponds to what most people think of when they talk about innate concepts. This does not mean that there is no development. All abilities develop. But, according to this perspective, children (or animals) come into the world able to make sense of certain aspects of their environments given only minimal experience (basic notions of physics, how to build webs if you're a spider, for example).

Architectural constraints (or **architectural innateness**) refer to ways in which the architecture of the brain is organized at birth. For example, some neurons are excitatory and others inhibitory, or neurons can differ in the amount of activation that is required for them to fire. At a somewhat higher level, neurons in a particular area of the brain might be more or less densely packed or have many or few connections with other local neurons. And at a higher level yet, different areas of the brain are connected with other areas of the brain, affecting the global organization of the organ. Architectural constraints limit the type and manner in which information can be processed by the brain, not because the brain comes equipped with innate representations (for example, what a grammar is), but because certain neurons/areas of the brain can only process certain types of information and pass it along to certain other areas of the brain. Thus, architectural constraints imply limits on what is processed, as do representational constraints. Unlike representational constraints, however, architectural constraints permit (or require) a high degree of learning to occur.

For example, the architecture of a particular area of the brain might be best suited for processing a certain type of information (language, for instance) but the architecture will change as a function of the quantity and quality of the information it receives. Structures in the brain are not preformed to "know" grammar, for instance, but are biased toward processing information about language and develop a grammar as a result of interactions with the world. Variants of architectural innateness have been proposed by several theorists under a variety of names (see Chapters 2, 4, 8, and 9). In general, I will use the term *architectural constraints* (or *architectural innateness*) to refer to situations in which there are limitations on how information can be processed.

Chronotopic constraints (or **chronotopic innateness**) refer to limitations on the developmental timing of events. For example, certain areas of the brain might develop before others. This would mean that early developing areas would likely come to have different processing responsibilities than would later developing areas. Similarly, some areas of the brain might be most receptive to certain types of experiences (to "learning") at specified times, making it imperative that certain experiences (exposure to patterned light or language, for example) occur during this "critical period" of development. For example, children around the world acquire language in about the same way and at about the same time. If, however, for some reason children are not exposed to language until later in life, their level of language proficiency is greatly reduced. The human brain appears to be prepared to make sense of language and this makes it easy for children to acquire the language that they hear around them. But such neural readiness is constrained by time. Wait too long, and the ability to acquire a fully articulated language is lost. The issue of developmental timing will be discussed in greater detail in Chapter 2 and with relation to language in Chapter 11.

Nature/Nurture and Developmental Contextualism

I have noticed two shifts in emphasis in the cognitive development field during the past decades, which at first glance might seem contradictory. The first is a greater emphasis given to the role of context in development (including cultural context). The second is a greater acknowledgment of the role of biological factors in development. In a field where nature and nurture have traditionally occupied opposite scientific, philosophical, and often political poles, seeing an increasing emphasis on both seems a contradiction, perhaps reflecting a field composed of mutual antagonists, each taking an extreme perspective to counterbalance the other. This is not the case, however. Rather, the current perspective on the dynamic transaction of nature and nurture is one in which biological and environmental factors not only can peacefully coexist but also are intricately entwined.

Let me provide one brief illustration of how biology and environment are viewed as separate, interacting components of a larger system. Richard Lerner (1991) has been a proponent of the **developmental systems approach** (or **developmental contextual model**). The basic contention of this model is that all parts of the organism (such as genes, cells, tissues, and organs), as well as the whole organism itself, interact dynamically with "the contexts within which the organism is embedded" (Lerner, 1991, p. 27). This means that one must always consider the organism-context as a unit and that there are multiple levels of the organism and multiple levels of the context. Figure 1-1 graphically presents the developmental contextual model, showing the many bidirectional influences between children, who are born with biological propensities and dispositions, and the contexts in which they find themselves. Perhaps more than anything else, this figure demonstrates the complexity of development. But of equal importance, it demonstrates the interactions that occur between the many levels of life, from genes and hormones to family and culture, and the fact that cultural effects cannot be meaningfully separated from their biological influences, and vice versa. The dynamic nature of development, which results from the interaction of a child at many different levels (genetic, hormonal, physical environment, social environment, self-produced activity, and so on) is a

theme that runs through most contemporary theories of development. (See discussion later in this chapter.) The developmental systems approach will be examined in greater detail in Chapter 2.

Stages of Development

One issue that has been the source of great debate among cognitive developmentalists is the extent to which development is stage-like in nature. When speaking of children, we frequently refer to **stages.** The "terrible twos" is a stage reserved for 2-year-olds, and we speak of a stubborn child who refuses to wear anything but his "Bob the Builder" underwear as being in a stage—a stage we hope will be past by wash day. In everyday parlance, we use the term *stage* to refer to a period during which a child displays a certain type of thought or behavior. Stages during childhood are not permanent but are transitory times as a child makes his or her way to adulthood. Stages are related to age. When we see children engaging in behavior appropriate to younger children, we often say that they have regressed to an earlier stage.

The epitome of stage theories in cognitive development belongs to Piaget. Piaget proposed four major stages of cognitive development. The earliest, which he called *sensorimotor,* typifies the hands-on problem solving of infants and toddlers. All later stages involve the use of mental representation, permitting children to represent objects and ideas through symbols such as language. Differences between these later stages are somewhat more subtle than the drastic differences between the infant and the symbol user, but they reflect striking differences in the quality of thinking just the same. When an apple is divided into four pieces, for instance, a 4-year-old will probably think that the result is more apple. The 8-year-old knows that this notion is nonsense.

As will be seen in the remainder of this section and throughout this book, not all age-related changes reflect stages of development. In fact, some developmentalists would go as far as saying that no aspect of development is truly stage-like. But there is

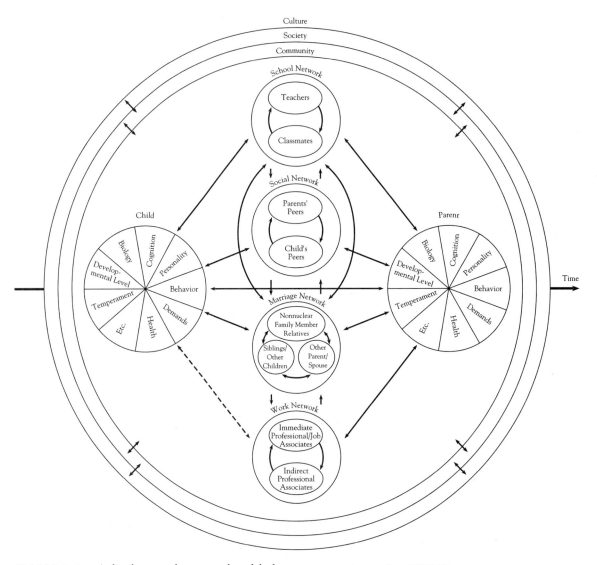

FIGURE 1-1   A developmental contextual model of person-context interaction. SOURCE: "Changing Organism-Context Relations as the Basic Process of Development: A Developmental Contextual Perspective," by R. M. Lerner, 1991, *Developmental Psychology, 27,* 27–32. Copyright © 1991 American Psychological Association. Reprinted with permission.

general agreement concerning what characteristics age-related changes must have for them to be considered indicative of stages. The disagreement lies not in what constitutes a stage but in whether or not development has these characteristics. John Flavell

(1971) listed several attributes of stages, including these:

a. Stages entail qualitative rather than quantitative differences.

b. The change from one stage to another is relatively abrupt; in other words, development is discontinuous.

c. Children's thinking within a stage is relatively even, or *homogeneous*. That is, all stage-related skills are integrated with one another, resulting in homogeneity of cognitive function, or similar cognitive functioning across a wide range of tasks.

Let us briefly examine these characteristics of stages.

Qualitative versus Quantitative Differences

Stage theories are based on the belief that children's thinking in each stage is qualitatively different from that in earlier or later stages. **Qualitative differences** are those of type, or kind. These can be contrasted with **quantitative differences,** which are differences in things that can be counted. Contrast, for example, the differences in how a 14-month-old and a 20-month-old play with a toy telephone. Most 14-month-olds play with the phone by seeing how it responds to them. They pull on the cord, pound indiscriminately on the buttons with their palms to hear the bell ring, and shake the receiver, swinging the rest of the toy around them. Most important to their play are the perceptual consequences of their actions on the toy. Within half a year, another approach to playing with this same toy can be observed. Most 20-month-old children recognize the phone as a toy that represents something else in the adult world, and they behave toward it accordingly. Although having few words, they pick up the receiver and "talk" into it, even though much of their talk is gibberish. They hold the phone to the ears of their parents, expecting them to play along and to say something into the phone. Even dogs and cats may be asked to play along with the phone game. The game can also be expanded to substitute other objects for the toy phone, such as a shoe or a banana. Underlying these differences in play are the ways in which children conceptualize objects and interact with them, and these differences seem to be qualitative in nature.

Problems arise when we try to define what constitutes a qualitative change. The differences between the perceptually based play of the 14-month-old and the symbolically based play of the 20-month-old certainly appear to be qualitative. The older child doesn't just do more with the toy or do it faster than the younger child does; the entire nature of the play is different. The same can be said for the difference between the 4-year-old and the 8-year-old who hold different beliefs about an apple as a function of how many pieces it is cut into. In other words, when one cannot see, on the surface, how the different approaches to a problem vary quantitatively, they must vary qualitatively. Qualitative differences are subjective ("It certainly looks like a different type of behavior to me") and reflect our inability to describe the change in ways that can be easily quantified.

Yet, does the surface appearance of a qualitative change mean that the mechanisms underlying development also vary qualitatively in nature? Remember that cognition deals with unobservables. Behavior serves only as the outward manifestation of what we are really interested in. Perhaps, for instance, changes in the amount of information that children can consider at any one time are responsible for the drastically different behaviors observed in the 4-year-old and the 8-year-old described earlier. Four-year-olds know that 4 is greater than 2. They also know that any particular object can be divided into pieces and, in some cases, be put back together again. Yet, these are different pieces of knowledge, and coordinating them at one time requires greater memory capacity than they can muster. Or possibly it takes them so long to process one piece of information that by the time a second piece needs to be considered, it is too late. The first piece has been dealt with and is lost from their immediate memory. The 8-year-old, by comparison, can hold onto two thoughts at once and can think about things quickly enough that the first item of information is still available by the time the second piece comes into consciousness. Such changes in the amount of information that can be remembered and the speed with which that information can be processed are quantitative. It is possible that these or related quantitative changes, which can change gradually and in linear fashion, are responsible for the apparent qualitative and nonlinear changes that are observed in overt behavior (see Courage & Howe, 2002).

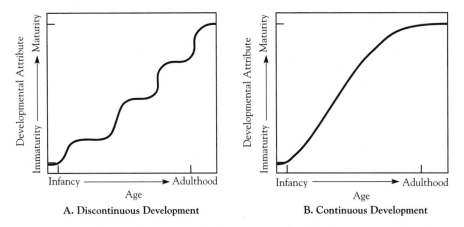

FIGURE 1-2 Stage, or discontinuity, theorists propose that development proceeds in a step-like fashion (a), with qualitative changes from one stage to the next occurring abruptly. Nonstage, or continuity, theorists propose that development proceeds in a continuous fashion (b), with quantitative changes occurring gradually over time.

The issue of the extent to which cognitive development is qualitative or quantitative is much debated. Many argue that it is both (Flavell & Wohlwill, 1969). Surely many changes within a stage are quantitative in nature. A 30-month-old girl plays with the toy telephone in much the same way as the 20-month-old does, yet she uses more words and skills (such as knowing how to dial and to mimic real phone conversations) than does the younger child. The two children are doing the same type of thing, but the older child is doing it better. More controversial is whether the underlying causes of cognitive change are quantitative or qualitative.

Continuity versus Discontinuity

Stated simply, stage theories propose that changes from one stage to another are reasonably abrupt, representing **discontinuity** rather than **continuity.** According to these theories, there is not much transition period from one stage to the next, so the qualitatively different behaviors appear suddenly and function at maturity from their onset. Furthermore, all stage-related skills make the jump at once. Note that as defined here, discontinuity refers to a sudden change in observed functioning and not necessarily

to the changes that underlie the intelligent behavior. Figure 1-2 graphically illustrates the distinction between discontinuous (stage-like) development and continuous (nonstage-like) development.

The developmental patterns in Figure 1-2 reflect regular enhancements with age, regardless of whether such enhancements take the form of stage-like discontinuities or gradual and continuous changes. Children become more competent with age, reaching maturity in adolescence or early adulthood. Developmental function need not follow such a pattern, however, and some important aspects of cognitive development seem to take a very different course.

One alternative can be described as reflecting **developmental invariance** and is depicted in Figure 1-3. In this case, cognitive skill does not improve steadily over childhood, but reaches adult competence early in life and remains stable thereafter. Such a developmental function typifies many sensory capabilities that approach adult levels in infancy or early childhood. There has also been much recent speculation that some basic cognitive skills, such as the knowledge of the permanence of objects—for years believed to develop gradually during the first two years of life—have a much earlier onset. Some of these

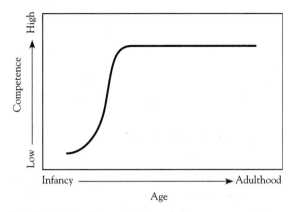

FIGURE 1-3 Some cognitive abilities mature early in life and are stable during development, reflecting developmental invariance.

ideas and the research associated with them will be discussed in Chapters 8 and 9.

Other abilities can actually decline over childhood. For example, although infants can discriminate a wide range of language sounds, by adolescence this ability has declined and it becomes difficult for adolescents to hear many of the sounds produced in some foreign languages. (See the discussion of infant phoneme discrimination ability and language acquisition in Chapter 11.) And some aspects of development clearly do decline through adulthood and old age. For example, the speed with which people can process information shows a steady, age-related decline beginning in middle age (Kail & Salthouse, 1994). So there is no one developmental pattern; rather, different mental abilities show different patterns of change, depending on when during the life span they are observed.

Homogeneity of Cognitive Function

Stage theories propose that all stage-related functions are well integrated, so that how children solve one problem is similar to how they solve other problems. A 2-year-old acts like a 2-year-old in all she says and does, and an 8-year-old is every inch an 8-year-old in all his activities. In other words, cognition is relatively uniform, or *homogeneous*, within an

individual. Many developmental psychologists would agree with the general statement that cognition is highly integrated within a given child at any one time. But development is not quite as even as some stage theorists would have us believe. It is not unusual for a child to excel at one intellectual skill but be average or even below average at others. Some 6-year-olds, for example, seem to know all there is to know about dinosaurs: their eating habits, their approximate sizes, and the types of armament they had. These same children might find it difficult to remember their phone numbers or to brush their teeth every morning. Another child might do very well at reading and the language arts in general but have great difficulty in mastering the basics of mathematics. Motivation is certainly one reason for some discrepancies of these types. Yet, it is not uncommon to find less glaring differences in many children. Children, as well as adults, often have pockets of expertise that are seemingly inconsistent with the rest of their cognitive skills. Also, for any given skill, a single child can show great variability in the level at which that skill is displayed, depending on the specific context. Many stage theories have difficulty explaining these discrepancies. In general, there is substantial **homogeneity of cognitive function** but not quite as much as classic stage theorists propose.

One task of cognitive development researchers is to explain how development can appear so even most of the time and for most tasks and yet so uneven at other times and for other tasks. But how much homogeneity is necessary before one can comfortably declare that it's enough to warrant a stage? Unfortunately, psychologists do not agree on this point, and that's a problem. What one psychologist sees as evenness, and thus stage-like, another sees as uneven (or at least not even enough), thus violating one condition for "stageness." Also, how homogeneous a child's cognitive abilities are depends on where one looks (Flavell, 1982). First, a certain level of homogeneity is imposed by limits in children's information-processing capacity. Although a given child's cognitive skills can vary, there is a limit of cognitive sophistication beyond which he or she cannot function. This limit, presumably dictated by maturational factors, expands with age but, at any given point in development, restricts the range of cognitive competencies that a child can display. (See Chapter 5 and a discussion of Fischer's theory in Chapter 4.)

Second, the type of cognitive tasks psychologists tend to study are relatively demanding, and such challenging tasks might yield greater heterogeneity of function than would the more mundane tasks that constitute most of children's daily cognitive encounters. Children's cognition appears to be relatively even to an unobtrusive observer because most of the things children do are highly routinized. We see unevenness in their abilities primarily when children's cognitive competencies are pushed to their limits.

Third, there might be more homogeneity of function during the *initial* cognitive treatment of a problem and more variability in how information is handled later in the task. For example, given a set of written problems to solve, most adults and older children begin by reading the problems, attempting to discern what the nature of the task will be. What happens after this "reading stage" is more likely to vary among individuals as a function of many factors. Similarly, when faced with a very difficult problem, children might adopt a "fall-back" strategy that they use consistently. For example, when given single-digit addition problems, children might resort to counting by ones on their fingers, even though they had solved the same problems just seconds earlier and could just "retrieve" the answer. In other words, how homogeneous cognitive function is seems to be a function of where one looks for it.

I do not want to give the impression, however, that stages are solely in the mind of the perceiver even though, admittedly, stages are not easy to identify. To constitute a stage, the cognitive ability under study must go through discontinuous, qualitative changes, and related cognitive abilities must also be relatively even within a child at any single time. Based on this definition, some developmental changes seem clearly to be nonstage-like in nature, as we'll see throughout this book. However, other age-related changes come closer to fitting the bill for a stage. More important than labeling developmental change as being "stage-like" or not is gaining an

understanding of the nature of the change. Whether we choose to use the term "stage" to describe a pattern of change will influence how we think about development, but the pattern itself is important—not the name we give it.

Dynamic Systems Approaches to Development

One approach to describing stage-like changes in development is provided by dynamic systems theories. *Dynamic systems theorists* propose that development involves the continuous and bidirectional interaction between all levels of organization, from the molecular to the cultural and that complex cognitive or behavioral characteristics *emerge* from the spontaneous interaction among simpler components (Lewis, 2000; Thelen & Smith, 1998). A **dynamic system** can be defined as a set of elements that undergoes change over time as a result of interactions among the elements. As such, dynamic systems approaches are not unique to development, but can be applied to any system that changes over time. In fact, dynamic systems theories were originally formulated to account for physical systems and are popular in the disciplines of physics, chemistry, and biology. Within psychology, dynamic systems theories have been used to explain brain functioning (Edelman, 1987), motor control (Kelso, 1995), and attitude change (Vallacher, Read, & Nowak, 2002), among many other topics. Within developmental psychology, dynamic systems approaches have been applied to learning to walk (Thelen & Smith, 1994), language development (van Geertz, 1994), and Piagetian stage transitions (van der Maas & Molenaar, 1992), among other topics.

Perhaps the central idea behind dynamic systems theories is the concept of **self-organization.** Esther Thelen and Linda Smith (1998) define self-organization as the process whereby "pattern and order emerge from interactions of the components of a complex system without explicit instructions either in the organism itself or from the environment" (p. 564). That is, order or structure in cognitive development (such as the linguistic ability to form the past tense, or being able to keep both the height and width of a container in mind when evaluating its volume) is not innately specified, waiting only for the right maturational conditions to be activated; nor is it simply the product of acquiring new knowledge (that is, learning). Rather, higher-level forms of cognition emerge from the self-initiated activity of the organism in interaction with all levels of its environment. According to Marc Lewis (2000), self-organization means that "structure does not have to be imported into a system from outside, as presumed by learning approaches, nor preordained from within, as presumed by nativist approaches. Structure is emergent" (p. 39).

Let me provide an example of emergence from meteorology, taken from Thelen and Smith:

> In certain meteorological contexts, clouds form into thunderheads that have a particular shape, internal complexity, and behavior. There is clear directionality to the way thunderheads emerge over time . . . But there is no design written anywhere in a cloud . . . that determines the final community structure. There is no set of instructions that causes clouds . . . to change form in a particular way. There are only a number of complex physical . . . systems interacting over time, such that the precise nature of their interactions leads inevitably to a thunderhead . . . We suggest that action and cognition are also emergent and not designed. (1994, p. xix)

But the type of changes brought about by self-organization, whether we're dealing with thunderheads or cognitive development, are not straightforward. In fact, one characteristic of dynamic systems is that changes are *nonlinear* in nature. When a system changes linearly, the magnitude of the effect is proportional to the magnitude of the cause. So, for example, one might expect that giving children one extra word to keep in memory while performing a second task (for example, identifying tones that are played over headphones as high or low) would result in a corresponding decrease in performance on the second task. Keeping one word in mind may decrease performance by 10%, two words by 20%, three words by 30%, and so on. However, changes of most interest to dynamic systems theorists

are those that are nonlinear, such that the magnitude of change in one variable is *not* proportional to the change in another. For instance, perhaps giving children in our hypothetical experiment four words to keep in mind reduces their performance to zero. The change from three words to four was abrupt and nonlinear—the proverbial straw that broke the camel's back. Similarly, children may acquire individual "facts" about a concept, but not until they have accumulated a sufficient number of such facts can they reorganize their knowledge base, producing a more complex structure. Or relatedly, children may be able to remember a series of five or six words without using any particular strategy (they "just remember them"). But once the list nears 10 words, say, children must reorganize their approaches to the problem, possibly by implementing a strategy of rehearsal or by remembering together words from the same category (for example, all the animal words). Thus, small changes in one factor can sometimes result in large changes in another factor.

Given the essential unpredictability of how individual elements will self-organize to produce new levels of functioning, the impression one can get is that dynamic systems are truly chaotic and that as far as explaining or understanding development, such impressions may be right, but they're not very helpful. Despite the impression of chaos, however, dynamic systems theories of human development are able to identify recurrent patterns or structures. Dynamic system theorists speak of recurrent, or stable patterns, as *attractors*. For example, all children eventually understand that an object covered by a cloth doesn't disappear into oblivion but continues to exist in time and space. Such stable states will be attained by all, or most, children given a certain level of maturation and experience and are not easily modified, or perturbed. These states do change eventually, of course (that's what development is all about), as elements interact and, through self-organization, the "system" (for example, a child's understanding of some physical phenomenon) moves toward another attractor, or more stable state. This movement from one stable state to another is called a *phase transition*.

As with stages, phase transitions refer to changes in functioning that are relatively abrupt, or discontinuous, and refer, essentially, to qualitatively similar ways of functioning. For instance, normal walking has associated with it a certain speed, gait, and coordination of the limbs. When one or more factors change, however, the system is "perturbed," such that the various components no long function smoothly together. For instance, if one walks faster or starts walking down a steep incline, maintaining a constant gait becomes difficult unless some changes in overall locomotive pattern are also made. At these points, there is instability and variability in performance, and subtle changes can move the system (in this case, the walker) into one of two forms (for example, walking, or jogging). There comes a point when "the system" (here, the various integrated components involved in bipedal locomotion) makes the phase transition from walking to jogging because maintaining the coordination among elements within the system given the new parameters becomes difficult unless a new level of organization is implemented. (Think of Olympic speed walking as an example. The pace is faster than regular walking, but the gait and coordination are much more like walking than running, and it's very unnatural. People do it, but without substantial deliberate control, the system—in this case the walker—would make the transition into the more "natural" running.)

Phase transitions can be used to describe changes at a variety of levels, including major stage changes. For example, van der Maas and Molenaar (1992) proposed that transitions between major Piagetian stages (see Chapter 4) can be described as phase transitions. As children acquire more information about their surroundings, they must coordinate that information to form a coherent understanding of their worlds. But as they gather more information, contradictions arise (for example, taller people are not always older than shorter people), and this produces instability in the cognitive system (or "disequilibrium in their structures," to use Piaget's terminology). During this period, children's performance is variable and eventually leads to a new, more stable structure. (Piaget referred to this process

FIGURE 1-4 Examples of a matrix problem. Children were to select the picture on the right that best completed the visual analogy. In this example, the correct answer is the small light-gray bird facing left. SOURCE: From Siegler, R. S., & Svetina, M. (2002). A microgenetic/cross-sectional study of matrix completion: Comparing short-term and long-term change. *Child Development, 73,* 793–809. Reprinted with permission of the Society for Research in Child Development.

as *equilibration*, and it will be discussed in more detail in Chapter 4. The point here is that such stage transitions can be described using concepts from dynamic systems theory.) Note, however, that a phase transition is not identical to a transition from one state to another. A phase transition refers to a sudden change from one state (or phase, or mode of functioning) to another, whereas a stage transition would include a number of different phase transitions over a wide range of tasks or domains.

As another example, consider children's problem solving on a visual analogy task (Siegler & Svetina, 2002). Six- to 8-year-old children were shown an incomplete matrix of pictures, similar to the example shown in Figure 1-4. In the top row on the left side is a picture of a large light-gray mouse facing right and a picture of a large light-gray bird facing right. Below them is a single picture of a small, light-gray mouse facing left. Children were to select from a group of six pictures on the right the one that best completed the analogy, in this case a small, light-gray bird, facing left. Although some children were able to solve these problems from the beginning, many were not. Of these, many began by making what Siegler and

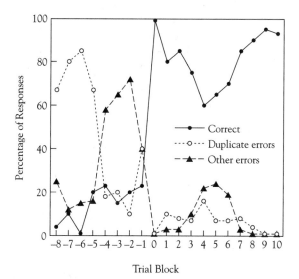

FIGURE 1-5 Pattern of responses on the matrix problem as a function of when children first achieved perfect (100%) performance on a set of three trials (trial block 0). Negative trial blocks (–8 through –1) correspond to the sets of trials preceding the trial block on which perfect performance was first attained, and positive trial blocks (1 through 10) correspond to sets of trials following the trial block on which perfect performance was first attained. SOURCE: From Siegler, R. S., & Svetina, M. (2002). A microgenetic/cross-sectional study of matrix completion: Comparing short-term and long-term change. *Child Development, 73,* 793–809. Reprinted with permission of the Society for Research in Child Development.

Svetina called "duplicate errors," selecting an object that was identical to the one in the problem (in this case, a small, light-gray mouse facing left). But several trials *before* they eventually learned how to solve the problems correctly, their pattern of errors changed. They generally stopped making duplicate errors and made other types of errors, apparently selecting randomly. But, just as suddenly, they made the transition to correct responding. This pattern of performance is shown in Figure 1-5. In the figure, trial block 0 corresponds to the set of three trials on which children first performed at 100% accuracy. As can be seen, by definition, performance here was perfect and continued to be high (although not perfect)

for all subsequent trial blocks (blocks 1 through 10). But on the trial blocks preceding block 0, performance was more variable. As can be seen, children made mostly duplicate errors on the earliest trials (blocks –8 to –5), but these declined abruptly and "other errors" increased just as abruptly on the four trial blocks immediately before block 0 (blocks –4 to –1). Stated in the language of dynamic systems theory, a period of instability and variable performance preceded a phase transition to a new level of organization, or to a new phase.

Much as Darwin's concept of natural selection (see Chapter 2), the concept of self-organization is not tied to a particular content but can be use to explain changes in any complex system. Thus, dynamic systems theories can serve as broad meta-theoretical accounts that can be adopted by researchers investigating a wide range of topics. The common ground on which developmental scientists with diverse interests can stand is the belief that development is a process of *emergence* rather than one of growth or learning. Although cognitive developmentalists who apply the often highly mathematical tools of dynamic systems theories to their areas of interest are still a minority, most believe in the dynamic nature of change and adopt, at some level, the metaphor of dynamic systems to explain development. This perspective will be implicitly (and sometimes explicitly) applied throughout the remainder of this book.

Domain-General versus Domain-Specific Abilities

As described previously, stage theories assume that cognition is homogeneous, or even, for children within a stage. Implicit in such an assumption is that a general mechanism controls cognition across all domains. Thus, domain-general theories assume that at any point in time, a child's thinking is influenced by a single set of factors, with these factors affecting different aspects of cognition (that is, different domains of thought) equally. One does not need to be a stage theorist, however, to believe in **domain-general abilities.** Development can progress through quantitative mechanisms (for example, increased memory capacity, faster speed of processing), with such mechanisms affecting all aspects of cognition.

In contrast to domain-general accounts of cognitive development are theories that postulate **domain-specific abilities.** Knowing a child's ability for one aspect of cognition might tell us nothing about his or her level of cognitive ability for other aspects of thinking because different cognitive domains are controlled by different mind/brain functions. At the extreme, domain-specific theories propose that different areas of the brain affect different aspects of cognition, with these areas being unaffected by what goes on in other areas of the brain.

The idea of the independence of different cognitive functions is best reflected in the work of philosopher Jerry Fodor (1983). Fodor proposed the concept of **modularity** in brain functions, meaning that certain areas of the brain are dedicated to performing specific cognitive tasks (such as processing language). These modules represent special-purpose systems that are "informationally encapsulated" (or "cognitively impenetrable"), meaning that other parts of the mind/brain can neither influence nor access the workings of the module. Many modules are proposed to be innate, part of the neural network an infant is born with and the result of millions of years of evolution; other modules can be developed as a result of experience and become encapsulated over time. Fodor proposed that the outputs of these modules become available to a central information processor (a domain-general mechanism), but the activity of this central processor does not affect the domain-specific modules. Although Fodor's idea of domain-specificity in human cognition has been challenged (Elman et al., 1996; and see Fodor, 2000, for a revision of his earlier ideas), it remains a dominant perspective within cognitive psychology.

Robbie Case (1992) put the controversy between domain-general and domain-specific theorists succinctly: "Is the mind better thought of as a general, all-purpose computing device, whose particular forte is general problem solving? Or is it better thought of as a modular device, each of whose modules has evolved to serve a unique biological function that it performs in its own unique and specialized way?" (p. 3). As we'll see in Chapters 4 and 5, the predominant theories of cognitive development throughout the 20th century were domain-general ones. Domain-specific theories arose primarily because of the failure of the domain-general theories to account for the heterogeneity of cognitive function that is frequently observed in development. Some of these will be discussed in Chapters 4, 5, and 9.

Some compromises between these two approaches are possible and likely necessary. For example, many researchers have shown that children think differently as a function of how much background knowledge they have in a particular domain. So, for example, chess experts show better memory spans for the positions of chess pieces than for sets of digits (Chi, 1978), and soccer experts show greater comprehension for soccer stories than for nonsoccer stories (Schneider, Körkel, & Weinert, 1989). Yet, such differences in cognitive performance as a function of background knowledge (that is, such domain-specificity) can be explained by domain-general mechanisms. Children who are experts use fewer of their general information-processing resources in thinking about information from their domain of expertise than they do in thinking about information from other areas, accounting for their uneven performance without postulating innate, modular brain structures (Bjorklund, 1987a; see Chapter 6).

Modularity implies inflexibility, in that the individual is constrained to process certain information in certain ways. This can be good, increasing the likelihood that complex information will be properly processed and understood. In discussing the benefits of constraints for infants, Annette Karmiloff-Smith (1992) states, "they enable the infant to accept as input only those data which it is initially able to compute in specific ways. The domain specificity of processing provides the infant with a limited yet organized (nonchaotic) system from the outset" (pp. 11–12). But the hallmark of human cognition is flexibility. Our species has come to dominate the globe, for better or worse, because we are able to solve problems that biology could not have imagined, and we have developed technological systems that expand our intellectual powers (such as writing, mathematics, and computers). Such cognition could not be achieved by a totally encapsulated mind/brain, and of course no domain-specific theorist proposes this degree of modularity. What we must keep in mind is the certainty that both domain-general and domain-specific abilities exist and be cautious of claims that postulate otherwise.

The Stability and Plasticity of Intelligence

Given that a particular level of intellectual competence has been established, to what extent will it remain constant over time? Will a precocious infant become a bright 3-year-old and later a talented adult? Or is it just as likely that a below-average 5-year-old will become an above-average high-school student, and a sluggish infant a whiz-kid computer jock? Once patterns have been established, what does it take to change them? Can they be modified by later experience? How plastic, or pliable, is the human intellect?

The stability and plasticity of intelligence are related. **Stability** refers to the degree to which children maintain over time their same relative rank order in comparison with their peers in some aspect of cognition. Does the high-IQ 3-year-old maintain her position in the intellectual pecking order at age 8 or 18? **Plasticity** concerns the extent to which children can be shaped by experience. More specifically with respect to cognition, once a pattern of intellectual ability is established, to what extent can it be altered? Is our cognitive system highly flexible, capable of being bent and re-bent, or, once an intellectual pattern has been forged, is it relatively resistant to change?

For the better part of the 20th century, psychologists believed that individual differences in intelligence were relatively stable over time and not likely to be strongly modified by subsequent environments. These views were held both by people who believed that such differences were mainly inherited and by those who believed that they were mainly a function of environment, but for different reasons. People on the "nature" side assumed that intelligence was primarily an expression of one's inheritance and that this expression would be constant over one's lifetime. People on the other side of the fence emphasized the role of early experience in shaping intelligence. Experience was the important component affecting levels of intelligence, with experiences during the early years of life being most critical.

Jerome Kagan (1976) referred to this latter view as the *tape recorder model* of development. Every experience was seen as being recorded for posterity, without the opportunity to rewrite or erase something once it has been recorded. Evidence for this view was found in studies of children reared in nonstimulating institutions (Spitz, 1945). Infants receiving little in the way of social or physical stimulation showed signs of retardation as early as 3 or 4 months of age. These deleterious effects became exacerbated the longer children remained institutionalized, and they were maintained long after children left the institutions (Dennis, 1973). The finding of long-term consequences of early experience was consistent with Freudian theory, which held that experiences during the oral and anal stages of development (from birth to about 2 years) have important effects on adult personality. This also seems to be the opinion shared by the media and general public.

Evidence of the permanence of the effects of early experience was also found in the animal literature. For example, Harry Harlow and his colleagues demonstrated in a series of classic studies that isolating infant rhesus monkeys from their mothers (and other monkeys) adversely affected their later social and sexual behaviors (Harlow, Dodsworth, & Harlow, 1965). Without steady interaction with other monkeys during infancy, young monkeys grew up lacking many of the social skills that facilitate important adaptive exchanges such as mating, cooperation with others, and play. Furthermore, their maladaptive behaviors apparently remained stable over the life of the animals.

Exceptions were found, however, and many began to believe that these exceptions were actually the rule. In one classic study, for instance, infants believed to be mentally retarded were removed from their overcrowded and understaffed orphanage to an institution for the mentally retarded (Skeels, 1966; see discussion of this study in Chapter 16). There they received lavish attention by women inmates, and within the course of several years, these children demonstrated normal levels of intelligence. In other work, isolated monkeys were placed in therapy sessions with younger, immature monkeys on a daily basis over a six-month period. By the end of therapy, these isolates were behaving in a reasonably normal fashion and could become integrated into a laboratory monkey troop (Suomi & Harlow, 1972). Each of these studies demonstrates plasticity by a young organism and resilience concerning the negative effects of early environments.

Kagan (1976) proposed that one reason to expect resilience is that development does not proceed as a tape recorder. Rather, development is transformational, with relatively drastic changes occurring between adjacent stages. During these times, the "tapes" are changed. Alternatively, methods of representing and interpreting the world change, so that the codes of the earlier tapes may be "lost" to the child. The tapes of our infancy might still reside in our heads, but we've lost the ability to play them or, maybe, the ability to understand the code in which they were written. In this view, plasticity should be the rule rather than the exception, especially for the experiences of infancy and early childhood.

Note that from this perspective we would not predict that all forms of behavior or cognition are modifiable. If the cognitive ability in question does not go through transformations in its development, there is every reason to expect that early patterns will be maintained. That is, cognitive abilities that change quantitatively over time, and not qualitatively, should show relative stability. The level of performance might change, but, given regular, continuous changes in developmental function, there is every reason to expect children to maintain their same rank order. Similarly, if an environment responsible for establishing a particular pattern of behavior (for example, a nonstimulating institution) remains relatively constant over time, there is no reason to expect remarkable changes in children's mental functioning. (These issues will be examined in greater depth in Chapter 16.)

One important thing to remember here is that, yes, stimulation and experience are important in the early years of life, but so is later experience. Al-

though early intellectual stimulation is important to get children off to a good start, later experiences are necessary to maintain that positive beginning. And although most children who start life in nonstimulating circumstances remain there, enhancements in intellectual skills are apt to occur for such children if the environments change for the better. This does not mean that there is infinite plasticity in cognitive development, but merely that early experience (just as biology) is not necessarily destiny and that change is as much a characteristic of human cognition as is stability.

Changes That Occur in Cognitive Development

As we'll see throughout this book, cognitive development is not a monolithic process. Many aspects of cognition change during development. Some of these changes are in basic processes, such as speed of information processing. Others, however, are more large-scale or global, and these global changes have been the focus of major theories of cognitive development. I believe that global changes in cognitive development can be reduced to two primary areas: how objects and events in the world (and in the mind/brain) are represented, and the degree to which the child can intentionally control learning and problem solving.

Changes in Representation

One key issue that all theories of cognitive development must address concerns age differences in how children represent experience. There is more than one way to represent a thing, and children of different ages seem to use different ways of representing their worlds. Adults, as well, use a variety of techniques to represent knowledge. While providing directions to my house to someone over the phone, for instance, I must convey the route to my home verbally, through a language code. But how is it represented in my head? What is the nature of the **representation?** I might think of the route I take by generating visual images of the buildings and landmarks I pass and convert those into words. In fact, what I have done in the past is to sketch a map and then transform that map into words that can be understood by my listener. What the person on the other end of the phone must do is encode the information. At one level, my friend might attend only to the sounds of the words I speak, encoding the acoustic properties of the words. If he does, he will probably be late for dinner. More likely, he will attend to the semantic, or meaning, features of the words. Once a basic meaning has been derived, however, he might convert the message to a mental (or physical) map, realizing that he will be better able to find my house if the relevant information is in the form of a visual image.

How children represent knowledge and how they encode events in their world change developmentally. Traditional theories have proposed that infants and toddlers much younger than 18 months are limited to knowing the world only through raw perception and their actions on things, with little or no use of symbols. This position has been questioned recently, with new research showing that even infants have access to some symbol systems (see Gelman & Williams, 1998; Spelke & Newport, 1998). Some researchers have even suggested that abstract, symbolic representation is innate, in that even newborns reveal behavior requiring seemingly symbolic representation, such as imitation of facial gestures (Meltzoff & Moore, 1985). Much of this research will be discussed in Chapters 8 and 9.

Most cognitive developmentalists agree that there are age differences in how children represent their world, and that these differences are central to age differences in thinking. These researchers disagree, however, about the nature of these differences and whether they are quantitative or qualitative in nature. Can children of all ages use all types of symbols, and do they simply use them with different frequencies? Or does representation develop in a stage-like manner, with the more advanced forms of symbol use

being unavailable to younger children? Research and theory pertinent to these and other issues related to changes in representation are central to the study of cognitive development, and they will be discussed in the pages ahead.

Changes in Intentional Control

Much cognitive development (and educational) research is concerned with how children solve problems. Much of what interests cognitive developmental psychologists is how children go about finding solutions to complex problems that might have multiple paths to a solution. For example, how do children solve a puzzle, how do they go about remembering a grocery list, or how do they study for a history exam? Problem solving begins in infancy, but the problems children face and their solutions become more complicated with age.

One central concern of cognitive developmentalists has been the degree to which children of different ages can intentionally guide their problem solving. Much research on this topic has addressed the use of strategies. **Strategies** are usually defined as deliberate, goal-directed mental operations that are aimed at solving a problem (Harnishfeger & Bjorklund, 1990a). We use strategies intentionally to help us achieve a specified goal. Strategies can be seen in the behavior of infants. Six-month-olds alter how hard they swing at mobiles over their cribs to yield slightly different movement from the inanimate object. Eighteen-month-old toddlers will deliberately stack boxes one on top of another so that they can reach the kitchen shelf and the chocolate-chip cookies. These are no less willful strategies than is the rhyming mnemonic the sixth-grader uses to remember how many days there are in each month or the plan the 15-year-old uses as she plays all her trump cards first in a game of bridge. Yet, strategies do change with development, and children seem increasingly able to carry out successful strategies as they grow older. One key research question in cognitive development concerns changes in the strategies children use and the situations in which they use them.

Although children around the world increasingly display goal-directed problem-solving behavior, this is especially evident for children from technologically advanced societies in which formal schooling is necessary to become a successful adult. Much of what children learn in school can only (or best) be acquired by deliberate study. This contrasts with how children in cultures without formal schooling often learn complicated tasks. Much of what children in all cultures learn about their world they acquire incidentally, without specific intention and sometimes without specific awareness. This type of learning and development is important also, and recent research, particularly in the area of memory development, has recognized this (see Chapter 10).

Although I said that there were two major issues that encompass almost all aspects of cognitive development (representation and intentionality), a third issue concerns all cognitive developmentalists, and that is the mechanisms responsible for change. Although we can observe changes in how children represent their world and see evidence of enhanced intentional, goal-directed behavior with age, as scientists, we very much want to know the causes of these changes. Thus, description of change is not enough, although it is a necessary start. Perhaps the principal goal of cognitive developmentalists is to discover the underlying mechanisms of change, and much of the research in the remainder of this book addresses this issue.

Another goal for many cognitive developmentalists is to produce research that can be applied to real-world contexts. For example, issues about the stability and plasticity of intelligence have direct applications to the remediation of mental retardation and to some learning disabilities (Chapter 15). Understanding how children learn to use strategies of arithmetic, memory, and reading are directly pertinent to children's acquisition of modern culture's most important technological skills (Chapters 6, 10, and 14). As you'll see in Chapter 10, research on factors that influence children's recollection of experienced or witnessed events have immediate relevance to the courtroom, where children have increasingly been called to testify. Understanding the normal de-

velopment of both basic (and unconscious) cognitive processes as well as forms of higher-order (and conscious) cognition, provides insight into the causes of some learning disabilities, be it in math and reading (Chapter 14), or perhaps as a result of Attention Deficit Hyperactivity Disorder (ADHD) (Chapter 5). And although extensions to the schoolhouse or clinic may be the most obvious applications of cognitive development research and theory, I believe perhaps the greatest application is to an appreciation of children, in general, particularly when they are your own.

Overview of the Remainder of the Book

As I mentioned earlier in this chapter, two themes have come to dominate cognitive developmental thinking over the past decade or so: (1) an increasing emphasis on the biological basis of development, and (2) an increasing emphasis on the sociocultural influence on development. These seemingly contradictory trends are actually quite compatible and are the focus of Chapters 2 and 3. In Chapter 2, I discuss the biological basis of cognitive development. This chapter was written for the beginning student, so a solid background in biology is not necessary to understand the material in the chapter. The chapter focuses on models of biology-environment interaction and on the development of the brain, as well as on new ideas (evolutionary psychology) and new approaches (neuroimaging) to the study of cognitive development. Chapter 3 presents the sociocultural perspective of cognitive development, emphasizing the theorizing of Lev Vygotsky and his contemporary followers.

The following two chapters are devoted to major theoretical approaches to cognitive development research. In Chapter 4, I describe the theory of Jean Piaget. Piaget has unquestionably been the most influential person in the cognitive development field, and any appreciation of contemporary research requires an understanding of the theory that more than any other has stimulated interest in children's thinking. The chapter discusses the principles and assumptions of Piaget's theory and describes the four major stages of development he proposed. Because of the impact he has had on the field of cognitive development, his work and theory will surface continually in other chapters of the book. I also discuss major neo-Piagetian theories in Chapter 4, including the ideas of Kurt Fischer, and "theory theories" of development.

Chapter 5 examines information-processing approaches to children's thinking, particularly basic-level information-processing mechanisms. Information-processing accounts of cognition replaced Piaget's theory as the most popular approaches to the study of cognitive development and present an important alternative to Piagetian theory. Chapter 6 examines the development higher-level cognitive operations, specifically strategies.

The next seven chapters examine specific topics in cognitive development. Chapter 7 deals with perception. Much of the information in this chapter relates to perceptual abilities in infancy, although perceptual abilities in childhood are also examined. Chapter 8 examines spatial cognition, from infancy through childhood, concluding with a look at data and theory about the frequently found gender differences in spatial cognition. Chapter 9 addresses developmental differences in representation, looking at research demonstrating greater representational knowledge and abilities in infants and young children than was previously believed. Included in this chapter are discussions of infants' imitative abilities, young children's understanding of how one object can "stand for" another, and children's theories of mind. Chapter 10 looks at memory and includes topics ranging from parents' roles in "teaching" children how to remember, implicit memory, to forgetting, infantile amnesia, and children as courtroom eyewitnesses. Chapter 11 is devoted to language, examining children's acquisition of a first and second language, communication, and the developmental relationship between language and thought. Children's problem solving, including rule acquisition, and analogical, formal, and scientific reasoning, are examined in Chapter 12. Chapter 13 examines certain aspects of social cognition. The term *social cognition* covers many diverse subjects, and I

don't pretend to have examined most of them here. Among the topics included in this chapter are Albert Bandura's social cognitive theory, Kenneth Dodge's social information-processing theory, the development of self-concept, perspective taking, and the cognitive bases of gender identification.

Chapter 14 is a bridge between Chapters 2 through 13, which deal primarily with developmental function, and Chapters 15 and 16, which deal primarily with individual differences. Chapter 14 examines the development of and individual differences in two important technological skills, reading and arithmetic, along with other aspects of the role of schooling on cognitive development, including cross-cultural differences in cognition and academic performance, the role of schooling on intelligence, and the benefits and detriments of academic preschools and enrichment programs.

Chapters 15 and 16 each deal with individual differences in intelligence. Chapter 15 examines basic approaches to the study of intelligence, including the psychometric, information-processing, and Piagetian approaches. I also include some alternative perspectives on intelligence, including Robert Sternberg's triarchic theory and Howard Gardner's theory of multiple intelligences. Chapter 16 looks at the stability of intelligence over time and examines issues relating to the heritability of intelligence. Recent findings from behavior genetics, as well as work that examines environmental influences on establishing, maintaining, and modifying intellectual functioning, are discussed in this chapter.

The book ends with a brief epilogue, which attempts to abstract several "truths," or generalizations, about cognitive development.

Summary

The study of cognitive development involves the regular, age-related changes in children's cognition over time, referred to as *developmental function*, as well as *individual differences* in such cognition.

Cognition refers to the acquisition and manipulation of knowledge. It includes conscious, effortful processes, such as those involved in making important decisions, and unconscious, automatic processes, such as those involved in recognizing a familiar face, word, or object. Cognition cannot be observed directly but must be inferred from behavior.

Development refers to changes in *structure* or *function* over time, with such a relationship being conceived as *bidirectional* in nature (*structure* ↔ *function*). Development has its roots in biology, and its course is relatively predictable. Yet, within any given age or stage, there are individual differences in children's thinking, with the organism-environment interaction being critical for an understanding of the course of development. Although development is often viewed as being progressive, children's immature cognitions might provide them with some adaptive advantages.

With respect to the nature/nurture issues, extreme views of both *nativism* (a belief that all intellectual abilities are innate) and *empiricism* (a belief that all intellectual abilities are a result of experience) have been rejected, and replaced by a belief in the bidirectional relation of biological and experiential factors, with children playing critical roles in their own development. Three different types of innate constraints have been proposed: *representational*, referring to innate representations; *architectural*, referring to innate characteristics of neurons and their connections with other groups of neurons; and *chronotopic*, referring to maturational (timing) constraints. Biological and environmental factors are seen as interacting in bidirectional relationships, as reflected by the *developmental systems approach*.

Changes between *stages* of development are said by stage theorists to be qualitative rather than quantitative in nature. *Qualitative differences* are those of type, or kind, whereas *quantitative differences* are those of amount or speed. Shifts from one stage to another are theorized to occur abruptly, reflecting *discontinuity* rather than *continuity* in development. Stage theorists posit that children's abilities are highly integrated within a stage. Many (but not all) cognitive developmentalists agree that there is substantial *homogeneity of cognitive function*, although not as much homogeneity as predicted by many stage theories. Cognitive development does not always increase gradually (or discontinuously) over time but in some domains might reach adult levels early, with a skill showing *developmental invariance*.

Dynamic systems theories propose that new levels of organization (such as stages) emerge as a result of the *self-organization* among lower-level elements within a system. As such, development is viewed not as the product of learning or of innately specified information in the genes but, rather, as the process of emergence.

Most traditional approaches to cognitive development have posited *domain-general abilities*, although recent research has shown that many aspects of cognition and its development are *domain-specific* in nature, with some forms of cognition being *modular*.

Stability refers to the degree to which children maintain their same rank order relative to their peers over time. *Plasticity* refers to the extent to which individuals can be shaped by the environment. For most of the 20th century, it was believed that intelligence is relatively stable over time and that experiences later in life cannot greatly affect patterns of intelligence established earlier. More recent research suggests that some characteristics—but not others—are stable and that human intelligence can be substantially modified under certain circumstances. It is important to consider the issues of stability and plasticity along with issues of developmental function.

Among several other important theoretical issues, the two most critical are developmental differences in *representation* and the extent to which children are able to intentionally control their problem solving through *strategies*.

Key Terms and Concepts

cognition
development
structure
function

bidirectionality of structure and function
(structure ↔ function)
developmental function
individual differences
nativism
empiricism
representational constraints (or representational
innateness)
architectural constraints (or architectural
innateness)
chronotopic constraints (or chronotopic
innateness)
developmental systems approach (developmental
contextual model)
stages
qualitative versus quantitative differences
continuity versus discontinuity of development
developmental invariance
homogeneity of cognitive function
dynamic systems
self-organization
domain-general abilities
domain-specific abilities
modularity
stability
plasticity (of cognition and behavior)
representation
strategies

Suggested Readings

Bjorklund, D. F., & Green, B. L. (1992). The adaptive nature of cognitive immaturity. *American Psychologist, 47,* 46–54. This article presents the argument that some aspects of infants' and young children's immature thinking are adaptive and that attempts to accelerate development should be carefully thought out before being implemented.

Elman, J. L., Bates, E. A., Johnson, M. H., Karmiloff-Smith, A., Parisi, D., & Plunkett, K. (1996). *Rethinking innateness: A connectionist perspective on development.* Cambridge, MA: MIT Press. This book discusses issues related to the concept of innateness as it relates to developmental psychology. Although numerous aspects of development are discussed, most discussion is related to brain development and language development. The authors present a connectionist (computer modeling) perspective, but the book is valuable even for those who want to avoid such approaches.

Flavell, J. H. (1992). Cognitive development: Past, present, and future. *Developmental Psychology, 28,* 988–1005. This article presents a brief history of thought in cognitive development, current issues, and predictions for research in the future.

Lewis, M. D. (2000). The promise of dynamic systems approaches for an integrated account of human development. *Child Development, 71,* 36–43. This short article presents the major concepts of dynamic systems as they are applied in developmental psychology. For a more in-depth discussion, the reader is directed to the chapter by Thelen and Smith in the 1998 *Handbook of Child Psychology.*

InfoTrac® College Edition

For additional readings, explore InfoTrac College Edition, your online library. Go to http://www.infotrac-college.com/wadsworth.

Biological Bases of Cognitive Development

For some time now, I've begun including lectures on the biological basis of cognitive development in my undergraduate class, discussing brain development and the evolution of mental abilities. Invariably, one or two students will approach me after class and ask why we need to know anything about biology to understand children's thinking. They didn't sign-up to be psychology majors to study biology.

The question, actually, is not a trivial one. For much of the 20th century, social and behavioral scientists interested in cognition gave only lip service, at best, to biology. The mind might emanate from the brain, but understanding the brain was not seen as a prerequisite to understanding the mind. In fact, there existed in the social and behavioral sciences what can be called *biophobia* and an implicit belief that acknowledging biology was akin to rejecting the influence of environment or culture on behavior, something at odds with the central theme of the social sciences (see Tooby & Cosmides, 1992). The study of cognition was essentially isolated from the study of the brain.

Things have clearly changed. The new field of cognitive science takes as a given the close connection between mind and brain. As philosopher John Searle (1992) states, "Mental phenomena are caused by neurophysiological processes in the brain and are themselves features of the brain. . . . Mental events and processes are as much part of our biological natural history as digestion, mitosis, or enzyme secretion" (p. 1). Moreover, cognitive scientists are not only concerned with immediate biological causes (for example, how the brain affects behavior), but also with factors that influenced the evolution of human cognition.

Looking at the biological basis of cognition and its development does not mean that one ignores the psychological level. Biology and psychology provide different levels of analysis. Much as psychology and anthropology present different pictures of human behavior (one at the level of the individual and the other at the level of the culture), so too do biology and psychology. Moreover, just as concepts in biology must be consistent with the known facts of chemistry, so also must concepts in psychology be consistent with the known facts of biology. Thus,

proposing theories of mind that are inconsistent with what we know about physiology or evolution cannot lead to a productive theory of cognition (see Cosmides, Tooby, & Barkow, 1992).

But psychology cannot be reduced to biology. Knowing how nerve cells function will not tell us all we need to know about how we think. The concepts of psychology, while being consistent with the concepts of biology, represent a different level of analysis. Developing a theory of the brain is important, of course, but it is not enough. Having a theory of the brain does not obviate having a theory of the mind. Cognitive psychology is not just something to do until the biologists get better at their trade. Developmental psychologists should not blindly accept everything that biologists propose, but they should be mindful of the biological causes of cognitive development and formulate theories and design experiments accordingly (Bjorklund, 1997b).

In this chapter, I first provide a look at ideas from evolutionary theory and how such Darwinian ideas can contribute to an understanding of the developing modern child. In the next section, I examine a couple of developmental theories that take biology seriously, particularly the relation between genetic/biologic factors and environmental/experiential factors. I then provide a brief overview of brain development. In this, and in later chapters, I will comment on the relation between brain and cognitive development. Although no one ever doubted that the brain was the seat of cognition, only recently, with the emergence of the field of **developmental cognitive neuroscience,** have brain-cognition relations in development been taken seriously (Byrnes & Fox, 1998; Nelson, 2001; Nelson & Bloom, 1997). Developmental cognitive neuroscience takes data from a variety of sources— molecular biology, cell biology, artificial intelligence, evolutionary theory, as well as conventional cognitive development—to create a picture of how the mind/ brain develops. As will be made clear soon, contemporary biologically based theories of development do not hold that "biology is destiny" but, rather, deal with the classic nature/nurture controversy by explaining how genes and environments interact to produce a particular pattern of development.

Because most research in cognitive development over the last century essentially ignored biological causation, most of what is covered in the rest of the book is at the psychological rather than the biological level. However, I firmly believe that we will develop an understanding of cognitive development only by taking biology seriously, and reference to biological factors will be made throughout the remainder of the book.

Evolution and Cognitive Development

What is the adaptive value of particular cognitive abilities? How might cognitive abilities have a different adaptive value at different times in development? In what contexts should certain cognitive abilities develop? How do some evolved human characteristics, such as bipedality or prolonged immaturity, affect the ontogeny of cognition? Developmentalists ask these questions relating to evolution.

When biologists speak of **evolution,** they (usually) mean the process of change in gene frequencies in populations over many generations that in time produces new species. Modern evolutionary theory had its beginnings in the ideas of Charles Darwin, whose 1859 book *The Origin of Species* represents one of the grandest ideas of science. The book made an immediate impact on the scientific community and is considered by many today to be one of the most important books ever written. The crux of the theory is that many more members of a species are born in each generation than will survive. They all have different combinations of inherited traits; that is, there is substantial *variation* among members of a species. Conditions in the environment for that particular generation cause some members of that species to survive and reproduce whereas others do not, a process that Darwin referred to as **natural selection.** The inherited traits of the survivors will be passed on to the next generation of that species, whereas the traits of the nonsurvivors will not. Over the course of many generations, the predominant traits of a species will change by this mechanism. The major principle

of Darwin's theory is *reproductive fitness*, which basically refers to the likelihood that an individual will become a parent and a grandparent.

Darwin's theory has gone through some substantial modifications during the last century or so, the most significant being the inclusion of modern genetic theory into formulations of evolution. Among scientists today, the *fact* of evolution is not questioned, although some lively debates center on the *mechanisms* of evolution (see Gould, 2002). Despite controversies, evolutionary theory is the backbone of modern biology, and because human cognition and behavior are rooted in biology, evolutionary theory should be the backbone of modern psychology.

Evolutionary theory has had an influence on developmental psychology since its beginnings. Some of the early giants of developmental psychology were greatly influenced by evolutionary theory, among them James Mark Baldwin, G. Stanley Hall, and Jean Piaget. From time to time during the last century, scientists have emphasized the importance of having knowledge of evolutionary theory for developing knowledge of children's thinking (for example, Fishbein, 1976). This is one of those times. Within the past decade, a number of developmentalists have made explicit proposals for looking at child development from an evolutionary perspective (see Bjorklund & Hernándz Blasi, in press; Bjorklund & Pellegrini, 2002; Bugental, 2000; Geary, 1998; Geary & Bjorklund, 2000; Weisfeld, 1999), including cognitive development (Bjorklund, 1997b; Geary & Bjorklund, 2000).

One thing that evolutionary theory provides is a framework for interpreting all aspects of behavior and development. It does this, in part, by providing an explanation for *how* a particular mechanism came about (through natural selection), but also a possible explanation of *why* this mechanism evolved. In my early training, I was taught not to ask "why" questions. Scientists ask "how" questions, for example, "How do children come to appreciate that other people have perceptions and ideas other than their own?," not *why* do they develop this ability. Evolutionary theory provides answers to both the "how" and "why" questions. The "how" is through natural selection over evolutionary time, in that children who could not learn to see the perspectives of another person did not grow up to have children of their own. Of course, this is not a sufficient answer to "how" this ability develops in individual children (see Chapter 9 on the development of theory of mind), but it does provide a mechanism for how it developed in the species. The "why" suggests that this ability was likely important for survival, or that it was *adaptive*. Children who could understand the perspective of another were able to anticipate other people's actions and act accordingly. Such *adaptationist* reasoning must be used cautiously, of course. Not all aspects of present-day life were necessarily adaptive for our ancient ancestors. Some aspects might have been neutral, some associated with other characteristics, and others just not sufficiently maladaptive to result in extinction. But having a theory that provides a framework for asking why a particular behavior or pattern of development is present can help us develop a better understanding of human nature and to ask better "how" questions.

Evolutionary theory is currently influencing cognitive development in at least two ways. The first is through the newly developed field of **evolutionary psychology** (Barkow, Cosmides, & Tooby, 1992; Buss, 1995), and its offshoot *evolutionary developmental psychology* (Bjorklund & Pellegrini, 2002; Geary & Bjorklund, 2000). This field explains human behavior through evolutionary theory; evolutionary theorists ask "why" questions and provide answers about adaptive fit to environments. It is important to understand that what might have been adaptive to our ancestors 100,000 or one million years ago might not be adaptive to us today. Our preference for sweets and fat is a good case in point. Although these foods would have been rare and much valued sources of energy to our ancient ancestors, they are easily available to people from postindustrial cultures today and are largely responsible for our high incidence of heart disease (Nesse & Williams, 1994). Many cognitive mechanisms can be seen similarly, and, alternatively, many of the technological problems we must solve as modern humans are only centuries old at most and have no specific mechanisms that have evolved to solve them.

The second way evolutionary theory is influencing current research and theory in cognitive devel-

opment is by applying selectionist explanations to current phenomenon (Cziko, 1995; Siegler, 1996). Rather than speculating about what environmental conditions might have been two million years ago or assuming what the adaptive value of a particular behavior might have been, these theorists use Darwin's idea of natural selection to explain how the brain or the mind develops. I will examine briefly each of these approaches in the following sections, and we will encounter evolutionary interpretations of patterns of development throughout the remainder of the book.

Evolutionary Psychology

Evolutionary psychologists have suggested that cognitive psychology is the missing link in the evolution of human behavior. Leda Cosmides and John Tooby (1987) proposed that information-processing mechanisms evolved and "these mechanisms in interaction with environmental input generate manifest behavior. The causal link between evolution and behavior is made through psychological mechanisms" (p. 277). According to Cosmides and Tooby, adaptive behavior is predicated on adaptive thought, at least in humans. Natural selection operates on the cognitive level—information-processing programs evolved to solve real-world problems. How do I tell friend from foe? When do I fight and when do I flee? From this viewpoint, it becomes fruitful to ask what kind of cognitive operations an organism must have "if it is to extract and process information about its environment in a way that will lead to adaptive behavior" (Cosmides & Tooby, 1987, p. 285). From an evolutionary perspective, we must ask, What is the purpose of a behavior and the cognitive operations that underlie that behavior? What problem was it designed to solve?

It is also important in the realm of cognitive development to remember that cognitive processes *develop* and that the problems infants and children face are different from those faced by adults. Researchers can fruitfully ask how children's cognitions are adapted to the cultural contexts in which they find themselves, rather than to the contexts experienced by adults (Bjorklund, 1997a; Turkewitz & Kenny, 1982). For example, what type of information should helpless infants be attentive to? Might some information that is of vital importance to them be less important to older children and adults, and vice versa?

Also, evolutionary theory suggests that most psychological mechanisms evolved to accomplish specific adaptive functions. That is, rather than affecting general intelligence, for example, Darwinian algorithms affect very specific cognitive operations, such as face recognition or the processing of certain types of social relationships. This suggests that infants, children, and adults have evolved some cognitive abilities to deal with specific problems, and that such abilities will be independent of other intellectual skills (that is, they will be *modular*, as discussed in Chapter 1). This perspective, that evolution has shaped human cognition with a set of domain-specific brain modules, is captured by Steven Pinker's (1997) statement: "The mind is organized into modules or mental organs, each with a specialized design that makes it an expert in one area of interaction with the world. The modules' basic logic is specified by our genetic program. Their operation was shaped by natural selection to solve problems of the hunting and gathering life led by our ancestors in most of our evolutionary history" (p. 21). Although a number of developmental psychologists who take an evolutionary perspective also believe that important domain-general mechanisms (for example, speed of processing, ability to inhibit thoughts and actions) have also experienced pressures from natural selection (Bjorklund & Kipp, 2002; Geary & Huffman, 2002), most concur that many important evolved psychological mechanisms are specific to a narrow range of contexts (that is, are domain-specific in nature).

Implicit in the idea that there are domain-specific mechanisms, is that there are *constraints* (representational, architectural, and chronotopic, see Chapter 1) on learning (Gelman & Williams, 1998). Constraints imply restrictions, and restrictions are usually thought of as being bad. Human cognition is exceptional for its flexibility, not for its restrictiveness. But constraints, from this perspective, *enable* learning, rather than hamper it. Children enter a world of

sights, sounds, objects, language, and other people. If all types of learning were truly equiprobable, children would be overwhelmed by stimulation that bombards them from every direction. Instead, the argument goes, infants and young children are constrained to process certain information in "core domains" (such as the nature of objects, language) in certain ways. They come into the world with some idea of how the world is structured, and this leads to faster and more efficient processing of information within specific domains. According to Gelman and Williams, "From an evolutionary perspective, learning cannot be a process of arbitrary and completely flexible knowledge acquisition. In core domains, learning processes are the means to functionally defined ends: acquiring and storing the particular sorts of relevant information which are necessary for solving particular problems" (1998, p. 600).

One way of thinking of how the mind is structured has been presented by David Geary (1998; 2001; Geary & Bjorklund, 2000), who proposes that what evolved is a set of hierarchically organized, domain-specific modules that develop as children engage their physical and social worlds. Geary's model is shown in Figure 2-1. As can be seen, there are two overarching domains—*social and ecological*—with each consisting of two more-specific domains (*individual* and *group* for social, and *biological* and *physical* for ecological), each of which, in turn, consists of more-specific domains. Geary acknowledges that this list of domains is not complete (for example, there is no numerical domain listed here, which Geary believes exists), and one could argue about the organization of some of these domains (for example, should "language" be organized within the social domain, or is it best conceptualized as a separate domain?). Nonetheless, Geary's organization reflects one that is consistent with the dominant perspective of evolutionary psychologists (Buss, 1995; Tooby & Cosmides, 1992; Pinker, 1997) and captures much of the developmental data.

Despite the belief that many evolutionarily influenced cognitive abilities are domain-specific in nature, one should not lose track of the fact that human cognition is amazingly flexible. This implies that what evolved in *Homo sapiens* are not highly

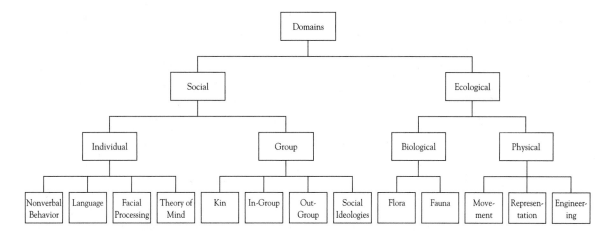

FIGURE 2-1 Proposed domains of mind. SOURCE: From *Male, female: The evolution of human sex differences* (p. 180), by D. C. Geary (1998), Washington DC: American Psychological Association. Copyright © 1998 by the American Psychological Association. Reprinted with permission.

specific approaches to problems, but genes and cognitive mechanisms that are sensitive to different environments and yield different outcomes (phenotypes) in different contexts that are (or would have been in ancient environments) adaptive to local conditions. Such mechanisms become more specific and finely tuned during development, primarily as a result of experience. And humans, more than any other mammal, have time to gather the experience that will be necessary to function optimally as an adult. In fact, evolutionary developmental psychologists have emphasized the importance of our species' extended childhood for cognitive development (Bjorklund & Pellegrini, 2002). Humans spend a greater proportion of their lifespans as juveniles than other any primate species does. There are great dangers associated with delaying reproducing, and, the argument goes, there must therefore be some substantial benefits to survival for this prolonged period of immaturity to have been selected for. Although there is no single answer to the questions of "Why do humans have such an extended juvenile period?," one reason proposed by many evolutionary developmental psychologists is that the long period of youth is necessary for children to master the complexities of human societies and technologies (Bjorklund &

Bering, 2003; Kaplan et al., 2000). This perspective argues that, because of the variety of social and physical environments in which people live (both presently and in our evolutionary past), human cognition must be flexible, adapted not to a highly specific environment, but to a broad range of potential environments, reflecting the diversity of social groups around the globe and throughout our species' history. To do this requires a long period of apprenticeship, as well as a large brain capable of flexible learning and cognition.

Another insight relevant to cognitive development and to education derived from evolutionary psychology is the idea that much of what we teach children in school is "unnatural" in that it involves tasks never encountered by our ancestors. For example, although our species has apparently been using language for tens of thousands of years, reading is a skill that goes back only a few thousand years, and only during the past century have a majority of people on the planet become literate. Geary (1995) has referred to cognitive abilities that were selected for in evolution, such as language, as **biologically primary abilities,** and skills that build on these primary abilities but are principally cultural inventions, such as reading, as **biologically secondary abilities.**

Biologically primary abilities are acquired universally and children typically have high motivation to perform tasks involving them. Biologically secondary abilities, on the other hand, are culturally determined, and tedious repetition and external pressure are often necessary for their mastery. It is little wonder that reading, a supposed "language art," and higher mathematics give many children substantial difficulty.

It is important to emphasize here that an evolutionary account of development is *not* one of biological determinism. That is, although evolution works through changing frequencies in genes within the population, natural selection requires a dynamic interaction between organisms and their environments. Organisms choose environments, the very act of which modifies those environments. Environments, in turn, affect the organism, by "selecting" some behaviors that "match" the environments over others. Because of this dynamic interaction between organisms and environments, we must evaluate organisms' interactions with their environments if we want to understand adaptation and cognitive development. Thus, this position rejects any simple notion of biological determinism (for example, "genes cause behavior") on cognitive development, intelligence, or the educability of children.

Selectionist Theories of Cognitive and Brain Development

The major tenets of Darwin's theory of natural selection are simple: Organisms produce more offspring than can survive (known as *superfecundity*), there is variability among offspring, and offspring that are better adapted to their environment survive, that is, organisms are "selected" by the environment. Actually, organisms that don't adapt well to their environments die, so there is both positive selection (survival) and negative selection (death). Other than explaining human evolution, how can such concepts be applied to human cognitive development?

The key here is *variability*, not so much between individuals (although this is obviously important), but *within* a single individual. **Selectionist theorists** propose that people possess a wide range of behaviors or cognitions (that is, there is substantial variability), and they emit these behaviors or thoughts in certain environments. Those behaviors or cognitions that are adaptive increase in frequency (that is, survive), and those that are not adaptive decrease in frequency (and may eventually "die").

From this perspective, cognitive development can be seen as a process of children trying out different behaviors or cognitive operations (the availability of which changes with age)—and keeping those that work (that the environment "selects") and dropping those that don't work (that the environment does not "select" or "selects" against) (Cziko, 1995; Siegler, 1996). New cognitive operations emerge during development, but these new operations coexist with older (and often simpler) cognitive operations and "compete" with one another for use to solve problems. Those that solve problems effectively increase in frequency, and those that do not decrease in frequency. Robert Siegler's (1996) *adaptive strategy choice model* is perhaps the best-developed contemporary selectionist theory of cognitive development, and I will discuss it in some detail in Chapter 6.

Selectionist theories are also being applied in brain development. Here, neurons, rather than organisms, behaviors, or cognitive operations, are generated in great number and variability (Changeux & Dehaene, 1989; Edelman, 1987). Neurons that "fit" well with their surrounding environments (in this case, other neurons) survive, and those that do not fit die. This approach to brain development will be discussed later in this chapter.

Evolutionary theory provides an overarching perspective of human psychological functioning, including development. Evolutionary thinking is part of the cognitive-science perspective that has influenced the study of human cognition and cognitive development during the past two decades. Understanding that our brains and minds evolved to solve specific problems, that the problems faced by infants and children were (and remain) different than those faced by adults, and that the principles of natural selection can be applied not only to changes over evolutionary time but also to changes over a lifetime, can provide us with a better perspective on human nature and human development.

Models of Gene-Environment Interaction

All self-respecting developmentalists believe that development is the result of an interaction between genetic/biologic factors and environmental/experiential factors. There is really no other alternative. Some theorists are more explicit about the nature of the interaction than others, however, and in this section, I will examine two approaches that examine gene-environment interactions and their consequences for development. Each approach posits that the child is an active agent in his or her own development, that development proceeds through the bidirectional effect of structure and function, and that the context in which development occurs is as important as the genes the individual inherits. The two approaches are the *developmental systems approach* (or *developmental contextualism*), as advocated by Gilbert Gottlieb (1991a; 2000; Gottlieb, Wahlsten, & Lickliter, 1998), Richard Lerner (1991), Susan Oyama (2000), and others (see Li, 2003; Lickliter, 1996; Turkewitz & Devenny, 1993), and a theory based on research in behavioral genetics, the *genotype → environment theory* as presented by Sandra Scarr and Kathleen McCartney (1983; Scarr, 1992, 1993). Although debate between theorists in these two camps can be vigorous (see Moore, 2001; Scarr, 1993), for our purposes, the difference between the two approaches can be seen as a matter of degree.

The Developmental Systems Approach

The Concept of Epigenesis

The **developmental systems approach** (so called because it views development as occurring within a system of interacting levels) is centered around the concept of **epigenesis.** Epigenetic phenomena have been defined as "any gene-regulating activity that doesn't involve changes to the DNA code and that can persist through one or more generations" (Pennisi, 2001, p. 1064). Epigenesis involves the action of genes, of course, but also the action of RNA, proteins, neurotransmitters, neurons, and so on, all in interaction with the "environment," broadly defined. Central to the concept of epigenesis is the activity of the organism itself in influencing its own development. According to Oyama, "Fate is constructed, amended, and reconstructed, partly by the emerging organism itself. It is known to no one, not even the genes" (2000, p. 137). Along similar lines, Gottlieb defined epigenesis as "the emergence of new structures and functions during the course of development" (1991a, p. 7) and states that epigenesis reflects a bidirectional relationship between all levels of biological and experiential variables, such that genetic activity both influences and is influenced by structural maturation, which is bidirectionally related to function and activity. This relationship can be expressed as follows:

genetic activity (DNA ↔ RNA ↔ proteins) ↔ structural maturation ↔ function, activity.

According to Gottlieb, "Individual development is characterized by an increase of complexity of organization (that is, the emergence of new structural and functional properties and competencies) at all levels of analysis (molecular, subcellular, cellular, organismic) as a consequence of horizontal and vertical coactions among the organism's parts, including organism-environment coactions" (1991a, p. 7).

The point here is that functioning at any level influences functioning at adjacent levels. For example, genes clearly direct the production of proteins, which in turn determine the formation of structures, such as muscle or nerve cells. But activity of these and surrounding cells can turn on or off a particular gene, causing the cessation or commencement of genetic activity. Moreover, experience in the form of self-produced activity or stimulation from external sources can alter the development of sets of cells.

From this perspective, there are no simple genetic or experiential causes of behavior; all development is

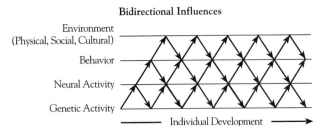

FIGURE 2-2 A simplified schematic of the developmental systems approach, showing a hierarchy of four mutually interacting components. SOURCE: From *Individual development and evolution: The genesis of novel behavior* by G. Gottlieb. Copyright © 1991 by Oxford University Press, Inc. Used by permission of Oxford University Press, Inc.

the product of epigenesis, with complex interactions occurring among multiple levels. This bidirectional approach to development is expressed in Figure 2-2. This figure suggests that we can never understand development merely by looking for genetic effects or for environmental effects; to understand development, we must look at the organism-context relationship (Lerner, 1991). Mark Johnson (1998), in his review of the neural basis of cognitive development, makes this point especially clear: "Since it has become evident that genes interact with their environment at all levels, including the molecular, there is no aspect of development that can be said to be strictly "genetic," that is, exclusively a product of information contained in the genes" (p. 4).

This position should be reminiscent of dynamic systems theories that were discussed in Chapter 1. The developmental systems approach *is* a dynamic systems theory, one that is specific to development. As such, new structures and function emerge during development by means of self-organization through the bidirectional interactions of elements at various levels of organization (that is, genes, RNA, neurons, overt behavior, and so on). As Gottlieb has stated, "the cause of development—what makes development happen—is the relationship between the . . . components, not the components themselves. Genes in themselves cannot cause development any more than stimulation in itself can cause development" (1991a, pp. 7–8).

If the relations expressed in Figure 2-2 approximate reality, there should be substantial plasticity in

development. Yet, it is undeniable that development is constrained by one's genes. Because our parents were humans, we develop in a way that a chimpanzee embryo can never develop (and vice versa). However, environments also constrain development. Genes will be expressed differently in different environments, yielding different patterns of development.

An example of how the effects of genes vary in different environments was provided in a study by Avshalom Caspi and his colleagues (2002), who examined the relationship between possessing a particular copy of a gene and child maltreatment on children's subsequent antisocial and violent behavior. Monoamine oxidase A (MAOA) is an enzyme that metabolizes several types of neurotransmitters in the brain. Research with both laboratory animals and humans has indicated that knocking out the gene responsible for the production of MAOA (which is located on the X chromosome) results in elevated levels of aggression. Low versus high levels of MAOA (or MAOA activity) are believed to reflect different genotypes. That is, different versions of the MAOA gene, or different alleles, are associated with different levels of MAOA activity. Using data on boys from a longitudinal study in New Zealand, Caspi and his colleagues examined the relationship between childhood maltreatment and MAOA activity (low versus high) on antisocial behavior. Their results are shown in Figure 2-3. As can be seen, boys who had been maltreated as children subsequently engaged in more antisocial behavior than nonmaltreated boys did, but this effect was especially strong

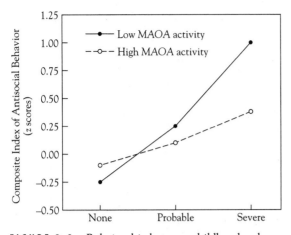

FIGURE 2-3 Relationship between childhood maltreatment (none, probable, severe) and *MAOA* activity (low versus high) on antisocial behavior. SOURCE: Adapted from Caspi, A., McClay, J., Moffitt, T. E., Mill, J., Martin, J., Craig, I. W., Taylor, A., & Poulton, R. (2002). Role of genotype in the cycle of violence in maltreated children. *Science, 297* (2 August), 851–854. Copyright © 2002 American Association for the Advancement of Science. Reprinted with Permission.

for children with low *MAOA* activity. Perhaps equally important, *MAOA* activity itself was not associated with high levels of antisocial behavior. Levels of antisocial behavior were high only for those low-*MAOA*-activity children who experienced probable and (especially) severe maltreatment. This study makes it clear that even genes clearly associated with known specific biochemical and behavior outcomes are expressed differently in different environments and that proposing that any gene is "for" a particular phenotype (for example, the *MAOA* gene is "for" aggression) is overly simplistic and misguided.

But if there is so much plasticity in development, why do almost all members of a species (human or otherwise) develop in a species-typical pattern? The answer is that a child (or a puppy or a chimp) inherits not only species-typical genes, but also a species-typical environment. This is expressed in Robert Lickliter's statement, "the organism-environment relationship is one that is structured on both sides. That is, it is a relation between a structured organism *and* a structured environment. The organism inher-

its not only its genetic complement, but also the structured organization of the environment into which it is born" (1996, pp. 90–91). For example, ducks begin life in eggs, usually surrounded by other eggs, with their mother staying close by them before they hatch. They are able to hear and vocalize before hatching, and it turns out that these abilities contribute to an important aspect of posthatching behavior. Under normal conditions, when baby ducks, shortly after hatching, are put into a large container and hear the maternal call of two species of birds— their own and another—they invariably approach the call from their own species. They seem "instinctively" to know what their own species sounds like and to move toward that sound, something that makes good sense in the wild. However, when experimental procedures are performed so that the embryonic duck in the egg does not hear its mother or any of its siblings and its own vocal chords are temporarily prevented from functioning so that it can produce no sound itself, it fails after hatching to show the species-typical pattern of approaching the call of its own species (see Gottlieb, 1991b). In other words, prehatching experience, particularly hearing its own self-produced vocalizations, plays a major role in posthatching species-typical behavior. The reason that nearly all ducks approach the species-typical call after hatching is that nearly all ducks inherit not only the genetic disposition to make such a selection but also the species-typical environment that provides the necessary experiences for such a pattern to develop. Viewing development from this perspective provides a new meaning for the term *instinctive*. A behavior or function that is inborn in almost all members of the species might be instinctive, but if so, we must consider both the species-typical genes and the species-typical environment as factors contributing to that behavior.

What results such as these indicate is that behaviors (here related to infant-mother attachment) that are found in almost all normal members of a species are influenced by often-subtle characteristics of the environment. Psychological mechanisms at the human level can be viewed similarly. Strong species-universal biases may exist for certain behaviors, but how any particular behavior or mechanism is expressed will depend on the experiences of the individual at certain times in development.

This is fine for ducks, but how does this relate to human cognitive development? The idea is that human children develop in species-typical environments, both prenatal and postnatal, and that experiences in these environments may direct development in species-typical ways. Take, for example, a proposal by Gerald Turkewitz (1993) concerning the functioning of the two hemispheres of the brain. The brain is composed of two sections, called **hemispheres,** which are connected by a large bundle of nerves called the corpus callosum. Although similar, the two hemispheres are not identical. Each hemisphere controls the opposite side of the body, with one hemisphere typically predominating over the other, resulting in a left- or right-side preference. For example, there are far more right-handed people in the world than left handers, which reflects a hemispheric asymmetry, with the left hemisphere (which controls the right side of the body) being dominant relative to the right (which controls the left side of the body). Such an asymmetry is found even in neonates, with newborns turning their heads to the right more often than to the left. Also, newborns process speech sounds more effectively when the sounds are presented to the right ear (and thus left hemisphere) than when they are presented to the left ear, further demonstrating hemispheric asymmetries. However, the right hemisphere seems to be more involved in recognizing faces, another important ability for human infants to have.

What is the origin of these asymmetries? Turkewitz (1993) proposes that they have to do with the timing of brain development and the nature of prenatal auditory experiences. Turkewitz presents evidence that the right hemisphere begins developing before the left hemisphere, but that later in prenatal development, the left hemisphere catches up and surpasses the right in size and complexity. Early in development, when the right hemisphere is developing most rapidly, because of characteristics of the uterine environment and the relatively undeveloped state of the fetus's auditory system, the most salient auditory signals for a fetus are internally generated sounds, such as gastrointestinal gurglings and cardiovascular noises

(that is, the heartbeat and the sound of pumping blood) produced by the mother. These are hardly important sounds for such a cognitively flexible and social species as *Homo sapiens*. As gestation proceeds and the fetus's auditory system improves, externally produced noises become more salient, particularly maternal speech. This is when the left hemisphere is developing most rapidly. Turkewitz suggests that it is the interaction of the timing of development (faster development for the right hemisphere early and for the left hemisphere late) with auditory experiences (clearer signals from external speech sources later in development) that causes hemispheric asymmetries. Because the left hemisphere is developing most rapidly when maternal speech is most salient, it develops a specialty for processing speech. This leaves the right hemisphere "unspecialized," so to speak. This means that after birth, when vision is possible, "the right hemisphere would be relatively unengaged and available for processing the facial information. In this way the right hemisphere could begin to develop a specialization for dealing with facial information" (Turkewitz, 1993, p. 136).

Turkewitz's proposal is intriguing. It suggests that asymmetries observed in infancy (and expressed later in visual and language processing in adults) have their origins in prenatal experiences, in interaction with genetically paced maturation. Turkewitz may be wrong, but the argument is logically sound and consistent with what we know about development, and aspects of his hypothesis are testable.

As another example, take the perception of pain. Despite its obvious discomfort, perceiving painful stimuli "properly" is clearly adaptive. Might experiences early in life alter how the brain is organized for perceiving pain? This question was experimentally addressed in neonatal rats (Ruda et al., 2000). Neurons in the spinal cords of rats develop during embryonic and early postnatal times, typically a time when rat pups are protected by their mother from painful experiences. When newborn rats were exposed to painful stimulation, however, the nerve circuits that respond to pain were permanently rewired, changing the way they responded to sensory stimulation, making the animals as adults more sensitive to pain. Only within the past 20 years have physicians bothered giving young human infants anesthesia for some medical procedures, believing that their perception of painful stimuli was minimal. These findings suggest that such unexpected stimulation, even if the infants seem not to perceive it as acutely painful, can alter the species-typical course of development in an adverse way.

Developmental Timing

As any comedian will tell you, timing is everything. In the developmental systems approach, the timing of a particular event during development can influence substantially what effect that event will have on development.

Perhaps the concept most central to the issue of the timing of development is that of a **critical period.** The critical period for a specific skill or ability is the time in development (usually early in life) when it is most easily acquired. If a requisite experience occurs outside of this critical period (either too early or too late), the target skill will not be readily acquired or possibly not acquired at all. (The term *sensitive period* is sometimes used rather than *critical period* to reflect the fact that although the organism is most sensitive to a particular event at a particular time, similar or perhaps more intense experiences later in development can still have considerable influence on development. For the sake of simplicity, I will use the term *critical period* throughout this chapter.) Figure 2-4 depicts the idea that a behavior is most easily acquired during a critical period. Researchers have suggested that many aspects of human cognitive development can be described as critical periods (see Bornstein, 1989; Ceci, 1996), with language being perhaps the clearest example (Lenneberg, 1967; Newport, 1991). Both a first and second language are acquired more easily when learned in early childhood. Although adolescents and adults can learn a second language, it is usually only with great difficulty, and they rarely attain the facility in that language observed when it is learned during childhood. (More will be said about a critical period for language acquisition in Chapter 11.)

Examples of the significance of timing of perceptual experience come from research by Lickliter

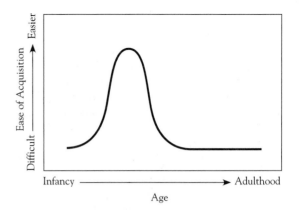

FIGURE 2-4 Some cognitive abilities, such as language, might be most easily acquired during a critical period in (usually early) development.

(1990), working with auditory and visual stimulation of bobwhite quails. Like ducks, bobwhite quails approach the maternal call of their own species shortly after hatching. As demonstrated earlier by Gottlieb, this phenomenon has been attributed to auditory experiences the birds have before hatching. But, Lickliter reasoned, this is caused not just by the *presence* of auditory experiences before hatching, but also by the *absence* of other sensory experiences, following an argument originally made by Turkewitz and Kenny (1982). Turkewitz and Kenny noted that the sensory systems in infants of many species function poorly at birth. Such inefficient functioning is actually adaptive, however, in that it protects the infant from sensory overload, permitting it to deal with small bits of simplified stimuli, making it easier for the immature being to make sense of its world. Also, poor functioning in one sensory system (vision, for example) might permit an earlier developing sensory system (hearing, for example) to develop without undue competition for neural resources.

This is exactly the logic that Lickliter adopted for his study with bobwhite quails. As in all vertebrates, hearing develops before vision (Gottlieb, 1971). Lickliter argued that the slower development of vision in bobwhite quails allows the auditory system to develop without competition from the visual system. What would happen if quails were given extra visual experience before hatching? One possibility is that it might hinder important aspects of auditory development, such as showing a preference for the maternal call.

Lickliter (1990) developed a procedure whereby he removed part of the eggshell and provided visual experience to bobwhite quails two to three days before hatching. Control quails had the end of the egg opened but received no visual experience. This ensured that the behavior of the experimental birds would not be caused by removing part of the eggshell, per se, but by the additional visual experience the chicks received. Lickliter then tested those birds in an auditory preference test in which the birds were placed in an oval container with speakers at opposite ends. From one speaker came the maternal call of a bobwhite quail and from the other speaker came the maternal call of a chicken. The researchers observed which speaker, if either, the chicks approached.

The results of this experiment are shown in Figure 2-5. As can be seen in the figure, the control birds demonstrated the species-typical pattern when tested, with nearly all the birds showing a preference for the maternal call of their own species (that is, approaching the speaker from which the bobwhite quail call came). This was not the case for the birds that had the extra visual experience, however. A majority of these birds showed no preference or approached the speaker producing the maternal call of a chicken! I should note that these animals displayed greater visual discrimination abilities. That is, the prehatching visual experience resulted in enhanced visual abilities but at the expense of auditory abilities, which are important in their early development of attachment.

This and other studies (see Bjorklund, 1997a) clearly demonstrate that the timing of perceptual experience is critically important, and that earlier experience is not always better experience. This is worth remembering for human infants. Might their sensory limitations actually be adaptive, and might extra stimulation in one modality interfere with development in other modalities? Or consider a related question: Is early learning always beneficial? Might providing an infant with too much stimulation or "learning tasks" too soon in development have a negative effect?

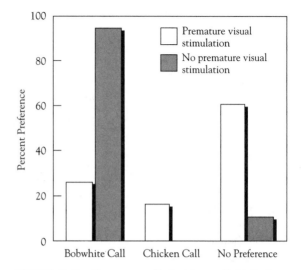

FIGURE 2-5 Percentage of bobwhite quail chicks that approached the bobwhite maternal call, the chicken maternal call, or showed no preference as a function of whether they received premature visual stimulation or not. SOURCE: Adapted from R. Lickliter (1990), Premature visual stimulation accelerates intersensory functioning in bobwhite quail neonates. *Developmental Psychobiology, 23,* 15–27.

There is little research on this issue. In one study conducted on infant monkeys, Harry Harlow (1959) began giving monkeys training on a discrimination-learning task at different ages ranging from 60 to 366 days. For example, monkeys were to choose which of several stimuli that varied in several dimensions (size, shape, color, and so on) was associated with a prize. Beginning at 120 days of age or older, monkeys were given a more complicated learning task. Monkeys' performance on these more complicated problems is shown in Figure 2-6 as a function of the age at which they began training. Chance performance for these problems was 50%. As can be seen, monkeys that began training early in life (at 60 and 90 days) never solved many more than 60% of the problems and soon fell behind the monkeys that began training later (at 120 and 150 days of age). That is, despite having more experience with the problems, the early-trained monkeys performed more poorly than the later-trained monkeys. Harlow concluded,

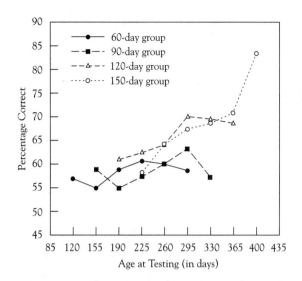

FIGURE 2-6 Discrimination learning set performance for monkeys as a function of age at which testing was begun. SOURCE: H. Harlow, (1959, December). The development of learning in the Rhesus monkey. *American Scientist*, 459–479. Reprinted with permission.

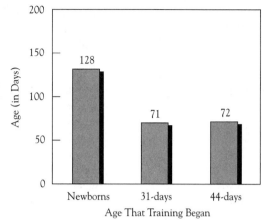

FIGURE 2-7 Age at which infants reached the criterion as a function of when training was begun. SOURCE: Adapted from Papousek, H. (1977). The development of learning ability in infancy (Entwicklung der Lernfähigkeit im Säuglingsalter). In G. Nissen (Ed.) *Intelligence, learning, and learning disabilities (Intelligenz, Lernen und Lernstörungen)* (pp. 75–93). Berlin: Springer-Verlag.

There is a tendency to think of learning or training as intrinsically good and necessarily valuable to the organism. It is entirely possible, however, that training can be either helpful or harmful, depending upon the nature of the training and the organism's stage of development. (1959, p. 472)

In the only research with human infants that I am aware of related to this idea, Hanus Papousek (1977) conditioned infants to turn their heads to a buzzer or a bell. Training began either at birth or at 31 or 44 days of age. Infants who began training at birth took many more trials before they learned the task (814 trials) than did infants who began later (278 and 224 trials for the 31- and 44-day-old infants, respectively). Figure 2-7 shows the age (in days) at which infants reached the criterion on this conditioning problem as a function of when they began training. Similar to Harlow's results with monkeys, infants who began at birth required more days to learn the task than did the infants who began at an older age.

Although there has been almost no research with human infants on the topic of "sensory overstimulation," researchers have speculated that some of the deficits experienced by premature infants are caused by exposure to too much sensory information too soon. Neonatologist Heidelise Als (1995) suggests that the early sensory stimulation that premature infants experience might adversely affect brain development by requiring them to process perceptual stimulation that they would not normally deal with for several more weeks (see also Lickliter, 2000). As in the research with quail chicks, the result might be enhanced performance later in life in some domains, but at the expense of functioning in others, which often leads to forms of learning disabilities. Als notes that these deficits are often accompanied by accelerated development or enhanced abilities in other areas as well, such as in mathematics. This idea is provocative, although still speculative. But it is consistent with the idea that the timing of developmentally sensitive periods in the brain are correlated with the species-typical timing of perceptual experiences. When stimulation exceeds the species-typical schedule, patterns of development will be affected accordingly.

These findings do not mean that infants (or preemies) should not be given adequate stimulation, or that early learning is maladaptive. It's unlikely that learning experiences such as infants in the Papousek study had would have any long-term effects. Many more infants in the world are potentially subject to receiving too *little* rather than too much stimulation. However, the research does suggest that stimulation far in excess of the species norm can adversely affect later learning and that there might be no benefit to beginning a learning task very early in life (Bjorklund, 1997a).

More generally, the differential timing of maturation in various areas of the brain influences how the brain becomes organized. For example, Jeffrey Elman et al. (1996) proposed that early developing brain regions effectively serve as filters for later developing areas. The type and manner in which these early developing areas can process information determines in a very real sense the type and way later developing areas can process information. These can be potent constraints on brain development, what I referred to in Chapter 1 as *chronotopic constraints*. From this perspective, it is not content that is inherited (representational constraints) but, rather, the timing of events, and this timing is largely responsible for the species-typical patterns of brain and cognitive development that we see.

The Genotype → Environment Theory

Related to the developmental systems approach are several theories that stem from the field of **behavior genetics,** which studies genetic effects on behavior and complex psychological characteristics such as intelligence and personality (Plomin et al., 1997; Scarr, 1992). These theories have attracted much attention among mainstream developmentalists, partly because they use human behavioral outcomes such as personality or IQ scores as data rather than generalizing results from ducks, rats, or bobwhite quails to humans. This is also a reason for the substantial controversy the approach has produced.

Academic psychologists have long been reluctant to accept a strong influence of genetics on human behavior. The argument against a genetic influence on behavior goes something like this: If we are what our genes determine us to be, then there is little hope of modifying the human spirit or human behavior through environmental intervention. If genes affect not only blood type and eye color but also behavior, personality, and intelligence, biology truly is destiny.

Yet, biology rarely dictates anything in an absolute way. As illustrated by Figure 2-2, all genetic effects are moderated by environmental ones. Even the genes for eye color must be expressed in a developing embryo, which is exposed to uncountable environmental factors as a result of its own development. The fact that genes influence behavior does not mean that environment plays only an inconsequential role. To deny the significant role of genetics in behavior is to place one's head in the sand, but to proclaim that genetics determines our personalities, intellects, and behavior is to seriously misinterpret reality.

Genotype → Environment Effects

One of the most influential theories from behavior genetics with respect to cognitive development is Scarr and McCartney's **genotype → environment theory.** Basically, Scarr and McCartney's proposal is that one's genotype (one's actual genetic constitution) influences which environments one encounters and the type of experiences one has. Their basic contention is that *genes drive experience*. One's genetic makeup determines how one organizes one's world. Thus, environment does play a significant role in shaping intellect, but a person's inherited characteristics largely determine what those experiences are and how they are perceived.

Figure 2-8 presents a schematic of Scarr and McCartney's model of behavioral development. A child's phenotype (his or her observed characteristics) is influenced both by the child's genotype and by his or her rearing environment. The child's genotype is determined by the genotype of his or her parents. The parents' genotype also influences the environment. Parents' genetic characteristics affect the types of environments they feel most comfortable in. In this model, however, the child's genotype has an impact on the environment, which affects the

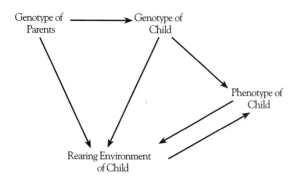

FIGURE 2-8 Scarr and McCartney's model of behavioral development. SOURCE: Adapted from "How People Make Their Own Environments: A Theory of Genotype-Environment Effects," by S. Scarr and K. McCartney, *Child Development*, 54, 424–435. Copyright © 1983 The Society for Research in Child Development, Inc. Adapted with permission.

TABLE 2-1 Three types of genotype → environment effects in Scarr & McCartney's Genotype → Environment Model

Passive:	Biological parents provide both genes and environment for child. Passive effects *decrease* with age.
Evocative:	Temperamental characteristics of child evokes responses from others. Evocative effects remain *constant* with age.
Active:	Children seek out environments consistent with their genotypes. Active effects *increase* with age.

child's development. Thus, characteristics of the child, as well as the rearing environment and genetic contributions of the parents, influence the course of development.

Scarr and McCartney posit three types of genotype → environment effects that vary in influence over the course of development (see Table 2-1). They are *passive, evocative,* and *active.* Passive effects occur when genetically related parents provide the rearing environment of the child. When biological parents rear a child, the effects of genetics and environment cannot be separated because the people who provide the genetic constitution for a child also provide the environment. The influence of passive effects is proposed to decline with age.

Evocative effects occur when the child elicits responses from others that are influenced by his or her genotype. For example, an irritable child is responded to differently than is a well-tempered child, and the type of attention received by an infant who likes to cuddle is different from that received by an infant who does not want to be held. During early childhood, an attentive and cooperative child receives more positive interactions from parents and teachers than does an uncooperative, distractible

child. Evocative effects presumably remain constant throughout development.

Active effects occur when one's genotype affects the type of environments one chooses to experience. A person actively selects an environment in which he or she feels comfortable. For example, children interested in competitive sports would likely seek other like-minded children to play with that would be very different from the type of people sport-phobic children would seek out. Accordingly, people with different genotypes choose to interact in different environments and thus have different experiences that influence their development. Active effects increase with age as children become increasingly independent of their parents and able to select their own environments.

How does Scarr and McCartney's model relate to cognitive development? For one thing, this model suggests that parents' environmental influence on children should be greatest during the early childhood years and decrease with age as active genotype → environment effects increase. Evidence for this position comes from an adoption study by Scarr and Weinberg (1978). They reported that the average correlations of the IQs of samples of adopted siblings (that is, genetically unrelated children living together) measured in early childhood ranged from .25 to .39. This means that there was a moderate level of similarity between the IQs of biologically unrelated children growing up together, a reflection of an environmental influence on IQ. However, the correlation of the IQs for adopted siblings measured late in adolescence was 0! This means that knowing the IQ of one child would not help you predict to any degree the IQ of his or her adopted sibling. The predictive power is zero. The results reflect the fact that the longer these genetically unrelated siblings lived together, the less alike in IQ scores they became. Similar findings of reduced correlations of IQs with age have been reported for dizygotic (nonidentical) twins. Correlations of the IQs of dizygotic twins computed during the preschool years ranged from .60 to .75 but were reduced to .55 when measured later in childhood (Matheny et al., 1981). In fact, siblings in general become less alike in most respects the older they get (McCartney, Harris, & Bernieri, 1990). Following Scarr and McCartney's model, passive genotype → environment effects, as reflected by the type of environments parents provide for their children, decrease with age, and active genotype → environment effects increase; as they get older, children are increasingly able to select environments that suit their particular needs, and such selection is determined primarily by one's genotype.

But then, do genes *cause* intelligence? Interestingly, Scarr and McCartney's theory ends up giving the environment a substantial role in directing development. Genotype causes a child to choose certain environments, environments that are compatible with the child's genetic constitution, and the experiences in these environments shape the child's cognition (and other important psychological characteristics). From this perspective, one's genes serve to select "appropriate" environments, but experience is actually responsible for crafting the intellect (see also Bouchard et al., 1990). (The heritability of intelligence is discussed in greater detail in Chapter 16.)

Scarr and McCartney's model illustrates how genetic and environmental factors might interact to produce different patterns and levels of intelligence. What is particularly attractive about this model is its consideration of developmental effects. Genetic and environmental effects are not viewed as constants but as dynamic factors that have different effects on intelligence at different points in time. This theory, in effect, postulates a transaction between developmental function and individual differences. As children become more autonomous with age, the influence of genetic and environmental factors on individual differences changes.

"Good Enough" Parents

Scarr expanded her initial position and proposed that "ordinary differences between families have little effect on children's development, unless the family is outside of a normal, developmental range. Good enough, ordinary parents probably have the same effects on their children's development as culturally defined super-parents" (1992, p. 15). In other words, because of the strong influence of genotype → environment effects, individual differences in parenting should have little consequence for children's development. Although this is a logical extension of the original theory, it takes the theory to an extreme that many contemporary developmental psychologists don't like; several psychologists have criticized the theory harshly (see Baumrind, 1993; Jackson, 1993).

As we'll see in Chapter 16, differences in how children are reared are related to individual differences in their levels of intelligence and academic achievement. Scarr's point, reiterated and expanded in a response to her critics (Scarr, 1993), is that children around the world grow up to be productive (and reproductive) members of their societies despite considerable differences in child-rearing practices. A behaviorally flexible species that required high-quality parenting for survival would likely be extinct before too long. Thus, the species evolved so that children could tolerate great flexibility in childrearing practices and still grow up to be "normal."

But Scarr's critics are not concerned with this level of development. They point out that differences in parenting style and opportunities make a tremendous difference in the eventual outcome of a child (Baumrind, 1993), and **"good enough" parents** are just not good enough for a sizable minority of children in our society. Scarr (1993) concurs. Children who lack opportunities and experiences associated with the dominant culture will show intellectual and social detriments relative to children in the majority culture. Scarr notes that these effects can often be ameliorated by education.

The difference between Scarr and her critics seems primarily to be one of focus: Scarr is taking an evolutionary perspective, looking at how individual children become functioning members of the species; her critics are focusing instead on individual differences among children within a culture. Each level is important and each is legitimate, but it is easy for the two camps to argue right past one another, certain that the other camp is missing the point, when in reality they are each talking about different levels of human functioning.

In support of both Scarr and her critics is research on "resilient" children—children who develop social and intellectual competence despite growing up in impoverished and "high-risk" environments (Masten & Coatsworth, 1998). Why do some children from the worst environments "make it," whereas others flounder? Perhaps the single most important factor is competent parenting, starting early in life. This fact is consistent with Scarr's critics, who point out that individual differences in how parents interact with their children is essential to their eventual success. However, Masten and Coatsworth point out that, although many parents do fail to provide adequate warmth and support for their children, it does not take extraordinary efforts to raise a competent child, even in unfavorable environments. "Through the process of evolution, parenting has been shaped to protect development; nature has created in ordinary parents a powerful protective system for child development" (Masten & Coatsworth, 1998, p. 213).

Both the developmental systems approach and the genotype → environment model posit continuous, bidirectional interactions between biologic and environmental factors in development. There are some important distinctions between the two approaches, centering mainly around the degree to which outside experience, influenced by one's genes, modifies the organism versus the degree to which a biological organism shapes its own development through epigenetic processes. Much vigorous debate could and has been generated based on these distinctions. But the critical point for our purposes is that these two models take the transaction of biologic and environmental factors seriously, making it clear that we need to give more than lip service to the interaction of the multiple factors that produce development. This is more easily said than done, but these approaches demonstrate how biology and environment can be included in serious scientific models that help us put development in proper perspective.

The Development of the Brain

The human brain is perhaps the most marvelous invention in the universe. Unlike the brains of any other species, ours provides us with self-awareness and a behavioral flexibility that has allowed us to create culture and to adapt to a limitless diversity of environments. Other animal brains are quite impressive, but only the human brain has led to language, mathematics, physics, and art.

Differences in thinking between humans and other mammals are, of course, directly related to differences in their brains. But the human brain does not have any special structures that other mammals don't have. The major differences between human brains and those of other mammals is primarily in the greater amount of area that is devoted to the cerebral cortex and the extended period of postnatal growth.

At birth, the human brain weighs about 350 grams—25% of its eventual adult weight of about 1400 grams. Compare this to overall body weight. At birth, an infant weighs only about 5% of what he or she will weigh as an adult. Stated another way, the brain accounts for about 10% of the overall body weight of a newborn, while accounting for only about 2% of the overall body weight of an adult. By 6 months, the brain weighs 50% of what it will in adulthood; at 2 years about 75%; at 5 years, 90%; and at 10 years, 95% (Tanner, 1978). In contrast, total body weight is about 20% of eventual adult weight at 2 years and only 50% at 10 years. So the brain, which grows rapidly before birth, continues its rapid development postnatally. The rapid postnatal growth of the brain and head relative to the body in

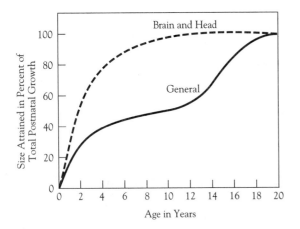

FIGURE 2-9 Growth curves for the brain and head and the body in general. SOURCE: Adapted from "The Measurement of the Body in Childhood," by R. E. Scammon. In J. A. Harris, C. M. Jackson, D. G. Paterson, R. E. Scammon, (Eds.), *The Measurement of Man*, University of Minnesota Press, 1930.

general is depicted in Figure 2-9. From this perspective, babies are brainy creatures indeed. But from another point of view, the brain of a newborn is grossly underdeveloped. Although the brain works effectively enough to direct basic physiological functions (breathing, wake/sleep cycles), it cannot control coordinated movement and it cannot perform the mental operations so characteristic of our species. Despite its size, the infant brain is far from the organ it will become.

The human brain, directly or indirectly, is responsible for controlling all aspects of behavior, from respiration and digestion to learning, and our most advanced forms of cognition. Our concern here is with the portion of the brain most associated with thought, the neocortex, or cerebral cortex. The neocortex is the most recent structure to appear in evolutionary time, associated primarily with mammals, having its greatest manifestation in primates and especially humans (MacLean, 1990). Other areas of the brain—such as the limbic system, which is the seat of emotion—are also important and significantly influence human behavior, but the neocortex—particularly the *frontal lobes* (sometimes referred to as

the prefrontal lobes) of the neocortex—provides the characteristics that we most associate with humanness. I will discuss briefly certain aspects of the neocortex and its development later in this section.

Our knowledge of brain development and its relation to cognition has increased substantially during the past decade, primarily because of new technologies that permit the imaging of brain activities (Casey & de Haan, 2002; Johnson, 1998; Posner et al., 2001). These **neuroimaging techniques** include, among others, *high-density event-related potentials*, which are a form of *electroencephalography* (EEG) measurements that permits the detailed recording of brain activity when children solve cognitive tasks or are presented with specific stimuli; *positron emission tomography* (PET) and *single photon emission tomography* (SPECT), in which radioactive materials are injected into participants and changes in radioactivity are used to reflect glucose consumption in specific areas of the brain; and *functional magnetic resonance imaging* (fMRI), which is a noninvasive technique that measures blood flow to the brain while children are performing cognitive tasks. There are, of course, limits to such methods, but these and related new technologies promise that a new understanding of the relation between brain and cognitive development will be soon upon us. But we must first examine the basic building block of the brain—the neuron.

Neuronal Development

The brain, and the nervous system in general, is a communication system. Electrical and chemical signals are transmitted from one **neuron,** or specialized nerve cell, to another. Estimates of the number of neurons in the mature human brain vary from 10 billion to more than 100 billion. Each neuron is connected to hundreds, and in many cases thousands, of other neurons via **synapses,** which are the small spaces between neurons through which messages are passed. The result is many trillions of connections among neurons.

Figure 2-10 presents a drawing of a neuron. The main part of the neuron is the cell body, which contains the nucleus. Extending from the cell body are

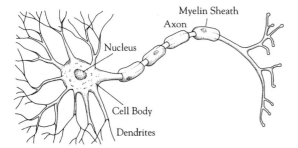

FIGURE 2-10 Primary structures of the neuron.
SOURCE: From *Looking at Children: An Introduction to Child Development*, by D. F. Bjorklund and B. R. Bjorklund, 1992. Belmont, CA: Wadsworth, p. 127.

many protractions, one of which is called the **axon,** a long fiber that carries messages away from the cell body to other cells. The other, more numerous fibers are called **dendrites,** which receive messages from other cells and transfer them to the cell body. Unlike most other cells in the human body, neurons are not compressed together but are separated. As mentioned earlier, the tiny spaces between the dendrites of one cell and the axon of another are called synapses. Electrical messages flowing down the axon of one cell cause the release of certain chemicals, called **neurotransmitters,** into the synapse. Neurotransmitters, which include dopamine, acetylcholine, and serotonin, move across the space between the cells and are "read" at the dendrites of the adjacent cell, which convert the message back to an electrical signal and pass it on to its cell body. So two neurons do not actually touch one another, but pass their information chemically through the small gaps that separate them. Conditions at the synapse (amount of and type of neurotransmitters available) affect the transmission of the messages among neurons.

Proliferation, Migration, and Differentiation

Neurons go through at least three stages of development (Spreen, Risser, & Edgell, 1995). The first stage is referred to as **proliferation,** which is the process of cell division by mitosis. Proliferation occurs early in development, during the prenatal period. It was once

believed that the seventh month after conception essentially marked the end of neuron production. However, relatively recent research in both laboratory animals (Gould et al., 1999) and humans (Eriksson et al., 1998) indicates that new neurons are produced at least in some areas of the brain, specifically the hippocampus, a structure that has been implicated in the formation of new memories. However, the extent to which the production of new neurons occurs in humans, and the role it plays in development and aging, are still highly speculative as of this writing.

The second stage in neuronal development is **migration.** Once produced, the cells migrate, or move, to what will be their permanent position in the brain, where they collect with other cells to form the major parts of the brain. Not all cells migrate at the same time, but most cells have arrived at the final position in the brain by five months after conception (Spreen et al., 1995). Obviously, it is important that cells destined to be in a certain part of the brain be where they are supposed to be. Mistakes do occasionally happen, however, and faulty neural migration has been found to be associated with a variety of human disorders, including some forms of dyslexia (reading disabilities), schizophrenia, fetal alcohol syndrome, and methylmercury poisoning, among others (Nowakowski, 1987).

The third stage in neuronal development is **differentiation** (or *cytodifferentiation*). Once at their final destination, neurons begin to grow in size, produce more and longer dendrites, and extend their axons farther and farther away from the cell body. Synapses are created during this stage. When an axon meets an appropriate dendrite from another neuron, a synapse is formed.

Synaptogenesis and Selective Cell Death

The process of synapse formation, or **synaptogenesis,** is rapid during the early years of life when the brain is first becoming organized. Synaptogenesis continues throughout life, as the brain changes in response to new information, although the rate at which new synapses are formed is never as great as it is during those pre- and postnatal months when the brain is growing most rapidly. Synapse formation is perhaps more rapid in the months immediately following birth, but the peak of synapse formation varies for different parts of the brain. For example, a burst of synapse formation in the visual cortex beginning about 3 or 4 months peaks between 4 and 12 months. At this time, the visual cortex has about 50% *more* synapses than there are in the adult brain. A similar pattern is found in the prefrontal cortex (the "thinking" part of the brain), but the peak number of synapses is not attained until about 24 months of age (Huttenlocher, 1994).

At this point, the infant brain has many more synapses and neurons than it needs, and a process of cell and synaptic pruning begins. Actually, the pruning had begun late during the prenatal period in a process known as **selective cell death.** Cell death and synaptic pruning occur at different rates for different parts of the brain. For example, the adult density of synapses for the visual cortex is attained between 2 and 4 years of age; in contrast, children continue to have more neurons and synapses than do adults in the prefrontal areas into their teen years (Huttenlocher, 1994). Dendritic branching seems to follow a somewhat different pattern. The dendrites of many neurons increase in diversity from infancy to adulthood (Quartz & Sejnowski, 1997; see Figure 2-11).

Rises and Declines in Neural Development

The pattern just described for synaptogenesis is one of rapid development (that is, synapse creation) followed by a decline in the number of synapses (and neurons). Other aspects of brain development show a similar rise and decline over childhood. For example, evidence indicates that the basic metabolism of the brain (the rate at which it uses energy) increases sharply after the first year of life and peaks at about 150% of the adult rate between the ages of 4 and 5 years (Chugani, Phelps, & Mazziota, 1987). Evidence for this comes from studies using PET scans, which measure the amount of glucose uptake in the resting brain. After age 5 or so, the rate of glucose consumption slows down, reaching adult levels at about age 9 years. Thus, not only do infants and children have more neurons and synapses than adults,

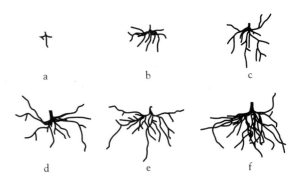

FIGURE 2-11 Drawings of basal dendrites of layer V human pyramidal cells: (a) newborn; (b) 3 months; (c) 6 months; (d) 15 months; (e) 24 months; (f) adult. SOURCE: Schade, J. P., & van Groenigen, W. B. (1961). Structural organization of the human cerebral cortex. I. Maturation of the middle frontal gyrus. *Acta Anatomica, 47*, 72–111. Reprinted with permission.

but their brains are also working harder (or at least using more calories) than those of adults.

In addition to changes in the actual structure of the neurons, developmental changes occur in the presence of various neurotransmitters. Neurotransmitters are chemicals that are found in the synapses that promote the electrical/chemical communication between cells. Several of these show increases followed by decreases over infancy and childhood, similar to the changes seen in synapses. These include glutamate, GABA, and serotonin (Johnson, 1998).

What function might there be in this rise and fall in several aspects of brain development? One proposal is that the hypermetabolism seen during the preschool years might be necessary for the rapid learning that occurs during this time (Elman et al., 1996). (Think of how children's language development proceeds from uttering only single words around 10 months to speaking in long paragraphs by age 3 or 4.) Preschool children also have more neurons and synapses than older children, and, I think it's fair to say, more to learn that is truly "new." These elevated levels of synapses and neurotransmitters also surely afford greater plasticity should brain damage occur.

Why the slowdown in later childhood into adulthood? I have no good answer for this other than to suggest that the tasks that must be solved by the older brain apparently require a different organization, needing less flexibility in number of neurons and perhaps synapses (much of what the brain will need to process "automatically" has already been established by 4 years of age) but greater differentiation in dendritic branching.

Myelination

Not all aspects of neuronal development show the "rise and decline" pattern, however. Some processes show only increases over early development, and one such important characteristic is **myelination. Myelin** is a fatty substance that surrounds the axons of neurons and promotes faster transmission of electrical signals. Compared with unmyelinated fibers, myelinated nerve fibers fire more rapidly, have lower thresholds of sensitivity to stimulation, and have greater functional specificity, meaning that there is less "leakage" of electrical impulse, so that only the target set of neurons are likely to get activated.

The process of myelination is a gradual one, beginning during the prenatal months and continuing into adolescence and beyond. Figure 2-12 shows the schedule of myelination for various parts of the human brain. The thin line on the left denotes when myelination for that brain structure begins, and the thicker line on the right denotes when myelination has reached adult levels. Note that myelination begins prenatally for the sensory system, with most sensory structures being completely myelinated within the first year. This corresponds to the well-developed sensory abilities of human infants and the adultlike sensory capacities they possess long before they can speak. Myelination of the motor areas follows closely, with most of these brain structures being completely myelinated before the second year. Again, this corresponds to the development of motor abilities in young children, most of whom are walking before their second birthdays. The final areas, which are labeled the integrative systems, correspond to the higher brain areas and are involved in complex cognition. Here a slower development of myelination is seen, continuing well into adolescence and adulthood (see Korner, 1991; Yakovlev & Lecours, 1967).

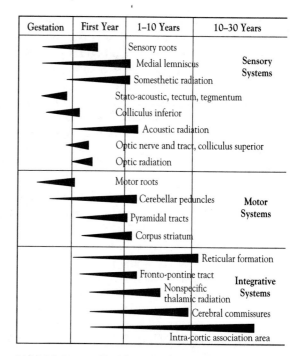

FIGURE 2-12 Developmental pattern of myelination for different areas of the human brain. SOURCE: "The Myelogenetic Cycles of Regional Maturation of the Brain," by P. I. Yakovlev and A. R. Lecours. In A. Minkowski (ed.), *Regional Development of the Brain in Early Life*. Copyright © 1967 Blackwell Scientific Publications, Ltd. Reprinted with permission.

Although only relatively gross assessments can be made, changes in degree of myelination in the integrative brain areas during childhood and adolescence are associated with changes in complex mental processes, such as language, planning, and attention (Lecours, 1975). One reason proposed for this relation is that faster transmission of nerve impulses is afforded by fully myelinated nerves. Speed of processing plays an important role in cognition and cognitive development (see Chapter 5), and it is likely that age-related changes in myelination contribute significantly to these cognitive changes. Also, because increased myelination results in less "leakage" of signals between neurons, there is less interference. This has also been suggested as an important component of cognitive development, with older children showing greater resistance to interference (Dempster, 1993) or greater abilities to inhibit irrelevant cognitive signals (Diamond & Taylor, 1996; Harnishfeger & Bjorklund, 1993), resulting in broad changes in overall cognitive competencies. The correlation between cognitive development and levels of myelination is seen in monkeys as well as in humans (Gibson, 1991). Although the sequence of myelination provides a rough index of general brain development, it is an imperfect one. Neurological functioning begins before myelin appears on nerves, and specific loss of myelin does not always result in the expected loss of function in diseases such as multiple sclerosis (see Korner, 1991).

The amount of myelination is influenced, to some extent, by experience. Research has shown that animals given extra or atypical experience (for example, swimming for rats) or prevented from having species-typical experience (for example, raising kittens or mice in the dark) have corresponding increases or decreases in degree of myelination (see Korner, 1991). However, the amount of change in myelination resulting from these enriching or depriving experiences is relatively small (about 10 to 20%), suggesting that the developmental rate of myelination is largely under maturational control. Nevertheless, as Melvin Korner (1991) points out, the effect of experience on myelination, although small compared with that attributed to genetic control, is significant, and "mutual interaction of biology and experience must always be considered to be the rule" (p. 191).

How Do Young Brains Get Hooked Up?

I have described briefly the process of synaptogenesis and related development of neurons, such as myelination. But how do brains actually get wired? That is, what mechanisms are responsible for building a brain that eventually will be able to recognize faces, solve arithmetic problems, talk, and read? Perhaps the position accepted implicitly by most brain scientists throughout most of the 20th century was that the brain becomes specialized, and complex cognition thus arises, through intrinsic genetic and bio-

chemical mechanisms. In other words, genes dictate the formation, migration, and differentiation of neurons, with experience serving only to "fine tune" the brain. Few developmental neuroscientists believe this today, arguing instead that brain development involves an extended process that is greatly influenced by postnatal experience (Johnson, 2001).

The Role of Experience in Brain Development

With respect to the survival of neurons and the process of synaptogenesis, William Greenough and his associates (Greenough, Black, & Wallace, 1987) proposed that specific experiences produce neural activity that in turn determines which of the excess synapses will survive (see also Black et al., 1998; Johnson, 1998, 2001; Nelson, 2001). The nervous system of animals (including humans) has been prepared by evolution to expect certain types of stimulation, such as a three-dimensional world consisting of moving objects. Greenough and his colleagues referred to the processes whereby synapses are formed and maintained when an organism has species-typical experiences as **experience-expectant processes** (or **experience-expectant synaptogenesis**); as a result, functions will develop for all members of a species, given a species-typical environment. Early experience of merely viewing a normal world, for example, is sufficient for the visual nervous system to develop properly. Those neurons and connections that receive the species-expected experience live and become organized with other activated neurons, and those that do not receive such activation die. Thus, although the infant comes into the world prepared and "prewired" for certain experiences and to develop certain abilities, these abilities are substantially influenced by experience. What is hardwired seems to be a susceptibility to certain environmental experiences rather than the circuitry for detailed behaviors themselves (a form of architectural constraints discussed in Chapter 1).

Examples of experience-expectant processes can be seen in research that restricts the species-typical perceptual experiences of an animal. For instance, cats or rats reared in total darkness or in the absence of patterned light later have difficulty making simple visual discriminations. That is, because they were not exposed to visual stimulation early in life, when later provided with visual experience they act as if they cannot see or at least do not see normally (Crabtree & Riesen, 1979). In humans, cataract patients who suddenly gain sight via surgery have difficulty making simple visual discriminations. For example, for several weeks after surgery, they can tell the difference between a square and a triangle only by counting the corners (Senden, 1960). Visual abilities for both animals and humans improve with time, although the longer the period of deprivation, the less reversible are the effects (Crabtree & Riesen, 1979; Timney, Mitchell, & Cynader, 1980).

The behavioral effects of sensory deprivation are reflected in changes at the neuronal level. For example, when a kitten's eyes first open, about half of the neurons in the visual cortex respond selectively to direction of movement or orientation of a stimulus (that is, firing only when an object in their visual field moves in a certain direction or is in a particular orientation, such as diagonal lines or straight lines). Usually, after several weeks of normal visual experience, all the cells in the visual cortex become sensitive to the orientation of a stimulus or to direction of movement. Following the arguments of Greenough and his colleagues, this is what the cells are "expected" to do, given species-typical experiences. But when kittens are prevented from seeing any patterns (that is, when they experience only homogeneous light without any objects to see), the cells of the visual cortex make fewer connections with other cells and gradually lose their sensitivity to orientation. Experience (or lack of experience) changes the structure and organization of the young brain, even for something as basic as vision. As with behavior, recovery of normal neuronal structure and responsivity following exposure to pattern light occurs, although the amount or degree of recovery declines with longer periods of deprivation (Blakemore & Van Sluyters, 1975; Cynader, Berman, & Hein, 1976).

Greenough and his colleagues proposed a second process of synapse development, which they called **experience-dependent processes** (or **experience-dependent synaptogenesis**). In this case, connections among neurons are made that reflect the unique experiences of an individual, rather than the experiences that all members of a species can expect to have. In both cases, the overproduction of neurons enables an individual to make connections (and thus store information) that reflect his or her particular environment. When certain experiences are not had—when the world does not cause certain neurons to be activated and synapses to join—the neurons die.

Bennett Bertenthal and Joseph Campos (1987) relate the ideas of Greenough and his colleagues to the old nature/nurture issue and the question of whether infants come into the world fully prepared by biology or as blank slates. Bertenthal and Campos write, "What determines the survival of synaptic connections is the principle of use: Those synapses activated by sensory or motor experience survive; the remainder are lost through disuse. For Greenough et al., then, experience does not create tracings on a blank tablet; rather experience erases some of them" (p. 560).

Related to the ideas of Greenough and his colleagues are *selectionist models* of neural development that propose, essentially, that many more neurons are produced than can ever survive, and that these neurons "compete" with one another for use (Changeaux & Dehaene, 1989; Edelman, 1987). For example, Gerald Edelman proposed the concept of **neural Darwinism,** in which groups of neurons are in constant competition with one another, each attempting to recruit adjacent neurons to their group and thus perform a particular function. Groups that receive the most stimulation develop strong synapses, are able to recruit more neurons to their group, and thus survive. What determines which groups flourish and which decline? One important factor is use. Neurons and groups of neurons are selected because they perform important tasks frequently, making them more likely to be used in the future. Because different groups are constantly competing for the same cells, changes in patterns of activation can result in changes in brain organization. Eventually, relatively stable patterns are achieved, but the process is an adaptive one, with the synaptic connections developing as a function of the types of information the young organism receives. Thus, through a process of activity-dependent competition, experience sculpts the brain into its final form.

Weak Initial Biases Are Strengthened by Experience

Related proposals of brain development have been made by Mark Johnson (2000) and Charles Nelson (2001), among others. Both Johnson and Nelson propose that infants are born with biases to process some information more effectively than other information, what I referred to as architectural constraints in Chapter 1. These biases are related to particular areas of the brain (that is, they are relatively domain-specific), but they are weak, just strong enough to ensure that some forms of information (language, for instance) are processed more efficiently by specific parts of the brain than others. Children's brains become increasing specialized, as, through repeated experience, areas of the brain gradually limit the range of information they respond to. From this perspective, there are few areas in the brain that, at birth, are "implanted with knowledge," what I referred to as representational innateness in Chapter 1 (see also Quartz & Sejnowski, 1997). Infants may be born with "innate" biases, but such biases are incomplete and require experience (much of it the experience-expectant type) before they are functioning at a high level.

Evidence for this position can be found in a series of experiments dealing with the development of face processing (de Haan, Oliver, & Johnson, 1998; Johnson & de Haan, 2001). For example, adults process inverted and upright faces differently, reflected by differences in reaction times and activation of different neural pathways, as revealed by patterns of event-related brain potentials (obtained from EEG recordings). Adults show, however, this differentiation only for faces from their own species; they do not show any systematic difference in the processing of inverted and upright monkey faces. In contrast, 6-month-old infants, like adults, process inverted and upright faces differently, but they do so for *both* human and monkey faces, suggesting that cortical processing of faces becomes more specialized with age and experience, specifically for the processing of human faces. In related research, adults and 9-

month-old infants looked longer at novel (unfamiliar) human faces than at familiar human faces, but looked equally long at novel and familiar monkey faces. In contrast, 6-month-olds looked longer at novel than at familiar faces for both human and monkeys (Pascalis, de Haan, & Nelson, 2002). Pascalis et al. proposed, "that the ability to perceive faces narrows with development, due in large measure to the cortical specialization that occurs with experience viewing faces. In this view, the sensitivity of the face recognition system to differences in identity among the faces of one's own species will increase with age and with experience in processing those faces" (p. 1321). (More will be said about the development of face processing in Chapter 7.)

The message here is that early brain development is not exclusively under genetic control, consistent with the developmental systems approach discussed earlier. Certainly, genes determine what the basic structure of the brain will be. But experiences play an important role in shaping the precise circuitry of the brain. From electrical and chemical activities of the growing nerve cells before birth, to the information obtained through the senses after birth, the brain becomes organized by information it receives and by its own activation as much as or more than by the instructions emanating from the genes.

The Development of the Neocortex

When most people think of the brain, they think of what's on the surface, a convoluted series of lobes. This is the **neocortex,** or **cerebral cortex,** which is a multilayered, sheet of neurons, only 3 to 4 millimeters thick, that surrounds the rest of the brain. Figure 2-13 provides a lateral view of the brain; all structures shown except the cerebellum and the spinal cord are part of the neocortex. Of course, there is much more to the brain than the neocortex, but because the neocortex is the part of the brain primarily associated with thinking, it is the only major part of the brain that I will discuss in this chapter.

The neocortex consists of two approximately equal halves, or hemispheres, connected by a thick mass of nerves called the **corpus callosum.** The neo-

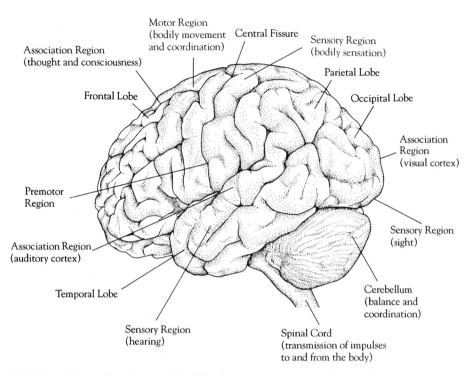

Motor Region
(bodily movement
and coordination)   Central Fissure   Sensory Region
(bodily sensation)

Association Region
(thought and consciousness)

Parietal Lobe

Frontal Lobe

Occipital Lobe

Association
Region
(visual cortex)

Premotor
Region

Sensory Region
(sight)

Association Region
(auditory cortex)

Cerebellum
(balance and
coordination)

Temporal Lobe

Sensory Region
(hearing)

Spinal Cord
(transmission of impulses
to and from the body)

FIGURE 2-13   A lateral view of the left side of the human brain showing the major structures. All but the cerebellum and the spinal cord are part of the neocortex. SOURCE: D. F. Bjorklund and B. R. Bjorklund, 1992. *Looking at Children: An Introduction to Child Development.* Belmont, CA: Wadsworth, p. 129.

cortex can be further divided into regions. Primary areas such as the various sensory regions directly receive information from the senses. Other primary areas, such as the motor regions, send instructions directly to muscles. Secondary areas consist of regions that integrate information and have many connections with other areas of the brain. These are the association (or thought) regions and are responsible for our more complex mental functioning.

Let me provide a research example of the connection between development of the prefrontal lobes of the neocortex and cognitive development. Development of the prefrontal lobes in humans is rapid between birth and about 2 years of age. The prefrontal lobes are proposed to be involved in many acts of "higher" cognition, but one important function of the prefrontal lobes appears to be in the inhibition

of responses (Fuster, 1989; see Chapter 5 for a more in-depth discussion of the role of the frontal lobes in inhibition). For example, for some tasks children must *not* execute a previously acquired response (that is, they must inhibit that response) so that they can make a new response. One such task is Piaget's A-not-B object permanence task. (See Chapter 4 for a more in-depth discussion of object permanence.) On this task, infants watch as a toy is hidden in one of two wells. The infants are distracted for a delay period, after which they are allowed to retrieve the toy. Over trials, the hiding place is changed to well B following a series of correct retrievals from well A. Piaget reported that infants younger than 12 months have great difficulty performing this task, and typically look for the hidden object at the A location, where they were successful previously.

Adele Diamond (1985) tested 25 infants in the A-not-B task, beginning at about 7 months and continuing until 12 months of age. She reported that the delay between hiding and searching that was necessary to produce the A-not-B error increased with age at a rate of about 2 seconds per month. That is, 7.5-month-old infants would search for the hidden object at the erroneous A position following only a 2-second delay. By 12 months of age, infants made the error only if approximately 10 seconds transpired between the hiding of the object and the beginning of the search.

Although such research suggests that memory might be a factor in infants' performance, Diamond believes that the more important factor is infants' ability to *inhibit* prepotent responses in solving the A-not-B task. Diamond (1991) proposes that during the first year, infants' prefrontal lobes develop gradually, which results in their becoming increasingly able to inhibit their behavioral responses. Despite "knowing" that the object was hidden at location B, young infants cannot stop themselves from executing a response that has been correct in the immediate past. They have learned a response, and before they can learn a new one, they must inhibit the old one. This ability develops over the first year, with girls showing faster progress than boys, suggesting more rapid maturational development of the prefrontal cortex in girls than boys through this age period (Diamond, 1985). That maturation of the prefrontal cortex is involved in performing this task has received support from a study by Martha Bell and Nathan Fox (1992). They recorded EEG activity from the frontal lobes of 7- to 12-month-old infants performing the A-not-B tasks and found changes in EEG patterns as a function of age and delay.

Age-related changes in brain structure and function associated with changes in cognition and behavior are not only observed in infancy and early childhood, but also later in life. It will likely not surprise you to learn that major changes in brain organization occur in adolescence. Adolescence is a time of substantial change in behavior and thinking. Although some, such as Piaget (see Chapter 4), have noted the advent of adult-like cognitive abilities, a more common description of adolescent thought and behavior centers around a new self-centeredness, emotional instability, and increases in risk-taking and the seeking of novelty (see Spear, 2000). Not surprisingly, these behavioral changes are also associated with changes in the brain. Linda Spear (2000) reviewed some of these brain changes, and they include the formation of new neural connections but also the relatively rapid loss of others. Most prominently affected are the frontal lobes. The frontal lobes actually decrease in relative size during this time, and the organization of the frontal lobes, as reflected by neural imaging studies (Luna et al., 2001), also changes substantially. In addition, there are changes in the distribution of various neurotransmitters, with some decreasing substantially in both the frontal cortex and the limbic system, an area of the brain associated with emotion.

These changes, characteristic to varying degrees of other adolescent mammals, are likely adaptive, in that the emerging adult must seek independence from his or her parents, experiment with new environments, and establish a place in his or her social group. That there is a species-typical pattern of brain changes associated with such behavior should not be surprising. But what we have here is only correlation, and the correlation is far from perfect. Although many adolescents experience the storm and strife one might expect from a radical restructuring of the brain, others do not. There is a species-typical pattern of changes in cognition and behavior in adolescence, but there is also much variability. I am convinced that the brain mediates all such behavior, but we must keep in mind that brain development is a dynamic process, influenced by both internal and external factors, rather than the simple consequence of the "unfolding" of a genetic blueprint.

The Brain's Plasticity

Plasticity, discussed in Chapter 1, refers to the ability to change. To what extent can new synapses be formed and different parts of the brain take over a function intended for another part of the nervous system? Put another way, plasticity also refers to the potential outcomes that are possible for a single neuron, bundle of neurons, or larger brain structure. Given certain experiences at certain times during life, how might these cells become organized? Implicit in the theorizing of Johnson (2000), Nelson (2001), and Greenough and his colleagues (1987) is the concept of plasticity. In the research reviewed earlier, the brain of infants was described as being only weakly specialized, with experience modifying greatly its eventual organization. This is an example of plasticity. But what about after infancy? Recall that in studies of face processing, infants by 9 months of age showed a similar pattern to that of adults (Pascalis et al., 2002), suggesting that, at least for some functions and areas of the brain, an adult-like organization is in place relatively early. Areas dealing with other functions obviously require more time before they take on adult-like functions, but once organized, how easily can brains be reorganized?

Neuronal Plasticity

There is apparently little or no plasticity in the production of new neurons, at least in the cerebral cortex. New neurons in the hippocampus are generated throughout life, but evidence of neourogenesis in the cortex in humans and other mammals is scarce. With a few exceptions, a newborn comes into the world with more neurons than he or she will ever need. From birth on, there is a loss of neurons (that is, cell degeneration)—a rapid loss during infancy and a gradual decline thereafter.

The picture is different for the formation of new synapses. Although it was believed not too many years ago that synapse production is limited to infancy, contemporary research indicates that new synaptic connections can be formed throughout life (see Greenough et al., 1987). What causes new synapses to form? The answer is experience. Perhaps the most convincing evidence of the effects of experience on brain structures comes from studies providing environmental stimulation for laboratory animals, mostly rats and mice. In studies dating back to 1949 (Hebb, 1949), researchers have raised groups of laboratory animals in environments constructed to be enriched or stimulating and compared their brain development and learning ability with those raised

in environments considered deprived (Hymovitch, 1952; Turner & Greenough, 1985). Enriched environments usually included animals raised together in large cages that were filled with a variety of objects with which they could interact. Various platforms, toys, and mazes filled some of the cages—not too dissimilar from the cages one might buy for the family gerbil.

These experiments have shown that rats and mice raised in enriched environments are superior at a wide range of complex tasks, such as maze learning. The differences in learning ability between enriched and nonenriched animals are of a general nature, with the most likely explanation for these effects being that "the groups differ in the amount of stored knowledge upon which they can draw in novel situations" (Greenough et al., 1987, p. 547). Concerning changes found in their brains, enriched animals have heavier and thicker neocortexes, larger neurons with more dendrites, and importantly, more synaptic connections. In one study, enriched rats had 20 to 25% more synapses per neuron in their visual cortexes than did rats raised in individual cages (Turner & Greenough, 1985). And these effects are not limited to infant animals; the behavioral and brain benefits of living in a stimulating environment are found even when experienced by older animals (Greenough et al., 1986).

Synaptic plasticity is greatest in infancy. With age and experience, neurons and synapses that were formed prenatally or in infancy die, and with their death connections that could have formed are now impossible. Thus, experience serves not only to create new connections, but also to make other ones impossible or less likely. Even though with age the plasticity to form new synapses decreases, it does not disappear; we retain substantial neural plasticity throughout life. What does change is the degree to which experience can change the brain and the intensity of the experience needed to produce change.

Let me make it clear that losing plasticity should not be viewed completely negatively. As a result of genetic programming and experience, neurons become dedicated, or committed to certain functions, effectively eliminating plasticity. This commitment affords greater efficiency of processing, permitting sets of neurons to specialize. For a species such as humans, who have long life spans and must deal with a large diversity of social circumstances, retaining some plasticity into adulthood is necessary, but there is much about human life that does not change substantially over time and circumstances, and individuals are best served by a nervous system that early in life commits neurons to basic functions.

Recovery of Function from Brain Damage

Perhaps the best-known evidence for the plasticity of the nervous system comes from case studies of people who have experienced brain damage and exhibit deficits in physical or mental functioning. These studies document the process of readjustment these people go through and the differences their ages make to their readjustment.[1]

The most studied type of brain damage of this sort concerns the areas of the brain controlling language. Since the 19th century, numerous reports have indicated that children who experience brain damage to the language areas of their left hemispheres before they are able to speak are eventually able to attain more advanced levels of language than are older children or adults who experience similar brain damage (Annett, 1973; Woods & Carey, 1979). Likewise, left-hemisphere brain injury for children who can already talk can produce an initial loss of language ability, but in many cases language is recovered and the child talks again at normal or near-normal levels. Studies conducted on adults have not found the same degree of recovery (see Witelson, 1985). Full recovery of language, even in young children, is rare, however, showing that the human brain is not completely plastic, even early in life (Witelson, 1987). Yet, the evidence clearly shows that "there is a remarkable functional plasticity for language functions following brain damage in childhood in that the eventual cognitive level reached is often far beyond that observed in cases of adult brain damage, even those having extensive remedial education. These results attest to the operation of marked neural plasticity at least in the immature brain" (Witelson, 1987, p. 676).

This might lead one to believe that, if one must have brain damage, do it early, for a young brain is more likely to recover normal function than an older brain. This is the so-called Kennard principle, and although it holds for many types of brain damage, it is not true in all cases (Robertson & Murre, 1999). In fact, when the focus of damage is to an area of the brain that is involved with more general cognitive functioning rather than with a specific cognitive ability such as language, the reverse is often true (Levine, 1993; Witelson, 1987). Evidence reviewed by Bryan Kolb and Ian Whishaw (1990) from both animal and human research demonstrates that younger children and animals show more permanent deficits than older children and animals do after brain damage to the frontal lobes, areas associated with general processes, such as IQ, brain size, and some species-typical behaviors. For example, in one study, brain damage before the age of one resulted in lower IQs for children than did similar brain damage that occurred after a child's first birthday (Riva & Cazzaniga, 1986); another study reported greater reductions in IQ for children who suffered brain damage before the age of 5 than for those who suffered similar injury after 5 (Kornhuber et al., 1985). In research with rats, Kolb and Whishaw (1981) reported that brain lesions inflicted shortly after birth resulted in a smaller adult brain (about 25% smaller) than did lesions inflicted on adult animals (about 12% smaller).

What is the reason for this pattern? In some instances, early insults affect how large portions of a brain system will develop, making the consequences of early injury very severe. Likewise, the damage may interfere with learning, resulting in delayed development of cognitive skills. Again, such loss is especially apt to occur when the skill under question is a general one. Yet, in other cases, early brain insults can be compensated for by a pliable system that is not yet set in its ways and can adjust to unexpected changes. This is most apt to occur when the skill under question is highly specified, as in language. The relationship between age at injury and degree of plasticity for specific and general skills is shown in Figure 2-14. As can be seen, the degree of plasticity observed is a

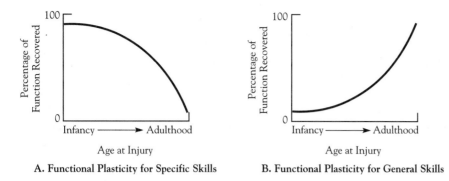

A. Functional Plasticity for Specific Skills   **B. Functional Plasticity for General Skills**

FIGURE 2-14   Theoretical relationship between age when brain damage is suffered and recovery of function depending on whether the brain injury affects a specific skill (such as language) or a more general skill (such as intelligence or planning). SOURCE: Adapted from "Neurobiological Aspects of Language in Children," by S. F. Witelson, 1987, *Child Development, 58*, 653–688. Copyright © 1987 The Society for Research in Child Development, Inc. Adapted with permission.

function not only of age at injury but also of the nature of the brain injury.

Slow Growth and Plasticity

Through much of the 20th century, it was believed that if children suffered severe deprivation for much more than their first year of life, they were destined to a life of mental retardation and psychopathology. More recently, both human and animal work has clearly shown that this is not true (Clark & Hanisee, 1982; Suomi & Harlow, 1972). When the course of a young child's or young animal's life changes drastically, patterns of development can also be radically altered.

Let me provide one research example of the reversibility of the effects of negative early experience here. (The topic is discussed in greater detail in Chapter 16.) With the political turmoil in Southeast Asia during the 1970s, many abandoned and sickly children were subsequently adopted by American families. Generally, follow-up interviews of adopted Asian children who were malnourished and socially deprived as infants revealed that their intellectual and social development was at or above normal by early childhood (Clark & Hanisee, 1982; Winick, Meyer, & Harris, 1975). In the 1982 study by Audrey

Clark and Jeanette Hanisee, for example, 25 adopted Asian children were given a test of verbal intelligence, the Peabody Picture Vocabulary Test (PPVT), and a test of social competence, the Vineland Social Maturity Scale (VSMS). The average age of the children at the time of testing was 44 months, and all the children had been in their adoptive homes for at least 23 months before testing. Before being adopted, most of the children had experienced physical and psychological deprivation. Sixteen of them were reported to have been malnourished sometime during infancy, with many displaying dehydration and muscle weakness. Despite their inauspicious beginnings, the children fared exceptionally well on the tests of verbal and social competencies. The national average on both the PPVT and the VSMS is 100. The adopted children's average scores were 120 on the PPVT and 137 on the VSMS. These children, impoverished and malnourished as infants, showed no residual signs of their early deprivation within two years of having been placed in upper-middle-class homes.

This plasticity of behavior and intelligence is attributed, in part, to the slow growth of the brain. As noted earlier in this chapter, although the human brain is large relative to the rest of the body at birth, it continues to grow well into early adulthood. This prolonged immaturity provides humans the time necessary to master the complexities of social life. But it also provides the opportunity to change behavior and to acquire novel patterns later in life. Seen in this light, the extended immaturity of the human nervous system provides opportunities for behavioral flexibility and plasticity unsurpassed by any other species (see Bjorklund & Pellegrini, 2002).

An immature brain means a slow and inefficient brain. Partly because of the extent of myelination and partly because of a paucity of experience, young children process information more slowly than older children do (see Kail, 1991). This slower speed of processing translates directly into less-efficient processing (Case, 1985; Dempster, 1985). This overall slower speed means that more of the younger children's processing is effortful in nature, in that it uses substantial portions of their limited mental resources (Hasher & Zacks, 1979; see Chapters 4 and 5). In contrast, more of older children's and adults' cognitive processing is automatic, in that it can be done quickly without conscious awareness and requires little or none of one's limited mental capacity. In other words, young children must work harder mentally to obtain the same results that older children can achieve.

This inefficiency has its drawbacks, of course. You can't teach much of a complex nature to young children, you can't expect them to gain as much from experiences as older children do, and they can't be relied on to make many important decisions on their own. Despite the obvious disadvantages of a slow and inefficient brain, it also has its benefits. According to Bjorklund and Green,

> Because little in the way of cognitive processing can be automatized early, presumably because of children's incomplete myelination, they are better prepared to adapt, cognitively, to later environments. If experiences early in life yielded automization, the child would lose the flexibility necessary for adult life. Processes automatized in response to the demands of early childhood may be useless and likely detrimental for coping with the very different cognitive demands faced by adults. Cognitive flexibility in the species is

maintained by an immature nervous system that gradually permits the automization of more mental operations, increasing the likelihood that lessons learned as a young child will not interfere with the qualitatively different tasks required of the adult. (1992, pp. 49–50)

This should not be seen as implying that the effects of early social or physical deprivation can always be reversed. As will be seen in later chapters, early experiences (or lack of them) can have relatively permanent, negative consequences. The experiences of infancy and toddlerhood establish patterns of behavior that can potentially influence the accomplishments of later years, particularly when those experiences are stable over childhood. But the inefficiency of the young brain does offer children some protection from the perils of an early damaging environment.

Developmental Biology and Cognitive Development

As the field of cognitive psychology evolved into cognitive science, people interested in mental functioning became increasingly aware of the need to coordinate the psychological level of explanation with the biological level. A similar realization is occurring now in the field of cognitive development. For example, James Byrnes and Nathan Fox (1998) reviewed some of the new neuroscience techniques and research findings from the developmental neurosciences and concluded that we are on the threshold of a new revolution, equivalent to the cognitive revolution. Admittedly, the presentation in this chapter is cursory, but I believe that it provides a foundation for the proper understanding of the ontogeny of human thought.

Many more topics could have been considered in this chapter. For example, hormones apparently play a major role in influencing cognition. Prenatal hormones are known to influence the brain and how later information is processed. More specifically, the class of male hormones called androgens are said to "masculinize" the brain, affecting certain sex differences in thinking (for example, spatial ability), as well as how sexual signals are processed (that is, sexual orientation) (see Money, 1988). Some research examining the role of prenatal exposure to male hormones in children's sex typing (specifically, toy preference) will be discussed in Chapter 13. The field of behavior genetics has also blossomed in the past two decades, looking at the role of genetics in such diverse behaviors as alcoholism, religiosity, intelligence, learning disabilities, and amount of television viewing (see Plomin, DeFries et al., 1997). I will examine some of the data and claims of behavior genetics in Chapter 16 when looking at individual differences in intelligence. I will also include contemporary neuroscience research in discussing a variety of other aspects of cognitive development, from social cognition, to information processing and memory, and I hope that this chapter will have served as an adequate introduction for placing this new brain-based research into perspective.

By acknowledging the importance of biological factors to cognitive development, I do not mean to suggest that the future of the field lies in biology. But having an idea of both the neural and evolutionary causes of behavior and development will help the psychologist ask better research questions and achieve a better understanding of development. For example, knowledge of the developmental relationship between brain and behavior has important implications not only for theories of cognitive development but also for societal practices. How pliable is human intelligence? When, in development, can children most benefit from certain educational experiences? Is earlier always better, or are there certain sensitive periods for particular experiences distributed throughout development?

The study of cognition, including its development, has gone through substantial changes since its beginnings in the 1950s. We cannot be certain what the future will hold, but it seems certain that part of the new paradigm will be closer attention to the biological bases of cognition and cognitive development.

Summary

Developmental psychology has become increasingly concerned with the biological causes of cognition. Although psychology provides a different level of analysis than biology does, concepts in psychology must be consistent with the known facts in biology. The new field of *developmental cognitive neuroscience* takes data from a variety of sources—molecular biology, cell biology, artificial intelligence, evolutionary theory, as well as conventional cognitive development—to create a picture of how the mind/brain develops.

Darwin's idea of variation and *natural selection* remains the cornerstone for theories of *evolution*. Proponents of *evolutionary psychology* believe that information-processing mechanisms have evolved in response to specific environmental pressures, equipping humans to solve specific problems; however, evolutionary developmental psychologists believe that domain-general mechanisms have also been modified over time as a result of natural selection. A distinction has been made between cognitive skills such as language that have been selected for in evolution (called *biologically primary abilities*) and those, such as reading, that are primarily determined by culture (called *biologically secondary abilities*). Other researchers have developed *selectionist theories*, based on Darwin's concept of natural selection, to account for cognitive and brain development.

The *developmental systems approach* centers around the concept of *epigenesis*, a bidirectional relationship between all levels of biological and experiential variables, such that genetic activity both influences and is influenced by structural maturation, which is bidirectionally related to function and activity. Organisms inherit not only a species-typical genotype but also a species-typical environment, and species-typical experiences early in life can greatly influence the course of development. Timing of experience can be crucial for development. Many early perceptual and cognitive abilities are governed by *critical periods*, those times in development when certain skills or abilities are most easily acquired.

Scarr and McCartney's *genotype → environment theory* proposes that genes drive experience. Based chiefly on research in *behavior genetics*, they describe three kinds of genotype → environment effects: passive, which occur when biological parents rear the child; evocative, which occur when characteristics of the child elicit responses from others; and active, which occur when children select environments in which they choose to interact. Passive effects decrease in influence over time, whereas active effects increase. Data supporting this theory show that parents' environmental influence on their children's intelligence is greatest during the early years and wanes as the children approach adolescence. Because of substantial influence of active genotype → environment effects, Scarr proposed that *"good-enough" parents* are sufficient to raise a child.

New *neuroimaging techniques*, such as high-density event-related potentials, positron emission tomography (PET), single photon emission tomography (SPECT), and functional magnetic resonance imaging (fMRI), are providing new knowledge about brain functioning and development.

The nervous system consists of *neurons*, which transport chemical and electrical signals. Neurons consist of a cell body, *axons*, long fibers that carry messages away from the cell body to other cells, and *dendrites*, more numerous fibers that receive messages from other cells and transfer them to the cell body. Electrical messages are transmitted through *synapses*, facilitated by various *neurotransmitters*. Neurons go through at least three stages of development: *proliferation*, *migration*, and *differentiation*. The formation of synapses (*synaptogenesis*) occurs during this last stage. Synapse formation is rapid during prenatal development and continues to be rapid during the early months of life. A complementary process of *selective cell death* also occurs, with many neurons dying. Nearly all the neurons an individual will ever have are produced by early infancy, although synaptogenesis occurs throughout life. *Myelin* is a fatty substance that surrounds axons, promoting faster transmission of electrical signals. Different areas of the brain begin and end the process of myelination at different times, and degree of *myelination* is related to certain sensory, motor, and intellectual levels of development. Ex-

tent of myelination is also influenced by experience, but apparently less so than is the structure and function of neurons.

Some neural connections are made by all members of a species, given normal experiences (*experience-expectant processes*), whereas other connections are made because of the unique experiences of an individual (*experience-dependent processes*). Neurons live (and form synapses with other neurons) or die as a function of use, with groups of neurons apparently competing with one another to recruit other neurons, a process referred to as *neural Darwinism*. Evidence suggests that areas of infants' brains are only weakly specialized for processing certain information (for example, language), but become more domain-specific in nature as a result of experience.

The *neocortex* (or *cerebral cortex*) is divided into two *hemispheres* that are connected by the *corpus callosum*. Neuronal *plasticity* has been most clearly demonstrated in studies with animals, including rearing animals in deprived or enriched environments. With age, the plasticity needed to form new synapses declines, but it does not disappear. Examination of the recovery of function after brain damage shows that, at least for damage to areas of the brain that control specific abilities such as language, plasticity is greater the earlier the damage occurs. Humans' prolonged immaturity contributes to our behavioral plasticity and to children's abilities to overcome the effects of deleterious early environments.

Note

1. Before proceeding, I must mention some problems that are inevitable when using brain-damage research to understand brain function. These include the facts that (a) brain damage can rarely be narrowed to one area; (b) brain damage frequently involves complications beyond that of simple lesions; (c) disorders following brain damage might not reveal how the brain functions normally; and (d) lesions in one area of the brain can lead to changes in other areas of the brain (Fuster, 1989). Nevertheless, despite these, and other, reservations, much can be learned about brain functioning from studying brain damage, especially when viewed in combination with other sources of data.

Key Terms and Concepts

developmental cognitive neuroscience

evolution

natural selection

evolutionary psychology

biologically primary abilities

biologically secondary abilities

selectionist theories

developmental systems approach
   (developmental contextual model)

epigenesis

hemispheres

critical (sensitive) period

behavior genetics

genotype → environment effects

"good enough" parents

neuroimaging techniques

neuron

synapse

axon

dendrites

neurotransmitters

proliferation (of neurons)

migration (of neurons)

differentiation (of neurons)

synaptogenesis

selective cell death

myelination

myelin

experience-expectant processes
   (or experience-expectant synaptogenesis)

experience-dependent processes
   (or experience-dependent synaptogenesis)

neural Darwinism

neocortex (or cerebral cortex)

corpus callosum

plasticity (of the brain)

Suggested Readings

Cziko, G. (1995). *Without miracles: Universal selection theory and the second Darwinian revolution*. Cambridge, MA: MIT Press. This book examines the historical, philosophical, and scientific basis of selectionist theories, especially as applied to human cognition.

Geary, D. C., & Bjorklund, D. F. (2000). Evolutionary developmental psychology. *Child Development, 71*, 57–65. This is a brief article introducing the basic tenets of evolutionary developmental psychology, particularly as it relates to cognitive development. For a more in-depth look at evolutionary developmental psychology, see Bjorklund and Pellegrini's book *The Origins of Human Nature: Evolutionary Developmental Psychology* (2002, American Psychological Press).

Gottlieb, G. (2000). Environmental and behavioral influences on gene activity. *Current Directions in Psychological Science, 9*, 93–102. This short article concisely presents the basic ideas of the developmental systems approach. Gottlieb is a major proponent of this perspective, and interested readers may want to refer to his 1997 book, *Synthesizing nature-nurture: Prenatal roots of instinctive behavior* (Mahwah, NJ: Erlbaum).

Johnson, M. H. (1998). The neural basis of cognitive development. In D. Kuhn & R. S. Siegler (Vol. Eds.), *Cognition, perception, and language* (Vol. 2) (pp. 1–49), in W. Damon (Gen. Ed.), *Handbook of child psychology* (5th ed.). New York: Wiley. Although a few years out of date given the speed with which research in developmental cognitive neuroscience is progressing, this chapter represents a through review of contemporary research on the neuronal basis of children's cognitive development.

Scarr, S. (1993). Biological and cultural diversity: The legacy of Darwin for development. *Child Development, 64*, 1333–1353. Scarr presents a relatively detailed account of her genotype → environment theory here, emphasizing the importance of an evolutionary theory to developmental psychologists. This paper is a response to critics of her theory (by Baumrind and by Jackson, same issue), and Scarr is careful to be precise about her theorizing.

InfoTrac College Edition

For additional readings, explore InfoTrac College Edition, your online library. Go to http://www.infotrac-college.com/wadsworth.

3

The Social Construction of Mind: Sociocultural Perspectives on Cognitive Development

In the opening chapter, I stated that there were two obvious trends in cognitive development during the past decade or so. The first trend was an increased emphasis on the biological basis of development. The second was an increasing emphasis on the social construction of cognition—the perspective that how children learn to think is governed largely by the culture in which they grow up. I hope, after reading Chapter 2, you agree that the "new view" of how biology influences psychological development gives experience a substantial role to play. But this is not the same as believing that the social environment plays a critical role in shaping development. For example, most researchers who examine the biological basis of development rarely investigate the social environment in detail and rarely see cognitive development as "constructed" by the social environment.

This is exactly the view that proponents of the **sociocultural perspective** of development take. Sociocultural psychologists believe that how we develop, particularly how we learn to think, is primarily a function of the social and cultural environment in which we are reared. This viewpoint emphasizes what makes people different thinkers rather than what we all, as human beings, share in common. Traditional views of cognitive development, such as Jean Piaget's (discussed in detail in the following chapter), emphasized *cognitive universals*—aspects of development that characterize all children in all parts of the world in essentially the same ways. For theorists like Piaget, and other contemporary theorists such as Sandra Scarr, whose ideas of "good enough" parents were discussed in Chapter 2, individual differences in the environments children grow up in certainly affect their views of the world, but they do not affect the "big picture" of cognitive development much. Certainly, children growing up in an information-age society will have different things to think about than will children growing up in a hunter-gatherer society, but, according to theorists such as Piaget, each will solve problems relevant to their daily lives using species-typical cognitive mechanisms that develop according to a species-typical schedule. Sociocultural theorists see cognitive development very differently.

The overriding theme of this chapter is that cognitive development is inseparable from its cultural context. Culture is transmitted to children by their parents and other members of society. Within the adult-child interchanges of daily life, children's intellectual processes are developed to handle the tasks and problems pertinent to their particular surroundings. Parents might not be conscious of their instructional techniques, but cultural practices of child rearing are usually well suited for the type of life children can expect to face as adults. Sociocultural theory addresses how children come to understand and function in their social world. From the sociocultural perspective, how children understand their physical world "is embedded within knowledge of the sociocultural world . . . and it is the latter that enables and guides the former" (Nelson, 1996, p. 5). This should not be taken to mean that scientists with a sociocultural perspective give biology short shrift in influencing cognitive development. Most do not, but they realize that neurologically influenced, species-typical cognitive abilities emerge in species-typical social environments. This is captured in Mary Gauvain's (2001) statement that "cognitive development is an active constructive process that involves beings who are evolutionarily predisposed to live and learn in social context with other 'like-minded' beings. They are like-minded in terms of both the neurological system available and the social requirements that are in place" (p. 63).

The current interest in sociocultural perspectives in contemporary developmental psychology can be traced to the rediscovery of the ideas of the Russian psychologist Lev Vygotsky (1962, 1978) (see Gauvain, 2001; Hernández Blasi, 1996; Rogoff, 1990, 1998; Wertsch & Tulviste, 1992). Vygotsky, writing in the 1920s and 1930s, emphasized that development is guided by adults interacting with children, with the cultural context determining largely how, where, and when these interactions take place. Vygotsky proposed that cognitive development occurs in situations where a child's problem solving is guided by an adult. For Vygotsky and his contemporary followers, cognitive development progresses through the collaborations of members of one generation with another. Children's development is embedded within a culture and proceeds as they are guided through life in collaboration with others. Elaborating on this perspective, Barbara Rogoff views development as a process of *transformation of participation*. From this perspective,

> Evaluation of development focuses on how individuals participate in and contribute to ongoing activity rather than on "outcome" and individuals' possessions of concepts and skills. Evaluation of development examines the ways people transform their participation, analyzing how they coordinate with others in shared endeavors, with attention to the purposes and dynamic nature of the activity itself and its meaning in the community. The investigation of people's actual involvement and changing goals in activities becomes the basis of understanding development rather than simply the surface to try to get past. (1998, p. 18)

From this perspective, it is clear why Vygotsky and modern sociocultural theorists propose that it is impossible to evaluate the individual without also considering other significant people and institutions in the community.

The Role of Culture in Cognitive Development

Vygotsky proposed that we should evaluate development from the perspective of four interrelated levels in interaction with children's environments—ontogenetic, microgenetic, phylogenetic, and sociohistorical. **Ontogenetic development** (or ontogeny), development of the individual over his or her lifetime, is the topic of this book and the level of analysis for nearly all developmental psychologists. **Microgenetic development** refers to changes that occur over relatively brief periods of time, such as the changes that one may see in a child solving addition problems every week for 11 consecutive weeks (Siegler & Jenkins, 1989), or even the changes in the use of memory strategies that children use over five different trials during a 20-minute session (Coyle & Bjorklund, 1997). This is obviously a finer-grained

analysis than that afforded by the traditional ontogenetic level. **Phylogenetic development** (or phylogeny) refers to changes over evolutionary time, measured in thousands and even millions of years. Here, Vygotsky anticipated the current evolutionary psychology perspective, believing that an understanding of the species' history can provide insight into child development. Finally, **sociohistorical development** refers to the changes that have occurred in one's culture and the values, norms, and technologies such a history has generated. For example, children growing up in Western nations today have received a legacy of literacy, computers, and a legal and "human rights" tradition that influences their development in ways that children growing up in other cultures without literacy, computers, or Western values can't even imagine (and vice versa).

Vygotsky's claim that multiple aspects of a child's endowment (genetic, cultural) must be viewed in interaction makes his theory reminiscent of the developmental systems approach discussed in the previous chapter (see Tudge, Putnam, & Valsiner, 1996). Vygotsky stressed the need to understand how changing organisms develop in changing environments. Focusing only on the individual or only on the environment could not provide an adequate explanation of development (Hernández Blasi, 1996). However, what modern-day researchers have emphasized most about Vygotsky's ideas is his belief that development can only be meaningfully studied in the social and cultural context in which it occurs.

Tools of Intellectual Adaptation

Vygotsky claimed that infants are born with a few *elementary mental functions*—attention, sensation, perception, and memory—that are eventually transformed by the culture into new and more sophisticated mental processes he called *higher mental functions*. Take memory, for example. Young children's early memorial capabilities are limited by biological constraints to the images and impressions they can produce. However, each culture provides its children with **tools of intellectual adaptation,** which are methods of thinking and problem-solving strategies that children internalize from their interactions with more competent members of society that permit children to use their basic mental functions more adaptively. Thus, children in information-age societies might learn to remember more efficiently by taking notes, whereas their agemates in preliterate societies might have learned other memory strategies, such as representing each object they must remember by tying a knot in a string or by tying a string around their fingers to remind them to perform a chore. Such socially transmitted memory strategies and other cultural tools teach children how to use their minds—in short, *how* to think. And because each culture also transmits specific beliefs and values, it teaches children *what* to think as well.

A subtle difference in cultural tools of intellectual adaptation that can make a noticeable difference on children's cognitive task performance can be found in how a language names its numbers. For example, in all languages, the first ten digits must be learned by rote. However, after that, some languages take advantage of the base-ten number system and name numbers accordingly. English does this beginning at 20, (twenty-one, twenty-two, and so on). However, the teen numbers in English are not so easily represented. Rather, 11 and 12 also must be memorized. Not until 13 does a base-ten system begin (three + ten = "thirteen"), and even then, several of the number names do not correspond to the formula digit + ten. "Fourteen," "sixteen," "seventeen," "eighteen," and "nineteen" do, but the number names for "thirteen" and "fifteen" are not as straightforward (that is, they are not expressed as "three-teen" and "fiveteen"). Moreover, for the teen numbers, the digit unit is stated first ("fourteen," "sixteen"), whereas the decade unit is stated first for the numbers 20 through 99 ("twenty-one," "thirty-three"). Thus, the number system becomes very regular in English beginning with the 20s.

Other languages, such as Chinese, have a more systematic number-naming system. In Chinese, as in English, the first ten digits must be memorized. However, from this point, the Chinese number-naming system follows a base-ten logic, with the name for 11 translating as "ten one," the name for 12 translating as "ten two," and so on. The Chinese and English languages are similar beginning at 20, and both use the base-ten logic once the "hundreds" are reached.

Kevin Miller and his colleagues (1995) reasoned that differences in the number-naming systems between English and Chinese might be associated with early mathematical competence, specifically counting. They tested 3- through 5-year-old children in Champaign-Urbana, Illinois, and Beijing, China. They asked each child to count as high as possible. Differences between the Chinese and U. S. sample are shown by age in Figure 3-1. As can be seen, there were no cultural differences for the 3-year-olds, but the Chinese children began to show an advantage by age 4, and this advantage was even larger at age 5. Further analyses indicated that cultural differences were limited to the teens decade. Although almost all children could count to 10 (94% of the American children and 92% of the Chinese children), only 48% of the American children could count to 20, compared with 74% of the Chinese children. Once children could count to 20, there were no cultural differences for counting to 100. These findings indicate how differences in the naming-number system of a language can contribute to early differences in a cognitive skill. This early difference in a *tool of intellectual adaptation* might contribute to later differences in mathematical abilities found between Chinese and American children (see Chapter 14).

The relevance of tools of intellectual adaptation to cognitive functioning is not limited to subtle differences between languages or to comparisons between high-tech and stone-age cultures, but can be seen within and between modern societies today. The 20th century saw the invention of many new tools of intellectual adaptation, but perhaps the one that will have the most profound impact is the personal computer. Like it or not, there is a global economy and "information" is a valuable commodity. To a great extent, access to computers and the ability to use them easily differentiates those cultures that will experience economic boom versus bust in the 21st century, and, within a culture, such as mainstream America, those who will reap the greatest benefits

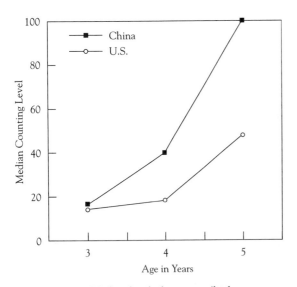

FIGURE 3-1   Median level of counting (highest number reached) by age for Chinese and U.S. preschoolers. SOURCE: Miller, K. F., Smith, C. M., Zhu, J., & Zhang, H. (1995). Preschool origins of cross-national differences in mathematical competence. *Psychological Science, 6*, 56–60. Reprinted with permission.

that an information-age society has to offer. Being computer literate not only affects what jobs we have and thus our income, but, just as reading and writing did centuries before, influences how one learns, how (and what) one remembers, and how one solves problems. In a sense, we are in the midst of a natural experiment, in which a new tool of intellectual adaptation has been introduced, and we should not be surprised if, in decades to come, we are a different-thinking people than we were before the computer revolution.

In sum, Vygotsky claimed that human cognition, even when carried out in isolation, is inherently *sociocultural* because it is affected by the beliefs, values, and tools of intellectual adaptation transmitted to individuals by their culture. And because these values and intellectual tools can vary substantially from culture to culture, Vygotsky believed that neither the course nor the content of intellectual growth was as "universal" as Piaget and others had assumed.

The Social Origins of Early Cognitive Competencies

Vygotsky viewed young children as curious explorers who are actively involved in learning and discovering new principles. However, he placed little emphasis on *self-initiated* discovery, choosing instead to stress the importance of *social* contributions to cognitive growth. For example, Vygotsky believed that higher psychological processes (those involving self-awareness) have a social origin, developing first on the social plane and only later becoming internalized and developing on the psychological plane (Wertsch & Tulviste, 1992). Vygotsky referred to this dual-nature of cognitive development as the **general genetic law of cultural development.** According to Vygotsky (1981, p. 163), "Any function in the child's cultural development appears twice, or on two planes. First it appears on the social plane, and then on the psychological plane. First it appears between people as an interpsychological category, and then within the child as an intrapsychological category. This is equally true with regard to voluntary attention, logical memory, the formation of concepts, and the development of volition." According to Wertsch and Tulviste (1992), cognitive processes such as memory are not understood as characteristics of individuals but, rather, as functions that can be carried out either between people or internally. Such processes can be viewed as *socially constituted cognitive activity* (Gauvain, 2001), which is "individual thinking that has embedded within it the contributions of the social world" (p. 41). Children learn to use the symbols or the representational tools of the social community, regardless of whether they are sharing a memory with another person, for example, or contemplating a problem "in their head."

Following this logic, Vygotsky believed that to understand cognitive development, psychologists should not focus on individuals as they execute some context-independent process (as Western psychologists have traditionally done) but should examine individuals as they participate in culturally valued activities.

It is not always practical, of course, to assess children's thinking in "naturalistic" settings (the loss of experimental control can limit greatly what one can say about the mechanisms underlying cognition). However, to the extent that children's thinking is applied to solve real-world problems (and what else is cognition for, and why else would we want to know about it?), an understanding of cognitive development requires that one have an appreciation of the "larger social and cultural context that provides meaning and purpose" for children's cognitions (Gauvain, 2001, p. 28).

According to Vygotsky, many of the truly important "discoveries" that children make occur within the context of cooperative, or collaborative *dialogues* between a skillful tutor, who might model the activity and transmit verbal instructions, and a novice pupil, who first seeks to understand the tutor's instruction and eventually internalizes this information, using it to regulate his or her own performance.

To illustrate collaborative (or guided) learning as Vygotsky viewed it, imagine Miguel, a 4-year-old, trying to put together a jigsaw puzzle. His early attempts get him nowhere. His mother notices his difficulties and sits down beside him and offers some assistance. She first suggests that Miguel look for the corner pieces, selecting one and showing Miguel. Next, she suggests that Miguel look for other edge pieces, starting with those that match the patterns and colors of one of the corner pieces. Miguel selects several pieces, tries to put them together, and on his third attempt finds a piece that fits. Miguel continues to look for other pieces, but becomes frustrated. His mother then selects two pieces, places them close together and says, "See if these two fit." Miguel puts them together, smiles, and continues to look for other pieces. Miguel's mother gives him a few words of encouragement and continues to help Miguel when he runs into trouble. But Miguel is getting the hang of it, and his mother's assistance is needed less and less. This kind of social interaction, claimed Vygotsky, fosters cognitive growth.

The Zone of Proximal Development

How? First, Miguel and his mother are operating in what Vygotsky called the **zone of proximal development**—defined as the difference between a child's "actual developmental level as determined by independent problem solving" and his or her level of "potential development as determined through problem solving under adult guidance or in collaboration with more capable peers" (Vygotsky, 1978, p. 86). It is in this zone in which sensitive instruction should be aimed and in which new cognitive growth can be expected to occur. Miguel obviously becomes a more competent puzzle-solver with his mother's help than without it. More important, he will internalize the problem-solving techniques that his mother uses in collaboration with him and will ultimately use them on his own, rising to a new level of independent mastery. In other words, children can best learn to solve problems at a level between their current ability and their ability when assisted by an adult. Within this zone, adults can do the most effective teaching. One important thing to remember here is that the skills of the child continue to develop, requiring modifications by the adults. Thus, the sociocultural approach is by necessity dynamic—ever changing—with both adults and children progressing as a result of their repeated transactions (Saxe, Guberman, & Gearhart, 1987).

Related to the concept of zone of proximal development is the concept of **scaffolding** (Wood, Bruner, & Ross, 1976). Scaffolding occurs when experts are sensitive to abilities of a novice and respond contingently to the novice's responses in a learning situation, so that the novice gradually increases his or her understanding of a problem. Scaffolding will be most effective when done in the zone of proximal development and occurs any time a more expert person tailors his or her interactions to guide a child to a level near the limits of his or her performance, not just in formal educational settings. The behavior of Miguel's mother in the earlier example reflected scaffolding and working in the zone of proximal development.

Evidence of scaffolding can be seen in a study in which mothers were instructed to teach their 5-year-old children how to play a board game involving the use of dice to compute moves (Bjorklund, Hubertz, & Reubens, 2004). In this research, kindergarten children played a board game of "Chutes and Ladders" with their mothers, with the spinner being replaced by a pair of dice. Children had to compute their moves by adding the numbers on the two dice. To what extent did mothers help their children add or attempt to teach their children arithmetic strategies in the process of playing the game? Mothers' behavior often varied with the competence of their children. For children who were using fact retrieval and mental arithmetic spontaneously (that is, who did not have to count out loud or on their fingers to arrive at an answer), mothers usually provided little support or advice, as little or none was needed. In contrast, mothers of less arithmetically competent children often prompted their 5-year-olds to count the dice, modeled or instructed use of simple addition strategies (for example, counting all the pips on the dice) and often re-represented the problem by holding up their fingers to correspond to the pips on the dice. Some mothers used these overt procedures more on the early trials and gradually declined their use of specific prompts and instructions as their children took more responsibility for solving the "problem" on their own. In other words, these mothers were "working in the zone of proximal development" to teach their children simple arithmetic strategies in the context of a social game.

There was variability in the degree of scaffolding shown by different mothers, of course. Let me provide one example from this research of a particularly effective mother. On her first move, 5-year-old Yolanda threw the dice and just stared at them, said nothing, and then looked at her mother. Her mother asked, "How many is that?" Yolanda shrugged her shoulders, and her mother said, "Count them." Yolanda shrugged again, and her mother then pointed to the dots on the first die saying, "One, two, three," then to the dots on the second die, saying "four, five. You have five. Now you count them." Yolanda complied, pointing to each dot as she counted out loud, and then moved her piece on the board. The mother then threw the dice and asked Yolanda, "How many do I have?" Yolanda shrugged her shoulders, her mother counted the dots on the dice out loud and then said, "You count them," which Yolanda did. The next five turns went very much the same, with Yolanda professing not to know

what to do and her mother modeling counting and then directing Yolanda to count the dots on the dice. On the sixth move, Yolanda counted the dots on the dice immediately after her mother's request (no shrug and no modeling of counting by mother) and did the same on her mother's turn. Her mother then hesitated on the next several turns before asking Yolanda how many dots she had. Eventually, Yolanda threw the dice and counted the dots herself spontaneously, without any prodding from her mother, and continued to do so, on both her and her mother's turns, throughout most of the game. The mother corrected Yolanda when she made mistakes counting, but she became less directive as Yolanda took more of the responsibility for the game herself.

Contrast the behavior of Yolanda's mother with that of Darrell's mother. Darrell would roll the dice and begin counting each pip on the dice, starting with the die closest to him ("one, two, three") and then continuing to count the pips on the second die ("four, five, six, seven, eight"). While he was counting, his mother would interrupt him and instruct him to count from the larger number, a more sophisticated strategy. For example, when the child rolled a "6 and 5" and started counting the dots, the mother would interrupt him by saying, "No, Darrell, start counting from the six here" pointing at the six and saying, "you know this is six." The child would start over counting each pip on the dice, asking his mother to stop. This continued throughout the game with mom rolling the dice during her turn and modeling retrieval of arithmetic facts (for example, "3 plus 4 is 7,"), which was apparently beyond this child's capability to execute on his own. Darrell usually ignored his mother's demonstrations and instructions and, as a result, showed no improvement in arithmetic strategy use over the course of the sessions.

All the responsibility for determining the extent of adult involvement is not on the adult. Both adults and children jointly determine the degree to which children can function independently. For example, children who are less able to solve problems on their own will elicit more support from adults than will more capable children. More skilled children need less adult support, or scaffolding, to solve a problem (Plumert & Nichols-Whitehead, 1996).

I have been careful not to use the word "competence" in describing children's problem-solving abilities. In Vygotsky's sociocultural perspective, learning and development are the result of interacting in specific culturally defined tasks that have specific rules. Unlike other theories of cognitive development (for example, Piaget's), "competence" is not an absolute level beyond which a child cannot exceed but, rather, is task specific (Fischer & Bidell, 1998; Laboratory of Comparative Human Cognition, 1983). A child can show a high level of ability on one highly practiced task but be much less adept on a very similar, perhaps even objectively less-demanding, task. A child's level of intellectual functioning is always evaluated by performance on specific tasks or in specific culturally determined situations.

Apprenticeship in Thinking and Guided Participation

Adults' interactions with children vary depending on their culture. Although child rearing in all cultures can take advantage of the zone of proximal development, what is taught will depend on what roles the child is expected to play eventually in society. Rogoff (1990; Rogoff et al., 1993) has viewed the transaction between children and adults as reflecting an *apprenticeship in thinking,* with novice children improving their "skills and understanding through participation with more skilled partners in culturally organized activities" (1990, p. 39). All the responsibility for the apprenticeship is not placed on the adults, however. Children might actively place themselves in positions to learn, prompting adults to increase the level of instruction as children become increasingly competent.

Rogoff developed the concept of **guided participation** to extend Vygotsky's idea of the zone of proximal development. The zone of proximal development has typically been applied to situations where there is explicit instruction between an older, more skilled teacher, and a younger, less knowledgeable learner. Rogoff uses the term *guided participation* to refer to adult-child interactions, not only during explicit instruction, but also during the more routine activities and communication of everyday life. Guided participation is "the process and system of involvement of individuals with others, as they communicate and engage in shared activities" (Rogoff et al., 1993, p. 6). Guided participation focuses on day-to-day activities in children's lives, such as doing chores, watching television, and eavesdropping on parents. Rogoff believes that children's cognitions are shaped during such mundane activities as much as or more so than in more formal educational settings.

The idea of an apprenticeship or guided participation might seem reasonable in cultures where children are integrated early into the daily activities of adult life, such as among the agrarian Mayans of Guatemala and Mexico, or the !Kung of Africa, whose hunting and gathering lifestyles have remained virtually unchanged for thousands of years. But this idea is not as easily grasped for a culture such as our own. Many school-age children do not even know what their parents do for a living and might not have seen their parents in action at their jobs. Moreover, children are generally excluded from adult activities, being segregated from adults much of the day. Other children around the world, for example, sleep in the same room or even the same bed as their parents throughout childhood, and babies never leave home unless they are strapped to their mothers' backs.

Many aspects of cognitive development in information-age cultures have been shifted from parents to professional educators, whose job it is to teach important cultural knowledge and skills to children. Yet, much learning certainly transpires between parent and child in postindustrial societies, particularly during the preschool years; in many ways, these transactions are designed to prepare children for the schooling that will follow. For example, formal education in the United States, Europe, and Japan involves children's responding to adults' questions when the adults already know the answers. It also involves learning and discussing things that have no immediate relevance—knowledge for knowledge's sake. Such context-independent learning, foreign to many cultures, is fostered in infancy and early childhood in our own culture. For example, as will be discussed in Chapter 10 on memory, parents of young children frequently prompt them to name objects or to recall recent events (Gauvain, 2001; Rogoff, 1990). Take, for instance, the following interchange between 19-month-old Brittany and her mother:

Mother: "Brittany, what's at the park?"

Brittany: "Babysing."

Mother: "That's right, the babyswing. And what else?"

Brittany: [Shrugs.]

Mother: "A slide?"

Brittany: [Smiling, nods yes.]

Mother: "And what else is at the park?"

Brittany: [Shrugs.]

Mother: "A see . . ."

Brittany: "See-saw!"

Mother: "That's right, a see-saw."

This type of interchange is not at all unusual for a mother and a child from mainstream America, and it is a good example of Vygotsky's zone of proximal development. Brittany, in this case, is learning to recall specific objects with her mother's help but also is learning the importance of remembering information out of context (mother and daughter are in their living room at the time, miles from the park). Brittany is learning that she can be called on to state facts to her mother that her mother already knows. She is also learning that she can depend on her mother to help provide answers when she is unable to generate them herself. Table 3-1, from Gauvain (2001, p. 111), provides a list of some of the functions that such "shared remembering" between parent and child can have on memory development.

Another way parents in postindustrial cultures prepare their children for formal education is by talking to them. In the United States and most of the developed world, parents talk to their young children, including them as conversational partners. Although the type of language environment children are exposed to does influence their language development (Hoff, 2000), children around the world acquire language at about the same time, even in

TABLE 3-1 Some functions of shared remembering in children's memory development.

- Children learn about memory process, for example, strategies.
- Children learn ways of remembering and communicating memories with others, for example, narrative structure.
- Children learn about themselves, which contributes to the development of the self-concept.
- Children learn about their own social and cultural history.
- Children learn values important to the family and the community, that is, what is worth remembering.
- Social solidarity is promoted.

SOURCE: Adapted from Gauvain, M. (2001). *The social context of cognitive development.* New York: Guilford, p. 111.

cultures where children are "seen and not heard." But children who are not included as conversational partners by adults might not be prepared for the type of language interaction used in school. These children might become proficient users of language in their own community, while being perceived as language deficient in school (Rogoff, 1990).

Another school-related skill that might be associated with parent-child conversations is reading. We know that reading to children is an important predictor of children's later reading ability (see Chapter 14). There are substantial differences in how frequently preschool children are read to (see Adams, Treiman, & Pressley, 1998), and differences in how children are read to can have important implications for later language, and possibly reading, development. For example, Grover Whitehurst and his colleagues (1988) trained parents of 2- and 3-year-old children in a technique of *interactive story reading.* Instead of just reading to the children, parents were told to stop every so often and to ask open-ended questions (such as "What is Eeyore doing?") and were encouraged to expand on their children's responses, suggest alternative possibilities, and to make the questions progressively more challenging as children's understanding increased. A control group of parents was simply asked to read to their children. Analysis of tape recordings of the sessions indicated that the parents in the two groups did read to their children equally often and that parents in the experimental group followed the interactive story reading instructions. After one month of such reading, children in the experimental group were 8.5 months more advanced than were children in the control group on a measure of verbal expression, despite the fact that the two groups were equal at the beginning of the study. In later research, similar, though somewhat less substantial, gains were observed for a group of low-income 2-year-olds attending a public daycare facility in Mexico (Valdez-Menchaca & Whitehurst, 1992). The effect, it seems, is quite robust and demonstrates that the way in which parents or teachers read to young children—ways that take into consideration children's understanding of the task and encourage their active participation—facilitates their subsequent language development and prepares them for life in a literate society. (For an example of interactive story reading, see the excerpt from Tudge, Putnam, & Valsiner [1996] in "Assessing Cognitive Development from a Sociocultural Perspective" later in this chapter.)

Is it just reading to children that prepares them for life in a literate society, or might talking to children also be related to later reading skills? Apparently so, but not all types of talking are equally effective at fostering later reading ability. Elaine Reese (1995) recorded conversations between mothers and their preschool children and related aspects of these conversations to children's understanding of print at 70 months of age. Most children were just beginning kindergarten, so few were actually reading. Children's understanding of print and prereading skills were assessed by their familiarity with letters and their ability to identify simple words (such as *cat* and *no*), a test of vocabulary, their knowledge about how books are read (front to back, with sentences running from left to right), and their ability both to comprehend and to produce coherent stories. Reese reported that mothers' conversations with their children about past events, especially when including elaborations of those events and associations with other events, was a good predictor of children's sub-

sequent print skills (see discussion of emergent literacy in Chapter 14). Reese proposed that mothers provide scaffolding by increasingly involving their children in collaborative conversations. According to Reese (1995), "a tentative conclusion that can be drawn from this study is that children who participate to a greater degree in early adult-child conversations may be honing different abilities from those children who allow the adult to direct the interaction" (p. 402).

Play is another area in which parents and older siblings guide children's development. One particularly important type of play for our purposes is **symbolic play.** Symbolic play is essentially pretending and can be solitary (for example, the child pretending that a chair is a car) or cooperative (for example, a child pretending that he's the driver of the car and his mother is a passenger). Symbolic play has been viewed by many as requiring mental representation and as an indication of children's general cognitive development (Piaget, 1962). According to Marc Bornstein and his colleagues (1996), "In symbolic play, young children advance upon their cognitions about people, objects, and actions and in this way construct increasingly sophisticated representations of the world" (p. 2923).

But how do parents, or more expert siblings and peers, contribute to children's symbolic play development? It seems that young children are more likely to engage in symbolic play when they are playing with someone else rather than alone and that mothers in particular bring out high levels of symbolic play in their children (Bornstein et al., 1996; Youngblood & Dunn, 1995). Consistent with Vygotsky's idea of a zone of proximal development and Rogoff's idea of guided participation, young children who interact with a more skilled partner who structures the situation appropriately for them, advance in their skills faster than when such support is not provided. Evidence for this comes from a study in which mothers and their 21-month-old children were videotaped during play sessions (Damast, Tamis-LeMonda, & Bornstein, 1996). Many mothers adjusted their level of play to that of their children's or slightly above the level their child was displaying. And mothers who knew more about play development were more likely to increase the level of play with their children than were less knowledgeable mothers, and thus provided appropriately challenging play interactions. Other research with 2- and 3-year-old children indicated that children were much more apt to look at an adult immediately after performing a symbolic action in play rather than an instrumental action, reflecting, according to the authors, the essential social nature of symbolic play (Striano, Tomasello, & Rochat, 2001).

Why might it be important to facilitate symbolic play? Children learn about "people, objects, and actions" through symbolic play, and research indicates that such play might be related to other aspects of cognitive development. Researchers have found a relationship between the amount of cooperative social play preschoolers engage in (often with a sibling or parent) and later understanding of other peoples' feelings and beliefs (Astington & Jenkins, 1995; Youngblood & Dunn, 1995). An understanding that other people have thoughts, feelings, and beliefs other than one's own reflects what has been called a *theory of mind* and will be discussed in Chapter 9. Developing an advanced theory of mind is necessary if children are to succeed in any society, and it appears that the guided participation afforded by parents, siblings, and other more expert partners during symbolic play contributes to this development.

Although the process of guided participation may be universal, how it is carried out varies as a function of how children are perceived and treated in a culture. Rogoff and her colleagues (1993) proposed that different parent-child interactions (that is, differences in the nature of guided participation) occur in different cultures. Rogoff et al. made contrasts between two general types of cultures: (1) cultures such as ours, where beginning in the preschool years children are often segregated from adults and receive much culturally important information and instruction outside of the context of skilled activity (that is, in school); and (2) cultures where children are in close contact most of the day with adults and observe and interact with adults while they perform culturally important activities. Rogoff and her associates observed 14 families with toddlers in each of four communities, two where culturally important infor-

mation is transmitted mainly out of context, through formal schooling (Salt Lake City, United States, and Keçiören, a middle-class community in Turkey), and two where culturally important information is transmitted mainly in context (the Guatemalan Mayan town of San Pedro, and Dhol-Ki-Patti, a tribal village in India). Rogoff and her colleagues observed toddlers and their caregivers doing routine activities (for example, feeding, dressing), while playing social games (for example, peek-a-boo, finger games) and while playing with novel objects (for example, a clear plastic jar with a small doll inside, an embroidery hoop, a jumping jack—a marionette that kicks its legs when its bottom string is pulled and the top string is held). Following are examples of guided participation in each of the four communities.[1]

Salt Lake City. A 21-month-old boy and his mother, exploring a glass jar that contains a peewee doll:

> Sandy's mother held the jar up and chirped excitedly, "What is it? What's inside?" and then pointed to the peewee doll inside. "Is that a little person?" When Sandy pulled down on the jar, she suggested, "Can you take the lid off?"
>
> Sandy inspected the round knob on top and said, "Da ball."
>
> "Da ball, yeah," his mother confirmed. "Pull the lid," she encouraged, and demonstrated pulling on the knob. "Can you pull?" Sandy put his hand on hers, and they pulled the lid off together triumphantly. "What's inside?" asked his mother, and took the peewee out. "Who is that?"
>
> Sandy reached for the lid, and his mother provided running commentary. "OK, you put the lid back on." And when Sandy exclaimed "Oh!" his mother repeated "Oh!" after him. When Sandy lost interest, his mother asked with mock disappointment, "Oh, you don't want to play anymore?" and suggested, "We could make him play peek-a-boo."
>
> When Sandy took the peewee out, she asked, "Where did she go?" and sang, "There, she's all gone," as she covered the peewee with her hands, "Aaall gone." (p. 81)

Keçiören, Turkey. A 14-month-old girl and her mother, playing with an embroidery hoop.

A mother introduced a game in which she and her 14-month-old daughter, Lamia, took turns putting the embroidery hoop on each other's head and then dropping it on the floor. The mother created a sense of pretend excitement by saying, "Ay ay ay . . . ," each time they dropped the hoop. This was followed by joint laughter. The game became explicitly pretend when the mother put the hoop on Lamia's head, making the girl look like a bug with the handles of the hoop sticking out like antennas. The older brother chipped in, saying, "Lamia is a bug, Lamia became a bug." "What kind of a bug?" asked the mother in a coquettish way. "A lady bug," the mother and brother said simultaneously. (p. 136)

Dhol-Ki-Patti, India.   An 18-month-old girl and her mother, playing with a jumping jack.

Roopa was not holding the top and bottom strings taut enough to cause the jumping jack to jump, so her mother took Roopa's hand in her own, grasped the bottom string with both hands, and pulled on the string twice, saying, "Pull here, pull here," as she demonstrated. She then released her hold of Roopa's hand to enable Roopa to do it on her own.

But the jumping jack fell to the ground because Roopa was not holding it tight. The mother, quick to help, lifted the jumping jack as Roopa reached for it. Twice again, she pulled on the bottom string with her left hand, repeating, "Pull it here." Then she released her hold, letting Roopa take the object. She held her hands close to (but not touching) Roopa's, ready to help if necessary. (p. 114)

San Pedro, Guatemala.   A 19-month-old boy and his mother, playing with a jumping jack.

The mother used a firm manner of placing the child's hands on the strings to mark the importance of holding firmly onto them, positioning the jumping-jack toy in a position that indicated to the child to hold the bottom string lower, and tapping the child gently on the arm, indicating not to pull the string so hard. (p. 71)

Although toddlers and caregivers in all communities interacted in ways permitting all participants to develop an understanding of the task at hand and their own participation in the task, there were important differences between the middle-class and more traditional communities. Parents in Salt Lake City and Keçiören placed a greater emphasis on verbal than nonverbal instruction, with the adults providing a good deal of structure to foster children's involvement in learning, including praise and other techniques to motivate children. The middle-class parents also frequently instructed their children in specific tasks. In contrast, parents in the Mayan and Indian villages used more explicit nonverbal communication and rarely directly instructed their children in a particular task. In these communities, children are rarely segregated from adults; because children are around adults most of the day, they can observe competent adult behavior and interact with adults while they perform the important tasks of their society. Rogoff and her colleagues reported that observation skills are more important and better developed in the traditional than the middle-class communities, with children in traditional communities being better at attending to relevant adult behavior. The acquisition of mature culturally appropriate behaviors via observation has been termed **legitimate peripheral participation** (Lave & Wenger, 1991), and, although adults seemingly play a less active role than in guided participation, it is nonetheless an important component in an apprenticeship in thinking.

The findings of Rogoff and her colleagues make it clear that there is no single path to becoming an effective member of society, but that, depending on the demands of one's particular community, different forms of guided participation are apt to be used. One form is not necessarily better than another. It depends on how a competent adult in a society is supposed to behave.

It is easy to think of cognitive development as something that "just happens" exactly the same way for children worldwide. After all, evolution has provided humans with a unique nervous system, and the center of our flexible intelligence is the brain. Yet, intelligence is also rooted in the environment, particularly in the culture. Understanding how cultural beliefs and technological tools influence cognitive development through child-rearing practices helps us better comprehend the process of development and our role as adults in fostering that process.

Assessing Cognitive Development from a Sociocultural Perspective

From the perspective of the researcher, how can one effectively measure how a child and a more experienced partner interact in a particular context? One must look at the characteristic of the context (some contexts might constrain the possible interactions more than others), the child, and the more experienced partner, all in interaction with one another. It is not enough to assess what the child does and then independently assess what the experienced partner does. All factors must be evaluated together. Let me provide an example of such an interaction by examining what happens in a joint-reading activity between a 4-year-old child, whom we'll call Rose, and her mother (adapted from Tudge, Putnam, and Valsiner, 1996, pp. 215–216).

For her regular bedtime story, Rose chose *Mike Mulligan and the Steam Shovel* for her mother to read. (The text of the story is placed in quotation marks.)

Mother: "Mike Mulligan and the Steam Shovel." [She turns the page.]
Rose: "To Mike."
Mother: Good. "Mike Mulligan had a steam shovel. A beautiful red steam shovel. Her name was . . ."? [Mother pauses.]
Mother: What was her name?
Rose: "Marianne."
Mother: Marianne. "Mike Mulligan was very proud of Marianne."
Mother: "It was Mike Mulligan and Marianne and some others who cut through the high mountains so that trains could go through. It was Mike Mulligan and Marianne and some others who lowered the hills and straightened the curves to make the long highways for the automobiles."
Rose: [Pointing to the picture.] And the holes for um er for the er um cars.
Mother: Yep, there are some holes for the cars to go through. "It was Mike Mulligan and Marianne and some others who smoothed out the ground and filled the holes to make the landing fields for the airplanes."
Mother: Rose, look at this airport. What do you think is strange about that airport? [Rose looks at the picture.]

Mother: Have you ever been to an airport that looked like that? [Rose shakes her head, indicating No.] What's different about that airport? Why does it look different from the airports we've been to?
Rose: Got houses.
Mother: It's got houses, but that wasn't what I was thinking of. But that's true. I was thinking that the airports that we've been to, the airplane landing is a long rectangular-shaped road called a landing strip, a runway. Is that what this one looks like?
Rose: [Shakes head, No]
Mother: No. What's different about this one?
Rose: Don't know.
Mother: It's round! Have you ever seen . . . been to an airport where the airplane landed on a round road?
Rose: No.
Mother: [Laughs] Pretty strange. Oooh, look at that.
Mother: "Then along came new gasoline shovels, and the new electric shovels and the new diesel motor shovels and took all the jobs away from the steam shovels. Mike Mulligan and Marianne were . . ." [pauses and looks down at Rose]
Rose: " . . . very sad."
Mother: Why were they sad?
Rose: Because they um, because, because um all the um gasoline shovels and all the [looks at mother] . . . shovels and all the mo . . . the motor shovels took all the jobs away from her.
Mother: Aaaah [sad]. That's right.
Mother: "All the other steam shovels were sold for . . ." [pauses]
Rose: " . . . junk."
Mother: " . . . or just left out in old gravel pits just to rust away."

What would one look at in this interaction to describe it in terms of a social constructivist perspective? First, the two are working toward the same goal (joint reading of the story) and seem to be jointly attending to the task. The two partners are also generally responsive to one another. This is obviously a familiar routine for mother and child, and each knew what to expect of the other. The two are not sharing equally in the load, however. The mother takes the lead in most of the exchanges. Although we have a dyadic (two-way) interaction, the relations are not symmetrical. In this case, mother is doing most of the work, although that might change over time as

Rose's reading improves. Note also that although the mother is contributing more to the interaction, Rose is not a passive participant. She selected the book, responded appropriately when her mother requested, and interjected her own comments at times. The mother seems to be providing adequate scaffolding for her daughter. When the context was clear, she requested that her daughter fill in parts of the text, but read most of the text for Rose.

Implications for Education

Vygotsky's theory has some rather obvious implications for education. He stressed active rather than passive learning and took great care to assess what the learner already knows, thereby estimating what he or she is now capable of learning. Teachers in Vygotsky's classroom would favor guided participation in which they structure the learning activity, provide helpful hints or instructions that are carefully tailored to the child's current abilities, and then monitor the learner's progress, gradually turning over more of the mental activity to their pupils. Teachers can also arrange **cooperative** (or collaborative) **learning** exercises in which students are encouraged to assist each other; the idea here is that the less competent members of the team are likely to benefit from the instruction they receive from their more skillful peers, who also benefit by playing the role of teacher (Palinscar, Brown, & Campione, 1993).

Is there any evidence that Vygotsky's guided-learning approach might be a particularly effective educational strategy? Consider a study by Lisa Freund (1990), in which she had 3- to 5-year-olds help a puppet decide which furnishings (for example, sofas, beds, bathtubs, and stoves) should be placed in each of six rooms of a dollhouse that the puppet was moving into. Children were first tested to determine what they already knew about proper furniture placement. Then each child worked at a similar task, either alone or with his or her mother (Vygotsky's guided learning). Then to assess what they had

learned, children performed a final, rather complex, furniture-sorting task. The results were clear. Children who had sorted furniture with help from their mothers showed dramatic improvements in sorting ability, whereas those who had practiced on their own showed little improvement at all, even though they had received some corrective feedback from the experimenter (see also Diaz, Neal, & Vachio, 1991; Rogoff, 1998).

Similar advances in problem-solving skills have been reported when children collaborate with peers rather than working alone (Azmitia, 1992; Fleming & Alexander, 2001), and the youngsters who gain the most from these collaborations are those who were initially much less competent than their partners (Manion & Alexander, 1997; Tudge, 1992). David Johnson and Roger Johnson (1987) conducted a meta-analysis of 378 studies that compared achievement of people working alone versus cooperatively and found that cooperative learning resulted in superior performance in more than half of the studies; in contrast, working alone resulted in improved performance in fewer than 10% of the studies.

There appear to be several reasons why cooperative learning is effective:

1. Motivation seems to be enhanced when children work on problems together (Johnson & Johnson, 1989).
2. Cooperative learning requires that children explain their ideas to one another, persuade, and resolve conflicts. These all require children to examine their own ideas more closely and be able to articulate them so someone else can understand them. Related to this are the results of a study in which fourth-grade children were given scientific reasoning problems to solve, either in pairs or alone, with some asked to talk aloud while solving the problems and others given no special instructions about talking aloud (Teasley, 1995). Did working in pairs or talking aloud make any difference in children's performance? Children who worked in pairs and talked aloud generated better hypotheses than did children who did not talk aloud. This result suggests that collaborative

learning leads to improved problem solving not simply because of the collaboration per se, but because collaboration increases "the likelihood that children would engage in the kinds of talk that support learning" (Teasley, 1995, p. 218).

3. Children are more likely to use high-quality cognitive strategies and metacognitive approaches during cooperative learning (Johnson & Johnson, 1989), which results in generating ideas that no one in the group would likely have generated alone.

Peer collaboration is not the cure-all, however, that the results of some of these studies might seem to imply. Performance is not always enhanced by cooperative learning (Pine & Messer, 1998). In fact, when older peers are compared with parents as partners in cooperative learning exercises, parents usually are the more effective collaborators (Ellis & Rogoff, 1986; Gauvain, 2001). For example, when peers work together on complex problems that involve planning and the use of strategies for their solutions, they tend not to talk as much as adults do about strategies and the task, are concerned about coordinating their actions (for example, who's turn is next, who should decide what), and interactions are sometimes influenced by dominance relationships that can interfere with learning opportunities (see Gauvain, 2001; Radziszewska & Rogoff, 1988). Thus, although peer cooperative learning often has advantages over learning a similar task alone, it is not a panacea, and typically does not result in as much learning as when an adult works with a child.

Performance on cooperative learning tasks also varies as a function of the competency of the "expert" in the pair. When the more competent peer lacks confidence or does not modify his or her behavior appropriately for the less-skilled peer (that is, does a poor job at scaffolding), achievement is usually no better than when working alone (Tudge, 1992).

As with other aspects of sociocultural theory, the effectiveness of cooperative learning will vary with culture. American children, accustomed to competitive and "do your own work" classrooms, seem to have particular difficulties adjusting to the shared-decision making found in cooperative learning (see Rogoff, 1998), although they get better at cooperative decision making with practice (for example, Socha & Socha, 1994). As the structure of schools change to support peer collaboration, with teachers' roles being that of active participants in the children's learning experiences rather than simply directors of it, the benefits of cooperative learning correspondingly increase (see Rogoff, 1998).

One interesting finding about cooperative learning is that young children will sometimes remember the behaviors of others as their own, an error of *source monitoring*—the ability to determine the origins of one's knowledge, memory, or beliefs. For example, Mary Ann Foley and Hilary Ratner had children make a collage with an adult, with the child and adult taking turns putting pieces on the collage (Foley & Ratner, 1998a; Foley, Ratner, & Passalacqua, 1993). After completing the collage, children were unexpectedly asked who had put each item on it, themselves or the adult. Foley and Ratner were interested in *attribution errors*—would children falsely attribute a piece to themselves that the adult had actually put on (an "I did it" error), or vice versa (a "You did it" error, when the child had actually placed the piece on the collage but said the adult had)? Four-year-olds made a disproportionate number of "I did it errors," attributing actions to themselves that adults had actually performed. The children tended to re-code the actions of the adults as their own. Foley and Ratner suggested that this bias might lead to better learning of the actions of others, partly because misattributing others' actions to oneself could cause children to link the actions to a common source (themselves) and thus produce a more integrated and easily retrievable memory. In support of this, Ratner, Foley, and Gimpert (2002) reported that 5-year-old children who performed a collaborative task with adults (place furniture in a doll house, as in the study by Freund [1990] discussed earlier) made many "I did errors"; however, these children later showed greater memory for the location of the furniture in each room than did children in a non-collaboration group. Thus, collaboration led to greater learning, but not in a way that might have been expected. Rather, young children's immature cognitive systems resulted in a high number of source-monitoring errors, which actually resulted in better learning (Bjorklund, 1997a).

Sociocultural Theory and Cognitive Development

The focus of sociocultural theory is unabashedly the social environment. But one need not reject any idea of looking at biological factors to adopt a sociocultural perspective. Contemporary sociocultural theorists clearly view development as occurring in a system of interacting levels (Gauvain, 2001; Rogoff, 1998), including the child and his or her behavior, people interacting with the child, other people in the immediate environment, and the school, the family, and the community. But there is the recognition that children's brains evolved to fit with children's environments, and those environments just happen to be essentially social in nature (Gauvain, 2001). In fact, as someone who didn't start out as a big fan of the sociocultural approach, I am sometimes surprised to see just how much of an advocate of this perspective I've become. One of my scholarly interests is in the role of development in human cognitive evolution, and I've argued that it was the confluence of big brains, an extended juvenile period, and life in a socially complex group that motivated the evolution of human intelligence; *Homo sapiens*' intellectual prowess evolved first in the social realm, in response to pressures to deal with other members of our species (Bjorklund & Bering, 2003; Bjorklund & Kipp, 2002). Although this is not the place to discuss these ideas in any detail, the account I favor is one in which the social environment played a central role in the evolution of human cognition and continues to play a central role in human cognition development.

I think it is easy to espouse belief in the idea that development is the result of multiple levels of causation, each interacting in a bidirectional way. It is more difficult to practice such a belief, however. I don't doubt that some researchers taking a sociocultural approach *do* view any mention of biological causation as unnecessary, and I believe some people who focus more on biological causation see the environment as nothing much more than a place for the genes to express themselves. And, at times, it is certainly convenient to talk about a pattern of development or a characteristic of a child as being primarily "environmental" or "biological" in origin, even though we know that *all* characteristics are the product of a complex interaction of bidirectional effects at multiple levels of organization. There are surely some spirited debates ahead for developmental scientists concerning *how* biological and sociocultural mechanisms interact to produce a developing child. But there should not be any debates concerning *if* they do. In my opinion, and in the opinion of probably most leading developmental scientists, one cannot look at human development independently of culture. Humans' social, emotional, and cognitive abilities evolved for life in a human group. And such a perspective is not at odds with other, more biologically oriented, models of development. Rather, models describing how the specific social environment in which a child lives influences development must be integrated with theories such as those presented in Chapter 2 on the biological bases of development. Only by studying children, with their genetic and congenital characteristics, in dynamic interaction with their environment, including the larger culture, can a complete understanding of development be attained.

Summary

Sociocultural perspectives of cognitive development hold that a child's cognition is constructed by the social environment. Contemporary sociocultural theories are based on the ideas of Soviet psychologist Lev Vygotsky, who proposed that development should be evaluated from the perspective of four interrelated levels in interaction with children's environments—*ontogenetic, microgenetic, phylogenetic,* and *sociohistorical*. Each culture transmits beliefs, values, and preferred methods of thinking or problem solving—its *tools of intellectual adaptation*—to each successive generation. Thus, culture teaches children what to think and how to think about it.

According to Vygotsky's *general genetic law of cultural development*, cognitive function occurs on two planes, first on the social, between individuals, and only later is internalized by the child. Children acquire cultural beliefs and problem-solving strategies in the context of collaborative dialogues with more skillful partners as they gradually internalize their tutor's instructions to master tasks within their *zone of proximal development*. Related to the concept of the zone of proximal development is *scaffolding*, which occurs when experts are sensitive to abilities of a novice and respond contingently to the novice's responses in a learning situation, and *guided participation*, which refers to adult-child interactions, not only during explicit instruction, but also during the more routine activities and communication of everyday life. Children also acquire important cultural behaviors by working along side and simply observing more skilled members of the community, termed *legitimate peripheral participation*.

Different cultures prepare their children for adult life differently. For example, in modern Western societies, parents talk to children extensively and prepare them for the types of tasks they will encounter in schools; in more traditional societies, adults are less likely to use language and more likely to demonstrate certain abilities to their children.

Sociocultural theory has been applied to educational settings, suggesting that *cooperative (or collaborative) learning* results in improved learning relative to when children solve problems on their own. Research has found that cooperative learning often produces better performance than individual learning does, but characteristics of the participants and the schools affect how beneficial cooperative learning is.

Note

1. From "Guided participation in cultural activity by toddlers and caregivers," by B. Rogoff, J. Mistry, A. Göncü, C. Mosier, 1993, *Monographs of the Society for Research in Child Development*, 58 (Serial No. 236, No. 8). Copyright ©1993, The Society for Research in Child Development, Inc., Reprinted with permission.

Key Terms and Concepts

sociocultural perspective
ontogenetic development
microgenetic development
phylogenetic development
sociohistorical development
tools of intellectual adaptation
general genetic law of cultural development
zone of proximal development
scaffolding
guided participation
symbolic play
legitimate peripheral participation
cooperative (collaborative) learning

Suggested Readings

Gauvain, M. (2001). *The social context of cognitive development*. New York: Guilford.   This book presents an up-to-date authoritative yet highly readable account of research and theory from the sociocultural perspective. The first set of chapters discusses mainly theory, whereas the second set of chapters presented sociocultural research in areas of "higher mental functions," including the acquisition of knowledge, memory, problem solving, and planning.

Miller, K. F., Smith, C. M., Zhu, J., & Zhang, H. (1995). Preschool origins of cross-national differences in mathematical competence. *Psychological Science*, 6, 56–60. This paper presents a good example of a study examining how cultural differences in "tools of intellectual adaptation" (in this case, how different languages represent numbers) can influence children's cognitive performance. It demonstrates how subtle differences between two cultures can have unexpected intellectual differences.

Rogoff, B. (1990). *Apprenticeship in thinking: Cognitive development in social context*. New York: Oxford University Press.   I was a slow convert to the sociocultural perspective of development, but Rogoff's book made me see the light. Rogoff provides the right mix of theory and data to provide a convincing argument for taking seriously Vygotsky's concept of the zone of proximal development as well as her own important contribution of the idea of guided participation.

Tudge, J., Putnam, S., & Valsiner, J. (1996). Culture and cognition in developmental perspective. In R. B. Cairns, G. H. Elder, Jr., & E. J. Costello (Eds.), *Developmental Science* (pp. 190–222). New York: Cambridge University Press.   This chapter presents an excellent account of the sociocultural perspective as involving a dynamic relation between the culture and a child's developing cognition.

Wertsch, J. V., & Tulviste, P. (1992). L. S. Vygotsky and contemporary developmental psychology. *Developmental Psychology*, 28, 548–557.   This article, written as part of a series to commemorate the intellectual giants of developmental psychology, presents a brief overview of Vygotsky's ideas and how they have influenced contemporary developmental psychology.

InfoTrac College Edition

For additional readings, explore InfoTrac College Edition, your online library. Go to http://www.infotrac-college.com/wadsworth.

4

Piaget and the Neo-Piagetians

Jean Piaget (1896–1980) has had a greater impact on the field of developmental psychology than any other person in the brief history of our science. The self-proclaimed experimental philosopher formulated a grand theory of intelligence that made children themselves, rather than their environment or their genetic constitution, the primary force in the development of thought. Piaget changed the way we look at children. Following Piaget, we no longer view the child as an incomplete adult. Piaget taught us that children's thinking at any age reflects a unique way of interpreting the world. Development is more than the simple acquisition of skills and knowledge. The 4-year-old is not just a smaller model of the 12-year-old who merely lacks the experience and knowledge of his older peer. Rather, in addition to quantitative differences in what these two children know (that is, differences in amount, degree, or speed), there are qualitative differences in how they know it (that is, differences in form, or type). Because of Piaget's work, it is difficult for us today to conceive of the child as a passive organism, shaped and molded by environmental pressures. At any given developmental level, children are seekers of stimulation who act on their environment as much as their environment acts on them.

Most contemporary theorists start with Piagetian theory (or at least phenomena brought to light by Piaget) and attempt to build on the edifice Piaget and his colleagues established in more than 50 years of work. Many cognitive developmentalists hold great reverence for Piaget's theory because of the impact it has had on the field of developmental psychology (see Brainerd, 1996). Although the number of active researchers today who are strict adherents of Piaget's theory is relatively small, familiarity with Piaget's theory is essential for understanding cognitive development as it is studied today.

Some Assumptions of Piaget's Theory

Piaget was a stage theorist. He believed that cognition develops in a series of discrete stages, with children's thinking at any particular stage being qualitatively dif-

ferent from that which preceded it or that which will follow it. (See Chapter 1 for a discussion of what constitutes a developmental "stage.") In other words, Piaget did not view cognitive development as the gradual accretion of knowledge or skills. Rather, he viewed cognitive development as a series of transformations, with children's thinking going through abrupt changes over relatively brief periods of time. Despite his belief in the discontinuous nature of changes in children's thinking, Piaget believed that the functions underlying cognitive development are continuous. New abilities do not just pop up but emerge from earlier abilities. Given this underlying continuity, Piaget hypothesized transition, or preparatory phases between stages—brief times when a child can have one foot in each of two qualitatively different cognitive worlds.

Piaget also believed that the mechanisms of cognitive development are domain general. Children come into the world with a general, species-typical nervous system, without being specially prepared to acquire any one type of information more than another. Thus, all intellectual accomplishments of infancy, for example, are governed by a general developmental function. Infants' mastery of early language, knowledge of objects, imitation abilities, and problem-solving skills are all interrelated and are the products of changes in a single cognitive system.

Before describing Piaget's account of children's thinking at each stage of development, I must introduce several assumptions Piaget made concerning the nature of development. One concept central to Piaget's theory is that of structures.

Structures

According to Piaget, cognition develops through the refinement and transformation of mental structures (Piaget & Inhelder, 1969). **Structures** are unobservable mental systems that underlie intelligence. In a sense, all cognitive psychologists are concerned with unobservables and examine behavior only to achieve an understanding of what goes on in the head. *Structuralism*, however, is a specific orientation within cognitive psychology, and an appreciation of what

Piaget meant by structures is essential for understanding Piagetian theory.

Unfortunately, it is easier to develop an appreciation of structures than it is to define them precisely in a way that the uninitiated can comprehend. Structures are most simply viewed as some enduring knowledge base by which children interpret their world. Structures, in effect, are representations of reality. Children know their world through their structures. Structures are the means by which experience is interpreted and organized. For Piaget, cognitive development is the development of structures. Children enter the world with some reflexes by which they interpret their surroundings, and what underlies these reflexes are structures (or more properly, **schemes**).[1] As development progresses, structures change.

Intrinsic Activity

A second central thesis of Piagetian theory is the idea that the child is intrinsically active. Children are not passive creatures, waiting to be stimulated by their surroundings before they behave. Rather, they are active initiators and seekers of stimulation. Of course, when Piaget spoke of a child being intrinsically active, he was actually referring to a property of structures. Structures are intrinsically active and must be exercised so that they can be strengthened, consolidated, and developed. Structures are most active when they are newly acquired, as any parent of a young child who has just learned a new game (such as rolling a ball back and forth with Daddy) can attest.

Intrinsic activity in children can be viewed as curiosity. Children are not content with what they already know but seek to know more. Although a child can be enticed to acquire certain information through external rewards, such exogenous reinforcements are not necessary to motivate learning and development. The motivation for development is within the child; children are the movers and shakers of their own experiences and thus are primarily responsible for their own development. Piaget made the child not only the focus of development but also

its major perpetrator. Environmental and genetic sources play a role in influencing development as well, of course, and Piaget most explicitly believed that development is the result of an interaction between a biologically prepared child and his or her environment. Nevertheless, unlike most of his contemporaries, Piaget placed his emphasis squarely on the child.

Consistent with his focus on the child as the primary "cause" of development, Piaget emphasized that the role of teachers should not be to *instruct* children (that is, to transmit knowledge) but, rather, to provide opportunities for them to *discover* knowledge. According to Piaget, "Children should be able to do their own experimenting and their own research. Teachers, of course, can guide them by providing appropriate materials, but the essential thing is that in order for a child to understand something, he must construct it for himself; he must reinvent it" (Piaget, 1972, p. 27). Piaget believed that the authority status of teachers actually hampered learning. "It is despite adult authority, and not because of it, that the child learns. And also it is to the extent that the intelligent teacher has known to efface him or herself, to become an equal and not a superior, to discuss and to examine, rather than to agree and constrain morally, that the traditional school has been able to render service" (Piaget, 1977, cited in Rogoff, 1998, p. 38).

As these quotes indicate, Piaget did not believe that children learn much from interacting with adults. This is quite different from the sociocultural perspective of Vygotsky. Piaget saw development as a process of discovery (as did Vygotsky), and Piaget believed discovery isn't possible if one is instructed by an authority figure. Piaget felt more kindly, however, to the role of peers in influencing cognitive change. Peers are of equal status, and the mind develops through the inevitable conflict that occurs when children interact with one another. Other children's ideas conflict with a child's own, causing disequilibration, which children seek to resolve. Because peers are equal in status, they must work together to resolve these conflicts, and cognitive development is the consequence.

The Constructive Nature of Cognition

Related to the concept of intrinsic activity is Piaget's belief that cognition is a constructive process. According to Piaget, when children act on their world, they interpret the objects and events that surround them in terms of what they already know. For Piaget, there is no such thing as objective reality. We interpret the world through our own personal perspective, and reality is a construction based on the information in the environment and in our heads. Piaget believed that our current state of knowledge guides our processing, substantially influencing how (and what) new information is acquired. In other words, the world is not out there for everyone to perceive in exactly the same manner. Knowing is an active, constructive process—an interaction between the environment and the active individual.

This position, known as **constructivism,** is not unique to Piaget. Constructivist viewpoints have been adopted by numerous psychologists dating back to Bartlett (1932) and can be found in the work of contemporary researchers describing the memories of both adults (Loftus, 1992) and children (Nelson, 1996). However, Piaget's constructivist position has a distinct developmental perspective. If reality is a construction, children at different developmental levels must surely construct different realities. The same event experienced by a 2-, 7-, and 14-year-old will be interpreted very differently by each. This is not only because of differences in the amount of knowledge they possess (that is, quantitative differences), but also because of differences in the quality of that knowledge (that is, qualitative differences). For a formerly 3-year-old who believes that cattle is cattle, there is little no difference between a cow and a bull. Wearing different clothes means him, and placing girls' clothes on him convinced the 3-year-old. Naming something doesn't quarter of this. But for Piaget, reality is not an absolute; it is a construction based on our current

Functional Invariants

Piaget used the term **functional invariants** to describe processes that characterize all biological systems (including intelligence) and operate throughout the life span. Piaget proposed two functional invariants: organization and adaptation.

Organization

Through the process of **organization,** every intellectual operation is related to all other acts of intelligence. Thus, one structure does not exist independently of other structures but is coordinated with them. Such a concept is consistent with Piaget's domain-general view of cognitive development. Similarly, organization is the tendency to integrate structures into higher-order systems or structures. For example, a week-old infant has one scheme for sucking and another for hand and arm movements. It doesn't take long, however, for these two schemes to become coordinated, resulting in a thumb-sucking scheme. Thumb sucking is not innate but represents the organization of two initially independent schemes into an integrated, higher-order scheme (even if these schemes become coordinated before birth).

Adaptation

The second functional invariant in Piaget's theory is **adaptation.** In its simplest form, adaptation is the organism's tendency to adjust its structures to environmental demands. Piaget defined two aspects of adaptation: assimilation and accommodation. Basically, **assimilation** is the incorporation of new information into already-existing schemes. Assimilation is not a passive process; it often requires that children modify or distort environmental input (hence, one source of cognitive errors) so that they can incorporate it into their current schemes. Assimilation is not the mere registration of a stimulus but the active construction of external data to fit the child's existing schemes.

Given Piaget's assumption of intrinsic activity, it is the nature of schemes to be active and sometimes

Maturation & building of schemas, assimilation

- Theory of mind
Cognitive ability not quite formed.

individuality - maturation
should grasp at 4.

used for no apparent reason. Piaget proposed that the application of a scheme for no apparent reason is an example of *functional assimilation*. If schemes are to develop, they must be used, so schemes are applied to objects in the world merely for the sake of exercise. Functional assimilation is most easily observed in infancy, with infants applying inborn reflexes to objects. According to Piaget, the "reflex is consolidated and strengthened by virtue of its own functioning" (Piaget, 1952, p. 32).

Complementary to assimilation is the process of **accommodation,** in which a current scheme is changed to incorporate new information. Accommodation occurs when children are confronted with information that cannot be interpreted by current cognitive schemes. Accommodation is obviously an active process, resulting in the modification of existing schemes as a result of those schemes' interaction with the environment.

Knowledge is constructed by these complementary processes of assimilation and accommodation. Actually, Piaget viewed knowledge as an activity and not a state, per se. Hans Furth (1969) interpreted Piaget's position concerning the acquisition of knowledge by suggesting that knowledge "can be viewed as a structuring of the environment according to underlying subjective structures [assimilation] or as a structuring of the subject in living interaction with the environment [accommodation]" (p. 20).

As a simple example of assimilation and accommodation, consider the grasp of an infant. Babies will reflexively grasp objects placed in the palms of their hands. This grasping scheme can be applied to a variety of objects that fit easily into the infant's hand. So grasping the handle of a rattle, daddy's finger, or the railing of a crib all involve (primarily) assimilation. The infant is incorporating information into an existing scheme. If the same infant is presented with a small ball, some small modifications in hand movements are required if the infant is to "know" this new object and successfully apply the grasping scheme to it. These modifications constitute (primarily) accommodation, permitting the infant to incorporate new data by slightly changing current schemes.

Assimilation and accommodation also describe the functioning of older children. The 2-year-old who calls all men "Daddy," for example, is using the verbal label she acquired to refer to her father to refer to all adult males (assimilation). She must learn to restrict her use of the term *Daddy* to her father and develop new terms for other men (accommodation), lest she cause her mother embarrassment. Likewise, many college students reading this chapter will need to alter their way of thinking about children and development to make sense of Piagetian theory. Piaget is not easily assimilated, and much accommodation is typically required before his theory is understood and appreciated.

Piaget stressed that every act of intelligence involves both assimilation and accommodation. However, some actions involve a predominance of one over the other. For example, Piaget proposed that play is the purest form of assimilation, with children modifying the information in the environment to fit their make-believe actions. Conversely, Piaget proposed that there is a relative predominance of accommodation in imitation, with children adjusting their schemes to match those of a model.

For Piaget, children enter the world possessing the functional invariants of organization and adaptation, with little, if anything, else pre-specified. Thus, counter to neo-nativists, children are not specifically "prepared" to process some information more readily than others, but rather, they actively construct knowledge, chiefly through the mechanisms of assimilation and accommodation. Piaget made his position on this matter clear, stating, "Fifty years of experience have taught us that knowledge does not result from a mere recording of observations without a structuring activity on the part of the subject. Nor do any a priori or innate cognitive structures exist in man; the functioning of intelligence alone is hereditary and creates structures only through an organization of successive actions performed on objects" (1980, p. 23).

Equilibration

Piaget stated that at least four major factors contribute to development: (1) maturation, the gradual unfolding of genetic plans; (2) the physical environment, the child's actions on objects in his or her world; (3) social transmission, the knowledge abstracted from people in the environment; and (4) equilibration, a concept unique to Piagetian theory. Piaget proposed that the first three factors are not sufficient to explain development and that development can only be understood when maturation, the physical environment, and social transmission are integrated with the concept of equilibration.

Equilibration refers to the organism's attempt to keep its cognitive structures in balance. This concept explains the motivation for development; it is meant to answer the questions "Why should we develop at all?" and "Why do cognitive structures change?" When a child encounters some information that does not match his or her current schemes, an imbalance, or disequilibrium, results. The child experiences cognitive incongruity, with the new information not quite fitting his or her current state of knowledge. States of disequilibrium are intrinsically dissatisfying, and there is an attempt to reinstate equilibrium.

How is this equilibration achieved? According to Piaget, equilibration is achieved by altering one's cognitive structures. That is, given the disconfirming information, accommodation can occur, with the child slightly modifying current schemes to match the environmental data. As a result, a new and more stable structure develops. This new structure is more stable because fewer intrusions will set it into a state of disequilibrium than the immediately previous structure was vulnerable to.

Discrepant information is not always dealt with in such a way as to produce cognitive change (that is, by accommodation). If new information is too discrepant from a child's current schemes, for example, accommodation becomes impossible and assimilation becomes unlikely. The alternative is to ignore (that is, not act on) the information, thus returning the structures to their original state. For instance, a first-grader given algebra problems to solve will likely remain in a state of disequilibrium only briefly, realizing very soon that he or she hasn't the foggiest idea what these symbols mean, and will go on to something else.

Another alternative is to distort the new information by assimilation, making it compatible with the old structures. In this case no qualitative change in the structures occurs, only a possible broadening of the original schemes. Nevertheless, the environmental intrusion is dealt with effectively, although it might not appear that way to an outsider. For example, the same algebra problem given to a 12-year-old will likely be recognized as a math problem, and the child might apply his or her basic arithmetic schemes to derive an "answer." Such an answer will likely be wrong, but distorting an algebra problem to an arithmetic one can re-establish a temporary equilibrium. The equilibration process is schematically represented in Figure 4-1.

Let me provide one more example of how the equilibration process might work. A 3-year-old in the bathtub is confronted for the first time by a bar of soap that floats. The child has no scheme for floating soap. Toy boats float, but soap sinks. This new information produces cognitive incongruity, or a state of disequilibrium. The child can distort somewhat the characteristics of the soap in her mind and assimilate it into her "toy boat" scheme. She also has the option of hiding it under the washcloth and pretending it was never there. Her third option is to modify her current "soap" scheme by accommodating this new information and changing slightly her knowledge of soaps.

Accommodation, and thus the attainment of more stable structures, is most apt to occur when the new information is only slightly discrepant from current structures. Information that exactly matches current structures can be assimilated into those structures, and information that is too different from what a child already knows is likely to be either distorted or ignored. Regardless, children remain active operators on their environments throughout and following the re-establishment of equilibrium.

Stages of Development

Piaget divided cognitive development into four major stages, or periods: sensorimotor, preoperations, concrete operations, and formal operations. A brief description of the major characteristics of children's

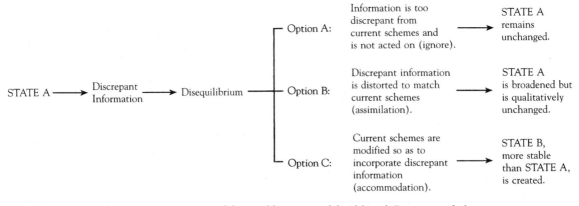

FIGURE 4-1 A schematic representation of the equilibration model. Although Piaget specified that equilibration involves accommodation (option C), options A and B reflect ways in which children may achieve temporary states of stability.

thinking during each of these stages is provided in Table 4-1. Piaget insisted that the order in which children progress through these stages is invariant and culturally universal; stages cannot be skipped. So, from a Piagetian perspective, a precocious 8-year-old who has mastered analytic geometry acquired these skills by going through the same stage sequence as her adolescent peers, but she went through them at a faster rate.

This assumption of the invariant order of stages is a direct consequence of Piaget's belief that development is *epigenetic* in nature—that it proceeds gradually, with later developments being based on earlier developments (see discussion of epigenesis in Chapter 2). According to Piaget (1967), a new cognitive skill does not arise fully formed. Rather, it has a history, in that the structure that underlies the new skill is a transformation of an earlier structure. Nothing starts out fully formed. Thus, the abstract reasoning of the adolescent, according to Piaget, can be traced back to the overt actions of the infant. A child cannot display reasoning at the concrete operational level until he or she has mastered the prerequisites at the preoperational level. In a sense, development at earlier stages is preparatory for development at later stages; "new" structures do not suddenly appear, nor do they lie dormant until the proper level of maturation has been achieved. Rather, in Piagetian psychol-

ogy, "new" structures are new only in the particular form or organization that they take. Each current structure can be traced to earlier, more primitive structures, which were necessary for the attainment of the more advanced structure. Piaget referred to this characteristic of development as **hierarchization.**

The Sensorimotor Stage

The first major stage in Piaget's theory is the **sensorimotor stage,** or sensorimotor period, which lasts from birth to approximately 2 years of age (Piaget, 1952, 1954, 1962). During this period, children's intelligence is limited to their own actions. During their first 18 months or so, children develop some complex problem-solving skills, but they do this without the benefit of mental representation. They know the world only by their direct actions (both sensory and motoric) on it.

During the first two years, cognition is transformed in two major ways. First, there is a progression from an action-based to a symbol-based intelligence—from sensorimotor to representational thinking. Second, there is a related change in personal perspective. Young infants, asserted Piaget, are unable to differentiate themselves from the external world; all the universe is one, with themselves at the center. By the

TABLE 4-1 Characteristics of major periods in Piaget's theory.

Period and approximate age range	Major characteristics
Sensorimotor: birth to 2 years	Intelligence is limited to the infant's own actions on the environment. Cognition progresses from the exercise of reflexes (for example, sucking, visual orienting) to the beginning of symbolic functioning.
Preoperations: 2 to 7 years	Intelligence is symbolic, expressed via language, imagery, and other modes, permitting children to mentally represent and compare objects out of immediate perception. Thought is intuitive rather than logical and is egocentric, in that children have a difficult time taking the perspective of another.
Concrete operations: 7 to 11 years	Intelligence is symbolic and logical. (For example, if A is greater than B and B is greater than C, then A must be greater than C.) Thought is less egocentric. Children's thinking is limited to concrete phenomena and their own past experiences; that is, thinking is not abstract.
Formal operations: 11 to 16 years	Children are able to make and test hypotheses; possibility dominates reality. Children are able to introspect about their own thought processes and, generally, can think abstractly.

end of the sensorimotor stage, not only are infants able to distinguish themselves from the objects they act on, but they also realize that these objects have an existence independent of their actions on them. In general, during infancy, children increasingly move from cognition centered on their immediate actions to cognition that displaces them in time and space from the things they wish to think about.

Piaget divided the sensorimotor stage into six substages. As with Piaget's theory in general, infants progress through these increasingly complex substages in an invariant sequence, with the successful accomplishments of earlier substages being the basis for the accomplishments of later substages. Central to each substage is children's problem-solving skills, particularly the extent to which they display intentionality, or **goal-directed behavior,** and this will be the focus of my description of Piaget's sensorimotor substages. A brief description of the major characteristics of children's intelligence at each sensorimotor substage is presented in Table 4-2.

There are many more specific cognitive accomplishments of the sensorimotor stage besides general problem solving. Two of the most studied, both by Piaget and others, have been children's acquisition of a sense of object permanence (the belief that objects exist independent of one's perceptions or actions) and imitation. I will outline Piaget's accounts of the development of object permanence and imitation following a general description of the substages of the sensorimotor stage. Contemporary research on these two topics, much of it questioning Piaget's interpretation if not his descriptions, is presented in Chapters 8 and 9.

Substages of the Sensorimotor Stage

Substage 1: The use of reflexes (birth to 1 month). Infants enter the world with a set of inherited action patterns, or reflexes, through which they interpret their experiences. Piaget used the term *reflex* broadly, so that infant reflexes include not only obvious behaviors such as sucking and grasping but also more subtle behaviors such as eye movements, orientation to sound, and vocalization. This is where intellectual development begins, for, according to Piaget, the child first makes contact with the world via these **basic reflexes,** acquiring knowledge of objects in the environment that later will serve as the basis for more complex accomplishments.

During this first substage, infants are primarily engaged in applying inherited reflexes to objects. If an object "fits" infants' reflexes (or, more appropriately, the schemes underlying these reflexes), they apply them to the object, assimilating it into their existing schemes. However, accommodation also occurs during the first weeks of life. For example, Piaget (1952)

TABLE 4-2 Characteristics of the sensorimotor substages in Piaget's theory.

Substage and approximate age range	Major characteristics
Substage 1 (basic reflexes): birth to 1 month	Cognition is limited to inherited reflex patterns.
Substage 2 (primary circular reactions): 1 to 4 months	Infant acquires first adaptations, extends basic reflexes; reflex is activated by chance (for example, thumb comes in contact with lips, activating sucking reflex); infant attempts to reproduce reflex, resulting in acquisition of new, noninherited behavior (thumb sucking) that can be activated at the infant's discretion; initial occurrence of behavior is by chance, so need follows action.
Substage 3 (secondary circular reactions): 4 to 8 months	By chance, infant causes interesting event in environment to occur (for example, infant kicks mattress, causing mobile over crib to move) and tries to re-create event; beginning of control of objects and events external to infant; as in previous stage, initial occurrence of interesting event is by chance so need follows action.
Substage 4 (coordination of secondary circular reactions): 8 to 12 months	Infant uses two previously acquired schemes in coordination with each other to achieve a goal; first sign of need preceding action, or goal-directed behavior, is exhibited.
Substage 5 (tertiary circular reactions): 12 to 18 months	Infant discovers new means through active experimentation, develops new techniques to solve problems; goal-directed behavior is exhibited, but entire problem-solving process is conducted by overt trial and error; intelligence is still limited to child's actions on objects.
Substage 6 (mental combinations): 18 to 24 months	Infant shows first signs of symbolic functioning; infant is able to represent events in environment in terms of symbols (for example, language, imagery); problem solving can now be covert.

made careful observations of his son, Laurent, who was adjusting to nursing. Piaget noted how Laurent would suck his hand or a quilt even when not hungry, the reflex being released by almost anything that touched his lips. Piaget also observed that Laurent's ability to locate the nipple and nurse successfully improved gradually over the first three weeks of life, as he learned to apply his sucking reflex selectively to the nipple (rather than to the skin surrounding the nipple) when hungry.

Piaget's observations tell us a number of things about the cognitive abilities of infants during the first month of life. First, during this time infants are highly restricted in what they can know. Behaviors are elicited by environmental events over which they have little control, and the range of their schemes is highly limited. Second, although active, young infants do not act on their environment to ob-

tain specific outcomes. In other words, according to Piaget, they cannot separate need from action and thus cannot be said to behave intentionally. Third, Piaget's observations demonstrate adaptation by infants. This adaptation involves the assimilation of objects into inherited schemes and the accommodation of those schemes.

Substage 2: Primary circular reactions (1 to 4 months). In this second substage of the sensorimotor period, reflexes are extended so that new patterns of behavior are acquired that were not part of the basic biological apparatus with which the child was born. However, these new acquisitions are still based on innate reflexes and so do not reflect new behaviors, per se. What they do reflect is the accommodation of reflex schemes to the environment. In other words, infants can modify their reflexes as a result of the environment, reflecting what can be easily recognized as learning.

The basic mechanism for this change in behavior is the *circular reaction*, a concept first introduced by the American psychologist James Mark Baldwin (1895). Most simply stated, circular reactions are acquired, repetitive behaviors. **Primary circular reactions** are the first class of these patterns to be observed in development and the only ones that are based on hereditary reflexes. Piaget discussed these first circular reactions primarily with regard to sucking, vision, hearing, vocalizations, and grasping. For example, Piaget detailed how Laurent, between 1 month 1 day and 1 month 21 days, acquired the ability to suck his thumb. The initial contact between Laurent's hand and his mouth was by chance. That is, babies don't start out by thinking, "Gee, I'd like to suck my thumb. I wonder how I should go about it?" Rather, in the process of random activity or activity directed toward a biological outcome (for example, nursing), reflexes are fortuitously activated. However, once his thumb or fingers were in his mouth, sucking occurred. Laurent repeatedly attempted to re-create the experience, gradually coordinating his arm, hand, and finger movements with his mouth until he had established the ability to suck his thumb whenever (presumably) he pleased.

What significance do such observations have concerning the development of intelligence? The significance is the advancement that this represents beyond the previous substage. In substage 1, infants are primarily victims of their environment. They actively assimilate objects to reflexive schemes, but the exercise of these reflexes depends on the chance occurrence of a stimulus that fits with a hereditary action pattern. In substage 2, infants show the first primitive signs of intentionality—of initiating a scheme that although composed of reflexes is itself not inherited. That is, once infants acquire the ability to suck their thumbs, that behavior is theirs to use whenever and wherever they please.

Substage 3: Secondary circular reactions (4 to 8 months).

As previously mentioned, a circular reaction is a repetitive behavior. Unlike primary circular reactions characteristic of substage 2, **secondary**

circular reactions are not based on reflexes but represent the first acquired adaptations of new (that is, not reflexive) behaviors.

The establishment of secondary circular reactions is similar in form to the establishment of the earlier primary circular reactions. With no intention beforehand, babies cause something interesting to happen and attempt to re-create the interesting event. A major difference between primary and secondary circular reactions is that for the former, the interesting events are based on reflexes and thus necessarily centered on the infant's body. In contrast, for secondary circular reactions, interesting events are found in the external world. This is especially true of visual events, although Piaget discussed secondary circular reactions for other schemes, particularly grasping and hearing.

Let me provide an observation of my own. My daughter, Heidi, at 4 months of age, was lying in her playpen. She did not seem particularly interested in any of the toys that surrounded her, although she was awake, alert, and active. Strung over her head was a "crib gym," a complex mobile with parts that spin when they are hit. I had spun the objects for her on several occasions, and when I did, Heidi seemed to like it. But today was to be different. While flailing her arms and legs, she hit the mobile, causing it to spin. She happened to be looking at the mobile, and its movement caught her attention. She suddenly stopped and stared intently at the moving object over her head. It ceased moving, and she began to shake her arms and legs, to squirm, and finally to cry. Again she hit the mobile, and again she froze and quieted, staring straight ahead at the wonderful event she had caused.

My daughter did not start out to spin the mobile. Her hand made contact while, from the point of view of an adult observer, she was randomly moving her limbs. The result of her act was an interesting visual event. She had caused a change in an object she was looking at and tried to reproduce that outcome. Although she apparently realized, at some level, that she was responsible for the change, babies do not have a well-developed sense of cause and effect. As such, she presumably did not know whether it was the movement of her legs, the turn of her head, or her vocalizations that made the difference. (In fact,

Piaget [1954] observed that infants at this stage will attempt to exert control over objects and events in their world without an awareness of the necessity of physical contact between agent and object.) However, through a trial-and-error process, she reduced her options concerning what exactly she did that made the interesting event occur, and she eventually gained control over the situation.

Substage 4: Coordination of secondary circular reactions (8 to 12 months). The intentionality observed during substage 3 is limited in at least two respects. First, the initial relation between an infant's behavior and environmental outcome occurs by chance. The "need" of hitting a mobile to watch it move, for example, arises from the chance discovery of this phenomenon, and not vice versa. Second, the infant's need seems to be mainly that of repetition—that is, the need to activate a scheme. The goal of a secondary circular reaction appears to be its own exercise. A major change in intentionality is found in substage 4, in that the need now precedes the act. That is, we have for the first time goal-directed behavior and the beginning of the differentiation between means and ends (that is, cause and effect).

This means/ends separation is first accomplished by the coordination of two previously acquired secondary schemes to obtain a specific goal. Previously, a secondary circular reaction was executed only for its own sake; now, with the **coordination of secondary circular reactions,** one circular reaction can be used in the service of another.

Piaget suggested that one of the simplest coordinations is that of removing an obstacle to retrieve a visible object. Piaget (1952) provided a lengthy description of experiments in which he placed obstacles, such as his hand, between his son, Laurent, and some desired objects. Laurent acquired the ability to brush aside his father's hand to obtain a desired goal. Laurent was able to use one well-established scheme (striking) so that another scheme could be activated (reaching, grasping, and retrieving an object).

Substage 5: Tertiary circular reactions (12 to 18 months). As with coordination of secondary circular reactions, **tertiary circular reactions** are charac-

terized by clear means/ends differentiation. Need precedes action. However, unlike infants in substage 4, infants during this substage are not restricted to applying previously acquired and consolidated schemes to achieve a goal. Rather, when faced with a problem, children can now make subtle alterations in their existing schemes that are directly related to obtaining a solution to their conundrum. This, Piaget stated, reflects a process of active experimentation.

Piaget (1952) provided the example of his daughter Jacqueline attempting to get a long stick through the bars of her playpen. The intent is there from the beginning, but it is only through a process of trial and error that the stick is successfully maneuvered between the bars and into the playpen. Piaget noted his daughter's surprise when some of her attempts failed, and the gradual accommodations she made before she mastered the problem successfully.

Along with their new intellectual tools come increasing locomotive abilities. By 12 months of age most babies can get around well, be it on two limbs or four, and this combination of increased locomotor and cognitive skills results in a child who is apt to be into everything. Children of this age often show a peak in curiosity. They want to know what makes things tick, and more importantly, how *they* can make them tick. They are explorers and adventurers. Is it possible to unravel the toilet paper, getting it all into the toilet without breaking the paper? How does one get into the bathroom sink? Isn't it interesting how by turning one knob the music becomes so much louder? Adults are often perplexed about why 15-month-olds find dog food and kitty litter so fascinating, why they are so interested in electric sockets and wastebaskets, and why they insist on climbing out of their high chairs and manipulating and mouthing everything on the kitchen table.

Although children during this substage are wonderful problem solvers, their intelligence, according to Piaget, is still basically limited to physical actions on objects. They know objects by acting on them and cannot yet make mental comparisons or represent objects and events symbolically. These children solve problems by a trial-and-error process, with all their trials available for public examination. So, for example, if a 15-month-old wants to see if her brother's tricycle fits beneath the coffee table, she will have to do it by physically attempting to place it under the table. It makes no difference that the tricycle rises a foot above the table. She cannot simply examine the two objects and discern that one is too big to fit under the other. She can learn this, however, by attempting it, although it may take several such tries before she concludes what, to an adult, is obvious.

Substage 6: Invention of new means through mental combinations (18 to 24 months). Until substage 6, development through the sensorimotor stage is relatively continuous, with behavior patterns acquired at one substage being superimposed on those of earlier substages. In contrast, the transition between substages 5 and 6 is more drastic and discontinuous. Symbolic functioning is first seen during this last sensorimotor substage, according to Piaget. Children show the first glimmer of mental representation, of being able to think about objects without having to directly act on them. With the advent of mental representation, the process of children's problem solving is no longer totally in the open. Trial-and-error procedures can occur covertly in the head, producing what appears to be sudden comprehension or insight. New means can be invented through **mental combinations.**

Piaget proposed that the *symbolic function* is expressed by language, deferred imitation, gestures, symbolic play, and mental imagery. (Piaget made it clear that the most obvious demonstration of the symbolic function, language, was made possible by the advent of the symbolic function, and not vice versa.) These varied mental abilities arise alongside the more action-based forms of intelligence during the latter part of the second year. During this substage, the cognitions of the sensorimotor stage begin to be internalized as representational thought, setting the stage for a revolutionary change in the nature of human intelligence.

The Development of Object Permanence

If a tree falls in the middle of the forest and no one is there to hear it, is there any noise? Young infants, presuming, of course, that they could communicate their answer to us, would answer this perennial philosophical question very easily. Their answer would be no, for there can be no noise unless someone is there to perceive it. But the young infant would go on to say that there is also no tree and no forest. Nothing exists unless it is directly perceived, or, more precisely, unless it is personally perceived by them.

This hypothetical philosophical discussion illustrates Piaget's concept of object permanence or, more appropriately, the lack of object permanence. **Object permanence** refers to the knowledge that objects have an existence in time and space independent of one's perception or action on those objects. For infants who lack object permanence, out of sight is literally out of mind. Object permanence is obviously a cognitive skill necessary for normal intellectual functioning in all human cultures, and this has been one of the most investigated cognitive contents of Piaget's infancy theory. Understandably, Piaget discussed the development of object permanence in the context of his broader theory of sensorimotor intelligence (Piaget, 1954).

Piaget stated that during the first two substages of the sensorimotor stage (from birth to approximately 4 months), objects are understood only as extensions of infants' actions. Objects have no reality for babies independent of their perceptions or actions upon them. For example, a 2- or 3-month-old follows his mother with his eyes, but when she leaves his visual field, he continues to gaze at the point where he lost sight of her, not anticipating her reappearance at another location.

The first semblance of object permanence appears during the third sensorimotor substage (approximately 4 to 8 months). Infants now attempt to retrieve an object that "disappears," although only if the object is still partially visible. For example, babies at this stage fetch a toy that has been partially covered by a cloth, apparently realizing that the entire toy exists under the cloth even though they can see only a portion of it. They do not search, however, for a toy that is completely hidden, even if the hiding occurred right before their eyes. An exception to this behavior seems to be that late in this substage, infants search for a completely hidden object if they are moving in that direction when the object is hidden. So, for example, a 6-month-old infant playing with a favorite toy does not attempt to retrieve that toy when her father places it under a blanket while she is watching. She does retrieve it, however, if she is reaching for the toy in front of her as Dad places the blanket over it.

By substage 4 (approximately 8 to 12 months), infants can retrieve a completely hidden object. To do this, they must be able to use one scheme (removing an obstacle) in the service of another (retrieving a desired object), which, according to Piaget, is the major cognitive accomplishment of this substage. However, object permanence is not yet complete, for if an object is hidden in one location and then later moved to a second, all while the child is watching, the infant searches at the first location and often acts quite surprised not to find the desired object.

Let me provide an observation for what has been termed the *A-not-B* object-permanence task. At approximately 10 months, my daughter Heidi was seated in her high chair, having just completed lunch. She was banging her spoon on the tray of the chair when it fell to the floor to her right. She leaned to the right, saw the spoon on the floor, and vocalized to me; I retrieved it for her. She began playing with the spoon again, and it fell to the right a second time. She again leaned to the right, saw the spoon on the floor, and vocalized until I returned it to her. Again, she played with the spoon, and again it fell to the floor, but this time to her left. After hearing the clang of the spoon hitting the floor, Heidi leaned to the right to search for the spoon, and she continued her search for several seconds before looking at me with a puzzled expression. Heidi had been watching the spoon at the time it fell. Thus, when it fell the third time, she had both visual and auditory cues to tell her where it must be. But she searched where she had found the vanished object before. She trusted her past experience with the fallen spoon more than her perceptions. At this age, children still understand objects by their actions on them, in these cases by their prior actions.

In substage 5 (approximately 12 to 18 months), infants can solve problems like the one just described. What they cannot yet do, however, is solve

what Piaget called *invisible displacements*. In invisible displacements, an object is hidden in one container and then hidden under another container out of the vision of the observer. An example from Piaget will help clarify this task:

> Jacqueline is sitting on a green rug playing with a potato which interests her very much (it is a new object for her). She says "po-terre" [pomme de terre] and amuses herself by putting it into an empty box and taking it out again. . . . I then take the potato and put it in the box while Jacqueline watches. Then I place the box under the rug and turn it upside down, thus leaving the object hidden by the rug without letting the child see my maneuver, and I bring out the empty box. I say to Jacqueline, who has not stopped looking at the rug and who has realized that I was doing something under it: "Give papa the potato." She searches for the object in the box, looks at me, again looks at the box minutely, looks at the rug, etc., but it does not occur to her to raise the rug in order to find the potato underneath. During the five subsequent attempts the reaction is uniformly negative. . . . Each time Jacqueline looks in the box, then looks at everything around her including the rug, but does not search under it. (1954, p. 68)

To solve invisible displacement problems, according to Piaget, children must be able to mentally represent objects, something that is not found until the last sensorimotor substage, beginning around 18 months.

Imitation During the Sensorimotor Stage

Imitation refers to matching one's behavior to that of a model. True imitation is not reflexive but is voluntary and selective, involving the modification of one's own behavior in accordance with that of a model. Piaget believed that imitation is the purest example of accommodation. Piaget (1962) did not view imitation as a unique cognitive phenomenon but, rather, proposed that imitation is primarily a function of the development of general intellectual abilities during the sensorimotor stage.

In substage 1 (birth to 1 month), infants are limited to interpreting the world through their inherited reflexes. During this first substage, some imitation-like behavior can be seen, but it is reflexive in nature and not true imitation. For example, a baby may begin crying when she hears the cries of other babies. Although this response could reflect merely an annoyance at being disturbed by the aversive wailing of nursery-mates, Piaget suggested that infants may confuse the cries of others with their own, thus eliciting crying in a reflexive manner.

During substages 2 and 3 (1 to 8 months), sounds that infants can already make are repeated for their own sake (primary circular reactions), and such reactions can be prolonged by the presence of a model displaying the same behavior as the infant. In these cases, the baby initiates a behavior that is mimicked by the adult, which in turn activates the baby to continue that behavior. Piaget's description of such interaction with his daughter will help illustrate this phenomenon: "I noted a differentiation in the sounds of her laughter. I imitated them. She reacted by reproducing them quite clearly, but only when she had already uttered them immediately before" (1962, p. 10). Piaget referred to this behavior as *mutual imitation*, with the infant imitating the adult who is imitating her. The imitation is exact, but only to the extent that the adult imitates the infant exactly. This, again, is not true imitation, for nothing new is acquired by the imitative-like behaviors observed here, with this pre-imitation representing primarily the assimilation of previously acquired circular reactions.

Piaget first observed true imitation in substage 4 (8 to 12 months). Children in this substage can imitate behaviors for which they receive no visual or auditory feedback, such as facial gestures. Infants can see the movements of their own fingers or hear their own voices when they attempt to imitate a hand gesture or a sound produced by another person, but they cannot see themselves imitate an adult's grimace or pout. Piaget referred to these unseen actions as *invisible gestures*. Infants in this substage are also now able to acquire new behaviors by imitation. Before this substage, infants' matching is limited to schemes they have previously acquired. Accommodation begins to predominate over assimilation. Although new behaviors are learned through imitation, the model's behavior must be very similar to what a child

can already produce if it is to give rise to imitation. Patterns that are too discrepant from a child's current schemes are not good candidates for imitation.

The process of true imitation begun during substage 4 continues in substage 5 (12 to 18 months). Piaget contended that imitation becomes more systematic and exact at this time. It becomes more deliberate and is more accommodative to the model than at previous substages. Nevertheless, the differences between imitation in substage 4 and in substage 5 are of degree rather than kind.

In both substages 4 and 5, children are limited to imitating a model in the model's presence. They are unable to observe a model and delay imitation for any length of time. Delayed, or **deferred imitation** is the hallmark of Piaget's sixth sensorimotor substage (18 to 24 months). With the advent of mental representation, children can observe a model and mentally code the behavior as images or "suggestions of actions" (Piaget, 1962, p. 62). With mental representation, events can be coded symbolically and retrieved later. Piaget provides an interesting example of deferred imitation:

> [Jacqueline] had a visit from a little boy of [one year, six months], whom she used to see from time to time, and who, in the course of the afternoon, got into a terrible temper. He screamed as he tried to get out of a play-pen and pushed it backwards, stamping his feet. J. stood watching him in amazement, never having witnessed such a scene before. The next day, she herself screamed in her play-pen and tried to move it, stamping her foot lightly several times in succession. The imitation of the whole scene was most striking. Had it been immediate, it would naturally not have involved representation, but coming as it did after an interval of more than twelve hours, it must have involved some representative or pre-representative element. (1962, p. 63)

In addition to being able to defer imitation, the substage 6 child can mentally practice a behavior before actually imitating it. The trial-and-error process involved in the substage 5 child's imitation of a model can now be accomplished covertly. Accordingly, a substage 6 child's first public attempt at imitation is likely to be more accurate than that of a substage 5 child, primarily because the trial-and-error process of the latter child is all overt.

Replications of Piaget's Sensorimotor Sequence

There has been no lack of research or alternate theories concerning the development of intelligence over the sensorimotor stage. One of the largest research projects to provide a test of Piaget's theory of infant development is that of Ina Uzgiris and J. McVicker Hunt (1975). Based on the observations of Piaget (1952, 1954, 1962), Uzgiris and Hunt developed a test of sensorimotor intelligence that assessed the development of circular reactions, object permanence, imitation, space, and causality. One major contribution of this work was their demonstration of interobserver reliability. A major complaint with Piaget's observations was that they were highly subjective. Uzgiris and Hunt developed items that could be scored reliably by independent examiners. The average agreement between different examiners' evaluations of infants' performance on this scale was an impressive 96%.

In addition to demonstrating that Piagetian tasks could be standardized, the sequence of sensorimotor accomplishments that Uzgiris and Hunt found in their cross-sectional sample was much as Piaget described. A number of other, smaller-scale studies investigated the sequential nature of sensorimotor accomplishments (including object permanence and imitation), and most of these studies confirmed the basic Piagetian substage sequence (Kaye & Marcus, 1981; Kopp, Sigman, & Parmelee, 1974). The consistency of the research findings led Uzgiris (1983) to claim that the "available literature on infant functioning during the sensorimotor period demonstrates that an orderly sequence of achievements is manifested in the formation of a number of competencies. The regularity of these sequences and their high correlation with chronological age are among the most consistently reported findings" (p. 182).

Despite the replicability of the substage sequence as presented by Piaget, much new research, using methodologies quite different from that of Piaget, has challenged the accuracy of Piaget's account of in-

fant intelligence. Most of this work has proposed that infants have far more knowledge and abilities than Piaget attributed to them. For example, research by Peter Willatts (1990) has shown that infants are better problem solvers and have a more developed sense of causality than Piaget proposed (see Chapter 12). Other research has shown that even very young infants have some relatively sophisticated ideas about the permanency of objects (Baillargeon, 1987; Spelke, 1991), infants can solve the A-not-B object permanence tasks at a much younger age than Piaget proposed (Reznick, Fueser, & Bosquet, 1998), are capable of imitating facial gestures shortly after birth (Meltzoff & Moore, 1985), and possess at least rudimentary symbolic abilities before their first birthdays (Gelman & Williams, 1998; Spelke & Newport, 1998). Piaget's observations were not wrong; he just did not take a close enough look at the phenomena under study. Much of this research will be discussed in Chapters 8 and 9. For now, it is important to understand the basic sequence of development described by Piaget and his belief that such development reflects domain-general changes in cognitive development.

The Development of Operations

With the advent of symbols, children's thinking becomes uniquely human. We might not be the only thinking species, and other species may occasionally use symbols (Savage-Rumbaugh et al., 1993), but the intellectual prowess that language, imagery, and deferred imitation provide us makes humans different from any other creature on the planet. In comparing the intellectual abilities of a 12-month-old infant, a 3-year-old child, and a 21-year-old adult, most would agree that the 3-year-old and the 21-year-old are more alike, cognitively speaking, despite their vast age difference. But no one would mistake a 3-year-old and 21-year-old as intellectual equals. Despite the fact that both the young child and the adult possess and use symbols, there are many differences in their cognitions.

The three stages that follow the sensorimotor stage are all similar in that the child has symbolic (that is, mental representational) abilities, but they differ in how children are able to use these symbols for thought (Piaget & Inhelder, 1969). Piaget labeled these three stages **preoperations,** describing children's thinking between the ages of 2 and 7 years, **concrete operations,** occurring between the ages of 7 and 11 years, and **formal operations,** characterizing the advent of adult thinking beginning about 11 years of age (see Table 4-1). As the names denote, each stage is characterized by operations, or in the case of preoperations, the lack of them. Most of Piaget's work beyond the infancy period dealt, in one way or another, with the development of operations.

Operations are particular types of cognitive schemes, and they describe general ways that children act on their world. Piaget specified four characteristics of operations. First, they are mental, and thus require the use of symbols. Not all symbol users possess operations, however, as is apparent in Piaget's description of preschool children as preoperational.

Second, operations derive from action. Operations can be thought of as internalized actions. This should not be surprising given Piaget's belief that every form of cognition has its origins in earlier forms. With respect to operations, a child's overt actions for a particular cognitive function (counting, for example) serve as a necessary basis for the internalization of that process. Children will first count on their fingers or physically line up red checkers with an equal number of black checkers, discovering through action that the one-to-one correspondence between red and black checkers remains the same no matter where they start counting or how they arrange the pieces.

A third characteristic of operations is that they exist in an organized system. Piaget referred to this concept of overall integration as *structures d'ensemble* or **structures of the whole.** Piaget believed that all cognitive operations are integrated with all other operations, so that a child's cognition at any particular time should be relatively even, or homogeneous. This assumption has provoked substantial controversy, and data pertinent to this issue will be presented in this and subsequent chapters.

A fourth aspect of operations is that they are logical in that they follow a system of rules, the most critical of which are those of **reversibility.** Reversibility comes in two types: **negation** (or **inversion**) and **compensation** (or **reciprocity**). The negation rule states that an operation can always be negated, or inverted. For example, in arithmetic, subtraction is the inverse of addition. If 5 plus 2 equals 7, then 7 minus 2 must equal 5. Such a rule would seem to be obviously critical in children's learning basic arithmetic. (This brings to mind the 6-year-old who proudly announced to his mother that he learned that day at school that 3 plus 2 equals 5. After praising him for his new knowledge, his mother asked him how much 2 plus 3 equaled, and the child answered that he didn't know; he hadn't learned that one yet.) The compensation rule states that for any operation, there exists another operation that can compensate for the effects of the first. For example, if water is poured from a short, fat glass into a tall, thin glass, the increased height of the water level in the second glass is compensated by a decrease in the breadth of the water.

The following sections give a general account of Piaget's description of the thought of preoperational, concrete operational, and formal operational children. Some specific cognitive contents of these periods are also discussed, and both Piagetian and non-Piagetian research are examined. Many other topics relating to the development of operations in Piaget's theory will be discussed in later chapters.

The Transition from Preoperational to Concrete Operational Thought

Piaget described preoperational thought, although based on symbols, as lacking the logic characteristic of concrete operations. By this, Piaget meant that operations do not generate contradictions. In contrast to concrete operational children, preoperational children are greatly influenced by the appearance of things, and their thought is said to be *intuitive.* Thus, young children are less affected by what, according to logic, must be and more affected by what, according to appearance, seems to be.

The example of conservation. Perhaps giving an example is the easiest way to explain the distinction between preoperational and concrete operational thought. **Conservation,** the realization that an entity remains the same despite changes in its form, is the sine qua non of concrete operations. For Piaget, conservation is not just a convenient task to illustrate cognitive differences among children but represents the basis for all rational thinking (Piaget, 1965). The concept of conservation can apply to any substance that can be quantified, and conservation has been studied with respect to length, number, mass, weight, area, and volume. In general, Piaget's conservation tasks take the following form:

$$A = B$$
$$B \rightarrow B'$$
$$A \,?\, B'$$

In words, the equivalence between A and B is first established (for example, two balls of clay). Object B is then transformed while children watch (for example, rolling one ball of clay into a sausage). The children are then asked to judge the equivalence of the transformed object with the initial, unchanged object, and to provide a justification for their decision. Basically, children must realize that the quantitative relation between the two objects remains the same despite changes in appearance of one.

Piaget's conservation-of-liquid task is illustrated in Figure 4-2. A child is presented with two identical glasses containing equal amounts of water. A third glass is introduced that is taller and thinner than the original two containers. The water in one of the original glasses is then poured into the third, taller glass, all while the child watches. The water level in the new glass is, of course, higher than the water level in the original glass because of its narrower width. The child is then asked if the two glasses have the same amount of water in them and to justify his or her answer.

Most 5-year-old children answer by saying no, the amounts of liquid are not the same anymore—there is more water in the new, taller glass. Ask them why this is so, and they will point out the difference in the height of the water. They will ignore the fact that the shorter glass is wider, and if this is pointed out to them, they will either dismiss it as insignificant, or in some cases, actually change their minds

"Is there the same amount of water in the two glasses, or does one have more?"

Water is poured from one of the original glasses to a taller, thinner glass.

"Is there the same amount of water in the two glasses now, or does one have more? Why?"

FIGURE 4-2 Piaget's conservation-of-liquid problem.

and tell you that there is more water in the shorter glass because it is so fat. They will admit that the water in the two glasses was the same to begin with, and they do not believe that anyone is playing a trick on them. The difference in appearance between the water levels in the two glasses is too great for them to believe that the same amount of water is contained in both.

In contrast, most 8-year-olds given the same problem tell you that the two glasses still contain the same amount of water. When pressed to explain why, they say that all you did was pour the water from one glass to the other, and that you could just as easily pour it back to confirm equivalence. If you ask them "Why do they look so different then?" they will likely comment that although the water level is much higher in the tall, skinny glass, it is much wider in the short, fat glass, and that the difference in height is made up by the difference in width. Children's responses to such questions are important, for in conservation problems, it is not sufficient just to provide the correct answer to demonstrate concrete operations; a justification that involves the concept of reversibility is also necessary.

This example demonstrates the intuitive thinking of the preoperational child. There really seems to be more water in the tall, skinny glass. In fact, most objective adults would probably concur, although we know that this cannot be so. The young child's intuitive approach to the problem leads to some contradictions. What happens when the water in the tall glass is returned to its original container? Most preoperational children will tell you that the water in the two glasses is now the same as it was to begin with. The contradiction, however, is one of objective fact; there is no apparent contradiction to the child. Some cognitive discrepancy (disequilibrium) may be experienced by slightly older and cognitively more advanced children, who realize that something is not quite right but can't figure out exactly what it is. For Piaget, these children are in a transition phase between preoperations and concrete operations. Their cognitive structures are thrown into states of disequilibrium, and within a short time they will make the accommodations necessary to achieve conservation. No such disequilibrium is experienced by younger children, as they assimilate the information to their preoperative schemes.

With a few mainly laboratory-based exceptions, conservation is not something that children are taught. The notion of conservation develops gradually, and once it is acquired, most children assume that they always thought that way. Ask most 8-year-old conservers if they ever in their lives thought the glass with the higher water level had more water, and they will answer "No" and often give you a funny look to think an adult would ask such a question.

An operational knowledge of conservation does not develop simultaneously for all properties of material; conservation of some properties develops before others. Piaget referred to this phenomena as *horizontal décalage*. When children acquire the concept of conservation for one property, they do not realize that the same general principle applies to other properties. Piaget claimed that the order in which conservation is acquired for different properties is constant across children. Thus, conservation of number is acquired before conservation of mass, and

these are acquired before conservation of weight, which precedes the conservation of volume. Other researchers have generally confirmed this pattern of development (for example, Brainerd & Brainerd, 1972; Uzgiris, 1964).

It's worth noting here that Piaget's concept of horizontal décalage implicitly acknowledges that there is variability in development and that a child's thinking will not always be at the same level for all related contents. But even here, he tried to show how there is regularity in this variability, with the order in which the various types of conservation are mastered being acquired in an invariant order. Thus, although Piaget did not ignore heterogeneity, or unevenness, in cognitive development, his emphasis was clearly on what was universal and invariant.

Conservation and cultural differences. Although the developmental sequence of attaining conservation is apparently universal, there are individual differences in the rate at which conservation, and other concrete operational abilities, are achieved. Piaget acknowledged that the social environment plays a role in cognitive development, although the role was a relatively minor one. Piaget proposed that the course of cognitive development is universal—that children in all cultures around the world will progress through these stages in the same order. However, the rate at which these cognitive accomplishments are achieved can vary as a function of the social environment, and this was the main (though not exclusive) role Piaget gave to culture in influencing cognitive development.

Cultural differences in the rate of attaining conservation have been repeatedly observed, with most studies finding a slower rate of development for nonschooled children relative to schooled children (Dasen, 1977). Yet, these cultural differences in rate of development might be attributed less to differences in the actual competence of these children than to cultural differences in the nature of the tasks and how they are administered. For example, in many studies, children from traditional cultures were tested either through interpreters or in their second or third language (see Nyiti, 1982). This contrasts sharply with the way American or European children are tested and makes it difficult to interpret differences in performance found between these groups.

In a study of conservation, Raphael Nyiti (1982) compared two cultural groups of Canadian children: Europeans (white and English speaking) and Micmacs (an American Indian people of eastern Canada). The Indian children attended school, where they learned English but spoke their native language (Micmac) at home. Both the European and Indian children were given a series of conservation tasks, following standard Piagetian procedures. The European children were all tested in English. The Indian children were divided into two groups, with half being tested in English by a European and the other half being tested in Micmac by a Micmac. There was no difference in how the European and Indian children performed the tasks when tested in their "home" language—European children in English and Indian children in Micmac. When the Indian children were tested in English by a European examiner, however, they gave much shorter and less complete answers and were significantly less likely to be classified as conservers than their European counterparts were. These results suggest that certain aspects of cognitive development as described by Piaget are universal and that concepts such as conservation develop on a predictable schedule in all cultures (Nyiti, 1982). This truism can be overlooked, however, if one is not mindful of the cultural context in which performance is assessed.

Reversibility. Piaget's description of children's performance on conservation tasks illustrates the importance of the concept of reversibility. Preoperational children, stated Piaget, are unable to apply the reversibility rules of negation or compensation to arrive at correct solutions to conservation problems.

Preoperational and concrete operational children differ in ways other than reversibility, however. Generally, Piaget described preoperational children as being more influenced by their immediate perceptions, more egocentric, and less apt to identify transformational relations between events, all relative to concrete operational children. Each of these factors is discussed briefly in the following sections.

Perceptual centration versus decentration. Preoperational children's perception is said to be *centered*, in that they attend to and make judgments based on the most salient aspect of their perceptual fields. They are highly attentive to particular portions of a perceptual array and often are unable to integrate various parts into a whole. In the conservation-of-liquid problem discussed earlier, their attention is directed only to the difference in height of the water levels, and they are unable (according to Piaget) to coordinate the two dimensions of height and width simultaneously. In contrast, concrete operational children's perception is said to be *decentered*, in that they can divorce themselves from specific aspects of a perceptual array and attend to and make decisions based on the entire perceptual field. Unlike their younger peers, they can consider two dimensions at once, partly because they are not so highly focused on one dimension that differences in the other escape their awareness.

The role of perceptual **centration** and **decentration** in young children's performance on conservation-of-liquid tasks is illustrated nicely in an experiment cited by Jerome Bruner (1966). In this experiment, children were presented with different-sized, clear beakers and asked to pour water from one beaker (for example, a skinny one) into a second beaker (for example, a fat one). However, a screen shielded the second beaker so that the children could not see the resulting water level. When asked whether there was still the same amount of water in the second beaker as was in the first, most children gave conservation responses. When the screen was removed revealing the difference in water level relative to the original beaker, almost all 4-year-olds who had given a conservation response when the beaker had been screened changed their minds. They could not ignore the discrepancy in the size of the beakers or of the height of the water levels; they confessed to being in error previously and gave a nonconservation judgment.

Perceptual centration is not limited to young children's performance on laboratory tasks but is reflected in their everyday thinking. For example, Piaget (1969a) noted that preoperational children often use height as a means of estimating age. Take, for example, the 5-year-old who told her 35-year-old, 4-foot-11-inch mother that she was the "youngest mommy in the whole neighborhood." In actuality, she was the shortest mommy in the whole neighborhood, and, if truth be known, one of the oldest among her daughter's friends.

This age-height relation was illustrated in an experiment by Thomas Kratochwill and Jane Goldman (1973). In their study, children between the ages of 3 and 9 years were shown realistic photographs of people from four age groups: infants, children, adolescents, and middle-aged adults. The size of the person's image in the photograph was varied, so that some people in the photos were 3 inches tall and others 5¼ inches tall. Children were given pairs of photos and asked to select the picture of the older person. Overall, the percentage of correct responses increased with age, but more interestingly, younger children were more apt than older children to choose incorrectly the taller, younger figure (for example, 5¼ inch picture of an infant versus a 3-inch picture of an adolescent). This doesn't mean that preschool children cannot evaluate the age of a person based on other factors such as facial characteristics. In fact, when children are not distracted by size and height cues, they can (Montepare & McArthur, 1986). Yet, when height cues are present, young children have a difficult time ignoring them, despite often obvious age differences based on other characteristics.

Egocentricity. In general, Piaget described preoperational children as being more egocentric than older, concrete operational children. Piaget used the term **egocentricity** to describe young children's intellectual perspective. Young children interpret the world through preoperative eyes and generally assume that others see the world as they do. Their cognition is centered around themselves, and they have a difficult time putting themselves in someone else's shoes. They, of course, are less egocentric than the sensorimotor child, who knows objects and events only by direct action on them. Yet, young children are more self-centered in cognitive perspective than concrete operational children.

According to Piaget, this egocentric perspective permeates young children's entire cognitive life, in-

fluencing their perceptions, their language, and their social interactions. For example, 6-year-old Jamal assumes that all children in the first grade have older siblings and can never be the eldest child in their family. Jamal is in first grade and he has an older brother; therefore, all first-graders, if they have siblings at all, must have older siblings. Or consider, for example, my encounter with a neighbor child when I, and he, were about 6. Maurice asked about the ages of my parents, and I told him I wasn't sure, but I knew that my mother was older than my father. Maurice quite emphatically told me that that was impossible. "Daddies are *always* older than mommies. It's the law." That evening, I talked to my parents and was told that my mother was indeed a few months older than my father, and that this was perfectly legal in the state of Massachusetts. Maurice's assertions were related to the structure of his own family. His father was about 15 years older than his mother, and Maurice assumed that *all* fathers must be older than *all* mothers. (There is also the fact that my father was nearly a foot taller than my mother, so that Maurice's egocentrically based belief in age differences between mothers and fathers may have been further influenced by his centering on the difference in height between my parents.)

Don't be misled, however, into believing that preschool children are so self-centered as to be impervious to others in their environment. They can identify and empathize with the emotions of others (Hoffman, 1975) and realize that they possess knowledge that others do not share. In fact, research during the last three decades has indicated that Piaget underestimated the perspective-taking abilities of young children, and that egocentricity is far from an all-or-none matter.

The bulk of research on egocentricity has concentrated on three topics: (1) young children's abilities to take the visual perspective of others, (2) communication, and (3) social perspective-taking. Communication will be discussed in Chapter 11, and social perspective taking will be discussed in Chapter 9 under the topic of theory of mind and in Chapter 13 on social cognition. For visual perspective-taking, Piaget and Barbel Inhelder's (1967) study of the three-mountain task served as the beginning of a long line of research. In this task, children were seated in front of a three-dimensional display of three mountains. The mountains differed in size, color, and form, with each having a different object on its peak (a red cross, a snow cap, or a small house). A doll was then moved to different locations around the display, and the children were to select from a set of pictures the one that corresponded to the doll's point of view. Piaget and Inhelder reported that most children younger than 8 years old were unable to determine how the doll viewed the array, but instead gave egocentric responses, choosing pictures that represented their *own* view of the mountains. That is, children stated that the doll saw what they saw.

Piaget and Inhelder's three-mountain task has been criticized as being unusually difficult, and later research showed that children will respond without egocentrism when provided with less complicated visual displays (Borke, 1975; Newcombe & Huttenlocher, 1992). John Flavell and his colleagues (Flavell, Everett et al., 1981; Masangkay et al., 1974) refined Piaget's original conceptions concerning visual perspective taking and proposed two developmental levels of knowledge about visual perception. At level 1, children are able to determine that another person might see something that he or she does not. This is reflected in a task where children are familiarized with a card having a different picture on each side (for example, a dog and a cat). The card is held upright between the child and the experimenter, and the child is asked what the experimenter sees. Children as young as 2.5 years can consistently provide nonegocentric responses to these types of questions, indicating that they realize that other people have perceptions different from their own. In fact, Harriet Rheingold, Dale Hay, and Meredith West (1976) observed the pointing behavior of toddlers, and reported that 18-month-old children will point to objects in their surroundings to direct an adult's attention to the objects. These young children wish to share their visual experiences, realizing that their perceptions are not necessarily the same as those of another.

In contrast to level-1 perspective taking, level 2 involves the knowledge that an object that is simultaneously viewed by two people can give rise to different visual impressions. At level 2, children realize *how* another person might view the same object they are looking at and understand that the two views might differ. This is reflected by a task in which a picture is placed on a table so that it is right side up for the child but upside down for the experimenter seated on the opposite side of the table. The child is asked how the experimenter sees the picture. This is a more difficult task, and children typically do not solve level-2 tasks consistently until 4 or 5 years of age. Nevertheless, the level-2 tasks used by Flavell and his colleagues seem to be simplified versions of Piaget's three-mountain task and indicate that the difficulty of the task greatly influences children's visual perspective-taking abilities.

Like most other aspects of preoperational thought, the young child's egocentricity is viewed as ineffective, which, in most situations, it is. However, there might be some adaptive advantage to a young child's egocentricity (Bjorklund, 1997a; Bjorklund & Green, 1992). From a global perspective, young children should be self-centered and less concerned with the thoughts, feelings, and behavior of others. They are universal novices and need to learn the complicated ways of their culture, making a self-centered perspective for young children likely beneficial from a Darwinian perspective. For instance, research with both adults and children has shown that when information is related to oneself (for example, when one is asked to determine how words on a list or events in a story relate to oneself), it is remembered better than when no self-referencing is done (Kail & Levine, 1976; Mood, 1979). Young children's tendencies to relate new information to themselves might thus give them a learning advantage, making egocentricity beneficial and not detrimental for the young child (Bjorklund & Green, 1992; Mood, 1979).

The Development of Class Inclusion

Piaget examined many aspects of cognitive development, some of which have been discussed here and others will be discussed in other chapters. Perhaps the most studied Piagetian indicator of differences between the preschool and school-aged child, other than conservation, is **class inclusion.** Class inclusion involves the knowledge that a class must always be smaller than any more inclusive class in which it is contained. In a typical class-inclusion problem, children are given several examples from two subordinate categories of a single superordinate category (for example, seven pictures of dogs and three pictures of cats). They are then asked whether there are more dogs or more animals; in other words, they are asked to make a comparison between a subordinate set (dogs) and its superordinate set (animals). Although preschool children can easily make correct numerical judgments when comparing two subordinate sets (for example, dogs versus cats), correct responses on class-inclusion problems using Inhelder and Piaget's procedures are not found reliably until late childhood or early adolescence (see Winer, 1980).

Inhelder and Piaget's description of the development of class inclusion has generally been replicated using variants of their original tasks (Winer, 1980). As with other aspects of Piaget's theory, however, there has been considerable controversy concerning the nature of the task itself and young children's class-inclusion abilities. For example, the questions posed to children in class-inclusion problems have been criticized as being a bit bizarre. Why would any well-meaning adult ask a child if there are more dogs or more animals? It is an unusual question and can easily be misinterpreted by children. Research by Charles Brainerd and Peter Kaszor (1974) indicated, however, that children who had failed class-inclusion problems rarely misinterpreted the questions. Moreover, there was no relation between children's abilities to recall the class-inclusion questions and their performance on the task.

Children's difficulty in dealing with subordinate and superordinate concepts can be seen in other situations in which potentially confusing questions are not a problem. For instance, my daughter Heidi at 6 years of age called me at work one day to talk.

"Is Julie visiting you today?" I asked.
"Which Julie?" Heidi asked. "Julie my friend or Julie my cousin?"
"Julie your friend," I said.
"No," she replied.

"Then your cousin's there?"
"No, she's not here either."

When I initially posed the question, she was not able to respond because I did not specify which Julie. She could field a question about Julie her friend or Julie her cousin, but I had to make up my mind which one I wanted to know about. She could not deal with the larger set of Julies, in general.

As is the case for much of Piaget's work, evidence indicates that children much younger than hypothesized by Piaget can solve class-inclusion problems under some circumstances. Even 3- and 4-year-olds have been shown to solve class-inclusion problems after being trained and to generalize this training to similar problems (Siegel et al., 1978; Waxman & Gelman, 1986). Other researchers have influenced children's performance by making the differences between the two subordinate categories more distinctive. For example, techniques that have increased children's likelihood of recognizing the difference in size between the superordinate and subordinate sets involve simply enumerating the items in each subclass (Brainerd & Kaszor, 1974), making the superordinate set visually salient (Wilkinson, 1976), requiring them to graphically represent hierarchies (through drawings or construction of graphs) (Greene, 1991), and making sure that children are highly familiar with the concepts used in the task. For example, several researchers have presented children with standard class-inclusion problems but have varied the typicality of the subordinate categories used (Carson & Abrahamson, 1976; Lane & Hodkin, 1985). Category typicality refers to differences in how representative various items are of their superordinate category (Rosch, 1975). Both adults (Rosch, 1975) and children (Bjorklund, Thompson, & Ornstein, 1983) evaluate some members of natural language categories as being better examples of those categories than are other members (see discussion of category typicality in Chapter 11). With respect to class inclusion, several researchers (Carson & Abrahamson, 1976; Lane & Hodkin, 1985) reported better performance when category-typical items were used as exemplars. For example, children were more likely to answer class-inclusion problems correctly when presented with pictures of robins and blue jays (both typical examples of birds) than when presented with pictures of chickens and ducks (both atypical examples). In other words, the children's knowledge of category relations influenced their class-inclusion decisions, indicating that children's abilities to deal simultaneously with subordinate and superordinate relations is not absolute but varies as a function of their knowledge of the category relations used in the task.

The Transition from Concrete to Formal Operational Thought

Children in the concrete operational stage are impressive thinkers. Given a set of data, they can arrive at an answer (generally) free of contradictions. They can solve reasonably complex problems, as long as the general form of the problem and of the solution are previously known to them. Their thought is directed to the objects and events in their immediate experience, and "thinking about things" suffices to get most people through most of the routine tasks of everyday life. However, most of us also recognize that a change takes place in early adolescence. Children no longer are tied to thinking about concrete objects. Their thought can roam to discover or invent objects, events, and relations independent of their previous experiences. Their thinking is no longer restricted to things, but can be applied to itself. As one Piagetian scholar put it: "Concrete operations consist of thought thinking about the environment, but formal operations consist of thought thinking about itself" (Brainerd, 1978a, p. 215).

Hypothetico-deductive reasoning. The benchmark of formal operations is what Piaget referred to as **hypothetico-deductive reasoning** (Inhelder & Piaget, 1958). Deductive reasoning, which entails going from the general to the specific, is not, in itself, a formal operational process. Concrete operational children can arrive at a correct conclusion if they are provided with the proper evidence. However, their reasoning is confined to events and objects with which they are already familiar. "Concrete" operations are so named because children's thinking is lim-

ited to tangible facts and objects and not to hypotheses. Formal operational children, on the other hand, are not restricted to thinking about previously acquired facts but can generate hypotheses—what is possible is more important than what is real.

Thinking during the formal operational period can be done solely on the basis of symbols, with no need for referents in real life. Although this might bring to mind a person whose head is perpetually in the clouds and who cannot carry on a conversation without getting into metaphysics, this was not Piaget's intention. Rather, we have a person who is not tied to facts in his or her thinking but can postulate what might be as well as what is. The formal-operational thinker can generate ideas of things not yet experienced, accounting for the novel (to the child) and often-grand ideas adolescents generate concerning morality, ethics, justice, government, and religion. Adolescents are entering, cognitively, the adult arena and ponder many of the weighty issues of the day without having had to experience directly the things they think about. The theories of most adolescents are naive because of their limited knowledge, but Piaget believed these children are flexing their mental muscles, using their newly acquired symbolic skills to deal with ideas rather than with things.

Hypothetical thinking is also critical for most forms of mathematics beyond arithmetic. If $2x + 5 = 15$, what does x equal? The problem does not deal with concrete entities such as apples or oranges but with numbers and letters. Mathematics in general is based on hypotheses and not necessarily in reality. Let y be 22; or let it be 7, or –12, or 45 degrees, or the cosine of angle AB. Once provided with a premise, formal operational thinkers can go on to solve the problem. They don't ask, "Is y *really 22?*" It is an arbitrary, hypothetical problem, and one that can be answered only if it is approached abstractly, using a symbol system that does not require concrete referents.

Thinking like a scientist. In addition to developing deductive reasoning abilities, Piaget theorized that formal operational children are able to think inductively, going from specific observations to broad generalizations. **Inductive reasoning** is the type of thinking that characterizes scientists, where hypotheses are generated and then systematically tested in experiments. By controlling for extraneous or potentially confounding factors, experiments lead to conclusions about nature. Inhelder and Piaget (1958) used a series of tasks to assess scientific reasoning, one of which, the pendulum problem, I will discuss briefly.

In the pendulum problem, children are given a rod from which strings of different lengths can be suspended. Objects of varying weight can be attached to the strings. The apparatus for this problem is shown in Figure 4-3. The children are shown how the pendulum operates (one places a weighted string on the rod and swings it) and are asked to determine the factors responsible for the speed with which the pendulum swings (the rate of oscillation). The children are told that in addition to varying the length of the string and the weight of the object attached to it, they can drop the object from varying heights (for example, high versus low) and alter the force of the push they give the object when initially propelling it. Thus, in attempting to solve the problem of the oscillating pendulum, the children can consider four possible factors (string length, weight of object, height of release, and force of push), with several levels within each factor (for example, three lengths of string; four weights of objects). The children are given the opportunity to experiment with the apparatus before providing an answer to the question of which factors are responsible for the pendulum's rate of oscillations. The correct answer is the length of the string—short strings swing faster than long strings, regardless of all other factors.

How might a scientist go about solving this problem? The first step is to generate a hypothesis. It doesn't matter if the hypothesis is correct or not, merely that it be testable and yield noncontradictory conclusions. This initial step is within the ability of concrete operational children. The next step is what separates the concrete from the formal operational thinkers—the testing of one's hypothesis. The trick is to vary a single factor while holding the others constant. For example, a child might examine the rate of oscillation for the 100-gram weight in combination with all the other factors (that is, short string, high release, easy push; short string, high release,

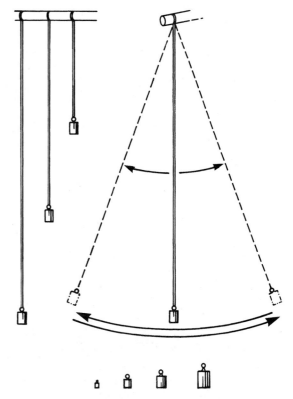

FIGURE 4-3 The apparatus for the pendulum problem. Children are to determine what factors or combination of factors are responsible for the rate at which the pendulum oscillates. SOURCE: "The Pendulum Problem" from *The Growth of Logical Thinking from Childhood to Adolescence*, by B. Inhelder and Jean Piaget. Copyright © 1985 Basic Books. Reprinted with permission

hard push; short string, low release, short push, and so on). This can then be done for other weights, until the child has tested all of the various combinations. Table 4-3 presents the 16 possible combinations and their outcomes for a pendulum problem involving four factors and two levels for each factor (long versus short string; heavy versus light weight; low versus high release; easy versus hard push).

Concrete operational children often get off to a good start on this problem but rarely arrive at the correct answer. Their observations are generally accurate (which is not the case for preoperational children), but they usually fail to isolate relevant

TABLE 4-3 Possible combinations and outcomes of the pendulum.

Weight of object	Height of drop	Force of push	Length of string	
			Short	Long
Light	Low	Easy	Fast	Slow
		Hard	Fast	Slow
	High	Easy	Fast	Slow
		Hard	Fast	Slow
Heavy	Low	Easy	Fast	Slow
		Hard	Fast	Slow
	High	Easy	Fast	Slow
		Hard	Fast	Slow

variables and will arrive at a conclusion before exhaustively testing their hypotheses. For example, children might observe that the pendulum swings fast with a short string and a heavy weight and conclude that both string length and weight are jointly responsible for rate of oscillation. According to Inhelder and Piaget (1958), not until formal operations can children test their hypotheses correctly and arrive at the only possible, logical conclusion. More will be said about scientific reasoning in Chapter 12.

Thinking About Thinking. A further formal operational characteristic involves the ability to examine the contents of one's thought. Concrete operational thinkers have available to them some powerful problem-solving skills. But, according to Piaget, they are not able to reflect on the content of their thinking to arrive at new insights. Concrete operational children gain knowledge from the outside world but cannot learn anything new by contemplating what

they already know. In contrast, formal operational children can acquire new information as a result of internal reflection. Piaget (1971) used the term **reflective abstraction** to refer to "a rearrangement, by means of thought, of some matter previously presented to the subject in a rough or immediate form" (p. 320). In other words, formal operational children can reflect on knowledge they already possess and, without needing additional information from the external environment, arrive at a previously unknown truth. Reflective abstraction is thinking about thinking and might allow a child to apply more readily information that he or she knows to new situations, or to discover alternative cognitive routes to solving old problems.

Egocentricity in Adolescence. One interesting observation Piaget made about adolescents that ties their cognition to that of much younger children concerns egocentricity. Egocentricity is usually associated with preoperational thought. Piaget defined egocentrism broadly as an inability to decenter, however, and proposed that adolescents demonstrate their own form of centration.

Piaget stated that adolescents are concerned about their future in society and often with how they might transform society, but many of the grand social and political ideas of adolescents conflict with the beliefs or attitudes of others (particularly people in authority). Adolescents also might believe that these abstract ideas are unique to them, making them impatient with the "stodgy and simple-minded" ideas of their elders. This view changes as the adolescent approaches adulthood, and many of us can identify with Mark Twain, who professed to be impressed by how much his father had learned between Twain's 14th and 21st birthdays.

Adolescence is a time when young people are trying to leave childhood behind and adopt adult roles, an attempt that often results in extreme self-consciousness. Adolescents' self-centered perspectives result in the mistaken belief that other people are as concerned with their feelings and behavior as they are, which only enhances their self-consciousness. David Elkind (1967; Elkind & Bowen, 1979) hypothesized that adolescents feel that they are constantly "on stage" or playing to an **imaginary audience.** This hypothesis has been confirmed in several studies, where adolescents' responses to potentially embarrassing situations and their tendencies to reveal aspects of themselves to others were related to age and formal operational abilities (Elkind & Bowen, 1979; Gray & Hudson, 1984). Although there are some discrepancies in the findings, the effect of the imaginary audience seems to peak in early adolescence and to decline as formal operational skills increase.

Elkind also proposed that the egocentrism of adolescence leads to what he called the **personal fable,** a belief in one's uniqueness and invulnerability. This is reflected in the often-reckless behavior of adolescents and the belief that bad things happen only to other people (for example, "I won't get pregnant," or "I can get off the tracks before the train gets here") (Arnett, 1992).

The risk-taking behavior that springs from adolescents' personal fables clearly has its drawbacks, but it might also have some adaptive value, just as preschool children's egocentricity might. For example, teenage egocentricity ensures that adolescents will experiment with new ideas and generally behave more independently (Bjorklund & Green, 1992). Many of these experiences will be beneficial to adult functioning and might hasten the entry into adult life. Many parents do not welcome such independence, for the negative consequences of much adolescent risk taking are real, but the end result for most adolescents of their egocentricity might be adaptive in the long run.

The State of Piaget's Theory Today

Piaget is a giant in the field of human development. As one scholar quoted by Harry Beilin (1992) put it, "assessing the impact of Piaget on developmental psychology is like assessing the impact of Shakespeare on English literature or Aristotle on philosophy—impossible" (p. 191). What does Piaget's theory, initially formulated more than three-quarters of a century ago, tell us about development today? Piaget continues to influence contemporary developmentalists. His work is cited more frequently by developmental researchers than that of anyone else. But much of the interest Piaget has generated has been criticism rather than praise. Does this theory paint an accurate picture of cognitive development, or is it ready to be relegated to the historical archives? Obviously, I would not commit an entire chapter to this theory if I did not think it had substantial merit. But 40-some years of intense investigation (some would say 40 years of Piaget bashing) has shown that Piaget's theory is not the final word.

Before detailing the criticisms of Piaget's theory, however, I think it is appropriate to acknowledge some of the lasting contributions that the man and the theory have made to developmental psychology.

Piaget's Contributions

Here is a list of the major contributions that Piaget made to the field of cognitive development. The list is based, in part, on an assessment of Piaget's contributions made by several prominent researchers, written in honor of the centennial of Piaget's birth (Brainerd, 1996; Elkind, 1996; Fischer & Hencke, 1996; Flavell, 1996; Gopnik, 1996; Kessen, 1996; Siegler & Ellis, 1996):

1. Piaget founded the field of cognitive development as we know it. The study of children's thinking has focused on high-level, cognitive tasks, very different from the emphasis on basic-level and mainly unconscious cognition that has characterized the study of adult cognition. Because of Piaget, cognitive development is a unique field to itself, and not simply the application of ideas and methods developed in the study of adult cognition to children.

2. The child is an active, self-motivated agent, playing an important role in his or her own development. This is reflected by Piaget's idea of constructivism, which might seem obvious to anyone today who has seriously considered the nature of cognitive development, but was an innovation

of Piaget and counter to the dominant perspective of his time.

3. Piaget's equilibration model was one of the first attempts to explain, rather than just describe, the process of development. Despite the many years since Piaget originally formulated this model, only recently have psychologists taken seriously the challenge to explain, rather than just describe, developmental transitions (Case, 1992; Fischer, 1980; Siegler, 1996).

4. Piaget introduced many interesting and useful concepts to cognitive development, including *scheme, object permanence, egocentrism, centration, decentration,* and *conservation,* among many others. Accompanying these concepts were many experimental tasks used to assess them, many of which are still used by psychologists today.

5. Piaget provided a highly memorable description of cognitive development that gave a relatively accurate picture of how children of different ages think. Piaget's description of development still captures much of the richness and uniqueness of children's thinking. Most preschool children do take a relatively egocentric perspective of the world and their attention is centered on the obvious physical characteristics of stimuli. Most concrete operational children cannot engage in introspection about their own thought processes, they don't think hypothetically, and they rarely approach problems in a scientific way. Children can, under certain circumstances, be trained or biased to think in a more advanced way, but such training is usually limited and rarely transforms the child into a totally different type of thinker. In other words, Piaget's description of intellectual development has ecological validity in that it depicts well the day-to-day functioning of most children.

6. Piaget's influence extended beyond the field of cognitive development to other areas of development (social, emotional), and, importantly, to education.

7. Piaget made more important empirical discoveries, on a wider range of topics, than any other developmental psychologist, and he is not likely to be displaced from this lofty seat of honor soon.

8. Finally, Piaget asked important questions and drew literally thousands of researchers to the study of cognitive development. And as often happens when heuristic theories such as Piaget's are repeatedly scrutinized, some of his research led to new insights while pointing to problems with his original ideas. We now turn to some of these problems.

Competence or Performance?

Piaget believed that he was assessing children's competencies—their actual abilities. Research cited earlier concerning young children's visual perspective taking (for example, Borke, 1975) clearly demonstrates that children often have greater mental skills than Piaget attributed to them. Other researchers have shown that children who do not spontaneously solve problems in a concrete operational way can be trained to do so. For example, although scientists have replicated the stages involved in the acquisition of conservation proposed by Piaget (Brainerd & Brainerd, 1972), many have demonstrated that children as young as 4 years of age can be trained to conserve by way of a variety of techniques (Brainerd & Allen, 1971; Gelman, 1969), and more recent research has reported success in training children with mental retardation to conserve (Hendler & Weisberg, 1992). The magnitude of training effects is greater for older than for younger children, with few studies revealing convincing evidence that 3-year-olds can be trained to conserve (Field, 1987). In a review of the conservation training literature, however, Dorothy Field (1987) concluded that 76% of all studies successfully induced conservation in preschool children, with a smaller percentage of these studies demonstrating generalization to other materials and transfer over delayed (one week or longer) periods.

Despite the impressive training and transfer effects shown by numerous researchers for conservation, the training effects are confined to the laboratory. Will 4-year-old children who are taught to conserve in the lab be convinced that they have the same amount of sandwich regardless of whether it is cut into two pieces or four? Much recent work in cognitive development has been concerned with context specificity —the extent to which cognitive competence is limited to a specific context (Ceci, 1996)—and future research should investigate whether conservation training can be generalized beyond the laboratory and into the homes and schools of children.

Training studies have not been limited to teaching preoperational children conservation and other concrete operational tasks but also have been used to teach formal operational reasoning to concrete operational children. Many of the observations of adolescent thinking made by Inhelder and Piaget (1958) have been replicated by others using their original problems (Lovell, 1961) as well as modifications of their experimental tasks (Kuhn & Brannock, 1977). As with Piaget's research on concrete operations, however, subsequent research has indicated that Piaget underestimated children's intellectual abilities in many ways. Children much younger than proposed by Inhelder and Piaget have been shown to display formal operational reasoning under some conditions. Subtle differences in how the instructions are given or in the task materials influence the likelihood that children will successfully perform formal operational tasks (Danner & Day, 1977; Slater & Kingston, 1981), and several researchers have demonstrated that concrete operational children can be trained to solve formal operational problems (Adey & Shayer, 1992; Stone & Day, 1978). In general, research has indicated that young children have greater competencies with respect to some formal operational abilities than Inhelder and Piaget originally proposed, although they will display these competencies only under limited conditions.

In other situations, however, research has shown that Piaget's account of formal operations greatly overestimates how adults actually think (Capon & Kuhn, 1979; Kuhn et al., 1977). For example, Noel Capon and Deanna Kuhn (1979) investigated whether adults tend to use formal operational abilities in a practical task. These researchers interviewed 50 women in a supermarket and asked them to judge which of two sizes of the same product was the better buy. For example, one task involved two bottles of garlic powder: a smaller bottle containing 1.25 ounces

(35 grams) selling for 41 cents, and a larger bottle containing 2.37 ounces (67 grams) selling for 77 cents. The women were provided with pencil and paper that they were told they could use if they wished and asked to justify their explanations. The most direct way to arrive at the correct answer is to compute the price per unit of weight for each product and to compare the two. This involves reasoning about proportions, which Inhelder and Piaget (1958) said was a scheme characteristic of formal operations. Fewer than 30% of the women used a proportional reasoning strategy, and at least 50% of the women used a strategy that yielded inconclusive evidence at best and was just as likely to be wrong as right. For instance, some women used a subtraction strategy, saying, for example, "With the bigger one you get 32 more grams for 36 more cents," concluding that the bigger one was thus the better buy. Others merely relied on their past experiences, making statements such as "The big one must be cheaper" without providing any justification for the statement. In general, formal operational reasoning was not observed for a majority of these women. This does not mean that these adults would not have displayed formal reasoning under some other conditions, but it does suggest that formal operations are not typical of adult thought in general.

As this research reflects, American adults do not often reason at the formal level, and apparently there are some cultures—particularly those where formal schooling is rare or nonexistent—in which no one solves Piaget's formal-operational problems (Cole, 1990; Dasen, 1977).

Why do some people fail to attain formal operations? P. R. Dasen's (1977) cross-cultural research provides one clue: They might not have had sufficient exposure to the kinds of schooling that stress logic, mathematics, and science—experiences that Piaget believed help the child to reason at the formal level (Cole, 1990). Indeed, Steven Tulkin and M. J. Konner (1973) found that preliterate Bushman hunters who fail Piaget's problems often do reason at the formal level on at least one task—tracking prey. Clearly, this is an activity of great importance to them that requires the systematic testing of inferences and hypotheses.

Piaget's picture of adult intelligence is one of a reasonable, systematic, and logical thinker. Few psychologists who study adult cognition share this picture. We adults, in general, are not nearly as logical and systematic in our thinking as Piaget would have us be. We take shortcuts, make estimates, and arrive at conclusions before exhausting all possible combinations of elements or considering all the facts. Formal operations as described by Piaget might reflect the best adults can do, but they are not characteristic of how grown-ups deal with real-world problems on a daily basis.

Questioning the Mechanisms of Development

Training studies not only demonstrate that children can perform at more advanced levels than Piaget proposed but have also suggested some very non-Piagetian mechanisms for developmental change. For example, in a pioneering conservation-training study by Rochel Gelman (1969), preschool children were required to ignore irrelevant dimensions of a problem (such as where two rows of dots begin or end) and focus instead on the relevant dimension (for example, the number of dots in a row). By learning to focus on the proper dimension, children were able to solve conservation problems and to generalize their acquired skill to other materials. Such research indicates that young children have the competence to solve conservation problems, but that limitations of other cognitive or perceptual abilities prevent them from displaying this competence under some circumstances. This challenges Piaget's very notion of structures, stages, and operations.

The concepts of operations and stages imply substantial integration. Piaget's "structures of the whole" principle is concerned specifically with the organization of operations. Yet, discrepancies in cognitive abilities are found both within a given child and between different children, indicating that cognitive functioning is not as homogeneous, or even, as Piaget proposed. A particular child may display a highly egocentric attitude in one situation, for example, but show impressive perspective-taking skills in another.

Such contradictory findings challenge Piaget's notion of stages of development that represent qualitatively unique forms of thinking, with transitions between stages reflecting discontinuities in development (see Brainerd, 1978b; Courage & Howe, 2002). As Flavell (1978) has written, "However much we may wish it otherwise, human cognitive growth may simply be too contingent, multiform, and heterogeneous—too variegated in developmental mechanisms, routes, and rates—to be accurately characterized by any single stage theory of the Piagetian kind" (p. 187).

Yet, homogeneity of cognitive function is a relative thing. Although most researchers concur that cognitive development is not as even as Piaget proposed, most children's thinking most of the time can be described as well-integrated and relatively homogenous. For example, Robbie Case (1992) acknowledged that children's thinking is more heterogeneous than proposed by Piaget and likely governed by many domain-specific mechanisms; nonetheless, he still believes that some important aspects of cognition are likely under the influence of a domain-general mechanism, much as proposed by Piaget, and are relatively even. In summarizing his work, Case (1992) stated that "at each successive developmental level, children possess a more complex general conceptual representation of their quantitative world, and . . . this general representation enables them to assemble a variety of more specific executive control structures to meet the requirements of particular tasks" (p. 352). In other words, stages, or levels, do exist, are relatively well integrated, and do influence greatly children's thinking. Just not quite as much as Piaget proposed.

In sum, Piaget's account of development does not fully capture what actually occurs. New theories are needed to account for some of the discrepancies researchers have found in Piaget's theory. Some of these theories, based on information-processing approaches, will be discussed in Chapter 5. Before looking at these approaches, however, I would like to examine briefly three contemporary neo-Piagetian approaches that adopt some of Piaget's ideas about the nature of development while addressing some discrepancies that have arisen between Piaget's theory and new data. These are the theories of Kurt Fischer, the "theory theory" as presented by Alison Gopnik and Andrew Meltzoff, and Annette Karmiloff-Smith's representational redescription theory.

Neo-Piagetian Theories

Fischer's Skill Theory

Fischer (1980; Fischer & Bidell, 1991, 1998) was perhaps the first major neo-Piagetian theorist to consider seriously the issue of heterogeneity and variability of cognitive function. Fischer's approach was to blend what would seem on the surface to be two incompatible theories: Piaget's cognitive development theory and B. F. Skinner's behaviorism (and more recently, Vygotsky's sociocultural approach). Fischer takes as his starting point the position that development is the result of a dynamic interaction between a child and the environment. Piaget, of course, made the same assumption, but Piaget gave the environment only a small role in affecting development. Piaget believed that the child actively interacts with the environment and is the principal "cause" of development. Fischer takes the environment more seriously than did Piaget. The consequence is a theory that gives more equal weight to the contributions of the child and of the environment in influencing development and a theory that predicts greater heterogeneity of cognitive function than Piaget proposed.

Fischer theorizes that children develop *skills* (or *dynamic skills*). Fischer defines a skill as "a capacity to act in an organized way in a specific context (Fischer & Bidell, 1998, p. 478), making skills both action based and context specific. Consistent with sociocultural theory (see Chapter 3), skills are also culturally defined. An important aspect of Fischer's theory is that skills are seen as jointly defined by the organism and the environment. Thus, only skills that are exercised in the most supportive of environments will be developed to their highest level. To the extent

that a child's environment encourages development of various skills equally, there will be homogeneity (or evenness) of cognitive function. That is, if the environment is relatively homogeneous with respect to supporting all of a child's skills, development will proceed evenly. To the extent that one's environment is heterogeneous, however, with some skills being exercised more consistently or receiving more support than others, development will be relatively uneven. Because the world in which most children live is not homogeneous with respect to opportunities to develop different skills, Fischer assumes, quite contrary to Piaget, that heterogeneity of cognitive function is the rule rather than the exception.

Fischer proposes that skills show an invariant developmental progression (à la Piaget) with respect to optimal level of performance. **Optimal level** refers to the maximum level of complexity of a skill that the individual can control, or, in other words, the best performance that a child can show, working on his or her own. Children's level of performance can exceed this optimal level when they are supported by a more skilled partner through the process of scaffolding (see Chapter 3). In fact, Fischer states that it is inappropriate to think of a child as "possessing" a fixed level of a skill. Rather, one's dynamic skills are always changing as a people adjust and reorganize their skills in response to situations in the environment. Consistent with Fischer's position that skills are jointly defined by the environment and the child, he proposes that the optimal level of performance is realized only for those skills practiced in the most supportive of environments.

Skills are also self-organizing, in that they change as other skills change (a single skill can involve many different aspects of psychological functioning) and as a function of experience. Skills become coordinated with other skills and, as a result, produce qualitatively new systems.

Such change is not random, however. Although there is substantial variability in skills (and thus development) both between and within individuals, skills nonetheless develop in a step-by-step sequence of ten hierarchical levels, with these levels being grouped into three tiers (sensorimotor, representational, and abstract). Each tier reflects the

TABLE 4-4 Outline of levels in Fischer's skill theory.

Hierarchical level	Tier	Cyclical level	Characteristic structure	Estimated age range of emergence
1		1	Single	3 to 4 months
2		2	Mapping	7 to 8 months
3	Sensorimotor skills	3	System	11 to 13 months
4	————————	4 = 1	System of systems	20 to 24 months
5		2		4 to 5 years
6	Representational skills	3		6 to 7 years
7	————————	4 = 1		10 to 12 years
8		2		14 to 16 years
9	Abstract skills	3		18 to 20 years
10		4		24 to 26 years

SOURCE: Adapted from "Processes of Cognitive Development: Optimal Level and Skill Acquisition," by K. W. Fischer and S. L. Pipp. In R. J. Sternberg (Ed.), Mechanisms of Cognitive Development. Copyright © 1994 W. H. Freeman and Company. Adapted with permission of the author.

general type of information that a child can control. In the *sensorimotor tier* (approximately 3 to 24 months), children's skills are limited to their actions on and perceptions of objects in their environments. In the *representational tier* (approximately 2 to 12 years), children can represent concrete objects mentally, and in the *abstract tier* (approximately 12 to 26 years), they can combine representational sets so that objects can be thought of as general, intangible attributes. Each tier consists of four levels, with the highest skill level of one tier (for example, sensorimotor, level 4) corresponding to the first level of the next tier (for example, representational, level 1). A brief outline of Fischer's levels is presented in Table 4-4.

How Does Fischer's Theory Differ from Piaget's?

By stressing the role that the environment plays in the development of skills, Fischer's theory acknowledges the significance of experience far more than Piaget's does. Fischer's ten hierarchical levels and the cyclical, predictable nature of development are certainly reminiscent of Piaget, however, and Fischer's

concept of optimal level is consistent with contemporary information-processing viewpoints (see Chapter 5). What, then, is the contribution of this theory, and how is it similar to and different from other formulations, particularly that of Piaget?

Contrasts between Fischer's and Piaget's theories can most readily be made with respect to the basic structures of their theories: *skills* and *schemes*. Schemes are structures by which the child knows the world. Schemes are based on action and, for Piaget, are the things that do the assimilating and accommodating. Schemes develop from earlier schemes and have a high degree of generality in that they are integrated with one another (structures of the whole) and thus result in a high degree of homogeneity of cognitive function. Skills are also structures by which a child knows the world, and, like schemes, they are based in action and develop from earlier acquired skills. Similarly, skills are relatively well integrated and are characterized by the type of representations a child can control (sensorimotor, representational, abstract). Unlike schemes, however, most of a child's skills are never at the same level at a given time. Development of skills is induced by the environment in dynamic interaction with the child, and only skills that are induced most consistently operate at their optimal level in a child.

Both schemes and skills are viewed as developing from simpler to more complex states of organization. For Piaget, schemes are organized into stages, whereas for Fischer, skills are organized into levels and then tiers. The major difference between the two theorists is that Piaget's stages reflect a high degree of generality and characterize the child. A child *is* a concrete operational thinker or *is* in the sensorimotor period. In contrast, levels characterize skills that are specific to particular objects and tasks. In Fischer's theory, children are not described as being at level 4 or at level 7. One can specify the optimal level of performance that a child is able to achieve, but this does not reflect a classification of the child. Accordingly, the range of expected behaviors for a given child is very broad, especially in comparison with the high degree of generality predicted for children at a particular stage in Piaget's theory.

One further difference is that unlike Piaget, Fischer maintains that there are several different developmental routes to any particular outcome. That is, although all skills are based on earlier skills, it is not necessary for all children to progress through the same sequence of skills in exactly the same order. This is due partly to the great variability that exists in cognitive functioning. For example, a child might have achieved a level-5 skill for conservation of length but have level-6 skills for the more-practiced conservation of number and solids. The child might coordinate these two level-6 skills to arrive at a level-7 skill and can then abstract the rule for level-7 conservation of length without ever having attained the level-6 skill for this particular content (Fischer, 1980).

Age-Related Changes in Brain and Cognitive Development

Like all modern theorists, Fischer believes that changes in brain development directly underlie changes in cognitive development (Fischer & Bidell, 1998; Fischer & Rose, 1996). For example, Fischer examined data looking at changes in brain growth over childhood and noted that it is not continuous but occurs in spurts that correspond quite nicely to

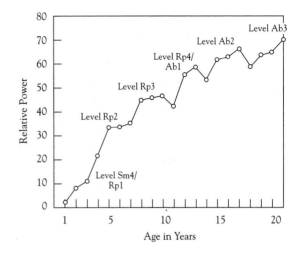

FIGURE 4-4 Development of relative power in alpha EEG in occipital-parietal area (see text). Labels in figure denote levels in Fischer's skill theory. Changes in relative power correspond to changes in levels in Fischer's theory. SOURCE: Fischer, K.W., & Rose, S. P. (1996). Dynamic growth cycles of brain and cognitive development. In R.W. Thatcher, G. R. Lyon, J. Rumsey, & N. Krasnegor (Eds.) *Developmental neuroimaging: Mapping the development of brain and behavior* (pp. 263–279). Reprinted by permission from Elsevier.

the various levels of his theory. He also noted that developmental changes in EEG functioning (Thatcher, 1996), which measures the activity of the brain rather than simply its physical growth, correspond well with his levels of development. Figure 4-4 presents a summary of changes in the relative power of a type of EEG wave in the occipital-parietal area of the brain. Relative power refers to the percentage of energy in one particular type of EEG wave (here, the alpha band) relative to energy in all EEG bands. The higher the value, the more powerful is the alpha band. As can be seen from the figure, the relative power of the alpha band increases with age, but not in a straight line. Rather, it increases in spurts, with those spurts corresponding to levels of cognitive development in Fischer's theory. The labels on the figure denote specific transitions between levels. (For example, "Level Sm4/Rp1" corresponds to the fourth sensorimotor level, which is the same as the first representational level, "Level Rp2" corresponds to the second level of the representational tier, and so on.) Fischer believes that changes in EEG power, particularly in the frontal lobes, "plays a central role in cementing together skill systems to form a new unit at the beginning of a new tier" (Fischer & Rose, 1996, p. 271). Fischer observed other cyclical changes in brain development that are associated with cognitive development (for example, hemispheric changes and changes in EEG power from the front-to-back of the brain), but, for our purposes, it is sufficient to note that aspects of Fischer's theory can be tied to developmental changes in brain functioning.

Theory Theories of Cognitive Development

A growing group of developmental psychologists view infants and children as having sets of innate theories that they modify during childhood until their understanding of the world is like that of adults in their culture. In many respects, these theories are very different from Piaget's, particularly in their proposals that children possess substantial innate knowledge or processes and that there is no domain-general set of logical structures as Piaget believed. But in another way, many *theory theorists* see themselves as the inheritors of Piaget's tradition. This is because they see cognitive development as being a constructive process much as Piaget did, with mechanisms of change that are not so dissimilar from those proposed by Piaget.

First, I should state that there is no one "**theory theory**" of cognitive development. A variety of researchers have adopted the general framework to describe different aspects of cognitive development, including many of the accomplishments attained in infancy (Baillargeon, 1994; Gopnik & Meltzoff, 1997), children's acquisition of concepts (Keil, 1998; Wellman & Gelman, 1998), and children's understanding of how people's minds work (Perner, 1991; Wellman, 1990), some of which will be discussed in later chapters. Perhaps the best general description of the theory theory of cognitive development can be found in Alison Gopnik and Andrew Meltzoff's (1997) book, *Words, Thoughts, and Theories.*

Advocates of the theory theory propose that the process of cognitive development is similar, or perhaps identical to, the process of scientific discovery. An initial theory is tested (experimentation) and revised when the old theory can't explain the new data. Children use these theories to predict, interpret, and explain the world, just as scientists do. In fact, Gopnik and Meltzoff suggest that scientific reasoning is not a *late* invention (either in evolutionary time or over the course of childhood), but has long characterized our species and infants and children. The nature of theories and how they're tested might change in adulthood, but the basic processes of theory generation, theory testing, and theory change are characteristics not just of people in white lab coats, but of children from birth. According to Gopnik and Meltzoff, "It is not that children are little scientists but that scientists are big children. Scientific progress is possible because scientists employ cognitive processes that are first seen in very young children" (p. 32).

What is very different from Piaget's theory is that theory theorists believe that infants come into the world with knowledge or processing constraints for particular domains. This perspective, often referred to as a **neonativism** or **structural-constraint theory,** is at odds with Piaget's contention that cognitive development is a process of construction. How can the idea that the mind is specifically prepared to think—to have innate knowledge—be compatible with the idea that development is a process of constructing reality from previous cognitive structures in interaction with the world? Theory theorists attempt to integrate these two ideas, resulting in an approach that is simultaneously neo-Piagetian and neo-nativist.

Neonativists propose that cognitive processes that Piaget proposed undergo gradual, constructivist development are actually innate and await only the requisite motor or sensory skills for their demonstration. Two good examples of such abilities are object permanence and imitation. As we saw earlier in this chapter, Piaget proposed that both knowledge of objects and imitation develop gradually during infancy, following the six-stage sequence of the sensorimotor period. From his epigenetic perspective, Piaget believed that the mature forms of these skills are acquired late in the second year of life (or later) and are the result of transformations from earlier skills. Recent research has shown, however, that very young infants can demonstrate reasonably sophisticated levels of object permanence and imitation when the tasks are modified to reflect their limited motor abilities. Such findings indicate to some researchers (Spelke & Newport, 1998) innate cognitive knowledge that does not develop through constructive processes. (These lines of research are discussed more fully in Chapters 8 and 9.)

Along these lines, some neonativists argue that little, if anything, develops—that development is not a constructive process but, rather, that infants are born with innate knowledge for interpreting the world (representational innateness as discussed in Chapter 1; see Spelke, 1991). For example, this approach proposes that knowledge of objects (object permanence), language, and space are innate, requiring only the proper environmental stimuli for them to be demonstrated (see Mandler, 2000; Spelke & Newport, 1998). Such knowledge is proposed to be domain specific and to impose constraints on the child, in that the mind/brain is designed to process certain types of information in certain ways, meaning that there is not infinite flexibility in what is learned (thus the name *structural-constraint theory*). Stated more positively, these constraints make it easier for the child to learn certain things, such as language (Gelman & Williams, 1998).

Theory theorists rarely take this strong perspective. Rather, they advocate that the innate constraints will be very general in nature (architectural innateness as discussed in Chapter 1). Gopnik and Meltzoff propose a *"starting-state" nativism*, in contrast with a representational innateness (or, in their terms, modularity nativism). The starting-state perspective holds that children are born with sets of rules for operating on particular representations. However, the rules and the representations they generate are altered by experience. Thus, domain-specific mechanisms constrain what and how information can be processed, but development is still a constructive process with both the content (for example, knowledge of objects) and processes of operating on that content changing with experience.

How should development proceed from a theory-theory perspective? According to Gopnik and Meltzoff, "We will typically see a pattern in which the child holds to a particular set of predictions and interpretations for some time; the child has a particular theory. Then we may expect a period of disorganization, in which the theory is in crisis. And finally, we should see a new, equally coherent and stable theory emerge" (1997, p. 63). This to me is reminiscent of Piaget's equilibration model, discussed earlier in this chapter. Gopnik and Meltzoff make no explicit comparison between the process of change they propose and Piaget's equilibration model (although they do make it clear that the mechanisms of their two theories are different), but the transition from one stable theory to another, following a period of disorganization, is similar to Piaget's idea of changes from one set of structures to another, following a period of disequilibration.

One question that is fair to ask of the theory-theory approach to cognitive development is that if development is the process of testing and changing theories, why do children all over the globe end up with basically the same adult theories of the world? Experience plays an important role in this formulation, and experiences will surely vary considerably for children growing up in information-age societies from those growing up in traditional hunter-gatherer societies. And of course, adults in these cultures do differ considerably in their thinking, but their understandings of the physical and social world are remarkably similar. How can a theory theory explain such similarity of cognitive functioning?

Consistent with the formulations of evolutionary developmental psychologists (Bjorklund & Pellegrini, 2002; Geary, 1998), Gopnik and Meltzoff propose that children around the world are born with the same initial theories and that they possess powerful mechanisms to revise current theories when they are faced with conflicting evidence. That is, all infants start with the same ideas about how the world works and modify these theories as they grow. They also try to solve the same problems about how the physical and social world works, and they get similar information at about the same time in their lives. Remember that children inherit not only a species-typical genome but also a species-typical environment (Gottlieb, 2000). They are prepared by biology to make sense of their world, and human culture ensures that their evolved processing constraints have a chance to work by presenting them with an environment that humans and their ancestors have experienced for hundreds of thousands of years.

Karmiloff-Smith's Representational Redescription Theory

Karmiloff-Smith (1991, 1992) has developed a theory of cognitive development that incorporates many of the assumptions of the theory-theory approach just discussed. She believes that the human infant is biologically constrained to process certain classes of stimuli that are relevant to human existence, including knowledge of physical objects, space, cause and effect, and language, all topics studied by Piaget and proposed by him to develop through active constructivism. Karmiloff-Smith proposes, however, that nativism and constructivism need not be mutually incompatible concepts. Rather, nativism describes the initial state of human cognitive development but "does not preclude a constructivist approach with respect to subsequent development" (1991, p. 173). She also states that a constructivist approach need not require a domain-general, stage-like perspective as offered by Piaget.

The centerpiece of Karmiloff-Smith's theory is **representational redescription,** a process whereby the mind re-represents its own representations (see Mandler, 1992, for a similar account of redescription in infancy). This ability to make representations of representations makes the human mind distinct from the minds of all other species. Karmiloff-Smith believes that much special-purpose knowledge (for example, knowledge related to physical objects, language, and cause and effect) is modular in nature, being activated by specific environmental stimuli and, as described by Jerry Fodor (1983) (see Chapter 1), inaccessible to other parts of the cognitive system. Such knowledge, proposes Karmiloff-Smith, is similar to the knowledge possessed by other species

(for example, the knowledge spiders have about making webs); it is complex, procedural knowledge, which must reside somewhere in the brain but is not available to conscious evaluation and is not easily modified. Humans go beyond this level of representation by the process of representational redescription, making certain aspects of knowledge available to other parts of the cognitive system.

Karmiloff-Smith proposes that knowledge gets into a child's brain in three ways. Some knowledge is innately specified, other knowledge is gained through interaction with the environment, and yet other knowledge is arrived at by the process of representational redescription. Representational redescription involves the process whereby the mind uses knowledge it already possesses by re-representing its own internal representations. According to Karmiloff-Smith, "human development crucially involves the passage from representations that constitute knowledge in the mind to representations that acquire the status of knowledge to other parts of the mind" (1991, p. 175). From this perspective, representational redescription is seen as similar to Piaget's concept of *reflective abstraction*, whereby children discover new information by examining the contents of their own minds (that is, introspecting). Whereas Piaget proposed that reflective abstraction is a characteristic of formal operational thinking, Karmiloff-Smith sees representational redescription as involving a series of levels, beginning at the implicit (I) level and progressing through levels of increasing explication (E1, E2, and possibly E3). Levels E1, E2, E3 all involve representational redescription.

Knowledge represented at the implicit level is unavailable to other aspects of the cognitive system and unavailable to consciousness. In other words, it is modularlike, reflecting efficient, innate procedures for dealing with specific information. For example, neonates' knowledge of physical objects or infants' and young children's knowledge of linguistically relevant stimuli would be represented at the implicit level. There is no redescription here, and this knowledge, impressive as it may be, is similar to the knowledge a spider has about making a web, a blue jay has about building a nest, or a newborn goat has about avoiding falling off cliffs.

Related to this is the idea that implicit learning (acquiring new knowledge without explicit awareness) is an early developing ability. For example, research has shown that 6- and 10-year-old children learn serial sequences of responses (that is, learning which of several responses follows one another) as well as adults do, despite having no explicit (verbalizable) knowledge of what they have learned (Meulemans, Van der Linden, & Perruchet, 1998). Similarly, implicit memory (memory without awareness) has also been proposed to be an early developing ability that shows little improvement across childhood (see Chapter 10).

At the E1 level (first level of explication), knowledge can be redescribed so that it is made available to other cognitive systems. However, this knowledge is not yet conscious. For example, as young children master language, they are able to ignore aspects of the external stimuli and to focus on the internal meaning of language, which they use to formulate linguistic theories. Young children are very good, for example, at determining what is and is not a grammatical sentence—but they can rarely tell you why this is the case. The fact that this knowledge is unavailable to conscious awareness makes the E1 level similar to what other theorists might still call implicit (Clements & Perner, 1994). The important distinction here is that knowledge is made available to other cognitive systems, even if not to consciousness.

For knowledge to be conscious requires additional redescription (level E2), and for it to be verbalized so that the knowledge can be shared with others requires a still further level of redescription (E3). For example, Karmiloff-Smith (1979) describes English-speaking children's correct usage of the articles *a* and *the* during the preschool years. Certainly by 5 years of age, children know the rules for using *a* and *the*, but not until 9 or 10 years of age do they become consciously aware of the rules. According to Karmiloff-Smith, not until this time are children able to redescribe their representations so that these representations are available to consciousness as well as to other cognitive systems.

Redescriptions can get much more complicated and abstract than a conscious knowledge of simple grammatical rules. The process of generating theories in science, philosophy, politics, or everyday social interaction requires going far beyond the data given and often involves re-representing information initially available to once insular, modularlike cognitive systems. (Although Karmiloff-Smith distinguishes between E2 and E3 levels of representation, she notes that no research has focused on the E2 level—conscious access without verbal report. Her writings thus concentrate on E3 representations, although she sometimes refers to a combination of E2 and E3 levels, E2/3.)

For Karmiloff-Smith as for Piaget, children are intrinsically active, spontaneously building theories about how the world works. Building these theories involves taking advantage of both acquired and innate knowledge. Theory building, then, accomplished by the process of representational redescription, is a constructive process. But stages of representation that are observed are more likely to be domain specific than domain general as in Piaget's theory. There is, for example, no such thing as a "stage E1 child." Rather, any given child will have knowledge represented at a variety of levels, both within and between domains. Nevertheless, because knowledge can be available to consciousness through the explication processes involved in representational redescription, some aspects of cognition and development can be domain general in nature.

Karmiloff-Smith retains many of Piaget's assumptions regarding the process of development (constructivism, intrinsic activity, levels of representation) while recognizing the significance of innate knowledge for early cognitive functioning and that neither cognition within an individual child nor the course of development for children as a group is as homogeneous as Piaget proposed.

Summary

Jean Piaget's theory of intellectual development has had a profound impact on how we view children, their thinking, and their development. Piaget believed that abstract *structures* or *schemes* within the child underlie intelligence and that cognitive development is the development of structures. Piaget viewed the child as being *intrinsically active* and thus largely responsible for his or her own development. He believed that cognition is a constructive process (a belief known as *constructivism*) and that our current state of knowledge influences how we perceive and process new information. Piaget believed that cognitive development is domain general in nature and that all cognitive abilities develop together as a result of a single underlying set of mechanisms.

Piaget described the *functional invariants* of *organization* and *adaptation* as processes that are characteristic of all biological systems (including intelligence) and operate throughout the life span. Organization is an organism's tendency to integrate structures into higher-order systems or structures. Adaptation is the process of adjustment the organism goes through in response to the environment. This process has two complementary components. *Assimilation* is the structuring of environmental input to fit a child's current schemes, and *accommodation* is the structuring of the child's schemes to match environmental data. Piaget proposed *equilibration* as a mechanism for development. When confronted with information that cannot be assimilated into existing structures, one enters a state of cognitive incongruity, or disequilibrium. When disequilibrium is resolved by accommodation, a new, more stable structure results. Piaget stressed that equilibration is an active process, even when structures are relatively stable.

Piaget postulated four major stages, or periods, of cognitive development. He hypothesized that stages are (1) qualitatively different in form from each preceding or following stage; (2) culturally universal, so that all children progress through them in a single, invariant order; and (3) based on earlier, more primitive cognitive structures (*hierarchization*).

During the *sensorimotor stage* (from birth to about 2 years), children's thinking is limited to their own actions on objects. Piaget described six substages during the sensorimotor period. During the earliest substages, cognition is limited to inherited reflexes (*basic reflexes*, substage 1) and simple extensions of these reflexes (*primary circular reactions*, substage 2). In-

fants are capable of developing new (that is, not reflexive) behaviors in substage 3 with the advent of *secondary circular reactions*. *Goal-directed behavior* is seen first in substage 4 (*coordination of secondary circular reactions*), with clear means/ends differentiation occurring in substage 5 (*tertiary circular reactions*). Infants become capable of *mental combinations* (mentally representing environmental events) in substage 6. Piaget described the development of *object permanence* and imitation in the context of his broader theory of sensorimotor development.

Sometime between 18 and 24 months, children begin to use symbols, exemplified by language, imagery, symbolic play, and *deferred imitation*. From this point on, development consists of the acquisition of operations. Piaget described three major periods between the ages of approximately 2 and 16 years: *preoperations* (between 2 and 7 years), *concrete operations* (between 7 and 11 years), and *formal operations* (between 11 and 16 years). Piaget proposed four characteristics of *operations*: (1) mental, (2) derived from action, (3) integrated with one another (*structures of the whole*), and (4) reversible. Piaget specified two types of *reversibility: negation* (or *inversion*) and *compensation* (or *reciprocity*).

Piaget described the thought of preoperational children as being intuitive, in contrast with the logical thought of concrete operational children. He proposed that preoperational and concrete operational children differ on several factors. Most critically, the thought of preoperational children lacks reversibility, the benchmark of operations. Piaget described the perception of preoperational children as being *centered* on the most salient aspects of a perceptual array, in contrast with the *decentered* perception of concrete operational children. Preoperational children are said to be *egocentric*, in that they have a difficult time seeing the perspective (visual, communicative, or social) of another. Although Piaget described concrete operational children as less egocentric, recent research has indicated that even preschool-age children can easily take the perspective of another in certain situations.

Differences between preoperational and concrete operational children are displayed on many tasks, the most critical of which is *conservation*. Conservation represents the cognitive constancy of quantitative relations and refers to the knowledge that the quantity of a substance remains the same despite a perceptual transformation of that substance. *Class inclusion* refers to the knowledge that any subordinate category (dogs, for example) can be no larger than its superordinate category (animals, for example). Piaget found that children typically do not solve class-inclusion problems until late in childhood, although non-Piagetian research has found that class-inclusion performance is influenced by a variety of factors and, under some circumstances, is displayed by younger children.

The major factor in the transition from concrete to formal operations is the advent of *hypothetico-deductive reasoning*. With this type of reasoning, thinking can be done solely in terms of symbols, without need for referents in real life; the child can think about what is possible as well as what is real. Piaget described the formal operational child as being able to think like a scientist, or to use *inductive reasoning*. Formal operational children are able to think about thinking, or to reflect on the outcome of their own thought (*reflective abstraction*). Adolescents display a form of egocentrism reflected in their feeling they are constantly "on stage" or playing to an *imaginary audience*, and a belief in their uniqueness and invulnerability, which Elkind referred to as the *personal fable*.

Although Piaget's account of the development of operations has generated tremendous interest for more than seven decades, research investigating his account has often been critical. Non-Piagetian research indicates that Piaget often underestimated the cognitive competencies of children; children have typically been found to be more competent than Piaget proposed, and numerous studies have demonstrated that children can be easily trained to display both concrete and formal operational abilities. Young children can display sophisticated cognitive processing in certain situations and, in general, are less homogeneous in cognitive functioning than Piaget proposed.

Fischer's skill theory integrates aspects of Piagetian theory with aspects of behaviorism in an attempt to account for the unevenness of cognitive function within a stage-like framework. Fischer proposed that

there is an *optimal level* of performance, and a child's skills will be at that level only for those skills that are most consistently supported by the environment. *Theory theories* combine ideas from *neonativism* (or *structural constraint*) and Piaget's constructivism, proposing that cognitive development progresses by children generating, testing, and changing theories about the physical and social world. Karmiloff-Smith adopts a neo-nativist perspective, arguing that much knowledge and many skills are present at birth or shortly thereafter and do not involve the constructive processes proposed by Piaget. Development beyond early infancy is constructive in nature, however, with the process of *representational redescription* being the principal mechanism of cognitive development. Karmiloff-Smith proposes four levels of representation: implicit (I) is unavailable to other cognitive systems and thus unavailable to consciousness; levels E1, E2, and E3 (explication levels 1, 2, and 3) all involve representational redescription, with the latter two reflecting conscious and verbalizable knowledge.

Note

1. At this point, some comment is appropriate concerning Piaget's use of the term *structure* and of the related term *scheme*. When discussing broad theoretical or philosophical issues, Piaget used the term *structure* to refer to any system within the child that underlies intelligence. However, when discussing a particular system reflecting some specific knowledge, Piaget used the term *scheme*. Schemes reflect children's knowledge at all stages of development. When referring to some specific cognitive content, Piaget reserved the term *cognitive structure* to reflect a special type of scheme—those characterized by mental representation. By this definition, the organization that underlies sensorimotor intelligence is not in the form of cognitive structures but in the form of schemes. In the remainder of this chapter I will use the term *scheme* whenever referring to the abstract organization that underlies some specific knowledge. I will use the term *structure* when referring to general aspects of Piaget's theory or his philosophical positions. In either case, both terms are used to represent the abstract knowledge that underlies children's intelligence.

  One further comment is in order here. Early translations and reviews of Piaget's work used the terms *schema* and *schemata* rather than *scheme* or *schemes*.

Piaget had slightly different meanings for these terms and commented that the translations using schema were inaccurate (Piaget & Inhelder, 1969). To be consistent with Piaget's original intention, I will use the term *scheme* rather than *schema* throughout this and other chapters.

Key Terms and Concepts

structures
schemes
intrinsic activity
constructivism
functional invariants
organization
adaptation
assimilation
accommodation
equilibration
hierarchization
sensorimotor stage
goal-directed behavior
basic reflexes
primary circular reactions
secondary circular reactions
coordination of secondary circular reactions
tertiary circular reactions
mental combinations
object permanence
deferred imitation
preoperations
concrete operations
formal operations
operations
structures of the whole (structures d'ensemble)
reversibility
negation (inversion)
compensation (reciprocity)
conservation
centration
decentration
egocentricity
class inclusion
hypothetico-deductive reasoning
inductive reasoning
reflective abstraction
imaginary audience
personal fable
optimal level
theory theories
neonativism (structural-constraint theory)
representational redescription

Suggested Readings

Brainerd, C. F. (1996). Piaget: A centennial celebration. *Psychological Science*, 7, 191–195. This is the introductory article to a special issue of *Psychological Science* devoted to commemorating the centennial of Piaget's birth. Piaget's many contributions are summarized in the articles in this issue, written by prominent cognitive developmental psychologists, documenting that Piaget's influence and legacy lives on.

Fischer, K. W., & Bidell, T. (1998). Dynamic development of psychological structures in action and thought. In R. M. Lerner (Vol. Ed.), *Theoretical models of human development*, (Vol. 1) (pp. 467–561), in W. Damon (Gen. Ed.), *Handbook of child psychology* (5th ed.). New York: Wiley. This chapter presents an updated version of Fischer's skill theory. It emphasizes the dynamic aspect of cognitive development and reflects a greater awareness of sociocultural influences than earlier versions of the theory.

Flavell, J. H. (1982). On cognitive development. *Child Development*, 53, 1–10. This paper, based on the author's presidential address to the Society for Research in Child Development, addresses the important question "How stage-like is cognitive development?"

Gopnik, A., & Meltzoff, A. N. (1997). *Words, thoughts, and theories*. Cambridge, MA: MIT Press. Gopnik and Meltzoff present their version of a theory theory of cognitive development, focusing primarily on development in infancy and young children. This is a clear presentation of the basic ideas behind theory theories of cognitive development.

Karmiloff-Smith, A. (1991). Beyond modularity: Innate constraints and developmental change. In S. Carey & R. Gelman (Eds.), *The epigenesis of mind: Essays on biology and cognition* (pp. 171–197). Hillsdale, NJ: Erlbaum. This is the abbreviated version of Karmiloff-Smith's theory, but one that should give the reader a good feel of the important concepts of her influential ideas.

Piaget, J. (1952).*The origins of intelligence in children*. New York: Norton.   This is Piaget's first book in his series of three on infant cognition and presents many of the central concepts of his theory of sensorimotor intelligence. It was the first book by Piaget I ever read, perhaps accounting for my fondness for it.

Piaget, J., & Inhelder, B. (1969).*The psychology of the child*. New York: Basic Books.   This book by Piaget and his long-time collaborator presents a brief overview of Piaget's theory in Piaget's own words. One word of caution: It is difficult to read works by Piaget before reading works written by others about Piaget.

InfoTrac College Edition

For additional readings, explore InfoTrac College Edition, your online library. Go to http://www.infotrac-college.com/wadsworth.

5

Information-Processing Approaches

Although Piaget's approach to cognitive development stands as the major theoretical contribution of the past century, the computer as a model for how children handle knowledge has also contributed substantially to our understanding. During the 1950s and 1960s, developmental psychologists began looking at changes in children's thinking in terms of a computer metaphor. Like computers, humans can be viewed as information-processing systems. From this perspective, cognitive development can be seen as reflecting changes in either *hardware* (or "structure," such as the capacity of memory systems and the speed with which information is processed through the systems) or *software* (or processes, such as children's access to and ability to use strategies or other learning devices) or both. From their inception more than 40 years ago, information-processing approaches have strongly influenced theory and research in developmental psychology, challenging and eventually replacing Piagetian theory as the major perspective in cognitive development.

Few, if any, cognitive psychologists truly believe that the human mind/brain works like a computer. In fact, the more we learn about how the brain works, the more we realize how much *not* like a computer it is. Brains function like dynamic systems (see Chapter 1), with new levels of functioning emerging as a result of the interactions among lower-level units (e.g., neurons). To the extent that cognition emanates from brains (and we all believe it does), the mind, too, should function like a dynamic system and not like a digital computer. Despite this, information-processing approaches to cognition have provided us with a language and a set of concepts that guide the way we think about thought and its development. Terms and concepts used throughout this book, such as encoding, storage, working memory, speed of processing, and strategies, all derive from information-processing theories. And, although the mind may not work exactly as such theories propose, they give us a way of asking and answering questions related to cognition and its development. For these reasons, a basic understanding of the information-processing approach to cognitive development is every bit as essential to understanding the field as is a familiarity with Piaget.

In this chapter, I cover a diverse set of topics related to developmental differences in how children process information. Some topics involve age differences in the hardware, or structure, of the information processing system, such as the capacity of various memory stores, the different ways memories can be represented, or the role that knowledge base, the content children possess about a topic, influences cognition. Other topics relate more to developmental differences in the software, or the processes, that children engage in when solving problems. As you'll see, it is impossible to fully separate structure from process, and most of the processes discussed in this chapter are those closely related to age differences in structure, often referred to as *basic-level processes*, including age differences in speed of processes and inhibition. "Higher-level" cognitive processes, often referred to as *strategies*, will be the topic of Chapter 6.

Assumptions of Information-Processing Approaches

There is no single information-processing theory of cognition or cognitive development. Rather, information-processing theories are built on a set of assumptions concerning how humans acquire, store, and retrieve information. Perhaps the most obvious assumption of information-processing approaches is that people process information. Processing refers to mentally acting on information to know it. We can act on an external stimulus to make sense of it (such as the writing on this page), or we can act on information that already resides in our heads. These mental actions can be referred to as operations, processes, procedures, strategies, information-processing components, or programs. Each of these terms refers to mental actions taken by the individual to make sense of "input," or, in other words, to think.

Limited Capacity

Central to information-processing approaches is the idea of **limited capacity.** We can deal with only so much information at any single time. Theorists have used a variety of metaphors for capacity, including a space metaphor (one has only so much mental space in which to store or operate on information), an energy metaphor (one has only so much energy to allocate to storage or the execution of cognitive operations), and a time metaphor (one can only perform operations so fast). So, for example, most of us have enough mental space to walk and chew gum at the same time. Add to these operations a nontrivial arithmetic problem, however, and a change in our rate of gum chewing or walking will be discerned. We have added something else to do, and doing it will interfere with the execution of other operations.

Traditionally, the assumption of limited capacity has implied that cognition is *domain general*, so that all types of mental operations—chewing gum, walking, reading, and solving algebra word problems—use the same limited pool of mental resources. In this way, information-processing approaches are similar to Piaget's theory. As we'll see later in this chapter, however, this assumption has been challenged, and some information-processing theories have been modified to accommodate evidence of domain-specific cognitive abilities. I think it is fair to say that most capacity theorists today assume that there are multiple capacities or resources, although the number of such resources and the extent to which they influence many versus a limited number of cognitive tasks is much debated (Kail & Salthouse, 1994).

The Information-Processing System

Another assumption of information-processing approaches is that information moves through the system. The pathways between input and storage can be depicted schematically with a flowchart such as the one in Figure 5-1. Typically, processing is viewed as occurring serially, with the product of one stage of processing serving as the input for the next stage, and so on until some final response or decision is made. The initial multistore models of the sort shown in the figure were first suggested as theories of memory (Atkinson & Shiffrin, 1968). At the risk of oversimplification, it may be said that these theories assume that information from the external world is initially represented, perceptually intact, in **sensory registers.** There is a separate sensory register, or *sensory store*, for each sense modality (for example, vision, audition), and they can presumably hold large quantities of information—but only for a matter of milliseconds. From this initial registration, information is passed through to the **short-term store,** where capacity is smaller but the representations are more durable, lasting for seconds. The short-term store has also been referred to as *primary memory, working memory*, or the *contents of consciousness*. Our short-term store makes contact with the world, holding information long enough for us to evaluate it. We apply strategies, or control processes, for remembering or solving problems in the short-term store. The short-term store is where we live, mentally. Its capacity is limited, however, and if something is not done to information once it is in the short-term store, it will be lost. If we apply some cognitive operation to the information in the short-term store, that information is transferred to the **long-term store,** where presumably it is retained indefinitely.

Representation of Knowledge

How is information represented in long-term memory? Endel Tulving (1985) proposed that information in the long-term store can be represented in one of two general ways: declarative memory and nondeclarative memory. **Declarative memory** refers to facts and events and comes in two types: episodic and semantic memory. **Episodic memory**—literally, memory for episodes—can be consciously retrieved, such as what you had for breakfast this morning, the gist of a conversation you had with your mother last night, and the Christmas visit to your grandparents when you were 5 years old. Such memory is sometimes called **explicit memory,** which refers to the fact that it is available to conscious awareness and can be directly (explicitly) assessed by tests of recall or recognition memory. **Semantic memory** refers to our knowledge of language, rules, and concepts. So, for instance, the meaning of the term "democracy" or the rules for multiplication are examples of semantic

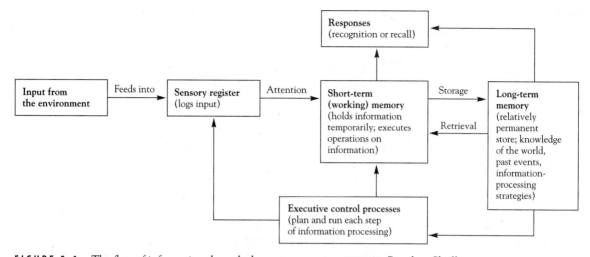

FIGURE 5-1 The flow of information through the memory system. SOURCE: Based on Shaffer, D. R. (1996). *Developmental Psychology: Childhood and Adolescence* (4th ed.) Pacific Grove, CA: Brooks/Cole, as adapted from "Human Memory: A Proposed System and Its Control Processes," by R. C. Atkinson & R. M. Shiffrin, 1968, in K. Spence and J. T. Spence (Eds.), *The Psychology of Learning and Motivation: Advances in Research and Theory* (Vol. 2), Copyright © 1968 by Academic Press, Inc.

memory. You might remember learning the definition of "democracy" and the rules for multiplication in the fourth grade—an example of episodic memory—but your actual knowledge of these terms and rules are examples of semantic memory.

The second general type of memory has been termed **nondeclarative,** or **procedural memory.** Nondeclarative memory refers to knowledge of procedures that are unconscious. For example, some have argued that the learning and memory observed in classical and operant conditioning are unconscious, as are many familiar routines once they have become well practiced (such as tying one's shoe). Such memory is sometimes called **implicit memory,** which refers to the fact it is unavailable to conscious awareness ("memory without awareness") and can be assessed only indirectly (that is, you just can't ask someone to remember something they know only implicitly). Implicit memory is similar to the implicit level of representation proposed by Annette Karmiloff-Smith (1992), discussed in the previous chapter. (Implicit memory will be discussed in greater detail in Chapter 10.)

In addition to tapping different "types" of memories, there is also evidence that different areas of the brain are involved in declarative and nondeclarative memories (Schacter, 1992). This supports the argument that memory is not a single phenomenon (that is, domain-general) but, rather, a set of domain-specific mental operations that may show different patterns of developmental function. More will be said on this issue in Chapter 10.

Automatic and Effortful Processes

Cognitive theorists assume that mental processes can be placed on a continuum relative to how much of one's limited capacity each process requires for its execution (Hasher & Zacks, 1979). At one extreme are **automatic processes,** which require none of the short-term store's limited capacity; at the other extreme are **effortful processes,** which require the use of mental resources for their successful completion. In addition to not requiring any mental effort, truly automatic processes are hypothesized (1) to occur

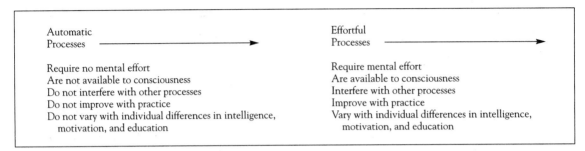

FIGURE 5-2 A hypothetical continuum of cognitive processes.

without intention and without conscious awareness, (2) not to interfere with the execution of other processes, (3) not to improve with practice, and (4) not to be influenced by individual differences in intelligence, motivation, and education (Hasher & Zacks, 1979). In contrast, effortful processes, which have also been called strategies or control processes, are hypothesized to (1) be available to consciousness, (2) interfere with the execution of other effortful processes, (3) improve with practice, and (4) be influenced by individual differences in intelligence, motivation, and education. The automatic-effortful continuum of mental processes is illustrated in Figure 5-2.

Although it is easy to conceive of effortful processes (after all, they are available to consciousness), it is less easy to appreciate automatic processes, precisely because we cannot reflect on them. One process that has been proposed to be automatic is *frequency of occurrence* judgments (Hasher & Zacks, 1979). When people perform some task—for example, determining whether they recognize pictures of familiar and unfamiliar faces—they are rarely consciously aware of how frequently different faces appear. Yet, when later asked to make decisions about frequency of occurrence (for instance, by being shown pairs of pictures and asked to select which member of a pair has been shown more often), people are amazingly accurate in their judgments, despite their lack of conscious awareness. What is interesting is that there are few age differences in frequency of occurrence judgments, with kinder-

garten children often being as accurate as adults (Hasher & Zacks, 1979).

Some interesting research relates the degree of effortful processing to glucose consumption in the brain. For example, Richard Haier and his colleagues (1992) used PET scans, which measure the amount of glucose used in different areas of the brain while performing cognitive tasks. (See Chapter 2.) The researchers reported that the amount of glucose consumption declined as adult participants became more effective at solving a problem. In other words, as processing became less effortful (as defined in cognitive terms) it required less energy (as defined by glucose consumption), illustrating a direct connection between changes in the efficiency of cognitive performance and efficiency in brain functioning. In other research, higher ability people were shown to have lower glucose consumption when solving problems than lower ability people have (Haier et al., 1988), suggesting that brighter people use less energy when executing a task than less-bright people. This finding was supported in a study that showed that when high- and low-ability participants are given problems of comparable difficulty (that is, the problems are selected specifically to match the ability of each individual), the high- and low-ability people use comparable amounts of energy (as measured by glucose consumption) (Larson et al., 1995). Thus, one way of thinking about individual differences in cognitive ability is that higher-ability people process information with less effort (literally with less glucose consumption) than less-able people.

Many information-processing accounts of development include **executive functions**—the processes involved in planning and monitoring what we attend to and what we do with this input (Zelazo et al., 1997). Although it is tempting to view an executive as a little person (homunculus) residing in one's head making decisions based on stored knowledge and incoming perceptual information, such a view is not necessary (nor appropriate). Although we cannot yet specify precisely *how* such decision making occurs, current theory holds that such higher-level cognition emerges because of self-organization processes in dynamic systems. Admittedly, such a phrase conceals a good bit if ignorance of the details of the underlying procedures, but by defining executive functions in this way, examining their development, and looking at how individual differences in executive functioning relate to performance on cognitive tasks, much can be learned about children's thinking and possibly ways to enhance it through educational intervention.

Aspects of planning and decision making that involve such executive functions apparently involve the prefrontal cortex, in that damage to this area of the brain results in characteristic disorders in decision making (Fuster, 1989; Luria, 1973). Similarly, maturationally paced differences in the development of the prefrontal lobes have been associated with age-related changes in problem solving (Barkley, 1997; Dempster, 1993). Children's ability to solve many everyday problems involves establishing a goal, planning a course of action, executing the desired strategies, and monitoring their progress toward their goal, all of which have been described as aspects of executive functioning.

We sometimes refer to such executive control processes as **metacognition**—knowledge of one's cognitive abilities and processes relating to thinking. Our executive functions are thought to be largely under voluntary control and are, in fact, what most clearly distinguish human information processors from computers. Unlike computers, we decide what to attend to, we select our own strategies for retaining and retrieving this input, we call up our own "programs" for solving problems, and, last but not least, we are often free to choose the very problems that we will attempt to solve. Clearly, we humans are rather versatile information processors indeed. For every type of cognition (attention, memory), there is a corresponding type of metacognition (meta-attention, metamemory). For the most part, metacognition will be discussed with its corresponding cognition in later chapters in the book.[1]

Information-Processing Perspectives on Development

Given the brief framework just outlined, where should a psychologist with an information-processing point of view look for developmental differences in children's thinking? One place to look is semantic memory, or children's knowledge base in general. Many developmental psychologists have examined age differences in the structure of children's language concepts, and these differences will be discussed in Chapter 11. However, the benchmark of information-processing theories is the idea of limited mental capacity, and psychologists have searched for age differences that would explain developmental changes in children's thinking. There are apparently no capacity limitations to the long-term store. (Children's ability to store and subsequently retrieve information from the long-term store will be the focus of Chapter 10.) When looking for developmental differences in capacity, most researchers have limited their search to the short-term store and to differences in speed of processing.

The Short-Term Store

Traditionally, the capacity of the short-term store has been assessed by tests of **memory span** that measure the number of (usually) unrelated items that can be recalled in exact order. Presentation of items is done rapidly (usually one per second), so there is minimal time for the application of strategies to aid recall. A child's memory span is considered a reflection of the size of the short-term store, or the capacity of working memory. Norms from the digit-span subtests of the Stanford-Binet and Wechsler IQ scales show a regular increase with age. Similar findings have been provided by Frank Dempster (1981), who reported, for example, that when digits are used, the memory span of 2-year-olds is about two items; of 5-year-olds, about four items; of 7-year-olds, about five items; and of 9-year-olds, about six items. The average memory span of adults is about seven items. Figure 5-3 shows the highly predictable growth of the memory span for digits (digit span) for children from age 2 years through adulthood.

Evidence for developmental differences in the capacity of the short-term store comes from a study by Nelson Cowan and his colleagues (1999) assessing **span of apprehension,** a term coined by George Sperling (1960) to refer to the number of items that people can keep in mind at any one time or the amount of information that people can attend to at a single time. Sperling found that the span of apprehension for adults was about four items. This is lower than the average adult memory span of seven items because factors such as focused attention, knowledge of the to-be-remembered information, and encoding strategies can affect memory span when items are presented more slowly. (See later discussion.)

Does the span of apprehension represent an absolute capacity of the short-term store, and does it increase with age? In the critical condition in the study by Cowan et al. (1999), first-grade and fourth-grade children and adults played a computer game. Over earphones, they also heard series of digits that they were to ignore. Occasionally and unexpectedly, however, they were signaled to recall, in exact order, the most recently presented set of digits they had heard. Participants were not explicitly attending to the digits, making it unlikely that they were using any encoding strategies to remember them. Thus, performance on this task seems to be a fair test of span of apprehension. Average span of apprehension was about 3.5 digits for adults, about 3 digits for fourth-graders, and about 2.5 digits for first-grade children. Cowan and his colleagues interpreted these significant age differences as reflecting a true

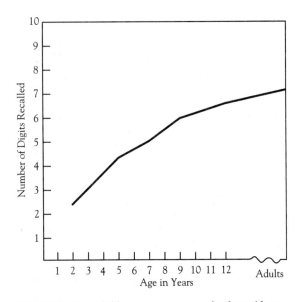

FIGURE 5-3 Children's memory span for digits (digit span) shows regular increases with age. SOURCE: "Memory Span: Sources of Individual and Developmental Differences," by F. N. Dempster, 1981, *Psychological Bulletin, 89,* 63–100. Copyright © 1981 American Psychological Association. Reprinted with permission of the author.

developmental difference in the capacity of the short-term store. According to Cowan et al., there seems to be an underlying difference in capacity, as reflected by differences in the span of apprehension, that serves as the foundation for age differences on memory span tasks.

Despite these impressive and robust findings, researchers have seriously questioned the idea that the capacity of the short-term is the only (or even most important) source of age differences on memory span tasks. For example, in one often-cited study, a group of graduate students at the University of Pittsburgh was given two simple memory tests. On one, they were read a series of numbers quickly (about one per second) and were asked to recall them immediately in exact order. On a second test, they were briefly shown chess pieces on a chessboard in game-possible positions (again, about one chess piece per second) and then given the pieces and asked to place them at their previous positions on the board. Their perfor-

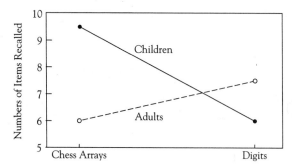

FIGURE 5-4 The average memory span for digits and chess arrays by chess-expert children and college-educated adults. SOURCE: Adapted from "Knowledge Structures and Memory Development," by M. T. H. Chi. In R. Siegler, (Ed.), *Children's Thinking: What Develops?* Copyright © 1978 Lawrence Erlbaum Associates, Inc. Reprinted with permission.

mance on these tasks was compared with that of a group of 10-year-olds. In all fairness, these were not typical 10-year-olds—they were all chess experts, winners of local tournaments or members of chess clubs. When memory for the chess positions was tested, the children outperformed the adults. This finding is probably not surprising, given the expert status of the children. But the critical question is how they did when remembering the numbers. Does being a chess expert cause one's memory capabilities to improve overall, or was the children's remarkable performance limited to what they knew best? The results supported the latter interpretation. The adults, despite being outdone by the children when memory for chess positions was tested, were superior to the children when the test stimuli were numbers. The results of this experiment, conducted by Michelene Chi (1978), can be seen in Figure 5-4 (see also Schneider et al., 1993).

These findings indicate that having a detailed knowledge base in a particular domain facilitates memory for information from that domain but not necessarily for information from other areas. But how does being an expert in a subject such as chess result in improved memory span? Some researchers have proposed that age and individual differences in memory span may be caused by developmental differences

in the use of *strategies* such as rehearsal (repeating the items to oneself) or chunking (recoding two or more items into a single memory unit). However, Dempster (1981, 1985) and others have questioned both the capacity and strategy hypotheses regarding developmental changes in memory span. Concerning the role of strategies in memory span, Dempster concluded, "research offers little evidence that strategic variables are a source of span differences, even though several—rehearsal, chunking and retrieval strategies—appear to be sources of performance differences in other tasks" (1981, pp. 78–79). Of ten strategic and nonstrategic variables investigated by Dempster, only one—ease of item identification—appeared to be a major source of developmental differences in memory span.

Ease of item identification relates to speed of processing: how quickly can a child identify an item? Speed of identification is an indication of processing efficiency; the faster an operation can be completed, the less mental effort it presumably requires for its execution. In work by Chi (1977), 5-year-olds required more time to identify photographs of faces than did adults and showed corresponding differences in memory span for the faces. When the amount of time that adults were permitted to view the faces was limited, however, Chi reported drastic reductions in age differences in memory span. Thus, although maturational differences in the capacity of the short-term store appear to be small (few psychologists would say nonexistent), maturational differences in speed of processing, which in turn affects memory span, are more substantial (Kail, 1993).

A distinction is often made between short-term memory and **working memory,** with the former involving only the storage of information held in the short-term system, whereas the latter involves storage capacity and the capacity to transform information held in the short-term system (Schneider & Pressley, 1997). Digit-span tasks described earlier assess the capacity of short-term memory. An example of a working-memory task can be found in the research of Linda Siegel and Ellen Ryan (1989). They gave children sets of incomplete sentences, requiring them to supply the final word (for example, "In the summer it is very _____"). After being presented with several such sentences, children were asked to recall the final word in each sentence, in order. Such a test requires not only the short-term storage of information, but also some mental work dealing with the to-be-remembered information. Similar to the findings reported for digit span, reliable age differences in working memory are found, although working-memory span is usually about two items less than a child's short-term memory span (Case, 1985).

Alan Baddeley and Graham Hitch presented one popular account of working memory and its development (Baddeley, 1986; Baddeley & Hitch, 1974). According to the Baddeley and Hitch model, working memory consists of a central executive that stores information, and two temporary systems, one for coding verbal information called the **articulatory loop,** and another for coding visual information, which is referred to as the visuo-spatial scratch pad. (Because there has been relatively little developmental research on the visuo-spatial scratch pad, my discussion here will focus on the articulatory loop.) Figure 5-5 presents a simplified model of the working memory system as Baddeley and Hitch think of it. According to the theory, age differences in verbal memory span (for example, recall of digits or words) are primarily caused by developmental differences in the articulatory loop. On verbal span tasks, phonological information is stored in the articulatory loop. These verbal representations (or memory traces) decay rapidly but can be maintained in working memory by verbal rehearsal. Although age differences in the rate that information decays in working memory have been reported (see Cowan, 1997), most researchers believe that age differences in rehearsal rate is the primary reason for developmental differences in memory span. The faster one rehearses, the more memory traces one can rehearse, the more information that can be kept active in working memory, the more one can remember.

Baddeley and Hitch assume that the articulatory loop involves a literal subvocalization process, with people saying the items to themselves. One factor that influences rehearsal rate is word length. Longer words require more time to say, thus leaving less time to rehearse other words before they decay and are lost from working memory. There is good evidence

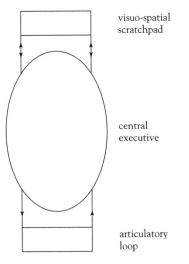

FIGURE 5-5 A simplified version of Baddeley and Hitch's working memory model. SOURCE: Baddeley, A. D. (1983). Working memory. *Philosophical Transactions of the Royal Society, B302,* 311–324. Reprinted with permission of the Royal Society.

from the adult literature that such a process (or one very like it) actually occurs (see Baddeley, 1986, for an extensive review). In the developmental literature, research has shown a relationship between the speed with which children can say words and memory span. With age, children are able to read or say words at a faster rate, and memory span increases accordingly (Hulme et al., 1984; Chuah & Maybery, 1999). Figure 5-6 presents data from a study by Charles Hulme and his colleagues (1984) showing a very regular, age-related relationship between speech rate (that is, how fast people can say the words) and the number of words recalled on a word-span task. Older children and adults have a faster rate of speech than younger children do, and their memory spans vary accordingly.

It is interesting to note that differences in digit span have been found as a function of the language a person speaks. For example, Chinese speakers have considerably longer digit spans than English speakers do; this difference is apparent as early as age 4 and extends into adulthood (Chen & Stevenson, 1988; Geary et al., 1993). This cultural effect seems to be caused by differences in the rate with which number

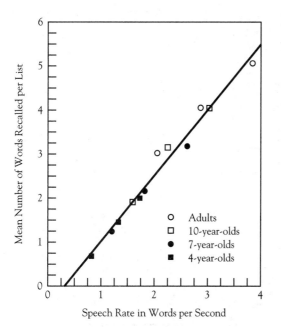

FIGURE 5-6 The relationship between word length, speech rate, and memory span as a function of age. As speech rate increases, more words are recalled, with both speech rate and words recalled increasing with age. SOURCE: "Speech Rate and the Development of Spoken Words: The Role of Rehearsal and Item Identification Processes," by C. Hulme, N. Thomson, C. Muir, and A. Lawrence, 1984, *Journal of Experimental Child Psychology*, 38, 241–253. Copyright © 1984 Academic Press. Reprinted with permission.

words (one, two, and so on) in the two languages are spoken. Languages such as Chinese with relatively short number words that can be articulated quickly enable longer digit spans than do languages such as English with relatively long number words that are articulated more slowly (Chen & Stevenson, 1988). In fact, in one study with bilingual children, children had longer digit spans in their *second* language (English) than their first (Welsh). This counterintuitive finding was because number words can be articulated more rapidly in English than in Welsh (Ellis & Hennelley, 1980). Thus, the greater digit spans of Chinese relative to American children, for example, seem not the result of some inherent cognitive or educational superiority for the Chinese children but, rather, the

result of the language they speak. From a Vygotskian perspective (see Chapter 3), the number words in a language are a "tool of intellectual adaptation," provided by the culture that influences cognition.

What seems central to the various accounts of age differences in memory span is **speed of processing.** For example, Dempster's (1981) review of the literature concluded that the only factor influencing memory span is speed of item identification, and the research performed in the Baddeley and Hitch tradition similarly demonstrates that speed of speech articulation plays a central role in children's memory spans. Research has shown that both of these factors affect children's memory spans, but that neither factor alone adequately accounts for developmental differences in working memory (Henry & Millar, 1991; Hitch & Towse, 1995). Speed of processing must be considered along with other factors, such as children's familiarity with the to-be-remembered information. Nonetheless, age differences in speed of processing seem to be critically related to age differences in working memory and thus to cognitive development in general.

Speed of Processing

With respect to overall speed of processing, young children require more time, and thus presumably use more of their limited capacity, to execute most cognitive processes than do older children (Dempster, 1981). In a series of studies, Robert Kail (1991, 1997) reported that the general developmental changes in processing speed are similar across different tasks. In Kail's studies, participants ranging in age from 6 to about 21 years were given a series of reaction-time tasks. For example, in some experiments participants were presented with a pair of letters in different orientations and were to determine as quickly as possible whether the two letters were identical or mirror images of each other. To do this, participants had to mentally rotate one letter into the same orientation as the other. In a name-retrieval task, the participants were shown pairs of pictures and asked to determine whether they were physically identical or had the same name (for

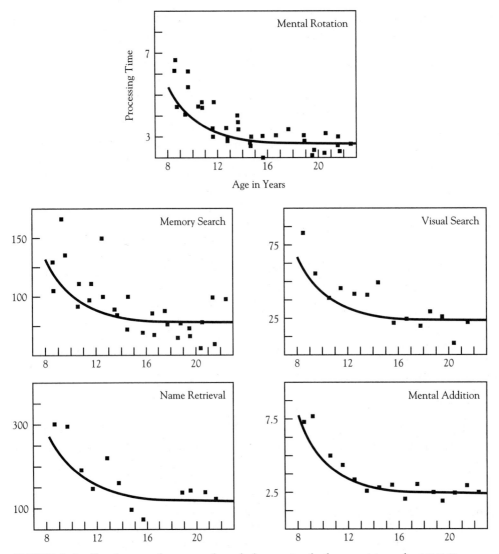

FIGURE 5-7 Developmental patterns of speed of processing for five cognitive tasks. SOURCE: "Development of Processing Speed in Childhood and Adolescence," by R. Kail. In H. W. Reese (Ed.), *Advances in Child Development and Behavior, 23*, 151–187. Copyright © 1991. Reprinted with permission from Elsevier.

instance, different examples of a banana, one peeled and one unpeeled). Patterns of responses over these two, and several other tasks were highly similar, with reaction times becoming faster with age (see also Hale, Fry, & Jessie, 1993; Miller & Vernon, 1997). Figure 5-7 presents the pattern of reaction times across age for a variety of tasks used in Kail's experiments. Note that despite substantial differences in the task requirements and the length of time it takes to perform the tasks (processing time for some tasks is measured in milliseconds, others in seconds), all show essentially the same pattern of changes in reaction time across age. Recent research has even shown a similar (though not identical) age trend in reaction time over the first year of life (Canfield et al., 1997; Rose et al., 2002), and between 22 and 32 months of age (Zelazo, Kearsley, & Stack, 1995).

Kail interpreted these findings as reflecting age-related increases in the amount of processing resources available for the execution of cognitive operations. Kail acknowledged that knowledge (such as that possessed by a chess expert) influences speed of processing, and thus levels of performance on cognitive tasks, but he argued that maturationally based factors are primarily responsible for age-related differences in speed, and thus efficiency, of processing (see Kail & Salthouse, 1994).

Developmental and individual differences in knowledge cannot be dismissed as playing only a minor role in differences in speed of processing, though. The relationship between knowledge, speed, and cognitive performance has been demonstrated repeatedly (Chi, 1977). People process familiar information faster (and thus with less mental effort) than they do less familiar information, and children are relatively unfamiliar with much of what they encounter in their everyday world. With age, they become more experienced and, in the process, quicken their speed of responding. As Robert Kail and Timothy Salthouse (1994) point out, however, although knowledge can substantially affect speed of performance on many tasks, the effects of knowledge appear to operate in a similar way for people of different ages. Thus, underlying individual and developmental differences in knowledge are maturationally based neurological differences, which, in combination, determine speed of processing and availability of mental capacity.

What is the nature of those maturationally based changes that are proposed to underlie age-related changes in speed of processing? They might involve the myelination of nerves in the associative ("thinking") area of the brain. As noted in Chapter 2, myelin is a fatty substance that surrounds nerves and facilitates transmission of nerve impulses. Whereas myelination of most sensory and motor areas of the brain is adultlike within the first several years of life, myelination of the associative area is not complete until the teen years and beyond.

Capacity and Cognitive Development

The findings of Dempster, Kail, and others reporting age-related changes in speed of processing concomitant with age-related changes in cognitive task performance are consistent with theories attributing changes in cognitive development to changes in general information-processing capacity (Halford, 1982; Pascual-Leone, 1970). In fact, the first widely regarded neo-Piagetian theories were those that viewed stage-related changes as caused by differences in information-processing capacity. This tradition is exemplified by the theorizing of Juan Pascual-Leone (1970, 2000; Pascual-Leone & Johnson, 1999) and Robbie Case (1974, 1985, 1992). I discuss aspects of Case's theory in the next section (specifically his ideas about age differences in the efficiency of processing); in this section, I outline briefly the principal ideas behind Pascual-Leone's theory.

Piagetian Stages as Reflecting Changes in Capacity

The central concept behind "limited capacity" theories is that stages reflect "the endogenous growth of maturationally driven mental attention mechanisms (Pascual-Leone, 2000, p. 843). So, for example, Pascual-Leone hypothesized age-related changes in memory capacity, called **M-space** (or M-capacity). A child's cognitive capacity is represented by M, which is a combination of a constant, called a, which is shared by all children, and a variable, labeled k, which changes with age. Thus, for any given child, mental capacity can be expressed as $M = a + k$, with the value of k increasing with age. Increments in k are, to Pascual-Leone, representative of transitions between Piagetian stages.

M-space reflects the number of items one can hold in short-term memory at a given time. It is assessed by *working-memory tasks*, similar to those described earlier. As an example of a working-memory task used in this type of research, consider the counting-span task (Case, Kurland, & Goldberg, 1982), in which children are shown arrays of blue and red dots. They must count the red dots on the page and remember that number. They are then shown a second page of blue and red dots, must count the red dots on that page, and then recall, in order, the number of red dots on the first page and the number of red dots on the second page. This continues until a child can no longer recall the correct sequence of dots he or she counted. The more pages of dots children can remember in order, the higher their M-space is.

Pascual-Leone proposed that the number of separate concepts a child can manipulate simultaneously is limited by M-space (that is, the amount of space available for cognitive processing). Seen in this light, the transition from preoperational to concrete operational thought, for example, involves an increase in M-space with a concomitant increase in the problem-solving capacity of the child (see Table 5-1). Because the constant a is identical for all children, estimations of M are done through factor k. Pascual-Leone theorized that k corresponds to the amount of capacity required to deal with peripheral aspects of a task such as instructions and strategies. More specifically, k refers to the number of problem-solving schemes that a child can coordinate at any point in time. Thus, from Table 5-1, an early preoperational child can coordinate $a + 1$ schemes, a late preoperational child $a + 2$ schemes, and so on. Basically, with age, children can keep more things in mind at once. As capacity expands (as reflected by performance on working-memory tasks), children are increasingly able to consider new strategies or ideas and thus change stages. In Piaget's conservation problems, for example, young children typically make their decisions on the basis of a single dimension ("The water level's so high in this one that there must be more water in it"). To solve conservation problems, children must realize that a change in one dimension (height of water, for example) is compensated by a corresponding change in another dimension (width). From a point of view such as

TABLE 5-1 M-space as a function of age and developmental level (adapted from Case, 1974).

Piagetian substage	Age (years)	Modal value of $M(a+k)$
Early preoperational	(3–4)	$a + 1$
Late preoperational	(5–6)	$a + 2$
Early concrete	(7–8)	$a + 3$
Late concrete	(9–10)	$a + 4$
Early formal	(11–12)	$a + 5$
Middle formal	(13–14)	$a + 6$
Late formal	(15–16)	$a + 7$

Pascual-Leone's, young children cannot keep two dimensions in mind at once. They can shift their attention from one dimension to another, but they do not have sufficient information processing capacity to coordinate two dimensions simultaneously. Although Pascual-Leone's is one of the earliest theories to apply ideas from information-processing approaches to Piagetian theory, such approaches, in modified form, continue to be popular (Case, 1992; de Ribaupierre & Bailleux, 1995; Pascual-Leone & Johnson, 1999).

Developmental Differences in the Efficiency of Processing

Capacity theories as exemplified by Pascual-Leone and his colleagues, essentially proposed that children's performance on tasks such as conservation can be accounted for by how much information they can hold in mind at a given time. These theories propose a domain-general set of cognitive resources that children allocate to various cognitive operations that increase with age. Unmodified, such domain-general models have a difficult time explaining results such as those reported by Chi (1978), where chess-expert children had a greater memory span for chess positions than did adults, but not when digits served as stimuli. Some cognitive feats seem to be domain specific, with skills in one domain not generalizing to other domains.

How can a theory that postulates a domain-general pool of resources account for such findings? More contemporary theories propose age differences not so much in *absolute* capacity (although such differences surely exist), but in the *efficiency* with which children use the mental capacity they have available to them (Case, 1985; Kee, 1994). One influential theory of cognitive development that considers age differences in the efficiency with which information is processed is that of Case (Case, 1985, 1992, 1998). Case proposed age-related declines in the amount of mental effort required to execute a cognitive process. Some of this improvement can be attributed to maturation. However, within each maturational stage (Case proposed four such stages, reflecting the type of representation children could handle), children become increasingly adept at acquiring information and using strategies. This ability, in turn, fosters greater efficiency, resulting in heightened speed of processing.

Case distinguished between **storage space** and **operating space** when conceptualizing memory processes. Storage space is the mental space that an individual has available for storing information; operating space is the mental space that can be allocated to the execution of intellectual operations. Case also defined **total processing space** as the sum of storage and operating space.

Case proposed that there is a developmental decrease in the amount of operating space required for the execution of cognitive processes with a concomitant increase in operational efficiency. Simply put, as each new developmental skill is mastered and becomes practiced, the increase in processing efficiency frees attention (or processing space) for coordinating new strategies. Developmental changes in operating and storage space are displayed in Figure 5–8. Case's theory is illustrated in a study that assessed the independent contributions of storage space and operating efficiency to memory performance (Case et al., 1982). Storage space was measured by counting the number of items that children (ranging in age from 3 to 6 years) recalled under conditions that minimized the effects of memory strategies (for example, working-memory tasks). Operating efficiency was reflected by the speed with which a set

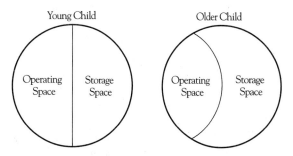

FIGURE 5-8 With age, children process information more efficiently, requiring less operating space and leaving more storage space.

of cognitive operations, such as identifying items, could be performed. Case and his associates predicted that there would be a relationship between operational efficiency (as reflected by speed of identification) and storage space (as reflected by how much was remembered). Children who were slow in identifying items (thus requiring substantial amounts of operating space) should realize lower levels of memory performance for those items. The data supported this prediction, showing a relationship between storage space and operating efficiency that was also related to age. Furthermore, when the processing speeds of college students were reduced by changing the task so that they no longer benefited from being able to say the words quickly (unfamiliar nonsense words were used), their level of memory performance was comparably reduced. The results of this study are graphically presented in Figure 5-9. As processing efficiency increased (as reflected by speed of processing), memory performance also increased. When adults were given a task reducing their processing efficiency to a level comparable to that of 6-year-olds, their memory performance was similarly modified. These results are similar to those reported by Hulme et al. (1984), who examined the relationship between word length, articulatory speed, and memory span (see Figure 5-6).

Few theorists today argue that there is a single set of resources that influence all aspects of cognition. Yet, much research and many theorists support the possibility that a general-processing mechanism, in

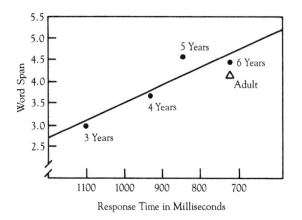

FIGURE 5-9 The relation between word span and speed of word repetition at age levels from 3 to 6 years and adulthood. Younger children were generally slower to identify words and had shorter word spans than older children did. When the identification times of adults were slowed to levels comparable to those of 6-year-olds, they showed a corresponding deficit in word span. SOURCE: "Operational Efficiency and the Growth of Short-Term Memory Span," by R. Case, D. M. Kurland, and J. Goldberg, 1982, *Journal of Experimental Child Psychology, 33,* 386–404. Copyright 1982. Reprinted with permission from Elsevier.

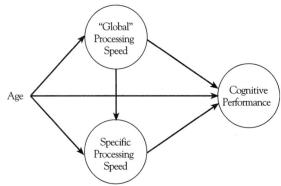

FIGURE 5-10 Model showing the possible relationships among age, global processing speed, specific processing speed, and cognitive performance. SOURCE: Adapted from "Processing Speed as a Mental Capacity," by R. V. Kail and T. A. Salthouse, 1994, *Acta Psychologica, 86,* 199–225. Copyright © 1994 by Elsevier Science Publishers BV. Adapted with permission.

combination with more specific mechanisms, plays a substantial role in cognitive development. Although capacity models are frequently expressed in terms of space, energy, or efficiency metaphors, they can also be expressed as a time metaphor. Older children require less time to process information than younger children do. This is reflected by age differences in speed of processing, discussed earlier. If we view speed of processing as a direct indication of capacity, we can avoid some definitional problems associated with resource theories using metaphors of mental space or mental energy. (Although glucose consumption [Haier et al., 1998], as indicated by PET scans, is a pretty direct measure of energy expenditure.)

Kail and Salthouse (1994) proposed such a developmental theory; they suggest that a global processing-speed mechanism influences cognitive performance either directly (faster global processing results in enhanced performance) or indirectly by influencing the speed with which more domain-specific processing mechanisms (such as rehearsal) are executed. Each of these phenomena (global processing speed, specific processing speed, and cognitive performance) can be influenced by other factors associated with age (such as maturational changes in the brain or increased knowledge). Figure 5-10 illustrates the hypothetical relationship between these factors. Based on evidence of regular age-related changes in speed of processing (discussed earlier), Kail and Salthouse (1994) proposed that speed of processing is a *cognitive primitive*, or a basic aspect of the human cognitive architecture, much like the central processing unit of a computer is a basic part of the machine's hardware. Differences in this capacity change with age in regular ways and influence much cognitive functioning by limiting how much (or how quickly) information can be handled at any one time. Yet, age differences in speed of processing do not account for all age differences in cognitive performance. As Figure 5-10 shows, factors associated with age may directly influence cognitive functioning independent of processing speed, or age may affect task-specific processing speed. So although speed of processing is not everything, Kail and Salthouse (1994), like other capacity theorists, propose that it is perhaps the most important single factor underlying cognitive development.

Attention as Resources

One concept closely associated with information-processing approaches to cognition and development is that of *attention*. We all know what is meant by attention. In everyday parlance, we use the term interchangeably with *concentration*. When we tell a child to "pay attention," we usually want that child to concentrate on the task at hand and not to let his or her mind wander to other things. One assumption about attention is that it consumes limited mental resources. Thus, age differences in the ability to attend to, or to focus one's attention on, a particular stimulus or task have been presumed to reflect differences in the availability of and ability to allocate limited mental resources. Thus, attending to some task has often been seen as equivalent to allocating one's limited resources to that task. Yet attending means more than merely consuming limited resources. Developmental differences in attention have been examined for a variety of phenomena, including the extent to which children can sustain their focus on tasks, as well as their abilities to switch their focus between competing stimuli, to focus selectively on some stimuli to the exclusion of others, and to apply strategies for selective attention. The latter two topics will be discussed in Chapter 6 on strategies. Here, I will briefly examine developmental differences in sustaining attention. Issues related to switching attention and resisting interference will be discussed later in this chapter.

One aspect of attention involves sustaining one's focus on a particular task—that is, paying attention. To some extent, we can measure this even in infancy, with some babies staying "on task" better than others do. There is some interesting evidence that variations in attention in infants and toddlers (1- and 2-year-olds) predict attention in early childhood (3.5 years) (Ruff et al., 1990). Such a finding suggests that some common factor may underlie individual differences in attentiveness, both in infancy and childhood, and may make possible the prediction of attention disorders from measurements in infancy.

The ability to sustain attention becomes increasingly important for children beyond infancy, and there is ample evidence that children's attention spans, the length of time for which they can sustain focused attention, increases with age. For example, Holly Ruff and Katherine Lawson (1990) observed children between the ages of 1 and 4.5 years during free play. They noted a regular increase in focused attention during play over this time and attributed such increases, in part, to improved abilities to inhibit extraneous information. In other research, children between the ages of 30 and 54 months were given a series of tests of sustained visual attention, for example, attention during play, while watching television, and during a reaction-time task (Ruff, Capozzoli, & Weisberg, 1998). For each measure, attention increased with age, although it differed among the tasks, with attention during play and for television viewing developing earlier than attention during the reaction-time task. Also, there were only low to moderate correlations among the tasks, indicating that individual differences in attention were relatively domain specific in nature, tied to particular contexts.

One area where issues of sustained attention may have some social and educational implications concerns young children's attention to television shows. It is widely believed that children's comprehension of television is fragmented and passive, promoting a passive attitude toward thinking in general (Singer, 1980). However, there is evidence that young children can and do sustain attention to television shows, although the degree of attention varies with the comprehensibility of the program (Anderson & Lorch, 1983). For example, in a study by Elizabeth Lorch and Victoria Castle (1997), 5-year-old children watched special shows of *Sesame Street*. Some of the segments in the shows had been altered to make them less comprehensible by dubbing them in a foreign language, whereas others were intact (more comprehensible). Children were told to "watch and enjoy" the shows. However, they also were asked to press a button every time a loud buzzer went off, and to do this as fast as they could. This was a *secondary* task (viewing the TV show being the *primary task*), and reaction times to press the buzzer were used as an indication of how much attention they were showing to the TV program. The longer it took them to press the button, the more attention they were presumably paying to the television show.

Lorch and Castle reported that children paid more attention to the television show when more versus less comprehensible segments were showing, and that, when watching the shows, they devoted more attention to the more comprehensible segments. That is, they had slower reaction times to the secondary task when watching the more meaningful shows than the less meaningful shows, or when not looking at the TV at all. Also, the longer children sustained their attention to the meaningful segments (sustaining attention for 15 seconds or longer), the slower were their reaction times on the secondary task, implying that they were devoting more attention to the TV program. In general, children paid substantial attention to meaningful TV programs, implying active, rather than passive processing of the show's content, and they may become more actively involved (cognitively) the longer they continuously attend to the show.

Learning How *Not* to Respond: Inhibition and Resistance to Interference

To this point, the cognitive processes I have discussed all involve some process of activation. Children must *encode* information, *hold* it in short-term store, *rehearse* it in the articulatory loop, and do this all as fast as possible if performance is to be optimal. There should be no surprise here, for thinking is nothing if not an active process, and one important point of cognitive development would seem to be that children can do "more" thinking "more effectively" with age. Well enough. But sometimes what one *doesn't* do is as important to effective thinking as what one does. Sometime people must inhibit thoughts and action if they expect to get a job done. Of course, "not doing" something is actually a very

active process itself, so I have perhaps misled the reader a bit to make a point—that point being that sometimes inhibiting processes are just as important as activating them and that these abilities change during development.

Inhibition is an old concept in psychology and refers "to an active suppression process, such as the removal of task-irrelevant information from working memory" (Harnishfeger, 1995, p. 188). With the rise of information-processing theory, however, concepts of inhibition temporarily fell out of grace, being seemingly incompatible with the computer metaphor of mind. As gaps in information-processing theory became apparent, theorists looking at both adult cognition and cognitive development re-examined the role that inhibition might play in human thought. A theory of cognition that examines only "activation" is going to have only part of the picture. And the role of inhibition might be especially important, or obvious, in children.

Many of children's cognitive errors and their everyday "problem" behaviors come from things they do despite instructions otherwise (for example, "I didn't mean to trip Josh when he walked up the aisle, it just happened"). The basic idea at its simplest is that, with age, children are increasingly able to inhibit prepotent (primary) and often inappropriate mental or behavioral responses from both internal and external sources and that these improved skills permit the more efficient execution of other cognitive operations.

Related to the concept of inhibition is **resistance to interference,** which refers to "susceptibility to performance decrements under conditions of multiple distracting stimuli" (Harnishfeger, 1995, p. 188–189). Resistance to interference, for example, is shown on dual-tasks, when performing one task (chewing gum or watching television) interferes with performance on a second task (walking or doing one's homework), or in selective attention, when one must focus on "central" information (one's homework) and ignore "peripheral" information (the story line of the sitcom on television). (The development of selective attention will be discussed in the next chapter.) Inhibition and resistance to interference have often been treated as reflecting the same underlying mechanisms, which is likely true, but the two concepts, although highly related, are not synonymous. Nevertheless, they do seem to have a similar neurological locus and to follow the same developmental function, and so I will discuss them in this section as reflecting a single set of processes.

Neurological Locus

Inhibitory and resistance-to-interference processes are related to the functioning of the frontal lobes of the neocortex (or the prefrontal cortex—see Chapter 2). The frontal lobes of the neocortex have many projections to other areas of the brain, including the limbic system, the "emotional" part of the brain. The prefrontal cortex is one of the last areas of the brain to reach full maturity. Development of the frontal lobes in humans is rapid between birth and about 2 years of age. Another, less pronounced growth spurt occurs between about 4 and 7 years, with subsequent growth being slow and gradual into young adulthood (Luria, 1973).

Much evidence for the role of frontal lobes in inhibition in humans comes from cases of brain damage. Humans with frontal lobe damage have difficulty with planning and concentration. Frontal lobe dysfunction has been implicated in some psychiatric syndromes, such as obsessive-compulsive disorder (Malloy, 1987). One test that demonstrates the difficulty frontal-lobe patients have with interference is the Wisconsin Card Sorting Test (WCST). The WCST consists of cards on which are depicted different objects (such as squares, stars, and circles) that vary in color and number (see Figure 5-11). The participants' task is to sort the cards into specified categories (that is, according to color, number, or shape), which is reinforced by the examiner. Without specifically informing the participant, the examiner then switches reinforcement to another category. For example, the initial category may be number, in which case participants would be reinforced for sorting all the target cards with four items on them under the cue card consisting of four circles, all the cards with three items on them under the cue card with the three crosses, and so on, regardless of the color or

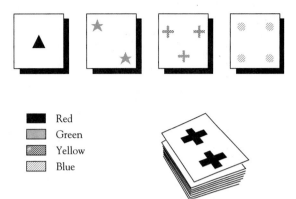

FIGURE 5-11   The Wisconsin Card Sorting Test.
SOURCE: "Some Effects of Frontal Lobotomy in Man," by B. Milner. In J. M. Warren & K. Akert (Eds.), *The Frontal Granular Cortex and Behavior.* New York: McGraw-Hill, 1964.

shape of the items on the cards. The examiner may then switch from number to shape, so that all target cards are now to be placed with the cue card consisting of the same shape (stars with stars, triangles with triangles, and so on), with color and number being irrelevant. Participants are corrected after a mistake, so they should presumably be able to learn a new classification scheme after only a few trials. Normal people do exactly this. However, patients with lesions in the frontal lobes do poorly on this task, often finding it difficult to make a new response (Milner, 1964). This reflects an inability to inhibit a previously acquired response. Based on these and related findings, it has become clear that the frontal lobes play a central role in the selection and regulation of behavior by inhibiting previous responses and fostering resistance to interference from extraneous stimuli (see Dempster, 1993; Luria, 1973).

More recent research using neuroimaging techniques has further pinpointed the neurological locus of age-related differences in inhibition. Beatriz Luna and her colleagues (2001) administered a series of tasks that required the suppression of context-inappropriate responses to people ranging in age from 8 to 30 years. They reported that adult-like abilities to inhibit inappropriate responses developed gradually and were correlated with patterns of brain activity. Using fMRI techniques, Luna et al. found that the prefrontal cortex was more active on these inhibition tasks in adolescents than in either children or adults. Thus, developmental changes in task performance were *nonlinearly* related to underlying brain activation, with adolescents still demonstrating both behavioral and neurological immaturity relative to adults.

Developmental Differences

Because we know the frontal lobes develop during infancy and childhood, we should expect corresponding changes in the ability to inhibit irrelevant information and to resist interference, and ample evidence demonstrates just that. Recall, for example, the research by Adele Diamond (1985), discussed in Chapter 2, in which infants' performance on A-not-B object-permanence tasks was related to development of the prefrontal lobes (see also Bell & Fox, 1992). Likewise, many of the tasks that adults with frontal lobe damage have difficulty performing also show improvements with development. For example, age differences are found in performance on the WCST, with young children performing much the way adults with frontal lesions perform (Chelune & Baer, 1986).

In a task that is essentially a simplified version of the WCST, children are given a set of cards with each card depicting one of two objects (a red boat or a blue rabbit, for example). Children first sort the pictures into groups on the basis of one dimension (shape, for example, boats versus rabbits), and then, after several trials, are told that the rules have changed and they must now sort the pictures on the basis of the other dimension (color, red versus blue) (Zelazo, Frye, & Rapus, 1996). Although 3-year-old children can easily sort the pictures into groups by either color or shape, they almost always fail on the "switch" trials, when the rules change from sorting by shape to color (or vice versa). Instead, they continue to sort the cards as they had previously, despite being able to articulate the rule. Philip Zelazo and his colleagues attribute this failure to 3-year-olds' in-

ability to reflect on their knowledge, something that develops between the ages of 3 and 5 years (Zelazo et al., 1997) (see further discussion of this and related tasks in Chapter 12). Zelazo might be correct about this, but it also seems clear that one of the difficulties these young children have is inhibiting the activation of the previously correct rule (boats go here, rabbits go there), despite seemingly knowing better.

Children's ability to regulate their behavior (which involves inhibiting undesired behavior as well as executing desired behavior) improves with age (see Kochanska et al., 1996; Luria, 1961). This includes using language to guide their behavior (see Luria, 1961; Vygotsky, 1962), with young children often displaying the same problems shown by adults with frontal lesions. For example, preschool children show the same difficulty in performing tasks in which verbal instructions contradict a more salient routine as do patients with frontal lobe lesions, such as the task in which participants are to tap once each time the examiner taps twice, and tap twice each time the examiner taps once (Diamond & Taylor, 1996). Similarly, in the day-night task, children must say "day" each time they see a picture of the moon and "night" each time they see a picture of the sun, which is very difficult for preschoolers, presumably because they cannot inhibit the response to say the highly associated word (for example, "day") with its corresponding picture (that is, the sun). Young children's difficulties are eliminated when they are requested to pair unrelated words (for example, "dog" and "pig") with the pictures (Diamond, Kirkham, & Amso, 2002). Young children's difficulties inhibiting their behavior to language can be seen even in simple games such as "Simon Says." Preschool and early school-age children make many inhibitory errors in this game, making responses to verbal commands even though Simon didn't say so; simplifying the game helps, but young children still make many more inhibitory errors than older children do (LaVoie et al., 1981; Reed, Pien, & Rothbart, 1984).

Children also have a difficult time inhibiting their speech. For example, in research in which children were to name out loud only certain pictures on a page (for example, animals) but not say the names of distractor items (for example, people), kindergarten children showed no evidence of inhibiting their responses. They mentioned the distractor items as frequently on trials when they were told not to mention them as on trials when they were told to mention them (Kipp & Pope, 1997). (This reminds me of a verbally precocious 4-year-old who was telling a story to his parents about his day at school and then, in the middle of the story, suddenly started talking about a TV show he had recently seen. The child paused briefly and then said, "Oops, I just interrupted myself." He couldn't keep the distracting thought about the TV show from intruding on his story about his day at school.)

Changes in inhibitory processes over childhood have been related to a number of cognitive tasks. For example, children's ability to selectively forget information is affected by their ability to keep the to-be-forgotten information out of mind. Older children are better able to execute these inhibitory processes than are younger children (Harnishfeger & Pope, 1996; Lehman et al., 1997; see Wilson & Kipp, 1998). Age differences in selective attention (to be discussed in Chapter 6) can be explained by young children's difficulty ignoring task-irrelevant stimuli. Although task instructions make it clear that they are to attend only to the central stimuli and ignore peripheral stimuli, they have a difficult time doing so (see Ridderinkhof, van der Molen, & Band, 1997). And young children's difficulty in inhibiting some behaviors (such as pointing to where an object is hidden) might impede their ability to deceive others in some situations (Carlson, Moses, & Hix, 1998; see Chapter 9).

Katherine Kipp Harnishfeger and I (Bjorklund & Harnishfeger, 1990; Harnishfeger, 1995; Harnishfeger & Bjorklund, 1994) proposed a model of inefficient inhibition in working memory to account for the influence of inhibition mechanisms on cognitive development. The central idea in this model is that differences in the ability to keep task-inappropriate information out of working memory influences task performance. We suggested that young children not only have difficulty ignoring task-irrelevant stimuli in their environment, but they also have a difficult time keeping task-irrelevant "thoughts" out of working memory. We proposed that the greater amount of

task-irrelevant information in working memory for young children results in greater "cognitive clutter," which effectively reduces functional working-memory space (see Lorsbach & Reimer, 1997).

Thomas Lorsbach, Gerilyn Katz, and Amy Cupak (1998) provided evidence for this by modifying a procedure initially used to assess inhibition mechanisms during text processing in younger and older adults (Hamm & Hasher, 1992). Third-grade, sixth-grade, and college students heard passages that initially led to a particular interpretation (for example, Mike and his mom were watching butterflies). During the second half of the passage, the story either continued as expected or the interpretation switched (they were actually watching birds). Participants were given memory tests to determine whether they still had the idea of butterflies (now disconfirmed) in their minds at the end of the story. Adults were able to "forget" about the initial, now disconfirmed, interpretation (that is, butterflies), keeping this irrelevant information out of working memory. Third- and sixth-grade-children were much less likely to do this. In other words, whereas adults were able to inhibit the irrelevant interpretation (butterflies) and focus only on the relevant interpretation (birds), the children had a more difficult time inhibiting the irrelevant information, resulting in cognitive clutter in their working memory.

Dempster (1992, 1993) has focused on age differences in resistance to interference, such as reflected by children's performance on selective attention tasks and the Wisconsin Card Sorting Test described earlier. Dempster sees resistance to interference as a basic-level process that is central to understanding cognitive development. However, this resistance to interference is not a unitary construct. Although Dempster believes that the frontal lobes are involved in most cases of resistance to interference, he contends that there are at least three separate types of interference phenomena, each with its own developmental course. The hypothesized relation between age and sensitivity to interference is shown in Figure 5-12 for the motor, perceptual, and linguistic domains.

As can be seen from the figure, sensitivity to motor interference is greatest early in life. Such high sensitivity to motor interference would

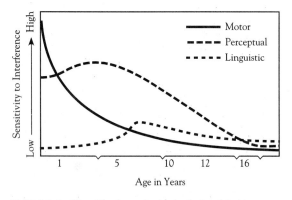

FIGURE 5-12 The hypothesized relationship between age and sensitivity to motor, perceptual, and linguistic interference. SOURCE: "Resistance to Interference: Developmental Changes in Basic Processing Mechanisms," by F. N. Dempster. In M. L. Howe & R. Pasnak (Eds.), *Emerging Themes in Cognitive Development, Vol. I: Foundations*, p. 19. Copyright © 1993 Springer-Verlag, New York, Inc. Reprinted with permission.

account for infants' behaviors on A-not-B object-permanence tasks (Diamond, 1985; see Chapter 2). Infants might know that an object was hidden at location B, but they cannot prevent themselves from reaching toward location A. Children's ability to inhibit responses increases over infancy and childhood, as reflected by the greater motor control children acquire during the elementary school years (which can be seen in playing a game of "Simon says," for example).

Sensitivity to perceptual interference shows a more gradual decline over late childhood and early adolescence. This, Dempster proposes, is reflected by young children's perception being stimulus bound, or, following Piaget, being perceptually centered. For example, in the conservation-of-liquid task, preschool children cannot ignore the differences in height of the two containers. Their perception is centered on the most salient aspect of the perceptual array and they base their decisions on this aspect. According to Dempster, children during Piaget's preoperational period cannot easily resist perceptual sources of interference (see Houdé & Guichart, 2001).

Dempster suggests that sensitivity to linguistic interference remains relatively constant over development, peaking during early childhood, when language begins to play an increasingly important role in guiding problem solving (Vygotsky, 1962). This increase in sensitivity to linguistic interference corresponds to the decrease seen in sensitivity to perceptual interference, suggesting a change in the underlying representational system.

Inhibition (and resistance to interference) has been thought of as a basic-level process, much as working memory and speed of processing are. Might a single, underlying mechanism influence all these tasks? For example, perhaps what we're seeing here is an effect caused by the ability to execute mental operations quickly (whether those operations are to activate processes or to inhibit them). This question was assessed by Guido Band and his colleagues (2000), who evaluated age difference in changes in reaction times on a series of tasks that required either activation or inhibition of mental operations. Similar to findings of Kail (1991) and others, Band et al. reported age differences in the speed with which operations could be activated, with the pattern of reaction times suggesting a single, global mechanism underlying development. The pattern of reaction times for the 5-, 8-, and 11-year-olds and adults in the study associated with inhibition also followed a single developmental function, but one different from that observed on the activation tasks. That is, activation and inhibition tasks followed different developmental trajectories, suggesting different underlying mechanisms.

Acknowledging that inhibitory processes play an important role in cognitive development seems to be an important step forward in helping us arrive at a better understanding of children's thinking. But such a perspective should be seen as supplementing information-processing views of development rather than replacing them. Age changes in inhibition may *permit* certain other abilities to be expressed, but they do not seemingly *cause* them to develop. Improvements in inhibitory control may thus play a *permissive* role in cognitive development, with a certain level of inhibitory control being necessary before other specific abilities can develop. Along similar lines, Bjorklund and Kipp (1996, 2002) have specu-

CARTOON 5-1   Young children often have a difficult time not saying whatever is on their minds.
SOURCE: © Baby Blue Partnership. Reprinted with special permission of King Features Syndicate.

lated that improvement in inhibition abilities in our hominid ancestors played a permissive role in human cognitive evolution. The ability to inhibit aggressive and sexual responses is critical in any human group for successful social interaction to take place. Once such social-cognitive inhibition abilities were in place, the brain areas associated with them could be co-opted for other purposes, such as selective attention, increased concentration necessary for tool use, and possibly even language.

Inhibition and Attention Deficit Hyperactivity Disorder (ADHD)

Following our discussion of developmental differences in inhibition and resistance to interference, it may seem obvious that inhibition deficits may also describe children who have particular difficulty staying "on task" in school. In recent decades, the phenomenon of **attention deficit hyperactivity disorder (ADHD)** has gained substantial attention, with children (and adults) with this disorder displaying hyperactivity, impulsiveness, and great difficulty sustaining attention. The incidence of ADHD in the

United States is approximately 3–7% of the childhood population and is more common in boys than in girls, with between about a third to a half of cases of childhood ADHD persisting into adulthood (see Barkley, 1998). Children with ADHD are more likely to experience school problems, including poor academic performance, grade retention, suspensions, and expulsions than are non-ADHD children and are also at greater risk for delinquency, substance abuse, and troubled social relationships in adulthood (see Barkley, 1997).

Russell Barkley (1997) has proposed that the principal cause of ADHD is deficits in behavioral inhibition. According to Barkley, behavioral inhibition involves the ability to inhibit a prepotent response, to stop an ongoing response, and to resist interference, much as it was described in earlier sections. Behavioral inhibition, claims Barkley, influences working memory, self-regulation of emotion, internalization of speech, which is critical in directing problem solving and reflecting upon one's behavior, and in what Barkley calls reconstitution, which involves the "creation of novel, complex goal-directed behaviors" (p. 72). Given the importance of these abilities for cognition and successful day-to-day functioning, children with deficits in behavioral inhibition would be especially disadvantaged.

There is ample support for Barkley's contention that children with ADHD also show deficits in these areas. For example, children with ADHD (a) do more poorly on working memory tasks (Mariani & Barkley, 1997); (b) are less proficient at imitating lengthy sequences of actions (Mariani & Barkley, 1997); (c) have a poorer sense of time (Barkley et al., 1997); (d) are more adversely affected by delay (Songua-Barke et al., 1992); (e) are more likely to be described as irritable, hostile, and excitable (see Barkley, 1990), and (f) are less likely to use strategies on memory tasks (August, 1987), all relative to non-ADHD controls (see Barkley, 1997, for a review).

Although ADHD clearly interferes with successful functioning, especially in venues requiring sustained and focused attention such as school, less extreme individual differences in behavioral inhibition exist among children and adults, and people on the "high end of normal" may not always be at a disadvantage. For example, Harnishfeger and Bjorklund (1994) speculated that creativity may be fostered by a more "uninhibited cognition," in which multiple interpretations of an event are active in working memory at a given time, so that nonobvious relations and meanings among items can be discovered. This can be seen in the person who creates puns, which requires identifying an unintended, and often nonobvious, meaning for a word or phrase. Granted, the punster may not be viewed as the height of intellectual or creative genius, but such an ability to keep and evaluate multiple meanings in mind at once, coupled with an above-average general intelligence, may be necessary for true creativity.

Some have speculated that some children diagnosed with ADHD may merely be highly active children within the "normal range" of functioning, but who have a difficult time adjusting to the "sit still and listen" regime of school (Panksepp, 1998). Others have suggested that high activity levels and frequent switching of attention may actually be beneficial in some environments and was adaptive to our hunter/gatherer ancestors (Jensen et al., 1997). For example, the benefits of having individuals in a group who constantly scanned the horizon for signs of predators or prey would seem to be obvious. One must be cautious, however, in taking these arguments too far. As Sam Goldstein and Russell Barkley (1998) comment, it is unlikely that any person with a true case of ADHD would be at an advantage in any environment, modern or ancient. However, one must keep in mind that schools are a recent invention for our species and that "normal" levels of activity and playful behavior, especially as displayed by preadolescent boys, although sometimes interfering with ideal educational practices, may not, in-and-of-themselves, be signs of pathology.

The Role of Knowledge Base in Cognitive Development

Domain-General Mechanisms and Context-Specific Effects

As traditionally conceived, information-processing accounts of cognition and development are domain general. Each person is seen as having a limited mental capacity to apply to a variety of problems, and processes or strategies that function in one context are expected to function well in other contexts. However, one of the consistent findings in cognitive development research during the past three decades has been the *domain specificity* of children's thinking. There are many examples in the literature and in everyday life of children performing one cognitive task like a champ while performing other seemingly similar tasks like a chump. The memory-span performance of chess-expert children reported by Chi (1978), discussed earlier in this chapter, is a perfect example.

How can such evidence of domain specificity be reconciled with the domain-general assumptions of the information-processing approach? A perspective that preserves the fundamental assumptions of information-processing approaches is to postulate that the amount of knowledge an individual already has in his or her mind/brain relating to the to-be-processed information affects how that information is operated on. From this viewpoint, the amount of knowledge one possesses influences how new information is stored and integrated into one's previous knowledge and the speed and efficiency with which information is processed. Cognition, then, acts in a domain-specific fashion while operating with domain-general mechanisms.

Age differences in knowledge, or in one's **knowledge base,** have been given a central role by some researchers in cognitive development. For example, Susan Carey (1985) has written, "the acquisition and reorganization of strictly domain-specific knowledge . . . probably account for most of the cognitive differences between 3-year-olds and adults" (p. 512). Young children are novices at most tasks, having less knowledge than older children about the to-be-processed information and about what it is they are supposed to do on the task itself. To what extent are young children's less sophisticated cognitive skills a function of limits on their abilities to process information on the one hand, or limits on their knowledge about information relevant to the task, on the other? Let me provide the general answer to this question at the start: Processing and knowledge cannot be understood independently of one another. How a person of any age processes information is a function of the prior knowledge that person possesses. Much like the relationship between structure and function, the relationship between processing and knowledge is bidirectional.

Experts and Novices

Although domain-specific cognitive processing and abilities can be found in people of any age, such differences are exaggerated when comparing experts and novices for some specific domains, such as chess, physics, or soccer. By studying differences in thinking, memory, or problem solving between experts and novices, we can get a clearer picture of how one's knowledge base affects cognition and its development (see Schneider, 1993).

One advantage experts have over novices seems to be in how easily they can group domain-relevant information. For example, research with children (Chi, 1978; Schneider et al., 1993) and adults (Chase & Simon, 1973) has found that chess experts process chess information faster than do novices and are able to recognize familiar grouping patterns, or "chunks," of chess pieces, whereas novices rely on remembering the position of individual pieces. This greater "chunking" ability effectively increases the memory span of the experts. Importantly, the memory-span advantage of chess experts for chess positions disappears (or becomes greatly reduced) when chess pieces are placed on the board in random, rather than in game-possible, positions (Chase & Simon, 1973; Schneider et al., 1993).

Related to experts' chunking ability, experts are more likely to categorize facts related to their area of expertise in terms of higher-level concepts than are novices (Chi, Feltovich, & Glaser, 1981; Johnson & Mervis, 1998). For example, Chi and her colleagues (1981) assessed the way adults who were either physics experts or novices classified physics problems. They reported that the experts classified problems with respect to underlying principles, whereas the novices were more apt to use superficial characteristics of the problems (the meanings of individual words or diagrams) as a basis for classification. Such higher-level classification for experts than for novices is not restricted to adults (Johnson & Mervis, 1994; McPherson & Thomas, 1989). For example, in a study by Sue McPherson and Jerry Thomas (1989), 10- to 13-year-old expert and novice tennis players were evaluated for their performance and knowledge of tennis. As in the research with adults, child tennis experts focused on higher-level concepts and had more connections among concepts than novices did, and this differential knowledge base affected actual tennis performance. According to McPherson and Thomas (1989), novices approach tennis problems in a general manner and as a result process tennis-related information more slowly and "must keep active in memory the features of the problem and the very general goal of finding a way to solve it" (p. 209). Just as knowledge of chess affects how experts and novices play the game, so too does knowledge of tennis affect how children make decisions during a match and how they execute their sport skill. Note that such knowledge may not always be conscious. Children, or adults, may be able to reflect on their knowledge when asked (or may not), but it is unusual for an expert to be keenly aware of "how" they are operating on a problem while they are engaged in it.

Let me provide an example that illustrates the powerful role that knowledge can play on thinking and the disconnect between "knowing" and "doing." Stephen Ceci and Jeffrey Liker (1986, 1988) examined the intellectual profiles of expert racetrack handicappers. Ceci and Liker identified two groups of men who attended the racetrack nearly every day. One group was classified as experts, who were especially skilled at predicting the odds for any given horse when the race begins. The nonexperts were far from amateurs but were not as accurate as the experts at predicting odds. The men were administered IQ tests and were asked to handicap both real and imaginary races. Through statistical analyses of the men's solutions, Ceci and Liker identified a seven-way interactive model that experts used to predict how fast a horse would run the final quarter mile. None of the men could verbally describe this model, but the statistical analyses demonstrated quite clearly that the experts were using the model to arrive at their estimates. The specifics of these algorithms are beyond the scope of this book (and my expertise at handicapping races), but the message is that they were complex. Ceci and Liker generated a score reflecting how well the experts used this model and correlated it with IQ. The result was a correlation of –.07, which basically means that there was no systematic relationship between IQ and skill on this complex task. IQ was useless in predicting how well the men would do on this task.

Ceci (1993) extended these results by contrasting a low-IQ (IQ = 81) expert who had a fifth-grade education with a high-IQ (IQ = 121) expert who had a master's degree in mathematics education on a simulated task that required the men to predict the price of stocks and bonds. The algorithm used for comput-

ing prices on this task was the same one that the experts used in handicapping races (although they weren't told this). Ceci reports that the performance of the two men gradually became better than chance over 600 trials, but that there was no difference between the high-IQ and the low-IQ expert. That is, having a high IQ yielded no advantage when the men had to generalize their skill to another context.

Despite the influence that knowledge has on developmental differences, however, it is likely that cognitive development is not equivalent to knowledge development. For example, in studies where knowledge is equated between younger and older children (Barnes, Dennis, & Haefele-Kalvaitis, 1996; DeMarie-Dreblow, 1991), age differences in performance are rarely eliminated. How knowledge is connected to other pieces of knowledge will affect how it is accessed and used to solve problems. Knowledge, however, is important. How much we know influences how we process information, which clearly influences how we perform.

Fuzzy-Trace Theory

A relatively new theory cast, very broadly, within the information-processing framework is fuzzy-trace theory, as proposed by Charles Brainerd and Valerie Reyna. I say "cast, very broadly, within the information-processing framework," because, although most of the concepts Brainerd and Reyna adopt—such as encoding, short-term memory, memory traces, interference, and the very notion of processing itself—are those found in standard information-processing theory, they reject the "mind-like-a-computer" approach of information processing (as well as the logical, structuralist approach of Piaget). In their place, Brainerd and Reyna suggest the metaphor of **intuitionism,** in which people prefer to think, reason, and remember by processing inexact, "fuzzy" memory representations rather than working logically from exact, verbatim representations. In a nutshell, according to Brainerd

TABLE 5-2   Some assumptions of fuzzy-trace theory and their relation to cognitive development.

---

1. Gist extraction and the fuzzy-to-verbatim continua

Basic Assumption: People extract fuzzy, gistlike information from the stimuli and events they experience, following the reduction to essence rule. Traces for an event exist on a fuzzy-to-verbatim continuum. At one extreme are fuzzy traces that are vague, degenerated representations that maintain only the sense or pattern of recently encoded information. At the other extreme are verbatim traces, which are elaborated, exact representations of the recently encoded information.

Age Differences: Young children's memory is specialized for encoding and processing verbatim information; with age, their ability to extract gist improves.

2. Fuzzy-processing preference (intuition)

Basic Assumption: People prefer to reason, think, and remember intuitively, processing fuzzy rather than verbatim traces.

Age Differences: There is a shift in the reliance on verbatim and gist traces, sometime during the elementary school years, with children becoming increasing facile processing gist traces. Processing of verbatim traces declines in efficiency during adolescence.

3. Output interference

Basic Assumption: As people make responses, output interference occurs and interferes with subsequent processing.

Age Differences: Young children are more sensitive to the effects of output interference than are older children or adults.

---

and Reyna, most cognition is intuitive, in that it is based on "fuzzy representations (senses, patterns, gists) in combination with construction rules that operate on those representations" (Brainerd & Reyna, 1993, p. 50). Brainerd and Reyna refer to their approach as **fuzzy-trace theory** and have applied it to a wide range of cognitive contents (Brainerd & Reyna, 1993, 2002).

Fuzzy-trace theory makes several basic assumptions about aspects of cognitive processing, as well as about how these aspects of processing vary with development. I will first mention each of the assump-

tions and then discuss how they relate to cognitive development. Table 5-2 outlines these assumptions.[2]

Assumptions of Fuzzy-Trace Theory

At the core of fuzzy-trace theory is the idea that memory representations (or memory traces) exist on a continuum from literal, verbatim representations to fuzzy, imprecise, gistlike traces. Take, for example, a transitive-inference problem in which children are shown a series of sticks varying in length. Stick A is 20 centimeters long, stick B is 20.5 centimeters long, and stick C is 21 centimeters long. The children are shown each of two adjacent pairs of sticks (A and B; B and C) and asked to judge which item of each pair is longer. They then are asked to decide whether stick A or stick C is longer, without having seen these two particular sticks together and without being allowed to make a visual comparison of their lengths. Verbatim traces would correspond to the actual lengths of the sticks (expressed, perhaps, in the form of visual images). Fuzzy or gistlike traces would be of a less exact form, such as "C is long, B is not long and not short, A is short" or "The sticks get taller to my right." Either of these forms of representation can be used to solve the problem. Fuzzy-trace theory poses such questions as these: Which representation is cognitively easier? Which representations do people actually use? and, important for us, What develops?

An important assumption in fuzzy-trace theory is the idea that gist can exist at several different levels for the same information (for example, "A is short, C is long" and "The sticks get taller to my right"), and a single event will be represented in short-term memory by a number of different traces, from exact **verbatim traces** to a variety of inexact **fuzzy traces.** Moreover, these various traces are independent of one another. That is, gist traces are not simply the result of the deterioration of verbatim traces.

A central assumption of fuzzy-trace theory is that people of all ages prefer to use fuzzy traces when solving problems, although this preference does vary with age (see later). Brainerd and Reyna refer to this as the **reduction to essence rule.** Fuzzy traces cannot always be used to solve a problem, but, according to Brainerd and Reyna (1990), "it is a natural habit of mind to process traces that are as near to the fuzzy ends of fuzzy-to-verbatim continua as possible" (p. 9). In other words, there is a bias in human cognition toward thinking and solving problems intuitively rather than logically.

Fuzzy and verbatim traces differ in important ways. First, relative to verbatim traces, fuzzy traces are more easily accessed and generally require less effort to use. Also, verbatim traces are more susceptible to interference and forgetting than are fuzzy traces. For example, when a shopper is comparing the prices of two sweaters at two stores, he or she will quickly forget the exact prices of the sweaters. More resistant to forgetting, however, will be the less-precise information that the sweater at Sears was cheaper than the comparable sweater at J. C. Penney. If your problem is to decide which sweater is the better buy, you can rely on the degraded, fuzzy knowledge of the relative prices of the two sweaters. If, however, you are required to write a check for one of the sweaters, you will need the verbatim information, and in that case, it would be helpful if you wrote the price down, for it is unlikely that you will have remembered the exact price.

A final assumption of fuzzy-trace theory has to do with the role of **output interference** and how it varies with development. Brainerd and Reyna hold that the act of making responses produces output interference that hinders subsequent performance. This is similar to the theorizing of Dempster (1993) discussed with respect to inhibition and interference approaches to cognitive development. According to Brainerd and Reyna, output interference occurs in two forms: scheduling effects and feedback effects. Scheduling effects are caused by the serial nature of response systems. Although people can perform several different cognitive operations simultaneously (that is, in parallel), responses are made serially, that is, one response at a time. This leads to a parallel-to-serial bottleneck at output, or response competition, with the various possible responses competing for priority of execution. Once a response is made,

Brainerd and Reyna propose, irrelevant feedback is generated "that reverberates through the systems, degrading performance as it goes . . . [and] introducing noise into working memory" (1990, p. 29). These researchers theorize that the "noise" in working memory competes with task-relevant information, reducing performance; this is similar to what the inhibition theorists (Bjorklund & Harnishfeger, 1990; Hasher & Zacks, 1988) propose.

Developmental Differences

How does processing of fuzzy and verbatim traces vary with development? Fuzzy-trace theory makes specific predictions, some of which have been confirmed by research. First, there are age differences in gist extraction. Early in life, children are biased toward storing and retrieving verbatim traces. They do extract gist, of course, but relative to older children and adults, young children are biased toward the verbatim end of the continuum. A verbatim → gist shift occurs sometime during the early elementary school years, with children now showing a gist bias. Thus, the memory system for processing verbatim information should develop earlier than the system for processing fuzzy, gistlike information. Moreover, the memory system used for processing verbatim information should decline relatively early in development, likely during adolescence or young adulthood.

Evidence from a variety of sources supports the idea that preschool and early school-age children are more biased toward encoding and remembering verbatim traces, whereas older children, like adults, are more prone to encode and remember gist traces (Brainerd & Gordon, 1994; Marx & Henderson, 1996). For example, in research by Brainerd and Gordon (1994), preschool and second-grade children were given simple numerical problems. In one problem, children were given the following background information: "Farmer Brown owns many animals. He owns 3 dogs, 5 sheep, 7 chickens, 9 horses, and 11 cows." They were then asked a series of questions, some requiring verbatim knowledge for their correct answer, such as "How many cows does Farmer Brown

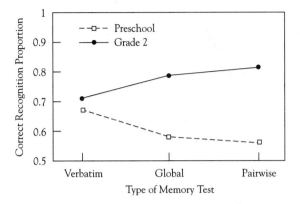

FIGURE 5-13 Proportion of correct recognition responses for verbatim, global, and pairwise problems for preschool and grade-2 children. SOURCE: Brainerd, C. J., & Gordon, L. L. (1994). Development of verbatim and gist memory for numbers. *Developmental Psychology, 30,* 163–177. Copyright © 1994 by the American Psychological Association. Reprinted with permission.

own, 11 or 9?" and others requiring only gist information, such as "Which of Farmer Brown's animals are the most, cows or horses?" (called global) and "Does Farmer Brown have more cows or more horses?" (called pairwise). The results of this experiment are shown in Figure 5-13. They found that preschool children were better at remembering the verbatim numbers than the numerical gist, whereas the reverse was true for second-graders.

Note that the theory does *not* say that young children are better at processing or remembering verbatim traces than older children are; the ability to deal with *both* verbatim and fuzzy traces improves with age. Young children merely start with a bias toward processing verbatim relative to gist traces; this tendency shifts with age, as children are increasingly biased to processing at the fuzzy end of the continuum, all while overall processing effectiveness, for both types of traces, improves.

Consistent with the theorizing of the inhibition and resistance to interference theorists discussed earlier (Harnishfeger & Bjorklund, 1993; Dempster, 1993), age differences have been found in sensitivity to output interference, with younger children being more adversely affected than older children. Recent support for this contention has come from studies of selective attention (for example, Ridderinkhof et al., 1997), including research that has used developmental differences in evoked brain potentials on tasks involving interference (Ridderinkhof & van der Molen, 1995). One reason for young children's greater interference sensitivity is their reliance on verbatim traces, which are more susceptible to interference than fuzzy traces are.

Fuzzy-trace theory has been useful in explaining some phenomena in the child developmental literature, among them the often-inconsistent findings in research examining reasoning-remembering relationships and age differences in eyewitness testimony and suggestibility, the latter of which will be discussed in Chapter 10. In addition, fuzzy trace theory has also predicted and discovered at least one new phenomenon. On free-recall tests with repeated trials, participants tend to recall words with weaker memory representations (words that have not been recalled frequently before) before recalling words with stronger representations (words that have been recalled frequently before), and this effect varies with age. This pattern is opposite both to common sense and predictions made by standard information-processing theory, yet is explained by Brainerd and Reyna's *cognitive triage theory*, which is a subtheory within fuzzy-trace theory (Harnishfeger & Brainerd, 1994). Without going into detail about the theory here, suffice it to say that cognitive triage explains this phenomenon chiefly by output interference effects in interaction with the strengths of the memory traces. The ability of a theory to predict new and often counterintuitive phenomena is often used as a yardstick of that theory's scientific merit, and although the phenomenon that cognitive triage explains might not be as pragmatically important as explaining age differences in eyewitness suggestibility, it certainly enhances the credibility of the theory. Note also that fuzzy-trace theory accomplishes all this without the need to postulate higher-level mechanisms such as strategies or metacognition. Fuzzy-trace theory is, rather, based on basic-level processes.

Connectionist Perspective of Developmental Change

During the past two decades, psychologists have come increasingly to use computer simulations to test their theories. The use of computer simulations in cognitive psychology is not new. For a long time, it has been recognized that being able to simulate a phenomenon means that one must define quite precisely the various factors believed to be involved in any form of processing, resulting in a better (more detailed) model (see Elman et al., 1996; Klahr & MacWhinney, 1998). However, a particular type of modeling, which has implications for how we view the relation between innate and environmental factors in development, has emerged: **connectionist models.** Connectionist models, often referred to as *neural networks,* or *parallel distributed processing (PDP)* networks, attempt to simulate aspects of neural (that is, brain) processing. At their heart, connectionist models are *associationistic models,* with connections between individual units being the basis for computations (just as connections between individual neurons are the basis of processing in the nervous system). Units (or nodes) in a connectionist network can be of different types. First, there are input nodes that receive information from some external source. Other nodes may receive input only from other nodes (just as interneurons receive input only from other neurons). Output nodes "produce a response." Connections between nodes can be excitatory (when node *a* activates node *b*, node *b* increases in its energy level) or inhibitory (when node *a* activates node *b*, node *b* decreases in its energy level). Different nodes can have different *weights*, such that more or less energy (activation from other nodes) is required for it to become active. These weights can change as a function of "experience" (that is, the history of patterns of activation that nodes receive). Figure 5-14 shows a very simple connectionist network. Unlike other computer simulations that involve symbol manipulation, processing is performed in parallel in connectionist networks, with many nodes being activated at any one time.

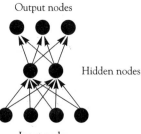

Output nodes

Hidden nodes

Input nodes

FIGURE 5-14 A simplified connectionist network with four input nodes, two "hidden" nodes, and three output nodes.

So how can a model that consists only of connections among simple nodes tell us anything about development and how nature and nurture interact in development? (For more detailed descriptions see, Elman et al., 1996 and Plunkett et al., 1997.) First, a connectionist model starts out with a certain *architecture*—a set of nodes, some inhibitory and some excitatory—that relate the input the model receives (that is, "experience") to the output the model produces (that is, a response to a certain task). This beginning architecture can be thought of as corresponding to what a child brings into the world (or brings to a particular task). The architecture might, for example, be structured so that it responds to objects that move at a certain frequency, or to regularities observed when hearing a series of past-tense verbs (most, in English, have an "ed" added to the end of the root verb).

But if a connectionist system is only a specified architecture, there is no development. The architecture would dictate the relation between the input and output (perhaps with many different layers of intervening nodes), and that would be that. What is crucial in any connectionist network are *learning algorithms*. These learning algorithms change the architecture as a result of the experiences (the pattern of activation) the system receives. In other words, connectionist systems learn by changing the architecture (analogous to changing the brain). They have rules that dictate how changes in the input and the output are related.

Connectionist systems are usually *trained*. That is, they are given some input, make some output, and then receive feedback about the correctness of their responses. For example, if a connectionist system were to simulate performance on an A-not-B object-permanence task, the system would get positive feedback if it "searched" in the B location on the critical B trial, but get negative feedback if its output was to search at the previous A location. A successful simulation will mirror how real children solve the problem. In this case, the simulation should initially make perseverative errors on the A-not-B task, show the same pattern of errors infants make (for example, make different responses under different conditions of delay), and eventually make the correct response. To do this, the model must have one architecture at the beginning and a different one at the end that are like the mental architectures of the younger and older infant, respectively, and a learning algorithm that matches, at some level, the process of learning infants go through as they gradually come to solve the A-not-B problem. Of course, just because the computer programmer was smart enough to write a program that mimics how infants solve these problems doesn't mean that that's the way infants actually do it, but it's an impressive start.

Connectionist models often are used to test hypotheses generated by *dynamic systems theories*, as discussed in Chapter 1. Interactions among individual nodes produce patterns of behavior that could not be easily predicted from examining the individual units. In fact, one important aspect of connectionist models is that they are a bit unpredictable. This is because the architecture and learning rules interact such that they produce *emergent properties*. Depending on the initial architecture, the learning rules, and the information the network receives, different architectures and different patterns of responses will emerge, just as individual differences in children's responses to any task will differ as a function of individual biological and experiential differences. Such emergent properties often take the form of what developmentalists have traditionally viewed as stage transitions, with relatively abrupt changes over a brief period. However, such changes can also be viewed as examples of *nonlinear change*, so that changes in a target behavior do not show gradual, incremental changes over time but, rather, demonstrate a rapid change in the target behavior over relatively brief periods (such as the rapid increase in children's vocabularies sometime during their second and third years).

What connectionist models, and dynamic systems theories in general, do is avoid the idea of innate concepts or ideas (representational innateness). Rather, what is innate is the general architecture and some basic learning algorithms (architectural innateness), which might be, as the neo-nativists propose, domain specific, but not necessarily. But, unlike neo-nativists (for example, Spelke & Newport, 1998), connectionist theorists do not propose that children are born with specific concepts. Connectionist models have been applied quite successfully to several areas of development (see Elman et al., 1996; Plunkett et al., 1997), but have been especially influential in the study of language development. Here, connectionist accounts of language development are contrasted with more "traditional" explanations offered by Noam Chomsky and his followers, which take a decidedly nativist account. (See the discussion of these different approaches in Chapter 11.) I provide no more than this brief sketch of connectionist models here. I introduce it here only to demonstrate a potentially valuable tool to assess developmental change, one that purports to be able to "explain" some of the new evidence of symbolic sophistication in infants and young children (to be discussed in Chapters 8 and 9) without having to resort to the concept of representational innateness.

Summary

Information-processing approaches to the study of cognition emphasize the flow of information through a *limited capacity* processing systems, specifically the *sensory registers*, the *short-term store*, and the *long-term store*. The long-term store consists of *declarative memory*, which includes *episodic* and *semantic memory*, and is proposed to be available to consciousness (*explicit*) and is often contrasted with *nondeclarative*, or *procedural memory*, which is unavailable to consciousness (*implicit*). Cognitive operations are conceptualized as existing on a continuum with *automatic*, or effortless, *processes* at one extreme and strategic, or *effortful processes* at the other. Information-processing theories are concerned with the acquisition and manipulation of knowledge. Many information-processing accounts of development include *executive functions*, which are involved in planning and monitoring what we attend to and what we do with this input. Executive functions that monitor selection of strategies and task performance are sometimes referred to as *metacognition*.

Reliable age-related differences are found on tasks assessing *memory span*, *span of apprehension*, and *working memory*. According to one popular model, working memory consists of a central executive that stores information, and two temporary systems, one for coding verbal information called the *articulatory loop*, and another for coding visual information, referred to as the visuo-spatial scratch pad. Reliable age differences are also found in *speed of processing*, which is related to age differences on the various span tasks.

Early neo-Piagetian theories emphasized age-related changes in mental capacity, as reflected by Pascual-Leone's concept of *M-space*. As capacity expands (as reflected by performance on working-memory tasks), children are increasingly able to consider new strategies or ideas and thus change stages. Age differences in efficiency of processing, rather than absolute differences in capacity, have been proposed to account for developmental differences in children's thinking. Older children require less *operating space* for the execution of cognitive processes than younger children do, leaving more *storage space* available for the execution of other cognitive operations. *Total processing space* reflects the combination of operating and storage space. The ability to sustain attention requires the use of limited resources and shows improvements over the preschool years.

Theories postulating age-related changes in *inhibition* and *resistance to interference* propose that infants' and children's difficulties inhibiting responses or to resist internal and external sources of interference contribute significantly to cognitive development. Neurological evidence suggests that development of the frontal lobes is important in the development of inhibition and resistance to interference. Several researchers have presented evidence of age-related changes in inhibition and resistance to interference and propose that these differences account for development of performance on a wide range of cognitive tasks, including selective attention, memory, and verbal tasks. Deficits in behavioral inhibition have been implicated in *attention deficit hyperactivity disorder (ADHD)*, with children diagnosed with ADHD showing poor performance on a range of tasks requiring inhibition.

It is becoming increasingly clear that what children know, or their *knowledge base*, plays an important role in how they process information. Recent data indicate that a child's domain-specific knowledge, acquired continuously throughout development, accounts for many of the adult/child differences observed in cognition.

Brainerd and Reyna's *fuzzy-trace theory* suggests *intuitionism* as a metaphor for cognition. Fuzzy-trace theory assumes that memory representations exist on a continuum from *verbatim* to *fuzzy*, or gistlike traces. People generally prefer to think with fuzzy rather than verbatim traces, following the *reduction to essence* rule, but this develops, with young children showing more of a verbatim bias than do older children. Processing of verbatim traces is relatively good in young children but declines in efficiency during adolescence. Fuzzy-trace theory assumes that *output interference*, resulting from scheduling effects and feedback effects, causes deterioration of performance and that younger children are more susceptible to the effects of output interference than older children or adults are.

Connectionist models are computer models that simulate aspects of development through repeated activation of associated nodes. Connectionist models begin with learning algorithms and a certain architecture (meant to be analogous to brain structure) that is modified through "experience." These models reflect dynamic systems and have been successful in modeling certain aspects of development (particularly language development). They also purport to explain some of the new evidence of symbolic sophistication in infants and young children without having to resort to the concept of representational innateness.

Notes

1. The perspective that I've presented in this chapter could be considered to reflect the "soft-core" approach of information processing. It takes the "mind-as-a-computer" metaphor loosely and proposes that cognitive development involves changes in what and how (and how quickly) children process information. I have not taken a "hard-core" perspective of information processing, one that uses various types of computer simulations and formal models to describe and explain cognitive development (Klahr & MacWhinney, 1998). From my point of view, the formal modeling of cognitive development is an important tool, and developmental scientists who do such modeling make important contributions to our understanding of children's intellectual development. However, in a book that is already too long as far as my editor is concerned, I decided not to discuss these models here, with the exception of a short section on connectionist modeling at the end of the chapter. The interested reader is referred to an excellent chapter by David Klahr and Brian MacWhinney (1998).
2. A fourth assumption of fuzzy trace theory is that short-term memory is reconstructive. However, because the theory predicts few developmental differences in reconstructive processes, this aspect of the theory will not be discussed here.

Key Terms and Concepts

limited capacity
sensory registers
short-term store
long-term store
declarative memory
episodic memory
explicit memory
semantic memory
nondeclarative memory
procedural memory
implicit memory
automatic processes
effortful processes
executive function
metacognition
memory span
span of apprehension
working memory
articulatory loop
speed of processing
M-space
storage space
operating space
total processing space
inhibition
resistance to interference
attention deficit hyperactivity disorder (ADHD)
knowledge base
intuitionism
fuzzy-trace theory
verbatim traces
fuzzy traces
reduction to essence rule
output interference
connectionist models

Suggested Readings

Harnishfeger, K. K. (1995). The development of cognitive inhibition: Theories, definitions, and research evidence. In F. Dempster & C. Brainerd (Eds.), *New perspectives on interference and inhibition in cognition*. New York: Academic Press. Harnishfeger reviews theory and research dealing with age differences in inhibition and resistance to interference and how these processes relate to cognitive development.

Kail, R. V., & Salthouse, T. A. (1994). Processing speed as a mental capacity. *Acta Psychologica, 86,* 199–225. This article presents research and theory relating to age differences in speed of processing, both over childhood and into old age, and the developmental relation between speed of processing and performance on a host of cognitive tasks.

Plunkett, K., Karmiloff-Smith, A., Bates, E., Elman, J. L., & Johnson, M. H. (1997). Connectionism and developmental psychology. *Journal of Child Psychology and Psychiatry, 38,* 53–80. This article presents a relatively high-level introduction to connectionism and developmental psychology. For an expanded view, see Elman et al. (1996), *Rethinking Innateness,* in the recommended readings of Chapter 1.

Reyna, V. F., & Brainerd, C. J. (1995). Fuzzy-trace theory: An interim synthesis. *Learning and Individual Differences, 3,* 27–59. This article presents a summary of fuzzy-trace theory by the theory's originators.

InfoTrac College Edition

For additional readings, explore InfoTrac College Edition, your online library. Go to http://www.infotrac-college.com/wadsworth.

6

Learning to Think on Their Own: The Role of Strategies in Cognitive Development

Four-year-old Dexter had pushed his father's patience too far.

"Dexter," said his father, "I want you to go over to that corner and just *think* about all this for a while."

Instead of following his father's orders, Dexter stood where he was, not defiantly, but with a confused look and quivering lips, as if he were trying to say something but was afraid to.

"What's the matter now?" his father asked, his irritation still showing.

"But, Daddy," Dexter said, "I don't know *how* to think."

Obviously, 4-year-old Dexter did know how to think. He just didn't know that he did. The term "thinking" has associated with it specific meaning for most people. People think when they need to solve a difficult problem, whereas something that can be done easily and automatically is said to be done "without thinking." As adults, we know what we mean when we refer to thinking, but obviously, as this story illustrates, young children do not have the same understanding of mental processes as adults do.

In the previous chapter, I discussed the principal characteristics of information-processing approaches to cognitive development. But I only dealt with a part of the picture, specifically the "hardware" that develops with age (for example, the short-term store) and basic-level processes, as reflected by working memory, speed of processing, and inhibition mechanisms. Such processes are at the core of any information-processing approach, and the development of these abilities affects performance on nearly every type of task children (or adults) are likely to encounter. But other types of processes are also investigated from an information-processing perspective, and these are higher-level operations over which children have considerable control and that in everyday language would be classified as a form of "thinking." Such cognitive operations are usually called **strategies** and are defined as goal-directed operations used to aid task performance. Strategies are usually viewed as being deliberately implemented, nonobligatory, and potentially available to consciousness (Harnishfeger & Bjorklund, 1990a; Siegler, 1996). And strategies develop.

In Chapter 1, I mentioned that one of the major issues of cognitive development concerns how children gain intentional control over their cognition and problem solving. One way of investigating this question is to look at the development of strategies and the knowledge that children have about using such strategies, a form of metacognition. Both topics will be examined in this chapter. Strategies will play a central role throughout much of the remainder of this book, particularly in Chapter 12 on problem solving.

The Development of Strategies

Strategies are relevant to most aspects of cognitive development. For example, in memory development, commonly used strategies include rehearsing information and grouping to-be-remembered items by conceptual categories (for example, remembering all the outfielders on a baseball team in one group and all the pitchers in another). In mathematics, simple strategies of addition include counting on one's fingers and mental counting (for instance, for the problem 3 + 2 = ?, mentally starting with 3 and counting up two to arrive at 5). Strategies can be much more complicated and involve an evaluation component, a form of metacognition. For example, in reading, one must occasionally determine how well the recently read information is being understood. In all cases, the strategy is used to achieve some cognitive goal (remembering, adding, comprehending).

I have tried to show throughout this book the universal side of cognitive development; children's thinking changes in relatively predictable ways for children across the globe, although the content of what is learned and the emphasis of how things are learned may vary considerably from culture to culture (see discussion of the sociocultural approach in Chapter 3). The same could be said about strategies. Children in all cultures will use deliberate, planful, procedures to solve some of the problems they encounter in their day-to-day lives, the nature of the problems varying with one's culture. However, most of the strategies studied by developmental psychologists have *not* been for contents found in all cultures or faced by most children throughout history; rather, most research in strategy development has focused on contents especially relevant for children in schooled societies such as our own. Children in schooled societies must learn information that our ancestors never could have dreamed of—to read, to learn by rote the multiplication tables, to learn how to compute the velocity and acceleration of a falling body, and to recall, in correct order, all the presidents of the United States or the monarchs of England. Such learning is usually deliberate, requires much mental effort, and is invariably learned in school. Children are expected to master these tasks without any reason other than "the teacher said to," and children from schooled cultures learn to do so with little questioning. This is often referred to as learning "out of context," or **context-independent learning.** Of course, children in information-age cultures have good reasons for learning such information, and context-independent learning is necessary for success in the modern world. And I believe that the cognitive underpinnings of strategy development are, indeed, universal. But it's worth keeping in mind that most of the tasks to be described in this chapter may be relevant only to children in literate societies. Granted, this includes the vast majority of children in the world today, but it has only been a matter of centuries (perhaps decades) that this is so. Context-independent learning is an evolutionarily novel phenomenon, but one that is vital to success in modern cultures.

Mediational and Production Deficiencies

During the 1960s, it became obvious to cognitive developmental researchers that young children (usually preschoolers) typically do not generate and use the types of strategies that older children do. If strategies are so important to developmental differences in cognition, researchers reasoned, instructing a young child to use a strategy that is characteristic of an older child should result in changes in the younger child's cognitive performance.

Research using the logic of **training studies** flourished during the 1960s and 1970s and is still alive and well today. A three-step developmental progres-

sion of children's use of strategies was proposed. Early in development, children do not spontaneously generate a strategy to help them solve a task, and when they are shown a strategy, they are unable to use it to guide their performance. This inability is called a **mediational deficiency** (Reese, 1962), meaning that a potentially effective strategy does not mediate task performance for young children. Presumably, these children do not have the mental apparatus to effectively use the strategy. For slightly older children (or for slightly simpler strategies), the imposition of a strategy results in improvement in task performance. In these cases, children do not *produce* the strategies spontaneously, but when shown what to do, they are able to follow instructions with corresponding improvements. Thus, they still have a **production deficiency** (Flavell, 1970); that is, they have the mental ability to use strategies but for some reason do not produce them without prompting. The stage of production deficiency is followed by a stage in which children produce strategies on their own without needing to have them imposed by an outsider.

Much cognitive developmental research through the 1970s focused on young children's production deficiencies (see Harnishfeger & Bjorklund, 1990a, for a brief history of research in strategy development). Many of the phenomena associated with concrete operations introduced by Jean Piaget were examined from the viewpoint of production deficiencies. Demonstrations abounded, with researchers showing that 4-, 5-, and 6-year-olds could be taught to conserve (Gelman, 1969) and to take the visual perspective of another (Borke, 1975). Memory research used training studies extensively, demonstrating that under some conditions young children could be trained to use reasonably complex strategies such as rehearsal, organization, and imagery, although the effect of such training was often short-lived (see Schneider & Bjorklund, 1998, 2003). It became clear that young children could be trained to use many of the strategies previously thought to be available only to older children. Tasks often had to be greatly simplified, and a trained 4-year-old rarely performed as well as an untrained 12-year-old, but younger children obviously had greater competence than psychologists had believed.

By showing that certain strategies could be taught to young children, researchers also illuminated something of the nature of what happens spontaneously in development. Thus, training studies were not done solely for their own sake (that is, to train children because they could be trained), but as a way of learning about the normal process of development.

What Are Production-Deficient Children Doing?

The emphasis on production deficiencies and their laboratory remediation resulted in a science that had a good deal to say about what older children do and about how to train younger children to resemble older children (at least in the laboratory). But the science had little to say about what young children do spontaneously. If young children are not using strategies (unless we train them), what are they doing? More recently, developmental psychologists have concentrated on what production-deficient children do on their own. The answer is, basically, that they are also strategic. Preschool children, who do not spontaneously conserve liquid or organize sets of pictures according to familiar categories (such as animals, tools, and vegetables), nevertheless do things to help them perform tasks (see Wellman, 1988, for a review). These strategies often result in incorrect answers, but they are strategies nonetheless.

As an example, consider age differences in children's performance on class-inclusion problems, discussed in Chapter 4. Children are presented with two subsets of objects (for example, 6 dogs and 4 cats) and asked if there are more members of the more numerous subset than the superset ("Are there more dogs or more animals?"). Preoperational children tend to fail these problems, stating, in this case, that there are more dogs than animals, whereas by 8 or 9 years of age, most children can answer the question correctly. Is there any systematic way that children of different ages solve such problems? Might younger children's approach reflect the use of a less effective strategy than that of older children rather than a totally deficient understanding of the concept? One interesting study by Ann McCabe and her colleagues (1982) found qualitative differences in how children of dif-

ferent ages solved these problems. The researchers gave standard class-inclusion problems to children ranging in age from 3 to 8 years. They reported that the 7- and 8-year-olds performed the best, followed by the 3- and 4-year-olds, with the 5- and 6-year-old children performing the worst! This somewhat anomalous finding was explained in terms of how children of different ages had approached the task. The 3- and 4-year-olds failed to discern any rule governing task performance and so responded randomly (that is, astrategically). As a result, they were correct on about 50% of the trials. In contrast, the 5- and 6-year-olds had figured out a rule (that is, a strategy) for solving the task and followed the rule consistently. As it happened, however, the rule (pick the larger of the two subordinate sets) produced consistently wrong answers. The oldest children also had a rule for guiding their problem solving, and, for most of the children, the rule yielded correct solutions.

Preschool children also use simple, and presumably more effective, strategies in real-world settings. For instance, assessing memory strategies in naturalistic settings (for example, children's homes), Judy DeLoache, Ann Brown, and their colleagues have reported strategies for children as young as 18 months (DeLoache & Brown, 1983; DeLoache, Cassidy, & Brown, 1985). The procedure involves a hide-and-seek game, in which a toy (a stuffed animal, for example) is hidden in one of several locations in a child's home. Following delays of several minutes, the child is asked to retrieve the toy. DeLoache and Brown reported that young children engage in strategic behavior during the delay periods, including looking or pointing at the hiding location and repeating the name of the toy. In more recent research, 3- and 4-year-old children played a game of "store," in which they had to fill customers' vegetable orders (Cohen, 1996). To complete these orders, children could use a variety of strategies including addition (add a potato to an array), subtraction (take a potato away from an array), and recognizing that no changes in an array had to be made to fill the order. These young children used a full range of the possible strategies and became more efficient (that is, made fewer moves to fill an order) with practice. These results make it clear that production deficien-

PHOTO 6-1 Apparatus used in studies of children's attentional strategies by Patricia Miller and her colleagues. SOURCE: Courtesy of Patricia Miller.

cies are relative. Even very young children use strategies; the strategies that they use tend to be simple and to increase in efficiency with age.

Following these findings, it seems clear that preschool children engage in some planning that warrants being called strategic. Still, their strategies lack the effectiveness of the procedures used by older children and often may not aid task performance at all. However, Henry Wellman (1988) asserts that preschoolers' strategies are every bit as goal-directed and performance-influencing as the strategies of older children are and that they are used in a wide range of situations. Recent findings support Wellman's interpretation, although we must be careful not to attribute too much in the way of strategic competence to the preschool child, for cognitive skills are clearly more effective and more easily observed in older children.

Utilization Deficiencies

Until recently, it was generally accepted that children progress from a mediational deficiency to a production deficiency and then finally are able to produce effective strategies on their own. But researchers have seriously questioned this progression

and observed a phase in strategy development in which young children use a strategy, sometimes as effectively as older children, but experience no benefit in performance. This phase in strategy development, first identified by Patricia Miller and her colleagues (Miller, 1990; Miller & Seier, 1994) has been termed a **utilization deficiency.** Most experiments performed by Miller and her colleagues involve children's use of a selective-attention strategy (DeMarie-Dreblow & Miller, 1988; Miller et al., 1986). Children (usually between 3 and 8 years old) are shown a series of boxes with doors on top arranged into two rows of six columns (see Photo 6-1). On half of the doors are pictures of cages, meaning that those boxes contain pictures of animals. On the remaining doors are pictures of houses, meaning that those boxes contain pictures of household objects. Children are told to remember the location of one group of objects, either the animals or the household objects. They are also told that they can open any doors they wish during a study period. Children's strategies can be examined by looking at the doors they choose to open during this study period.

The most efficient strategy, of course, is to open only those doors that have a drawing of the relevant category. In a series of experiments, Miller and her colleagues found a developmental sequence in strategy use. In the first phase, preschoolers show no selective strategy, usually opening all the doors on the top first and then all the doors on the bottom, regardless of what picture is on the door. In the second phase, children use the selective strategy, but only partially: they still open many irrelevant doors. In the third phase, children use the strategy (that is, open mainly the relevant doors), but the strategy does not help them remember the locations of the items. This third phase constitutes a utilization deficiency. Not until the fourth phase, usually late in the preschool years, are children able to use the strategy and to benefit from its use.

Utilization deficiencies have since been documented in older children for more complex strategies of memory (Ackerman, 1996), reading (Gaultney, 1995), and analogical reasoning (Muir-Broaddus, 1995), among others. Moreover, reviews of earlier research indicate that utilization deficiencies are very common, at least for memory strategies. For example, Miller and Wendy Seier (1994) reported strong or partial evidence of utilization deficiencies in more than 90% of all experiments examining children's spontaneous use of memory strategies. Similarly, utilization deficiencies have been found in more than 50% of memory training studies conducted over a 30-year period (Bjorklund et al., 1997).

Let me provide an example of a utilization deficiency in a memory training study my colleagues and I did (Bjorklund et al., 1994). We trained groups of third- and fourth-grade children in the use of an organizational memory strategy in a *sort-recall task*. Children were given sets of randomly arranged words printed on cards that could be organized into familiar language categories (for example, tools, animals, vegetables). They were given two minutes to study the cards and told that they could do whatever they wanted with the cards during this time to help them remember. The cards were then removed and they were asked to remember as many words as they could, out loud, in any order that they liked. When remembering such lists, older children and adults spontaneously sort words into groups during the study period, and at recall they tend to remember the words from the same category together. The degree to which people sort or recall items according to the

list categories is assessed by *clustering* scores, with higher scores reflecting greater use of an organizational strategy. In Phase 1, children were given a list of words with only the standard instructions to remember as many as they could. In Phase 2, children were presented with a new list of words and received specific instructions in the use of an organizational strategy, both at sorting ("Put words that are alike or go together in some way in the same group") and at recall ("Try to remember words together that are alike or go together in some way"). The near extension trial followed immediately, with children given a new list of words and "standard" instructions ("Remember any way you want"). Children were seen one week later for a far extension task, again with a new list of words and standard instructions.

Would children take advantage of the strategy instructions they were given by increasing how much they remembered? Would they then transfer the strategies to new sets of materials? And, if so, would the memory advantage of using the strategy transfer as well? Results from one training condition in this experiment are shown in Figure 6-1. Organization at sorting and at recall (clustering) was measured by the adjusted ratio of clustering (ARC) score, with a maximum score of 1.0 and 0 as chance. As can be seen, levels of recall, sorting, and clustering all increased significantly from the baseline phase to the training phase. So the answer to our first question is affirmative: children did learn the instructed strategy and improved their memory performance accordingly. Performance on the two extension phases for sorting and clustering was quite similar. Children maintained their high levels of strategy use, both during sorting and at recall. Thus, the answer to the second question is also affirmative: children transferred the strategy they had learned to new materials. But the same cannot be said for levels of recall. Children showed a decline in recall, comparable to their baseline levels, in Phases 3 and 4. That is, they displayed a utilization deficiency, using a strategy but experiencing no immediate benefit from it.

If strategies are so important to children's cognitive performance, why should they sometimes *not* benefit from them? And when strategies don't do them any good, why do they bother using them?

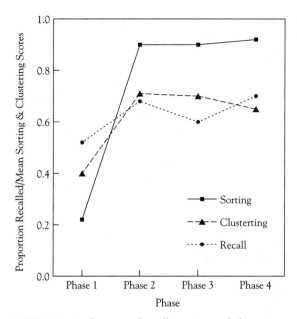

FIGURE 6-1 Patterns of recall, sorting, and clustering for trained children. SOURCE: Bjorklund, D. F., Schneider, W., Cassel, W. S., & Ashley, E. (1994). Training and extension of a memory strategy: Evidence for utilization deficiencies in the acquisition of an organizational strategy in high- and low-IQ children. *Child Development, 65,* 951–965. Reprinted with permission of the Society for Research in Child Development.

There is surely no single reason for utilization deficiencies. But perhaps the factor that is most responsible for utilization deficiencies, especially in young children, is lack of mental resources. By definition, strategies are effortful to use (see discussion in Chapter 5), and children who use a strategy may not have enough mental resources left over to devote to solving the problem at hand (Bjorklund & Harnishfeger, 1987; Miller et al., 1991). (This issue will be the focus of a later section of this chapter, "The Cost of Strategy Use.") Other factors that are likely involved include children's lack of awareness that the strategy use is not helping them. That is, they may possess poor metacognition and fail to realize that all the extra effort they are putting in isn't resulting in any benefit. (Metacognition will be discussed later in this chapter.) This may not always be such a bad thing, however. Children who practice strategies eventually

get good at them and their task performance does indeed improve. That is, utilization deficiencies are often short lived (Bjorklund, Coyle, & Gaultney, 1992). If young children realized how poorly they were doing, they might stop using the strategy and, although saving themselves some effort in the short term, could hinder their overall effectiveness in the long term. Finally, children may use a new strategy just for the sake of novelty (Siegler, 1996). Although, from an adult perspective, the number one reason to use a strategy is to improve task performance (that's what strategies are "for," after all), this may not reflect the child's point of view. Trying something new may be a goal unto itself, and the fact that it does not improve performance may be relatively unimportant to children.

Earlier researchers typically dismissed their findings of young children using strategies but not benefiting from them, rarely discussing such results in their papers. It appears now, however, that such a finding is not a quirk or experimental error, but the typical pattern of strategy development. Yet, despite the general acceptance of utilization deficiencies, the concept is controversial (see Waters, 2000), and the conditions under which it is observed (or not observed) have yet to be clearly established. For example, in a series of experiments, Thomas Coyle and I (Bjorklund et al., 1992; Coyle & Bjorklund, 1997) gave children in the second, third, and fourth grades a series of sort-recall trials with *different* sets of categorized items on each adjacent trial. Children were said to display a utilization deficiency if they demonstrated a significant trial-to-trial increase in *clustering* (recalling categorically related items together) without a corresponding improvement in recall. Using this criterion, evidence of utilization deficiency was observed for children of all the ages tested, with some children displaying a subsequent improvement of recall on later trials, illustrating that the utilization deficiency phase was relatively short lived (Bjorklund et al., 1992).

Other more recent research has obtained different patterns of results. For example, Matthias Schlagmüller and Wolfgang Schneider (2002) examined changes in third- and seventh-grade children's strategy use in a sort-recall task over nine weeks. Unlike

Bjorklund, Coyle, and their colleagues, Schlagmüller and Schneider used categorical *sorting* during the study period (that is, the degree to which children sorted the list material by categories during the study phase) as their strategy measure. They reported a low incidence of utilization deficiency, in direct contradiction to the Bjorklund and Coyle findings for the same-aged children. A number of procedural differences between these two sets of studies preclude an easy resolution of the discrepancy of the findings, but the most obvious one is the use of a measure of strategic functioning. Whereas Bjorklund and Coyle used a measure of output organization (clustering in recall) as an indication of strategy use, Schlagmüller and Schneider used a measure of input organization, sorting, during the study phase. Thus, it appears that finding utilization deficiencies depends on what strategies one looks at. As we'll see in later sections of this chapter, children use multiple strategies on a single task, and what you find (that is, utilization deficiencies or not) may depend on which strategies you look at.

The Development of Memory Strategies

Children's strategies have been investigated for a wide range of topics, but no area has focused as much on strategies as has memory development. In fact, from the inception of contemporary research on memory development in the late 1960s through the 1980s, most researchers focused on **memory strategies,** or **mnemonics.** Developmental researchers have studied a variety of memory strategies, and here I review briefly the two most investigated: **rehearsal,** in which a child repeats the target information, and **organization,** in which the child combines different items into categories, themes, or other units.

Rehearsal

The study most responsible for the interest in strategy development (and memory development more generally) was published in 1966 by John Flavell and his colleagues (Flavell, Beach, & Chinsky, 1966). Children in kindergarten and the second and fifth grades were shown a set of pictures that they were asked to remember. Following the presentation, a 15-second delay allowed the children to prepare for the recall test. An experimenter, who was trained to identify lip movements corresponding to the words the children were trying to remember, watched the children's mouths. Flavell and his associates reported age-related increases in recall with corresponding increases in the amount of rehearsal. Eighty-five percent of the fifth graders displayed evidence of some spontaneous rehearsal, whereas only 10% of the kindergarten children did so. Furthermore, within a grade level, children who had rehearsed more recalled more, on average, than did children who had rehearsed less. These findings led the researchers to conclude that rehearsal is a powerful mnemonic that increases with age, with the frequency of rehearsal (the absolute number of times one rehearses) determining memory performance.

Later research by Peter Ornstein, Mary Naus, and Charles Liberty (1975) questioned Flavell's frequency interpretation. These researchers used an *overt rehearsal procedure* with children in grades three, six, and eight. In this procedure, children are presented with a series of words to recall, with several seconds between each successive word. During this interval, the children are told they must repeat the most recently presented word at least once, and, if they wish, they may practice any other words they like. Thus, rehearsal is made obligatory (they must "rehearse" at least one word once during each interval), and the experimenters can determine exactly what the children are doing. Using this procedure, the researchers found no differences in the frequency of rehearsal across the three grade levels. Despite this equivalence in quantity of rehearsal, age differences in recall persisted, a perplexing finding given the interpretation of the earlier study by Flavell and his colleagues. However, Ornstein and his associates reported differences in the quality, or *style*, of rehearsal.

Typical rehearsal protocols for a third- and an eighth-grade child are shown in Table 6-1. The number of words actually rehearsed is similar for the two children, but the style of rehearsing is very different. The younger child includes only one or, at best, two unique words per rehearsal set. (A rehearsal set refers

TABLE 6-1 Typical rehearsal protocols for an eighth-grade child and a third-grade child. Note the use of cumulative rehearsal by eighth graders and the more passive rehearsal style by third graders.

Word presented	Rehearsal sets	
	Eighth-grade child	Third-grade child
1. Yard	Yard, yard, yard	Yard, yard, yard, yard, yard,
2. Cat	Cat, yard, yard, cat	Cat, cat, cat, cat, yard
3. Man	Man, cat, yard, man, yard, cat	Man, man, man, man, man
4. Desk	Desk, man, yard, cat, man, desk, cat, yard	Desk, desk, desk, desk

SOURCE: Ornstein, P. A., Naus, M. J., & Liberty, C. (1975). Rehearsal and organizational processes in children's memory. *Child Development, 46,* 818–830. Copyright © The Society for Research in Child Development, Inc. Reprinted with permission.

to the words repeated during the interstimulus interval.) The researchers referred to this method as a **passive rehearsal** style. In contrast, the older child includes several different words per rehearsal set, a style labeled **active,** or **cumulative.** The child repeats the most recently presented word and then rehearses it with as many other different words as possible. From these and other data, Ornstein and his colleagues asserted that the important developmental changes are in style rather than frequency of rehearsal (see also Guttentag, Ornstein, & Siemans, 1987).

A causal relationship between differences in the frequency and style of rehearsal and age differences in memory performance has been demonstrated in training studies. Preteenage children trained to use a cumulative rehearsal strategy display elevated levels of recall (Cox et al., 1989; Ornstein, Naus, & Stone, 1977). Thus, young children can be trained to use a rehearsal strategy, resulting in increases in memory performance (although age differences are rarely eliminated). What differs in development is children's inclination to implement a strategy, rather than their

ability to use it (that is, a *production deficiency*). This general pattern is not unique to rehearsal but, as will be seen, typifies other strategies as well.

Organization

One reason that active rehearsal benefits memory might be that conceptual relations are noticed among items that are rehearsed together (Ornstein & Naus, 1978). *Organization* in memory refers to the structure discovered or imposed on a set of items that is used to guide subsequent performance. In attempting to remember what groceries one must buy at the store, for example, we benefit by organizing the information by categories (dairy products, meats, vegetables) or meals (food necessary for pot roast, food necessary for Saturday's barbecue).

In a typical study of organization and recall, children are given a randomized list of items that can be divided into categories (several instances of furniture, tools, and occupations, for example). When the children recall the items, will they remember different ones from the same category together, even though they were not originally presented together? As discussed earlier in this chapter, recalling items from the same category together has been referred to as *clustering,* and adults who display high levels of clustering in their recall typically remember more than do adults displaying lower levels of clustering. Developmentally, levels of recall and clustering usually increase with age, with preschool children's clustering often being at chance levels (see Schneider & Bjorklund, 1998).

Organization in memory can be measured more directly by giving children the opportunity to sort items into groups before recall (a *sort-recall* task). For example, Harriet Salatas and John Flavell (1976) presented first graders with a set of 16 pictures, four each from four different categories (for example, animals, clothing, toys, and tools). The experimenter named each picture, identified the categories, and placed the pictures randomly on a table in front of the children. The children were told that they would be asked to remember the pictures later on and that they should put them together in a way that would help them recall the pictures. Following a 90-second study period, the children were asked to remember as many of the pictures as they could. Although the instructions would seem to bias children to organize (that is, physically sort) the items for recall, only 13 of 48 children (27%) organized the pictures according to categories to a significant degree. Other studies, requiring children to sort items before recall with instructions similar to those used by Salatas and Flavell ("Make groups that will help you remember"), report that children as old as 8 years often fail to organize items on the basis of meaning but, rather, place items into groups randomly. Older children are more likely to group items by meaning and, as a result, realize higher levels of recall (Best & Ornstein, 1986; Hasselhorn, 1992). Yet, when the instructions are modified, stressing to children that they should make their groups on the basis of meaning, even preschoolers comply and demonstrate enhanced levels of memory performance (Lange & Jackson, 1974; Sodian, Schneider, & Perlmutter, 1986).

Other experiments, more explicitly training children to use an organizational strategy, have also yielded positive results. Young children, under certain instructional conditions, use an organizational strategy and display elevated levels of memory performance (Black & Rollins, 1982; Lange & Pierce, 1992). In other words, young children are capable of organizing information for recall, but they generally fail to do so spontaneously. As with rehearsal, training children to use an organizational strategy rarely eliminates age differences, and, under most conditions, young children fail to generalize the strategy to new situations or new sets of materials (Cox & Waters, 1986).

The impression one gets when looking at the memory strategy literature is that children show regular and gradual changes in strategy use (rehearsal or organization) with time. Most data looking at age-related changes in strategy use, however, are cross-sectional in nature, with different children of different ages being tested to assess developmental differences. Although there are many benefits to cross-sectional studies (their economy in time, effort, and expense being their foremost values), they cannot adequately test developmental hypotheses. Only longitudinal studies can do this. Unfortunately, there

have been very few longitudinal studies of basic strategic processes. An exception is the Munich Longitudinal Study on the Genesis of Individual Competencies (LOGIC) (Sodian & Schneider, 1999; Weinert & Schneider, 1992), which followed children between the ages of 4 and 18 years and evaluated performance on sort-recall tasks as part of their assessments. Beate Sodian and Wolfgang Schneider (1999) observed changes in strategy use over time by individual children and noted that only about 8% of the children showed a gradual improvement in the use of organizational memory strategies (sorting items into categories and clustering), with 81% "jumping" from chance sorting or clustering scores at one test interval to near perfect scores at the following measurement point. Thus, although cross-sectional data can give the impression of a gradual change in strategic functioning over childhood, longitudinal data indicate that, for most children, the transition from astrategic to strategic, at least for organizational memory strategies, occurs relatively quickly, and at different ages for different children.

Strategies of Attention

When children must inspect something or make comparisons among objects, how do they allocate, or spend, their attention? Do children attend to some parts of a display more than to others? Do they compare two objects carefully before declaring them the same or different? Are there age differences in what they do? Stated another way, what strategies of attention do children use when they must examine a stimulus or set of stimuli? Classic work on developmental differences in children's attentional strategies was conducted by Elaine Vurpillot (1968; Vurpillot & Ball, 1979). In these studies, children were shown pictures of pairs of houses (see Figure 6-2). The children's task was to tell whether the windows in the two houses were the same or different. While they were making their decisions, a camera concealed behind the picture recorded their eye movements. Vurpillot found that preschool children rarely looked at all the windows before making a judgment. For example, when there were 12 windows in the two

FIGURE 6-2 Stimulus materials used in research on attentional strategies. Children's eye movements are recorded as they determine whether the houses in each pair are the same or different. SOURCE: "The Development of Scanning Strategies and Their Relation to Visual Differentiation," by E. Vurpillot, 1968, *Journal of Experimental Child Psychology*, 6, 632–650. Copyright © 1968 Academic Press. Reprinted with permission from Elsevier.

houses, 4- and 5- year-olds, on average, made a decision after looking at only 7 of the 12 windows. Children 6 to 8 years old, however, looked at between 10 and 12 of the windows, on average. Not surprisingly, the older children, who used a better strategy, were more apt to be correct in their judgments than were the less strategic preschoolers (Vurpillot & Ball, 1979).

Research by Miller and her colleagues, discussed earlier with respect to utilization deficiencies, has similarly shown improved attentional strategies during the preschool years. In this work, children are instructed to study and remember only a subset of items, hidden in clearly marked boxes (for example, they are asked to remember only the animals, which are hidden in boxes with cages marked on them). Most 3-year-olds open all boxes, both relevant (those with cages on them) and irrelevant (those with houses on them). Slightly older children begin to use a systematic strategy, but children do not typically use a selective strategy on this task consistently until after 6 years of age (DeMarie-Dreblow & Miller, 1988; Miller et al., 1986).

Another form of attentional strategies is reflected in tasks of **selective attention.** Selective attention is the ability to focus only on chosen stimuli and not to be distracted by other "noise" in the environment. Because children must identify and select what to attend to, I consider selective attention to reflect strategic abilities. In general, selective attention abilities increase with age, with young children giving a disproportionate amount of attention to information irrelevant to the task at hand and not enough attention to important information (Lane & Pearson, 1982).

Selective attention in children has been extensively studied using tests of **incidental learning.** In a typical experiment, children are shown pairs of pictures like those in Figure 6-3. One member of each pair is designated as central, and the children are told to remember it for later on. The other is designated as incidental and the children are told that they can ignore it (Hagen & Stanovich, 1977). Following stimulus presentation, the children are asked to recall the central stimuli and, as would be expected, the older they are, the more they recall. Then, the children are asked to recall the incidental stimuli—the ones they were supposed to ignore. Age differences are much smaller for the incidental recall. In fact, after about age 11, the amount of incidental information remembered actually decreases (Hagen & Stanovich, 1977). This means that when instructed to remember one set of items and ignore another, younger children have more difficulty with both. From results such as these, researchers have concluded that older children are better able to allocate attention in accordance with task demands and that they can store information more efficiently than younger children do (Schiff & Knopf, 1985). Teachers and parents need to recognize the possibility that young children's seeming inability to learn prescribed lessons might be because they are filling their minds with incidental learning.

Other researchers have emphasized the role that age differences play in the ability to exert inhibitory control in developmental differences in selective attention. For example, in research with adults and 5- to 12-year-old children (Ridderinkhof & van der Molen, 1995), participants were shown target arrays (central stimuli) with arrows pointing either to the left or the right. Participants held a bulb in each hand and were to squeeze the bulb in their right hand for a right facing arrow and the bulb in their left hand for a left-facing arrow. The target arrows were surrounded either by (1) incidental arrows (that children were told to ignore) that faced in the same direction as the target arrows, (2) incidental arrows that faced in the opposite direction, or (3) diamonds, that served as neutral stimuli.

The length of time it took children to squeeze the bulb, depending on whether the distractor arrows were pointing in the same or opposite direction as the target arrows (all relative to the time it took to squeeze the bulb in the neutral "diamond" condition) was measured. The longer it took children to squeeze the bulb, relative to the neutral condition, the greater interference (and the poorer their selective attention) was proposed to be. Children's brainwave patterns were also recorded. Ridderinkhof and van der Molen reported a reduction

FIGURE 6-3 Stimulus materials used in central-incidental memory tasks. Children are instructed to attend to one stimulus class of pictures (the animals, for example) and are later tested for memory of both the central (animals) and incidental (household items) stimuli. SOURCE: "Strategies for Remembering," by J. W. Hagen. In S. Farnham-Diggory (Ed.), *Information Processing in Children*, p. 68. Copyright © 1972. Academic Press. Reprinted with permission from Elsevier.

in interference effects with age, as measured both by patterns of hand squeezes and brain waves. Based on their findings, the researchers concluded that age-related differences in inhibition account for much of the data and that this is related to developmental differences in the maturation of the frontal cortex (see also Ridderinkhof, van der Molen, & Band, 1997).

The Cost of Strategy Use

One speculation is that executing strategies requires substantial mental effort and that young children do not have enough information-processing resources to execute the strategy and still perform other aspects of the task as well. That is, strategy use has a cost in mental effort, and young children exert so much of their limited resources executing the strategy that they do not retain sufficient mental capacity to perform other aspects of the task efficiently.

Katherine Kipp Harnishfeger and I demonstrated this possibility in a dual-task memory experiment (Bjorklund & Harnishfeger, 1987). Third- and seventh-grade children were instructed in the use of an organizational memory strategy (remembering all the words from a category together). In addition, the children were required to tap an index finger on the space bar of a microcomputer as fast as they could. Their tapping rates during the memory training were compared with their rates during a baseline period when no memory task was given and during a free-recall memory task for which no training instructions had been provided. Decreases in tapping rate during the memory tasks were used as an indication of how much mental effort the children were expending on the tasks. The more slowly the children tapped (relative to when they were performing no memory task), the greater the mental effort required to perform the memory task was presumed to be. That is, the more mental effort required for the memory task, the more interference (measured by the decreased tapping rate) there should be on the secondary, tapping task.

We reported that both the third- and seventh-graders showed increased interference as a result of the training, relative to the free-recall task. Furthermore, both groups later used the strategy that they had been shown during training. This use was indicated by increased clustering in recall, with children remembering words from the same category together. Only the seventh-grade children, however, showed a corresponding improvement in the number of words they recalled, relative to the free-recall task. The third-graders remembered no more words as a result of the training than they did when no memory instructions had been given, despite the fact that they used the strategy and expended greater amounts of mental effort. We interpreted these results as indicating that the third-graders used too much of their limited mental capacity in executing the strategy to have enough left over for other aspects of the memory task, such as retrieving specific words. Strategies are supposed to provide greater efficiency in processing, and

had the third-grade children mastered the strategy to a greater degree, their memory performance would probably have improved. Nevertheless, under the conditions of this experiment, their memory performance did not improve. Similar findings and interpretations have been reported for rehearsal (Guttentag, 1984), simpler attentional strategies (Miller et al., 1991), and a more complex elaboration memory strategy (Rohwer & Litrownik, 1983).

Strategies are effortful. Young children process information less efficiently than older children do, making them less likely to use a strategy spontaneously and less likely to benefit from the imposition of a strategy. Cognitive processing becomes more efficient with age, allowing children to execute more strategies and to use them with greater effectiveness.

Knowledge and Strategies

I discussed in Chapter 5 the relation between what children know, or their **knowledge base,** and how they perform on cognitive tasks. For example, the research with chess-expert children by Michelene Chi (1978) demonstrated that when someone knows a lot about a specific topic, memory span for information *in one's area of expertise,* but not beyond it, is significantly enhanced. Perhaps the relationship between knowledge and processing is most easily seen with respect to strategies. According to Daniel Kee (1994), "Most researchers acknowledge that strategic processing is dependent on the availability and accessibility of relevant knowledge" (see also Bjorklund, Muir-Broaddus, & Schneider, 1990; Rabinowitz & Kee, 1994). The primary reason hypothesized for this relationship is that having a detailed, or elaborated, knowledge base results in faster processing for domain-specific information, which in turn results in more efficient processing and greater availability of mental resources. The relationship between knowledge and strategy use has been demonstrated for a variety of domains, including mathematics (Ashcraft, 1990), reading (Daneman & Green, 1986), text comprehension (Schneider, Körkel, & Weinert, 1989), problem solving (Chi, Feltovich, & Glaser, 1981), communication (Furman & Walden, 1990), memory

(Ornstein, Baker-Ward, & Naus, 1988), and forming inferences (Barnes, Dennis, & Haefele-Kalvaitis, 1996), among others.

A memory experiment by Daniel Kee and Leslie Davies (1990) provided one particularly straightforward demonstration of the interrelationship between knowledge, strategy use, mental effort, and task performance. These researchers used the dual-task procedure described earlier to assess the relationship between mental effort and knowledge base in the use of a memory strategy in 10- and 11-year-old children. Changes in rate of finger tapping as a function of strategy use and familiarity of the to-be-learned information were used as a measure of the mental effort required to perform the memory strategy. The children were given pairs of words and asked to form an association between them, so that when they were presented with the first word in a pair they would be able to remember the second word (this is referred to as a *paired-associates task*). The children were instructed to use an *elaboration strategy* to help them learn the pairs. Elaboration consists of generating a relationship between paired items; for example, if the two words were arrow and glasses, an effective elaboration strategy might be to generate an image or the statement "the arrow smashes the glasses" (see Kee, 1994; Pressley, 1982).

Kee and Davies (1990) generated two types of lists for the children to learn. One list consisted of "accessible" pairs (for example, stairs-tower, cowboy-ranch, pig-mud); these were pairs of items for which children would have substantial background knowledge, making it easy for them to generate elaborations. The other list consisted of "inaccessible" pairs (for example, ticket-knee, frog-chair, cake-valley); these were pairs of items for which children would have few pre-established associations, making the generation of elaborations more difficult (that is, more effortful).

The results indicated that the children remembered fewer of the inaccessible than the accessible pairs, showing that prior knowledge has an effect on how well one remembers. Moreover, the children expended more mental effort, as reflected by the reduction of tapping rate when performing the elaboration strategy, for the inaccessible than for the accessible

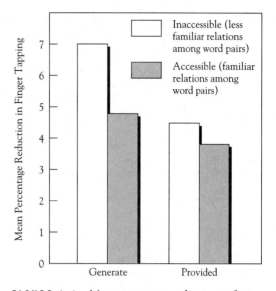

FIGURE 6-4 Mean percentage reduction in finger tapping as a function of accessibility for subjects in the dual-task memory experiment by Kee and Davies. SOURCE: From "Mental Effort and Elaboration: Effects of Accessibility and Instruction," by D. W. Kee and L. Davies, 1990, *Journal of Experimental Child Psychology, 49,* 264–274. Copyright © 1990 Academic Press. Reprinted with permission.

pairs. Differences in memory performance and mental effort between the accessible and inaccessible lists were greatly reduced, however, when the children were provided with the elaborations (the provide condition), rather than having to generate them themselves (the generate condition). The difference in mental effort between the generate and provide conditions in this experiment is shown in Figure 6-4. The mental effort associated with having to generate elaborations for relatively unfamiliar pairs of items directly affected how children used the strategy and how much they remembered.

But *how* does knowing a lot (or a little) about the task materials influence performance? This will vary with the nature of the task, but knowledge should influence task performance in some general ways. I examined the role of knowledge on children's strategic memory performance (Bjorklund, 1987a) and proposed three ways in which knowledge may enhance children's performance, some of which are directly related to strategies: (1) by increasing the accessibility of specific items (item-specific effects), (2) by the relatively effortless activation of relations among sets of items (nonstrategic organization), and (3) by facilitating the use of deliberate strategies. Research examining each of these alternatives is reviewed briefly next.

Item-Specific Effects

Item-specific effects are most easily observed when children are asked to recall sets of unrelated items (for example, *apple, army, clock, day, dress, flower, hammer, snow*). Recall typically improves with age, but there are no corresponding improvements in measures of organization (Ornstein, Hale, & Morgan, 1977). One interpretation of these findings is that individual items are more richly represented in the semantic memories of older children than in those of younger children, resulting in greater ease of retrieval. This interpretation is bolstered by studies using lists of unrelated items that are chosen because of their meaningfulness for children of different ages. In these studies, groups of children first evaluate words by how meaningful each one is to them. From these ratings, recall lists are constructed that are balanced in meaningfulness over several ages, thus eliminating age differences in knowledge for the information to be remembered. Under these conditions, age differences for short lists of words are eliminated (Chechile & Richman, 1982; Ghatala, 1984).

Nonstrategic Organization

Concerning nonstrategic organization, I suggested that much of the improvement seen in children's recall of categorically related material over the school years can be attributed to age-related increases in the relatively automatic (effortless) activation of semantic memory relations (Bjorklund, 1987a; Bjorklund et al., 1990). For instance, highly associated words (for example, *dog* and *cat, hand* and *glove, mouse* and *cheese*) are processed faster and are more likely to be

sorted together by 5- and 6-year-old children than are nonassociated words that are categorically related (for example, *dog* and *lion, cheese* and *milk, hand* and *head*). Older children show efficient processing for both highly associated and nonassociated categorically related words (McCauley, Weil, & Sperber, 1976). When highly associated words are used on memory tests, levels of recall and clustering are high for both younger and older children. When associative strength is low among categorically related words, however, only older children show elevated memory performance (Frankel & Rollins, 1985; Schneider, 1986). One reason proposed for this effect is that semantic relations between high associates are activated with relatively little expenditure of mental effort, resulting in retrieval that appears organized (all the high associates are recalled together) but does not require the use of a deliberate strategy.

In other studies, age differences in recall have been eliminated or greatly reduced when children have detailed knowledge about the information they are asked to remember (Bjorklund & Zeman, 1982; Lindberg 1980). For example, Barbara Zeman and I (Bjorklund & Zeman, 1982) asked children in first, third, and fifth grades to recall the names of their classmates. Age differences in class recall were small and were significantly less than age differences found for lists of categorically related words (see Figure 6-5). Furthermore, children's recall of their classmates' names was not random but typically was highly organized (by seating arrangement, reading groups, sex, and so on). Yet, when queried about their use of strategies, most of the children in all grades were unaware of using any special technique to remember the names. We proposed that the classmates' names represented a well-established knowledge base, with relations among names being activated with relatively little effort. Thus, a strategy was not necessary for successful retrieval. In other words, although the outcome of the children's recall appeared to be strategic (highly organized retrieval), the processes underlying their performance were not but, rather, represented the relatively automatic activation and retrieval of relations among items in memory.

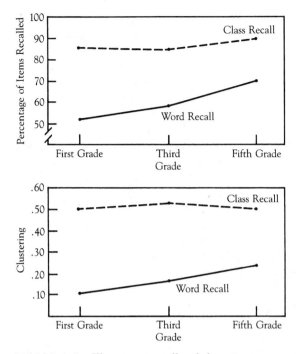

FIGURE 6-5 The average recall and clustering on class- and word-recall tasks by children in first, third, and fifth grades. SOURCE: Bjorklund, D. F., & Zeman, B. R. (1982). Children's organization and metamemory awareness in their recall of familiar information. *Child Development, 53,* 799–810. The Society for Research in Child Development, Inc.

Facilitating Strategies

Another interpretation for our findings is that the elaborated knowledge base that the children had for their classmates' names allowed them to use memory strategies efficiently. In fact, we proposed this possibility for the oldest children, who might have identified categorical relations in their recall while retrieving names on the basis of the relatively automatic activation of semantic memory relations and then continued to use this fortuitously discovered strategy for the remainder of their recall ("Hey, all those kids sit in the same row. I think I'll remember the rest of the kids by where they sit"). Peter Ornstein and his colleagues have championed this position, proposing that an elaborated knowledge base

for sets of items allows the effective use of mnemonics (Folds et al., 1990; Ornstein et al., 1988). The researchers propose that the use of memory strategies is facilitated by the automatic execution of certain parts of a task, even in very young children. Later in development, when children have a more sophisticated knowledge base and more experience, entire problem-solving routines can become automated. In support of this, several studies have demonstrated that children (and adults) more readily acquire strategies, both spontaneously and through training, and generalize a learned strategy to a new set of materials, when more familiar rather than less familiar stimulus items are used (Best, 1993; Rabinowitz, Freeman, & Cohen, 1992).

The relationship between knowledge, strategies, and task performance is a complicated one and centrally important to cognitive development. What is important to remember is that what and how much one knows influences how and how well one thinks. With age, children acquire more knowledge and, simply as a result of these quantitative increases, process information differently. Because knowledge affects processing, children (and adults) think differently about topics on which they have detailed knowledge versus those on which they have less knowledge, thus accounting, in part, for the often-observed phenomenon of domain specificity.

Strategies and Metacognition

In Chapter 5, I defined **metacognition** as the knowledge of one's cognitive abilities. Every type of cognition has a corresponding type of metacognition; that is, metamemory, meta-attention, meta-comprehension, and so on. Metacognition implies that a person is self-aware of his or her thinking. That is, someone with metacognitive awareness should be aware of the cognitive operation he or she is engaged in and perhaps how successful his or her attempts at solving a particular problem are. Strategies as I defined them earlier in the chapter almost require a degree of metacognitive awareness. If strategies are available to consciousness, it implies that children "know" (that is, are self-aware) of using them. At one level, this is true, but this still leaves much room for variability. Children differ greatly in the degree to which they know what strategies they have available in their cognitive arsenal, their relative effectiveness, when they are needed and when they are not, and in monitoring task performance. These various factors can influence strategy use and effectiveness, and, not surprisingly, they each develop.

Metacognition can be divided into types: *declarative* and *procedural* (Schneider & Lockl, 2002). **Declarative metacognition** refers to the explicit, conscious, and factual knowledge a person has about the characteristics of the task he or she is performing, one's own weak and strong points with respect to performing the task, and the possible strategies that could be used on the task. (Compare this with explicit memory as discussed in Chapter 5.) For example, for simple addition problems, are children aware of their own abilities to add and subtract numbers? Do they realize that computing sums may be easier if they use some external aids, such as their fingers or pips on a pair of dice, rather than having to do the computation in their heads? Do they know that they can derive an answer to the problem by counting all the numbers (for example, for the problem 3 + 2 = ?, saying, "1, 2, 3, . . . 4, **5**"), by counting from the larger number (for example, saying "3 . . . 4, **5**"), or, in some cases, "just knowing" the answer ("**5!**")? In contrast to declarative metacognition is **procedural metacognition,** which refers to the knowledge about when strategies are necessary ("Do I need to do something special to remember this telephone number?), as well as monitoring how well one is performing on a task (see Schneider & Pressley, 1997).

Meta-Attention

Metacognition generally improves with age, with young children generally being more out of touch with cognitive abilities than are older children,

specifically when it comes to using strategies. Let me begin with an examination of **meta-attention,** children's knowledge of their attentional abilities. As noted earlier in this chapter, young children tend to use ineffective attentional strategies and often attend as much, or more, to task irrelevant stimuli as to task relevant ones. Might such performance be attributed (or at least related) to deficits in meta-attention? Well, yes, and no. Even though 4-year-olds generally cannot overcome distractions when performing selective-attention tasks, they are apparently aware that distractions are a problem, for they realize that two stories will be harder to understand if the storytellers speak simultaneously rather than taking turns (Pillow, 1988). In contrast, 3-year-olds would just as soon listen to stories told simultaneously as to have the storytellers take turns. In other research, Patricia Miller and Michael Weiss (1982) asked 5-, 7-, and 9-year-olds to answer a series of questions about factors known to affect performance on an incidental-learning task (that is, a task like the "animals and objects" test described earlier). Although knowledge about attentional processes generally increased with age, even the 5-year-olds realized that one should at least *look first* at task-relevant stimuli and then *label* these objects as an aid to remembering them. The 7- and 10-year-olds further understood that one must *attend selectively* to task-relevant stimuli and *ignore* irrelevant information to do well on these problems.

At other times, however, young children seem unaware that paying attention is something special. Flavell and his colleagues (Flavell, Green, & Flavell, 1995a) asked 4-, 6-, and 8-year-old children a series of questions about attention. For example, if a woman were examining a set of decorative pins so that she can select one as a gift, what would be on her mind? Would she be focusing just on the pins, or might she have other things on her mind as well? Whereas almost all 8-year-olds and most 6-year-olds were aware that the woman would be thinking primarily about the pins and not likely thinking about other things, few 4-year-olds had this insight. It's as if they do not realize what is involved in selective attention. By 8 years of age, children's understanding of attentional focus was about as good as that of adults.

Metamemory

As another example, consider **metamemory.** In a pioneering study of children's metacognition abilities, Mary Anne Kreutzer, Catherine Leonard, and John Flavell (1975) asked children in kindergarten and the first, third, and fifth grades a series of questions about memory. For example, the children were asked if they ever forget things, if it would be easier to remember a phone number immediately after being told the number or after getting a drink of water, and if learning pairs of opposites (for example, boy/girl) would be easier or harder than learning pairs of unrelated words (for example, Mary/walk), all forms of declarative metacognition. Some kindergarten children asserted that they never forgot things, and fewer than 50% believed that phoning the friend immediately would yield more accurate recall. About half of the kindergarten and first-grade children believed that the arbitrary pairs would be just as easy or easier to learn as the opposites.

Let me relate an anecdote about how young children can be out of touch with their memory performance. I was conducting a memory test with a 5-year-old boy. I showed him 16 pictures of familiar objects from four categories (fruit, tools, body parts, and animals), which he had two minutes to study. After the two minutes, I asked him a few questions as a simple distraction task ("How old are you? When's your birthday?"), and then asked him to remember as many of those picture as he could, out loud, in any order that he wanted. The child did not hesitate but said quickly "cow, hammer, screwdriver, apple," and just as quickly stopped, and sat quietly waiting for me to say something. After sitting silently for about 10 seconds, I asked him "Can you remember any more of the pictures?," and he looked incredulously at me and said, "You mean there were *more* pictures?" This child had told me all he could remember of the list, and as far as he was concerned, his recall was perfect. His ability to monitor his performance (procedural metamemory) would (one hopes) improve considerably in the years to come.

More specifically with respect to strategies, are children aware that strategies are necessary to perform a task well and of the relation between using strategies and task performance (procedural metacognition)? Not surprisingly, young children are often unaware of simple strategies they can use to solve problems, or at least they are not conscious that such techniques can be useful when they are given a specific task. For example, children who are aware of the connection between strategies such as rehearsal and organization and memory performance often remember more information than do children who do not posses such awareness (Justice et al., 1997). Furthermore, young children who have been taught a strategy are often unaware that using it facilitated their memory performance. This is illustrated in an experiment by Barbara Ringel and Carla Springer (1980). They trained first-, third-, and fifth-grade children to use an organizational strategy. The children were given pictures and instructed to sort them into groups by meaning and to use the groupings to help them remember the pictures. Each group of children showed improved memory performance after training (relative to an earlier baseline phase). The children were then given a third memory task to assess transfer of training. After completing training but before beginning the transfer list, some of the children were provided with explicit feedback concerning their improved performance on the task, whereas others were not. The fifth-grade children transferred the organizational strategy to the new task under all conditions, whereas there was no evidence of significant transfer for any group of first graders. For the third-grade children, however, feedback made a difference. Those third graders who had received feedback concerning their memory performance transferred the organizational strategy to a new set of pictures. Third graders receiving no feedback did not, but, for the most part, reverted to a nonstrategic style characteristic of their pretraining behavior. In other words, knowing how well they were doing influenced the third-graders' generalization of a strategy. The older children, apparently being better able to assess their own progress, did not require such feedback to transfer the strategy, and the younger children either were unable to transfer the strategy or at best needed more intensive instructions before generalization would take place. Other researchers have emphasized the role of metamemory in the effectiveness of strategy use and transfer, demonstrating that training in memory monitoring or other aspects of metamemory is responsible for the effectiveness and maintenance of strategy training (Ghatala et al., 1986; Melot, 1998).

Given the impressive findings of the training studies, it seems reasonable that improvements in metacognitive knowledge must be causally related to improvements in cognitive behavior, or metacognitive knowledge → cognitive behavior. Yet, an argument can be made that metamemory knowledge grows out of memory behavior, or cognitive behavior → metacognitive knowledge. That is, children perform cognitive strategies effectively and, as a result, acquire knowledge about strategies.

John Cavanaugh and John Borkowski conducted research aimed at elucidating the relationship between metacognitive (specifically metamemory) knowledge and cognitive (specifically memory) behavior in development by administering extensive memory and metamemory interviews to children in kindergarten and the first, third, and fifth grades (1980). Cavanaugh and Borkowski reported that both metamemory knowledge and memory behavior increased with age but that, within a grade level, there was little significant relationship between the two factors. That is, knowing a child's level of metamemory knowledge did not predict well his or her level of memory performance when age was held constant.

Other research has shown that the relation one finds between metamemory and memory depends on the age of the child and the nature of the questions (Cantor, Andreassen, & Waters, 1985; Schneider & Pressley, 1997). For example, studies looking at metamemory/memory relations in sorting and elaboration tasks do not yield strong connections between the two factors until the elementary school years (Lange et al., 1990), and not consistently until about age 10 (Hasselhorn, 1992). When the task is simple and the metamemory questions are highly related to successful task performance, however, even preschool children show a significant relationship between metamemory knowledge and memory behavior. For example, Schneider and Sodian (1988) asked 4- and 6-year-old children to remember 10 objects that they placed in each of 10 play houses. Each house was associated with a picture of a person (for example, doctor, farmer, policeman, soccer player, sailor), and some of the items were related to the people (for example, syringe, tractor, police car, soccer ball, and ship), whereas others were not (for example, comb, letter, key, flower, and lamp). For both the 4- and 6-year-olds, children who were aware of the importance of associating the objects (syringe, tractor) with the people (doctor, farmer) performed better on the memory test. Thus, the relation between metamemory and memory is significant even for 4-year-olds when the task is sufficiently simplified and the metamemory questions are immediately pertinent to the memory behavior.

In general, the research evidence points to a bidirectional relationship between metacognitive knowledge and cognitive behavior (Schneider & Bjorklund, 1998). Metacognitive knowledge can result in improved cognitive performance, which, in turn, results in enhanced metacognitive knowledge. Metacognition is obviously an important component in children's cognitive development. However, research findings suggest that metacognitive competence is as much a consequence as it is a cause of competent cognitive behavior, the two being intimately entwined, and that this relationship varies as a function of age and task variables. Also, metacognition interacts with other factors. For example, as we noted earlier, children who are experts in a domain will perform better in that domain than will less-expert children. However, expert children's cognitive performance will be greatest when they also have substantial metacognitive knowledge (Schneider, Schlagmüller, & Visé, 1998).

I will have more to say about metacognition with respect to specific types of cognition in other chapters in the book. For now, it's important to keep in mind that possessing and using strategies are not enough to ensure competent performance. Being aware of when to use strategies, which ones to use, and how effective the strategies you're using are will all influence task performance.

Culture and Strategies

Cultures clearly differ in the extent to which they support and encourage particular strategic activities (Kurtz, 1990; Mistry, 1997). For example, the memory strategies of rehearsal and organization are especially helpful to children from Western industrialized societies, whose school activities involve a great deal of rote memorization and list learning. Yet, these same strategies might not be so useful to unschooled children from nonindustrialized societies, whose most important memory tasks might involve recalling the location of objects (water, game animals) in a natural setting or remembering instructions passed along in the context of proverbs or stories.

For example, in list-learning experiments, Western children rely heavily on strategies acquired at school and clearly outperform their unschooled peers from nonindustrialized societies (Cole & Scribner, 1977; Rogoff & Waddell, 1982). The picture is much different, however, when the memory task is embedded in a meaningful and structured context. When tests are structured so that people must recall organized prose (as in a story) or items from spatially organized arrays (as in familiar scenes), few cultural differences in memory performance are found (see Rogoff, 1990).

Not all cultural differences in strategic functioning are between children in schooled and nonschooled societies. For example, studies have linked differences in American and German attitudes toward intellectual development to differences in memory strategy use (Carr et al., 1989; Kurtz et al., 1990). In these studies, second- and third-graders in Germany and the United States were trained to use a memory strategy (specifically, to recall related items together in clusters). Before training, children were given a battery of tests assessing their verbal and nonverbal intelligence, academic self-esteem, metamemory, spontaneous use of strategies, and attributional beliefs about learning (whether they attributed success and failure to luck, their own effort, or some inherent ability). Children's parents and teachers also answered questionnaires regarding their beliefs about children's academic success or failure and the extent of instruction in or encouragement of strategic thinking that occurred in the home and at school.

An initial finding was that the German children were significantly more strategic on their own than the American children were, although the American children did benefit from the memory training. Despite the German children's superiority on the memory task, however, the American children had more positive academic self-esteem and were more apt to attribute academic outcomes to effort (that is, hard work) than the German children were, something that has been associated with enhanced academic achievement (Borkowski & Turner, 1988; Dweck & Leggett, 1988). The German children, on the other hand, were more apt to believe that their success or failure in school-related tasks was due to ability (that is, inborn traits). Moreover, American children who believe in effort perform better than American children holding other views, and German children who believe in natural ability perform better than German children who hold other views (Kurtz, 1990). This shows that when studies of American children report that belief in effort is related to higher academic achievement, it is culturally dependent—holding only for that culture. Different patterns of performance are found for children from different cultures.

The source of this cultural difference in strategy use and attribution of success can be traced to the behaviors and attitudes of children's parents and teachers. German parents give children more direct strategy training, buy them more games that require strategic thinking, and check their homework more than do American parents. German teachers reported more direct strategy instruction than did American teachers (Carr et al., 1989; Kurtz et al., 1990). German parents and teachers were more likely to attribute children's academic performance to ability, whereas their American counterparts were more likely to attribute it to effort.

How Do Children's Strategies Develop?

Siegler's Adaptive Strategy Choice Model

The foregoing discussion might give the idea that for any given task, children use one strategy and perhaps with time and practice eventually begin using another, more efficient strategy. Such a perspective reflects how a good deal of strategy research during the last 40 years was done, looking at changes in a single strategy over relatively brief periods of time. This perspective is an overly simplified one, however. Recent research has shown that children use a variety of strategies to solve a single problem, sometimes several strategies at a single time. Evidence for multiple and variable strategy use has been found everywhere it has been looked for, including arithmetic (Alibali, 1999), scientific reasoning (Schauble, 1990), memory (Fletcher & Bray, 1997), spelling (Rittle-Johnson & Siegler, 1999), and conservation (Church & Goldin-Meadow, 1986), among others (see Siegler, 1996).

Robert Siegler's (1996, 2000) **adaptive strategy choice model** best exemplifies this perspective of multiple- and variable-strategy use. I discussed Siegler's model briefly in Chapter 2 in the section on "Selectionist Theories of Cognitive and Brain Development." Basically, Siegler adopts the idea of natural selection from Darwin's theory of evolution and applies it to cognitive development. Stated most simply, Siegler proposes that, in cognitive development, children generate a wide variety of strategies to solve problems and, depending on the nature of the task and the goals of the child, certain strategies are "selected" and used frequently, whereas others that are less effective are used less often and eventually decrease in frequency (Siegler, 1996; Siegler & Jenkins, 1989).

The technique Siegler and his colleagues used to assess children's multiple strategy use has been re-ferred to as the **microgenetic method** and involves looking at developmental change within a single set of individuals over short time intervals—days or weeks, usually (see Miller & Coyle, 1999; Siegler, 2000). This method is based on research and theory of Vygotsky, discussed in Chapter 3, in which important changes in development can occur over relatively brief periods. Not all aspects of development (cognitive or otherwise) fit this bill, so one must be careful in selecting phenomena to study and to assess children who are most susceptible to changing how they think over relatively short intervals. But cognitive strategies are good candidates for examination from a microgenetic perspective, and research following Siegler's general approach has produced some interesting results.

But to what extent do changes observed in microgenetic studies reflect those found during longer developmental periods? For example, are the same types and patterns of changes found in microgenetic studies, when children are given many opportunities to solve certain problems over a period of weeks, found when such problems are assessed via longitudinal or cross-sectional methods, over intervals of years? Although it is doubtful that patterns of microgenetic and longitudinal changes would be identical for most phenomena, they may be for some. For example, in the study by Siegler and Matija Svetina (2002), discussed briefly in Chapter 1, 6-, 7-, and 8-year-old children were given matrix problems to solve over seven sessions, with an average of 3 to 5 days between most sessions. As you may recall, children were given a matrix like the one shown in Figure 1-4 on page 16 in Chapter 1: on the right-hand side, in the top row is a picture of a large light-gray mouse facing right and a picture of a large light-gray bird facing right. Below them is a single picture of a small, light-gray mouse facing left. Children were to select from a group of six pictures the one that best completed the analogy, in this case a small, light-gray bird, facing left. Different patterns of change were observed both between sessions within individual children (microgenetic comparisons) and between children of different ages (6 to 7 years, cross-sectional comparisons). Table 6-2 presents factors that changed and how they changed in

TABLE 6-2   Microgenetic and cross-sectional changes in matrix task.

| | Observed changes | | |
Variable	Over sessions (1–7)	Over age (6–7) years	Match
1. Total % correct	Increase	Increase	+
2. % Form correct	No change	No change	+
3. % Orientation correct	Increase	Increase	+
4. % Size correct	Increase	Increase	+
5. % Color correct	No change	No change	+
6. % Form cited	No change	No change	+
7. % Orientation cited	No change	Increase	–
8. % Size cited	No change	No change	+
9. % Color cited	No change	No change	+
10. Predominant error	Duplicates	Duplicates	+
11. Stability over time	Yes	Predicted	+
12. Transfer to conservation	Yes	Yes	+

SOURCE: Siegler, R. S., & Svetina, M. (2002). A microgenetic/cross-sectional study of matrix completion: Comparing short-term and long-term change. *Child Development, 73*, 793–809. Reprinted with permission of the Society for Research in Child Development.

the microgenetic and cross-sectional samples. Most of the changes refer to types of responses children made (for example, making responses based on the size of the items or orientation of the items). As can be seen, of the 12 factors investigated, 11 showed the same pattern of change in both samples, suggesting to Siegler and Svetina that patterns of change observed in microgenetic studies are highly similar to those found during longer periods of development and may reflect the same underlying mechanisms of change.

Basically, Siegler sees multiple strategies existing within a child's cognitive repertoire at any one time, with these strategies competing with one another. Early in development or when a child is first learning a new task, relatively simple strategies will "win" most of the time. With practice and maturation, the child will use other, more effortful but more efficient strategies more frequently. Thus, Siegler believes that development does not occur in a steplike fashion but, rather, as a series of overlapping waves, with the pattern of those waves changing over time. Figure 6-6 presents Siegler's wave approach to cognitive de-

velopment. Multiple strategies are available to children at every age, but which strategies are used most frequently changes with age.

Perhaps the single most investigated topic using the microgenetic method and following Siegler's adaptive strategy choice model is simple arithmetic. For example, in learning to add, children frequently use a strategy that involves counting out loud both addends, called the *sum strategy* (for example, for 5 + 3 = ?, saying "1, 2, 3, 4, 5 [pause], 6, 7, **8.**"). A more sophisticated strategy, called the *min strategy*, is to begin with the larger addend (in this case, 5) and count up from there (for example, saying "5 [pause], 6, 7, **8.**"). A still more sophisticated strategy, known as *fact retrieval*, is "just knowing" the answer—retrieving it directly from long-term memory without having to count at all (for example, simply saying "8" to the question "How much is 5 + 3?"). When looking at group data, one gets the impression that children progress from using the sum strategy to using the min strategy to using fact retrieval. Yet closer examination reveals that individual children use a variety of these strategies at any one time: the frequencies

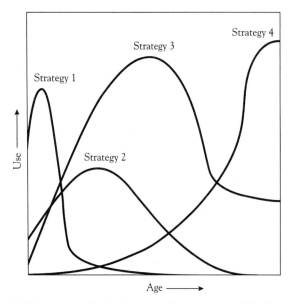

FIGURE 6-6 Siegler's strategy choice model of development. Change in strategy use is seen as a series of overlapping waves, with different strategies being used more frequently at different ages. SOURCE: Adapted from Siegler, 1996; thanks to Robert Siegler.

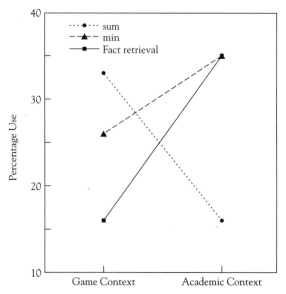

FIGURE 6-7 Percentage of strategy use for the three main strategies, sum, min, and fact retrieval for the game and academic contexts. SOURCE: Bjorklund, D. F., & Rosenblum, K. E. (2002). Context effects in children's selection and use of simple arithmetic strategies. *Journal of Cognition and Development, 3,* 225–242. Copyright © 2002 Lawrence Erlbaum Associates, Inc. Reprinted with permission.

with which these strategies are used vary with age. (More will be said of children's arithmetic strategies in Chapter 14.)

Let me provide an example of multiple strategy use from some research Kristina Rosenblum and I did on kindergarten children's simple arithmetic strategies when computing moves from dice while playing the board game "Chutes and Ladders" (Bjorklund & Rosenblum, 2002). Children calculated moves based on the throw of two dice, so the possible combinations ranged from 1 plus 1 to 6 plus 6. We also gave children more standard verbal math problems as they would receive in school following the game (for example, "How much is 3 plus 4?"). The most frequently used strategies were the sum, min, and fact retrieval, as discussed earlier, but it was rare for any child to use one strategy only, and the frequency with which these strategies were used varied with the context (game versus academic context). Children used an average of 2.65 different strategies during the

game context and 2.89 during the academic context. Interestingly, the distribution of these strategies varied with context. Figure 6-7 presents the percentages that each of these three strategies was used in both the game and academic contexts. As can be seen, there was substantial variability. Note that sum, the least sophisticated strategy, was used most often in the game context, but it was used least often in the academic context. The strategies children used also varied with the particular problem they received. Table 6-3 presents all the possible combinations of dice rolls in the experiment (from 1 + 1 to 6 + 6) and the modal (most frequently used) strategy for each combination. The numbers in parentheses correspond to the difference between the two addends for each problem. For most of the doubles (that is, 6 + 6; 5 + 5) children used fact retrieval, and for the

TABLE 6-3 Modal strategy used for various addition problems in the game context. (Difference between the two addends presented in parentheses.)

sum		min		Fact retrieval	
6 + 5	(1)	6 + 3	(3)	6 + 6	(0)
6 + 4	(2)	6 + 2	(4)	5 + 5	(0)
5 + 4	(1)	6 + 1	(5)	4 + 4	(0)
5 + 3	(2)	5 + 2	(3)	3 + 3	(0)
4 + 3	(1)	5 + 1	(4)	2 + 1	(1)
4 + 2	(2)	4 + 1	(3)	1 + 1	(0)
3 + 2	(1)				
3 + 1	(2)				
2 + 2	(0)				

SOURCE: Bjorklund, D. F., & Rosenblum, K. E. (2002). Context effects in children's selection and use of simple arithmetic strategies. *Journal of Cognition and Development, 3,* 225–242. Copyright © 2002 Lawrence Erlbaum Associates, Inc. Reprinted with permission.

TABLE 6-4 Modal strategy used for various addition problems in the academic context. (Difference between the two addends presented in parentheses.)

sum		min		Fact retrieval	
4 + 2	(2)	6 + 5	(1)	6 + 6	(0)
		6 + 4	(2)	6 + 1	(5)
		6 + 3	(3)	5 + 5	(0)
		6 + 2	(4)	5 + 1	(4)
		5 + 4	(1)	4 + 4	(0)
		5 + 3	(2)	4 + 1	(3)
		5 + 2	(3)	3 + 3	(0)
		4 + 3	(1)	3 + 1	(2)
		3 + 2	(1)	2 + 2	(0)
				2 + 1	(1)
				1 + 1	(0)

SOURCE: Bjorklund, D. F., & Rosenblum, K. E. (2002). Context effects in children's selection and use of simple arithmetic strategies. *Journal of Cognition and Development, 3,* 225–242. Copyright © 2002 Lawrence Erlbaum Associates, Inc. Reprinted with permission.

problems with large differences between the addends (that is, differences of 3, 4, and 5), min was the modal strategy that was used. For all other problems, sum was used most frequently. This pattern was very different in the academic context (see Table 6-4), with min and fact retrieval serving as the modal strategy about equally often. Fact retrieval tended to be used for all doubles (as in the game context) and when the smaller addend was a 1. Thus, not only do children use multiple and variable strategies in a task, but they are highly sensitive to factors within the testing context.

Other examples of children's multiple strategy use come from experiments assessing memory development. For example, Kate McGilly and Siegler (1990) gave children in kindergarten, second grade, and fourth grade a serial-recall task (remember a list of digits in exact order). McGilly and Siegler observed the strategies the children used and later questioned them about their strategy use. They reported that the children used a variety of strategies on these tasks (single word rehearsal, repeated rehearsal), with any given child using a combination of strategies over re-

peated trials. That is, multiple strategy use was the rule rather than the exception. In other research, Brian Cox and his colleagues (1989) demonstrated that third-grade children given instructions to sort words into groups by meaning not only improved their memory performance but also used more sophisticated *rehearsal* techniques. That is, improvements in one strategy (organization) led to improvements in another strategy (rehearsal), which in turn led to greater levels of memory performance. Moreover, on some tasks, children use a variety of different strategies on a single trial, often switching the combination of strategies they use from trial to trial (Coyle & Bjorklund, 1997). This is illustrated in a sort-recall memory study in which children could use as many as four different strategies on any one trial (sorting words into groups, naming categories, and rehearsing words during the study period and showing high levels of clustering at recall). Figure 6-8 presents the number of trials (maximum = 5) on which children in the second, third, and fourth

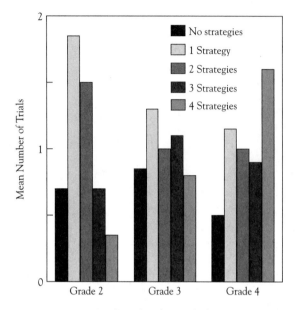

FIGURE 6-8 Number of trials on which no strategy, one strategy, two strategies, three strategies, or four strategies were used, by grade. SOURCE: Coyle, T. R., & Bjorklund, D. F. (1997). Age differences in, and consequences of, multiple- and variable strategy use on a multitrial sort-recall task. *Developmental Psychology, 33,* 372–380. Copyright © 1997 by the American Psychological Association. Reprinted with permission.

grades used 0, 1, 2, 3, or 4 strategies. As you can see, the general pattern was for children at all grades to use more than one strategy per trial, although older children did, on average, use a greater number of strategies per trial than younger children did.

More will be said about Siegler's account of strategy development later in this book, particularly in Chapter 14, examining age differences in arithmetic strategies. Siegler believes that age differences in how strategies are selected and used reflect an important way of viewing cognitive development that differs from conventional Piagetian and information-processing models. Perhaps the most important message from Siegler's work is that children use strategies *selectively* and *adaptively,* and that at any point in time and for any given task, children have a variety of strategies available to them. The issue facing cog-

nitive developmental psychologists is not whether children are being strategic. Rather, we are seeking to discover what strategies and combination of strategies children of different ages use and how the simpler strategies used by young children develop into the more sophisticated and effective strategies used by older children and adults.

Variability and Change

I have noted how children use multiple and variable strategies, but what do we really mean by "variability," and might it be little more than "noise," that is, random fluctuation that really has little if anything important to do with children's strategy development? In the context of Siegler's adaptive strategy choice model, variability refers to fluctuations in the strategies children use from one trial to another. For instance, will children use the sum strategy on one trial and min on the next two, followed by fact retrieval, and so on, or might they use sum on the first 20 trials, and then suddenly switch to min and stick with it for the remainder of the task? There is clearly more variability in the first pattern than the second. Coyle (2001) has analyzed variability in children's and adults' strategy use and found two general patterns of change and relationships between these patterns and levels of task performance. Coyle referred to one type of strategy variability as **strategy diversity,** which refers to the number of different strategies a person uses on a task (for example, sum and min, 2 strategies, or sum, min, fact retrieval, and "guessing," four strategies), and the second as **strategy change,** which refers to the number of trial-by-trial changes people make in the strategies they use. Take, for instance, a child who, on six consecutive arithmetic problems, uses sum on the first three and min on the second three. Contrast this with another child who used sum on trials 1, 3, and 5, and min on trials 2, 4, and 6. Both children used the same number of strategies (and thus show comparable levels of strategy diversity), but the second child displayed much higher levels of strategy change. One method of quantifying just how much strategy change exists is to figure out the maximum amount of trial-to-trial switches that are possible (which is the total number of trials minus one, or in this case, 6 − 1 = 5) and divide that into the number of strategy changes that were observed. In the first case, the child displayed just one trial with a strategy change (from sum to min on trials 3 to 4), for a strategy change score of .20 (1 divided by 5); in the second case, the child displayed the maximum change, with changes on each trial transition, for a strategy change score of 1.0.

Coyle analyzed findings from a series of experiments that assessed both strategy diversity and strategy change and found these two measures were each related to task performance, but in different ways and that the relationships varied with age. For example, strategy diversity was positively associated with task performance for children (the more strategies children used the better their performance tended to be), but not for adults. The reverse pattern was observed for strategy change: High levels of strategy change were associated with poorer performance for adults but not for children. Coyle (2001) interpreted this pattern as reflecting a two-step developmental process: "Early in development, the primary developmental task is to acquire, and experiment with, new strategies . . . Because development proceeds at different rates for different individuals, individual differences in the acquisition of new strategies is considerable. . . . Later in development, nearly all individuals have in their repertoires a complete set of strategies . . . ; their task now is to learn to apply these strategies consistently. Thus, variation in the consistency with which strategies are used, not the number of different approaches used, is primarily predictive of [task performance for adults]" (p. 354).

Variability is not necessarily random, either. Recall in Chapter 1 our discussion of phase transitions and the example from Siegler and Svetina (2002), in which children displayed more variability in their solutions to a problem immediately before changing to consistently getting the right answer. In that study, most errors early on were what Siegler and Svetina called "duplicate errors," selecting an alternative that was the same as in the base problem (see

Figure 1-5 in Chapter 1). This changed to making mostly "other errors" for the three trial blocks preceding a switch to consistently correct performance. This period of instability immediately before a change from using one strategy (in this case, one that consistently produced wrong responses to one that consistently produced correct ones) is characteristic of a phase transition in dynamic systems theories (see Chapter 1) and has been found for other strategies (Kelso, 1995).

Implicit Strategy Use

Can strategies ever be implicit, out of our conscious awareness? We may not always be aware of the strategies we are using, but part of the definition of strategies I provided earlier made it explicit that strategies are at least *available* to consciousness. Recent research by Robert Siegler and Elsbeth Stern (1998), however, has caused a reconsideration of this aspect of strategies. In their experiment, second-grade children were given a series of arithmetic problems of the following form: a + b − b = ?, for example, 37 + 16 − 16 = ? Most of you will recognize that there is a shortcut to solving such problems. Because the b term is both added to and then subtracted from the a term, they cancel each other out. Thus, the answer can be arrived at quite quickly, merely by stating the a term (37 in this example). The problem can also be solved by direct computation, of course (for example, 37 + 16 = 53; 53 − 16 = 37), which takes considerably longer.

Siegler and Stern tested a group of second-grade children during eight sessions on problems like these. Children's reaction times to solve each problem were recorded, and, after every trial, they were asked how they went about solving the problem. Although none of the children was using the shortcut strategy during the first session, most were using it, at least occasionally, by the end of the experiment. Siegler and Stern noted that latencies to solve the problems tended to be either very fast (4 seconds or less) or quite long (8 seconds or more). When children answered the problems quickly (under 4 seconds) they never showed evidence of computation, whereas they were almost always observed to compute the solution on problems when they had the longer latencies.

By recording both latencies to solve problems and explanations, Siegler and Stern were able to classify children's strategy use into several categories: (a) *computation,* in which children took a long time and were observed to compute (or said they computed) the solution; (b) *shortcut strategy,* in which children responded quickly and reported using the shortcut strategy; and (c) *unconscious shortcut strategy,* in which children responded quickly, showed no signs of computation, but claimed *not* to have used the shortcut procedure. Siegler and Stern reported that 88% of the children used the unconscious shortcut strategy before using the shortcut strategy. Nor was it the case that these children just lacked the verbal ability to express their ideas. Most of these children later used the shortcut strategy and provided adequate verbal descriptions of it. What these data suggest is that knowledge of the shortcut strategy was initially implicit (not available to consciousness), and only later became explicit.

Other evidence is consistent with Siegler and Stern's findings. For example, Susan Goldin-Meadow and her colleagues (Church & Goldin-Meadow, 1986; Alibali & Goldin-Meadow, 1993) have shown that children often reveal more sophisticated strategies in their gestures than in their speech. For example, some children given a conservation of liquid task to solve referred to differences in height in their (erroneous) verbal explanations, but referred to differences in width with their hands. Children who made such mismatches were more likely to benefit from subsequent training than were those whose verbal explanations and gestures matched. These findings indicate that implicit processes, such as those hypothesized by Annette Karmiloff-Smith (1992) and others (see discussion in Chapter 4), play an important role in the development of explicit processes such as strategies. Transitions from one strategy to another might not occur with a sudden burst of awareness (an "aha experience"), but might first be expressed only implicitly, before an explicit, and pre-sumably more flexible, level of strategy use is realized. Such findings can also be interpreted from a dynamic systems perspective, with the "unconscious strategies" reflecting some instability (or at least inconsistency) in children's approach to the problems, which tends to precede a phase transition.

Strategies in the Classroom

I'd like to think that all (or nearly all) aspects of cognitive development have some practical utility, but this seems to be especially the case for strategies. Many aspects of cognition develop because of children's normal day-to-day interaction with their environment. Change happens when no one (even the child him- or herself) is watching. Strategies are different. Although children often discover strategies on their own in the process of performing a task (Siegler & Jenkins, 1989), many important cognitive strategies are explicitly taught in school (Moely et al., 1992; Pressley & Woloshyn, 1995). As such, knowledge of how strategies develop and factors that influence their use can be of great practical value for the educator or parent of a school-age child.

But how much explicit strategy instruction do children get in school? This, of course, will vary from school to school and teacher to teacher, but it may surprise you to learn that strategy instruction is rarely on the top of most teachers' "to do" list. In a classroom observational study, Barbara Moely and her colleagues (1992) reported that teachers in kindergarten through sixth grade taught a wide range of strategies that varied with the age of the child and the nature of the task. These included rote learning for simple repetitive tasks, elaboration, imagery, and self-checking, among others. Despite the diversity of strategies taught, Moely and her colleagues (1992) reported that the absolute frequency of strategy instruction was low. For example, specific strategy instruction was observed on an average of fewer than 3% of the teacher observations, with teachers providing some general instruction about how to deal with a task strategically in 9.5% of the observations. In fact, 10% of the teachers observed in this study provided no strategy instruction at all. When focusing specifically on math instruction, however, second- and fifth-grade teachers were found to provide strategy or metacognitive instruction in nearly half of the observation intervals (Moely, Santulli, & Obach, 1995). Thus, strategy instruction in school varies with the teacher, the task, and the age of the children, with teachers generally providing children with instruction that is age-appropriate (that is, neither too simple nor too complicated for them to understand).

Strategy instruction is more likely to occur for some subjects than for others and especially for children just beginning to tackle a new challenge. For example, teachers (and parents) often give children specific instruction in simple arithmetic strategies, teaching them, for instance, in how to use the min strategy ("Start with the bigger number, 6, and then count from there, 7, 8, 9"), and provide quite explicit directions about how to decode letters and printed words into spoken sounds and language (Pressley & Woloshyn, 1995). Strategy instruction occurs less frequently for higher-level cognitive tasks, such as reading comprehension, yet researchers have extensively investigated such strategies with known positive effects of instruction on children's performance (Gaultney, 1995; Mastropieri & Scruggs, 1991). In their book, *Cognitive Strategy Instruction*, Michael Pressley and Vera Woloshyn (1995) present a variety of strategies for teachers to use in facilitating children's learning. For example, when discussing reading comprehension, they provide examples of the following strategies: summarization (abstracting the gist of a text), mental imagery (constructing mental images), self-generation of questions (teaching children to generate their own questions and answers), question-answering strategies (questions provided by the teacher or textbook author), story grammar (using the narrative structure of a text to generate questions), and activating prior knowledge (making use of what the reader already knows to aid comprehension of new material), among others.

The goal of strategy instruction is to make children into effective learners. Pressley, Borkowski, and Schneider, have developed the **good information processing model** (Pressley, Borkowski, & Schneider, 1989; Schneider & Pressley, 1997) to describe how efficient learners function. The model is based on the idea that good memory, and good thinking in general, is based on a combination of factors, including strategies, the knowledge base, metamemory, capacity, and motivation, many of which were discussed earlier in this chapter. These factors never operate alone (that is, one cannot truly understand how children use strategies without considering the other factors as well); rather, efficient information processing is the product of an interaction of these components. Moreover, each of these processes depends on consciousness, attentional capacity, and working memory.

Using this model, Pressley and his colleagues propose three stages in which knowledge is acquired via instruction: (1) children are taught by teachers or parents to use a strategy, and with practice they come to learn the attributes and advantages of the strategy (*specific strategy knowledge*). Children who experience stimulating school and home environments will be exposed to more strategies, which will broaden their specific strategy knowledge. (2) Teachers demonstrate similarities and differences of various strategies within a domain (for example, summarization versus self-generation of questions for reading comprehension), permitting children to make comparisons among strategies (*relational knowledge*). (3) At this point, children recognize the general utility of being strategic, leading to *general strategy knowledge*. As a result, children learn to attribute successful learning outcomes to the effort they expend using a strategy, and they also acquire higher-order skills such as selecting and monitoring strategies appropriate for the task (*metacognitive acquisition procedures*). The model's core assumption is that such higher-order skills—and attributional beliefs about the utility of strategies—are important for producing generalized thinking and problem-solving skills.

Having a theory of what constitutes "good information processing," based on years of careful

TABLE 6-5   General model of how to teach strategies.

Teach a few strategies at a time, intensively and extensively, as part of the ongoing curriculum; in the beginning, teach only one at a time, until students are familiar with the "idea" of strategy use.

Model and explain each new strategy.

Model again and re-explain strategies in ways that are sensitive to aspects of strategy use that are not well understood. (The students are constructing their understanding of the strategy, refining the understanding a little bit at a time.)

Explain to students where and when to use strategies, although students will also discover some such metacognitive information as they use strategies.

Provide plenty of practice, using strategies for as many appropriate tasks as possible. Such practice increases proficient execution of the strategy, knowledge of how to adapt it, and knowledge of when to use it.

Encourage students to monitor how they are doing when they are using strategies.

Encourage continued use of and generalization of strategies, for example, by reminding students throughout the school day about when they could apply strategies they are learning about.

Increase students' motivation to use strategies by heightening student awareness that they are acquiring valuable skills that are at the heart of competent functioning with learning tasks.

Emphasize reflective processing rather than speedy processing; do all possible to eliminate high anxiety in students; encourage students to shield themselves from distraction so they can attend to the academic task.

SOURCE: Pressley, M., & Woloshyn, V. (1995). *Cognitive strategy instruction that really improves children's academic performance* (2nd edition). Cambridge, MA: Brookline Books. Reprinted with permission.

experimental research, makes the job of applying it to the classroom a bit easier. Yet, knowing the research literature and converting it to lesson plans is often more easily said than done. Although methods of instruction will vary depending on the age of the child and the specific strategy that is being taught, Pressley and Woloshyn (1995) provide a general model for how to teach strategies, which is summarized in Table 6-5.

Summary

Strategies are defined as deliberately implemented, nonobligatory operations that are potentially available to consciousness and used to improve task performance. Most of the strategies investigated by developmental psychologists have been especially relevant for children from schooled societies, where *context-independent learning* is emphasized. Children's strategies have been extensively examined in *training studies*, in which young children who do not use a strategy spontaneously are instructed to use one. Children who cannot benefit from strategic instruction are said to illustrate a *mediational deficiency*. Slightly older children can benefit from a strategy when instructed but do not produce one spontaneously; they have a *production deficiency*. Even production-deficient children use strategies spontaneously, however, although these strategies are not very sophisticated and might not facilitate performance. Children frequently display a *utilization deficiency*, using a strategy without experiencing any benefit from its use.

The development of *memory strategies*, or *mnemonics*, has been much investigated, with the use of strategies such as *rehearsal* and *organization* increasing with age. Young children tend to use a *passive rehearsal strategy*, rehearsing only a few unique words at a time, whereas older children are more apt to use an *active*, or *cumulative*, rehearsal strategy, rehearsing several different words at a time. Developmental differences in attentional strategies have also been found, with young children being less systematic in their visual inspection of objects than older children are. *Selective attention* has most often been studied using *incidental learning* tasks. Older children are better able to ignore incidental information than are younger children. Strategies are costly in mental resource use, and children who have greater knowledge for the materials they are dealing with often use strategies more effectively. Strategies are effortful to use, requiring a significant portion of a child's limited mental resources. Three types of influences of *knowledge base* have been proposed: item-specific effects, nonstrategic organization, and facilitating strategies.

Metacognition, an awareness of one's cognitive abilities, plays an important role in the use and effectiveness of strategies and can be divided into two general types. *Declarative metacognition* refers to explicit, conscious, factual knowledge about person or task variables. *Procedural metacognition* refers to knowledge about when strategies are necessary, as well as monitoring one's progress on a task. Metacognitive knowledge increases with age, as reflected by studies examining *meta-attention* and *metamemory.*

Cultural differences also play an important role in the use of strategies, with children from schooled societies being more strategic on list-learning tasks than children from nonschooled societies are. Differences between German and American children are also found in the extent to which they use strategies, their attributions of success and failure on cognitive tasks, and the amount of strategy training teachers and parents provide children.

Children actually use a variety of different strategies to solve any given problem, and such multiple- and variable-strategy use is explained by Siegler's *adaptive strategy choice model,* which proposes that children have a variety of strategies available to them at any one time and that these strategies "compete" for use, with strategies changing in frequency over time. Changes in strategies are usually assessed via the *microgenetic method,* with children's task performance being assessed repeatedly over relatively brief periods. Strategy variability has been divided into two general types, *strategy diversity,* which refers to the number of different strategies people use, and *strategy change,* which refers to the extent to which people change strategies over trials. Each correlates with task performance, but the nature of the relations vary with age. Evidence indicates that children sometimes have implicit knowledge of strategies before explicit knowledge.

Classroom teachers instruct children in the use of a variety of different strategies, although the absolute level of strategy instruction in school is often low. The *good information processing model* serves as a framework for strategy instruction and proposes that efficient learning is based on a combination of factors including strategies, knowledge base, metamemory, capacity, and motivation.

Key Terms and Concepts

strategies
context-independent learning
training studies
mediational deficiency
production deficiency
utilization deficiency
memory strategies (mnemonics)
rehearsal
organization
passive rehearsal style
active style
cumulative style
selective attention
incidental learning
knowledge base
metacognition
declarative metacognition
procedural metacognition
meta-attention
metamemory
adaptive strategy choice model
microgenetic method
strategy diversity
strategy change
good information processing model

Suggested Readings

Bjorklund, D. F., & Miller, P. H. (Eds.) (1997). New themes in strategy development. Special Issue of *Developmental Review,* 17, December issue. This special edition of the journal *Developmental Review* contains summaries of research in children's strategy development, including an article by Bjorklund, Miller, and colleagues looking at utilization deficiencies, one by Siegler and colleagues presenting his strategy choice model, and articles looking at longitudinal studies of strategy use, computer models of strategy use, and children's strategy use from a sociocultural perspective.

Kee, D. W. (1994).   Developmental differences in associative memory: Strategy use, mental effort, and knowledge-access interactions. In H. W. Reese (Ed.), *Advances in Child Development and Behavior* (Vol. 25). San Diego: Academic Press. This chapter provides an excellent review of research looking at the interaction of knowledge, mental effort, and strategy use in development.

Pressley, M., & Woloshyn, V. (1995).   *Cognitive strategy instruction that really improves children's academic performance* (2nd edition). Cambridge, MA: Brookline Books. This book, written for educational psychologists and teachers, applies basic research in strategy development to the classroom. It provides specific examples of teaching strategies to children for reading and reading comprehension, vocabulary, spelling, writing, mathematics, science, and "learning facts." This is a great book for anyone considering a career in teaching.

Siegler, R. S. (2000).   The rebirth of learning. *Child Development, 71*, 26–35. This short paper presents some of the basic ideas of Siegler's adaptive strategy choice model, including how to use the microgenetic method to study children's learning.

InfoTrac College Edition

For additional readings, explore InfoTrac College Edition, your online library. Go to http://www.infotrac-college.com/wadsworth.

Infant Perception

All cognition begins in perception. Before we can make comparisons between two objects, categorize sets of items, retrieve a fact, or create an image, we must have the basic data from the external world with which to work. We can, of course, think about things without the need of actually perceiving the things we think about. We can create mental images of objects we've never seen (or that never existed) and auditory images of sounds we've never actually heard. Cognition is thus not a simple extension of perception. Nevertheless, most of what we think about consists of objects, words, or other messages that we received, in one form or another, through our senses.

Early developmental research in perception dealt with issues of basic sensory abilities (for example, whether babies can see and hear). Research questions have expanded during the past 40 years, however. How is it that infants learn to discriminate the sounds of their language? What perceptual biases, if any, are they born with that make the learning process easier? How do infants come to recognize their mothers and, eventually, other people? How do they categorize experience? These questions deal with perception during infancy, and although developmental psychologists have not ignored perceptual development during childhood (see Gibson & Spelke, 1983), most research in the area has focused on the infant, and this is the body of work that I review here.

Perceptual functioning in human infants is viewed today as an active process. Remember throughout this chapter that the infant is an active participant in the process of acquiring and interpreting perceptual information. Also, keep in mind that infants are learning through their perceptions. They are gaining knowledge, and this knowledge is being added to and is transforming their prior knowledge.

Basic Perceptual Abilities of Young Infants

Not all that many years ago, well-informed people believed that infants enter the world unable to perceive sights and sounds. When I was teaching my first child development class as a graduate student in the early 1970s, I stated that newborn infants can "see," meaning that they can tell the difference between two visual displays. A middle-age woman informed me that I was wrong; infants cannot see. She had had four children, and her obstetrician and pediatrician had both told her that her babies were functionally blind at birth and that they "learned" to see during their first month of life. Newborns are far from mental giants, but they do enter the world able to perceive information with all their senses. Furthermore, babies have some perceptual biases. Some sights, sounds, and smells are inherently more pleasing to them than others, and they learn to prefer other sensations in the first weeks of life.

Most research on infant perceptual development has been done on audition (hearing) and vision. This is partly because of the importance of these two senses for human information processing and because vision in particular, shows substantial development during the first year of life. Research on other senses has also been conducted, of course. For example, although it was once believed that newborns were relatively insensitive to pain, more recent research clearly demonstrates that they do indeed perceive pain (Delevati & Bergamasco, 1999), and some evidence indicates that, for extremely low birth weight (ELBW) infants, their response to pain is affected by repeated painful episodes, which are often necessary for preterm infants (Grunau et al., 2001). When tested at 8 months of age, the number of invasive procedures ELBW infants had from birth was associated with reduced facial and heart rate reactions to pain (blood collection). (Recall from Chapter 2 the research with rats that demonstrated that painful experiences during the pre- and neonatal periods was associated with increased sensitivity to pain in adulthood (Ruda et al., 2000).) Newborns also respond to another skin sense, that of touch, or tactile stimulation. Actually, research with both animals and human preterm infants indicates that tactile stimulation is important in promoting normal growth and development. For instance, research has shown that very small preterm infants who receive extra tactile stimulation gain more weight, spend more time awake, and display more advanced cognitive and motor skills than do normally treated preterm babies (see Schanberg & Field, 1987).

The chemical senses (olfaction and taste) tend to develop early, and are quite well developed shortly after (and even before) birth. For example, babies can discriminate among a wide variety of odors early in life (Steiner, 1979), and they develop preferences for certain odors within the first week. In a study by Macfarlane (1975), for example, 6-day-old nursing babies were able to discriminate the odor of their mothers from those of other women. Mothers wore breast pads in their bras between nursings. Two breast pads—one from the baby's mother and the other from another woman—were placed on either side of an infant's head. Although there were no differences in infants' behaviors in this situation at 2 days of age, by day 6 babies were turning to their own mother's pad more often than to the pad of another woman. That is, not only can babies discriminate odors, they quickly learn to make associations with odors and to modify their behavior accordingly. In more recent work using a procedure similar to that of Macfarlane, researchers reported that infants develop a preference for the odor of milk versus amniotic fluid (which they had been living in for 9 months) by 4 days (Marlier, Schaal, & Soussignan, 1998) and that bottle-fed, 2-week-old infants preferred the breast odor of a lactating female to that of a non-lactating female (Makin & Porter, 1989).

Some Methodologies Used to Assess Infant Perception

How can a psychologist tell if an infant can see or hear something? That is, how can we determine if an infant can tell the difference between a bull's eye and a checkerboard pattern, for example, or between her mother's voice and that of another woman? This basic problem hampered serious investigation of infants' perceptual abilities for years, but the solution is really quite simple. What one must do is to find some behavior that an infant can control and use that behavior as an entry into what babies can perceive. For

example, in the research just presented, researchers took advantage of babies' abilities to turn their heads in one direction or another to determine if they could discriminate and develop a preference for certain odors (Macfarlane, 1975).

"This Sucks": Using Infant Sucking to Provide Insight into Infant Perception

Another behavior that very young infants can control is sucking. How might researchers use this behavior to tell if babies can discriminate between two different auditory signals? Anthony DeCasper and Melanie Spence (1986) used infants' ability to regulate their sucking to ask just this question and whether infants were learning something about the outside world while still in utero. DeCasper and Spence asked pregnant women to read aloud one of three passages twice a day during the last six weeks of their pregnancies. Shortly after birth, the neonates were tested for which passage, if any, would have more reinforcing value. Headphones were placed over the babies' ears, and various passages were played to the infants. Nonnutritive sucking (that is, sucking on a pacifier) was assessed as a function of which passage was being played. First, a baseline sucking rate was determined for each baby (that is, how rapidly the infant sucked on a nipple when no passage was being played). Changes in the babies' rate of sucking then determined whether they heard a familiar passage (the one their mothers had read during pregnancy) or a novel passage (one their mothers had not read). Some infants heard the familiar passage when they increased their sucking rate, whereas the contingency was reversed for other infants. The general finding was that the familiar passage was more reinforcing than the novel passage. That is, infants were more likely to alter their sucking rate to hear the familiar passage than to hear the novel passage. Furthermore, the reinforcing value of the passage was independent of who recited it, an infant's mother or another woman. These results present unambiguous evidence of prenatal conditioning to auditory patterns. The infants were able to discern the auditory characteristics (the rhythm and sound pattern) of these often-repeated passages, and the researchers were able to determine this by associating the various passages with changes in a behavior that infants could control themselves, that is, sucking rate.

Visual Preference Paradigm

The simplest (and first) technique to test infants' *visual* discrimination abilities was developed by Robert Fantz (1958, 1961). He placed alert babies in a looking chamber. Series of visual stimuli were placed in front of infants' eyes, and an observer peeking through a hole in the chamber above the infant recorded which stimuli the baby looked at the most. If groups of infants spend significantly more time gazing at one pattern than another, it can be assumed that they can differentiate between the two patterns and prefer to look at one relative to the other. If they couldn't tell the difference between the paired stimuli, there would be no difference in their looking behavior. Using this **visual preference paradigm,** Fantz was able to show that babies less than 1 week old can tell the difference between stimuli such as a schematic face, a bull's-eye pattern, and an unpatterned disk (see Figure 7-1).

Habituation/Dishabituation Paradigm

A somewhat more complicated procedure is often used to evaluate infants' perception, memory, and concepts, and this is the *habituation/dishabituation* paradigm. **Habituation** refers to the decrease in response as a result of repeated presentation of a stimulus. The first day on the job in a noisy factory, for example, produces increased levels of physiological stress (heart rate, blood pressure). After a week in this environment, however, levels of stress decline, even though the noise remains. This is habituation. **Dishabituation** (sometimes referred to as release from habituation) occurs when, following habituation, a new stimulus is presented that increases level of responding. If we switch from factory A to factory B, for instance, levels of physiological stress rise, even though the new factory is no louder than the

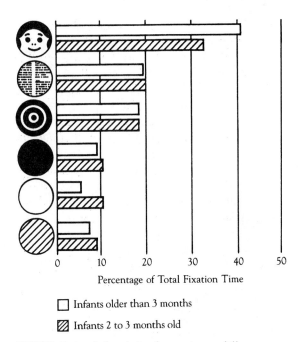

Percentage of Total Fixation Time

□ Infants older than 3 months

▨ Infants 2 to 3 months old

FIGURE 7-1 Infants' visual attention to different patterns. SOURCE: "The Origin of Form Perception," by R. L. Fantz, 1961, *Scientific American, 204,* 66–72. Copyright © 1961 Scientific American, Inc. All rights reserved. Reprinted with permission.

old one was. The noises are different, causing an increase in responding, or a release from habituation.

How does this phenomenon relate to infant perception? The amount of time babies look at visual stimuli (or orient to auditory stimuli) is analogous to the worker's physiological reactions to loud noise. The longer infants are exposed to a visual stimulus, the less time they spend looking at it. Habituation is said to occur when an infant's looking time is significantly less than it was initially (often defined as when visual fixation to the stimulus is 50% of what it was on the early trials). At that point, a new stimulus is presented. If attention (that is, looking time) increases from the level of immediately before, dishabituation is said to occur. A typical habituation/dishabituation curve is shown in Figure 7-2.

What does such a pattern mean? First, it demonstrates that infants can discriminate between the two stimuli. Babies might not prefer one to the other, but

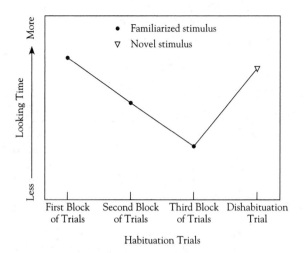

FIGURE 7-2 An example of results from a habituation/dishabituation experiment on infant visual attention. The amount of looking time decreases with repeated presentation of the same stimulus (habituation) but increases with the presentation of a new stimulus (dishabituation).

that they respond to the new stimulus with increased attention indicates that they can tell the difference between the two. This paradigm is very useful in determining infants' discrimination abilities when researchers are using stimuli for which babies might not have a decided preference. Habituation and dishabituation also indicate memory. Infants are making a discrimination between one stimulus that is physically present and another that is present only in memory. They are not choosing between two stimuli that are before them, but between one stimulus that is in front of their eyes and another that is only in their minds.

Using this procedure, evidence of habituation/ dishabituation (and thus rudimentary memory) has been found for newborns for vision (Friedman, 1972), haptic perception (identifying an object by active touch) (Streri, Lhote, & Dutilleul, 2000), and even in 32-week-old fetuses for vibroacoustic stimuli (Sandman et al., 1997). In one of the first studies to demonstrate this in newborns, Steven Friedman (1972) habituated 1- to 3-day-old infants to one visual pattern and then, immediately after

habituation, showed the babies a novel pattern. These neonates displayed the classic increase in responding to the new stimulus, indicative of memory (be it ever so brief).

One word of caution about Friedman's results is in order, however. Of 90 newborns initially tested, 50 were excluded for reasons such as crying and falling asleep. Of the 40 remaining, only 29 displayed dishabituation. Thus, only 32% of the original sample demonstrated the habituation/ dishabituation phenomenon. Dropout rates have been lower in some more recent studies. (For example, of the 34 newborns tested by Alan Slater et al. (1991), only 10 (29%) were excluded for fussiness and related problems.) The high dropout rate challenges the generalizability of Friedman's (and others') findings. What Friedman's results indicate is that visual memory is within the capability of many human newborns, although the possibility exists that many infants do not possess such memory until several weeks after birth.

These are not the only methods used to assess infant perception. But these methodologies have been used for more than 40 years to evaluate what babies can perceive and what they know, and most of the research reviewed in this chapter, and much discussed in the next, used variants of these well-developed techniques.

Auditory Development

Homo sapiens, as other primates, is a visual species. However, we also depend on hearing for acquiring much information about our world. Although language can be transmitted through visual signs, the primary means of communication involves audition, and deaf children often experience significant retardation if they do not learn language through an alternate means (sign language) early in life.

Auditory perception is well developed in the newborn. Infants appear to be more sensitive to high-frequency than to low-frequency tones (Trehub,

Schneider, & Endman, 1980), and this might explain their seeming preference for the voices of women. As with smell, infants less than 1 week old have been shown to recognize their mothers on the basis of sound (DeCasper & Fifer, 1980; Spence & Freeman, 1996). For example, Anthony DeCasper and William Fifer (1980) measured the rate at which 1- to 3-day-old infants sucked on a pacifier. They then conditioned the babies to alter their sucking rate (faster for half of the babies and slower for the other half) to the tape-recorded voices of their mothers and of an unfamiliar woman. DeCasper and Fifer reported that these young infants varied their sucking rates to hear their mothers' voices, indicating that they not only could discriminate the voices of their mothers from that of other women but also acquired a distinct preference for the voices of their mothers in a matter of days.

I noted in the preceding section that infants who heard stories being read to them by their mothers during the last six weeks of pregnancy were able to discriminate between that story and another, and preferred the one their mother had read to them (DeCasper & Spence, 1986). These findings indicate not only that the auditory system in newborns is working well but also that babies are learning some things about the outside world while still in utero. Moreover, more recent research following the same design as that of DeCasper and Spence reported changes in heart rate to familiar and novel passages among third trimester fetuses, unambiguously indicating that learning occurs before birth (DeCasper et al., 1994).

Let me provide another, admittedly anecdotal, piece of evidence for what is likely prenatal auditory learning. The mother of a healthy, 9-pound newborn reported an unusual preference for her daughter. The baby would nurse only from one breast, despite the fact that the mother expressed milk equally well from both breasts. It was the left breast, the one over the mother's beating heart, a sound the baby had heard from the time her auditory system began to function several months after conception. The baby would nurse from the left breast only and inevitably fall asleep, presumably being soothed, not only by

the milk she was consuming, but also by the familiar sound she was hearing.

Speech Perception

One particularly interesting aspect of infant auditory perception is the extent to which it is attuned to language. The basic units of speech are called **phonemes,** and evidence indicates that infants come into the world with the ability to perceive most, if not all, of the phonemes found in all human languages (see Aslin, Jusczyk, & Pisoni, 1998), suggesting substantial biological preparation for infants to learn language (but see Kuhl, 1987, for a counter interpretation).

Like colors, phonemes (such as "ba" and "pa") can be arranged on continua, with gradual changes between them. For example, there is a range of sounds that we hear as "pa" and another range that we hear as "ba." Despite this continuum, we categorize phonemes into distinct groups. For example, we tend to hear either a "pa" sound or a "ba" sound, and not some hybrid of the two of them. And most of us agree on the point at which "ba" ends and "pa" begins, just like we agree on the division between orange and red. The gradual changes in phonemes (and in colors) are considered physical, and the dichotomies we perceive are considered perceptual.

Peter Eimas and his colleagues (1971) presented 1-month-old infants with one physical example of the "ba/pa" continuum until they had decreased the rate at which they sucked on a pacifier (habituation). The researchers then replaced the phoneme with another example along the "ba/pa" continuum. If the infants perceive the new sound as being from the same phonemic category as the previous sound (both "ba," for instance), they should continue to habituate (that is, decrease their sucking). This is because even though the sound is physically different from the one they heard before, it is just another example of the sound they had just heard repeatedly (that is, just another "ba"). If, however, they recognize this new sound as being from a different phonemic category (a "pa" rather than a "ba," for example), they should increase their sucking rate (dishabituation). Using this technique, Eimas and his colleagues found that very young infants, like their parents and older siblings who already possess language, can categorize phonemes. They hear either "ba" or "pa," and the dividing line they make between the two is the same as older members of their species make.

Other studies have used reinforcement techniques to assess infants' abilities to discriminate among phonemes. For example, Cameron Marean, Lynne Werner, and Patricia Kuhl (1992) reinforced 2-, 3-, and 6-month-old infants by the activation of a mechanical toy for turning their heads when they heard a change from one vowel sound to another (either "A" to "I" or vice versa). This technique showed that even 2-month-olds were able to make the discrimination, despite changes in other auditory characteristics (that is, in the voice of the individual speaking). In related work, evidence suggests that even newborns classify vowel sounds much as adults do (Aldridge, Stillman, & Bower, 2001) and that infants form *prototypes*, or "best examples," for sound categories. Infants identify vowel sounds representing a range of "good" examples of a vowel prototype while not identifying "less good" examples of the same vowels (Grieser & Kuhl, 1989).

If infants can discriminate basic phonemes shortly after birth, how is it they acquire the language sounds peculiar to their mother tongue? English-speaking adults have a difficult time discriminating phonetic contrasts that occur in Czech but that are not found in English. Yet, babies from English-speaking homes have little difficulty with these contrasts, suggesting that they were born with the ability (Trehub, 1976). Other studies have similarly shown that infants can make discriminations among speech sounds that are not found in their mother tongues and that their parents cannot make (Lasky, Syrdal-Lasky, & Klein, 1975; Werker et al., 1981). In other research, Rebecca Eilers and her colleagues reported that 6- to 8-month-old infants from English-speaking homes were unable to discriminate some phonetic contrasts that are found in Spanish but not in English (Eilers, Gavin, & Wilson, 1979). Babies from homes where Spanish was spoken had no trouble

with such contrasts. What these and other data suggest is that babies can make some sound discriminations that adult speakers of their language communities cannot make; with time, babies lose the ability to make these contrasts because they rarely hear them (see Colombo, 1986).

Why should children lose this seemingly valuable ability? The flexibility to learn the sounds of any possible human language has a great adaptive advantage, of course, but keeping this flexibility beyond a certain age likely is not adaptive. Once our ancestors learned one language, there was likely little need (or opportunity) to become proficient in another language. Thus, it makes more sense for the brain to dedicate neurons to processing the sounds it hears early in life. The alternative would give individuals more flexibility, but likely less proficiency in perceiving or producing any one language.

Speech perception is more than the ability to detect phonemes, of course, but involves the discrimination of individual words. And perhaps the word that young infants hear most frequently is their own name. Denise Mandel, Peter Jusczyk, and David Pisoni (1995) asked "at what age can infants recognize the sound of their own name?" They used a reinforcement technique (infants turned their heads to hear a name spoken, either their own or one of three other names) to test this. Infants 4.5 months old spent more time listening to their own names than to other names, regardless of whether the other names had the same stress pattern as their own (for example, "Johnny" versus "Abby") or a different stress pattern (for example, "Johnny" versus "Elaine"). These findings indicate that infants are able to recognize frequently heard sound patterns at least by 4.5 months of age.

Music Perception

Although humans are especially prepared to process language, we also seem to be well prepared to process music. For example, some evidence suggests that young infants can imitate the pitch, loudness, melodic contour, and rhythm of their mothers' songs.

Moreover, specific types of brain damage affect musical abilities, suggesting that the ability to perceive and produce music is rooted in evolution and biology (see Gardner, 1983).

Many aspects of music perception appear to be adultlike very early in infancy. For example, babies seem to respond to changes in melody, rhythmic pattern, and redundancy much the same way adults do and seem to be able to distinguish "good" from "bad" melodies (see Trehub, Trainor, & Unyk, 1993; Schellenberg & Trehub, 1999). Examples of telling the difference between "good" (regular or natural) musical patterns and "bad" (irregular or unnatural) musical patterns are particularly impressive, given the diversity of human musical systems. Carol Krumhansl and Peter Jusczyk (1990) demonstrated this by having 4.5- and 6-month-old infants listen to segments of Mozart minuets. Some of the segments had pauses inserted at the end of each musical phrase (natural), whereas other segments had pauses inserted in the middle of phrases (unnatural). Infants learned to control which music they heard—natural or unnatural—by turning their heads in the direction of the speaker playing the music they preferred. Overall, infants spent more time listening to the natural than to the unnatural versions, with 22 of 24 6-month-olds and 20 of 24 4.5-month-olds showing this pattern. Other research has shown that infants as young as 6 months old prefer tones related by simple ratios (what most adults consider to be consonant, or pleasant sounding) over dissonant sounds (as is found in atonal music) (Trainor & Heinmiller, 1998; Schellenberg & Trehub, 1996). Given these infants' lack of musical experience, the results of these experiments suggest that music appreciation might not require a college class to attain but is a basic characteristic of the human nervous system.

Other research has shown that infants are prepared to hear more than just Western music; they are able from an early age to distinguish regular from irregular patterns in culturally different music systems. For example, in one study, infants and adults were played series of notes based on Western scales and Javanese pelog scales (Lynch et al., 1990). The formal description of these two musical systems is beyond the scope of this book (and my expertise); suffice it to say that the underlying scales differ considerably. Adults and 6.5-month-old infants heard well-tuned or out-of-tune patterns of both types of music and were asked to distinguish between the two. The infants, of course, weren't asked to "tell" the difference, but an operant-conditioning paradigm was used in which infants were rewarded for turning their heads to out-of-tune series. The adults, who merely raised their hands for an out-of-tune series, were better able to distinguish between in-tune and out-of-tune patterns in the Western music than in the Javanese music, reflecting the influence of experience on their musical perception. (The adults were American and all familiar with the Western but not the Javanese system.) The infants, however, were equally good at distinguishing the out-of-tune series for both the Western and Javanese patterns, "suggesting that infants may be born with an equipotentiality for the perception of scales from a variety of cultures" (Lynch et al., 1990, p. 275). That is, just as children are capable of and biologically prepared for acquiring any human language, they seem also to be prepared for acquiring any system of music.

The Development of Visual Perception

When can infants begin to make sense of their visual world? When, for example, can they discriminate between two visual stimuli or form visual concepts? We, like our primate cousins, are a visual species. Survival during our prehistoric past would have been unlikely for a visually impaired child. Vision gives us information about both near and distant objects that touch and hearing cannot easily provide. Spatial cognition is an important "higher order" skill (see Chapter 8), and such thinking is based on vision. Perhaps because of the importance of vision to the species, or perhaps because we're better at thinking of ways of testing vision, visual perception has been the most studied sense in psychology, both in children and adults.

Vision in the Newborn

Newborns can perceive light, as demonstrated by the pupillary reflex (constriction of the pupil to bright light and dilation to low levels of illumination). However, **accommodation,** or focusing, of the lens is relatively poor at birth, regardless of the distance an object is from an infant's eyes, and most of what newborns look at they see unclearly (Banks, 1980). But development of the muscles of the lens is rapid, and under favorable stimulus conditions, accommodation is adult-like by as early as 3 months of age.

Newborns will visually track a moving object, but their eyes will not necessarily move in harmony. **Convergence** refers to both eyes looking at the same object, an ability apparently not possessed by newborns (Wickelgren, 1967). Convergence and **coordination** (both eyes following a moving stimulus in a coordinated fashion) improve during the first months of life and are adultlike by 6 months (Aslin & Jackson, 1979).

Studies attempting to determine the *acuity* of infants, or the ability to see clearly, have yielded varied results, depending on the technique used. Acuity improves substantially during the first year of life, but is very poor at birth (Kellman & Banks, 1998). With normal acuity for adults being 20/20 (one can see at a distance of 20 feet what a personal with "normal" vision can see at 20 feet), estimates of newborn acuity range from 20/400 to 20/600 (Slater, 1995), making the neonate legally blind in most states.

An important reason for newborns' poor vision is the underdeveloped state of their foveas, the area of the retina where there is the highest concentration of cones (color perceiving cells that provide the clearest vision). Although the fovea of a newborn is larger than that of an adult, individual cells are arranged differently, cells vary in size and shape, and the cones are more widely distributed in the foveas of newborns relative to adults. This makes the cones of newborns much less sensitive to light than those of an adult—by some estimates by a difference of 350 to 1 (Kellman & Banks, 1998).

Do newborns see the world in color, the way adults do? Although newborns might not be color

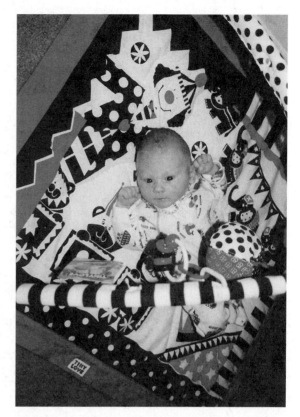

PHOTO 7-1   Young infants' attention is attracted by high contrast. (Photo by Barbara Bjorklund)

blind, they apparently do not perceive much in the way of color. When differences in brightness are controlled, infants can't discriminate between a wide range of colors until about 8 weeks of age (Allen, Banks, & Schefrin, 1988). Research has shown newborns can likely discriminate between the colors red and white, but cannot differentiate blue, green, and yellow from white (Adams, Courage, & Mercer, 1994). In general, newborns seem to process color information the same *way* adults do, but color vision itself is extremely poor (Adams & Courage, 1998).

The research just cited indicated that newborns can discriminate differences in intensity of light, can track a moving object, and likely can see differences between contrasting colors (see Photo 7-1). But what really interests most cognitive psychologists is the question of what infants can see: Can they tell the difference, for example, between a checkerboard pattern and a bull's-eye? I described in the earlier section on methodology a simple procedure developed by Fantz (1958) in which infants are shown two pictures and the time they look at the various stimuli is noted. If the stimuli chosen are sufficiently different, even very young infants will show a preference for one over the other, demonstrating by their differential looking time that they can tell the difference between the two stimuli. Because of the relatively poor acuity of young infants' vision, stimuli must be reasonably discrepant before discriminations can be made, but newborns do make such discriminations (Slater, 1995).

Primary and Secondary Visual Systems

Babies come into the world prepared to see. But more important yet is that they are biologically prepared to look at some things more than at others. The shift from attention based primarily on physical stimulus features to attention based on psychological characteristics reflects underlying changes in the organization of the visual nervous system. Gordon Bronson (1974) cited behavioral and anatomical evidence suggesting that babies' vision during the first month of life is controlled by the **secondary visual system.** This system, which mediates visually guided behavior in simple animals, appears to be better developed in human newborns than is the more sophisticated but phylogenetically younger **primary visual system.** Bronson's interpretation is that vision during the first few months of life is qualitatively different from subsequent vision. The earliest visual processing (the secondary visual system) is under the control of subcortical portions of the brain, and it has different functions than does later visual processing, which is controlled chiefly by cortical brain structures (the primary visual system). These differences in brain control of vision account for developmental changes in visual preferences observed during the first 2 or 3 months of life.

According to Bronson, processing with the primary visual system is done by the fovea, permitting the careful analysis of stimulus properties. With repeated exposure, infants can encode salient features of a stimulus, which serve as the basis for perceptual representations (or schemas). In other words, the primary visual system provides information concerning *what* a stimulus is. The secondary visual system operates mainly in the visual periphery (that is, nonfoveally) and orients the infant toward a stimulus, providing information concerning *where* a stimulus is.

Bronson proposed that the primary visual system begins influencing babies' vision at about 2 months, and as visual experiences accumulate, they increasingly affect what infants choose to look at. According to Bronson,

> As memories accrue there is an increasing ability to utilize prior experience for the guidance of visual regard, and hence gaze no longer will be largely limited to the most salient aspects of a configuration. Around the third month babies are able to examine diverse aspects of a stimulus in a series of repeated refixations, and the development of this intentional scanning enables the infant to encode entire patterns where previously only isolated elements were recorded (for example, it is now a face that is smiled at, not just a pair of eyes). (1974, p. 874)

Many parents can recognize this change. Babies during the first couple of months seem to stare at things, even if those things (such as eyes) happen to be located on a human face. By 3 or 4 months, however, many parents get the feeling that their baby is really looking at *them.* This feeling fits well with the research data, although, as we'll see later in this chapter, there seems to be something special about the human face, perhaps even for newborns.

More recent research has shown that Bronson's position is overstated. Although perhaps most of a newborn's visual processing is performed by subcortical brain areas, some limited cortical activity occurs in neonates. Changes in visual processing during the first several months of life appears *not* to be in the form of a relatively abrupt transition from the secondary to primary system, as Bronson proposed; rather, the changes are more gradual in nature (Johnson, 1998). Nevertheless, Bronson's (and others') description of the human newborn as having an immature visual system remains undisputed.

As I discussed in Chapter 2, the immaturity of the infant visual system might have an adaptive value. Recall the argument of Gerald Turkewitz and Patricia Kenny (1982), who suggested that the limited sensory abilities of young infants might protect them from sensory overload. Newborns must begin the process of constructing a coherent mental world, beginning with virtually no knowledge of the external world. Their sensory limitations might help them reduce the amount of information they have to deal with and thus aid them in constructing a simplified, comprehensible world.

The Development of Visual Preferences

What a baby, or anyone else for that matter, likes to look at depends on a variety of physical stimulus characteristics as well as psychological characteristics. Physical characteristics such as movement, amount of contour or contrast, complexity, symmetry, and curvature of the stimulus affect our looking behavior from a very early age. Familiarity and novelty, which determine the psychological significance of a stimulus for us, also affect the visual preferences of young infants, but these "psychological" factors increasingly influence infants' attention between 2 and 4 months; until this time, babies' visual attention is affected chiefly (but not exclusively) by physical stimulus features.

Movement is a potent stimulus characteristic influencing infants' visual attention. Everything else being equal, babies look more at a moving stimulus than at a comparable stimulus that is stationary. In an experiment by Marshall Haith (1966), newborns sucked on a nipple while watching a light display. On some trials, the light moved, tracing the outline of a triangle. Babies decreased their sucking on these trials, relative to those when the light did not move, indicating increased attention to movement.

Infants are also attracted to areas of high contrast, as reflected by the outline, or contour, of an object. In a pioneering study, Philip Salapatek and William Kessen (1966) assessed the visual scanning of newborns. Infants less than 1 week old were placed in a modified looking chamber with a white triangle

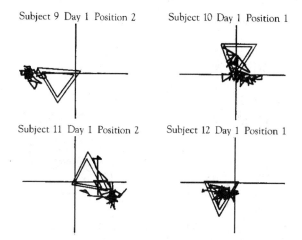

FIGURE 7-3 Examples of scanning patterns of newborns. SOURCE: "Visual Scanning of Triangles by the Human Newborn," by P. Salapatek and W. Kessen, 1966, *Journal of Experimental Child Psychology, 3,* 155–167. Copyright © 1966 Academic Press. Reprinted with permission from Elsevier.

painted on a black background situated before their eyes. The infants' eye movements were recorded and were contrasted with those when the triangle was not visible. Examples of the scanning patterns of the newborns when the triangle was present are shown in Figure 7-3. As can be seen, the infants' visual fixations were centered near the vertices of the triangles, the areas of most contrast. More recent research has indicated substantial individual variability in newborn scanning, with many infants during the first 6 weeks of life showing no systematic visual attention to stimulus contours; much of this variation has been attributed to differences in infant neurological maturity at birth (Bronson, 1990). By about 2 months, however, infants in the Bronson (1990) study were able to consistently direct their attention toward stimulus contours. Work by Salapatek and his colleagues (Maurer & Salapatek, 1976; Salapatek, 1975) indicated that infants at 1 month of age direct their attention primarily to the outside of a figure and spend little time inspecting internal features. Salapatek referred to this tendency as the **externality effect.** By 2 months, however, most of infants' fixations are on internal stimulus features. An example

Scanning by a 1-month-old   Scanning by a 2-month-old

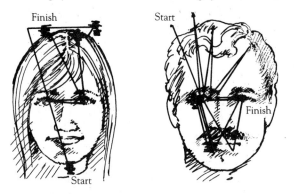

FIGURE 7-4 Examples of visual scanning of faces by 1- and 2-month-old infants. SOURCE: Adapted from Shaffer, D. R. (1993). *Social and personality development* (3rd ed.). Pacific Grove, CA: Brooks/Cole.

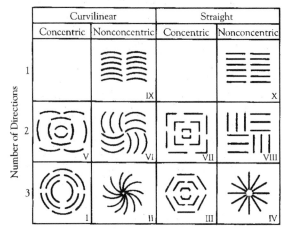

FIGURE 7-5 Examples of stimuli used to assess infants' preferences for curvature. SOURCE: "Infant Visual Fixation: The Effect of Concentricity, Curvilinearity, and Number of Directions," by H. A. Ruff and H. G. Birch, 1974, *Journal of Experimental Child Psychology, 17,* 460–473. Copyright © 1974 Academic Press. Reprinted with permission from Elsevier.

of scanning patterns of 1- and 2-month-olds is shown in Figure 7-4.

Infants' preference for and processing of symmetrical forms have been shown for vertical stimuli. Although there seems to be no preference for *vertical symmetry* until the latter part of the first year, infants as young as 4 months process vertically symmetrical stimuli (stimuli that are the same on the left and right sides) more efficiently than vertically asymmetrical or horizontal stimuli (Bornstein, Ferdinandsen, & Gross, 1981). Efficiency of visual processing in these studies was measured by rates of visual habituation, the decrease in attention as a result of repeated exposure to a stimulus. Four-month-old infants acquired information about vertically symmetrical stimuli more effectively than about asymmetrical or horizontal information as reflected by their faster rates of habituation (that is, they looked at the symmetrical stimuli less on later trials than they looked at asymmetrical or horizontal stimuli). According to Marc Bornstein and his colleagues, "The results . . . support the view that verticality has a special status in early perceptual development. . . . Whether innate, early maturing, or based on experience, the special quality of verticality generally may derive from the importance of the vertically symmetrical body and face" (1981, p. 85).

Another physical stimulus feature of importance is that of curvature, or *curvilinearity*. Some of Fantz's original work demonstrated infants' preferences for curved stimuli, such as a bull's-eye, over linear (that is, straight-line) stimuli of comparable contour (Fantz, 1958). Holly Ruff and Herbert Birch (1974) similarly observed a preference for curvilinear stimuli in 3- and 4-month-old infants, but they also found a preference for concentric stimuli, even if composed of straight lines (see Figure 7-5). This preference for curvature was reported even in a sample of newborns (Fantz & Miranda, 1975), although only when the stimuli differed in their outer perimeter (recall the externality effect).

Attention to the Human Face

Infants' preferences for physical features such as curvilinearity and vertical symmetry may largely account for babies' more general bias to attend to faces. Some of the earliest work in infant visual preferences revealed that babies of 4 months and older demonstrate a preference for the human face over other nonface-like stimuli (Fantz, 1961). In Chapter 2, I discussed more recent research that showed that babies initially have a weak bias to attend to faces, which becomes stronger with age and experience. For example, whereas both adults and 6-month-old infants process upright and inverted faces differently, revealing what appears to be an appreciation of what the proper orientation of faces is "supposed" to be, adults show this bias only for human faces; 6-month-olds show it both for human and monkey faces (de Haan, Oliver, & Johnson, 1998). Although this and related research (Pascalis, de Haan, & Nelson, 2002) make it clear that the processing of faces develops during infancy, might there be a bias to attend to faces present shortly after birth? Such a bias would not be surprising, for there is likely no single visual stimulus that is of greater importance to a human infant than that of the face of another member of his or her own species. Human infants are highly dependent on their parents for support and protection for a far longer time than are other mammals, and human infants' survival is made more likely by the strong social attachment they establish with their parents. Given this, it makes sense from an evolutionary perspective for infants to be oriented to the most social of stimuli, the human face.

Research following Fantz's pioneering work pushed back the age at which infants show a preference for face-like stimuli to the newborn period. For example, Mark Johnson and his colleagues demonstrated that newborns can distinguish between face-like and nonface-like stimuli (Johnson et al., 1991; Morton & Johnson, 1991). These studies did not use a visual preference paradigm, however. Rather, they showed infants different head-shaped stimuli, moving each stimulus across the babies' line of visual regard. Investigators measured the extent to which the infants followed each moving stimulus (1) with their eyes and (2) by turning their heads. Using these measures, studies have reported significantly greater eye or head movement to face-like stimuli than to nonface-like stimuli for infants ranging in age from several minutes to 5 weeks old. Figure 7-6 presents the results of one such study (Johnson et al., 1991). More recent research using related methodologies

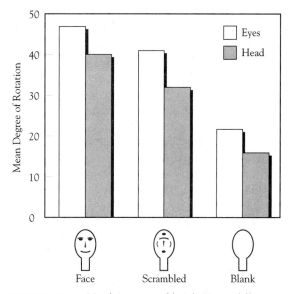

FIGURE 7-6 Newborn eye and head turns in following different stimuli. SOURCE: "Newborns' Preferential Tracking of Faces and Its Subsequent Decline," by M. H. Johnson, S. Dziurawiec, H. D. Ellis, and J. Morton, 1991, *Cognition, 40,* 1–19. Copyright © 1991 Elsevier Science Publishing Co., Inc. Reprinted with permission.

has found special attention for face-like stimuli for newborns (Easterbrook et al., 1999; Mondloch et al., 1999).

Such evidence suggests that infants are born with some notion of "faceness" and will attend to such stimuli more than to others. Based on the results of their own studies plus those of others, John Morton and Mark Johnson concluded, "it can now be accepted with some degree of confidence that neonates find slowly moving faces with high-contrast definition particularly attractive stimuli" (1991, p. 172). These researchers go on to caution that this does not mean that newborns understand the conceptual meaning of a face, merely that they prefer to visually track face-like rather than nonface-like patterns.

Morton and Johnson (1991) developed a two-process theory for infant face preference. An initial process is accessed primarily through subcortical pathways, and this controls newborns' tracking of faces. This system is responsible for human newborns' preference for the human face, but because of limited sensory capabilities, infants are not able to learn about features of faces until about 8 weeks of age. Beginning about this time, this system loses its influence over infants' attention to faces, and the second process, which is under the control of cortical circuits, begins to take over. The functioning of this system depends on cortical maturation and experience with faces during the first two months of life, as infants begin to build a representation that enables them "to discriminate the human face from other stimuli and especially from faces of other species" (p. 178). More recent research by Paul Quinn and Peter Eimas (1996) has shown that 3- and 4-month-old infants are able to use cues from the faces of animals (dogs and cats, for example) to identify not only specific individuals, but which species an animal is. That is, they are able to acquire a category for "dogs" versus "cats" based on facial features, an ability that is consistent with Morton and Johnson's ideas.

Some evidence suggests, however, that even newborns might be able to make discriminations among faces, looking longer at faces of their mothers than of other women, for example (Bushnell, Sai, & Mullin, 1989). In related research, Gail Walton, N. J. Bower, and T. G. Bower (1992) reported that 12- to 36-hour-old infants would vary their rate of sucking more to see a picture of their mother's face than that of another woman. This suggests not only that newborns can tell the difference between faces and nonfaces, but also that they learn a preference for their mothers' faces shortly after birth. This bias toward faces and the early-developing ability of preferring familiar faces may be evolutionarily quite old. Similar patterns have been reported for an infant gibbon (a lesser ape), who displayed a preference for looking at faces in general and a preference for familiar faces specifically by 4 weeks of age (Myowa-Yamakoshi & Tomonaga, 2001).

One interesting discovery about infants' preference for faces is that babies find some faces more interesting than others, specifically faces that adults classify as being attractive. For example, Judith Langlois and her colleagues (1987) asked college men and women to judge the attractiveness of adult Caucasian women from photographs. From these ratings,

photographs of eight attractive and eight less attractive faces were selected, although the distribution of attractiveness was relatively normal (that is, there were no extremely attractive or unattractive faces). The photographs were selected so that all women had neutral expressions, had medium to dark hair, and did not wear glasses. In one part of the study, 2- to 3-month-old and 6- to 8-month-old infants were shown pairs of faces varying in attractiveness (one attractive and one less attractive face), and their looking time was measured. Both the younger and older infants spent significantly more time looking at the attractive faces than at the unattractive faces, with approximately two-thirds of the infants showing a preference for the more attractive faces. Furthermore, the preference for the more attractive faces was unrelated to how attractive an infant's mother was judged to be. More recent research has shown that this bias toward attractive faces is found even in newborns (Slater et al., 1998). Other research has shown that this preference extends across sex, race, and age of the modeled face; 6-month-olds consistently show a preference for attractive faces of both men and women, of both black and white adult females, and of 3-month-old infants, despite the fact that the infants had little or no experience with some of these classes of faces (Langlois et al., 1991).

One possible explanation for these findings is that attractive faces have more of the physical stimulus characteristics that attract infant attention than do unattractive faces. For example, attractive faces might be more curvilinear, concentric, and vertically symmetrical than unattractive faces (see earlier discussion). From this perspective, infants' preference for faces is simply a by-product of their preference for many of the physical features that happen to be characteristic of faces. Facial symmetry may be the most important factor here, for it is perhaps the single most potent determinate of attractiveness in adults (Gangestad &Thornhill, 1997). Evolutionary psychologists have indicated that symmetry is a sign of physical (Gangestad & Thornhill, 1997) and psychological (Shackelford & Larsen, 1997) health, making it possible that a preference for facial symmetry may have been selected for in evolution in selecting mates. Although mate selection is not on the minds of infants, the preference may be a general one, which is weak early in life but becomes stronger with experience. However, evidence suggesting that preference for attractive faces involves more than simply symmetry comes from work with newborns, who displayed a preference for (that is, looked longer at) upright attractive versus less attractive faces but not for the same faces presented upside down (Slater et al., 2000).

The finding that newborns' preference for attractive faces is limited to upright stimuli, suggests that they might be born with a schema, or abstract representation, of a human face and that attractive faces (in the proper orientation, that is, upright) match that schema better than unattractive ones. But how could such a scheme be represented in the brain of a newborn baby? Some evidence indicates that attractive faces are those that reflect the "average" of a range of facial features (for example, average nose length, average distance between the eyes); that is, for both men and women, attractive faces are in essence average faces in the features they possess (Langlois & Roggman, 1990). This would make sense from an evolutionary perspective. If attention to faces is important in forming social relations in early infancy, and thus to survival, the best bet would be to have an attentional bias toward "average" features (even if the combination of these "average" features results in an attractive, and thus "above average" face). More recent research has found a relationship between attractiveness and averageness not only for human faces but also for pictures of dogs, birds, and wristwatches (Halberstadt & Rhodes, 2000). This suggests the possibility that the preference for "average" faces is built, in part, on a mechanism for averageness in general, rather than a domain-specific mechanism exclusively for faces. Regardless of the reason, the data of Langlois and her colleagues indicate that what was once believed to be a learned preference (attractiveness) might have its basis in biology.

The face is a complicated stimulus with many defining features, but one that has attracted much attention (both of infants and researchers) is the eyes. For example, newborns prefer to look at faces with eyes opened (Batki et al., 2000), and mutual gaze

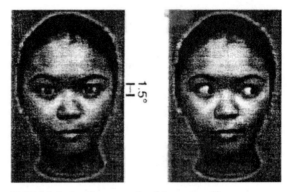

FIGURE 7-7 An example of the types of faces newborns saw. SOURCE: Drawings adapted from Farroni, T., Csibra, G., Simion, F., & Johnson, M. H. (2002). Eye contact detection in humans from birth. *Proceedings of the National Academy of Science, 99,* 9602–9605.

(eye contact between two people) plays a critical role in social interaction. Recent research has shown that even newborns are sensitive to eye gaze and are more attentive to faces gazing at them than when the eyes are averted (Farroni et al., 2002). For instance, Teresa Farroni and her colleagues (2002) sat infants between 24 and 120 hours old in front of two photographs of the same female face. One face had a direct gaze whereas the other face had its eyes averted to either right (for about half of the babies) or to the left (for the other half). Figure 7-7 shows an example of the type of faces babies saw. A flashing light attracted infants' attention, and then the two pictures were presented, side by side. Farroni and her colleagues reported that the newborns were more likely to orient toward the gazing face and spent significantly more time looking at the face with the direct gaze than at the picture with the averted eyes. A follow-up experiment with 4-month-olds demonstrated that infants showed enhanced neural processing, as indicated by patterns of brain activity (event-related potentials from EEGs) when viewing faces with direct versus averted gazes. Farroni et al. concluded that infants' preference for direct gaze "is probably a result of a fast and approximate analysis of the visual input, dedicated to find socially relevant stimuli for further processing" (p. 9604).

Research from a variety of perspectives using a variety of methodologies has illustrated that infants, from birth, are oriented toward faces, or face-like stimuli. This makes sense from an evolutionary perspective; it is also consistent with the speculation of Fantz, who wrote more than 40 years ago that infants' preferences for face-like patterns may "play an important role in the development of behavior by focusing attention to stimuli that will later have adaptive significance" (1961, p. 72).

Psychological Stimulus Characteristics

The face, of course, is a psychologically important stimulus, but it seems that infants' attention to faces and face-like stimuli early in life is based primarily on their physical properties. Movement, contour, complexity, symmetry, curvature, and attractiveness continue to affect the attention of people throughout life. Beginning sometime around 2 to 4 months, however, the psychological characteristics of a stimulus—that is, the stimulus's familiarity or novelty—exert an increasing influence on whether and for how long it will be attended to. The fact that a stimulus's familiarity or novelty influences infants' attention implies some sort of memory for the stimulus event. For a stimulus to be regarded as familiar, it must be contrasted with some previous mental representation of that stimulus; that is, it must be contrasted with a stimulus that was previously known. Similarly, to be novel, a stimulus has to be slightly different from something that the perceiver already knows (Rheingold, 1985).

The increased importance of familiarity and novelty to infants' visual preference between 2 and 4 months of life is consistent with Bronson's (1974) theory of secondary and primary visual systems and Morton and Johnson's two-level system for attending to faces. That is, the nervous system goes through some changes (from primary subcortical to cortical control), permitting the retention of experiences and formation of long-term memories. Infants during the first two months of life are not functioning only at the subcortical level, of course. (Recall evidence that infants 12 to 36 hours old prefer to look the faces of

their mothers versus the faces of other women, Walton et al., 1992.) But their visual cortices are immature, limiting intentional visual control and the retention of visual memories (Johnson, 1998).

Jerome Kagan (1971) proposed that beginning around 2 months, infants form **schemas,** or sensory representations and that the similarity of a stimulus to previously formed schemas determines attention. A schema is not an exact copy of a stimulus but is "a representation of an event that preserves the temporal and spatial arrangement of its distinctive elements without necessarily being isomorphic with the event" (Kagan, 1971, p. 6). Kagan proposed the **discrepancy principle** to explain infants' attention to novel stimuli. Infants are most attentive to stimuli that are moderately discrepant from a schema. A stimulus that differs slightly from what a baby already knows (for example, a bearded face when the infant is familiar with nonbearded faces) is likely to maintain attention, whereas a highly familiar stimulus (a nonbearded face) or a highly discrepant one (a model of a face with its features scrambled) is likely to receive less of an infant's attention.

Robert McCall and his colleagues provided support for the discrepancy principle (McCall, Kennedy, & Appelbaum, 1977). In their experiments, infants between 2 and 4 months old were familiarized with stimuli and were later shown new stimuli that varied in their similarity to the originals. The researchers reported an inverted-U relationship between attention and similarity of the new stimulus to the standard (see Figure 7-8). Stimuli that were highly similar to the original and those that were highly discrepant received less attention than those that were moderately discrepant from the standard. This preference for novelty implies that some representation of the original stimulus (a schema) was retained and was used to guide subsequent visual processing.

Kagan's discrepancy principle, and much experimental data, such as those presented by McCall and his colleagues, suggest that once infants have the ability to form long-lasting visual memories, they use those memories, or schemas, as a standard and direct their attention to stimuli that are somewhat novel to them. However, it has long been known that, under some circumstances, infants actually prefer to attend

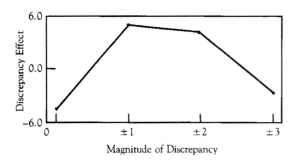

FIGURE 7-8 The relative amount of looking time (discrepancy effect) as a function of the magnitude of the discrepancy for 10-week-old infants. SOURCE: "Magnitude of Discrepancy and the Distribution of Attention in Infants," by R. B. McCall, C. B. Kennedy, and M. I. Appelbaum, 1977, *Child Development, 48,* 772–785. Copyright © 1977 The Society for Research in Child Development, Inc. Reprinted with permission.

to familiar, and not novel, stimuli (Courage & Howe, 1998; Rose et al., 1982). In general, a preference for familiarity typifies the preference for younger infants, but also for older infants in the early phases of visual processing. For example, Susan Rose and her colleagues (1982, Experiment 2) showed that groups of 3.5- and 6.5-month-old infants initially showed a preference for familiarity, followed by no preference, and eventually a preference for novelty (see also Courage & Howe, 1998 for similar results with 3-month-olds). In a similar vein, Richard Bogartz and his colleagues (Bogartz & Shinskey, 1998; Bogartz, Shinskey, & Speaker, 1997) proposed that infants will prefer to look at familiar stimuli when processing is in its early stages. It takes time to create and store memory representations, so infants should prefer attending to familiar stimuli until memory representations are well developed. Once a stable memory representation has been formed, an infant's preference should switch to a novel stimulus. A similar model of infants' preference for familiar and novel stimuli was provided by Loraine Bahrick and Jeffrey Pickens (1995; Bahrick, Hernandez-Reif, & Pickens, 1997) and has been supported by evidence from the auditory mode (Spence, 1996), in

addition to the visual modality. (Bogartz's ideas will be discussed further in Chapter 8 when examining representation in infancy.)

Intermodal Integration

Although we often think of each sense as being distinct from all others, as adults we do a great deal of coordinating information between senses. We direct our vision to a loud noise, and we can identify our slippers by touch alone when we are awakened in the middle of the night by a barking dog outside our window. To what extent is such sensory integration available to infants, and how can we interpret such integration when we observe it? At one level, **intermodal** (that is, between senses) **integration** (or **intersensory integration**) is present at birth. Newborns move their heads and eyes in the direction of a sound, as if they wish to see what all the noise is about. In a series of experiments examining the effects of sound on visual scanning in newborns, Morton Mendelson and Marshall Haith (1966) found that the presence of sound increased infants' visual attentiveness. The researchers suggested that this response to sound increases the likelihood that infants will discover something to look at.

Elizabeth Spelke provided an interesting demonstration of intermodal integration in young infants (1976). Spelke showed 4-month-old infants two films on side-by-side screens. On one screen was a film of a woman playing peekaboo; on the other screen was a hand holding a stick and striking a block of wood. A single sound track was played, corresponding either to the peekaboo or the drumming video. The babies somehow figured out which sound track went with which screen, devoting more looking time to the screen that matched the sound. That is, these 4-month-old infants realized that certain sound sequences go with certain visual displays and visually attended to those displays that provided such a match (see also Bahrick, 2002; Lewkowicz, 1992).

In somewhat related work, Loraine Bahrick and John Watson (1985) investigated 5-month-olds' ability to integrate proprioceptive (relating to perception of body movements) and visual information. The babies were seated in infant seats equipped with a type of tray that prevented them from seeing their legs. Two video screens were placed in front of the infants. One screen displayed the infant's own legs; that is, the picture was transmitted live. On the other screen was a film of the legs of another infant (or in one experiment, the same infant's legs from a session recorded earlier). Thus, for one display (the contingent display), the movement of infants' legs was contemporaneous with their actual movement, whereas for the other display (the noncontingent display), the movement of legs was independent of the infants' current activity. Bahrick and Watson reasoned that if infants are able to integrate proprioception (as reflected by their own leg movements) and vision, they should be able to discriminate between the two films and spend more time looking at one than the other. This was their finding. In three experiments, 5-month-olds spent, on average, 67% of their time looking at the noncontingent display. Presumably, the lack of contingency between their leg movements and those seen on the video produced some discrepancy, and this resulted in increased attention to the noncontingent display. In a fourth experiment, Bahrick and Watson tested 3-month-olds and found no overall preference for either the contingent or the noncontingent display. They concluded that proprioceptive-visual integration is well established by 5 months and that the ability to detect the congruency between one's movements and their visual representation plays a fundamental role in an infant's perception of self, possibly underlying the development of visual self-recognition (discussed in Chapter 13). Other researchers, using a similar design that varied the spatial orientation of the images that infants saw, report that even 3-month-old infants can detect the congruence between their actual leg movements and a video image of those movements (Rochat & Morgan, 1995), suggesting that this might be an early developing ability.

A seemingly more complex intermodal feat concerns **intermodal** (or **cross-modal**) **matching.** In intermodal matching, a child must be able to recog-

nize an object initially inspected in one modality (touch, for example) through another modality (vision, for example). Rose and her colleagues (Rose, Gottfried, & Bridger, 1981) have shown that 6-month-old babies can perform visual-tactual integration. The infants were presented an object (either through touch alone or vision alone) for 60 seconds (familiarization phase) and were later presented a small set of objects through the alternative mode (transfer phase). The researchers reported that the infants spent more time exploring the novel objects (by manipulating or gazing at them) than the familiar ones during the transfer phase. That is, the babies showed dishabituation by examining the novel stimuli more than the familiar ones, even though familiarization was done in a different sensory modality. Other studies using similar methods have demonstrated intermodal matching for 4- to 6-month-old infants (Streri & Spelke, 1989).

Other research has shown that infants can make judgments of numerosity between two different sensory modalities. For example, 6- to 9-month-old infants were simultaneously shown arrays of two or three objects and heard either two or three drum beats. Infants looked significantly longer at the visual array corresponding to the number of drumbeats (Starkey, Spelke, & Gelman, 1990). This finding is particularly interesting, in that 3-year-old children have difficulty making audio-visual matches, that is, selecting visual arrays consisting of the same number of discrete auditory signals (Mix, Huttenlocher, & Levine, 1996). The lack of continuity between the performance of 6-month-old infants and 3-year-old children may reflect how this knowledge is represented and accessed. The infants' knowledge was represented *implicitly* and assessed via a looking-time procedure. In contrast, the preschool children's knowledge was assessed via an *explicit* task. It is likely that cross-modal judgments early in life can only be made through implicit cognition and that such knowledge does not become available to conscious awareness until much later in development.

In related research, Andrew Meltzoff and Richard Borton (1979) reported visual-tactual integration in infants less than 1 month old. In their study, the infants were familiarized with one of two pacifiers (a

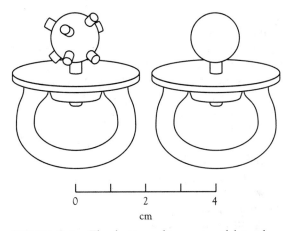

FIGURE 7-9 The shapes used in cross-modal matching study with 1-month-olds to assess tactual matching. SOURCE: "Intermodal Matching by Human Neonates," by A.N. Meltzoff and R.W. Borton, 1979, *Nature, 282,* 403–404. Copyright © 1979 Macmillan Magazines Ltd

gration in infants (Lewkowicz, 2000; Lickliter & Bahrick, 2000). Perceptual experience begins before birth, and the specific experiences a fetus or embryo receives can alter its development, including the ability to integrate information between senses. For example, I discussed in Chapter 2 research by Robert Lickliter (1990), in which exposure to pattern light before hatching augmented bobwhite quails' subsequent visual abilities but was detrimental to some important auditory skills (identifying their species' call). Although space limitations prevent me from discussing these ideas in any detail, what's important to keep in mind when seemingly advanced abilities are observed in very young infants, is that these skills are not preformed and functioning without the benefit of prior experience; rather, such skills are constructed from the interaction of genes and environment, broadly defined, which begin prenatally and continue throughout life.

sphere or a sphere with knobs, as shown in Figure 7-9) and later shown three-dimensional models of the two pacifiers. In two experiments, the infants looked significantly longer at the visual display that corresponded to the pacifier they had orally (but not visually) inspected seconds earlier. The findings of Meltzoff and Borton have been confirmed by some researchers (Gibson & Walker, 1984) but not by others (Maurer, Stager, & Mondlach, 1999).

Is intermodal integration innate? Although research clearly indicates that intermodal abilities improve with age (see Lewkowicz, 2000, for a review), even newborns are capable of recognizing the equivalence between stimuli in two different modalities (a bright light and loud sound, for instance, Lewkowicz & Turkewitz, 1980). Yet, it does not mean that such abilities are innate, at least not in the way that term is typically used. The developmental systems approach, introduced in Chapter 2, argues that all traits develop as a result of the bidirectional interaction between different levels of organization within the organism and that normal prenatal experiences are crucial in determining species-typical patterns of development. Such arguments have recently been made for intermodal inte-

Category Representation

Babies have distinct preferences for what they look at and display a rudimentary form of visual memory, as reflected by the effects that novelty and familiarity have on their preferences. As important as these basic processes are, our ability to deal effectively with new information would be hopelessly impaired if we did not form *categories*. By the process of categorization, one can treat objects that are perceptually different as being the same kind of thing. Uncle Joe, Aunt Mary, Mommy, Daddy, and the stranger on the street are all unique individuals, but at one level they're all the same: they're all people. Our ability to categorize allows us to reduce an enormous diversity of information into manageable units. A 6-month-old given a new stuffed animal, rattle, or bottle can identify each object and act toward it accordingly, even though he or she has never seen the object before. Each object is similar to something the child already knows, and the objects can be categorized and dealt with easily. The process of categorization is ubiquitous, permeating every aspect of our intellectual life, and the origins of categorization can be found early in infancy.

How Is Categorization Measured?

One technique that has been used to assess infants' perceptual categories is the habituation/dishabituation paradigm, discussed earlier in this chapter. How can this paradigm be used to assess infants' categories, or concepts? One way is by varying the stimuli that are presented during the habituation trials. Rather than habituating infants to a picture of a face of a single individual (Sally), for example, pictures of different individuals can be presented (Sally, Maria, Barbara, and Teresa). In both the single- and multiple-face cases, the amount of response declines with repeated exposure (that is, habituation). In the former case, infants are habituated to a specific stimulus (Sally), and in the latter case, to a category of stimuli (women's faces). After habituation has occurred, a new female face can be presented (Elizabeth). Infants who were habituated to a single face should recognize this new face as a novel stimulus and increase their attention to it (that is, show dishabituation). In contrast, infants who were habituated to women's faces in general should recognize it as just another example of a woman's face and continue to habituate. That is, even though they have never seen this face before, they should categorize it as familiar and direct relatively little of their attention to it.

The procedure and results just described are similar to those reported by Leslie Cohen and Mark Strauss for a group of 30-week-old infants. Cohen and Strauss interpreted their findings as evidence that such infants can abstract "appropriate conceptual categories regarding the human face" (1979, p. 422). By continuing to habituate to the new stimulus, infants are, in effect, telling us that although the face is perceptually different from anything they have seen before, it is similar in general form to what they already know. They are telling us that they have acquired a category for female faces.

Research during the past 30 years has shown that infants as young as 3 months old can organize objects into perceptual categories during relatively brief experimental sessions (Eimas & Quinn, 1994; Younger & Gotlieb, 1988). For example, in a series of experiments by Peter Eimas and Paul Quinn (1994), 3- and 4-month-old infants were habituated to a series of pictures of either horses or cats. Following habituation, the infants were shown a pair of new pictures, one from the habituated category (a "new" picture of a horse, for instance) and one from a different, but related category (a zebra or giraffe, for instance). Note that both pictures on these test trials were "new" to the infants, in that they had never been shown the specific picture of this horse before, nor of any giraffe or zebra. However, if they had formed a concept of "horse," they would recognize the new picture of a horse as "just another horse" and thus look longer at the giraffe (or zebra) than at the horse. This, in fact, is what Eimas and Quinn found. Infants formed categories of horses that were distinct from zebras, giraffes, and cats, and they formed categories of cats that were distinct from horses and tigers. However, these babies were not able to distinguish between cats and female lions, indicating that the perceptual similarity between cats and female lions is too great for infants of this age to form separate categories of them, at least with this little experience. But when 3- and 4-month-old infants were given more experience with cats before being tested for category formation, they were able to make the "cat versus female lion" categorical distinction (Quinn & Eimas, 1996), indicating that perceptual category formation for "natural" categories is quite well developed early in life.

In more recent research, Quinn and Eimas (1998) included humans as well as a potential category for 3- and 4-month-old infants. They found that when infants were familiarized with pictures of humans, they later included not only novel pictures of humans as members of that category (that is, continued to habituate to pictures of humans), but also pictures of horses and fish, but not cars. That is, they treated horses and fish as if they were human. The reverse, however, did not hold, for when infants were familiarized with pictures of horses, they did not include humans in their categorizations (that is, they dishabituated to pictures of humans). What does this pattern mean? Quinn and Eimas suggested that babies already have experience interacting with humans, and that the "human" category serves as an anchor for interpreting other animals. After being familiarized with pictures of humans, other animals will share many of the same characteristics with humans, so that infants will initially classify nonhuman animals as human. Because they are less familiar before the experiment with nonhuman animals, the reverse is not true. Then, they learn the characteristics of "horses," for instance, but don't later mistake humans (or cats) for horses. Quinn and Eimas speculated, "the incorporation of nonhuman animal species into the categorical representation of humans may be the process that allows for the development of a representation of animals in general" (1998, p. 171). By 7 months, however, infants seem able to distinguish between humans and other mammals, showing dishabituation to nonhuman mammals following habituation to humans (Pauen, 2000).

It's worth asking "What are these categorization experiments really assessing?" If 3-month-old infants habituate to a category of vehicles, for example, and then dishabituate to pictures of animals (Arterberry & Bornstein, 2001), does this mean that they came into the laboratory with these categories "in mind," and that the experimenter is discovering how they classify their world? Or rather, do these results indicate that infants are able to distinguish physical features of items that correlate with one another (for example, four legs of mammals, certain characteristics of faces) and discover for themselves the categories in the minds (and the stimuli) of the experimenters (Oakes & Madole, 2000)? In most experiments, there is likely a little bit of both going on. At one level, these experiments reveal something of the processes underlying infants' categorization. What type of features do they attend to in order to form categories? How much overlap, or correlation among features, is necessary for them to treat two different members of a concept as the same? From this perspective, it would be foolhardy to assume that 3-month-olds have a concept of "vehicles," but more sensible to assume that they are able to identify the perceptual similarity among the different pictures of vehicles to form a category, one they formed in the course of the experiment. But then again, even 3-month-olds have substantial perceptual experiences. Although they may never have seen a giraffe, their parents may have shown them pictures of such bizarre animals in books, and to assume that their behavior in the laboratory is independent of their past experience is equally foolhardy (Quinn, 2002). In general, results from infant categorization studies reveal something about both the content of children's categories and the processes by which such content is acquired. It takes careful experimentation, however, to know which is which. In the next section, I discuss more specifically one process by which infants form categories.

The Structure of Infants' Categories

When infants form categories, how do they do it? One popular way of describing adult concepts is through category prototypes. A **category prototype** is an abstract representation of a category. It reflects the central tendency, or "best example," of a category. Items that share many features in common with the prototype are said to be typical category exemplars (for instance, *robin* for the category *birds*), whereas items that share fewer features with the prototype are said to be atypical category exemplars (for instance, *ostrich* for the category *birds*) (see Rosch, 1975; Chapter 11).

Several researchers have demonstrated that infants form category prototypes much as adults do. The dot patterns in the first column of Figure 7-10 present the prototypes used in a study by Younger and Gotlieb (1988). The dot patterns to the right reflect examples of stimuli generated from the prototype. Some of these stimuli represent "low" distortion from the prototype (that is, they are very similar to the prototype), whereas others represent "medium" and "high" distortion from the prototype. Three-, 5-, and 7-month-old infants were habituated to sets of dot patterns that varied in degree of distortion from the prototype (that is, either low, medium, or high levels of distortion). None of the infants ever saw the prototypes. After habituation, babies were shown pairs of stimuli. In one comparison, infants were

shown one of the stimuli they had just been familiarized with (an "old" stimulus) and the prototype from
which that "old" stimulus had been generated. Remember that infants had never seen the prototype
before, only stimuli generated from it. What would
babies look at longer? In general, babies looked at
the "old" stimulus longer than the prototype. They
acted as if the prototype were a familiar stimulus,
even though they had never seen it before. This is a
clear indication that infants as young as 3 months
old are able to form categories based on prototypes,
much as adults do. However, there was variation between infants of different ages. Three-month-olds
only formed categories when they were familiarized
with dot patterns that represented "good form," such
as the cross (first row) in Figure 7-10. Five-month-
olds formed categories for both "good" and "intermediate" forms (the middle row in Figure 7-10), but not
"poor" forms (the bottom row in Figure 7-10),
whereas 7-month-olds formed categories for all three
types of stimuli. That is, it is easier for young infants
to form categories for perceptual arrays with "good"
form (highly regular with bilateral symmetry) than
"poor" form, even though the rules of creating exemplars from the prototypes are the same for the various
types of categories.

The experiment by Younger and Gotlieb (1988)
is a good example of research investigating *how* infants form categories, or the processes involved in
category formation. But the particular patterns of
dots they showed infants have little connection with
stimuli or categories these babies encounter in their
everyday lives. Will the same processes of category
formation be in play when infants are shown examples from categories they may, indeed, have some experience with? That is, do babies form categories of
real-world stimuli and do prototypes play a role in
such category formation?

The answer seems to be "yes." In research using
more "natural" categories, Kenneth Roberts and
Frances Horowitz (1986; Roberts, 1988) showed that
9-month-old infants formed a category for the concept birds when habituated to highly typical exemplars of the category (for example, *sparrow*, *robin*,
and *blue jay*). There was no evidence of concept formation, however, when atypical exemplars served as

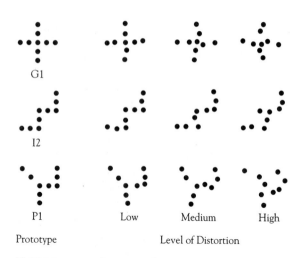

FIGURE 7-10 Prototype dot patterns showing "poor"
(P), "intermediate" (I), and "good" (G) form. SOURCE:
Younger, B., & Gotlieb, S. (1988). Development of categorization skills: Changes in the nature or structure of
infant form categories? *Developmental Psychology, 24,*
611–619.

the habituation stimuli (for example, *turkey, ostrich,*
and *chicken*). Like young children, infants are more
apt to identify or form a category when provided
with typical, rather than atypical, category exemplars
(Anglin, 1977). The findings of these experiments
are enlightening, suggesting that the categorization
process of infants is qualitatively similar to that of
older children and adults.

However, although infants and older children
both seem to use prototypes in forming categories,
the processes may not be identical. Research with
verbal preschool children indicates that they form
categories first at the basic level (for example, dogs
versus cats versus horses) and only later form categories at the superordinate level (for example, mammals versus vehicles versus furniture). (Some of this
research will be discussed in Chapter 11.) In contrast, research with infants indicates that they are
able to discriminate superordinate-level categories
(for example, mammals versus vehicles) before they
distinguish between basic-level categories (for example, cats versus dogs) (Mandler & McDonough,
1993). Differences in how categories are assessed, the

use of language by the older children, the specific stimuli used in an experiment, and, of course, the amount of experience children have with the categories in question, all influence the difference we see between infants and children (see Oakes & Madole, 2000; Quinn, 2002). But there do seem to be some common processes at work, which begin in early infancy and seemingly continue throughout life.

Color Categories

Although languages vary greatly in the number of terms they have to describe colors, people in all cultures seem to perceive colors similarly. When people are given color chips to categorize into a specified number of groups, the outcomes are highly similar regardless of whether the person doing the sorting has 11 different basic color words in his or her language or only 2 (Heider, 1972).

The interesting developmental question is "Do infants categorize colors as adults do, or is there an age-related progression in the categorization of color?" I mentioned earlier that newborns seem to possess the rudiments of color vision (Adams et al., 1994), but that such color vision is limited to large stimuli and particular parts of the color spectrum. Bornstein and his colleagues investigated the question of color categorization using the habituation/dishabituation paradigm with slightly older infants (Bornstein, Kessen, & Weiskopf, 1976). Four-month-olds were habituated to a color patch corresponding to a light wavelength of 480 nanometers. Adults classify this color as blue. After habituation, the infants were presented with one of two different color patches, one corresponding to a wavelength 30 nanometers greater than the habituated stimulus (510 nanometers) and one corresponding to a wavelength 30 nanometers less than the habituated stimulus (450 nanometers). The two posthabituation stimuli were comparably discrepant from the standard stimulus but in opposite directions. Adults classify the 450-nanometer wavelength as blue, just as they classify the 480-nanometer wavelength. But they classify the 510-nanometer wavelength as green. Thus, were adults to be subjects in this ex-

periment, they would show dishabituation (increased visual attention) to the 510-nanometer wavelength because they classify it as a color different from the standard blue. However, they would continue to habituate to the 450-nanometer wavelength of light because, although it is comparably different in physical characteristics from the standard, it is perceived only as a different shade of the same color (both blue).

How did the babies respond? The 4-month-old infants showed the same categorization responses as adults, habituating to the 450-nanometer stimulus and dishabituating to the 510-nanometer stimulus. The researchers reported similar results for other color boundaries. Although these findings do not prove that the way humans categorize the color spectrum does not change during development, they are strong evidence for that position.

Infant Perception: A Successful Past and a Bright Future

Much has been learned about infant perception during the past 40 years. Actually, this has been one of the great success stories of developmental psychology. Researchers have discovered an amazing number of basic facts about how infants perceive their world. But this does not mean that we have learned all there is to know, or that we have a proper understanding of these facts. Haith (1993), a leading researcher in the field of infant perception, cautions us not to become too complacent with our newfound knowledge, or to attribute too much in the way of sophisticated cognition to infants. For example, researchers are all too likely to view infant perceptual skills as all-or-none: Either babies can discriminate faces or they can't; either they show a preference for novel stimuli or they don't. This, Haith states, is too simplistic. Infants, like older children, show considerable variability in perceptual skills, behaving more competently in some contexts than others. Rather than asking when a particular ability is first seen in development, it makes more sense to take a truly developmental perspective, asking what the course of development is for any particular ability and under what conditions an infant will display a specific skill.

This is related to a second issue. Simply describing a perceptual ability tells us nothing about what the infant uses it for. Haith argues that we must take a more functional view of perceptual skills in infancy, asking, "how the baby applies his or her perceptual skills and knowledge in the real world" (1993, p. 364). We know much about basic infant perceptual abilities, and we will learn more when we examine what impact those abilities have on an infant's life.

Finally, Haith discusses what he calls the "species gap." The methods, theories, and concepts used for assessing infant perception are completely different from those used for assessing perception in childhood. The result is that we treat infants as if they were members of a different species. What we need are methods and theories that take a wider view of perceptual development, integrating what we know about infants' perception with what we know about perception in children and adults.

Haith's comments are less criticisms of work that has been done than they are suggestions for future directions. One must start somewhere, and developmental psychologists have made a very good start, indeed, in assessing the perceptual abilities of infants. But there is more to know, and future researchers must adopt slightly different ways of thinking if scientific progress is to continue.

Summary

From birth, infants actively use their perceptual systems to acquire information from their surroundings. By 1 week of age, babies can discriminate their mothers from other women by smell and by the sound of their voices. A number of techniques have been used to assess infants' perceptual abilities, including changes in their sucking rate to different stimuli, the *visual preference paradigm*—in which differences in the amount of time infants spend looking at two stimuli is used to infer that they can discriminate between the stimuli and prefer to look at one versus the other—and the habituation/dishabituation paradigm. *Habituation* occurs when infants' looking time diminishes as a result of repeated presentation of a stimulus. *Dishabituation*, or release from habituation, occurs when looking time increases with the presentation of a new stimulus. Habituation and dishabituation to visual stimuli are found for some newborns and reflect both discrimination and memory.

Newborns show a preference for high-pitched voices, and this preference might have its origins in the womb. Young infants can discriminate among *phonemes* and categorize language sounds much as adults do and appear to be biologically prepared to perceive music.

Vision is not well developed at birth, although the abilities of *accommodation* of the lens, *convergence*, and *coordination* improve rapidly during the first six months. From birth, infants look longer at some stimuli than others, indicating that they can discriminate between the stimuli and have preferences. Developmental differences in the organization of the visual nervous system have been proposed to account for changes in infants' visual preferences during the first several months of life. At birth, the phylogenetically older *secondary visual system* is functioning better than is the more sophisticated *primary visual system*. During the first month of life, infants tend to direct their attention to the outside of a figure, which is referred to as the *externality effect*. Among the physical characteristics of a stimulus that attracts infants' visual attention are movement, contour and contrast, certain levels of complexity, vertical symmetry, curvature, and attractive faces. Very young infants also seem to have a bias toward attending to the human face.

Beginning around 2 months of age, infants' attention is increasingly influenced by psychological factors such as the familiarity or novelty of a stimulus. Infants form long-term sensory representations, or *schemas*, which are representations of events that preserve the temporal and spatial arrangements of elements of events. Kagan proposed the *discrepancy principle* to explain infants' preferences for novel stimuli, stating that stimuli that are moderately discrepant from a previously acquired schema are most likely to be attended to.

Intermodal (or *intersensory*) *integration* refers to the coordination of information from two, or more, sensory modalities and may be present at birth, or shortly thereafter. *Intermodal* (or *cross-modal*) *matching* refers to the ability to recognize a stimulus initially inspected in one modality (vision, for example) through another modality (touch, for example), and this ability may also be present at birth or shortly thereafter.

Using the habituation/dishabituation paradigm, researchers have been able to demonstrate that infants can form categories and do so much the same way that older children and adults do. Infant categories are formed around *category prototypes,* which is an abstract representation reflecting the central tendency, or "best example" of a category.

Key Terms and Concepts

visual preference paradigm
habituation
dishabituation
phonemes
accommodation (of the lens)
convergence (of the eyes)
coordination (of the eyes)
secondary visual system
primary visual system
externality effect
schema
discrepancy principle
intermodal (intersensory) integration
intermodal (cross-modal) matching
category prototype

Suggested Readings

Haith, M. M. (1993). Preparing for the 21st century: Some goals and challenges for studies of infant sensory and perceptual development. *Developmental Review, 13,* 354–371. Haith briefly reviews the state of the art in infant perceptual development and suggests directions for the future. These include taking a more continuous, developmental perspective of infant perception, integrating ideas about infant perception with those about older children, looking more at the brain basis of perceptual development, and increasing the emphasis on applying research findings to at-risk populations.

Kellman, P. H., & Banks, M. S. (1998). Infant visual perception. In D. Kuhn & R. S. Siegler (Vol. Eds.), *Cognitive, language, and perceptual development,* Vol. 2 (pp. 103–146). In W. Damon (General Editor), *Handbook of child psychology.* New York: Wiley. This chapter reviews the basic research on infant visual perception. Written by two leaders in the field, it is an authoritative and often detailed account of how babies see.

Lewkowicz, D. J. (2000). The development of intersensory temporal perception: An epigenetic systems/limitations view. *Psychological Bulletin, 126,* 281–308. This paper reviews much of the literature on intermodal, or intersensory, integration, in infancy and provides a dynamic, epigenetic model for how such integration develops.

Morton, J., & Johnson, M. H. (1991). CONSPEC and CONLERN: A two-process theory of infant face recognition. *Psychological Review, 98,* 164–181. This paper reviews the small set of studies concerned with face recognition during the first few months after birth and provides a model proposing that infants are born with some innate information about faces as well as a "program" that guides them in learning about the facial features of others.

Quinn, P. C. (2002). Category representation in young infants. *Current Directions in Psychological Science, 11,* 66–70. This article presents a brief up-to-date review of research in infants' category representation, by one of the leading experimentalists on the topic.

InfoTrac College Edition

For additional readings, explore InfoTrac College Edition, your online library. Go to http://www.infotrac-college.com/wadsworth.

8

Spatial Cognition

Where does perception end and cognition begin? That's actually a trick question because there is no simple, agreed-upon answer. The topic of this chapter is **spatial cognition,** which refers to the processing of visual information in terms of spatial relations. So defined, some aspects of spatial cognition, particularly those displayed by preverbal infants, may be difficult to distinguish from some of the topics described in the previous chapter as examples of "visual perception." I admit to this ambiguity, but I believe that the topics covered in this chapter do provide a coherent picture of children's developing abilities to understand and represent space. Representation is important here, for spatial relations are an important way in which children mentally code, or represent, their world.

This chapter is appropriately situated between chapters on perception and representation and reflects the interacting nature of cognition at multiple levels. As a textbook author, I must make some distinctions and divide cognitive developmental phenomenon in some sensible way. Otherwise, you, the reader, would have a very difficult time making heads or tails out of the bounty of research findings in this extensive field (and the book would seem to be a rambling collection of experiments, hypotheses, and theories, as my students sometimes find my lectures). Classifying is something we humans do to make sense of our world, and cognitive processes are no exception. But the reality is that the developing mind/brain makes no such distinctions, and processes that we call "perceptual" interact in complicated ways with what we consider to be "higher-order" processes. Perhaps it's good to have a topic such as spatial cognition to help us see these connections and to appreciate that cognition is actually a seamless cloth with we—the observers and interpreters—making distinctions that nature does not.

In this chapter, I review research on spatial cognition beginning in infancy with depth perception and babies' knowledge of objects and then examine the seemingly more complicated spatial cognition and its development in older children. In addition to an interest in the development of these abilities, psychologists have long noted and been pressed to explain gender differences in spatial cognition. Although the conventional wisdom is that this is an area of male expertise, that, as you'll see, is only part of the picture.

The Development of Spatial Abilities in Infants and Toddlers

When we think of spatial cognition, what often comes to mind are relatively complicated tasks such as reading maps, finding the "hidden object" within a complex visual scene, or mentally rotating figures. These are all forms of spatial cognition and involve the mental representation of spatial relations to solve problems. But not all spatial tasks are so complex, and even infants display often-impressive spatial cognitive abilities. For example, Paul Quinn (1994) repeatedly showed 3-month-old infants displays in which a dot was presented in one of several locations below a solid bar. (Other infants were habituated to dots consistently presented above a bar.) Infants eventually decreased their looking time to the displays (that is, they habituated) and were then shown two new stimuli, one in which a dot was presented in a new location, but still below the bar, and another in which a dot was presented above the bar. Infants had seen neither stimulus before, so both were literally "new." Yet, the display with the dot below the bar was similar to other below-the-bar stimuli infants had seen on the habituation trials. Would the babies recognize this as "just another below-the-bar stimulus" and continue to habituate, indicating that they had acquired a spatial concept (dot above versus below the bar)? Yes indeed. Although infants increased their looking time to the dot-above-the-bar display, recognizing it as a novel stimulus, they treated the never-before-seen dot-below-the-bar display as if it were familiar. That is, they had formed a perceptual category (recall our discussion of infant categorization in Chapter 7), this time based strictly on spatial relations.

Depth Perception

One area of infant visual perception that has received considerable attention over the years is **depth perception.** At what age and under what conditions can infants discriminate visual patterns denoting depth? One reason for interest in the topic is that the ability to perceive depth appears to be present immediately for some species that are able to locomote shortly after birth, including chickens and goats (Walk & Gibson, 1961). Are human babies born with the ability to discriminate depth, or does the discrimination of depth require experience? One factor that is important for depth perception concerns binocular cues. Because the two eyes are separated by several centimeters, the message one eye receives is slightly different from that received by its partner. This disparity produces information that is important for evaluating an object's distance from us. One ability critical to binocular depth perception is that of **bifoveal fixation,** the ability of the foveas of the two eyes to focus on the same object simultaneously. Richard Aslin (1977) tested bifoveal fixation in 1-, 2-, and 3-month-old infants. A target was moved past the infants' eyes at one of two constant speeds, and eye fixations were photographed. Aslin reported that the infants' eyes did not consistently converge on the targets until 2 months and did not do so without delay until 3 months. Thus, binocular cues to depth perception are not likely to be functioning well until the second or third month of life.

Another reason for the interest in the development of depth cues is their importance in early locomotion. Many parents tell of their 8-month-old infants crawling off the side of the bed, sometimes to be caught by a watchful parent and sometimes not. What cues must infants recognize to avoid falling, and when and how do they develop? An apparatus designed to test these questions is the *visual cliff* (Walk & Gibson, 1961). The visual cliff consists of a glass-topped table with a board across its center. On one side of the board, the infant sees a checkerboard pattern situated directly under the glass. This is referred to as the "shallow" side. On the other side the checkerboard pattern is several feet below the glass. This is referred to as the "deep" side (see Photo 8-1).

PHOTO 8-1 An infant on a visual cliff. Infants who can perceive depth will crawl to their mothers across the "shallow" side but not across the "deep" side. (Topman/ The Image Works)

Infants who can crawl (usually beginning around 7 or 8 months) are placed on the center board and called by their mothers from either side of the cliff. Will infants ignore the visual cues of depth on the "deep" side and crawl to their mothers, or will they fuss and refuse to traverse the "deep" side? Infants who crawl to their mothers on the "shallow" side but not on the "deep" side are said to be able to discriminate depth.

In general, early findings of Walk and Gibson indicated that babies rarely crawled to their mothers over the "deep" side. These findings suggest that once infants can crawl, they display fear, suggesting that little learning is necessary. However, more recent research by Bennett Bertenthal, Joseph Campos, and their colleagues found that the tendency to show fear on the visual cliff was related to the extent of previous locomotor experience (Bertenthal, Campos, & Barrett, 1984; Bertenthal, Campos, & Kermoian, 1994). Infants with more locomotive experience were more likely to show fear than were their less-experienced peers, suggesting that such experience is related to depth perception.

Because tests of depth perception using the visual cliff require that an infant be able to crawl, the apparatus would seem to be inappropriate for assessing depth perception in younger infants. However, Campos and his colleagues used the visual cliff with babies who had not begun to crawl (2 and 3.5 months) and were able to determine that locomotor experience is not necessary for the perception of depth (Campos, Langer, & Krowitz, 1970). The infants were placed on the center board of the cliff and their heart rates were measured. They were later placed on the "deep" side, and changes in their heart rates were assessed. Increases in heart rate reflect stress, and the older infants in this study who were placed on the "deep" side of a visual cliff showed such a rise, indicating that they could discriminate depth and that they feared it, despite their lack of crawling experience. Younger infants in the study, however, showed a *decrease* in heart rate relative to baseline when placed on the "deep" side. Decreases in heart rate reflect increased visual attention. Such a finding suggests that young infants can discriminate depth but have not yet learned to fear it.

Self-Produced Movement and the Development of Spatial Cognition

In an interesting study of depth perception, the locomotive experience of one group of infants who did not yet crawl was enriched by letting them get around in walkers (Bertenthal et al., 1984). Unlike their noncrawling agemates who did not use walkers, the walker babies showed fear of heights (reflected by heart-rate acceleration when placed on the "deep" side of a visual cliff), indicating that the experience in the walkers accelerated the development of depth perception. These findings and others like them (see Bertenthal et al., 1994) suggest that there might be something about self-propelled movement that facil-

itates depth perception, or more specifically wariness of heights. This implies that perceptual systems do not develop in isolation but rather in coordination with motor systems. Bertenthal and his colleagues (1994) suggest that the "active control of locomotion, unlike passive locomotion, demands continuous updating of one's orientation relative to the spatial layout. This information is provided through multimodal sources, such as visual and vestibular coding of angular acceleration. With locomotor experience, changes in angular acceleration detected by the visual system are mapped onto analogous changes detected by the vestibular system. Fear or avoidance [on an apparatus such as the visual cliff] ensues when the expected mapping between visual and vestibular information is violated" (p. 142).

Perhaps the best-known research dealing with self-propelled movement in perception is that of Richard Held and Alan Hein (1963) with kittens. In this classic study, kittens were raised in a darkened room and had visual experience only during training and testing. Pairs of kittens of the same age were used, one given normal visual-motor experience and the other given visual experience without associated motor experience. To do this, a special training apparatus was developed, shown in Figure 8-1. To train a pair of kittens, one (the active kitten) was harnessed to walk around the brightly decorated track and one (the passive kitten) was placed in a gondola to have identical visual experiences without the associated motor feedback. That is, although both kittens had the same visual experience, and both had motor experience in their darkened room, only the active kitten had visual experience concomitant with movement. After training, both kittens were tested on the visual cliff to determine if they showed a preference for sides. The passive kittens showed no preference for sides, indicating a lack of depth perception. By contrast, the active kittens consistently chose the "shallow" side, indicating that they could perceive depth.

In more recent research with human infants and toddlers, locomotive experience was related to aspects of spatial cognition other than depth perception. For example, in one study (Kermoian & Campos, 1988), 8.5-month-old infants were divided

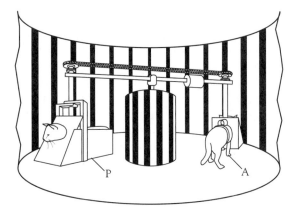

FIGURE 8-1 The apparatus used in Held and Hein's study of the effects of locomotor experience on visual perception. The "active" kittens could locomote around the chamber, while the "passive" kittens could not, although they had comparable visual experiences. SOURCE: Adapted from "Movement-Produced Stimulation in the Development of Visually Guided Behavior," by R. Held & A. Hein, 1963, *Journal of Comparative and Physiological Psychology, 56,* 872–876, American Psychological Association.

into three groups: (1) prelocomotive (that is, not yet crawling), (2) prelocomotive but with walker experience, and (3) locomotive (that is, crawling). The infants were then tested with a series of tasks in which they had to retrieve an object hidden under a cloth. Infants with locomotive experience, either by crawling or in a walker, showed more advanced performance on the object-retrieval task than the non-crawlers did. Moreover, there were no differences in performance between the crawlers and the walkers, suggesting that it is the locomotor experience and not maturation that is responsible for the advanced spatial memory. Other research has similarly shown advantages in certain aspects of spatial cognition associated with self-produced locomotion for infants, although these effects tend to be limited to specific abilities (Arterberry, Yonas, & Bensen, 1989; Bai & Bertenthal, 1992). For example, self-produced locomotion is associated with infants' ability to search for a hidden object after the infant is moved (that is, hiding the object in a container, then moving the in-

fant 180 degrees before permitting him or her to search), but not after the container is moved (Bai & Bertenthal, 1992). These findings suggest that the effects on spatial cognition of self-produced locomotion are domain specific rather than domain general.

The findings of Held and Hein with kittens and of Bertenthal, Campos, and their colleagues with children make it clear that spatial cognition does not simply develop as a result of maturation or visual experience, but along with motor experience. This research points to the importance of studying the development of the whole child and not just looking at one system in isolation from other aspects of development.

Knowledge of Objects

A basic question in infant spatial cognition concerns what they know about the nature of objects—for example, the extent to which they understand that physical objects follow the basic Newtonian laws of physics. (Must everything that goes up eventually come down?) The trick in demonstrating object knowledge in very young infants is to test behaviors appropriate to their developmental level. For example, it is impossible to assess object retrieval in 3- and 4-month-old infants because of their limited motor skills. Most researchers looking at early infant abilities have used variants of the habituation/dishabituation procedure, described with respect to infant perception and attention in Chapter 7. Basically, infants are shown an event repeatedly until their attention to it diminishes to a certain level (habituation). They are then shown an alternative event, and changes in their level of attention are examined. As demonstrated in Chapter 7, following habituation, young infants will increase their attention (that is, show dishabituation) when a new stimulus is presented. The experimenter must be clever enough to take advantage of this characteristic of infant attention and to use it to infer knowledge of objects that previously went undetected.

Object Constancy

Perhaps the most basic form of spatial cognition concerns infants' understanding of the constancy of physical objects in time and space. **Object constancy** refers to the knowledge that an object remains the same despite changes in how it is viewed. For example, when we see an object, a table, for instance, at a certain distance, it makes a specific impression on the retinas of our eyes. As we move away from the table, that image on the back of our eyes gets smaller, but we continue to perceive the table as maintaining a constant size and shape. We don't act as if the table is changing before our eyes; although the literal sensation changes, we maintain a type of perceptual constancy in our minds.

This would seem to be a very basic form of spatial cognition, and in fact, it is possessed, to varying degrees, even by newborns. For example, newborns are habituated to an object of a particular size and then shown one of two new objects: the same object but as seen from a different distance, and a new object of a different size, but presented so that the retinal image it projects is the same as the retinal image projected by the original habituated object. If infants possess size constancy, they should continue to habituate to the same object/different distance, even though the actual retinal image is different. If they do *not* possess size constancy, they should dishabituate to the same object at a different distance and habituate to the new object that produces the same retinal image. Newborns display the former pattern, displaying a degree of size and shape constancy that, although not quite adult-like, indicates that human infants are well-prepared at birth for making sense of physical objects (Slater, Mattock, & Brown, 1990).

Yet, despite this precocial ability, older children sometimes reveal what appears to be a surprising ignorance of size and shape constancy. For example, I recall sitting with 4-year-old Brendan recently, looking at planes flying overhead. "How do they get so small?" he asked. "Huh?" was probably my response, and he went on to wonder how, big planes like he sees at the airport can get so tiny when they go up in the air. He seems not to have realized that the plane stays the same despite the vastly changing retinal image it projects as it soars away. Brendan is not unique in his confusion, for I have heard other people tell of their children's mystification of the "amazing shrinking abilities" of airplanes. ("When do we get small?" asked

one preschool child of her mother on her first airplane trip. This child figured out that if the plane gets smaller, so, too, must the people in it.) What we seem to have here is a discrepancy between the implicit knowledge of the infant, assessed by looking-time or operant conditioning procedures, and the explicit, verbalizable knowledge of the older child. Granted, in most of children's everyday experiences, they behave as if objects maintain their size and shape despite changes in retinal image. Yet, for extraordinary events (extraordinary in that they were unlikely to be experienced by our ancestors hundreds of thousands or even millions of years ago), such as rapidly moving, large flying objects, the appearance of a change in size seemingly overpowers their intuitive knowledge of object constancy, reflecting a disconnect between what they know implicitly and what they know explicitly.

Even adults' well-developed notions of size constancy can be overridden if they experience an event totally foreign to them. This is illustrated by Colin Turnbull's account of an African Pygmy's first trip out of the forest and his first experience with seeing a herd of buffalo crossing a wide plain in the distance:

> [When Kenge] saw the buffalo, still grazing lazily several miles away, far below . . . he said "What insects are those?" At first I hardly understood; then I realized that in the forest the range of vision is so limited that there is no great need to make an automatic allowance for distance when judging size. . . . When I told Kenge that the insects were buffalo, he roared with laughter and told me not to tell such stupid lies. . . . As we got closer, the "insects" must have seemed to get bigger and bigger. Kenge . . . kept his face glued to the window, which nothing would make him lower. . . . I was never able to discover just what he thought was happening—whether he thought that the insects were changing into buffalo, or that they were miniature buffalo growing rapidly as we approached. His only comment was that they were not real buffalo, and he was not going to get out of the car until we left the park. (1961, pp. 252–253)

Knowing That Objects Are Continuous, Solid, and Require Support

Another form of basic spatial cognition in infancy concerns the Gestalt concept of continuation. For example, Figure 8-2 shows a solid rectangle with two bars extending from its top and bottom. Adults infer that the rectangle is occluding a solid bar, although no solid bar is actually seen. Will infants make the same inference? How can one tell? One way is by repeatedly showing infants the stimulus until their attention to it decreases (habituation), and then showing them a picture of a solid bar, in the same orientation as the partial bars in the original stimulus. If they increase their attention to this stimulus, they would be treating it as if it is novel; this would be an indication that they had *not* inferred that the two partial bars in the original stimulus were connected. If, however, when shown the solid bar they show little interest in it (that is, they continue to habituate), they would be treating it like an "old" stimulus, one they've gotten tired of looking at. But it is not literally the "same old thing," but a different physical stimulus. If they treat it like an "old" stimulus, it would be because they have inferred that the rectangle in the original stimulus was occluding a solid bar.

When doing experiments like this, how do babies respond? Infants 4 months of age treat the solid bar as if it were an old stimulus (that is, they continue to habituate), but only for moving stimuli (as shown by the arrows in Figure 8-2), not for stationary stimuli (Johnson & Aslin, 1996; Kellman & Spelke, 1983). Elizabeth Spelke (1985) speculated that this is an indication that infants are born with the notion of the persistence, coherence, and unity of objects. They "know," at some level, that objects are continuous in space. However, more recent research indicates that 2-month-old (Johnson & Aslin, 1995) and 4-month-old (Eizenman & Bertenthal, 1998) infants will show evidence of inferring object unity in some, but not other situations, and that newborns *increase* their attention to the solid bar (Slater et al., 1990), suggesting that babies are likely *not* born with this knowledge.

Spelke and her colleagues have conducted other studies consistent with the interpretation that infants as young as 2.5 months of age have a knowledge of the solidity and continuity of objects (the fact that a moving object continues on its path), and more recently Renée Baillargeon and her colleagues

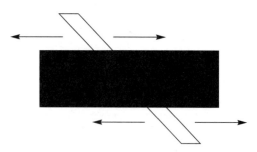

FIGURE 8-2 Example of Gestalt continuation.

have investigated young infants' understanding of support (an object must be supported or it falls), collisions (an object that is hit by another object moves) (Baillargeon, Kotovsky, & Needham, 1995), and containment (a larger object cannot fit into a smaller object) (Aguiar & Baillargeon, 1998).

Let me provide an example from Baillargeon's work on the development of infants' understanding of support, using the **violation-of-expectation method,** in which infants' reaction to an unexpected event is used to infer what he or she knows. Baillargeon and her colleagues (1995) showed infants possible and impossible events reflecting the notion of support (see Figure 8-3). A gloved hand would push a box that sat atop a platform from left to right. In the possible event, the box stopped while firmly situated on the platform. In the impossible event, the box was pushed until only 15% of it rested on the platform. How did babies react to the impossible event? If they understand that objects need to be supported lest they fall, they should show "surprise" and increased looking time when observing the impossible event. The youngest infants (3-month-olds) weren't surprised. As long as the box maintained some contact with the platform, they acted as if they expected it to remain on the platform and not to fall. Beginning about 4.5 months, the amount of contact between the box and the platform becomes important, and by 6.5 months, infants expect that the box will fall unless a significant portion of it is in contact with the platform.

How can one interpret these findings? According to Baillargeon, infants originally believe that any

FIGURE 8-3 Example of possible and impossible events for object support. SOURCE: Baillargeon, R. (1994). How do infants learn about the physical world? *Current Directions in Psychological Science, 3,* 133–140. Reprinted with permission.

contact between two objects is enough for one to support the other. Only when there is no contact between two objects do they expect gravity to take over. Their concept is progressively revised with experience, however, until they eventually arrive, quite early in life, at an adult-like concept of support. Baillargeon (1994; Baillargeon et al., 1995) provides evidence that other aspects of infants' knowledge of objects develop in a similar sequence from all-or-none to a progressively mature understanding of objects.

There is an interesting aside to the work demonstrating infant's often-substantial knowledge of support and solidarity. Recall my comments about the discrepancy between infants' (even newborns') appreciation of object constancy and that of the preschooler ("How does the plane get so small?"). This discrepancy is also found for an understanding of support and solidity. For example, in search tasks, in which children must find an object hidden in one of several locations, 2-year-olds generally fail to display knowledge of these concepts, unlike their younger 6-month-old counterparts (Berthier et al., 2000; Hood, Carey, & Prasada, 2000). For example, Bruce Hood and his colleagues (2000) showed groups of 2- and 2.5-year-old children a ball being dropped onto a stage behind a screen. The screen was removed to reveal the ball resting on the floor of the stage (Experiment 1). After the children witnessed this three times, the experimenter placed a cup on the floor of the stage, a shelf over the cup, and then a second cup on that shelf. This is illustrated in Figure 8-4. The screen was then replaced and the ball was dropped behind the screen again. The children then saw the two cups, one on the shelf and one on the stage floor, and were asked to retrieve the ball. If they possessed a sense of solidarity, as presumably 6-month-old infants do using looking-time procedures, they should search in the upper cup. However, if their sense of solidarity is not fully developed, they should be just as likely to search in the cup on the floor of the stage, particularly since that is where they had successfully retrieved the ball three times before. Hood et al. (2000) reported that only 40% of the 2-year-olds searched in the upper cup, whereas this percentage rose to 93% for the 2.5-year olds.

This perplexing result, suggestive that infants have a more sophisticated understanding of spatial relations than 2-year-olds, is likely due to the very different nature of the tasks (Keen, 2003). Older children must demonstrate an explicit (that is, conscious) understanding of solidarity and support in the search tasks, whereas the looking-time tasks used with infants require only implicit knowledge. Consistent with Annette Karmiloff-Smith's (1992) theory (see Chapter 4), implicit knowledge develops before explicit knowledge. As such, postulating that infants who look longer at an "impossible" than at a "possible" event have the same type of knowledge that older children have for the phenomenon under question (here, support) is likely unwarranted. What young infants appear to posses, or develop early, is implicit knowledge, which likely cannot be used as flexibly as explicit knowledge. This is an issue we will encounter for other phenomena, later in this chapter and in other chapters in this book.

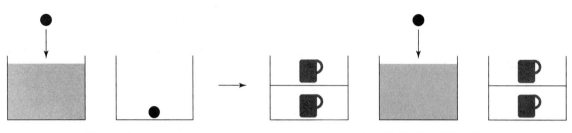

Familiarize × 3   Introduce Shelf + Cups, Then Search

FIGURE 8-4   The apparatus and procedure used in study by Hood et al. with 2- and 2.5-year-old children. Children watched as a ball was dropped behind the screen and saw that it rested on the floor. A shelf and two cups were then added to the stage, and the ball was dropped again behind the screen. Children were then asked to retrieve the ball. SOURCE: Hood, B., Carey, S., & Prasada, S. (2000). Predicting the outcomes of physical events: Two-year-olds fail to reveal knowledge of solidity and support. *Child Development, 71*, 1540–1554. Adapted with permission of the Society for Research in Child Development.

Object Permanence

Perhaps the most studied aspect of infant spatial cognition is that of **object permanence,** the belief that objects have permanence in time and space. As you may recall from our discussion of Jean Piaget's account of sensorimotor intelligence (Chapter 4), infants will not search for a hidden object until about 8 months and will fail the A-not-B object-permanence task until about 12 months. Infants slightly younger than 8 months may retrieve a hidden object when they are in the process of reaching for it when it was covered, but this more likely reflects an inability to inhibit a prepotent response (Diamond, 1985) rather than demonstrating object permanence. Despite the robustness of these observations, growing evidence indicates that infants as young as 3.5 months have far more knowledge of objects than Piaget proposed, suggesting to some that this knowledge is innate (that is, representational innateness, Spelke & Newport, 1998).

Evidence of object permanence in very young infants is probably best exemplified by Baillargeon's work (1987; Baillargeon & De Vos, 1991) using the violation-of-expectation method, much as was done in her work on understanding support. In Baillargeon's experiment (1987), infants 3.5 and 4.5 months of age were habituated to a moving screen (see Figure 8-5). The screen was rotated 180 degrees,

from being flat in a box with its leading edge facing the infant, rising continuously through an arc until it rested in the box with its leading edge farthest away from the infant. Once habituated to this event, infants in the experimental group were shown a colorful wooden block with a clown face painted on it, placed to the rear of the flat screen. In the "impossible event" condition, the screen was rotated upward (exactly as in the habituation trials), which, in the process, obscured the wooden block from the infant's sight. When the screen reached 90 degrees, the wooden block was removed, out of the view of the infant. The screen then continued its downward rotation until it lay flat. The screen was then rotated upward again and the wooden block was replaced, again unbeknownst to the infant, so that it reappeared once more when the screen was being rotated toward the infant. From the infant's perspective, such a series of events (the continuous movement of the screen, despite the presence of an obstacle) should have been impossible and violated the infant's expectation of what should have happened. If the wooden object were real in space and time, the screen should have stopped when it reached it. This, in fact, is what infants did see on some trials (the "possible event"), with the screen stopping at the point at which it should have, given that there was an object on the other side. If the infants believed that the wooden block continued to exist, they

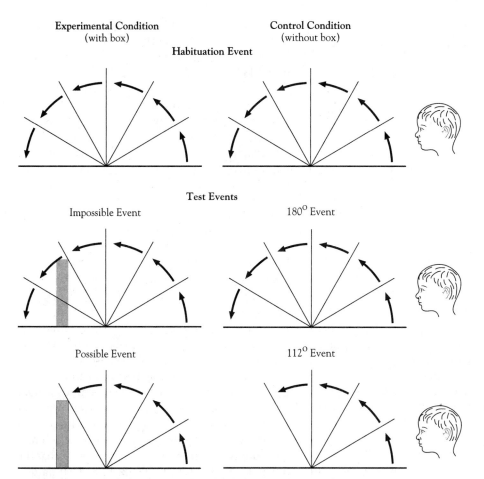

FIGURE 8-5 The habituation and test (dishabituation) events shown to infants in the experimental and control conditions in the object-permanence experiment by Baillargeon. SOURCE: From "Object Permanence in 3½- and 4½-month-old infants," by R. Baillargeon, 1987, *Developmental Psychology, 23*, 655–664. Copyright © 1987 American Psychological Association. Reprinted with permission.

should have shown surprise or increased looking time at the "impossible event" relative to the "possible event." Infants in the control condition saw the same sequence of screen movements but were never shown the wooden block. Thus, these infants had no reason to express surprise. Infants in all conditions received four test trials.

The results of this experiment for the 4.5-month-old infants are graphed in Figure 8-6. As can be seen, the infants in the experimental condition

looked significantly longer at the "impossible event" than at the "possible event." For the experimental infants, there was apparently nothing surprising about the "possible event," but they knew that something was amiss when the screen failed to stop. No differences in looking time were found for the infants in the control condition. Similar findings were reported for 3.5-month-old infants (Baillargeon, 1987, Experiments 2 and 3; Baillargeon & De Vos, 1991).

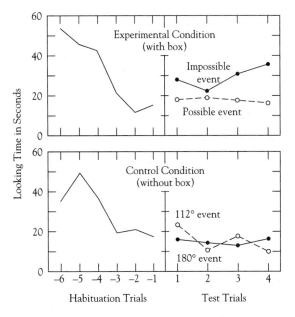

FIGURE 8-6 Looking times of infants in the experimental and control conditions during habituation and test trials in Baillargeon's experiment. Note the increased looking time for the infants in the experimental condition during the test trials for the impossible event. SOURCE: "Object Permanence in 3½- and 4½-month-old infants," by R. Baillargeon, 1987, *Developmental Psychology*, *23*, 655–664. Copyright © 1987 American Psychological Association. Reprinted with permission.

The most straightforward interpretation of these results is that the infants believed that the block continued to exist even though it was out of their sight, and they were surprised when the screen failed to stop. Their performance in the "impossible event" condition reflects not only a knowledge of the permanence of objects, but also a knowledge that one solid object cannot pass through another (see discussion of solidarity earlier).

Other research using looking-time measures has shown that 5-month-olds code the spatial location of hidden objects (Newcombe, Huttenlocher, & Learmonth, 1999). For instance, babies watched as an object was buried in a sandbox. After a 10-second delay, the object was dug out. This was repeated four times. On the fifth occasion, instead of digging up

the object at the location where it had been hidden, the experimenter dug out the object from a different location (as near as 6 inches from where the first had been hidden). Babies looked significantly longer at these "trick" trials than the previous trials, suggesting that they had coded the specific location of the objects. In a final experiment in this study, infants were not surprised (that is, did not look longer) when a *different object* was retrieved from the sand. This finding suggests that spatiotemporal characteristics may play a central role in defining objects to young infants, with shape and color being unimportant.

One very interesting aspect of the findings of the study by Nora Newcombe and her colleagues (1999) is that toddlers usually fail an analogous hiding task. In this task, toddlers watch as an object is hidden in a sandbox, they then move to the opposite end of the box and are asked to retrieve the object. Not until 21-months of age can children solve this problem reliably (Newcombe et al., 1998), calling into question what exactly are the skills involved in solving these simple spatial tasks (Newcombe, 2002). Maybe the act of moving around the sandbox makes the task too demanding of children's limited mental resources or disrupts their memory, accounting for the discrepancy. Similar to the argument I made earlier about the discrepancy between infants' and toddlers' understanding of support, it is possible that the difference between the implicit and explicit natures of the two tasks is responsible for the different findings. Children may possess an understanding of spatial relations at first only implicitly (Karmiloff-Smith, 1992), with explicit understanding, as reflected by an overt search task, being displayed only later in development.

Is Infants' Object Knowledge Innate?

Knowledge of the constancy, continuity, solidity, and permanence of objects is obvious to adults, but why should it be obvious to 3.5-month-old infants? One interpretation of these findings is that, counter to Piaget, such knowledge is not constructed from earlier knowledge but is part of the mental apparatus with which infants are born. That is, infants come into the world with substantive beliefs (representational innateness) about objects. This *neonativist* perspective was introduced when I described Karmiloff-Smith's theory in Chapter 4. Writing about young infants' knowledge of continuity and solidity, Spelke (1991) proposed that such knowledge "may derive from universal, early-developing capacities to represent and reason about the physical world. These capacities may emerge in all infants whose early growth and experience fall within some normal range. They may enable children to infer how any material body will move in any situation" (pp. 160–161). Spelke and her colleagues (Spelke, 1994; Spelke et al., 1992) have proposed that there are three core principles of innate knowledge about objects that infants possess: *cohesion*, the idea that objects have boundaries and that their components stay connected to one another; *continuity*, the idea that an object moves from one location to another in a continuous path and cannot be in the same place as another object; and *contact*, the idea that one object must contact another object to make it move. Infants' development of their ideas about cohesion, continuity, and contact develop with experience, but, according to Spelke, babies possess *core knowledge* (representational innateness) about these domains from birth.

A related idea is that infants do not possess innate beliefs about objects but, rather, come into the world with highly constrained mechanisms for dealing with objects (architectural innateness). This perspective can still be considered one of neonativism, for it suggests specific constraints that make it easier for the infant to learn. But it is *processes*, rather than knowledge per se, that are innate. This is a type of "starting-state" nativism as proposed by Alison Gopnik and Andrew Meltzoff (1997) in their theory theory discussed in Chapter 4, and reflects Baillargeon's perspective (Baillargeon, 1994; Baillargeon et al., 1995). According to Baillargeon, infants initially form a preliminary all-or-none concept about a phenomenon. Only later, with experience, is this concept modified and results in an adult understanding.

Not everyone believes that the new research findings truly reflect advanced symbolic functioning or innate knowledge, of any type. For example, Kurt Fischer and Thomas Bidell (1991) argue that any particular infant skill should not be viewed in isolation, but in the context of overall development. Rather than asking, for instance, when infants "really" have object permanence, Fischer and Bidell suggest that developmental researchers should ask more fruitful questions, including these: "What is the developmental sequence of object knowledge from earliest infancy through early childhood? How is the development of this sequence related to developments in other domains? How is it constrained by the nature of perceptual and sensorimotor processes, which are partly regulated by the genome, and by environmental inputs? How are such constraints evident at various points in developmental sequences?" (1991, pp. 223–224). These are similar to the arguments Marshall Haith (1993) made regarding infant perceptual abilities (see Chapter 7).

On a more fundamental level, Richard Bogartz and his colleagues (Bogartz & Shinskey, 1998; Bogartz, Shinskey, & Speaker, 1997) argued that it is not necessary to attribute innate knowledge of physical objects to account for the findings of studies that use infants' looking behavior as an indication of what they know. Bogartz and his colleagues "assume that young infants cannot reason, draw inferences, or have beliefs" (1997, p. 411) and "that the infant does not enter the world with [knowledge of objects] nor does it acquire such knowledge of physical laws in the first 6 months of life" (p. 412).

How, then, can one explain the data if there are no innate conceptual or processing constraints? Bogartz and his colleagues suggest that young infants come into the world with a set of mechanisms for processing perceptual information and that infants acquire knowledge of objects through perceptual experience (much as Piaget proposed). The nature of perceptual processing produces looking patterns that Baillargeon, Spelke, and others interpret as "innate knowledge." According to Bogartz and his colleagues, infants' perceptual processing "consists of analysis of the immediate representations of events, the construction in associative memory of the transformations of these immediate representations, abstraction of their forms, and the comparison of immediate perceptual representations to the representations stored in memory" (Bogartz et al., 1997, p. 411). All this processing takes time. In habituation/dishabituation tasks, infants look at familiar stimuli because it takes time to store memory representations. Novel events (that is, impossible events in the studies described earlier) take even more time because initial encoding of the stimuli needs to be done. Infants show a preference for looking at the novel (impossible) over the familiar (habituated and possible) event simply because more processing is required to make sense of the former than the latter event. There is no need to postulate innate knowledge of physical laws, only laws about how infant perception and memory work.

There has been much debate about the nature of early spatial cognition. Some researchers propose that some important aspects are domain-specific and modular in nature, implying a form of nativism (Spelke & Newport, 1998); others propose that processes, rather than core knowledge, are innate (Gopnik & Meltzoff, 1997); and still others propose that infants' and toddlers' spatial skills are influenced by more domain-general mechanisms, perhaps the same that influence the processing of quantitative information (Newcombe, 2002). Although I believe that humans, and others species, have been prepared by evolution for processing spatial information (a form of architectural constraints), such constraints require substantial input from the environment to develop properly during early childhood.

Spatial Cognition Beyond Infancy

Spatial cognition shows substantial improvements during the preschool years and into the school years. These more advanced forms of spatial cognition are sometimes divided into three broad categories: *spatial orientation, spatial visualization,* and *object and location memory.* **Spatial orientation** refers to how people understand the placement of objects in space with themselves as the reference point. Spatial-orientation tasks include those in which participants are asked to distinguish geographic directions in an unfamiliar lo-

cale or to draw their way from point A to point B on a map. In contrast, **spatial-visualization** tasks involve visual operations, such as mentally rotating a figure or adjusting a tilted object to bring it to an upright position. **Object and location memory** is tested by having participants remember objects and their location from a spatial array. Both developmental and gender differences have been reported in each of these areas.

Spatial Orientation

Age differences in spatial orientation are found reliably on a variety of tasks. For example, Linda Anooshian and Douglas Young (1981) asked three groups of children—first- and second-graders, fourth- and fifth-graders, and seventh- and eighth-graders— to point a telescope at landmarks surrounding their own neighborhoods. Even the youngest children performed well above chance on this task, indicating that they had formed a spatial representation of their neighborhoods.

In other research, children are required to form "cognitive maps" to find their way around an area or to construct a model of an area. In one study, kindergarten, second-grade, and fifth-grade children walked repeatedly through a large model town consisting of buildings, streets, railroad tracks, and trees (Herman & Siegel, 1978). Following the walks, the children were asked to re-create the layout from memory. Performance increased with age. Similar age-related improvements in the formation of cognitive maps have been found between 3- and 5.5-year-old children, although the spatial representations were poorly integrated for both the younger and older children (Herman, Shiraki, & Miller, 1985).

Rather than forming cognitive maps from one's experience, other research has examined children's abilities to use two-dimensional maps to locate objects in space. In general, preschoolers have a difficult time using maps, even when dealing with familiar environments (Liben & Yekel, 1996), although the ability to use maps improves by age 6 (Sandberg & Huttenlocher, 2001). In an interesting study examining preschool children's ability to use spatial information (that is, simple maps) to locate hidden objects,

David Uttal and his colleagues (2001) showed 3-, 4-, and 5-year-old children a 10- x 10-foot yellow carpet with 27 cups placed on the it. Children were told that stickers would be hidden under some of the cups, and they would be asked to find them. To help them find the stickers, they would be shown on a map where the stickers were hidden. There were 10 trials, with one sticker hidden on each trial. Children were given three tries per trial to locate the sticker. After explaining the task, the experimenter took the child behind a screen while an assistant hid a sticker, and she showed the child a map of the carpet and cups. The map consisted of 27 small circles corresponding to the location of each cup. For half the children, lines were drawn connecting the circles, whereas no lines were drawn for the other children. Figure 8-7 shows the maps used in this experiment, along with the location where each of the stickers was hidden. As you can see, the cups were placed in such a way that, when the lines are connected, there is an unmistakable image of a dog. Would children be able to take advantage of this information to help them use the map to find the stickers? The answer is yes, at least for the oldest children. Correct performance increased with age, but seeing the lines on the map only helped the 5-year-olds, who performed significantly better when the dots were connected than not. This effect was not significant for the two groups of younger children. (In fact, the 3-year-olds actually performed slightly better in the no-lines condition.) In a later experiment, the dog image was replaced with a random array of dots, so that connecting them produced no familiar image (see Figure 8-8). Here, 5-year-olds performed no better when having the lines drawn as not, indicating that it was not just having lines drawn, per se, that made the differences but, rather, seeing a familiar picture that they could use as a guide was responsible for their improved performance. In other words, seeing the dog helped children to identify and think about relations among the elements of the map. The research shows that even 5-year-olds (but not 3- and 4-year-olds) are capable of using maps to locate objects under some conditions.

Maps not only serve as a way of evaluating children's spatial ability, but using maps may also affect how children think of large-scale space. That is,

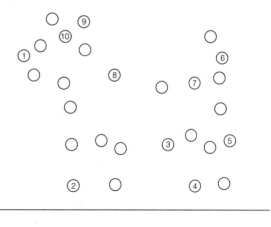

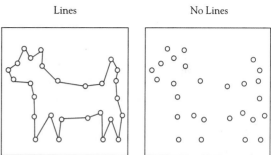

FIGURE 8-7   The pattern of cups on the 10- x 10-foot carpet and the hiding location of each sticker (top), and the maps children saw in the Lines and No Lines conditions, Experiment 1. Note that the configuration of dots produces an image of a dog. SOURCE: Uttal, D. H., Gregg, V. H., Tan, L. S., Chamberlin, M. H., & Sines, A. (2001). Connecting the dots: Children's use of a systematic figure to facilitate mapping and search. *Developmental Psychology, 37,* 338–350. Copyright © 2001 by the American Psychological Association. Reprinted with permission.

maps can be viewed as a *tool of intellectual adaptation* that a culture affords its members to think about important aspects of their environments (Vygotsky, 1978, see Chapter 3). The relation between maps and spatial development is thus reciprocal: children's developing spatial skills influences their ability to use maps, but the very process of using maps influences spatial cognition (Uttal, 2000). According to Uttal, "Maps provide a cognitive tool that helps children extend their reasoning about space in a new way. Over time, children can internalize the tool and

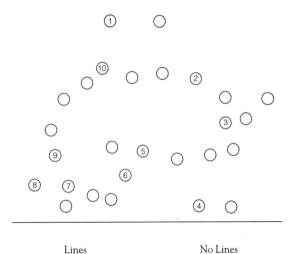

Lines   No Lines

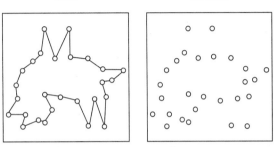

FIGURE 8-8 The pattern of cups on the 10-foot-square carpet and the hiding location of each sticker (top), and the maps children saw in the Lines and No Lines conditions, Experiment 3. Note that the configuration of dots produces no coherent image. SOURCE: Uttal, D. H., Gregg, V. H., Tan, L. S., Chamberlin, M. H., & Sines, A. (2001). Connecting the dots: Children's use of a systematic figure to facilitate mapping and search. *Developmental Psychology, 37,* 338–350. Copyright © 2001 by the American Psychological Association. Reprinted with permission.

think about space in map-like ways, even if they are not looking at a map at the time" (2000, p. 249). Tentative evidence for Uttal's position is found in an experiment in which 4- to 7-year-old children were asked to learn which of six animals went with each of six rooms in a life-sized playhouse (Uttal & Wellman, 1989). One group of children was given a simple map, with each room represented by a box that contained a picture of the animal. A control group of children was shown a series of flash cards, with the picture of one animal on each of six cards. Children in both the map and control groups learned perfectly the six animals that went with the playhouse. They then were walked through the playhouse and were asked to anticipate which animal would be found in each room. Although both groups of children had learned perfectly the list of animals, the children in the map group performed significantly better than children in the control group. Why did the children in the map group do so well? Uttal and Wellman argued that the experience with the map changed the way they represented space, allowing them to more easily see spatial relationships among elements. Thus, consistent with arguments made previously in this chapter, the development of spatial cognition is influenced not only by endogenous (internal, or maturational) factors, but also by children's experience in the real world. In this case, a cultural invention, that is maps, not only permits children (and adults) to apply their spatial skills to solve problems, but also influences how those skills develop.

Spatial Visualization

Age differences have also been reported for spatial-visualization tasks. For example, tasks that purportedly assess **field dependence/field independence (FD/FI)** involve such analytic/spatial skills. The concept of field dependence/field independence has its origins in adult perception. Herman Witkin and his associates (Witkin et al., 1962; Witkin et al., 1954) showed that some people have a difficult time perceiving component parts of a visual field separately from the whole. Witkin referred to such people as *field dependent*. In contrast, others could analyze the perceptual field into its discrete parts. Witkin referred to these people as *field independent*. An example of a task that assesses the FD/FI dimension is one in which a person must find a figure embedded in a larger picture. A couple of items from the Children's Embedded Figures Test are shown in Figure 8-9. Field-independent people discover the hidden object much more quickly than field-dependent people do. In other words, the perception of field-dependent

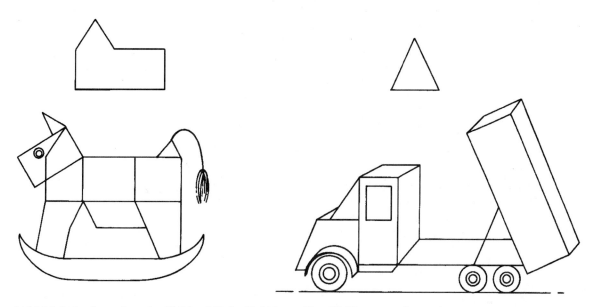

FIGURE 8-9 Items from the Children's Embedded Figures Test. Children are to locate the geometric form on top within the figure below. SOURCE: From *Children's Embedded Figures Test,* by S. A. Karp and N. Konstadt. Copyright © 1971 by Consulting Psychologists Press, Inc. Reprinted with permission from the author.

people is influenced by the entire perceptual field, so that they find it difficult to analyze any specific component within the field. Field-independent people are less affected by the global characteristics of a display and find it easier to discover the individual parts that make up the whole.

There is a general developmental trend toward increasing field independence—older children and adults take less time to identify objects in the Embedded Figures Test than younger children do (Witkin, Goodenough, & Karp, 1967). Witkin and his colleagues (1967) reported longitudinal results from a sample of males, followed from age 10 to 24 years. They found a steady change toward field independence from 10 to 17 years, with performance stabilizing at this point, showing no further improvement when participants were tested at 24 years of age. Although people become more field independent with age, reflecting changes in developmental function, individual differences in FD/FI are relatively stable over time, with field-dependent children becoming field-dependent adults (Witkin et al., 1967).

Developmental differences have been reported for other tests of spatial visualization. For example, robust age differences are found on *mental rotation tasks* (see Figure 8-10), in which a person must mentally rotate a visual stimulus to determine if it matches another stimulus (see Halpern, 1992). Another relatively simple test of spatial visualization that has consistently yielded gender differences is Piaget and Inhelder's (1967) water-level problem (see Figure 8-11). In this problem, children are shown tipped bottles and asked to imagine the water level if the bottles were half-filled with water. The correct answer involves knowledge of the horizontality of the water level; that is, the participants should indicate (usually by drawing a line) that the level of the water would be horizontal across the bottle. In Piaget and Inhelder's work, preoperational children had difficulty with the task, often indicating that the water level would be parallel to the bottom of the bottle and not parallel to the ground. Although Piaget and Inhelder's data suggested that knowledge of invariant horizontality develops in late childhood, other

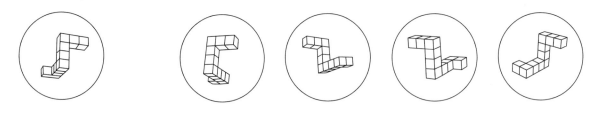

Correct answers: The first and second

FIGURE 8-10 Example of problem from the Vandenberg Test of Mental Rotation. Participants must select alternatives from the four on the right that are the same as the one on the left, only rotated (Correct answers: the first and second). SOURCE: Vandenberg, S. G., & Kuse, A. R. Mental rotations, a group test of three-dimensional spatial visualization. *Perceptual and Motor Skills,* 1978, 47, 599–604. © Perceptual and Motor Skills 1978.

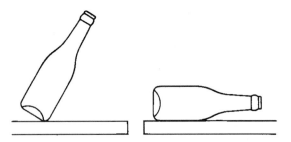

FIGURE 8-11 A water-level problem. Participants are to draw the water line in each bottle to represent how it would look if it were half-filled with water.

researchers noted that many adolescents and young adults continue to have difficulty with the concept (see Kalichman, 1988; Vasta & Liben, 1996).

Object and Location Memory

Several authors have proposed that memory for spatial location, or object and location memory, is an early developing ability, and, unlike other aspects of spatial cognition, one that shows relatively little change with age. I admit that this is a controversial claim, for most studies examining age differences in spatial memory find differences, although the magnitude of such differences is relatively small (Park &

James, 1983; Schumann-Hengsteler, 1992). But some studies report no developmental differences. For instance, a study by Norman Ellis, Eileen Katz, and Jeffrey Williams (1987) used recall and reconstruction tasks with people ranging in age from 3 years to elderly adults. Ellis and his colleagues reported no developmental improvements in memory for location, with the exception of *higher* performance for 3- and 4-year-old children in one condition. Other research has examined the performance of children and adults on the game *Concentration* (or *Memory*), where participants must find matches to cards placed face down on a table by turning over two cards on each turn (Baker-Ward & Ornstein, 1988; Schumann-Hengsteler, 1989). Children as young as 5 years of age performed as well as adults and sometimes better, at least on early trials when strategies were less important. Older children and adults eventually outperformed the younger children, but the location memories for young children were nonetheless impressive, and age differences were substantially less than those found on most other memory tasks (Schneider & Pressley, 1997).

Thus, we cannot say that location memory is *better* in younger than older children or that there are no development improvements in such memory. We can say, however, that young children have impressive memories for the location of objects and that this memory skill seems, at least, to undergo less development than other memory abilities.

Gender Differences in Spatial Cognition

Although the job of developmentalists is to describe and explain age-related changes in functioning, sometimes reliable individual differences are also found and pique researchers' attention as much, or more, than developmental difference. This has been the case for spatial cognition. In fact, some of our culture's most familiar gender stereotypes relate to spatial cognition. Women, for example, are alleged to have difficulty using maps, especially when one must turn the map (that is, mentally rotate it) to find where one is and where one wants to go. (This disability afflicts some men, your author included. I do just fine as long as both the map and I are facing north. But rotation of either the map or me leaves me confusing my left from my right. This less-than-exceptional mental rotation ability had me heading west to the outskirts of the Everglades at midnight one evening, when my destination was east near the Atlantic Ocean.) And men are supposed victims of the "Where's the mayonnaise, Honey?" syndrome, in which they stare into a crowded refrigerator searching futilely for the mayonnaise, which their wives find with little difficulty. (I plead guilty to this fault, as well.) Do these stereotypes have any basis in reality? Like all stereotypes, they do not describe the abilities of all men or all women (or perhaps even most of them), but does the research literature suggest at least a general trend in that direction?

In general, the answer is yes, with many of the gender differences being found early and persisting into adulthood. For example, gender differences in spatial orientation are frequently found, favoring males, beginning in the preschool years (Anooshian & Young, 1981; Levine et al., 1999). Males tend to perform better than females do on tasks that involve manipulating spatial relations (Baenninger & Newcombe, 1995; Casey, 1996), finding their way through physical (or virtual) environments (Moffat, Hampson, & Hatzipantelis, 1998; Silverman et al., 2000), and making (Matthews, 1987) and using (Dabbs et al., 1998; Gibbs & Wilson, 1999) maps. Gender differences are not always found at all ages,

however, and other studies have failed to find any differences between males and females on spatial-orientation tasks (Allen, Kirasic, & Beard, 1989; Uttal et al., 2001).

One explanation for gender differences, when they are found, has to do with familiarity with the environment. For example, Nancy Hazen (1982) controlled for preschool children's exposure to the test environment and reported no gender differences in a spatial-orientation task. Thus, although age differences are robust on spatial-orientation tasks, gender differences are less so, but when gender differences are found, they invariably favor males.

Gender differences are perhaps the greatest on tests of spatial visualization. On the Embedded Figures Tests (see Figure 8-9) girls are more influenced by the background (that is, they are more field dependent) than boys are (Harris, 1978; Witkin et al., 1967). And gender differences favoring males have been reliably found for mental rotation tasks (see Figure 8-10) (Casey et al., 1995), block design tasks (Livesey & Intili, 1996), and Piaget and Inhelder's water-level task (see Figure 8-11) (see Kalichman, 1988; Vasta & Liben, 1996).

Let's take a closer look at the gender differences on the water-level task, which, at first glance, would seem to be a relatively simple problem. Participants are to draw a line on the bottles corresponding to how the water level would look. Performance is evaluated by the extent to which the lines deviate from the horizontal. Although performance for both males and females increases with age, female adolescent and college students consistently draw lines that deviate more from the horizontal than same-aged males do. Early attempts to train women to improve their performance on water-level tasks were not successful (Thomas, Jamison, & Hummel, 1973), although subsequent research demonstrated that female children and adults can improve their performance on horizontality problems when the task demands are modified or when they are given explicit information about the concepts dealt with in the tasks (Liben & Golbeck, 1980, 1984). These findings indicate that females have the ability to construct mature spatial representations and that some of the gender differences on these tasks "reflect males' and females' differential knowledge of the relevant physical phenomena" (Liben & Golbeck, 1984, p. 605).

Hoben Thomas and Geoffrey Turner (1991) examined age and gender differences on the water-level task from a novel perspective. Participants ranged in age from 6.5 years to college age and were given a series of water-level tasks. Although the researchers obtained the typical age and gender differences in task performance, they found that children did not gradually become more competent at this task. Rather, at every age and for both males and females, there were two kinds of performers: those who solved the tasks correctly and those who did not. Thus, age differences were not caused by children becoming increasingly accurate with age but, rather, by age-related changes in the distribution of accurate versus inaccurate performers. That is, individual differences (for both sexes) in performing the water-level task were not a matter of degree but could be better described as a dichotomy between accurate and inaccurate performers. At all age levels, there was a higher proportion of accurate male performers than accurate female performers (see also Sholl & Liben, 1995; Thomas & Lohaus, 1993).

Although gender differences in spatial cognition have been consistently found, the absolute magnitude of those differences is small. One way of evaluating the size of such differences is to conduct a **meta-analysis**—a statistical technique that allows an investigator to evaluate the magnitude of a significant effect across a large number of studies. Janet Hyde (1981) performed such an analysis, reanalyzing the findings of spatial cognition studies initially reviewed by Eleanor Maccoby and Carol Jacklin in 1974. Hyde reported that differences in spatial ability attributed to the gender of the child accounted for less than 5% of the difference in performance. Other meta-analyses have reported similar findings. For example, Marcia Linn and Anne Petersen (1985) reported that only between 1% and 5% of differences in spatial abilities can be attributed to gender, depending on the particular task. One exception Linn and Petersen noted was mental rotation, in which males of all ages performed better than females did. Robert Rosenthal and Donald

FIGURE 8-12 The initial stimulus array shown to participants in a test of object and location memory. SOURCE: "Sex Differences in Spatial Abilities: Evolutionary Theory and Data," by I. Silverman and M. Eals. In J. H. Barkow, L. Cosmides, and J. Tooby (Eds.), *The Adapted Mind: Evolutionary Psychology and the Generation of Culture*, p. 537. Copyright © 1992 by Oxford University Press. Used by permission of Oxford University Press, Inc.

Rubin (1982) similarly reported small differences between the sexes in their meta-analysis, but also reported that the size of effect diminished across the years, with females showing a substantial gain in cognitive performance (relative to males) in recent years. One exception to this trend is mental rotation, which has shown no diminution in the gender difference over the years (Masters & Soares, 1993).

Not all spatial ability tasks favor males. As the "Where's the mayonnaise?" syndrome suggests, females seem to be better at tasks that assess memory for location. In laboratory studies, females are better than males are at remembering the locations of each item in an array of objects, with this ability increasing with age for both sexes (Cherney & Ryalls, 1998; Silverman & Eals, 1992). For example, in a series of experiments with participants ranging in age from 8.5 years to college adults, Irwin Silverman and Marion Eals (1992) reported better memory for objects and for object location by females than by males. In several of their experiments, participants were shown an array consisting of a variety of objects, as depicted in Figure 8-12. Sometime later, they were shown a

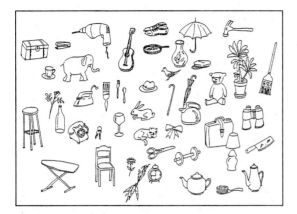

FIGURE 8-13 The stimulus array with objects added. Participants were to cross out all items not found in the original array. SOURCE: "Sex Differences in Spatial Abilities: Evolutionary Theory and Data," by I. Silverman and M. Eals. In J. H. Barkow, L. Cosmides, and J. Tooby (Eds.), *The Adapted Mind: Evolutionary Psychology and the Generation of Culture*, p. 538. Copyright © 1992 by Oxford University Press. Used by permission of Oxford University Press, Inc.

larger array, as depicted in Figure 8-13, and were to cross out all items that were not in the original array. At all ages tested, females performed better than males. When asked about the correct location of items (for example, where in an array a particular item was originally located), females again performed better than males, although differences were not significant until adolescence (see also Kail & Siegel, 1977). For what it's worth, as part of a class assignment, I regularly ask my students to test males and females of different ages using Silverman and Eals' stimuli. And although there is clearly overlap in the distributions, in every semester in which students have performed these informal experiments, females have always outperformed males.

Explaining Gender Differences in Spatial Cognition

How can these gender differences in spatial ability be explained? Myriad factors have been proposed to explain these differences, including differential experi-

ence for males and females, genetics, prenatal hormones, and evolutionary accounts (see articles in Halpern, 1995). Not surprisingly, the most sophisticated explanations consider interactions of biological and experiential factors during development. For example, the **bent-twig model,** originally proposed by Julia Sherman (1978), posits that males are biased from early in life toward activities involving spatial cognition, such as block building, carpentry, and activities involving throwing and catching objects. Because of these biases, they spend many more hours over childhood in these activities than girls. Thus, whatever gender differences in spatial abilities existed early in life attributable to biological factors, the differential experience of boys relative to girls in activities emphasizing spatial cognition increase this difference. For example, differences in children's abilities to form cognitive maps of large-scale environments is associated with differences in experience with the environment (Hazen, 1982); across a wide range of cultures, boys tend to have a larger exploration range than girls, and, as a result, may acquire more information about their physical surroundings than girls do (Matthews, 1992).

Research examining the "differential-experience" portion of the bent-twig hypothesis has shown that spatial abilities in women are related to personality measures of masculinity (Newcombe & Dubas, 1992; Signorella, Jamison, & Krupa, 1989). One reason for the relationship between masculine personality characteristics and spatial abilities might have to do with the types of activities girls engage in (Baenninger & Newcombe, 1995). For example, Newcombe and her colleagues found that differences in spatial experience accounted for observed differences in spatial performance (Newcombe, Bandura, & Taylor, 1983). They created a list of everyday activities that might occur in a population of high school and college students. In the first part of the study, college students were asked to classify the activities as masculine, feminine, or neutral. The raters typically selected those tasks judged to have high spatial content as masculine and as having more male participants (see Table 8-1). Subsequently, the researchers found small but significant gender differences among college students on a psychometric test with strong spatial components.

TABLE 8-1 Examples of masculine, neutral, and feminine activities.

Masculine	Neutral	Feminine
touch football	bowling	figure skating
baseball	softball	field hockey
basketball	advanced tennis	gymnastics
darts	table tennis	ballet
hunting	diving	disco dancing
skateboarding	drawing	embroidery
shooting pool	sculpting	knitting
car repair	photography	baton twirling
electrical circuitry	navigating in a car	tailoring
sketching house plans	marching in a band	touch typing

SOURCE: Adapted from Newcombe, Bandura, & Taylor, 1983

Newcombe and her colleagues also reported a significant correlation between spatial activities and aptitude scores, particularly for females; that is, the more spatial activities one engages in, the greater one's spatial ability is likely to be (see also Newcombe & Dubas, 1992; Signorella et al., 1989).

Working with preschool children, Jane Connor and Lisa Serbin (1977) similarly reported differences in spatial play activities between boys and girls. These researchers further reported that the amount of boys' spatial play correlated significantly with their performance on the Block Design subtest of the Wechsler Intelligence Scale for Children and the Preschool Embedded Figures Test, suggesting that gender differences in play activity are partly responsible for boys' generally greater spatial skills. Although other studies have found smaller differences in spatial play between preschool boys and girls and no significant relation between spatial play and spatial cognition (Caldera et al., 1999), a meta-analysis of published studies through the mid-1990s reported significant relations between children's spatial cognition and locomotor experiences, with these effects being greater during early childhood than during the infancy and toddler periods (Yan, Thomas, & Downing, 1998).

M. Beth Casey presented a very specific version of the bent-twig hypothesis (1996; Casey, Nuttall, & Pezaris, 1999). Casey extended a model originally developed by Marian Annett (1985), which proposed a genetic basis for handedness and brain laterality. According to Annett, most people inherit a "right-shift factor" that causes them to be right handed and to have the language center of the brain located in the left hemisphere. Evidence indicates that females show left-hemisphere dominance more than males do. This greater left-hemisphere dominance influences language abilities positively and spatial abilities negatively. People who inherit two dominant genes for this right-shift factor are said to be *homozygous* for this trait, whereas people who inherit one dominant and one recessive gene for this factor are said to be *heterozygous* for this trait. There is, for some traits, a *heterozygous advantage*; in this case, Annett proposed that people who inherit both the dominant and recessive genes for the right-shift factor (those who are heterozygous for the right-shift factor) should have an advantage in spatial abilities over those who inherit two dominant genes (those who are homozygous for the right-shift factor).

How can one tell if one is hetero- or homozygous for this trait? There is no sure-fire way, but one good estimate is the number of close relatives one has who are right-handers versus left-handers or ambidextrous. People whose close relatives are all right handed are likely homozygous for the right-shift trait and should thus have relatively good verbal skills and relatively poor spatial skills. People who have some close relatives who are not right handed are more likely to be heterozygous for the right-shift factor and, thus, be better at spatial skills.

Casey's model takes Annett's right-shift factor hypothesis and proposes that this genetic predisposition interacts with environmental factors. Specifically, people who are heterozygous for the right-shift factor and who have extensive spatial experience, should have high spatial skills, whereas those who are homozygous for the right-shift factor or those who have minimal spatial experience, should have low spatial ability. She made these predictions specifically for right-handed females and tested her model (which is shown in Figure 8-14) in a series of studies.

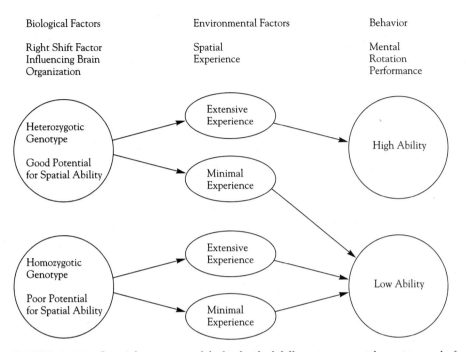

Biological Factors Environmental Factors Behavior

Right Shift Factor Spatial Mental
Influencing Brain Experience Rotation
Organization Performance

FIGURE 8-14 Casey's bent-twig model of individual differences on spatial cognition tasks for right-handed females. SOURCE: Casey, M. B. (1996). Understanding individual differences in spatial ability within females: A nature/nurture interactionist framework. *Developmental Review, 16,* 241–260. Used by permission of Elsevier.

In one study, Casey and Mary Brabeck (1989) evaluated mental rotation performance in a group of college women (some with and some without nonright-handed close relatives) who were either math or science majors (and thus presumed to have substantial spatial experience) with college women who were not math or science majors (and thus presumed to have fewer spatial experiences). Casey and Brabeck's prediction was that heterozygous women with more spatial experience (math and science majors with some close relatives who were not right handed) would perform better on the mental rotation task than all other groups, and this was what they found. There was no difference in spatial abilities among the homozygous, heterozygous, or left-handed women who were not math or science majors; for the math and science majors, the left-handers and the homozygous right-handers performed comparably, and both did worse than the heterozygous, right-handed women did.

Casey's model has its critics (Halpern, 1996), but even her critics believe that the bent-twig model, in general form, is an appropriate one for investigating differences both between and within genders for spatial (and mathematical) differences.

An Evolutionary Hypothesis of Gender Differences in Spatial Cognition

Although I am confident that some complex combination of biological and environment factors, such as those proposed by the bent-twig model, will account for most gender differences in spatial cognition, another level of analysis might prove useful: an evolutionary approach. One hypothesis is that the patterns of gender difference we find (better male performance on some tasks, better female performance on others) reflect our evolutionary history and the different demands placed on males and females during the past million years or so (Geary, 1998; Silverman & Eals, 1992). In small groups of hunters and gatherers, men were likely responsible for hunting large game, requiring accurate throwing, eye-hand coordination, and long-distance travel, which required spatial orientation skills. Women most likely stayed near camp, where they tended to children and gathered food, the latter requiring fine-motor capabilities and the recognition of small perceptual differences (to distinguish between edible and poisonous berries, for example), which relate to object-location memory. The different evolutionary pressures led to different spatial skills that remain with us today (better spatial visualization abilities for males and better object and location memory for females).

It is admittedly difficult to test such hypotheses, eliminating other interpretations of the data. Nevertheless, a number of research projects have attempted to do just that, examining different types of spatial ability and comparing the patterns to what would be predicted from the theory. Although most published research investigating this issue has presented results consistent with the evolutionary hypothesis (Dabbs et al., 1998; Silverman et al., 2000), it is still a bit early to state that the gender differences we see in spatial cognition have been selected over the course of human evolution. Yet, these are provocative ideas, and testing them, regardless of whether they are found to be supported by the data or not, will lead to an improved understanding of spatial cognition, its development, and the nature of gender differences.

The Development of Spatial Abilities in Perspective

On the one hand, we should be quite amazed at the impressive level of spatial cognition children are able to demonstrate at a very early age. Even newborns have some notion of the constancy of objects, and by 6 months babies seem to have acquired the rudiments of what objects are all about—their continuity, solidity, need for support, and even their permanence in time and space. Yet, we also saw how changing the task demands leads to a very different impression of what young children seem to know about objects. Two-year-olds, when administered tasks that require a more explicit response than the looking-time behavior required of infants, often seem to lack the very knowledge their 6-month-old counterparts display. Thus, there is much development of spatial cognition going on during the first few years of life, although I am convinced that it is based on a system prepared by eons of evolution and these basic abilities will emerge pretty much the same and on the same developmental schedule for most members of the species, given a species-typical environment. Spatial cognition gets much more complicated than dealing with the physical properties of objects, and seemingly is affected more by the experiences that children have, as reflected by the use of maps and possibly gender differences on spatial orientation, visualization, and object-location tasks. Thus, spatial cognition serves as a good model for cognition development in general. Abilities exist on a variety of levels (implicit and explicit), infants are "prepared" to process some classes of information more readily than others, and age-related changes in these abilities are significantly influenced by experience, some of which all normal humans will have and others of which will be unique to individuals (or individuals within a culture).

Let me provide one last thought about spatial cognition. Although we may not easily admit it, most of us are "specieists," believing that there is something special about humans compared with other animals. Although I think such a position is mostly justified when discussing cognition, that does not mean that every aspect of our cognition is superior to those of other animals. Actually, a point worth keeping in mind is that animals have evolved cognitive and behavioral abilities well suited to their particular ecological niches, and ranking the abilities of one species from high to low relative to others is a meaningless endeavor. Yet, when we use humans as the standard, as we specieists are sometimes wont to do, we are often surprised at how wimpy our abilities are compared with those of supposedly "inferior" animals. This is the case for spatial cognition. For example, the migratory behavior of many birds, insects, fish, and reptiles is far more complex than that shown by the typical human. And although people (particularly women) may be able to remember the location of many objects situated in space, this pales in comparison with the spatial memory of the Clark's nutcracker, birds that store seeds in the fall and return months later to retrieve them. Observations of these birds have demonstrated that they can store as many as 33,000 seeds in more than 6,600 locations and recover most of them months later (Hauser, 2000). So just as we need to keep in perspective the impressive abilities that infants seem to posses, it is sometimes good to realize that *Homo sapiens* are not always at the top of the heap when it comes to cognition.

Summary

Spatial cognition refers to the processing of visual information in terms of relative to spatial relations. *Depth perception* is affected by infants' ability to fixate both eyes on the same target (*bifoveal fixation*), which develops within the first three months. Research using the visual cliff demonstrates that crawling infants will not crawl onto the "deep" side, although the tendency to do so is related to the amount of crawling experience an infant has had. Other research has shown the importance of self-propelled movement in the development of visual perception in infancy.

Even newborns display evidence of *object constancy*, the knowledge that an object remains the same despite changes in the how it is viewed. Evidence has been accumulating for an early understanding of the physical properties of objects in infancy. By using variations of the *violation-of-expectation method*, which is based on habituation/dishabituation procedures, researchers have demonstrated evidence of *object permanence* far earlier than Piaget had proposed. However, in some cases, using tasks tapping explicit cognition, older children fail to show the same knowledge displayed by infants using looking time, challenging the nature of early object knowledge.

Spatial cognition continues to develop during childhood, with age differences being found on tasks of *spatial orientation*, which measure how people understand the placement of objects in space with themselves as the reference point, and *spatial visualization*, which involves the mental manipulations of visual stimuli, such as performing mental rotation, solving embedded-figures problems, and as reflected by performance on *field dependence/field independence (FD/FI)* tasks. Age differences are often smaller on tasks assessing *object and location memory*.

Results from *meta-analyses* have shown that gender differences favoring males are generally (but not always) found on tests of spatial orientation and spatial visualization, and differences favoring females are found on tests of object and location memory. The *bent-twig model* explains gender differences as an interaction between biological and experiential factors. Explanations based on evolutionary psychology have also been proposed to account for some observed gender differences in spatial cognition.

Key Terms and Concepts

spatial cognition
depth perception
bifoveal fixation
object constancy
violation-of-expectation method
object permanence
spatial orientation
spatial visualization
object and location memory
field dependence/field independence (FD/FI)
meta-analysis
bent-twig model

Suggested Readings

Baillargeon, R. (1994). How do infants learn about the physical world? *Current Directions in Psychological Science*, 3, 133–140. Baillargeon, one of the most innovative researchers in the area of infants' object knowledge, presents a review of research examining the development of such knowledge, much of it from her own laboratory.

Casey, M. B. (1996). Understanding individual differences in spatial ability within females: A nature/nurture interactionist framework. *Developmental Review, 16,* 241–260. This article presents the bent-twig hypothesis and reviews research from the author's laboratory testing (and supporting) the hypothesis.

Newcombe, N. S. (2002). The nativist-empiricist controversy in the context of recent research on spatial and quantitative development. *Psychological Science, 13,* 395–401. This article reviews research on spatial cognition in infants and young children and examines the arguments that these early developing abilities are modular in nature and innate, or rather under the influence of more domain-general mechanisms. The question of the nature of infants' and young children's knowledge is central to developmental psychology, and this article does a good job reviewing the arguments and some of the data for two specific contents (spatial and quantitative cognition).

Uttal, D. H. (2000). Seeing the big picture: Map use and the development of spatial cognition. *Developmental Science, 3,* 247–286. In this paper, Uttal reviews some of the research on how people represent and use maps, the development of this ability, and the possible role that using maps may have on the development of spatial cognition.

InfoTrac College Edition

For additional readings, explore InfoTrac College Edition, your online library. Go to http://www.infotrac-college.com/wadsworth.

Representation

One of the central issues in cognitive development concerns the nature of **representation.** How do children of different ages represent their world? Age differences in representation have been central to Piagetian and neo-Piagetian theories. For example, Jean Piaget, Kurt Fischer, and Robbie Case each proposed developmental stages in representational abilities, progressing from sensorimotor, through symbolic, to abstract representation, and Annette Karmiloff-Smith proposed developmental differences in the use of implicit and explicit representations, with the central mechanism of her theory being the redescription of representations. Information-processing approaches have traditionally been less concerned about stages of representation but have nonetheless held that how children represent information influences subsequent processing. For example, Charles Brainerd and Valerie Reyna's fuzzy-trace theory holds that information is represented along a verbatim-to-fuzzy continuum, and how any particular event is encoded will affect how it is remembered and used to solve problems.

In this chapter, I examine different aspects of children's developing abilities to symbolically represent their worlds. I begin with infancy, where there is much debate about when and to what extent infants can use symbols. The remainder of the chapter focuses on changes in representational abilities and preferences during childhood, particularly during the preschool years. This includes children's abilities to use external objects such as pictures and models as symbols, distinguishing between appearance and reality and between reality and fantasy, and differences in how children classify objects.

Mental Representation Through Infancy

The transition from the curious, hands-on-everything toddler to the contemplative, speaking child is a remarkable one indeed. Until very recently, few argued with Piaget's claim that infants represent information differently than do older children. According to Pia-

get, infants during their first 18 months or so represent objects and events by means of self-produced action (including perceptual "action"). They cannot mentally try out a behavior before executing it and cannot make mental contrasts between stimuli. Infants are not capable of symbolic representation until they are 18- to 24-months old. However, during the last two decades, considerable dissent has been forming concerning the symbolic abilities of infants, and I will explore some of this research in the sections to follow. But first, let's look at the changes in representation and behavior that Piaget and others observed beginning late in the second year of life.

Expressions of the Symbolic Function

According to Piaget, the **symbolic** (or, more properly, the **semiotic**) **function** has its origins in sensorimotor operations. This view is consistent with Piaget's epigenetic and constructivist positions, discussed in Chapter 4, which posit that every form of cognition is constructed from earlier, more primitive functioning. The symbolic function is expressed through a variety of mechanisms, including **deferred imitation,** language, **symbolic play,** and **mental imagery.**

Piaget's observations of *deferred imitation* were discussed in Chapter 4. Deferred imitation refers to observing a model and imitating the model's behavior after some significant period. To do this requires not only that children pay attention to a model but also that they store a mental representation of the target behavior and retrieve that representation from memory at the appropriate time. This, stated Piaget, requires the use of symbols, which is not usually seen until about 18 months. More recent research on deferred imitation, suggesting a much earlier onset than proposed by Piaget, will be discussed later in this chapter.

Language is the most obvious form of the symbolic function. Although most children start uttering individual words by 10 to 12 months, not until 18 months or so do they put two words together into simple sentences. Piaget recognized language as a useful means by which people express their knowledge. But he was firm in his belief that we use language *because* we are symbolic, and not vice versa. In other words, language is a symptom of the symbolic function and not its cause. Language development and the developmental relation between language and thought are the topics of Chapter 11.

Symbolic play is basically the game of pretending and was discussed briefly in Chapter 3. The parents of most 2-year-olds can give examples of symbolic play. The 18-month-old who holds his mother's shoe to his ear and says "Hello" or the 2-year-old who feeds her doll imaginary cereal and scolds her for playing with her food, for example, are endearing to adults and reflect a child's increasingly sophisticated cognitive system.

Mental imagery is the internal representation of an external event. Although it is most easily thought of in terms of vision, Piaget used imagery to refer to mental representations of information from any sensory modality (for example, hearing or kinesthesia). According to Piaget, mental images are the result of internalized imitation. Imagery is not merely an exact copy of the perception of an object but is an active re-creation of a perception.

Few developmental psychologists would argue with the idea that children's cognition changes drastically toward the symbolic sometime between the ages of about 18 and 30 months of age. But a growing body of evidence suggests that infants and young children are far more sophisticated than Piaget proposed. What Piaget (and millions of parents) observed is real—no one is questioning his observations. But when one looks more carefully—designing experiments to better assess what infants and young children know, not just what they spontaneously show—there is evidence that Piaget underestimated the knowledge and symbolic abilities of the sensorimotor child. To some (Fischer & Bidell, 1991), such evidence reflects only that Piaget had the timetable wrong; the order of stages is still the same, as are the processes underlying development. Others (Gelman & Williams, 1998; Spelke & Newport, 1998) see such evidence as indicating that the process of development is very different from that described by Piaget.

What Do Infants Know?

In this section, I examine some of the evidence for claims of greater knowledge/symbolic ability in infants and toddlers than Piaget recognized. I summarized research on what infants know of objects in the previous chapter. As you will recall, research using looking-time measures (violation of expectation, habituation/dishabituation) has shown that infants possess more knowledge about the physics of objects than Piaget proposed (such as object permanence); however, such knowledge can best be described as *implicit*, and often seems independent from the later *explicit* knowledge of objects displayed by the preschool child. In this section, infants' abilities to imitate and their basic concept of number will be examined. As you'll see, the findings provide interesting and sometimes controversial evidence for symbolic functioning in the preverbal child.

Neonatal Imitation

Research into **neonatal imitation** has generated perhaps more controversy about possible symbolic representation in early infancy than any other topic. Piaget (1962) initially noted that infants do not imitate "invisible gestures" such as facial expressions until about 12 months of age. This observation, and Piaget's description of the development of imitation in general, went unchallenged until a 1977 report by Andrew Meltzoff and M. Keith Moore, demonstrating imitation of facial expressions by 6- to 21-day-old babies. Photo 9-1 shows examples of the facial gestures modeled to infants in this experiment and responses by infants. The number of tongue protrusions and mouth openings that infants made in response to an adult model were counted from video recordings of the sessions and contrasted with the number of each gesture made during the baseline periods (that is, when no gestures were modeled). Meltzoff and Moore reported that infants made significantly more tongue protrusions to the tongue model than to the open-mouth model or during baseline. Similar patterns of results were found for mouth opening. Meltzoff and Moore interpreted

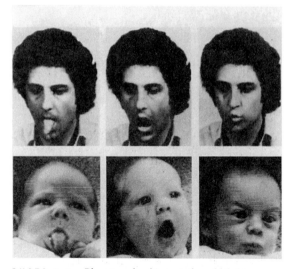

PHOTO 9-1 Photograph of 2- to 3-day-old infants imitating (a) tongue protrusion, (b) mouth opening, and (c) lip protrusion demonstrated by an adult experimenter. SOURCE: Meltzoff, A. N., & Moore, M. K. (1977). Imitation of facial and manual gestures by human neonates. *Science, 198,* 75–78.

these results as clear evidence for selective imitation of facial gestures during the first month. Other researchers have similarly reported imitation of tongue protrusions and other facial gestures in infants during the first two months of life (Legerstee, 1991; Meltzoff & Moore, 1992), with several researchers reporting imitation in newborns (Field et al., 1982; Vinter, 1986) (for a review, see Anisfeld, 1991).

The effect is somewhat elusive, however, and several experimenters have failed to replicate early imitation using procedures similar to those Meltzoff and Moore used (Anisfeld et al., 2001; Kaitz et al., 1988). Moreover, imitation of facial gestures actually declines during the first year of life. For the most-studied facial gesture of tongue protrusion, most investigators who have examined infants of different ages report a peak in imitation sometime during the first two months, followed by a decline within weeks to chance values (Abravanel & Sigafoos, 1984; Jacobson, 1979). This is indeed perplexing, in that we have what appears to be a sophisticated cognitive phenomenon that actually decreases in frequency

over a very brief period. The only exception to this decrease in facial imitation over time was reported by Meltzoff and Moore (1992), who assessed 2- and 3-month-old infants' responses over several trials. They, too, failed to find any evidence of facial imitation on the initial trial but did find imitation by these "older" infants on later trials.

How can neonatal imitation be explained? Meltzoff and Moore (1977, 1985) suggested that modeling effects during early infancy could be attributed to (1) learning; (2) selective imitation, guided by the integration of information from one sensory modality (vision) with information from another (proprioception derived from self-initiated movements); or (3) an innate releasing mechanism, where reflex-like responses are elicited by a specific set of stimuli.

Meltzoff and Moore suggest that learning is an unlikely candidate to explain early imitation. The most compelling reason for rejecting a learning or reinforcement interpretation is that infants only hours old will match certain facial expressions to those of an adult (Field et al., 1982; Vinter, 1986). It is unlikely that such young infants would have had sufficient experience to "learn" these responses.

The second interpretation is the one Meltzoff and Moore favor. They propose that the matching behavior observed in the early weeks of life is true imitation. Newborns are able to coordinate information from two senses. They can visually observe a stimulus, store an abstract representation of that stimulus, and compare it shortly thereafter with a proprioceptive representation (that is, their own movements). This position holds that newborns possess the ability to integrate information from two senses (that is, they possess intermodal integration, see Chapter 7). Meltzoff and Moore (1985) refer to this as **active intermodal mapping.** If one accepts this interpretation, it advances the ability to coordinate two sensory modalities to a period many months earlier than that suggested by Piaget. Such an interpretation is not without some additional empirical support. As discussed in Chapter 7, for example, research has demonstrated tactual-visual transfer of information in 4- to 6-month-olds (Streri & Spelke, 1989), and Meltzoff and Borton (1979) reported visual-tactual integration in infants less than 1 month old.

Yet, if the imitation observed in very young infants is selective and is accomplished by active intermodal mapping, why does it seemingly disappear only months after its appearance? The third alternative, that neonatal matching behavior is attributed to an innate releasing mechanism, attempts to account for the decline in imitation over the first six months (Abravanel & Sigafoos, 1984; Jacobson, 1979). **Innate releasing mechanisms,** or **fixed-action patterns,** are inherited sets of behaviors elicited by specific sets of stimuli without prior environmental experience (Tinbergen, 1951).

The idea that neonatal imitation can best be explained as a fixed-action pattern is at odds not only with Meltzoff and Moore's theorizing but also with Piagetian theory. Piaget's epigenetic approach holds that nothing comes from nothing, that every structure has its genesis in earlier structures. A corollary to this view is that every form of early intelligence serves as preparation for later forms of intelligence. Thus, early reflexes, although they may eventually drop out of the child's repertoire, serve as a basis for later, more advanced cognitive functioning. This is clearly seen in Piaget's description of imitative-like responses during the first three sensorimotor stages. The interpretation of early imitation as a fixed-action pattern is counter to Piaget's view in that this reflexive matching behavior, which has the appearance of a legitimate cognitive function, need not lead to more advanced forms of imitation. Rather, the behavior disappears without specifically preparing the child for subsequent intellectual accomplishments.

What function might neonatal imitation play, then, if it is not preparation for later cognitive development? One interpretation is that such responses play a specific role in survival for the infant at that time, and that time only, and that they disappear when they are no longer needed (Bjorklund, 1987b). R. W. Oppenheim (1981) has referred to such phenomena as **ontogenetic adaptations.** He argues that the young organism lives in a very different world from the adult, requiring different behavioral or neurological organization to cope with life. Such organization might not be the basis for later development but, rather, might be present only for survival at that time and in that specific environment. Sandra Jacobson (1979), for example, suggested that tongue protrusions might be functional in early nursing. I (Bjorklund, 1987b) suggested that the neonatal imitation might play a role in early social development. The matching of adult facial gestures by the infant might help maintain social interaction between the two, with these reflexes declining when infants are better able to intentionally direct their gaze and control their head and mouth movements to social stimulation, somewhere between the second and fourth months of life (Cairns, 1979). In a similar vein, Maria Legerstee (1991) suggested that early imitation serves as a form of prelinguistic communication. Tentative support for these positions was provided by Mikael Heimann (1989), who found a relationship between imitation in newborns and mother-infant social interactions at 3 months of age; infants who showed high levels of neonatal imitation had more social interactions with their mothers three months later.

Meltzoff and Moore (1992) have a different but related idea. They propose that the decrease in facial imitation seen beginning about 2 months of age is caused by the increasing social orientation of infants. Beginning about this time, infants initially respond to people by playing social games. These games make it difficult to discern imitation responses, making it appear that they disappear. However, when proper controls are used, as in Meltzoff and Moore's (1992) repeated-trials procedure, facial imitation is still found in 2- to 3-month-old infants. Meltzoff and Moore (1985) further argue against the view of neonatal imitation as a fixed-action pattern, writing that infants' imitative responses are not strongly stereotyped, as would be expected if they were governed by innate releasing mechanisms. Also, Meltzoff and Moore note that infants have been shown to imitate a large number of different gestures and that it is not reasonable to propose a different reflex for each gesture. (But see Anisfeld et al. [2001], who reported neonatal imitation for some, but not other, facial gestures.)

Deferred Imitation

Initial research by Piaget (1962), and later research by others (McCall, Parke, & Kavanaugh, 1977; Uzgiris &

Hunt, 1975), demonstrated that infants do not display deferred imitation until they are about 18 months old. Piaget believed that deferred imitation is a reflection of the symbolic function. Children must observe a model, store a representation of the model's behavior in memory, and retrieve that memory representation later when attempting to reproduce the behavior. (Recall the example of Piaget's daughter who demonstrated deferred imitation of a temper tantrum at 16 months.) Given his theory, 18 to 24 months is the perfect time to see this behavior.

Evidence that deferred imitation might occur earlier surfaced in 1985, with the publication of papers by Meltzoff (1985) and by Eugene Abravanel and Herbert Gingold (1985). The basic procedure used in these, and later, studies involves showing infants some novel behavior, often with a new toy. For example, an infant may observe a model picking up a dumb-bell-shaped toy and taking one end off in a particular way (Meltzoff, 1988a). Sometime later, the infants are again shown the toy and their behavior is observed. If they show the novel behavior (in this case, taking apart the toy in a specific way) more frequently than do children who are given the toy for the first time, this is good evidence for deferred imitation. In other words, because other children who have never seen the toy before rarely take it apart, the fact that children who have seen it taken apart do so implies that they learned this behavior from watching the model, rather than that taking the toy apart is just something that children normally do when playing with it.

The initial studies by Meltzoff (1985) and Abravanel and Gingold (1985) reported deferred imitation for 12- and 14-month-old infants over delays ranging from 10 minutes to 24 hours. Later research has extended these findings, reporting deferred imitation for 14-month-olds for novel behaviors after delays of one week (Meltzoff, 1988a), after a five-week period for 9-month-olds (Carver & Bauer, 1999), and after 24 hours for 6-month-olds (Collie & Hayne, 1999). Other research has found evidence of deferred imitation in preverbal toddlers for as long as one year (Bauer et al., 2000; Meltzoff, 1995). Levels or quality of deferred imitation are typically greater for older

than for younger infants (Abravenal & Gingold, 1985; Meltzoff, 1985), and few would claim that the imitation abilities of a 12-month-old infant can compare with those of a 20- or 24-month-old child.

Moreover, toddlers will imitate not just adults but also other toddlers and televised models. One study reported deferred imitation (over 2 days) in 14-month-old children who watched the novel behavior of another 14-month-old, indicating the potential role of peers as models for very young children (Hanna & Meltzoff, 1993). Another study found deferred imitation (over 24 hours) in 12- to 18-month-olds for behaviors modeled by an adult on television (Meltzoff, 1988b). This latter finding indicates that young children can learn from two-dimensional displays and that toddlers can potentially acquire new behaviors from viewing television.

Is deferred imitation a type of explicit, or declarative, memory? Recall from Chapter 5, *explicit* memory is contrasted with *implicit* memory. The former represents a deliberate attempt to remember and is potentially available to conscious awareness, whereas the latter is often referred to as "memory without awareness." Most researchers who have investigated deferred imitation in older infants believe it to be a form of nonverbal explicit memory (Bauer, 1997; Collie & Hayne, 1999). If so, it would be using the same type of representational system used by older children on verbal memory tasks (see Chapter 10 on memory).

How can one tell the difference between explicit and implicit memory in preverbal children? Perhaps one can't definitively, but support for this argument comes from a study of adult amnesiacs. These people are unable to perform typical declarative memory tasks (memory with awareness) but do perform well on implicit memory tasks (memory without awareness). How do they perform on deferred imitation tasks? Just like they do on the declarative memory tasks—they fail them (McDonough et al., 1995). These findings suggest that deferred imitation tasks tap the same memory system as do declarative tasks used with older children (for example, "Tell me what you had for breakfast this morning") and "that the neurological systems underlying long-term recall are present, in at least rudimentary form, by the beginning of the second year of life" (Schneider & Bjorklund, 1998, p. 474).

Early Number Concepts

Perhaps one of the more surprising, and still controversial, claims made recently about infants' symbolic abilities is that 5-month-olds can effectively add and subtract simple sets of numbers. It has been known for some time that very young infants can detect differences in numerosity—that is, tell the difference between two arrays that differ in the number of objects they contain (Antell & Keating, 1983; van Loosbroek & Smitsman, 1990). But this is far removed from the claim that infants can perform simple addition and subtraction.

How would one ever test such a claim? Karen Wynn (1992) was the first to assess this possibility, using the violation-of-expectation method that has been so useful in assessing infants' cognitive abilities. The logic behind Wynn's procedure is similar to that used by René Baillargeon (1987) discussed in the previous chapter. Baillargeon showed infants "possible" and "impossible" events concerning the physical existence of objects and inferred their knowledge of object permanence based on their attention to the various events. In Wynn's experiment, 5-month-old infants were shown a sequence of events that involved the addition or subtraction of elements. Two of these sequences are shown in Figure 9-1. One sequence (the "possible outcome") led to the conclusion that 1 + 1 = 2; the other sequence (the "impossible outcome") led to the conclusion that 1 + 1 = 1. Infants sat in front of a stage and watched as one object was placed in it (step 1 in Figure 9-1). A screen was then raised, hiding the object (step 2 in Figure 9-1). The infant then watched as a second object was placed behind the screen (steps 3 and 4 in Figure 9-1). The screen was then lowered, revealing either two objects (the "possible outcome") or one object (the "impossible outcome"). If infants have some primitive concept of addition, they should be surprised and thus spend more time looking at the "impossible outcome." This was exactly what oc-

curred, both for the addition problem shown in Figure 9-1 and for a simple subtraction problem (2 − 1 = 1). Others have replicated these findings (Simon, Hespos, & Rochat, 1995; but see Wakeley, Rivera, & Langer, 2000 for an exception).

How can these results best be interpreted? Infants seem not to be making only a perceptual discrimination between two arrays (that is, telling the difference between an array with one item in it and another with two). Rather, when they watch as one item is added to another behind a screen, they expect to see two items when the screen is dropped. This requires a certain level of object permanence and memory, but also some rudimentary ideas about addition. They must infer that the second object was added to the first, without actually seeing that this was done (recall that the screen occluded their vision).

Of course, infants are not adding in the way young children add (even if they wanted to, they don't have sufficient motor coordination to count on their fingers). One interpretation of what infants seem to be doing is **subitizing,** which is quantifying small numbers of items without conscious counting. For example, when looking at playing cards, one immediately "knows" how many clubs, diamonds, hearts, or spades are on the card by looking at the configuration of objects (at least up to six). Direct counting is not necessary, nor is it necessary to actually read the number in the corner of the card. One can arrive at the correct number of items by subitizing. Based on Wynn's findings, 5-month-old infants seem to be able to do something similar, at least for the quantities of one and two. However, other researchers question Wynn's interpretation, suggesting that babies are not responding on the basis of *number* but, rather, on the basis of total amount of *substance* present (Mix, Huttenlocher, & Levine, 2002). In other words, infants are not doing primitive (and unconscious) addition and subtraction, but rather are responding to changes in the amount of "stuff" that is present in the various arrays. For example, rather than reflecting infants' abstract understanding of integers (that is, there should be "1" or "2" objects behind the screen), performance on such tasks may be based on representations of the actual objects (for

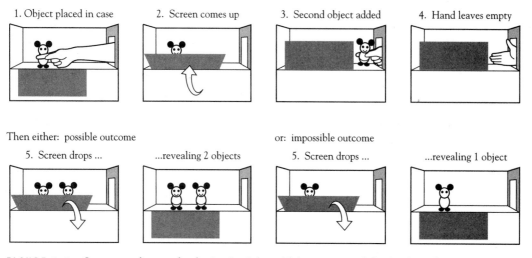

1. Object placed in case   2. Screen comes up   3. Second object added   4. Hand leaves empty

Then either: possible outcome   or: impossible outcome

5. Screen drops ...   ...revealing 2 objects   5. Screen drops ...   ...revealing 1 object

FIGURE 9-1   Sequence of events for the 1 + 1 = 2 (possible) outcome and the 1 + 1 = 1 (impossible) outcome from the experiment by Wynn (1992). SOURCE: "Addition and Subtraction by Human Infants," by K. Wynn, 1992, *Nature, 358,* 749–750. Copyright © 1992 Macmillan Magazines Ltd. Reprinted with permission from *Nature.*

example, ♥ versus ♥♥ suggesting that decisions are based more on perceptual than conceptual relations (Uller et al., 1999; see Mandler, 2000).

This line of work is provocative and, regardless of interpretation, suggests substantially greater quantitative knowledge in young infants than was previously believed, although it does not justify the conclusion that babies are born knowing basic arithmetic or that infants and toddlers should be able to learn complicated mathematics given the proper instructions. Although the nature of their numerical competencies might not be fully known, it seems relatively certain that it is not the equivalent of the abilities found in children only a few years older.

What Is Infant Cognition Made Of?

The gospel according to Piaget held that infant cognition is sensorimotor in nature. Infants know their world through raw sensation and their direct actions on objects. Slowly, during the first two years of life, cognition is changed, transformed (constructed) into symbol-based thought, permitting the child to con-

ceptualize the world in a new way. There is little debate that cognition and behavior do change during these years of life. Brain growth is more rapid during the first two years than at any other time in postnatal life. Cognitive differences between the 10-month-old and the 2-year-old are dramatic, obvious to anyone who takes the time to look. Yet, increasing evidence indicates that the huge changes in overt behavior that are apparent to all might be masking much smaller changes in underlying competencies. Infants seem to know a lot about their physical world from birth, or shortly thereafter, are able to use simple symbol systems to remember events over extended periods, and may even be able to do simple computations.

Some of these skills may be domain specific in nature. In Chapter 7, we saw that very young infants can recognize faces and perhaps are even born with a prototype for the human face (as reflected by their preference for "attractive" faces; see Langlois et al., 1987). Such skills are likely limited to face identification and recognition and do not generalize to other aspects of cognition. Similarly, knowledge of addition and subtraction might be domain specific, with the symbolic skills underlying simple computation being unavailable to other conceptual systems. Similar arguments have been made for neonatal imitation (Bjorklund, 1987b; Legerstee, 1991), which might function as a fixed-action pattern and serve a restricted role in early social development.

Other aspects of young infants' cognitions might be more domain general in nature. For example, the symbolic abilities underlying deferred imitation of novel events seem not to be restricted to any particular domain of knowledge. In a similar vein, Catherine Sophian (1997) has suggested that innate structures are more like tools that might be best suited for some contents (understanding objects, for example) but can also be used flexibly for other purposes (see also Gelman & Williams, 1998).

Do these new findings require a full-scale replacement of Piagetian ideas of sensorimotor development? Meltzoff (1990) apparently thinks so. In reviewing his and other people's research on cognitive development over infancy, Meltzoff concluded that "in a very real sense, there may be no such thing as an exclusively 'sensorimotor period' in the normal human infant" (p. 20, italics in the original). Jean Mandler (1992, 2000) takes a similar, though somewhat less drastic position. Mandler interprets the wealth of new information about infant cognition as requiring new theories. She has suggested a model similar to the one described in Chapter 4 by Karmiloff-Smith (1992), in which infants redescribe their perceptions (presumably including both the sensory and motor representations of the traditional sensorimotor stage) into conceptual form. Such conceptual knowledge can coexist with the type of knowledge Piaget described. It is not necessary to posit substantial amounts of innate knowledge, Mandler suggests. According to Mandler (1992), from the first few months of life, infants are able to abstract certain types of perceptual information and redescribe it into conceptual form. Such redescription, rather than having a late onset, develops alongside sensorimotor functioning.

Who's right? We can't yet answer that question, and perhaps one group doesn't have to be wrong for the other group to be right. Cognitive development does not follow a single course for all aspects of intelligence, and it is possible, and I believe likely, that infants' cognition is multiply determined. Infants might possess some innate knowledge (representational constraints), some innate processing mechanisms (architectural constraints), but at other times their behavior might be better explained by referring to more domain-general perceptual and memory mechanisms, rather than to highly constrained domain-specific processes. And most likely, infants' brains are structured so that domain-specific constraints (both representational and architectural) and domain-general mechanisms interact (see Bjorklund & Pellegrini, 2002).

There is much excitement in infant research these days. Regardless of which interpretation one prefers, I think most researchers would agree that infants have far greater conceptual abilities than was previously believed, and every year we learn something else that infants know or can do. We should not lose sight, however, of what infants cannot do. There is no evidence, for example, that infants can be taught arithmetic, reading, or chemistry. Infancy is still a special time, and the infant mind remains far different from the mind that resides in the 3-year-old child. Remembering the limits of infant cognition is sometimes difficult when we look at all the things infants can do, but it is a thought we shouldn't lose.

Learning to Use Symbols

The term "symbol" as used in this and previous chapters has generally referred to some mental representation of a physical object or event. But in everyday parlance, symbol also refers to external referents for objects and events. For example, a picture or a photograph of an object is a stand-in for the real thing—it is a concrete, yet symbolic representation of an object that is not physically present. Likewise, scale models, such as a miniature room complete with doll-sized furniture, can serve as a symbolic representation of a larger, real room. Similarly, some things are not exactly what they seem. The ubiquitous refrigerator magnet attests to this. Cookies, candy bars, and many other "real" things are in actuality only magnets that look like something else. At a more abstract level, the letters and numbers so central to our technological culture are not what they seem to be but, rather, are symbols necessary for reading and computation. Judy DeLoache (1987; DeLoache & Marzolf, 1992) has referred to the knowledge that an entity can stand for something other than itself as **representational insight.** Representational insight extends beyond the abilities required for object permanence or deferred imitation. When can children understand and effectively use external forms of representation, such as pictures and models, and what does this tell us about their representational development?

In this section, I examine three areas of research related to young children's use of external symbols. The first is the research of DeLoache and her colleagues looking at children's abilities to use pictures and scale models as representations for the real things. The second is research examining children's abilities to distinguish the differences between the appearance and reality of objects, and the third area examines young children's ability to distinguish imagining and experiencing.

Young Children's Interpretation of Pictures and Models

How do children come to understand that pictures and models are symbols for other things? Judy De-Loache and her colleagues have been investigating this question, and their studies have produced some interesting and, at first look, counterintuitive findings (DeLoache, 2000; DeLoache & Marzolf, 1992). In DeLoache's studies, 2- and 3-year-old children are asked to find a toy hidden in a room. Before searching for the object, they are shown a picture or scale model of the room, with the location of the hidden object made obvious in the picture or model. For example, children are shown a scale model of a room, with the experimenter hiding a miniature toy behind a chair in the model. The miniature toy and the model chair correspond to a large toy and a real chair in the adjoining real room. Children are then asked to find the toy in the room (retrieval 1). After

searching for the toy in the room, they return to the model and are asked to find where the miniature toy was hidden (retrieval 2). If children cannot find the large toy in the room (retrieval 1) but can find the miniature toy in the scale model (retrieval 2), their failure to find the large toy cannot be because they forgot where the miniature toy was hidden. A better interpretation would be that the children cannot use the model in a symbolic fashion.

The results of one such experiment with 2.5- and 3-year-old children are graphed in Figure 9-2 (De-Loache, 1987). As can be seen, 3-year-olds performed comparably in both retrieval tasks, indicating that they remembered where the miniature toy was hidden and used the information from the scale model to find the large toy in the real room. The younger children showed good memory for where the miniature toy was hidden (retrieval 2 in the figure) but performed very poorly when trying to find the large toy in the real room (retrieval 1 in the figure). This pattern of results suggests that 2.5-year-old children failed to recognize that the scale model was a symbolic representation of the large room. Recalling DeLoache's definition of representational insight as realizing that one entity can stand for another, it appears that on the scale-model task, 3-year-olds possess representational insight whereas 2.5-year-old children do not.

A similar pattern of results was found when pictures of a room were used, with an experimenter pointing to the location in a picture where the toy was hidden (DeLoache, 1987, 1991). The primary difference between the picture and scale-model experiments was that the picture task was solved by 2.5-year-old children but not by 2-year-olds. Thus, when pictures are used as symbols, 2.5-year-olds demonstrate representational insight. Such competence is not achieved until 3 years of age, however, when a scale model is used.

Why should children perform more poorly using the scale model than the pictures? If I had been asked to make a prediction of which task would be the easier, my guess would have been exactly the reverse. The model, being a more concrete stimulus, is more like the real room, and thus, it would seem, less symbolic sophistication would be required to use it to

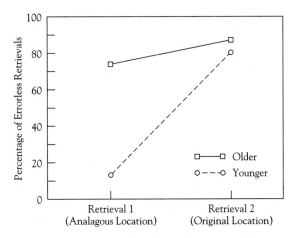

FIGURE 9-2 The number of errorless retrievals (correctly locating the hidden toy) for 2.5- (younger) and 3-year-olds (older) on a model task. Retrieval 1 involved locating the real toy in the real room; retrieval 2 involved locating the miniature toy in the model. SOURCE: "Rapid Change in the Symbolic Functioning of Very Young Children," by J. S. DeLoache, 1987, *Science, 238,* 1556–1557. Copyright © 1987 American Association for the Advancement of Science. Reprinted with permission.

guide behavior. In fact, when young children are given toy objects versus pictures of objects to use in memory and simple problem-solving tasks, they usually perform better with the objects, not the pictures (Daehler, Lonardo, & Bukatko, 1979). Such was not the case with DeLoache's study, of course, and she proposed that one reason for the pattern of results was related to children's difficulty in thinking about an entity in two different ways at the same time, or what she refers to as **dual representation** (or **dual orientation**). A model, she argues, is an object worthy of attention all by itself. A picture, by contrast, is itself uninteresting, with its primary purpose being to represent something else. When models are made less interesting and less concrete, or when pictures are made more salient, performance should change.

This is exactly what DeLoache found. When models were viewed through a window, 2.5-year-olds' performance increased substantially relative to the standard model task. Likewise, when 3-year-olds were allowed to play with the model before the hiding

task, their performance significantly *decreased.* Making the model *less* salient for the 2.5-year-olds (by requiring that they view it through a window) enabled them to more easily represent the model as both an object and a model; making the model *more* salient for the 3-year-olds (by encouraging them to play with it) made it more difficult for them to treat it as a representation for something else, and their performance deteriorated. A similar result was found when pictures were made more salient. For example, rather than showing children a picture of the room, the experimenters showed them a picture of an object (a chair, for instance), with the miniature toy hidden behind the picture. This manipulation increased the saliency of the picture as an object and should have made it more difficult for young children to treat it as a symbol. This was precisely the case, with none of the 2.5-year-olds in this study successfully finding the large toy in the real room (DeLoache, 1991).

If dual representation is the key here, as DeLoache proposes, what would happen if young children had to use a model to find a hidden toy *without* dual representation? How can this be done? DeLoache, Kevin Miller, and Karl Rosengren (1997) convinced children that a "shrinking machine" (an oscilloscope with flashing lights and computer-generated sounds) could actually shrink a room, something that the 2.5-year-old children easily believed. They were then given the "hiding" test as in previous research. First, a toy was hidden in the large room. Then the room was "shrunk" and the child searched for the toy in the miniaturized model. Their performance this time was exceptional. Whereas children who were given the standard (no shrinking room) instructions successfully found the toy on only 19% of all trials (about what one would expect by chance), children who searched in the shrunken (model) room were correct nearly 80% of the time. Why the difference? DeLoache and her colleagues reasoned that the children believed that *the miniaturized room was the same room as the larger room;* it was not a model, and thus not a symbol. In this case, as far as the children were concerned, dual representation was not necessary.

The ability to use one object to represent another is the essence of what we mean when we refer to symbol use. At a very basic level, we see this ability in very young children, most easily perhaps in symbolic play. For example, an 18-month-old might hold a shoe to her ear and pretend that it's a phone, or a 20-month-old child might place a napkin on his head and parade around the living room drawing attention to his "hat." In these cases, one object is being used as a symbol for another. But this is not quite what DeLoache means when she refers to representational insight. It is not enough to use an object as a symbol; one must know that the object can be both a symbol (for example, a representation of a room) and an object (for example, a model) at the same time. DeLoache and Donald Marzolf make this point nicely, stating, "Young children are capable of responding to a single entity either concretely, as an object itself, or abstractly, as a representation of something else. It is very difficult for them to do both at once, that is, to achieve dual representation" (1992, p. 328).

Recent research has documented the development of dual representation for children's understanding of one common symbolic entity—pictures. DeLoache and her colleagues (1998) presented pictures of objects to children between the ages of 9 and 19 months in the United States and the Ivory Coast. The youngest children in both countries initially touched the pictures as if they were real objects, sometimes even trying to pick them off the page. By 19 months of age, children in both countries realized that the pictures represented something else: They now point at the depicted objects rather than try to manipulate them. DeLoache and her colleagues propose that infants' initial uncertainty about pictures causes them to explore them, which gradually results in their acquisition of the concept of "picture" and the understanding that they represent something else.

The Appearance/Reality Distinction

Adults know very well that things are not always what they appear to be. We realize that the appearance of an object does not necessarily correspond to its reality. This is not knowledge we are born with but knowledge that has a developmental history. One problem that tests our ability to make this

appearance/reality distinction is the conservation-of-liquid task used by Piaget. When water is poured from a short, stout glass into a tall, skinny one, the amount of water appears to have increased. We know, of course, that in reality the amount of water is the same. We also know that children much younger than 7 years are not cognizant of this fact.

As discussed in Chapter 4, conservation is the knowledge that quantitative relations between objects remain the same despite irrelevant perceptual transformations. A more basic form of the appearance/reality distinction concerns the knowledge that *qualitative* relations between objects remain the same despite some perceptual transformation. Quantitative properties have to do with amount, as in number, length, weight, or volume; in comparison, qualitative properties have to do with characteristics of type or form. For example, children would demonstrate qualitative constancy if they realized that their parents' car remained the same despite being painted. Piaget (1968) referred to such knowledge as reflecting **identity.** Identity and conservation are similar in that both involve a form of cognitive constancy, a realization that an entity remains unchanged despite changes in appearance. However, Piaget asserted that constancies involving qualitative properties do not require reversibility but merely a dissociation of the permanent and variable properties of an object. As such, qualitative constancies are developed during the preschool years. In fact, Piaget (1968) contended that object permanence is the first qualitative identity, being achieved between 18 and 24 months of age.

In 1969, Rheta De Vries published a pioneering study of qualitative identity in which children 3 to 6 years of age were familiarized with a trained cat named Maynard. In one condition, after the children petted Maynard, he was fitted with a realistic dog mask. Although the children did not actually see the mask being placed on Maynard, the cat's body and tail remained in full view of the children during the transformation. They were then asked questions concerning the identity of the animal: "What kind of animal is it now? Would this animal eat dog food or cat food? Does it bark or meow?" In general, 3-year-olds frequently believed that the mask had actually changed the identity of the animal, whereas most 5- and 6-year-olds believed that changes in the appearance of the animal had not altered its identity. De Vries referred to this type of qualitative constancy as *generic identity*.

In addition to her research involving changing the appearance of animals, De Vries also interviewed children about their beliefs about people wearing masks and about the constancy of gender as a result of certain irrelevant changes (for example, boys wearing dresses). Again, she reported that 3-year-olds tended to believe that changes in appearance result in changes in identity. This can account for young children's sometimes puzzling responses to costumes worn both by others and by themselves. For example, it is not uncommon at Halloween for 2- and 3-year-old children to be excited about wearing a costume, only to become distressed when the masks are placed over their faces or when they look at themselves in the mirror. Wearing a Bob the Builder outfit is one thing, but wearing the mask is another story. Not all transformations of personal identity are so upsetting, however, as is evidenced by the number of scraped elbows and knees on children who wear their Batman underwear, tie capes around their necks, and jump from tables and fences, convinced they can fly. These children's behaviors are consistent with the belief that a significant change in appearance results in a change in identity.

Let me provide an anecdote to illustrate young children's thinking about how appearance can influence reality. Three-year-old Nicholas sometimes spent the night with his grandparents, who would take him to preschool the following morning. Nicholas especially liked to ride with his grandfather because he drove a somewhat battered, stick-shift Chevy, which Nicholas called "Papa's car." Nicholas's grandmother, however, drove only cars with automatic transmissions, and thus she was unable to take Nicholas to school in Papa's car. One morning when Grandma was about to drive Nicholas to school, he said, "Grandma, dress up like a man this morning. Put on Papa's shirt and wear his hat." When asked why he wanted her to do that, he responded, "Then you can take me to school in Papa's car." Nicholas had a problem and attempted to solve

it by changing his grandmother's appearance, which he believed would transform her temporarily into a man and give her the ability to drive a stick-shift car. More will be said in Chapter 13 concerning children's belief in the constancy of gender as a function of behavior or dress.

In related research, John Flavell and his colleagues have extensively investigated young children's knowledge about the distinction between appearance and reality (Flavell, Green, & Flavell, 1986; Taylor & Flavell, 1984). In some experiments, children were presented with a realistic-looking fake rock made of sponge, or watched as white milk was poured into a red glass. The children were then asked two questions. The first concerned what the objects looked like, "how they look to your eyes right now." The second concerned the actual identity of the objects, "how they really and truly are." Somewhat surprisingly, Flavell and his colleagues reported that most 3-year-olds could not solve these seemingly simple problems. Their errors tended to be of two types: *phenomenism errors* and *intellectual realism errors*. Phenomenism errors typically occurred when appearance/reality tests involving color were used. Children stated, for example, that the milk looked red and "really and truly" was red. In contrast, intellectual realism errors were more likely to occur on tasks involving objects that looked like something they were not. For example, children would say that the fake rock was indeed a sponge and looked like a sponge. In general, when children erred, they did so by giving the same answer to both questions.

Before assuming that 3-year-olds cannot solve appearance/reality tasks, John Flavell, Frances Green, and Eleanor Flavell (1986) simplified their problems. Children were acquainted with an experimenter, for example, and watched as she put on a soft plastic mask; then they were asked who the person in the mask "really and truly" was. For other tasks, they were asked questions about objects that had uncharacteristic sounds or smells (for example, socks that smelled like peanut butter). The 3-year-olds' performance on these simplified tasks was surprisingly poor, and in a subsequent study, explicit training in making the appearance/reality distinction did little to improve their performance. Later research similarly failed to "teach" 3- and 4-year-olds the appearance/reality distinction (Taylor & Hort, 1990), reflecting that young children's difficulty is not caused by a simple, easily remedied misunderstanding about the nature of the task. Given these findings, Flavell and his colleagues (1986) concluded that 3-year-olds "truly did not understand [the appearance/reality distinction], even minimally" (p. 23).

There is at least one exception to this pattern of failure, and that is when children are encouraged to participate in an act of deception. When 3-year-old children are induced to play a trick on someone (for example, "Let's trick Sally and make her think that this sponge really IS a rock, and not just a sponge that looks like one"), many are quite capable of doing so (Rice et al., 1997). Also, 3-year-olds' correct performance is higher when nonverbal appearance/reality tasks are used (Sapp, Lee, & Muir, 2000). These findings indicate that young children's knowledge of the appearance/reality distinction is not an all-or-none thing but develops during the preschool years.

Flavell and his colleagues (1986) speculated about the factors that can mediate children's development of the appearance/reality distinction. One likely candidate is **dual encoding.** Three-year-olds' inability to differentiate between the appearance of an object and its actual identity might stem, in part, from their difficulty in representing an object in more than one form at a time. That is, young children might focus on one aspect of a stimulus (its appearance or its actual identity) and give the same answer, based on either appearance or reality, regardless of the question asked. Thus, on the one hand, if the change in color is more salient to a child, the object *looks* red and *is* red (phenomenism error). If, on the other hand, the identity of the object is more salient, it *is* a sponge and *looks like* a sponge (intellectual realism error). Young children cannot act on multiple representations of an object simultaneously. With increasing age they become more adept at dual encoding, but not until later childhood or early adolescence can they "think about notions of 'looks like,' 'really and truly,' 'looks different from the way it really and truly is,' and

so on in the abstract, metaconceptual way that older subjects can" (Flavell et al., 1986, p. 59).

The findings and interpretation of Flavell and his colleagues are similar to those DeLoache (1987; DeLoache & Marzolf, 1992) reported with respect to dual representation for pictures and models. Recall that DeLoache found that 2- and 2.5-year-old children had difficulty representing a model or a picture as both an object and a symbol simultaneously. DeLoache's findings support Flavell's contention that dual encoding/representation is an important step in preschool children's representational development. Together, the findings of Flavell and DeLoache suggest that there is not a single dual representational ability that emerges at a single time and affects thinking across all tasks. Rather, this ability appears to develop gradually from ages 2 to 5, being found early (2.5 years) in some circumstances (using pictures as symbols), a bit later (3 years) in others (using models as symbols), and later yet (4 to 5 years) in other situations (making the appearance/reality distinction).

Distinguishing Between Imagined and Real Events

Related to the appearance/reality distinction is children's ability to distinguish what they imagine from what they experience. In other words, do children realize that thinking or imagining something is distinct from actually doing or experiencing something? At one level, it is clear that even young children know the difference between imagining and doing. For example, although dreams can seem quite real to people of any age, apparently even 3- and 4-year-olds know the difference between dreams and reality, although many 3-year-olds seem to believe that the same dream is experienced by different people (Woolley & Wellman, 1992), and that dreams are highly controllable (Wooley & Boerger, 2002). Also, several researchers have shown that 4- and 6-year-olds can easily distinguish between real and pretend items (Golomb & Galasso, 1995; Harris et al., 1991). For example, when a pencil is placed on a table in front of a child, 4-year-olds can state that both they and a person sitting opposite them can see the pencil. When asked to close their eyes and imagine a pencil, however, they can state quite correctly that the person sitting across from them cannot see the imagined object.

The ability to distinguish between an imagined and an experienced event seems to develop with age. For example, although 3-year-olds can often distinguish between seeing and imagining an object, this ability does improve with age (Woolley & Bruell, 1996), and many 3-year-olds believe that imagined events reflect reality (Woolley & Wellman, 1993). By age 4, children know very well the distinction between information gained from imagining (that is, without perceptual experience) and from perceptual experience.

Yet, the ability to make the distinction between imagined and experienced events is far from complete by age 4. For example, in research evaluating developmental differences in **source monitoring**—the awareness of the origins of one's memories, knowledge, or beliefs—children and adults are asked to perform certain actions (for instance, "touch your nose") or to imagine performing certain actions (for instance, "imagine touching your nose") (Foley & Ratner, 1998a). The ability to distinguish imagined from real actions improves during the preschool years (Sussman, 2001; Welch-Ross, 1995), but even 6- and 7-year-olds have greater difficulty making such distinctions than older children or adults do (Foley & Ratner, 1998; Parker, 1995). When children make errors they usually claim that they had performed an action they had actually only imagined. Thus, for young children, imagination can easily be remembered as reality. Interestingly, young children are often as good as adults at distinguishing something they said or did from something that someone else said or did (but not always; see Foley & Ratner, 1998; Foley, Ratner, & Passalacqua, 1993, discussed in Chapter 3 for counter examples in collaborative learning). Children's greatest difficulty comes from distinguishing between self-generated action and self-generated imagining.

Related to distinguishing real from imagined events is the distinction between fantasy and reality.

Young children seem to have a difficult time differentiating between what is real and what is fantasy. Young children are more apt to believe in fantasy figures such as superheroes, monsters, Santa Claus, and the Tooth Fairy (the latter two of which adults heartily promote) than are older children, and they are prone to interpret events they don't understand as magic (Rosengren & Hickling, 1994). For example, Karl Rosengren and Anne Hickling (1994) asked 4- and 5-year-old children how certain objects could be changed (for example, "How can you make this piece of string look different?"), and most provided answers based on physical mechanisms ("Cut it in two."). Children were then shown some magic tricks (for example, putting two pieces of string together to make one piece), and asked for their explanations for the transformations. Whereas most 5-year-olds explained the changes as tricks that anyone could learn, many 4-year-olds explained them as magic that could only be performed by a magician.

Young children's tenuous grasp of the distinction between fantasy and reality is seen in experiments by Paul Harris and his colleagues (1991). As noted earlier, these researchers demonstrated that 4- and 6-year-olds could easily distinguish between real and imagined objects. For example, when asked to imagine that there was either a bunny or a monster in a box on a table in front of them, few children had any difficulty with the task; most stated quite clearly that the bunny or the monster was pretend and not real. But this knowledge was tenuous for many of the children. For example, after asking children to imagine a bunny or a monster in the box, the experimenter said she had to leave the room for a few minutes. Four of 12 4-year-olds who had imagined a monster in the box became frightened and wouldn't let the experimenter leave. No child who was asked to imagine a bunny became frightened. When the experimenter returned and questioned the children, nearly half of both the 4- and 6-year-olds admitted to wondering whether there was indeed a monster or a bunny in the box. Perhaps imagining made it so. That is, although nearly all the children admitted that the bunny or the monster was make-believe at the beginning of the experiment, many had second thoughts at the end. Harris and his colleagues view this contradiction between children's beginning and final beliefs as a reflection of the uncertain state of young children's knowledge of fantasy versus reality. "Our general explanation is that when children imagine a creature such as a monster or rabbit in a box they start to wonder whether there is such a creature in the box, and they cannot completely discount that possibility. Thus, children's imagination increases the subjective likelihood that certain fantasy creatures might become encountered" (1991, p. 121). These results help explain why young children are often frightened by imagining bogey men in the closet or monsters under their beds. Although at one level they know the difference between imagined and real, at another level they possess a belief in magic, making the fantasy-reality distinction a tenuous one.

Let me provide an anecdote to illustrate young children's uncertainty about what is real and what is fantasy. Four-year-old Jeffrey was very impressed with the Disney movie *The Lion King*. He knew the cartoon was fiction, of course, and was quite aware that lions and hyenas can't actually talk. He was especially impressed with the character of Simba, the young lion cub and star of the movie. "Simba was so sad when his father died," he said. "Boy, what a good actor he is. He *really* looked sad." Jeffrey knew that this was fiction and that the characters were not real. But he still got confused. He was so impressed with the skills of the cartoon "actor" who played the role of Simba.

But how different are children from adults regarding magical thinking? Jaqueline Woolley (1997) thinks not too much. Children are more likely to attribute unfamiliar events to magic and to believe that "just wishing" can make something come true. But such thinking does not disappear at adolescence or adulthood. The belief systems of most cultures include supernatural beings who intervene in the physical world on a regular basis and who can be beseeched to intervene on people's behalf. Many adults are highly superstitious. They believe that blowing on dice before a roll will produce a good outcome, knocking on wood will prevent a bad outcome, and breaking a mirror will result in bad luck.

Belief in the paranormal approaches 50% among American adults, including faith healing, demonic possession, and astrology. Thus, the tendency to provide a magical explanation for phenomenon for which we have no known physical explanation is not unique to children. One likely reason for children's greater tendency to believe in fantasy is knowledge. Older children and adults know more about how the physical world works and know the domains in their culture where belief in supernatural explanation is accepted (for example, religion) and where it is not (for example, David Copperfield's illusions).

Children's Theory of Mind

During the last two decades, the topic of children's **theory of mind** has become immensely popular. In general, the phrase "theory of mind" is used to refer to children's developing concepts of mental activity. A theory of mind is more than just a collection of concepts, however. Theory implies some coherent framework for organizing facts and making predictions. (See the discussion of theory theories in Chapter 4.) Having a theory of mind implies recognizing different categories of mind, such as dreams, memories, imagination, beliefs, and so on, and having some causal-explanatory framework to account for the actions of other people (that is, to explain why someone behaves as he or she does). For example, Henry Wellman (1990) believes that adults' theory of mind is based on **belief-desire reasoning.** Basically, we explain and predict what people do based on what we understand their desires and beliefs to be—that is, by referring to their wants, wishes, hopes, and goals (their desires) and to their ideas, opinions, suppositions, and knowledge (their beliefs). Such belief-desire reasoning is depicted in Figure 9-3. Basically, this is what researchers mean when they talk about children developing a theory of mind: To what extent do children have a coherent explanatory "theory" to understand, predict, and explain behavior?

Developmental differences in theory of mind are reflections of developmental differences in how chil-

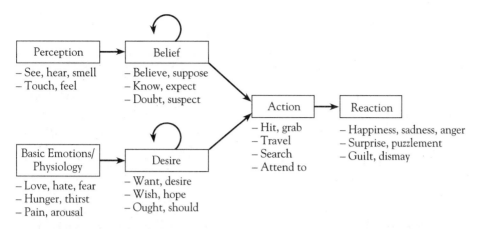

FIGURE 9-3 A simplified scheme depicting belief-desire reasoning. SOURCE: *The Child's Theory of Mind,* by H. M. Wellman. Copyright © 1990 Massachusetts Institute of Technology Press. Reprinted with permission.

dren represent the world—in this case, the mental world. In fact, most research examining children's ability to distinguish between appearance and reality (Flavell et al., 1986) or between imagining and experiencing (Harris et al., 1991) could properly be classified as theory-of-mind research (see Flavell & Miller, 1998).

One aspect of theory of mind concerns children's developing knowledge of what it means to think and to perform other aspects of cognition, a topic related to metacognition as well as to representation (Flavell, Green, & Flavell, 1998; Schwanenflugel, Henderson, & Fabricius, 1998). For example, Flavell and his colleagues (1998) asked 5-, 9-, and 13-year-old children and adults a series of questions related to mental uncontrollability. For instance, will a child who hears a strange noise automatically wonder what that noise is, even if he or she doesn't want to, and is it possible to go for three days without thinking about anything? Adults and older children understood that the mind "has a mind of its own" better than younger children. That is, they understood that the mind will sometimes "think" about things even if the person has no interest in thinking about it (the source of an unexpected noise, for example) and that one cannot avoid thinking for an extended period. Although younger children sometimes understand

"I KNOW WHAT I THINK, BUT WHAT'S IMPORTANT IS WHAT MY MOM THINKS I THINK!"

CARTOON 9-1 Knowing that someone else has thoughts and being able to infer those thoughts has important social and intellectual implications. SOURCE: DENNIS THE MENACE® used by permission of Hank Ketcham and © 1990 by North America Syndicate.

these facts of mental life, they are much less likely to make these claims than adolescents and adults are. Children's understanding of the controllability of mental states improves during the elementary school years (Flavell & Green, 1999), as does children's understanding of different categories of thinking, such as memory, comprehension, attention, and inference (Schwanenflugel et al., 1998).

The aspect of theory of mind that has spawned the most research, however, concerns children's abilities to "read the minds" of others (Perner, 1991; Wellman, Cross, & Watson, 2001). To what extent do young children understand that the perceptions, knowledge, and thoughts of others are different from their own? Children's representation of others and of themselves as thinkers is vitally important to our species' way of life. Cooperation, competition, and social interaction in general as we know it would be radically different if we did not develop a theory of mind and the ability to "read" the minds of others. I believe that one reason for the popularity of this topic is its significance for understanding the human condition.

The Development of Mind Reading

When and how do children come to appreciate that other people have beliefs and desires, often different from their own, that motivate their behavior? To assess this question, researchers have developed tasks in which children must predict what another person will do or state, or what another person thinks, in an effort to determine what young children know about the minds of others.

False Belief

The most frequently used tool to assess children's theory of mind is the **false-belief task,** first developed for use with chimpanzees (Premack & Woodruff, 1978). In a standard false-belief task (first used with children by Wimmer & Perner, 1983), children watch as candy (or some other treat) is hidden in a special location (in a box, for example). Another person—for example, Maxi—is present when the treat is hidden but then leaves the room. While Maxi is out of the room, the treat is moved from the box to another container. When Maxi returns, will he know where the treat is hidden? The results of using variants of this standard task are relatively straightforward. Most 4-year-old children can solve the problem, stating that Maxi will look where the candy was originally hidden. Three-year-olds, in contrast, generally cannot solve the problem, stating that Maxi will look for the candy in the new hiding place, apparently not realizing that Maxi is not privy to the new information (Wellman et al., 2001). This pattern is not confined to European and North American children but is apparently universal, being observed among the children of Baka pygmies living in the rain forests of Cameroon (Avis & Harris, 1991; Tardif & Wellman, 2000; see, Lillard, 1998, for a discussion of cultural variations in theories of mind).

Why do 3-year-olds fail at the false-belief task? For one thing, they seem not to remember what they originally believed before any switch was made (Gopnik & Slaughter, 1991; Zelazo & Boseovski, 2001). For example, in a modification of the false-belief task, called the "Smarties" task, developed by G.-Juergen Hogrefe, Heinz Wimmer, and Josef Perner (1986), children are shown a box of "Smarties" (a type of candy in a distinctive box, with which British children are highly familiar) and asked what they think is in the box. Naturally, they say "Smarties." The box is then opened, revealing not candy but pencils. Children are then asked what they originally thought (that is, what they believed was in the box before being shown the contents), as well to predict what another child (who is not privy to the trick) will think is in the box. The first question assesses children's memory for their initial belief (referred to as **representational change**), whereas the second question assesses their ability to understand false belief. The correct answer to both of these questions, of course, is "Smarties," but most 3-year-olds say "pencils" to both questions; that is, they seem to forget their initial belief. Alison Gopnik and Virginia Slaughter (1991) found that this memory deficit is not a general one but is specific to beliefs. Three-year-olds have little difficulty remembering their past images, perceptions, or pretenses. They have particular difficulty, however, remembering their past beliefs.

If young children's problem with false-belief tasks is not one of general memory, what can account for their poor performance? Perner (1991), among others, has proposed that 3-year-old children lack the conceptual structures necessary to solve problems dealing with beliefs. In other words, they have a *representational deficit* and do not possess a true theory of mind.

One possibility, originally proposed by Wimmer and Perner (1983), is that young children have difficulty with contradictory evidence. They cannot deal with two representations of a single object (the candy in location 1 and in location 2) simultaneously. This is similar to the *dual-encoding* (or *dual representation*) *hypothesis* Flavell and DeLoache proposed to explain representational differences between younger and older preschoolers. Basically, this position argues that young children will fail in situations where they must consider two different beliefs or representations for one target.

Support for this position comes from a study by Alison Gopnik and Janet Astington (1988) in which they assessed 3-, 4-, and 5-year-old children's performance on a series of tasks, each requiring the children to deal with contradictory evidence: false belief, appearance/reality distinction (Flavell et al., 1986), and representational change (remembering their past beliefs). The results of this study are graphed in Figure 9-4. As can be seen, performance on each of the three tasks varied with age, consistent with the idea that a single, domain-general mechanism underlies preschool children's representational abilities.

Other researchers have suggested that young children have the underlying representational abilities, but they lack some specific cognitive skills. For example, Douglas Frye, Philip Zelazo, and Tibor Palfai (1995) proposed that young children cannot easily switch their perspectives from one focus to another. In the task used by Frye and his colleagues, children are told to sort pictures into one of two piles on the basis of color, for instance ("All the red cards go in this pile, all the blue cards go in that pile"), and

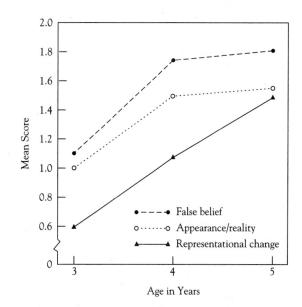

FIGURE 9-4 Average scores on false-belief, appearance-reality, and representational change questions for 3-, 4-, and 5-year-olds. Note the similar pattern of developmental change for each task. SOURCE: "Children's Understanding of the Representational Change and Its Relation to the Understanding of False Belief and the Appearance-Reality Distinction," by A. Gopnik & J. W. Astington, 1988, *Child Development, 59*, 26–37. Copyright © 1988 The Society for Research in Child Development. Reprinted with permission.

then, after several trials of this, they are told to now sort the cards by the objects depicted on them ("Now put the *boats* in this pile and the *cars* in that pile"). Despite being able to articulate the rule, most 3-year-olds continue to sort the cards by the previous dimension (color). They can state the rule, but have a tough time switching from one dimension to another. Frye and his colleagues believe that this is the deficit that young children have on false-belief tasks. Young children have a difficult time switching between their beliefs and that of another person.

Related to this interpretation is the idea that young children have a general lack of **executive functions** (Carlson & Moses, 2001; Perner & Lang, 2000; see Chapter 5). Executive functions refer to cognitive abilities involved in planning, executing, and inhibiting actions. Of the various components of executive function related to theory of mind, inhibition mechanisms have received the most attention (Bjorklund & Kipp, 2002; Perner & Lang, 2000). Cognitive inhibition was discussed in Chapter 5 and refers to the ability to inhibit certain thoughts and behaviors at specified times. With respect to theory of mind, many tasks require children to inhibit a dominant response to "pass" the task. For example, Joan Peskin (1992) showed preschool children a series of stickers, some more attractive than others. She then introduced "Mean Monkey," a hand puppet controlled by the experimenter, who played a game with the children. Mean Monkey would ask the children which of the stickers they really wanted and which stickers they did not want; he then selected the children's favorite sticker, leaving them with the least desirable ones. By 4 years of age, children understood the dynamics of the interchange and quickly learned to tell Mean Monkey the opposite of their true desires. Younger children rarely caught on and played most of the game telling Mean Monkey the truth and not getting the stickers they wanted. Similarly, in research by James Russell and his colleagues (1991), 3-year-old children were shown a series of windows, some of which had treats in them. To get the treat, the children had to select the nontreat window. Children had a difficult time doing this, and repeatedly failed to get a treat, seemingly being unable to inhibit their "pick-the-treat" response.

Do other factors contribute to children's developing theory of mind? One interesting finding is that 3- and 4-year-old children's performance on false-belief tasks is related to family size (Perner, Ruffman, & Leekam, 1994; Jenkins & Astington, 1996). Children from larger families perform false-belief tasks better than do children from smaller families. Why should there be a relation between family size and theory-of-mind reasoning? One explanation has to do with the role of siblings. The type of interaction provided by siblings facilitates developing a sophisticated theory of mind. Jennifer Jenkins and Janet Astington (1996) have shown that family size is particularly important for children with low linguistic skills. Apparently, having siblings can compensate for delayed language development in influencing performance on false-belief tasks. More recent research indicates that it is only having *older*, not younger, siblings that has a facilitative effect on theory-of-mind reasoning (Ruffman et al., 1998). Ted Ruffman and colleagues believe that having older siblings stimulates pretend play, which helps younger children represent "counterfactual states of affairs," which is a necessary skill for solving false-belief tasks. Although siblings may be important, they are not necessarily more effective tutors than adults. Charlie Lewis and his colleagues (1996) administered a series of theory-of-mind tests to 3- and 4-year-old children and found that the number of adults that children interact with daily is the best single predictor of a child's performance on theory-of-mind tasks.

Denise Cummins (1998) suggested an alternative explanation based on dominance theory. Siblings are always competing for resources, with older siblings typically having the advantage because of their greater size and mental abilities. Younger children would be motivated to develop whatever latent talents they have to aid them in their social competition with their older siblings, and developing an understanding of the mind of his or her chief competitor sooner rather than later would certainly be to the younger child's advantage. A similar argument can be made for interacting with older peers.

Despite the impressive evidence that most 3-year-old children cannot solve false-belief tasks, there is evidence that 3-year-olds do solve other tasks that seemingly require an understanding of other minds, challenging the representational-deficit hypothesis. In one particularly interesting study, Wendy Clements and Josef Perner (1994) evaluated children's *implicit* understanding of false belief. In this study, children ranging in age from 2 years 5 months to 4 years 6 months were told a story about a mouse named Sam who had placed a piece of cheese in a specific location (Location A) so that he could get it later when he was hungry. While Sam was sleeping, Katie mouse found the cheese and moved it to another place (Location B). When Sam woke up, he said, "I feel very hungry now. I'll go get the cheese." Children were then asked, "I wonder where he's

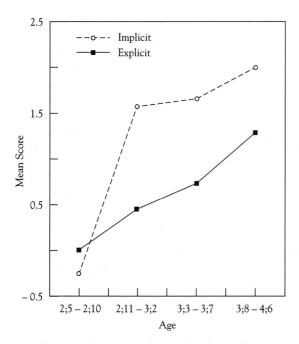

FIGURE 9-5 Average implicit and explicit understanding scores on false-belief task by age. SOURCE: Clements, W. A., & Perner, J. (1994). Implicit understanding of belief. *Cognitive Development*, 9, 377–395.

going to look?" The answer most older children should give is Location A, where he originally hid it, whereas most younger children should say Location B, reflecting their lack of understanding of false belief. This is the standard, or explicit, false-belief task, and this was the pattern of results that Clements and Perner found. However, Clements and Perner also recorded where children *looked*, at Location A or Location B. This is an *implicit task*, requiring no verbal response and presumably no conscious awareness. Now, all but the youngest children showed high levels of correct responding (that is, they looked at Location A). Figure 9-5 shows the average explicit and implicit understanding scores, based on children's performance on the tasks in this experiment. This finding has since been replicated (Clements, Rustin, & McCallum, 2000; Garnham & Ruffman, 2001), and a similar finding has been reported for infants' performance on A-not-B object-permanence tasks, with infants *looking* at the right location before

searching at the right location (Ahmed & Ruffman, 1998). What these findings imply is that by about 3 years of age children have a well-developed *implicit* understanding of false belief that exceeds their explicit (verbalizable) knowledge. These findings are reminiscent of results discussed in this and previous chapters suggesting that infants and children develop implicit understanding of many cognitive phenomena before they develop explicit understanding.

In other research, the first inkling of a theory of mind has been found in 18-month-old toddlers (Repacholi & Gopnik, 1997). In this study, 14- and 18-month-old infants were first tested for their preference for two types of food (Pepperidge Farm Goldfish and raw vegetables). They then watched as a woman tasted the two types of food. She expressed disgust for one type and happiness for the other. The woman then placed her hand, palm up, between the two bowls of food and said, "Can you give me some?" What did the infants do? The 14-month-olds gave the woman the type of food *they* liked, regardless of what food the woman liked. In contrast, the 18-month-olds were more likely to give the woman the food she had expressed a preference for, independent of whether it was what they liked best. That is, whereas the 14-month-olds responded egocentrically, the 18-month-olds did not, but recognized that their likes were different from those of another person.

Deception

One research area that has produced compelling evidence that young children have knowledge of the beliefs of other people concerns *deception*. When young children play tricks on others, they sometimes seem to be aware of what the other person does and doesn't know. Deception is an important skill in its own right. Deception is perhaps the consummate political skill, useful in love, war, and poker games. In fact, some theorists have speculated that early hominids' abilities to deceive may have contributed significantly to the evolution of intelligence in our species (Bjorklund & Harnishfeger, 1995; Humphrey, 1976). But deception also reflects knowledge of other minds. If children are so egocentric in perspective that they assume that if they know something (for example, where an apple is hidden) other people must know it, too, they will see trying to deceive as fruitless. Deception is only reasonable when a person (the deceiver) knows something that another person (the deceived) doesn't know; only then can attempts be made to mislead or conceal information. Thus, deception is another indication that a child is able to "read" another's mind.

Observations by many parents would suggest that 2- and 3-year-old children frequently practice (sometimes successfully, sometimes not) deception. For example, 3-year-old Carmen had gotten into her mother's make-up and spilled powder over the top of the bureau. She found a handkerchief and covered up the offending mess, acting as if nothing had ever happened. In this case, the ruse did not work. Kate Sullivan and Ellen Winner relate an example of more successful deception by a 2-year-old. The child pretended to cry when his aunt said that she could not come over to play with him. When she relented, the child turned to his mother and said, "I tricked her. I made her think I was sad so she would come" (1991, p. 160).

These observations have been supported by empirical science. For example, Michael Chandler, Anna Fritz, and Suzanne Hala (1989, 1991) assessed deception in hide-and-seek tasks in children ranging in age from 2.5 to 4 years In these studies, children were introduced to a hiding task involving several containers placed on a white surface made of a washable oilcloth material (see Figure 9-6). A puppet hid various pieces of "treasure," making footprints on the cloth from the start box to the container in which the treasure was hidden. A sponge was available that could be used to wipe up the puppet's footprints. After ensuring that the children understood the basics of the game, one of two experimenters (E1) left the room, and the remaining experimenter explained to the child that he or she should help the puppet hide the treasure so that E1 wouldn't be able to find it. The hide-and-seek game went on for several trials, with the sponge being taken away on later trials so that the puppet's footprints could not be wiped off. If children didn't

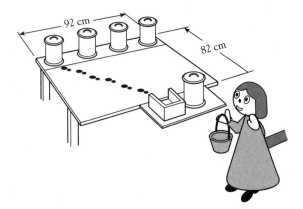

FIGURE 9-6 Illustration of the hide-and-seek game used in research by Chandler and colleagues. The puppet would hide a "treasure" in one of the four containers, leaving footprints tracing her path. SOURCE: "Small-Scale Deceit: Deception as a Marker of Two-, Three-, and Four-Year-Olds' Early Theories of Mind," by M. Chandler, A. S. Fritz, and S. Hala, 1989, *Child Development, 60,* 1263–1277. Copyright © 1989 The Society for Research in Child Development. Reprinted with permission.

think of it themselves on these later trials, they were shown how false tracks could be made (that is, tracks leading to the wrong container). The question of interest was the extent to which children would use a variety of deception strategies to make it difficult for E1 to find the treasure.

Several different types of deception were scored. The simplest involved withholding information— for example, by making sure that E1 was out of earshot before commenting on the hiding strategy they would use. Another involved destroying evidence by wiping away the tracks, leaving no sign of the path that the puppet took in hiding the treasure. A third involved openly lying—for example, telling E1 to look in an incorrect container. A fourth involved leaving a false trail of footprints leading to an incorrect container. The most sophisticated deceptive strategy involved a combination of both destroying the correct trail and laying a false one.

Table 9-1 shows the proportion of 2-, 3-, and 4-year-olds who used the various deceptive strategies. As can be seen, children of all ages used deception,

TABLE 9-1 Percentage of 2-, 3-, and 4-year-olds using various deceptive strategies.

Deceptive strategy	Age Years		
	2 (n = 10)	3 (n = 20)	4 (n = 20)
Withholding evidence	80	90	100
Destroying evidence	50	60	80
Lying	30	60	55
Producing false trails without destroying evidence	20	35	20
Destroying evidence and producing false trails	50	25	50

SOURCE: "Small-Scale Deceit: Deception as a Marker of Two-, Three-, and Four-Year-Olds' Early Theories of Mind," by M. Chandler, A. S. Fritz and S. Hala, 1989, *Child Development, 60*, 1263–1277. Copyright © 1989 The Society for Research in Child Development. Reprinted with permission.

with no age differences between the three groups. Chandler and his colleagues concluded that these findings "leave little room for doubt that even children as young as 2.5 are already capable of engaging in a variety of well-crafted deceptive practices, best interpreted as strategies aimed at instilling false beliefs in others" (1989, p. 1274).

In a related study (Hala & Chandler, 1996), 3-year-olds were asked to play a trick on a person (Lisa) by moving some biscuits from their distinctive jar to a hiding place, so that Lisa would be fooled. When later asked where Lisa will look for the biscuits and where she will think the biscuits are, children who helped plan the deception performed quite well. In contrast, children who merely observed the experimenter planning the deception or who planned a nondeception themselves, did not perform so well. Rather, they were more likely to answer this false-belief task erroneously, stating that Lisa would look for the biscuits in the new hiding place. In other words, when they planned to deceive someone, they were later able to take the perspective of that person; when they were not actively involved in the deceit, however, they performed egocentrically, stating that

the unsuspecting person would look for the biscuits where the children knew them to be.

In other research, Sullivan and Winner (1993) reported that 3-year-old children can solve the "Smarties" false-belief task (discussed earlier), but only when they are asked to actively trick another person. When the same task is used but without the "trick" instructions, 3-year-olds perform poorly. Sullivan and Winner (1993) interpreted these findings as indicating that 3-year-olds can understand false belief when it is embedded within a deceptive context. More recent research has similarly shown that 3-year-olds are able to use deception successfully under some situations (Carlson, Moses, & Hix, 1998).

Unfortunately, the picture is not as simple as the research by Chandler and his colleagues and Sullivan and Winner suggests, with more than a little room for doubt, at least according to some researchers. Most other studies report little evidence that children much under 4 years of age use deception in a way that reflects "mind reading" (Peskin, 1992; Sodian et al., 1991). For example, Beate Sodian and her colleagues (1991) reported that 3-year-olds were just as likely to use a deceptive strategy whether they were asked to mislead a competitor or help a collaborator (although Hala et al., 1991, report evidence that 3-year-olds can use a deceptive strategy selectively). Subtle differences in the way the deception tasks are performed seem to make a big difference in whether children younger than 4 years use deception selectively or not.

Do Three-Year-Olds Have a Theory of Mind?

What can we make of the often-contradictory evidence concerning young children's theory of mind? There is actually much that the various researchers agree on. Three-year-olds seem to have a limited knowledge of other minds. In some circumstances, particularly involving deception or when implicit tasks are used, even 2.5-year-old children seem to be aware that they have knowledge not possessed by others. But young children's theory of mind, or belief-desire reasoning, is tenuous at best.

In general, there have been two camps of theory-of-mind researchers (Wellman et al., 2001). Members of the first camp argue for early competence, proposing that 3-year-olds (and perhaps even younger children) possess the same basic competence as older children, but overly demanding tasks, confusing questions, or information-processing limits prevent them from displaying this competence in most situations. Members of the second camp propose that there is real conceptual change during the preschool years, that is, age-related differences in performance on false-belief tasks are the result of "genuine changes in children's conceptions of persons" (Wellman et al., 2001, p. 671). To differentiate between these two positions, Henry Wellman, David Cross, and Julanne Watson (2001) conducted a meta-analysis including 178 separate false-belief studies. They reported a substantial age effect in every analysis performed and found patterns of change generally consistent with the conceptual change position. That is, although different task and instruction variables did influence young children's performance, there was little evidence that 3-year-old children possess the conceptual understanding to perform false-belief tasks. According to the authors, "early competence accounts that claim apparent development during the ages of 3 to 5 years are solely the products of overly difficult tasks masking young children's essentially correct understanding of belief are not substantiated in several key regards" (p. 678).

Theory of Mind, Evolved Modules, and Autism

Some theorists have proposed that theory of mind evolved during the course of human evolution and is the basis of our social intelligence (Baron-Cohen, 1995; Leslie, 1994). The social complexity of human groups demands attention to the actions of fellow members, and having an idea of the beliefs and desires of others would provide a tremendous political advantage for anyone trying to predict the actions of other members of a group, or of rival groups. Consistent with the premises of evolutionary psychology (see Chapter 2), the cognitive and brain mechanisms underlying theory of mind have been proposed to be domain specific and modular in nature, rather than resulting from some domain-general ability. Thus, the theory goes, our ancestors developed specific skills relating to mindreading, and these skills are relatively independent of more general cognitive abilities.

One modular-type theory of theory of mind was presented by Simon Baron-Cohen (1995), who proposed four separate, interacting modules involved in mindreading that develop during infancy and early childhood. The earliest developing module is the *intentionality detector (ID)*, which interprets moving objects as having some volition or intention. For example, an object that is moving toward an individual might be perceived as an agent with some intention toward that individual (for instance, it wants to harm me, to be near me). All animals that have nervous systems likely possess this very primitive skill. The second module is the *eye-direction detector (EDD)*, which has three related functions: It detects the presence of eyes or eye-like stimuli, determines whether the eyes are looking toward it or toward something else, and infers that if an organism's eyes are looking at something, then that organism sees that thing. In other words, this module is responsible for our belief that knowledge is gained through the eyes (both ours and the eyes of others). According to Baron-Cohen, these first two modules develop between birth and 9 months of age. The third module is the *shared-attention mechanisms (SAM)*. Whereas the ID and EDD involve only two objects/individuals (that is, dyadic interactions/representations), the SAM involves triadic (three-way) interactions/representations. For example, if person A is looking at object B, and person C can see the eyes of person A and can see object B, person C can come to the conclusion that "You (person A) and I (person C) are looking at the same thing (object B)." This module develops between 9 and 18 months. Finally, the *theory of mind module (TOMM)* is roughly equivalent to the belief-desire reasoning described earlier and is reflected by passing false-belief tasks. This develops between the ages of about 18 to 48 months.

I will not describe here the evidence Baron-Cohen provides for each of these modules, but refer the reader to Baron-Cohen's (1995) book. But what support is there that these abilities are modular? Recall from Chapter 2 that modular abilities are domain-specific and relatively independent of other cognitive abilities (such as general intelligence). What evidence does Baron-Cohen have for this claim? His primary source of evidence is that the more advanced forms of mindreading (SAM and TOMM) are typically absent in one particular class of childhood psychiatric disorder, autism. Autism is a relatively rare (between 4 and 15 children per 10,000) but severe disorder characterized by social and communication disabilities. These children (and later adults) often seem to be in a world of their own and have a difficult time in most forms of social interaction. Baron-Cohen claims that the primary deficit of these children is an inability to read minds, or what he calls **mindblindness.** Evidence for this comes from studies in which autistic children are presented with false-belief and other theory-of-mind tasks and consistently fail them, despite performing well on other, nonsocial tasks. This is in contrast to children with mental retardation, such as Down Syndrome, who perform the theory-of-mind tasks easily, despite often doing poorly on other tasks that assess more general intelligence. Most autistic children are able to perform well on the simpler tasks requiring the ID or EDD modules, but fail tasks involving the SAM and especially the TOMM modules. According to Baron-Cohen, autistic children are unable to understand other people's different beliefs, and as a result, the world consisting of humans must be a confusing and frightening one, even for those children who are functioning at a relatively high intellectual level.

More recently, Baron-Cohen and his colleagues (1999) have demonstrated deficits in theory of mind in three highly successful autistic (Asperger syndrome) adults, despite above-average performance on tests related to IQ and executive functioning and reasoning, further bolstering the independence of theory of mind and general intelligence. Recent research has shown that neurophysiological deficits in people with autism are located in the same brain region (left frontal lobe) as is normal adults' processing on theory-of-mind tasks (Sabbagh & Taylor, 2000),

further suggesting the domain specificity of theory-of-mind abilities. Additional support for the modular view is found in behavioral genetic research. Claire Hughes and Alexandra Cutting (1999) reported substantial genetic influence on theory-of-mind tasks among 199 pairs of 3-year-old same-sex twins. Importantly for the domain-specificity perspective, most of this genetic effect was independent of a general measure of verbal ability, consistent with the idea that theory of mind is not simply a function of general intellectual functioning.

Although much research needs to be done to specify the different components involved in children's developing theories of mind, research with autistic children provides evidence that the ability is relatively independent of other cognitive skills and is consistent with the evolutionary psychological account that the skill is modular and evolved to solve the problems of dealing with other members of our own species in social settings. This does not mean that there are not domain-general skills, such as executive function, that also influence the development of theory of mind. Both domain-specific and domain-general skills surely exist and interact with one another (Bjorklund, Cormier, & Rosenberg, in press). But the evidence Baron-Cohen and others present for the modularity of theory of mind, along with research on theory of mind in great apes (Bjorklund et al., in press; Tomasello & Call, 1997), suggests that social intelligence may have played a significant role in human cognitive evolution.

Classification

At the center of the great and near-great stage theories of cognitive development is the idea of changes in the nature of mental representation between the preschool and school years. Piaget, Fischer, and Case all attest to the symbolic nature of thinking by the 2- and 3-year-old child, but all concur that thinking changes qualitatively sometime between 5 and 7 years of age. Piaget and the neo-Piagetians generally agree on the nature of the representational change. Piaget believed that preschool children's thinking is intuitive rather than logical in nature; moreover, their thinking is perceptually centered and based more on perceptual than abstract, or conceptual, features.

Researchers have long been interested in the transition in representation that occurs during this time, and evidence from a variety of sources indicates changes in children's representation from (1) perceptual to conceptual properties of stimuli, and (2) schematic to conceptual/taxonomic categorical properties. The term **schematic** as used here refers to representing objects in terms of real or potential interactions with other items. Thus, a tractor may be thought about in terms of what it does (plows fields, pulls heavy equipment), who interacts with it (farmers), and where it is found (on farms, in barns), rather than in terms of its conceptual or taxonomic category (vehicle; similar to cars). Each form of representation reflects something important about an object, but which representation comes to mind first (perceptual, schematic, or conceptual) or which one we find easier to use in our thinking will influence how we think and what conclusions we're likely to reach when considering a problem.

In this section, I will review research mainly from classification tasks that reflect some of these changes in representation during early and middle childhood. (Other research using classification tasks will be examined in Chapter 12 on problem solving.)

Classification Style

Classification refers to the grouping of objects on the basis of some set of characteristics. In many classification experiments, children are given a set of objects, pictures, or words and asked to group them so that items that are alike or go together in some way are grouped together. Following sorting, children are usually asked to justify their groupings. By examining the composition of and justifications for their groupings, one can infer how children represent sets of items and the type of relations they use for categorizing diverse stimuli.

Although age-related changes in classification can be described in a variety of ways, four general phases in classification can be identified. The earliest phase, typifying most 2- and some 3-year-olds, I have labeled **idiosyncratic classification** (also called *fiat equivalence* or *random classification*). Children group items together, usually in pairs, and either fail to provide a reason for their groupings or provide one that is independent of any physical or conceptual characteristics of the stimuli (Inhelder & Piaget, 1964). For example, a child might sort pictures of a dog and an apple together, and when asked why he or she made such a grouping, answer, "Because a dog barks and you can eat an apple." Alternatively, the child might simply label each object or state, "I like dogs and I like apples." This latter explanation may seem to reflect a grouping on the basis of likes and dislikes, but such a child will probably give the same justification for all pairings.

In a second phase, labeled here **perceptual classification,** children group items on the basis of perceptual characteristics. For example, table and chair go together because they both have four legs, or elephant and car go together because they're both big, or frog and tree go together because they're both green. Perceptual justifications are found mainly in the groupings of 3- and 4-year-old children but are also found in the classifications of older children.

Complementary classification (also called *functional*, *schematic*, or *thematic classification*) typifies the groupings of slightly older children. Nancy Denney described groupings based on complementary relations as those "composed of items that are different but share some interrelationship either in the subject's past experiences or in the experimental situation" (1974, p. 41). For example, dog and apple go together because dogs can eat apples, or barn, tractor, and farmer go together because a farmer can drive a tractor into a barn. Complementary justifications increase in incidence during the preschool years and typically are replaced by conceptual justifications some time between the ages of 6 and 9 years.

Finally, **conceptual classification** (also called *similarity*, *taxonomic*, *nominal*, or *categorical classification*) dominates the groupings of older children. I use this term to mean groupings based on similar category membership (for example, membership in categories such as animals, furniture, clothing) or shared function (for example, both birds and airplanes fly). Conceptual justifications can be found in the classifications of preschool children, but they increase in frequency between the ages of 6 and 10 years. The use of conceptual classification seems to be related to formal schooling (see Denney, 1974).

There is other evidence of a schematic-to-conceptual shift in development, including research examining age differences in how children define words (Denney, 1974), word associations (Emerson & Gekowski, 1976), cued recall (Ackerman, 1986), errors in recognition memory (Scott, Serchuk, & Mundy, 1982), and children's specification of relations existing among a series of items (Anglin, 1970). For example, when preschool children are asked to define words, they typically describe a function for the word (for instance, "A hoe is for digging"), whereas older children more typically provide a category name (for instance, "A hoe is a type of garden tool") or a synonym (for instance, "A hoe is like a shovel") (Denney, 1974). Similarly, on word-association tasks, in which children are read a word and are to say the first word that comes into their minds, older school-age children, like adults, usually provide a response word of the same conceptual class as the stimulus word (for example, car: truck; dress: pants). Preschool and early school-age children are more likely to provide a complementary response, stating a function of the stimulus word (for example, car: drive) or one that "goes with" the stimulus word (for example, dress: girl) (Emerson & Gekowski, 1976).

Cross-Cultural Differences in Classification

Evidence for Denney's "schooling" hypothesis is found in research examining the thinking of people from traditional cultures, where the shift from complementary to conceptual classification, as defined here, is typically not found (Cole & Scribner, 1977). Soviet psychologist Alexander Luria (1976) studied the thinking styles of people from a remote area of Uzbekistan in the 1930s. Following are excerpts from Luria's study that reflect complementary classification similar to that shown by 5- and 6-year-olds from technologically more advanced cultures. In these examples, the participant was shown four pictures and was to choose the one that was different. This is known as an oddity problem.

> **Subject: Rakmat, age thirty-nine, illiterate peasant from an outlying district; . . . He is shown drawings of the following: hammer-saw-log-hatchet.**
>
> "They're all alike. I think all of them have to be here. See, if you're going to saw, you need a saw, and if you have to split something you need a hatchet. So they're all needed here."

> **We tried to explain the task by another, simpler example: "Look, here you have three adults and one child. Now clearly the child doesn't belong in this group."**
>
> "Oh, but the boy must stay with the others! All three of them are working, you see, and if they have to keep running out to fetch things, they'll never get the job done, but the boy can do the running for them. . . . The boy will learn; that'll be better, then they'll be able to work well together." [p. 55]

> **Subject is then shown drawing of: bird-rifle-dagger-bullet.**
>
> "The swallow doesn't fit here. . . . No . . . this is a rifle. It's loaded with a bullet and kills the swallow. Then you have to cut the bird up with the dagger, since there's no other way to do it. . . . What I said about the swallow before is wrong! All these things go together." [pp. 56–57]

The classification responses of this uneducated adult are reminiscent of the responses of 5-year-olds. However, one must be cautious not to make value judgments concerning the thinking of people from traditional cultures. The thinking of the people described in Luria's study was well suited for their environment, and, in some ways, may be more advanced than our own. The demands of their world were different, requiring a different cognitive system. They did not have to worry about a monetary system of checks, automatic tellers, and credit cards, whereas we do. Human cognitive abilities are flexible. In fact,

Luria noted that the thinking of these people became more conceptual as a result of formal education, reflecting the plasticity of human intelligence, even in adults.

Other research has shown that people from traditional cultures are able to classify objects according to conceptual criteria—they just don't think that it's a very intelligent way of doing things. For instance, in a study of Kpelle farmers from Liberia, adults consistently sorted objects into functional groups (for example, *knife* with *orange; potato* with *hoe*), rather than into conceptual categories (for example, *potato* and *orange; hoe* and *knife*). Functional grouping, many farmers stated, was the wise way to do it. When asked how a fool would do the task, the farmers classified the objects into neat conceptually based piles, exactly as Westerners do (Glick, 1975).

Phases Not Stages

The developmental trend in classification described here is not stage-like. Although a preference for conceptual classification is usually observed in children 8 or 9 years of age, for example, some studies find this preference even in preschool-age children (Osborne & Calhoun, 1998), and complementary schemes continue to be used by older children and adults when the stimuli and task demands call for them (Greenfield & Scott, 1986). Thus, people over a broad age range have available to them a variety of relations by which to classify objects. What changes in development seems to be the tendency for various forms of relations to be used, with conceptual relations being used in a wider range of contexts with increasing age.

The use of alternative classification styles is not limited to older children and adults. Although one would not expect many conceptually based groupings in the sortings of 3-year-olds, children at least as young as 4 and 5 years use a variety of these classification schemes. Let me provide an example of a not-too-atypical 5-year-old who used an interesting mixture of styles in a single sorting task. The child was given 16 black-and-white line drawings of familiar objects that could, from an adult's perspective, be grouped into four categories (animals, clothes, food, and tools). He was told to put the drawings into groups so that "pictures that are alike or go together in some way are grouped together." He spontaneously provided justifications for his groupings as he sorted. This child grouped all items into pairs, although this was not a requirement of the task. His first pair was corn and banana, and they went together, he said, because they are both yellow (perceptual). Horse and pants go together because a cowboy needs pants to ride a horse (complementary); saw and shovel go together because they both have sharp points (perceptual); coat and shirt go together because you wear them (conceptual); pie and hat go together because they're both round (perceptual); hammer and screwdriver go together because they're both tools (conceptual); and rabbit and milk go together because they're both white (perceptual), and squirrel and cat go together because a cat can chase a squirrel (complementary). This child had more perceptual justifications than is usual for a 5-year-old, but his mixture of justifications is typical for children of this age.

An example from another 5-year-old reflects the mixture of classification styles for children of this age, as well as their creativity and lack of planning. This child's first group consisted of the items shovel, saw, screwdriver, and hammer, and her justification was that they are all tools (conceptual). Next, she placed cat, rabbit, and milk together and said that cats and rabbits drink milk (complementary); horse and corn go together because a horse eats corn (complementary); hat and coat go together because you wear them (conceptual); and squirrel and banana go together because a squirrel might eat a banana (complementary). The child was then left with three pictures, and rather than not including them in any group or rethinking some of her earlier categories, she paused and then placed pants, shirt, and pie together and said, "Well, you've got to get dressed to eat dessert." This last example shows children's tendencies to follow instructions to make groups even if it means being inventive. It also reflects young children's lack of planning. This child did not look at all the pictures first and then decide the best categorization plan. Rather, she noticed salient relations among items and formed her groups on an item-by-item basis. Older children, with more foresight, would not be left with squirrel and banana or shirt, pants, and pie. Age differences in planning are discussed further in Chapter 12.

The diversity of classification judgments made by the same child indicates that these styles reflect, for the most part, preferences by the child. For example, children alter their sorting styles as a function of changes in procedures or instructions. A clear example of the preference basis of children's classification styles is found in a study by Sandra Smiley and Ann Brown (1979). Children were to choose which of two pictures went best with a standard picture. One of the alternatives was related to the standard on the basis of complementary relations (for example, for needle, thread), whereas the other alternative was related on the basis of conceptual relations (for example, for needle, pin). Most selections of preschool and first-grade children reflected complementary relations. In contrast, fifth-grade and college students showed a marked preference for conceptual relations. In a second experiment, kindergarten children were successfully trained to make selections based on conceptual relations. One day after training, however, the children were tested again, and their bias for complementary classification had returned. Thus, young children can easily be trained to use conceptual relations, but they revert to their preferred mode when given the opportunity to do so.

In other research using a similar task, young children actually showed a preference for a conceptual classification strategy over a thematic/complementary one (Blanchet, Dunham, & Dunham, 2001). In this study, 2-, 3-, and 4-year-old children were given a standard picture and three alternatives. They were told to pick the alternative that "goes with" the standard picture. The alternatives consisted of (1) a *basic-level taxonomic* match—a different example of the *same kind of thing* (for instance, two different examples of dogs or two different examples of keys); (2) a *thematic* match (for instance, a bone for the standard dog, a door for the standard key), and (3) an ir-

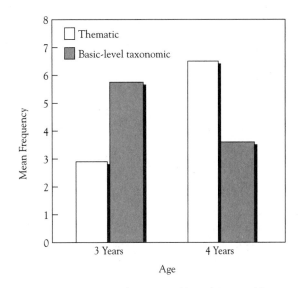

FIGURE 9-7 Mean frequency of 3- and 4-year-old children's thematic and basic-level taxonomic choices. SOURCE: Adapted from Blanchet, N., Dunham, P. J., & Dunham, F. (2001). Differences in preschool children's conceptual strategies when thinking about animate entities and artifacts. *Developmental Psychology, 37,* 791–800. Copyright © 2001 by the American Psychological Association. Adapted with permission.

relevant match (for instance, a fountain pen for the dog, a wheel for the key). Note that the basic-level taxonomic choice is the only one that is conceptually related to the standard. It is a member of the same superordinate category (for example, both dogs are animals), but, more important, they are different members of the same basic-level categories. Nicole Blanchet and her colleagues reported that 2-year-olds' selections were apparently random, choosing equally often the taxonomic, thematic, and irrelevant alternatives. In contrast, the 3- and 4-year-old children's choices were selective, but for different alternatives. These are shown in Figure 9-7. As can be seen, 3-year-old children selected the taxonomic alternatives more often than the thematic, with this being reversed for the 4-year-olds. Thus, preschool children's seeming preference for thematic over conceptual relations as a basis for classifying objects holds true only when higher-level conceptual categories are involved. Young children actually prefer to classify items on the basis of conceptual relations when such relations are at the basic level. More will be said about basic-level categories in Chapter 11 when I discuss natural language categories.

The classification research suggests that, although children may have preferences for how they group together sets of objects, these preferences are not set in stone for any given child, and, although they change with age, they do not have the quality of stages, with a given child using a variety of different classification relations within a single task. This pattern is consistent with Robert Siegler's (1996) observations that children use a variety of strategies on any cognitive task, with developmental changes being best described not as stage transitions but as changes in the frequency with which different strategies are used (see Chapter 6). This research also reveals the difficulty of divorcing content (as reflected by the nature of children's representation) from process (as reflected by strategy use).

Summary

Representation is the way in which objects, events, and experiences are encoded or represented in the mind. Traditionally, representation during infancy has been referred to as sensorimotor, in that objects and events are known by action associated with those objects (either activity inherent in the object itself or the child's action on the object). Sensorimotor representation is replaced by mentalistic, symbolic representation (the *symbolic*, or *semiotic*, *function*) sometime around 18 to 24 months of age, as reflected by *deferred imitation*, language, *symbolic play*, and *mental imagery*.

Neonatal imitation has been observed, with Meltzoff and Moore attributing this phenomenon to *active intermodal mapping* and thus seeing it as a reflection of symbolic functioning. Others observe that neonatal imitation typically disappears by about 2 months and suggest that it reflects an *innate releasing mechanism (fixed-action pattern)* and an *ontogenetic adaptation*, serving a specific function at a particular time in development, rather than a reflection of symbolic ability. Evidence for deferred imitation has been found as early as 6 months of age, which has been interpreted as reflecting symbolic functioning. By using variations of the violation-of-expectation method, researchers have demonstrated evidence for simple arithmetic in infants (for example, by *subitizing*), although there is great debate in how to interpret these findings.

The knowledge that an entity can stand for something other than itself has been referred to as *representational insight*. DeLoache and her colleagues have investigated the development of representational insight in children by examining how they deal with scale models and pictures. Whereas children as young as 2.5 years old show representational insight when pictures are used, not until age 3 do children show representational insight with models. DeLoache proposed that *dual representation* (or *dual orientation*) is required before children can show representational insight.

Young children have a difficult time distinguishing between an object's appearance and its actual identity (*appearance/reality distinction*). This is reflected in children's abilities to make judgments of *identity*, which Piaget defined as knowledge that qualitative properties do not change the identity of an object. Flavell and his colleagues speculated that children must be able to engage in *dual encoding* before this distinction can be made. Although 3- and 4-year-old children can distinguish between imagined and experienced events, this distinction is tenuous, with preschoolers often thinking that make-believe objects can become real by imagining them as real. Young children also often show *source-monitoring* errors, confusing whether they had imagined or experienced an event.

Theory of mind refers to children's developing concepts of mental activity, both their own and others'. Adults' theory of mind is based on *belief-desire reasoning*, understanding that one's behavior is motivated by what one believes (knows) and desires (wants). Concerning children as "mind readers," 3-year-olds usually fail *false-belief tasks* and show poor memory for their earlier (erroneous) beliefs (*representational change*). Some explanations for young children's poor performance on false-belief tasks are that children lack the requisite representational abilities and have poor *executive function*, including poor inhibitory skills. Children seem to show greater theory of mind abilities when deception is involved. Theory of mind has been proposed by Baron-Cohen to be modular (domain-specific) in nature. Evidence of this comes from the general inability of children with autism to read minds, which has been referred to as *mindblindness*.

The nature of children's symbolic representation varies during childhood, with preschool children being especially attentive to *schematic representations* whereas older children are more attentive to *conceptual relations*. In *classification* experiments, children sort sets of objects so that items that are alike or go together in some way are grouped together. Four different phases in children's classification can be identified: (1) *idiosyncratic*, (2) *perceptual*, (3) *complementary (schematic)*, and (4) *conceptual*. These classification phases do not have the quality of stages, and children can easily be trained to use a more advanced style than they use spontaneously. Even adults frequently use complementary schemes in certain situations.

Key Terms and Concepts

representation
symbolic (semiotic) function
deferred imitation
symbolic play
mental imagery
neonatal imitation
active intermodal mapping
innate releasing mechanisms (fixed action patterns)
ontogenetic adaptations
subitizing
representational insight
dual representation (dual encoding, dual orientation)
appearance/reality distinction
identity
source monitoring
theory of mind
belief-desire reasoning
false-belief task
representational change
executive functions
mindblindness
schematic representation
classification
idiosyncratic (fiat equivalence, random) classification
perceptual classification
complementary (functional, schematic, thematic) classification
conceptual (similarity, taxonomic, nominal, categorical) classification

Suggested Readings

Baron-Cohen, S. (1995). *Mindblindness: An essay on autism and theory of mind.* Cambridge, MA: MIT Press. In this short and highly readable book, Baron-Cohen presents an evolutionary psychological account of theory of mind, and supports his idea that theory of mind is modular in nature with research on autistic children, whom, Baron-Cohen proposes, are "mindblind," in that they are not able to read the minds of other people and, thus, find themselves in a social world they do not understand.

DeLoache, J. S. (1995). Early understanding and use of symbols: The model model. *Current Directions in Psychological Science, 4,* 109–113. DeLoache provides a brief and easily comprehensible account of her research and theory about preschool children's developing understanding of symbols.

Mandler, J. (1998). Representation. In D. Kuhn & R. S. Siegler (Eds.), *Cognition, perception, and language,* Vol. 2 (pp. 255–308). In W. Damon (Gen. Ed.), *Handbook of child psychology.* New York: Wiley. Mandler provides an excellent review of research on representation in infancy and the debate concerning the nature of infants' representation. Another chapter in this volume that discusses infant representation is M. M. Haith & J. B. Benson, "Infant cognition" (pp. 199–254).

Wellman, H. M., & Gelman, S. A. (1998). Knowledge acquisition in foundational domains. In D. Kuhn & R. S. Siegler (Eds.), *Cognition, perception, and language*, Vol. 2 (pp. 523–574). In W. Damon (Gen. Ed.), *Handbook of child psychology*. New York: Wiley.   In addition to discussing representation in infancy, this chapter also provides a good overview of children's early "psychological theories" (theories of mind), as well as their "biological theories" (theories about animate and inanimate things). Another chapter in this volume that discusses representation during childhood (theory of mind and appearance/reality distinction) is that of J. H. Flavell and P. H. Miller, "Social cognition" (pp. 851–898).

InfoTrac College Edition

For additional readings, explore InfoTrac College Edition, your online library. Go to http://www.infotrac-college.com/wadsworth.

Memory Development

A 4-month-old looks longer at a new picture than at one he has seen repeatedly, a 3-year-old recounts her class field trip to a bakery, a 7-year-old lists for her mother the names of all her classmates in preparing to send Valentine's Day cards, and a high school sophomore attempts to remember everything his father asked him to get at the corner store. Each of these diverse activities has at least one thing in common: memory. The 4-month-old can recognize a new stimulus only if he has some notion that it is different from a previously experienced but currently unseen stimulus. The memory requirements for the three older children are more demanding, but all involve retrieving from memory some previously stored information.

Memory is not a unitary phenomenon. Information must be encoded and possibly related with other information known to the individual. What knowledge already resides in memory influences the ease with which new information is stored and later retrieved. Furthermore, few acts of cognition do not involve memory. Classification, problem solving, and decision making all require the retrieval of previously stored information.

To make matters even more complex, memory can refer to the contents of one's mind (one's memories) or to the process of bringing that information to consciousness. The contents of memory can be *declarative*, or *explicit*, so that a person can consciously reflect on what he or she knows, or it can be *nondeclarative* (procedural), or *implicit*, unavailable to conscious evaluation. Moreover, there are two general types of declarative memory: *semantic memory*, which refers to the long-term repository of language terms, their definitions, and their relations to one another; and *episodic memory*, which refers to memories for events or episodes. For example, the definition for the word "avuncular" is part of my semantic memory, but my recollections of the events surrounding my learning the word (preparing for the Graduate Record Exam) are part of my episodic memory.[1] Most of this chapter will deal with explicit, episodic memory, although we will also look at research into implicit memory.

Concerning the process of remembering, researchers have specified different operations by which information in our minds can be retrieved. The most

basic form of retrieval is **recognition,** in which a stimulus is presented to a person and he or she must merely signify whether that stimulus is new (not experienced previously) or old. Young children often show very high levels of recognition memory, and in some situations, age differences in recognition memory are quite small, causing some to assert that this ability changes little with development (see Perlmutter & Lange, 1978). However, recognition is not purely automatic, and developmental differences in children's application of what they know to the task at hand have also been reported for this form of memory (Dirks & Neisser, 1977).

More demanding in terms of self-activation is *recall*, in which some information is not currently perceived but must be retrieved from memory. Retrieval can be prompted by a specific environmental context or cue (**cued recall**), or the reminder might be general or be internally generated (**free recall**). An important developmental consideration in retrieving information from memory is the degree to which children will use information they have available to them. In general, recall (especially free recall) requires more self-initiation and application of prior knowledge than recognition does.

The distinction between cued-recall and free-recall memory in young children can be appreciated when one attempts to get some information from a young child. Such a question as, "How was school today?," is apt to bring a response of "Fine." More detailed information can be forthcoming, however, if more specific questions are asked. For example, a 5-year-old boy who spent the afternoon with his grandparents seeing his first play, "Little Shop of Horrors," was asked by his mother, "Well, how was your afternoon?" The child replied, "OK." The mother persisted, "Well, did you have a good time?" The child said, "Yeah." However, when prompted by his grandmother ("Tell your mother about Audrey II, the plant"), he provided great details, telling how the plant ate some of the main characters, talked, sang, and how it took three people underneath it to make it move. The child had a wealth of information, but it could only be accessed when specific cues were provided.

Memory development is one of the oldest, continuously researched topics in the field of cognitive development. But how it is researched today and the theoretical focus of researchers is much different than it was 30 years ago. How much children remember is influenced greatly by developmental differences in basic information-processing abilities of encoding, storage, and retrieval, and by the strategies they use to intentionally learn information. These topics were the primary focus of researchers in the past, and were discussed previously in some detail in Chapters 5 and 6, but there is an increasing awareness today that memory is used *for* specific purposes and *in* specific social contexts (Kuhn, 2000; Ornstein & Haden, 2001). It is not enough merely to assess children's memory behavior in one context, particularly a context devoid of social meaning. How and what children remember depends on a host of dynamically interacting factors that vary over time. Despite the wealth of information we have about children's memory today, we are just beginning to develop an appreciation for the factors and contexts that influence children's memory performance and the development of those abilities.

In this chapter, I examine research and theory dealing with the development of memory in children. The topics of short-term (working) memory and strategic memory were discussed in earlier chapters and I will not review them here. I will open the chapter with an examination of the memory development in infancy, followed by a look at children's implicit memory. Children's memories for events will then be examined, specifically autobiographical memory. Research examining children as eyewitness, and the factors that influence their suggestibility, will be reviewed in some detail. This will be followed by the topics of the consistency and stability of memory, and finally, the flip side of remembering, forgetting.

Memory Development in Infancy

Babies obviously remember things. The questions of interest are when and under what conditions infants demonstrate memory and how long these memories last. Research examining infants' search behavior, as reflected by object permanence tasks (see Chapters 4 and 8), indicates age changes in memory during the first year (Diamond, 1985). Recall Adele Diamond's findings that the amount of delay necessary to yield the A-not-B error increased with each successive month between 7 and 12 months of age. Although Diamond proposed that developmental differences in the ability to inhibit a prepotent response were partly responsible for this effect, she also acknowledges that such results reflect age changes in memory during this six-month period (Diamond, Cruttenden, & Neiderman, 1994).

Preference for Novelty as an Indication of Memory

The bulk of research assessing infant memory, particularly in the early days of research, used variants of the habituation/dishabituation paradigm discussed in previous chapters. To review, infants' attention to a stimulus declines as a result of repeated presentation of a stimulus (habituation) but returns to its previously high levels when a new stimulus is presented (dishabituation). Such a finding not only indicates that infants can discriminate between the two stimuli but also implicates memory, in that the discrimination is being made between one stimulus that is physically present and another that is present only memorially. In a related procedure, infants are familiarized with a stimulus and later shown two stimuli: the original, familiarized stimulus and a novel one. As in the habituation/dishabituation paradigm, preference for the novel stimulus is (usually) taken as evidence of memory for the original. Using these **preference-for-novelty paradigms,** memory for visual stimuli has been found for some newborns. Research by Steven Friedman (1972) illustrated that some newborns demonstrate dishabituation (discussed in Chapter 7), although other research suggests that this ability likely characterizes only the more maturationally advanced neonates. Nonetheless, basic visual memory is an early developing ability, certainly within the capacity of most infants within their first months of life.

Perhaps the most influential work demonstrating memory in infants using the preference for novelty paradigm is that of Joseph Fagan (1973, 1974). One study showed that 5- and 6-month-old babies formed visual memories following brief exposures (5 to 10 seconds) and that these memories lasted as long as 2 weeks (Fagan, 1974). Fagan's procedures have been widely used by researchers, and recent work has suggested a relationship between individual differences in preference for novelty during infancy and childhood memory and intelligence. This research will be examined in Chapter 16.

More recent research has shown that even 1-month-old infants demonstrate relatively long-lived memories. For example, in one study the mothers of 1- and 2-month-old infants read their babies one of two nursery rhymes over the course of two weeks. Infants were then brought into the laboratory and their preferences for the familiar versus a novel nursery rhyme was tested. This was done by permitting infants to hear either the familiar or a novel nursery rhyme by modifying their sucking on a pacifier (for example, increase sucking rate to hear one rhyme, decrease to hear the other). After a 3-day delay between the time infants last heard their mothers read the familiar nursery rhyme and being tested in the lab, even 1-month-old babies showed a preference for the familiar rhyme, indicating memory for the auditory event (Spence, 1996).

It's worth noting here that infants' preference in Melanie Spence's (1996) study was for the familiar stimulus, not for the novel one. Yet, to demonstrate memory, all that is required is that infants show a decided preference for one stimulus or the other. As I noted in earlier chapters, infants' preferences for novel versus familiar objects/events varies as a function of their age and stage of learning in a task, among other factors (Bogartz & Shinskey, 1998). For example, Mary Courage and Mark Howe (2001) showed 3.5-month-old infants a stimulus for 30 seconds and then tested their preference for the old (familiar) versus a new (novel) stimulus after delays of 1 minute, 1 day, and 1 month. The researchers reported a preference for novelty after the 1-minute delay, no preference after 1 day, and a preference for familiarity after 1 month (see Figure 10-1). Following the theorizing of Loraine Bahrick and Jeffrey Pickens (1995), Courage and Howe interpreted

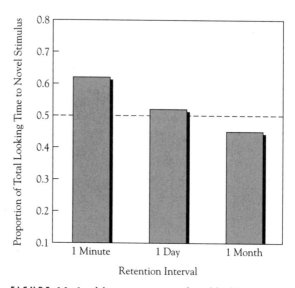

FIGURE 10-1 Mean proportion of total looking time infants directed to the novel stimulus during the 1-minute, 1-day, and 1-month delays. Chance is .5. Mean looking time significantly greater than chance reflects a preference for novelty. Mean looking time significantly less than expected by chance reflects a preference for familiarity. SOURCE: Courage, M. L., & Howe, M. L. (2001). Long-term retention in 3.5-month-olds: Familiarization time and individual differences in attentional style. *Journal of Experimental Child Psychology, 79,* 271–293. © 2001 Elsevier. Reprinted with permission.

these findings as indicating that infants' attention to novel versus familiar stimuli varies as a function of the strength of the familiar information in long-term memory at the time of testing. Infants will attend more to novel stimuli when memory traces are strong (after the 1-day delay) and attend more to familiar stimuli when the memory traces are weak (after the 1-month delay). Null effects (that is, neither a preference for the novel nor familiar stimuli) reflect a transition phase in which both stimuli compete equally for attention.

Conjugate Reinforcement Procedure

Other research by Carolyn Rovee-Collier and her colleagues has used conditioning techniques, demon-

PHOTO 10-1 An infant connected to a mobile in an experiment to assess memory used by Carolyn Rovee-Collier and her colleagues. (Thanks to Carolyn Rovee-Collier)

strating retention over relatively long periods for very young infants (see Rovee-Collier, 1999; Rovee-Collier & Gerhardstein, 1997 for reviews). In their **conjugate reinforcement procedure,** a ribbon is tied to an infant's ankle and connected to a mobile that is suspended over the crib (see Photo 10-1). Infants quickly learn that when they kick their feet the mobile moves, and they soon make repeated kicks, controlling the movement of the mobile overhead. In a typical experiment, for the first 3 minutes the ribbon is not connected to the mobile, so that kicks do not cause it to move (baseline nonreinforcement period). This is followed by a 9-minute reinforcement period in which the ribbon and mobile are connected, and infants quickly learn to kick to make the

mobile move. What will happen when the infants are hooked up to the apparatus hours or days later? Will they resume kicking (even when the ribbon is not connected to the mobile), or will their level of kicks be comparable to that observed during the 3-minute baseline? If the kicking rate is high on these delayed trials, it reflects memory; if it is low, it reflects forgetting.

Rovee-Collier and her colleagues have used this procedure successfully with infants as young as 2 months of age. For example, Margaret Sullivan, Carolyn Rovee-Collier, and Derek Tynes (1979) varied the delayed memory test between 48 hours and 336 hours (2 weeks) with 3-month-old infants. The researchers reported no forgetting by these young infants for as much as 8 days, and some babies displayed memory for the full 2-week interval. In related work, retention of conditioned responses during a 2-week period was obtained for infants as young as 8 weeks, although evidence of memory was obtained only under optimal conditions (distributing training over several sessions) (Vander Linde, Morrongiello, & Rovee-Collier, 1985). These results indicate that young infants can remember events over long intervals, although these skills do improve over the first several months of life. (More will be said on infants' long-term memories in the next section.)

More recent research by Rovee-Collier and her colleagues has focused on the role of context in infants' memories. How similar must the learning environment and testing environment be for babies to show retention? This was assessed in a study in which different aspects of the learning environment (in this case, the playpens in which the infants were tested) were changed between time of learning and time of testing (Rovee-Collier et al., 1992). Six-month-old infants were tested in the standard way, but the testing situation was made very distinctive. Infants sat in an infant seat that was placed in a playpen. The sides of the playpen were draped with a distinctive cloth (for example, yellow liner with green felt squares). Some infants were tested 24 hours later with the same cloth, whereas others were placed in the playpen that was draped with a blue liner and vertical red felt strips. The results of this experiment are presented in Figure 10-2 (expressed

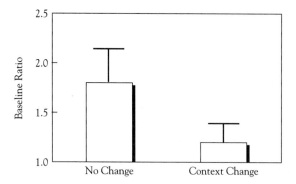

FIGURE 10-2 Mean baseline ratios for 6-month-old infants in a No Change (control) condition and a Context Change condition. The higher ratio for infants in the No Change condition reflects greater retention of the behaviors that were learned 24 hours earlier. SOURCE: Adapted from Rovee-Collier, C., Schechter, A., Shyi, C.-W. G., & Shields, P. (1992). Perceptual identification of contextual attributes and infant memory retrieval. *Developmental Psychology, 28*, 307–318.

as kicking rate during testing relative to kicking rate during baseline). As can be seen, infants in the "No Change" condition demonstrated significantly better retention of the learned behavior than infants in the "Context Change" condition, indicating the important role that context plays in reinstating infants' memories.

Rovee-Collier et al. (1992) performed six other experiments, varying different aspects of the context. They concluded that infants do not respond to the context "as a whole" but, rather, seem to process individual components of a context. For instance, changes in visual patterns (for example, strips versus squares) or reversal of the foreground and background (for example, yellow liner with green squares versus green liner with yellow squares) disrupted memory, but changes in color did not (for other examples, see Bhatt, Rovee-Collier, & Shyi, 1994; Fagen et al., 1997). Rovee-Collier and Gary Shyi (1992) speculated that infants' reliance on specific aspects of a context prevents them from retrieving memories in "inappropriate" situations. This may be especially important for infants with poor inhibitory

abilities, who would be apt to retrieve previously acquired memories (actions) in a wide range of often-inappropriate situations unless there were some potent constraints on the memory system (such as context specificity). The role of inhibitory factors in infant cognition has been addressed by several researchers, most notably Diamond, and this work was discussed in Chapter 2.

One interesting study by Rovee-Collier and her colleagues (Gulya et al., 1998) demonstrated that 3-month-olds can remember arbitrary sequences, something that is seemingly important in learning language. In their study, infants were hooked up to a series of three mobiles, one at a time. Infants were seen again 24 hours later. Some infants were first cued with the first mobile they had seen and then hooked up to the second mobile (that is, these two mobiles were presented in the same serial order they had been presented the previous day). Other infants were first cued with the third mobile they had seen the day before followed by the second mobile (that is, the serial order of presentation was different than the previous day). Infants who received the mobiles in the same serial order on the two days demonstrated significantly more kicking when hooked up to the second mobile than those who received the mobiles in a different serial order than the day before. This is clear evidence that 3-month-old babies are able to remember a three-item arbitrary sequence for a 24-hour period. (Researchers using a very different paradigm have similarly shown that 8-month-olds can learn, very quickly, arbitrary patterns of syllables, again, critical for language acquisition [Aslin, Saffran, & Newport, 1998].)

How Long Do Infants' Memories Last?

Rovee-Collier and her colleagues have used conjugate reinforcement procedures to assess age-related changes in long-term memory in infants. For example, in addition to the mobile task, they developed the *train task*, which uses the same logic as the mobile task but is appropriate to use with older babies. In the train task, infants sit in front of a display that

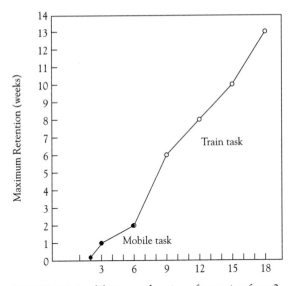

FIGURE 10-3 Maximum duration of retention from 2 to 18 months of age. Filled circles show retention on the mobile task, and open circles show retention on the train task; 6-month-olds were trained and tested on both tasks. SOURCE: Rovee-Collier, C. (1999). The development of infant memory. *Current Directions in Psychological Science*, 8, 80–85. © 1999 Blackwell Publishers. Reprinted with permission.

includes a miniature train set. They can learn to move the train around the set by pressing a lever in front of them, and retention is tested as it is in the mobile task, with infants sitting in front of the display after a delay and the rate with which they press the lever (when it is now not connected to the train) is measured. With these two comparable tasks, it is now possible to ask "how long do memories last for infants of different ages?" Figure 10-3 presents the maximum number of weeks that infants between 2 and 18 months of age demonstrated retention under standard conditions. As can be seen, the duration of infants' memories showed gradual but steady increases with age, reflecting a continuously developing memory system.

Another task that has been used to assess infants' long-term memory is deferred imitation, discussed in Chapter 9 on representation. As you will recall, in most experiments, infants watch as an experimenter demonstrates some novel behavior with an unfamiliar toy. At some later time, they are given the toy. If they display the novel behavior more than does a control group of infants who had not previously been shown the toy, it implies that they formed a long-term memory for the action. The results of recent research are quite striking, showing that infants form long-term memories for these novel actions that can last as long as one year (see Bauer, 1997; Meltzoff, 1995). These results suggest that preverbal infants and toddlers do represent events in their long-term memories, and, under the right conditions, can access those memories months later.

But, just as Rovee-Collier and her colleagues found using conjugate reinforcement procedures, there are age differences in how long babies are able to retain the actions they observe. For example, Patricia Bauer and her colleagues (Bauer, 2002; Bauer et al., 2000, 2001) showed infants a series of three-step sequences. (For example, the model placed a bar across two posts, hung a plate from the bar, and then struck the plate with a mallet.) After delays ranging from 1 to 12 months, the babies were given the objects and the incidence of deferred imitation was noted. About half of 9-month-olds tested displayed imitation of simpler two-sequence actions after a 1-month delay, and these infants required at least three exposures to the events to achieve this level of performance. Rate of deferred imitation increased substantially for 13-, 16-, and 20-month-old infants, with older infants demonstrating higher levels of deferred imitation during each delay interval than younger infants did (Bauer et al., 2000). Figure 10-4 shows results of long-term retention as a function of age of infant and length of delay from this study. These findings are similar in form to those Rovee-Collier reported and illustrate that infants are able to form long-term memories early in life, and that the ability to retain these memories increases gradually during the first two years. Moreover, as discussed in Chapter 9, deferred imitation is believed to be a type of recall, which requires the retrieval of specific information in the presence of a cue. This is a form of explicit, or declarative, memory, which, until relatively

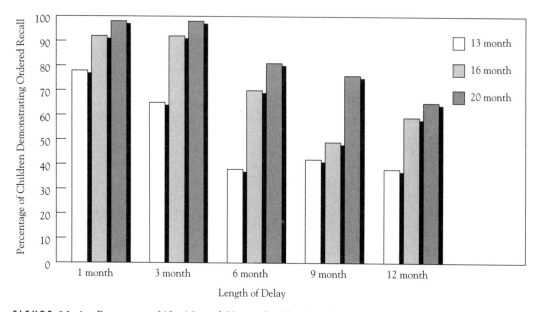

FIGURE 10-4 Percentage of 13-, 16-, and 20-month-old infants displaying deferred imitation of three-step sequences as a function of length of delay. SOURCE: Data from Bauer, P. J., Wenner, J. A., Dropik, P. L., & Wewerka, S. S. (2000). Parameters of remembering and forgetting in the transition from infancy to early childhood. *Monographs of the Society for Research in Child Development*, 65 (Issue no. 4, Serial No. 263). Figure from Bauer, P. J. (2002). Long-term recall memory: Behavioral and neuro-developmental changes in the first 2 years of life. *Current Directions in Psychological Science, 11*, 137–141. © 2002 Blackwell Publishers. Reprinted with permission.

recently, was believed to be unavailable until language is acquired. Based on recent research, some claim that explicit memory, like its supposedly more primitive cousin implicit memory, is "on line" from the earliest stages of life (Howe, 2000; Rovee-Collier, 1999).

The pattern of deferred imitation shown by infants between 6 months and approximately 2 years is consistent with what is known about brain development during this time (C. Nelson, 1997). Long-term memory requires the integration of brain activity from multiple sites, including the hippocampus, which develops early, and the prefrontal cortex and structures within the temporal lobe, which are much slower to develop. The early developing hippocampus presumably underlies the deferred imitation of simple actions by 6-month-olds (Collie & Hayne, 1999), but other brain areas must mature before infants can retain more complicated information for longer periods. Not until the second year of life do

these systems (hippocampus, prefrontal lobe, temporal lobe) begin to coalesce, with development continuing well into the third year. The relatively gradual development of these brain structures correlates with the relatively gradual improvement in long-term retention of infants during this same period (Liston & Kagan, 2002; Bauer et al., 2000).

Infantile Amnesia

The results of Rovee-Collier, Bauer, and their colleagues indicate that infants do indeed form long-term memories. This is a new finding, and one that, on the surface, contradicts the phenomenon of **infantile amnesia,** the seeming inability to recall information from early childhood. Such amnesia is bothersome not only to researchers, but also to some parents. For example, my wife and I used to write a

CALVIN & HOBBES

CARTOON 10-1 Most people cannot remember anything from the first few years of their lives, but this does not mean that this information is being repressed. SOURCE: CALVIN AND HOBBES © Watterson. Reprinted with permission of UNIVERSAL PRESS SYNDICATE. All rights reserved.

column for a parenting magazine and would occasionally get letters from concerned parents. One letter was from a woman who was worried because her 10-year-old son could remember very little from his preschool days. She said that she and her husband had always tried to be good parents but thought her son's inability to remember things from early childhood was an indication that either they hadn't done a very good job after all, or worse yet, they had done a truly terrible job and her son was repressing this painful period of his life. We wrote back to the woman, assuring her that her son's inability to remember events much before his fourth birthday is quite normal and that just because her child can't remember his experiences from this age doesn't mean that they didn't have an impact on him.

It is not just memories from infancy that escape us. For the most part, we are unable to remember much of anything before the age of 3.5 or 4 years (Pillemer & White, 1989; Usher & Neisser, 1993). Moreover, most of us have a few memories for events that happened between the ages of about 3 and 6 years, but very few in comparison with what we can remember from after this time (Pillemer & White, 1989). What we lack specifically are **autobiographical memories,** which refer to personal and long-

lasting memories, which are the basis for one's personal life history (K. Nelson, 1996).

JoNell Usher and Ulrich Neisser (1993) studied this lack of memory for the early years by questioning college students about experiences they had had early in life—experiences such as the birth of a younger sibling, a stay in the hospital, a family move, or the death of a family member. To assess recall, a series of questions was asked about each event the person had experienced (for example, Who told you your mother was going to the hospital to give birth? What were you doing when she left? Where were you when you first saw the new baby?) The percentage of questions college students could answer increased substantially the older the person was when he or she had experienced the event. Usher and Neisser concluded that the earliest age of *any* meaningful recall was about 2 for the birth of a sibling or a hospitalization and age 3 for the death of a family member or a family move.

Of course, many people do claim to have memories from infancy, some from birth (or before). But are these memories to be trusted? I, for example, have one very vivid memory, stemming from my first year of life. My memory is of me as a sick baby. I had the croup (something like bronchitis). When I recall this memory I can feel the congestion in my chest, hear the vaporizer whir, smell the Vicks VapoRub, and see the living room of my grandparents' house while looking through the bars of my crib. The memory is like a multisensory snapshot. I have no story to tell, only the recall of an instant of my life as a sickly baby. My mistake was relating this vibrant and personally poignant memory to my mother. She listened carefully and then told me that I had never had the croup; my younger brother Dick had the croup as an infant. I was about 4 years old at the time. My "memory" was a reconstruction—and of an event I had only *observed*, not one I had actually *experienced*. Most memories of infancy, it seems, are like mine—reconstructions of events that never happened, or happened but what one is remembering is the retelling of the event by other people. But back to our earlier question: Does this inability to retrieve memories from infancy contradict the new research findings of long-term retention in early infancy?

Why Can't We Remember Events from Infancy and Early Childhood?

Sigmund Freud (1963) was the first to speculate on the reason for infantile amnesia, proposing that the events of infancy and early childhood are rife with sexual overtones toward one's mother and are just generally so traumatic that they are actively repressed. We protect our adult egos, claimed Freud, by preventing these disturbing memories from rising to consciousness.

Few scientists today agree with Freud's interpretation. Other, more cognitively based interpretations propose the possibility that (a) information is not stored for long-term retention before about 2 years of age and (b) that information is encoded differently by infants and toddlers than by older children and adults (see White & Pillemer, 1979). The first possibility seems unlikely. As we've seen, research using the deferred-imitation procedure (Bauer, 2002; Meltzoff, 1995) discussed earlier in this chapter and in Chapter 9 has shown that infants between 6 and 16 months of age can encode and retain a simple experience for as long as one year.

The second alternative, that information is encoded differently during the early and later years of life, is consistent with observations made by Jean Piaget and others that the nature of representation changes from infancy to early childhood and then again (although less drastically) somewhere between the ages of 5 and 7 years. The minds that resided in our heads when we were infants are no longer there, replaced by minds that process symbols, especially verbal ones. We reconstruct memories through adult schemes and representations, which are not suitable for events encoded in infancy and early childhood. For example, the memories tested in infancy all involve recall of action patterns, whereas the recall assessed in childhood and adulthood involve verbal recall, using language. Perhaps the inability of converting the motor memories into verbal ones prevents children from recalling events from infancy.

Some evidence for this argument has recently been presented (Bauer, Wenner, & Kroupina, 2002; Simcock & Hayne, 2002). For example, Gabrielle Simcock and Harlene Hayne (2002) showed children ranging in age from 27 to 39 months sequences of actions and interviewed them 6 and 12 months later, both for their verbal and nonverbal memory of the events. Despite having the verbal ability to describe their previous experience, none of the children did so spontaneously. To the extent that children did talk about these prior events, they did so only if they had the vocabulary to describe the event *at the time of the experience*. That is, children who were more verbally sophisticated at time of initial testing tended to verbally recall some aspects of the event (Bauer et al., 2002), but children were seemingly not able to translate earlier preverbal experiences into language. According to Simcock and Hayne, "children's verbal reports were frozen in time, reflecting their verbal skill at the time of encoding, rather than at the time of test" (2002, p. 229).

Such an interpretation can account for our inability to retrieve memories from infancy, but 3- and 4-year-old children are clearly verbal and would presumably represent information in a similar symbolic form as adults. The fact that 3- and 4-year-old children can recount verbally events that happened many months or even years ago suggests that this interpretation cannot be the entire answer (Fivush & Hamond, 1990).

Several new explanations for infantile amnesia have been proposed. For example, several authors have suggested that for autobiographical memories to be laid down and later retrieved, there needs to be a sense of self (the "auto" in autobiographical) (Fivush, 1988; Howe & Courage, 1993). Research has shown that the sense of self develops gradually during the preschool years (see discussion of the development of self-concept in Chapter 13), and that, although young children have "memories," the experiences of early childhood occurred when the sense of self was poorly developed, thus providing no anchor for such events. Unless events can be related to the self, they cannot be retrieved later.

Another alternative is that infantile amnesia is merely a consequence of the child's developing information-processing system (Leichtman & Ceci, 1993). Following the tenets of fuzzy-trace theory (Brainerd & Reyna, 2002; see discussion in Chapter 5 and later in this chapter), Michelle Leichtman and Stephen Ceci proposed that there is a developmental shift in how events are represented, with young children encoding events primarily in terms of verbatim (precise) memory traces, whereas older children rely more on gist (less precise) traces. Verbatim traces are more susceptible to forgetting than gist traces are. Thus, the heavy reliance on the highly forgettable verbatim traces makes memories from infancy and early childhood unavailable. Gist traces become increasingly available by the early school years, about the time when more memories can be retrieved. Leichtman and Ceci also note that children are becoming increasingly facile with language at this time, using it not just for communication but as a representational system (K. Nelson, 1996; Vygotsky, 1962) and that these improved linguistic skills also likely contribute to improved autobiographical memory.

Other theorists have proposed changes in language and how language is used as an explanation for the phenomenon of infantile amnesia (Fivush & Hamond, 1990; K. Nelson, 1993, 1996). This was illustrated in Simcock and Hayne's (2002) research, which showed that 2- and 3-year-old children were not able to translate a preverbal memory into language 6 months later. But language is not fully developed by 3 years of age, and other language-related changes may further influence children's ability to remember events from their past. Young children, in trying to understand and predict their world, are attentive to routines and embed novel events in terms of these routines (for example, what happens at breakfast; what happens on a trip to the grocery store). Such memories, ensconced as they are in routines, are not very distinctive and thus not easily retrievable later on. Even when events *are* distinctive, however, young children do not necessarily know how to organize them in a memorable form. As I'll discuss in more detail later in this chapter, children "learn" to remember through interactions with adults. Adults provide the cues and structure for children to form narratives—stories for embedding events and later for remembering them. Only after being guided by adults can children learn to code memories and realize that language can be used to share memories with others.

Katherine Nelson makes this point especially clear:

> The claim here is that the initial functional significance of autobiographical memory is that of sharing memory with other people, a function that language makes possible. Memories become valued in their own right—not because they predict the future and guide present action, but because they are shareable with others and thus serve a social solidarity function. I suggest that this is a universal human function, although one with variable, culturally specific rules. In this respect, it is analogous to human language itself, uniquely and universally human but culturally —and individually—variable. (1993, p. 12)

Nelson's claim suggests that infantile amnesia might not be so significant in its own right, as Freud believed, but rather reflects an important transition in human cognition. This transition is based on everyday adult-child interaction and the developing language system and transforms the child into an individual who has a personal past that can be shared with others. This does not preclude the possibility that changes in the self-system (Howe & Courage, 1993) or in the information-processing system (Leichtman & Ceci, 1993) do not also play an important role. My guess is that they do. The most recent theorizing of Nelson, Howe and Courage, and Leichtman and Ceci suggest that infantile amnesia reflects important changes occurring during early childhood—changes that permit autobiographical memory and that truly separate our species from all others.

Infantile Amnesia and Hypnotic Age Regression

But are memories from infancy and early childhood really gone, or are they just not retrievable by our conscious minds? What about hypnosis? Don't psychologists often use hypnosis to help people remember "forgotten" or "repressed" memories, and doesn't that sometimes include remembering events from one's early childhood? Yes, indeed, between 20% and 34% of psychotherapists report using hypnosis to help their patients "recall the unrecallable" (Lynn et al., 1997), and that sometimes includes memories from early childhood. But is it accurate and are these memories real? In general, people under hypnosis often do recall more details about an event than do people not under hypnosis, but many of these details turn out to be false (Erdelyi, 1994).

In hypnotic age regression, adults are hypnotized and "brought back" to an earlier age. In doing so, will the adults now truly think like they did as children and will they remember events from their childhoods better than nonhypnotized people? Michael Nash (1987) reviewed more than 60 years of this literature, and his answer is a definitive "no." For example, in research in which adults are regressed to the preschool years and then given Piagetian tasks such as conservation (see Chapter 4), they act more like adults who are asked to *pretend* to solve the problem like a 4-year-old would than like an actual 4-year-old child. In one study, adults were regressed to 3 years of age and asked to identify objects such as dolls, blankets, or teddy bears that were of particular importance and comfort to them at that time (Nash et al.,

1986). The parents of both hypnotized and control participants were contacted to confirm the subjects' recollections. The hypnotized people were substantially *less* accurate in identifying favorite objects from their early childhoods than were the controls. The reports of the hypnotized participants matched those of their parents just 21% of the time, whereas the hit rate for the controls was 70%.

People who experience age regression might have the feeling of recalling a "real" memory. However, how confident one is in the veracity of a memory, unfortunately, does not always predict the truth of the memory. There is no evidence that hypnotic age regression can succeed in retrieving "repressed," or simply forgotten memories from childhood, despite many people's claims to the contrary.

Implicit Memory

The memory infants show in the preference for novelty task or in Rovee-Collier's conditioning experiments do not seem to require conscious awareness. Typically, conscious awareness has been a prerequisite for explicit, or declarative, memory, with the "unconscious" memories of infants typically being classified as a form of **implicit memory.** (But see Howe, 2000, and Rovee-Collier, 1999, for arguments against this distinction.) Even the memory displayed through deferred-imitation tasks, which some interpreted as clear evidence of explicit memory (Bauer, 2002), is interpreted otherwise by others (K. Nelson, 1996). Implicit memory is "memory without awareness" (see Schacter, 1992), and it is not limited to preverbal infants and toddlers but occurs also in older children and adults.

The distinction between implicit and explicit memory has more than heuristic value, for the two types of memories seem to be governed by different brain systems as revealed by research with people with brain damage (Schacter, 1992; Schacter, Norman, & Koustaal, 2000). For instance, the hippocampus is involved in transferring new explicit information from the short-term store (the "location" of immediate awareness) to the long-term store. People with damage to the hippocampus can acquire a new skill as a result of repeated practice but will have no awareness of ever learning such skills. For example, Brenda Milner (1964) reported the case of H.M., a patient with hippocampal brain damage. H.M. was given a mirror-drawing task over several days, in which he had to trace figures while watching his hand in a mirror. H.M.'s performance was quite poor initially but improved after several days of practice, despite the fact that he had no recollection of ever performing the task before. The enhancement of performance as a result of practice is a reflection of intact implicit (procedural) memory, whereas H.M.'s failure to recall previously performing the task is a reflection of a lack of explicit memory.

There has been relatively little developmental research on implicit memory, but what research has been done presents a consistent picture. Although substantial age differences are found on tests of declarative memorization, few age differences are found when implicit memory is tested (Billingsley, Smith, & McAndrews, 2002; Vinter & Perruchet, 2000). One procedure used to assess implicit memory in children involves the use of fragmented pictures. Here, a fragmented picture is presented and children are asked to identify it. This is very difficult to do initially, but as more of the picture is completed, it becomes increasingly easier to identify the object. In experiments using this task, children are shown the series of degraded pictures and later given another task involving those pictures. Do children perform this second task better (faster or more accurately) for pictures they had previously seen, despite the fact that they might not remember seeing those pictures before? The answer is generally "yes," and, more important, there are few age differences in magnitude of the effects (Drummey & Newcombe, 1995; Hayes & Hennessy, 1996).

Let me provide an example of a study using this procedure. Brett Hayes and Ruth Hennessy (1996) showed 4-, 5-, and 10-year-old children a series of pictures on one day and asked the children to identify them or to answer some questions about each item (for example, "What would you use an X for?"). Two days later, the children were shown some of the previous pictures and some new ones to identify in a fragmented-picture task. Children were also asked if they had remembered seeing each picture two days earlier. Although older children identified more pictures than did the younger children, the *priming effect* (that is, the degree to which children identified "old" pictures sooner than "new" pictures) was equal for children of all ages. Also, there was no relation between how many pictures children of any age recognized (their explicit memory) and priming effects (their implicit memory). In other words, although children exhibited substantial differences in explicit memory, no developmental differences were found in implicit memory.

One interesting study of implicit memory involved showing 9- and 10-year-olds pictures of preschool children, including some who had been their classmates 4 and 5 years earlier (Newcombe & Fox, 1994). Children were asked to determine whether each picture they were shown was that of a former classmate (an explicit recognition memory task); changes in the electrical conductance of their skin was also recorded. Greater changes in skin conductance for former classmates' pictures relative to pictures of unfamiliar children was used as a reflection of implicit recognition memory (that is, requiring no conscious awareness). Not surprisingly, children's performance was relatively poor on both the explicit and implicit tasks (although greater than expected by chance, indicating some memory of both the explicit and implicit types). However, there was no difference in skin conductance between children who performed well on the explicit task and those who performed poorly. This suggests that even the children whose performance on the explicit memory task was no greater than chance still "recognized" as many of their former classmates as those children who had performed better. This pattern of data indicates that some children "remembered" (implicitly) more than they "knew" (explicitly). Eunhui Lie and Nora Newcombe (1999) have reported similar results of greater implicit than explicit recognition of former classmates, using a different method of implicit memory.

These findings suggest that implicit memory is an early developing ability, perhaps more related to the development of semantic memory than to episodic memory (Tulving, 1987). Some theorists have speculated that implicit memory is under the control of automatic rather than effortful processes (Jacoby, 1991) and, following the theorizing of Lynn Hasher and Rose Zacks (1979, see Chapter 5), that these processes show little development across childhood (Newcombe et al., 2000). Actually, the procedures used to assess memory in infants (habituation/dishabituation and conditioning techniques) are likely more similar in nature to the tests used to assess implicit memory in older children than are the tests used to assess explicit memory. Recall from Chapter 7 Marshall Haith's (1993) comments of the need to bridge the gap between cognition in infancy and cognition in childhood by developing new research techniques and theories. Research using implicit memory techniques might be that bridge. In this spirit, Jayne Ausley and Robert Guttentag suggested, "research using indirect [implicit] methods of memory assessment with children probably does provide a real avenue of continuity with infancy research, because these tests do not require an awareness of the previous occurrence of events for successful performance" (1993, p. 254).

The Development of Event Memory

Much of what we remember is for *events*, things that happen to us during the course of everyday life. Unlike implicit memory, **event memory** is explicit. We are aware that we are remembering. For most aspects of event memory, however, we did not specifically *try* to remember the event when we experienced it. In other words, for most event memories, the encoding of the event was unintentional. Because we did not intend to learn new information, our unintentional memory is not influenced by the use of deliberate encoding strategies, which accounts for much of the age differences observed on intentional memory tasks. (See discussion of strategic memory in Chapter 6.) Rather, memory representations can be laid down involuntarily as part of ongoing activity, and

several researchers have speculated that, in some cases, such "naturalistic learning" could actually produce higher levels of memory performance than would more deliberate memorization attempts, especially for young children (Istomina, 1975; Piaget & Inhelder, 1973).

The issue at hand is when and how it is that children remember the experiences of their everyday lives. How are these memories organized? How long do they last? And how is it that children acquire them?

A young child must master many aspects of memory if he or she is to remember important events. First, an event must be attended to and perceived. Then, the child must make some sense of that event so that it can be represented in his or her mind and recalled later on. If a child doesn't attend to the important aspects of an event or cannot make sense of what he or she experienced, there is really nothing to remember. One important thing to remember is that young children pay attention to different aspects of events than adults do and do not necessarily know what aspects of an event are important and which are trivial. For example, as adults, we know that the purpose of a baseball game is to watch the players on the field play ball. We automatically pay less attention to the field maintenance staff, the players on the bench, and most of the other spectators. However, young children don't always select the "right" things to pay attention to. At a baseball game, they might spend more time watching the hot dog vendors, the batboys, and the second base ump. What they remember of the game will thus be very different than what an older child or adult remembers.

It is also worth noting that event memory is *constructive* in nature. Event memory does not involve the verbatim recall of a list of facts or the memorization of lines, like an actor in a play. Rather, we recall the gist of the message and in the process, we transform what was actually said or done. That is, we interpret our experiences as a function of what we already know about the world, and our memory for events is colored by previous knowledge (Bartlett, 1932). Memory, in general, is not like a tape recorder. True, we sometimes do retain verbatim information and use that information to construct stories. But the tales we tell about our lives are best thought of as constructions, based on our actual experiences, our background knowledge of the things we are trying to remember, our information-processing abilities, and the social context in which the remembering is being done.

Script-Based Memory

What is it that young children remember? One thing they tend to remember well is recurring events—what typically happens on a day-to-day basis. Katherine Nelson and her colleagues have demonstrated that preschool children tend to organize events in terms of **scripts,** which are a form of schematic organization with real-world events organized in terms of their causal and temporal characteristics (Nelson, 1993, 1996; Fivush, 1997). For example, a "fast-food restaurant" script might involve driving to the restaurant, entering the restaurant and standing in line, ordering, paying the cashier, taking the food to the table, eating, and then throwing away the trash before leaving. Children learn what "usually happens" in a situation, such as what happens at snack time at school, at a birthday party, or at a fast-food restaurant, and remember novel information in the context of these familiar events.

Substantial research demonstrates that even very young children organize information temporally in a script-like fashion (Bauer, 1997; Fivush, Kuebli, & Clubb, 1992) and that such schematic organization for events doesn't change appreciably into adulthood (see Fivush & Hudson, 1990; K. Nelson, 1996, for reviews of this literature). Perhaps even more impressive is the evidence that even preverbal infants use temporal order to remember events. Patricia Bauer and Jean Mandler (1989, 1992) tested infants ranging in age from 11.5 to 20 months on imitation tasks. The toddlers were shown a sequence of events (for example, putting a ball in a cup, inverting a smaller cup on top of the larger one, and shaking the cups) and later given the opportunity to interact with the materials again. Bauer and Mandler reported that the children re-enacted the sequence of events in the same temporal order they had been shown. This finding argues for the existence of a script-style memory organization long before children are able to talk.

Young children's tendencies to organize information following familiar scripts seems to result in their tendency *not* to remember much in the way of specific (that is, nonscript) information. For example, Robyn Fivush and Nina Hamond (1990), asked 2.5-year-old children specific questions about recent special events, such as a trip to the beach, a camping trip, or a ride on an airplane. Rather than recalling the novel aspects of these special events, the children were more apt to focus on what adults would consider routine information. Take, for instance, the following conversation reported by Fivush and Hamond between an adult and child about a camping trip. The child first recalled sleeping outside, which is unusual, but then remembered very routine things:

> *Interviewer:* You slept outside in a tent? Wow, that sounds like a lot of fun.
> *Child:* And then we waked up and eat dinner. First we eat dinner, then go to bed, and then wake up and eat breakfast.
> *Interviewer:* What else did you do when you went camping? What did you do when you got up, after breakfast?
> *Child:* Umm, in the night, and went to sleep.
> (1990, p. 231)

It seems strange that a child would talk about such routine tasks as waking up, eating, and going to bed when so many new and exciting things must have happened on the camping trip. But the younger the child, the more he or she might need to embed novel events into familiar routines. According to Fivush and Hamond, everything is new to 2-year-olds, and they are in the process of learning about their surroundings.

Why should young children's memory be so tied to recurring events? One way to answer this question is to ask what the function of memory is for young children. Nelson (1996, in press) has taken such a functional view (consistent with ideas from evolutionary psychology discussed in Chapter 2) and believes that memory has an adaptive value of permitting children to predict the likelihood of events in the future. Basically, by remembering the likelihood of an event's occurrence in the past, one can predict its likelihood of occurring in the future. From this perspective, some events (recurring ones) are more likely to be remembered than are others (single events). According to Nelson, "Memory for a single, one-time occurrence of some event, if the event were not traumatic or life-threatening, would not be especially useful, given its low probability. Thus, a memory system might be optimally designed to retain information about frequent and recurrent events—and to discard information about unrepeated events—and to integrate new information about variations in recurrent events into a general knowledge system" (1996, p. 174). Nelson makes the point that memory for routine events makes it possible for infants to anticipate events and to take a part in, and possibly control of, these events. There is no such pay-off for a novel event, and thus it makes sense to forget it.

But children do eventually remember specific events, not just some generalized event memory. In fact, although 2- and 3-year-old children may rely heavily on scripts, they have been shown to remember specific information for extended periods (Hamond & Fivush, 1991; Howe, 2000). Hamond and Fivush presented research that demonstrates how long memories for specific events can last (1991). They interviewed children 6 or 18 months after the children had gone to Disney World. Children were either about 3 or 4 years old when they visited Disney World. All children recalled a great deal of information about their trip, even after 18 months. The older children recalled more details and required fewer prompts (cues) to generate recall than did the younger children. Nevertheless, recall for this single, special event was quite good, even though it did not fall nicely into a familiar routine.

The Role of Parents in "Teaching" Children to Remember

Hamond and Fivush also noted that children who talked more about the trip with their parents recalled more information about the trip. This suggests that parents can play an important role in children's early remembering, a point that has recently been made by several theorists (Fivush, 1997; Ornstein & Haden, 2001) and is consistent with the theorizing of Lev Vygotsky (1978) and the sociocultural perspective discussed in Chapter 3 (Rogoff, 1998). For example, Judith Hudson has argued that children learn how to remember by interacting with their parents, that "remembering can be viewed as an activity that is at first jointly carried out by parent and child and then later performed by the child alone" (1990, p. 172). In most families, Hudson proposes, parents begin talking with young children about things that happened in the past. They ask questions such as, "Where did we go this morning?," "What did we see at the zoo?," "Who went with us?," and "What else did we see?." From these interchanges, children learn that the important facts to remember about events are the whos, whats, whens, and wheres of their experiences. Through these conversations with their parents, they are learning to notice the important details of their experiences and to store their memories in an organized way that will be easily retrieved when needed.

In studying these interchanges between parents and preschoolers, Hudson found that parents do more than just ask the right questions. They also give the right answers when the child can't remember, showing children how the conversation should go. Young children generally show low levels of free recall, but can remember much more when specific cues are presented. In fact, Fivush and Hamond stated, "young children recall as much information as older children do, but they need more memory questions in order to do so" (1990, p. 244). By asking repeated questions to children, adults are structuring the conversation, showing children how "remembering" is done. Moreover, by providing the missing information, children also learn that their parents will help them out when they can't seem to retrieve the information called for.

A good example of this was a conversation I overheard while riding on the Metro in Washington, D.C. A young mother and her 19-month-old daughter, Tanya, were returning home after a trip to the zoo.

Mother: Tanya, what did we see at the zoo?

Tanya: Elephunts.

Mother: That's right! We saw elephants. What else?

Tanya: (shrugs and looks at her mother)

Mother: Panda bear? Did we see a panda bear?

Tanya: (smiles and nods her head)

Mother: Can you say "panda bear?"

Tanya: Panda bear.

Mother: Good! Elephants and panda bears. What else?

Tanya: Elephunts.

Mother: That's right, elephants. And also a gorilla.

Tanya: Go-rilla!

Hilary Ratner (1984) illustrated the importance of these parent-child conversations. She observed 2- and 3-year-old children interacting with their parents at home and recorded the number of times the mother asked the child about past events. She then tested the children's memory abilities. The children who showed better memory abilities at that time, and also a year later, were those whose mothers had asked them many questions about past events. Other research has shown that mothers who provide their preschool children with more evaluations of their memory performance, and who use more elaborative language when talking about memory with their children, have children who remember past events better than do children with less elaborative mothers (Reese, Haden, & Fivush, 1993). That is, after making a statement about some previous event (for example, "Then we ate the cake"), elaborative mothers are more likely to provide comments that confirm or negate a child's statement (such as "That's right," "Yes," or "No") than less elaborative mothers are.

In other research, mothers and their young children engaged in three novel events, one when children were 30 months, a second at 36 months, and a third at 42 months (Haden et al., 2001). Children were tested for their memory of each event 1 day and 3 weeks following each episode. The events were carried out in children's homes and involved the investigator setting up props and asking the mother and child to carry out an elaborate make-believe activity. For example, for the "camping event" the mother and child first loaded supplies in a backpack, hiked to a fishing pond, caught a fish with a fishing rod and net, moved to their campsite where they found sleeping bags, pots, pans and utensils, which they used to cook and eat their food. The frequency with which mothers and children jointly carried out these activities, and the degree to which language was involved during the execution of the task, were observed and related to children's subsequent memory performance. First, and not surprisingly, children's overall memory performance increased with age and was greater for the 1-day than the 3-week delay. Most pertinent for our discussion here was the relation between mother-child activities during the event and children's later recollections. Features of the events (for example, putting food in the backpack) that were jointly handled and talked about by the mother and child were better remembered than were features that were handled and talked about only by the mother, or jointly handled by the mother and child but not discussed. This result clearly points out the important role of joint activity, guided by the mother, including the use of language, in fostering young children's event memory.

The results of recent research point to the interactive role of parents and children in the process of "learning" how to remember. Thus, remembering becomes a cultural phenomenon, consistent with the ideas of Vygotsky and others who propose a sociocultural perspective of development (see Chapter 3). Parents teach children how to construct narratives (that is, create stories) in which to embed the important things that happen to them. This, in turn, allows children to share their experiences with others. This is a practice characteristic of parents in postindustrial societies, such as ours, but it is not universal. For example, Mary Mullen and Soonhyung Yi (1995) examined how frequently Korean and American mothers talked to their 3-year-old children about past events and reported that the American mothers talked about the past with their young children nearly three times as often as the Korean mothers did. This is consistent with reports that American children talk about past events more than Korean children do (Han, Leichtman, & Wang, 1998) and that American adults report earlier childhood memories than do Korean adults (Mullen, 1994). This suggests that early language experience contributes to the onset of autobiographical memory, consistent with the argument made by K. Nelson (1996).

It is also worth noting that there are differences in the event memories reported by girls and boys. When asked to remember information about earlier experienced events, girls tend to remember more information than boys do (Haden & Reese, 1994; Reese, Haden, & Fivush, 1996) but not always (see Lewis, 1999; Weber & Strube, 1999). For example, in a study by Catherine Haden and Elaine Reese (1994), children between the ages of 40 and 70 months participated in several sessions in which their mothers, fathers, or an experimenter asked them to recollect about salient events that had occurred in the recent past. Regardless of who interviewed the children (that is, their mothers, fathers, or the experimenter), girls remembered more details about past events than boys did. These gender differences were related to ways in which parents converse with their sons and daughters about the past. Girls generally received more evaluations of their memory responses than boys. These findings suggest that the roots of females' greater event memory lie early in development and might be partly because of the way parents talk to boys and girls during attempts at remembering, with daughters being encouraged to embellish their memories more than sons are. Other research indicates that mothers talk to their male and female preschool children about different topics. For example, Dorothy Flannagan, Lynne Baker-Ward, and Loranel Graham (1995) reported that in their conversations about school, mothers talked to their sons more about learning and instruction, whereas they tended to talk to their daughters more about social interactions. Thus, there are differences both in how parents talk to boys and girls about remembering events and in what they are asked to remember, both of which seemingly affect what and how well children remember.

Children as Eyewitnesses

One topic in event memory that has attracted substantial research attention lately concerns the reliability of children as eyewitnesses. How reliable is children's testimony? How much do they remember, and for how long? How suggestible are children? Can a persuasive interviewer make children say things that didn't really happen, and can faulty interviewing techniques actually result in children believing they were victims of a crime (or witnesses to a crime) when it never happened? These are not just questions for the justice system, but also for psychologists because they deal with the nature of children's developing memory systems and the construction of a particular kind of event memory.

In the following sections, I review research and theory about children as eyewitnesses and the degree to which their testimonies and their memories are subject to change. In the first section, I review age differences in children's eyewitness reports when no one is trying to change their minds. That is, what do children remember and what factors influence their memory when they are asked to report what they witnessed or experienced? In a second section, I investigate the large literature on age differences in suggestibility. How susceptible are children to suggestion and to what extent will they change their answers or their memory representations as a result of suggestive questioning?

But first, let me provide a general framework for making sense of this research literature. Children's eyewitness testimony and suggestibility, as event memory in general, are influenced by a host of interacting factors. Which factors are most important? Can we specify how the various factors will interact to predict performance? And can we be confident enough in our conclusions to inform the legal system? Marc Lindberg (1991; Lindberg, Keiffer, & Thomas, 2000) has suggested three major categories of factors that we should consider in evaluating studies of children's eyewitness memory and suggestibility, which are presented in Figure 10-5. The first category in Lindberg's scheme is *memory processes*,

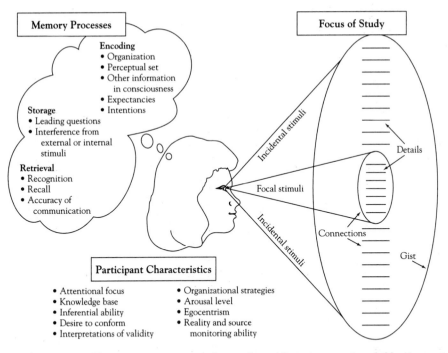

FIGURE 10-5 Three major interacting classes of variables in interpreting children's eyewitness memory and suggestibility. SOURCE: Lindberg, M. A. (1991). An interactive approach to assessing the suggestibility and testimony of eyewitnesses. In J. Doris (Ed.), *The suggestibility of children's recollections: Implications for eyewitness testimony* (pp. 47–55). Copyright © 1991 by the American Psychological Association. Reprinted with permission.

and these concern the different memory operations of encoding, storage, and retrieval. *Encoding* refers to children's representation of an event and how children respond to information they receive before the event. For example, how are children influenced by being told that someone they are about to meet is a "bad boy" or prone to breaking things? *Storage* refers to information provided to participants after witnessing an event. This may be in the form of suggestive questions ("He spilled chocolate milk over the book, didn't he?"), or post-event information, which includes any experiences that intervene between witnessing an event and recollecting it. *Retrieval* refers to manipulations at time of testing. For example, how is memory tested? With open-ended (free-recall) questions, cued-recall questions, or recognition? How are these questions posed? Lind-

berg refers to the second category of his taxonomy as *focus of the study*, by which he means the type of information that is being assessed. For example, is the interviewer concerned with psychologically and legally central (or focal) information (who did what to whom, critical in determining innocence or guilt in court), or is peripheral (incidental) information also important? (What color pants was the man wearing? How tall was the girl?) Similarly, is the memory for gist information or for details, or verbatim information (as in fuzzy-trace theory's description of memory traces, Brainerd & Reyna, 2002)? And finally, one must consider *participant factors*. Here developmental level and the associated social, emotional, and cognitive skills of children are important. Also of potential importance are personality characteristics of the participants, their level of stress at time of the event (or at time of retrieval), their past experiences with a situation, and their more general knowledge of the things they witness. No single study will include all relevant factors from this taxonomy, but it is worthwhile to keep these categories in mind, if for no other reason than to remember that understanding children's eyewitness memory is not child's play.

Age Differences in Children's Eyewitness Memories

Although there is much variability from study to study, most investigations of children's eyewitness memory begin by showing children a video of some event, having them observe some activity in their school, or involving them personally in an activity. Usually, children are not told that they will be asked to remember what they view. Later, often minutes after the event but in some cases days or weeks later, children are asked what they remembered (for example, "Tell me what happened in the video you saw" or "Tell me what happened in your classroom yesterday morning"). This is essentially a request for free recall. Typically, children will then be asked some more specific recall questions (for example, "What was the girl in the video wearing?" or "What did the man who came into your class yesterday morning do?"), which constitute cued recall. Often, children will be asked some recognition memory questions (for example, "Was the girl wearing a white t-shirt?" or "Did the man play with the teddy bear?"). In some studies, the same or similar questions may be repeated, and in others, questions are often intentionally suggestive, sometimes directing children to a "correct" answer ("Did the man play nicely with the teddy bear?") and sometimes leading to an "incorrect" answer ("Did the man rip the book?"). There are, of course, many variations, depending on the purpose of the study, but in most cases, children's memories for specific events are probed, often with the purpose of seeing how likely children are to change their answers or to be swayed by leading questions posed by an in-

terviewer (see Ceci & Bruck, 1995, 1998; Qin et al., 1997 for reviews).

How Much Do Children Remember, and How Accurate Are They?

First, how much do children of different ages remember shortly after witnessing an event? When examining immediate (that is, within the same experimental session) free recall, substantial age differences are found (Ornstein, Gordon, & Larus, 1992; Poole & White, 1995). How much is remembered differs from study to study, but preschool children typically recall only a small proportion of information from an event to free-recall questions. Although young children recall very little information, what they do recall is highly accurate and central to the event, if there are no suggestions or coaching (Goodman, Aman, & Hirschman, 1987; Poole & White, 1995). For example, in a video involving a boy and a girl in a park, with the boy stealing a bike, young children typically recall the bike theft, but are much less apt than older children or adults to mention in their free recall descriptions of the participants, characteristics of the bicycle, or things about the setting (Cassel & Bjorklund, 1995). Thus, young children's free recall is typically low, accurate, and about central aspects of an event.

When children are provided general cues (for example, "Tell me what the girl looked like"), they recall more information, as you would expect. However, in addition to remembering more *correct* facts, they also tend to remember some *incorrect* "facts" as well, reducing the overall accuracy of their recall (Bjorklund et al., 1998; Goodman et al., 1994).

When children do falsely remember information to cues, does this actually change their memory representations? Will these children, when interviewed later, remember this misinformation again? The answer to this seems to depend on several factors, including the amount of time between the initial and later interviews. With delays of only several weeks or less, children seem *not* to recall their earlier false memories (Cassel & Bjorklund, 1995). But when delays are longer (Poole, 1995) or when children are merely asked to recognize, rather than recall, information (Brainerd & Reyna, 1996; Brainerd, Reyna, & Brandse, 1995), these false memories tend to persist, and might even be *more* resistant to forgetting than true memories (Brainerd & Mojardin, 1999).

These counterintuitive findings have been interpreted in terms of fuzzy-trace theory (Brainerd & Poole, 1997; Brainerd & Reyna, 2002; see Chapter 5). According to the theory, correct recognition is based on literal, or verbatim, memory traces, which are more susceptible to forgetting than are less-exact fuzzy, or gist, traces. In contrast, false recognition must be based on gist traces because there are no verbatim traces for false memories. Gist traces are more resistant to forgetting than verbatim traces are, and thus the gist-based false memories become more likely to be remembered over long delays than the more easily forgettable verbatim-based true memories.

How Long Do Memories Last?

Although most studies have not assessed the long-term recollections of children, several have investigated children's memories of specific events for periods ranging from several weeks to two years (Flin et al., 1992; Salmon & Pipe, 1997). The results of these studies are not totally consistent, but a picture emerges of greater age differences in the accuracy of recall with increasing delays. Accuracy, as used here, does not refer to "how much" was remembered but, rather, to the ratio of incorrect-to-correct information remembered. Children who recall very little, for example, but correctly recall that amount, have perfect accuracy. In contrast, a child who recalls a substantial amount of both correct (accurate) and incorrect (inaccurate) information, might demonstrate more recall, but less accuracy.

First, with delays of about one month or less, children of all ages and adults remember about the same proportion of accurate and inaccurate information as they did originally (Baker-Ward et al., 1993; Cassel & Bjorklund, 1995). Age differences in recall accuracy are found with longer delays, however. For example, Rhona Flin and her colleagues (1992) reported that both 6-year-olds and adults recalled as much accurate information after a 5-month delay as they had originally, but the 6-year-olds' recall was *less accurate* than the adults. Thus, the ratio of incorrect-to-correct recall became higher for the children than for the adults during the 5-month period (see also Poole & White, 1993). The conclusion from these studies is that age differences in accuracy are found, but only when memory is assessed after extended delays. Fuzzy-trace theory (Brainerd & Reyna, 2002, see Chapter 5) explains these findings by the greater rate of trace decay of verbatim (exact) relative to gist traces. Verbatim traces, favored by younger children, deteriorate more rapidly than the gist, or fuzzy traces favored by older children, resulting in greater loss of information over delays and corresponding increases in erroneous recall. These are the same arguments that have been used to explain the phenomenon of infantile amnesia (see earlier discussion). The verbatim traces favored by infants and young children are especially susceptible to deterioration, making it highly unlikely that these memories would be available years after their original encoding (Leichtman & Ceci, 1993).

Factors Influencing Children's Eyewitness Memory

A host of factors, other than age and length of delay, have been found to influence the amount and accuracy of children's eyewitness memories. For instance, among many other factors, children with high IQs show higher levels of eyewitness recall than do their lower-IQ peers (Roebers & Schneider, 2001), children given incentives to be accurate in their recall are indeed more accurate than children not given incentives (Roebers, Moga, & Schneider, 2001), intermediate levels of stress (when experiencing the event) seem to facilitate recall of an event relative to overly high or low levels of stress (Bahrick et al., 1998), and children who have emotionally supportive mothers who discuss upcoming medical procedures with them, recall less inaccurate information about the procedure than children with less sympathetic or talkative mothers (Goodman et al., 1994,

1997). Two sets of factors that have substantial influences on children's eyewitness reports are children's background knowledge for the event (Ornstein & Greenhoot, 2000) and characteristics of the interview (Ceci, Bruck, & Battin, 2000).

The role of knowledge. We saw in Chapters 5 and 6 that knowledge has a potent role in children's working memory and strategic memory, so we should not be surprised that it also plays an important role in eyewitness memory (Ornstein & Greenhoot, 2000; Stein, Wade, & Liwag, 1997). For example, children's recollections of stressful and invasive medical procedures are related to their knowledge of the procedures; children who know more about the procedure remember more accurate information (Clubb et al., 1993) and recall less inaccurate information (Goodman et al., 1994).

Yet, although knowing a lot about an event (that is, how actions in an event are "supposed to go") is usually associated with increased memory accuracy, knowledge can sometimes be a double-edged sword. For example, in a study of 4- and 6-year-old children's recall of a mock physical examination, Peter Ornstein and his colleagues (1998) included some typical, expected features in the exam (for example, the doctor listened to the children's hearts with a stethoscope, looked into their ears), but also included some atypical, unexpected features (for example, the doctor measured children's head circumference, used alcohol to wipe their belly buttons). In addition, some expected features were omitted from the exams (for example, measuring blood pressure, looking in children's mouths). Children were interviewed about the exam immediately and after a 12-week delay. They were first asked open-ended questions ("Tell me what happened during your check-up"; "Tell me what the doctor did to check you"), followed by increasingly specific questions ("Did the doctor check any parts of your face?"; "Did the doctor check your eyes?"). In addition to being asked questions about what really did happen during the exam, children were also asked specific questions about things that did *not* happen. For example, children for whom the doctor did *not* check their ears would be asked, "Did the doctor look into

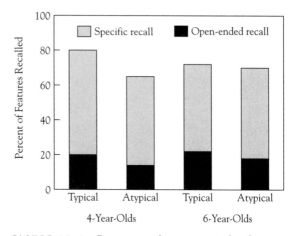

FIGURE 10-6 Percentage of present-typical and present-atypical features recalled correctly in response to open-ended and specific questions for 4- and 6-year-old children, 12-week assessment. SOURCE: Ornstein, P. A., & A. F. Greenhoot, "Remembering the distant past: Implications of research on children's memory for the recovered memory debate." In D. F. Bjorklund (Ed.), *False-memory creation in children and adults: Theory, research, and implications.* © 2000 Lawrence Erlbaum Associates, Inc. Reprinted with permission. Based on data in Ornstein, P. A., K. A. Merritt, L. Baker-Ward, E. Furtado, B. N. Gordon, & G. F. Principe (1998). Children's knowledge, expectation, and long-term retention. *Applied Cognitive Psychology, 12,* 387–405.

your ears?" Some of the questions referred to events that are likely to occur in an exam, such as looking into children's ears, whereas others were for events that were unlikely to occur, for example, "Did the doctor give you some stitches?."

How did the children do? The results for the 12-week assessment of this study are shown in Figures 10-6 and 10-7. The first figure reports the percentage of correct responses for the 4- and 6-year-old children for the present-typical and present-atypical features (that is, aspects of the exam that children actually experienced), separately for the open-ended and specific questions. As can be seen, children of both ages recalled more typical features correctly than atypical features, for both types of questions. This reflects the positive effects of knowledge base. This was not the first medical exam for any of the children, and they

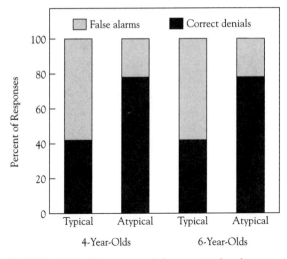

FIGURE 10-7 Percentage of absent-typical and absent-atypical features to which children responded with correct denials and false alarms for 4- and 6-year-old children, 12-week assessment. SOURCE: Ornstein, P. A., & A. F. Greenhoot, "Remembering the distant past: Implications of research on children's memory for the recovered memory debate." In D. F. Bjorklund (Ed.), *False-memory creation in children and adults: Theory, research, and implications.* © 2000 Lawrence Erlbaum Associates, Inc. Reprinted with permission. Based on data in Ornstein, P. A., K. A. Merritt, L. Baker-Ward, E. Furtado, B. N. Gordon, & G. F. Principe (1998). Children's knowledge, expectation, and long-term retention. *Applied Cognitive Psychology, 12,* 387–405.

presumably had a script for what usually happens in such an exam. As a result, features that are typically found in medical exams, based on children's past experiences, were more likely to be remembered than atypical features. But there was a negative side to knowledge, and this is reflected in the results displayed in Figure 10-7. Correct denials (the dark portion of the bars in Figure 10-7) refer to children correctly stating that an event did not happen. ("Did the doctor give you stitches? No.") As can be seen, children were more likely to correctly reject these nonevents for the atypical features. False alarms (the white portion of the bars in Figure 10-7) refer to children *incorrectly* agreeing that an event happened when it did not. ("Did the doctor look into your ears?

Yes.") Here, both the 4- and 6-year-old children were more likely to erroneously say that these events did indeed happen when they were typical rather than atypical features of a physical exam. Knowing what usually happens caused children to falsely remember what did happen, at least when their memory was tested 12 weeks after the event.

Characteristics of the interview. Not surprisingly, how children are interviewed can greatly affect what they remember and the accuracy of their recollections (Ceci et al., 2000). The type of questions asked, for example, influences what children remember. As I noted earlier, young children tend to recall relatively little to open-ended, free-recall questions ("Tell me everything that happened when the man came into your classroom."), but what they do recall tends to be highly accurate. Children recall more when given neutral cues, but the accuracy of their recall declines (that is, they also recall more false information). Interviewer characteristics, such as whether the interviewer is warm and supportive, or high status (such as a police officer), influences the accuracy of children's memory, as does the use of any special recall-facilitating technique or props. For example, many forensic interviews make use of anatomically correct dolls when questioning children who are suspected of being victims of sexual abuse. Does the use of such dolls increase the accuracy of children's reports? Maggie Bruck and her colleagues (1995) interviewed 3-year-old children following a routine medical exam (that is, these children were *not* suspected child-abuse victims). Half of the children received a genital exam by the doctor and half did not. Immediately after the examination, children were shown an anatomically correct doll and they were asked "Did the doctor touch you here?," pointing to the genital area of the doll. Only about half of the children who did receive the genital exam answered correctly, whereas about half of those who did not receive a genital exam also said "yes." When simply asked to "show on the doll" how the doctor had touched their genitals or buttocks, only 25% of the children who had received the genital exam responded correctly, and 50% of the children who were not give such an exam falsely showed anal or genital touching. Similar results have been reported by other researchers (Gordon et al., 1993), calling into question the use of anatomically correct dolls, at least with young children.

Another factor that can influence children's recollection of an event is the number of times they are asked questions. It is very common in legal matters for witnesses to be asked the same or similar questions repeatedly. Does such questioning affect children's memory, or at least what they say to an interviewer? Several researchers have reported that when young children are asked the same or similar questions in a single session, they are more likely to change their answers than older children are (Cassel, Roebers, & Bjorklund, 1996; Warren, Hulse-Trotter, & Tubbs, 1991). One reason for children's greater tendencies to change their answers is that they might interpret a repeated question as evidence that the interviewer was dissatisfied with their first answer and that another, different answer must be more correct.

However, asking the same or similar questions repeatedly does not always lead to greater "mind changing" and inaccurate recall. For example, Debra Poole and Lawrence White (1991) reported slightly lower levels of accurate recall as a result of repeated questioning in a single session for 4-, 6-, and 8-year-old children and adults (because of boredom, they speculated), but no corresponding increase in inaccurate information (which was low to begin with). Several other studies have reported *higher* levels of accurate recall when children are given repeated opportunities to remember events over different sessions (Baker-Ward, Hess, & Flannagan, 1990; Fivush & Hamond, 1989). This is a well-known phenomenon termed **hypermnesia** (see Howe & Brainerd, 1989), in which the total amount remembered increases when people attempt to recall the target information repeatedly. In fact, Charles Brainerd and Peter Ornstein state, "Perhaps the most fundamental principle of memory is that repetition facilitates performance" (1991, p. 15). However, others, using similar experimental designs, report no appreciable changes in amount of accurate or inaccurate free recall (compared with cued recall) as a result of repeated questioning over different interviews (Cassel & Bjorklund, 1995). Thus, repeated questioning can sometimes reduce accurate recall, can

sometimes enhance it, and can sometimes make no difference. Obviously, several factors are responsible for the effects of repeated questioning on children, but, when the questions are *not* misleading (that is, they do not suggest a specific, inaccurate fact) and care is taken to ensure that children understand the nature of the questions, they can enhance amount remembered. This caused Poole and White to state, "Because repetition elicits additional information and is a relatively innocuous procedure when appropriate questions are used, sweeping recommendations to avoid repetition are not warranted" (1995, p. 42).

Age Differences in Suggestibility

Perhaps the single most investigated area of eyewitness testimony in both the adult and child literatures concerns suggestibility (see Ceci & Bruck, 1995, 1998, for reviews). To what extent are children susceptible to suggestion? Research has shown that people of all ages report more inaccurate information when misleading questions are posed (that is, questions suggesting incorrect "facts"). The question for developmentalists, and for the legal profession, include "are children more suggestible than adults, what factors influence their suggestibility, and how can we maximize memory accuracy and minimize suggestibility?"

The general consensus to the question, "Are children more suggestible than adults?" seems to be "yes." In an extensive review of the literature, Ceci and Bruck concluded, "There do appear to be significant age differences in suggestibility, with preschool children being disproportionately more vulnerable to suggestion than either school-age children or adults" (1993, p. 431). Most investigators looking for age differences in suggestibility have found it, although in varying degrees and sometimes only under certain circumstances (Ackil & Zaragoza, 1995; Bruck et al., 1995).

How Do Children Respond to Misleading Questions?

Let me provide an example from research that asked children different types of suggestive (leading) ques-

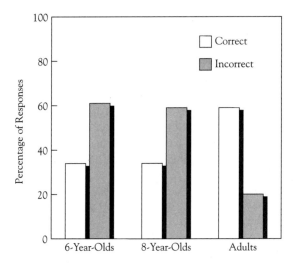

FIGURE 10-8 Percentage correct and incorrect responses by age to misleading questions. SOURCE: Based on data from Cassel, W. S., & Bjorklund, D. F. (1995). Developmental patterns of eyewitness memory and suggestibility: An ecologically based short-term longitudinal study. *Law & Human Behavior, 19,* 507–532.

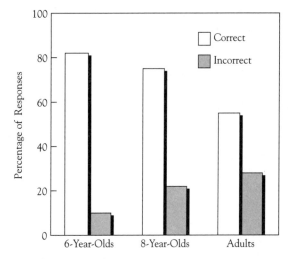

FIGURE 10-9 Percentage correct and incorrect responses by age to positive-leading questions. SOURCE: Based on data from Cassel, W. S., & Bjorklund, D. F. (1995). Developmental patterns of eyewitness memory and suggestibility: An ecologically based short-term longitudinal study. *Law & Human Behavior, 19,* 507–532.

tions. William Cassel and I (1995) showed groups of 6- and 8-year-old children and college adults a brief video of a boy and a girl in a park, with the boy eventually taking the girl's bike without permission. Participants were interviewed 15 minutes after viewing the video, and again 1 week and 1 month later. During these later interviews, participants were given either sets of misleading questions, suggesting things that did not happen (for example, "The girl said it was okay for the boy to take her bike, didn't she?"), or positive-leading questions, suggesting things that did indeed, happen (for example, "The girl told the boy not to take the bike, didn't she?"). Figures 10-8 and 10-9 present some of the results for the 1-week interview. As can be seen, the 6- and 8-year-olds tended to follow the lead of the interviewer, agreeing both with the misleading questions (Figure 10-8), and thus getting more wrong than the adults did, and with the positive-leading questions (Figure 10-9), and thus getting more right than the adults did. In fact, as can be seen in Figure 10-8, both the 6- and 8-year-olds had more incorrect than

correct responses to the misleading questions, whereas the reverse was true for the adults.

In the 1-month interview, participants were first asked sets of leading questions by one examiner suggesting one interpretation (either misleading or positive-leading) and then immediately thereafter asked a second set of questions by a second examiner, asking for the *opposite* interpretation (misleading if positive-leading had been asked first, and vice versa). How would children respond to, in some cases, the same question they had just been asked, but with an opposite "spin"? The answer is that children often changed their minds. For example, when asked about the color of the bike, 71% of the 6-year-olds who had agreed with the suggestion of the first interviewer later changed their answers to comply with the suggestion of the second interviewer. The corresponding percentages for the 8-year-old children and adults were 53% and 35%, respectively. For the more critical central question, of whether the girl had given the boy permission to take her bike, 42% of the 6-year-old children changed their answers in response to the second interviewer, whereas only 7% of 8-year-olds and 12% of adults did so. These results make it clear that younger children are highly susceptible to the suggestion of an adult interviewer, modifying their answers, it seems, to suit the desires of whomever is interviewing them.

Yet, despite the ease with which young children can be led to give answers consistent with the suggestion of any adult, are their memories actually changed as well, or only their answers? Research that has asked children misleading questions over repeated interviews indicates that such repetition will indeed cause some children to report the incorrect information in later tests of free recall and recognition, particularly information that is peripheral, or incidental to the event. Such findings indicate that suggestive questioning changes not only children's answers but also their memories. Yet, in many other cases, children who follow the lead of an interviewer fail to incorporate that misinformation in their subsequent free recall of the event, especially information that is central to the event, suggesting that it is far easier to change children's answers with such questions than to change their minds (see Bjorklund, Brown, & Bjorklund, 2002).

Gail Goodman and Allison Clarke-Stewart (1991, Experiment 6) illustrated the extent to which young children's reports of a witnessed event can be swayed and the extent to which they will stick to their interpretation. Preschool children watched a man posing as a janitor who either cleaned and arranged some toys, including a doll, or played with the toys in a somewhat rough and inappropriately suggestive manner. About an hour later, the janitor's "boss" interviewed the children about what they had seen. Of primary concern here is the situation in which children watched the janitor merely cleaning the toys although it was suggested to them that he had actually been playing with the toys improperly instead of doing his job. If a child in this situation initially did not agree with the interviewer's suggestion, subsequent leading questions were asked, with each question becoming increasingly stronger in its suggestion (that is, more explicitly suggesting misbehavior). Two-thirds of these children eventually followed the interviewers' suggestions, although it did not correspond to what they had seen. Moreover, when their parents questioned the children at the end of the session, all stuck with the story that they had given the interviewer. In sum, when suggestions and accusations were strong and persistent, young children were easily led and did not alter their newfound interpretations when later questioned by their parents.

In other research, Leichtman and Ceci (1995) assessed the effects of negative stereotyping and suggestion on preschool children's recollections of an event that happened at their school. An unfamiliar person, Sam Stone, came into children's classrooms, talked to the teacher, sat with the children during the reading of a story and made a comment about the story ("I know that story; it's one of my favorites!"), walked around the classroom, and finally left the room, waving good bye to the children. Children in the *stereotype* condition were given information about Sam Stone before his visit that depicted him as accident prone and irresponsible ("That Sam Stone is always getting into accidents and breaking things!"). Children in the *suggestion* condition were interviewed several times after Sam Stone's visit and given misinformation about the visit (Sam ripped a book and soiled a teddy bear when he visited). Children in the *stereotype-plus-suggestion* condition received both the negative stereotype before Sam Stone's visit and the misinformation afterward, and children in the *control* condition received neither the stereotyped information nor the misinformation about Sam.

Ten weeks after the visit, the children were given an open-ended interview about what happened the day Sam Stone visited the classroom. Leichtman and Ceci (1995) reported that children who had been given the stereotypes made a modest number of false statements about Sam in the interview (relative to children in the control condition), and that children in the suggestion condition made a substantial number of false reports. The highest levels of false reports about Sam's visit, however, came from children who received both the stereotyped information before and the misinformation after the visit; 46% of 3- and 4-year-old children and 30% of 5- and 6-year-old children said that Sam had either ripped a book or soiled a teddy bear, or both. The percentage of erroneous responses increased to 72% and 44% for the younger and older preschoolers, respectively, when children were asked specific follow-up questions concerning whether Sam had ripped a book or soiled a teddy bear.

Why are younger children often more susceptible to the effects of misinformation and suggestion than older children are? One explanation comes from fuzzy-trace theory, as discussed earlier (Brainerd & Poole, 1997; Brainerd & Reyna, 2002). Because verbatim traces deteriorate rapidly, they may not be available when post-event information is provided or when suggestive questions are asked. Thus, the erroneous information has an excellent chance of being incorporated with "real" memories and becoming indistinguishable from them. Similarly, it would seem that young children's elevated rates of erroneous information to unbiased cues (that is, questions that ask for more information but do not attempt to bias a child's answer one way or the other) might be the result of their greater reliance on verbatim traces.

Many factors influence suggestibility in children. For example, social factors, such as a desire to comply with adult requests, surely play a role in children's greater suggestibility (Bjorklund et al., 1998). Children are more likely to comply with the suggestion of a high-status versus a low-status person (Ceci, Ross, & Toglia, 1987); children's background knowledge for the witnessed event influences their performance (Ornstein et al., 1998), as does the number of times an event is experienced (Powell et al., 1999). Much research has investigated how other aspects of children's cognitive development influence suggestibility. For example, developmental and individual differences in working memory and inhibitory control are related to suggestibility in children (Ruffman et al., 2001), preschool children who perform better on theory of mind tasks tend to be less suggestible than are children with poorer theory-of-mind abilities (Welch, 1999), and children and adults with better metacognitive skills are more accurate in suggestive interviews than are their less-metacognitively sophisticated peers (Roebers, 2002).

One topic that has received considerable attention is that of **source monitoring.** Source monitoring refers to being aware of the source of information one knows or remembers. For example, did a particular experience happen to them, a friend, or did they see it on TV?

This can be particularly important in cases of eyewitness testimony. "Was the information that the boy stole the bike something I saw, or something someone told me?" Research has shown that preschool and early school-age children often have difficulty monitoring the source of their memories (see discussion in Chapter 9). For example, children sometimes have difficulty determining whether they actually performed an act or just imagined it (Foley, Santini, & Sopasakis, 1989) and often incorrectly remember that an action carried out by another person during a joint activity was actually performed by them (Ackil & Zaragoza, 1995; Foley, Ratner, & Passalacqua, 1993; see discussion in Chapter 3). When young children make errors in such situations, they are much more likely to attribute an action to themselves that someone else actually did than vice versa. Findings such as these have caused some researchers to propose that young children's increased susceptibility to suggestion might be caused largely by their difficulty in monitoring the source of what they know (Ceci & Bruck, 1995). Recent research supports these speculations, showing that 6-year-olds who are poor at source monitoring are more prone to the effects of suggestion (Mazzoni, 1998). Moreover, children who are given some source-monitoring training (for example, training in distinguishing between events they experienced directly versus events they heard about in a previous interview) make fewer false statements to misleading questions (Thierry & Spence, 2002), although some researchers have found this effect only for older (7- and 8-year-old) children and not for preschoolers (Poole & Lindsay, 2002).

Another reason contributing to young children's suggestibility might be their beliefs that their memory is invulnerable to suggestion. For example, Julia O'Sullivan, Mark Howe, and Tammy Marche (1996) interviewed preschool, first-grade, and third-grade children about factors that might influence their memories. Although children of all ages believed that central aspects of a story would be more likely to be remembered than would be peripheral details, only the third-grade children believed that their memories would be susceptible to suggestion. The preschool and first-grade children were confident that suggestion from a parent or sibling would not affect their recollection of an event.

False-Memory Creation

How easy is it to create a false memory in a person? Asking children misleading questions about an event they have seen can cause children to confuse the source of the information, thinking that the misinformation was actually something they experienced and not just something they heard someone else say (Ackil & Zaragoza, 1995). But how easy is it to actually get children, or adults, to believe an event happened to them that never really did?

Elizabeth Loftus and her colleagues first investigated this with adults (Loftus & Pickrell, 1995). College students were interviewed about four events that had supposedly happened to them in childhood (based on reports of parents and older siblings). One event, being lost in a mall at age 5, never actually occurred. The students were asked to write as much about each event as they could remember. They remembered, on average, 68% of the true events; they also "remembered" 25% of the false events, sometimes vividly (see also Oakes & Hyman, 2000).

It seems that preschool children are even more susceptible to creating false memories than are adults. Ceci and his colleagues (1994) used a similar technique to that used by Loftus and interviewed children throughout an 11-week period about events that might have happened to them. For example, children were asked if they ever remember getting their finger caught in a mousetrap. The percentage of false reports (that is, recalling something about the event) for the 3- and 4-year-old children and the 5- and 6-year-old children in this study, over the 11-week period, is shown in Figure 10-10. Although few children admitted to experiencing these false events in the initial interviews, by the conclusion of the study, more than 50% of the preschool children and about 40% of 5- to 6-year-olds assented that these events did indeed happen and often provided substantial detail about the events. Moreover, many children continued to believe that these events actually happened even after being told by the interviewers and their parents that the events were just made up. It seems that false memories of plausible but extraordinary events are relatively easy to put into young children's minds.

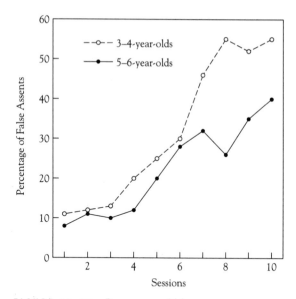

FIGURE 10-10 Percentage of false reports over sessions for 3–4-year-olds and 5–6-year-olds. SOURCE: Ceci, S. J., Loftus, E. F., Leichtman, M., & Bruck, M. (1994). The role of source misattributions in the creation of false beliefs among preschoolers. *International Journal of Clinical and Experimental Hypnosis, 62,* 304–320. © 1994 by Sage Publications, Inc. Reprinted by permission.

Plausibility is an important factor here. Even though getting one's finger caught in a mousetrap might be an event that few children have ever actually experienced, it is one that "could" happen in many households. Kathy Pezdek and Danelle Hodge (1999) demonstrated that about one-third of 5- to 7-year-old children "remembered" being lost in a mall (which they had not been), whereas only one of 19 children (about 5%) "remembered" being given an enema. Although most of these children knew what an enema was, the event was implausible. If such an embarrassing and invasive event had happened to them, they certainly would have remembered.

Field Studies and Recommendations to the Legal System

The investigations described in the previous sections are laboratory studies. Researchers know what children witnessed or experienced, and researchers often manipulated some aspect of the experience or characteristics of the interview to see what would happen. Such studies are relevant to the issue of the validity of children's testimony in cases of child abuse to the extent that they are analogous, in some way, to the experiences that abused children have or to how such children are interviewed. For example, studies examining children's recollections of invasive medical procedures involve bodily contact and discomfort, making them analogous to instances of child abuse (Ornstein et al., 1997). Other studies attempt to construct forensic interviews to be similar to those that abused children would experience (Bruck et al., 1995). Such studies afford control of variables that are difficult, if not impossible, to control in real life. However, there is always the question of the ecological validity of the studies. How do we know that children who experience child abuse behave in the same way? This is where field studies, interviewing children who are suspected victims of child abuse become important (Lamb & Thierry, in press). Of course, field studies lack control of important factors, and one does not know for certain what children actually experienced. But the combination of laboratory and field studies can provide greater insight into the reliability and accuracy of children as witnesses.

Do the factors that influence children's testimonies in laboratory studies similarly affect children's testimonies in field studies? For the most part, the answer is "yes." In general, in studies with children who are suspected victims of abuse, younger children remember less information than do older children, memory performance declines over delays, open-ended questions apparently produce more accurate information than do more specific cued questions, and suggestive questions increase levels of inaccurate information (see Lamb & Thierry, in press). However, field studies have also shown that young children can often recall more information about abuse than many laboratory studies would suggest when nonsuggestive open-ended prompts are used (Sternberg et al., 2001).

Has the abundance of research on the topic during the past decade led to changes in how children are interviewed by legal professionals? The answer is "yes." Many of the interview techniques previously used by people when interviewing suspected victims of child abuse turned out to be highly suggestive and the statements of the children highly questionable (Ceci & Bruck, 1995; Poole & Lamb, 1998). In recent years, a number of protocols have been designed to help those in the legal profession to interview children, getting the most accurate information possible (see Poole & Lamb, 1998, for reviews). For example, the National Institute of Child Health and Human Development (NICHD) protocol incorporates research findings from both laboratory and field settings (Lamb, Sternberg, & Esplin, 1998). It provides children with practice in recalling detailed accounts of events, it admonishes children to tell the truth, to say, "I don't know" when they are uncertain, and to correct the interviewer when they are uncertain. Following is the sequence of phases recommended by the NICHD guidelines (adapted from Poole & Lamb, 1998, pp. 98 & 99):

1. Introduction of parties and their roles
2. The "truth and lie ceremony" (warning the child of the necessity to tell the truth)
3. Rapport building
4. Description of a recent salient event
5. First narrative account of the allegation
6. Narrative accounts of the last incident (if the child reports multiple incidents)
7. Cue question (for example, "You said something about a barn. Tell me about that.")
8. Paired direct-open questions about the last incident
9. Narrative account of first incident
10. Cue questions
11. Paired direct-open questions about the first incident
12. Narrative accounts of another incident that the child remembers
13. Cue questions
14. Paired direct-open questions about this incident
15. If necessary, leading questions about forensically important details not mentioned by the child
16. Invitation for any other information the child wants to mention
17. Return to neutral topic

Note that the interview calls for the use of open-ended (free recall), cued, and even leading questions, where necessary, but that the child is always first encouraged to provide a narrative (open-ended) account of each incident that he or she experienced before resorting to cued and, if necessary, leading questions.

Research into the development of event memory in general, and eyewitness testimony specifically, has been one of the most investigated areas in cognitive development. We have learned a lot in a relatively short period, but we have also learned that there is no simple answer to any of the questions that we may ask. As I noted in the beginning of this section, we must consider the interaction of many different factors in evaluating children's eyewitness memory (Lindberg, 1991; Lindberg et al., 2000). Researchers have generally done this, and the result has been increased knowledge of both theory and practice.

Consistency and Stability of Memory

With a chapter titled "Memory," your expectation may be that we are talking about a single cognitive skill. Memory can be tapped in different ways (recognition, recall), can occur in different situations (event memory, school- or laboratory-type tasks), and can involve deliberate strategies or be indirect and unintentional, but the implication is that there is a single, underlying "memory" ability. This, of course, is an empirical question, and there is every reason to believe that the phenomenon we call "memory" is not a domain-general skill but, rather, comprises different domain-specific abilities.

Is "Memory" a Domain-General Faculty or a Set of Domain-Specific Abilities?

The way to assess this question is to administer different memory tasks to children and note the intertask correlations. That is, do children who do well

on one memory task perform well on others, and do children who perform poorly on one task perform poorly on others? Early developmental studies using this technique reported relatively high correlations among tasks, with the correlations increasing with age (Cavanaugh & Borkowski, 1980; Kail, 1979). These studies used strategic, laboratory tasks, discussed in Chapter 6, and the results suggest that not only is there a general memory ability, but there is also a general strategy ability, at least for children 8 years and older. (Recall that young children show little spontaneous strategic behavior, at least on the tasks used in these investigations.)

Later research used a wider variety of tasks, including laboratory tasks such as digit span and sort-recall, and "everyday" memory tasks, such as story recall (Kurtz-Costes, Schneider, & Rupp, 1995; Schneider & Weinert, 1995). These studies reported lower intertask correlations, suggesting that deliberate memory could better be thought of as a set of specific abilities rather than as a domain-general faculty. For example, Beth Kurtz-Costes and colleagues (1995) administered a set of 12 memory tasks to 5-, 7-, and 9-year-old children, including several reflecting everyday activities (for example, remember to remind the interviewer of something at the end of the session; "shopping" for items at a store), school-related tasks (for example, remembering a geography "lesson"; recalling a story), and laboratory tasks (sort-recall and paired associates). The researchers reported little intertask consistency among the 12 tasks at any age, with only slightly more correlations reaching statistical significance than would be expected by chance. The average correlations among tasks did increase slightly with age (average correlations = .07, .08, and .13 for 5-, 7-, and 9-year-olds, respectively), but, overall, little developmental differences were observed.

In related research, Wolfgang Schneider and Franz Weinert (1995) expanded the type of tasks given to children, including a variety of memory-span tasks (word span, sentence span), sort-recall, and several story-recall tasks. As part of a longitudinal study, Schneider and Weinert assessed the intertask correlations in the same group of children at

4, 6, 8, and 10 years of age. Schneider and Weinert reported few developmental patterns. But they did find relatively high intertask correlations among the two span tasks and the two story-recall tasks. That is, consistency was high only when the parallel measures of story recall and word span were used. Like the results of Kurtz-Costes and her colleagues, these findings are consistent with the position that there is no unitary "memory" construct, and little change in the relationship among memory tasks with development.

How Stable Is Memory Performance over Time?

One issue that interests developmental psychologists is *stability*. In this case, stability refers to maintaining the same rank order with respect to ability over time. That is, will children who remember well at one age also remember well on a similar task several years later? Research investigating stability requires longitudinal assessment, and such expensive and laborious work has rarely focused on basic cognitive processes such as memory. One notable exception is the Munich Longitudinal Study on the Genesis of Individual Competencies (LOGIC) (Sodian & Schneider, 1999; Weinert & Schneider, 1992), which has followed children through a 10-year period and made extensive assessments of memory performance.

When looking at the stability of children's performance on a sort-recall task, Schneider and Weinert (1995) reported relatively low long-term stability, with correlations of recall, sorting (the degree to which participants sort items into categories), and clustering never exceeding .20 over four-years time and .39 over a two-year period. Table 10-1 presents the pattern of correlations for different intervals and at different ages from the LOGIC sample. The column labeled "short-term stability" presents correlations between tasks given to the same children within a two-week period. The high correlations here suggest that children's performance is stable when tests are given over very brief intervals, suggesting that the tests themselves are reliable. What is not reliable is performance over longer periods.

Schneider and Weinert (1995) noted that long-term stability is higher for other memory tasks, however. For example, the correlations over a two-year period for sentence span, word span, and several measures of story recall were usually quite high (most in the .40 to .70 range). Schneider and Weinert suggested that the lower stabilities for the sort-recall tasks, in comparison with the memory-span and story-recall tasks, is related to the substantially greater strategic component required for the sort-recall tasks. That is, stability is relatively high for tasks involving relatively little in the way of deliberate strategic functioning (memory span and story recall), but lower when strategies play a crucial part in task performance.

TABLE 10-1 Stability of memory performance over time (long-term and short-term stability) obtained for strategy and recall measures for the sort-recall task from the Munich Longitudinal Project.

Variable	Two-year stability (4–6)	Two-year stability (6–8)	Two-year stability (8–10)	Four-year stability (4–8)	Six-year stability (4–10)	Short-term stability
Recall	.36	.29	.39	.20	.16	.68
Sorting	.17	.12	.07	.08	.02	.85
Clustering	.12	.16	.12	.08	.19	.64

SOURCE: Schneider, W., & Weinert, F. E. (1995). Memory development during early and middle childhood: Findings from the Munich longitudinal study (LOGIC). In F. E. Weinert & W. Schneider (Eds.), *Memory performance and competencies: Issues in growth and development*. Hillsdale, NJ: Erlbaum. Reprinted with permission from the author.

Forgetting

All the information presented in this chapter to this point has dealt with remembering. But each of us is familiar with another side of memory—**forgetting.** Forgetting refers to failing to remember some information that one knew, or had previously remembered, some time earlier. Forgetting is not the same as never knowing. If a child is given 20 words to remember and recalls only 10 of them, the remaining 10 were not forgotten. They were never learned. Forgetting would occur when, some time following the initial test, the child was asked again to remember as many of the 20 words that he or she had seen earlier. If of the 10 words the child had originally remembered, only 5 were recalled again, we could say that the child forgot 5 words, or 50% of what he or she had remembered earlier.

Until recently, forgetting was not much studied by developmental psychologists. Forgetting was a relatively popular topic earlier in the last century, but fell out of favor, partly because forgetting did not fit well with the computer metaphor of information-processing models and because early studies reported few developmental differences in forgetting. It seemed that once something was learned, people of all ages were equally likely to remember (or forget) it (see Howe & Brainerd, 1989, for a review of the early research).

More recent research by Howe, Brainerd, and their colleagues questioned this interpretation, stating that most earlier studies were methodologically flawed in one way or another (Brainerd, 1997; Howe & O'Sullivan, 1997). Some of the flaws included using measures that are not sensitive to developmental differences (for example, recognition rather than recall measures), ceiling effects in forgetting rates (that is, everyone forgot almost everything, making meaningful analyses impossible), and a failure to control for differences in initial levels of learning (that is, older children learned more initially than did younger children, giving them more to forget).

Howe, Brainerd, and their colleagues addressed these methodological problems by requiring that children of all ages learn the target information to a specified criterion (usually perfect recall). Once accomplished, children were tested again for the target material using recall measures, often days and weeks later (Howe, 1991). Under these conditions, age differences in forgetting are found, with younger children forgetting at higher rates than older children and adults. Research using a variant of this paradigm has even been done with preverbal toddlers, with the finding that 12-month-olds showed higher rates of forgetting than did 18-month-olds (Howe & Courage, 1997).

Although most forgetting experiments of the type described used lists of words, several have used stories as stimuli (Howe, 1991; Marche & Howe, 1995). For example, Howe (1991) reported that second-grade children remembered more information than kindergartners did about a story after delays of both 2 and 9 days, illustrating greater forgetting for the younger relative to the older children (remember that all children learned the story to criterion).

In other research, Cassel and I (1995) showed kindergarten, second grade, and college students a brief video and asked for their immediate recall of events in the video. After recalling all they could, participants were given a set of cues for items they had not remembered in free recall. Participants were tested for free-recall of the events in the video again one week and one month later. When considering only information people remembered initially in *free recall*, forgetting rates during the 1-week and 1-month sessions were comparable at all grades (about 50%). Forgetting rates were higher for information that was remembered originally to the cues, with the adults showing better retention (less forgetting) than the children. These results are consistent with the claims of Howe and Brainerd that developmental differences in degree of initial learning affect later forgetting. Information that adults and the children remembered in free recall was best (and equally) retained one week and one month later by all participants. Age differences were found only for the less salient information; adults were better able to retain information they had retrieved only to the experimenter's cues than the children were. Thus, age differences in forgetting are found for less salient information (Cassel & Bjorklund, 1995) and when all participants learn the to-be-remembered information perfectly (Brainerd, 1997), the latter being a situation that is rarely found in everyday life. Age differences in forgetting are less apt to be found, however, in some more "realistic" situations, when levels of initial memory vary with age. These results illustrate that answering the question "Are there age differences in forgetting?" is not an easy one. To a large extent, it depends on where one looks.

One reason that has been proposed for age differences in forgetting (when they are found) has focused on developmental differences in how information is encoded. This possibility was discussed earlier in this chapter in our discussion of children's eyewitness memories. Younger children are more likely to encode information in terms of literal, verbatim memory traces, whereas older children are more likely to encode information in terms of less-precise, gist memory traces (Brainerd & Reyna, 1990; Leichtman & Ceci, 1993). Verbatim traces, favored by the younger children, are less resistant to decay, thus producing higher forgetting rates for younger relative to older children. Age differences in verbatim and gist encoding are a central theme of fuzzy-trace theory (Brainerd & Reyna, 2002) and were discussed in some detail in Chapter 5.

Summary

Memory is multifaceted, involving a host of other cognitive operations, and it is involved in all complex forms of thinking. Memory can refer to the process of bringing information to consciousness or to the contents of memory. *Recognition* is generally good in young children, although age changes in recognition are found when the task demands become difficult or when children can apply their world knowledge to assist them in the recognition process. More substantial age differences are found for *free recall*. Children's recall is higher on *cued-recall* tasks, with younger children needing more specific cues before recalling information.

Infants display memory in habituation/dishabituation and *preference-for-novelty paradigms* shortly after birth. Conditioning techniques, particularly *conjugate reinforcement procedures*, have been used to demonstrate memory in infants as young as 3 months for periods as long as 2 weeks, with infants' memories in these situations being greatly influenced by context effects. Deferred-imitation tasks have shown that older infants can retain information over relatively long periods, with infants' long-term memory for actions increasing gradually over the first two years of life. *Infantile amnesia* refers to the inability to recall information from infancy and early childhood. Current theories about the reason for infantile amnesia focus on the development of self-concept, developmental differences in how information is encoded, and changes in children's use of language to communicate their memories to others. The use of hypnotic age regression is not successful in retrieving memories from infancy.

In contrast to explicit, or intentional memory, few age differences are observed for *implicit memory*, when there is no conscious intention to remember something.

Young children's *event memory* is based on *scripts*, a form of schematic organization with real-world events organized by their causal and temporal characteristics. Children's early memories are for general routines and not for specific *autobiographical* experiences. Parents "teach" children how to remember by interacting with them and providing the structure for putting their experiences into narratives.

Recent research in event memory has focused on children as eyewitnesses. Age differences are found in the amount of information children remember, but what young children do recall tends to be accurate and for central components of an event. The accuracy of children's event memory is influenced by a host of factors, including their knowledge for the event they experienced and characteristics of the interview, such as the use of anatomically correct dolls and the use of repeated questions, although repeatedly recalling events can sometimes result in an increase in recall, termed *hypermnesia*. Recent research has documented that young children are generally more susceptible to misleading questions (suggestions) and misinformation than are older children and can easily be caused to form false memories. Many factors influence children's suggestibility, including deficits in *source monitoring*, with children confusing the source of information they know or remember.

Research has shown that memory is best conceptualized as a set of different, domain-specific skills rather than as a single mental faculty. There is relatively little stability of strategic memory, but greater short-term stability (2 years) for less obviously strategic tasks such as memory span and story recall.

Age differences in *forgetting* are typically found when researchers control for differences in levels of initial learning.

Note

1. *avuncular:* Of, pertaining to or resembling an uncle (*The American Heritage Dictionary of the English Language*).

Key Terms and Concepts

recognition
cued recall
free recall
preference-for-novelty paradigms
conjugate reinforcement procedures
infantile amnesia
autobiographical memory
implicit memory
event memory
scripts
hypermnesia
source monitoring
forgetting

Suggested Readings

Bauer, P. J. (2002). Long-term recall memory: Behavioral and neuro-developmental changes in the first 2 years of life. *Current Directions in Psychological Science, 11,* 137–141. This article presents a concise review of the latest work looking at memory in infants and young children using elicited and deferred imitation tasks.

Brainerd, C. J., & Reyna, V. F. (2002). Fuzzy-trace theory and false memory. *Current Directions on Psychological Science, 11,* 164–169. This brief article presents the basic tenets and findings of fuzzy-trace theory as applied to the creation false memories in children and adults.

Ceci, S. J., & Bruck, M. (1998). Children's testimony: Applied and basic issues. In I. E. Sigel & K. A. Renninger (Vol. Eds.), *Child psychology in practice* (Vol. 4) (pp. 713–774). In W. Damon (Gen. Ed.), *Handbook of child psychology.* New York: Wiley. This chapter presents an historical review and the latest research on children's eyewitness memory and suggestibility, including summaries of important legal cases in which children's testimony played a central role.

Cowan, N. (Ed.) (1997). *The development of memory in childhood.* London: London University College Press. This book includes 12 chapters written by leading researchers and theorists on various topics of children's memory, including infant memory, strategies, event memory, metamemory, and children's eyewitness testimony, among others. The chapters were written with an undergraduate audience in mind.

Nelson, K. (1996). *Language in cognitive development: The emergence of the mediated mind.* New York: Cambridge University Press. This book presents Katherine Nelson's theory on the role of language in cognitive development and in the process reviews research on the development of event and autobiographical memory.

Schneider, W., & Pressley, M. (1997). *Memory development between 2 and 20* (2nd ed.). Mahwah, NJ: Erlbaum. This is a thorough review of memory development, from the beginning of psychology through the mid 1990s, written by two of the leading researchers in the field. This book is written for the professional researcher and advanced student.

InfoTrac College Edition

For additional readings, explore InfoTrac College Edition, your online library. Go to http://www.infotrac-college.com/wadsworth.

Language Development

Human beings' use of language, more than any other single ability, is what most obviously distinguishes us from all other animals. Children around the globe acquire language without formal instruction. Language belongs to the class of abilities that are too important to be relegated to our conscious awareness and "free will" (Spelke & Newport, 1998). Some scientists believe that the evolution of language made human thought possible (Bickerton, 1990; Nelson, 1996). Although a few nonhuman primates have shown simple language abilities (see Savage-Rumbaugh et al., 1993), none has approached the level found in all normal humans. And despite the universality of language (that is, all groups of people possess it and develop it at about the same age), the language people learn depends on what is spoken around them. Language is thus strongly influenced both by humans' general biological inheritance and by the uniqueness of the environments in which they grow up.

In this chapter, I examine some of the fascinating and often controversial research and theory related to language development. In the first section, I consider what exactly language is and how it differs from other communication systems. I then provide a brief sketch of children's developing language abilities, from cooing and babbling to communicative competence. Next I investigate some of the major theoretical perspectives of language development, particularly contrasting *nativist theories*, which hold that the mechanisms and structures underlying language acquisition (specifically the acquisition of syntax, or grammar) are largely innate, and *social-interactionist theories*, which hold that the social environment plays a substantial role in language development. This is followed by a brief look at gender differences in language development and, finally, a look at the developmental relationship between language and thought.

What Makes a Communication System a Language?

Humans are not the only species to have a complex communication system, but, by some definitions, we are the only species to have language. Most linguists, I think, would agree on the following features as typifying language: **arbitrariness, productivity, semanticity, displacement,** and **duality** (Brown, 1973; Lyons, 1978).

1. *Arbitrariness.* Any pattern of sound (that is, any word) can refer to anything that the speakers of a language choose to have it refer to. A word is not inherently related to the concept it represents. For example, in English we refer to the bright yellow ball in the daytime sky as the "sun," and the "lesser light" of the evening as the "moon." The words themselves are arbitrary, having nothing to do with the objects themselves. If we wished to, we could agree to reverse the names, as some groups of people sometimes do. (For instance, the word "bad," when used in the right context with the proper pronunciation, has a positive, not a negative, connotation to it.)

2. *Productivity.* Languages are *creative*, or generative. Speakers of a language can produce an infinite number of sentences using only a finite set of words. A language does not consist of a specific set of sentences that are to be memorized. Rather, language has a system of rules (syntax, or grammar) that permits a speaker to produce and understand sentences that have never been uttered before.

3. *Semanticity.* Semanticity refers to the fact that language can represent objects, actions, events, and ideas symbolically.

4. *Displacement.* Language has the ability to displace the speaker and the listener from the here and now. People can talk about objects and events that are outside of their immediate context, both in time and space. Language permits us to talk about the past or the future and to know about events or objects that are miles away.

5. *Duality.* Duality refers to the fact that language is represented at two levels: *phonology*, the actual sound that a speaker produces, and the underlying abstract, meaning of language, reflected by the *syntax* (rules of putting words together) and *semantics* (meanings of those words and concepts).

Describing Children's Language Development

The concept of duality implies that there are at least two different *aspects* of language, but in fact there are at least five different aspects: phonology, morphology, syntax, semantics, and pragmatics, and they all develop. In this section, I first provide a brief description of early language development, primarily to give readers some context in which to interpret what follows. I then look at the five aspects of language just mentioned and provide a more in-depth description of children's development for each aspect.

A Brief Description of Early Language Development

Infants' earliest vocalizations are cries, but they begin cooing and babbling between 2 and 4 months of age. Children typically say their first words late in their first year of life or shortly thereafter. Early words are sometimes only recognized by family members and usually refer to people in the family ("Mama," "Dada"), or important objects. Most of the first 50 or so words that children acquire refer to familiar people, toys, and food (Nelson, 1974), and this is apparently true across different languages (Caselli et al., 1995).

At about 18 to 24 months, children know a few dozen words and begin putting them together, a few at a time, into short sentences or phrases. Again, the words they know are those that are important to them, such as actions (what happened), possession (what belongs to whom), location (where people and objects are), recurrence (requesting "more" or "again"), naming (familiar people and objects), and nonexistence ("all gone") (de Villiers & de Villiers, 1979).

Another way toddlers get the most meaning from their limited language abilities is by using gestures and intonations to supplement their sparse sentences. "MOMMY!" can be a clear cry of distress, whereas "Mommy?" can be the initiation of a light conversation. Add a little hand waving and an empty cup and "Mommy" becomes a request for a drink refill. And coming from behind a chairback, "Mommy" can be the beginning of a round of peek-a-boo. Take, for example, the toddler who gets his mother's attention by climbing up next to her on the sofa, putting one hand on each of her cheeks, and turning her face toward his as he finally says "Cookie?" And another 2-year-old who tells her parents that she doesn't want any more milk by giving a negative head shake as she says "More milk."

Although children at this age express limited words and ideas, they are capable of understanding much more. It is estimated that by the time children speak their first words, they understand approximately one hundred (Benedict, 1979). This brings us to the distinction between **productive language,** the language that children can actually produce, or speak, and **receptive language,** the language that children can understand. Receptive language exceeds productive language, with this distinction beginning early in infancy and persisting into adulthood (Hirsh-Pasek, Golinkoff, & Naigles, 1996). For instance, in one study, 16- to 18-month-old toddlers were able to tell the difference between sentences such as "Where is Big Bird washing Cookie Monster?" and "Where is Cookie Monster washing Big Bird?," although most of the children were able to produce "sentences" only one word in length (Hirsh-Pasek & Golinkoff, 1991).

When children get beyond the two-word phase, they do so mostly by including only those words that convey the most meaning and omitting the "little" words that make language easy to understand but that are not absolutely necessary for comprehension. For example, a child might say "Daddy give milk me" or "Amy me go Grandma's?" rather than "Give me the milk, Daddy," or "May Amy and I go to Grandma's?" When heard in context, the meanings of these abbreviated sentences are straightforward. Children are economical in their word choice, using only the concrete and high-information words that are most important in conveying meaning. Such speech has been described as **telegraphic,** in that it is accomplished much as telegrams were once written, including only the high-content words and leaving out all the ifs, ands, and buts.

During the three years from age 2 to age 5, children's language develops from baby talk to adultlike communication—surely an impressive feat to anyone who has tried to learn a second language during adulthood. Yet, children accomplish this with little formal instruction, only their day-to-day interactions with language-using adults and older children.

Children increase their vocabularies dramatically during these years, learning an average of a dozen new words a day. By school age, children know between 8,000 and 14,000 words (Carey, 1978). At the same time, they increase the length and content of their sentences.

Phonological Development

Phonology refers to the sounds of a language. Our unique anatomy permits us to make a wide range of sounds that can be combined into sequences of words. There are age-related changes in the tongue, mouth, and position of larynx in the throat, and these physical differences mean that the sounds that infants and children are able to produce change over time (Stoel-Gammon & Menn, 1997).

Infants begin cooing and laughing between 2 and 4 months, and these vocalizations increase until 9 to 12 months, when they decline and one-word utterances begin (see Table 11-1). Sounds made during babbling vary widely, including both sounds heard in the baby's native language and sounds that are not. Babbling sounds change with age. All this caused some early theorists to conclude from diary studies that babbling served as an exotic smorgasbord of universal language sounds from which infants selected those they heard in the language being spoken around them, while gradually eliminating those they didn't hear (Jakobson, 1968). This popular theory is still cited today by some, but research findings have not supported it. Babbling does not contain all the sounds found in human language, only a small subset (Locke, 1983; Oller, 1980). The developmental changes in babbling reflect anatomic changes in the vocal apparatus more than they reflect approximations toward the sounds of one's native tongue (Ingram, 1989).

It has been suggested that babbling plays a more important role in language development than just a poor attempt at spoken words (Sachs, 1977). Bab-

bling might serve as a way to relate socially with family members long before the cognitive system is able to appreciate the intricacies of language. In addition, there is evidence that although the *sounds* of babbling don't gradually approximate speech, the *intonation* of babbling does. Infants begin to "converse" in many ways that do not involve words but, rather, the conventions of speech. Infants develop the ability to take turns (Snow & Ferguson, 1977), match the speaker's tone of voice, pause between strings of syllables, end phrases with upward or downward inflections (Tonkova-Yompol'skaya, 1969), and match the pitch of adults speaking to them—higher for mother, lower for father (Lieberman, 1967).

But, is babbling truly a component of language, using the same neurological structure that later "real" language does? Or is it simply the infant exercising his or her vocal apparatus? Siobhan Holowka and Laura Ann Petitto (2002) investigated this question. In most adults, language is principally localized in the left hemisphere of the brain, which controls the right side of the body. When adults are engaged in linguistic tasks, mouth openings are generally greater on the right-hand side (and thus controlled by the language-dominant left hemisphere) compared with when adults are engaged in nonlinguistic tasks, such as smiling, when mouth openings are greater on the left-hand side (and thus controlled by the right hemisphere). According to Holowka and Petitto, "If babbling is fundamentally linguistic in nature, then left hemispheric specialization should be reflected in right mouth asymmetry while babbling. If babbling is fundamentally motoric in nature, then equal hemispheric participation should be reflected in equal mouth opening while babbling" (2002, p. 1515). To test this, they videotaped 10 babies (5 from English-speaking parents and 5 from French-speaking parents) between the ages of 5 and 12 months, while making three types of expressions, babbles, non-babbles, and smiles. Holowka and Petitto reported that all babies opened their mouths to the right side when babbling, opened their mouths to the left side when smiling, and there was no significant left-right difference when they made non-babbling sounds. These findings suggest that brain lateralization for language is present before children's first words, and

TABLE 11-1 Developmental stages of infants' babbling.

Stage 1: *Reflexive crying and vegetative sounds (0 to 8 weeks)*

Infants in stage 1 cry as a reaction to a distressed state and make various vegetative sounds associated with feeding and breathing, such as burps, coughs, and sneezes. The vocal tract of these young infants closely resembles that of nonhuman primates; their tongue fills their oral cavity and their larynx is high in their neck (which permits them to breathe and swallow simultaneously). This leaves little room for making different sounds. As the infant's head and neck grow, a greater variety of sounds become possible.

Stage 2: *Cooing and laughter (8 to 20 weeks)*

Infants at this age begin to make pleasant noises, especially during social interactions. These are mostly vowel sounds such as "oooh" and are termed cooing because they resemble the sounds made by pigeons. A few of the sounds will also contain some consonants such as *g* and *k*. Crying decreases and takes distinct forms that convey meaning to caregivers—discomfort, call, and request. Sustained laughter appears.

Stage 3: *Vocal play (16 to 30 weeks)*

This is a transition between cooing and true babbling. Infants begin to utter single syllables with prolonged vowel or consonant sounds.

Stage 4: *Reduplicated babbling (25 to 50 weeks)*

True babbling sounds appear, such as "bababa" and "nanana." Consonant-vowel patterns are repeated, and playful variations of pitch disappear. This type of vocalization is not just a response to caregiver's social interaction, but often occurs when no one is present. Deaf infants, although going through the first three stages, do not engage in true babbling at this time (Oller & Eilers, 1988).

Stage 5: *Jargon (9 to 18 months)*

Babbling consists of many nonrepeated consonant-vowel patterns. Jargon babbling is strings of sound filled with a variety of intonations and rhythms to sound like meaningful speech. Infants at this stage often sound as if they are carrying on their end of a conversation, with their intonations sometimes sounding as if they reflect questions or explanations, but their "words" are only babble sounds.

SOURCE: Stark, R. (1978). Features of infant sounds: The emergence of cooing. *Journal of Child Language*, 5, 1–12; and Stoel-Gammon, C., & Menn, L. (1997). Phonological development: Learning sounds and sound patterns. In J. Berko Gleason (Ed.), *The development of language* (4th ed.). Boston: Allyn & Bacon.

that babbling is more than motor exercise but reflects infants' "sensitivity to and production of patterns in the linguistic input" (p. 1515). (These findings also suggest that, like adults, infants' *emotional* expressions, reflected here by smiling, may be controlled principally by the right hemisphere.)

Speech perception (as opposed to production) was discussed in Chapter 7. To reiterate briefly here, very young infants can perceive *phonemes*, the basic sound units of language, and they categorize them much as adults do. Young infants can also discriminate between the sounds of many different languages, something that their parents cannot do. Over time, however, infants lose the ability to tell the dif-

ference between sounds that are not found in their mother tongue. Thus, infants' auditory systems seem prepared to make sense of human speech, although their audition is modified over childhood as a function of what language sounds they hear.

Morphological Development

Morphology refers to the structure of something—in the case of language, the structure of words. Counter to what you might think, the word is *not* the smallest unit of meaning in a language. In English, for example, we add sounds to words to make them past tense (add *ed*), to express the present progressive (add *ing*), or to make a word plural (add *s*), and these word endings are also units of meaning. The smallest unit of meaning in a language is called a **morpheme,** and there are two types. **Free morphemes** can stand alone as words, such as "fire," "run," or "sad." In contrast, **bound morphemes** cannot stand alone but, rather, are attached to free morphemes. They convey meaning by changing the free morpheme they are attached to. These include the rules for making nouns plural (add an *s*), for making a verb past tense (add an *ed*), as well as prefixes (*un*likable) and suffixes (like*ness*). The average number of morphemes a child uses in a sentence, or the **mean length of utterance (MLU),** is a good measure of how far a child has developed linguistically. MLU is measured by recording a child's speech during a period and computing the average number of morphemes (both free and bound).

Roger Brown (1973) identified many of the morphemes used in children's early language and analyzed the speech of three unacquainted children (Adam, Eve, and Sarah) to determine the order in which these morphemes appear in development. He found 14 morphemes that occurred in almost the same order for the three children in his sample (see Table 11-2). Later research by Jill and Peter de Villiers (1973) extended these findings to 21 other preschoolers and found a high correlation between their sample and Brown's.

As can be seen from Table 11-2, many of the morphemes children learn are word endings. Once children learn these rules, they tend to apply them, even when it is not correct. For example, 2- and 3-year-olds learn that adding -*ed* to a verb makes it past tense and -*s* to a noun makes it plural. Although this may be generally true, there are many irregular verbs and nouns (especially in English), and although words such as *goed* (or *wented*), *drinked, runned, feets* (or *footes*), and *mices* follow the rules, they are incorrect. Children make these kinds of mistakes even when they have previously used the proper irregular word forms (for example, *went, drank, ran, feet,* and *mice*). This phenomenon is referred to as **overregularization** and usually begins around 20 months of

TABLE 11-2 Mean order of acquisition of 14 morphemes for three children.

Morpheme		Example	MLU per child		
			Adam	Eve	Sarah
1.	Present progressive	sing*ing*, walk*ing*	2.5	2.5	2.5
2. & 3.	In, on		2.5	2.5	2.5
4.	Plural, regular	apples, shoes	2.5	3.0	2.0
5.	Past, irregular	*went, saw*	3.0	4.0	2.5
6.	Possessive	Eve's, hers	3.5	2.5	2.5
7.	Uncontractable copula	The dog *is* big.	3.0	4.0	3.0
8.	Articles	*a, the*	3.5	4.0	3.0
9.	Past, regular	talk*ed*, throw*ed*	4.0	3.0	4.0
10.	Third person, regular	he run*s*, she swim*s*	4.0	4.0	3.5
11.	Third person, irregular	he *does*, she *has*	3.5	4.0	4.0
12.	Uncontractable	I *am* going.	4.0	4.0	4.0
13.	Contractable copula	The dog's big.	4.0	4.0	4.0
14.	Contractable auxiliary	I'm going.	4.0	4.0	4.0

SOURCE: Brown, R. (1973). *A first language: The early stages,* pp. 271, 274. Cambridge, MA: Harvard University Press. Copyright © 1973 by the President and Fellows of Harvard College. Reprinted by permission

age. Children continue to overregularize words throughout the preschool years, although beginning around 3 they are increasingly likely to use the irregular forms of verbs and nouns properly (Marcus, 1995; Marcus et al., 1992). Children have learned a rule for regular words and generalize it to irregular words. Apparently, having a history of being understood is not as potent a motivator for using a certain form of language as is the acquisition of a rule and its generalization to all situations where it might apply. This phenomenon is not limited to children learning

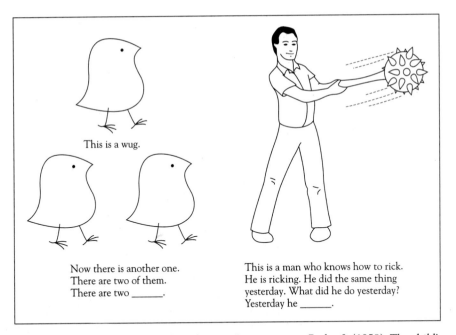

This is a wug.

Now there is another one.
There are two of them.
There are two _____.

This is a man who knows how to rick.
He is ricking. He did the same thing
yesterday. What did he do yesterday?
Yesterday he _____.

FIGURE 11-1 Two examples from the "wug" test. SOURCE: Berko, J. (1958). The child's learning of English morphology. *Word, 14,* 150–177. Reprinted with permission.

English, but has been found in a wide variety of languages, suggesting that children around the world approach the problem of language acquisition in a similar way (Slobin, 1970).

How can you know whether children understand the morphological rules of their language? One technique that has been quite successful is the "wug test" (Berko, 1958, see Figure 11-1). Children are shown a series of unfamiliar objects (for example, "This is a *wug*.") or pictures of people performing unfamiliar actions (for example, "This man knows how to rick.") For the "wug" example, children are then shown two of these creatures and told, "Now there are two of them. There are two _____." If children know the regular rules for making plurals, they will say "wugs." When shown a picture of a man who knows how "to rick," when asked what he did yesterday, children who know the rules will say that "he ricked," and if they know the rules for the present progressive, they will say that currently "he is ricking" (Marcus et al., 1992).

Syntactic Development

Syntax is the knowledge of sentence structure, or grammatical rules—rules for how words are combined into sentences and how sentences are transformed into other sentences. Competent speakers of a language can use the same set of words to create very different meanings by applying basic grammatical rules. For example, the sentence, "The man drove the car," can be made negative ("The man didn't drive the car"), transformed to pose a question ("Did the man drive the car?"), or expressed in the passive voice ("The car was driven by the man"). If you followed these simple transformations of these English sentences, it means that you know the underlying structure, or syntax, of English. You might not be able to pass a freshman test of English grammar, but you implicitly know the rules. These rules might not be part of your explicit (declarative) knowledge. Few of us can actually state the rules used for transforming an active declarative sentence into a question or to the passive voice, but nonetheless, we are all linguistic experts when it comes to actual performance. Our syntactic expertise is so good that we can even recognize grammatical sentences that contain nonsense words. For example, the sentence "The golup was pudaded under his limnex" is meaningless because "golup," "pudaded," and "limnex" are all meaningless. But because you are an expert at English syntax, you know that the subject of the sentence is "golup" (and that it is animate and masculine), that "pudaded" is a verb, specifically an action that was done to the "golup," and a "limnex" is something (a noun) possessed by the "golup," possibly a body part. Not bad for nonsense.

The question central to language acquisition has been the acquisition of syntax. How is it that children make sense of the jumble of sounds that surround them to eventually discover the underlying rules of language? Although each of the world's 4,000 plus languages might have some unique features to them, they all also have some things in common with one another. That is, they all possess, at some "deep level" some common aspects of syntax (see Maratsos, 1998; Pinker, 1994). I will discuss some of these seemingly universal aspects of syntax later in this chapter.

One way of assessing syntactic development is to look at common grammatical forms and see how children of different ages use them. I examine briefly young children's development of negatives, questions, passive sentences, and relating events in sentences.

Negatives

Early in the preschool years, children learn the power of negatives. Actually, many problems during the so-called "terrible twos" spring from children's new knowledge that they can have thoughts and wishes that don't necessarily reflect those of their parents and that they can express them by using negatives. Early use of negatives involves tacking "n" words onto positive sentences, as in "No drink milk" or "Not bath, Mommy." They sometimes add the negative to the end of a sentence, as in "Drink milk no."

Following this stage, the negative term is moved inside the sentence next to the main verb, for example,

"I no do it" or "She no go." Eventually, children learn to use auxiliaries much as adults do and as reflected in sentences such as, "I don't want to do it," and "She can't have it." These later, more sophisticated negatives are also associated with longer sentences.

Questions

Questions develop from adding a raised intonation at the end of declarative sentences, such as "Aaron go outside, Mommy?" to more adultlike forms such as "Can I go outside, Mommy?." Sometime during the third year, the "wh" questions begin: "Where Daddy?," "What's this?" and the all-too-common, "Why?."

More significant to developmentalists is the child's growing ability to answer "wh" questions. Different "wh" words refer to different parts of speech—*who, what,* and *where* refer to people, objects, and locations and are easily answered by young toddlers. For example, "Where's Mommy?" requires a simple response of "Outside" or "In the kitchen." In contrast, *when, which, how,* and *why,* require more difficult concepts and greater language ability. For example, asking a toddler "When did Daddy go to work?" or "Why did you leave the door open?" could result in great frustration for both adult and child (de Villiers & de Villiers, 1978).

Passive Sentences

Late in the preschool years, around age 5 or 6, children learn about passive sentences. With active sentences, the word order tells the story: "John hit the ball." Passive sentences take away that cue—"The ball was hit by John"—and young preschoolers get confused (Goodz, 1982). Interestingly, children first learn to interpret passive sentences when the verb refers to some observable event, such as "The horse was kicked by the cow." Later they learn passive sentences with less observable verbs, such as "Tommy was remembered by the teacher."

Relating Events in Sentences

Around the age of 3, children can relate two ideas by connecting them with *and.* They no longer have to string together short phrases such as "I went outside. I played on the swing." Now they can say, "I went outside and played on the swing." Later they can use other conjunctions such as *but, because,* and *while,* which gives them new ways to express more complex relationships between ideas than just tacking them together with "and" (de Villiers & de Villiers, 1978). There is quite a different meaning to "Mommy got mad and Daddy was late" and "Mommy got mad because Daddy was late."

Syntactic development does not stop at age 5, of course, but the differences between the grammar used by 6- and 7-year-olds and adults are subtle and minor. For instance, school-age children still must master subject-verb agreement (for example, "They were going" instead of "They was going") and the use of personal pronouns (for example, "He and she went" instead of "Him and her went"). But in general, the basic grammatical structure of school-age children's sentences varies little from that of adults.

How do children master this seemingly overly complicated task? The syntax of a language seems far more complex than young children's meager cognitive skills can handle. Yet, during their first five years, most children become linguistic experts in their mother tongue. On top of all this, children learn language despite the fact that the speech that they hear is imperfect, or "degenerate," filled with errors, incomplete sentences, and mumbled words. Somehow, children take the imperfect language that surrounds them and weave a theory of language (that is, syntax) that corresponds to that which their parents speak. This, among other evidence, has caused many to propose that the learning of syntax has a strongly innate basis to it (see later section on Nativist Perspectives).

Semantic Development

Semantics refers to meaning, specifically the meaning of language terms. "Meaning" here, however, refers to more than just a simple definition. Words refer to concepts or objects, but are also related to other concepts or objects. For example, children must learn not only that "dog" refers to a four-legged

family pet called Spot, but to other perceptually similar creatures, who themselves are members of the larger group of "mammals" and "animals." Children must also learn that the word "dog" does not refer to horses, goats, or pigs and that it might be related to other objects such as cats and fire hydrants, although not in the same way it is related to animals.

The Word Spurt

Perhaps the simplest indication of children's semantic development is the number of words they know. Children speak their first words at about 10 to 12 months of age and learn new words at a rate of about 8 to 11 per month. However, at about 18 months of age, or when children have about 50 words in their active vocabulary, the rate at which they learn new words increases substantially, to between 22 and 37 words per month (Benedict, 1979). This has been termed the **word spurt.** Most of the words children learn during this time are nouns, often labels for objects. (This is the time when children frequently ask "What's that?," as they point to every new object they see.) Although there has been some debate about whether all children have this word spurt (Goldfield & Reznick, 1990), most children observed seemed to display such a spurt, although the age at which they show a spurt varies considerably (Mervis & Bertrand, 1994).

Recent research indicates that infants in their second year of life spontaneously look at objects for familiar words. This ability increases in efficiency between 15 and 20 months of age, and the oldest children are about as fast as adults at doing this (Fernald et al., 1998). In other words, children in the latter part of their second year are getting faster at understanding the words they hear. Other research has shown that even children 12 to 17 months old are learning new words at a rapid rate, but for their *receptive* vocabulary (words they can recognize) rather than for their *productive* vocabularies (Schafer & Plunkett, 1998). This all indicates that toddlers' word spurt doesn't appear out of nowhere, but has its beginnings in pre-speaking processing.

What accounts for children's rapid acquisition of words, specifically nouns, during this time? Some have speculated that children have a set of specific language-processing constraints that kick in at this time to make word learning easy (Carey, 1978; Mervis & Bertrand, 1994). Carey (1978) labeled the process underlying the word spurt as **fast mapping.** Fast mapping refers to the ability to learn new words based on very little input (that is, few opportunities to learn the words), although children's understanding of words acquired through fast mapping are usually fragmented and incomplete. Carolyn Mervis and Jacquelyn Bertrand (1994) demonstrated fast mapping in children by showing children between the ages of 16 and 20 months a set of objects, one of which was unfamiliar to them (for example, a garlic press). They were asked to pick out the items, one at a time, and were given a nonsense word for the unfamiliar item (for example, "May I have the bliff?"). Only some of the children were able to learn new words for these unfamiliar items after only a few exposures (the "fast mappers"). These children were found to have larger vocabularies than did the children who did not learn words for these novel items. This latter group of children was seen several months later, after they had gone through their word spurts, and now they, too, showed the ability to "fast map." These results indicate that the word spurt is associated with a special processing ability, reflected by fast mapping, in which children map novel words to novel objects for which they do not yet have a name.

Constraints on Word Learning

But how do children figure out what the words spoken by others refer to? When a child sees a white, long-eared object, hopping across the lawn, and her father points and says, "See the rabbit," how does the child know what he is referring to? Is it the animal itself, the color of the animal, the long ears, the act of hopping, or perhaps the phenomenon of an object moving across one's lawn? There, of course, must be a lot of trial-and-error learning in acquiring the meaning of words, yet once children begin their word spurts, they learn words with great speed, suggesting that there are some **lexical constraints** on word learning, such that children do not consider all possibilities each time they hear a new word (Markman, 1994).

One proposed constraint is the **whole-object assumption.** Children assume when hearing a word that it refers to the whole object and not to some part of that object. Thus, the child is not likely to think that "rabbit" refers to color, or long ears, or pattern of movement when her father shouts the word. Another proposed constraint is the **taxonomic assumption,** with children assuming that words refer to things that are similar. For example, after associating the word "rabbit" with the white, long-eared creature that hopped across her back yard, a child should assume that the short-eared, brown animal sitting in the pet store window also goes by the same name. And finally, the **mutual exclusivity assumption** holds that different words refer to different things, so that the word "rabbit," for example, would not overlap with the word "mouse." For instance, when children are given a novel word and asked to select a referent for that word, they pick the objects they do not already have a word for, realizing, apparently, that the new word is not a synonym for a word they already know, but must refer to a distinct (mutually exclusive) object. For example, in studies by Ellen Markman and Gwyn Wachtel (1988), 3-year-olds who knew the word for "cup" but not for "tongs," were asked to "Show me the dax." Eighty percent of children selected the tongs, presumably believing that "dax" refers to the novel object rather than being another word for "cup."

Others have suggested that what children are actually doing is being sensitive to the social cues that adults provide in conversation. For example, children attend to a speaker's gaze and gestures, are sensitive to emotional and behavioral cues and to a speaker's intentions when figuring out the referent of an utterance (Baldwin, 1993; Diesendruck & Markson, 2001). Most likely, children use multiple cues, including lexical constraints and social cues, and are also influenced by general mechanisms of memory and attention and conceptual knowledge in deciding what a novel vocal utterance refers to (Bloom, 2000; Hollich, Hirsh-Pasek, & Golinkoff, 2000).

The point that is most critical for our discussion here is that children are *prepared* to learn words. Whether this preparation comes in the form of lexical constraints or is a by-product of their developing social cognition, children seem *not* to experience language as random noise. Rather, their cognitive systems (or social cognitive systems) are ready to make sense of the connection between things they hear and things they see, making the process of word learning much easier than it would be in the absence of such constraints.

Overextensions and Underextensions

Often, the errors children make in using words provide us with a good indication of their level of semantic development. Researchers who have analyzed these early errors find that one common pattern is to use **overextensions**—stretching a familiar word beyond its correct meaning (Thompson & Chapman, 1977). For example, children might use the word *doggie* to describe all four-legged creatures, even Daddy when he is on his hands and knees (whether barking or not). Many developmental psychologists argue against the concept of error in children's early language use, pointing out that practices such as using overextensions result in having adults provide the correct words and can be very effective learning devices. For example, although children might use the word *doggie* to label a kitten or a horse, when given a set of pictures and asked to choose which one is a doggie, they usually perform well (Thompson & Chapman, 1977). By overextending the word "doggie," however, they often get some expansion or clarification from adults (for example, "That's not a doggie, that's a kitty"), thus receiving more information about language than they would have gotten had they remained silent.

At other times, children will make **underextensions**—for example, claiming that only their pet Lucy Starbright is a "cat" and that other felines must go by another name. Underextensions indicate that children's boundary for a category is too restricted. During childhood, children learn to classify words and concepts as adults in their culture do. This process doesn't stop in childhood, however, but continues throughout life. It is likely that none of us has exactly the same meaning for all common concepts used in our native language (Nelson, 1996). That speakers of a language are able to make sense of what others say most of the time, however, suggests that most of us have very similar interpretations for the words we use. Both the number of words we know and our understanding of these words change during development. Children go from three or four words in their vocabularies at age 1 to more than 10,000 words by age 6 (Carey, 1978). In fact, most changes in language development beyond the age of about 5 are not in syntax or phonology, but in semantics in the form of vocabulary growth. However, just because a child is able to use a word doesn't mean that he or she has the same understanding as an adult, and in the following section, we will look at the development of children's word meanings.

The Development of Word Meanings

The representation of the meanings of words has been referred to as *semantic memory*, the long-term repository of language terms, their definitions, and their interrelations with other entries in memory (see Chapter 5). (However, just how distinct this type of knowledge is from our general repository of world knowledge is under debate; see Schwanenflugel, 1991.) We can think about word meaning in a variety of ways. One way of describing semantic memory is through **feature-list models.** Feature-list models of semantic memory hold that language concepts (or words) can be defined by lists of characteristics or features they possess. Most feature-list theories of adult semantic memory hold that features are differentially weighted, with some being more important for the definition of a word than are others (Rosch & Mervis, 1975; Smith, Shoben, & Rips, 1974). Thus, in development, children must learn to use features in the way adults do. Given that young children might emphasize different features of a word or concept than adults do (for example, perceptual, schematic), children must not only acquire new features for words but also reorganize the weights they give to words.

In a study in which children and adults were asked to rate the importance of features for defining a word (for example, how important to the concept *cheese* are the features "made with milk," "melts," "found near mice"), kindergarten and second-grade children made no differentiation among the various features, whereas fourth-grade children and adults did. That is, with age, children learn to give more weight to features that are more centrally associated with a given concept (Schwanenflugel, Guth, & Bjorklund, 1986).

Along these same lines, there is some evidence that preschool and early school-age children give too much emphasis to features that are only *characteristic* of a concept (for example, "tropical" for the concept *island*, or "ugly and mean" for the concept *burglar*) and less emphasis to features that are *defining* for a concept (for example, "surrounded by water" for island, or "steals something" for *burglar*). For instance, 5-year-old children in an experiment by Frank Keil and Nancy Batterman (1984) were likely to say that a smelly, mean old man with a gun in his pocket who took one's television set was a robber, even though their parents did not want the set anymore and had told the man he could have it. However, a friendly, cheerful woman who gave the children a hug was not declared to be a robber, even though she removed their toilet bowl and took it without permission. Other research suggests that it is not so much that children give more emphasis to characteristic than to defining features but, rather, they give more weight to the many characteristic features in the description (Schwanenflugel et al., 1986). The more features there are, the more important, taken together, they become.

The Development of Natural Language Categories

Some aspects of semantic memory can be described in terms of categorical relations. Meaningful objects are related to other meaningful objects and can be referred to as belonging to one or more categories. All languages have terms to serve this function. **Natural language categories** refer to categorical terms that a language uses to describe and group a large number of words and concepts. Many natural language categories are hierarchical in nature. So, for example, *collie* is a language category term that includes all creatures of a particular canine breed. A more inclusive category term is *dog*, which includes

all collies and many other breeds that are not collies. From here, our language provides us with terms of increasing inclusiveness, from *pets* or *canines* to *animals*. If one wanted to get technical about it, one could list the biological species, genus, family, class, and so on of which Fido is a member, with each step up the ladder being more inclusive than the one preceding it. Such language categories are obviously very important in communicating and classifying information. However, their development requires more than just learning the term; what children must learn is what characteristics an object must have to qualify for membership in a language category and when to use the term.

Two- and 3-year-old children obviously have some understanding of terms for broad, superordinate categories such as *animals*, *clothes*, or *food*. They use these words occasionally (for example, "Dresses are girls' clothes, not boys'"), and they seem to comprehend their meaning when used by an adult (for example, "Stop playing with your food!"). Yet, there are many superordinate category terms that young children typically do not use (most 3-year-olds do not speak of *vehicles*, *weapons*, or *tools*), and we must be careful not to attribute adult meaning to children's language categories (Nelson, 1996).

Basic-level categories. Eleanor Rosch, Carolyn Mervis, and their colleagues (Mervis & Rosch, 1981; Rosch et al., 1976) proposed that young children's early categories are not at the superordinate level but, rather, include objects that have similar overall configurations (for example, cars and chairs but not vehicles and furniture). As we saw in Chapter 7, infants can form primitive concepts for sets of objects that are perceptually similar (see Cohen & Younger, 1983; Reznick & Kagan, 1983). Rosch and her colleagues (1976) referred to such groupings as **basic-level categories.**

In a series of experiments, Rosch et al. (1976) demonstrated that 3- and 4-year-old children were easily able to categorize sets of objects at the basic level, whereas few could organize items according to more superordinate categories. The children were shown sets of three pictures and asked to point to the two pictures "that are alike, that are the same kind of thing." In some triads, two of the pictures were examples from the same basic-level category (for example, two different types of cats or cars). In other triads, the pictures were from different basic-level categories but from the same superordinate category (for example, a car and a train—both vehicles—or a cat and a dog—both animals). Both the 3- and 4-year-old children had no difficulty identifying the category membership of objects from the same basic-level categories. The 4-year-olds also performed well when matches were based on superordinate category relations; in contrast, the 3-year-olds' performance was at chance values for these latter problems. A similar developmental trend was observed in a more demanding sorting task, where children grouped pictures that went together or were alike in some way. Kindergarten and first-grade children easily grouped items according to basic-level categories, but only half of these children were able to sort items by superordinate category membership.

Perhaps even more impressive is evidence that children appear to be cognizant of basic-level categories well before their second birthdays, before they have language terms for these concepts. For example, in some experiments, 15- to 18-month-old toddlers are presented with sets of objects that can be grouped into two basic-level categories. For instance, Alison Gopnik and Andrew Meltzoff (1992) gave children four brightly colored human figures and four flat yellow rectangles. The children were then told simply to "play with these things" or "fix them up." At 15 months of age, children will serially touch all the items from one basic-level category and then touch all the items from the second category. At 18 months, many children actually sorted the two sets of items into discernible groups, picking up and moving objects so they are grouped with "their own kind" (Gopnik & Meltzoff, 1992; Sugarman, 1983). This, of course, occurs long before children can group items into superordinate categories and reflects the fact that young children do have some basic categorical knowledge very early in life, before they have words for these concepts.

The development of category prototypes. Other researchers have suggested that children acquire sets of

features that characterize specific members of a category and gradually integrate these features to develop a higher-level, taxonomic concept. For instance, Jeremy Anglin (1977) proposed that children abstract the general features of a category and form a **category prototype.** As mentioned in Chapter 7, a category prototype is a mentalistic representation reflecting the most typical or best examples of that category. Forming such a prototype involves abstracting features possessed by most or all members of the category and ignoring features that are idiosyncratic to specific members and do not characterize the category as a whole. For example, one's prototype for *dog* probably includes four legs, fur, a tail, a certain shape of head, and a certain size. Your hairless Chihuahua may be your favorite dog, but with its tiny size and lack of fur, it is unlikely that it resembles your prototype for dog.

Anglin suggested that children's prototypes develop from their experiences with specific members of the category. In defining a category, Anglin suggested, young children often rely on visual imagery and their recollection of specific experiences with particular instances of the category. For instance, Sharon, at 4 years 7 months, described a dog as something that has "soggy ears that go, that hang down," that "goes 'ruff,'" and that "chases cats" (1977, p. 205). Her definition of *dog* is based on specific experiences with them. Eventually, as children's experiences with the real world increase, their knowledge becomes broader and their categories more closely resemble those of adults.

Related to the idea of category prototypes is that of **category typicality.** Rosch and her colleagues (Mervis & Rosch, 1981; Rosch, 1975) proposed that some items are more representative of the prototype than others are. Items that are highly typical of a category have more features in common with the category prototype than do less typical items. For example, both socks and shirt are appropriate examples of the category of clothing, but most adults would say that shirt is more typical of their idea of clothing than socks are. In other words, not all category members are created equal, with some items being more representative of our idea of a category than others. Adults show high intersubject agreement in their ratings of items in terms of typicality

(Rosch, 1975), and differences in the typicality of category items influence adults' performance on a variety of cognitive tasks (Keller & Kellas, 1978).

The questions of importance here are how children achieve an adult understanding of natural language categories and what role category typicality plays in this development. In studies where children are asked to select from a set of pictures or words all the examples of a specified category (for example, "Pick out all the pictures of clothes, things you can wear"), young children usually choose most of the items that adults judge to be highly typical of the category (for example, shirt and pants), but they often fail to include many items that adults judge to be less typical of the category (for example, gloves, hat, and tie) (Anglin, 1977; Bjorklund, Thompson, & Ornstein, 1983). Moreover, when children are asked to rate category items by typicality ("goodness of example"), children's ratings become progressively more adultlike with age (Bjorklund et al., 1983).

Children are apparently sensitive to differences in category typicality at a very early age. In one set of experiments, toddlers as young as 13 months were more likely to group sets of prototypical items together (examples from both superordinate [for example, *animals*] and basic-level [for example, *dogs*] categories) than sets of items consisting of less typical items (Bauer, Dow, & Hertsgaard, 1995), and 12-month-olds will look at typical (for example, a robin) but not atypical (for example, ostrich) objects when given the category name (for example, bird) (Meints, Plunkett, & Harris, 1999). (See further discussion of infants classifying objects on the basis of typicality in Chapter 7.) Other researchers, using a variety of cognitive tasks, have reported developmental differences in the semantic representation of category-typical and category-atypical items (Whitney & Kunen, 1983). In general, these researchers assert that age differences in how children process category information occur because children reorganize their semantic concepts with age, realizing that some features are more important than others in defining items (see Bjorklund, 1985, for a review).

Thus, although children's natural language categories can be described as prototypes much as adults' categories can, the nature of the prototypes changes.

Children include fewer items as appropriate category members, with more typical exemplars being incorporated into children's category structures before less typical items. Furthermore, children's prototypes seem to be structured slightly differently from those of adults, with children emphasizing different features in defining natural language categories. Differences are most apparent during the preschool years and are greatly minimized (although not eliminated) by the time a child is 10 or 11 years of age (Bjorklund et al., 1983; Whitney & Kunen, 1983).

The Development of Scripts

Most research in semantic development has been concerned with how children define individual items and how those items are combined into language categories. An alternative view of semantic development has been presented by Katherine Nelson and her colleagues, who have suggested that early language categories are based on functional, or schematic, relations among words rather than conceptual, or taxonomic, relations (Nelson, 1996). More specifically, Nelson has suggested that children's early language categories are schematically organized, in that they are based on relations typifying real-world scenes, stories, and events (for example, what is involved in eating at a restaurant; objects and events dealing with sailing a ship) rather than more abstract conceptual categories (for example, fruits, vegetables, vehicles). Children's representations can be expressed in terms of **scripts** (Schank & Abelson, 1977). Scripts are a form of schematic organization, with real-world events "organized in terms of temporal and causal relations between component acts" (Nelson, 1983, p. 55). For example, a "going to bed" script might include brushing one's teeth, putting on pajamas, getting a drink of water, having Daddy read a story, and being tucked into bed.

Nelson and her colleagues have argued that superordinate language categories such as *food, animals,* and *clothes* have their origins in earlier acquired, schematically based scripts (Lucariello, Kyratzis, & Nelson, 1992; Nelson, 1983). Certain items are more likely to be found in specific scripts than are other items. So, for instance, a breakfast script is likely to include eating toast, cereal, or pancakes and drinking orange juice, milk, or cocoa. Much less likely to be found in a breakfast script would be French fries, ice cream, beer, or macaroni and cheese. Thus, in a particular script, several different items can be included, each of which would satisfy the conditions of the script. *Slot fillers* are items that could successfully complete the script (for example, juice and cocoa). Nelson has suggested that context-free, superordinate categories develop from these **slot-filler categories.**

This hypothesis was tested in a memory experiment by Joan Lucariello and Katherine Nelson (1985). Children's recall of sets of words was compared using lists consisting of items from different superordinate categories (animals, food, clothes) and lists consisting of items from script-derived categories, or slot-filler categories (zoo animals, lunch food, clothes you put on in the morning). Children remembered significantly more items from the slot-filler categories than from the superordinate categories. Based on these and other findings (Lucariello et al., 1992), Lucariello and Nelson asserted that children's early superordinate knowledge might be restricted to slot-filler categories, which have a more cohesive structure than superordinate categories do. Lucariello and Nelson proposed that these schematically based groupings serve as the beginning for broader, context-free natural language categories.

Other researchers have failed to find such a difference between script-based, slot-filler categories and superordinate categories in preschool children, proposing, rather, that young children's semantic memories are organized in terms of both schematic and taxonomic relations very early in life (Blewitt & Krackow, 1992; Blewitt & Toppino, 1991). The results of Lucariello and Nelson's (1985) memory study is explained not by young children's bias to encode information in terms of slot-filler categories, but because items in most slot-filler categories are highly typical of their categories and are often highly associated with one another. When typicality and associativity are controlled for, the memory advantage afforded by slot-filler categories disappears (Krackow & Gordon, 1998, but see Lucariello, 1998, for a different opinion of these findings). The position that young children's semantic memory is organized along both schematic and taxonomic relations (and by typicality and associativity) seems to be an eminently reasonable one, given that even toddlers display knowledge of basic-level categories (see the earlier discussion). However, as I noted before, young children's knowledge of superordinate categories goes through considerable development and their tendency to use superordinate category knowledge will be limited only to those categories for which they have an elaborated representation (Bjorklund, 1985). Thus, although schematic and superordinate category knowledge surely resides side by side in the minds of young children, much of their thinking, remembering, and reasoning is likely based on the more readily available schematic relationships, rather than on the more slowly developing superordinate category knowledge.

Pragmatics

How we actually use language in a social context, or the ability to use language to get things done in the world, is referred to as **pragmatics.** *Pragmatics* refers to knowledge about how language can be used and adjusted to fit different circumstances, such as using different tones when speaking to a teacher versus an agemate. Knowing the phonology, morphology, syntax, and semantics of language does one little good in communicating unless one can use language appropriately in a social context.

Children must learn a number of conversational principles to become effective communicators (Grice, 1975). Children must learn that messages need to have the right *quantity* of information, or be at the proper level of description. For example, a mother might request of her son that he "put the plates on the table." Such a message is likely at the proper level of abstraction to be understood. It would be unnecessary and inappropriate for the mother to say, "Open the kitchen cupboard door, remove a dish, using two hands, and take it into the dining room, and place it at the head of the table where your father usually sits. Repeat the procedure for the place where I usually sit, where your sister usually sits, and where you usually sit." At the other extreme, an instruction to "prepare the table for dinner" might not have enough information in it, especially if the job of putting out silverware usually fell to the boy's sister. Not surprisingly, children are more likely to provide too little rather than too much information.

Good messages should have other characteristics, such as being truthful (except for jokes and sarcasm) and relevant to the present context. Also, speakers need to realize the importance of taking turns. Monologues do not make for good conversation.

Beginning early in life, children learn these various conversation principles. For example, toddlers know to watch their listener for signs that they are being understood (Wilcox & Webster, 1980), they know they must be close to their listener to be heard and that if they are not close to their listener they need to speak louder (Wellman & Lempers, 1977), and they know to clarify their speech when they are being misunderstood (Shwe & Markman, 1997). A responsive listener provides a speaker with nonverbal cues such as nods, gazes, and smiles, and he or she says "yes" and "uh-huh" at appropriate times to make it clear that the message is being understood. These skills increase with age, but even 2-year-olds use many of these tactics when listening to an adult (Miller, Lechner, & Rugs, 1985). Children also learn that, depending on the context, sometimes a question is not really a question. For example, when a father says, "How many times do I have to tell you to leave that alone?" and "Why do you insist on carrying that blanket everywhere?," children learn that the question is a rhetorical one and does not require a serious answer. Children learn from the speaker's tone of voice that these are really statements because even young preschoolers seldom mistake them for real questions (de Villiers & de Villiers, 1978). The reverse is also true: sometimes questions can be hidden in statements, such as asking a babysitter for a bedtime extension by stating, "Mommy always lets me watch 'The Simpsons'" (Reeder, 1981).

Speech Registers: The Case of Black English

One aspect of pragmatics involves using different styles of speech in different situations. For example, children use one style of speech when at home or with their friends and another, more formal style when in school. These different styles are referred to as **speech registers** (Warren & McCloskey, 1997).

When the speech registers, or codes, children use at home and the ones they are expected to use in school differ considerably, there is the potential for educational difficulties. Usually, children from middle-class families speak a "standard" version of the language that is similar to the more formal style used in school. In contrast, children from less affluent homes often speak a nonstandard version of the language that is often appreciably different from the one used in school (for example, Bernstein, 1971). In the United States, this distinction between social (or home) language and school language among native speakers is often more obvious for children whose home language is described as **Black English** (or more recently as *Ebonics*).

Black English is familiar to most Americans. Although it is used mostly by African Americans, not all African Americans speak it, and many non–African Americans do, so the term can be somewhat misleading. Black English has some special rules of pronunciation and syntax (see Table 11-3), the most obvious to many speakers of standard English being the use of the verb "to be." Unlike standard English, this verb is often not conjugated (for example, "We be" or "She be" rather than "We are" or "She is"), and sometimes is dropped from a sentence entirely. For instance, the verb "to be" can be left out if the sentence refers to a one-time or unusual occurrence of an event, as in the sentence, "He playing tennis" for a person who doesn't usually play tennis. But if the sentence refers to a recurrent event, the verb "to be" is included in the sentence. So for example, "He be playing tennis," describes a person who regularly plays tennis and is playing tennis at this moment (Warren & McCloskey, 1997). Black English is *not* a simplified or inferior linguistic form of standard English. For the most part, the two share common vocabulary and syntax, both are syntactically complex, and both are used to express complicated ideas and emotions (Heath, 1989).

Despite the linguistic legitimacy and complexity of Black English, it is not the language of the schools, nor of the mainstream American market-

TABLE 11-3 Sample differences between standard English and Black English.

Pronunciation and word forms

Consonant Substitutions:	/d/ for initial /th/	"Dey" for "They"
	/f/ or /t/ for final /th/	"toof" for "tooth"
	/v/ for medial /th/	"muvver" for "mother"
Consonant Deletions:	medial /r/	"doing" for "during"
	medial /l/	"hep" for "help"
	final consonants	"doe" for "door"
Syllable Contractions:		"spoze" for "suppose"
Stress on First Syllable in (some) Bisyllabic Words:		"Po'-lice" for "Police"
Hypercorrection:		"Pickted" for "picked"
		"2 childrens" for "2 children"

Sentence structure	*BE*	*SE*
Multiple Negation:	"I ain't done nothing"	"I have not done anything"
Aspect:	"He be crazy"	"He's (usually) crazy"
	"He crazy"	"He's crazy (right now)"

Nonmarking or nonmatching of verb with subject

	"She do all the work"	"She does all the work"
	"Two girl wearing hats"	"Two girls wearing hats"
Double Subjects:	"My daddy, he works . . ."	"My daddy works . . ."
Perfective *Done*:	"You done lost your mind"	"You have (already) lost your mind"

SOURCE: Warren, A. R., & McCloskey, L. A. Language in social contexts. In J. Berko Gleason (Ed.),
The development of language (4th ed.). Published by Allyn and Bacon. Copyright © 1997 by Pearson Education.
Reprinted by permission.

place. This means that teachers, who usually speak standard English, will often not understand children who speak Black English, and vice versa. Such children can have a difficult time reading text or comprehending directions expressed in standard English. As a result, they might be unjustly classified as less bright than children who speak standard English. For instance, the language abilities of children who speak Black English are often underestimated when they are tested using standard English (Adler, 1990; Wheldall & Joseph, 1986).

There has been substantial debate about how best to instruct children whose home language is Black English. Should they be taught using Black English, the dialect they know best, or should they be taught using standard English, the dialect, or register, of the marketplace? Most young speakers of Black English do learn some aspects of standard English and use it in school (DeStefano, 1972). For example, in one study (DeStefano, 1972), the classroom speech of 8- to 11-year-old African American children contained more components of standard English than did their speech out of school, indicating that elementary school children are able to switch between social (Black English) and school (standard English) registers. Yet, many African American adolescents tend to *increase* their use of Black, compared with standard, English, as use of Black English becomes an important part of their social identity (Delpit, 1990).

The debate about how to educate children whose home language register is different from the language register used by teachers is a controversial one, involving social and political aspects, as well as linguistics and educational ones, and no simple answer can, or will, be offered here. But one important thing to remember is that Black English, or any other regional dialect, is not a linguistically inferior language relative to standard English, just as modern English is neither inferior nor superior to the Elizabethan English used by Shakespeare. One must also keep in mind that, despite Black English's linguistic equivalency to standard English, its use can hinder educability and the opportunity to partake fully in the American economy. Black English is more than just a different language register; it is also a different dialect with some different syntactic and phonological rules compared with standard English. One's language also identifies its user as a member of a social group, and children and adolescents might be reluctant to give up their language style merely for the sake of doing well in school. Ideally, children would master both dialects, just as children might ideally acquire a second language, and have the flexibility to switch between them as the context demands. In such a situation, different dialects would then truly become different registers, to be used when and where appropriate.

Communicative Competence

Although children may have acquired the basic structure of language and know enough words to make most of their wants and feelings known by age 5 or 6, their ability to communicate effectively continues to increase with age. All types of language knowledge (phonology, morphology, syntax, semantics, and pragmatics) are combined in a package called **communicative competence** (Hymes, 1972). Generally, as children—or, indeed, adults—participate in varied contexts, they become communicatively more competent.

Despite the seeming communicative sophistication of many preschoolers, effective communication between adult and child, or between child and child, is variable. Many messages within the grammatical competence of a child are simply not understood. Also, young children often have difficulty in conveying exactly the right message and are frequently unaware that their message was inadequate. To some extent, their difficulties in communicating effectively can be attributed to other aspects of their cognitive development, in particular to a tendency to assume that other people understand the world exactly as they do.

Communication and Egocentrism

For years, research and theory in communicative development followed the interpretation of Jean Piaget (1955), who proposed that young children's speech is *egocentric* and *presocial*. In social situations, young children attempt to communicate with others, but their egocentric view of the world often results in speech that does not get the message across to a listener. This failure often does not bother preschool children, however, because in many cases they are unaware that the message is not being comprehended. Such egocentric speech can be observed in young children in a variety of contexts. Listen to the phone conversation of a 4-year-old. When the voice on the other end of the receiver asked Alese, "What are you wearing today?" Alese responded, "This," while looking down and pointing at her dress. This apparently is not an atypical phone conversation for a preschooler (see Warren & Tate, 1992, for other examples). The conversation of two 5-year-old boys playing together in a sandbox can be interesting. "I drive my truck over here, and then I drive beside your plane and I fill it up with stuff," says one child. In the meantime, the other is saying, "My plane's coming in for a landing. I drop bombs on your truck and crash into it. Boom!" Such a "conversation" would not be taking place if each child were alone. However, what one child says has little to do with the comments of the other. The two boys are talking "with" each other but not necessarily "to" each other. Piaget labeled such egocentric exchanges **collective monologues.**

Metacommunication

But do children have any idea that they are sometimes not being understood, or that the message they are receiving from someone else is unclear? Research by John Flavell and his associates (Beal & Flavell, 1982; Flavell et al., 1981) indicated that children 5 years of age and younger seem to recognize an inadequate or ambiguous message but seldom act on their uncertainty, behaving as if the message had been understood loud and clear. When kindergarten children were provided with ambiguous instructions for making a block building, for instance, they often looked puzzled and hesitated in selecting the appropriate block. Yet, when their building was completed, these children said that it was just like the model (which it was not) and that the instructions had been adequate for reproducing the model (which they had not). Carole Beal and John Flavell found that children's poor performance on these tasks could not be attributed to memory or attentional failures. Rather, their problems were a result of metacognitive deficits; they had "a poor understanding of message quality and its role in determining the success or failure of a communication" (1982, p. 48).

Another **metacommunication** skill involves children's abilities to monitor their own speech. Again, young children tend to display deficits in this area of metacommunication (for reviews see Shatz, 1983; Whitehurst & Sonnenschein, 1985); their speech includes a greater incidence of omissions and ambiguities and requires greater contextual support to be comprehended than the speech of older children does.

One way of assessing children's self-monitoring abilities is to examine the frequency with which they correct their speech by repeating, by including new information, by telling the listener to forget the last thing that was said until later, and so forth. Mary Ann Evans (1985) studied such *verbal repairs* in the speech of kindergarten and second-grade children during classroom "show and tell" sessions. Evans reported that the incidence of verbal repairs was significantly greater for the second-grade children than for the kindergartners, occurring for 19% of all the utterances for the older children compared with only 7% for the younger. The following is an example of a story by a second-grade girl that includes several verbal repairs:

> We went to—uh me and Don went to Aunt Judy's. And . . . and uh my brother came down on Fri— Friday night, Uh there was a acc—came on the train, And there was an accident. And they thought uh . . .

that uh . . . the—there was an accident with a—a van, And they thought—there was pig's blood in it. And they thought there was somebody hurt. But it was the pig. (Evans, 1985, p. 370)

Evans proposed that the high incidence of self-repairs for the second-grade children relative to the kindergartners reflected an increased ability by the older children to monitor their speech. Evans suggested that as communication skills increase from this point through childhood, the ability to plan and organize one's thoughts improves, resulting in a reduction of verbal repairs into adolescence (Sabin et al., 1979). Thus, the incidence of verbal repairs is low in young children's speech because of poor self-monitoring skills, increases during middle childhood as children become increasingly aware of the effectiveness of their speech in conveying a message, and then decreases as other skills such as planning improve.

Despite the ample evidence of young children's poor communication skills, preschoolers' language is not as egocentric as Piaget and other early researchers believed. In fact, several researchers have reported clearly nonegocentric use of language in the communication attempts of young children. For example, in Evans' (1985) study of speech repairs just cited, many 5-year-olds displayed at least limited self-monitoring abilities. In other research, Marilyn Shatz and Rochel Gelman (1973) observed the speech of 4-year-old children when they talked to adults, to other 4-year-olds, or to 2-year-olds. Shatz and Gelman found that these children modified their speech to the 2-year-olds, using different tones of voice and shorter sentences, much as adults do. Other research has demonstrated that preschool children show greater metacommunicative competence when the messages are embedded in familiar scripts, such as a trip to the grocery store (Furman & Walden, 1990). Findings such as these, among others (Nadig & Sedivy, 2002; Warren-Leubecker & Bohannon, 1989), suggest that young children have substantial metacommunication skills. As with many newly acquired skills, however, communication abilities seem to develop first in highly specific, familiar situations and are easily disrupted. With age, children display their communicative skills in increasingly diverse contexts, generalizing what they know to new and unfamiliar settings.

Some Theoretical Perspectives of Language Development

The question of how children learn to speak their mother tongue has fascinated philosophers back at least to the time of the ancient Greeks. Yet, only in the past 50 years or so did serious scientific study of language acquisition begin. Here, I am referring to theories or perspectives on the acquisition of *syntax*, the underlying structure of language. Although there can still be considerable debate on how children come to learn the meaning of specific words, the most heated and complicated debates have arisen over how children learn the grammatical rules (that is, the syntax) of language. I do not intend to cover the intricacies of theories of syntax development in great detail, but merely to describe some of the major points of the dominant perspectives so that the reader can get a general idea of how children approach the seemingly complicated task of learning to talk (see Bloom, 1998; Maratsos, 1998).

In very general terms, three major types of theories have been postulated to account for language acquisition: behavioral theories, nativist theories, and social interactionist theories. Behavioral theories were popular in the early and middle part of the last century and proposed, basically, that children learn language like they learn any other complex behavior, through the principles of classical and operant conditioning (Skinner, 1957). Behaviorists emphasized the role of parents as models of and reinforcers for language. The behaviorists actually paid relatively little attention to children, who for generations had been producing perfectly understandable original sentences and phrases they could not have possibly learned through conditioning and imitation, such as "all-gone sticky" to announce that their hands have been washed.

Many claims of the behaviorists have not stood the test of time. For example, although words can be learned through conditioning principles in the laboratory, there is little evidence that parents use such structured techniques at home; yet almost all children are fluent in their native language before they reach school age. Other research has shown that parents seldom comment to children about the grammatical correctness of their spoken messages, only the meaningfulness of them (Brown & Hanlon, 1970), and although new words are obviously learned by imitation, new grammatical forms (such as plurals or the past tense) are typically not imitated until children are able to produce them spontaneously (Bloom, Hood, & Lightbown, 1974). All this makes it very unlikely that a behavioral theory of language development is adequate. Thus, one way in which children apparently do *not* learn the syntax of their mother tongue is through the conventional rules of classical and operant conditioning.

This does not mean that the environment in general and parents specifically do not play a role in children's language acquisition. Children are not born with the knowledge of a specific language, but learn to speak the language that is spoken around them, often *to* them. But traditional behavioral accounts are clearly not adequate. What are the alternatives? Nativist theorists propose that children are biologically prepared to learn language and do so with special, innate learning mechanisms, not through some domain-general set of learning devices as proposed by the behaviorists. Social interactionist theorists blend aspects of the behavioral and nativists perspectives, granting that humans are specially prepared to acquire language, but that aspects of the environment, especially parents, also might be specially prepared to foster language acquisition, although not to the extent that Skinner and his behaviorist colleagues once believed.

In the following sections, I outline some of the theory and data associated with nativist and social interactionist theories of language acquisition. This account is admittedly a cursory one, and readers who would like to pursue some of the ideas mentioned in this section are encouraged to seek some of the references listed in Suggested Readings at the end of the chapter.

Nativist Perspectives on Language Development

Contemporary nativist perspectives on language development can trace their beginnings to the work of Noam Chomsky (1957). Chomsky reviewed B. F. Skinner's (1957) book *Verbal Behavior* in the journal *Language* and wrote, "I can find no support whatsoever for the doctrine . . . that slow and careful shaping of verbal behavior through differential reinforcement is an absolute necessity" (Chomsky, 1959, p. 42). Chomsky's ideas were as radical in one direction as Skinner's were in the other. Instead of viewing language as something taught, produced by the child's environment, Chomsky insisted that it is something innate, produced by the child's biology. Chomsky believed that language, as we commonly use the term, is only one part of this process—the **surface structure.** Infants hear this being spoken around them and end up being able to speak it themselves within a few years. However, no simple rules of learning or conditioning account adequately for this acquisition because the language children hear is too complicated and often too ambiguous for them to discern the rules. Chomsky suggested that another mechanism is necessary to explain why children have the ability to sample the surface structure of the language being spoken around them and then produce it fully and fluently by the age of 3, even creating sentences that they could not have heard before.

Chomsky believed that a second structure of language exists, the **deep structure**—the underlying meaning of language. This is a more gut-level understanding of language, a "species-specific characteristic . . . latent in the nervous system until kindled by actual language use" (Sacks, 1989, p. 81). According to Chomsky, all human languages share this deep structure and it is an innate concept in humans, much like the concepts of time and space.

Chomsky believed that humans possess a mental organ, much like a heart or liver, that is dedicated to language use and is located in the brain. This innate neural device (the **language acquisition device**, or **LAD**) imposes order on incoming stimuli. This is not a totally novel concept. As Chomsky points out,

a similar function has been found for the visual cortex; it orders incoming visual stimuli into meaningful patterns before passing them on to higher levels of the brain.

Chomsky's ideas about the innateness of language derive from linguistic theory. Other support for the nativism school of thought is less specifically linguistic in nature. For example, nearly 40 years ago Eric Lenneberg (1967) argued that language is a special human ability (that is, not just a result of "learning") that has a strong biological basis. Lenneberg noted several characteristics of language as support for this contention, among them:

1. *Language is species specific.* Humans are the only species to possess it. Apes can be taught simple sign language comparable with that of a 2-year-old child (Savage-Rumbaugh et al., 1993), and other species certainly do communicate complicated ideas (such as bees' ability to communicate the location of pollen-rich flowers), but, at least as human linguists define it, only humans possess language.

2. *Language is species uniform.* All normal members of the species possess language. Moreover, the complexity of a language is not related to the complexity of a culture's technology. That is, the language of "primitive" people is no more or no less complicated, on average, than is the language of people from information-age societies (Pinker, 1994).

3. *Language is difficult to retard.* Except for children raised in closets or in other severely deprived situations, nearly all children learn to speak. This is true for many severely retarded children, whose language is often far in excess of their more general intellectual abilities.

4. *Language develops in a regular sequence.* Children around the world acquire language in about the same way at about the same time. This is similar to the universal sequence of motor development.

5. *There are specific anatomical structures for language.* The structure of the mouth and throat are unique to our species and specially suited for the task of speaking. Equally critical, areas in the

brain are dedicated to different aspects of language, and damage to specific areas of the brain can result in a very specific type of *aphasia,* or language disability.

6. *There are language disabilities that are genetically based.* Specific language disorders run in families, suggesting that there is a genetic basis for these disorders, with some apparently being controlled by a dominant gene (Gopnik & Crago, 1991).

All this is well and good, but how does this give us a better picture of how children actually learn to talk? What it does is place language in the realm of important, species-uniform skills that was likely selected in human evolution for its survival value. But saying that language is based in biology, by itself, doesn't tell us a whole lot. We need to look at more specific theories and research to get a better picture of how it is that children acquire language. I do this briefly in the next two sections. First, I look at evidence for universal grammar that all children begin life with and modify until it resembles the language spoken around them. I then look at research suggesting that there is a critical period for language—a time when the child is biologically prepared to learn language.

Universal Grammar and Language Development

Following the nativist ideas of Chomsky, most linguistic theorists today believe that children around the world acquire language so easily because they possess at birth a "mental organ," specially designed to perform the job of learning language. In addition to this mental organ (the LAD), infants also have at birth some primitive "knowledge" about the structure, or syntax of language. This is **universal grammar,** which consists of the basic grammatical rules that typify all languages. Having this "theory of syntax" in their heads from the beginning of life, children do not have to learn all the rules of their language. Rather, they have to examine the language that surrounds them, see how it fits with the universal grammar that resides in their brains, and make

the appropriate modifications so that their innate theory of syntax comes to match the theory that people around them use.

Children, of course, don't actually "know" any language (universal or otherwise) at birth, but they have a set of *principles* and *parameters* that guide their interpretation of speech. Parameters, as used here, refers to aspects of a grammar that vary across languages. For example, although all languages have subjects, some languages require that proper sentences state the subject (as in the English, "I love you"), whereas in other languages the subject can be expressed as part of the verb, eliminating the necessity of stating the subject (as in the Spanish, "Te amo"). This is a parameter, and children must learn whether their language requires the subject explicitly stated (as in English) or not (as in Spanish). One piece of evidence for universal grammar is that English-speaking children's early sentences often resemble those of languages that don't require an explicit subject. This is reflected in children's statements such as "Helping Mommy" or "make a house" (Bloom, Lightbown, & Hood, 1975).

The many similarities across languages argue for a universal grammar. For example, all have extensive vocabularies divided into part-of-speech categories that include nouns and verbs; words are organized into phrases that follow a similar underlying rule system (called the X-bar system); all permit movement of grammatical categories, such as the subject-auxiliary inversion used to form declarative sentences in English into questions (for example, "You are going" transformed to "Are you going?"); and all use word prefixes or suffixes for verbs and nouns (for example, adding the "ed" to make a verb past tense) (Hoff, 2001; Pinker, 1994). The similar way and rate that children around the world acquire many of the same grammatical forms is further evidence for a universal grammar.

One source of evidence that children will create a grammatical system based on some universal principles comes from **pidgins** and **creoles** (Bickerton, 1990). When a group of people with a variety of native languages are taken from their homes and transported to a foreign land where they are not given the opportunity to participate in the majority culture or to learn the language of their new homeland, they develop a communication system termed a *pidgin*. Pidgins combine several languages at a rudimentary level and are used to convey necessary information within the group and between the group and its "hosts." Word order is often highly variable and there is little in the way of a grammatical system. (Bickerton proposed that pidgins might be similar in form to the protolanguage spoken by our ancient ancestors.) But pidgins can quickly transform into true languages in the hands (or mouths) of children. Derek Bickerton (1990) documented (based on historical evidence and his own studies of Hawaii creole) how the children of pidgin speakers take the remnants of their parents' language and create a fully developed language in only one generation—a language termed a *creole*. Thus, rather than acquiring language in the typical sense, these children *create* a language. Although there might not be an easy interpretation of this phenomenon, the creation of a creole by children suggests that they possess an innate grammar and use it to "correct" the fragmented pidgin spoken by their parents and convert it into a true (and new) language.

Recent evidence consistent with this hypothesis comes from a study of several cohorts of children creating Nicaraguan Sign Language (Senghas & Coppola, 2001). Deaf education in Nicaragua began only in the 1970s, with deaf children before this time having little contact with one another. There was also no recognized form of Nicaraguan Sign Language for children to be taught. Such a language began to emerge, however, in the Managua school for the deaf and was well developed by the late 1990s. Ann Senghas and Marie Coppola (2001) tested deaf Nicaraguan signers who had first been exposed to Nicaraguan Sign Language as early as 1978 (Cohort 1) or as late as 1990 (Cohort 2) and examined changes in early linguistic structures in the newly emerged sign language. They found that Nicaraguan Sign Language was systematically modified from one cohort of children to the next, with children aged 10 years and younger generating most of the changes. In other words, sequences of children created a new sign language from the incomplete forms used by their predecessors.

Is There a Critical Period for Learning Language?

Almost without exception, adults learn things more easily than children do. This is hardly surprising. This truism is apparent in our school system. Children first starting school are not expected to master complicated material. In fact, some schools of thought argue that expecting too much in the way of intellectual mastery for young children is not only foolish but also emotionally harmful (Elkind, 1987). Young children just don't have the mental capacity to acquire and understand information that an older child or adult has.

But there is at least one major exception to this, and that is language development. Children are better than adults at acquiring both first and second languages. The cognitive system of the child is seemingly not less efficient in any respect than the adult's when it comes to language learning; rather, it is well suited to the demands, making immaturity highly adaptive for the important human ability of acquiring language. This has suggested to many that there is a *critical*, or *sensitive period* for learning language—that children must be exposed to language early in life if they are ever expected to master it.

Lenneberg (1967) was the first vocal proponent of a critical period for language acquisition. With age, the nervous system loses its flexibility, so that by puberty, the organization of the brain is fixed, making language learning difficult. In support of Lenneberg's claim, John Locke (1993) states that there are four types of evidence for a sensitive period for language acquisition. First, there are cases of people who were socially deprived or isolated during infancy and early childhood, who typically demonstrate only a tenuous mastery of language (particularly syntax) (Curtiss, 1977).

The second and largest body of evidence for a sensitive period comes from studies involving second-language learning, with eventual proficiency in the foreign tongue being related to the age of first exposure. For example, Jacqueline Johnson and Elissa Newport (1989) tested 46 native Chinese or Korean speakers who had immigrated to the United States and learned English as a second language. These people had arrived in the United States at ages ranging from 3 to 39 years and had lived in the United States between 3 and 26 years when they were tested (all were educated adults). Johnson and Newport reported that their subjects' proficiency in English was related to the age at which they arrived in the United States, not to the number of years they had been speaking the language or to formal instruction. Figure 11-2 graphs average scores on a test of grammatical competency (having people determine whether or not a sentence is properly grammatical or not) as a function of age of arrival in the United States. As can be seen from the figure, people who learned their second language early in childhood showed greater proficiency as adults than did people who learned their second language later in childhood. In fact, people who arrived in the United States between the ages of 3 and 7 years had grammatical proficiency comparable with that of native speakers. Although it might not be surprising that one maintains an accent when the second language is not learned until the teen years, these data demonstrate that the same holds true for syntax.

A third source of evidence for a sensitive period comes from deaf children who are not exposed to any formal language, spoken or signed, until late in childhood or adolescence. Newport (1990) performed studies with such a population of deaf people, evaluating their proficiency in American Sign Language as a function of when they were first exposed to it. The logic here is similar to that in the Johnson and Newport study (1989), except in this study, American Sign Language is these people's first language, not their second. Newport reports results similar to those she found for second-language learning: Grammatical proficiency is related to age of first exposure to sign language and not to the number of years one has been using the language.

The fourth type of evidence concerns recovery of language function after specific brain damage. Some of this research was discussed in Chapter 2. Basically, when the language areas of the left hemisphere are

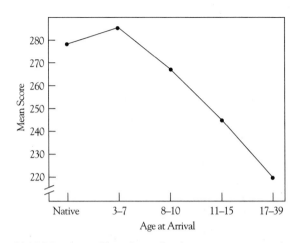

FIGURE 11-2 The relationship between age at arrival in the United States and total number of correct answers on a test of English grammar (data from Johnson & Newport, 1989, as reported in Newport, 1991). SOURCE: "Critical Period Effects in Second Language Learning: The Influence of Maturational State on the Acquisition of English as a Second Language," by J. S. Johnson and E. L. Newport, 1989. *Cognitive Psychology, 21*, 60–99. Copyright © 1989 Academic Press. Reprinted with permission.

damaged early in life, much plasticity is observed, with other areas of the brain taking over the language function of the destroyed area. This plasticity is reduced with age (see Witelson, 1987).

Some interesting research indicates differences in the organization of the brains between bilingual people who learned their second language in early childhood versus in adolescence or adulthood (Kim et al., 1997). In this study, brain images were taken of "early" and "late" bilinguals while they silently recited brief descriptions of events from the previous day. For people who had learned their second language in childhood, the same areas of their brains "lit up" regardless of whether they were using their first or second language. In contrast, different parts of the brains of the "late" bilinguals were activated when using their first versus second language. Both the "early" and "late" bilinguals in this study reported comparable fluency in their second languages, so differences in language ability between these two groups is not likely the cause of this effect. Rather, these results suggest that different parts of the brain, and thus likely different cognitive processes, are involved when a second language is learned early in childhood rather than later.

Although there is still much to be learned about the nature of language acquisition, it is clear that the cognitive system of the young child is especially suited to language learning—both of a first and second language. This ability is gradually lost over childhood, and although adults are able to acquire a second language, they rarely attain the same proficiency that is achieved when language is acquired in childhood.

But why is language learning easier early in life than later? There has been much speculation over the years, with recent data providing researchers with evidence permitting them to go beyond interesting speculation to real (if still preliminary) theories.

The "Less Is More" Hypothesis

One hypothesis concerning why young children are better at language acquisition than are older children and adults focuses not so much on their advanced cognitive abilities for processing language as on their cognitive limitations (Newport, 1991). For example, Newport (1991) has proposed that the cognitive limitations of infants and young children simplify the corpus (the body of language they process), thus making it easier to learn the complicated syntactical system of any human language. Newport's **"less is more" hypothesis** is based on the ideas of Gerald Turkewitz and Patricia Kenny (1982), who proposed that perceptual limitations in infancy are adaptive in that they allow one sensory system to develop (hearing, for example) without having to compete for neural resources with another, usually later-developing system (vision, for example). (Turkewitz and Kenny's ideas of the advantage of perceptual immaturity in infancy, along with some research examples, were discussed in Chapter 2.) The principal application of these ideas to language acquisition is that children's limited information-processing abilities reduce the complexity of what they must master, resulting in easier initial acquisition. With success and time, maturationally paced abilities gradually increase, as does language learning.

Newport observes that children in early stages of language learning start out slowly, actually more slowly than do adults learning a second language. This is partly because children perceive and store only component parts of complex stimuli. Their speech starts with single morphemes (usually a single syllable), and they gradually increase the syntactic complexity and the number of units they can control. This is true not only in spontaneous speech but also in imitation. The result is that children are able to extract only limited pieces of the speech stream. But, claims Newport, because of their limited cognitive abilities, the simplified language that they deal with makes the job of learning language easier. Adults, in contrast, begin learning a second language faster than do children, producing more complex words and sentences. This is because adults more readily perceive and remember the whole complex stimulus. But the advantage is short lived. They extract more of the language input but are then faced with a more difficult problem of analyzing everything all at once. As a result, adult learners often fail to analyze aspects of language they have acquired in a rote-like fashion, limiting the eventual proficiency they are apt to attain.

Newport (1991) presents the result of a simulation, in which a computer program was given aspects of language to "learn." The "language-learning" mechanism of the computer program was constant, but the size of the input filter was varied, which effectively limited how much the computer program could keep in memory at any one time. This is essentially equivalent to varying the size of a child's short-term store. In the simulation, the input filter became less restricted over repeated trials, similar to the effect that maturation has on the size of the short-term store in developing children (Dempster, 1981). Newport reported that the restricted filter did result in the loss of data for morphology (the smallest units of word meanings, including word endings that denote pluralization and verb tense), making initial learning worse than when a less restricted input filter was used. However, there was greater loss at the whole-word level than at the morphology level (indicating that prefixes and suffixes were often retained). Importantly, the restricted filter resulted in an improvement in the signal-to-noise ratio (that is, the ratio of relevant linguistic information to irrelevant background information). There was also greater loss of data from accidental co-occurrences than from systematic co-occurrences of form and meaning. This means that with the less restricted filter (reflecting a larger short-term store), many language-irrelevant associations were retained, which impeded rather than facilitated language learning. Newport concluded, "overall, then, a learning mechanism with a restricted input filter more successfully acquired a morphology; the same learning mechanism with a less restricted filter, or with no filter at all, entertains too many alternative analyses and cannot uniquely determine which is the better one" (1991, p. 127). Jeffrey Elman (1994) reached a similar conclusion, using a very different connectionist type of computer simulation. Elman used the metaphor "the importance of starting small" to describe his findings and suggested that the critical period for language acquisition involves the developmental delay of certain abilities rather than the loss of some language-specific capabilities. Preliminary empirical support for the "importance of starting small" position comes from evidence that adults learn an artificial grammar faster when presented with smaller units of the language (Kersten & Earles, 2001).

There seems to be little debate that children are especially prepared to learn language. In other words, most people who have thought deeply about the issue believe that the nativist perspective has something going for it. However, there is considerable debate about the role that the social environment plays in language acquisition in interaction with children's innate disposition. Clearly, language is acquired in the social context of a mother-child relationship, with infants being oriented to people and the sounds that people make. Language is used to soothe and orient infants, serving as an effective communication system long before any words can be understood (Fernald, 1992; Locke, 1993). What role does the social environment play? Is it enough for children just to hear adult language that surrounds them to acquire language, or is more social input required (or at least beneficial)? In the following section, I examine some claims of people who advocate a social-interactionist perspective of language acquisition, believing that social factors cannot be separated from biological ones in explaining the development of this uniquely human ability.

Social-Interactionist Perspectives of Language Development

Most contemporary theorists who adhere to a social-interactionist perspective believe that the nativists have most of the story right. There is an overwhelming (though not unanimous) belief that humans are specially prepared to acquire language, that something akin to universal grammar exists, and that there is a critical period for language. Despite this near consensus, some theorists see the social environment as playing a more important role than some of the more vocal proponents of the nativist camp believe. This interactive perspective is well illustrated in the theorizing of Jerome Bruner (1983). He rejected the idea that language is encountered willy-nilly by the child and that the innate LAD abstracts rules from this shower of spoken language. Instead, Bruner believes that language is carefully presented to children by the people around them. Not only is the content selected for the child's current abilities, but the presentation is executed to provide the best possible chance of learning. According to this *social-pragmatic view* of language acquisition, "children's initial skills of linguistic communication are a natural outgrowth of their emerging understanding of other persons as intentional agents" (Carpenter, Nagell, & Tomasello, 1998, p. 126). Language is viewed as a powerful social-cognitive tool, used to manipulate other people's attention. It is based on more primitive social processes, such as shared joint attention, which makes language possible.

In this section, I review research on the role of child-directed speech and how the way adults talk to infants and young children might contribute to language acquisition. I will then examine one specific theory of neurolinguistic development that takes an explicitly social-interactionist perspective.

Child-Directed Speech

Anyone who has listened to adults, especially mothers, talking to babies, knows that it is a special type of speech that is *not* used when talking to other adults. In everyday parlance, this is termed "baby talk" ("Hi big girl! How is my baby today? Huh? How is Mama's little angel? Did we just go for a walk? Did you and mommy just walk around the block? We did, didn't we? Did you see the kitty? Huh? Did we see the little kitty?").

The speech that mothers, and others, use with infants and young children is special. It is simpler and more redundant than the speech they use with their older children. Such speech was originally termed *motherese* (Snow, 1972), and subsequent research revealed additional properties, showing that mothers typically talk to their young children using high-pitched tones, exaggerated modulations, simplified forms of adult words, many questions, and many repetitions (see Hoff, 2001). When "motherese" was found to be used by fathers and 4-year-old children, the new term became **child-directed speech,** or **infant-directed speech** when directed specifically to infants, and it was suggested that this special form of speech is connected with some innate language-transmittal mechanism found in adults—the counterpart to Chomsky's LAD. (Bruner [1983] suggested that adults have a device in their brains that responds to infants and young children by automatically altering speech to a more understandable form, and he even suggested an appropriate name, **language acquisition support system,** or **LASS.**)

Prosodic features of child-directed speech.

Beginning in the late 1970s and early 1980s, a new phase of research focused on the prosodic features of speech, or **prosody,** the ups and downs of the tones and the rhythms of the sounds we make. Instead of counting repetitions or comparing words used in infant-directed (I-D) speech versus adult-directed (A-D) speech, researchers used instruments to measure the acoustic features of different types of speech. I-D speech, compared with A-D speech, was found to have a higher mean frequency, a wider range of frequencies, and a greater incidence of rising frequency contours. In other words, when mothers talk to infants, they use higher tones of voice in general, more high and low tones, and more tones that move from low to high (Fernald & Mazzie, 1991).

Using this acoustic comparison method, mothers in other cultures were studied as they interacted with their infants, and these same general prosodic features were found for Latvian, Comanche, Mandarin Chinese, Japanese, Sinhala, Russian, Thai, and Swedish mothers (see Fernald, 1992; Fisher & Tokura, 1996; Kitamura et al., 2002; Kuhl et al., 1997). In a study of French, Italian, German, Japanese, British, and American families, Anne Fernald and her colleagues (1989) demonstrated typical I-D speech versus A-D speech differences for both mothers and fathers. Not all cultures use the same exaggerated style of I-D speech as American mothers (and fathers) frequently do, but as the list of cultures mentioned suggests, some aspects of infant-directed speech might be universal (Fernald, 1992; Kuhl et al., 1997).

Why do people use I-D speech when talking to babies? One reason seems to be that this is the way babies "want" to be spoken to. They are more attentive to adults who speak to them using I-D rather than A-D speech. For example, 4-month-old infants who have been conditioned to turn their heads to one side or the other to select which of two tapes they will listen to, will turn their heads to hear I-D speech rather than A-D speech. There is even evidence that 1-month-old infants show a preference for I-D speech (Cooper & Aslin, 1990, 1994).

One interesting study examined mothers of deaf infants signing to their babies and to their deaf friends (Masataka, 1996). Similar to the findings for spoken language, the mothers signed more slowly, used more repetitions, and greater exaggerations of movements to their deaf infants than to their deaf adult friends. Moreover, like hearing babies, the deaf infants paid greater attention and made more affective responses to infant-directed signing than to adult-directed signing. In a follow-up study, Nobuo Masataka (1998) demonstrated that *hearing* babies, who had never been exposed to sign language, were also more responsive to the greater exaggerations found in infant-directed sign language than to adult-directed sign language, suggesting that this effect is not modality specific.

Other studies have shown that when I-D speech styles are used, young infants can discriminate between words that have very slight differences in sounds (Moore, Spence, & Katz, 1997). For example, research has shown that 1- to 4-month-old infants can discriminate among three-syllable sequences (such as "ma*ra*na" versus "ma*la*na") if the words are spoken using the exaggerated style of I-D speech (Karzon, 1985). For instance, in these examples, the middle syllables would be accented ("ma-**ra**-na" and "ma-**la**-na") in I-D speech, which would not be the case in normal adult-to-adult speech (see Trehub, Trainor, & Unyk, 1993). Babies this age cannot tell the difference between the two words when they are spoken in normal A-D speech.

In related work, Daniel Stern and his colleagues (Stern, Spieker, & MacKain, 1982) found that mothers of 2-, 4-, and 6-month-old babies used rising intonations when they wished to *get* a baby's attention and down-up-down phrasing (as in the "malana" example earlier) when wishing to *maintain* an infant's attention. The results of these and other studies suggest that babies are born ready to process certain types of language, and it is no coincidence that the sing-songy type of speech babies best understand is the same kind of speech that adults and children seem compelled to produce in the presence of an infant.

The role of child-directed speech. Earlier theories about child-directed speech centered on mothers' roles as teachers of language for their children (Hoff-Ginsburg, 1985). Individual differences in how mothers converse with their 1- and 2-year-old children have been found to be related to early aspects of language development (see Hoff, 2000). For example, the use of *expansions* (expanding a statement that a child made), repetitions, and questions, all frequent in child-directed speech, has been shown to be related to children's language development. The relation between mothers' speech and children's lan-

guage development is not straightforward, however, with different aspects of mothers' speech influencing different aspects of their children's language development at different times. Nevertheless, it seems clear that mothers are indeed "teaching" their children something important about the syntactic properties of language, even if that "something" cannot be easily specified.

Infant-directed speech seems also to serve other types of development at much earlier ages. Stern and his colleagues (1983) showed that the prosodic features of mothers' I-D speech peak when the infant is 4 months old, almost half a year before the infant shows any sign of understanding specific words. This has led to the alternative interpretation that I-D speech plays a role not only in syntactic development but also in the emotional relationship between infant and caregiver. Fernald (1992) suggested that by using specific tones, the mother regulates the infant's emotions, behavior, and attention and conveys her own emotional state to her infant. Fernald divided I-D speech into four different acoustical patterns, all of which are used by British, American, German, French, and Italian mothers when talking to their 12-month-old infants. These patterns are used to convey the mother's approval, express prohibition, ask for attention, and provide comfort to the infant. Such nonverbal communication is important in developing secure mother-infant attachment, and, according to Locke, "Spoken language piggybacks on this open channel, taking advantage of mother-infant attachment by embedding new information in the same stream of cues" (1994, p. 441). Although children do not need a secure attachment to develop language, there is evidence that maltreated toddlers have significant delays in language acquisition (Cicchetti, 1989). Fernald's claim is that the evolutionary origins of language may stem from mothers attempting to regulate the emotions of their infants, something that I-D speech continues to do today (see also Trainor, Austin, & Desjardins, 2000).

In the previous section examining the critical period for language acquisition, the importance of "starting small" was emphasized. Children's limited information-processing abilities might limit the amount of information they can process, which might make the task of acquiring language easier. But if young children acquire language best by "starting small," this is apparently accomplished not only because of their limited cognitive abilities but also with the help of adults (Bjorklund & Schwartz, 1996). Adults around the world talk to children using highly repetitive and greatly simplified child-directed speech. As children's language competencies increase, so too does the complexity of language addressed to them. Thus, in the early phases of language acquisition, children receive a highly simplified language corpus. As Richard Schwartz and I noted, "Such modified language, accompanied with young children's limited information-processing abilities, results in children receiving a much reduced body of linguistic evidence from which to extract the phonological, syntactic, and semantic rules of their mother tongue" (Bjorklund & Schwartz, 1996, p. 26). I should also note that there is a large variation in the amount of speech adults in different cultures direct toward infants, yet children from cultures that address little speech directly to children still acquire language pretty much "on schedule," making it unlikely that child-directed speech is necessary for language acquisition.

The significance of using simplified child-directed speech for language acquisition is illustrated by anecdotal evidence that simply being exposed to adult-directed speech is not sufficient to learn a first or second language. For example, a hearing child of deaf parents, who was confined to his home because of poor health, learned sign language from his parents but could neither speak nor understand spoken English by the age of 3, despite frequently watching television (Moskowitz, 1978). In another example, Dutch children who regularly watched (and frequently preferred) German television often failed to understand the programs and did not achieve appreciable control of German (reported in Snow et al., 1976). Not only does watching and listening to television provide no opportunity for social (and language) give and take, but the language heard on television consists almost totally of adult-directed

speech and not the modified (and simplified) child-directed speech that children typically receive from adults.

Research examining the role that child-directed speech plays in development makes it clear that although infants might be biologically prepared to acquire their mother tongue, language development is embedded within the social-emotional context of the family. Language development cannot be properly understood unless it is viewed as part of the broader human developmental perspective (see Locke, 1993).

Locke's Theory of Neurolinguistic Development

Locke (1997) has formulated a neurolinguistic theory of language acquisition that emphasizes the interplay of biologically paced and experiential factors. Locke proposed that there are four neurologically based phases of language acquisition, with the initial phase beginning before birth and the final phase beginning at about 3 years of age and extending into the years beyond. These phases overlap one another to a significant degree (that is, they are not stages, with one replacing the preceding one), and children are receptive to different types of linguistic information and perform different types of linguistic operations at different phases (see Table 11-4).

Locke calls the first phase *vocal learning*. While still in utero, infants are aware of and react to the prosody (that is, the rhythmic characteristics) of their mothers' voices. Anthony DeCasper, Melanie Spence, and their colleagues (DeCasper & Spence, 1986; Spence & Freeman, 1996) have demonstrated that infants are "learning" something about the language that their mothers speak during the last several weeks (or more) before birth. Moreover, infants show a preference (apparently present at birth; Mehler et al., 1988) for listening to their mother tongue over foreign languages and are responsive to the emotional tone of language (see Fernald, 1992; Locke, 1993). During this phase, infants are predisposed by their biology to orient to people who are talking and to respond to such behavior. Thus, this early phase is

TABLE 11-4 Phases and processing systems, and neural cognitive mechanisms associated with the development of linguistic capacity, along with the corresponding areas of language in Locke's neurolinguistic theory.

Age of onset	Developmental phases and systems	Neurocognitive mechanisms	Linguistic domains
Prenatal	Vocal learning	Specialization in social cognition	Prosody and sound segments
5–7 months	Utterance acquisition	Specialization in social cognition	Stereotyped utterances
20–37 months	Analysis and computation	Grammatical analysis mechanism	Morphology Syntax Phonology
3+ years	Integration and elaboration	Social cognition and grammatical analysis	Expanded lexicon, automatized operations

SOURCE: Locke, J. L. (1997). A theory of neurolinguistic development. *Brain and Language, 58*, p. 268. Copyright © 1997, reprinted with permission from Elsevier and the author.

actually one of social cognition that sets the stage for later language development.

While the child is still learning about prosody, the second phase, which Locke refers to as *utterance acquisition*, begins at 5 to 7 months of age. Included during this phase are not only children's first words but also short phrases that sometimes sound like simple sentences ("Time to go to bed"). Although the young children using such phrases sound grammatically sophisticated, Locke considers the phrases to be *formulaic*, in that they were acquired by rote memorization and do not involve any grammatical analysis. During this phase, children are acquiring words and simple phrases from listening to others. This represents the acquisitive, or storage, phase of language development. Children have a set of "starter" utterances that they can use in restricted contexts, effectively increasing the quality (if not quantity) of their interactions with adults.

Beginning about 20 months is the *analysis and computation* (or *utterance analysis*) phase. This is the first grammatical phase, in that an internal (that is, neurologically based) system acts on the language information stored during phase 2 and imposes some (syntactic) structure on it. Although the mechanisms involved in this third phase are seemingly innate (akin to the mechanisms of Chomsky's language acquisition device), they can only operate on infor-

mation already in long-term memory. Thus, if for some reason a child has not acquired a sufficient body of language utterances, there will be nothing to analyze. According to Locke, "The structure analysis system locates recurring elements within and across utterances, and thereby learns the rules by which utterances are to be synthesized and parsed" (1997, p. 273). Perhaps the clearest evidence of this phase is found in the overregularization of irregular verbs and noun plurals, discussed earlier in this chapter (for example, "runned," "goed," "mouses").

Locke proposes that the rapidly expanding lexicon, acquired during phase 2, prompts the grammatical processes during this third phase to come into operation. Evidence for this comes from research demonstrating a positive relationship between total vocabulary and grammatical sophistication in a group of 20-month-old toddlers (Bates, Bretherton, & Snyder, 1988; see discussion of the relation between vocabulary growth and syntactic complexity below). Not surprisingly, this reflects a bidirectional relationship between structure and function, with what one knows influencing how (and perhaps whether) one processes information.

Locke refers to the final phase as *integration and elaboration*, beginning about 3 years of age. Now, as a result of the child's acquiring some basic grammatical rules, new information can be readily organized,

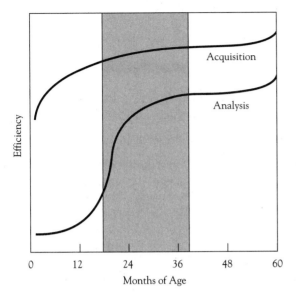

FIGURE 11-3 Age changes in the acquisition and analysis phases in Locke's neurolinguistic theory. The shaded area is a critical period in which utterance acquisition must reach a certain level of efficiency to fully activate and stabilize an utterance-analytic mechanism that is intrinsically "ready" to respond to experience. SOURCE: Locke, J. L. (1997). A theory of neurolinguistic development. *Brain and Language, 58,* 280. Copyright © 1997, reprinted with permission from Elsevier and the author.

making it easier to acquire new words (thus effectively extending the efficiency of utterance acquisition). This is similar to the facilitative effects that an elaborated knowledge base has on subsequent learning and memory (see Chapters 8, 10, and 12). Because children now have rules for classifying language terms and forms, new information can be readily acquired, resulting in the creation of larger vocabularies.

But how does Locke's theory help explain the fact that young children are better at learning language than older children and adults are? Figure 11-3 shows age-related changes in the efficiency of utterance acquisition (phase 2) and utterance analysis (phase 3). The shaded area in the figure reflects a critical period in which a certain level of utterances have to be acquired for the analysis and computation mechanisms

to work efficiently. According to Locke, if children have not acquired a sufficiently large body of language utterances by the time the analysis-and-computation phase kicks in, language learning will be hampered. The efficiency of utterance acquisition is in high gear by 12 months and continues to be high through the preschool years. In contrast, the efficiency of utterance analysis starts low, and begins to peak at about 20 months, only after a high level of acquisition efficiency is attained (that is, after children have acquired a relatively large number of words). This figure shows what is proposed to happen in normal development. The two systems (utterance acquisition and utterance analysis) are functioning at high levels of efficiency together for nearly a two-year period. This results in the acquisition of basic grammatical forms, which serve as the foundation for the integration-and-elaboration phase, leading to mature language use.

But what happens if a child is not exposed to a sufficiently large body of language utterances or if the utterance acquisition system is not operating at peak efficiency early in development? This alternative is shown in Figure 11-4. Now, when the utterance analysis system is ready to kick in, there is little stored information to operate on. As a result, little in the way of analysis and computation is done during this critical period, and efficient analysis actually decreases following this critical period of language development (reflected by the shaded area in Figure 11-4). According to Locke, "the critical phase for grammatical analysis, timed by unidentified endogenous factors, expires soon. When the lexically delayed [children] finally have enough words, neurodevelopmental conditions no longer favor instatement of grammatical capability. A child who has not realized a sizable lexical increase by about 24 months is therefore at developmental risk, for his analytic-computational capability may not turn all the way on" (1977, p. 288).

By extending the logic of Locke's model, one can see why people who are not exposed to a language until later in life are apt to have difficulty acquiring syntax (Curtiss, 1977). Their utterance analysis system is no longer functioning at peak efficiency. Thus, although individual vocabulary items can still be

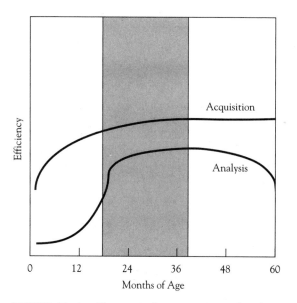

FIGURE 11-4 Changes in the acquisition and analysis for the lexically delayed child. Because the utterance-acquisition phase is behind schedule, by the time there are enough utterances to enable the utterance-analysis mechanisms to produce grammar, the optimal time has passed. SOURCE: Locke, J. L. (1997). A theory of neurolinguistic development. *Brain and Language, 58,* 289. Copyright © 1997, reprinted with permission from Elsevier and the author.

acquired, using these utterances as a basis for grammar is less easily done because the period of highest efficiency for the utterance analysis system has long since passed.

Locke provides evidence from a variety of sources, including language-delayed children, cases of brain damage, neurological organization for language, and cross-species comparisons, to support his theory. He emphasizes that early language development is supported by biologically based dispositions in infants to orient them to language and the people who speak it. He is explicit that language development involves the bidirectional relation between biologically paced changes and the social environment: "All phases in the induction of linguistic capacity are affected by interactions between neuromaturational events and social stimulation" (1997, p. 279). He recognizes that language is an inherently social phenomenon and

that its beginnings can be found as much in social and emotional responding as in perceptual and cognitive abilities.

The Relation Between Lexical and Syntactic Development: Is a Grammar Module Necessary?

Locke's theory addresses the relation between lexical and syntactic development, proposing that a certain level of utterance acquisition (that is, a certain vocabulary size) needs to be achieved before utterance analysis can begin. In other words, children have to know a certain number of words before their "grammar module" kicks in.

Related to Locke's hypothesis is the observation of the close relation of vocabulary size and grammatical complexity during the preschool years (Bates, 1999; Bates & Goodman, 1997), which is illustrated in Figure 11-5 (from Bates, 1999). Elizabeth Bates and her colleagues have demonstrated this relation in longitudinal and cross-sectional studies, in late talkers and early talkers, in children with Down Syndrome and Williams Syndrome, in children with language disorders, in people with brain damage, and for a variety of languages (see Bates, 1999; Bates & Goodman, 1997). The relation between vocabulary size and syntactic complexity is stronger than the relation between age and syntactic complexity, making it unlikely that age alone is the common underlying factor (see also Robinson & Mervis, 1998).

Do these data support Locke's hypothesis? Yes, in a general way I believe they do, but they also suggest that the connection between vocabulary size and syntactic complexity might be more direct than what Locke proposes. According to Locke, children must attain a certain number of lexical items before their utterance-analysis module can function properly. Thus, the theory is still based on the idea of children having a domain-specific grammatical organ (something like Chomsky's LAD), consistent with nativists' viewpoints. Bates and her colleagues argue that the strong relation between vocabulary and syntactic development argues against the need for a "grammar module" (that is, against representational

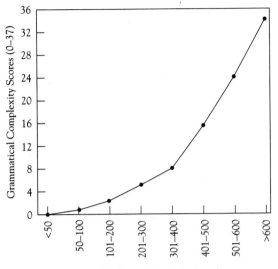

FIGURE 11-5 Grammatical complexity increases as a function of the size of children's vocabularies. SOURCE: Bates, E. (1999). On the nature of language. In R. Levi-Montalcini, D. Baltimore, R. Dulbecco. & F. Jacob (Series Eds.) & E. Bizzi, P. Calissano, & V. Volterra (Vol. Eds.), *Frontiere della biologia [Frontiers of biology]*, *The brain of Homo sapiens*. Rome: Giovanni Trecanni.

innateness). Rather, as vocabulary increases, grammar emerges from a need to organize the growing corpus. According to Bates and her colleagues, words and grammar are two sides of the same coin, developing together, with changes in one affecting changes in the other. It is not necessary to hypothesize separate innate modules, à la Chomsky, to account for the data. Rather, they propose a connectionist approach (see Chapter 5), in which grammar emerges out of the acquisition and analysis of individual words (Elman et al., 1996). Such an approach still hypothesizes that there are innate constraints that influence how language items are processed (architectural constraints), but it avoids the idea of a specific grammar module that has a ready-made theory of syntax that children will discover just by being exposed to language. Instead, through adjustments that children make as they acquire words (changing weights in the connectionist model, see

Chapter 5), grammar emerges without the need of specific, innate structures. I will not attempt to elaborate on this model here, but mention it only to demonstrate that there are other reasonable alternatives to the nativist view of language acquisition, in which there are innate constraints on how language is processed (architectural constraints) without having to resort to the idea of innate modules (representational constraints).

But is there really that much of a difference between the approach that Bates and her colleagues are proposing and that of, say Locke? At one level, no, but at another level, yes. Both models view language as different from other forms of cognition and suggest that children are prepared to learn language—that is, they are born with some language-specific constraints. However, nativist perspectives propose that different aspects of language development are relatively independent. Even Locke, who proposes that a certain level of lexical development is necessary for the grammar module to work properly, sees children as being born with a domain-specific syntactic device. The perspective taken by Bates and her colleagues differs in that they see language acquisition as emerging gradually without the need of a highly specific grammar module but through the dynamic interaction between a brain with innate processing constraints and a language-speaking world. This view is more consistent with the developmental systems perspective introduced in the first two chapters of this book. Which perspective is right, or at least closer to the truth? I have my biases, but don't claim to have *the* answer; I do know that there will be some lively debates on this issue, at least in some academic circles, during the next decade.

Gender Differences in Language Acquisition

There is a persistent belief that females are better than males at language and language-related skills. For example, girls and women are believed to be better readers than boys and men are, with this difference appearing early and lasting into adulthood. Research pertinent to this question will be examined in Chapter 14. Here, I will review research concerning possible gender differences in the acquisition of a first language.

Some researchers have reported faster rates of language acquisition for girls (Bornstein & Haynes, 1998; Galsworthy et al., 2000), although other studies have failed to observe any significant gender differences (McCarthy, 1954), and some find a difference favoring young girls for spontaneous speech but not on standardized tests (Morisset, Barnard, & Booth, 1995). In related research, Michael Lewis and his colleagues reported greater vocalization by infant girls than boys. For example, 3-month-old girls were found to vocalize more than boys in response to their mother's invitation to "talk" (Lewis & Freedle, 1973), and infant girls between the ages of 3 and 13 months vocalized more to facial stimuli than did boys of the same age (Lewis, 1969). In a meta-analysis summarizing the effects in more than 30 studies that looked at differences in how mothers talked with their sons and their daughters, Campbell Leaper, Kristin Anderson, and Paul Sanders (1998) reported moderate gender differences, with mothers talking more and using more supportive speech with their daughters than with their sons. Other research has shown that mothers talk about different things with their sons than with their daughters. For example, examining the emotion talk of women to their 2-, 3-, and 4-year-old children, mothers were more apt to explain emotions to boys rather than just to label them, but they showed no difference in the use of explanations and labels with their daughters (Cervantes & Callanan, 1998). Of equal interest, even the youngest girls in this study talked about emotions quite frequently and as often as older girls. In contrast, emotion talk was less frequent for the youngest boys but increased with age.

Others have proposed that the gender differences sometimes found in language acquisition are related to cultural factors. For example, there is evidence that in Greece, where boys are valued more than girls, boys rather than girls are more vocally responsive (Roe et al., 1985). Perhaps the gender differences favoring girls found in the United States can be attributed to different ways in which girls and boys are spoken to rather than to endogenous factors. Recall from Chapter 10 on memory development that parents use a more elaborative conversation style with their daughters than with their sons when prompting them to remember past events (Haden & Reese, 1994). Such differences are related to gender differences in event memory (girls' being better than boys') and are consistent with the hypothesis that differences in cultural practices are responsible, in part, for gender differences in rate of language acquisition (Roe et al., 1985).

However, some gender differences in early language are found that are *not* related to differences in how parents talk to boys and girls. Catherine Haden, Rochel Haine, and Robyn Fivush (1997) reported that girls between 40 and 70 months of age produced longer and more structured narratives than did boys of the same age; however, unlike other aspects of language presented to boys and girls, there were no differences in how parents used narratives to talk about past experiences with their sons and daughters. These results indicate that girls are more advanced in their narrative production than boys are and that a simple socialization explanation cannot adequately account for these differences. Similarly, in a behavior-genetics study examining more than 3,000 pairs of 2-year-old twins (Galsworthy et al., 2000), gender differences favoring girls were found (although they accounted for only 3% of the variance). Interestingly, the heritability of verbal ability was higher for the boys than for the girls. In other research, 18- and 24-month-old girls had significantly larger vocabularies than boys did, and this difference was related to exposure to fetal testosterone: the greater exposure to testosterone (a male hormone) prenatally, the smaller a child's vocabulary tended to be (Lutchmaya, Baron-Cohen, & Raggatt, 2002).

As of this writing, the question of gender differences in language acquisition is unanswered. Research suggests that girls might be more vocal than boys early in infancy and that this difference leads to a subsequent advantage in learning a first language. However, other research suggests that whatever small advantage in language acquisition girls do hold is a function of cultural practices, with boys in some cultures displaying the typical "feminine" pattern of faster language acquisition we've come to expect in our culture.

Language and Thought

Although most laypeople would concur that language is not only a system of communication but an important vehicle for thought, most theorists of language would likely disagree. Language is used to *express* thought, both to others and to ourselves, but it is not thought itself (Pinker, 1994). Some developmental psychologists have taken a different perspective. For example, theorists such as Bruner (1966) argued that the ability to use language as a conceptual tool transforms a child's thinking during early childhood. Moreover, the use of language in social situations facilitates this transformation. Knowledge of the physical world is imbedded in the social world, and language is a universal mechanism for communicating and thus structuring knowledge. Perhaps more to the point, language is used to communicate ideas and thoughts (that is, mental representations) between people, and language structures these mental representations. This perspective is probably best represented by the work of Katherine Nelson (1993, 1996) and was discussed with respect to the development of autobiographical memory in Chapter 10. Along similar lines, Soviet psychologist Lev Vygotsky (1962) proposed that language directs much of children's intelligent behavior, with the relationship between language and thought changing developmentally, and I now turn to this line of research.

Vygotsky (1962) believed that thought and speech have different roots in development, with the two initially being independent; that is, thought is prelinguistic, and speech is preintellectual. In development, however, thought and speech merge, with thought becoming verbal and speech rational. This developmental relationship between language and thought, particularly during the stages where the two cross, has attracted the interest of psychologists.

DENNIS THE MENACE

"I'M GONNA HAVE TO STOP THINKIN' OUT LOUD."

CARTOON 11-1 Young children often have a difficult time keeping their thoughts to themselves. SOURCE: Dennis the Menace ®, used by permission of Hank Ketcham and © 1986 by North America Syndicate.

Vygotsky was particularly interested in the role of **egocentric speech** in affecting children's thought. Egocentric speech, or **private speech,** as it is commonly referred to, can be thought of as speech-for-self. This overt language is carried out with apparent satisfaction even though it does not function to communicate. Private speech can be observed both when children are alone and in social settings. Vygotsky believed that private speech plays a specific role in affecting children's thought and problem solving. Language can guide children's behavior (and thus their thought), but young children cannot yet use language covertly, "in their heads." To benefit from the self-regulatory function of language, young children must essentially talk to themselves, using their speech to guide thought and behavior. With development, the self-regulatory function of language changes so that children can direct their behavior using **inner speech.** In other words, private speech serves as a **cognitive self-guidance system** and then goes "underground" as covert verbal thought. (Vygotsky contrasted his position with that of Piaget [1955], who believed that private speech plays no functional role in cognitive development but is merely symptomatic of ongoing mental activity.)

Several studies have assessed aspects of Vygotsky's theory of private speech, and most generally find support for his ideas. For example, Laura Berk (1986) observed first- and third-grade children during daily math periods for four months. Various forms of private speech were recorded (for example, task-irrelevant, self-stimulating speech; task-relevant, externalized speech; and task-relevant, external manifestations of inner speech such as lip movements), as well as other aspects of their overt behavior (movement, pointing to objects to help them add) and measures of their task performance (daily math papers and achievement and IQ tests). Berk reported high levels of private speech in this sample of children that changed with age. The self-guidance function of private speech varied with age and eventually gave way to covert, inner speech. Most of the children's task-relevant externalized speech was used to guide their problem solving, with third-graders using more internalized forms of speech (for example, inaudible mutterings, lip and tongue movements) to facilitate their performance. The total amount of private speech was positively related to intelligence at grade 1 but not at grade 3, an indication that brighter children begin to use private speech to guide their problem solving earlier than less bright children and also stop sooner, as thought goes "underground" as inner speech (see also Berk & Landau, 1993; Kohlberg, Yaeger, & Hjertholm, 1968).

Also consistent with Vygotsky's claims, children rely more heavily on private speech when facing difficult rather than easy tasks, when deciding how to proceed after making errors (Berk, 1992), and their performance often improves after turning to self-instruction (Behrend, Rosengren & Perlmutter, 1989; Berk & Spuhl, 1995). Moreover, private speech does eventually go "underground," progressing from words and phrases, to whispers and mutterings, to inner

speech (Bivens & Berk, 1990), although the use of private speech on problem-solving tasks persists into adolescence, even though such speech is not associated with improved task performance for these older children (Winsler, 2003).

In addition to the developmental trend in private speech, there is evidence that young children might not even believe that inner speech is possible. Instead, they believe that a person cannot "talk to herself" and think at the same time. When preschool children are prompted to use inner speech (for example, "Silently think about how your name sounds"), they are just as likely to say that they had a *picture* of their name in their heads while thinking as to say that they said their names in their heads (Flavell et al., 1997).

In general, although some discrepancies from Vygotsky's theory have been reported, the existing research suggests that there is indeed a developmental relationship between language and thought, along the lines that Vygotsky and his colleagues hypothesized.

Summary

Several features typify language, including *arbitrariness* (any word can be used to express any concept), *productivity* (language is "creative"), *semanticity* (language can represent objects, actions, events, and ideas symbolically), *displacement* (ability to displace speaker from the here and now), and *duality* (language is represented at two levels: phonology and syntax).

Children usually speak their first words around 10 months. Their *productive language* (what they can speak) is less than their *receptive language* (what they can comprehend), and early sentences are *telegraphic*, including only the high-content words.

Children's language development can be described on several dimensions, including *phonology, morphology, syntax, semantics,* and *pragmatics. Phonology* refers to the sounds of language and is first reflected in infants' babbling, which varies initially as a function of physical anatomy and later as a function of the language infants hear.

Morphemes (both *free* and *bound*) are the smallest unit of meaning in a language. Children learn rules and *overregularize* irregular words to fit these rules (forming words such as "goed" and "mouses"). The average number of morphemes used in a sentence, or the *mean length of utterance (MLU)*, is a good indication of the language complexity of a preschool child.

Syntactic development progresses quickly during the preschool years and is reflected in regular age-related changes in forming negatives, asking questions, using the passive voice, and relating events in sentences.

Semantic development refers to the development of word meaning. Around 18 months of age, children experience a *word spurt,* in which the rate of new word learning (mostly nouns) increases rapidly. This has been attributed to *fast mapping,* in which children are able to learn novel words with minimal input. Researchers have proposed the existence of *lexical constraints* to make word learning easier. These include the *whole-word assumption,* the *taxonomic assumption,* and the *mutual exclusivity assumption.* Infants and young children also likely make use of social cues of speakers, such as gazes, to help them identify the referent to words. Early in development, children often make *overextensions,* applying a word beyond its correct meaning (calling all four-legged animals "dog"), but sometimes make *underextensions,* incorrectly restricting the use of a term. Semantic memory can be described using *feature-list models,* with the number and type of features children use to define words changing with age.

Natural language categories comprise items that are related by some set of features and that can be referred to by a single language term (for example, dogs, pets, animals). Young children are able to categorize *basic-level* objects (for example, cars, chairs, dogs) and only later categorize by more superordinate categories (for example, vehicles, furniture, animals). One factor influencing the formation of superordinate natural language categories is that of *category typicality.* Some items are more representative of the *category prototype* than others are. Children tend to learn the category membership of more-typical items before that of less-typical items, and their judgments of category typicality vary with age. Aspects of children's semantic memories seem to be schematically organized by *scripts.* Nelson has proposed that broad-based superordinates (such as food) have their basis in context-specific, script-related, *slot-filler categories* (such as things you eat at breakfast).

Pragmatics refers to knowledge about how language can be used and adjusted to fit different circumstances. Even young children are aware of some basic aspects of pragmatics, although there are also substantial improvements with age. *Speech registers* refer to a distinct style of speaking that is used only in specific contexts (for example, when talking to children, when talking in school). For example, *Black English*—a dialect of American English used mostly (but not exclusively) by members of the African American community—is characterized by some special rules of pronunciation and syntax.

Communicative competence refers to the various types of language knowledge (phonology, morphology, syntax, semantics, and pragmatics) that are combined in a package to yield effective communication. Preschool children often display poor communication and *metacommunication* skills, being less aware of factors that influence comprehension of messages than older children are, and sometimes speak in *collective monologues,* with children speaking "with" one another, but not necessarily "to" one another.

Behavioral theories of language (syntax) acquisition have generally been discredited and replaced by nativist and social-interactionist theories. Nativist theories follow the theorizing of Noam Chomsky, who proposed language has both a *surface* and a *deep structure,* that children are born with a *language acquisition device (LAD),* and all that is needed for language acquisition is exposure to speech. Nativists propose there is an innate *universal grammar* that contains the basic syntactic structure of all human languages. Both a first and second language are learned more easily by younger than by older children, suggesting a critical period for language learning. Some support for the nativist position comes from children creating *creoles* from *pidgins* after only one generation. Newport's *"less is more" hypothesis* suggests that young children's cognitive limitations actually make it easier for them to acquire a first or second language than for older children or adults to do so.

Social-interactionist theorists examine the interplay between language, cognitive, and social development. Young infants are responsive to human speech and are especially responsive to *infant-directed* (or *child-directed*) *speech*, which includes a distinctive type of *prosody*, or rhythm. Bruner suggested that adults have an innate device that causes them to respond to infants and young children with child-directed speech, which he called the *language acquisition support system*, or *LASS*. Locke proposed a theory of neurolinguistic development involving four overlapping and interactive stages: vocal learning, utterance acquisition, analysis and computation, and integration and elaboration. Differences in the timing of peak efficiency of these stages accounts for the performance of some language-delayed children. Bates and her colleagues similarly proposed that there is a direct relation between a child's vocabulary size and syntactic complexity, and that one need not postulate a "grammar module" (representational innateness) to account for the acquisition of grammar.

Gender differences in language acquisition favoring girls have occasionally been found, but there is evidence that different cultural practices regarding how boys and girls are treated play an important role in possible gender differences in language acquisition.

Vygotsky proposed that *egocentric*, or *private*, *speech* has a special role in guiding children's thinking and behavior. Young children's private speech serves as a *cognitive self-guidance system* and is eventually replaced by covert verbal thought, or *inner speech*. Recent research provides support for Vygotsky's theory.

Key Terms and Concepts

arbitrariness
productivity
semanticity
displacement
duality
productive language
receptive language
telegraphic speech

phonology
morphology
morphemes
free morphemes
bound morphemes
mean length of utterance (MLU)
overregularization
syntax
semantics
word spurt
fast mapping
lexical constraints
whole-object assumption
taxonomic assumption
mutual exclusivity assumption
overextensions
underextensions
feature-list models (of semantic memory)
natural language categories
basic-level categories
category prototype
category typicality
scripts
slot-filler categories
pragmatics
speech register
Black English
communicative competence
collective monologues
metacommunication
surface structure
deep structure
language acquisition device (LAD)
universal grammar
pidgins
creoles
"less is more" hypothesis
child-directed speech
infant-directed speech
language acquisition support system
    (LASS)
prosody
private (egocentric) speech
inner speech
cognitive self-guidance system

Suggested Readings

Bates, E., & Goodman, J. C. (1997). On the inseparability of grammar and the lexicon: Evidence from acquisition, aphasia and real-time processing. In G. Altman (Ed.), Special issue on the lexicon, *Language and Cognitive Processes, 12,* 507–586.   This article presents the position that the development of grammar and vocabulary cannot be viewed as separate phenomena and suggests an alternative account of the development of grammar, one that does not require a universal grammar as proposed by Chomsky and his followers.

Berko Gleason, J. (Ed.) (1997). *The development of language* (4th ed.). Boston, MA: Allyn & Bacon.   This book consists of 11 chapters, each written by experts in the field on various topics of language development, including phonology, morphology, semantics, syntax, and pragmatics. The chapters provide more detailed accounts of the various areas of language development than afforded here.

Hoff, E. (2001). *Language development* (2nd ed.). Belmont, CA: Wadsworth.   This textbook presents an overview of all aspects of language development, from linguistic theory to brain development.

Pinker, S. (1994). *The language instinct: How the mind creates language*. New York: Morrow.   This popular book (but *not* a book of pop-psychology) presents the nativist position of language acquisition perhaps more clearly and thoroughly than any other source. Whether you agree with Pinker's arguments or not, it provides an excellent look at the issues and data dealing with the child's acquisition of language.

Senghas, A., & Coppola, M. (2001). Children creating language: How Nicaraguan Sign Language acquired a spatial grammar. *Psychological Science, 12,* 323–326. This is a report of a research project looking at children's "spontaneous" invention of a sign language. In addition to providing fodder for debates about the nature of language development, it is an excellent demonstration of a "naturalistic experiment."

InfoTrac College Edition

For additional readings, explore InfoTrac College Edition, your online library. Go to http://www.infotrac-college.com/wadsworth.

Problem Solving
and Reasoning

ife is full of problems that we seek to solve. Problems and their attempted solutions start early. Infants will strive to retrieve a fallen toy, overcoming obstacles along the way. The problems we face, and their solutions, become more complicated as we get older, but they all have certain things in common. We say that someone is solving a problem when there is a specific goal in mind that cannot be attained immediately because of the presence of one or more obstacles. We solve problems by learning rules or by using (sometimes discovering) one or more strategies. Sometimes a problem takes several attempts before it is solved, and we must be able to evaluate our progress toward the goal, if, for no other reason, to know when the problem has been solved. Thus, the four basic requirements of problem solving are goals, obstacles, strategies for overcoming the obstacles, and an evaluation of the results (DeLoache, Miller, & Pierroutsakos, 1998).

Much of what we have covered in this book to this point can be considered to be in the realm of problem solving. The classic tasks of conservation and classification, for example, are problem-solving tasks. Arithmetic problems, which will be discussed in Chapter 14, are clearly problem-solving tasks. So are the strategies that were discussed in Chapter 6. To some extent, many tasks assessing memory are problem-solving tasks, with the goal being to remember as much as one possibly can. In this chapter, I describe children's general problem-solving abilities, beginning in infancy. This will be followed by a brief section on planning. The remaining part of the chapter will be devoted to a special type of problem solving, reasoning.

Problem Solving

The Development of Problem Solving

When do children first solve problems? Based on our definition of what constitutes **problem solving** (having a goal, obstacles to that goal, strategies, and evaluation of results), infants cannot be said to solve problems until they demonstrate some sense of **goal-directed behavior.** Recall from our discussion of Jean Piaget's theory of sensorimotor development (see Chapter 4), goal-directed behavior requires that "need precede action." That is, infants do not discover an interesting outcome fortuitously (for example, hitting a mobile with their arms) but, rather, first seek to achieve a specific goal (move a mobile) and then act accordingly. This is also the beginning of cause and effect (means-end) thinking. Infants must realize that they must do something quite specific (make physical contact with the mobile) before the mobile will move.

Piaget proposed that infants are not able to accomplish this until about 8 months of age, during the substage of coordination of secondary circular reactions. At this time, infants can use one behavior *strategically* in the service of another (for example, push aside a cloth to retrieve a toy hidden underneath). Thus, following from Piaget's classic work, we can say that problem solving begins at least during the latter part of the first year of life.

But must infants wait that long to solve simple problems? Infants younger than 8 months can clearly learn to control aspects of their environments to make interesting things happen (Rovee-Collier & Gerhardstein, 1997; Lewis, Alessandri, & Sullivan, 1990). For example, infants 2 to 8 months of age learned to pull a lever to see a color picture of a baby's face and to hear an accompanying song (Lewis et al., 1990). Even the youngest infants learned to pull the lever to get the reinforcement and became angry when the lever pulls no longer produced the interesting outcome. But the study by Lewis et al., although it had a specific goal to be achieved, does not have all the classic aspects of problem solving. The only obstacle was infants learning the association between their behavior and the outcome, and there seems to be no explicit strategy involved. True problem solving, involving means-end action sequences, seems not to be found until about the time Piaget originally proposed (the latter half of the first year).

Peter Willatts (1990) performed some interesting experiments demonstrating means-end problem solving in infants. In one study, 6-, 7-, and 8-month-old infants were placed on a table. In front of the infants was a long cloth with a toy placed on the cloth, out of the infants' reach. Here's a goal (get that toy) and an obstacle (it's out of reach). The solution is to strategically use one behavior (pull the cloth toward them) to achieve the goal (get the toy). How did the infants do? The 6-month-olds often retrieved the toy, but their behavior was not always intentional. Instead of pulling the cloth to them and fixing their attention on the toy, these youngest infants often simply played with the cloth, looked away from the toy, and, after a while, the toy finally was in their reach. By 8 months of age, infants were much less apt to play with the cloth. They grabbed the cloth and immediately began pulling it to bring the toy closer to them. They kept their fixation on the toy and quickly and efficiently brought the toy within their grasp, often holding out a hand in anticipation of the toy's arrival. The 7-month-olds fell between the 6- and 8-month-olds.

Although means-end problem solving might be within the capacity of infants as young as 7- and 8-months of age, it does not mean that children will display such behavior on more complicated tasks. Merry Bullock and Paul Lütkenhaus (1988) illustrated this in an interesting study in which children between the ages of 15- and 35-months were asked to perform one of several tasks, for example, stacking blocks to copy a house built by an adult. The youngest children (average age, 17 months) showed little specific goal-directed behavior. They did play with the blocks and built "something," but there was little evidence that they kept the goal of building a house in mind during their activities. In contrast, most 2-year-olds were able to keep the goal in mind and build the house. These children also did a good job of monitoring their performance (evaluating the results of their behavior). Almost all of these children made at least one correction, and 85% of the 2-year-olds stacked all the blocks correctly on at least one trial. The reactions of the children to their problem-solving attempts also revealed their evaluations of their behavior toward achieving their goal. Only about a third (36%) of the 17-month-olds showed some clear sign of emotion to their performance (smiling or frowning), whereas 90% of the older children (32-month-olds) did so.

The tasks the children need to solve get more complicated as they get older, and so their problem-solving abilities must also improve. One factor that has been found to have a significant impact on problem solving is knowledge. The more one knows about a particular topic or the more familiar one is with the context, the more sophisticated problem solving will be. Let me provide an example for learning the rules behind a computer game. Stephen Ceci (1996) proposed that context influences how people approach and solve problems. Ceci defines context as the way in which a problem is represented in long-term memory; that is, it consists of what a person knows about a task, including the reason for performing it. Ceci (1996) reported an experiment in which 10-year-old children were asked to predict where, on a computer screen, an object would land by using a joystick to mark on the screen the next position of the object. The object varied in size (big or small), color (dark or light), and shape (square, circle, or triangle), producing 12 combinations of features (two sizes × two colors × three shapes). A simple algorithm was written so that (1) squares would move upward, circles downward, and triangles would stay on the horizontal; (2) dark figures would move to the right and light figures to the left; and (3) large objects would move diagonally from lower left to upper right, whereas small objects would move in the opposite direction. So, for example, a large, light square would move upward, leftward, and from the lower left to the upper right.

Figuring out how the object would move (that is, where it would be on the next trial) seems like it would be a difficult task for children (as well as for adults), and it was. The children were given 15 sessions with the task, with 50 trials per session. Some children were simply asked to predict where the object would move on each trial. Other children were told that this was a video game, the purpose of which was to capture flying animals. The three shapes were changed to a butterfly, a bee, and a bird. These children were told to use the joystick to place the "butterfly net" so that they could "capture the prey" on each trial. The algorithm (that is, the rule by which the target moved on each trial) was identical in both conditions.

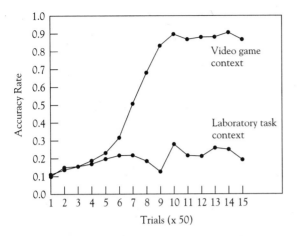

FIGURE 12-1 Children's mean proportion of accurate predictions of the position of a moving object in a video game versus laboratory context. SOURCE: From Stephen J. Ceci, *On intelligence . . . more or less: A bioecological treatise on intellectual development,* © 1990, p. 39. Reprinted by permission of Prentice Hall, Englewood Cliffs, New Jersey.

The results of this study are graphed in Figure 12-1. As can be seen, the two groups started out similarly, performing relatively poorly over the first five sessions. However, the children in the video-game context then took off, performing at levels approaching 90% by the ninth session. In comparison, the children given the laboratory context continued to perform poorly, never really improving on the task during the 15 sessions. Discovering the algorithm depended on the mental context in which the problem was presented. The rules were the same for all children, but the context, a form of knowledge, influenced greatly children's problem-solving performance.

Problem Solving as Inducing and Using Rules

One way of thinking about children's problem solving is considering their acquisition and use of *rules*. Rules specify relations between two or more variables and are usually thought of as "if . . . then" statements ("If condition A exists, make response X; if condi-

tion B exists, make response Y") (Zelazo & Jacques, 1997). One tradition in developmental psychology has focused on children's acquisition of the rules of formal logic ("If *p* then *q*," and so on), which will be discussed in a separate section later in this chapter. The second concerns children inducing, or discovering, a rule as a result of experience and using these rules to solve problems (DeLoache et al., 1998).

When Can Children Induce Rules?

When can children induce rules for solving a problem from experience? One simple task that requires the discovery of a rule is an *oddity problem*. This will be familiar to any readers who grew up watching *Sesame Street* and the game "One of these things is not like the other." In this game, and in oddity problems in general, people must figure out which object is different, or odd, relative to the others in the set. These problems can be very simple, based on perceptual similarity (for example, § § ¥) or more complex, based on conceptual similarity (for example, tiger, elephant, blue jay; or Brainerd, Gopnik, Karmiloff-Smith).

Oddity tasks can even be administered to preverbal children and animals. In these cases, children are shown a series of problems and receive a food reward when they select the correct (odd) item. William Overman and his colleagues (1996) used such an oddity task, showing toddlers from 16 months of age through adults series of three objects, two of which were the same (Experiment 1). When children selected the odd object, they received a food reward. This was a difficult task for toddlers (16 to 31 months of age), even more difficult for the preschoolers (32 to 60 months of age), but relatively trivial for participants 6 years of age and older. Yet, most of the toddlers (16- to 31-month-olds) did eventually learn the task, although it took them several hundred trials, and most children of all ages quickly solved the problems when given verbal instructions (Experiment 2).

It is interesting that the lack of verbal instructions (that is, performing the task using nonverbal procedures as is done when testing animals) was particularly detrimental for children between the ages of about 2.5 and 5 years of age. Other researchers

(Inhelder & Piaget, 1964) have reported similar findings, which have been interpreted as indicating that younger children approach oddity problems differently than older children do (see Overman et al., 1996). Obviously, the approach the 2.5- to 5-year-old children used was ineffective. It appears that these preschoolers' reliance on language made inducing a rule based solely on behavior very difficult, whereas the problem was simple enough for older children and adults to figure out without being told explicitly what to do. That these children were able to solve the problem easily as soon as they were told the rule ("Pick the one that's different") indicates that they can apply this rule across different problems, but just have a difficult time inducing a rule based on behavior alone.

Rule-Assessment Approach

Much of cognitive development can be viewed as a process of inducing rules to solve problems. Many problems share some of the same underlying features, and thus require the application of very similar rule systems. For example, many of the problems Piaget developed involved children learning about the physical world and, according to Piaget, require children to learn a set of logical rules to solve the problems. Although each problem would have something unique about it, a universal set of cognitive structures develops to handle these problems.

Robert Siegler (1976, 1981) developed a rule-based model of cognitive development to explain many of the concepts that children acquire over childhood initially described by Piaget and others. In his **rule-assessment approach,** cognitive development is characterized by the acquisition of increasingly powerful rules for solving problems. Let me provide a description of the rule-assessment approach for the balance-scale problem (Siegler, 1976, 1981). For this problem, children are shown a balance scale, similar to that shown in Figure 12-2. Weights are then placed on the two sides of the scale, and children must predict which side of the scale will fall (if either). Children must consider not only the number of weights on the two sides, but also their distance from the midpoint. Weights farther

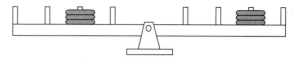

FIGURE 12-2 Example of a balance-scale task. The scale would be locked and weights would be placed on the two sides and children were to predict which side, if either, would fall.

away from the midpoint will have a greater impact on the movement of the scale than will weights closer to the midpoint. Siegler discerned four rules children used on this task. Children using Rule 1 consider only a single dimension: the amount (number) of weights on each side. Thus, children who use Rule 1 should say that the side with the most weights should fall, regardless of where those weights are placed. This will lead to some correct predictions, but also to some incorrect predictions. Children using Rule 2 similarly predict that the side with the most weights will drop, but when the number of weights is equal on both sides, they then consider the distance from the scale's midpoint. With Rule 3, children use both the weight and the distance dimensions; they predict that the side with either more weights *or* greater distance from the center will go down. If one side has more weights and the other side has greater distance, they muddle through the problem. Finally, children using Rule 4 make the appropriate computations of weight and distance, thus deriving the correct answer regardless of how the weights are distributed across the scale.

Siegler (1976) reported that 88% of children 5 to 17 years of age consistently applied one (or several) of these four rules in solving balance-scale problems. Most 5-year-olds used Rule 1, whereas 9-year-olds most often used Rules 2 or 3. Adolescents (13 to 17 years of age) usually used Rule 3, with very few children ever using the most sophisticated Rule 4. Perhaps somewhat surprisingly, most college students also rely on Rule 3, with only a minority of them using the most sophisticated Rule 4 (and the only one that will consistently produce a correct answer) (Siegler, 1981). This use of systematic rules breaks down on the balance-scale problem when younger children are tested. Siegler (1981) reported that none of the 3-year-olds he tested, and only about half of the 4-year-olds, used any discernible rule. The problem was apparently beyond their comprehension, and they were unable to generate even the simplest rule (more weights win) to solve these problems. Other studies have confirmed this sequence (Amsel et al., 1996; Jansen & van der Maas, 2002), and Siegler (1981) reports similar sequences following similar rules for a variety of tasks (for example, probability judgment, conservation, judging the projection of shadows).

Siegler (1996; Siegler & Chen, 2002) has since modified his view of children's problem solving, proposing that, instead of a stage-like progression, children have a variety of strategies available to them to solve problems at any one time, and that these strategies "compete" for use. (See the discussion of Siegler's *adaptive strategy choice model* in Chapter 6.) There is much evidence in the recent problem-solving literature to suggest that Siegler is right, and support for his model from the realm of arithmetic will be discussed in Chapter 14.

Learning to Follow Rules

Philip Zelazo and his colleagues have focused on pre-school children's ability to follow simple sets of rules and propose that following relatively arbitrary sets of rules is a reflection of consciousness and cognitive self-control (Zelazo, 2000; Zelazo et al., 1997). In an early experiment, Philip Zelazo and J. Steven Reznick (1991) gave children between the ages of 31 and 36 months of age a sorting task to complete. Children were shown sets of pictures and given two rules to follow: "If it's something found *inside* the house, then it goes in this box. If it's something found *outside* the house, then it goes in that box." Pictures included a variety of objects, some of which were obviously "inside" things (bed, TV), and others that were obviously "outside" things (snowman, plane). Children were also given a "knowledge" task. Now, instead of having to sort each object into one of two boxes, they were shown each card and simply asked, "Is this something found inside the house or is it found outside?" All children performed well on the knowledge

task (that is, they answered correctly when asked if an object belonged "inside" or "outside"). However, only the oldest children (36 months) could put this knowledge into action, sorting the cards correctly into boxes. In contrast, the younger groups of children (31- and 33.5-month-olds) did not sort items correctly, despite "knowing" to which category each item belonged. Later research indicated that 32-month-old children similarly failed the sorting task (and passed the knowledge task) despite having each item labeled ("This is a bed, where does it go?"), being reminded of the rules ("Remember, if it goes inside, then you put it here, and if it goes outside you put it here"), and receiving feedback and rewards for correct responding (Zelazo, Reznick, & Piñon, 1995).

These findings indicate that 36-month-old children can follow an arbitrary rule system, whereas younger children have a difficult time doing so, despite *knowing* the rules. However, 3-year-old children's ability to follow and coordinate rules is far from fully developed. This is indicated by experiments using the *dimensional card-sorting task*, discussed briefly in Chapter 5 (Zelazo, Frye, & Rapus, 1996). In this task, children are shown sets of cards that vary on two dimensions. Figure 12-3 provides an example of the cards used in these experiments. Children are shown two target cards, a yellow car and a green flower, for instance. When playing the color game, they are told that all the yellow cards go here (with the yellow car) and all the green cards go there (with the green flower). Children then are given a series of test cards (for instance, yellow flowers and green cars), and are asked to sort them by color. This most children do easily. Then children are told they are going to play a new game, the shape game. (For half the children the shape game is played first, and for the other half, the color game is played first.) In the shape game, children are to place cars in this box (with the yellow car) and flowers in that box (with the green flower). These are called *switch trials* because the rules have been switched (from sorting on the basis of color to shape, or vice versa). Now, most 3-year-old children fail, continuing to sort the cards according to the original dimension. Yet, when asked what the new rule is, most can easily and correctly tell the experimenter. That is,

Target Cards

Test Cards

FIGURE 12-3 Dimensional card-sorting task. Children are to sort cards initially by one dimension (color) and later by a second dimension (shape). SOURCE: Zelazo, P. D., Frye, D., & Rapus, T. (1996). An age-related dissociation between knowing rules and using them. *Cognitive Development, 11,* 37–63. Copyright © 1996, reprinted with permission from Elsevier.

like the 32-month-olds for the simpler task (Zelazo & Reznick, 1991), 3-year-olds can verbalize the rule but cannot execute it. By 4 years of age, most children do fine on both tasks.

Why do children have difficulties on these tasks, and what develops so that by 4 and 5 years of age most children can follow simple rule systems relatively easily? One thing to look at on these tasks is the type of errors children make. Children tend to persist in making responses they had learned earlier, termed *perseverative errors* (Zelazo et al., 1995; Zelazo et al., 1996), and this suggests that one source of their problem is poor inhibitory control (Harnishfeger & Bjorklund, 1993). That is, children have learned a response in this context and have a difficult time not making that response (sort by color) when the rules change (now sort by shape). Although I'm convinced that children's developing inhibitory abilities play a role in their use of rules, it cannot be the entire answer. For example, Zelazo and his colleagues (1996, Experiment 2) reported that 3-year-olds made perseverative errors on the dimensional card-sorting task after only one trial on the original dimension. That is, it was not necessary for children to acquire a well-learned response before they made errors on the switch trials.

What, then, accounts for the development of rule use during the preschool years? According to Zelazo and his colleagues, children gain increasing conscious control of their problem solving, and this is captured by the **cognitive complexity and control (CCC) theory** (Zelazo, 2000; Zelazo & Frye, 1997). Much like the distinction between implicit and different levels of explicit representation in Annette Karmiloff-Smith's (1992) theory (see Chapter 4), Zelazo and Frye propose that there are age-related changes in the complexity of rule systems that children can represent. According to Zelazo et al. (1997), developmental differences in *reflection* give children increased control of their behavior and cognition. "Reflection is defined as a recursive process whereby the contents of consciousness become an object of consciousness so that they can be operated on and modified . . . [H]igher order rules mediate reflective awareness of lower order rules and make possible the deliberate selection of lower order rules for use. In the absence of a higher order rule, children will perseverate on whichever lower order rules are most compelling" (1997, p. 221). In other words, children acquire rules early on and can follow them in certain situations. But coordinating rules requires greater conscious reflection, and this develops during the preschool years. It is interesting to see the parallel in development between rule use that Zelazo and his colleagues reported and theory of mind research discussed in Chapter 9. Although speculative, it appears that a single representational system might underlie cognition in these seemingly different areas.

Tool Use

People solve many of the problems they encounter by using tools. Actually, tool use is so common in problem solving that it's easy to take its use for granted. We are one of only a handful of species that uses tools to any significant degree. Not that long ago tool use was considered a defining feature of *Homo sapiens*. We now know that many other species use tools to solve problems and that chimpanzees, like humans, actually make tools (for example, the sticks used in termite fishing) (Whiten et al., 1999). This does not lessen, however, the significance of tool use in humans, and given its significance, it's a bit surprising that the development of tool use has not received more research attention. By the time children are 3 or 4 years old, they are using many of the tools a culture offers on a regular basis, such as forks, spoons, chopsticks, pencils, hammers, or scissors. As such, the origins of tool use must be sought in infancy and the preschool years. How is it that children come to use other objects (that is, tools) to solve problems? What factors are involved in early tool use, and how might they relate to the cognitive functioning both in infancy and in later childhood?

As discussed earlier in the chapter, infants are solving problems and displaying goal-directed behavior well before their first birthdays. And as was illustrated in Willatts' research (1990) reported previously, infants will manipulate one object (pulling a blanket toward them) to achieve a goal (obtaining a toy that was on the far end of the blanket). But can we actually say in this case that infants were using the blanket as a tool? After all, the toy was already on the blanket. That their behavior was goal directed is clear, and they obviously used one behavior (pulling on the blanket) in the service of another (obtaining the toy). But I would hesitate to call this a demonstration of tool use. Yet, children's eventual use of tools to solve problems may have its origins in infants' manipulation of their physical world.

Jeffrey Lockman recently articulated this position, arguing, "the origins of tool use in humans can be found during much of the first year of life, in the perception-action routines that infants repeatedly display as they explore their environments" (2000, p. 137). According to Lewis, tool use develops continuously during infancy and early childhood and should be thought of as the gradual process of discovery and exploration, rather than resulting from the emergence of new representational skills; it develops from infants' interactions with objects in the real world (for example, seeing what objects "do," hitting two objects together), often to obtain some perceptual outcome, such as noise. In the process, children learn how objects relate together, and learn,

often through trial and error, how best to manipulate one object (a spoon, for example) in relation to other objects (various types of food, for example) to achieve specific goals (getting food to one's mouth).

The Development of Tool Use in Young Children

According to Piaget (1954), the first signs of tool use in infants are seen around their first birthdays. But subsequent research indicated that infants are able to use tools earlier than Piaget proposed. Most tool-use research with infants and young children uses a variant of the lure-retrieval task, first developed by Wolfgang Köhler (1925) for use with chimpanzees, in which a desired object is placed out of the child's reach and a number of potential tools are available to use to retrieve the object. Infants as young as 9 and 10 months of age are able to use tools to solve lure-retrieval problems, although performance is influenced by features such as physical proximity (performance is greater when the tool is close to the target item) and perceptual similarity (performance is greater when the tool and lure are of contrasting colors and textures) (Bates, Carlson-Luden, & Bretherton, 1980).

In a study with slightly older children by Zhe Chen and Robert Siegler (2000), 1.5- and 2.5-year-old children were shown an out-of-reach toy and a sets of toy tools, only one of which could be used to get the toy. The set up for their experiments is shown in Figure 12-4. As can be seen from the figure, only one tool, the rake, was both long enough and had the appropriate shape to retrieve the toy. Children sat with their parents and, for three consecutive trials, an experimenter urged them to get the toy. If they did not retrieve the toy after these trials, some children were given hints about using the tool (hint condition), whereas others saw the experimenter retrieve the toy with the appropriate tool (model condition). Children were then given a second (and third) set of trials using different tools and toys.

First, although older children (about 30 months) were more likely to use the tools to retrieve the toy before any instruction (hint or model) than were

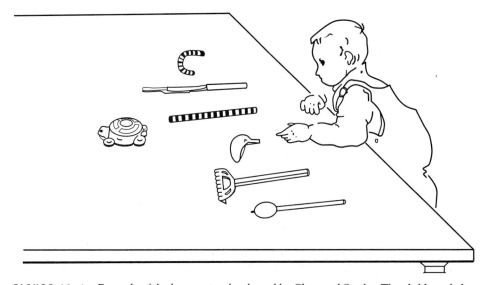

FIGURE 12-4 Example of the lure-retrieval task used by Chen and Siegler. The child needed to choose the appropriate tool (here, the rake) to retrieve that toy (here, the turtle). SOURCE: Chen, Z., & Siegler, R. S. (2000). Across the great divide: Bridging the gap between understanding of toddlers' and older children's thinking. *Monographs of the Society for Research in Child Development* 65 (Issue no. 2, Serial No. 261). Reprinted with permission of the Society for Research in Child Development.

younger children (about 21 months), even these older children retrieved the toy successfully only 15% of the time. However, following the hint or modeling, even the youngest group of children used the tool to retrieve the toys.

Chen and Siegler also examined the types of strategies children used to get the toy. The *forward strategy* involved the children leaning forward to reach the toy with their hands, the *indirect strategy* involved turning to their parents for help, and the *tool strategy* involved using one of the tools. Figure 12-5 shows changes in strategy use over the three trials (1, 2, and 3 in the figure) on each of the three problems (A, B, and C in the figure). As can be seen, the incidence of tool use increased over the problems, although children continued to use the forward strategy on the same trials they used the tool strategy. Thus, these young children, although not spontaneously using tools to retrieve the out-of-reach toy initially, could do so easily after receiving a simple

hint or demonstration and generalized their new-found skill to a similar, but new, task.

As these results illustrate, young children can learn to use tools by instruction (the hint condition) or through social learning (the modeling condition). However, as we'll see in greater detail in the next chapter, not all social learning is created equal. For example, preschool children who watch a model use a tool to solve a problem will imitate the target behavior and continue to do so even when those behaviors do not produce functional outcomes (Nagell, Olguin, & Tomasello, 1993; Whiten et al., 1996). This suggests that the children may not understand the intention of the adults for using these tools, but were merely mimicking the modeled behavior. A recent experiment by Stephen Want and Paul Harris (2001) suggests that this interpretation may be true for the youngest children, but likely not for older preschoolers. In their study, 2- and 3-year-old children watched as an adult attempted to remove a

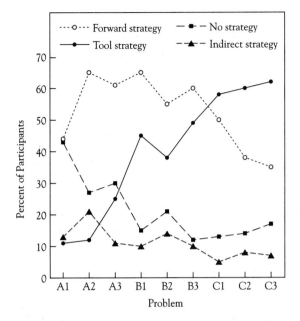

FIGURE 12-5 Percentage of children who used each strategy on the pretraining trials of the Chen and Siegler (2000) study. SOURCE: Chen, Z., & Siegler, R. S. (2000). Across the great divide: Bridging the gap between understanding of toddlers' and older children's thinking. *Monographs of the Society for Research in Child Development 65* (Issue no. 2, Serial No. 261). Reprinted with permission of the Society for Research in Child Development.

treat from a tube using a stick to push the treat out the end of the tube. Successful retrieval depended on which side of the tube the stick was inserted: If the model (or child) inserted the stick from the wrong side, the treat fell through a hole and was lost. When children were shown both a correct and incorrect solution to the problems, 3-year-olds were later able to imitate the actions to get the treat. Two-year-old children, in contrast, were essentially at chance on this task, suggesting that they did not fully understand the relationship between the model's actions with the tool and the outcome, but simply copied the behavior of the model (mimicry), resulting in chance performance. Thus, even though young children can learn to use a tool, success at solving a problem depends on other factors, such as understanding the relation between behavior with the tool and various outcomes.

Tool Use and Object-Oriented Play

Many factors influence children's tool use, with social factors (that is, modeling or instructions) being important. But recall from the Chen and Siegler (2000) study that few 1- and 2-year-old children spontaneously used the tools placed in front of them to retrieve the out-of-reach object, although older children were somewhat more likely to use a tool than were younger children. Recall also Lockman's contention that children's tool use is an outgrowth of the their "perception-action routines that infants repeatedly display as they explore their environments" (2000, p. 137). Might there be a relationship between children's interaction with objects, as seen during play, for instance, and tool use? Some researchers have thought so, proposing, for example, that object-oriented, or constructive, play should enhance problem solving by creating a flexible cognitive set whereby children learn that materials can be used in a variety of ways and by helping them develop generalized approaches for solving problems (e.g., Bruner, 1972; Cheyne & Rubin, 1983). In a similar vein, Peter Smith proposed that object manipulation and exploration may prepare children to use tools "over and above what could be learnt through observation, imitation, and goal-directed practice" (1982, p. 151).

Is there any evidence for this position? Several studies using a lure-retrieval task report that children who had the opportunity to play with the tools before being exposed to the task performed better than did children not given such an opportunity (Cheyne & Rubin, 1983; Simon & Smith, 1983). However, this effect could be due simply to familiarization with the specific objects to be used as tools in the later lure-retrieval task rather than to object-oriented play, per se. In a study that examined children's object-oriented play in a free-play session with different materials than those used on the lure-retrieval task, 3-year-olds who engaged in more object-oriented play also showed better performance on the tool-use task, supporting the relation between object-oriented play and tool use (Gredlein, Bjorklund, & Hickling, 2003). What's also interesting is that several studies have found that boys engage in more object-oriented play than girls do (see Geary, 1998), and they also tend to perform better on simple tool-use tasks, at least initially (Chen & Siegler, 2000; Cheyne & Rubin, 1983). Some have speculated that the gender difference observed in object-oriented play and its hypothesized relation to tool use is an old one that was selected over evolutionary time to accommodate males' greater use of tools in hunting. According to Geary, "From this perspective, the sex difference in manipulative and exploratory object-oriented play reflects an evolved bias in children's activities, so that boys, more so than girls, play in ways that elaborate the skeletal competencies associated with the engineering modules and later tool use" (1998, p. 238).

Children seem to use tools to solve problems soon after the first glimmers of goal-directed behavior appear. As problem-solving abilities in general, children's effective use of tools increases with age and is influenced by a host of factors, including perceptual similarity and physical proximity (Bates et al., 1980), social learning skills (Want & Harris, 2001), and possibly even their tendencies to engage in object-oriented play (Gredlein et al., 2003). But once children learn about tools, tool use seems to become part of children's basic toolkit of problem-solving skills and an essential component of human cognition.

Planning

An important part of problem solving is *planning*. In many complicated problems, several steps must be executed before a goal can be reached. There is little planning involved for an 8-month-old, whose goal is to get a toy by pulling on a cloth. But as the problems get more complicated, so does the need for planning. For example, in the Bullock and Lütkenhaus study (1988) discussed earlier, children had to plan which blocks they would select first and which

needed to be used only later. The problem had several aspects, and although a trial-and-error procedure might have eventually produced a correct answer, it rarely did for the youngest children.

Planning is difficult for young children, and they rarely do it, or at least rarely do it well. There are many reasons for this, associated with children's limited cognitive abilities. Shari Ellis and Robert Siegler (1997) listed several reasons for young children's generally poor planning abilities:

1. Planning often requires inhibition of currently active behavior. As you may recall from our discussion of the development of inhibition/resistance from interference in Chapter 5, these abilities increase with age, with preschool children often having difficulty inhibiting an ongoing activity (Harnishfeger & Bjorklund, 1993).

2. Planning takes time, and children often prefer to do a task quickly than to do it accurately. This, in part, might be facilitated by adults' reactions to children's problem-solving attempts. Adults often praise children for the attempt, telling them that they have performed better than they actually have. Related to this, children's goals in solving a problem might not be identical to that of an adult, and they might not have the metacognitive ability to evaluate how successfully they achieved their goal, tending to overestimate their performance (Bjorklund, 1997a).

3. Planning is often viewed as difficult, time-consuming, and subjectively unpleasant. This is true not only for children but also for adults. Planning is a special type of strategy (or metastrategy), and strategies are used when people cannot solve a problem using less effortful procedures. If you have reason to believe that the solution to a problem will "just come to you" as you fiddle with the components (such as putting your new barbecue grill together without reading the instructions), then why spend the time planning? A plan (as many strategies) should be used only when solving the problem can't be done without one.

4. When children do generate a plan, they are not always successful. Why spend the time and effort when the outcome is uncertain?

5. It might be more fun to "wing it." Problem solving can present novel activities for children, and the implementation of a plan might make the process less enjoyable.

Such a description makes it seem as if young children approach problems in a willy-nilly fashion, and if they're lucky, eventually bump into the right solution. There is a bit of trial-and-error learning in most problem solving, but rarely are children's approaches to a problem completely random. Children tend to select problem-solving strategies that are appropriate (if not always optimal) for the task at hand, and often modify their strategies as they progress through the problem (Siegler, 1996). However, young children rarely demonstrate the forward-looking approach that older children and adults often do when solving a complicated problem.

Preschool children do show signs of some planning in some situations, of course. For example, several studies have asked preschoolers to "plan" a trip to a grocery store (Gauvain & Rogoff, 1989; Hudson, Shapiro, & Sosa, 1995). In one study, children were asked to get several items from a model grocery store (Gauvain & Rogoff, 1989). Most 5-year-olds did an efficient item-by-item search, but older children were more likely to display signs of explicit planning by looking through the entire store and then searching for specific objects based on where they believed they would be located. The result was a more effective search. In other research, Judith Hudson and her colleagues (1995) asked 3-, 4-, and 5-year-olds to plan a trip to a grocery store (or to the beach). Children were also told of potential mishaps that could occur (you forgot to bring your shopping list) and asked how they might remedy or prevent the situation. Hudson et al. reported that recognizable plans were relatively rare for the 3- and 4-year-olds, but quite common for the 5-year-old children. Age differences were also found both in children's responses to remedy and prevent a mishap. Children of all ages were able to suggest some remedy to a potential problem (although the number of plans to remedy mishaps did increase with age), but very few 3- and 4-year-old children suggested plans to prevent a mishap. Only the 5-year-old children made a substantial number of prevention plans.

In other research, 4- and 5-year-old children were asked to plan a route through a large space to retrieve a set of objects as quickly as possible (Fabricius, 1988). Children were familiarized with the space and then asked to retrieve the objects "the quick way." Fabricius concluded that the 5-year-old children engaged in *forward search*, in which a person envisions a series of moves that will achieve a partial solution. In other words, 5-year-olds had a plan that permitted them to foresee the consequences of their moves and thus made relatively few "backtracking" moves during their search. The 4-year-olds were less apt to do this, and when they did engage in forward search, they did so inconsistently.

One example of a task where planning is important is the Tower of Hanoi problem. The three-disk version of this problem is illustrated in Figure 12-6. Children are shown a structure with three pegs, with three different sized disks on one peg (the one to the far left, for instance). The task is to get all the disks to the peg on the opposite side by moving only one disc at a time and obeying the rule that a larger disk cannot be placed on a smaller disk. This task can be solved in seven moves, which are indicated by the arrows in Figure 12-6. It would seem that planning is important in solving this problem. Having an idea in mind ahead of time (or figuring one out soon after the task begins) seems to be associated with the likelihood of finding the right solution quickly.

Several researchers have emphasized that the first move children make on the Tower of Hanoi task is important and reflects and influences their planning on the task (Klahr & Robinson, 1981). However, Gary Fireman (1996) failed to find any relation between making the optimal first move (move number 2 in Figure 12-6) and later success on the three-disk problem with first- and second-grade children. Children who never solved the problem were just as likely to make a correct first move as were children who eventually solved the problem within the 3-minute time limit. Does this mean that planning is actually *not* important in the Tower of Hanoi problem? Not at all. This is a difficult task for children of this age, and most of the planning on this task seems to come after a few moves are made as children

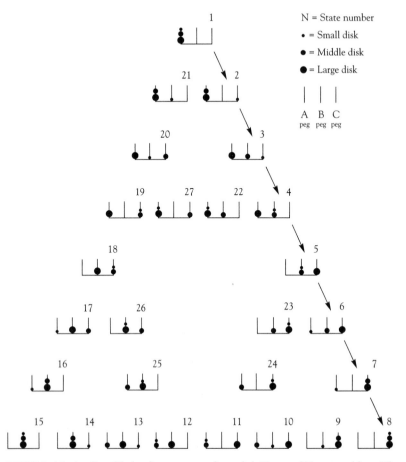

FIGURE 12-6 Possible legal moves on a three-disk Tower of Hanoi problem. The arrows on the far right show the most efficient solution path. SOURCE: Fireman, G. (1996). Developing a plan for solving a problem: A representational shift. *Cognitive Development*, *11*, 107–122. Copyright © 1996, reprinted with permission from Elsevier.

become familiar with the problem and the range of strategies they have available to them to solve the problem. Before planning could occur, children needed to learn, in a hands-on way, the constraints associated with the problem. According to Fireman, at the start of the task "children were not concerned with the strategy of reducing the problem depth or attaining a subgoal. Instead, children's initial actions explored the range of legal and illegal moves. Apparently, the children had to experience the instructions in action, despite their initial, sponta-

neous declaration that they understood the goal of the problem" (1996, p. 120). Planning for these children came only after becoming acquainted with the problem.

Rudiments of planning may be found in early childhood, but even older children and adults are often reluctant to engage in planning (Chalmers & Lawrence, 1993). In general, planning is a late developing ability and many of us, adults as well as children, approach many problems with as little planning as possible.

Reasoning

Reasoning is a special type of problem solving. Reasoning usually requires that one make an *inference*. That is, to reason, one must go beyond the information given. It is not enough to figure out the rules associated with some game. That's problem solving, but not necessarily reasoning. In reasoning, one must take the evidence presented and arrive at a new conclusion based on that evidence. The result is often new knowledge (DeLoache et al., 1998).

We use some forms of reasoning in our everyday lives, and we are so accustomed to thinking this way that we are often unaware of it. Other types of reasoning are highly formalized (termed *formal reasoning*), which most of us do not engage in regularly, and when we do we are certainly conscious of it. In the following sections, I discuss three types of reasoning: analogical reasoning, formal reasoning, and scientific reasoning.

Analogical Reasoning

Perhaps the type of reasoning that people are most familiar with is **analogical reasoning.** Analogical reasoning involves using something you already know to help you understand something you don't know yet. Analogical reasoning involves **relational mapping**—the application of what one knows about one set of elements (the relation of A to B) to relations about different elements (the relation of C to D). Classic analogical reasoning problems are stated A:B :: C:?. For example, *dog* is to *puppy* as *cat* is to ?. The answer here, of course, is *kitten*. By knowing the relation between the first two elements in the problem (a *puppy* is a baby *dog*), one can use that knowledge to complete the analogy for a new item (*cat*). Analogies are thus based on *similarity relations*. One must understand the similarity between dogs and cats and puppies and kittens if one is to solve this analogy.

How basic is analogical reasoning to cognitive development? Is it an early or late developing ability? How well adults are able to solve analogies is related

to general intelligence as measured by IQ tests (Sternberg, 1985), and one advantage gifted children have over nongifted children is in their ability to solve analogies (Muir-Broaddus, 1995). This suggests that it is a complex skill that is influenced by a variety of other cognitive abilities and does not peak early in life. According to Piagetian theory (Inhelder & Piaget, 1958), analogical reasoning is a sophisticated ability that is not seen until adolescence. Others, however, have proposed that analogical thinking serves as the basis for other reasoning and problem-solving tasks (Halford, 1993), and might be present at birth (Goswami, 1996).

How can there be such divergence of opinion about when analogical reasoning is first seen in development? Part of the problem lies in the nature of the problems children are asked to solve. In cases when successful problem solving is not seen until late childhood or adolescence, the problems often involve objects or concepts with which children are unfamiliar. Perhaps more than any other factor, knowledge of the objects and relations among objects in analogical reasoning problems is paramount in determining whether a child will solve or fail to solve a problem. Other factors also contribute to a child's success on analogical-reasoning problems, including memory for the premises, availability of mental resources, representation of the relations, and metacognitive knowledge (see DeLoache et al., 1998; Gentner, 1989). In the following section, I review children's ability to solve analogical-reasoning problems and look at some of the factors that contribute to this developmental progression.

Analogical Reasoning in Young Children

Analogical reasoning involves using what you know about solving one problem to solve a related problem. One would expect this ability to increase with age, as knowledge, mental capacity, memory, and other factors increase with age, but there is no a priori reason that this ability should not be present very early in life. In fact, Usha Goswami (1996) has proposed the **relational primacy hypothesis,** proposing that analogical reasoning is available early in infancy.

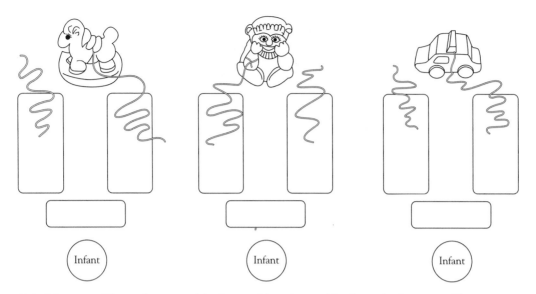

FIGURE 12-7 The configuration of the three problems 1-year-old infants solved. SOURCE: Chen, Z., Sanchez, R. P., & Campbell, T. (1997). From beyond to within their grasp: The rudiments of analogical problem solving in 10- and 13-month-olds. *Developmental Psychology, 33,* 790–801. Copyright © 1997 by the American Psychological Association. Reprinted with permission.

In one of the few experiments to assess analogical reasoning in infants, Zhe Chen, Rebecca Sanchez, and Tammy Campbell (1997) tested 1-year-old infants (Experiment 1). The basic task involved placing a desirable toy out of reach of the infant, with a barrier between the baby and the toy. Two strings, one attached to the toy and one not, were also out of the infant's reach, but each string was on a cloth that *was* within reach. To get the toy, the infants had to pull the cloth toward them and then pull the string attached to the toy. (This is similar to the task described earlier by Willatts [1990].) There were three similar tasks, although the toy, the barrier, and the color of the cloth varied among the three tasks. These are illustrated in Figure 12-7. If infants did not solve the problem after 100 seconds, their parents modeled the correct solution for them. The primary research question concerned whether, after solving an initial problem, either with or without parental modeling, would the infants see the similarity with the later problems and be more apt to solve them? That is, would infants use analogical reasoning to solve the subsequent problems?

Few children solved the first problem spontaneously (most required help from a parent). However, the percentage of infants solving the problems increased from 29% for the first problem, to 43% for the second, and 67% for the third (Experiment 1). Infants' problem solving was also rated for "efficiency," with higher scores reflecting a greater goal-directed approach, compared with a trial-and-error approach to the problem. As can be seen in Figure 12-8, efficiency increased steadily over the three problems.

The research by Chen and his colleagues (1997) reveals that 1-year-olds are able to use the similarity between tasks analogously to solve problems. However, this is very different from the classic problems used in research. The first study to demonstrate analogical reasoning in young children using a more traditional task was performed by Keith Holyoak, Ellen Junn, and Dorrit Billman (1984). In their study, preschool and kindergarten children had to move some gumballs in one bowl on a table to another, out-of-reach bowl, without leaving their chairs. The children had various objects available to them that they

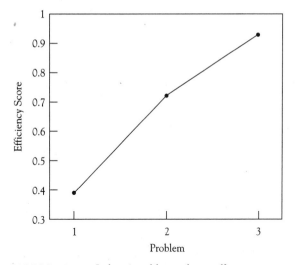

FIGURE 12-8 Infants' problem-solving efficiency scores. SOURCE: Chen, Z., Sanchez, R. P., & Campbell, T. (1997). From beyond to within their grasp: The rudiments of analogical problem solving in 10- and 13-month-olds. *Developmental Psychology, 33,* 790–801. Copyright © 1997 by the American Psychological Association. Adapted with permission.

could use to solve the problem, including scissors, an aluminum cane, tape, string, and a sheet of paper. Before solving the problem, children heard a story about a genie who had a similar problem. The genie's problem was to move some jewels from one bottle within his reach to another bottle, out of his reach. One way in which he solved this problem was to roll his magic carpet into a tube and pass the jewels down the tube into the second bottle. Another solution that other children heard was to use his magic staff to pull the second bottle closer to him. (This latter solution is analogous to the lure-retrieval task discussed in the section on tool use.) After hearing the stories, children were told to think of as many ways that they could to solve *their* problem—to get the gumballs from one bowl to another. About half of the preschool and kindergarten children solved the "magic staff" problem, and the remainder did so after a hint. That is, these 4.5- to 6-year-old children were able to reason by analogy. However, they were less successful with the "magic carpet" analogy, suggesting that

young children's performance on analogical reasoning tasks is highly dependent on the similarity between objects. The "magic staff" and the aluminum cane were more perceptually similar to one another, Holyoak and his colleagues argued, than were the "magic carpet" and the sheet of paper, making the former analogy easier to use than the latter for these young children. But the basic finding that preschool children could use the similarity in one story to solve an analogous problem suggests that such reasoning is well within the capability of these children, counter to the traditional Piagetian position.

Not all similarity is perceptual, however. Sometimes the similarity between objects is *relational*. Usha Goswami and Ann Brown (1990) illustrated this by showing 4-, 5-, and 9-year-old children sets of pictures of the A:B :: C:? type. Children were given four alternatives and had to choose which of the four best completed the analogy. Figure 12-9 shows an example of a problem used in this study. In this problem, children must discover the relation between bird and nest (a bird lives in a nest) and find the proper match for dog (here, doghouse). Chance performance on this task was 25%, and children of all ages performed greater than expected by chance (59%, 66%, and 94% correct for the 4-, 5-, and 9-year-olds, respectively). Note that children were not solving the problem based on *perceptual similarity*. The bird and dog look nothing alike, nor do the nest and the doghouse. To solve this problem, they must do so on the basis of *relational similarity*—the relation between the A and B terms (bird and nest) is used to find the best match for the C term (dog). This is clearly a more advanced form of analogical reason than that demonstrated by the 1-year-old infants in Chen et al.'s (1997) study.

However, children might not have been using analogical reasoning to solve this problem. Maybe they were simply selecting the item that "went best with" the dog. This apparently was not the case, however. Children in a control group were asked exactly this question: pick the one that "goes best" with the C term (in this case, dog). When asked to do this, children were no more likely to select the analogical choice (doghouse) than to select a high associate (bone). Thus, children's performance on the

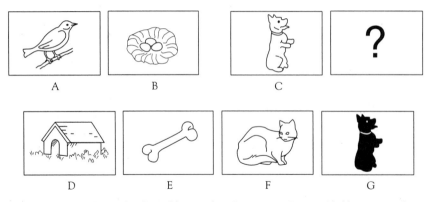

FIGURE 12-9 Example of a problem used in Goswami & Brown. Children must select from the set of pictures in bottom row (pictures D through G) the one that best completes the visual analogy on the top row. (The correct answer is D.) SOURCE: Goswami, U., & Brown, A. L. (1990). Higher-order structure and relational reasoning: Contrasting analogical and thematic relations. *Cognition, 36,* 207–226. Reprinted with permission of Elsevier Science.

analogical-reasoning task cannot be attributed to responding on the basis of strictly associative or thematic relations but, rather, reflects the use of true analogical reasoning.

The type of errors they made indicated that at least some young children were solving these problems using true analogical reasoning. For example, Goswami reported a 4-year-old child, Lucas, who, after seeing the *bird:nest :: dog:?* problem, figured out what the answer should be without seeing the alternatives. However, what he figured was wrong. "Lucas first told us that the correct solution was *puppy*. He argued, quite logically, 'Bird lays eggs in her nest . . . dog—dogs lay babies, and the babies are—umm— and the name of the babies is puppy'" (1996, p. 102). Lucas quickly changed his mind when he saw that a puppy was not among the alternatives, rethought the problem, and identified the "lives in" relation. However, his first idea was also relational. He had simply identified a type of relation (*type of offspring*) different than that identified by the experimenters. Successful analogical reasoning requires identifying the "right" relation, but there can be many different relations existing between sets of items, and, outside of the laboratory or classroom, there might not be clear-cut "right" and "wrong" answers.

Factors Affecting Children's Analogical Reasoning

According to Goswami's (1996) analogical primacy view, the ability to reason by analogy is present in infancy. Even if we accept such a position, however, many factors influence children's success on any given task. For example, Graeme Halford (1993) has proposed that analogical reasoning develops in a stage-like fashion reminiscent of Piaget, based on the availability of mental resources. A child's ability to symbolically represent concepts and relations will also affect whether and how a child will use analogical reasoning (see DeLoache et al., 1998).

Analogical reasoning and relational shift. Related to how children represent a problem are the types of relations they identify and base their reasoning on. For example, although Goswami and Brown's research (1990) indicates that young children *can* use analogies based on relational similarity, it does not mean that they do so easily, especially when they can form analogies based on perceptual similarity. Dedre Gentner (1989) has argued that a **relational shift** occurs in the development of analogical reasoning, in which young children are more likely to focus on perceptual similarity, whereas older children and adults focus more on relational similarity in solving problems. For example, infants and young children are more influenced by the surface similarity of objects, such as an object's shape. Older children, on the other hand, are more tuned to the underlying relation between sets of objects. For example, the better performance of the preschool children for the "magic staff" than for the "magic carpet" analogy in Holyoak and his colleagues' (1984) study was attributed to the greater perceptual similarity between the magic staff and the aluminum cane available to solve the "gumball" problem than between the magic carpet and the sheet of paper (for other examples, see Daehler & Chen, 1993; Pierce & Gholson, 1994). When there is a conflict between object similarity and relational similarity, young children's ability to use relational similarity is hindered (see Goswami, 1996).

Knowledge. One factor that affects whether children will use relational similarity to solve an analogical-reasoning problem is knowledge, or familiarity. How familiar are children with the underlying relations used to make the analogy? Remember, the function of analogical reasoning is to use something you know to help you understand something you don't know. From this perspective, analogical reasoning can only make sense if a child is familiar with the base relation. You might get a better understanding of the human nervous system, for example, if you see it as analogous to electrical circuits. But if you know nothing about electrical circuits, it won't help you understand the nervous system at all, no matter how well developed your analogical reasoning abilities are. I think it is fair to say that all major theorists acknowledge the importance of knowledge and familiarity on the development of analogical reasoning, although they might disagree on the exact role that knowledge plays in such development (see DeLoache et al., 1998; Goswami, 1996).

Goswami (1995) illustrated the role of familiarity by using a familiar children's story as the basis for analogical reasoning. Goswami used *Goldilocks and the Three Bears* ("The Daddy Bear has all the big things, the Mummy Bear has all the medium-sized things, and the Baby Bear has all the tiny things") to help children make *transitive mappings.* A transitive relation involves at least three objects varying in some dimension, such as length. If object A is longer than object B, and object B is longer than object C, then object A must be longer than object C (that is, A > B > C). Can young children use the transitive relation on one dimension as a basis for mapping transitive relations on another dimension? Or, stated somewhat differently, can children map the transitive relation from one dimension (the Daddy, Mummy, and Baby bear) to another (size, for instance)?

In Goswami's (1995) study, 3- and 4-year-old children were asked to use the relation in the Goldilocks story (Daddy Bear > Mummy Bear > Baby Bear) to classify objects that differed in quantity (a lot versus a medium amount versus a little of pizza, candy, or lemonade), or to rank order (three levels) certain phenomena on the basis of loudness (footsteps), pitch (of voices), temperature (of porridge), saltiness (of porridge), width (of beds), or height (of mirrors). Four-year-olds generally performed well on all these tasks, using the Three Bears analogy to map onto other dimensions. Three-year-olds did less well, although they performed above chance levels on most tasks, indicating that they, too, could use the familiar (perhaps less familiar to them than to the 4-year-olds) story as a basis for making analogical relations.

Metacognition. To what extent is explicit awareness of the relations between entities on analogical reasoning tasks important in solving problems? Can children think analogically but be unable to articulate what they are doing? Might such knowledge be *implicit,* and unavailable to consciousness? It certainly appears that the knowledge that the infants in the Chen et al. (1997) study had was implicit. These preverbal children's metacognitive understanding of the problem and their solutions to them was likely nonexistent. How important is metacognitive knowledge for analogical reasoning during childhood?

That analogical relations can be explicit to young children was illustrated by the example of 4-year-old Lucas discussed earlier, who generated an analogical relation (albeit an incorrect one) for the *bird:nest* ::

dog:? problem before seeing the alternatives. Successful training of analogical reasoning is often best accomplished when children receive explicit instruction about the rationale behind the training (Brown & Kane, 1988; Daehler & Chen, 1993), much as has been found in the training of memory strategies (see Chapter 6). This suggests, not at all surprisingly, that knowing what one is doing (that is, having metacognitive knowledge) facilitates analogical reasoning.

Ann Brown, Mary Kane, and their colleagues did one set of studies relevant to metacognitive knowledge (Brown & Kane, 1988; Brown, Kane, & Long, 1989), assessing children's **learning to learn** on a series of analogical reasoning tasks. Learning to learn refers to improvements in performance on new tasks as a result of performance on earlier tasks, during which time children learn a general rule or approach to problems. That is, participants learn a general set of rules that they can apply to new tasks, so that performance on later tasks is enhanced relative to performance on earlier tasks.

In Brown and Kane's studies, preschool children were given a series of problems similar to the "magic carpet" story used by Holyoak and his colleagues (1984). For example, some children were first given the genie problem. If they did not solve it, they were told about how rolling the "carpet" could be used to transport the jewels. They were then given a similar problem (the Easter Bunny needing to transport eggs by using a rolled up blanket), and then a third (a farmer transporting cherries using a rolled-up rug). Children who received this series of problems and were given the solution to a problem when they failed showed a large learning-to-learn effect. For the "rolling" solution, 46% of the children used analogical reasoning to solve the second problem, and 98% of the children did so for the third task. This compares with a control group, who received the three sets of "rolling" problems but who did not receive the hints. They showed only 20% transfer after the first problem and 39% after the second.

Does a learning-to-learn effect have to involve metacognition? Not necessarily. But some of the children's comments suggested that their improved performance on the later problems was the result of their awareness of analogical reasoning strategies. For example, one 4-year-old child in the Brown and Kane study, after solving two "rolling" problems, commented at the beginning of the third problem: "And all you need to do is get this thing rolled up? I betcha!" (1988, p. 517). Brown and Kane (1988) commented that children had developed a mind-set to look for analogies, expecting to extract some general rule to solve problems and to be able to use knowledge they acquired in one context elsewhere.

Formal Reasoning

To this point, we have examined children's informal reasoning, or the type of reasoning children might use in their everyday lives (even if the problems are invented by a psychologist). Informal reasoning is contrasted with formal reasoning. According to Judy DeLoache, Kevin Miller, and Sophia Pierroutsakos, "In **formal reasoning,** the *form* of an argument, not its semantic content, is crucial. Logical, not empirical, truth matters: The internal consistency of a set of premises and the conclusion drawn from them is all that counts, not whether or how they map onto the real world" (1998, p. 804). Why should such decontextualized reasoning be of interest to developmental psychologists, who are ostensibly concerned about children's intellectual development in the real world? The answer is that formal-reasoning ability has long been viewed as a hallmark of adult, and especially scientific, thinking. This is seen clearly in Piaget's account of adolescent thinking (Inhelder & Piaget, 1958). It is no accident that Piaget called this final stage of cognitive development *formal operations* (see Moshman, 1998). **Conditional reasoning** is the term typically used for problem solving when people must make logical inferences "whose truth value depends entirely on the supposed truth of given, and possibly arbitrary, premises," and, according to Henry Markovits and Pierre Barrouillet "is one of the clearest examples of a cognitive capacity that differentiates human and nonhuman species" (2002, p. 5).

Piaget proposed that not until 11 or 12 years of age is formal reasoning first seen and that the thinking of adults (and older adolescents) corresponds to a certain type of logical operation—specifically, **propositional logic.** Propositional logic is a form of symbolic logic that involves two or more factors (conventionally, P and Q), with each factor having two possible values (for instance, true or false). Take, for example, two coins, a penny and a dime. Each coin has two and only two possible values, heads and tails. In flipping these coins we have four possible combinations: both the penny and the dime are heads (P and Q), the penny is heads and the dime is tails (P and not Q), the penny is tails and the dime is heads (not P and Q), and both the penny and the dime are tails (not P and not Q).

These four alternatives can themselves be combined, resulting in 16 outcomes that are referred to as the 16 binary operations.[1] Piaget proposed that these correspond to mental operations characteristic of formal operational thought. One of these operations, implication, is found frequently in human discourse and is expressed as "P implies Q." This means that Q is true if P is true, or P implies Q "if and only if no interpretation makes [P] true and [Q] false" (Quine, 1972, p. 40). In everyday language, implication is expressed in "if . . . then" statements. Tests of implication usually take the following form:

1. If there is a P, then there is a Q.
2. There is a P.
3. There is a Q.

Subjects are to determine the validity of the third statement, which in this example is true. Conversely, there is the invalid form of implication, and tests of this are usually expressed as follows:

1. If there is a P, then there is a Q.
2. There is no P.
3. There is no Q.

In this case, the third statement is not necessarily true, for although P implies Q, the initial premise does not require that "not P implies not Q." For example, "If John passes calculus, then he will take his girlfriend out to dinner." Given this statement, the girlfriend can expect dinner if John passes calculus. Should John fail, however, dinner is not necessarily out of the question.

Based on observations from a variety of experimental tasks and the verbal reports of their participants, Inhelder and Piaget concluded that concrete operational children are unable to use the 16 binary operations to solve problems, whereas formal operational thinkers can use each of the 16 operations as the tasks demand.

A substantial amount of research has generally supported Piaget's view that formal, logical reasoning is not observed for most preadolescent children and increases during the teenage years (Markovits & Vachon, 1989; Müller, Overton, & Reene, 2001). But what about adults? Do *we* really think this way? Apparently not, at least not most of the time. For example, Scott Paris (1973) assessed the ability of children and adults to comprehend statements of propositional logic, including "if . . . then" implication statements. Paris reported that even 7-year-olds could answer correctly valid implications, for instance, "If there is a P, then there is a Q. There is a P. There is a Q" (true or false?). However, both 7-year-olds and adults performed poorly on the invalid implications, for example, "If there is a P, then there is a Q. There is no P. There is no Q" (true or false?). That is, concrete operational children cannot solve invalid forms of implication, but neither can college students. Rather, like children, adults tend to interpret the reasonableness of the problem ("John didn't say anything about taking his girlfriend out to dinner if he fails.").

Yet, as Paris (1973) demonstrated, even young children can reason logically for some problems in some situations. J. Hawkins and colleagues (1984) provided an interesting example of this by presenting verbal syllogisms to 4- and 5-year-old children. Syllogisms are problems that require deductive reasoning (a characteristic of formal reasoning) and are of the form:

1. Socrates was a man.
2. All men are mortal.
3. Socrates was mortal.

On such problems, participants are to discern the truth of the third statement given the first two. Note that the truth value of the third statement is based solely on the content of the first two, not on the basis of what one knows to be true of the real world. (Remember, formal reasoning is based on the *form* of the problem.) Piaget proposed that to solve syllogisms, the conclusions drawn from the premises "must be held to be true only by reason of the premises and quite independently of the empirical truth of these premises" (Piaget, 1969b, p. 32). Hawkins and his colleagues presented preschool children with syllogisms of three types: (1) *fantasy*, involving imaginary characters of which the children had no knowledge (for example, "Every banga is purple"); (2) *congruent*, in which the premises were consistent with children's world knowledge (for example, "Bears have big teeth"); and (3) *incongruent*, in which the premises were in contradiction to the children's knowledge (for example, "Glasses bounce when they fall"). Here are examples of a fantasy, congruent, and incongruent syllogism:

Fantasy Syllogism
    Every banga is purple.
    Purple animals sneeze at people.
    Do bangas sneeze at people?

Congruent Syllogism
    Bears have big teeth.
    Animals with big teeth can't read books.
    Can bears read books?

Incongruent Syllogism
    Glasses bounce when they fall.
    Everything that bounces is made of rubber.
    Are glasses made of rubber?

The children were given eight problems of each type, with some children being presented the set of fantasy problems first and others being presented the fantasy problems second or third.

In keeping with Piaget's observations, children consistently failed the incongruent problems (13% correct). They were not able to ignore what they know about the world in answering these questions. In other words, they were not able to think "formally," using only the *form* of the problem to generate an answer. Children's performance was excellent, however, for the congruent problems (94%). But such performance does not require any reasoning at all. Children could have used their world knowledge to answer the question ("Do bears read books? Of course not!"). In fact, when children's justifications of their answers to the congruent problems were ex-

amined, most of them (81%) were described as *empirical*, with reference being made to their practical world knowledge. Very few of their justifications were classified as *theoretical* (10%), in which reference was made only to the information presented in the problem.

But what about the fantasy questions? Here, performance is independent of children's past knowledge. The fantasy questions were about hypothetical characters, requiring, it would seem, formal reasoning. Children's performance on the fantasy problems was very high, particularly when these problems were presented first (94% correct). The percentage of correct answers was lower on these problems when the congruent or incongruent problems preceded them (66% correct). Furthermore, children's justifications on the fantasy problems were likely to be classified as theoretical when the fantasy problems were presented first (58%), although nontheoretical explanations predominated when the fantasy problems were presented later in the session (92% nontheoretical explanations).

One interpretation of these findings is that 4- and 5-year-old children possess rudiments for formal reasoning. However, this study also reveals the tenuous nature of such reasoning in young children. They consistently failed the incongruous problems. When their real-world knowledge conflicted with the *form* of the problem, they almost always went with what they know (generally not a bad strategy to follow). Yet, when imaginary characters were used, young children's responses and their justifications were indicative of formal reasoning (see also Markovits & Vachon, 1989). Nevertheless, children were easily biased away from such deductions when the fantasy problems were preceded by the congruent or incongruent problems. Obviously, formal reasoning is not well established in young children and is displayed only under optimal conditions. (Compare this with Fischer's skill theory, discussed in Chapter 4.)

Scientific Reasoning

Not all logical reasoning is decontextualized. Logic comes in handy frequently in everyday life, especially if you happen to make your living being a scientist. I discussed scientific reasoning briefly in Piaget's model of formal operations (Chapter 4). **Scientific reasoning** involves generating hypotheses about how something in the world works and then systematically testing those hypotheses. Basically, one uses scientific reasoning by identifying the factors that can affect a particular phenomenon (the rate at which a pendulum oscillates, as in the example provided in Chapter 4, for instance), and exhaustively varying one factor at a time while holding the other factors constant. Recall that Piaget proposed that scientific reasoning is not found until adolescence (Inhelder & Piaget, 1958). Subsequent research has not always supported Piaget's theories, but it is generally agreed that scientific reasoning is a late-developing ability that is not easily demonstrated by many adults (Kuhn, Amsel, & O'Loughlin, 1988). [Recall, however, that "theory theory" accounts of development propose that something akin to theory testing, and thus scientific reasoning, characterizes even infants and young children (Gopnik & Meltzoff, 1997).]

Let me provide an example from research by Deanna Kuhn and her colleagues (1988), who presented hypothetical information about the relation between certain foods and the likelihood of catching colds to sixth- and ninth-grade students and to adults of varying educational backgrounds. Participants were first interviewed to determine which foods they thought might be associated with colds. Then, over several trials, they were given a series of foods (for example, oranges, baked potatoes, cereal, Coca-Cola), each associated with an outcome (cold or no cold). Some foods were always associated with getting a cold (baked potatoes, for instance), some were always associated with not getting colds (cereal, for instance), and others were independent of getting colds (that is, sometimes they were associated with getting colds, and sometimes not). At least one outcome was consistent with a participant's initial opinion about the "healthiness" of a food, and one inconsistent with it.

Scientific reasoning involves hypotheses, but what is most crucial about the scientific method is that it involves *evidence*. Maybe you have grown up believing that eating chicken soup will make you healthy, but science requires that evidence, when available, be used to provide an answer. Initial responses on these questions were usually based on prior beliefs, but as more evidence accumulated, most adults increased their decisions based on that evidence. The adolescents, however, were much less apt to consider evidence in their decisions, but instead relied more frequently on extra-experimental beliefs (for example, "The juice makes a difference because my mother says orange juice is better for you"). In fact, 30% of the sixth graders never made a single spontaneous evidence-based response. Yet, when asked how they knew one food did or didn't have an effect, most participants of all ages were able to provide an evidence-based answer, although children were still less likely to do so than adults. This indicates that reasoning from evidence is something that sixth graders can do, but that they choose not to do spontaneously. It's also worth noting that the adults did not perform perfectly on these problems either. Only the most highly educated adults (philosophy graduate students) consistently solved these problems using the evidence that was presented.

Scientific reasoning can improve with practice. Several researchers have given participants of varying ages sets of scientific problems to solve in repeated testing sessions (Kuhn et al., 1995; Schauble, 1996). In these studies, participants' performance improved over sessions and generalized to different scientific problems (for example, from determining what factors affect the speed of a car to determining what factors influence school achievement). However, although participants of all ages showed improvements over sessions, preadolescent children showed fewer gains than adults did.

Some evidence even suggests that elementary school children can be trained to use scientific reasoning with explicit instruction and transfer such strategies to new tasks. Zhe Chen and David Klahr (1999) trained second-, third- and fourth-grade children to use the "control of variables strategy" (CVS), which essentially involves setting up experiments so that contrasts are made between experimental conditions, one at a time. This is essential in being able to assess a scientific hypothesis properly. Chen and Klahr provided children with both explicit training,

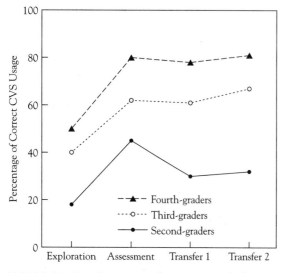

FIGURE 12-10 Percentage of correct control of variables strategy (CVS) usage by phase and grade for children receiving both explicit training and probes.
SOURCE: Chen, Z., & Klahr, D. (1999). All other things being equal: Acquisition and transfer of the control of variables strategy. *Child Development, 70,* 1098–1120. Reprinted with permission of the Society for Research in Child Development.

in which children received direct instruction in how to use the CVS, and implicit training via the use of probes, in which children were asked systematic questions about factors in the experiments as they were conducting them. Children performed hands-on experiments, testing, for example, factors that influence how far a ball will travel down an inclined plane (such as degree of the slope, surface of the ramp, length of the ramp, and type of ball). To assess transfer of training, children were then given new problems, one and two days after training. Figure 12-10 presents the percentage of correct CVS usage for the condition in which children received both direct training and probes, separately for second-, third-, and fourth-grade children. The exploration phase in the figure can be considered a baseline, whereas the assessment phase reflects children's performance on the training trials. As can be seen, all groups of children improved as a result of training, although the improvement for the second graders

was only marginally significant. Perhaps more critically, both the third- and fourth-grade children continued their high level of CVS use on the one- and two-day transfer tests. These results indicate that elementary school children can, indeed, learn to use scientific reasoning to solve problems and generalize them to new tasks. However, when some of the third- and fourth-grade children were tested again seven months after training, only the fourth-graders showed any long-term benefits of training, indicating that the instruction given to the younger children was not sufficient to have lasting effects.

An inability to reason scientifically, however, does not mean an inability to be interested in scientific phenomena, and parents seem to recognize this by talking to their children about scientific topics, at least in some contexts. For example, Kevin Crowley and his colleagues (2001) looked at interactions between parents and their preteen children related to scientific reasoning while exploring interactive science exhibits in museums. Crowley et al. reported that parents often talked to their children about how to select and encode relevant information. Interestingly, although the amount of talk directed to sons and daughters was comparable, parents were more likely to provide scientific explanations to boys than to girls.

Why do children, adolescents, and many adults perform so poorly on scientific reasoning problems? Kuhn and her colleagues (1988) argued that scientific reasoning involves thinking *about* theories rather than just working with them. In other words, scientific reasoning requires a high level of metacognition. Scientific reasoning requires integrating theories (or hypotheses) with data (or evidence). When the two agree, there is little problem. Problems occur when hypotheses and evidence are in conflict. Kuhn (1989) has speculated that children (and many adults) take one of two extreme approaches to theory-data conflicts: *Theory-bound children* distort the data to fit the theory, whereas *data-bound children* focus not on the global theory to explain their results but, rather, on isolated patterns of results (to avoid conflict with the theory).

Although poor metacognition might be the overarching reason for peoples' difficulties with scientific reasoning, it is not the only one. Children and adolescents often do not conduct effective experiments; they frequently fail to vary one factor systematically, or they come to a decision before all possible factors have been tested. Children, and to a lesser extent adults, have a positive-results bias. They put more weight on results that produce good outcomes (for example, good academic performance, good health) than on results that yield negative outcomes (see De-Loache et al., 1998). Adolescents' preexisting beliefs also strongly influence their scientific reasoning. Outcomes that are consistent with their prior beliefs are quickly and uncritically accepted, whereas evidence counter to their beliefs are regarded more critically (Klaczynski, 1997; Klaczynski & Narasimham, 1998).

In general, the "big" picture of scientific reasoning painted by Barbel Inhelder and Jean Piaget (1958) nearly 50 years ago has not drastically changed. Scientific reasoning is rarely found in children. What the new research indicates, however, is that scientific reasoning is only occasionally found in adolescents and adults without specific training. Given these findings, it makes good sense for university-level psychology students to take a course in research methods, where the logic of experimental design is made explicit. College students are clearly capable of such thinking, but we should not be surprised that it does not come spontaneously or easily to them.

Summary

Problem solving involves having a goal, obstacles to that goal, strategies for overcoming the obstacles, and an evaluation of the results. Infants show signs of true *goal-directed behavior* and problem solving in the latter part of the first year. Problem solving improves during the preschool years and is influenced by how much knowledge the problem solver has about the task to be solved or the context in which the task is embedded.

Some forms of problem solving involve the discovery or induction of rules. Preverbal toddlers can learn rules for simple oddity problems, especially when they are accompanied by language instructions. In the *rule-assessment approach*, cognitive development is characterized by the acquisition of increasingly powerful rules for solving problems. Although the rule-assessment approach describes reasonably well the development of many tasks (for example, balance-scale problem, conservation), children typically use a variety of strategies for any particular problem, as exemplified by Siegler's adaptive strategy choice model. Zelazo and his colleagues have focused on children's developing ability to follow rules, and they report that young children often fail to use a rule even though they can demonstrate knowledge of the rule. This is especially apparent when the rules governing a task change (for example, from sorting cards by color to sorting cards by shape). *Cognitive complexity and control (CCC) theory* proposes that there are age-related changes in the complexity of rule systems that children can represent and that developmental differences in conscious awareness give children increased control over their behavior and cognition.

Tool use is observed during the first year of life, although it is influenced by many factors, including perceptual similarity, proximity of tools to desired object, and social-learning abilities. Tool use is associated with children's object-oriented play, with some research indicating that boys engage more in such play than do girls and also show greater initial performance on tool-using tasks than girls do.

Planning is an important aspect of problem solving, but is a relatively late-developing phenomenon. Some reasons for young children's frequent failure to plan include poor inhibition abilities, a bias toward speed over accuracy, that planning is difficult and time consuming and does not always improve task performance, and that it may be more fun to solve novel problems without planning. Planning improves during the preschool years, and most 5-year-olds display planning for simple tasks.

Reasoning is a special type of problem solving that requires that one make an inference. *Analogical reasoning* involves *relational mapping*—the application of what one knows about one set of elements to relations about different elements. The *relational primacy hypothesis* proposes that analogical reasoning is available early in infancy. Although there is some evidence for this in preschoolers, young children have difficulty with more traditional analogy problems, although they are able to solve them in some situations. Similarity (perceptual and relational) between different aspects of a problem plays an important role in solving analogies. There appears to be a *relational shift* in the development of analogical reasoning, in which young children are more likely to focus on perceptual similarity, whereas older children and adults focus more on relational similarity in solving problems. Other factors that influence children's success at analogical reasoning are knowledge for the relations on which the analogy is based, and metacognition, or a conscious awareness of the basis on which one is solving a problem. The role of metacognition in analogical reasoning has been assessed using *learning-to-learn* tasks, in which children are given a series of different problems and abstract a general rule to apply to new tasks.

In *formal reasoning* the form of an argument, not its semantic content, is crucial. Piaget proposed that formal reasoning is the hallmark of adult cognition and was reflected by adolescents' and adults' use of *conditional reasoning*, or *propositional logic*, a form of symbolic logic that involves two or more factors (conventionally, P and Q), with each factor having two possible values (for instance, true or false). Counter to Piaget's theory, adults do not frequently show propositional logic. Preschool children under certain situations can demonstrate other forms of formal reasoning, such as syllogisms, when statements in a problem do not contradict their world knowledge.

Scientific reasoning involves generating hypotheses about how something in the world works and then systematically testing those hypotheses. Scientific reasoning is also a late-developing ability, partly because of the metacognitive difficulty involved in reasoning about theories.

Note

1. The sixteen binary operations of propositional logic following Inhelder and Piaget (1958) are (1) Affirmation: All combinations are possible, for example,

P and Q, P and not Q, not P and Q, and not P and not Q are all possible; (2) Negation: No combinations are possible; (3) Conjunction: P is true and Q is true; (4) Incompatibility: P is never true if Q is true, and vice versa; (5) Disjunction: P is true or Q is true (or both are true); (6) Conjunctive Negation: P is false and Q is false; (7) Implication: P implies Q; (8) Nonimplication: P does not imply Q; (9) Reciprocal Implication: Q implies P; (10) Negation of Reciprocal Implication: Q does not imply P; (11) Equivalence: The effect of P is equal to the effect of Q; (12) Reciprocal Equivalence: The effect of P is not equal to the effect of Q; (13) Affirmation of P: P is true independent of Q; (14) Negation of P: P is false independent of Q; (15) Affirmation of Q: Q is true independent of P; (16) Negation of Q: Q is false independent of P.

Key Terms and Concepts

problem solving
goal-directed behavior
rule-assessment approach
cognitive complexity and control (CCC) theory
reasoning
analogical reasoning
relational mapping
relational primacy hypothesis
relational shift
learning to learn
formal reasoning
conditional reasoning
propositional logic
scientific reasoning

Suggested Readings

DeLoache, J. S., Miller, K. F., & Pierroutsakos, S. L. (1998). Reasoning and problem solving. In D. Kuhn & R. S. Siegler (Vol. Eds.), *Cognitive, language, and perceptual development*, Vol. 2 (pp. 801–850), In W. Damon (Gen. Ed.), *Handbook of child psychology*. New York: Wiley. This chapter presents a comprehensive review of the developmental literature of problem solving and reasoning, extending beyond the topics covered in this book.

Goswami, U. (1996). Analogical reasoning and cognitive development. In H. W. Reese (Ed.), *Advances in child development and behavior* (Vol. 26) (pp. 92–138). San

Diego: Academic Press. This chapter provides an excellent review of research examining analogical reasoning in children. Much of the review focuses on Goswami's own research, which is substantial, influential, and interesting.

Kuhn, D., Amsel, E., & O'Loughlin, M. (1988). *The development of scientific thinking skills*. San Diego: Academic Press. This book provides an excellent overview of research on the development of scientific reasoning, as well as presenting the authors' own innovative work.

Want, S. C., and Harris, P. L. (2001). Learning from other peoples' mistakes: Causal understanding in learning to use a tool. *Child Development, 72*, 431–443. This paper presents two studies of tool use in young children. It illustrates how such studies can be done and some of the social-learning factors associated with the development of tool use.

Zelazo, P. D., & Jacques, S. (1997). Children's rule use: Representation, reflection and cognitive control. *Annals of Child Development, 12* (pp. 119–176). London: Jessica Kingsley Press. This chapter provides a review of children's rule-following, beginning with classic Soviet work by Luria and his colleagues, and concluding with the contemporary research of Zelazo and his colleagues.

InfoTrac College Edition

For additional readings, explore InfoTrac College Edition, your online library. Go to http://www.infotrac-college.com/wadsworth.

13

Social Cognition

As a cognitive psychologist, I tend to believe that most aspects of human behavior are a function, to some significant degree, of one's cognitions. I find this especially easy to believe for the social behavior of children. Children can be only as social as their level of cognitive functioning will permit. One cannot expect children to behave in a socially appropriate way if they cannot understand the social relationships among individuals and the ramifications of behaving in one way as rather than another. **Social cognition** refers to cognition about social relationships and social phenomena. Nonsocial cognition deals with words, numbers, maps, images, and inanimate objects in general; such "hard," or "cold," cognition can be contrasted with the "soft," or "warm," cognition that involves thinking about people and their relationships with one another.

Many of a child's day-to-day activities involve interactions with people. These interactions require thought. Children must make evaluations of social situations and must understand their relationships with other people in a particular context. This requires an appreciation of who they are as social beings and who their fellow interactants are. It involves anticipating the thoughts and feelings of others and the execution of social "strategies." These strategies can be aimed at facilitating the formation of relationships, such as mother-infant attachment or playground friendships, or the successful completion of some cooperative task, such as jumping rope or playing baseball.

It could be argued, I believe, that social cognition is actually the most basic type of cognition because of its importance to everyday functioning. Many have argued that competing and cooperating with conspecifics (fellow members of our own species) might have been the single most powerful force in the evolution of human intelligence (Alexander, 1989; Humphrey, 1976). I would argue that understanding ourselves and others is just as important today as it was in our evolutionary past. Although we can employ our intellect today to figure out how to use computers, automatic teller machines, and VCRs, we remain a social species, and our social "thinking" likely still has the greatest impact on us on a day-today basis.

There are few narrow topics in cognitive development. Research into memory, perception, and language involves many subtopics, with numerous facets to each. The number of topics subsumed under the rubric of social cognition, however, is even greater. Any thinking involved in any social setting or about any social phenomenon is a potential area of inquiry. And there is not necessarily a hard line drawn between social and nonsocial cognition. For example, much of the research I reviewed on theory of mind in Chapter 9 could have just as easily been included in a chapter on social cognition (see Flavell & Miller, 1998).

I will not attempt to provide a representative review of the topics in developmental social cognition. Rather, I have selected six topics to review, in varying degrees of detail, hoping to provide a flavor of developmental social cognition, how the research is done, and how it is relates to nonsocial cognitive development. In the sections to follow, I first define and describe various forms of social learning and their development. I then review three broad theories of developmental social cognition: Albert Bandura's social cognitive theory, Michael Tomasello's cultural learning theory, and Kenneth Dodge's social information processing model. I then review research on the development of self, and the cognitive bases of gender identification.

Social Learning

Forms of Social Learning

At its simplest, **social learning** refers to the acquisition of social information and behavior. A narrower definition of social learning refers to "situations in which one individual comes to behave similarly to others" (Boesch & Tomasello, 1998, p. 598). Most child developmentalists have usually assumed that if children acquire some behavior by observation, the mechanism is imitation. However, imitation is only one rather sophisticated form of social learning, and it is worthwhile distinguishing between different forms of social learning. Table 13-1 lists several mechanisms by which social learning can occur, most of them identified by comparative (animal) psychologists to explain the behavior of their subjects, but the list is equally applicable to human children (see Bjorklund & Pellegrini, 2002; Want & Harris, 2003). **Local enhancement** occurs when an individual notices activity at a particular location (for example, children digging in the sand, recovering sea shells), moves to that location, and, in a process of trial and error, discovers a useful behavior (for example, using one's fingers to sift sand). More sophisticated mechanisms include **mimicry,** the duplication of a behavior without any understanding of the goal of that behavior, and the cognitively more sophisticated processes of **emulation** and true imitation, or **imitative learning** (Tomasello, 2000).

Emulation (sometimes referred to as *goal emulation*) refers to understanding the goal of a model and engaging in similar behavior to achieve that goal, without necessarily reproducing the exact actions of the model (Tomasello, 2000). For example, child A may observe child B sifting sand through her fingers to search for seashells. Child A may then start searching through sand with his hands, but tossing handfuls of sand that separates sand from the shells. Unlike in mimicry (or imitative learning), the child does not reproduce the behaviors of the model but, rather through a trial and error process, achieves the desired goal he had observed another child attain. In contrast to emulation, imitative learning, according to Tomasello and his colleagues (Tomasello, 2000; Tomasello, Kruger, & Ratner, 1993), requires the observer to take the perspective of the model, to understand the model's goal, and to repeat important portions of the model's behavior. From this viewpoint, imitative learning is not the mindless matching behavior of an unsophisticated organism, as in mimicry, but reflects rather sophisticated cognitive processing.

Age Differences in Social Learning

I discussed the development of imitation during infancy in Chapter 10, particularly deferred imitation,

TABLE 13-1 Different forms of social learning.

Local enhancement: An individual notices activity at a particular location, moves to that location, and, in a process of trial and error, discovers a useful behavior.

Mimicry: The duplication of a behavior without any understanding of the goal of that behavior.

Emulation: One individual observes another interacting with an object to achieve a specific goal. The first individual then interacts with the object attempting to attain the same end but does not duplicate the same behavior as the model to achieve that goal.

Imitative learning: Reproduction of observed behavior to achieve a specific goal. This requires an understanding of the goal that the model had in mind, as well as the reproduction of important components of the observed behavior.

which was used as an indication of memory in preverbal infants. However, most researchers examining observational learning in children have used the term "imitation" quite broadly and have not differentiated between the various forms of social learning. In fact, when looking closely at observational learning in infants and young children, the picture gets quite complicated (see Want & Harris, 2003). For example, several researchers have noted that infants will faithfully reproduce the actions of a model, even when those actions are irrelevant to attaining a goal (Nagell, Olguin, & Tomasello, 1993; Whiten et al., 1996). This was illustrated in a study in which an experimenter displayed one of two sets of action to 2-year-old children using a rake to retrieve an out-of-reach object. The children copied the actions of the adults, even when a more effective way of solving the problem was possible (Nagell et al., 1993). In another experiment, Andrew Whiten et al. (1996) showed 2- to 4-year-old children a clear box with a desirable object inside. The box contained a series of bolts and a latch, and an experimenter modeled several ways (of many) the box could be opened and the reward obtained. Children tended to copy the exact actions of the model, even though other, more direct routes to opening the box were available. Children also copied nonfunctional or redundant actions. These patterns of data suggest that young children engage in mimicry, but not true imitation.

But perhaps such results reflect little of young children's cognitive abilities. Infants and young children copy the often-arbitrary behaviors of adults, without any external motivation. Maybe the mimicry observed in these studies reflects children's motivation to maintain a social interaction and reveals little about their cognitive capabilities, per se. That infants and toddlers seem to appreciate the *intention* of a model, something necessary for true imitation, suggests the plausibility of this interpretation. In one study, 18-month-old children watched adults perform actions on objects (Meltzoff, 1995). Sometimes the actions were successful (for example, picking up a dumbbell-shaped object, pulling on the wooden cube on one end and removing the cube) and sometime they were not (for example, the model's hand slips off the end of the cube, failing to remove it from the dumbbell). Compared with infants in a control group who did not see a demonstration of the dumbbell, children in both the successful and unsuccessful conditions removed the cube on the end of the dumbbell when given the chance. They appeared to understand what the model *intended* to do to achieve an inferred (but not witnessed) goal. In a second experiment, 14- and 18-month-old infants watched as either a person or a mechanical device acted on an object (for example, a person removing the cube end of a dumbbell or a vice-like machine pulling on one end of the dumbbell to remove the cube). Infants who watched the person were twice as likely to copy the actions than infants who watched the mechanical device, suggesting that by 14 months of age, infants understand that people (but not inanimate objects) have intentions (goals) that are sometimes worthy of imitating (see also Carpenter, Akhatar, & Tomasello, 1998; Carpenter, Call, & Tomasello, 2002).

Do Chimpanzees "Ape"?

People have a tendency to think of imitation as a lesser cognitive skill—something unimaginative adults, small children, and even animals do. This might be true of unimaginative adults and small children, but it is not true of animals (Whiten & Ham, 1992). Very little in the way of object imitation (important in tool use) is observed even in our close relatives the chimpanzees (Tomasello et al., 1987). Given the substantial cognitive abilities of chimpanzees, this is somewhat surprising.

Michael Tomasello, Sue Savage-Rumbaugh, and Ann Kruger speculated that one reason for chimps' failure to display imitative learning readily is that "unlike human children, they do not develop in a social environment in which adult conspecifics are constantly encouraging their attention to objects, intentionally teaching them how to use objects as tools, and rewarding them for imitating actions on objects" (1993, p. 1689). In other words, human children's imitation of actions on objects is fostered by their social environment, whereas the different structure of chimpanzee social environments is not conducive to imitation. Such an interpretation makes imitation not only an important cognitive tool for social learning but also a cognitive ability that emerges from a uniquely human social context.

Tomasello and his colleagues (1993) evaluated their idea by testing mother-reared chimpanzees (that is, chimpanzees reared by their own chimpanzee mothers), human-reared (enculturated) chimpanzees, and 18- and 30-month-old human children on a series of object-imitation tasks. The social experiences of the enculturated chimps were similar to those of the children; Tomasello and his associates hypothesized that such experiences should foster imitative learning. They reported that the mother-reared chimpanzees were much poorer at immediate imitation than were either the enculturated chimps or the human children, who did not differ from one another. The findings for *deferred imitation* were even more interesting and are shown in Figure 13-1. Somewhat surprisingly, the enculturated chimpanzees actually showed greater deferred imitation (two days after observing the actions) than did the children (see also Bering, Bjorklund, & Ragan, 2000; Bjorklund, Yunger, Bering, & Ragan, 2002). These findings indicate that chimpanzees possess the rudimentary cognitive skills for object imitation but rarely express it in species-typical

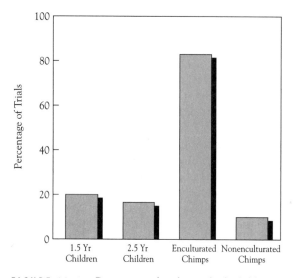

FIGURE 13-1 Percentage of trials on which children and apes displayed deferred imitation. SOURCE: Tomasello, M., Savage-Rumbaugh, S., & Kruger, A. C. (1993). Imitative learning of actions and objects by children, chimpanzees, and enculturated chimpanzees. *Child Development, 64,* 1688–1705. Reprinted with permission of the Society for Research in Child Development.

situations. When provided with a human-typical rearing environment, however, the abilities appear, comparable with those observed for 30-month-old children. Such experience does not (nor ever could) make a chimpanzee think like a human, but the rearing conditions of these animals did change their cognitions substantially.

These findings are consistent with the developmental systems approach discussed in Chapter 2 (Gottlieb, 2000), in that species-atypical environments can produce species-atypical behaviors, in this case humanlike imitation in chimpanzees. For human cognitive development, these results point to the necessity of considering the role of the social environment when examining the development of a cognitive ability. These findings also hint at possible developmental mechanisms for the evolution of human cognition (Bjorklund & Bering, 2003; Bjorklund & Pellegrini, 2002).

Social Cognitive Theory

One of the most influential theories in developmental psychology during the past 40 years has been Albert Bandura's **social learning theory,** renamed **social cognitive theory** by Bandura to reflect a more mentalistic approach. Initial formulations of social learning theory (Bandura & Walters, 1963) were based on extensions of models of classical and operant conditioning, popular throughout most of this century in American psychology. It became apparent, however, that explicit reinforcement was not necessary for children (and adults) to learn about their social world. Rather, people learn much about their world simply by watching. As the field of cognitive psychology developed during the 1960s and 1970s, Bandura incorporated many cognitive principles, transforming his theory into a cognitive one in which children learn about important social relationships by watching (Bandura, 1986, 1989; Bussey & Bandura, 1999).

There are many similarities between the ideas expressed in social cognitive theory and those expressed by Jean Piaget (as discussed in Chapter 4). For example, similar to Piaget, Bandura believes that children affect their environment as much as their environment affects them, selecting and creating the world in which they live. Bandura refers to this interaction between children and their environment as **reciprocal determinism,** with children determining how others respond toward them as much as they are influenced by others. Bandura proposes that there are complex interactions between children's thoughts, feelings, and behaviors and the external environment. How children feel or think about something will affect their behavior. Likewise, their behavior in certain situations will influence their thought. Each of us tries to make sense of our behavior, and often we change our thinking and beliefs to be in line with our actions. Children's behavior will influence how other people in the environment perceive and act toward them, which will, of course, affect their thinking and behavior. Thus, Bandura proposes a process of causation that gives serious attention to the internal states of children (their thoughts and emotions), their observable behaviors, and the perceptions and actions of others.

Factors Involved in Observational Learning

Bandura proposed five capabilities that contribute to children's learning about their social world and their place in it, each of which develops (see Table 13-2): (1) symbolization, (2) forethought, (3) self-regulation, (4) self-reflection, and (5) vicarious learning. The first capability, that of **symbolization**, means that we can think about our social behavior in words and images. This is necessary for us to be aware of various aspects of our actions. The capability of **forethought** means that we are able to anticipate the consequences of our actions and the actions of others. This future-time perspective motivates behavior. **Self-regulation** involves adopting standards of acceptable behavior for ourselves. These include aspirational standards (hoped-for levels of accomplishment) as well as social and moral standards. A capacity for **self-reflection** allows us to analyze our thoughts and actions.

The final capability, that of **vicarious learning,** is the cornerstone of social cognitive theory. Children need not receive specific reinforcement for their behavior to learn; rather, they learn much social behavior merely by observing others. This places **observational learning** at the center of Bandura's theory.

Bandura proposed four subprocesses that govern observational learning: attentional processes, retention processes, production processes, and motivational processes. Information must be attended to, coded in memory, stored, and retrieved, and the behavior must be performed at the appropriate time. Each of these processes changes with age, and a failure in any one process (retention, for example) rules out successful observational learning. Children do not need to physically imitate a model to have learned from observing the model. Children might have learned all they need to know from observing but never have the motivation to produce the behavior.

TABLE 13-2   Capabilities involved in Bandura's social cognitive theory and the four subprocesses of observational learning.

Key cognitive capabilities

Symbolization: The ability to think about social behavior in words and images.

Forethought: The ability to anticipate the consequences of our actions and the actions of others.

Self-regulation: The ability to adopt standards of acceptable behavior for ourselves.

Self-reflection: The ability to analyze our thoughts and actions.

Vicarious learning: The ability to learn new behavior and the consequences of one's actions by observing others.

Subprocesses of observational learning

Attentional processes

Retention processes

Production processes

Motivational processes

Following Bandura's theory, after children have attended to a model and formed a mental representation of the behavior, they must convert that representation to action. Yet, children observe some things that they do not have the motoric ability to reproduce. For example, although a 5-year-old boy may have watched and mentally practiced the behaviors involved in driving a car, because of his short arms and legs (among other things), he is physically unable to produce the behaviors he has observed. Despite such obvious shortcomings, young children frequently overestimate their imitative abilities. They have watched a behavior being performed and believe that "seeing is knowing." (More than one parent has been shocked to see his or her young child behind the wheel of a moving car.) In a study in which mothers recorded the imitative attempts of their preschoolers, children overestimated their imitative abilities 55% of the time—stating that they were capable of imitating a behavior when they were not. Cases of underestimation were rare, occurring on only 5% of the observations (Bjorklund, Gault-ney, & Green, 1993). Young children have great confidence in their own abilities. To improve obser-vational learning, children must learn to monitor and compare their actions with their symbolic repre-sentations and to correct mismatches. As these pro-duction processes improve with age, the difference between what children know and what they can pro-duce declines (Bandura, 1989).

The Development of Self-Efficacy

The concept of **self-efficacy,** the extent to which a person views himself or herself as an effective indi-vidual, plays a central role in Bandura's theory. Self-efficacy develops through experience. Children evaluate the effectiveness of their own actions, com-pare it with the actions of others, and are told by others how their behavior meets certain standards. Children who believe they are competent (even if they are not) develop feelings of positive self-efficacy. Conversely, when self-efficacy is poor, people tend to behave ineffectually, regardless of their actual abili-ties (Bandura, 1997). Developing feelings of positive self-efficacy has important consequences for chil-dren's social, emotional, and intellectual develop-ment (Bandura et al., 1996). One should not think of self-efficacy as a general characteristic of a child. Rather, self-efficacy (and the related concept of self-worth) is specific to a domain and a task (Harter, Waters, & Whitesell, 1998). A child can have a pos-itive sense of self-efficacy for playing baseball, for ex-ample, but a poor sense of self-efficacy for doing long division.

The development of self-efficacy begins early, as infants learn that they can exert some control over their environment. Beginning around 3 or 4 months, babies learn that their actions have consequences—that if they kick their feet, the mobile over the crib will move and if they smile and coo their parents will smile and talk back to them. Infants who have expe-rienced some control over their environments are better able to learn new behaviors (Finkelstein & Ramey, 1977). Mary Ainsworth and her colleagues have proposed that parents' responsiveness to their infants' attempts to communicate their needs gives the infants some sense of control over their parents and is related to later social and cognitive develop-ment (Ainsworth et al., 1978).

With the development of language and other symbols, children are able to reflect on their new so-cial and intellectual abilities and evaluate what others tell them about their skills. Initially, the fam-ily provides children with feedback on their effec-tiveness. As children approach school age, their peer group becomes a valuable source of information, and school itself is a potent agent in forming children's self-efficacy. Children learn through daily experience with teachers and peers that they are good at some tasks and not so good at others (Bandura, 1997).

Although children learn self-efficacy through ex-perience, developing a positive sense of self-efficacy is facilitated by a generally optimistic (and unrealis-tic) opinion of their own abilities. Preschool chil-dren think that they can remember more items, communicate more effectively, perform tasks better, and imitate a model more accurately than they ac-tually can (Bjorklund et al., 1993; Plumert, 1995). Young children's beliefs that they know more than they actually do and can do more than they actually can provides them with positive perceptions of their own skills. This positive sense of self-efficacy might encourage children to attempt things that they would not try if they had a more realistic idea of their abilities. In other words, their cognitive imma-turity, as reflected by their unrealistic assessments of their abilities, can actually facilitate development rather than hinder it (Bjorklund, 1997a; Bjorklund & Green, 1992). (However, it also poses some prob-lems. For example, Jodie Plumert (1995) reports that 6-year-olds who consistently overestimate their physical abilities are more accident prone than less optimistic children are.)

This point is made by Deborah Stipek and her colleagues (Stipek, 1984; Stipek & Daniels, 1988), who found that young children can make relatively accurate predictions of how other children are likely to perform on school-like tasks but are overly opti-mistic in predicting their own future performance. Stipek suggested that this overly optimistic self-perception is due to **wishful thinking,** a concept originally introduced by Piaget (1930): Children wish for A's on their report cards; therefore, they expect A's. By the third or fourth grade, children's assessments of their own abilities move closer to reality, and they are able to tell the difference between what they wish would happen and what they can reasonably expect to happen.

Stipek believes that this tendency to overestimate their own abilities enhances children's self-efficacy and gives them the confidence to attempt things they would not otherwise try. Some preliminary evidence suggests that brighter 3-year-olds overestimate their abilities (on an imitation task) more than less-bright 3-year-olds do, suggesting an adaptive value of overestimation in young children (Bjorklund et al., 1993). Stipek proposed that rather than trying to make young children's self-assessments more accurate, we should "try harder to design educational environments which maintain their optimism and eagerness" (1984, p. 53). The positive consequences of overestimation are not limited to the preschool years. Recent research has shown, for example, that 8- to 11-year-old children who overestimated their capabilities had better school performance than did less optimistic children (Lopez et al., 1998).

Bandura's ideas have been applied to many different contents, the majority of which are more social in character than cognitive. As a cognitive psychologist, however, I believe that knowledge, be it of inanimate objects, of other people, or of one's self, is mentally represented and operated on by a set of cognitive mechanisms. Bandura's approach to development acknowledges this, blurring the distinction between what is social and what is cognitive, recognizing that it is all governed by the same nervous system.

Cultural Learning

Why are children so good at social learning, particularly when other species, even chimpanzees, are much less adept? According to Tomasello and his colleagues (Tomasello, 2000; Tomasello, Kruger, & Ratner, 1993), the principal reason has to do with the ability to take the perspective of others to understand their *intentions*. Tomasello argues that what sets humans apart from other species is **cultural learning**—the transmission of acquired information and behavior both within and across generations with a high degree of fidelity. Although it can be argued whether other species, such as chimpanzees, have something akin to human culture (Boesch, 1993; Whiten et al., 1999), no other species communicates the lessons of one generation to another, thus passing on the ways and traditions of the group, as effectively as humans do. Tomasello argues that at the center of humans' impressive cultural-learning abilities is perspective taking. According to Tomasello and his colleagues, "In cultural learning, learners do not just direct their attention to the location of another individual's activity; rather, they actually attempt to see a situation the way the other sees it—from inside the other's perspective, as it were" (1993, p. 496). They do not just learn from others but through others.

Tomasello et al. propose three stagelike forms of learning in humans that develop during childhood: imitative learning, instructed learning, and collaborative learning. Each subsequent form of social learning is based on a more sophisticated type of perspective taking than the previous form. Together, these three forms of learning constitute cultural learning. Not all human learning, of course, fits into one of these three categories. Much of what a person or animal learns is not "cultural" in nature. What is unique about cultural learning is that it requires the learner to be able to take the perspective of another.

Imitative Learning

Imitative learning, as discussed previously, occurs when the learner internalizes something of the model's behavioral strategies and intentions for executing the behavior. This requires perspective taking. What is the goal of a particular behavior? Why is the model engaging in these actions? For any act of modeling to be considered imitative learning, a child must do more than simply to mimic a behavior displayed by another; one must also appreciate the purpose or *intention* of that behavior. For example, if an infant observes a person opening a jar and then proceeds to make similar hand motions, this may not be imitative learning. Does the infant realize that the purpose of the behavior is to open the jar? If not, the infant might make the twisting motions without applying adequate pressure to remove the lid. According to the theory, imitative learning occurs only if the learner has an understanding of the purpose of the behavior.

Although we've seen earlier that even neonates will imitate facial gestures (Meltzoff & Moore, 1985), nothing new is learned in these situations, and infants certainly do not need to have an understanding of the intentional state of the model (that is, why the model is engaging is such behavior). According to Tomasello and his colleagues, imitative learning is first seen during the latter part of the first year, when infants begin to imitate language sounds and actions with objects (Abravanel & Gingold, 1985).

Instructed Learning

If imitative learning were the only form of cultural learning, human culture and cognition would be much less complex than we know it to be. A more sophisticated form of cultural learning, requiring more sophisticated perspective taking, is **instructed learning.** Here, teaching is involved, with a more accomplished person instructing a less accomplished person. But not all cases of instruction qualify for instructed learning. Instructed learning requires that "children learn about the adult, specifically, about the adult's understanding of the task and how that compares with their own understanding" (Tomasello et al., 1993, p. 499). What distinguishes instructed learning from other aspects of "learning from instruction" is that in the former, children will reproduce the instructed behavior in the appropriate context to regulate their own behavior. That is, as in imitative learning, children must understand the purpose of the behavior—the adult's purpose when he or she initially taught the behavior. Children must internalize the adult's instruction, not just re-

peat a behavior on demand. Thus, a child who is taught to bounce a ball off the wall and into the wastebasket has learned a complicated trick. But it is a trick that can be acquired by a monkey and is not the same as learning that putting a ball in a basket in certain situations is a goal to a game. Each is learning through instruction, but only the latter is instructed learning.

According to Tomasello and his colleagues, self-regulation is the best evidence of instructed learning. Self-regulation refers, basically, to self-control—a person's ability to purposefully direct his or her own behavior in the pursuit of some goal. Effective self-regulation requires the monitoring of one's actions and progress toward the goal (forms of metacognition). It is also reflected in children's self-regulated speech—their use of self-produced language to direct their problem-solving behavior (see Chapter 11). Tomasello and his colleagues proposed that such self-regulation and the associated metacognitive competence are not present until about the age of 4. Moreover, this age is when, according to some, children first demonstrate a theory of mind (see Chapter 9), in that they can solve the false-belief task, demonstrating that they realize that other people can have different knowledge and a different perspective from their own. This last point is critical, for true instructed learning requires that the learner appreciate the perspective of the teacher. According to Tomasello and his associates, "To learn from an instructor culturally—to understand the instruction from something resembling the instructor's point of view—requires that children be able to understand a mental perspective that differs from their own, and then to relate that point of view to their own in an explicit fashion" (1993, p. 500).

Collaborative Learning

In both imitative and instructed learning, an adult or more accomplished person passes on information to a child or less accomplished person. Although in instructed learning the teacher might modify his or her behavior in accordance with the behavior of the student, the direction of effect clearly moves from the

TABLE 13-3 Major characteristics of three types of cultural learning.

Cultural learning process	Social-cognitive ability	Concept of person	Cognitive representation
Imitative (9 months)	Perspective taking (e.g., joint attention, social referencing)	Intentional agent (0 order)	Simple (other's perspective)
Instructed (4 years)	Intersubjectivity (e.g., false-belief task, intentional deception)	Mental agent (1st order)	Alternating/coordinated (other's and own perspective)
Collaborative (6 years)	Recursive intersubjectivity (e.g., embedded mental-state language)	Reflective agent (2nd order)	Integrated (dyad's intersubjectivity)

SOURCE: Tomasello, M., Kruger, A. C., & Ratner, H. H. (1993). Cultural learning. *Behavioral and Brain Sciences, 16,* 495–511. Copyright © 1993 Cambridge University Press. Reprinted with the permission of Cambridge University Press

teacher to the student. This is not the case in the third form of cultural learning, **collaborative learning.** Collaborative learning involves two (or more) individuals, with neither being an authority or expert. Rather, collaborative learning occurs in the process of peer interaction, when two people work together to solve a common problem (see further discussion of collaborative, or cooperative, learning in Chapter 3). Tomasello and his colleagues point out that collaborative learning is different from imitative and instructional learning in that it is a process of cultural creation rather than cultural transmission.

What type of perspective taking is required for collaborative learning to occur? According to Tomasello and associates, collaborative learning requires that a child be able to represent his or her peer as a reflective agent, capable of reflecting on his or her own thoughts and the thoughts of fellow interactants. An example of reflective, or recursive, representation is when a child understands not only that another person can have a different point of view from his or hers, but also that the other person can think about other people's perspectives. For example, "Tom thinks that I think Jessie is a jerk" is a form of recursive thinking. This is necessary for collaborative learning, which often occurs in the midst of disagreement and conflict. For example, children must be able to evaluate and comment on another child's criticism of their previous suggestion if collaborative learning and the creation of a new joint perspective is to take place. Each participant needs

to be able to think of the other participant as being a reflective thinker—as being able to reflect back on his or her past arguments and the arguments made by other participants—if a single solution to a problem is to be reached. According to Tomasello and his colleagues, this is first achieved during the early school years, between 6 and 7 years of age.

Table 13-3 summarizes the major features of each of the three types of cultural learning according to Tomasello, Kruger, and Ratner.

The ideas of Tomasello and his colleagues have much in common with those of Josef Perner, Henry Wellman, and others who have examined young children's representations of other minds (discussed in Chapter 9). The degree to which children can "read the minds" of other people—understand their beliefs, intentions, and mental states—varies developmentally and serves as the cognitive basis for effective social interaction. Tomasello and his colleagues take this perspective a bit further, integrating it with a Vygotskian sociocultural perspective, in proposing that how children conceive of people with whom they interact "is an integral component of the basic learning process" (Tomasello, Kruger, & Ratner, 1993, p. 502).

Although there is some lively debate concerning whether we are the only species to possess the perspective-taking skills necessary to display cultural learning as Tomasello and his colleagues suggest (Boesch, 1993), I think it is fair to say that no other species is in the same ballpark as *Homo sapiens* when it comes to cultural learning. What Tomasello, Kruger, and Ratner's theory does is place human cognition and its development within the realm of social cognition. Our unmatched behavioral and intellectual flexibility finds its origins not so much in tool use, spatial ability, abstract mathematical reasoning, or even language, but in social cognition. Many contemporary theorists of human evolution propose that our unique intelligence evolved because of the need to cooperate, compete, and understand other members of our own species. The theory of Tomasello and his associates regarding the ontogeny of cultural learning takes this point seriously, arguing that what is unique about human intelligence is to be found in social cognition.

Social Information Processing

Social cognitive theorists have adopted many of the tenets of information processing. Social information must be encoded, compared with other pertinent information, and retrieved so that social interactions run smoothly. The more skillfully social information is processed, the more socially competent a child is seen to be. Kenneth Dodge and his colleagues have postulated a theory that describes the mental processes involved in evaluating social information (Crick & Dodge, 1994; Dodge, 1986; Dodge et al., 1986; see also Rubin & Krasnor, 1986). Dodge's original model of social exchange in children is shown in Figure 13-2.

As can be seen in the model, there are five major units of social interaction. The first is the social stimulus, or cue. This is the information that a child must process. For example, a shove by another child, a smile, a scowl, a pout, and an invitation to join a game are all social signals that must be interpreted. The second unit of the model is a child's social information processing of these cues. A child must make sense of the social cues and decide how to respond. More will be said of this unit shortly. Once a child evaluates the information, he or she must emit some social behavior (unit 3). Does the 6-year-old enter the play group by jumping in the middle of an ongoing game, ask if she can play, too, or just stand

to the side, waiting to be asked? This behavior serves as a social stimulus for a child's peers, who make some judgment of the child (unit 4), and then act themselves (unit 5). (The model has been reformulated to include a sixth stage between the representation and search processes in which children clarify their goals in the situation [Crick & Dodge, 1994]. The reformulated model refines the theory but does not substantially change it. The basic model has been quite successful in accounting for a wide range of children's social behaviors.)

Of major concern here is the part of Dodge's theory dealing with **social information processing.** How do children make sense of social information to select a proper social response? Dodge postulated five sequential steps of information processing that are necessary for competent social functioning:

1. *Encoding.* The child must first encode the social stimulus. This requires that the child be properly attentive and adequately perceive the social signal. The child must know what cues are important to encode. For a child entering an already established group, for example, whether he is greeted by a smile or a frown is an important social cue. Less critical are things such as what the other children are wearing or that Kevin needs a haircut.

2. *Interpretation.* Once encoded, the social information must be interpreted. What does this information mean? To determine meaning, children must compare this information with what they already know. What does it mean if the child is greeted by smiles? This will depend on what this child knows about the smiles of others in similar situations. "When I approach a group of kids I know who are already playing a game, smiles are usually a sign of welcome. But when Marvin smiles at me, it usually means he's going to trip me the first chance he gets." Children develop rules for interpreting social signals. These rules are probably not conscious and are executed in a matter of microseconds.

3. *Response search.* Once an interpretation has been made, a child must decide what his or her next move is. Children must generate a variety of re-

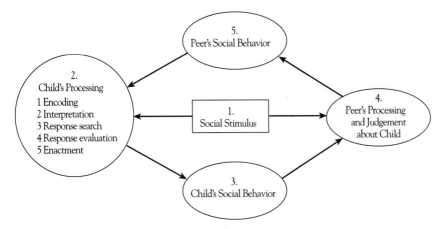

FIGURE 13-2 Dodge's model of social exchange in children. SOURCE: From "Social Competence in Children," by Dodge et al., 1986, *Monographs of the Society for Research in Child Development*, 51 (Serial No. 213). Copyright © 1986 The Society for Research in Child Development, Inc. Reprinted with permission

sponse alternatives. Do they join the group? If so, by what means? Do they approach the playground bully, walk around him, think of something clever to say, or run away? With age, children have a greater number of more sophisticated options from which to choose, which should contribute greatly to behaving in a socially competent fashion.

4. *Response evaluation.* Once responses have been generated, they must be evaluated. Does it make sense to approach the bully, hitting him before he hits me, or might one of the other options be wiser? To what extent can children anticipate the consequences of their behavior, selecting the response alternative that will be most successful in the current situation?

5. *Enactment.* Finally, the child must execute the chosen response.

Dodge proposed that these steps are executed in order. However, steps of processing can be skipped. When they are, it is likely that socially incompetent behavior will result. The first response a child comes up with might not be the ideal response for the situation. If this response is not evaluated and found wanting, the resulting behavior will probably not ingratiate the child to his or her peers. Similarly, a

child might make a decision based on misinterpreted information. The quiet manner of a peer while studying may have been interpreted as an invitation to horse around, or the smile of the well-known bully may have been construed erroneously as a peace offering. Also, as mentioned earlier, the wrong information might be encoded. The cues may have been there, but they may have been ignored or missed because the child was attending to other more salient environmental or internal cues.

Dodge and his colleagues (1986) tested this model with respect to the social skill of peer-group entry—that is, entering an established group of other children. Children in kindergarten and the first and second grades were shown videotapes of two children playing a game and were asked a series of questions related to peer-group entry. The questions were selected so that each of the five aspects of Dodge's model of social information processing could be evaluated. After viewing the video, for example, the children were asked to imagine that they wanted to join the group. They were then asked how much the child on the left and then the child on the right from the video would like to play with them. Answers to these questions reflected the children's interpretation of social cues, step 2 of the model. The children were then asked the reasons for their decisions. Answers to this question indicated the children's use of specific cues from the videotapes in making their decisions, step 1 of the model (encoding). The children were then asked to think of as many ways as possible to join the group, step 3 of the model (response search). After this, the children viewed five scenarios consisting of the original video of two children playing followed by the arrival of a third child who attempted to join the group. The new arrival displayed one of five strategies for joining the group (competent, aggressive, self-centered, passive, or authority intervention). The children were then asked a series of questions concerning the potential effectiveness of each of the five strategies, to assess step 4 of the model (response evaluation). Finally, the children were asked to pretend that they wished to play with the experimenter and were told to "show me how you would ask me if you could play with me." This corresponded to step 5 of the model (enactment).

In a separate session, conducted one to two weeks later, each child was brought into a room in which two other children were already playing and was told to play with these children. Based on videotapes of these sessions and interviews with the children, each child's actual peer-group entry was evaluated.

The most important aspect of the results of this study concerns the prediction of children's peer-group entry (their actual social behavior) as a function of their skills at social information processing. In general, children who scored higher on the assessment of social information processing were rated as more successful at actual peer-group entry. Children who used presented cues (step 1), who generated competent and nonaggressive strategies in response to a hypothetical entry situation (step 3), who evaluated incompetent responses negatively (step 4), and who demonstrated high skill in enactment of responses (step 5) were relatively likely to perform competently and successfully in actual group entry (Dodge et al., 1986). Furthermore, Dodge and his colleagues reported that these skills were relatively independent of one another, suggesting that each contributes something unique to social judgment and

behavior rather than reflecting different aspects of a single social intelligence. Other researchers have tested the relation between children's competence for each of the five areas of social information processing and subsequent social behavior, and as Dodge et al. (1986), report modest relations (Dodge & Price, 1994; Slaby & Guerra, 1988).

The area in which social information processing theory has been most frequently applied is aggressive behavior (Coie & Dodge, 1998; Crick & Dodge, 1996). Research has found characteristic ways in which—at least some—aggressive children encode, interpret, search, evaluate, and enact social behavior. For example, highly aggressive children have been found to be less likely to recall relevant social cues from a videotape (Dodge et al., 1995) and to be more attentive to potentially aggressive cues (Gouze, 1987) than less aggressive children are. Concerning interpretation, highly aggressive children are more likely to interpret an ambiguous situation (for example, a peer spills water on you) as having an aggressive, rather than accidental, intent (Graham & Hudley, 1994) and interpret events with clearly benign intentions as hostile (Dodge et al., 1986) than less aggressive children. Concerning response search, aggressive children tend to generate more atypical and socially inappropriate responses than less aggressive children do (see Coie & Dodge, 1998) and have a difficult time inhibiting aggressive responses (Perry, Perry, & Rasmussen, 1986). Aggressive children perceive aggressive responses as socially appropriate and normative (Guerra, Huesmann, & Hanish, 1995), and believe that they can engage in aggression relatively easily (Perry et al., 1986). Although such a pattern does not reduce in any way the effect of other, more traditionally "social" factors, on aggression, it does point to the conclusion that how children process social information with respect to aggression is related to their own level of aggressive behavior.

The work of Dodge and his colleagues clearly points to the cognitive basis of social behavior. Complex social situations must be evaluated and thought about just as strictly "intellectual" situations must be contemplated. Theories of nonsocial information processing have specified routines (such as encoding and retrieval) and structures (such as the short-term store and semantic memory) with relative precision. Although there is still much debate concerning the particulars of nonsocial information processing, there is also much consensus. The field of social information processing is less advanced because it is more complicated. How can one specify the features of a social stimulus? How is social information represented in long-term memory? How is it retrieved? Can the concepts of the short-term store, schemas, and strategies, so useful for explaining nonsocial cognition, be successfully applied to social cognition? Social information processing is in its infancy. However, the work of Dodge and others (Rubin & Krasnor, 1986) represents an exciting beginning to research that will surely lead to a better understanding of the development of children's social lives.

The Development of a Concept of Self

Few mental concepts are more important to us than the personal sense of self. By **self-concept,** I mean the way a person defines himself or herself. Some theorists have speculated that a conscious awareness of oneself greatly influences cognitive development, particularly the use of goal-directed strategies (Bullock & Lütkenhaus, 1988). Others have stressed the significance of a sense of self for social and emotional development (Brooks-Gunn & Lewis, 1984; Gallup, 1979). Many believe that it is our well-developed sense of self that makes humans unique as a species. Some people have speculated that the development of self-awareness vaulted our hominid ancestors to full human cognition and social organization (Alexander, 1989). The significance of the concept of self for the developing person and for the species cannot be overstated.

How can we know if young children have a concept of self? If they are too young to talk, we cannot ask them and must infer self-awareness from their behavior. Piaget (1952), among others, proposed that infants only gradually come to recognize themselves as distinct from the objects around them, with the distinction becoming fully developed sometime around 18 to 24 months of age (see Chapter 4).

Perhaps one of the earliest indications of a self-concept is infants' ability to differentiate themselves from other people and objects. Infants during the first several months of life should be receiving various forms of proprioceptive, visual, and acoustic feedback from their behavior. This should give them some sense of "who they are," at least with respect to other people.

How can one determine this? One technique is to show infants pictures or videos of themselves along with pictures of videos of other infants or objects and assess their looking time (Bahrick, Moss, & Fadil, 1996; Legerstee, Anderson, & Schaffer, 1998). If infants "recognize" themselves, they should pay less attention (a novelty effect), or possibly more attention (a familiarity effect) to these other stimuli than to images of themselves (see the discussion of preference for novelty/familiarity effects in Chapter 7). If they can't tell the difference between images of themselves and those of other people or objects, there should be no differential attention to any of the stimuli. In experiments using variants of this technique, infants as young as 3 months of age were able to discriminate between images of themselves and same-aged infants (Legerstee et al., 1998; Rochat & Striano, 2002), suggesting a primitive form of self-recognition early in infancy. How do infants this young know what they look like? The most likely source of this self-knowledge is mirrors; infants as young as 2-months-old often have daily exposure to their image from mirrors (Bahrick, 1995), and so by 3 months of age, they recognize themselves as a familiar sight.

Still, the ability to differentiate one's self from the environment is a far cry from what we typically mean by a sense of self. Theorists have proposed that two types of self-concept develop in the first two years of life. The first type, which typifies infants from birth to about 15–18 months old, has been referred to as the *I-self* (Lewis, 1991) or the *implicit self* (Case, 1991). The I-self reflects what Lewis (1991) termed the "machinery of the self." There is no self-awareness of the I-self. There is a distinction between the self and others and a realization that "I can cause things to happen." This is contrasted with the *me-self* (Lewis, 1991) or *explicit self* (Case, 1991). The me-self requires a conscious (explicit) awareness of the self, or, as Lewis has stated, the "idea of me."

How can one tell if an infant has an explicit self rather than an implicit self? One technique that some people think captures the idea of an explicit self (or the me-self) is *visual self-recognition*. Children prove that they have a sense of self by recognizing themselves in a mirror. The procedure involves placing a mark on a child's nose or forehead and then seeing the child's reaction to his or her image in the mirror. Children's behavior in the marked condition is then compared with their behavior when there are no marks on their faces or to the behavior of other unmarked children. Children show the first signs of self-recognition beginning around 15 months by touching the mark on their face rather than touching the mirror (Lewis & Brooks-Gunn, 1979). Not all studies report mark-directed behavior this early (Schulman & Kaplowitz, 1977), but by 18 to 24 months this form of self-recognition is found in about 75% of all children tested. It is also found in the great apes—chimpanzees and orangutans (Gallup, 1979)—and dolphins (Reiss & Marino, 2001), but not in any other animal tested.

Our culture provides more ways than mirrors for children to identify themselves. For example, when do children show a sense of self in pictures or videos? Daniel Povinelli and his colleagues (Povinelli, Landau, & Perilloux, 1996; Povinelli & Simon, 1998) took Polaroid photos or videotaped preschool children while they played. Without the children knowing it, the experimenters placed large stickers on the children. How would children react when they saw themselves in the photos or on the video with stickers on their heads? Most 2- and younger 3-year-old children did not reach for the sticker on their heads, whereas most older preschoolers did. All children, however, removed the sticker when they looked at themselves in a mirror (Povinelli et al., 1996). These results suggest that children's developing sense of self develops gradually over the preschool years, as their ability to deal with different modes of representation (mirrors, photos, videos) develops (see also Zelazo, Sommerville, & Nichols, 1999).

The development of a sense of self, as reflected by self-recognition, has important consequences for emotional, social, and cognitive development. Brooks-Gunn and Lewis make this clear: "The acquisition of the self by the end of the second year not only facilitates the acquisition of social knowledge, but underlies social competence, peer relations, gender identity, and empathy" (1984, p. 234). The change from a helpless newborn, who seemingly cannot distinguish where he or she ends and the world begins, to a self-conscious child is a remarkable and important change indeed.

Mirror recognition is not the only sign of self-awareness that develops late in the second year. In one study, the ability to recognize oneself in a mirror was associated with the tendency to become embarrassed in certain situations, suggesting that both are related to the emergence of a child's concept of self (Lewis et al., 1989). But perhaps the most important indication of a sense of self can be gleaned from children's use of language. Late in the second year or early in the third year, many children begin using the personal pronouns *I, me, my,* and *mine,* thereby indicating a distinction between themselves and others (Lewis & Brooks-Gunn, 1979).

As was noted in Chapter 10 on memory, the development of a sense of self during the second and third years of life has been proposed as one reason for infantile amnesia—our inability to remember information from infancy and early childhood. What we fail to recall is autobiographical memory, and there can be no such memory (no "auto") unless there is a sense of self (see Howe & Courage, 1993).

Once children realize they are distinct from other people and objects, how can we determine how they think about themselves? One way of gaining some insight into children's self-concepts is simply to ask them to describe themselves. Preschool children generally describe themselves in terms of physical characteristics ("I'm strong," "I have brown hair," "I have blue eyes"), by their actions ("I run real fast," "I play baseball," "I walk my dog"), where they live, and who's in their family (Keller, Ford, & Meachum,

1978; Livesley & Bromley, 1973). Rarely do preschool children provide psychological descriptions of themselves (for example, "I'm happy," "I'm smart," "I'm friendly"). This self-definition in terms of physical characteristics is consistent with the Piagetian idea that children's thinking is concrete and tied to specific experiences. This picture does not change substantially during the early school years. As children approach adolescence, their thinking becomes more abstract, and so does the way they view themselves. Children are now more likely to define themselves in terms of psychological qualities—things they like and personality characteristics (Montemayor & Eisen, 1977). (For a more in-depth discussion of the development of self-concept over childhood, see Harter, 1998.)

Cognitive Bases of Gender Identity

Being male or female is a matter of biology. But behaving in a fashion consistent with societal views of masculinity and femininity and identifying oneself with males or females encompasses more than biology. This process of incorporating the roles and values of one's sex is referred to as **gender identification.** Our identification of ourselves as male or female has implications far beyond reproduction. Unlike other demarcations of social standing such as age, occupation, or marital status, our gender is one characteristic that remains constant throughout development. All societies make distinctions between the sexes, although outside of reproduction few if any universal roles or behaviors delineate the sexes. What is universal is the significance that gender has in defining who an individual is in society and the striving of children around the world to acquire an appropriate gender role.

Many factors contribute to children's gender identification (see Eagan & Perry, 2001). One important factor is their ability to understand gender as a concept and that gender remains stable over time and is consistent over situations. Whether a boy decides to identify with his father is related to what he understands about his gender, that of his father, and the continuity of his own gender over time. Children should not be expected to behave as if gender is important if they are not yet aware that differences among males and females exist and that their own gender is constant. Another important factor is children's knowledge of gender stereotypes. What information do they have about how boys and men and girls and women behave, and what consequences does this knowledge have for their own actions and attitudes? In the following sections, I review research on the development of gender constancy and gender schemas and how these cognitive factors relate to the societally important process of gender identification.

Gender Constancy

The Development of Gender Constancy

One of the first people to postulate a cognitive basis for gender identification was Lawrence Kohlberg (1966). He proposed that children's understanding of gender develops in the same way as their understanding of the physical world. According to Kohlberg, knowledge of gender follows Piaget's model of cognitive development, with children not having a mature notion of gender until the advent of concrete operations, beginning about 7 years of age.

Kohlberg proposed that a key cognitive accomplishment in the understanding of gender is that of **gender constancy**—the knowledge that gender remains the same despite changes in physical appearance. Rheta De Vries (1969) conducted one of the first studies to test this aspect of Kohlberg's theory as part of a larger study of the appearance/reality distinction, discussed in Chapter 9. De Vries reported that 3-year-olds believed that a person temporarily changes his or her sex when engaging in opposite-sex behavior or when wearing opposite-sex clothing. That is, boys who wear girls' clothes or play girls' games are, for the time being, girls.

The significance of dress in determining gender for young children is illustrated by an observation Stone and Church (1973) reported. A new family with a baby had moved into the neighborhood. When a 4-year-old girl was asked whether the baby was a boy or a girl, she responded, "I don't know. It's so hard to tell at that age, especially with their clothes off" (1973, p. 297). Another demonstration of gender being determined by dress came from my daughter, Heidi, when she was about 3. She declared that I could not wear a pink shirt because if I did, I would be a girl. The major difference between boys and girls, she said, is that girls wear pink and boys do not. Always fashion conscious, she added that both boys and girls could wear blue and yellow. Pink, it seemed, is the critical color.

Following De Vries's study, several researchers investigated the development of gender constancy in greater detail (Ruble, Balaban, & Cooper, 1981; Slaby & Frey, 1975). In a pioneering study, Ronald Slaby and Karin Frey (1975) interviewed children aged 2 to 5.5 years about their beliefs in the constancy of gender. In agreement with Kohlberg's theory, Slaby and Frey reported three components in the development of gender constancy: gender identity, gender stability, and gender consistency. Slaby and Frey defined **gender identity** as the ability to identify oneself as male or female and to accurately identify the gender of others. **Gender stability** refers to the knowledge that gender remains stable over time. Thus, little boys at some point come to believe that they will become fathers when they grow up, and little girls believe that they will become mothers. The questions the researchers asked made it clear that the children were expressing not just a preference but a necessity; for example, they asked boys: "Could you ever be a mommy when you grow up?" **Gender consistency** refers to the knowledge that gender remains the same despite changes in behavior or dress. The researchers tested this knowledge with questions such as: "If you wore boys' clothes, would you be a girl or a boy?" and "If you played girls' games, would you be a boy or a girl?" These questions might seem trivial to an adult, but answers by preschool children can be quite revealing (for example, "I can't wear girls' clothes, 'cause then I'd be a girl!").

Slaby and Frey reported an age-related developmental sequence, such that gender identity was ac-

quired before gender stability and gender stability was acquired before gender consistency (that is, identity → stability → consistency). Other researchers have confirmed this three-stage sequence, with gender identity being achieved, on average, by 2.5 years, gender stability by 4 or 5 years, and gender consistency by 6 or 7 years (Eaton & Von Bargen, 1981; Ruble et al., 1981). This sequence of development is not confined to North America or to industrialized countries but has also been found in traditional communities in Belize, Kenya, Nepal, and American Samoa (Munroe, Shimmin, & Munroe, 1984).

As with many other aspects of cognition in young children, performance can be helped or hindered by subtle changes in the task. For example, Warren Eaton and Donna Von Bargen (1981) asked preschool children gender-constancy questions pertaining to (1) themselves, (2) a same-sex child, and (3) an opposite-sex child. The children answered the questions relating to themselves at a more advanced level than they did the questions relating to a same-sex child; these latter questions were answered at a more advanced level than the questions relating to an opposite-sex child. In other words, young children become confident of the stability and consistency of their own gender before that of the gender of other children, particularly children of the opposite sex. These, and other research findings (for example, Szkrybalo & Ruble, 1999) indicate that seemingly subtle differences in how the gender-constancy task is administered can result in dramatic changes in children's responses. These findings indicate that beliefs about the constancy of gender are not well established until middle childhood. However, they also indicate that even preschoolers sometimes believe that gender is constant over time and situations. The range of situations in which they believe this, however, is limited and expands with age.

Consequences of Gender Constancy for Gender Identification

Why should knowing that gender is constant over time and over situations affect children's gender identification? For one thing, it makes little sense to learn the behaviors and roles of one gender if you are not certain that your own gender will remain the same.

Several researchers have compared attention to same-sex models for children who score high on tests of gender constancy (knowing that gender is stable or consistent over time), with children who seem unaware of either the consistency or stability of gender. In an early study, by Slaby and Frey (1975), preschool children were shown a 5.5-minute silent video depicting a man and a woman engaging in simple, separate activities. The man was on one side of the screen, and the woman on the other. As children watched the film, an observer recorded the amount of time they spent attending to the male and female models. Slaby and Frey reported that the high-gender-constancy children spent more time looking at the same-sex model than did the low-gender-constancy children, and this effect was stronger in boys than in girls. That is, the high-gender-constancy boys looked at the male model longer than did the other boys (108.2 seconds versus 63.0 seconds), and the high-gender-constancy girls looked more at the female model than did the other girls (86.8 seconds versus 63.8 seconds).

Other researchers have reported findings similar to those of Slaby and Frey. For example, in one study, 5-year-old boys who scored high on gender constancy spent more time viewing TV programs featuring a greater percentage of men than did boys who scored lower on a test of gender constancy; no such effect, however, was found for girls (Luecke-Aleksa et al., 1995).

In other research, Diane Ruble and her colleagues (1981) showed high- and low-gender-constancy children cartoons, complete with commercials of same-sex or opposite-sex children playing with a gender-neutral toy (a movie viewer). Children were later given the opportunity to play with the movie viewer, along with many other toys not shown in the commercial. The results of this study are shown in Figure 13-3. As can be seen, there was little difference between the high- and low-gender-constancy children when viewing a same-sex model. Differences were substantial, however, when the children viewed an opposite-sex model playing with the toy. The low-gender-

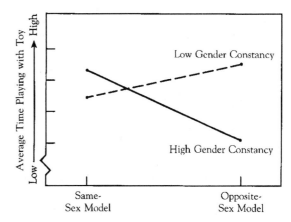

FIGURE 13-3 Average amount of time spent playing with a toy as a function of stage of gender constancy (high versus low) and sex of model in the commercial (same-sex versus opposite-sex). SOURCE: Adapted from "Gender Constancy and the Effects of Sex-Typed Television Toy Commercials," by Ruble, D. N., Balaban, T., & Cooper J., 1981, *Child Development, 52,* 667–673. Copyright © 1981 The Society for Research in Child Development, Inc. Adapted with permission.

constancy children showed no differentiation. They actually played with the movie viewer slightly more when they had seen an opposite-sex child in the commercial. Not so for the high-gender-constancy children: these children knew that gender remains constant over time and that there are certain things that boys do and other different things that girls do. When these young children thought that a toy was appropriate for an opposite-sex child (as reflected by the commercial), they avoided it. The important point here is that this distinction is not made until children have acquired the cognitive sophistication to know that gender is a stable characteristic.

Despite the impressive effects of some of these studies, not all studies looking for the influence of gender constancy of behavior have found it (see Ruble & Martin, 1998). One reason some studies fail to find relations between gender constancy and children's behavior may be attributed to overestimating children's knowledge of constancy. For example, some children may display *pseudoconstancy* (Ruble & Martin, 1998; Szkrybalo & Ruble, 1999), revealing high levels of gender constancy when answering forced-choice questions ("If John wore a dress, would he be a boy or a girl?" "A boy."), but illustrating less secure knowledge when asked to explain their answers. ("He's still a boy 'cause he has a boy's face," or "I don't know why"). In general, gender constancy does show regular increases with age and is (often) related to important gender-related behaviors.

Certainly there is more to the process of gender identification than strictly cognitive factors, but it is very likely that cognitive factors other than gender constancy might be involved in the process (see Ruble & Martin, 1998). In recent years, researchers have emphasized the role of knowledge of gender stereotypes as an important factor, with gender schemas playing a central role as the organizing mechanisms underlying children's gender knowledge.

Gender Schemas

Contemporary cognitive theories of gender identification have been based on the tenets of information processing, particularly the concept of schemas (Bem, 1981; Martin & Halverson, 1981). I discussed the concept of schemas in Chapter 7. A schema is a mentalistic structure consisting of a set of expectations and associations that guide processing with respect to a particular content. A **gender schema** influences how children process information about gender and serves as a way for them to organize information about sex. According to Carol Martin and Charles Halverson (1981), schemas develop primarily from observation. Sex is a salient characteristic in children's worlds, relating both to themselves and to others. It is thus used to organize information in place of other more subtle characteristics of a person or event that older and more knowledgeable children might use. Children use their developing gender schemas to evaluate the appropriateness of some behavior. When children can answer questions such as "Is this OK for boys to do?" positively, they attempt to acquire more information about the activity ("What are the rules of football? How do you throw a pass?").

Not surprisingly, children's knowledge of gender stereotypes increases with age. For example, when children are asked to determine whether a toy (a doll or a gun) or an activity (ironing shirts or driving a truck) is more appropriate for males or females, older children show a greater understanding of the cultural stereotypes than younger children (see Signorella, Bigler, & Liben, 1993, for a review). Also, when children are given the option that an activity or toy might be appropriate for both males and females, elementary school girls are more apt to choose such an activity or toy than boys are, reflecting greater flexibility regarding sex stereotypes in girls than in boys (see Ruble & Martin, 1998, for review).

In most studies assessing children's knowledge of gender stereotypes, concrete objects (for example, hammer, doll) or specific activities (for example, playing football, jumping rope) are used as stimuli. In addition to these objects and activities, however, genders come to have *metaphoric* meanings. Some objects or characteristics, which have no concrete association with either males or females, are nonetheless associated with one gender or the other. For example, most people would tend to associate "bear," "dog," and "angry" with males and "heart," "pink," and "flower" with females. When do children make such associations? Mary Leinbach, Barbara Hort, and Beverly Fagot (1997) developed a test to assess children's knowledge of metaphorical sex stereotypes. They tested children between the ages of 3 and 7 years and reported that children as young as 4 years of age consistently classified metaphorical items according to their "appropriate" gender stereotype, although this tendency increased with age. Three-year-olds, in contrast, rarely made such classifications. Also, Leinbach and colleagues reported that 4-year-old children who were high in gender constancy were more likely to classify sex-stereotyped metaphorical items "appropriately" than were 4-year-olds who scored low on a gender-constancy test.

A particular type of gender schema is the **gender script,** which is a temporally organized event sequence related to gender. Knowledge of such scripts should increase with age, with children presumably becoming more familiar with same-sex than with opposite-sex gender scripts. This was investigated in a study by Martha Boston and Gary Levy (1991). Preschool children were given a series of scrambled pictures that when placed in order would make a coherent event. Some of these events were stereotypically feminine (for example, doing laundry, preparing dinner in the kitchen), and others were stereotypically masculine (for example, building a birdhouse, barbecuing). Children were shown the pictures one set at a time and told to "put these in the order the way they would happen" (1991, p. 424).

First, older preschoolers were better able to sequence the pictures than were younger preschoolers, demonstrating an age-related increase in gender-script knowledge, although even the youngest children (3.5 to 4 years old) performed quite well at sequencing the pictures. Following the researchers' predictions, boys were more accurate at sequencing masculine activities than feminine activities. Contrary to predictions, girls showed no difference in the accuracy of sequencing the feminine and masculine activities.

One primary function of schemas is to organize information, making it more accessible in memory. Several researchers have demonstrated that children better remember information that is consistent with their sex stereotypes than inconsistent information (Bauer, 1993; Liben & Signorella, 1993). Perhaps the most impressive demonstration of this is Patricia Bauer's (1993) study with a group of 25-month-old toddlers. In her study, children were shown a series of six activities: two stereotypically masculine activities (for example, building a house), two stereotypically feminine activities (for example, putting a diaper on a baby), and two neutral activities (for example, having a birthday party). Children were then encouraged to imitate each activity, both immediately and following a two-week delay. The results were similar both for immediate and delayed imitation: Although there was no difference in successful imitation among the three types of activities for the girls, the boys showed greater imitation of the masculine and neutral activities than of the feminine activities. Moreover, the boys spent more time interacting with the props for the masculine and neutral activities than for the feminine activities. These results suggest

that, at least for boys, gender schemas are operating as early as 2 years of age, with boys avoiding traditionally feminine activities.

Although both boys and girls show a decided preference for same-sex toys and activities, and both boys and girls seem to remember and understand same-sex stereotypes better than opposite-sex stereotypes (Liben & Signorella, 1993; Martin, Wood, & Little, 1990), these effects generally appear earlier (as in the Bauer, 1993, study) and are more extreme (as in the Boston and Levy, 1991, study) in boys than in girls. Consistent with these observations, boys show sex-stereotyped toy preferences earlier than girls do (O'Brien & Huston, 1985) and avoid opposite-sex toys more than girls do (Fagot, Leinbach, & Hagan, 1986). One interpretation of these findings is that young boys are more strongly sex-stereotyped than are young girls (Bauer, 1993).

A developmental assessment of gender schemas and their relations to sex-stereotypic behavior was done by Lisa Serbin and Carol Sprafkin (1986). Because sex is a highly salient dimension, Serbin and Sprafkin hypothesized that young children would use gender to classify people and activities to a greater extent than older children would. Older children, whose knowledge of sex roles is greater and whose gender schemas are thus more elaborated, were expected to be more flexible in their classifications, relying less on gender and more on other characteristics of behavior. To assess this hypothesis, 3- to 7-year-old children were administered a gender classification task. In this task, the children were shown photographs of adults engaging in some routine activities. For example, one picture was of a man stirring a pot. The children were then shown three other pictures and were asked to choose the one that "went best" with the standard. One picture was of a man reading (same sex, different activity); children who chose this picture as going with the standard would be making a classification based on gender. A second picture was of a woman rolling dough (different sex, similar activity); children choosing this picture would be making their classification on the basis of type of activity. A third picture was of a woman sweeping (different sex, different activity); this was a control picture, and children who chose this alternative would presumably be responding randomly. The children were also administered tests of sex typing. For example, they were shown pictures of objects typically associated with males (hammer, shovel, baseball) and others typically associated with females (iron, needle and thread, baby bottle) and were asked who would use each object—boys, girls, or both. When children said that either boys or girls could use the object, they were later asked which sex would use it most. The extent to which children made sex-stereotypic responses was used as an indication of their knowledge of sex stereotypes.

Following the researchers' predictions, children's classifications of activities on the basis of gender declined with age. Three-year-olds chose the same-sex/different-activity picture 57% of the time. This percentage decreased to 20% for the 7-year-olds. Furthermore, children's gender classifications were significantly related to their knowledge of sex roles. Children who knew more about sex roles tended to make *fewer* classifications based on gender. In other words, as children's knowledge of sex roles expands, so do their gender schemas. The better established children's gender schemas are, the more flexible they become in interpreting gender differences, and the more tolerant they become of people engaging in cross-sex activities (Stoddart & Turiel, 1985). Thus, whereas a 4-year-old might be aghast that his sister's teenage boyfriend wears a dangling earring, the 7-year-old codes it only as an exception to the rule and realizes that it does not alter the "maleness" of the person.

There are many levels of gender identification, however, and even young children who have mastered only the rudiments of gender differences can behave in a more sex-typed fashion than do less knowledgeable children. For example, Beverly Fagot and her colleagues (1986) assessed the relationship between the ability of young children to identify pictures of males and females and their adoption of sex-typed behaviors. Children between the ages of 21 and 40 months were shown pairs of pictures (one of a male and one of a female) and were asked to identify the boys and girls (or men and women). The children were also observed in their preschool

classroom to obtain measures of sex-typed behaviors. Differences in aggression, interaction with same-sex peers, and play with sex-stereotyped toys (for example, blocks, trucks, and carpentry tools for boys) were measured. The researchers reasoned that 2- and 3-year-old children with greater knowledge of gender differences (as reflected by their ability to identify males and females) should show greater sex-typed behavior.

The results generally supported the researchers' hypothesis of a relationship between gender knowledge and sex-stereotypic behavior in young children. Children who could correctly apply gender labels to the pictures were more likely to play with same-sex peers, and girls who performed well on this task showed almost no aggression in the classroom. Aggression is more associated with males than with females, so preschool girls who showed low levels of aggression were assumed to be displaying more sex-appropriate behavior than were girls who showed more aggression.

Although most of the research cited so far suggests that children's knowledge of gender and gender stereotypes does not becomes apparent until into the third year of life, this would be an overstatement. Before their first birthdays, infants are able to discriminate between men and women, and by their second birthdays can identify themselves and other children as boys or girls. Table 13-4, adapted from Martin, Ruble, & Szkrybalo (2002), provides some of the gender-based knowledge that children demonstrate between 6 months and about 2 years of age. As can be seen, gender has been a salient category in children's lives from very early on, and it should not be surprising that they are quick to associate different behaviors and expectations from males and females, including themselves (once they identify which they are).

Gender Knowledge and Sex-Typed Behavior: Possible Predispositions

Based on what we've reviewed to this point, one would think that children's toy preferences would be related to their knowledge of gender stereotypes. This certainly seems to be true for older children

TABLE 13-4   Time line for early gender development.

Age	Gender-based knowledge and perception
6–8 months	Discriminate between voices of males and females
	Will habituate (reduce looking time) to one category of faces (male or female)
9–11 months	Discriminate between male and female faces
	Associate female faces with female voices
12–14 months	Associate female faces with female voices and male faces with male voices
18–20 months	Associate sex-stereotypic objects with "appropriate" gender (that is, associate male faces with male-stereotypic objects and female faces with female-stereotypic objects)
	Associate verbal labels (lady, man) with appropriate faces
24–26 months	Correctly identify pictures of boys and girls
	Imitate gender-related sequences
	Generalize imitation to appropriate gender (for example, using a male doll to imitate a masculine activity)

SOURCE: Adapted from Martin, C. L., Ruble, D. N., & Szkrybalo, J. (2002). Cognitive theories of early gender development. *Psychological Bulletin, 128,* 903–933.

(Ruble et al., 1981). But it does not appear to be true for children under 3 years old. For example, in the study by Fagot and her colleagues (1986) discussed earlier, toy preference (that is, which toys the children played with during school) was not related to the ability to identify males and females. Rather, boys and girls generally displayed a preference for sex-typed toys regardless of their level of gender knowledge. This finding is similar to that reported by David Perry, Adam White, and Louise Perry (1984), who found no relationship between young children's toy preferences and their knowledge of sex stereotypes for toys. Rather, children (particularly boys) showed a preference for same-sex toys before showing knowledge of which toys are usually for girls and

which are usually for boys. These results suggest that early toy and play preferences are not related to children's understanding of gender. Instead, these patterns might be the result of biological differences in activity and interactional styles between the sexes or to differences in the type of toys and activities adults introduce to children.

Support for a biological rather than an environmental basis for early toy preference comes from studies examining the relation between prenatal exposure to the male hormone androgen and later toy preference (Berenbaum & Hines, 1992; Berenbaum & Snyder, 1995). Children who had been exposed to high levels of androgen before birth (because of overproduction of androgen in the fetus's adrenal glands) were seen when they were between 3 and 8 years old and contrasted for their toy preference with groups of nonaffected boys and girls (Berenbaum & Hines, 1992). (In a nice methodological touch, the control children were sisters, brothers, or cousins of the affected children.) Children were brought into a playroom where stereotypically masculine, feminine, and neutral toys were available. As expected, for the control children, boys played more often with the masculine toys and girls played more often with the feminine toys. For the androgenized boys, there was no difference in their toy preferences from the control boys, although the affected boys spent somewhat greater time playing with the masculine toys than did the control boys (see Figure 13-4). In contrast, the androgenized girls demonstrated a strong masculine toy preference. As can be seen in Figure 13-4, the androgenized girls spent much more time playing with the masculine toys than did control girls, such that their masculine toy preferences were comparable with those of the boys. This pattern of toy preference was replicated in later research (Berenbaum & Snyder, 1995). More recent research has shown that levels of testosterone in pregnant women predicted later gender-role behavior in girls (but not boys) at 3.5 years of age; in contrast, other factors, including the presence of older brothers or sisters in the home, maternal education, and parents' adherence to traditional gender roles, did not predict subsequent gender role behavior (Hines et al., 2002). Along with the findings of Berenbaum and her colleagues, these

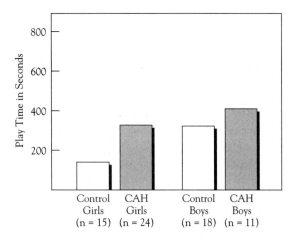

FIGURE 13-4 Average time spent playing with boys' toys for androgenized (CAH) and control boys and girls. SOURCE: Adapted from "Early Androgens Are Related to Childhood Sex-Typed Toy Preferences," by S. A. Berenbaum & M. Hines, 1992, *Psychological Science, 3*, p. 205. Copyright © 1992 Blackwell Publishers. Reprinted with permission.

results suggest that normal variation in levels of prenatal testosterone exposure contributes significantly to gender-related behavior in girls, at least during the preschool years.

These results, coupled with the findings that young children's toy preferences are not related to their knowledge of gender stereotypes, suggest that early toy preference is influenced more by biological than by cognitive factors. Sheri Berenbaum's studies suggest that exposure to prenatal androgen has a defeminizing effect on toy preferences, although extra androgen is apparently not necessary for boys to show this effect. This does not mean, however, that androgen has a direct effect on toy preference. (I seriously doubt that there is a part of the brain that causes us to find toy guns attractive and toy dolls unattractive.) One possibility is that the androgen influences activity level, temperament, or motor skills, which leads to a preference for more stereotypically masculine toys (Halverson & Waldrop, 1973; O'Brien & Huston, 1985).

These findings do not imply that children's gender-related behavior is biologically "fixed." Children around the world are exposed to a wide variety of culturally "appropriate" male and females models, and the social setting, more than anything else, determines what behaviors children will adopt for their own. But it should not be surprising that biology can predispose male and female children toward certain general types of behavior (males more to manipulation of objects and large-muscle activity, perhaps, and females to social relations). And it is interesting that boys tend to be more sex-typed (that is, approach and attend to male and avoid female activities/models) than females are. Might this also reflect a biological influence? Biology is not destiny, and, as has been made clear throughout this book, there are no pure biological or environmental factors on development. But acknowledging that some aspects of gender behavior are influenced by biological dispositions in interaction with a child's social environment can help us better understand the developmental process of gender identification.

Gender Knowledge, Sex-Stereotypic Behavior, and Intelligence

From a cognitive developmental viewpoint, gender is a concept that children acquire by the early school years. Accordingly, bright children should acquire the concept of gender (that is, what gender-appropriate behavior is) earlier than others do. This possibility was evaluated in a meta-analysis examining age, sex, and IQ effects in nearly 200 studies on children's gender schema knowledge (Signorella et al., 1993). The studies examined in this analysis included those that asked children to determine whether objects or activities were masculine or feminine (or both). Margaret Signorella and her colleagues found that children with higher IQ scores were more likely to make sex-stereotypic selections than were children with lower IQ scores (Signorella et al., 1993). (They also reported that children who watched more television made more sex-stereotypic selections, suggesting that children learn gender stereotypes as much from TV as from live people.)

Following these results, if knowledge of gender roles varies as a function of one's level of cognitive development, brighter children should behave in a sex-stereotyped way earlier than do average or below-average children. Jane Connor and Lisa Serbin (1977) investigated this possibility by observing 35 play activities of preschool children. Some of these activities had been evaluated by a sample of adults as being "traditionally masculine" (for example, playing with balls and trucks), others as being "traditionally feminine" (playing with dolls and kitchen utensils), and others as being neutral (playing with a blackboard and puzzles). The amount of time each child spent playing in each activity was recorded and children were assigned a score for sex-stereotypic activity. Boys who engaged mainly in masculine-rated activities, for example, would have high sex-stereotypic scores, whereas boys who engaged mainly in neutral or feminine-rated activities would have lower sex-stereotypic scores. Similar scores were computed for girls. In addition, the children were administered the vocabulary subtest of the Wechsler Preschool and Primary Scale of Intelligence (WPPSI). The results of this study indicated a strong relationship between preschool children's scores for sex-stereotypic activities and their scores on the vocabulary test. When controlling for the effect of age, the researchers found a correlation between sex-stereotypic play activities and vocabulary of .88 for boys and .81 for girls. In other words, preschool children who engaged in sex-stereotypic activities had higher vocabulary scores than did less sex-stereotypic children. These results are consistent with the position that brighter preschool children learn about gender and its significance before less bright children do and behave accordingly.

Children's Theories of Gender

The process of gender identification is a complex one, involving biological dispositions and culture-appropriate experiences. However, it also seems clear that cognitive differences among children contribute substantially to their developing identification with members of their own sex. Controversy does exist concerning how important cognitive factors are in gender identification (in comparison with

environmental and biological factors), as well as which aspects of cognitive development are most important. Moreover, once cognitive factors are given their due, there is the question of how gender knowledge in its various forms influences children's sex roles and behaviors. But there is little question that children's knowledge of gender roles and their understanding of the concept of gender are important for development.

Children realize early that gender is an important dimension and formulate theories concerning exactly what it is that differentiates the sexes. Many of these theories are wrong. For example, a 6-year-old boy noticing that my infant daughter had brown hair, just like his, asked if that meant "she will be a boy when she gets older." A 4-year-old eating at an Italian restaurant with his parents and another couple noticed that his father and the other gentleman had ordered pizza, whereas his mother had ordered lasagna. In the car on the way home, the child announced that he had figured it out: "Men eat pizza and women don't."

Once a child starts mingling with peers, what other children do largely determines what is viewed as appropriate male and female behavior, often independent of the wishes of that child's parents. For example, friends of mine refused to buy guns for their 3-year-old son and restricted the number of aggressive programs he watched on television. Nevertheless, the boy learned from his preschool peers that gun play is boys' stuff: he ran around the house pointing sticks, spoons, or fingers at people and saying "bang," despite constant reprimands from his parents. He had learned from other 3-year-olds one special thing that boys do and, over his parents' objections, was making it something that he did as well.

Children continually gain knowledge about what differentiates males and females in society, and with this knowledge they continually devise and test theories about sex differences (as suggested by "theory theories" of cognitive development, see Chapter 4). Their early theories are simplistic, based on the grossest of characteristics (clothing, for example), and often not even tangentially related to societal sex stereotypes. However, much like the scientist delving into a new field of inquiry, children discard old theories, try new ones, and eventually acquire the meaning of gender that is implicitly agreed upon by members of their society.

How "Special" Is Social Cognition?

Should social cognition be covered at all in a textbook on cognitive development, or does it more properly belong in books about social development? My opinion on this issue should be obvious, given the inclusion of this topic in this book. People use the same brains they use to solve analogical-reasoning problems or to compute the cost per ounce of laundry detergent to figure out what other people are thinking and how they themselves should best behave. Whereas people with faulty mathematical or scientific reasoning abilities will likely get along all right in the world, someone who lacks a well-developed sense of self, an ability to take the perspective of another, or who is ineffective at social information processing, is in for a tough time.

I mentioned in the introduction to this chapter that some people believe that human intelligence evolved in the form that it has chiefly to deal with other members of our species (Alexander, 1989). We are far more intelligent than necessary to eke out an existence on the African savannas. In fact, so are chimpanzees. Nicholas Humphrey (1976) suggested that most of humans' technological genius is absent from our daily lives. If alien anthropologists had observed Albert Einstein during a typical day, they would likely infer that that he had a "humdrum mind." But we do use our superior intelligence every-day when dealing with other people. We became the intelligent species not so much to cope with the demands of a hostile physical world, but to meet the demands of hostile members of our own species.

But this form of cognition, like all others, develops. Children are born prepared by evolution for a social world, but they do not have the requisite skills necessary to function effectively in that world. Their social intelligence unfolds, in part following a universal time line, much as Piaget proposed, but also varying as a function of the particular society they are born into. There is much variability among cultures, and children must have the cognitive skills to adapt to the particular environment in which they live. But what is common to all children across the globe is that they are part of a social species, and they develop the requisite intellectual skills necessary to live in such a world.

Summary

Social cognition is cognition about social relations and social phenomena. Many topics can be subsumed under the heading of social cognition. *Social learning* refers to the acquisition of social information and behavior. Different forms of social learning include *local enhancement, mimicry, emulation,* and *imitative learning.* Whereas both emulation and imitative learning involve the observer understanding the intention of the model, only imitative learning also includes reproducing many of the same actions of the model.

Bandura's *social cognitive theory* is an extension of earlier *social learning theory* and is mainly a theory about how children operate cognitively on their social experiences. Bandura postulated five capabilities that contribute to development, all of which change with age: *symbolization, forethought, self-regulation, self-reflection,* and *vicarious learning.* Bandura believes that children affect their environment as much as their environment affects them and referred to such interaction as *reciprocal determinism.* Following social cognitive theory, *observational learning* involves four subprocesses, each of which changes with development: attentional processes, retention processes, production processes, and motivational processes. *Self-efficacy* is the sense of control people have over their lives, beginning in infancy and developing during childhood. Young children tend to overestimate their abilities, which can be attributed, in part to *wishful thinking,* in which children fail to differentiate between their wishes and their expectations.

Tomasello and his colleagues proposed three types of *cultural learning* (*imitative learning*, *instructed learning*, and *collaborative learning*), each based on underlying perspective-taking abilities that develop during childhood.

Dodge proposed a model that adopts many of the tenets of contemporary information-processing approaches to explain children's social functioning. Dodge proposed five sequential steps of *social information processing* that are necessary for competent social behavior: (1) encoding of the social stimulus, (2) interpretation of the social information, (3) response search, in which children generate possible response alternatives, (4) response evaluation, in which children evaluate the potential effectiveness of the various alternatives, and (5) enactment, in which children execute the chosen response. Dodge and his colleagues have shown a relationship between the efficacy of children's social information processing and their social behavior, suggesting that how children process social information plays a significant role in their social competence.

A child's *self-concept* begins to develop in infancy, with mirror recognition being observed as early as 15 months for some children. Children's self-concept changes during childhood and is reflected in how they describe themselves.

Gender identification is the process of incorporating the roles and values of one's sex. Children's knowledge of *gender constancy* develops during the preschool years, with *gender identity* preceding *gender stability*, which precedes *gender consistency*. *Gender schemas* are mentalistic structures consisting of a set of associations and expectations related to gender. *Gender scripts* are a particular type of gender schema that are temporally organized event sequences related to gender. Gender schemas influence how children process information related to gender and are related to their knowledge of sex stereotypes and gender-related behavior. As children's knowledge of gender expands, their schemas change, resulting in a more sophisticated use of gender in classifying people and behavior. During the preschool years, intellectu-ally more advanced children tend to know more about sex stereotypes than less bright children do.

Key Terms and Concepts

social cognition
social learning
local enhancement
mimicry
emulation
imitative learning
social learning theory
social cognitive theory
reciprocal determinism
symbolization
forethought
self-regulation
self-reflection
vicarious learning
observational learning
self-efficacy
wishful thinking
cultural learning
instructed learning
collaborative learning
social information processing
self-concept
gender identification
gender constancy
gender identity
gender stability
gender consistency
gender schema
gender script

Suggested Readings

Bandura, A. (1989). Social cognitive theory. In R. Vasta (Ed.), *Annals of child development* (pp. 1–60). Greenwich, CT: JAI. This paper concisely presents the most recent formulation of Bandura's social cognitive theory. It deals with the central concepts of social cognitive theory (for example, symbolizing capacity, vicarious learning, and observational learning) and devotes several pages to the issue of self-efficacy.

Dodge, K. A., Pettit, G. S., McClaskey, C. L., & Brown, M. M. (1986). Social competence in children. *Monographs of the Society for Research in Child Development, 51* (Serial No. 213). This monograph presents Dodge's social information processing theory, along with the results of experiments testing the theory. Despite its being nearly 20 years old, I think it's the best source for getting the "big picture" of social information processing.

Harter, S. (1998). The development of self-representation. In N. Eisenberg (Vol. Ed.), *Social, emotional, and personality development*, Vol. 3 (pp. 553–617). In W. Damon (Gen. Ed.), *Handbook of child psychology.* New York: Wiley. Harter presents a thorough review of research and theory on the development of self-concept from infancy through adolescence, including research on self-evaluation.

Ruble, D. N., & Martin, C. L. (1998). Gender development. In N. Eisenberg (Vol. Ed.), *Social, emotional, and personality development*, Vol. 3 (pp. 933–1016). In W. Damon (Gen. Ed.), *Handbook of child psychology.* New York: Wiley. Ruble and Martin provide an up-to-date review of gender development, not only from a cognitive perspective, but also from social and biological perspectives. It is likely the best single source for a comprehensive review of issues, theory, and research on gender development.

Tomasello, M. (2000). Culture and cognitive development. *Current Directions in Psychological Science, 9*, 37–40. This concise presentation of Tomasello's position on cultural learning includes a discussion of some of the different forms of social learning.

InfoTrac College Edition

For additional readings, explore InfoTrac College Edition, your online library. Go to http://www.infotrac-college.com/wadsworth.

Schooling and Cognition

In the previous chapters, we have examined the development of basic cognitive abilities. These abilities, including perceptual discrimination, selective attention, memory, and language, are each modified by the contexts in which children develop. Yet some cognitive abilities seem to develop only in certain contexts, particularly school. Reading is perhaps the best example of this. Children learn to read using universal cognitive skills, but it is unheard of for an unschooled child in an illiterate culture ever to learn to read. We as a species did not evolve to read. Unlike language, reading is rarely acquired "spontaneously." Reading is understandably classified in educational circles as a language skill, but it is a very different language skill, acquired in a very different way, from a child's native tongue. Although all normal children learn to be proficient speakers of their native language, not all learn to be proficient readers, even with instruction.

Reading is perhaps the single most important technological skill in postindustrial cultures. Although one may be regarded as intelligent despite being illiterate, it is difficult to think of an illiterate person becoming educated in modern society. Educational success depends on reading proficiency and so does occupational success. One can sustain life and even support a family legally in our culture while being illiterate, but it is difficult, and few of the rewards of contemporary culture go to those who cannot read. And poor reading among American adults is not a rarity. It has been estimated that nearly one-quarter of American adults—between 35 to 50 million people—cannot read much beyond a third-grade level (see Adams, Treiman, & Pressley, 1998).

If reading is the number one technological skill in modern society, mathematical abilities must come in second. Verbal and quantitative skills constitute the two major subtests of the Scholastic Assessment Test (SAT), the Graduate Record Exam (GRE), and even most IQ tests (see Gardner, 1983). Although there is more to verbal and quantitative abilities than reading and mathematics, these are the core abilities. Unlike reading, basic mathematical skills can be acquired without formal schooling. However, beginning in preschool, children in postindustrial societies receive instruction in simple number concepts and

arithmetic, and math constitutes one of the primary subject areas in schools.

In this chapter, I review the development of reading and mathematical abilities. Both topics have been investigated mainly through information-processing theory, although Jean Piaget had much to say about children's early number concepts. Individual, gender, and cultural differences in these topics have been of great interest to educators and the public at large, and I devote considerable space to these issues. In the latter part of the chapter I look at several issues directly related to cognitive development and schooling. I selected these issues from the many topics that I could have included in this chapter primarily because I believe they are related to issues that we have already dealt with in this book or will deal with in the final two chapters. First, how does the effect of schooling influence cognitive development in comparison with the effect of age? Second, what is the effect of schooling on IQ? And finally, what are the costs and benefits of academic preschools for children from middle-class homes? Issues related to preschool education for children judged to be "at risk for mental retardation" will be discussed in Chapter 15.

The Development of Reading Skills

A Brief Overview of Learning to Read

Learning to read involves acquiring a set of skills that are built on the preceding skills. Jeanne Chall (1979) proposed five stages in the development of proficient reading, ranging from the prereading skills of the preschool child to the highly skilled reading of the adult.

In stage 0, covering the years before a child enters first grade, children must master the prerequisites of reading, most notably learning to discriminate the letters of the alphabet. By the time children enter school, many can already "read" some words, such as "Pepsi," "McDonalds," and "Pizza Hut." Their ability to recognize these popular symbols, flashed at them from the television and seen repeatedly on the road-side or the dinner table, indicates that they can tell the difference between patterns of letters, even if they are unable to sound out the words. Children's knowledge of letters and single words is generally better than it was several generations ago, partly because of the influence of children's television shows such as "Sesame Street."

Stage 1 covers children's first year of formal reading instruction. In first grade, children learn phonological recoding skills, the skills used to translate written symbols into sounds and thus words. This is followed in the second and third grades by stage 2, in which children learn to read fluently. By the end of the third grade, most school children have mastered the letter-to-sound correspondence and can read most words and simple sentences they are given. But reading is effortful for these children, in that the process of identifying individual words requires so much of their limited mental resources that they often do not comprehend much of what they read. They are still concentrating on what individual sets of letters mean and are not very skilled at putting the words together to abstract the broader meaning of the text.

(The transition from "reading by phonological decoding" to "reading individual words" is reflected in the statement of 7-year-old Nicholas, who impressed his grandmother with how well he was reading. "It's a trick, Grandma," he said. "I'm not really reading. I just see the word and I know it." Nicholas no longer had to sound out words to "know" them, and to him, this wasn't reading, it was a trick. Nicholas had "broken the code" as Paula Schwanenflugel (personal communication) says, and he was on his way to "reading to learn" rather than "learning to read.")

The change from "learning to read" to "reading to learn" begins in stage 3, spanning grades 4 through 8. Children can now more readily acquire information from written material, and this is reflected by the school curriculum. Children in these grades are expected to learn from the books they read. If children have not mastered the "how to's" of reading by fourth grade, progress in school can be difficult. Stage 4, beginning in the high school years, reflects truly proficient reading, with children becoming increasingly able to comprehend a variety of written material and to draw inferences from what they read.

Based on this brief description, it would appear that reading does not develop hand in hand with language. Rather, reading is built on a well-established language system and develops alongside general cognitive development.

Emergent Literacy

Although most children learn to read in school, most learn *about* reading in the home. They learn that arbitrary written symbols correspond to spoken language and convey meaning. They learn that language is used to communicate with others, as a memory reminder (writing down a phone number to call later), and for pleasure (Bialystok, 1996). In the United States and many other literate cultures in the world, books are written just for adults to read to children. Parents who share storybooks with their preschool children are teaching them much about reading and are preparing their children for success in a literate culture. (See the discussion in Chapter 3 on the sociocultural nature of early language and reading.)

But most preschool children do not read—not really. They might be able to identify Coca-Cola, Burger King, or Fruit Loops signs when they see them, but this is not really reading. Nevertheless, what children are learning during story times with a parent and in a household where reading is done frequently are skills that set the stage for true reading. The idea that there is a developmental continuum of reading skills, from those of the preschooler to those of the proficient reader, is referred to as **emergent literacy.** According to Grover Whitehurst and Christopher Lonigan, emergent literacy "consists of the skills, knowledge and attitudes that are presumed to be developmental precursors to conventional forms of reading and writing . . . and the environments that support these developments (for example, shared book reading . . .)" (1998, p. 849). Whitehurst and Lonigan (1998) list nine components of emergent literacy, which I discuss briefly here.

1. *Language:* Reading is obviously a language skill, and children need to be versatile with their spoken language before they can be expected to read it. However, skilled (and even early) reading requires more than just proficiency with spoken language. Reading does *not* seem to be simply a reflection of spoken language, with children with advanced language skills becoming children with advanced reading skills. For example, Catherine Crain-Thoreson and Philip Dale (1992) examined a group of early-talkers through several years and found virtually no relation between spoken language skills and literacy knowledge at age 4.5 years. Later reading, however, that involves "reading to learn," might be more sensitive to children's background knowledge, their vocabulary, and familiarity with complex grammar (Mason, 1992).

2. *Conventions of print:* Children exposed to reading in the home know the conventions of print. For example, in English, children learn that reading is done left-to-right, top-to-bottom, and front-to-back.

3. *Knowledge of letters:* Most children can recite their ABCs before entering school and can identify individual letters of the alphabet (although some children think "elemeno" is the name of the letter between "k" and "p"). Knowledge of letters is critical for reading. For example, research has shown that kindergarten children's ability to name letters predicts their later reading achievement scores (Schneider & Näslund, 1999).

4. *Linguistic awareness:* Children must learn to identify not only letters but also linguistic units, such as phonemes, syllables, and words. Perhaps the most important set of linguistic abilities for reading deals with phonological processing, or the discrimination and making sense of the various sounds of a language. More will be said about phonological processing in the following sections.

5. *Phoneme-grapheme correspondence:* Once children have figured out how to segment and discriminate the various sounds of a language, they must learn how these sounds correspond to written letters. Most begin this process during the preschool years, with letter knowledge and phonological

sensitivity developing simultaneously and reciprocally (Burgess & Lonigan, 1998).

6. *Emergent reading:* Many children pretend to read. They will take a familiar storybook and "read" one page after another, often "just like Daddy does," or will take an unfamiliar book and pretend to read, making up a narrative to go along with the pictures on the pages.

7. *Emergent writing:* Similar to pretend reading, children often pretend to write, making squiggles on a page to "write" their name or a story, or stringing together real letters to produce something they think corresponds to a story, a shopping list, or a note to Mom.

8. *Print motivation:* How interested are children in reading and writing? How important is it for them to figure out what the secret code is that permits adults to make sense of a series of marks on a page? Some evidence indicates that young children who are interested in print and reading have greater emergent literacy skills than less motivated children do (Crain-Thoreson & Dale, 1992). Children who are interested in reading and writing are more likely to notice print, ask questions about print, encourage adults to read to them, and spend more time reading once they are able.

9. *Other cognitive skills:* A host of individual cognitive skills, in addition to those associated with language and linguistic awareness, influence a child's reading ability. Various aspects of memory are very important, and some of these will be discussed.

Relations between any specific component of emergent literacy and later reading are sometimes difficult to establish. However, it is clear that families that provide "the whole package" of emergent literacy skills to their children have children who are better readers, both early in school and later, than do families that provide less of the package (Bialystok, 1996; Whitehurst & Lonigan, 1998). This has been confirmed by recent longitudinal studies that report significant relations between emergent literacy skills assessed during the preschool years and reading ability in elementary school (Lonigan, Burgess, & Anthony, 2000; Storch & Whitehurst, 2002).

As in other aspects of school performance, differences in reading are frequently found as a function of socioeconomic status (SES). Children from poverty homes are much more likely to encounter reading problems in school than are children from middle-income homes. The point I want to make here is that these SES differences do not begin in school, but in the home in the years before children begin formal reading instructions. Parents from lower-SES families are much less likely to read to their children, have fewer books in the house, and generally do not foster the emergent literacy skills that are so important in learning to read. Reading may be a highly technological skill, but its origins are in everyday family interactions. Does this mean that children's literacy skills are determined before they enter school? No, but their experiences at home do establish a foundation on which school instruction is based. And the quality of home environments tends to be stable. Children who receive intellectual support for literacy early in life can expect similar support later on. (See Chapter 16 for a discussion of the stability of intelligence.) This implies that children from homes in which emergent literacy is *not* fostered will likely not receive the kind of support during the elementary school years that is associated with proficient reading. However, it also suggests that if the amount or quality of support in the environment (both home and school) changes for the better, so, too, may children's reading abilities.

Cognitive Development and Reading

The Role of Phonological Processing in Identifying Words

Phonemic awareness. One early skill that predicts good reading in later years is **phonemic awareness.** Phonemic awareness is the knowledge that words consist of separable sounds. Such awareness is generally not available to preschool children. In one study, 4- and 5-year-olds were taught to tap once for each sound in a short word (Liberman et al., 1974). For instance, children would tap twice for "at" and three times for "cat." Although the children presumably understood the task, their performance was poor, with none of the 4-year-olds (and only a few of the 5-year-olds) performing it accurately. Although this task might seem trivial, it predicts children's early reading achievement quite well (Liberman & Shankweiler, 1977). Other aspects of phonological awareness (such as children's abilities to detect rhymes) also develop slowly during the preschool and early school years and predict remarkably well children's early reading skills (Gottardo, Stanovich, & Siegel, 1996; Wagner et al., 1997). This is also true in languages other than English (Lundberg, Frost, & Peterson, 1988; Schneider & Näslund, 1999), including Chinese, which includes a phonetic component in its characters (Chan & Siegel, 2001).

Research has shown that children's sensitivity to rhymes leads to awareness of phonemes, which in turn affects reading and also presumably makes it easier for children to recognize written words that both sound and look alike (for example, *cat* and *hat*) (Bryant et al., 1990). Other research has suggested that it is not children's sensitivity to rhymes, per se, that is the critical component to literacy, but rather the ability to segment phonemes (Muter et al., 1998). Valerie Muter and her colleagues tested a group of preschool children (average age, 4 years, 3 months) on rhyming and phonemic segmentation abilities. Tests of rhyming included asking children to identify pictures and then to pick out those that rhyme, and to produce words that rhymed with each of two words ("day" and "bell"). For one test of phonemic segmentation, children were shown a picture of an object (a cat, for instance), the interviewer provided the first two phonemes ("ca"), and children were asked to finish the word (in this case, say "t"). In another test, children were shown a picture and asked to say the word without the first phoneme (for example, "Bus without the /b/ says . . . ," with the correct response being "us"). The researchers reported that reading ability at the end of first grade was significantly related to preschool phonemic segmentation ability but not to rhyming ability (see also Hulme et al., 2002).

Not surprisingly, instruction in phonemic awareness relates to later reading ability. For example, kindergarten and first-grade children who are given explicit instruction in phonemic awareness display better early reading ability than do children not given such instruction (Cunningham, 1990; Schneider et al., 1997). Anne Cunningham states that the results from her training study argue against the idea that phonemic awareness is a consequence of learning to read. Rather, she proposes, as have others (Bryant et al., 1990), phonemic awareness is causally related to reading achievement, even in the early stage of learning to read.

Phonological recoding. The reason that phonological awareness is such a good predictor of early reading, of course, is that early reading generally involves sounding out words. This process of **phonological recoding** is the basis of the majority of reading instruction programs in the United States today (the **phonics** method). Children are taught the sound of each letter and how to combine these sounds, blending them into words.

Truly proficient reading is not done by sounding out each letter but rather by directly retrieving the meaning of the whole word from memory (whole-word or visually based retrieval). Think for a while about how you read. Very few college students sound words out, letter by letter; instead they simply know the meaning of a word when they see it. Adults and older children who read phonetically are not good readers. The amount of mental effort it takes to process a single word by this method is tremendous, making it unlikely that much meaning will be obtained from what is read. Yet without phonological recoding skills, we would be unable to read novel words (such as *defenestration*, defined as the act of throwing something out of a window); we would be limited to reading only words we have learned before. So it seems that phonological skills are necessary if one's reading ability is to advance.

The key to proficient reading is the process of *automatization*, the effortless retrieval of word meaning. Being able to access the meaning of words, expending little or none of one's limited resources in the process, is critical for skilled reading. When too

many mental resources are used just getting the meaning of individual words, too few resources are left to piece the words together and understand the greater meaning of the text. (Recall the discussion in Chapter 5 of the limited nature of mental resources.)

Robert Siegler (1996) developed the **adaptive strategy choice model** to describe how children read words. (Siegler has also applied his model to memory and arithmetic strategies, as discussed in Chapter 6 and later in this chapter.) According to Siegler, children's first choice of a strategy for word identification is that of visually based retrieval (or **fact retrieval**), done automatically (or nearly so). If children are not sufficiently familiar with the word to retrieve its meaning directly from long-term memory, they fall back to more effortful strategies, in this case, phonological recoding. As children become more experienced with the words they read and better able in general to automatize processing, reading becomes more proficient.

Phonological processing and reading disabilities. There is substantial evidence that perhaps the principal cognitive factor underlying reading disability, often referred to as **dyslexia,** is faulty phonological processing (Adams et al., 1998). Children are said to have a reading disability if they have great difficulty in learning to read despite an average intelligence. Stated another way, if a child's reading ability is substantially worse than his or her general intellectual ability would predict, that child is said to be reading disabled, or dyslexic.

Keith Stanovich (1988) proposed that phonological processing is a relatively modular function, little influenced by "higher," conscious cognitive structures. Thus, according to Stanovich's model, phonological processes should be independent of other, more general aspects of cognition, including IQ. There is evidence that this is the case. For example, Linda Siegel (1988) reported that reading-disabled children from a range of IQ levels have equal difficulty on phonological processing tasks. For instance, pseudoword reading requires children to read a sequence of pronounceable letters that do not make up an English word (for example, *joak, kake*). Related to pseudoword reading, phonological-lexical tasks re-

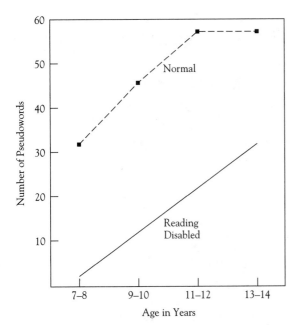

FIGURE 14-1 Accuracy of pseudoword reading as a function of age for normal and reading-disabled children. SOURCE: "The Cognitive Basis of Dyslexia," by L. S. Siegel. In R. Pasnak and M. L. Howe (Eds.), *Emerging Themes in Cognitive Development*, Vol. II: *Competencies*. Copyright © 1993 Springer-Verlag. Reprinted with permission.

quire children to determine which of two pseudowords sounds like a real word (for example, *kake, dake*). In Siegel's study, performance of reading-disabled children was poor on these tasks and did not differ among children as a function of IQ level.

Reading-disabled children's phonological-processing abilities improve with age, but these children typically start school with poorer phonological skills than do good readers and usually stay behind. For example, research by Siegel and her colleagues (Siegel, 1993; Siegel & Ryan, 1988) compared the phonological processing of groups of reading-disabled and nondisabled children between the ages of 7 and 14 years. As one test of phonological processing, children were asked to read pseudowords. The results are shown in Figure 14-1. As can be seen, older disabled readers were better at pseudoword reading than younger disabled readers were, demonstrating that

these skills were developing. However, the performance of 13- and 14-year-old disabled readers was comparable to that of 7- and 8-year-old nondisabled readers, reflecting significant retardation of this skill. Moreover, more recent longitudinal research suggests that phonological-processing abilities remain relatively stable over childhood (Storch & Whitehurst, 2002; Wagner et al., 1997), making early intervention all the more important.

Recent research using brain-imaging techniques has supported the interpretation that phonological problems are at the core of many reading disabilities. Sally Shaywitz and her colleagues (1998) gave adults with developmental reading disabilities (dyslexia) and non–reading-disabled adults a series of reading-related tasks that varied in the amount of phonological processing required to perform each task. Brain activation patterns, as measured by functional MRI (see Chapter 2), were observed between the normal and dyslexic readers. Shaywitz and her colleagues reported different brain-wave patterns for the normal and dyslexic readers, especially when the tasks required substantial phonological processing. Compared with the normal readers, the dyslexic readers showed underactivation in some portions of the brain (mainly posterior regions) and overactivation in others (mainly anterior regions). Underactive parts of the brain included those areas typically associated with phonological processing and cross-modal integration. In reading, cross-modal integration (see the discussion of cross-modal integration in infancy in Chapter 7) involves the translation of symbols in one modality (in this case vision, as in the letters and words on a page) into another modality (in this case audition, as in the sounds of letters and words). Shaywitz and her colleagues concluded that the patterns of brain activity of dyslexic readers "provide evidence of an imperfectly functioning system for segmenting words into their phonological constituents . . . and adds neurobiological support for previous cognitive/behavioral data pointing to the critical role of phonological analysis and its impairment in dyslexia" (1998, p. 2640).

Further evidence for the neurological basis of dyslexia comes from a study assessing brain activation patterns of dyslexics in Great Britain, France, and Italy (Paulesu et al., 2001). Eraldo Paulesu and his colleagues reported similar patterns of brain activity (PET) while reading for groups of English-, French-, and Italian-speaking dyslexics. Moreover, all three groups showed deficits in tests of phonological short-term memory, pointing, again, to problems in phonological processing as the basis for dyslexia. But there was an interesting catch in this study. Although dyslexics from the three languages did equally poorly in tests of phonological processing, only the English and French speakers showed problems in reading. The Italian dyslexic group displayed relatively good reading ability.

Why should this be so? The reason seems to be related to the specific language people speak, and specifically, the relationship between how a language is spoken and how it is written. The correspondence between spoken and written Italian is quite close. Italian uses 25 phonemes, and 33 combinations of letters are used to represent these sounds. In contrast, English uses 40 phonemes, but 1,120 different letter combinations are needed to completely represent these sounds. That is, English (and French) *orthography* (the structure of words) is irregular, making it difficult for children to learn the letter-sound correspondence in the language; in comparison, the orthography in languages such as Italian (and Finnish, for example) is highly regular, making it relatively easy to learn the letter-sound correspondence. As a result, dyslexia is diagnosed much more frequently in English than in Italian speakers (about twice the rate).

The relationship between children's reading ability and the degree to which the written language corresponds to the spoken language (that is, the degree to which a language is orthographically regular), can also be seen in research with nondyslexic readers. Figure 14-2 presents the percentage of children speaking and reading orthographically regular languages (Greek, Finnish, and Italian) and orthographically irregular languages (French, Danish, and Scottish English) who correctly read familiar real words and pseudowords (Goswami, 2002; Seymour, Aro, & Erskine, 2003). As can be seen, performance was nearly perfect for children reading languages with regular orthography, but much lower for children reading languages with irregular orthography.

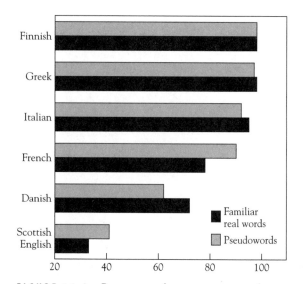

FIGURE 14-2 Percentage of correct responses of children reading familiar real words and pseudowords for orthographically regular languages (Finnish, Greek, and Italian) versus orthographically irregular languages (French, Danish, and Scottish English). SOURCE: Adapted from data in Seymour, P. H. K., Aro, M., & Erskine, J. M. (2003), 94, 143-174. Foundations of literacy acquisition in European orthographies. *British Journal of Psychology.*

What this research indicates is that the neurological basis of dyslexia is universal, likely the result of unknown genetic or prenatal anomalies; however, the likelihood that this particular neurological abnormality will adversely affect reading is a function of how closely the written language of one's culture corresponds to the structure of its spoken language. If we recall from Chapter 3 our discussion of the tools of intellectual adaptation a culture provides to its members, the relation between the structure of one's spoken and written language is another unexpected (at least to me) way in which one's cultures influences one's thought.

Comprehension

Reading involves more than just identifying words. Reading involves understanding language, including stories, instructions for assembling a VCR, and cognitive development textbooks, among other things. Children must relate the meaning of individual words and sentences to abstract the broader meaning that a written text intends. Such a process is referred to as **reading comprehension.**

The role of working memory in reading comprehension.

Reading comprehension is not a single process but a set of processes that must all be integrated to function smoothly. Individual words must be identified and related to other words in the sentence. One factor that limits children's comprehension is the amount of information they can hold in working memory at any one time. Meredyth Daneman and her colleagues proposed that it is necessary for information to be retained in working memory for as long as possible so that each newly read word in a passage can be integrated with the words and concepts that preceded it. Younger or less-proficient readers have less available mental capacity to store and maintain information in working memory because it is necessary for them to devote considerable capacity to the processes involved in identifying words and comprehension. Daneman and her colleagues showed that listening span, defined as the number of successive short sentences that can be recalled verbatim, correlates significantly with comprehension for people ranging from preschoolers to college students (Daneman & Blennerhassett, 1984; Daneman & Green, 1986).

As with phonological coding, differences in working-memory capacity differentiate disabled from nondisabled readers (Siegel & Ryan, 1989; Swanson, Ashbaker, & Lee, 1996). For example, Linda Siegel and Ellen Ryan (1989) gave normal and reading-disabled children, ranging in age from 7 to 13 years, a series of incomplete sentences, requiring them to supply the final word of each sentence. Sentences included the following: "In the summer it is very _____. People go to see monkeys in a _____. With dinner we sometimes eat bread and _____." After being presented two, three, four, or five such sentences, children were asked to repeat the final words, in order, that they had generated for each sentence. The results of the

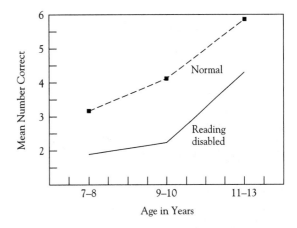

FIGURE 14-3 Performance on a working-memory task as a function of age for normal and reading-disabled children. SOURCE: "The Cognitive Basis of Dyslexia," by L. S. Siegel. In R. Pasnak and M. L. Howe (Eds.), *Emerging Themes in Cognitive Development*, Vol. II: *Competencies.* Copyright © 1993 Springer-Verlag. Reprinted with permission.

study are graphed in Figure 14-3. As can be seen, working memory improved for both the disabled and normal readers with age, but the disabled readers had shorter memory spans than the normal readers at each age level.

Individual differences in working memory are not only related to reading comprehension but also to writing ability. H. Lee Swanson and Virginia Berninger (1996) reported that working memory performance was a significant predictor of both reading comprehension and writing ability in groups of fourth-, fifth-, and sixth-grade children. However, Swanson and Berninger proposed that writing skills are related to a domain-specific set of working-memory operations, whereas reading comprehension is related to a more general set of processing resources.

The role of knowledge in reading comprehension.

Another critical factor in reading comprehension is the knowledge an individual has of the material being read. As discussed in earlier chapters, having detailed knowledge of a topic permits one to process information about that topic more efficiently (Bjork-lund, Muir-Broaddus, & Schneider, 1990). This is especially true in reading comprehension.

Richard Anderson and his colleagues (Anderson et al., 1984) defined reading as "a process in which information from the text and the knowledge possessed by the readers act together to produce meaning" (p. 8). In other words, "reading is a constructive process" (p. 9), in which the background knowledge that one brings to a text interacts with what is written on the page to produce understanding. Anderson and his associates cite considerable evidence from the research literature to support these claims. In one study, for example, second-graders who were equated in reading skill were tested for their knowledge of spiders and then given a passage about spiders to read (Pearson, Hansen, & Gordon, 1979). The children who knew more about spiders at the outset were better at answering subsequent questions about the passage, especially those questions that involved reasoning. Instructional efforts aimed at increasing background knowledge have also been found to enhance reading comprehension (Hansen & Pearson, 1983; Omanson et al., 1984). The relation between background knowledge and text comprehension will be explored further in Chapter 16.

In other research, the ease with which children could think of a sentence containing a word (referred to as *context availability*) predicted several aspects of word processing (word identification, determining whether a set of letters was a word or not) for second-, third-, and fifth-grade children, and for high- and low-ability readers in each grade (Schwanenflugel & Noyes, 1996). However, the effect of context availability was greater for younger and low-ability readers than for older and high-ability readers. Paula Schwanenflugel and Caroline Noyes suggested that young and low-ability readers have difficulty connecting low-context available words to their meanings, and the result is many reading errors. Although context availability might not be equivalent to "knowledge" as defined by Anderson and his colleagues (1984), it is, I argue, a function of word knowledge, and this research

demonstrates the importance of background knowledge not only for reading comprehension but also for reading individual words.

The role of monitoring on reading comprehension. Another factor related to reading comprehension is the ability to monitor one's understanding of a text and to adjust reading strategies accordingly (Brown & Smiley, 1978; Paris & Oka, 1986). Good readers easily recognize when they don't comprehend something they are reading. They then take the necessary action to rectify the situation. This can involve rereading a sentence, reading more slowly, checking back a few lines to see if some important information might have been missed, or perhaps consulting a dictionary. These are ideal skills; children do not approach them until the high-school years, and many people never develop them fully. In general, comprehension-monitoring skills improve with age and experience (Baker, 1985; Garner, 1990), and, importantly, they can be improved with instruction (Palincsar & Brown, 1984).

How to Instruct Children How to Read

The focus of this chapter is on children's developing cognitive abilities as they relate to important tasks, here reading. As such, I have chosen not to get involved in the often-heated debate of how best to teach children how to read. However, the topic should not be totally neglected, and I will briefly outline the two major approaches to reading instruction and comment on how the research evidence weighs in on this topic.

Basically (and simplistically), reading instruction can be thought of as either (1) a *bottom-up process,* with children learning the individual components of reading (identifying letters, letter-sound correspondence) and putting them together to achieve meaning; or (2) a *top-down process,* with children's goals, background knowledge, and expectations determining what information they select from text (see Adams et al., 1998). This latter is a constructivist perspective, reminiscent of Piaget's ideas. Surely, skilled reading involves both bottom-up and top-down processes, making any dichotomy artificial. However, reading instruction, particularly in the early grades, often emphasizes one over the other, and thus the dichotomy has some basis in reality.

Curricula that emphasize bottom-up processes are exemplified by the phonics method, discussed earlier. Here, children are taught specific letter-sound correspondence, often independent of any "meaningful" context. Curricula that emphasize top-down processes are exemplified by the **whole-language approach.** According to Marilyn Adams and her colleagues, "the whole language approach holds that learning is anchored on and motivated by meaning. Further, since meaning and meaningfulness are necessarily defined internally and never by pronouncement, learning can be effective only to the extent that it is cognitively controlled by the learner" (1998, p. 277). Thus, whole-language curricula emphasize reading interesting and meaningful text from the very beginning. Classrooms where whole language is taught are more apt to be student—rather than teacher—centered, have an integration of reading and writing within the overall curriculum, have an avoidance of drill, and are less likely to have rigid abilities groupings. All this sounds quite inviting, actually. However, many proponents of the whole-language approach "have steadfastly, adamantly, and sometimes vitriolically denied the value and rejected the practice of skills instruction, including phonics, and this has been a point of heated contention" (Adams et al., 1998, p. 277).

The research evidence reviewed earlier in this chapter should make clear the importance of basic-level (bottom-up) processing in learning to read. Phonological skills are the single best predictor of reading ability (and disability). These abilities do not develop spontaneously, but are acquired only with practice, and usually explicit instruction. Curricula that ignore phonics, regardless of how "meaningful" they make the experience of reading, are risking the literacy of many of their students. This is not to argue for a curriculum that has children reading only stories about "Dick, Jane, and their dog Spot." But it does argue for including some aspects of phonics in any reading instruction.

Gender Differences in Reading and Verbal Abilities

"Female superiority on verbal tasks has been one of the more solidly established generalizations in the field of gender differences," wrote Eleanor Maccoby and Carol Jacklin (1974, p. 75) in introducing their section on gender differences in verbal ability in their seminal book that set the stage for contemporary investigations of gender differences. Despite this strong opening statement, Maccoby and Jacklin followed with the observation that the magnitude of such differences is small and often insignificant, but when differences do appear in the data, they usually favor females.

The definition of verbal tasks can be quite broad. It typically includes tests of vocabulary, spelling, and reading comprehension, all topics closely associated with reading. As we saw in Chapter 11, gender differences in rate of language acquisition favoring girls are sometimes found (and sometimes not) but are small in magnitude. Gender differences in verbal tasks have been found more frequently, again favoring females, but, as we'll see, the differences are not always robust and they seem to be getting smaller over the years.

In this section, I examine research evidence concerning possible gender differences in reading and other verbal tasks. Are females really more verbal than males, and if so, what is the nature of this difference? One concern of most researchers interested in gender differences is their source. Is it possible to determine whether differences, when found, have a primarily biologic origin or can be traced primarily to environmental causes?

Gender Differences in Reading Ability

In reviewing research on gender differences, Diane Halpern concluded that females, on average, perform better than males do on "tasks that require rapid access to and use of phonological and semantic information in long-term memory, [and] production and comprehension of complex prose" (1997, p. 1091). There is no single reason for these gender differences, but the preponderance of boys who are classified as reading disabled is strong evidence for a biological basis for gender differences in reading ability. Boys are far more likely than are girls to be in special education classes for reading, and it is likely that most studies that have assessed gender differences in verbal abilities (including reading) have excluded reading-disabled children (Hyde & Linn, 1988). Thus, perhaps gender differences in general reading ability would be found to be greater were more low-scoring boys included in the testings. But, more to the point, the fact that many aspects of reading disabilities can be traced to basic cognitive abilities that are found early and tend to be stable over childhood suggests that there is a substantial biological component to reading disabilities.

Despite this evidence, what do gender differences in reading disabilities tell us about the nature of possible gender differences in the general population? Can we generalize our findings of gender differences from research with the learning disabled to normal populations, or are dyslexic children a qualitatively distinct subgroup? I don't have an answer to this question, but the fact that gender differences are so small in the normal population and that boys are so overrepresented in reading-disabled classes suggests that we must be cautious in generalizing from the dyslexic to the general population concerning the nature of gender differences.

Reading and the expression of feelings (both verbal tasks) are viewed as stereotypically female activities and might contribute to girls' superior verbal skills. Also, many of the stories in children's reading books are not inherently interesting to children (Blom, Waite, & Zimet, 1968), and there is evidence that boys are particularly motivated by the interest level of the reading material. For example, Steven Asher and Richard Markel (1974) reported that fifth-grade boys displayed better comprehension for stories of high interest than for those of low interest. This difference in reading level was much smaller for fifth-grade girls. Gender differences in reading ability were small and insignificant for high-interest stories but large and significant in favor of girls for low-interest stories (see Figure 14-4). Similar findings of a greater influence of topic interest on reading and

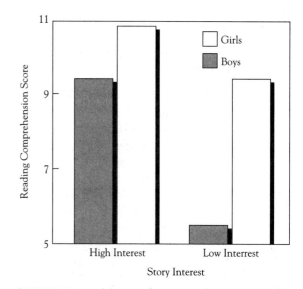

FIGURE 14-4 Mean reading comprehension scores for high- and low-interest stories for groups of fifth-grade boys and girls. SOURCE: Adapted from Asher, S. R., & Markel, R. A. (1974). Sex differences in comprehension of high- and low-interest reading material. *Journal of Educational Psychology, 66*, 680–687. Copyright © 1974 by the American Psychological Association. Adapted with permission.

academic performance for boys than for girls have been reported by several other researchers (Renninger, 1992; Schiefele, Krapp, & Winteler, 1992).

Meta-Analytic Studies of Gender Differences in Reading and Verbal Abilities

Maccoby and Jacklin's 1974 review of gender differences was primarily descriptive. That is, they reviewed the literature for studies that examined gender differences and computed a "box score" of the results, finding girls to be the "winners" more frequently than the boys were. This does not give us an idea of the magnitude of the effects, however. During the past 25 years or so, a new method—termed **meta-analysis**—has permitted researchers to better appreciate the magnitude of gender differences across a large number of studies. I discussed meta-analyses with respect to spatial cognition in Chapter 8. Meta-

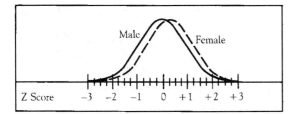

FIGURE 14-5 The idealized distribution of verbal ability for males and females. SOURCE: "How Large Are Cognitive Gender Differences? A Meta-Analysis Using v^2 and d," by J. S. Hyde, 1981, *American Psychologist, 36,* 892–901. Copyright © 1981 American Psychological Association. Reprinted with permission.

analysis provides an estimate of *effect size*, which is expressed in terms of how large the average differences between males and females are across the various studies, taking into consideration the overall amount of variability. An effect size of 1.0 would mean that the average male-female difference was one standard deviation in magnitude. If this were for IQ, for example, it would be equivalent to saying that the average difference between the sexes was about 15 points, which would be quite substantial. The statistic of effect size is used because it would be meaningless to compute mean performance across the many different studies, which used different measurements and often assessed different verbal tasks. By using the effect size statistic, differences in performance among different studies can be meaningfully combined.

The first meta-analysis of verbal gender differences was reported by Janet Hyde (1981), who examined 27 studies of verbal ability included in the original Maccoby and Jacklin review. Hyde reported an effect size of .24 (about one-quarter of a standard deviation, favoring females) and concluded that the gender of the child alone accounted for approximately 1% of the variance in verbal performance. In other words, these findings mean that the difference, although statistically significant, is small in absolute magnitude. To understand the magnitude of these differences, look at the idealized distribution of verbal skills for males and females graphed in Figure 14-5 (expressed as standard scores). We can see substantial overlap of

performance between the genders, and the absolute difference in the means are small.

Since the publication of Hyde's report, several other meta-analytic studies have been published, and they point to the same conclusion: Although gender differences in verbal abilities favoring females continue to be found, the effect size is small in an absolute sense, and, perhaps surprisingly, getting smaller (Feingold, 1988; Hyde & Linn, 1988; Marsh, 1989, but for a different interpretation of the data, see Hedges & Nowell, 1995). For example, Janet Hyde and Marcia Linn (1988) reviewed 165 different studies, involving 1,418,899 participants, and reported that the effect size, again favoring females, for studies published after 1973 was .10, or one-tenth of a standard deviation (compared with .23 for pre-1973 studies). In fact, since 1972, performance on the Scholastic Assessment Test (SAT)-Verbal has actually slightly favored males (mean scores = 437 for males and 425 for females, effect size = −.1086). This seems particularly anomalous, given the general belief among college students that females perform better on the SAT-Verbal than males do (Feingold, 1988).

What might be the reason for the decline in gender differences in verbal abilities between the sexes during the past 40 years, and for the actual reversal on the SAT-Verbal? One possibility, suggested by Hyde and Linn (1988), is that there has been an increase in the flexibility of gender roles beginning in the 1970s, with boys being encouraged to engage in activities previously reserved for girls. Another possibility is that test publishers during the past 30 years have been attempting to minimize gender differences in their tests, possibly accounting for the diminished gender differences in performance (Stanley et al., 1992). Although others question this interpretation (Feingold, 1988), it seems that changes in test construction are at least partly responsible for the small male superiority now found on the SAT-Verbal. The verbal portion of the SAT includes more technical and science-related topics than did earlier versions, and males likely have a better knowledge base for such material (Halpern, 1992; Hyde & Linn, 1988).

Based on the most recent meta-analyses, what can be concluded about gender differences in verbal skills? First, they do seem to exist but are so small on average that knowing the gender of a person would not help one predict how verbal he or she would be. Even if these differences are based in biology, the two sexes are biologically more alike in verbal abilities than they are different.

Children's Number and Arithmetic Concepts

Although the quintessential symbols of human cognition are probably found in language, a good case can be made for the primacy of number. Our tendency to quantify objects and events in our world is ubiquitous. The bulk of the technological advancements made during the past three centuries, and particularly in the last century, can be attributed to our species' quantitative skills. Although children develop a basic sense of number and mathematical relations without explicit instruction, most people's mathematical abilities are acquired through formal instruction. This is true even of simple arithmetic as well as more complicated mathematics.

In the following sections, I review aspects of children's earliest concepts of number and then take a brief look at the development of basic arithmetic skills. Although mathematical reasoning, in our culture, develops beyond arithmetic, most developmentally oriented research has focused on children's acquisition of arithmetic concepts, and I review this literature here. I then look briefly at characteristics of math-disabled children, followed by a look at cross-cultural differences in mathematical achievement. At the conclusion of this section, I examine the controversial topic of gender differences in mathematical ability. Do such differences exist? If so, how big are they, and what difference do they make?

Conservation of Number

Piaget (1965) believed that the concept of number is reflected in conservation. **Conservation-of-number** tasks follow the same basic procedures as all of Pia-

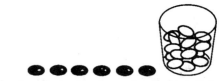

"Select from the jar the same number of white jelly beans as there are black jelly beans."

"Are there the same number of black jelly beans as there are white jelly beans?"

The row of white jelly beans is extended while the child watches.

"Are there the same number of white jelly beans as there are black jelly beans now? Which has more? Why?"

FIGURE 14-6 A conservation-of-number task.

get's conservation problems. Children are first shown a set of items—black jelly beans, for instance. The children are then asked to take white jelly beans from a container so that there are an equal number of black and white beans. Once the appropriate number of white beans has been selected (with assistance from the experimenter, if necessary), the beans are arranged in two rows, one black and one white (see Figure 14-6). While the children are watching, the experimenter spreads out the white jelly beans so that the line of white beans extends beyond the line of black beans. The children are then asked if the two rows still have the same number of jelly beans. If they answer no, they are asked which row has more, and why.

As with conservation in general, Piaget proposed three stages in the acquisition of the conservation of number. In stage 1, children are unable to consistently establish a one-to-one correspondence between the two sets of items. So, for example, stage-1 children select too few or too many white jelly beans or fail to arrange them in a one-to-one relationship with the black beans. When two equal sets of beans are established and one is modified, children say that the longer, less-dense row now has more beans in it, being unable to ignore the perceptual differences between the two rows. During stage 2, children can establish an "intuitive one-to-one correspondence" (Piaget, 1965) between the items in the two sets, but judgments of equivalence between the sets do not last long. Once the beans in one row are extended, the children say that there are more in the longer row. Only the stage-3 child (concrete operations) realizes that the number of beans does not change when one of the rows is elongated, but that changes in spatial extension of elements are compensated for by equivalent changes in the density of the elements.

Subsequent research, using variants of Piaget's original task, has generally replicated his observations, illustrating that (1) children are able to form a one-to-one correspondence before they can conserve; (2) young children make their evaluations on the basis of relative length, independent of other factors; (3) slightly older children sometimes consider density but do not coordinate the dimensions of length and density, thus failing to conserve in many situations; and (4) not until 7 or 8 years of age do children consistently pass conservation-of-number tasks (see Brainerd, 1978a).

Intuitive Mathematics

Arithmetic is one of education's three Rs, and thus a discussion of its development clearly belongs in a chapter devoted to schooling and cognition. But, just as language serves as a basis for reading (and writing), there are "cognitive primitives" that underlie arithmetic and other mathematical skills. Recall from Chapter 2 our discussion of David Geary's (1995) ideas about *biologically primary* and *biologically secondary abilities*. The former represent basic cognitive abilities that were selected during evolution to solve recurrent problems faced by our ancestors, are universal, and are acquired at about the same time and in about the same way by all normally developing children. In contrast are biologically secondary abilities

TABLE 14-1 Potential biologically primary mathematical abilities.

Numerosity

The ability to accurately determine the quantity of small sets of items or events without counting. In humans, accurate numerosity judgments are typically limited to sets of four or fewer items.

Ordinality

A basic understanding of *more than* and *less than* and, later, an understanding of specific ordinal relationships. For example, understanding that $4 > 3$, $3 > 2$, and $2 > 1$. For humans, the limits of this system are not clear, but it is probably limited to quantities < 5.

Counting

Early in development there appears to be a preverbal counting system that can be used for the enumeration of sets up to three, perhaps four, items. With the advent of language and the learning of number words, there appears to be a pan-cultural understanding that serial-ordered number words can be used for counting, measurement, and simple arithmetic.

Simple Arithmetic

Early in development there appears to be sensitivity to increases (addition) and decreases (subtraction) in the quantity of small sets. This system appears to be limited to the addition or subtraction of items within sets of three, perhaps four, items.

SOURCE: From D. C. Geary. (1995). Reflections of evolution and culture in children's cognition: Implications for mathematical development and instruction. *American Psychologist, 50,* p. 36.

that are built on biologically primary abilities, are specific to a particular culture, and often need tedious repetition and external pressure for their mastery. Most mathematics, of course, including simple arithmetic, are examples of biologically secondary abilities, but Geary (1995, 1996) proposed that the quantitative skills that children master in school are based on a set of biologically primary abilities, specifically numerosity, ordinality, counting, and simple arithmetic, which are defined briefly in Table 14-1.

Numerosity refers to the ability to determine quickly the number of items in a set without counting. This does not necessarily require understanding the difference between "two" and "three," for example, but only being able to discriminate consistently between the number of items within small arrays. We saw in Chapter 7 that infants are capable of making such discriminations (Starkey, Spelke, & Gelman, 1990), and it has been observed in many mammal and bird species (Davis & Pérusse, 1988), including cats, chimpanzees, and an African grey parrot.

Ordinality refers to a basic understanding of *more than* and *less than* relationships, and this, too, seems to develop in infancy. For example, in one study, 16-month-old infants were shown computer screens consisting of arrays of dots that varied in number. They were conditioned to point to either the smaller or larger of the arrays (Strauss & Curtis, 1981). For instance, an infant might be repeatedly shown arrays of three and four dots and reinforced for touching the array with three dots. Following training, babies were shown arrays with different numbers of dots, in the present example, two versus three dots. Which array will they point to? If they had learned merely to point to the absolute number of dots in an array, they should continue to point to the array with three dots in the transfer phase, but if they instead had learned an ordinal relationship (select the array with the smaller number of dots), they should point to the array consisting of two dots. Infants did the latter, suggesting they had learned an ordinal relationship.

Ordinality is clearly a more complex concept than numerosity, but again it does not seem to be unique to humans. In one interesting study with wild rhesus monkeys that had become accustomed to the presence of humans, it was shown that these animals do apparently have an understanding of *more than* and *less than* relations when small numbers are involved (Hauser, Carey, & Hauser, 2000). Researchers placed pieces of food, one at a time, under one of two distinctive containers as a monkey watched. The number of pieces of food in the containers always differed, varying from one to eight. After placing the food in the containers, the researchers then walked away and observed which container the monkey first approached. When the number of food pieces in the two boxes varied by only one, and the total number of food pieces in the most numerous box was not greater than four, the monkeys consistently approached the box with more pieces in

it. That is, for contrasts of 0 versus 1, 1 versus 2, 2 versus 3, and 3 versus 4, the monkeys consistently approached the box with the greater number of food pieces. For larger numbers the monkeys were less able to make the distinction of "approach the larger" first. These results suggest that monkeys do have a "natural" understanding of ordinality for small quantities, suggesting that human's ordinality skills are evolutionarily quite old.

Whereas numerosity and ordinality develop early in life, counting and simple arithmetic take longer to develop and show considerable change over the preschool and school years. And the amount of research devoted to these topics has been considerable. I discuss some of this research in the following two sections.

Young Children's Knowledge of Number: The Role of Counting

Although the methodologies used to assess numerosity and ordinality make it unlikely that most adults would recognize such abilities in their infants, by the time children can speak, they give the impression of having some concept of number. The 18-month-old might respond with a loud and definitive "Two!" when asked how many cookies he wants, and the 3-year-old might point at her dolls, saying "One, two, three, seven, nine, twelve-teen, three-teen, seventeen." Each is displaying some knowledge of number, yet neither is using numbers with the same consistency and meaning that a 7- or 8-year-old child is capable of.

How do children's conceptions of numbers develop? One popular non-Piagetian candidate for the precursor of number conservation is counting. Rochel Gelman and C. R. Gallistel (1978) extensively investigated children's early counting and have proposed five principles of counting:

1. *The one-one principle:* Each item in an array is associated with one and only one number name (such as "two").
2. *The stable-order principle:* Number names must be in a stable, repeatable order.
3. *The cardinal principle:* The final number in a series represents the quantity of the set.

4. *The abstraction principle:* The first three principles can be applied to any array or collection of entities, physical (for example, chairs, jelly beans) or non-physical (for example, minds in a room, ideas).
5. *The order-irrelevant principle:* The order in which things are counted is irrelevant.

Gelman and Gallistel (1978) referred to the first three principles as the "how-to" principles of counting and proposed that children as young as 2.5 years demonstrate knowledge of them under some circumstances. For example, in a counting experiment where 3-, 4-, and 5-year-old children were asked to discern the number of objects in a series of arrays, all groups of children used the one-one principle (that is, one unique number name per object), although performance deteriorated for the youngest children for arrays of six or greater. Let me provide an example of a 4-year-old child's difficulty applying the one-one rule. Brendan and his grandfather were playing a "catch" game, in which each took a specified number of steps backward before one threw a ball to the other. In playing, Brendan called his numbers aloud, one number per step. This began to break down, however, once the numbers got larger than five. He'd call out "One, two, three, four, five, six, seven, eight, nine," pausing between announcing some of the larger numbers. But although his counting slowed down when he reached six, his stepping didn't. By the time he got to "nine" he'd taken more than a dozen steps, violating the one-one rule of counting.

Gelman and Gallistel (1978) also reported that children who counted items in arrays used the stable-order principle; more than 90% of the 4- and 5-year-olds and 80% of the 3-year-olds used the same list of number words in the same order on all of their trials. The children sometimes used an idiosyncratic list of number words (for example, "one, two, six"), but they used this list consistently across arrays of varying size.

Children seem to have mastered the cardinal principle by age 4. For example, Karen Fuson and her colleagues demonstrated that after counting arrays of objects ranging in number from 2 to 19, 3- and 4-year-old children generally gave the last counting word they had spoken in response to the question "How many things are there?" (Fuson et al., 1985). This was true even for children who counted incorrectly, implying that accurate counting is not a requirement for attainment of the cardinal principle (see also Gelman, Meck, & Merkin, 1986). However, many 2- and 3-year-olds seem to have only a tenuous grasp of the cardinality principle (Bermejo, 1996). For example, children might correctly count a set of objects, "One, two, three, four, five," but, when asked how many objects are in the set, instead of stating the last number they counted ("five"), they often count again (Fuson, 1988). It's as if the purpose of the first count was independent of determining "how many" objects were in the set. Most of these children can come up with the correct answer, but that they seemed to think that a second count was necessary suggests that this knowledge is not well established.

In related research, Diane Briars and Robert Siegler (1984) investigated children's knowledge of the counting principles. These researchers asserted that children must induce which features of counting are critical and which are merely optional in enumerating an array, and they speculated that some children might believe that more is required for successful counting than is actually the case. In their experiment, 3-, 4-, and 5-year-old children watched a puppet counting and were asked to determine whether the puppet had counted properly. The puppet demonstrated (sometimes accurately and sometimes inaccurately) five features of counting, one of which was necessary for counting and four of which were optional. The necessary feature was that of word-object correspondence, which encompasses the first two principles of Gelman and Gallistel (one-one correspondence and stable order). The four optional features were that (1) adjacent objects were counted consecutively, (2) counting started from the end rather than the middle, (3) counting progressed from left to right, and (4) each object in an array was pointed to exactly once. Children's knowledge that word-object correspondence was critical in counting increased with age (30%, 90%, and 100% for the 3-, 4-, and 5-year-olds, respectively). However, 60% of the 5-year-olds also viewed other features, such as beginning to count at an end rather than in the middle and pointing to each object only once, as essential. In other words, young children learn the critical features of counting by 4 years of age but infer, from watching others, additional features that are characteristic of, but not necessary for, proper counting.

The relation between children's counting and conservation of number has been explored in several experiments. For instance, Karen Fuson, Walter Secada, and James Hall (1983) reported significantly higher levels of number conservation (69%) by 4- and 5-year-old children who were required to count the elements in both sets before judging which set, if either, was larger, than by children given a standard conservation-of-number task (14%).

In another experiment, Geoffrey Saxe (1979) administered a series of counting and conservation tasks to 4-, 5-, and 6-year-old children. On the counting tasks, the children were required to assess the equivalence of two rows of dots differing in length and, later, to select the same number of beads from a container as there were dots on a card. In each case, the task was constructed so that counting was necessary to yield the correct answer. The conservation tasks were similar to those used by Piaget, with beads in one row compressed on one trial and elongated on another. Saxe classified each child as conserving or not conserving on the conservation-of-number tasks and as prequantitative or quantitative on the counting tasks. The children were classified as prequantitative if they counted items in the arrays but did not use the results of counting to solve the problem. They were classified as quantitative counters if they used counting to aid their performance, although they might not have used exactly the same number words or order as adults conventionally do. Saxe found that no child who was prequantitative with respect to counting was also a conserver; in contrast, 22 children displayed sophisticated counting skills but were still unable to conserve (see Table 14-2). In related research, Catherine Sophian (1995) reports that children under 6 years of age do not conserve number when they are prevented from counting the arrays. These findings are consistent with the view that quantitative counting skills are

TABLE 14-2 Number of children classified jointly according to understanding of number concept (conservers versus nonconservers) and counting ability (prequantitative versus quantitative).

	Number concept	
Counting ability	Nonconservers	Conservers
Prequantitative	12	0
Quantitative	22	20

SOURCE: Adapted from "Developmental Relations Between Notational Counting and Number Conservation," by G. Saxe, 1979, *Child Development, 50,* 189–197. Copyright © 1979 The Society for Research in Child Development, Inc. Adapted with permission.

a necessary but not sufficient condition for the attainment of conservation of number.

In summary, young children do possess a limited knowledge of numbers, relations among numbers, and counting, but they are restricted to dealing with small quantities. As children's knowledge of numbers expands, they refine their number concept, discriminating between what is necessary and what is optional in dealing with numbers; and importantly, their ability to deal with large quantities increases and their belief in the invariance of number is applied more consistently across a wider range of tasks.

Children's Arithmetic Concepts

Clearly young children have some concept of number. They can count and can determine which of two quantities is the larger. And research discussed in Chapter 9 by Karen Wynn (1992) using the violation-of-expectation method suggested that even 5-month-old infants have some appreciation of addition and subtraction of small numbers. But when can children perform tasks of basic arithmetic such as addition and subtraction? These skills are not formally taught until the first grade in many schools, and from a Piagetian perspective, they require concrete-operational ability.

Piaget's Perspective on Children's Early Arithmetic

Piaget (1965) proposed that addition and subtraction require inversion reversibility, something that is not achieved (according to Piaget) until about 7 years of age. For example, if 5 + 3 = 8, then, by the logical rule of inversion, 8 – 3 must equal 5.

In one experiment, Piaget (1965) showed children an array of eight objects. The array was then modified; for example, it was divided into two equal sets of four objects and was then divided a second time into unequal sets (seven and one, for instance). Do children recognize the equivalence of these two groupings? In other words, do they know that 4 + 4 is the same as 7 + 1? As with conservation of number, Piaget reported three stages in children's early arithmetic abilities. In stage 1, characterizing 5- and 6-year-olds, the children typically relied on the spatial arrangement of the objects, erroneously asserting that there were different numbers of elements in the two combinations. In stage 2, the children could correctly solve the task, but only after counting the objects or establishing a spatial one-to-one correspondence between the items. The stage-3 children (7-year-olds) solved the problem without resorting to physical counting techniques. Without this understanding, according to Piaget, children cannot have a true comprehension of addition, although they can be taught to memorize certain formulas (for example, 2 + 3 = 5, but will they know what 3 + 2 equals?).

More recent research has questioned some of Piaget's interpretations and has demonstrated that even preschool children are able to handle simple addition and subtraction problems. Their approaches to addition and subtraction usually involve counting out loud, often with use of fingers or other objects. I discussed children's counting strategies in Chapter 6. The simplest strategy consists of counting from 1 to the first addend (in 3 + 5 = ?, the first addend is 3), then counting the second, then counting the two together (for example, "1, 2, 3 . . . 1, 2, 3, 4, 5 . . . 1, 2,

3 . . . 4, 5, 6, 7, 8"; or a bit more efficiently, "1, 2, 3 . . . 4, 5, 6, 7, 8"). This has been referred to as the **sum strategy,** and although it usually produces the correct answer, it takes a considerable amount of time to execute and is not very effective when large addends are involved (such as 23 + 16 = ?). A more economical counting strategy has been called the **min strategy,** and involves starting with the larger addend and then counting up from there—that is, making the *minimum* number of counts. For example, given the problem 3 + 2 = ?, a child would start with the cardinal value of the first number ("3") and continue counting from there ("4, 5"). Preschoolers use a variety of such rules to arrive at correct answers to simple addition and subtraction problems. These rules, however, almost always involve forward counting by ones of concrete objects, including fingers (Carpenter & Moser, 1982). Such addition and subtraction by counting can be successful for unpracticed combinations such as 14 + 1 = ? and 15 – 1 = ?, which is in violation of Piaget's tenet that true addition cannot be achieved by simple counting.

The Development of Mental Arithmetic

Sometime during the early school years, children's solutions to simple arithmetic problems become covert. They no longer rely on counting objects or their fingers but perform the calculations in their heads. At this point, knowing precisely what children are doing becomes more difficult because the only evidence of the mental processes underlying performance is the answers they give. However, children's arithmetic strategies can be inferred from how quickly they solve the problems. For example, if children are using the min strategy, their reaction times to solve problems will vary as a function of the second, smaller addend.

In fact, based on patterns of reaction times to solve simple addition problems, it has been demonstrated that children in the early elementary school years frequently use the min strategy (Groen & Resnick, 1977). In the min model (the mathematical model used to describe children's use of the min strategy), a mental counter is set to the first addend (in the problem 5 + 3 = ?, the counter would be set to 5). The counter is then increased by increments of one until enough have been added (here, 3). Children's reaction times to solve problems vary as a function of the second, smaller addend. Thus, for any individual child, arriving at an answer for 5 + 4 (thinking "5 . . . 6, 7, 8, 9") takes longer than arriving at an answer for 5 + 2 (thinking "5 . . . 6, 7") because the mental counter must tick off four times for the former problem but only two times for the latter. In other words, reaction times are proportional to the smaller, or minimum, number being added.

Some time during the elementary school years, children begin to use fact retrieval to answer simple arithmetic problems (see Ashcraft, 1990). When adults are given the problem 7 + 5 = ?, for example, they need not start at 7 and mentally increase this by 5 to arrive at the answer. Rather, the knowledge that 7 + 5 = 12 resides in long-term memory, and this fact can be retrieved just like any other fact in memory.

This shift in development from procedural (that is, counting) to retrieval-based techniques for solving simple arithmetic problems reflects changes in the efficiency of information processing. With age, children solve problems more quickly. This increased speed can be attributed to the fact that processes are becoming more automatic, requiring less of one's limited mental capacity for successful execution. First-graders' use of counting strategies is highly conscious and laborious in contrast with the fact retrieval of older children. However, even 5- and 6-year-olds apparently store and retrieve some arithmetic facts. For small whole-number problems (for example, 2 + 2 = ?), young children's performance is relatively rapid, indicating fact retrieval (Siegler & Shrager, 1984). With age and experience, more arithmetic facts become stored and can be retrieved with increasing ease, without the need of laborious counting procedures. Although children learn how to multiply later than they learn how to add, much of even third-grade children's multiplication seems to be based on fact retrieval (Koshmider & Ashcraft, 1991), likely as a result of memorizing the multiplication tables.

Arithmetic becomes more complex, of course, and as it does, children must rely again on procedural knowledge. When subtraction involves "borrowing" (as in 92 – 59 = ?) or addition involves "carrying" (as in 92 + 59 = ?), procedures are at first slow and difficult, but with practice they become more efficient. In general, the development of arithmetic competence can be described as involving an increase in the efficiency of both procedural knowledge and, most important, information retrieval (Ashcraft, 1990). Older children know more facts, can retrieve those facts more easily, and, when necessary, can use arithmetic procedures more efficiently than younger children can.

One factor that appears to be important in successful mental arithmetic is working memory (Passolunghi & Siegel, 2001). To arrive at a correct answer to a simple problem such as 7 + 5 = ?, children must hold the two addends in mind and execute the addition operation (either by retrieving the "fact," or through some counting method). John Adams and Graham Hitch (1997) have shown for groups of both English- and German-speaking children (ranging in age from about 7.5 to 11.5 years) that differences in memory span play a critical role in computation. Adams and Hitch also found a relation between the speed of adding the digits and both age and memory span, confirming the role of speed of processing in memory span discussed in Chapter 5.

Another factor related to children's successful use of arithmetic strategies is metacognition, as reflected by children's knowledge of the effectiveness and appropriateness of different strategies. For example, Martha Carr and Donna Jessup (1995) presented second-grade children with sets of arithmetic problems and metacognitive assessment in April and tested them again in June. Children were asked about the effectiveness of the strategies they used (for example, "Why did you use that way for this problem?"), and other questions about the appropriateness of the strategy (for example, "When do you use that way to get the answer?" and "Is there any time it's not a good idea to use that way?"). Carr and Jessup looked at changes in children's use of the min strategy, fact retrieval, and decomposition and the relation between changes in strategy use and metacognition. **Decomposition** consists of transforming the original problem into two or more simpler problems.

If the problem were 13 + 3 = ?, for example, a child might say, "13 is 10 and 3; 3 and 3 are 6; 10 and 6 are 16; so the answer is 16."

Children's use of the decomposition and fact retrieval strategies increased during the two-month period (although the *accuracy* of fact retrieval did not increase during this same time), and the use of the min strategy decreased over time. How did children's metacognitive knowledge in April predict their strategy use in June? Quite well for the decomposition strategy, but not well at all for the use of fact retrieval. Carr and Jessup reasoned that metacognition is important when strategy use is both effortful and in the early stages of being acquired, something that described the decomposition strategy well. It is less important, however, for highly automated and less effortful strategies, such as fact retrieval.

Is Children's Acquisition of Arithmetic Strategies Stagelike?

The impression one might get from this research is of a steady improvement in arithmetic strategy use, with children moving from the sum to the min to the fact-retrieval strategy in a regular, stagelike progression. Such a view is not entirely accurate, however. At any given age, children use a variety of strategies to solve arithmetic problems, although the average sophistication of their strategies increases with age (Ashcraft, 1990; Hopkins & Lawson, 2001).

Robert Siegler and his colleagues have demonstrated this in several studies. In one study, kindergarten and first- and second-grade children's reaction times to solve the problems were obtained from a video recording of the sessions (Siegler, 1987). Following completion of each problem, the children were asked what they had done to "figure out the answer to that problem." The problems were selected so that different patterns of reaction times among the problems were predicted by various models (for example, the min model, the fact-retrieval model, and a counting model).

Based on analyses of reaction times, errors, and verbal reports, Siegler discerned five general approaches to solving the addition problems. Four of these were the sum strategy, the min strategy, decomposition, and the fact-retrieval technique, as discussed previously. A fifth strategy was guessing. Most children used a variety of these strategies on the problems; 62% reported using three or more across the various problems. The min strategy was used most frequently, but even it was used on no more than 40% of the trials at any age. The older children were more likely to use the fact-retrieval and decomposition strategies than were the kindergarten children. In general, the children showed little homogeneity of strategy use in these addition problems. Siegler and Jeff Shrager (1984) reported similar findings for 4- and 5-year-olds. In their study, the use of strategies varied as a function of the difficulty of the problem. The harder the problem, the more likely the children were to use overt strategies such as counting on their fingers, rather than covert strategies such as fact retrieval.

Siegler and Eric Jenkins (1989) looked at the acquisition of the min strategy using a short-term longitudinal study (or a microgenetic approach, see Chapter 3). In this study, Siegler and Jenkins examined the development of arithmetic strategies in eight children over an 11-week period. Four- and 5-year-old children were selected who (1) could perform simple addition using counting methods but (2) never used the min strategy. Over 11 weeks, these children were given a series of addition problems to solve.

Siegler and Jenkins reported that all the children used multiple strategies. These included the sum, min, fact retrieval, and decomposition strategies discussed earlier, plus strategies such as finger recognition (putting up two fingers on one hand and three on the other and saying "five"), shortcut sum (similar to the sum), counting from the first addend (similar to min, but counting the larger addend), and guessing. The percentage of the most frequently used strategies can be seen in Figure 14-7. As can be seen, there was great variety in strategy use. Moreover, different children used different combinations of the strategies, so that any particular child used a unique mixture of the strategies in his or her solutions. (See similar findings that were reported for arithmetic and other strategies in Chapter 6.) Also,

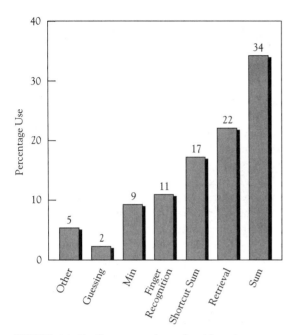

FIGURE 14-7 Percent use for each arithmetic strategy. SOURCE: Adapted from Siegler, R. S., & Jenkins. E. (1989). *How children discover new strategies*. Hillsdale, NJ: Erlbaum.

during the 11 weeks, the children's strategies tended to become more sophisticated, so that the children who started mainly by guessing or using the sum strategy progressed to using the min or fact-retrieval strategy more frequently.

One major aspect of the Siegler and Jenkins study was children's "discovery" of the min strategy. Remember that none of the children were using the min strategy at the beginning of the study. By the 11th week, seven of the eight children were using the min strategy, and six of these children were able to describe how they used it. It is interesting to note that the first time the children used the min strategy, and on the problem immediately before it, they took much longer than average to arrive at a solution. Siegler and Jenkins speculated that the longer times spent on these problems indicated that the children were experiencing conflict, or interference from alternative strategies and that new strategies require more mental effort than previously established ones.

Thus, the children required more time and did some hemming and hawing before arriving at an answer.

Siegler's adaptive strategy choice model, discussed earlier in this chapter with regard to reading and in Chapter 6, applies here as well. The model proposes that, in general, the various strategies that children know compete with one another (Siegler, 1996). Sometimes one strategy will win the mental competition (the min strategy, for example) and sometimes another strategy will win (fact retrieval, for example). With age, experience, and improved information-processing abilities, more sophisticated strategies are apt to win, so that min, on average, replaces sum, and later on, fact retrieval replaces min. But for new problems or problems with which children are less familiar, the older, more familiar, or fallback strategies often come up as the winners.

Thus, from Siegler's perspective, strategy development is not a simple matter of replacing older, less sophisticated strategies with newer, more powerful ones. Rather, multiple strategies reside side by side in one's mind and compete with one another for the chance to solve problems. There are age changes in which newer strategies are likely to win the competition, but old strategies never die—they just lie in wait for the chance to be used in cases where the newer strategy doesn't quite fit or fails to produce the correct answer.

Are Humans the Only Species That Can Add?

Although it may not have come as a big surprise to you that monkeys have some notion of numerosity or ordinality as discussed earlier (Hauser et al., 2000), it may come as a surprise that these primates can add, or at least display some ability comparable to simple addition. It did to me. Gregory Sulkowski and Marc Hauser (2001) illustrated this by evaluating the ability of free-living rhesus monkeys to subtract. Monkeys were shown food objects placed on two side-by-side stages. Screens then covered the stages, hiding the food from the monkey's vision. In some conditions, the experimenter removed food from behind the screens while the monkey watched. Although the monkey could not see how many pieces of food were behind each screen, it could keep track of how many pieces were removed. If monkeys can subtract, they should be able know which stage has the largest cache of food and approach that one first when the people back off and let the monkey approach. This is exactly what happened, so long as the number of items initially placed behind the screen did not exceed three.

In other research, a human-reared (enculturated) chimpanzee named Sheba was taught the Arabic numerals 1 through 8 (Boysen, 1993; Boysen & Berntson, 1989). When Sheba was shown a number on a video screen ("3," for example), she would have to point to an array containing three objects to receive a reward. In one set of experiments, one to four orange slices were placed at two of three sites in the laboratory. Sheba's task was to inspect the sites, return to a home base, and select the Arabic numeral that represented the sum of the orange slices. So, for example, if one site had one orange slice, a second had three, and the third had none, Sheba would have to select the Arabic numeral "4" to be correct. Sheba performed correctly on the first trial, requiring virtually no training. In a second experiment, the arrays of oranges were replaced by Arabic numerals. So instead of finding one and three orange slices at two sites as in the example above, she would find only the numerals "1" and "3." Sheba performed significantly above chance on this task beginning with the first experimental session. Sheba's simple arithmetic performance is comparable with the simple counting strategies observed for 3- and 4-year-old children, and suggests that simple human-like addition abilities can be used by at least some chimpanzees. This also suggests that the basic arithmetic abilities shown by human infants and young children may be evolutionarily old, making it less surprising that preschool children acquire basic numerical skills so easily.

Math Disabilities

When discussing the development of reading earlier in this chapter, I found it useful to examine cognitive differences between normal and reading-disabled children, partly because reading is such an important technological skill that reading disabilities are important in their own right, but also to provide additional support for the mechanisms that underlie "normal" development. One way of inferring that a process is important to development is to look at processing in children who show some disabilities. The same logic holds true for math disabilities.

Math-disabled children can be identified early (in kindergarten) and their progress in arithmetic followed. David Geary and his colleagues have taken this longitudinal approach and report that math-disabled children display two types of difficulties (Geary, 1993, Geary, Brown, & Samaranayake, 1991). First, these children show poor procedural skills, in that they use a more immature mix of arithmetic strategies than normal children do. Also, first-grade math-disabled children show poorer knowledge of the rules of counting. Using a procedure similar to the one described earlier by Briars and Siegler (1984) in which a puppet counts arrays either correctly or incorrectly, Geary and his associates found that math-disabled children demonstrated an immature understanding of counting. For example, many believed that adjacent items in an array had to be counted consecutively for the count to be correct. However, Geary and his colleagues note that the procedural skills of many kindergarten and first-grade math-disabled children approach those of their normal peers by the end of second grade. That is, with respect to using procedures, they catch up, suggesting that their deficit was a developmental delay.

The second source of difficulties for math-disabled children is a memory-retrieval deficit. Math-disabled children retrieve fewer facts from long-term memory (that is, they use fact retrieval less often), and when they do, they are often wrong. Moreover, simple practice at fact retrieval alone does not appreciably improve performance, and, unlike procedural difficulties, these deficits tend not to improve to the level of their agemates with time (see Geary, 1993).

One possible reason for these children's persistent problems with fact retrieval has to do with working-memory capacity. For example, Geary and his colleagues (1991) reported that the digit spans for math-disabled children (4.2 words) were about one word less than for nondisabled children (5.3 words).

This deficit might be the result of faster decay of information (that is, the memory representations might disappear more quickly in working memory for math-disabled children), of slower counting speed (recall from Chapter 5 that digit span is related to articulation rate), or of a slower domain-general speed-of-processing capacity (Bull & Johnston, 1997). Because these children make computation errors, they arrive at many incorrect answers, and these answers can become part of their long-term memory representations of arithmetic facts. Unfortunately, they are wrong.

The deficits shown by many math-disabled children are similar to those shown by many reading-disabled children. In fact, there is considerable overlap between the two populations. In a large-scale study of math disabilities, Nathlie Badian (1983) reported that 43% of math-disabled children were also classified as reading disabled, and that 56% of reading-disabled children were similarly classified as math disabled. Both math and reading disabilities seem to share a common problem—the inability to retrieve information efficiently from long-term memory. Math facts are thought to be represented in a semantic network system, much as word definitions are. Geary (1993) proposed that a single deficit underlies many math and reading disabilities. "At the cognitive level, this deficit manifests itself as difficulties in the representation and retrieval of semantic information from long-term memory. This would include fact-retrieval problems in simple arithmetic and, for instance, word-recognition and phonological awareness in reading" (1993, p. 356). In addition, phonological processing, so important in reading, also is implicated in mathematics. Children with better phonological processing skills tend to show better math computation ability (Hecht et al., 2001; Swanson & Sachse-Lee, 2001).

Yet, many children read just fine but have great difficulty in math, and vice versa. It appears that there is no single cause of math disability (or of reading disability, for that matter), and that some of these disabilities are domain specific in nature. However, the substantial overlap between the reading- and math-disabled populations suggests that some domain-general abilities are involved in these important technological skills, namely working-memory capacity and efficiency of retrieval from semantic memory.

Cultural Differences in Mathematics

Mathematics is truly the universal language (although many would give that distinction to love, I suppose). Regardless of one's native tongue, the rules of mathematics are the same all over the globe. However, most forms of mathematics beyond arithmetic are explicitly taught, at least in our culture. Yet, people from traditional cultures still have a need for basic arithmetic and other forms of mathematical problem solving. How do people from nonschooled societies acquire mathematics? How is it similar to and different from what happens in cultures such as ours where formal schooling is universal?

Differences in mathematical attainment also occur between different information-age cultures. In recent years, this has been brought to the public's attention by reports of substantial differences in mathematics performance between American children and college students and those from other information-age cultures, particularly those in East Asia. How different are Americans from East Asians in mathematical attainment, when do those differences appear, and what factors contribute to them? These issues will be discussed in the next section, following a brief examination of arithmetic in unschooled cultures.

Arithmetic in Unschooled Children

Research examining the arithmetic ability of nonschooled Brazilian children has shown that these children possess a high level of computational skill, but only when the problems are tied to real-life situations. For example, Terezinha Carraher, David Carraher, and Analucia Schliemann (1985) examined 9- and 15-year-old unschooled street vendors and gave them a series of arithmetic problems to solve. Problems that were imbedded in real-life contexts (for example, "If a large coconut costs 76 cruzeiros, and a small one costs 50, how much do the two cost together?") were solved at a much higher rate than were the same problems presented out of context (for example, "How much is 76 + 50?"). Carraher and associates reported that the children answered the context-appropriate questions correctly 98% of the time; in contrast, the out-of-context questions were answered correctly only 37% of the time. Reviewing their research on schooled versus nonschooled Brazilian children's mathematical reasoning, Schliemann (1992) stated that these children use mathematics to solve everyday problems, where mistakes have real consequences. This is contrasted with school learning, in which children are taught standardized procedures with little or no application. Schliemann (1992) concluded that unschooled street vendors (and unschooled people from other professions, such as brick layers and lottery bookies) develop a flexible arithmetic system and apply it appropriately within their work context, and that "unschooled people develop at work not only fixed procedures to solve specific problems but a conceptual and flexible understanding of the mathematical models applied to solve problems" (1992, p. 2).

In other research, Steven Guberman (1996) showed that Brazilian shantytown children frequently use their knowledge of currency to help them to solve school-type arithmetic problems. Also, interviews with children's parents indicated that parents adjusted the complexity of the purchases they asked their children to make depending on the perceived skill of the child. As children grew older and more arithmetically competent, parents presented them with more difficult real-world problems to solve (purchases to make). This is consistent with "working within the zone of proximal development," a concept developed by Lev Vygotsky (1978) and discussed in some detail in Chapter 3.

Academic Performance by American and Asian Schoolchildren

Evidence has been accumulating that American school children lag behind children from other industrialized countries in their academic knowledge, including mathematics (Baker, 1992; Stevenson & Lee, 1990). Figure 14-8 graphs mathematics test scores of first- and fifth-grade children from the United States (Minneapolis), Japan (Sendai), and Taiwan (Taipei) (Stevenson & Lee, 1990). As can be seen, the children from the United States performed more poorly than did the children from the two Asian cultures, with the differences being quite substantial as early as the first grade. The magnitude of the differences suggests that the Chinese and Japanese children are getting a better mathematics education than the American children, but that this gap is found so early points to differences in the home.

One possible reason for the early difference might be the greater digit spans for many East Asian relative to American children because of differences in the rate at which the number words can be articulated in the different languages (Geary et al., 1993; see the discussion in Chapter 5). But there are also early differences in the use of arithmetic strategies. Geary and his colleagues have examined differences in the arithmetic strategies used by Chinese and American first graders (Geary et al., 1996; Geary, Fan, & Bow-Thomas, 1992). The researchers reported that Chinese first-grade children used a more sophisticated mix of strategies, including decomposition. The Chinese children were also faster at retrieving an answer directly from long-term memory (that is, at fact retrieval) than the American children were. However, this speed advantage was apparently limited to retrieval of arithmetic facts and did not reflect an overall greater speed-of-processing advantage, for the Chinese and American children were equally fast at counting (recall, however, our discussion in Chapter 3 about Chinese preschool children being able to count to 20 before American children could [Miller et al., 1995]). Other research has shown that this advantage in the use of arithmetic strategies for Chinese relative to American children is present even before the start of formal schooling (Geary et al., 1993).

One might ask, "So what?" We're talking about the most basic of arithmetic abilities, which American children clearly master by the end of elementary school. But children's early arithmetical accomplishments set the stage for later achievements. Geary and his colleagues (1992) argue that "if the mastery of basic skills facilitates the acquisition of

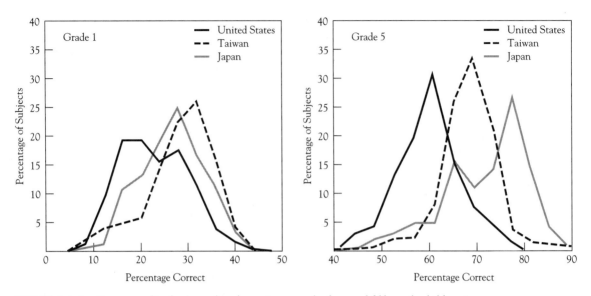

FIGURE 14-8 Frequency distributions of mathematics scores for first- and fifth-grade children in the United States, Japan, and Taiwan. SOURCE: "Context of Achievement," by H. W. Stevenson & S. Y. Lee, 1990, *Monographs of the Society for Research in Child Development, 55.* (Serial No. 221). Copyright © 1990 The Society for Research in Child Development, Inc. Reprinted with permission.

more complex mathematical concepts and procedures, then the results of the current study suggest that Chinese children will have a consistent 3- to 4-year advantage over their American peers in the development of mathematical cognition" (1992, p. 184).

What is the origin of these differences? One source of the difference is likely practice. Children who practice elementary computation more frequently are able to retrieve math facts more quickly from long-term memory and have greater opportunities to develop arithmetic strategies than do children who practice them less often (Geary et al., 1992). Harold Stevenson and his colleagues report that Chinese and Japanese children do indeed spend more time on mathematics, both in and out of the classroom (Fuligni & Stevenson, 1995; Stevenson & Lee, 1990). Thus, we have the very commonsense finding of practice makes perfect (or at least makes for enhanced performance), with children who practice arithmetic more frequently (Chinese and Japan-

ese children) performing better than children who practice it less frequently (American children).

But what causes this cultural difference in time invested in mathematics and the overall greater academic performance? Again, the answer is quite commonsensical: parents' attitudes and behavior regarding education and child rearing. Although American parents tend to believe that their children's academic performance is due to effort, this tendency to emphasize effort and hard work is even more obvious in Japanese and Chinese parents. Japanese mothers, for instance, are more likely to believe that their children's academic performance can be improved than are American mothers. These Japanese women also take personal pride in the success of their children (and shame in their failure) and require their children to establish regular study habits. They are less likely to be satisfied with their children's academic performance, and they set higher academic standards for their children than American mothers do. In addition, the Buddhist, Confucian, and Shintoistic traditions of Japan, which value order, intellectual growth, and social good, might contribute to a cultural setting that is geared for success in school.

Because of Japan's cultural traditions, children also spend more time in school and devote a higher percentage of their school time to academic material than do American children. For example, whereas the average school year in Minneapolis is 174 days, it is 230 in Taipei and 243 in Sendai (Stevenson & Lee, 1990). Recent research has shown that American kindergarten (Frazier, 1993) and first-grade children (Frazier & Morrison, 1998) show greater improvements in academic subjects as a result of attending an extended-year schooling program (210–230 days) rather than a school program of conventional length (180 days).

It's worth noting that American children of recent Asian descent perform better in school, on average, than do white or black native-born Americans (Chen & Stevenson, 1995). A major reason for this difference is the attitudes that Chinese American and Japanese American parents have toward education. For example, Chin-yau Lin and Victoria Fu (1990) compared the child-rearing practices of European American parents with those of Chinese parents from Taiwan and immigrant-Chinese parents living in the United States. Lin and Fu reported that both the immigrant-Chinese and the Taiwanese parents rated higher on parental control, encouragement of independence, and emphasis on achievement than European American parents did. In other research, Chinese American 7- and 8-year-old children spent more time doing homework and taking music lessons, spent less time playing organized sports, and had less free time than comparable European American children (Huntsinger, Jose, & Larson, 1998). The Chinese American parents also used more formal teaching methods for math and reading than did the European American parents. From these findings, we can see how cultural attitudes of Chinese American parents exert an influence on their children's educational attainment, which is likely responsible for the academic edge these children have in American schools.

One finding of note is that the Chinese versus American differences in arithmetic ability are a recent phenomenon. Geary and his colleagues (1996) administered a series of arithmetic tests to younger and older Chinese and American adults. For the young adults (college students), there was a significant difference favoring the Chinese over the Americans. There was no such cultural difference, however, for the older adults (most over 60 years old)—the older Americans performed as well in arithmetic as the older Chinese did. In fact, although the younger Chinese outperformed the older Chinese adults on arithmetic, the reverse was true for the American sample. Here, the older adults actually performed better then the younger adults. This suggests that whatever factors are responsible for the cultural differences in arithmetic, they are of recent origin.

Gender Differences in Mathematical Ability

When most people think of gender differences in academic abilities, perhaps the first area to come to mind is mathematics, with males generally being better than females. (The other area is verbal abilities, with the common wisdom being that females are generally more verbal than males, as discussed earlier in this chapter.) Such observations date back in the scientific literature to at least 1894, with Havelock Ellis's comments on male superiority on a host of cognitive tasks, and continue to be much studied today. What is the nature of gender differences in mathematical abilities? When, in development, are they observed? Are they a reflection primarily of inherited biology or of educational opportunities? Perhaps the best place to start looking for answers to some of these questions is Maccoby and Jacklin's 1974 review of gender differences. Maccoby and Jacklin reviewed the findings of 27 studies in which gender differences in quantitative (mathematical) ability had been assessed. Of the studies reporting significant differences between the sexes, most favored boys. Studies with preadolescent children, however, found either no gender differences in mathematics or small but significant differences favoring girls. Boys did not achieve quantitative superiority until 10 to 12 years of age, and after mid-adolescence, no findings were reported in which girls outscored boys.

Meta-Analysis of Gender Differences in Mathematics

Similar to what has been done evaluating gender differences in verbal abilities, researchers have used meta-analysis to evaluate the many studies looking at gender differences in mathematical ability. To reiterate, meta-analysis is a statistical technique that allows an investigator to evaluate the magnitude of a significant effect across a large number of studies. Differences between the sexes across studies are expressed in terms of effect size, with 1.0 corresponding to a difference equivalent to one standard deviation. Hyde (1981) reported the first meta-analysis of gender differences in mathematical ability, but more recent and extensive studies have since been published, each reporting similar results (Feingold, 1988; Hedges & Nowell, 1995; Hyde, Fennema, & Lamon, 1990; Marsh, 1989).

Take, for example, the meta-analysis Hyde and her colleagues (1990) reported, which included 100 studies and the data of 3,175,188 participants. Contrasts were made between males and females for elementary school children for simple arithmetic computation, and for high-school students, college students, and adults for performance on standardized tests. Several main conclusions can be stated:

1. Similar to the Maccoby and Jacklin (1974) findings, gender differences are small and often nonsignificant for arithmetic computation in elementary school, and what effect there is favors girls.
2. Significant differences in mathematics favoring males are first seen in high school, with this difference increasing some in college and adulthood (effect sizes = .29, .41, and .59 for high school, college, and adult samples, respectively).

3. The magnitude of the gender differences between males and females has declined during the past several decades (effect sizes: pre-1973 = .31; post-1973 = .14).
4. Gender differences are greater at the highest ability levels, with males much more likely than females to be represented among the top percentiles of mathematics ability.

Related to this last point are the results of meta-analyses by Alan Feingold (1992) and Larry Hedges and Amy Nowell (1995) looking at gender differences in variability—both studies reported that males are much more variable than females in their performance. This greater male variability has long been noted (Ellis, 1894) and is not limited to mathematics (Hedges & Nowell, 1995). These results suggest that for most of the population, there is much overlap and little real difference in mathematical abilities between males and females. Differences are most apparent at the extremes, particularly at the upper levels of performance.

Gender Differences at the Extremes

Differential representation of males and females in the top 5% of mathematics ability has been demonstrated most dramatically by Camilla Benbow and Julian Stanley (1980). These researchers examined the verbal and mathematics SAT scores of a group of seventh- and eighth-grade children selected to participate in a study of mathematically skilled youth conducted at Johns Hopkins University. The students were selected in a series of talent searches conducted between 1972 and 1979 and scored in the top 5% of students taking the exam. The data revealed consistent gender differences favoring boys. Further, the students were essentially equivalent in verbal SAT scores and in math-course background. Benbow and Stanley (1983) reported similar findings in a second investigation with a much larger number of students (nearly 40,000). In this second study, they found that the disparity between the sexes was greater at the higher ability levels. For example, the ratio of boys to girls scoring 420 or more on the SAT-Math was 1.5:1. In contrast, this boy-to-girl ratio was 4.1:1 for students scoring 600 or more, and 13:1 for the small number of students scoring 700 or more.

Source of Gender Differences in Mathematics

Benbow and Stanley's participants were selected in advance for exceptional math ability. It is possible that comparisons of scores in their sample have limited generalizability to the remaining 95% of the population. Moreover, their data reveal nothing about the sources of the observed gender differences in SAT scores. There is also no compelling reason to conclude that SAT scores reflect innate differences in aptitude or capacity. Actually, Lynn Fox (1976) underscored the fact that teachers, parents, and peers all have negative feelings about mathematically talented girls. Likewise, children's books, magazines, and the popular media often present females in stereotypic ways that militate against strong interest in mathematics.

Another alternative to explain gender differences on the SAT is that males and females differ in their background knowledge, including mathematics problem-solving strategies, and that differences in cognitive processing are responsible for the gender differences in test performance. James Byrnes and Sayuri Takahira (1993) assessed this possibility by giving 11th- and 12th-grade students SAT math problems to solve, a strategy questionnaire, and a test of background mathematical knowledge. The strategy questionnaire presented students with an SAT problem and several alternative strategies, from which they were to select the one they used to solve the problem. Table 14-3 shows one example. The knowledge test assessed knowledge of the concepts needed to solve SAT problems—for example, knowledge of what a tangent is. Byrnes and Takahira reported that males performed better than females did on the SAT problems and that they scored higher on the strategy and background knowledge tests. In fact, these two measures accounted for 50% of the variance in the SAT scores, and when participants' per-

TABLE 14-3 An example of a problem and the strategies listed for it. Participants are to choose which alternative they used for solving the problem.

Midpoint problem:

(1) On the number line above, which of the following is the coordinate of the midpoint of the segment PQ?

(a) $\dfrac{x}{2}$ (d) $2(x + 1)$

(b) $\dfrac{x + 1}{2}$ (e) $\dfrac{x(x + 1)}{2}$

(c) $x + \dfrac{1}{2}$

Problem/strategy	Percentage of subjects
1. I added the two points (x and x + 1) together and divided by 2.	56*
2. I multiplied the two points (x and x + 1) together and divided by 2.	17
3. I figured to get x + 1 and divided by 2.	6
4. I knew the answer had to be between x and x + 1. So, I substituted a number for x. I used each of these numbers to get the answers.	13
5. I just guessed.	6
6. Other (please explain).	2

*Sucessful strategy.

SOURCE: "Explaining Gender Differences on SAT-Math Items," by J. P. Byrnes and S. Takahira, 1993 *Developmental Psychology,* 29, 805–810. Copyright © 1993 American Psychological Association. Adapted with permission. (Original problem from November 1987 SAT exam, Educational Testing Service.)

formances on the strategy questionnaire and the knowledge test were controlled for statistically, gender differences were no longer significant. More recent research has similarly found high school and college males used mathematical strategies more flexibly than did females, largely accounting for gender differences on tests such as the SAT-Math and quantitative portion of the Graduate Record Exam (Gallagher et al., 2000).

It is unclear why males showed greater strategy and background knowledge than females did in the Byrnes and Takahira study. The number of high-school math courses taken and the grade-point average in those courses were comparable for the males and females in this study (although no information was obtained concerning the level of math courses taken). Byrnes and Takahira propose that the most likely reason for gender differences on the SAT involves a multitude of factors, including socialization, physiological, and cognitive factors. The researchers note, for example, that socialization factors play an important role in fostering an interest in mathematics, with interest, in turn, influencing cognitive arousal and selective attention (Renninger, Hidi, & Krapp, 1992).

Cindy Raymond and Camilla Benbow (1986) investigated this alternative by assessing the relationship between parental attitudes, gender typing, and mathematical ability for groups of adolescents scoring high on the quantitative and verbal portions of the SAT. Raymond and Benbow reported that mathematically talented students received greater parental encouragement in mathematics than did verbally talented students and that this pattern did not differ with sex. Related to this, the amount of encouragement in mathematics that children received was comparable for boys and girls, regardless of their area or level of talent (that is, high verbal or high math). Finally, mathematically talented girls were no more sex typed as masculine than were verbally talented girls, and there was no relationship between sex typing and SAT scores. Raymond and Benbow concluded that parental socialization practices during adolescence could not account for mathematical ability in this group of mathematically talented children.

One fascinating and educationally important finding in the new set of studies is the steady reduction of gender differences in mathematics ability since the 1960s. Why are gender differences in mathematics ability decreasing over time? The answer favored by many is that attitudes and curricula are changing, that gender roles are being viewed more flexibly (Hyde & Linn, 1988), and that girls are taking more mathematics courses than before (Marsh, 1989). Some evidence suggests that this is true. In Herbert Marsh's (1989) assessment of math performance of 14,825 students in the High School and Beyond project, much smaller gender differences in performance were found than in previous studies. This was associated with evidence that the boys and girls in the study had taken, on average, equal numbers of mathematics courses in high school. However, as noted earlier in this chapter in discussing the diminishing gender differences in verbal abilities, there is also evidence that test publishers during the past 25 years have been attempting to minimize gender differences in their tests, possibly accounting for the diminished gender differences in performance (Stanley et al., 1992), although this interpretation is questioned by others (Feingold, 1988). Whatever the reason, gender differences favoring males in high-school mathematics and beyond are still found, but they are relatively small in magnitude and getting smaller. The only exception to this statement concerns performance at the highest levels, where males are disproportionately represented.

What do mathematically gifted females do? It is perhaps worth looking at the exceptions to this phenomenon, the minority of females who fall within the top 5% in mathematics ability. What are these people like? Camilla Benbow, David Lubinski, and their colleagues (Benbow et al., 2000; Lubinski & Benbow, 1992; Lubinski, Benbow, & Sander, 1993) have followed a sample of mathematically gifted females (top 1%) from identification in seventh grade to adulthood. Compared with equally mathematically gifted males, the females tended to select different areas of study in college and different professions: The males were two to three times more likely to choose careers in engineering or the physical sciences than the females, who were more likely to pursue careers in biology, the social sciences, or the humanities.

Why this difference? One possibility is that there are still educational or occupational roadblocks for women in these traditionally male-dominated fields. However, Lubinski and Benbow proposed an alternative interpretation. They found that these mathematically gifted women are different from the mathematically gifted men in some noncognitive ways that could influence their choice of careers. For instance, in an assessment of values, gifted males gave higher ratings to theoretical issues than gifted females did. The reverse was true for ratings of social issues. Lubinski and Benbow (1992) reported that having strong theoretical values was positively associated with an interest in the physical sciences, whereas an interest in social values was negatively associated with such an interest. Basically, Lubinski and Benbow are proposing that other gender differences—possibly rooted in biology, possibly in socialization—contribute significantly to career choice, in addition to cognitive abilities. People choose a career not only because they think they will be good at it (that is, that they have the requisite intellectual abilities), but also because it fits their values and interests. This position is consistent with Sandra Scarr and Kathleen McCartney's genotype → environment model, suggesting that people select environments in which they feel comfortable.

The relation between spatial and mathematical abilities. Males show a consistent advantage on certain types of spatial cognition (but not other types; see the discussion in Chapter 8), and these spatial abilities are related to mathematical performance. For example, M. Beth Casey and her colleagues (1995) assessed spatial ability (using a mental-rotation task, see Figure 8-10 in Chapter 8) in groups of adolescents. They also obtained scores on the SAT-Math scores, reporting that males outperformed females on the mental-rotation task and on the SAT-Math for all but the lowest ability level. Moreover, performance on the mental-rotation task predicted SAT-Math scores for both males and females. And when participants' spatial performance was statistically controlled for, the gender difference on the SAT-Math was eliminated. That is, differences in spatial ability were responsible (at least in a statistical sense) for gender differences on mathematical performance.

Geary (1995, 1996) has similarly noted the relations between gender, spatial ability, and mathematical performance and has proposed an evolutionary account for gender differences in math performance. Basically, Geary proposes that, over evolutionary time, there has been selection pressure on human males to develop spatial abilities, primarily for the purpose of navigation (see similar arguments by Silverman & Eals, 1992 in Chapter 8). In development, gender differences in hormones and experiences (particularly in the types of play boys and girls engage in) foster differences in boys' and girls' abilities to process three-dimensional space, which are related to certain types of mathematical abilities.

Geary's proposal does not imply that females are not capable of advanced mathematics. But his proposal does suggest that boys and girls may possibly benefit from different types of educational curricula when it comes to mathematics (Geary, 1996) and reinforces the idea that individual and gender differences in spatial abilities could be the root of individual and gender differences in mathematics.

Schooling and Cognitive Development

There should be little question that schooling makes a difference in how a child thinks. In our day-to-day experience, children who attend school are brighter than children who don't, and children in more advanced grades are smarter than children in lower grades. But children in higher grades not only have had more school experience than have children in lower grades, they are also older. Does attending school actually make a difference in cognitive development beyond the effect of age?

Schooling versus Age Effects on Intelligence

The question of how schooling versus age influences intelligence has been addressed by examining the effects of years of education on intellectual performance while statistically controlling for age (Cahan

& Cohen, 1989) or, more frequently, by using the *cut-off method*, in which children who just missed the cut-off date for entering school are compared with children who are close to their age but just made the cut-off date. Thus, the two groups of children are nearly identical in age but differ in that the former group has had one more year of education than the latter group (Morrison, Griffith, & Frazier, 1996). For example, Sorel Cahan and Nora Cohen (1989) compared intelligence test scores and school achievement of fourth-, fifth-, and sixth-grade children. They reported significant effects of schooling; children in the higher grade scored better than children their same age in the lower grade. These findings clearly show that IQ and related cognitive skills are strongly associated with schooling. In this study, effects of both age and schooling were reported (that is, older children did better than younger children, and children with one more year of school did better than children without the extra year), but the effect of schooling was two to three times greater than the effect of age. In related research, kindergarten and first-grade children showed greater gains on tests of cognitive skills during periods when there was more academic information presented during school (between October and April) than for comparable time periods when less academic information was provided (from April to October) (Huttenlocher, Levine, & Vevea, 1998).

The results of this line of research may not be surprising. After all, we expect education to produce smarter children. But these findings force us to question the concept of intelligence as measured by IQ tests. IQ tests are age-based. The norms change as a function of age, not grade. (The construction of the logic behind IQ tests will be discussed in Chapter 15.) The results of the research cited here indicate that not only should age be considered in computing an IQ score, but so should school experience. Moreover, the idea that some intelligence tests can be "culture fair" (that is, used in any culture without yielding biased results) must be questioned. One of the tests Cahan and Cohen (1989) used was the Ravens' Progressive Matrices Test, a test that has been proposed to produce "an index of intellectual capacity whatever [a person's] nationality or educa-

tion" (Raven, Court, & Raven, 1975, p. 1). The effects of one year's schooling were found to be twice as large as the effects of one year of age on the Ravens' test, seriously challenging the fairness of such a test when assessing children from cultures where there is no formal education.

Other researchers, notably Frederick Morrison and his colleagues, have looked at age versus schooling effects for specific cognitive and educational abilities for children just beginning formal education. In Morrison's research, "old kindergarten" children, who just missed the school-entry cut-off date, are compared with "young first-grade" children, with contrasts typically being made at the beginning and end of the school year. Morrison and his colleagues report both schooling and age effects, depending on the particular skill that is being assessed. For example, one year of schooling has a greater effect than one year of age on (1) phonological awareness (Morrison et al., 1996); (2) free-recall memory, including simple strategy use (Morrison, Smith, & Dow-Ehrensberger, 1995; Morrison et al., 1996); (3) accuracy in mental arithmetic (Bisanz, Morrison, & Dunn, 1995); (4) the ability to understand complex sentences with longer subjects (Ferreira & Morrison, 1994); (5) knowledge of the alphabet (Christian et al., 2000); and (6) the ability to use causal structure (that is, connections between different pieces in a story) in recalling stories (Varnhagen, Morrison, & Everall, 1994). However, significant *age* effects have also been found for (1) subsyllabic segmentation (the ability to differentiate between sounds within one-syllable words; for example, for the word "grasp," being able to segment "gr" from "asp") (Morrison et al., 1996); (2) conservation of number (Bisanz et al., 1995); (3) the use of simple arithmetic strategies, such as fact retrieval and various counting methods (Bisanz et al., 1995); (4) gist recall of stories (Varnhagen et al., 1994); (5) the ability to understand the use of pronouns in sentences (Ferreira & Morrison, 1994); and (6) vocabulary, cultural knowledge, and general narrative skills (Morrison et al., 1996). Of course, for most academic abilities, significant effects are found for both school experience and age (Morrison, Griffith, & Alberts, 1997). And at least some of these effects are not unique to American schools and children, but have been reported for some aspects of arithmetic abilities in Japanese children (Naito & Miura, 2001).

The conclusion to draw from this research is that changes in different cognitive skills follow different developmental paths, reflecting a large degree of domain specificity. Some skills, such as phonemic awareness, free-recall memory, accuracy of mental arithmetic, and the abilities that underlie IQ test performance, are greatly affected by schooling experiences. Presumably, the experiences children have in school have a direct impact on these skills (for example, reading instruction affects phonemic awareness). However, other seemingly closely related skills, such as story recall, use of arithmetic strategies, and vocabulary, are more influenced by the presumably maturational and general (versus schooling-specific) experiences associated with age. According to Morrison and his colleagues (1996), this pattern reflects a substantial degree of specificity in the timing, magnitude, and nature of changes in cognitive abilities.

In other research, the effects of schooling on memory were investigated longitudinally, by following children enrolled in the academically demanding curriculum of the German Gymnasium (for university-bound students) versus the less demanding curricula of the Hauptschule ("main school") (Schneider, Knopf, & Stefanek, 2003). Wolfgang Schneider and his colleagues hypothesized that differences in memory performance between children in the more rigorous (Gymnasium) versus less rigorous (Hauptschule) programs would increase over time because of the greater demands on memory of the Gymnasium curriculum. The results did not confirm their hypothesis, however. Although the various memory measures were moderately correlated with IQ at all ages, and children in the higher-achieving schools showed greater performance than did children in the lower-achieving schools for all memory measures (free recall, text recall, and listening span), these differences were present at age 8, *before* children began their different curricula. Average performance for each memory measure increased with age, but the magnitude of the difference between the groups remained relatively constant. That is, memory differences existing among children at age 8 predicted which types of educational programs they would attend, but were not subsequently affected by their different educational experiences. Thus, general memory performance, at least from age 8 into adolescence, is influenced by age but not by differences in schooling experience.

The Effect of Schooling on IQ

The research contrasting the effects of one year of schooling versus one year of age demonstrates that schooling, indeed, plays a role in cognitive development, at least for some important skills. I suppose that this should not be surprising, given the evidence presented earlier in this and in previous chapters demonstrating substantial differences in mathematics, memory, and classification abilities for children from schooled versus nonschooled cultures. But the question of a relationship between schooling and intellectual functioning is not a trivial one. For example, to what extent does schooling affect IQ? Cahan and Cohen (1989) found that one year of schooling has a substantial effect on IQ, twice the size associated with one year of age. That schooling affects IQ indicates that an IQ score is greatly influenced by experiential factors and is not solely under the influence of genetic or other biological factors that are relatively impervious to societal-level effects. The effects of schooling on IQ have been studied for a number of years, and Stephen Ceci (1991, 1996; Ceci & Williams, 1997) has organized and reviewed this literature, making the point that schooling indeed has a powerful impact on IQ.

In addition to citing Cahan and Cohen's (1989) data as evidence for the influence of schooling on IQ, Ceci examined several additional areas of research pertinent to the schooling-IQ question, some of which I mention here.

1. Perhaps the most obvious approach to the question would be to compute correlations between years of education and IQ. When this is done, the correlations tend to be very high, usually higher than .60 and often in excess of .80. The effects

remain large even after controlling for differences in socioeconomic status.

2. There is a small but statistically significant drop in children's IQ over summer vacation. This drop is larger among children from low-income homes, probably because their summer activities have less resemblance to school activities than do those of children from more affluent homes.

3. Children who attend school intermittently, being frequently absent, have lower IQs than do children who attend school regularly. What is typically found in samples of frequently truant children is that IQ scores get lower with age. That is, children lose IQ points as they get older, partly because they increasingly fall behind in school. This reflects a cumulative deficit, with the result that the intellectual deficits increase with age. Similar cumulative deficit effects have been reported for children of parents in the lower versus middle socioeconomic stratum, in that the difference in IQ between the two groups becomes greater with age.

4. Children who enter school late show an IQ decrement relative to children who start school on time. In one study, children experienced, on average, a five-point IQ deficit for each year that their schooling was delayed.

5. Just as people who start school late have lower IQs, so, too, do people who drop out of school early. One study of Swedish males (Harnquist, 1968) reported a loss of 1.8 IQ points for each year of school not finished.

6. There is evidence that the quality and not just the quantity of schooling is important for IQ effects. For example, a study of African Americans who migrated from segregated and poor school systems in Georgia to better-quality systems in Philadelphia between World Wars I and II showed that children gained about one-half an IQ point for each year they were enrolled in the Philadelphia schools (Lee, 1951). However, it is difficult to measure quality of schooling, and other investigators question the connection between quality of school and IQ (Bouchard & Segal, 1985).

Taken together, the evidence is impressive that attending school influences one's IQ. Again, perhaps this should not be too surprising, in part because IQ tests, although purporting not to assess specific aptitudes, do tap general cultural knowledge (the information and vocabulary subtests on the Wechsler scales, for example, do this), much of which is learned in school. What seems inarguable is that whatever IQ tests measure, it is influenced greatly by the school experience.

The Costs and Benefits of Academic Preschools

The evidence presented in the preceding sections clearly shows that schooling has a powerful impact on cognitive development. People in schooled cultures think differently from people in nonschooled cultures, one year of schooling has a greater impact on cognition than does one year of age, and schooling influences IQ. All this, along with evidence that a longer school year likely produces cognitive gains, makes a compelling argument for extended education, at least in postindustrial societies. In fact, some people have looked at the evidence and concluded that intellectual gains could be even greater if formal education were to begin even earlier (Doman, 1984). If starting school at 5 is good, surely starting school at 4, 3, or even 2 is better.

This is an argument made by many educators and parents in the United States. Many families in the United States have a tendency to push their young children. Many preschool programs have academic curricula, preparing 3- and 4-year-old children for the rigors of school. These parents believe that if children can be taught the important skills used in reading and arithmetic in preschool, they will have an intellectual advantage when they enter kindergarten or first grade.

The logic follows from the evidence of the relation between schooling and cognition in older children and adults, but does it make sense for preschool children? Is there a single relation between the amount of formal education and intelligence for all ages? Or might the effects of formal schooling vary with the age of the child?

Evidence indicates that children who attend high quality child-care programs during the preschool years score higher on measures of cognitive ability during elementary school than do matched groups of children who do not attend preschool programs (Broberg et al., 1997). But quality child care does not necessarily mean academically oriented child care. In fact, several researchers and educators have seriously questioned the idea of academic instruction for preschoolers (Elkind, 1987; Sigel, 1987). David Elkind (1987), for example, states that academic programs for preschoolers amount to *miseducation*. Young children do not have the cognitive capacity to adequately master the academic skills of these programs, and the overall result is unnecessary stress with no long-term benefits.

Despite the importance of this issue, there has been surprisingly little research on it. Research by Marion Hyson, Kathy Hirsh-Pasek, and Leslie Rescorla (1990; Rescorla, Hyson, & Hirsh-Pasek, 1991) is a notable exception. In their study, 4-year-old children attending prekindergarten programs were assessed. Children were given tests of academic skills, creativity, social competence, and emotional well-being at the end of their prekindergarten program and again toward the end of their kindergarten year. Parents were also interviewed concerning their attitudes about education and their expectations for their children's academic achievement. The preschool programs were classified as high academic or low academic. High-academic programs stressed adult-directed instruction, whereas low academic programs did not but instead followed a "developmentally appropriate" curriculum (Bredekamp & Copple, 1997). Not surprisingly, parents who believed in adult-directed education tended to put their children in the more academically oriented preschools.

Table 14-4 presents children's scores on each of nine measures. The Academic Schools Test assessed school-related cognitive skills and was given at the end of the prekindergarten year; the Program for Auxiliary Services to Schools (PASS) is also a test of academic skills that was given at the end of the

TABLE 14-4 Comparison for child outcome variables for children who attended academic versus nonacademic preschools. The Academic Schools and PASS tests assessed school-related cognitive skills; the Ravens' Matrices is a nonverbal test of intelligence; the Harter and Pike scales assess self-concept. The Ravens' Matrices and Creativity/Originality tests were given only once before children entered kindergarten. The MYCATS was given only at the end of kindergarten.

Variable	High-academic mean score (n = 46)	Low-academic mean score (n = 44)
Academic Schools (Preschool)	45.61	43.84
PASS (Kindergarten)	7.91	8.60
Ravens' Matrices	63.70	63.27
Creativity/Originality	1.21	1.25
Harter & Pike (Preschool)	3.35	3.27
Harter & Pike (Kindergarten)	3.08	3.01
Test Anxiety (Preschool)	5.10	5.61
Test Anxiety (Kindergarten)	5.56	5.87
MYCATS (school attitudes)	13.15	14.00

SOURCE: Adapted from "Academic Environments in Preschool: Challenge or Pressure?" by M.C. Hyson, K. Hirsh-Pasek, and L. Rescorla, 1990, *Early Education and Development*, 1, 401–423, Wide Range, Inc.

kindergarten year; the Ravens' Matrices is a nonverbal test of intelligence; the Harter and Pike scales are tests of self-concept; the Measurement of Young Children's Attitudes Toward School (MYCATS) test assesses children's general feelings about school, their teachers, and their perceived difficulty and enjoyment of school; the purposes of creativity and test anxiety tests are self-evident. The Ravens' Matrices test and the creativity test were given only once, during the summer before children entered kindergarten. The MYCATS was given only at the conclusion of kindergarten.

As can be seen from the table, there were no significant differences in academic ability between the children who attended the high-academic and low-academic programs. Performance on the cognitive skills tests both at the end of preschool (Academic Schools) and at the end of kindergarten (PASS) was comparable, as was performance on the Ravens' Matrices test of intelligence. A small difference was found for test anxiety at the end of preschool, with children attending the academically oriented preschools showing greater test anxiety than children attending the developmentally appropriate programs.

Further correlational analyses showed some other small but interesting relationships. For example, the extent to which mothers endorsed adult-directed instruction for preschool children did predict academic skills during preschool, with mothers who favored formal instruction having children who performed better on the Academic Schools Test than did preschoolers who had mothers who did not endorse adult-directed instruction. There was no significant relation between mothers' endorsement of adult-directed instruction and academic skills in kindergarten, but this factor did correlate negatively with preschool measures of creativity. Thus, mothers scoring high on the adult-instruction scale tended to have children rated as lower in creativity. Also, the degree to which the preschools endorsed adult-directed practices was related to children's test anxiety at the end of kindergarten (the greater the emphasis on adult-directed practices, the higher was children's anxiety). Finally, children who attended the developmentally appropriate schools were more likely to have a positive attitude toward school than were children who attended the high-academic programs.

Hyson and her associates cautioned that most of these effects, although statistically significant, are small in magnitude. Nevertheless, the pattern is clear. In general, there were no long-term benefits of academically oriented preschool programs, and some evidence indicates that such programs might actually be detrimental. The researchers proposed two alternative interpretations of the data. The first points to the small differences between the schools, so that from a practical perspective the academic orientation of a school likely makes little difference in the long run. The second, stronger, interpretation of their data holds that an academic orientation provides no advantage and actually has some small negative consequences. Hyson and colleagues concluded that whichever interpretation is adopted, there seems to be no defensible reason for encouraging formal academic instruction during the preschool years. Rather, for most children from middle-class homes, cognitive development and creativity can best be fostered in a developmentally appropriate preschool program that considers children's limitations as well as their abilities. In the opinion of these researchers, "it may be developmentally prudent to let children explore the world at their own pace rather than to impose our adult timetables and anxieties on them" (Hyson et al., 1990, p. 421).

Although these results must be viewed as tentative, they are consistent with the perspective that cognitive development during the early years of life is best accomplished outside a formal, teacher-directed environment. A young child's cognitive system is immature, and because of this, learning and development might take place best in unstructured settings. The skills of young children are different from the skills of older children and might be ideally suited for the learning they need to do at this time in their lives (Bjorklund, 1997a; Bjorklund & Green, 1992). These findings argue that children ought not be hurried through a childhood that has purposes in and of itself.

Summary

Reading is perhaps the most critical technological skill for people in postindustrial societies. Chall has proposed five stages of learning to read: (a) the prereading skill of letter identification, (b) phonological recoding in the first grade, (c) fluent but effortful reading in grades 2 and 3, (d) "reading to learn" in grades 4 through 8, and (e) proficient reading in high school and beyond.

Emergent literacy refers to the skills, knowledge, and attitudes that are presumed to be developmental precursors to conventional forms of reading and writing and the environments that support these developments. There are at least nine components to emergent literacy, including language, knowledge of the conventions of print, knowledge of letters, linguistic awareness, phoneme-grapheme correspondence, emergent reading, emergent writing, print motivation, and other cognitive abilities, such as memory.

Phonemic awareness and *phonological recoding* are important skills for both beginning and later reading, with children with *dyslexia*, or reading-disability, generally having delayed phonological processing skills. *Reading comprehension* involves working memory and is influenced by one's knowledge base and monitoring skills, each of which develops over childhood.

Research has shown that reading-disabled children show deficits in working-memory capacity. Two broadly defined types of reading instruction have been used: *phonics*, which is a bottom-up system that emphasizes learning letter-sound correspondence, and the *whole-language approach*, which is a top-down system that emphasizes a reader's construction of meaning. Although reading surely involves both top-down and bottom-up processes, research evidence makes it clear that any reading program should include some instruction in phonics.

More boys than girls are classified as dyslexic, but differences in reading ability beyond dyslexic children are small, with boys being more influenced by text interest than girls are. *Meta-analyses* have found that females show an overall advantage in verbal abilities relative to males, although the magnitude of this gender difference has diminished during the last several decades.

Geary has proposed that some quantitative abilities develop early, are universal, and do not require instruction. Among these are *numerosity* (the ability to determine quickly the number of items in a set without counting), *ordinality* (a basic understanding of more than and less than relationships, counting small quantities), and simple arithmetic.

Children's concept of number has been studied in terms of *conservation of number*, following Piaget. Some researchers have focused on counting as a precursor to conservation of number. Children appear to acquire knowledge of counting gradually during the preschool years, and this knowledge precedes that necessary for conservation of number.

Research on children's arithmetic has concentrated primarily on the strategies children use to solve problems. Early arithmetic is done out loud, often on fingers. Children's early strategies include the *sum strategy*, with children counting all numbers, and the *min strategy*, with children beginning with the larger addend and counting up from there. More sophisticated strategies include retrieving addition and subtraction facts directly from long-term memory (*fact retrieval*) and *decomposition*, in which a problem is decomposed into simpler problems. Siegler has proposed the *adaptive strategy choice model*, which shows that children actually use a variety of arithmetic strategies, making it inappropriate to classify children as users of a single approach to solve arithmetic problems.

Math-disabled children typically display procedural deficits early but often catch up to their peers by second grade. Difficulties in storing and retrieving math facts from long-term memory persist, however, with deficits in working-memory capacity being a likely contributor to math disability.

The mathematics performance of unschooled children, although usually much poorer than that of schooled children, improves when their familiarity with the test materials and the context of testing are considered. Patterns of cognitive abilities vary as a function of culture even in those societies that require formal education, with different values and educational practices affecting children's academic performance.

Gender differences in mathematics favoring males are not typically found until high school, then increase slightly into college and adulthood. The absolute magnitude of these differences is small, however, and has been decreasing during the past 30 years. The largest gender differences are found among the most mathematically gifted, with boys being disproportionately represented.

Attending school enhances development of many cognitive skills beyond the effects of age, although age has a greater impact on development of other cognitive abilities. Evidence from a variety of sources suggests that schooling influences IQ. Middle-class children who attend preschool programs that stress academics demonstrate no long-term gains and have less positive attitudes about school than do children who attend nonacademic preschool programs.

Key Terms and Concepts

emergent literacy
phonemic awareness
phonological recoding
phonics
adaptive strategy choice model
fact retrieval
dyslexia
reading comprehension
whole-language approach
meta-analysis
conservation of number
numerosity
ordinality
sum strategy
min strategy
decomposition

Suggested Readings

Adams, M. J., Treiman, R., & Pressley, M. (1998). Reading, writing, and literacy. In I. E. Sigel & K. A. Renninger (Vol. Eds.), *Child psychology in practice*, Vol. 4 (pp. 275–355). In W. Damon (Gen. Ed.), *Handbook of child psychology*. New York: Wiley.   This chapter provides a review of the development of children's reading. The authors also examine the development of other educational topics, such as spelling and writing.

Benbow, C. P., Lubinski, D., Shea, D. L., & Eftekhari-Sanjani, H. (2000). Sex differences in mathematical reasoning ability at age 13: Their status 20 years later. *Psychological Science, 11,* 474–480.   This is the most recent follow-up study of gender differences in mathematically gifted boys and girls, 20 years after they were originally identified at age 13. This study looks at the educations, occupations, and personal values of these mathematically talented people and reveals that what one does with one's life is a function of more than intellectual ability.

Ceci, S. J. (1991). How much does schooling influence general intelligence and its cognitive components? A reassessment of the evidence. *Developmental Psychology, 27,* 703–722.   In this paper, Ceci provides a thorough review of the research examining the relationship between quantity and quality of schooling and intellectual functioning.

Ginsburg, H. P., Klein, A., & Starkey, P. (1998). The development of children's mathematical thinking: Connecting research with practice. In I. E. Sigel & K. A. Renninger (Vol. Eds.), *Child psychology in practice*, Vol. 4 (pp. 401–476). In W. Damon (Gen. Ed.), *Handbook of child psychology*. New York: Wiley.   This chapter reviews research and theory on children's developing mathematical abilities, covering topics of more advanced math as well as the basic number concepts and arithmetic discussed in this chapter. Ginsburg and his colleagues devote about half of their chapter to mathematical education, making this an excellent book for those interested in instruction.

Rescorla, L., Hyson, M. C., & Hirsh-Pasek, K. (Eds.). (1991). *Academic instruction in early childhood: Challenge or pressure?* San Francisco: Jossey-Bass.   This short edited volume (less than 100 pages long) presents a detailed description of the study by Hirsh-Pasek and colleagues of the effects of early academic instruction on children's development, along with five additional papers on this topic written by others.

InfoTrac College Edition

For additional readings, explore InfoTrac College Edition, your online library. Go to http://www.infotrac-college.com/wadsworth.

Approaches to the Study of Intelligence

Look at the fingers of your right hand. No two are alike. That's the way children are." This homily, attributed to a retired elementary school teacher, reflects the individuality of children.

To this point, my primary focus has been on developmental function, the form that cognition takes in the species over time. Theories and research on developmental function are concerned with cognition in the typical child at any given age or stage and the general processes that influence transitions from lower levels of cognitive functioning to more advanced levels. I have not ignored individual differences in earlier chapters; in fact, much of the research in the previous chapter on schooling dealt with individual differences. But individual differences take center stage in the last two chapters of this book, which concentrate on the origins and stability of individual differences in children's thinking.

At any given age, some children function better than others. Differences in rate of development are partly responsible. Johnny attains concrete operations a year ahead of Joey, but Joey will eventually catch up. Yet, within any given developmental level, some children solve most problems more efficiently than other children do despite the qualitatively similar form of their cognitions. How can such differences be conceptualized? How and why do these individual differences come about? Are they stable over time? What are the origins of these differences? This brings us to the concept of **intelligence.** If you were to ask a psychologist her specialty and she stated "the study of intelligence," she would probably be referring to individual differences in how people process information, or think. The term *intelligence* itself need not be used solely to reflect the nature of individual differences in thought. As the term is used today, however, investigations of intelligence are usually concerned with the magnitude, pattern, origins, or stability of individual differences in mental functioning.

Intelligence is an elusive concept. Most broadly, it refers to acting or thinking in ways that are goal directed and adaptive. This definition covers a lot of ground, allowing much leeway for theorists to sculpt their own meanings of the concept while still being understood by others. I am in general agreement with Robert Sternberg's definition of intelligence, as "the mental activities necessary for adaptation to, as well as shaping and selecting of, any environmental context . . . (I)ntelligence is not just reactive to the environment but also active in forming it. It offers people an opportunity to respond flexibly to challenging situations" (1997, p. 1030). Following this definition, intelligence is obviously a multifaceted phenomenon that no single test can likely tap. Several researchers have produced assessment tools that aim to assess some of the multiple aspects of intelligence described in this definition (Sternberg, Ferrari, & Clinkenbeard, 1996; Wexler-Sherman, Gardner, & Feldman, 1988), but the bulk of data, both historically and in contemporary research, has come from the testing, or *psychometric, approach,* with IQ tests being the measure most often associated with intelligence. Although much of this chapter concentrates on the theory and practice of IQ testing, even more total space is given to alternatives to the testing approach to intelligence. More specifically, I examine information-processing and Piagetian approaches to intelligence, followed by a detailed look at two popular alternative theories: Robert Sternberg's triarchic theory and Howard Gardner's theory of multiple intelligences. In the next chapter, I continue the discussion of intelligence, focusing on the extent to which intelligence is biologically and environmentally influenced, and the stability of intelligence over time.

The Psychometric Approach to the Study of Intelligence

The major approach to the study of individual differences in intelligence since the turn of the 20th century has been the **psychometric (or differential) approach.** Psychometric theories of intelligence have as their basis a belief that intelligence can be described in terms of mental **factors** and that tests can be constructed that reveal individual differences in the factors that underlie mental performance. Factors are related mental skills that (presumably) affect thinking in a wide range of situations. For example, a verbal factor can be tapped by tests assessing a variety of more specific verbal skills such as vocabulary and reading comprehension. An individual may possess a general facility with words and language concepts that influences his or her performance on most tasks involving the processing of language terms and concepts.

Factors of Intelligence

What constitutes a factor is determined by a statistical procedure known as **factor analysis.** In factor analysis, numerous test items are administered to people, and the resulting data are examined to see which items fit together well. Tests might show, for example, that the pattern of individual differences among people is very similar on vocabulary, reading comprehension, story completion, and verbal analogies. That is, people who score high on one of these tests usually score high on all of them, whereas people who score low on one usually score low on all of them. In contrast, performance on these test items might not correlate as highly with performance on items that involve rotating three-dimensional figures, solving maze problems, or quickly placing geometric forms in a form board, although these three tests might all correlate highly with one another. What do the first tests (vocabulary, reading comprehension, story completion, and verbal analogies) have in common? It is not difficult to conclude that all involve some aspect of verbal thinking, whereas the second set (3-D rotation, maze learning, and form-board performance) are all basically nonverbal and involve some form of spatial thinking. Accordingly, based on the results of the statistical analysis, an investigator can assume that two factors that account for individual differences among people are verbal ability and spatial thinking.

Patterns of performance are not always clear-cut, however. The extent to which sets of test items correlate with one another is a matter of degree. Only in

textbooks do we find perfect data that can be interpreted in only one way. Thus, how one defines mental factors is influenced not only by the data but also by one's theoretical and statistical perspective.

Determining the number and makeup of factors is a function of the items included on a test (you could not very well have a verbal component if no verbal items were included in your test) and the particular way you perform statistical analyses. Based on variants of the same form of analysis, the number of factors that have been proposed to account for human intelligence has varied considerably. On the one hand, Charles Spearman (1927) proposed that intelligence consists of only two kinds of factors. He viewed the most critical kind of factor as a general one, labeled **g,** that influences performance on all intellectual tasks. He saw the other kind of factors as specific ones that are not generalizable and that are each pertinent to only a single task. As such, these highly specific abilities are of little interest to psychologists trying to construct theories to explain individual differences among people. In other words, from Spearman's point of view, intelligence exists on a single dimension and is not some multifaceted phenomenon (that is, there is actually only one factor of intelligence, g). Intellectual functioning is relatively homogeneous, or even, across different tasks performed by a single person. Smart people are smart all the time (or most of the time, anyway), and dumb people are consistently dumb. (I will have more to say about the concept of g later in this and in the following chapter.)

At the other extreme, J. P. Guilford's (1988) **structure-of-the-intellect model** includes 180 unique intellectual factors organized along three dimensions. One dimension includes six forms of mental operations; a second includes five contents on which the operations function, and a third includes six possible products that result from applying a given operation to a particular content. Between the extremes of Spearman and Guilford lie theories such as L. L. Thurstone's (1938), which names seven "primary mental abilities":

1. *Verbal comprehension,* which includes vocabulary and reading comprehension.

2. *Verbal fluency*, as measured by tests that require rapid production of words ("Tell me as many names of animals that you can as quickly as you can").
3. *Number*, as reflected by arithmetic word problems.
4. *Spatial visualization*, measured by the mental manipulation of symbols or geometric forms.
5. *Memory*, evaluated by tests of recall for lists of words or of the ability to associate names with pictures of people.
6. *Reasoning*, as exemplified in analogies (for example, "Doctor is to hospital as teacher is to _____?").
7. *Perceptual speed*, involving the rapid recognition of symbols, such as crossing out all the 3s that are embedded in a string of numbers.

Also falling between the extremes is Raymond Cattell's (1971) theory, which recognizes both a general intellectual factor similar to Spearman's g and two second-order factors that he called **fluid abilities** and **crystallized abilities.** Basically, Cattell proposed that fluid intelligence is biologically determined and is reflected in tests of memory span and most tests of spatial thinking. In contrast, crystallized intelligence is best reflected in tests of verbal comprehension or social relations, skills that depend more highly on cultural context and experience. (See Stankov, 2000, for a series of papers discussing the latest work and theory of fluid and crystallized abilities.)

Despite this plurality of theories, the diverse models are not as discrepant as they appear on first examination. In fact, whether only a single factor or many factors make up intelligence is a matter of interpretation even within a given psychometric theory. Toward the end of his career, for example, Spearman acknowledged that group factors (such as verbal abilities) do exist along with a more general intellectual factor. Similarly, Thurstone conceded that his primary mental abilities typically do correlate with one another, suggesting a general factor of intelligence. Thus, despite their diversity, most psychometricians would agree that there is a general factor of intelligence but that there are also "lower-level" factors, reflective of more specific skills (Daniel, 1997). Differences among the various theorists seem to con-

centrate on the extent to which intelligence can be described by g or by other sets of lower-level factors.

The best evidence for the existence of g is what has been termed the **positive manifold,** the frequent finding of high correlations among scores on sets of cognitive tests that have little in common with one another in content or types of strategies used (see Daniel, 1997; Jensen, 1998). This is exactly what Spearman proposed earlier in the 20th century, and the finding is still with us.

Research has produced at least one interesting caveat to the positive manifold. Douglas Detterman and Mark Daniel (1989) found much higher correlations among scores on a variety of cognitive and intelligence tasks for low-IQ people than for high-IQ people. For example, in one study, adults with mental retardation (mean IQ = 67.5) and college students (mean IQ = 115.5) were given a battery of nine cognitive tasks and an IQ test. Detterman and Daniel correlated performance on the cognitive tasks with IQ and then examined the correlations of the scores on the nine cognitive tasks with each other. The correlations were considerably higher for the low-IQ group (.60 for IQ scores and .44 for the cognitive tasks) than for the high-IQ group (.26 for IQ scores and .23 for the cognitive tasks), which means that the cognitions of high-IQ people (in this case, college students) are more varied than the cognitions of low-IQ people.

There is no single interpretation of this finding, but Detterman (1987) proposed that intelligence is made up of several independent processes, although each of these is influenced by central (domain-general) processes. According to Detterman (1987), mental retardation is caused by a deficit in central processes, which in turn affects all other components in the cognitive system, producing relative homogeneity of cognitive function. When there is no central deficit, however, variability is more apt to be found in different components of intelligence, thus producing lower correlations. In other words, a certain level of domain-general central processing resources must exist for individual components of intelligence to operate adequately. Once that level is achieved, there will be substantial variability in cognitive task performance within a given person. However, if that level is not achieved, as is the case for the people with mental retardation, no individual component will receive enough in the way of processing resources to function well, resulting in relative homogeneity of cognitive functioning, and thus high correlations.

There is also some tentative evidence to suggest that the positive manifold develops. Thomas Price and his colleagues (2000) investigated the degree to which verbal and nonverbal cognitive abilities were related in early childhood. As I've just commented, verbal and nonverbal abilities tend to be highly correlated in later childhood and adulthood, suggesting that they are influenced by some general intellectual factor, such as *g*. However, in a sample of nearly 2,000 same-sex 2-year-old twins, correlations between verbal and nonverbal abilities were only of moderate magnitude. This suggested to the authors that cognitive abilities are relatively domain-specific in infancy and early childhood and become more molar, or domain-general, in nature as children get older.

Most psychometricians today adhere to some form of the **hierarchical model of cognitive abilities** (Carrol, 1993). Basically, this model postulates a series of relatively specific cognitive abilities, such as verbal, spatial, speed of processing, and memory, as shown in Figure 15-1. These abilities, however, are correlated with one another (recall the positive manifold), and are influenced by a second-order general factor, or *g*. Thus, this model suggests that, depending on how one looks at the data, one can find evidence for either domain generality (*g*) or domain specificity (separate verbal and spatial modules, for example), and both could be correct (Petrill, 1997).

In some interesting research using neural imagining techniques, John Duncan and his colleagues (2000) used positron emission tomography (PET) to examine which parts of the brain were most activated when adults performed a variety of cognitive tasks. These researchers compared verbal, spatial, and perceptual-motor tasks with high-*g* involvement (that is, those that loaded heavily on *g*) with low-*g* tasks (that is, those that did not load heavily on *g*). Counter to what you might expect, they found that the high-*g* tasks are associated with activation of a

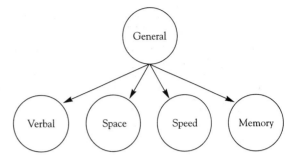

FIGURE 15-1 Hierarchical model of cognitive abilities. Intelligence is composed of specific cognitive abilities (for example, verbal, spatial, speed of processing, memory) that are intercorrelated and influenced by a higher-order general intellectual factor, *g*.

particular area of the brain, specifically the lateral frontal cortex. This yields the somewhat surprising conclusion that *g*, a measure of general intelligence, is highly localized in the brain, although a part of the brain that is involved in the functioning of a variety of cognitions and behaviors.

Psychometric theories have affected research and practice in psychology significantly during the twentieth century. For example, many of the achievement tests (designed to assess specific achievement in a topic, such as reading or mathematics, rather than general intelligence) administered regularly in American schools are based on extensions of Thurstone's multifactor theory. And researchers from a variety of theoretical perspectives continue to search for a general intellectual factor (Jensen, 1998) or to argue that the quest for *g* is fruitless (Ceci, 1996).

IQ Tests

Although mental testing has had a profound influence on psychologists' attempts to conceptualize the nature of intelligence, the greatest impact of mental testing has been **Intelligent Quotient (IQ) tests.** Intelligence testing is so widespread in our society that it is virtually impossible for a child to graduate from high school without having been administered at

TABLE 15-1   Three-level hierarchical model of Stanford-Binet.

g			
Crystallized abilities		**Fluid-analytic abilities**	**Short-term memory**
Verbal reasoning	**Quantitative reasoning**	**Abstract/visual reasoning**	
Vocabulary	Quantitative	Pattern analysis	Bead memory
Comprehension	Number series	Copying	Memory for sentences
Absurdities	Equation building	Matrices	Memory for digits
Verbal relations		Paper folding and cutting	Memory for objects

SOURCE: Adapted from the *Stanford-Binet Intelligence Scale:* (4th Edition) *Guide for Administering and Scoring,* by R. L. Thorndike, E. P. Hagen, and J. M. Sattler. Copyright 1986 The Riverside Publishing Company. Reprinted with permission.

least one IQ test and more than a dozen tests assessing more specific academic aptitudes.

IQ tests are less the result of psychometric theorizing than they are the instruments that produce the raw data for theory construction. IQ tests were developed at the turn of the 20th century in France by Alfred Binet and Theodore Simon. The original tests—and to a large extent even modern versions—were not based on explicit theory. Rather, they were constructed to assess school-related abilities and to differentiate among those children who could benefit from standard school instruction and those who would require special education. It would be inappropriate, however, to classify IQ tests as atheoretical. As will be seen later, modern IQ tests are based on certain concepts of what intelligence is. Nevertheless, pragmatic considerations of which items best differentiate children of a given age are critical in constructing IQ tests, causing some to question their contribution to understanding the underlying mechanisms of intelligence (Sternberg, 1985).

Numerous IQ-type tests are available today. Many are pencil-and-paper tests that can be administered to a group. The standard tests by which most are judged include the Stanford-Binet and the three intelligence scales developed by David Wechsler: the Wechsler Preschool and Primary Scale of Intelligence (WPPSI), the Wechsler Intelligence Scale for Children (WISC), and the Wechsler Adult Intelligence Scale (WAIS). These tests have been standardized on large samples and are individually administered by trained examiners using standardized procedures.

The **Stanford-Binet** was developed in 1916 by Lewis Terman, who made extensive revisions of Binet's original scale. The test has gone through revisions from time to time, the most recent one being in 1986 (Thorndike, Hagen, & Sattler, 1986). The current version consists of 15 subtests, organized in a three-level hierarchical model of the structure of intelligence. A general reasoning factor (*g*) is the most inclusive (see Table 15-1). The authors admit that the exact nature of this general ability is unclear but maintain that *g* reflects the type of intelligence that a person uses to solve problems that he or she has not been previously taught to solve.

There are three second-level factors: crystallized abilities, fluid-analytic abilities, and short-term memory. Crystallized abilities reflect cognitive skills used for solving verbal and quantitative problems. These abilities are greatly influenced by the environment, particularly school. Fluid-analytic abilities represent cognitive skills necessary for solving novel problems involving nonverbal stimuli; the knowledge necessary to solve such problems is not influenced substantially by academic experience. The short-term memory factor involves people's abilities to retain newly perceived information for a brief time and to hold information retrieved from the long-term store that is used in an ongoing task.

Three factors exist at the third level: verbal reasoning, quantitative reasoning, and abstract/visual reasoning. These factors are more specific and dependent on content than the first- or second-level factors are.

The **Wechsler scales** have similarly been revised periodically since their inception in the 1940s. The three scales are similar in that each consists of a series of subtests that are organized according to two larger factors: verbal and performance abilities. Following is a description of the verbal and performance subtests of the WISC (3rd edition) (Wechsler, 1991), with examples of the types of items included in each subtest. The specific examples provided here are *not* items from the WISC-III but are similar in form to items found on it.

Verbal IQ

Information: Children are asked questions assessing their general world knowledge, similar to the following: "How many pennies make a dime?" "What do the lungs do?" "What is the capital of Italy?"

Similarities: Children are read two words in pairs similar to the following and are to tell how they are alike: pear-peach; inch-ounce; snow-sand.

Arithmetic: Children are given arithmetic problems. The easiest involve counting, addition, and subtraction using physical reminders. A child might be shown a picture of nine trees and asked to cover up all but five. More complex problems are read aloud; for example, "Joyce had six dolls and lost two. How many dolls did she have left?" "Three girls had 48 cookies. They divided them equally among themselves. How many cookies did each girl get?"

Vocabulary: Children are read words and are to tell what each word means.

Comprehension: Children are asked questions assessing their knowledge of societal conventions and of appropriate behavior in a variety of situations: "What are some reasons we need soldiers?" "What are you supposed to do if you find someone's watch in school?" "Why is it important to have speed limits on roads?"

Digit Span: Children are read digits at a rate of one per second and are to repeat them back in exact order. This is followed by a test in which children must repeat the numbers in the reverse order from the order the examiner spoke them. This is an optional test.

Performance IQ

Picture Completion: Children are shown black-and-white pictures and are to determine what important part of each picture is missing.

Coding: Children are shown a key associating simple geometric figures (for instance, a triangle, a square, and a circle) with other symbols (a cross, a vertical line, and so on). Children are to mark the associated symbol below a set of randomly arranged figures as quickly as possible without skipping any. Bonus points are given for fast response times.

Picture Arrangement: Children are given a series of pictures in a mixed order and are to arrange them so that they tell a sensible story.

Block Design: Children are given nine cubes, colored red on two sides, white on two sides, and red and white on two sides. They are shown designs and are to reproduce them using the nine blocks. Bonus points are given for fast response times.

Object Assembly: Children are given pieces of a familiar object in a scrambled order. They are to put the pieces together to make the object. Bonus points are given for fast response times.

Symbol Search: Children are shown a target symbol (for example, $\neq$) and beside it a series of three symbols (for example, $\partial \infty ¥$, or $¥ \partial \neq$). Children must determine if the first (target) symbol is contained in the second (search) set of symbols. This is an optional test.

Mazes: Children are shown mazes drawn on paper and are to draw their way out of the maze with a pencil. This is an optional test.

Wechsler noted that the verbal/performance dichotomy reflects "two principal modes by which

TABLE 15-2 Examples of items on the Bayley Scales of Infant Development.

Items typifying infants between 1 and 3 months	Items typifying infants between 5 and 7 months	Items typifying infants between 9 and 12 months	Items typifying infants between 14 and 17 months
Responds to sound of bell.	Smiles at mirror image	Responds to verbal requests. (Can child perform some act upon request, such as waving in response to "bye-bye" or clapping hands in response to "pat-a-cake"?	Scribbles spontaneously (Will child attempt to scribble before it is demonstrated by examiner?)
Regards red ring. (Does infant attend to a red ring suspended by string 8 inches from infant's eye?)	Turns head after fallen spoon. (Does infant turn head in direction of a spoon that falls to the floor and makes a noise?)	Puts cube in cup on demand. (Will infant place a cube in a cup when asked to do so?)	Says two words. (Does child say two recognizable words during the interview?)
Vocalizes once or twice. (Does infant coo, gurgle, squeal during examination period?)	Shows interest in sound production. (Does infant intentionally use objects to make noise?)	Stirs with spoon in imitation. (Will infant imitate the examiner who makes a stirring motion in a cup?)	Shows shoes or other clothing. (Will child point to his or her shoes in response to question "Where are your shoes?")
Demonstrates circular eye coordination: red ring. (Does infant follow circular path of red ring moved above infant's eyes?)	Picks up cube deftly and directly. (Does child pick up small cube?)	Attempts to scribble. (After examiner demonstrates scribbling on a piece of paper, will infant attempt to scribble when given the chance?)	Builds a tower of three cubes.
Displays social smile. (Does infant smile or laugh in response to smile from examiner?)	Vocalizes four different syllables.	Turns pages of book.	Attains toy with stick. (When small toy is placed out of reach of child, will child use stick to attempt to attain it?)

SOURCE: Adapted from *Manual of the Bayley Scales of Infant Development* by N. Bayley, 1969. Copyright 1969 The Psychological Corporation. Adapted with permission.

human abilities express themselves" (1974, p. 9), while acknowledging that mental abilities could also be classified in other ways. In fact, in the 1991 revision of the WISC, scores for four factors can be derived: Verbal Comprehension (Information, Similarities, Vocabulary, Comprehension), Perceptual Organization (Picture Completion, Picture Arrangement, Block Design, Object Assembly), Freedom from Distractibility (Arithmetic, Digit Span), and Processing Speed (Coding, Symbol Search).

Although the youngest children who can be assessed using the Wechsler or Stanford-Binet scales are early preschoolers, psychometricians have not forgotten infants. Tests to assess infant intelligence have been developed with the same psychometric properties as IQ tests and yield a **developmental quotient (DQ).** Tests such as the Bayley Scales of Infant Development (Bayley, 1969, 1993), the Gesell Developmental Schedules (Gesell & Amatruda, 1954), the Neonatal Behavioral Assessment Scale (Brazelton, 1973), and their precursors are based on evaluations of individual differences in sensory and motor abilities. These tests have been well standardized, are reliable (that is, there is high test-retest and intertester agreement), and describe important differences among infants (McCall, Hogarty, & Hurlburt, 1972). Table 15-2 presents examples of items on the Bayley Scales of Infant Development (Bayley, 1969, 1st edition). I say more about DQ tests in Chapter 16.

Basically, IQ tests (and DQ tests) are standardized on large samples of people, and items that differentiate among people of a given age are retained, whereas items that do not (those that are too easy or too difficult) are eliminated. For each age assessed, the number of test items the average child passes is determined. For example, the number of items passed by 50% of the 8-year-olds in the standardization sample would reflect the number of items an average 8-year-old should be able to pass.

Historically, the relationship between the number of items passed and the age of the child was expressed as a quotient of one's **mental age** to one's chronological age (thus the term *intelligence quotient*, or IQ). A child's mental age corresponds to the number of items he or she passes. If a child passes the number of items equal to the number passed by an average 12-year-old, the child's mental age is 12 years. The child's mental age is then divided by his or her chronological age, and the result is multiplied by 100. Thus, a 10-year-old child with a mental age of 10 years has an IQ of 100 (10/10 × 100). A 10-year-old with the mental age of 9.5 years has an IQ of 95 (9.5/10 × 100), and a 10-year-old with a mental age of 12 has an IQ of 120 (12/10 × 100).

The concept of mental age has received substantial criticism (see Wechsler, 1974). One criticism of the concept is that a 7-year-old with a mental age of 10 and a 10-year-old with the same mental age are not, in reality, of comparable intelligence. They may have the same mental age with respect to test performance, but they do not have the same kind of minds. Also, a 5-year-old with a mental age of 6 has an IQ of 120; a 10-year-old with a comparable IQ has a mental age of 12. In the first case, the child's mental age is one year ahead of his chronological age; in the second case, there is a difference of two years.

These and other problems led test developers to abandon the concept of mental age and develop instead a **deviation IQ.** Children's performance is compared with that of children of their own age and not with the performance of older or younger children. Thus, tests can be constructed so that the statistical characteristics of IQ are the same at each age level. Modern tests are constructed so that IQ scores are distributed according to a normal distribution with specified statistical properties. The theoretical distribution of IQ scores for the WISC is shown in Figure 15-2. As can be seen, children with scores of 100 have IQs equal to or greater than 50% of the popula-

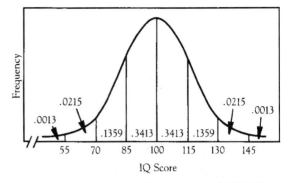

FIGURE 15-2 Theoretical distribution of WISC-III scores. The test is constructed so that 50% of all people at a given age will have IQ scores of 100 and below, and 50% will have scores of 100 and above.

tion. Children with scores of 115 have IQs equal to or greater than approximately 84% of the population. Thus, by knowing a child's IQ score, one knows where he or she stands with respect to intelligence relative to his or her agemates.

The renouncement of the concept of mental age and the use of the deviation IQ enable a more accurate comparison among children of a specified age. However, using the deviation IQ to express intelligence makes developmental contrasts difficult. IQ tests are not constructed to be a mechanism for understanding the development of intelligence. By using the deviation IQ, in fact, we hold developmental differences constant, so that we can make comparisons among agemates in the same way for children of all ages. As I noted earlier, this procedure has obvious advantages for making comparisons of children's intelligence. For the developmentalist, however, difficulties arise when changes in intelligence over time are of interest.

There is nothing magic about the IQ test itself. It does not necessarily measure innate intelligence, nor does it necessarily reflect a constant value that will typify an individual throughout life. In fact, although IQ does correlate significantly with academic success and occupational status (Brody, 1997), many argue that it is limited in the type of mental functioning it measures and that to view an IQ score as an indication of a child's "true" intelligence is misleading.

(See especially the discussions of Gardner's theory later in this chapter.)

Some Issues Regarding Standardized Tests

The remainder of this chapter deals with alternative approaches to the study of intelligence—basically, approaches that don't see IQ tests as the only or the best (or perhaps even a good) measure of intelligence. I think few people would argue that IQ tests are the last word in intelligence—that a score on a test accurately reflects one's true intelligence. But I think that most educators and scientists (but not all) who have given the subject serious thought would concur that IQ tests measure some aspect of intelligence, particularly as it relates to academic performance. I put myself in this large camp. But even in the area of predicting academic performance, IQ tests are far from perfect. For example, there has been much controversy about IQ testing of minority children, with critics arguing that the tests and the testing situation do not serve as fair assessments for such children. In a different but related vein, evidence indicates that some of the standardized achievement tests used in making college admission decisions, such as the SAT and the ACT, might not be tapping the skills they purport to tap. I will look briefly at these two issues here.

IQ Tests and Minority Children

Minority children in the United States consistently score lower on IQ tests than white, middle-class children do. In one respect, this should be expected because IQ tests do their best job predicting school success, and minority children often perform more poorly in school than their majority counterparts do. But does this mean that minority children are less intelligent than children from the majority? Posing this question requires one to evaluate what is meant by intelligence and the extent to which IQ tests assess it.

IQ tests, state many critics, are based on skills and knowledge deemed important by the majority culture. Children from minority homes might not share the same values or have access to the same knowledge that middle-class children do, making the test culturally biased. There is a strong movement today pushing the idea that intelligence can only be meaningfully assessed within the culture in which a child lives (Laboratory of Comparative Human Cognition, 1983; Miller-Jones, 1989). Thus, although IQ tests measure accurately some aspects of intelligence for children from the majority culture, they do not assess intelligence adequately for minority children. Moreover, the rigorously standardized nature of IQ tests might be a detriment to minority children because the tests must be administered in a constant format. The examiner cannot provide feedback to a child and usually cannot probe a child's answers to determine if he or she has more knowledge than reflected by an initial response. Minority children might have different expectations of what type of answers the examiner is looking for, and children's competencies will be masked by the requirements of standard test administration (Miller-Jones, 1989).

Dalton Miller-Jones (1989) provides several examples of how a 5-year-old black child's performance on an IQ test could be underestimated because of the standardized nature of the test:

> Tester: "How are wood and coal alike? How are they the same?"
> Child: "They're hard."
> Tester: "An apple and a peach?"
> Child: "They taste good."
> Tester: "A ship and an automobile?"
> Child: "They're hard."
> Tester: "Iron and silver?"
> Child: "They're hard." (p. 362)

These answers all earn a score of zero, but does this mean that the child does not know the conceptual relation between iron and silver or between an apple and a peach? By the rules of the test, no feedback can be provided, and the child must guess what type of answer the examiner wants. There is nothing incorrect about the child's answers to these questions, but they do not fit the test makers' conceptions. They also do not likely exhaust this child's knowledge of the relations between these objects, but the test format precludes finding this out.

Other aspects of test administration also influence minority children's performance on IQ tests. The testing situation, for example, with a child sitting quietly across the table from an adult and answering a series of questions, might be more familiar and comfortable to a middle-class child than to a lower-class or minority child. Also, in most testing situations, the examiner is a member of a different ethnic and social class than the minority child, adding further to the discomfort and novelty of the testing situation.

Not all agree that there is bias against minority children in mental testing, of course (Jensen, 1998). Despite all the criticism, the tests are cost efficient and widely accepted (though not universally) by both educational professionals and the public. Yet, most would argue that we could do a better job of assessing minority children's intelligence and achievement, and Miller-Jones (1989) makes five recommendations for improving minority assessment:

1. When assessing any area of intelligence, it is important to specify the cognitive processes that might be involved in the task or elicited by the stimuli.
2. Multiple tasks with different materials should be used with the same individual.
3. Tests must be appropriate for the culture from which the child comes.
4. The connection must be validated between the cognitive operations assessed by a test and the attainment of school-related concepts such as arithmetic and reading.
5. Procedures must be developed that permit an examiner to probe for the reasoning behind a child's answers.

Miller-Jones's advice is sound and applies to nonminority as well as to minority children.

Achievement Tests and Reading Comprehension

Although IQ tests are the crowning glory of the psychometric approach, achievement tests such as the Scholastic Assessment Test (SAT) and the American College Testing Assessment (ACT) have become a staple of the American educational system. The SAT and the ACT are taken by hundreds of thousands of college-bound students annually and consist of two major sections—the verbal and the mathematical—each assessing a variety of language and mathematical skills predictive of success in college.

One section of the verbal portion of both the SAT and the ACT is a reading comprehension test. On this test, students read short texts and then answer multiple-choice questions about them. These tests are designed to measure students' ability to read and understand English prose passages. But do they? In a series of experiments, college students were given the multiple-choice questions from reading comprehension sections of the SAT or the ACT and asked to guess the right answer without reading the text (Katz & Lautenschlager, 1994; Katz et al., 1990). Their performance was compared with that of a group of students who read the corresponding text before answering the questions and was related to their own performance on the entire verbal portion of the SAT.

The researchers reported that students not given the passages to read performed far better than expected by chance, and often nearly as well as students who actually read the passages. This was true for the ACT and several versions of the SAT. For example, in the study by Stuart Katz and Gary Lautenschlager (1994), correct performance of students who read the passages of one version of the SAT before answering the questions was 74.9%. Performance of students who answered the questions without reading the passages was 42.9%. Chance performance on this task is 20%. Similarly, for students taking the ACT reading comprehension test without reading the passages, correct performance was 48.9%. Students who read the passages scored 69.5%, with chance again being 20%. Students performed better when they read the passages, but "good guesses" resulted in performance substantially greater than expected by chance. Reading comprehension performance on both the SAT and ACT was related to how well students did on the overall verbal subtest of the SAT.

These findings suggest that performance on the reading comprehension sections of the SAT and

ACT is not tapping reading ability, per se, but rather some other general verbal abilities. It's worth noting that students performed much closer to chance (20%) when they answered reading comprehension questions without reading the passages on the Graduate Record Exam (GRE) (percentage correct = 27.1%) (Katz & Lautenschlager, 1994).

Few serious scientists believe that IQ tests reflect a "pure" measure of intelligence. Rather, intelligence is a multifaceted phenomenon that no single measure can adequately capture. However, IQ does predict reasonably well children's academic skills and later job-related performance, at least in the developed world (see Sternberg, Grigorenko, & Bundy, 2001), making it an important predictor of real-world functioning. But IQ tests are undeniably culturally determined, and the concept of general intelligence as measured by IQ, and its relevance to real-world functioning, is of questionable value, at best, in non-Western societies (Sternberg et al., 2001). Ideally, we would like to have measures that are truly universal, that can help to assess global theories that pertain to all members of the species. In the absence of such measures, I believe that IQ tests and related psychometric instruments assess important aspects of individual differences in mental abilities for children from Western societies and that the wealth of data obtained from such tests can be used to address important theoretical and practical questions related to individual differences in intellectual functioning. But there is more to intelligence than simply IQ, which I hope will be made clear in the remainder of this chapter.

Information-Processing Approaches to the Study of Intelligence

One criticism of the psychometric approach, and IQ tests specifically, is that test construction is based primarily on pragmatic considerations—which items discriminate reliably among children—and not on theoretical considerations (Sternberg, 1985). The factors that constitute intelligence are determined by statistical analyses and not because of any a priori model of intelligence. As I noted earlier, however, it would be unfair to say that IQ tests are atheoretical. Nevertheless, pragmatic considerations of selecting items that discriminate among children of a given age are still extremely important in choosing which items will be included on the tests. Thus, although IQ tests can assess individual differences in intelligence well, they are less successful at providing insight into the nature of the intelligence that underlies test performance. This is critical not just from the point of view of theory, but also for practice. For instance, Douglas Detterman and Lee Anne Thompson (1997) propose that the key to improving education (particularly special education) is an understanding of the basic cognitive abilities that underlie individual differences in intelligence. With such an understanding, educational interventions can be individualized, and only through such practices will children, especially those whose style of learning differs from that of the majority, reap the benefit of educational research.

Individual differences in cognitive abilities have been extensively studied from the information-processing perspective. In a sense, the same mechanisms used to describe developmental function from an information-processing perspective can be used to describe individual differences. Thus, for example, differences in how information is encoded, speed of processing, how easily information is categorized, and metacognition can all be sources of individual (as well as developmental) differences in thinking and intelligence.

When cognitive psychologists examine individual differences in children's thinking, they often make contrasts between groups known to vary on the basis of IQ (for example, normal children and children with mental retardation or gifted and nongifted children) or between children matched in IQ who differ on the basis of some academic ability (for example, good and poor readers or learning-disabled and nondisabled children). In such studies, researchers attempt to discover the underlying processes responsible for group differences in IQ, task performance, or academic skill. No attempt will be made here to assess the origins of mental retardation, learning and reading disabilities, or giftedness. The etiologies of these intellectual exceptionalities are interesting and important but would require separate chapters (or books) to investigate properly (although Chapter 14 discussed possible origins of reading and math disabilities). Rather, I examine differences in cognitive processing between exceptional and normal children to elucidate the nature of cognition in general and to discover educationally important differences in thinking among these groups of children. I look at a number of different aspects of cognitive processing that are implicated in intelligence, classified into two broad categories: basic-level processes, including speed of processing and working memory, and higher-level cognitive abilities, including strategies, knowledge base, and metacognition.

Basic-Level Processes

Basic-level processes include tasks of working memory and memory span (such as the digit-span task, versions of which are included in the Stanford-Binet and Wechsler IQ tests) and laboratory tests designed to measure people's response times as they make presumably simple decisions. These latter tasks include short-term memory scanning, retrieval of familiar words from the long-term store, and simple categorization tasks (see Jensen, 1998). The basic processes measured by these tasks are presumed to be closely related to physiological functioning and thus primarily under the influence of endogenous (and inherited) factors. Although a number of basic-level processing abilities have been touted as influencing individual differences in intelligence, including inhibition (e.g., Harnishfeger & Bjorklund, 1994; McCall & Carriger, 1993), resistance to interference (e.g., Dempster, 1993), and the ability to process novelty (e.g., Bornstein & Sigman, 1986; Sternberg, 1985), among others, most research has focused on two general mechanisms: speed of processing and

working memory, and I discuss research on these two topics here.

Speed of Information Processing

Older children perform most, if not all, aspects of information processing faster than younger children do (see Kail, 1991). Moreover, both children and adults show similar patterns of reaction times across a large variety of tasks (Kail & Salthouse, 1994). Similar differences in speed of retrieval between gifted and nongifted children (Saccuzzo, Johnson, & Guertin, 1994) and between learning-disabled (LD) and non–learning-disabled (non-LD) children (Ceci, 1983) have also been observed. The differences in memory performance between LD and non-LD children and between good and poor readers attributed to higher-order cognitive abilities (see later) might be mediated by differences in speed of processing. Some children might require more time to activate relevant concepts used on these memory and problem-solving tasks than other children do, which in turn requires greater expenditure of mental effort. The increased effort associated with the slower retrieval of language terms, for example, might be indirectly responsible for the less strategic approach of these children to the task and, thus, for their overall lower levels of performance.

In addition to distinguishing LD from non-LD children and good readers from poor ones, the efficiency of retrieval from long-term memory has been hypothesized to be an important component in individual differences in intelligence in the general population (Fry & Hale, 2000; Jensen, 1998). Most forms of intelligence require retrieving information in memory and acting on that information. Several researchers have reasoned that people who retrieve information quickly and efficiently will display an advantage on cognitive tasks, particularly verbal ones. Earl Hunt and his colleagues provided support for this position using a variety of experimental tasks. In one study, Hunt and his colleagues asked adults to verify category statements such as "A dog is an animal." They found that the time needed to confirm such simple statements correlated significantly with verbal ability (Hunt, Davidson, & Lansman, 1981).

Several reviews of the literature looking at evidence from both children and adults have found moderate correlations (between about −.30 and −.50) between speed of responding and intelligence, with faster responding (and thus presumably faster information processing) being associated with higher IQs (Fry & Hale, 2000; Jensen, 1998). Moreover, speed of information processing correlates significantly both with performance on timed tests, when speed is important, and on nontimed tests, when fast responding is irrelevant (Vernon & Kantor, 1986). This pattern of results, along with the evidence from the developmental literature indicating the role of speed of processing in cognitive development (Kail, 1991), suggests that speed of processing is an important component of individual differences in intelligence.

Individual differences in speed of processing are reliable but often small, and they point to important differences in intelligence at a microscopic level. Differences are often in milliseconds, and it may be wondered what the significance of a 50-millisecond (1/20th of a second) difference might be with respect to intelligence. Although such differences are small, they can be important indeed. Perhaps one of the most important cognitive skills for people in technological societies is reading. Small differences in rate of retrieving the meaning of a word or in integrating letters to form words can, over a very short time, result in substantial differences in reading rate and reading comprehension.

Working Memory

There seems little debate that speed of processing is an important component to general intelligence. But might there be other basic-level mechanisms that are equally or more important? Linda Miller and Philip Vernon (1996) proposed that working memory is a good candidate for a basic-level process that plays an important role in intelligence beyond the impact of speed of processing. Miller and Vernon (1996) tested children between 4 and 6 years of age. Children were administered the WISC and batteries of reaction-time and working-memory tasks. Not surprisingly, children became faster with age and working-memory span increased with age. Also, when general reaction time and memory factors were computed, the two were found to correlate significantly (−.44; the shorter the reaction time, the greater working memory tended to be). This is consistent with research reported in Chapter 5 on the relation between speed of item identification and memory span (Hulme et al., 1984). Reaction time was also significantly correlated with IQ at each age (overall correlation = −.42), as would be expected from the research reviewed earlier. The correlation between IQ and working memory, however, was even greater (.82), and remained significant even after the effects of reaction time and age were taken into consideration. Miller and Vernon concluded that, for children between the ages of 4 and 6 years, "memory accounts for significant variability in intelligence" (1996, p. 184). Reaction time, in contrast, has a smaller role in intelligence, at least once individual differences in working memory are taken into consideration.

This greater influence of working memory relative to speed of processing on intelligence may be age dependent, however. Working with individuals ranging in age from 7 years old through young adults (in contrast to the 4- to 6-year-old children tested by Miller and Vernon), Astrid Fry and Sandra Hale (1996, 2000) also found a strong relation between working memory and fluid intelligence, but, unlike Miller and Vernon (1996), reported that this effect was mediated mostly by the influence of speed of processing. Although the pattern of results of these and other studies (see Fry & Hale, 2000) differ somewhat as a function of the age of the children tested, it is clear that speed of processing, working memory, and intelligence are strongly interrelated, and, as pointed out by Fry and Hale (2000), they have nearly the same developmental function, suggesting a single underlying mechanism.

Higher-Level Cognitive Abilities

Speed of processing and working memory are clearly important components of intelligence. Yet, other more macro processes vary among people and probably contribute to individual differences in intelligence. Chief among these are strategies, knowledge base, and metacognition.

Strategies

Strategies allow people to plan the course of their cognitive operations, to anticipate the consequences of their acts and the acts of others. Given this view of strategies, it is not surprising that many researchers have proposed that strategies are a central aspect of intelligence (Bray, Fletcher, & Turner, 1996; Das, 1984). For example, J. P. Das has written, "What qualifies as intelligence may be the ability to plan or structure one's behavior with an end in view. The more efficient and parsimonious the plan is, the more intelligent the resulting behavior" (1984, p. 116).

Differences in strategy implementation have been hypothesized to explain the difference in task performance between children with and without mental retardation, between good and poor readers, between learning-disabled (LD) and nonlearning-disabled (non-LD) children, and between gifted and nongifted children For example, Richard Bauer (1979) gave 9- and 10-year-old LD and non-LD children a series of free-recall tasks. No group differences were found for the last several items on the lists. Recall for these last items was characteristically high and was attributed to children's emptying the contents of their short-term store, without the need of any specific strategy. In contrast, large group differences were noted in the recall of items from the beginning of the list. Recall of items from the beginning of a list has usually been interpreted as reflecting the use of strategies. In other words, the LD children differed from the non-LD children in strategy use but not in nonstrategic functioning. This interpretation was bolstered by the results of two subsequent experiments in which Bauer observed lower levels of categorical clustering (an indication of the memory strategy of organization; see Chapter 6) for the LD children. Similar observations have been made for poor readers, who likewise show lower levels of memory performance than do good readers of equal IQ (Dallago & Moely, 1980; Goldstein, Hasher, & Stein, 1983).

In other research, Jane Gaultney (1998) statistically equated the amount of strategy use on memory tasks between third-, fourth-, and fifth-grade LD and non-LD children and found that non-LD children benefited more from comparable strategy use than LD children did. That is, even when LD children were strategic (sometimes as strategic as non-LD children), they didn't reap the benefits of the strategy in memory performance compared with the non-LD children. This is an indication of a utilization deficiency (see Chapter 6), and Gaultney proposed that the LD children exerted more mental effort executing the memory strategies than the non-LD children did, and as a result had less mental capacity available for holding items in working memory.

Differences in strategy use are sometimes found to be a source of differences in task performance between gifted and nongifted children (Coyle et al., 1998; Gaultney, Bjorklund, & Goldstein, 1996). For example, in a series of free-recall experiments, Gaultney and her colleagues (1996) contrasted gifted and nongifted middle-school children for their use of memory strategies and found that gifted children consistently were more likely to be strategic than were their nongifted peers. One interesting finding of their study was that, despite the greater use of strategies by gifted than nongifted children, it was more important to task performance to be strategic for the nongifted children than for the gifted children. This is illustrated by looking at the average performance of children classified as strategic compared with those classified as nonstrategic for the gifted and nongifted children in this study. Figure 15-3 presents the mean difference in recall between the strategic children and nonstrategic children through five trials, separately for the gifted and nongifted children. The higher the score, the greater advantage to recall there was for being strategic.

The first thing to note is that all the scores are positive (from a little over 1 word to about 3.5 words remembered per trial). This means that, on average, it was always to a child's advantage to be strategic. But look at the difference between the gifted and nongifted children. Except for the first trial, it made a greater difference in amount recalled for the

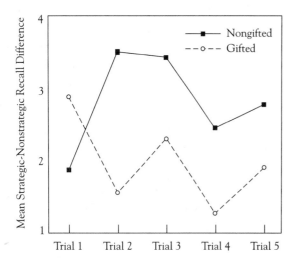

FIGURE 15-3   Mean strategic minus nonstrategic difference in recall for gifted and nongifted children at each trial. The higher the score, the greater the advantage for being strategic. SOURCE: Gaultney, J. F., Bjorklund, D. F., & Goldstein, D. (1996). To be young, gifted, and strategic: Advantages for memory performance. *Journal of Experimental Child Psychology, 61*, p. 51. Reprinted with permission.

nongifted children to be strategic than it did for the gifted children. That is, the difference between nongifted children who used a memory strategy and those who did not was quite large. This difference was much smaller for the gifted children.

Why should being strategic be more important for nongifted than gifted children? Gaultney and her colleagues (1996) proposed that many gifted children did not need strategies to perform reasonably well on this task. When nonstrategic gifted and nongifted children were compared, the gifted children did significantly better. Thus, Gaultney and her colleagues proposed that much of the superior performance of the gifted children was mediated by nonstrategic factors, including, perhaps, faster speed of processing and a more elaborated knowledge base.

Interestingly, the tendency of many gifted children to "just know" an answer, can sometimes have a negative side effect. For example, Katherine Kipp Harnishfeger and I (1990b) speculated that some gifted children have not needed to use deliberate learning and memory strategies during the elementary school years because they have been able to apprehend course material in a relatively automatic fashion. When the cognitive demands become more challenging in middle- or high-school, these children might be at a disadvantage relative to their lower-IQ but more strategic peers, accounting, in part, for some of the academic difficulties some gifted teenagers encounter. I have seen similar difficulties in some bright students making the transition from high school to college or from junior college to university.

In other research, David Geary and Sam Brown (1991) assessed gifted, nongifted, and mathematically disabled third- and fourth-grade children's selection and use of strategies in solving a series of addition problems. All the children used some combination of strategies to solve the problems, but the gifted children used the most mature mix of strategies, followed by the normal children and finally the mathematically disabled children. Geary and Brown concluded that the principal reason for the group differences in strategy use in this experiment was in children's long-term memory organization of basic addition facts. The gifted third- and fourth-grade children knew their basic math facts (9 + 7 = 16; 6 + 8 = 14) better than did the other two groups of children, permitting them to use more efficient strategies. In other words, one of the reasons for gifted children's more effective use of strategies was their greater knowledge base.

Knowledge Base

In an effort to make comprehensible the effects that various cognitive mechanisms have on intelligence and its development, psychologists, by necessity, categorize the various factors, to some extent separating the contribution one factor (e.g., working memory) has relative to others (e.g., strategies). This may give the impression that one can simply partial out variance associated with each factor, and identify "how much" each contributes to intelligence. This is, in fact, a reasonable research approach (e.g., Fry & Hale, 1996; Miller & Vernon, 1996), but one should not get the impression that, in reality, each cognitive factor makes its own independent contribution to overall intellectual functioning. Rather, the various factors are intricately entwined, affecting one another in complex ways that "partialling-out-the-variance" techniques cannot fully capture. One factor that seems to make an important contribution to all other factors, both basic and higher level, is *knowledge base*. What a person knows about the topic he or she is thinking or reasoning about greatly influences cognitive performance.

Just as developmental differences can be explained, in part, by differences in what a child knows (that is, in his or her knowledge base, see Chapters 6, 10, and 12), so can individual differences. For example, some researchers have suggested that memory differences between good and poor readers are more likely to stem from differences in knowledge base than from differences in strategy use. The semantic memories of poor readers are not as well developed as the semantic memories of good readers are, resulting in the inefficient retrieval of word meaning from long-term store and, thus, less effective processing of verbal information (Bjorklund & Bernholtz, 1986; Vellutino & Scanlon, 1985). Jean Bernholtz and I (Bjorklund & Bernholtz, 1986) illustrated this possibility by giving good and poor junior high school readers (average age = 13 years), matched for IQ, a series of concept and memory tasks. In a first session, children were asked to select examples from specified natural language categories (for example, birds, clothes, tools) and to rate each item in terms of how typical it was of its category. (Category typicality was discussed in Chapter 11.) In general, differences in judged typicality affect the performance of both children and adults on a variety of tasks, and children's judgments become more adultlike with age. We reported that the judgments of the 13-year-old poor readers resembled those of normal 9-year-olds and were less adultlike than were the ratings of the good readers. In other words, differences in the semantic memory organization of good and poor 13-year-old readers were found with respect to category typicality.

In later experiments (Bjorklund & Bernholtz, 1986), children were given sets of 12 typical and 12 atypical items to recall in any order they wanted. In one experiment, the typicality of the items was based on norms generated by adults (adult-generated lists).

In another experiment, the typicality of the items was based on each child's self-generated norms, obtained from the earlier session (self-generated lists). Significant differences in memory performance were observed only for the adult-generated lists. Recall was comparable between the good and poor readers when typical and atypical category items were selected based on each child's own judgments. Furthermore, measures of strategy use in these experiments (based on amount of clustering and latencies between the recall of words) indicated that the good readers were no more strategic than the poor readers were. Rather, their superior memory performance could best be attributed to differences in knowledge base. These results do not mean that there are no strategic differences between good and poor readers. Rather, the results indicate that differences in knowledge base contribute significantly to performance differences observed between these two groups of children and might be partly responsible for any apparent differences noted in strategy use.

In related research, Marcia Scott, Daryl Greenfield, and Esther Sterental (1986) reported differences in knowledge of familiar words between groups of 6- to 8-year-old LD and non-LD students. Children were presented with a series of four pictures from a single superordinate category (for example, banana, apple, strawberries, orange: fruit). Twelve superordinate categories were studied in all. The children were asked a series of questions concerning how the items were alike and different from one another. LD and non-LD children differed considerably on the number of responses they provided to these questions, revealing a difference in knowledge of familiar superordinate categories. That is, as in our study (Bjorklund & Bernholtz, 1986) of 13-year-old good and poor readers, a major difference between the LD and non-LD children was in their knowledge base for familiar language concepts.

One study that demonstrates the importance of knowledge base in learning and memory and its relation to IQ is that of Wolfgang Schneider, Joachim Körkel, and Franz Weinert (1989). German children in grades 3, 5, and 7 were evaluated for their knowledge of soccer and were classified as soccer experts or soccer novices. The children were also administered

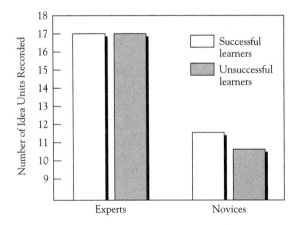

FIGURE 15-4 Number of idea units remembered about a soccer story for high- and low-aptitude soccer experts and soccer novices. In this case, being an expert eliminated any effect of academic aptitude (IQ) on performance. SOURCE: Adapted from data presented in Schneider, W., Körkel, J., & Weinert, F. E. (1989). Domain-specific knowledge and memory performance: A comparison of high- and low-aptitude children. *Journal of Educational Psychology, 81,* 306–312.

a series of intelligence tests, and these results, along with their school grades in math and German, were used to classify them as successful or unsuccessful learners. The children were then presented with a well-organized narrative text about soccer and were later asked to recall it. Amount remembered was computed by the number of idea units the children recalled about the story. Patterns of results with respect to expertise and IQ were similar for the children at each of the three grade levels and are summarized (averaged over grade) in Figure 15-4. As would be expected, memory performance was better for the soccer experts than for the soccer novices. However, the researchers reported no difference in performance between the academically successful learners and the unsuccessful ones. That is, being a good learner (and having a high IQ) did not result in better performance by either the expert or the novice children. Having a detailed knowledge of the subject matter was enough to yield high levels of memory performance. Similarly, having an impover-

ished knowledge of the subject matter was enough to yield low levels of performance, regardless of a child's level of IQ (see also Recht & Leslie, 1988; Walker, 1987). Although IQ might be related to academic performance, such as reading comprehension, what seems especially important for intelligent performance is knowledge. Children with substantial knowledge of a subject act smart when dealing with matter from that subject area, independent of their level of IQ.

This situation is admittedly not typical. In most contexts, successful learners do, of course, perform better than unsuccessful learners do. One important reason why this is so, however, is that successful learners generally know more about the things they are dealing with than unsuccessful learners do. Successful learners acquire information more readily and thus have a more elaborated knowledge base on which to base future learning. The more children know, the more easily they are able to learn and remember new information.

A detailed knowledge base does not always eliminate IQ effects, however. Wolfgang Schneider and I (1992; Schneider, Bjorklund & Maier-Brückner, 1996) classified high- and low-IQ second- and fourth-grade children as soccer experts and novices and gave them two sort-recall memory tasks. Children were given sets of written words to remember, which they could sort into categories before recalling them (see Chapter 6). On one task, sets of soccer-related words in one of four categories (soccer plays, equipment, players, parts of the field) were used as stimuli; in the second task, sets of words from familiar language categories were used (tools, fruits, mammals, vehicles—the nonsoccer list). As in the study by Schneider and his colleagues (1989) that examined story recall, experts remembered more than novices did from the soccer-related list (but not, of course, from the nonsoccer-related list). However, the effect of IQ was not eliminated in these studies, with high-IQ children remembering more than low-IQ children on both the soccer and nonsoccer lists, regardless of level of expertise. Schneider and I (1992) argued that intelligence played a greater role here than in the story-recall experiment because of the more deliberate encoding strategies used on sort-recall tasks. Expertise can reduce or eliminate the impact of intelligence (as measured by IQ) in some situations, but IQ will have a residual effect when explicit strategies, such as those used in sort-recall tasks, are called for.

Metacognition

One higher-level aspect of cognition that has been postulated as being significant to individual differences in intelligence is *metacognition,* a person's understanding of his or her own cognitive abilities. Basically, the brighter individuals of any age are those who possess the executive functions to monitor their task performance and to apply the techniques they possess to solve a problem. John Borkowski and his colleagues have suggested that differences in metacognition are a major cause of differences in strategy use and training effectiveness between children with and without mental retardation (Borkowski, Reid, & Kurtz, 1984), between reflective and impulsive children (Borkowski et al., 1983), between gifted and nongifted children (Borkowski & Peck, 1986), and between children within the normal range of intelligence (Carr, Borkowski, & Maxwell, 1991).

Borkowski and Virginia Peck (1986) instructed gifted and nongifted 7- and 8-year-olds to use an elaboration strategy or a simpler clustering strategy on a memory task. Children were later tested for transfer of the strategy to other memory problems. Elaboration involves creating a relationship between two items, so that the presentation of one item will elicit the recall of the other. For example, if I wanted to remember the pair of words *banana-coat,* I might form an image of a bunch of bananas hanging in a closet where I usually find my coat. Or I might think that a banana peel covers a banana in a way similar to how a coat covers my body. Although forming such relations may seem like a lot of work, the memory performance of both children and adults is facilitated by the use of an elaboration strategy (see Pressley, 1982; Chapter 6). For the children who received the clustering instructions (for example, "Try

to remember words from the same category together"), training was less explicit than it was for the children who were trained to use the elaboration strategy. Would both the gifted and nongifted children be able to benefit from the training, and would the extent of training affect the transfer of the strategy differently for the two groups of children?

Both the gifted and the nongifted children who were trained in the elaboration strategy learned it. Differences between the groups for this strategy became apparent during a generalization task, when the children were given different sets of problems to learn. The gifted children were more likely to generalize the strategy they had learned than were the nongifted children, with the extent of generalization being significantly related to scores on a battery of metamemory questions. For the clustering strategy, differences in training as well as transfer between the two groups of children were noted. The gifted children benefited more from the minimal training than did the nongifted children. This difference was extended to the transfer trials. That is, gifted children required less explicit prompting before they would learn a strategy and generalize it to new situations. According to Borkowski and Peck, because of their greater metamemory awareness, "gifted children realized the effectiveness of the strategy and applied it appropriately even without the aid of complete and explicit instructions" (1986, p. 193). Although gifted children apparently do not always show greater metacognitive awareness relative to nongifted children (see Alexander & Schwanenflugel, 1996; Alexander, Schwanenflugel, & Carr, 1995), when task performance is challenging, gifted children typically show greater metacognitive knowledge than their nongifted peers do (Kurtz & Weinert, 1989).

Although the picture is complex, information-processing models provide researchers with specific aspects of cognition to investigate as the source of intellectual differences among people and experimental methods to facilitate the search. Although my bias is certainly showing here, I believe that models that examine developmental changes in information processing are likely to produce important and exciting insights into the nature of individual differences in human intelligence (see Bjorklund & Schneider, 1996).

Piagetian Approaches to the Study of Intelligence

Information-processing approaches to individual differences in children's thinking have the advantage of reasonably well-developed theories and methods that can be applied for understanding intelligence. As with psychometric approaches, however, there is nothing inherently developmental about information-processing theories. One theory that is explicitly developmental in its orientation is Piaget's. Although Piaget himself did not apply his theory to individual differences, others have, and I now examine some of this research briefly.

Several researchers have demonstrated that individual differences on Piagetian tasks (for example, conservation, classification) predict academic ability. For instance, performance on batteries of Piagetian tasks has been shown to predict early (first- and second-grade) academic skills as well as or even better than standardized IQ tests do (Kingma, 1984; Lunzar, Dolan, & Wilkinson, 1976). In related research, Diana Byrd and Barry Gholson (1985) reported that degree of operativity (evidenced by performance on a series of conservation and classification tasks) was significantly related to the reading ability of second- and fourth-grade children. In fact, operativity was related to a variety of reading-related measures, including memory, metamemory, and metareading (knowledge about reading), although these other measures correlated only slightly with one another. These findings led Byrd and Gholson to conclude that developmental and individual differences in reading strategies are not mediated by memory skills or knowledge about memory strategies as much as they are by operative (that is, logical) abilities.

In other research, Deanna Kuhn (1976), testing middle-class children from the first through the seventh grades, failed to find a significant correspon-

dence between Piagetian task performance and IQ for her older groups of children. All the children were administered the WISC and a series of Piagetian tasks. The Piagetian tasks for the younger children (first through third grade) included class inclusion, seriation, conservation of amount, and multiple classification. The older children were given three tests of formal operational ability (Inhelder & Piaget, 1958), including the pendulum problem that was discussed in Chapter 4. Kuhn reported a significant relation between scores on the battery of Piagetian tasks and IQ for 6- to 8-year-olds (correlation = .69) but not for children approaching formal operations (correlation = .22). Kuhn suggested that the environmental factors causing children to excel on IQ tests are not the same as those affecting the rate of progress through Piagetian stages. Such environmental influences increase over time, Kuhn proposed, resulting in reduced correspondence between Piagetian and psychometric tests with advancing age.

Wolfgang Schneider and his colleagues (1999) observed an opposite pattern of correlations between Piagetian and psychometric tests. In their longitudinal study, correlations between preschool tests of cognitive ability (for example, conservation of number) and psychometric tests were low (average correlation = .24), whereas the relation between formal reasoning tests given in grades 4 through 6 and psychometric tests was higher (median correlation = .48). An additional and impressive finding in this study was the high correlations between psychometric tests given at ages 7 and 9 and formal and scientific reasoning tests given at ages 11 and 12 (median correlation = .51). In other words, psychometric and Piagetian-type tasks not only correlated significantly with one another when they were administered at the same point in time, but psychometric tests given during the elementary school years predicted logical reasoning abilities three to five years later.

Why the contradiction between the findings of the Schneider group and Kuhn? The tasks used by Schneider and his colleagues to assess preschool cognition reflect some of the earliest acquired cognitive accomplishments during this time (number conservation is typically the first conservation task children master), whereas those used by Kuhn reflect abilities usually acquired during the elementary school years (for example, class inclusion, multiple classification). One interpretation of these findings is that tasks that assess the transition from preoperations to concrete operations, as used by Kuhn, tap similar underlying cognitive abilities as do psychometric tests, whereas tasks that assess earlier-developing skills, such as those used by Schneider and his colleagues, tap cognitive abilities that are qualitatively different from those tapped by psychometric tests (Bjorklund, 1999). That is, the nature of early intelligence is more homogenous during the preschool years than it is by age 6 or 7 years.

In other research, Lloyd Humphreys and his colleagues examined the relationship between a battery of Piagetian tasks, Wechsler IQ tests, and academic ability for children of varying intellectual aptitudes (normal children and children with mental retardation) and ages (6 to 18 years) (Humphreys, 1980; Humphreys & Parsons, 1979; Humphreys, Rich, & Davey, 1985). Humphreys and his colleagues administered 27 different Piagetian tasks to the children. The tasks ranged from those that assessed early concrete operational abilities to those that evaluated formal operational skills. Correlations between the children's performance on Piagetian tasks and on Wechsler IQ tests were in excess of .80. Comparable results were reported when a subset of only 13 Piagetian tasks was selected. Humphreys also reported significant correlations between sets of Piagetian tasks and measures of academic achievement (correlations in excess of .70), only slightly lower than those found with verbal IQ. Furthermore, correlations between performance on these tasks and a general intelligence factor (g) were also high for most tasks, indicating to Humphreys that the battery of Piagetian tasks measures the same aspect of general intelligence as do psychometric tests. In general, there was a great deal of overlap among the Piagetian tasks, the Wechsler IQ scales, and measures of academic achievement. However, there were some differences between the tasks in the intellectual skills they assessed. Humphreys was not able to specify the nature of these differences, but he asserted that given the current data, each measure is a valid index of intelligence (Humphreys et al., 1985).

In comparison with researchers adhering to the psychometric and information-processing approaches, Piagetian researchers have done comparatively little work on individual differences in children's thinking. This is understandable given Piaget's emphasis on developmental function. What has been done, however, is encouraging. For example, the data of Kuhn (1976) and Schneider and his colleagues (1999) suggest that the relationship between the intelligence assessed by Piagetian measures and psychometrically measured intelligence can vary as a function of developmental level—that is, that the nature of intelligence changes with age, influencing patterns of individual differences. And Humphreys's work demonstrates that statistical analyses typically used with psychometric data can be applied successfully to Piagetian tests of intelligence. Piaget's theory has been a favorite of many educators for years, and standardized variants of Piagetian tasks, should they be developed, may be well received and used in the future.

Sternberg's Triarchic Theory of Intelligence

A theory of intelligence that has received substantial attention is Robert Sternberg's (1985) **triarchic theory.** The model includes three subtheories—the contextual, the experiential, and the componential—each of which is examined briefly.

The Contextual Subtheory

The **contextual subtheory** holds that intelligence must be viewed in the context in which it occurs. Intelligent behaviors for the middle-class American schoolchild might not be considered intelligent for the ghetto dropout or the unschooled Guatemalan farm boy. By defining intelligence in terms of real-world environments, Sternberg stresses the importance of the external as well as the internal world to intelligence. Such a definition also avoids the circularity of theories that basically define intelligence as a score on an IQ test (or a test of information processing). Sternberg proposes three processes of intelligence: *adaptation*, *selection*, and *shaping*. Adaptation is adjustment of one's behavior to achieve a good fit with one's environment. When adaptation is not possible or not desirable, a person can select an alternative environment in which he or she can adapt well. Failing to adapt to the whims of a new supervisor, for example, a person can choose to quit her job and select another. Or a child might find it difficult to get along with children in the neighborhood and instead become friendly with other children from school who do not live as close by. If for some reason a new environment cannot be selected, however, a person can attempt to shape the environment. The employee can try to convince her supervisor to change his ways or may go over his head to bring changes from above. The child can try to alter the behavior of his neighborhood peers by placating them with his mother's cookies or by inviting one child at a time over to play instead of inviting the entire group.

Although these three processes typify intelligence universally, what is required for adaptation, selection, and shaping will vary among different groups of people, so that a single set of behaviors cannot be specified as intelligent for all individuals. Also, what is deemed intelligent at one point in life might not be so judged later. For example, because children have less freedom than do adults to select new environments and are often powerless to shape significantly certain aspects of these environments, adapting to their uncomfortable surroundings might be the most intelligent option they have. Thus, whereas the school-phobic adult will select nonacademic environments, the 10-year-old child typically cannot, making adaptation the most intelligent choice.

Basically, the contextual subtheory is one of **cultural relativism.** Intellectual skills that are critical for survival in one culture might not be as important in another. Likewise, important intellectual skills within a culture can undergo some change from one generation to another. For example, arithmetic computation has unquestionably been a vital skill for people in technological societies. Wechsler noted

the significance of arithmetic to intelligence in the construction of the WISC and WAIS and their subsequent revisions: Each has an arithmetic subtest. Yet, with the widespread use of calculators, being able to add and subtract numbers quickly and accurately becomes a little less critical to everyday functioning. Although I would not care to say that arithmetic computation will become unimportant, in the generations ahead it will probably be viewed as much less critical to intelligence than it is today and, certainly, than it was a generation ago.

Sternberg is not the only person to propose a theory of intelligence that is culturally relative (see, for example, Laboratory of Comparative Human Cognition, 1983). Such theories have rightly been criticized, however, for preventing any general conclusions about the universal nature of human intellectual functioning. According to such theories, everything is relative, and thus intelligence can be studied only from the perspective of a particular culture or subculture. Sternberg avoids this problem by combining his contextual subtheory with the experiential and componential subtheories, which propose aspects of intelligence that are universal.

The Experiential Subtheory

The **experiential subtheory** is concerned with how prior knowledge influences performance on certain cognitive tasks. More specifically, the subtheory examines the ability to deal with novelty and the degree to which processing is automatized (that is, made to involve relatively little mental effort). Both skills are highly dependent on experience. A stimulus is novel only to the extent that it differs in some way from what is already familiar (Rheingold, 1985). Similarly, newly acquired processing skills are rarely executed effortlessly but, rather, require substantial expenditure of one's limited mental effort for their deployment. Only when a skill has been exercised frequently does it become automatized. Sternberg proposes that how people respond to novelty and the ease with which they can automatize information processing are important and universal aspects of intelligence.

The importance of such skills is apparent in any occupation. Good scientists must be able to apprehend quickly the relevant factors that are influencing whatever phenomenon they are concerned with. If scientists are to make major contributions to their field, however, they must also be able to devise clever ways of testing their hypotheses and to appreciate the significance of an unexpected result. These factors are important not only in the ivory tower but also in more worldly occupations. This importance was made apparent to me by an electrician who installed three ceiling fans in my home after two other electricians had failed. He quickly discerned what approach to take, and after nine hours of running into more obstacles than I knew existed in my walls and above my ceilings, he finished the task. After I expressed my appreciation for a job well done, the electrician commented: "Any yahoo can lay wire in a straight line. It only takes brains when things don't go as you planned."

The experiential subtheory suggests what tasks are good indicators of intelligence—namely, those that involve dealing with novelty or automatic processing for their successful completion. Many of the laboratory tasks of modern cognitive psychology are good candidates for assessing intelligence because they stress speed of responding, which is a good indicator of the extent to which processing has become automatized. For example, simple letter-identification tasks, in which people must respond as rapidly as possible to signal the presence of a specified letter, measure the degree to which processing for this over-learned code (the alphabet) is automatized. Similarly, word-identification tasks (deciding whether a letter string is a word or not) and category-identification tasks (deciding whether a word is a member of a specified category or not) also test automatic processing. More complex laboratory tasks such as solving analogies or syllogisms probably assess aspects of both automatic processing and response to novelty. Similarly, many items on psychometric batteries test the same processes as do lab tasks and, Sternberg asserts, are probably better estimators of intelligence. That is because these items are usually more difficult than the lab tasks, involving, on the average, greater degrees of novelty. Examples of psychometric test items that would fit Sternberg's experiential subtheory include picture arrangement ("Put these pictures together so that they make a story"), similarities ("How are television and education alike?"), and comprehension ("Why might it be important that Supreme Court judges be appointed and not elected?").

The Componential Subtheory

The **componential subtheory** is Sternberg's information-processing model of cognition. Sternberg (1997) argues that intelligence has a common core of mental processes that can be used in any environmental context or culture. These include recognizing the existence and defining the nature of a problem, representing information about the problem, devising a strategy for solving the problem, allocating sufficient mental resources to solve the problem, and monitoring and evaluating one's solution to the problem. How does one go about doing all these things? Basically, they require different aspects of information processing.

Briefly, Sternberg proposed three general types of information-processing components: metacomponents, performance components, and knowledge-acquisition components. *Metacomponents* are metacognitive abilities, involving the monitoring of task performance and the allocation of attentional resources. *Performance components* include encoding, mental comparison, and retrieval of information. And *knowledge-acquisition components* are the processes involved in gaining new knowledge and selectively acting on recently encoded information and information in one's long-term store. These three components interact so that deficits in any one component can result in deficits in any of the other components. Individual differences in any of these components reflect differences in how people process information and, thus, important differences in intelligence.

Following Sternberg's componential subtheory, why should intelligence increase with age? The major reason is growth in knowledge base. The knowledge-acquisition components provide a mechanism for a steadily increasing knowledge base. As the knowledge base increases, more sophisticated forms of knowledge acquisition are possible, which, in turn, further increase the knowledge base. The components lead to increases in knowledge, which lead to more effective use of the components, and so on. Similarly, feedback from the knowledge-acquisition and performance components to the metacomponents can result in improved metacognition. This leads to increased self-monitoring, which, in turn, results in the increased efficacy of the metacomponents. Again, feedback loops among the components lead to increased efficiency and, thus, a smarter individual. In general, the mechanisms that explain how intelligence develops in children are basically the same mechanisms that explain how a person becomes more effective at a particular task with increased experience.

Although the triarchic theory has three distinct parts, Sternberg stresses that they work together in an integrated fashion. Figure 15-5 illustrates this interaction. Starting with the bottom of the figure, we must first look at the information-processing components of intelligence and their interactions. We must realize, however, that these components can be applied to a broad range of situations, including those with which we are highly familiar (for which automatization is likely) to those with which we are highly unfamiliar, or novel. Finally, we must evaluate how these aspects of intelligence affect the external world, and how we adapt, select, or shape the contexts in which we live.

The Triarchic Theory Applied to Education

Each of the three subtheories of Sternberg's triarchic theory has a corresponding style of thinking associated with it. People strong relative to the contextual subtheory are skilled at *practical thinking* (using and applying information); people strong relative to the experiential subtheory excel at *creative thinking* (discovering, creating, and inventing); and people strong relative to the componential subtheory perform well at *analytical thinking* (analyzing, evaluating, critiquing). Sternberg also proposed that each of these

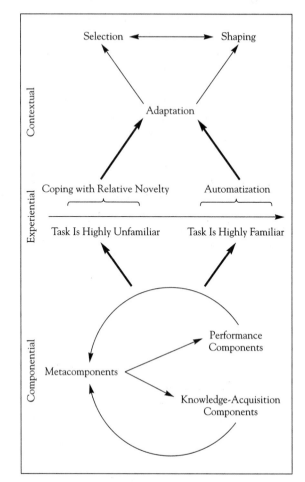

FIGURE 15-5 Relationships among the various aspects of the triarchic theory of intelligence. SOURCE: Sternberg, R. J. (1988). *The triarchic mind: A new theory of human intelligence.* New York: Viking. Reprinted with permission of the author.

three thinking abilities is relatively independent. That is, they are not hierarchically related to a factor of general intelligence (*g*).

If people do indeed have different intellectual patterns based around these three thinking styles, people who receive instruction that matches their preferred style should learn more easily than do people who receive instruction that does not match their preferred style. To assess this hypothesis, one must first gener-

TABLE 15-3 Examples of the instruction and assessment method based on the triarchic theory that might be used in a course in cognitive development.

Practical (contextual subtheory)

What are the implications of the fact of infantile amnesia for your life? For the legal system?

Creative (experiential subtheory)

Design an experiment to test a theory of infantile amnesia.

Analytical (componential subtheory)

Compare Freud's theory of infantile amnesia with Katherine Nelson's theory.

ate a test to assess thinking style, then develop a curriculum tailored to each style of thinking, and finally adequately assess how much was learned as a result of matched versus mismatched instruction. Sternberg and his colleagues (1996) did just that in a study with 199 gifted high-school students.

Gifted high-school students attended an intense, four-week summer college-level course in introductory psychology. Students' thinking style was evaluated as either practical, creative, analytic, or balanced (see later). All students were assigned the same textbook and attended the same morning lecture series. Instruction varied, however, during afternoon sessions, with students receiving instruction that either matched their preferred style (for example, analytic style–analytic instruction) or not (for example, creative style–analytic instruction). Examples of the type of tasks that would exemplify each of the three thinking-style types are shown in Table 15-3. Course performance was assessed by multiple-choice exams, homework assignments that evaluated practical, creative, or analytic thinking, and essay exams that asked for either practical, creative, or analytic responses.

Children were administered an abbreviated version of the *Sternberg Triarchic Abilities Test* (STAT). This test assessed the three basic types of thinking styles (practical, creative, analytic) for three types of content (verbal, quantitative, and figural), resulting in nine

subtests. Examples for each thinking style for the verbal content are (from Sternberg et al., 1996, p. 131):

- *Practical-Verbal:* Students were presented with some everyday problems in the life of an adolescent and asked to come up with a solution (for example, what would you do about a friend who has a substance-abuse problem?).
- *Creative-Verbal:* Students were given verbal analogies preceded by false premises (for example, money falls off trees). They had to solve the analogies as if the false premises were true.
- *Analytic-Verbal:* Students had to figure out the meaning of artificial words from a natural context. Students would see a novel word used in a paragraph and would have to infer the meaning of the word from the context.

Sternberg and his colleagues reported that the three subsections of the STAT (practical, creative, and analytic) were low to moderately correlated with one another. When factor-analytic techniques were applied to the data, nine factors emerged (one for each thinking-style × content combination). According to Sternberg and his colleagues, these findings indicate, "clearly, the STAT is not just another measure of Spearman's (1927) *g* (general ability)" (Sternberg et al., 1996, p. 134). The reason that most psychometric tests load heavily on *g* is likely because of the relatively narrow range of abilities tested—and not because it underlies *all* intellectual functioning.

Sternberg and his colleagues next correlated children's STAT scores with their performance in the course and found moderate but significant correlations between scores on each of the three subtests and course performance (correlations ranged from .24 to .42). More critical, however, was the performance of students whose thinking style matched the instruction they received. The results here were quite consistent: Students who received instruction matched to their thinking style performed significantly better than did mismatched students. Moreover, the same pattern of results was found not just for the homework and essay assessments (some of which would have matched children's thinking style), but also for the multiple-choice items.

In later research, Robert Sternberg, Bruce Torff, and Elena Grigorenko (1999) designed a social studies curriculum based on the triarchic theory for third-grade children (Study 1) and an introductory psychology curriculum for advanced eighth-grade children (Study 2). Unlike their earlier research (Sternberg et al., 1996), the curriculum involved all three aspects of thinking for all students. Course performance was contrasted among students who had the triarchic instructions, those who had special instruction in critical thinking, and those who received a "traditional" curriculum. The results of the research were consistent across the two studies: Students who received the triarchic instruction performed better, on a variety of dependent measures, than did children who received either the critical thinking or traditional curricula (although those receiving the critical thinking curriculum usually performed better than did those receiving the traditional one). And to top it off, third-grade children given the triarchic instruction enjoyed the course more than the other students did.

Sternberg's theory has been a popular one with psychologists and educators since its inception in the mid 1980s. The theory is based on solid experimental work (aspects of the componential and experiential subtheories have been well documented), and the latest research on applying the three subtheories (or three thinking styles) to instruction will do nothing but make the theory more popular. In sum, I believe that Sternberg's triarchic theory, or other multifaceted theories like it, will lead research on the nature of human intelligence in the decades ahead.

Gardner's Theory of Multiple Intelligences

Howard Gardner (1983, 1993, 1999) has proposed that intelligence is composed of separate components, or modules, much like the concept of factors used by the psychometric approach. Gardner's **theory of multiple intelligences** is different, however, because it relies heavily on neuropsychological evi-

dence for the existence of relatively independent "frames of mind." Gardner originally proposed seven such abilities, but has added one more and speculated about a ninth (Gardner, 1999): (1) linguistic, (2) logical-mathematical, (3) musical, (4) spatial, (5) bodily-kinesthetic, (6) interpersonal, (7) intrapersonal, (8) naturalist, and (possibly) (9) spirituality/existential. Linguistic and logical-mathematical intelligences are highly valued in technological societies such as ours, and people high in these types of intelligence are generally viewed as smart. Musical intelligence is usually associated with the composition or performance of music, and spatial intelligence involves the ability to perceive form, solve visual problems, and get around effectively in one's environment. Bodily-kinesthetic intelligence is reflected in control of one's body as epitomized by athletes of exceptional ability. The two forms of personal intelligence involve knowing how to deal with others (interpersonal) and knowledge of one's self (intrapersonal). Naturalistic intelligence concerns knowledge of the natural world (fauna and flora), and spiritual/existential intelligence deals with issues related to the meaning of life (and death), and other aspects of the "ultimate" human condition.

Gardner's claim is not that these are eight (or nine) different components of a single intelligence, but rather that these represent eight distinct intelligences, each being independent of the others. And there may be more. Gardner's proposal is for different, domain-specific forms of intelligence, the antithesis of *g*-based theories. For Gardner, each form of intelligence represents a modular, brain-based capacity. Gardner asserts that these various forms of intelligence are of different degrees of importance in different cultures and at different times in history. For example, in a hunting society, physical dexterity, an ability to locomote effectively, and an understanding of one's natural surroundings are more important than are numerical computation skills. In medieval Europe's apprenticeship system, emphasis was placed on bodily, spatial, and interpersonal abilities, whereas in today's Western society, 400 years later, the emphasis is on linguistic and logical-mathematical skills. Thus, Gardner views the cultural aspects of intelligence to be of utmost importance: different cultures value different types of intelligence. Moreover, Gardner argues that our society's reliance on IQ tests to classify children in terms of intelligence does a great disservice to many of them and to society itself. Because these tests emphasize linguistic and mathematical abilities, children gifted in other areas, such as working with their hands, are often "thrown on society's scrap heap," instead of receiving the education that could enhance their special abilities.

Criteria of an Intelligence

On what basis did Gardner select his list of intelligences? He lists a set of criteria that must be met for an ability to be considered an intelligence (although every criterion need not be met by an ability for it to be considered an intelligence).

Potential isolation by brain damage.   Ample evidence indicates that damage to specified areas of the brain can selectively impair language production or comprehension. Similar evidence abounds for mathematical, musical, and spatial abilities. There is even evidence that damage of the frontal lobes of the neocortex can leave general intellectual functioning unimpaired but produce a socially tactless individual, affecting interpersonal intelligence. The frontal cortex plays an important role in the inhibition of task-irrelevant and inappropriate responses (see Chapters 2 and 5), and many of those inappropriate responses that are no longer inhibited in social situations (Fuster, 1989).

The existence of savants and prodigies.   An intelligence is reflected by exceptionalities, and, thus, can be exhibited by savants and prodigies. *Savants* (sometimes called idiot savants) are people with mental retardation but who possess an exceptional talent in a single domain. Savants have been identified for a number of skills, most notably in mathematics and music. For example, some mathematical savants have an extraordinary facility with the calendar, being able to provide quickly the day of the week for any date in history (for example, September 14,

1522). Savants are perhaps most impressive when it comes to musical ability. There have been numerous newspaper articles and television stories about people with severe mental retardation who can play Beethoven piano sonatas after hearing them only once. Although these are impressive abilities, what is customarily lacking in savants is creativity. To my knowledge, there have been no musical savants who compose great music or who are great improvisers, only those with an outstanding ability to play back accurately what they have heard.

The *prodigy* is on the other side of the coin from the savant. A prodigy is a child with generally normal abilities in all but a small number of areas (usually one). Similar to savants, prodigies are most frequently found in the areas of mathematics and music. Wolfgang Amadeus Mozart was the quintessential musical prodigy. Raised in a musical family, he was playing instruments and composing music, while still a preschooler, at a level few humans ever attain. He was touring the great capitals of Europe by age 8, but aside from his musical prowess, Wolfgang was a normal boy. This is shown in an observation made in 1764 by Daines Barrington (cited in Gould, 1992), who was impressed by the 8-year-old Mozart's musical skill but also noted that music seemed to be the only area in which Mozart was exceptional:

> I must own that I could not help suspecting his father imposed with regard to the real age of the boy, though he had not only a most childish appearance, but likewise had all the actions of that stage of life. For example, whilst he was playing to me, a favorite cat came in, upon which he immediately left his harpsichord, nor could we bring him back for a considerable time. He would also sometimes run about the room with a stick between his legs by way of horse. (Gould, 1992, p. 10)

Why do savants and prodigies indicate multiple intelligences? Gardner believes that such exceptionalities reflect modular, brain-based skills and that such skills surely exist in the general population. The savant and the prodigy are only extreme examples of unevenness in abilities, but their existence suggests that the special skills they possess are domain-specific and can be found in lesser degrees of development in the vast normal range of the human population.

An identifiable core operation or set of operations.
Consistent with modern cognitive science, Gardner believes that each intelligence should have associated with it one or more basic information-processing operations, specialized to deal with a particular type of input (language, music, and so on). For example, sensitivity to pitch relations would be a core operation for musical intelligence, and the ability to imitate movements made by others would be central to bodily intelligence.

A distinctive developmental history, along with a definable set of expert end-state performances.
An intelligence must develop. Any skill that is present fully formed when it first appears does not qualify as a type of intelligence. Also, it must have an identifiable end-state—that is, a level of performance attainable by mature experts. We can certainly specify a developmental course and an expert end-state for most, if not all, of Gardner's intelligences. The gifted writer or speaker serves as the expert for linguistic intelligence, as does the mathematician for mathematical intelligence, the professional athlete or dancer for bodily intelligence, the composer or musician for musical intelligence, the visual artist or trail guide for spatial intelligence, perhaps the skilled politician or therapist for interpersonal intelligence, the philosopher for intrapersonal intelligence, the biologist, or possibly the hunter or farmer, for naturalist intelligence, and religious leaders for spiritual/existential intelligence. Some of these intelligences can have different developmental courses leading to slightly different expert end-states, with developmental milestones along the way from immature to mature performance.

An evolutionary history and evolutionary plausibility.
Why do humans possess these intelligences? Human intelligence is a significant part of the human condition and likely played an important role in the evolution of our species. As such, there should be some evolutionary history of an intelligence (and perhaps evidence of antecedents of these abilities in other species), and a plausible evolutionary explanation of how these intelligences may have been selected. We clearly share social skills and social organization with our primate cousins (see Byrne & Whiten, 1988), and spatial and bodily intelligence with most large mammals.

Even abilities that might be unique to humans, such as music (although this is debated), have an evolutionary plausibility. Music is an important part of contemporary humans' lives. We fall in love to music, praise God to music, and go to war to music. (I loved the line from a Woody Allen movie, directly related to this last point: "Every time I hear Wagner, I get the urge to invade Poland.") Although I find it hard to find phylogenetic antecedents to music (my guess is that it grew out of general language ability), it is easy to see how once the ability evolved, those who had control of music could have an important social advantage relative to others.

Support from experimental psychological tasks and from psychometric findings.
Psychologists from both the cognitive-experimental and psychometric approaches have been studying tasks that assess at least some of the eight intelligences, and findings from these literatures should reveal important individual differences. Psychologists have most often studied tasks assessing language, spatial, and mathematical abilities.

Susceptibility to encoding in a system.
One of the hallmarks of human cognitive functioning is that it is based on symbols. Ideally, an intelligence should have its own symbol system. This seems to be true for language, mathematics, and music, and perhaps for spatial and bodily intelligence.

As I noted earlier, each of these criteria does not have to be met for an ability to be classified as an intelligence. But these are the criteria that Gardner lists "by which each candidate intelligence can be judged" (1983, p. 66).

Multiple Intelligences and Education

Gardner argues for the exclusion of intelligence and aptitude tests from our schools because, as currently practiced, they measure only two types of intelligence and ignore other equally important types.

TABLE 15-4   Types of intelligences and examples of tasks used in Project Spectrum.

Type of intelligence	Tasks	Examples
Music	Production	Singing familiar and novel songs
	Perception	Identifying patterns of bell chimes
Language	Narrative	Telling a story from pictures on a storyboard
	Descriptive	Reporting a sequence of events
Numbers	Counting	Counting moves in a board game
	Calculating	Creating a notational system, performing mental calculations, and organizing number information in the context of a game
Visual arts	Drawing	Making pictures
	3-D	Working with clay
Movement	Dance	Responding to rhythm and performing expressive dance movements
	Athletic	Maneuvering through an obstacle course
Science	Logical inference	Playing treasure hunt games
	Mechanical	Using household gadgets
	Naturalistic	Observing, appreciating, and understanding natural phenomena in classroom "Discovery Area"
Social	Social analysis	Playing with scale model of classroom
	Social roles	Interacting with peers

SOURCE: Adapted with permission from Wexler-Sherman, C., Gardner, H., & Feldman, D. H. (1988). A pluralistic view of early assessment: The Project Spectrum approach. *Theory Into Practice, 27*, 77–83. Copyright © 1988 Ohio State University.

Gardner is not opposed to intellectual assessment in general, however. He advocates the development of measures that would evaluate all types of intelligence. He believes that such assessments should be done early so that intellectual strengths can be discovered and developed through education. Although Gardner believes that each form of intelligence has its origins in biology, he also believes that they are flexible and can be enhanced by education.

Gardner and his colleagues have implemented some of these ideas in a preschool program called Project Spectrum (Gardner & Hatch, 1989; Wexler-Sherman, Gardner, & Feldman, 1988). The curriculum for 4- and 5-year-old children is based on the various domains of intelligence in Gardner's theory. Assessment of children's abilities in each of these domains extends naturally from the curriculum, making the assessment ecologically valid for children. Children are given substantial freedom to explore within the preschool environment, being

encouraged, but never forced, to experience all the content areas. Based on observations in the preschool, 15 different subskill areas have been identified within the framework of Gardner's theory (see Table 15-4). Clear distinctions are noted among children in each of these areas, bolstering the claim that each represents a distinct form of intelligence (Wexler-Sherman et al., 1988).

Although there has not yet been a rigorous experimental test of Gardner's theory, preliminary results are available. Gardner and Thomas Hatch (1989) report two small-scale assessments of the theory—one with a group of 20 preschool children and another with a group of 15 kindergarten and first-grade children. An assessment procedure was developed to evaluate each of seven intelligences (the naturalist and spirituality intelligences had not been identified at the time of this assessment). For the preschoolers, Gardner and Hatch reported that children did not perform at the same level on the various tasks but, rather, showed distinct intellectual profiles, as predicted by the theory. Similar findings were reported for the kindergarten children. Among the first-grade children, however, the five first-grade girls showed no intellectual weaknesses and many strengths (only two first-grade boys were tested, too small a sample to warrant comment). Given the small sample sizes, no definitive conclusions can be reached, but the data, at least from the younger children, are consistent with Gardner's theory and indicate that an assessment measure can be constructed and that the theory is testable.

Evaluation of Gardner's Theory

Gardner's theory has attracted a lot of attention since its inception in 1983. I find that of all the theories of intelligence I discuss in class, Gardner's is usually my students' favorite. But the merits of a theory are not determined by popular vote. How does Gardner's account of intelligence stack up against other, more conventional accounts, or to Sternberg's triarchic theory? First, Gardner (1984) complains that Sternberg's account of intelligence is not sufficiently different from the psychometric account in that it leaves room for a general intellectual factor, not too dissimilar from Spearman's g. Sternberg (1984) countered that it is too early to compare the two theories because there have been no experimental tests of Gardner's theory itself. Is Gardner's theory, in fact, testable? Perhaps not easily. Gardner presents a framework about what is and what is not an intelligence. But even here, there is room for debate. For example, chess performance would fit many of the criteria set by Gardner to qualify as a candidate for an intelligence. There are chess prodigies, chess has a developmental history with an expert end-state, and chess ability perhaps meets other criteria (symbol systems, core set of operations). It does not have a plausible evolutionary explanation, however, and rightly seems not to be an intelligence. Also, Gardner's theory includes abilities that most people have not traditionally considered to be in the realm of intelligence. Musical talent has always been recognized as something special but usually as something distinct from intelligence. And although athletic ability and bodily control are certainly important human characteristics, they are not typically considered to be mental operations in the way that mathematical computation and verbal comprehension, which have been at the center of the definition of intelligence, are.

In many ways, Gardner's theory is an extension of the domain-specific theories of psychometricians such as Guilford. Gardner's considerable contribution has been getting people to look for evidence beyond psychometric testing, placing intelligence in the realm of both biology and culture, where it belongs. Gardner's ideas have been very influential, particularly in educational circles. Gardner might indeed find greater independence of intellectual abilities than g theorists typically find. But one reason for this might be that Gardner includes a broader range of intelligences than do conventional psychometric theorists. Thus, part of Gardner's appeal is his broader definition of intelligence. This may also be part of the difficulty in evaluating his theory.

The book is not closed on the nature of intelligence. Sternberg and Gardner make it clear that intelligence is a many-splendored thing—that any theorist who proposes that intelligence is a single phenomenon that influences all aspects of intellectual functioning equally is just not looking at the data (see also Ceci, 1996). Yet, the evidence of the positive manifold and the fact that basic processes do predict IQ test performance relatively well, for example, argue that there might be some general, cross-domain mechanisms that influence, to various degrees, most if not all cognitive task performance. I do not plan to provide my own theory of intelligence here. But it is clear to me that intelligence is multifaceted, with intellectual functioning varying considerably as a function of a person's knowledge and the context in which the cognitive operations were acquired and are assessed. Yet, certain aspects of information processing also appear to be domain general and will influence task performance to a significant degree in a variety of contexts. Factors such as motivation and practice are critically important, and, even at their best, measures of basic processing cannot account for all, or even most, of the variance in intellectual development. The most tenable position from my point of view is that some aspects of human intelligence are domain general in nature, whereas others are domain specific in nature. Even if I am right about this, there is much room for speculation about how much of intelligence is domain general and how much is domain specific.

Summary

Intelligence is generally understood to reflect goal-directed and adaptive functioning. The primary approach to the study of individual differences in intelligence has been the *psychometric* (or *differential*) *approach*. Intelligence is described in terms of *factors*, or sets of related abilities that can be discerned on tests by the statistical technique of *factor analysis*. The number of factors that has been proposed to constitute intelligence has varied considerably from 1 (Spearman's general *g* factor) to 180 in Guilford's *structure-of-the-intellect model*. *Fluid abilities* are biologically determined and reflected in tests of memory span and most tests of spatial thinking, whereas *crystallized abilities* are best reflected in tests of verbal comprehension or social relations, skills that depend more highly on cultural context and experience. The best evidence for the existence of *g* is the *positive manifold*, the fact that a person's performances on a variety of different cognitive tasks tend to be similar. Most psychometricians adhere to some form of the *hierarchical model of cognitive abilities* that postulates a series of relatively specific cognitive abilities, such as verbal, spatial, speed of processing, and memory. The impact of the psychometric approach has been most strongly expressed in *IQ tests*, which assess intellectual abilities relative to a normative population. The standard tests by which most are judged include the *Stanford-Binet* and the three *Wechsler scales* (WPPSI, WISC, WAIS). Infant intelligence has been expressed in terms of *DQ* (*developmental quotient*) *tests*. IQs were originally derived based on a ratio between *mental age* and chronological age. Modern tests have abandoned the concept of mental age and have developed the *deviation IQ*. Many researchers and theorists have argued that IQ tests are not theory based, they are limited in the type of mental functioning they assess, and they are culturally biased, with minority children often misinterpreting the testing situation.

Information-processing approaches to intelligence provide researchers with well-developed theories and methods for assessing individual differences in intelligence. Differences in speed of processing, working memory, strategy use, knowledge base, and metacognition have been suggested as the basis for individual differences in children's thinking. Developmental psychologists often use information-processing paradigms to explain differences in the thinking of children of different IQ levels (children with and without mental retardation) and children of comparable IQ but differential academic abilities (learning disabled versus nondisabled).

Several researchers have correlated children's performance on Piagetian tasks with academic performance and IQ and have generally found significant relations. The research seems to indicate that both Piagetian and psychometric tests assess the same general form of intelligence but that each also measures aspects of intelligence not measured by the other.

Sternberg's *triarchic theory* consists of three subtheories: *contextual*, *experiential*, and *componential*, each with a characteristic thinking style (practical, creative, and analytic). The contextual subtheory states that intelligence must be evaluated in the environment in which the individual lives, which, by itself, reflects a form of *cultural relativism*. The experiential subtheory proposes that how people deal with novelty and the extent to which they can automatize cognitive functioning are important aspects of intelligence. The componential subtheory describes the three universal information-processing mechanisms by which knowledge is acquired and manipulated. The theory is an attempt to go beyond earlier approaches by viewing intelligence from a wider scope.

Gardner's *theory of multiple intelligences* relies heavily on neuropsychological evidence and postulates eight distinct forms of intelligence: linguistic, logical-mathematical, musical, spatial, bodily kinesthetic, interpersonal, intrapersonal, and naturalistic. Gardner lists several criteria of an intelligence, including potential isolation by brain damage, the existence of savants and prodigies, an identifiable set of operations, developmental history, an evolutionary history and plausibility, support from experimental and psychometric tasks, and susceptibility to an encoding system.

Key Terms and Concepts

intelligence
psychometric (differential) approach
factors
factor analysis
g (Spearman's g, general intelligence)
structure-of-the-intellect model
fluid abilities
crystallized abilities
positive manifold
hierarchical model of cognitive abilities
IQ (intelligence quotient) tests
Stanford-Binet
Wechsler scales
DQ (development quotient) tests
mental age
deviation IQ
triarchic theory
contextual subtheory
cultural relativism
experiential subtheory
componential subtheory
theory of multiple intelligences

Suggested Readings

Bjorklund, D. F., & Schneider, W. (1996). The interaction of knowledge, aptitudes, and strategies in children's memory performance. In H. W. Reese (Ed.), *Advances in child development and behavior*, Vol. 26 (pp. 59–89). San Diego: Academic.   As the title indicates, this article reviews research looking at the interaction of knowledge, aptitude, and strategies on children's memory performance, and the authors conclude by stating that although domain-specific knowledge might be the single most important factor in intelligence, other domain-general and g-like mechanisms (possibly speed of processing and metacognition) also play a critical role in children's intelligent behavior.

Gardner, H. (Ed.). (1993). *Multiple intelligences: The theory in practice*. New York: Basic.   This book consists of a series of chapters, most of which were published earlier, presenting and assessing the theory of multiple intelligences. The first four chapters introduce the theory, and the remaining chapters deal with the theory's application (real and potential) to education.

Gould, S. J. (1981). *The mismeasure of man*. New York: Norton.   This very readable book provides a history of the research, theory, and politics of intelligence assessment. In addition to pointing out skeletons in the closets associated with IQ testing, Gould provides a good critique of the history and methods of the psychometric approach. Gould doesn't shy away from controversy and shows how science and politics can never be fully separated.

Jensen, A. R. (1998). *The g factor: The science of mental ability*. Westport, CT: Praeger.   Everything you always wanted to know about g but didn't know who to ask, from the most ardent contemporary advocate of g. This book provides a thorough examination of research and theory about general intelligence, although there is little discussion of developmental issues.

Sternberg, R. J. (1985). *Beyond IQ: A triarchic theory of human intelligence*. Cambridge: Cambridge University Press.   This is the long version of Sternberg's triarchic theory. I am recommending it because it covers all the bases, beginning with an introductory chapter that provides a critique of the standard psychometric approach and why a new theory of intelligence is needed in the first place.

InfoTrac College Edition

For additional readings, explore InfoTrac College Edition, your online library. Go to http://www.infotrac-college.com/wadsworth.

Origins, Modification, and Stability of Intellectual Differences

In the previous chapter, we looked at a variety of theories of intelligence. If I had to summarize the major issue that differentiates the various theories, I believe it would have to be the extent to which intelligence is viewed as a unitary phenomenon versus a multifaceted one. Essentially, this is the issue of whether intelligence is domain general or domain specific in nature.

This relatively esoteric issue has historically been tied to another issue that has considerable real-world application and that has provoked considerable controversy: the extent to which intelligence is inherited, determined primarily by one's genes, rather than being a matter of experience.

People who believe that intelligence is best represented by a unitary factor tend to believe that single factor is highly heritable—that is, people are born smart or not so smart, this is a stable characteristic across the life span, and this single factor permeates all aspects of one's intellectual life (Jensen, 1998). People who believe that intelligence is not a unitary factor but varies with the types of problems one encounters and with the context, tend to believe environmental factors determine the bulk of individual differences in intelligence—that is, our environments make us smart or not so smart, we can increase (or decrease) our intelligence through experience, and intelligence is not even stable across situations, let alone years (Ceci, 1996). These are socially and educationally important issues. How we view intelligence in terms of its origins (What are the seeds of intelligence?) and its modifiability (Can intelligence be enhanced through education, and if so, how much?) affects real-world decisions, particularly as they relate to education and one's occupation.

Given what's at stake, it's not surprising that people take strong, often emotional stands on the issue. But science should not be in the business of supporting or refuting a theory because it stirs strong emotions or is politically correct (or incorrect). Science is part of society and cannot be divorced from contemporary political and social forces; but the crux of science is objectivity, and, to the extent that we can, we must let the data speak for themselves, while being mindful of the social ramifications our results might have.

That being said, to what extent are individual differences in intelligence a function of nature versus nurture? As I mentioned in Chapter 1, developmental psychologists have long ago abandoned models that pitted "nature" versus "nurture" in explaining the course of the life span in favor of models that describe development as resulting from the continuous and bidirectional interaction of multiple factors, from the genetic through the cultural, over time (Bjorklund & Pellegrini, 2002; Gottlieb, 2000; Oyama, 2000). The proper question here is not *how much* of intelligence is attributable to nature (genes, biology) and *how much* to nurture (experience, environment) but, rather, *how do nature and nurture interact to produce a particular pattern of development or of intelligence?* This can best be accomplished by using models that seriously consider the transaction between biological and environmental factors. I introduced two of those models in Chapter 2 (the developmental systems approach and Scarr and McCartney's genotype → environment theory). Basically, these models propose that there is a bidirectional interaction between organismic factors (for example, genes, hormones) and environmental factors (for example, physical and social environment) and that the two are intricately entwined, making it impossible to evaluate one without considering the other (that is, a contextualist perspective). Yet even within these transactional models, there is considerable latitude for interpretation of which factors (genotype versus social environment, for example) play the major role in shaping development and intellect.

In this chapter, I examine some of the research relating to these issues. I first introduce a transactional approach to intelligence, a variant of the developmental systems approach introduced in Chapter 2. I then look at recent work in behavior genetics that argues for a strong role of genetics in intelligence. I follow this with research focusing on the role of environmental factors in influencing intelligence—in the establishment as well as the modification and maintenance of intelligence. Finally, I include a section on the stability of intelligence from infancy to young adulthood. There is no definitive conclusion at the end of this chapter—no bold statement saying what intelligence is and is not. But I hope the chapter will provide enough of both theory and data for students to appreciate better what is perhaps the most magnificent quality of our species—our intelligence.

A Transactional Approach to the Study of Intelligence

Chapters 1 and 2 introduced a general approach to studying development. This approach emphasized the bidirectionality of structure and function. Bidirectionality can be studied at many levels, of course, from the function of a firing neuron affecting its subsequent growth to the actions of a child influencing how significant others respond to him or her. I want to focus on this latter level now, examining the transaction between a child and people in his or her immediate environment and how this transaction might affect a developing intellect.

It has long been recognized that children play a critical role in their own development. Jean Piaget clearly recognized this, placing the child's mental and physical actions at the center of his theory. Yet throughout most of the 20th century, theorists who looked at the development of intelligence tended to view children as passive beings who are either constrained by their biology to develop in a certain way or shaped and molded by their environment (usually early environment). Little emphasis was given by theorists in either extreme camp to children themselves.

This began to change in the 1960s, with Richard Bell (1968) emphasizing the idea that parent and child have equal abilities to contribute to a social exchange and that each affects the other. This viewpoint holds that cognitive influences are transactional (Sameroff & Chandler, 1975; Sameroff & Suomi, 1996), for not only do parents act to produce behavior in their children, but children also modify their parents' behaviors.

The **transactional model** as proposed by Arnold Sameroff views the child's biological constitution (genotype in Figure 16-1) as having an organizing effect on the development of the child (phenotype in Figure 16-1). However, the child's environment

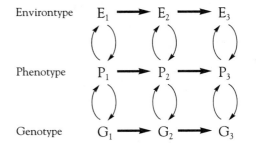

FIGURE 16-1 The transactional model of development, reflecting the continuous interaction of the child's constitution and the environment over time. SOURCE: Sameroff, A. J., & Suomi, S. J. (1996). Primates and persons: A comparative developmental understanding of social organization (pp. 97–120). In R. B. Cairns, G. H. Elder, Jr., & E. J. Costello (Eds.), *Developmental Science*. New York: Cambridge University Press. Reprinted with the permission of Cambridge University Press.

(environtype in Figure 16-1) also has an organizing effect on the child. What is critical in the transactional model are the *bidirectional* effects between the multiple levels of organization (compare this with the developmental systems approach described in Chapter 2 and Figure 2-1). The environment and child have reciprocating effects, which influence that child's biology, and so forth, and these factors continue to transact during development. From this viewpoint, then, *development is seen as the continuous and bidirectional interaction between an active organism with a unique biological constitution and a changing environment*. Although Sameroff initially used the transactional model primarily to explain the long-term effects of biological impairments during early infancy in different environments, the model, in general form, can be applied to explain parent-child interactions in a wide range of contexts.

The transactional model has been used to understand the nature of differences in intelligence among children as a function of socioeconomic status. Socioeconomic status (SES) is customarily defined in terms of level of family income, parents' occupational status, and years of parental education. Research has consistently shown that a significant portion of the differences in IQ and academic achievement among children can be attributed to SES factors (see Ceci, 1996); children from disadvantaged homes fare worse than children from more advantaged homes.

Variables such as SES do not influence children independently of other factors. Thus, there is a high correlation between SES and home environment, friend selection, neighborhood, academic expectation, and academic opportunities, among other factors. Arnold Sameroff and Michael Chandler (1975) proposed that some caretaking environments (middle-income homes) are more likely to produce intellectually and socially competent children than are others (lower-income homes). Furthermore, children who experience perinatal trauma (trauma at or around the time of birth) were proposed to be especially susceptible to nonsupportive caretaking, so that the negative consequences of early biological impairment are exacerbated in such environments. That is, Sameroff and Chandler proposed a transaction between infants' biological constitutions and their environment, as reflected by differences in SES.

Support for Sameroff and Chandler's model was provided by an examination of the outcomes of children experiencing stress at birth (oxygen deprivation, or anoxia) as a function of their SES level. Although differences in developmental level between normal and biologically impaired infants are obvious at birth in both lower- and middle-income groups, these differences are diminished and often eliminated by age 6 or 7 years in middle-income homes. In contrast, these differences are maintained or increase with age in lower-income homes. Sameroff and Chandler speculated that distressed infants—characterized by more aversive cries, slower attainment of social-developmental milestones such as smiling and vocalization, and a sickly appearance—receive different types of treatment in different environments. In reasonably affluent and well-educated families, these distressed children might receive lavish attention and stimulation, facilitating the amelioration of their impaired condition. In deprived, stressed, and poorly educated families, these same infant characteristics result in a pattern of reduced attention and stimulation and, thus, continued cognitive and social deficits. That is, there is a

transaction between parent and child, with the particular characteristics of the child interacting with the particular characteristics of the parents, yielding distinct patterns of development.

In a series of studies, P. Sanford Zeskind and Craig Ramey (1978, 1981) experimentally assessed the effects of different caretaking environments as a function of infants' biological status. Infants from poor, rural environments who had been classified as at high risk for mental retardation were assigned to one of two care-giving environments. Infants in one group received medical care and nutritional supplements and participated in an educationally oriented daycare program beginning at approximately 3 months of age (experimental group). Infants in a control group received the medical care and nutritional supplements but did not participate in the daycare program. Within each group, approximately half of the infants were classified as fetally malnourished at birth, whereas the remaining infants were described as biologically normal. Fetal malnourishment typically produces infants who are developmentally delayed and lethargic and who have aversive cries.

At 3 months of age, fetally malnourished infants in both the control and experimental groups had lower developmental scores on the Bayley Mental Developmental Index than the nonmalnourished (normal) infants did. However, Stanford-Binet IQ scores at 24 and 36 months demonstrated (1) overall higher IQ scores for the experimental than for the control children, (2) no difference in IQ scores between the normal and fetally malnourished infants in the experimental group, and (3) higher IQ scores for the normal than for the fetally malnourished infants in the control group. IQ scores at 36 months are shown for the four groups of children in this experiment in Table 16-1. In general, the pattern of IQ change observed in this experiment is similar to that Sameroff and Chandler (1975) observed, with the effects of a nonsupportive environment (the control group) being especially deleterious for the biologically distressed children.

Zeskind and Ramey also measured the degree of mother-child interaction in the home. They reported that in the experimental group there was no differ-

TABLE 16-1 Mean Stanford-Binet scores at 36 months for children in the Zeskind and Ramey study.

	Biologically normal	Fetally malnourished
Experimental (daycare) group	98.1	96.4
Control group	84.7	70.6

SOURCE: Adapted from Zeskind, P. S., & Ramey, C. T. (1981). Sequelae of fetal malnutrition: A longitudinal, transactional, and synergistic approach. *Child Development*, 52, 213–218. Copyright © 1981 The Society for Research in Child Development, Inc., Adapted with permission.

ence in the amount of maternal attention received by fetally malnourished and normal infants. In the control group, however, fetally malnourished infants received less maternal attention by age 24 months than the normal children did. Consistent with Sameroff's transactional interpretation, the researchers proposed that the increased responsivity of fetally malnourished infants receiving the educational day care resulted in increased attention from their mothers and a generally positive developmental outcome. In contrast, the withdrawn and sickly behavior of the fetally malnourished infants in the control group resulted in less maternal attention, exaggerating the injurious effects of their biological impairment.

Although the patterns reported here, while children were still participating in the enrichment program, are impressive and demonstrate the transaction of children's biology and environment in development, they do not mean that the effects of fetal malnutrition have necessarily disappeared. When environments change (as when children leave the enrichment program) patterns of interaction can also change and the residual effects of fetal malnutrition might return (Zeskind, 1996). But the pattern demonstrated by Zeskind and Ramey provides an elegant demonstration of the dynamic relation between children's biology and their environment over time and indicates that any simple interpretations of "biological causes" or "environmental causes" are likely wrong.

Most of the research we will examine in the remainder of this chapter does not fit as many of the pieces of the puzzle together as nicely as did the Zeskind and Ramey study. Some examine genetic factors and others examine detailed characteristics of the home environment, but it is the unusual study that carefully measures biological and environmental characteristics and has good experimental controls while assessing intelligence in natural contexts. Nonetheless, all the research presented here can be viewed from the perspective of the transactional model. Although the next several sections are roughly divided into accounts of genetic factors and environmental factors, never lose sight of the fact that intelligence (or any other aspect of cognitive development) is always a transaction between an active organism with its own biological dispositions and a changing environment.

Behavior Genetics and the Heritability of Intelligence

Behavior genetics examines patterns of individual differences in often-complex behaviors as a function of the genetic relationship between individuals. Stated simply, statistics are derived that provide estimates of the percent of variance, or differences in a trait, that can be accounted for by genetics, environment, and their interaction.

According to some, we have entered the age of *genomics*, a period when the entire human genome will be known and connections between genotypes and phenotypes will be elucidated (Venter et al., 2001). This is, indeed, an exciting time for biological science, and relationships between genes and behavior are continually being discovered, making anyone who claims that genetics are unimportant in explaining individual differences in complex behavior such as intelligence very much out of touch with contemporary science. However, one must be careful not to let this "genomicophelia" cause us to lose track of the fact that genes are only part (albeit a critical part) of a complex developmental system and that their expressions are governed by events surrounding them during development (Gottlieb, 2000; Oyama, 2000; see Chapter 2). Genes must be seen as interacting with their local environments, and thus genotype-phenotype relations should vary at different points in development and under different environmental conditions. Although not all researchers and theorists take this view, and there remain substantial disagreements among those who do (see Gottlieb, 1995; Scarr, 1995), many researchers have adopted a developmental behavior genetics perspective, and I review some of this literature as it relates to intelligence here.

The Concept of Heritability

Before we delve too deeply into the data of behavior genetics, some explanation concerning what is meant by the term **heritability** is appropriate here. Heritability is the extent to which differences in any trait within a population can be attributed to inheritance. Heritability is expressed as a statistic that ranges from 0 (none of the differences in a trait are attributed to inheritance) to 1.0 (100% of the differences in a trait are attributed to inheritance). It reflects the proportion of variance in an observed trait that is due to genetic variability.

Heritability is a population statistic, in that it describes average differences among people within a population. It does not refer to how much of any one person's intelligence (or height or personality characteristics) can be attributed to genetic factors, only what percentage of the difference in a trait within a specific population can be attributed to inheritance, on average.

For the purpose of illustration, assume that individual differences in height are due to only two factors: inheritance and diet. On an isolated island, every person receives 100% of his or her nutritional needs (no one receives less or more). The average height of men on the island is 6 feet. If you were to meet two men from this island, one being 6 feet 1 inch tall and the other being 5 feet 11 inches tall, 100% of the 2-inch difference in their height would be attributable to inheritance—in other words, her-

itability would be 1.0. The reason for this is that their environments (diets in this case) are homogeneous: no differences in environments exist. Thus, any difference in height between people must be attributable to inheritance.

What would happen if a famine hit the island, changing the diet of the people and thus the average height (from 6 feet to 5 feet 10 inches, say)? If the change were uniform (if, for example, everyone were getting 75% of his or her nutritional needs), the heritability would still be 1.0. Although the environment would have changed drastically, it would have changed equally for everyone. If the effects of the famine were not uniform, however, the heritability picture would change. If some people still received 100% of their nutritional needs, others 75%, and others only 50%, now when you met two men from the island who differed by 2 inches in height you would know that, on average, some proportion of this difference must be attributable to differences in diet; that is, heritability in this latter case would be something less than 1.0. The more heterogeneous, or variable, the environments are, the lower the heritability will be. Heritability is thus relative, varying with the environmental conditions in which people within the population live.

The concept of heritability is the same regardless of whether we are studying height or intelligence. One difference between concepts such as height and intelligence, however, is that of measurement. When we express height in inches or meters, we can be confident that the measure accurately reflects the underlying concept. There is less confidence with intelligence. In most studies examining the heritability of intelligence, IQ or other psychometric tests are used to measure intelligence. Thus, the findings of these studies more accurately pertain to the heritability of IQ (and usually *g*), with IQ being one (popular) index of intelligence.[1]

The statistical models underlying heritability are complicated and beyond the scope of this chapter (see Appendix B of Plomin, DeFries et al., 1997 for a discussion of the statistical models underlying estimates of heritability). Although, as traditionally conceived, these models assume that environmental and genetic effects are independent, more current models include effects assessing the interaction of genetic and environmental effects (G × E). For example, a certain characteristic might be more strongly expressed in one environment than another.

These models also consider the covariation of genetic and environmental effects, or genotype-environment correlations. In fact, Sandra Scarr and Kathleen McCartney's (1983) genotype → environment model discussed in Chapter 2 reflects such correlations. Thus, although it is not trivial to interpret results from behavior-genetic research in terms of the transactional model discussed in an earlier section (and patterns of correlations might not tell the entire story of genetic and environmental effects), most contemporary behavior geneticists would agree, I think, with the basic tenets of the transactional model presented earlier. This is not to say that behavior geneticists view the developing nature of intelligence the same way as do people such as Sameroff or Zeskind and Ramey, discussed in the previous section. However, both groups of scientists see intelligence as developing as a dynamical relationship between one's biological constitution and a changing environment and that this relation varies during development.

I should comment here that variance associated with genetic and environmental effects cannot be truly identified, as if each contributes something unique to the phenotype. As I've argued in earlier chapters, all development should be viewed as the product of the continuous bidirectional interaction of factors at multiple levels of organization, from the genetic through the cultural, making literal "partially-the-variance" techniques inadequate (see Moore, 2001). Nonetheless, I believe that this general approach of behavior genetics provides an estimate of how a particular trait is apt to vary as a function of genetic relatedness in known environments and, thus, provides useful information about the source of individual differences in a trait, including intelligence.

Elementary Cognitive Tasks and Intelligence

Elementary cognitive tasks (ECTs) are simple laboratory tests designed to measure people's response times as they make simple decisions. These include short-term memory scanning, retrieval of familiar words from the long-term store, and simple categorization tasks (Jensen, 1998). Some of these tasks were described in Chapter 15 in the discussion of information-processing approaches to individual differences. The basic processes measured by ECTs are presumed to be closely related to physiological functioning and thus primarily under the influence of endogenous (and inherited) factors.

Arthur Jensen and his colleagues, among others, have presented evidence that response times for several ECTs are significantly related to g-factor scores obtained from conventional psychometric tests (see Jensen, 1993, 1998). As noted in Chapter 15, significant relations have been found between basic-level cognitive tasks and verbal ability for both adults (Hunt, Davidson, & Lansman, 1981) and children (Fry & Hale, 2000). Following Jensen's argument, variations in these basic cognitive processes are probably inherited and are the basis for individual differences in intelligence. To bolster this contention, several researchers have demonstrated significant relationships between aspects of evoked brain potentials measured via electroencephalograph (EEG) apparatus and psychometrically measured intelligence (see Jensen, 1998).

Stephen Petrill, Lee Anne Thompson, and Douglas Detterman (1995) attempted to assess the genetic basis of performance on ECTs by administering a series of timed cognitive tasks to 287 monozygotic (genetically identical) and dizygotic (genetically nonidentical) twin pairs between 6 and 13 years of age. The correlation between decision times on the information-processing tasks and psychometrically measured intelligence had previously been found to be significant (correlation = −.42). Decision times also proved to be highly heritable. The correlation of decision times for the identical twins was .61, but was only .39 for the nonidentical twins. This resulted in a heritability of about 45 percent (see also McGue et al., 1984). Heritability for other cognitive tasks was lower, with the heritability of simple reaction times being zero. Nevertheless, the findings clearly reflect a strong genetic basis for overall speed of processing (decision time) on experimental cognitive tasks, and this speed component was strongly related to a general intellectual factor.

Even if speed of information processing is highly heritable, why should it correlate so strongly with psychometric measures of intelligence? Jensen states the dilemma: "It seems almost incredible that individual differences in reaction time (RT) in simple tasks that involve no intellectual content and are so easy as to be performed by most persons in less than 1 second should be correlated with scores on non-speeded, complex tests of reasoning ability, vocabulary, and general knowledge—the kinds of content that compose IQ tests" (1993, p. 53). Jensen (1993) proposed three possible brain-based reasons for the high correlations of reaction times with measures of *g*. First, speed of information processing might reflect speed of nerve transmission. Speed is important because of the brain's limited capacity to process information. Only so much can be done at once; faster processing will permit more to be done, and this will be true across domains. Second, there is evidence that people whose reaction times are more variable across trials have lower psychometrically measured intelligence (Eysenck, 1987). Third, the longer neurally encoded information can be maintained in immediate consciousness, the more efficient cognition will be. Thus, more durable memory traces, with information being retained longer in short-term memory, result in more effective information processing. Jensen acknowledges that the neurological aspects of his theory are still speculative but states that the theory is consistent with the empirical evidence showing a strong relation between speed of information processing and *g*.

Although the findings and theories regarding ECTs are intriguing and applauded by many, not all researchers are ready to accept them as conclusive or as representative of functioning on higher-level cognitive tasks. For example, Stephen Ceci (1996) argues that other important cognitive skills, such as strategic and metacognitive processes, are ignored in this research. Also, it is well established that response times on simple cognitive tasks can vary greatly as a function of a person's knowledge base. Response times are fast when decisions are made concerning very familiar information but slower when dealing with less familiar information (Case, Kurland, & Goldberg, 1982; Chi, 1977). Differences in knowledge base might be indirectly responsible for many of the group and individual differences observed in some of these experiments, and such differences might well be more a function of education and general experience than they are of genetics (see Chapter 15 and Ceci, 1996, for a compelling argument of this). As with most of the issues surrounding intelligence, the controversy continues, and clarification of these provocative ideas awaits future research.

Familial Studies of Intelligence

Most researchers in behavior genetics take the position that the primary influence of genes on intelligence is indirect. Genes do not necessarily make someone intelligent but, rather, influence behavior and the experiences an individual will have. For example, the genes of a child's parents influence how those parents behave toward the child, affecting a substantial part of that child's experiences, especially early in life. And children's own genotypes determine which situations they find comfortable and pleasing, which causes them to seek out some environments and to avoid others (Bouchard et al., 1990; Scarr, 1993). Thus, although genes surely influence things such as the rate of neural transmission or the durability of memory traces, which might have a direct effect on cognitive functioning (Jensen, 1998), their *indirect* effect, through the behavior of parents and of the children themselves, can have even greater consequences for the development of intellect. (Review Scarr and McCartney's genotype → environment theory in Chapter 2.)

The preponderance of research examining the heritability of intelligence has dealt with comparisons of IQ scores among people of varying genetic relationships (or **familial studies of intelligence**). If one holds a genetic theory of intelligence, the greater the genetic similarity between two groups of individuals, the higher the correlations of their IQs should be. One of two general approaches has usually been taken: adoption studies, in which the parents who rear the children are genetically unrelated to

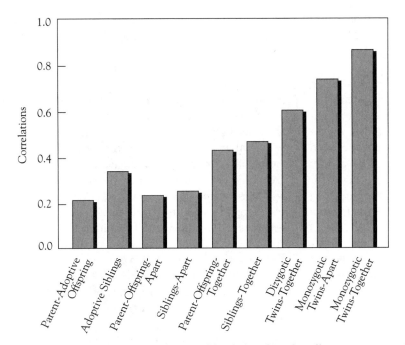

FIGURE 16-2 Average correlations of familial studies of intelligence. SOURCE: Adapted from data published by Bouchard, T. J., Jr., & McGue, M. (1981). Familial studies of intelligence: A review. *Science, 212,* 1055–1059.

them (Plomin, Fulker et al., 1997; Weinberg, Scarr, & Waldman, 1992) and twin studies, in which monozygotic twins, separated sometime early in life, are contrasted with dizygotic (nonidentical) twins and people of varying genetic relationships (Bouchard et al., 1990; Wilson, 1983).

Familial studies of intelligence have been conducted since the early part of the 20th century. However, evidence of falsification of data by Sir Cyril Burt, a prominent British psychologist and an important contributor to this literature, had caused many to question the reliability of the early findings. But several large-scale and tightly controlled adoption and twin studies have been conducted since the Burt fraud, and their findings are relatively consistent. Thomas Bouchard and Matt McGue (1981) reviewed 111 familial studies of intelligence, eliminating the studies by Burt and others that did not meet their methodological and statistical criteria. A summary of some of the average correlations from

this investigation is given in Figure 16-2. The results of several dozen additional studies during the past two decades have not altered the patterns shown in this figure (Plomin & Petrill, 1997).

Generally, the correlations increase as genetic similarity increases, implying a significant role for genetics in patterns of individual differences in intelligence. From these correlations, heritability estimates are derived. The easiest way to compute a heritability coefficient (H) is by using data from twin studies. The correlation (denoted as r) based on data from nonidentical twins is subtracted from the correlation based on data from identical twins, and the difference is doubled, or,

$$H = (r\ identical\ twins - r\ nonidentical\ twins) \times 2$$

If you take the correlations of the IQs of identical twins reared together shown in Figure 16-2 (.86) and those of nonidentical twins reared together (.60), the resulting computation is $H = (.86 - .60) \times 2 = .52$.

This means that the heritability of intelligence (at least based on this data set) is .52, or that 52% of the differences in intelligence between people is attributed to genetics.

Based on the dozens of studies that have been conducted during the past 25 years or so, a somewhat conservative conclusion would be that the heritability of IQ is approximately .50, meaning that, on average, 50% of the difference in intelligence between people in a population can be attributed to genetics (Plomin & Petrill, 1997). However, recall that heritability is a relative population statistic, meaning that it is subject to change across time and populations. So, for example, research has indicated that IQ has a higher heritability in adulthood than in childhood, is higher in North American whites than in North American blacks, and is higher in whites living in Great Britain than in whites living in America (see Ceci, 1993).

Developmental Differences in Heritability

Let's look at the relation between age and heritability of IQ, and let's start in infancy. Research by Petrill and his colleagues looked at the heritability of intelligence for infants who scored low on infant psychometric (*g*-loaded) tests (10th percentile or below, low-*g* infants) (Petrill et al., 1997), as well as those who scored high on psychometric tests (90th percentile or above, high-*g* infants) (Petrill et al., 1998) from the McArthur Longitudinal Twin Study. Infants were first tested at 14 months of age using the Bayley Scale of Infant Development, and again at 20, 24, and 36 months (with the Stanford-Binet being administered at the 36-month testing). For both groups of extreme infants, the correlations of IQs (or DQs) were higher for monozygotic than for dizygotic twins, reflecting the influence of inheritance, although this pattern varied with age. The difference between the correlations between the two twin groups was small and nonsignificant at 14 months for both the high- and low-*g* children. This reflects a small, nonsignificant genetic effect on infant intelligence at 14 months of age. The difference in the correlations between the monozygotic and dizygotic groups was

larger and significant at the 24- and 36-month tests for the high-*g* group and at 20 and 24 months for the low-*g* group, however, indicating significant genetic effects on intelligence. These findings indicate that both high- and low-levels of *g* (as reflected by extreme scores on psychometric tests) are significantly influenced by genetics late in infancy, with the genetic effect generally increasing into early childhood.

In other research using the adoption-study method, Robert Plomin, David Fulker et al. (1997) used longitudinal data to assess the similarity in IQ between adopted children and both their biological and adoptive parents at different ages. The researchers administered sets of cognitive tasks to children and to their adoptive and biological parents. Children were tested at 1, 2, 3, 4, 7, 12, and 16 years of age. The researchers contrasted the correlations between a general cognitive ability measure (derived from the set of cognitive tasks) between children and their adoptive and biological parents at the different ages tested. A control group of children who was raised by their biological parents was also included. The results of their study are shown in Figure 16-3. As can be seen, the correlations of cognitive ability between the children and their adoptive parents starts out low and declines during childhood, increasing a bit between the 14- and 16-year assessment. In contrast, the pattern of correlations between the children and their biological parents is very similar to that found for the control group (biological parents living with their offspring). The correlations increase steadily during the elementary school years, peaking in adolescence. Similar patterns were found for specific cognitive abilities (spatial ability, speed of processing, and recognition memory). This pattern reflects an increasing genetic influence on cognitive abilities as children move from childhood to their teen years.

The Role of the Environment in Behavior Genetic Analyses

If we accept the .50 heritability figure, this means that about 50% of the differences in IQ between people are attributable to *nongenetic* effects, namely

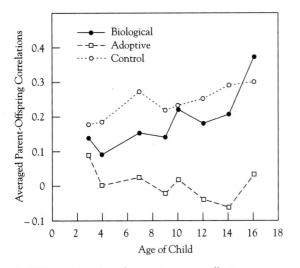

FIGURE 16-3 Age changes in parent-offspring correlations of cognitive abilities for adoptive children and the (a) biological parents, (b) their adoptive parents, and (c) a control group of parents and their biological offspring. SOURCE: Plomin, R., Fulker, D. W., Corley, R., & DeFries, J. C. (1997). Nature, nurture, and cognitive development from 1 to 6 years: A parent-offspring adoption study. *Psychological Science, 8*, 442–447. Reprinted with permission.

environment (Plomin & Petrill, 1997). In family comparisons, behavior geneticists typically consider the environmental effects of shared and nonshared environments. A **shared environment** is a home environment shared by different family members. A **nonshared environment** is an environment unique to an individual, not shared by a sibling, for instance. Thus, twins, for example, growing up in the same home at the same time would share the same family environment. Nontwin siblings growing up in the same family at different times would not share the same environment to the extent that twins do. As noted in Chapter 2, research has consistently shown that siblings become less alike the older they get and that this reflects the contribution of nonshared environments (McCartney, Harris, & Bernieri, 1990). Following the arguments of Scarr and McCartney (1983; Scarr, 1992, 1993), with increasing age, children's genotypes influence them to select their own environments, and the experiences they have in

those environments affect their intelligence. Thus, some portion of the nonshared-environmental effects can likely be attributed to indirect genetic effects (active genotype → environment effects in Scarr and McCartney's model).

Research has consistently found that the effects of shared environment on IQ are modest. In fact, in most behavior genetics models, *nonshared environmental effects* account for the greatest amount of nongenetic variance (Harris, 1995; McCartney et al., 1990; Turkheimer & Waldron, 2000). Nancy Segal (2000) developed the *virtual twin* method to illustrate this. Segal defined virtual twins as unrelated siblings of about the same age who grew up in the same family from early infancy. For example, two adopted siblings, or a biological child and an adopted child, less than 9 months apart in age, would be virtual twins. In such cases, they share the same family environment, similar to that shared by monozygotic or dizygotic twins, but are not related genetically. Segal reported a significant correlation between the IQs of the virtual twins (.26), but one that was substantially less than that found between monozygotic twins (.86), dizygotic twins (.60) or full siblings (.50), consistent with the argument that shared environments have only small effects on intellectual development.

It is too early to conclude, however, that shared environments have little impact on the development of intelligence. For example, Mike Stoolmiller (1999) proposed that the lack of effects of shared environments in adoption studies can be attributed to statistical anomalies, associated with restricted range of family environmental qualities in adoption studies. Adoptive parents are a selective group, and although they may differ in measures such as SES, few provide inadequate environments for their children. As a result, these studies greatly underestimate the degree of shared-family environment, and when this is taken into consideration, the amount of variance accounted for by shared-family environment increases substantially.

Behavior geneticists have also been criticized for simplifying the notion of "the environment," in part by not explicitly acknowledging the role that self-produced function may play in early development, by failing to objectively define specific aspects of children's environments that contribute to the characteristics under study, and by measuring only postnatal, and not prenatal environments (Gottlieb, 1995). When prenatal environments are evaluated, the effects of shared environments increase. B. Devlin, Michael Daniels, and Kathryn Roeder (1997) illustrated this in a meta-analysis of IQ studies. Devlin and his colleagues demonstrated that a mathematical model that included shared maternal (that is, *prenatal*) environment as a separate factor explained the variance in IQ performance significantly better than did traditional models that excluded this factor. In this model, 20% of IQ differences among twins was accounted for by shared-maternal environment, whereas shared-maternal environment accounted for only 5% of IQ differences among nontwin siblings. This pattern makes sense, given that twins share the womb concurrently, whereas nontwin siblings share it consecutively. Although a woman may maintain a common physiology and personal habits (in terms of diet, for example) from one pregnancy to another, the temporal separation between offspring, and the presumed differences through time in the physiological status of the mother, contribute to a lessening of the similarities of IQ among nontwin siblings.

It is easy to imagine many of the factors that may contribute to the maternal effects Devlin et al. reported. The brain grows rapidly during the prenatal period, and although there is substantial cognitive plasticity in postnatal intelligence, it should not be surprising that patterns of neural organization can be affected prenatally by factors impinging on the fetus. Individual differences in childhood intelligence have been reported as a function of malnutrition (Lukas & Campbell, 2000), exposure to drugs and other potential teratogens (Reinisch et al., 1995), alcohol and cigarette consumption (Olds, Henderson, & Tatelbaum, 1994), and lead poisoning (Baghurst et al., 1992), among others. Other research has shown the degree of bodily symmetry correlates positively with adult IQ (Furlow et al., 1997); bodily asymmetry is believed to be caused principally by prenatal stressors. Thus, more symmetrical (and higher-IQ) people likely experienced less stress in the womb than did less symmetrical (and lower-IQ) people,

providing another source of nongenetic, environmental variation in IQ.

These findings suggest that when behavior geneticists broaden their definition of the environment, as with the inclusion of a very general measure of prenatal environment in the Devlin et al. study, estimates of heritability decline as the contribution of experiential factors increase. This pattern is predicted by the developmental systems approach, with its emphasis on the continuing interaction of structure and function, at all levels of organization, beginning, not with birth, but with conception. Contemporary behavior geneticists are also recognizing such effects (Molenaar, Boomsma, & Dolan, 1993; Turkheimer, 2000).

The behavior genetics research I've reported here looks at correlations of IQs (or other tests of cognitive ability) as a function of degree of genetic similarity, and the conclusion is clear—the more similar two groups of people are genetically, the higher the correlation. But remember that correlations are independent of means, in this case, average levels of IQ scores. When looking at average levels of IQ, environment (as reflected, for example, by the average level of IQ in the parental home) can have a greater effect than biology. How can this be? How can there be such an overpowering genetic relation when looking at correlations and there be a strong environmental effect when looking at means?

Sandra Scarr and Richard Weinberg (1976; Weinberg et al., 1992) illustrated the combined impact of environment and genetics on intelligence in the transracial adoption study. Black children born primarily of parents from lower-income homes were adopted by white, primarily upper-middle-class parents. The average IQ of the adopted children who had been placed as infants in middle-income homes was found to be 110, 20 points higher than the average IQ of comparable children being reared in the local black community and comparable with the estimated IQs of their adopted parents. This effect demonstrates the potent influence of environment on IQ. However, the correlation between the children's IQs and their biological mothers' educational level (IQ scores were not available for the biological mothers) was significantly higher (.43) than was a similar correlation with the children's adoptive parents' educational level (.29).

The findings of this study appear paradoxical at first. How could the level of the children's IQ be more similar to that of their adopted parents, yet the correlation of their IQs be higher with the educational level of their biological mothers? To help understand this difference, keep in mind that correlations in this type of research reflect the degree to which knowing a parent's IQ (or equivalent) score will predict where a child's IQ will fall relative to other children in his or her particular group. Correlations of IQ are independent of level of IQ; correlations predict rank order and not mean level of IQ. In fact, the 20-point IQ difference between the children and their biological mothers could, theoretically, have been accompanied by a perfect correlation (1.0). In such a hypothetical situation, the child with the highest IQ of all the children (125, let's say) would have the biological mother with the highest IQ of all the mothers (105, let's say); the child with the next highest IQ (119) would have the biological mother with the next highest IQ (101), and so on until the child with the lowest IQ (82), who would have the biological mother with the lowest IQ (65). The correlation would be perfect, yet there would be, on average, a 20-point IQ difference between the children and their biological mothers.

In Scarr and Weinberg's study, the adopted children had all been placed in intellectually stimulating homes and had received similar treatment at the hands of their academically accelerating adoptive parents. Such stimulation was responsible for their relatively high levels of IQ in comparison with those of their biological mothers. Furthermore, given the similar patterns of experience that these children had, individual differences among the children were best predicted by genetics. When environmental conditions are relatively homogeneous, as they presumably were for the adopted children in Scarr and Weinberg's study, the best predictor of individual differences in intelligence is genetics. Prediction here refers to knowing a child's relative rank in a specified group of children (that is, where the child stands compared with his or her peers) and not to the actual level of IQ. When environments vary considerably (that is, are heterogeneous), differences in environments will play a more substantial role in affecting individual differences in intelligence (see later discussion). Thus, had the environments of the adopted families been more varied, chances are the correlations between the IQs of the children and their adoptive parents would have been greater. In other words, the heritability of intelligence is not constant but varies as a function of the similarity of environments among the people under study. As I noted earlier, however, nonshared-environmental factors increase in influence as children get older, which serve, essentially, to make the environments experienced by children more dissimilar to one another. Because these nonshared environments are influenced by their genetics (active genotype → environment effects), one would still expect the correlations of children's IQs with their biological parents to be high relative to those of adoptive parents during adolescence.

A recent study has explicitly assessed the interaction of genetics and environment on IQ using patterns of correlations derived from sets of siblings. David Rowe, Kristen Jacobson, and Edwin van der Oord (1999) obtained verbal IQ scores (from the Peabody Picture Vocabulary Test) from 3,139 sibling pairs, including sets of monozygotic and dizygotic twins, and adopted siblings. The siblings, all adolescents, were white, African American, and Hispanic and came from economically diverse backgrounds. Of particular interest to Rowe and his colleagues was the relation between education level of the children's parents and the heritability of IQ. The range of education of the parents was from no school to graduate or professional training. Rowe and his colleagues first computed correlations between siblings as a function of genetic relationship and found, similar to other research, that correlations increased as degree of genetic similarity increased. For example, the correlation of the monozygotic twins was .73, the correlation of full siblings was .39, and the correlation of unrelated siblings was .07. The researchers next used forms of regression analyses to obtain estimates of heritability and shared-environmental effects as a function of parental education.

For the overall sample, the researchers reported a heritability of .57 and an effect of shared environment of .13, which is similar to results reported by others. The patterns differed, however, when education level of the parents was considered. For adolescents in the low-education group (high school education or less), Rowe and his colleagues reported a heritability of .26 and an effect of shared environment of .23. In other words, both genetics and shared environment accounted for about one-quarter of the variability of differences in verbal IQ for the low-education group. In contrast, for the high-education group (greater than high-school education), the researchers reported a heritability of .74 and an effect of shared environment of 0. That is, heritability increased from about 25% for offspring of parents with less than a high-school education to about 75% for offspring of children with greater than a high-school education, with a corresponding decrease in the effects of shared environment (from about 25% to about 0%).

These findings indicate, consistent with the theorizing of others (Bronfenbrenner & Ceci, 1994; Scarr, 1992), that heritability increases with improved environmental conditions, here as reflected by level of parental education. This is because harmful environments might have a particularly strong influence on the development of certain traits, whereas, according to Scarr (1992), average or above average environments will have little impact beyond that contributed by genetics (recall Scarr's "good enough parents" from Chapter 2). Although we need not adopt Scarr's ideas of "good enough parents" to make sense of these data, the findings of Rowe and his colleagues indicate that environment and genetics do indeed interact and that these interactions can be found by using the methods of behavior genetics.

How Seriously Should We Take Heritability Studies of IQ?

At one level, the behavior genetics of intelligence is a highly esoteric topic, steeped in statistical models that most people don't even bother to try to understand. At a second level, however, it is the study of down-to-earth issues that most people have some opinions about and that affect social, economic, and educational policies. How much of one's intelligence is "in the genes"? And if the answer to that question is "quite a lot," what does it mean about educability and the modification of intelligence during development?

From time to time, the highly statistical analyses of behavior genetics are translated to the public at large and invariably a controversy ensues. In 1994 Richard Herrnstein and Charles Murray published *The Bell Curve*, in which they presented detailed analysis of a large longitudinal data base assessing the relation of IQ with occupation level, income, job disability, criminality, and welfare dependency, as well as ethnic and racial differences in IQ and what all this means for society. Their conclusion was that IQ is highly heritable, has a greater impact on the previously listed factors than any other single variable, and that social policy should be made with these "facts" in mind. Not surprisingly, there was an uproar from the academic, educational, and political communities against Herrnstein and Murray's claims (see Jacoby & Glauberman, 1995). Many critics claimed, not so much that the data Herrnstein and Murray reported were flawed, but that they erroneously equated IQ with intelligence (see discussions in Chapter 15) and confused correlation with causality (does low IQ cause one to have less education and lower income, or the reverse?).

I will not examine Herrnstein and Murray's claims here, nor attempt to support or refute them. The purpose of this chapter and the previous one is to provide a look at what intelligence is, its origins, and how it changes (or remains stable) over time. An important part of that picture comes from studies of the heritability of IQ. I am convinced that IQ tests assess something important for people from information-age societies, that the .50 heritability of IQ reported by behavior geneticists is real, and that this tells us something important about intelligence. However, I also believe that this is only part of the "intelligence" picture. Intelligence is a multifaceted thing, and I believe that a highly heritable general factor (*g*) can coexist with other aspects of intelligence (a position not all theorists of intelligence would agree with). Recall our earlier discussion of the transactional model. Biologically based abilities (or disabilities) will transact with the environment over time, yielding patterns of behavior and development that cannot be neatly described as "50% of the variance can be attributed to genetics." The main point I want to make here is that having an understanding of the various perspectives of the nature of intelligence is a good thing, not just for academics or students trying to pass a test, but for citizens of a modern democracy.

Experience and Intelligence

Undoubtedly, one's intellect is greatly influenced by experience. Even proponents of a strong genetic perspective such as Scarr (1993) argue that one's genotype has its greatest influence in terms of which environments a child explores and experiences. Others, however, argue that the environments in which children are reared and the experiences they have during childhood mold intellect, far more than do genetic influences (see Ceci, 1996).

In discussing experience and intelligence, it is useful to distinguish among the establishment, modification, and maintenance of intelligence. What factors are responsible for establishing intellectual competence? Once a certain level of intellectual functioning has been achieved, what is necessary to maintain that level? Finally, to what extent can an established level of intelligence be modified, either positively or negatively? Factors that influence the establishment of intelligence most certainly also exert an influence on its maintenance and modification. But it is important to recognize that these three aspects of the intelligence-experience relationship can be distinct. Once intellectual competence is established, the child will not necessarily maintain that same relative level of intelligence independent of his or her surroundings. That is, establishing some level of intellectual ability does not guarantee that

that level will be maintained or that it cannot be modified.

Establishing Intellectual Competence

Extremes in environments can have drastic effects on intelligence. Studies with laboratory animals clearly show that social, emotional, and intellectual functioning is greatly impaired when animals are raised in restricted environments (Greenough, Black, & Wallace, 1987). Although these lab experiments cannot be done with children, some naturalistic studies have been done in institutions and homes, assessing the consequences of growing up in impoverished environments.

Institutionalization Studies

Several **institutionalization studies** examined the effects of maternal deprivation, where infants had been separated from their mothers and raised in overcrowded and understaffed institutions (Dennis, 1973; Spitz, 1945). The results of such early living conditions were increased susceptibility to illness; retarded physical, mental, and social development (Provence & Lipton, 1962; Skeels, 1966); and, in some cases, death (Spitz, 1945).

For example, Wayne Dennis (1973) contrasted the outcomes of children reared in an orphanage in Beirut, Lebanon, called the Crèche, with those of infants placed in adoptive homes. The Crèche was a charity-run institution for illegitimate children. Infants received little direct stimulation in the form of play or other social interactions. The infants spent much of their day in small cribs without toys and with sheets covering the sides, limiting substantially what they could see. Life was more varied for older children, but opportunities for intellectual stimulation and the development of normal patterns of adult-child interaction were minimal. Furthermore, many of the primary caretakers were "graduates" of the Crèche themselves and were characterized by low IQ scores and a general unresponsiveness toward their young wards. Dennis reported that infants who remained institutionalized displayed signs of severe retardation within their first year and that their average IQs by age 16 ranged between 50 and 80. In contrast, infants leaving the Crèche for adoptive homes before the age of 2 years regained normal intellectual functioning, having average IQ scores of about 100. Children adopted following their second birthdays also demonstrated gains in intellectual performance, but they typically performed several years below their age level on all subsequent testings.

The effects of social deprivation appear early, within the first two or three months of life, reflected in infants' responses to simply being held. For example, Sally Provence and Rose Lipton describe 2- and 3-month-old institutionalized infants as feeling "something like sawdust dolls; they moved, they bent easily at the proper joints, but they felt stiff or wooden" (1962, p. 56). Signs of retardation and inappropriate social reactions to adults increased during the first two years, although these signs decreased some as children became able to move around on their own and were removed from nurseries to wards for older children (Provence & Lipton, 1962; Skeels, 1966).

The influence of spending their early years in institutions persisted years after children were removed from the foundling homes and placed in adoptive or foster homes. For example, Provence and Lipton (1962) followed into the preschool years a small group of institutionalized infants who had been placed in foster homes, most between 18 and 24 months of age. Provence and Lipton commented on the considerable resilience and capacity for improvement that these children showed, while noting that early institutionalization still caused long-term problems. These children, although relating to other toddlers, did not form strong personal attachments, either to other children or to adults. Their emotional behavior was described as "increasingly impoverished and predominantly bland. . . . One gained the impression on watching them that they had largely given up on their efforts to initiate a contact with the adult" (1962, p. 145). These children continued to improve, socially and intellectually, during the preschool years, so that many looked, on causal ob-

servation, like normal children. But closer examination revealed problems in forming emotional relationships, controlling impulses, developing language, and solving problems flexibly. In testing situations with adults, the children rarely sought assistance from their mothers, nor did they frequently turn to their mothers for comfort when distressed.

Research by Dennis, Provence and Lipton, and others like them are natural experiments and demonstrate how extremes in early environment can affect children's intellectual development. But such studies, although informative, lack the experimental rigor that psychologists like. (For example, there was no random assignment of children to an orphanage or to adoption.) Furthermore, such early deprived environments probably represent an extreme of child rearing and might not apply to the vast majority of parent-child interaction styles.

The Home Environment: Naturalistic Studies of Parent-Child Interaction

Beginning in the late 1960s, researchers began evaluating parent-child interaction patterns in the homes of young children. One of the more impressive longitudinal projects evaluating the quality of parent-child interactions and later intelligence was that conducted by Betty Caldwell, Richard Bradley, and their colleagues. They developed an inventory for assessing the quality of the home environment, called the Home Observation for Measurement of the Environment (HOME) scale (Caldwell & Bradley, 1978; Bradley, Caldwell, & Elardo, 1977). The **HOME scale** is divided into six subscales and is used to code aspects of a child's home environment that relate to intellectual development. Following are some sample items from the six subscales:

1. *Emotional and Verbal Responsivity of the Mother*
   a. Mother spontaneously vocalizes to child at least twice during visit (excluding scolding).
   b. Mother responds to child's vocalizations with a vocal or verbal response.
   c. Mother caresses or kisses child at least once during visit.

2. *Avoidance of Restriction and Punishment*
   a. Mother does not shout at child during visit.
   b. Mother neither slaps nor spanks child during visit.
   c. Mother does not interfere with child's actions or restrict child's movement more than three times during visit.
3. *Organization of the Physical and Temporal Environment*
   a. Someone takes the child to the grocery store at least once a week.
   b. When Mother is away, care is provided by one of three regular substitutes.
   c. The child's environment appears safe and free of hazards.
4. *Provision of Appropriate Play Materials*
   a. Child has a pull or push toy.
   b. Mother provides toys or interesting activities for child during interview.
   c. Mother provides toys for literature and music (books, records).
5. *Maternal Involvement with the Child*
   a. Mother tends to keep child within visual range and to look at him or her often.
   b. Mother "talks" to child while doing her work.
   c. Mother structures child's play period.
6. *Opportunities for Variety in Daily Stimulation*
   a. Father provides some care giving every day.
   b. Mother reads stories to child at least three times weekly.
   c. Child has at least three or more books of his or her own.

TABLE 16-2 Correlations between 54-month Stanford-Binet performance and scores on the HOME scale at 6 and 24 months.

	Correlations	
HOME subscale	*6 months*	*24 months*
1. Emotional and Verbal Responsibility of Mother	.27	.50**
2. Avoidance of Restriction and Punishment	.10	.28*
3. Organization of Physical and Temporal Environment	.31*	.33*
4. Provision of Appropriate Play Materials	.44**	.56**
5. Maternal Involvement with Child	.28*	.55**
6. Opportunities for Variety in Daily Stimulation	.30*	.39**
Total score	.44**	.57**
Multiple correlation[a]	.50*	.63**

[a]This represents the correlation of all HOME subscales with Binet scores.

*$p < .05$

**$p < .01$

SOURCE: Adapted from "The relation of infants' home environment to mental test performance at fifty-four months: A follow-up study," by R. H. Bradley and B. M. Caldwell, 1976, *Child Development, 47,* 1172–1174. Copyright © 1976 The Society for Research in Child Development, Inc. Adapted with permission.

Subsequent studies revealed moderate correlations (.30 – .60) between HOME scores and IQ measures (Bradley & Caldwell, 1976; Bradley et al., 1989; Espy, Molfese, & DiLalla, 2001). More specifically, mothers who were emotionally and verbally more responsive to their infants, who provided more play materials for their children, and who were generally more involved with their children during observations when their infants were 6 and 24 months of age had children with higher Stanford-Binet IQ scores at 54 months of age than did mothers who provided less stimulation for their youngsters (Brad-

ley & Caldwell, 1976). Table 16-2 presents the correlations between 6- and 24-month HOME scores and 54-month IQ scores for children in this study.

More recent research using the HOME scale has demonstrated that descriptions of the home environment during the first two years of life predict academic performance at age 11 reasonably well (Bradley, 1989). However, the picture is complicated. A beneficial early environment, for example, is not apt to have long-term consequences if later environments are less supportive. That is, when the childhood environment is stable, patterns of development are usually stable; when the childhood environment is constantly changing, patterns of intellectual development are also apt to change (Bradley, 1989). Thus, not only is a beneficial early environment important for sound intellectual development, but so is its stability—the beneficial environment also needs to be continuous.

Sameroff and his colleagues (Sameroff et al., 1993) made this point explicitly in a longitudinal study. Children from mainly lower-SES homes were administered IQ tests at 4 and 13 years of age. Children's home environments were also evaluated for risk factors (for example, family size, father absence, maternal education, maternal stress, maternal anxiety). First, Sameroff and his colleagues reported that a composite score of risk factors associated with each child's home life accounted for 34% of the variance in IQ scores at 4 years of age and 37% at 13 years of age. (This percentage increased to 50% at both ages when researchers used a more liberal measure of risk factors.) Thus, environmental risk contributed significantly to children's IQ; this remained true even after SES and mothers' IQ scores were taken into consideration. Second, the researchers reported that children's IQ scores at age 4 were significantly related with their IQ scores at age 13 (correlation = .72). However, environmental-risk scores were also highly correlated between age 4 and 13 years (correlation = .76). Thus, children living in nonsupportive and high-risk environments at age 4 were likely to be living in similar environments at age 13. It is exactly under such conditions that high correlations in IQs over time are expected.

More recent research has used the HOME scales, or measures like it, to examine further the connection between parenting behaviors and later intellectual development for a variety of populations. For example, Margaret Caughy (1996) examined the relation between several biological risk factors (low birth weight, length of hospitalization, rehospitalization during first year), environmental risk factors (low income, low maternal education, quality of the home environment as measured by a version of HOME Scale), and tests of mathematical and reading readiness in a group of 867 5- and 6-year-old children. Caughy reported a strong relation between

maternal education and HOME scores with both reading and mathematics performance. Not surprisingly, children from more intellectually supportive homes performed better on these tests. Also, biological risks (for example, low birth weight) adversely affected children's academic scores, although the impact of biological risk was not as great overall as that of environmental risk. And importantly, the children who were most adversely affected were those who experienced early health problems *and* who lived in impoverished environments as reflected primarily by low HOME scores. For example, children who were rehospitalized during their first year of life and came from homes with low HOME scores (indicating a nonsupportive intellectual environment) had significantly lower mathematics scores than did children who came from similar homes (that is, also having low HOME scores) but who were not rehospitalized. In contrast, rehospitalization did not affect academic scores for those children who came from homes with higher HOME scores (that is, a supportive intellectual environment). These findings are consistent with the transactional model described earlier and indicate that children living in nonsupportive homes are especially affected by biological risk.

Susan Landry and her colleagues (1997) illustrated the interaction between maternal behaviors and children's biological risks. In this study, 187 very low birth weight (VLBW) infants (less than 1600 grams at birth) and 112 full-term infants, all from lower SES homes, were followed longitudinally to 40 months of age. All these VLBW infants were at least three weeks "early" (that is, a gestational age of 36 weeks or less), and all had medical problems. Seventy-three of the VLBW infants were described as having high medical risk (high-risk group), whereas the remaining 114 were described as having low medical risk (low-risk group). Several maternal behaviors were coded at 6 and 12 months of age, and children were administered a test of language abilities, the Bayley Scale of Mental Development, and, at 36 months, the Stanford-Binet.

As would be expected, several aspects of maternal behavior predicted children's level of intellectual development. For example, mothers who frequently tried to maintain their child's interest or behavior in an ongoing activity had children with higher cognitive and language scores than did mothers who used maintaining strategies less often. Also, mothers who were restrictive, who used physical or verbal attempts to stop what their children were doing or saying, had children with lower cognitive and language scores. With respect to restrictiveness, the authors stated, "these results suggest that children whose early experiences are frequently interrupted with requests to stop doing something are not able to assume independence in their learning at a normal rate" (Landry et al., 1997, pp. 1049–1050).

Although the effect of restrictiveness was found for all groups of children, it was especially pronounced for the high-risk group. This restrictiveness style might send the message to children that they are not capable of controlling their own behavior or taking the initiative, and such a style seems to be particularly detrimental for high-risk children, who, because of their medical problems, are often more developmentally delayed than other VLBW children.

Naturalistic studies are generally consistent in their findings. Children who grow up in emotionally supportive homes and receive cognitively rich experiences tend to have higher IQs than do children growing up in high-risk homes who receive less intellectual stimulation (NICHD Early Child Care Research Network, 2002). But the type of experiences children receive and later intellectual performance is also related to characteristics of the children. The adverse effects of a nonstimulating environment are often exaggerated for high-risk children in particular (children with early health problems). There are a number of possible explanations for this latter fact. It might be that high-risk infants and children do not have the intellectual wherewithal to benefit from stimulating experiences. Alternatively, their biological impairment might result in different interaction patterns between themselves and their mothers, and this interaction pattern, with the children themselves contributing significantly to the transaction, produces a developmental course that is less than conducive to good intellectual functioning (recall the Zeskind and Ramey study).

I think that it is relatively easy to see how high-risk children can contribute to their own intellectual development in this way. It might be less obvious, however, to see how "normal" children also play a role in their own development. Jean Carew (1980) conducted a home observational study that considered the possible role of children in influencing their own development. Carew observed the behaviors of mothers and their children in their homes when the children were between the ages of 12 and 33 months and related her observations to children's IQ scores at 36 months. Carew reported that mothers' behaviors (for example, providing highly intellectual stimulation) when their children were between 12 and 27 months of age best predicted IQ level at 36 months. However, mothers' behaviors toward their children during the 30- to 33-month observation period were less predictive of IQ. During this time, solitary, child-initiated activities accounted for more of the individual differences in IQ level at 36 months than did mothers' behaviors. Similarly, in a Swedish longitudinal study, quality of the home environment predicted children's verbal abilities at age 40 months but not when children were tested at 101 months of age (second grade) (Broberg et al., 1997). These findings suggest that the direct influence of parents on children's behavior diminishes with age, as children take increasingly active roles in guiding their own development (see Scarr & McCartney, 1983). This is also consistent with the findings discussed earlier that the heritability of intelligence increases with age, as specific parental-environmental influences decline and genetic influences increase. This decline, of course, does not imply that how parents behave toward their children does not affect them after 30 (or 100) months of age. What must be kept in mind, however, is that children play a crucial role in influencing their own development at an early age and that parental influences must be evaluated as a continuous transaction between children and their parents, both of whom change as a result of the interactions.

Although the overall picture is somewhat murky, it is apparent that experiences during the preschool years set the stage for later intellectual accomplishments. Supportive and responsive environments tend to produce intelligent and competent children. It is impossible at this time to specify when, during childhood, these experiences are most important. Rather, from the available literature one can conclude that early experience is important, but so is later experience. Also, from infancy, children play an important role in their own development, helping to shape their own intellects. From a transactional perspective, we cannot put any numbers or percentages on how much of intellectual growth is influenced by nature versus nurture or how much is child-initiated or parent-initiated. From the current perspective, in fact, *how much* is the wrong question. The better question concerns how nature and nurture interact to yield a particular pattern of development, always keeping in mind that the child plays an active role in shaping his or her own life course.

Modification and Maintenance of Intellectual Functioning

It seems clear from the preceding discussion that individual differences in intelligence can be influenced by a child's early environment. A related series of questions concerns the modification of intelligence. Will the elevated or depressed IQ levels that are found in some populations still be present decades later, or can people's level of intellectual functioning be modified by subsequent experiences? In the section to follow, the modification and maintenance of intellectual functioning are considered for two related sets of conditions. First, to what extent are the intellectual deficits resulting from an impoverished early environment permanent? Can the deleterious effects of deprivation be ameliorated? And second, to what extent are the intellectual benefits resulting from enriched early environments permanent? Are intellectual skills that have been acquired during the preschool years maintained into later childhood?

Modification of Retardation Caused by Early Experience

As noted previously in this chapter, an early impoverished environment often results in reduced mental functioning. Based on the results of institutionalization studies of the type described earlier (Dennis,

1973; Spitz, 1945), it was once assumed that the deleterious effects of stimulus and social deprivation were permanent. Nevertheless, evidence suggesting the reversibility of the negative consequences of early deprivation has surfaced from time to time. Observations of children reared in relative isolation, for example, have indicated some plasticity of intellectual functioning with rehabilitation.

One of the best-documented studies of the mental growth of isolated children is that of Jarmila Koluchova (1976). A set of monozygotic twins who were physically and psychologically normal at 11 months experienced abuse, neglect, and malnutrition until discovered at 7 years 2 months. The children had no language and had an estimated mental age of about 3 years. They were placed in foster care and provided an educational program in the hope that they would attain some semblance of intellectual normalcy. The program was far more successful than originally expected; the twins had WISC scores of 93 and 95 by 11 years of age and of 101 and 100 by 14 years. Several other studies have similarly reported normal intellectual or language functioning following educational intervention for children initially classified as retarded because of neglect or isolation during the preschool years (see Clarke & Clarke, 1976). Related to these findings are reports of drastic changes in the intellectual performance of children from war-torn Southeast Asia in the 1970s adopted into American homes (Clark & Hanisee, 1982; Winick, Meyer, & Harris, 1975), which I discussed briefly in Chapter 2. It must be noted, however, that these are exceptions. Not all children who experience severe deprivation early in life show such reversibility as a result of later education (Curtiss, 1977).

Harold Skeels (1966) reported one controversial study concerning the reversibility of the negative effects of early experience. Skeels studied infants who were inmates of an orphanage. The orphanage was similar to many other Depression-era institutions, overcrowded and understaffed, and it was the type of institution that had been associated with reduced mental functioning by as early as 4 months of age (Spitz, 1945). During the course of several years, 13 children (10 girls and 3 boys) from the orphanage were transferred to a school for the mentally retarded and placed on the wards of the brighter women in-mates. These infants all showed signs of retardation at time of placement. Their IQ scores ranged from 35 to 89, with an average of 64.3. The average age at placement was 19 months, with a range from 7 to 36 months. These 13 children made up the experimental group. A contrast group was chosen from children who remained in the orphanage until at least the age of 4, 8 boys and 4 girls. The mean IQ score of the children in this group was 86.7 when first tested (mean age at first test = 16 months), with a range from 50 to 101.

The children in the experimental group received loving attention from the mentally retarded women. There was competition between wards to see who would have the first baby to walk or to talk. The attendants also spent much time with the youngsters. In almost every case, a single adult (inmate or attendant) became closely attached to a child, resulting in an intense one-to-one relationship that was supplemented by other adults. The experimental children remained in the institution for an average of 19 months and were then returned to the orphanage, with most being subsequently placed in adoptive homes. On their removal from the school for the mentally retarded, each child was administered an IQ test; the average score was 91.8, an increase of 27.5 points. The children in the contrast group were tested at approximately 4 years of age and had an average IQ score of 60.5 points, a decline of 26.2 points. The children were retested approximately 2.5 years later, with the experimental group having an average score of 95.9 and the contrast group an average of 66.1 (see Figure 16-4).

The results of this study are very impressive and demonstrate that toddlers characterized as severely retarded can realize significant gains in intelligence when placed in certain environments. Skeels extended his study, following these people into adulthood when they were between 25 and 35 years old. IQ tests were not given, but information was obtained concerning the occupational and educational levels of the participants, as well as information pertaining to their social adjustment. All 13 people in the experimental group had married, whereas only 2 of the 11 surviving members of the contrast group

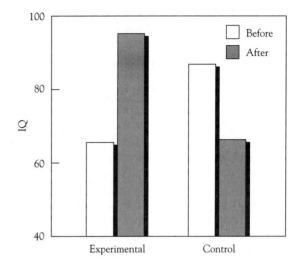

FIGURE 16-4 Average IQ scores before placement and two-and-one-half years after completion of program for children in the experimental and control groups. SOURCE: Adapted from data presented in Skeels, H. M. (1966). Adult status of children with contrasting early life experiences. *Monographs of the Society for Research in Child Development, 31* (Serial No. 105).

had married. The median number of years of formal education completed by the experimental group was 12 (that is, high school education), whereas the contrast group had completed a median of only 2.75 years. Most experimental participants or their spouses were employed in skilled or semi-skilled jobs. The range of socioeconomic status, based on income and occupation, was comparable with regional norms. In contrast, with one exception, people in the contrast group were in the lowest two socioeconomic levels. Four of the people in the contrast group remained institutional inmates, five held menial jobs such as dishwashers or cafeteria help, and only one had a skilled occupation (compositor and typesetter). IQ scores were available for some of the 28 children of the experimental participants and ranged from 86 to 125, with an average of 103.9. In general, people in the experimental group, who started life with a severe disadvantage, were normal by a variety of intellectual, occupational, and social standards.

The Skeels study demonstrates the potential plasticity of human intelligence. However, the study is not without its detractors. As an experiment, it leaves much to be desired. Skeels took advantage of a naturally occurring situation and assessed the effects of early environments within the constraints imposed on him by ethical and institutional considerations. As a result, there is much to fault with the methodology of the study, and although the study has been widely praised, its serious shortcomings have also been noted (see Longstreth, 1981).

One interpretation of the Skeel's study consistent with the transactional view of development popular today is that the intellectual immaturity of the women with mental retardation might actually have facilitated social interaction with the orphans, providing the children with stimulation they would not normally have received in the orphanage. In most situations, the characteristics of the severely retarded children in the experimental group would not produce lavish attention from adults. Most well-intending adults who direct their attention to a child expect some response in return. Children who are nonresponsive and generally lethargic tend not to elicit continued stimulation from adults, particularly adults from highly stressed homes (Sameroff & Chandler, 1975). This presumably would be especially true of overburdened members of an institution's staff. Because of the limited mental capacity of the inmates, however, their attention might have been repeatedly directed to the children even in the absence of appropriate responses. After prolonged stimulation, the children might have become more responsive and begun the climb back to normal intellectual functioning. That is, it is possible that the intellectual immaturity of the institutionalized women in the Skeels study matched the needs of the children.

Of course, highly responsive women of normal or above-normal intelligence could also have served as appropriate "therapists" for these children, as was apparently the case in the Asian adoption studies cited earlier (Clark & Hanisee, 1982). But this is not the type of experience that these children could have expected from the orphanage staff. Moreover, had the children remained in the institution for the mentally retarded for considerably longer, their intellectual gains would surely have been lost. As their intelligence increased, so would their needs for intellectual stimulation, quickly exceeding the boundaries of what the women with mental retardation could have provided.

In more recent times, after the fall of Ceausescu in communist Romania in 1989, hundreds of infants and young children were discovered in overcrowded and understaffed institutions, under conditions of nutritional and social deprivation at least as horrendous as those that existed in institutions during the early part of the last century (Kaler & Freedman, 1994). Many of these malnourished infants were adopted into advantaged homes across the globe. Some were adopted very early in life (0 to 6 months), whereas others were not adopted until after 2 or 3 years of age (O'Connor et al., 2000; Rutter et al., 1998). What happened to these children, all of whom were suffering from the effects of malnutrition and emotional neglect when adopted? Were they able to catch up, and, if so, by how much? What effect did age of adoption (or, stated another way, time spent institutionalized) have on their eventual recovery?

Research examining the course of development for Romanian children adopted in United Kingdom (UK) provides some preliminary answers to these questions (O'Connor et al., 2000; Rutter et al., 1998). Romanian children left their institutions for adoptive homes at ages ranging from a few months old to 42 months of age. For comparison purposes, they were classified into one of three groups: those adopted between 0 and 6 months, 7 and 24 months, and 25 and 42 months. These children were compared with a group of infants born in the UK and adopted by other UK parents. All the UK-born children were adopted between 0 and 6 months of age. All children were administered the McCarthy scale at 6 years of age. This scale produces a Global Cognitive Index (GCI) that has a population mean of 100 (like an IQ test).

The researchers reported remarkable recovery of cognitive abilities in all groups of Romanian adoptees. Despite the substantial developmental

TABLE 16-3 Scores on the General Cognitive Index (GCI) at age 6 for UK and Romanian children by the age they were adopted.

Nation	Age	GCI Scores
UK	0–6 mos	117
Romanian	0–6 mos	114
Romanian	6–24 mos	99
Romanian	24–42 mos	90

SOURCE: Adapted from O'Connor, T. G., Rutter, M., Beckett, C., Keaveney, L., & Kreppner, J. M., and the English and Romanian Adoptees Study Team. (2000). The effects of global severe privation on cognitive competence: Extension and longitudinal follow-up. *Child Development, 71,* 376–390.

delay that all the Romanian adopted children had demonstrated when first arriving to the UK, each group had mean GCI scores within the normal range (see Table 16-3). The average GCI score of the 0–6-month adopted Romania children was no different from that of the UK-adopted children. However, the scores did vary as a function of how long children had been institutionalized; children who had been institutionalized for 2 years or longer before being adopted had the lowest overall scores, and children who had been institutionalized for 6 months or less had the highest overall scores.

These findings indicate the remarkable resiliency of children to the effects of early deprivation, but also the long-term consequences of prolonged nutritional, social, and emotional neglect. One should not be surprised that children who experienced more than two years of extreme privation demonstrated some long-term effects. However, that many of these children were functioning above normal at 6 years of age is impressive, and we must wait for future research before we know if this group will show any subsequent gains.

Along similar lines, the short-term effectiveness of **compensatory education programs** has been well documented by several projects designed to provide preschool children from low-income homes with the intellectual skills necessary to do well in school (Klaus & Gray, 1968; Ramey, Campbell, & Finkelstein, 1984). Such programs have raised the IQ scores of high-risk children by 10 to 15 points during the program. These experimental programs, most of which were begun in the 1960s, varied considerably in the organization of their curricula, ranging from programs based on Piagetian theory to those using behavior modification techniques as advocated by B. F. Skinner. What most programs did have in common was an emphasis on language and problem-solving skills and a low student-teacher ratio, allowing substantial individual attention to children.

Generally, children in the more rigorous, highly structured programs demonstrated the greatest gains. In some studies, large gains in IQ level were noted relative to control children and to the children's performance before they entered the programs (see Barnett, 1995). In others, intervention began shortly after birth, with children demonstrating high IQ scores relative to control children at every age tested, thus never needing compensation for below-average intellectual achievement (Garber, 1988; Ramey et al., 1984). More will be said about the long-term effects of such intervention programs in the following section.

But before we move on, let us consider a final question relating to the reversibility of deleterious effects of early experience: At what age is plasticity lost? Unfortunately, we are not able to answer this question. We do know from animal research that plasticity is reduced with age and that we are most malleable as infants (see Chapter 2). Human development has been proposed to be highly *canalized* during the first 18 or 24 months of life, meaning that all children follow the species-typical path "under a wide range of diverse environments and exhibit strong self-righting tendencies following exposure to severely atypical environments" (McCall, 1981, p. 5). In other words, although infants might be adversely affected by early maladaptive environments, there is a strong tendency to return to a course of normalcy, given an appropriate environment. This plasticity is progressively reduced later in life, beginning as early as 18 or 24 months of age. In general, the earlier intervention is begun, the greater its chance of reversing an established behavior pattern, if for no other reason than older children and adults are more reluctant than younger children to accept the imposition of a drastically changed environment.

Maintenance of the Beneficial Effects of Early Experience on Intelligence

If the effects of a negative early environment can be reversed, what about the effects of a beneficial early environment? If intelligence can be modified for the better by experiences later in childhood, can a later-childhood environment also modify a child's intellectual functioning for the worse? For the most part, evidence of the long-term effects of positive environments comes from follow-up studies of preschool compensatory education programs. Although the initial reports of these programs were favorable, doubts concerning their long-term effectiveness began to surface shortly thereafter. The initial gains in IQ and academic performance shown by program graduates were slowly lost, and by the end of the fourth grade, levels of intellectual attainment were comparable between children who had participated in the programs and those who had not (Bradley, Burchinal, & Casey, 2001; Klaus & Gray, 1968). Figure 16-5 shows the typical pattern of IQ changes for graduates of preschool intervention programs.

Despite these findings, researchers were not ready to dismiss the influence of early compensatory education on the later intellectual functioning of high-risk children, and several investigators inquired into the long-term (from middle school and beyond) consequences of the preschool experience. Two of the more comprehensive investigations of the long-term effects of preschool compensatory education programs were reported by Irving Lazar and his colleagues (1982), who evaluated the effects of 11 experimental programs, and W. Steven Barnett (1995), who examined the effects of 36 model demonstration projects and large-scale public programs. The findings of the two studies were similar. Compensatory preschool programs had minimal long-term effects on IQ and academic achievement. Although the programs had an initial impact on children's IQ scores, few reliable differences were

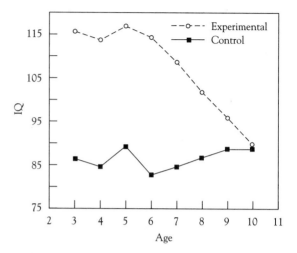

FIGURE 16-5 Typical pattern of IQ changes for experimental and control children during preschool program (2 to 6 years) and after.

found between experimental and control children by 10 years of age. Preschool graduates did score higher on some achievement tests than control children did, but this effect was not widespread.

More encouraging findings were found for school competence. For example, Lazar and his colleagues (1982) reported the median rate of assignment to special education classes was 13.8% for children who had participated in preschool programs and 28.6% for control children. Although less dramatic, there were also significant group differences in the percentage of children who were held back in grade. The median grade-retention rate was 30.5% for children in the control group and 25.8% for children who had participated in the preschool programs. Differences were also found in children's attitudes toward achievement. Program graduates were more likely to give achievement-related reasons for being proud of themselves, and the mothers of the experimental children felt more positively about their children and their likelihood of success than did the mothers of the control children.

There have been some exceptions to this general pattern, including the North Carolina Abecedarian Program (Campbell & Ramey, 1994; Campbell et al., 2001, 2002: Ramey et al., 2000). Children from rural

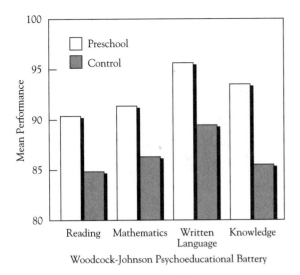

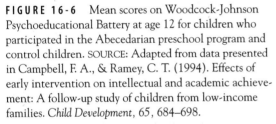

FIGURE 16-6 Mean scores on Woodcock-Johnson Psychoeducational Battery at age 12 for children who participated in the Abecedarian preschool program and control children. SOURCE: Adapted from data presented in Campbell, F. A., & Ramey, C. T. (1994). Effects of early intervention on intellectual and academic achievement: A follow-up study of children from low-income families. *Child Development, 65,* 684–698.

North Carolina, identified as at-risk for mental retardation, attended an educationally oriented daycare program beginning shortly after birth and continuing until they entered first grade. When tested at age 12, children who had attended the preschool program had significantly higher IQ scores (94) than did control children (88). Also, children in the preschool group scored consistently higher on a battery of academic tests (Woodcock-Johnson Psychoeducational Battery, see Figure 16-6). Many of these differences were maintained when participants were tested at age 21 (Campbell et al., 2002), although the effects were greater for women than for men. Similar effects of greater sixth-grade reading and math achievement for high-risk children who attended an urban preschool program relative to control children have also been reported (Reynolds et al., 1996).

The findings of the long-term benefits of preschool intervention are somewhat mixed. On the one hand, most (but not all) studies found that the intellectual benefits realized during the preschool years were lost when the program responsible for the gains was discontinued. Once intellectual competence is attained, it must be maintained. Apparently, the intellectual environment for most of the low-income children after leaving the program was not sufficiently supportive to maintain the level of intelligence established during the preschool years. On the other hand, several studies have reported long-term intellectual effects, and, taken together, there are several significant and important noncognitive benefits of compensatory education. The difference in assignment to special education classes alone represents a significant savings in tax dollars, justifying the cost of the preschool programs (Karoly et al., 1998). Furthermore, differences in grade retention (and presumably the probability of completing high school) and in personal and maternal attitudes suggest that program graduates will be more likely to succeed economically in the years to come than will children in the control conditions.

What if the compensatory preschool program had been extended into the early elementary school years? Might there then have been long-term effects of early education? Wesley Becker and Russell Gersten (1982) examined the academic performance of fifth- and sixth-grade children who had participated in Project Follow Through, a program designed to take over where the federally funded preschool Project Head Start left off. In Project Follow Through, low-income children are provided with compensatory education through the third grade. Becker and Gersten evaluated the effectiveness of five different Follow Through programs, comparing children's performance with that of control groups and with national norms on a series of achievement tests.

Children in the study had been administered portions of the Wide Range Achievement Test (WRAT) or the Metropolitan Achievement Test (MAT). Significant differences were found between the Follow Through and control children in both the fifth and sixth grades. Most striking were differences in reading level on the WRAT and differences on the spelling and math-problem-solving subscales of the MAT, all in favor of the Follow Through children. Of 180 statistical comparisons made between the control and

TABLE 16-4 Mean percentile ranks for children in Project Follow Through for subtests of the WRAT and the MAT.

Time of test	WRAT reading	MAT reading	MAT math	MAT spelling
Last year of Follow Through:				
Grade 3	63rd	38th	62nd	47th
After completion of Follow Through:				
Grade 5	53rd	22nd	29th	37th
Grade 6	38th	20th	27th	37th

SOURCE: Adapted with permission from "A Follow-up of Follow-Through: The Later Effects of the Direct Instruction Model for Children in Fifth and Sixth Grades," by W. C. Becker and R. Gersten, 1982, *American Educational Research Journal, 19,* 75–92. Copyright © 1982 American Educational Research Association.

the Follow Through children from the five different programs, 76 (42%) favored the Follow Through children, whereas only 2 (1%) favored the control subjects. Thus, compensatory education programs that are continued beyond the preschool years have beneficial effects on academic achievement.

Becker and Gersten also compared the performance of the Follow Through children on the WRAT and MAT with national norms. Mean percentile ranks for the Follow Through children for tests given in the third, fifth, and sixth grades are presented in Table 16-4. The percentiles are based on national averages for the WRAT and the MAT, with a score of 50 representing average performance. Tests given in the third grade reflect the children's performance while they were still participating in Project Follow Through, whereas scores in the fifth and sixth grades reflect performance two and three years after termination of the program.

The most striking aspect of these data is the steady decline in percentile standing as a function of grade. These high-risk children were performing close to or above the national average on three of these four tests in the third grade (the exception being MAT reading, 38th percentile). Two years after they had left Follow Through, only their WRAT reading scores were comparable to the national average, and by the sixth grade they had declined to the 38th percentile. These results indicate that although the Follow Through children maintained an academic advantage relative to matched sets of control children, they showed a decrement relative to national averages after leaving the program. Again, the social and educational benefits of the program are significant. However, as with the findings of Lazar and his associates (1982) and Barnett (1995), intellectual gains diminished once the children left the program.

How Modifiable Is Human Intelligence?

In general, the results of the studies reviewed in the previous sections indicate that the negative effects of early experience can be reversed and the beneficial effects of an early stimulating environment can be altered by experiences that follow it. Human intelligence is modifiable in both positive and negative directions. Intelligence is not something that once gotten is necessarily kept. Intelligence, as measured by IQ tests, reflects a person's intellectual functioning at a given time. Once established, intelligence (or any other complex behavior, for that matter) must be maintained. If the environmental supports responsible for establishing cognitive competence are removed, we should not be surprised that intelligence suffers.

The results of these studies reflect a flexible cognitive system that can be greatly modified by changes in the environment during childhood. However, the research cited can be criticized for not being representative of the way the world is structured for most children. Fortunately, few children spend their early years restricted to closets, and most children who are provided stimulating environments as preschoolers can expect comparably stimulating environments in the years to come. These studies indicate what *can* happen to levels of intelligence during childhood and not necessarily what actually *does* happen. Children's environments do change normally over time, such as the transition from home to school and a related shift from a family-centered to a peer-centered lifestyle. To the extent that these changes in environments do not represent major shifts in intellectual emphasis, levels of intelligence can be expected to be maintained. The more diverse the changing environments, the greater the change in level of intelligence that can be expected.

The Stability of Intelligence

We like to believe that the world we live in is relatively stable and predictable. This predilection includes some implicit beliefs concerning the stability of mental functioning. We have looked at the issue of stability briefly in earlier chapters in this book. For example, certain aspects of memory performance remain stable over time, whereas other aspects do not. But the primary arena for the study of stability of mental functioning has been the topic of intelligence. To what extent is intellectual functioning, as measured by IQ or other general assessments of intelligence, stable over time? Will a bright 5- year-old turn out to be an intelligent teenager, or is prediction of adolescent and adult intelligence from early childhood no more reliable than tossing a coin? And what about infancy? Is there any way that we can predict what level of intellectual functioning a child will attain from assessments in infancy? Traditionally, developmental psychologists have tended to believe in the stability of cognitive ability.

One reason for this perspective is that our profession specializes in investigating conditions in early life that predict later behavior or prepare the child for subsequent accomplishments. Despite our commonsense assumptions of the stability of intelligence and our professional biases that cause us to look for

stability over time, what is the evidence? To what extent are individual differences in intellectual functioning stable during infancy and childhood?

Defining Stability

Before looking at any evidence, let me define again what is meant by **stability.** Obviously, stability does not mean that intelligence stays the same over time. Of course, children get smarter as they get older. Rather, stability refers to the relative constancy of individual differences—the extent to which different children maintain their rank order over time in comparison with their peers. Is the valedictorian of her kindergarten class likely to be among the top students when her high school class graduates? Is the highly attentive 4-month-old likely to be a better reader than his less attentive peer? Stability in this sense is measured by correlations of rank order. If a group of children is given IQ tests at age 5, for example, they can be ranked in IQ score from highest to lowest. If that same group is tested again at age 10, we can compare the rankings of the children's IQ scores at the two ages. If the rankings are similar, the correlation will be positive and high. If there is no stability of individual differences in IQ scores between ages 5 and 10, the correlation will be close to 0. It is also possible, although seemingly unlikely, that the brightest children at age 5 will be, on the average, the least bright children at age 10, resulting in a negative correlation. Note that the correlations used to assess stability are unrelated to the actual level of performance. Correlations may be high, implying stability, although the average level of performance might have systematically increased (or decreased) for most members of the sample.

In the following sections, I examine research on the stability of individual differences in intelligence over time. For the most part, IQ data are used as a measure of intellectual functioning, although several studies are reported that used other measures of cognition. In addition to investigating stability of intelligence via cross-age correlations, I also examine patterns of change. That is, although there might be high correlations between measures of intelligence at two ages, that does not mean that intelligence has not changed during that period. In other words, the relationship between developmental function—patterns of change that characterize the species—and the stability of individual differences will be evaluated.

Predicting Later Intelligence from Tests in Infancy

One research topic in cognitive development that received much attention in the recent past has been that of predicting childhood IQ from measures taken in infancy. Before presenting this new research, let me provide a little necessary history.

Psychometricians have generally believed that intelligence is stable across time, including from infancy into childhood. In part, this prediction is based on the assumption that human intelligence can best be described as a unitary construct that varies in a continuous fashion over time. From a psychometric perspective, this is best described as a single general factor of intelligence, g. When developmental function is continuous and quantitative in nature, there is every reason to expect that individual differences will be stable (**continuity with stability**).

Testing such an hypothesis is relatively straightforward. Tests given in infancy are correlated with IQ tests given in childhood. The problem, of course, is developing tests that assess intelligence in infancy. Such tests have been around for nearly 60 years in the form of infant psychometric scales that produce a developmental quotient (DQ) with the same psychometric properties as IQ tests. Examples from one of these tests, the first edition of the Bayley Scale, were presented in Chapter 15. However, when babies who were given the Bayley and other scales are later administered IQ tests in early childhood, the correlations are disappointingly low. Prediction is only slightly greater for high-risk infants. Table 16-5 summarizes the results of studies examining the relationship between sensorimotor tests of development and later IQ scores for both normal and high-risk samples as a function of age of testing (both in infancy and in childhood). As can be seen, the corre-

lations are uniformly low; the average correlation between infant tests and IQ scores at age 6 years is only .11 for normal infants. Prediction is often considerably higher for infants scoring very low on the tests (for example, below 80), suggesting some power of these tests to predict pathology in limited situations (see McCall, Hogarty, & Hurlburt, 1972).

This should be very discouraging for people who believe the continuity-with-stability theory of intelligence, yet there is always the argument that the infant DQ tests are not sensitive enough, and new tests will eventually find the relationship. Others have looked at these data, however, and are not surprised. The reason for the low correlations is that development varies in a discontinuous way between infancy and childhood, with qualitative differences in the nature of intelligence. When developmental function is discontinuous (that is, relatively abrupt and qualitative in nature), there is no reason to expect stability. The bright sensorimotor child might become a bright preoperational child, for example, but because of the substantial difference in the nature of cognition between the infant and preschool child, such stability should not be expected.

This **discontinuity-with-instability** position was best articulated by Robert McCall and his colleagues (McCall, Eichorn, & Hogarty, 1977), who demonstrated using longitudinal data that there is little stability of individual differences in cognitive performance even across different stages in infancy, to say nothing of between infancy and later childhood. For example, McCall and his associates were able to identify five stages in cognitive development between birth and 3 years of age: birth to 2 months; 2 to 8 months; 8 to 13 months; 13 to 21 months; and 21 to 31–36 months. These correspond roughly to Piaget's stages of sensorimotor development, as outlined in Chapter 4. McCall and his colleagues found that there was substantial stability of individual differences (that is, high cross-age correlations) when comparing performance *within* a stage (for example, between 8 and 12 months), but much less stability (that is, low cross-age correlations) when comparisons were made *between* stages (for example, between 10 and 14 months). These data very nicely demonstrate continuity with stability for contrasts

TABLE 16-5 Median correlations between DQ test scores and later IQ test scores for normal and high-risk samples.

Infant test (months)	Normal sample				High-risk sample			
	Age at follow-up test (years)				Age at follow-up test (years)			
	3	4–5	6+	Mean	3	4–5	6+	Mean
3–4	.04 (4)*	.06 (2)	.07 (3)	.06	.14 (2)	.08 (4)	.07 (2)	.10
5–7	.25 (14)	.20 (5)	.06 (6)	.15	.27 (5)	.24 (13)	.28 (3)	.26
8–11	.20 (8)	.23 (5)	.21 (3)	.21	.29 (6)	.23 (10)	.29 (6)	.27
Mean	.16	.16	.11		.23	.18	.21	

*Numbers in parentheses represent number of studies in each median correlation.

SOURCE: Fagan, J. F., III, & Singer, J. T. (1983). Infant recognition memory as a measure of intelligence. In L. P. Lipsitt & C. K. Rovee-Collier (Eds.), *Advances in infancy research* (Vol. 2). Norwood, NJ: Ablex. Reprinted with permission.

within a cognitive stage and discontinuity with instability for contrasts *between* cognitive stages.

This, basically, is where the argument stood until the 1980s, when new research reported evidence of stability of intelligence from infancy to childhood. The evidence came from what to many was an unlikely source—measures of infant memory and attention. Recall from our discussions of infant perception and attention in Chapter 7 the habituation/dishabituation paradigm. Infants are presented a stimulus (a picture, for example) and their attention to that stimulus is noted (in this case, looking time). The same stimulus is presented repeatedly, with the typical finding that infant attention to the stimulus decreases. When attention to the stimulus decreases sufficiently (usually to 50% of what it was on the initial trials), the infant is said to have habituated to the stimulus.

This same technique has been used to assess recognition memory. Some time after habituation (minutes, hours, or even days), the infant is shown two stimuli, usually simultaneously. One of the stimuli is the same picture the infant had been habituated to earlier. The other stimulus is a new one. Memory is indicated if infants look at the novel stimulus more than at the habituated stimulus. They remember the old stimulus and are still tired of looking at it. This *preference-for-novelty* measure has been used exten-

sively and has revealed much about infant memory capacity. (See further discussion in Chapters 8 and 9.)

Psychologists began to look for relationships between individual differences in measures of infant attention/memory and childhood IQ. Joseph Fagan was the first person to systematically examine this relationship, which is fitting, given that he was a pioneer of the preference-for-novelty technique in assessing infant recognition memory.

In an early review, Joseph Fagan and Lynn Singer (1983) examined the results of previously published experiments concerning the prediction of childhood intelligence from infants' preferences for novelty by means of visual recognition, and they also reported the results of their own longitudinal study. The ages of infants assessed ranged from 3 to 7 months and assessments of childhood IQ for 12 sets of data ranged from 2 to 7.5 years. The range of correlations between infants' preferences for novelty and later IQ was .33 to .66, with a mean value of .44. That is, the stronger an infants' preference for novelty was (the more they looked at the novel versus the familiar stimulus), the higher their IQ during early childhood was apt to be. Compare this with the values given in Table 16-5, where average correlations between sensorimotor tests and IQ scores for normal infants ranged from .16 (for IQ tests given between the ages of 3 and 5 years) to .11 (for IQ tests given at age 6 and beyond). Similar results were later reported using habituation measures, with infants who habituate faster having higher childhood IQs (see Bornstein, 1989; Bornstein & Sigman, 1986).

Habituation and preference-for-novelty tasks have been used with hearing and touch as well as vision, and researchers have reported comparable correlations with childhood IQ when infants are tested in these other modalities (hearing—O'Connor, Cohen, & Parmelee, 1984; touch—Rose et al., 1991). Results are found both for full-term (Rose, Feldman, & Wallace, 1992; Slater et al., 1989) and preterm (Rose et al., 1989; Sigman et al., 1986) infants. Two more recent reviews of the literature have demonstrated the reliability of these findings. Marc Bornstein (1989) reported a median correlation between infant measures of habituation and childhood IQ of .49; the median correlation between preference for novelty and childhood IQ was .46. Robert McCall and Michael Carriger (1993) reviewed a total of 27 different studies and reported median correlations between infant measures and childhood IQ of .41 for habituation and .37 for preference for novelty. There have been nearly a dozen research papers published after the McCall and Carriger review, and in each case, significant correlations between infant cognitive measures and later IQ are reported (Dougherty & Haith, 1997; Thompson, Fagan, & Fulker, 1991).

The evidence just cited indicates that there is a moderate degree of continuity of developmental function and stability of individual differences from infancy to early childhood. Given these findings, how might continuity of developmental function be interpreted? Marc Bornstein and Marian Sigman (1986) examined several possibilities and concluded that the high correlations can best be explained by the continuity of an underlying process. This model proposes that a constant process underlies individual differences in both the allocation of infant attention and later performance on tests of intelligence. The question is, what might that process be?

Most researchers have assumed that habituation and preference for novelty involve information-processing mechanisms and that such mechanisms are stable in form during infancy and into childhood

(Bornstein & Sigman, 1986; Fagan, 1992; McCall & Carriger, 1993). For example, habituation and recognition memory involve encoding of a stimulus, storing it, categorizing it, comparing a present stimulus with a memory representation, and discriminating the old from the new stimulus. McCall and Carriger further suggest that the information-processing mechanisms underlying performance might be "the disposition to inhibit responding to familiar stimuli and to stimuli of minor prominence (e.g., low energy, static, etc.)" (1993, p. 77). Such a position is consistent with evidence presented in Chapter 5 of age-related differences in sensitivity to interference and the ability to inhibit prepotent responses. Such basic inhibitory abilities can play an important role not only in cognitive development (Bjorklund & Harnishfeger, 1990; Dempster, 1993) but also in individual differences in cognitive functioning (Harnishfeger & Bjorklund, 1994).

Another related aspect of information processing that might underlie both infant and childhood measures is the ability to process novelty. Particularly, the preference-for-novelty paradigm used for assessing recognition memory involves the handling of novel information. Unlike many of the sensorimotor skills assessed on infant scales of intelligence, these abilities are also characteristic of cognition in later life and, thus, might serve as a basis for the continuity of intelligence. Along similar lines, Robert Sternberg (1985) has argued that response to novelty is a major element of individual differences in intelligence that is constant across the life span (recall Sternberg's theory from Chapter 15). He proposes that how people react to novel situations is central to most definitions of intelligence. Even what Piaget called assimilation and accommodation, for example, are essentially means for dealing with novel environmental events. In a similar vein, Harriet Rheingold (1985) stressed the importance of novelty in development. She asserted that the development of behavior, including mental processes, can be viewed as a process of becoming familiar with our world (both internal and external). The child's task in development is "to render the novel familiar." Thus, like Sternberg, Rheingold sees the process of acquiring new knowledge—of rendering the novel familiar—

to be a central aspect of development that is continuous throughout life.

Let us return to an issue introduced earlier in this chapter. Does this new evidence of continuity with stability from infancy to childhood mean that there is a general factor of intelligence, or *g*? The data certainly seem to point in that direction. Fagan (1992) believes that the origins of intelligence can be found in the infant's ability to process information, and that such processing is tapped by habituation and recognition memory procedures. These basic-level information-processing abilities have a high heritability. This all suggests that there is a strong biological (genetic and possibly prenatal) basis for individual differences in intelligence. Fagan (1992) suggests that what underlies intelligence is best thought of as information-processing mechanisms rather than a mental factor; nevertheless, the relatively high prediction of later intelligence from infant measures is consistent with the continuity-with-stability position advocated by *g* theorists.

Recent evidence supports the idea of the stability of information-processing mechanisms that underlie tests both in infancy and childhood. For example, Susan Rose and Judith Feldman (1995) reported that visual recognition memory tests given at 7 months correlated significantly at age 11 years not only with IQ scores (correlation = .41) but also with perceptual speed (correlation = .38). In other work, Thomas Dougherty and Marshall Haith (1997) found infant visual reaction time (the time it took infants to begin an eye movement toward a picture after it appeared) taken at 3.5 months of age correlated significantly both with childhood IQ (correlation = .44) and with childhood (age 4) visual reaction times (measured similarly as they were in infancy; correlation = .51). These studies argue for cognitive continuity from infancy through childhood and that speed of processing is the likely component that underlies intellectual performance and is responsible, at least in part, for the stability observed.

But the correlations, although substantially higher than found with infant DQ tests, are far from perfect, and Fagan and others point out that individual differences in infant information processing do not consti-

tute the whole picture. For example, reliable differences in IQ scores are found between children of different races and different parental educational backgrounds in the United States. Yet, no differences have been found between children of different races or with different parental educational backgrounds on measures of recognition memory (Fagan, 1984). This suggests that experiential factors play a separate role in the establishment of intelligence.

Catherine Tamis-LeMonda and Marc Bornstein (Bornstein, 1989; Tamis-LeMonda & Bornstein, 1989) nicely illustrated the combined influence of basic information-processing abilities and environmental factors. They demonstrated that the quality of mother-child interaction predicted childhood intelligence at age 4 independent of infant habituation rates. In other words, how parents interact with their babies has an important influence on their children's intelligence beyond that measured by habituation rate. This means that intelligence is a multifaceted thing, and we must interpret any global pronouncements concerning its development very cautiously.

Intelligence is not a single, well-defined dimension. If a *g* factor does exist, it reflects only part of the picture. The work of Fagan, Bornstein, and others suggests that at least some aspects of intelligence vary continuously during infancy and childhood and are stable over time. Yet the earlier claim by McCall and his colleagues that intelligence during infancy changes in a discontinuous manner and is unstable over time is also likely true. The difference is that the various investigators are measuring different aspects of infant intelligence, with some aspects changing continuously and showing stability and others changing discontinuously and showing instability.

The Stability of IQ Scores During Childhood

Prediction of Adult IQ from Childhood Data

Although infant psychometric measures do not predict later IQ scores well, the stability of individual differences in intelligence as measured by IQ tests increases dramatically by age 2. Table 16-6 summarizes the findings of longitudinal studies by Nancy

TABLE 16-6 Cross-age correlations between IQ tests given in childhood and adult IQ scores.

Age of testing	Honzik, MacFarlane, and Allen (1948)	Bayley (1949)
1 year	—	−.14
2–3 years	.33	.40
4–5 years	.42	.52
6–7 years	.67	.68
8–9 years	.71	.80
10–11 years	.73	.87
12–13 years	.79	—
14–15 years	.76	.84

Bayley (1949) and M. P. Honzik, J. W. MacFarlane, and L. Allen (1948), and it presents the correlations between scores on intelligence tests given at various times during childhood and IQ scores as young adults (17 or 18 years of age). Whereas the correlations between intelligence tests given at 12 months and at 18 years are approximately 0, the correlations rise quickly by the beginning of the third year. The correlations with adult IQ scores rise rapidly until early childhood and are relatively stable from age 8 or so on. Claire Kopp and Robert McCall stated, "following age 5, IQ is perhaps the most stable, important behavioral characteristic yet measured" (1982, p. 39).

Why should there be such a high degree of stability in IQ scores during childhood, especially when predictions from infant psychometric tests are so poor? In all likelihood, the reason for the increased stability of IQ scores beginning around age 2 is the increasing similarity of the test items and of the nature of intelligence for children 2 years of age and beyond. Following Piaget, there is a qualitative change in intelligence occurring sometime between 18 and 30 months of age. Children become adept symbol users and will remain symbol users throughout their lives. IQ tests are constructed to reflect meaningful dimensions of intelligence for people of a given age, and, accordingly, the ability to retrieve and manipulate symbols is a central aspect of most if not all intelligence tests from the 2-year level onward. There

is thus a continuity of developmental function, to the extent that symbolic functioning is involved in measuring intelligence at all ages. Although continuity of developmental function does not necessitate stability of individual differences, it can be seen from the earlier discussion of IQ prediction from infancy data that such a relationship probably exists.

Patterns of IQ Change During Childhood

Despite the impressive stability of the rank order of IQ scores from the early school years, there is still room for change, particularly change in the level of IQ. Recall that correlations of rank order are statistically independent of average values. So, for example, the average level of IQ scores could vary substantially for a particular sample of children and affect the correlations of rank order only minimally.

Robert McCall, Mark Appelbaum, and Pamela Hogarty (1973) extensively examined patterns of IQ change during childhood. They analyzed IQ data from the Fels Longitudinal Study. In their study, the data of 80 people (38 males, 42 females) who had been administered a Stanford-Binet IQ test at 17 points in development (ages 2.5, 3, 3.5, 4, 4.5, 5, 5.5, 6, 7, 8, 9, 10, 11, 12, 14, 15, and 17 years) were examined for changes in level and pattern of IQ scores over time.

First, how much change, in IQ points, was observed? The range of IQ scores for a given child was obtained, and the difference between a child's highest score during the 17 testing sessions and his or her lowest score was computed. Note that this is not the difference between a child's IQ score at 17 years and his or her score at 2.5 years, but the difference between the highest and lowest scores a child received, independent of age. The average shift in IQ score for children in this sample was 28.5 points. The range for 21% of the children in this sample was 20 points or less, and 43% shifted between 21 and 30 points sometime between 2.5 and 17 years of age. Slightly more than one-third of the sample (36%) showed shifts of more than 30 points, with one child displaying an amazing increase of 74 points! Although such a drastic change is rare, other researchers have reported shifts of more than 50 points (Honzik et al.,

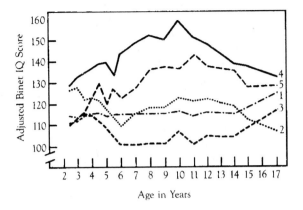

FIGURE 16-7   Mean IQ scores over time for five clusters of children. SOURCE: "Developmental Changes in Mental Performance," by R. B. McCall, M. I. Appelbaum, and P. S. Hogarty, 1973, *Monographs of the Society for Research in Child Development, 38* (Serial No. 150). Copyright © 1973 The Society for Research in Child Development, Inc. Reprinted with permission.

1948; Moore, 1967). In general, it's fair to say that, on average, IQ scores changed substantially during the 15-year period.

One potential problem with longitudinal studies is that children can become "test wise" because of repeated testings. It is possible that the large shifts in IQ scores observed in this study were the result of practice effects, with the children getting better at taking the tests with experience, and that this resulted in elevated levels of performance as they grew older. This explanation, although reasonable, was not supported by the data. McCall and his colleagues subjected the IQ scores to cluster analysis, a statistical technique that discerns common patterns among sets of data. Thus, children showing similar patterns of IQ change over time would be grouped together in a single cluster. The cluster analysis yielded five distinct patterns of IQ change, graphed in Figure 16-7. The first thing to note is that the general trend is not consistently increasing IQ scores with each subsequent testing, making unlikely the hypothesis that the large IQ shifts observed for this sample were caused by practice effects.

The largest group was cluster 1 (45% of the sample), with children displaying minimal systematic variation from a slightly rising pattern during childhood. Cluster 2 (11%) showed a sharp decline in IQ between the ages of 4 and 6 years, with a slight recovery in middle childhood, followed by a decrease in adolescence. Cluster 3 (13%) also showed a decline in IQ scores during the preschool years, followed by relatively stable performance from 6 to 14 years and an increase to age 17. Cluster 4 (9%) demonstrated a rapid rise in IQ scores, peaking between 8 and 10 years, followed by a comparably sharp decline. Cluster 5 (6%) showed a steady rise in IQ scores until age 8 or 10 years, much like the pattern for children in cluster 4, but displayed less of a subsequent drop in scores. The data for 16% of the sample followed no consistent pattern.

Note in Figure 16-7 that the children having the highest IQ scores (Cluster 4) also displayed the greatest amount of IQ change. This result is consistent with the findings of other investigators, who have similarly reported that very bright children tend to change more in test scores over time than do children with lower scores (Terman & Merrill, 1937). Along these same lines, it is interesting to observe that for the two groups of children showing the overall highest levels of IQ (clusters 4 and 5), scores increased until 8 or 10 years of age and then declined. Although speculative, one interpretation of this pattern is that at 8 to 10 years there is a transition in cognitive functioning (concrete to formal operations, for example) and that bright concrete operational thinkers, although making the transition to formal operations sooner than less bright children, do not maintain their high level of performance for this qualitatively different style of thought. McCall and his colleagues suggested another possible explanation, that children's intellectual performance during the early school years is under the direct influence of their parents, who emphasize acquiring basic skills in math and reading. As children grow older and develop interests outside the home, parents' influence on their intellectual functioning wanes, and IQ scores drop accordingly (compare with Scarr & McCartney, 1983).

McCall and his colleagues obtained some support for this latter position. As part of the Fels Longitudinal Study, children and their parents were evaluated on a variety of behavioral and attitudinal factors during the project. McCall and his associates examined aspects of parents' child rearing, including their attitudes toward discipline and academic achievement. The children having the highest overall IQ scores and showing the most change in test scores during childhood (clusters 4 and 5) were characterized by having parents who were classified as accelerating, in that they strove to increase their children's mental or motor development. These parents also tended to have clear household policies, were rewarding, and had medium to severe penalties for children's transgressions. The researchers described these parents as providing encouraging and rewarding environments with some structure and enforcement of the rules. These findings are consistent with the researchers' view that the children's increase in IQ scores during the early school years was due to the influence of their academically oriented parents. Children in the two clusters showing decreasing preschool IQ scores (clusters 2 and 3) tended to have parents who were minimally accelerating. Cluster-2 children were the least severely penalized, whereas cluster-3 children were the most severely punished of any group. The parents of children in cluster 1 showed a wide range of attitudes and behaviors.

The study by McCall and his colleagues (1973) indicates that substantial changes in IQ scores occur during childhood for some children. These findings should be considered relative to the very high stability of individual differences reported in the literature. How can rank order of individual differences be so high, yet actual levels of IQ vary so drastically for some children? One clue to this paradox can be found by again examining Figure 16-7. Note that the lines depicting IQ change for the five clusters remain relatively distinct during the 15-year period. After age 7, there are only two points at which any line crosses another. Thus, despite the substantial variability in IQ scores that these lines reflect, the rank order of the various clusters remained essentially unchanged for most testings. Moreover, recall again that the children who showed the greatest amount of change were high-IQ children. Because of the way IQ tests are constructed, a change in IQ score from 130 to 160 is not the same as a 30-point shift from 75

to 105. In the former case, a child's relative rank order changes from approximately the 97th to the 99th+ percentile. In both cases, a child would be brighter than all but a small minority of his of her agemates. In contrast, a change in IQ from 75 to 105 represents a change in relative rank order from about the 5th to the 63rd percentile, a change from borderline mentally retarded to slightly above normal! As the data indicate, changes of the former type are more common than are changes of the latter type, leaving the impression, both statistically and intuitively, that intelligence is relatively stable over time (McCall et al., 1973).

Has Intelligence Changed During This Century?

In discussing the stability and consistency of IQ scores over time, I have necessarily made use of longitudinal data, in which the same people are tested at different points in their development. But a related question about changes in IQ over time can be asked: Has the absolute level of intelligence, as measured by IQ, changed during the past century? If so, are we getting smarter or dumber? As I mentioned in Chapter 15, IQ tests are routinely restandardized. One reason for this is to keep the tests relevant for contemporary populations. Questions that might have been appropriate for people in 1930 can be meaningless for people in the year 2005. But, perhaps more critically, tests are restandardized so that the average remains at or about 100. If people start scoring higher or lower, on average, than 100, the test loses some of its statistical properties that makes it so valuable as an assessment tool.

There are several ways of evaluating whether average IQ scores have changed over historical time. One is to examine the scores of many people who take the same test at different times (for example, in 1960 versus in 1980). Another is to give people today versions of earlier IQ tests, standardized on samples decades before.

What prediction would you make? On the one hand, scores on standardized tests such as the SAT have been reported to decline during the past 40 years, and there has been much lament in the popular press about the "dumbing of America." Perhaps, then, IQ scores have gone down through the decades. On the other hand, more people are receiving both primary and secondary education than in decades past, and public health has improved considerably since the early years of the 20th century, so perhaps we're getting smarter.

The answer is that we're getting smarter, and that this phenomenon is not limited to the United States but is worldwide. The average increase in IQ is about 3 points per decade, which corresponds to more than a full standard deviation since 1940. This phenomenon has been termed the **Flynn effect,** after James Flynn (1987), the first person to describe the phenomenon systematically. (Interestingly, a similar gain in Piagetian formal operational abilities among adolescents has also been observed between the late 1960s to the mid 1990s [Flieller, 1999].)

How can this be explained? One explanation concerns more education for more people, which surely is a contributor to the change. However, the largest changes in performance are for *fluid abilities*, which are supposedly less influenced by education and cultural differences (see Chapter 15). That is, the type of cognitions that have changed the most are those *least* influenced by education and culture. Another explanation relates to better nutrition and health care. More people are healthy, thus fewer people score very low on IQ tests. A third speculation is that life has gotten more complex. We are constantly being bombarded with visual messages from television, but also from photographs and billboards. (These and other possible explanations of the Flynn effect are discussed in Neisser, 1998.)

If these gains reflect true increases in intelligence, they would reflect cultural changes of enormous magnitude. Flynn (1987) thinks otherwise. Surely, some aspects of intellectual functioning have changed. But the absurdity of a 30-point IQ increase since 1900 must cause one to ponder what the IQ test is actually measuring. The IQ test is a good measure of intelligence and permits us to know where a person stands relative to other people in his or her cohort. But the fact that IQ can change so substantially over historical time emphasizes the relative nature of the measure. This does not diminish its usefulness, but it does suggest that an IQ score is not "the" measure of a permanent and stable intelligence.

Summary

Issues concerning the heritability of intelligence are related to perspectives on whether intelligence is domain general or domain specific in nature, with domain-general (g) theorists typically believing that intelligence is primarily biologically based and stable over time. Most current theorists adopt some variant of a *transactional model* to studying the development of intelligence, emphasizing the interactive and bidirectional relations of children and their environments.

Heritability is a statistic that refers to the extent to which differences in a trait within a population are the result of inheritance. One approach to the heritability of intelligence has been to examine *elementary cognitive tasks (ECTs)*. Research has shown that response times on ECTs are related to psychometrically measured g, suggesting to some that these simple, and presumably highly heritable, cognitive operations are the basis for higher-order intelligence.

Familial studies of intelligence, comparing the IQs of people of varying degrees of genetic relations (monozygotic twins, adopted siblings), have been a major tool for assessing the heritability of intelligence. Studies show that the correlations of IQ between groups of people increase as genetic similarity increases. The current estimate of the heritability of IQ is about .50, meaning that, on average, 50% of the difference in IQ scores among people in a population can be attributed to inheritance. The heritability of IQ increases with age, attributed in part to a lessening of the effect of *shared environment* and a greater impact of *nonshared environment* on intelligence.

Early approaches to assessing the effects of experience on intelligence used human *institutionalization studies*, demonstrating that intellectual functioning can be seriously impaired under conditions of physical and social deprivation. Naturalistic studies of parent-child interaction, often assessing the quality of the environment using the *HOME scale*, generally find that mothers who provide their children with a variety of objects to play with and who are responsive have brighter children than do mothers who provide less intellectual stimulation. The effects of a nonstimulating environment tend to be especially detrimental for children with early medical problems. The role of the child in affecting the parent-child relation must also be investigated, with more competent children possibly eliciting more competent parenting. Because of age-related changes in children's abilities, the role of environmental factors in intellectual development is likely to be different at different times in development.

Early environmentally induced retardation can be reversed under certain conditions. Similarly, children from intellectually impoverished, low-income homes who receive cognitively enriched early experience through intensive *compensatory education* display immediate gains in IQ scores. However, follow-up data indicate that many of the gains manifested by these children are lost after the program ends. Once intellectual accomplishments are established, they must be maintained by subsequent environments. If the contexts of early, middle, and later childhood are highly similar, the relative level of intelligence is likely to be comparable across these years. Modifications in environment and experience, however, can foster modifications in intellectual attainments, for better or for worse.

Stability of intelligence is the degree to which the rank order of individual differences remains constant over time. Stability is evaluated by cross-age correlations, with high correlations reflecting stability of individual differences. Evidence from the psychometric literature indicates that the correlation between scores on sensorimotor tests given in infancy and IQ scores later in childhood is low. However, other research has shown significant correlations between measures of infants' preference for novelty and rate of habituation and later IQ scores. The findings suggest that infant intelligence is multifaceted, with some aspects presumably developing in a continuous fashion (*continuity with stability*) and others developing in a discontinuous fashion (*discontinuity-with-instability*).

Stability of individual differences in intelligence during childhood increases with age. These increases are attributed to age-related increases in the similarity of cognitive functioning between children and adults. Despite the high cross-age correlations, however, there are significant changes in level and pattern of IQ over age.

The *Flynn effect* refers to the systematic increase in IQ scores during the 20th century. Although speculative, changes in nutrition, health, and education and to a generally more complex visual environment have been hypothesized to account for this effect.

Note

1. Most of the research in behavior genetics (and in the studies to follow examining the effects of home environment) are not experimental in nature but correlational. Given the reliance on correlations for interpreting the findings of these studies, let me say a few words about correlations as they are used in the remainder of this chapter. Correlations measure the degree to which two factors vary. Correlations range from 1.0 (a perfect positive relation) to –1.0 (a perfect negative relation), with 0 being chance (no systematic relation). For example, we would expect a positive correlation between height and weight. Taller people, on average, are heavier than shorter people. There are many exceptions, so the correlation will not be perfect, but we would expect a correlation in the magnitude of .60 or .70. The correlation between weight and some measure of intelligence, however, should be close to zero. Among a group of adults, we would not expect heavy people to be more or less smart, on average, than light people.

   In familial studies of intelligence, the IQs (or speed of processing) of people of a known genetic relationship are correlated. For example, the IQs of sets of monozygotic twins might be obtained, and the score of each twin paired with his or her mate's. These scores can be contrasted with the IQs of randomly chosen, genetically unrelated people. In the latter case, the IQ of one person is paired at random with the IQ of another, and the correlation is computed. In the former case, a high correlation is expected, because the twins are genetically identical and grew up in the same home at the same time. In fact, the strong genetic position would predict a correlation of 1.0 even for monozygotic twins reared apart. In the case of the unrelated people, the correlation should be 0; knowing the IQ of one unrelated person does not help predict the IQ of another randomly selected person. Thus, the higher the correlation, the greater the relationship. These statistics are then used to infer the degree to which a characteristic is heritable (see later).

Key Terms and Concepts

transactional model
heritability
elementary cognitive tasks (ECTs)
familial studies of intelligence
shared environment
nonshared environment
institutionalization studies
HOME scale
compensatory education programs
stability
continuity with stability
discontinuity with instability
Flynn effect

Suggested Readings

Barnett, W. S. (1995). Long-term effects of early childhood programs on cognitive and school outcomes. *The Future of Children, 5* (No. 3, Winter).   This article presents an examination of the long-term effects of preschool compensatory educational programs and provides suggestions for future research and intervention.

McCall, R. B., & Carriger, M. S. (1993). A meta-analysis of infant habituation and recognition memory performance as predictors of later IQ. *Child Development, 64,* 57–79.   McCall and Carriger present an overview of research and theory relating to the prediction of childhood intelligence from infant measures of information processing (habituation and preference for novelty). McCall and Carriger's perspective emphasizes both possible biological as well as environmental factors in the prediction of childhood IQ from infancy.

Neisser, U., Boodoo, G., Bouchard, T. J., Boykin, A. W., Brody, N., Ceci, S. J., Halpern, D. F., Loehlin, J. C., Perloff, R., Sternberg, R. J., & Urbina, S. (1996). Intelligence: Knowns and unknowns. *American Psychologist, 51,* 77–101.   The authors of this article present the consensus of a task force of the American Psychological Association about what we know and don't know about intelligence. The task force and this paper were in response to the controversy following the publication of *The Bell Curve* by Herrnstein and Murray in 1994. The report provides a brief, even-handed view of many aspects of intelligence, including its definition, heritability, the influence of environment, and group differences.

Plomin, R., & Petrill, S. A. (1997). Genetics and intelligence: What's new? *Intelligence, 24,* 53–77.   Plomin and Petrill present a concise account of "what's new" in the behavioral genetics of intelligence. They take a decidedly developmental perspective, making this article particularly relevant.

Sameroff, A. J., Seifer, R., Baldwin, A., & Baldwin, C. (1993). Stability of intelligence from preschool to adolescence: The influence of social risk factors. *Child Development, 64,* 80–97.   This longitudinal study demonstrates the influence that various risk factors have on children's intelligence and the stability of both intelligence and risk factors over time.

InfoTrac College Edition

For additional readings, explore InfoTrac College Edition, your online library. Go to http://www.infotrac-college.com/wadsworth.

Cognitive Development:
What Changes and How?

Seven "Truths" About Cognitive Development

Diversity of Opinions, But a Single Science

This has been a long book, covering many topics from a variety of perspectives. Are there any general "truths" about cognitive development that can be succinctly stated, as in "Everything you wanted to know about cognitive development in 25 words or less"? Well, 25 words or less would be a bit too brief, but I will try, in 10 pages or less, to list several general "truths" of cognitive development as I see them, based on the information presented in this book. These "truths" are not self-evident, but have been derived from research and substantial thought during the past century. Although I've tried to be objective in presenting research and theory throughout the book (often accompanied with my own interpretations), I will present here *my* perspective of cognitive development rather than the "average opinion" of the field.

Seven "Truths" About Cognitive Development

I have identified seven "truths" that I think can be abstracted from reading the preceding 16 chapters. These truths are actually generalizations that I think are true about cognitive development, and I make no pretense that they have the authority of scientific law. Because the evidence for these "truths" has been presented throughout this book, I provided little or no empirical support for them here. Each of these issues was raised, directly or indirectly, in Chapter 1 and can be viewed as the general themes that ran throughout the book.

When reading the research-packed chapters of a book like this, it is easy to get lost in the details and miss the general themes, or "truths," that the details convey. And, quite honestly, I realize that general themes presented in an introductory chapter often do not have the organizing effect for students they are intended to have. The purpose of this epilogue is to re-introduce those themes; I hope that, after reading the book, these themes will make more sense and help the reader see cognitive development as a dynamic field tied together by some general "truths" that tell a coherent, but still developing, story.

1. Cognitive development proceeds through the dynamic and reciprocal transaction of a child's biological constitution (including genetics) and his or her physical and social environment (including culture).

This, to my mind, is the core assumption underlying development—all development. This is seen in the dynamic systems perspective introduced in Chapter 1, the developmental systems approach described in Chapter 2 on the "Biological Bases of Cognitive Development," and in the transactional model of development, as described in Chapter 16 when I explained how to think about the origins, maintenance, and modification of individual differences in intelligence. And this assumption has been emphasized throughout the book whenever I discussed the origins of developmental or individual differences in some cognitive ability.

This reflects the contemporary view of how nature and nurture interact to yield a particular pattern of development. From this perspective, children come into the world prepared by biology (and evolution) to make sense of the world. This biology, as reflected primarily by the organization of a child's brain, does not simply blossom but, rather, develops as a function of experience. For many phenomena, the brain has evolved to "expect" certain species-typical experiences and will develop in the same way at about the same time for children the world over, in all but extreme circumstances. However, equally important are specific aspects of children's physical and social environments that cause them to develop skills unique to them (or to that culture). Experience does not so much mold the mind as it interacts with genetic predisposition to move a child's thinking in one direction or another.

There are real biological constraints on cognitive development, although the strength of these constraints varies for different cognitive abilities. Some aspects of cognitive development, such as language and theory of mind, are based on cognitive skills fashioned by hundreds of thousands of years of evolution and seem to need only a "normal" human environment to be acquired. Others, such as reading and mathematics beyond simple addition and subtraction, are cultural inventions. We make use of cognitive skills that evolved for other purposes to learn to read and to do algebra, but this is only done in a highly supportive environment.

Despite the differences between cognitive skills such as language and reading (what David Geary referred to as biologically primary and biologically secondary abilities, respectively), all cognitive abilities develop through the continuous and bidirectional interaction between multiple levels of organization, from the genetic, through the nervous system, to the physical and social environment. The direction of causation is not one way. Biology (genetics) does not *cause* someone to acquire language or to excel on algebra word problems; neither does "environment" *cause* someone to understand that others have beliefs and desires different from one's own or to become a proficient reader. The only way to understand cognitive development is to look at the multiple levels of organization and the reciprocal interactions among them. This is why the emphasis on the biological bases of cognitive development, as exemplified by research in behavior genetics (Chapter 16) and developmental cognitive neuroscience (Chapter 2) is compatible with sociocultural perspectives of development (Chapter 3). Each alone provides only a part of the story. But the story only makes sense when the two parts are integrated—not put side by side, but viewed in continuous interaction with one another.

Central to the issue of the transaction of biological and social factors in development is the concept of *innateness*. As I mentioned in the Introduction, many developmental psychologists would prefer this term never be used, for it only makes people think of the false dichotomy of "nature versus nurture." But the concept will not go away, and in Chapter 1, I introduced three ways in which something can be "innate": representational innateness, architectural innateness, and chronotopic innateness. In each case, genetics provides some *constraints* on cognitive processing, making it easier to process certain classes of information (such as language), while limiting how the brain can process other information. Such constraints narrow the range of stimuli and situations

we can make sense of, but in the process make the job of learning about a human world easier for infants and children.

But what is the nature of these constraints? I presented research and theory throughout this book (but especially in Chapter 9 on representation) contrasting representational and architectural constraints (or innateness). Representational constraints refer to representations that are hardwired into the brain. Some have proposed that many accomplishments in infancy, such as knowledge of the physical properties of objects, reflect representational constraints. Interaction with the physical environment is necessary for development to occur, but little in the way of "learning," as traditionally conceived, is done. Researchers from the Chomskian tradition have proposed that language acquisition is governed by representational constraints of this nature (universal grammar). In contrast, architectural constraints refer to ways in which the architecture of the brain is organized at birth. For instance, some neurons are excitatory, others inhibitory; different neurons require different amounts of activation to fire; and they may have many or few connections to other sets of neurons, both within and outside their immediate area. Such constraints limit the way in which information can be processed, not because children are born with innate representations (for example, what a grammar is), but because certain neurons/areas of the brain are only able to process certain types of information and pass it along to certain other areas of the brain. At this level of innateness, the brain is "prepared" to process certain types of information, but subsequent structuring of the brain depends more on the specific experiences that children have than is the case with representational constraints.

From the research I reviewed throughout this book, I am convinced that both representational and architectural constraints (and chronotopic constraints, referring to the timing of development) exist. As of this writing, however, I believe that the constraints for most higher-order forms of cognition are likely of the architectural kind. Much of human cognition and development is universal, confirming a common human nature and possibly representational constraints. But the latest research in infant perception and representation seems to favor the prevalence of architectural constraints (see Chapters 7 and 8), and there is a lively debate among the various camps of psycholinguists about exactly this controversy (see Chapter 11). Not long ago, the debate about the nature of language acquisition seemed to have been settled, and the Chomskians (representational nativists) had won. Today, the arguments have been refined and vigorous discussion is on again.

2. Cognitive development is a constructive process, with children playing an active role in the constructions of their own minds.

We can trace this truth back to Jean Piaget, and, in some form or another, it is something that all cognitive developmentalists believe. Children are not passive creatures, waiting to be shaped by their environments; nor are they "victims" of their genetics, with cognitive abilities simply unfolding. Rather, children act on their environments, making sense of the world as they do. This "sense making" is a constructive process, in that children interpret objects and events in their world in terms of what they already know and thus *create* knowledge as much as they record it. This constructivist perspective is seen explicitly in a variety of theories, including Piaget's, the neo-Piagetian theories of Robbie Case and Kurt Fischer (Chapter 4); theory theories of cognitive development, including Annette Karmiloff-Smith's theory of representational redescription (Chapter 4) and theory of mind (Chapter 9); fuzzy-trace theory (Chapter 5); Katherine Nelson's account of autobiographical memory (Chapter 10); and reading comprehension (Chapter 14), among others. Children use their basic-level abilities to encode, categorize, and retrieve information, but actively organize that information to make sense of it. We are a "sense making" species, and this process is an inherently constructive one.

This does not mean, however, that we must take some postmodernist view that there is no objective reality, that every child constructs a reality that is unique to only him or her, or that it is fruitless to try to understand how another person thinks. There is a real world out there, and our sense organs evolved to perceive that world. Children learn to perceive (construct) the physical world in pretty much the same way regardless of where they are born. Again, our species-typical genome interacts with our species-typical environment to develop a prototypical human mind.

Yet, one's mind is also structured by the particular social environment in which we live. A child, in interaction with the social environment, will construct a mind that is well-suited to the specific cultural context in which he or she lives. For example, children in middle-class America (and elsewhere) "learn" to remember in a narrative style by the prompts their parents give them when recalling recent events (Chapter 10). Other cultures will provide other types of cognitive supports to their children (see Chapter 3), meaning that other types of cognition will develop.

There is much "structure" in cognitive development, from the constraints on what information the brain can process and how that processing can be done, to the organization of the physical and social environment that surrounds children from birth. Children actively construct a mental world within the bounds of these constraints. From this perspective, the child should not be viewed simply as the product of the interaction of genetic and environmental forces, but as an active biological and social agent who, by trying to make sense of the world, shapes his or her own cognitive development.

3. Cognition is multifaceted, and different cognitive skills show different patterns of developmental function and stability of individual differences.

Children get smarter as they get older. But *how* do they get smarter? What is the pattern of change during infancy and childhood, and do all cognitive abilities show essentially the same pattern? Developmental psychologists have spilled much ink debating this issue. Piaget, for example, proposed that development proceeds in a stagelike manner, with qualitative changes in thinking occurring relatively abruptly between stages. Other contemporary theorists, such as Case and Fischer, though loosening considerably the criteria for what constitutes a stage, also find qualitative, discontinuous changes in cognitive development. For example, these theorists, and many others, have observed reorganization in thought between infancy and early childhood, another change between the ages of 5 to 7 years, and again at adolescence. I think the data and interpretations of these and other theorists are compelling, and I have little reason to doubt that cognition, as they measure it, develops in a stagelike fashion. However, cognition is not a single, monolithic phenomenon. Rather, there are multiple aspects and types of cognition, each of which develops. And whereas some display patterns of discontinuities, where new skills and abilities emerge from the accretion or reorganization of earlier skills, others change in a more continuous and quantitative fashion. Children's information processing gets faster, their spans of apprehension increase, they acquire more knowledge, they can keep more irrelevant information out of working memory, and they have a greater number of problem-solving strategies to select from. Many of these abilities can be described as "basic-level processes," and from these simple, often-unconscious processes, significant differences in cognitive functioning emerge.

There is not one developmental function for cognitive development, but many. An important point to remember is that these various types of cognitions can develop independently of one another. That is, although different types of cognitive processing clearly interact, they often show different patterns of developmental function, with some developing in a gradual and continuous nature and others developing in a more abrupt, discontinuous way. And some skills might develop very early whereas related skills are slow to emerge. For example, in Chapter 10, we saw how implicit memory (memory without awareness) is quite good in young children and shows relatively little development in comparison with explicit memory (memory with awareness). Both memory skills can be used by the same child on a single task, and yet these skills can be at very different levels of proficiency. This is not a contradiction, but merely an indication that cognition is not a single "thing" that develops uniformly within a given child—but, rather, a collection of abilities, each having its own developmental schedule.

And the developmental schedule of a cognitive ability will influence patterns of individual differences, specifically the stability of individual differences over time. When should a child's cognitive ability, in comparison with that of his or her peers, remain stable over time, and when should we expect instability? By stability, I am referring to maintaining the same rank order in a cognitive ability over time. The answer one gets to this question depends on the pattern of developmental differences one observes. As we saw in Chapter 16 on intelligence, when the particular type of cognition under study changes in a qualitative way (such as representation from infancy to early childhood), there is little stability. Infants who score high on tests that can be described in Piagetian terms might or might not become high-IQ 3- and 4-year-olds. The reason is that the nature of intelligence measured by these tests changes in a qualitative way over time, and when there is discontinuity of developmental function (as one gets with qualitative, stagelike changes), there is instability of individual differences. However, when what underlies the cognitive tests changes in a quantitative way, such as speed or efficiency of processing, then stability of individual differences can be expected. When we have continuous developmental function (as we typically do when we have quantitative changes) we can expect stability of individual differences.

We thus should expect stability (and perhaps consistency) of cognitive ability when the underlying cognitive abilities are qualitatively the same from one time to another. In a similar way, when the environment that is "responsible" for establishing intellectual competence remains stable over time, one should expect stability of individual differences. Parents who provide an intellectually supportive (or nonsupportive) environment for their toddlers will likely provide similar support as their children get older. In other words, the kind of changes we see in children's thinking over time will vary both as a function of how the underlying (endogenous) cognitive ability changes and as a function of how the supportive social and physical environment (exogenous) changes over time.

4. Cognitive development involves changes in both domain-general and domain-specific mechanisms.

Consistent with the observation that different cognitive skills go though different patterns of change over time, some of those skills cut across a large number of domains and contents (domain general), whereas others are much more specific in nature (domain specific). But how can the two reside side by side? Either there are domain-general skills that permeate all cognitive tasks or there are not. Not necessarily. Some aspects of cognitive development, such as speed of processing or capacity of working memory, influence most complex cognitive tasks. This is seen in Piaget's stages, in resource theories of cognitive development (Chapter 5), and in the concept of g in individual differences in intelligence (Chapter 15). Yet, when we are able to measure these domain-general skills and relate them to cognitive task performance, we find that they account for only a portion of the variance (although often a major portion). The remaining portion of developmental or individual differences can sometimes be attributed to domain-specific abilities. Rather than seeing the two concepts as being antagonistic to one another, they can be seen as interacting. For example, I am convinced that there are domain-specific abilities (modules, if you like) for language acquisition. However, I also think that it's quite likely that language acquisition is facilitated by children's general level of information-processing abilities, for example, by how much information they can hold in working memory at any one time (see Chapter 11).

A domain-general ability does not have to account for everything to be real. And it doesn't have to influence *all* "higher-order" cognitive abilities. It is sufficient that a single cognitive phenomenon (such as speed of processing, for example) has comparable effects on multiple tasks for us to postulate that it is a domain-general ability. This does not negate the very real possibility of multiple cognitive abilities that are relatively independent of one another. Clearly, no single, domain-general ability subsumes all others. But it is also clear (to me, at least) that to postulate that the human mind consists of only a set of independent and "cognitively impenetrable" modules also misses the point. Multiple intelligences exist (whether of the type proposed by Howard Gardner in Chapter 15 or of some other classifications), but they coexist with one or more domain-general abilities. It is difficult at this time to specify the exact nature of this domain-general skill or skills, but patterns of re-sults from studies examining a diverse range of abilities make it clear that it (or they) exists.

5. Cognitive development involves changes in the way information is represented, although children of every age possess a range of ways in which to represent experiences.

What changes in cognitive development? To return to the issues raised in Chapter 1, one aspect of change has to be the way in which children represent their experiences. What are the differences in how children represent the world? We have seen many different perspectives on this. Piaget, and others, proposed that infants lack symbols, such as found in language and apparently used in deferred imitation. Instead, they represent the world as raw sensation and action. Others, however, point to evidence of simple symbolic functioning in even very young infants, as reflected by imitation of facial gestures by newborns and deferred imitation by infants in their first year of life.

But is this truly symbolic reasoning? Do results such as these mean that there are no qualitative changes in symbolic ability from infancy onward? I think not. Actually, it is often impossible to say when an infant or child "has" a specific skill. This is because children will sometimes display an ability when the task is highly simplified and they are provided with substantial support (hints, limited range of choices, social praise and guidance, and so on). What does it mean when we do experiments and find that 4-month-olds demonstrate some behavior consistent with knowledge of the permanence of objects or that 4-year-olds solve syllogisms when nonsense terms are used ("Every banga is purple")? Do 4-month-olds really "have" a concept of object permanence comparable with that of 18-month-olds and do 4-year-olds understand logical reasoning in the same way that adolescents do? No, I don't think so. But experiments like these do indicate that the development of many of these complex skills is not an all-or-nothing phenomenon. We should not be looking simply at "when" children can perform certain tasks but, rather, when they can perform them under certain conditions and what this says about the nature of the underlying representations and the mechanisms for their development.

This is illustrated not only in research in infancy, but also in research looking at representation in young children. Judy DeLoache's research on young children's understanding of models and pictures shows this "now they have it, now they don't" phenomenon, depending on how the task is constructed. Children's understanding of pretense, the appearance/reality distinction, deception, and theory of mind go through similar changes during the preschool years. These important changes affect how children behave in the real world on a daily basis. But the research also shows that how sophisticatedly children behave depends on where we look. For example, a finding I found particularly telling was that of Wendy Clements and Josef Perner (1994), who demonstrated that 3-year-old children failed the false-belief task when explicit knowledge was required (verbalizing the answer) but "passed" the task when only implicit knowledge was used as a measure (spontaneous looking behavior), much as is done in infancy research. So, can 3-year-olds solve false-beliefs tasks or can't they? Based on this research, there is no straightforward answer to the question, and this is true for most similar questions. What does seem apparent, however, is that the modal representational skills (those that children use most of the time) increase in sophistication with age and are used in an increasing number of contexts.

Figure E-1 presents the hypothetical relation between age and general cognitive abilities that I think captures the typical pattern of development for many (but certainly not all) types of cognition, including representation. Most of children's cognitive abilities occur within a relatively narrow range that increases with age. The hatch-marked areas in the figure reflect this. Yet, in a minority of situations, children perform at somewhat higher or somewhat lower levels, depending on the characteristics of the task, their motivation, and the amount of support they receive when performing the task. This perspective is consistent with a sociocultural viewpoint that proposes that there is a zone of proximal development within which instruction from a more experienced partner will benefit children's performance (Chapter 3). But you need not be a Vygotskian to note this de-

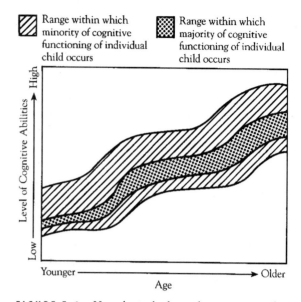

FIGURE E-1 Hypothetical relation between age and range of cognitive abilities. The majority of a child's cognitive functioning occurs within a relatively narrow range. However, a minority of children's cognitive functioning occurs within a substantially broader range. The absolute level of a child's cognitive functioning increases with age.

velopmental pattern. It is found not only in laboratory tasks but also in children's everyday lives.

6. Background knowledge, or knowledge base, has a significant influence on how children think.

One important component of "support" for children when solving almost any cognitive task is the background knowledge they have about the task. Knowledge is represented in children's minds, and the way that knowledge is represented might change in some qualitative ways with age. But strictly *quantitative* changes in knowledge play a substantial role in cognitive development. Some have proposed that, for most cognitive tasks, knowledge is what differentiates younger from older children. What a child knows affects greatly how a child thinks.

I believe that this latter statement is indisputable. Knowledge cannot be separated from processing, and the amount of knowledge a child possesses, how that knowledge is organized, and its ability to be accessed, will largely determine how well a child will solve a problem. From this perspective, children get smarter as they get older because they become more knowledgeable. We have seen the effects of background knowledge repeatedly throughout this book—on speed of processing, memory span (Chapter 5), strategies (Chapter 6), event memory (Chapter 10), language acquisition (Chapter 11), problem solving (Chapter 12), gender identification (Chapter 13), and reading and mathematics (Chapter 14). Increasing knowledge is one of the single most important factors in cognitive development.

However, knowledge itself is not enough. How a child organizes the knowledge he or she has is important to how that knowledge will be used, and although the amount of knowledge a child possesses will affect related cognitive processes, such as memory span and speed of processing, these basic-level abilities will also affect how an elaborated knowledge base is used. Again, we must always be cognizant of the interaction between different levels of organization.

How much a child knows has also been shown to be important in individual differences in cognition, or intelligence (Chapter 15). This is seen most clearly in Sternberg's theory of intelligence, but also in information-processing approaches. When children have detailed knowledge in some domain, their performance on tasks using that knowledge is often high regardless of their level of psychometric intelligence (that is, IQ). On other tasks, however, particularly those in which strategic functioning plays a critical role, knowledge can significantly facilitate performance, but it seems not to eliminate IQ-related differences.

I think the picture of the role of knowledge—long-term memory representations of events and "facts"—is relatively clear for both developmental function and individual differences. Differences in knowledge base account for much of the variance in performance on many cognitive tasks, with older and more intelligent children typically having more knowledge than do younger and less intelligent children. How much children know about a topic will influence how they process information about that topic and how readily they can acquire new information in that domain. But knowledge is not everything, and the effects of knowledge on task performance will vary with the nature of the task. Moreover, one cannot ignore that there are developmental and individual differences in the processes by which knowledge is acquired. These processes, and how they interact with the knowledge that a child possesses, must also be understood to get the full picture of cognitive development.

7. Children's problem solving becomes increasingly strategic with age; children have a broad selection of strategies to choose from, and they become more effective with age in their selection and monitoring of problem-solving strategies.

In one sense, this final "truth" of cognitive development is not very surprising. Quite obviously, children become better problem solvers with age. But what is important here is the *way* in which they become better problem solvers.

The core idea here, presented in Chapter 1, is that children gain greater intentional control over their problem solving as they get older. They become more strategic, in that they use a variety of different cognitive operations in the service of attaining a specific goal. These are "optional" operations, in that they are not required for performing the task, but they are executed presumably to enhance task performance. Even infants show goal-directed, strategic behaviors, although the complexity and effectiveness of these strategies increase with age.

Strategies are influenced by basic-level processes such as speed of processing and working memory, but they are also influenced by higher-order processes, such as metacognition. With age, children not only become more cognizant of the strategies they use but also of their effectiveness. Good metacognition is not always necessary for good cognition, but when problem solving is governed by the use of goal-directed strategies, task performance is considerably enhanced by knowing how well one is doing (that is, monitoring task performance) and assessing which strategies will be most effective and when. Such metacognitive abilities increase with age and are better developed in high-ability (gifted) children than in children of average or below-average intelligence.

Several points about strategic development are worthy of mention here. First, strategies are effortful. They deplete a child's limited mental resources for any given task (regardless of whether those resources are domain general or domain specific in nature). As such, there is a cost to using strategies. Sometimes that cost is expressed in an actual decline (or failure to enhance) task performance, a phenomenon known as a utilization deficiency. Similarly, when young children are taught strategies, which improve their performance, they often resort to their nonstrategic ways when given the opportunity to do so. The extra effort they put into the task is not worth the improved performance they get out of it. So strategies should not be used when they don't need to be, and children seem to realize this when, for example, they have detailed knowledge for a task that make strategies unnecessary.

Second, strategies do not develop in stagelike fashion. Rather, children seem to have multiple strategies available to them for any given task at any given time. This is best exemplified by Robert Siegler's adaptive strategy choice model, discussed in several chapters in this book (especially Chapters 6 and 14). The number of strategies available to a child increases with age, as does the effectiveness of the modal strategy that is used on any particular task.

Third, and closely related to the second point, there is much variability in strategy use. On some tasks, children will use several different strategies simultaneously (or successively) and on others will switch between different strategies on consecutive trials. This variability is important in development and is not just "noise" or "measurement error." For too long, psychologists have looked at only "average" patterns of performance and ignored within-child variability. Differences *between* individual children were often seen as important or interesting, but differences in cognitive functioning *within* a given child during brief periods were rarely seen as anything of great import. These differences are important, however. Qualitative changes, or at least changes in

modal strategies, can occur during times of high instability (high within-child variability), and less drastic changes might be influenced by the diversity of responses children make on a given task over repeated opportunities. Variability of responses creates novelty, and through novel responses to old problems new, and sometimes more effective, solutions are found.

Diversity of Opinions, But a Single Science

There is almost as much diversity among cognitive developmentalists as there is in children's cognitive development. The topics studied by cognitive developmentalists range from microprocesses such as speed of processing and memory span, to macroprocesses such as metacognition and theory of mind. Too often researchers who study one type of cognition (microprocesses) share little interest with those who study others (macroprocesses), and vice versa. For many who study microprocesses, looking at "the big picture" might be philosophically appealing, but scientifically fruitless. For example, although asking questions about metacognition and self-awareness can provide interesting descriptions of consciousness and its development, it leaves us with the feeling that the "ghost in the machine" is still in charge. In contrast, for many who study macroprocesses, to reduce cognitive development much below the level of conscious awareness or "meaning" results in an overabundance of details about children's performance on trivial tasks in unreal situations. Why bother? Similar disagreements exist among developmentalists who view a child's developing intellect to be a function primarily of his or her genetic inheritance with those who view the social environment as playing the predominant role in cognitive development. Disagreement among scientists in a field, particularly a field that still has a long way to go before becoming a mature science, is not a bad thing. In fact, it is a good thing, for disagreement stimulates theory construction and experimentation. What is bad, however, is if the proponents of different viewpoints of cognitive development talk past one another or, worse, ignore one another.

I think there are many "truths" about cognitive development. Both microprocesses and macroprocesses are worthy of study, as are the biological and social origins of development. Realizing that cognitive development occurs on multiple, interacting levels, and that the reality of macroprocesses such as self-awareness does not reduce the significance of microprocesses such as speed of processing (and vice versa), goes a long way to producing an integrated view of a child's developing mind. It is not just that "all these things are interesting and thus should be studied." Rather, cognitive development happens at a variety of levels, and we need to be cognizant of this and the interactions among the various levels to produce a true developmental science.

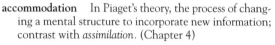

Glossary

accommodation In Piaget's theory, the process of changing a mental structure to incorporate new information; contrast with *assimilation*. (Chapter 4)

accommodation (of the lens) In vision, the process of adjusting the lens of the eye to focus on objects at different distances. (Chapter 7)

active intermodal mapping In Meltzoff and Moore's account of neonatal cognitive abilities, the ability to integrate information from two senses. (Chapter 9)

active rehearsal See *cumulative rehearsal*.

adaptation In Piaget's theory, the process of adjusting one's cognitive structures to meet environmental demands; includes the complementary processes of assimilation and accommodation. (Chapter 4)

adaptive strategy choice model Siegler's model to describe how strategies change over time; the view that multiple strategies exist within a child's cognitive repertoire at any one time, with these strategies competing with one another for use. (Chapters 6, 12, 14)

analogical reasoning Reasoning that involves using something one already knows to help reason about something not known yet. (Chapter 12)

appearance/reality distinction The knowledge that the appearance of an object does not necessarily correspond to its reality. (Chapter 9)

arbitrariness The fact that a word is not inherently related to the concept it represents. (Chapter 11)

architectural constraints (or architectural innateness) Ways in which the architecture of the brain is organized at birth; the type and manner in which information can be processed by the brain. (Chapter 1)

articulatory loop In Baddeley and Hitch's model of the short-term store, a phonological system that stores phonological information. (Chapter 5)

assimilation In Piaget's theory, the process of incorporating information into already existing cognitive structures; contrast with *accommodation*. (Chapter 4)

attention deficit hyperactivity disorder (ADHD) An inability to sustain attention, believed to be caused by deficits in behavioral inhibition. People with ADHD display hyperactivity, impulsiveness, show great difficulty sustaining attention, and are at high risk for academic difficulties. (Chapter 5)

autobiographical memory Personal and long-lasting memories that are the basis for one's personal life history. (Chapter 10)

automatic processes Cognitive processes that require no mental effort (or mental space) for their execution, and are hypothesized (1) to occur without intention and without conscious awareness, (2) not to interfere with the execution of other processes, (3) not to improve with practice, and (4) not to be influenced by individual differences in intelligence, motivation, or education. Contrast with *effortful processes*. (Chapter 5)

axon The long fiber of a neuron that carries messages from that cell to another. (Chapter 2)

basic-level categories Categories composed of objects that are perceptually similar. (Chapter 11)

basic reflexes In Piaget's theory, the first substage of sensorimotor development, in which infants know the world only by their inherited action patterns. (Chapter 4)

behavior genetics The study of genetic effects on behavior and on complex psychological characteristics such as intelligence and personality. (Chapter 2)

belief-desire reasoning The process whereby we explain and predict what people do based on what we understand their desires and beliefs to be. (Chapter 9)

bent-twig model Proposal that biological differences between males and females bias males to have different experiences than females and these differential experiences account for gender differences in spatial abilities. (Chapter 8)

bidirectionality of structure and function (structure ↔ function)   The reciprocal interaction of structure and function to produce a pattern of development. (Chapter 1)

bifoveal fixation   The ability of the foveas of the two eyes to focus on the same object simultaneously, critical to binocular depth perception. (Chapter 8)

biologically primary abilities   Cognitive abilities that have been selected for in evolution, are acquired universally, and children typically have high motivation to perform tasks involving them, such as language. (Chapter 2)

biologically secondary abilities   Cognitive abilities that build upon biologically primary abilities but are principally cultural inventions, and often-tedious repetition and external motivation are necessary for their mastery, such as reading. (Chapter 2)

Black English   A dialect of American English used mostly (but not exclusively) by members of the African American community, which is characterized by some special rules of pronunciation and syntax. (Chapter 11)

bound morphemes   Morphemes that cannot stand alone but are attached to free morphemes, such as the word endings "ed" and "ing" in English. (Chapter 11)

category prototype   An abstract representation of a category, reflecting the central tendency, or "best example," of a category. (Chapters 7, 11)

category typicality   The idea that some items are more representative of the category prototype than others. Items that are highly typical of a category have more features in common with the category prototype than do less typical items. (Chapter 11)

centration   In Piaget's theory, the tendency of preoperational children to attend to one aspect of a situation to the exclusion of others; contrast with *decentration*. (Chapter 4)

cerebral cortex   See *neocortex*.

child-directed speech   The specialized register of speech adults and older children use when talking to infants and young children. (Chapter 11)

chronotopic constraints (or chronotopic innateness)   Neural limitations on the developmental timing of events. (Chapter 1)

classification   The grouping of objects on the basis of some set of characteristics. (Chapter 9)

class inclusion   In Piaget's theory, the knowledge that a subordinate class (for example, dogs) must always be smaller than the superordinate class in which it is contained (for example, animals). (Chapter 4)

cognition   The processes or faculties by which knowledge is acquired and manipulated. (Chapter 1)

cognitive complexity and control (CCC) theory   Proposal that there are age-related changes in the complexity of rule systems that children can represent, and that developmental differences in conscious awareness give children increased control over their behavior and cognition. (Chapter 12)

cognitive self-guidance system   In Vygotsky's theory, the use of private speech to guide problem-solving behavior. (Chapter 11)

collaborative learning   In the theory of cultural learning of Tomasello et al., the third stage of cultural learning, which involves two (or more) individuals, with neither being an authority or expert, and occurs in the process of peer interaction when two people work together to solve a common problem; contrast with imitative learning, instructed learning; see also *cultural learning*. (Chapter 13)

collective monologues   Egocentric exchanges between two or more children with participants talking "with" one another, but not necessarily "to" one another, such that what one child says has little to do with the comments of the other. (Chapter 11)

communicative competence   Mastery of five aspects of language: semantics, syntax, morphology, phonology, and pragmatics. (Chapter 11)

compensation (reciprocity)   In Piaget's theory, a form of reversibility so there exists for any operation another operation that compensates for the effects of the first. (Chapter 4)

compensatory education programs   Programs designed to provide preschool children from low-income homes with the intellectual skills necessary to do well in school. (Chapter 16)

complementary (functional, schematic, thematic) classification   In classification tasks, the grouping together of items from conceptually different categories based on interrelationships in a person's past experiences or in the present situation; contrast with *idiosyncratic, perceptual*, and *conceptual classification*. (Chapter 9)

componential subtheory   In Sternberg's triarchic theory, an information-processing model of intelligence that includes three types of components: knowledge acquisition, performance, and metacomponents. (Chapter 15)

conceptual (similarity, taxonomic, nominal, categorical) classification   In classification tasks, the grouping together of items based on similar category membership or shared function; contrast with *idiosyncratic, perceptual*, and *complementary classification*. (Chapter 9)

concrete operations In Piaget's theory, the third major stage of cognitive development, in which children can decenter their perception, are less egocentric, and can think logically about concrete objects. (Chapter 4)

conditional reasoning A type of formal reasoning in which people make logical inferences whose truth value depends entirely on the supposed truth of given, and possibly arbitrary, premises. (Chapter 12)

conjugate reinforcement procedures Conditioning procedures used in memory research with infants, in which children's behaviors control aspects of a visual display. (Chapter 10)

connectionist models Computer models that simulate aspects of development through repeated activation of associated nodes. (Chapter 5)

conservation In Piaget's theory, the knowledge that the quantity of a substance remains the same despite changes in its form. (Chapter 4)

conservation of number In Piaget's theory, the knowledge that the number of items in an array remains the same despite changes in the form of the array. (Chapter 14)

constructivism The position, central to Piaget's theory, that people interpret objects and events that surround them in terms of what they already know, so that one's current state of knowledge guides processing, substantially influencing how (and what) new information is acquired. (Chapter 4)

context-independent learning Learning of a skill or strategy independent of a specific situation in which the skill will be applied. (Chapter 6)

contextual subtheory In Sternberg's triarchic theory, the idea that intelligence must be viewed in terms of the context in which it occurs. (Chapter 15)

continuity versus discontinuity of development The scientific debate over whether developmental change is gradual (continuous) or relatively abrupt (discontinuous). (Chapter 1)

continuity with stability The expectation and research finding that there is stability of individual differences in cognitive performance over time when the developmental function underlying performance is continuous and quantitative in nature; see also *continuity versus discontinuity of development*; *stability*; contrast with *discontinuity with instability*. (Chapter 16)

convergence (of the eyes) Both eyes looking at the same object. (Chapter 7)

cooperative learning Exercises in which students are encouraged to assist each other so that the less competent members of the team are likely to benefit from the instruction they receive from their more skillful peers, who also benefit by playing the role of teacher. (Chapter 3)

coordination (of the eyes) Both eyes following a moving stimulus in a coordinated fashion. (Chapter 7)

coordination of secondary circular reactions In Piaget's theory, the fourth substage of sensorimotor development, in which infants are able to coordinate two or more behavior patterns to achieve a goal. (Chapter 4)

corpus callosum A thick mass of nerves that connects the right and left hemispheres of the neocortex. (Chapter 2)

creoles Languages that develop when children transform the pidgin of their parents to a grammatically more complex "true" language. (Chapter 11)

critical (sensitive) period The time in development (usually early in life) when a certain skill or ability is most easily acquired. (Chapter 2)

cross-modal matching See *intermodal matching*.

crystallized abilities In Cattell's theory of intelligence, intellectual abilities that develop from cultural context and learning experience; contrast with *fluid abilities*. (Chapter 15)

cued recall In memory research, a task in which a participant recalls information after being given prompts or cues. (Chapter 10)

cultural learning The transmission of acquired information and behavior both within and across generations with a high degree of fidelity. The theory of Tomasello and colleagues proposes three stagelike levels of cultural learning, with each more advanced form being based on a more sophisticated type of perspective taking: imitative learning, instructed learning, and collaborative learning. (Chapter 13)

cultural relativism The idea that intellectual skills critical for survival in one's culture may not be important in another. (Chapter 15)

cumulative (active) rehearsal In memory research, type of rehearsal in which a person repeats the most recently presented word and then rehearses it with as many other different words as possible. (Chapter 6)

decentration In Piaget's theory, the ability of concrete operational children to consider multiple aspects of a stimulus or situation; contrast with *centration*. (Chapter 4)

declarative memory Facts and events stored in the long-term memory, which come in two types: episodic and semantic memory; see also *explicit memory*; contrast with *nondeclarative memory*. (Chapter 5)

declarative metacognition The explicit, conscious, and factual knowledge a person has about the characteristics of the task he or she is performing, one's own weak and strong points with respect to performing the task, and the possible strategies that could be used on the task. (Chapter 6)

decomposition An arithmetic strategy in which children transform the original problem into two or more simpler problems. (Chapter 14)

deep structure In Chomsky's theory, the grammatical organization and meaning that underlies all language; contrast with *surface structure*. (Chapter 11)

deferred imitation Imitation of a modeled act sometime after viewing the behavior. (Chapters 4, 9)

dendrites The numerous fibers of a neuron that receive messages from other neurons. (Chapter 2)

depth perception The ability to discriminate visual patterns denoting depth; see also *bifoveal fixation*. (Chapter 8)

development Predictable changes that occur in structure or function over the life span. (Chapter 1)

developmental cognitive neuroscience The perspective that takes data from a variety of sources—molecular biology, cell biology, artificial intelligence, evolutionary theory, as well as conventional cognitive development—to create a picture of how the mind/brain develops. (Chapter 2)

developmental contextual model See *developmental systems approach*.

developmental function The form that development takes over time. (Chapter 1)

developmental invariance Developmental pattern such that a cognitive skill does not improve steadily over childhood but reaches adult competence early in life and remains stable thereafter. (Chapter 1)

developmental systems approach (developmental contextual model) Perspective that views development as the result of bidirectional interaction between all levels of biological and experiential variables. (Chapters 1, 2)

development quotient tests (DQ) See *DQ*.

deviation IQ Method of constructing IQ scores that compares a child's performance to that of other children the same age; contrast with *mental age*. (Chapter 15)

differential approach See *psychometric approach*.

differentiation (of neurons) The final stage of neuronal development, in which neurons gain in size, produce more dendrites, and extend their axons farther away from the cell body. (Chapter 2)

discontinuity of development See *continuity versus discontinuity of development*.

discontinuity with instability The expectation and research finding that there is instability of individual differences in cognitive performance over time when the developmental function underlying performance is discontinuous and qualitative in nature; see also *continuity versus discontinuity of development*; *stability*; contrast with *continuity with stability*. (Chapter 16)

discrepancy principle The idea that infants are most attentive to slightly novel stimuli. (Chapter 7)

dishabituation The tendency to show renewed interest in a stimulus when some features of it have been changed; contrast with *habituation*. (Chapter 7)

displacement The fact that what one speaks about need not be limited to the immediate context. (Chapter 11)

domain-general abilities General, underlying cognitive abilities that influence performance over a wide range of situations (or domains); contrast with *domain-specific abilities*. (Chapter 1)

domain-specific abilities Cognitive abilities specific to one cognitive domain under control of a specific mind/brain function; contrast with *domain-general abilities*. (Chapter 1)

DQ (development quotient) tests A test of infant abilities, such as the Bayley Scales of Infant Development. (Chapter 15)

dual encoding See *dual representation*.

duality Refers to the fact that language is represented at two levels: *phonology*, the actual sound that a speaker produces, and the underlying abstract, meaning of language, reflected by the *syntax* (rules of putting words together) as well as *semantics* (meaning of those words and concepts). (Chapter 11)

dual orientation See *dual representation*.

dual representation (dual encoding, dual orientation) The ability to represent an object simultaneously as the object itself and as a representation of something else. (Chapter 9)

dynamic systems A set of elements that undergoes change over time as a result of interactions among the elements. Dynamic systems theories propose that developmental differences emerge as a result of the self-organization of lower-level elements. See *self-organization*. (Chapter 1)

dyslexia Reading disability, such that a person has difficulty in learning to read despite an average intelligence. (Chapter 14)

effortful processes Cognitive processes that consume some of the information-processing system's limited capacity and are hypothesized to (1) be available to conscious awareness, (2) interfere with the execution of other processes, (3) improve with practice, and (4) be influenced by individual differences in intelligence, motivation, or education; contrast with *automatic processes*. (Chapter 5)

egocentricity In Piaget's theory, the tendency to interpret objects and events from one's own perspective. (Chapter 4)

egocentric speech See *private speech*.

elementary cognitive tasks (ECTs)   Simple laboratory tests designed to measure participants' response times as they make presumably simple decisions; the low-level, or basic, processes measured by ECTs are presumed to be closely related to physiological functioning and thus primarily under the influence of endogenous (and inherited) factors. (Chapter 16)

emergent literacy   The skills, knowledge, and attitudes that are presumed to be developmental precursors to conventional forms of reading and writing and the environments that support these developments. (Chapter 14)

empiricism   Philosophical perspective that nature provides only species-general learning mechanisms, with cognition arising as a result of experience. (Chapter 1)

emulation   A form of social learning that refers to understanding the goal of a model and engaging in similar behavior to achieve that goal, without necessarily reproducing the exact actions of the model. (Chapter 13)

epigenesis   The emergence of new structures and functions during the course of development. (Chapter 2)

episodic memory   Long-term memory of events or episodes; contrast with *semantic memory*; see also *autobiographical memory*; *event memory*. (Chapter 5)

equilibration   In Piaget's theory, the process by which balance is restored to the cognitive structures through assimilation and accommodation. (Chapter 4)

event memory   Memory for everyday events, a form of episodic memory. (Chapter 10)

evolution   The process of change in gene frequencies in populations over many generations that in time produces new species. (Chapter 2)

evolutionary psychology   The field of study that explains human behavior through evolutionary theory. (Chapter 2)

executive function   The processes involved in regulating attention and in determining what to do with information just gathered or retrieved from long-term memory. (Chapters 5, 9)

experience-dependent processes (or experience-dependent synaptogenesis)   Processes whereby synapses are formed and maintained as a result of the unique experiences of an individual; contrast with *experience-expectant processes*. (Chapter 2)

experience-expectant processes (or experience-expectant synaptogenesis)   Processes whereby synapses are formed and maintained when an organism has species-typical experiences; as a result, functions (such as vision) will develop for all members of a species, given a species-typical environment; contrast with *experience-dependent processes*. (Chapter 2)

experiential subtheory   In Sternberg's triarchic theory, the subtheory concerned with how prior knowledge influences performance, specifically with the individual's ability to deal with novelty and the degree to which processing is automatized. (Chapter 15)

explicit memory   Memories that are available to conscious awareness and can be directly assessed by tests of recall or recognition memory; see also *declarative memory*; contrast with *implicit memory*. (Chapter 5)

externality effect   The tendency of young infants (1-month-olds) to direct their attention primarily to the outside of a figure and to spend little time inspecting internal features. (Chapter 7)

fact retrieval   In information-processing approaches to cognition, the retrieval of a fact directly from long-term memory without using effortful procedures. (Chapter 14)

factor analysis   A statistical technique used to define mental factors by analyzing results from intelligence tests. (Chapter 15)

factors   In psychometric approaches to intelligence, a set of related mental skills (such as verbal or spatial skills) that underlies intellectual functioning. (Chapter 15)

false-belief task   A type of task used in theory-of-mind studies, in which the child must infer that another person does not possess knowledge that he or she possesses (that is, that other person holds a belief that is false). (Chapter 9)

familial studies of intelligence   Studies in which some measure or measures of intelligence among people of a known genetic relationship are correlated; the extent to which performance varies as a function of genetic similarity is used as an indication of the heritability of that measure; see also *heritability*. (Chapter 16)

fast mapping   The ability to learn new words based on very little input. (Chapter 11)

feature-list models (of semantic memory)   Models of semantic memory that hold that language concepts (or words) can be defined in terms of lists of the characteristics or features they possess. (Chapter 11)

field dependence/field independence (FD/FI)   Thinking styles defined by the degree to which a person can perceive parts of a visual field separately from the whole. (Chapter 8)

fixed-action patterns   See *innate releasing mechanisms*.

fluid abilities   In Cattell's theory of intelligence, intellectual abilities that are biologically determined and reflected in tests of memory span and spatial thinking; contrast with *crystallized abilities*. (Chapter 15)

Flynn effect   The systematic increase in IQ scores (about 3 points per decade) observed over the 20th century. (Chapter 16)

forethought In Bandura's social cognitive theory, the ability to anticipate the consequences of one's actions and the actions of others. (Chapter 13)

forgetting The failure to retrieve information that one had retrieved on a previous attempt. (Chapter 10)

formal operations In Piaget's theory, the final stage of cognitive development, in which children are able to apply abstract logical rules. (Chapter 4)

formal reasoning The type of reasoning in which the *form* of an argument, not its semantic content, is crucial. (Chapter 12)

free morphemes Morphemes that can stand alone as a word, such as "dog," "chase," or "happy." (Chapter 11)

free recall In memory research, a task in which a participant recalls information without specific cues or prompts. (Chapter 10)

function In developmental psychology, action related to a structure, such as movement of a muscle, firing of a nerve, or activation of a mental representation; contrast with *structure*; see also *bidirectionality of structure and function*. (Chapter 1)

functional invariants In Piaget's theory, the processes of organization and adaptation that characterize all biological systems and operate throughout the life span. (Chapter 4)

fuzzy traces In fuzzy-trace theory, imprecise memory representations that are more easily accessed, generally require less effort to use, and are less susceptible to interference and forgetting than verbatim traces. (Chapter 5)

fuzzy-trace theory Brainerd and Reyna's theory that proposes that information is encoded on a continuum from verbatim to fuzzy, gistlike traces, and that developmental differences in many aspects of cognition can be attributed to age differences in encoding and in differences in sensitivity to output interference. (Chapter 5)

g (Spearman's g, general intelligence) In psychometric theory, the idea that intelligence can be expressed in terms of a single factor, general intelligence or *g*, first formulated by Spearman in the early 1900s. (Chapter 15)

Gardner's theory of multiple intelligences See *theory of multiple intelligences*.

gender consistency The concept that gender remains the same despite changes in behavior. (Chapter 13)

gender constancy The concept that gender remains the same despite changes in physical appearance, time, and behavior; includes gender identity, gender stability, and gender consistency. (Chapter 13)

gender identification The process of identifying oneself as male or female and adopting the roles and values of that gender. (Chapter 13)

gender identity The ability of children to identify themselves as either boys or girls. (Chapter 13)

gender schema A mentalistic structure consisting of a set of expectations and associations that guide processing with respect to gender. (Chapter 13)

gender script A particular type of gender schema that is a temporally organized event sequence related to gender. (Chapter 13)

gender stability The concept that gender remains the same over time. (Chapter 13)

general genetic law of cultural development The idea that cognition occurs on two planes, first the social, between individuals, and later the psychological, as it is internalized by the child. (Chapter 3)

general intelligence See *g*.

genotype → environment effects In Scarr and McCartney's theory, the proposal that one's genotype (genetic constitution) influences which environments one encounters and the type of experiences one has, or that genes drive experience. Three types of genotype → environment effects are proposed: passive, evocative, and active. (Chapter 2)

goal-directed behavior Means-end problem solving, seen first in the latter part of the first year. (Chapters 4, 12)

"good enough" parents The controversial proposal by Scarr that individual differences in parenting have little consequence for children's development and that "good enough" parents are adequate for proper development. (Chapter 2)

good information processing model A model based on the idea that effective learning is based on a combination of factors, including strategies, the knowledge base, metamemory, capacity, and motivation. (Chapter 6)

guided participation Adult-child interactions, not only during explicit instruction but also during the more routine activities and communication of everyday life; the process and system of involvement of individuals with others as they communicate and engage in shared activities; contrast with *zone of proximal development*; see also *sociocultural perspective*. (Chapter 3)

Guilford's structure-of-the-intellect model See *structure-of-the-intellect model*.

habituation The tendency to decrease responding to a stimulus that has been presented repeatedly; contrast with *dishabituation*. (Chapter 7)

hemispheres The two approximately equal halves of the neocortex. (Chapter 2)

heritability The extent to which differences in any trait within a population can be attributed to inheritance. (Chapter 16)

hierarchical model of cognitive abilities   The model that proposes that intelligence is composed of specific cognitive abilities (for example, verbal, spatial, speed of processing, memory) that are intercorrelated and influenced by a higher-order general intellectual factor, *g*. (Chapter 15)

hierarchization   In Piaget's theory, the fact that each current structure can be traced to earlier, more primitive structures, which were necessary for the attainment of the more advanced structure. (Chapter 4)

HOME scale   The Home Observation for Measurement of the Environment scale, a scale developed by Bradley, Caldwell, and Elardo that provides a detailed analysis of parental behavior and characteristics of the home environment that are hypothesized to be associated with intelligence. (Chapter 16)

homogeneity of cognitive function   Assumption in stage theories that a child's cognition is relatively homogeneous, or even, across different tasks and contexts. (Chapter 1)

hypermnesia   In memory research, the net increase in recall over repeated trials. (Chapter 10)

hypothetico-deductive reasoning   In Piaget's theory, a formal operational ability to think hypothetically. (Chapter 4)

identity   In Piaget's theory, realizing that qualitative properties of an object can change without changing the nature of that object (for example, realizing that a car remains the same despite being painted); contrast with *conservation*. (Chapter 9)

idiosyncratic (fiat equivalence, random) classification   In classification tasks, the grouping together of items without justification related to any physical or conceptual characteristics of the stimuli; contrast with *perceptual, complementary*, and *conceptual classification*. (Chapter 9)

imagery   See *mental imagery*.

imaginary audience   Expression of adolescent egocentrism, with adolescents feeling that they are constantly "on stage," or playing to an imaginary audience. (Chapter 4)

imitative learning   In the theory of cultural learning of Tomasello et al., the first stage of cultural learning, which occurs when the learner internalizes something of the model's behavioral strategies and intentions for executing the behavior; contrast with *instructed learning, collaborative learning*; see also *cultural learning*. (Chapter 13)

implicit memory   Memory without awareness; implicit memory can be assessed only indirectly. (Chapters 5, 10)

incidental learning   Acquiring knowledge about noncentral aspects of a task or situation. (Chapter 6)

individual differences   Differences in patterns of intellectual aptitudes among people of a given age. (Chapter 1)

inductive reasoning   The type of thinking that goes from specific observations to broad generalizations and, in Piaget's theory, is characteristic of formal operational thought. (Chapter 4)

infant-directed speech   The specialized register of speech adults and older children use when talking specifically to infants. (Chapter 11)

infantile amnesia   The inability to remember events from infancy and early childhood. (Chapter 10)

inhibition   The ability to prevent making some cognitive or behavioral response. (Chapter 5)

innate releasing mechanisms   Inherited sets of behaviors elicited by specific sets of stimuli without the need of prior environmental experience. (Chapter 9)

inner speech   In Vygotsky's theory, the covert language used to guide thought. (Chapter 11)

institutionalization studies   Studies of the effects of minimal human contact on children reared in institutions. (Chapter 16)

instructed learning   In the theory of cultural learning of Tomasello et al., the second stage of cultural learning, involving a more accomplished person instructing a less accomplished person; instructed learning requires that children learn about the adult, specifically about the adult's understanding of the task and how that compares with their own understanding; contrast with *imitative learning, collaborative learning*; see also *cultural learning*. (Chapter 13)

intelligence   Acting or thinking in ways that are goal-directed and adaptive. (Chapter 15)

intermodal integration   The coordination or integration of information from two or more senses. (Chapter 7)

intermodal (cross-modal) matching   The ability to recognize an object initially inspected in one modality (touch, for example) via another modality (vision, for example). (Chapter 7)

intersensory integration   See *intermodal integration*.

intrinsic activity   In Piaget's theory, the assumption that babies are born ready to make contact with their environment and that cognitive structures, by their very nature, seek to be active. (Chapter 4)

intuitionism   In fuzzy-trace theory, the tendency of people to prefer to think, reason, and remember by processing inexact, "fuzzy" memory representations rather than working logically from exact, verbatim representations. (Chapter 5)

inversion   See *negation*.

IQ (intelligence quotient) tests Aptitude tests, such as the Stanford-Binet and Wechsler scales, that are intended to measure aspects of intellectual functioning. (Chapter 15)

knowledge base The general background knowledge a person possesses, which influences most cognitive task performance. (Chapters 5, 6)

language A communication system, seemingly unique to humans, that possess the features of arbitrariness, productivity, semanticity, displacement, and duality. (Chapter 11)

language acquisition device (LAD) In Chomsky's theory, the hypothetical construct possessed by all humans at birth enabling them to acquire language. (Chapter 11)

language acquisition support system (LASS) The idea proposed by Bruner that adults and older children have learning devices that interact with children's language acquisition devices (LAD). (Chapter 11)

learning to learn Performance on later tasks is enhanced as a result of performance on earlier tasks, in which a general set of rules or approaches to a problem is acquired. (Chapter 12)

legitimate peripheral participation From sociocultural theory, the idea that children acquire mature, culturally appropriate behaviors simply by observation of skilled members of their community. (Chapter 3)

"less is more" hypothesis Newport's hypothesis that the cognitive limitations of infants and young children may serve to simplify the body of language they process, thus making it easier to learn the complicated syntactical system of any human language. (Chapter 11)

lexical constraints Constraints that facilitate word learning in young children by limiting the possible interpretations that an utterance is likely to have. See *whole-object assumption, taxonomic assumption,* and *mutual exclusivity assumption.* (Chapter 11)

limited capacity The concept that one's information processing ability is restricted (that people can only do so many things at any single time). Metaphors for capacity include mental space, mental energy or effort, and time. (Chapter 5)

local enhancement A form of social learning that occurs when an individual notices activity at a particular location, moves to that location, and, in a process of trial and error, discovers a useful behavior. (Chapter 13)

location memory See *object and location memory.*

long-term store In information-processing approaches to cognition, the large and presumably permanent repository of information in the brain. (Chapter 5)

M-space In Pascual-Leone's theory, a measure of mental capacity, reflecting how many concepts a child can keep in mind simultaneously. (Chapter 5)

mean length of utterance (MLU) A measure of language development defined by the average number of meaningful language units (root words and endings) a child uses at any one time. (Chapter 11)

mediational deficiency The inability of young children to use a strategy even if it is taught to them; contrast with *production deficiency* and *utilization deficiency.* (Chapter 6)

memory span The number of items a person can hold in the short-term store, assessed by testing the number of (usually) unrelated items that can be recalled in exact order. (Chapter 5)

memory strategies See *mnemonics.*

mental age Level of mental functioning (in years) as measured by the number of items passed on an intelligence test, formerly used in determining IQ scores; contrast with *deviation IQ.* (Chapter 15)

mental combinations In Piaget's theory, the final substage of sensorimotor development, a transition between the action-oriented world of the infant and the symbol-oriented world of the child. (Chapter 4)

mental imagery The internal representation of an external event. (Chapter 9)

meta-analysis A statistical technique that allows an investigator to evaluate the magnitude of a significant effect across a large number of studies by providing an estimate of effect size, expressed in terms of how large average differences between targeted groups are across the various studies, taking into consideration the overall amount of variability. (Chapters 8, 14)

meta-attention Knowledge of factors that influence one's attention. (Chapter 6)

metacognition Knowledge about one's own thoughts and the factors that influence thinking. (Chapters 5, 6)

metacommunication Knowledge of the adequacy of one's own communication abilities. (Chapter 11)

metamemory Knowledge of one's own memory abilities and the factors that influence memory. (Chapter 6)

microgenetic development In Vygotsky's sociocultural theory, changes that occur over relatively brief periods of time, in seconds, minutes, or days, as opposed to larger-scale changes, as conventionally studied in ontogenetic development. (Chapter 3)

microgenetic method A research methodology that looks at developmental change within a single set of individuals over relatively brief periods (days or weeks, usually). (Chapter 6)

migration (of neurons) The movement of neurons to their permanent positions in the brain, most of which is completed during the prenatal period. (Chapter 2)

mimicry A form of social learning that involves the duplication of a behavior without any understanding of the goal of that behavior. (Chapter 13)

mindblindness A deficit in theory of mind, characteristic of people with autism, in which a person cannot read the minds of others. (Chapter 9)

min strategy An arithmetic strategy in which children faced with an addition problem start with the largest addend and count up from there. (Chapter 14)

mnemonics (memory strategies) Effortful techniques used to improve memory, including rehearsal, organization, and elaboration. (Chapter 6)

modularity Concept that certain areas of the brain are dedicated to performing specific cognitive tasks. (Chapter 1)

morphemes Meaningful language units. (Chapter 11)

morphology In the study of language development, the knowledge of word formation. (Chapter 11)

motherese See *child-directed speech.*

multiple intelligences See *theory of multiple intelligences.*

mutual exclusivity assumption A type of lexical constraint in which children believe that different words refer to different things. (Chapter 11)

myelin A sheet of fatty substance that develops around the neurons to promote faster transmission of electrical signals through the nervous system. (Chapter 2)

myelination The development of myelin around neurons, which proceeds at different rates in different areas of the brain. (Chapter 2)

nativism Philosophical perspective that human intellectual abilities are innate. (Chapter 1)

natural language categories Language terms that include a wide range of exemplars; most natural language categories are hierarchical in nature (for example, animal; canine; dog). (Chapter 11)

natural selection In Darwin's theory of evolution, the idea that more individuals are produced in a generation than can usually survive, and that variations in individuals make some members of a species more fit than others and thus more likely to survive to reproduce; according to Darwin, natural selection is the primary mechanism for evolution. (Chapter 2)

negation (inversion) A form of Piagetian reversibility such that any operation can always be negated, or inverted. (Chapter 4)

neocortex The outer layer of the brain, which gives humans their highly developed intelligence. (Chapter 2)

neonatal imitation The ability of newborns to reproduce some behavior, such as a facial expression, that they have seen in others. (Chapter 9)

neonativism (structural constraint theory) The idea that much cognitive knowledge, such as object concept and certain aspects of language, is innate, requiring little in the way of specific experiences to be expressed, and that there are biological constraints, in that the mind/brain is designed to process certain types of information in certain ways. (Chapter 4)

neural Darwinism Edelman's theory that groups of neurons are in constant competition with one another, each attempting to recruit adjacent neurons to their group and thus perform a particular function. (Chapter 2)

neuroimaging techniques New technologies that permit imaging of brain activities, including high-density event-related potentials, positron emission tomography (PET), and functional magnetic resonance imaging (fMRI). (Chapter 2)

neuron Nervous system cell through which electrical and chemical signals are transmitted. (Chapter 2)

neurotransmitters Chemicals in synapses that serve to transmit electrical impulses between neurons. (Chapter 2)

nondeclarative, (or procedural) memory Knowledge in the long-term store of procedures that are unconscious; see also *implicit memory*; contrast with *declarative memory*. (Chapter 5)

nonshared environment Aspects of an individual's environment that are unique to that individual, not shared by a sibling, for instance. (Chapter 16)

numerosity The ability to determine quickly the number of items in a set without counting. (Chapter 14)

object and location memory A form of spatial cognition that involves locating and remembering objects in arrays. Unlike other forms of spatial cognition, object and location memory tends to be better in females than in males and shows relatively little improvement over development. (Chapter 8)

object constancy The knowledge that an object remains the same despite changes in the how it is viewed. (Chapter 8)

object permanence The knowledge that objects have an existence in time and space independent of one's own perception or action on those objects. (Chapters 4, 8)

observational learning The ability to learn about the world simply by watching, central to Bandura's social cognitive theory; according to Bandura, observational learning includes four subprocesses: attentional processes, retention processes, production processes, and motivational processes. (Chapter 13)

ontogenetic adaptations Behaviors that play a specific role in survival for an individual at one time only and then disappear when they are no longer needed. (Chapter 9)

ontogenetic development   Development of the individual over his or her lifetime. (Chapter 3)

operating space   In Case's theory of working memory, the mental space that can be allocated to the execution of intellectual operations. (Chapter 5)

operations   In Piaget's theory, particular types of cognitive schemes that are mental (that is, require symbols), derive from action, exist in organized systems (structures of the whole), and follow a set of logical rules, most importantly that of reversibility. (Chapter 4)

optimal level   In Fischer's theory, the maximum level of complexity of a skill that the individual can control. (Chapter 4)

ordinality   A basic understanding of *more than* and *less than* relationships. (Chapter 14)

organization (in memory research)   The structure discovered or imposed upon a set of items that is used to guide memory performance. (Chapter 6)

organization (in Piaget's theory)   The idea that every intellectual operation is related to all other acts of intelligence. (Chapter 4)

output interference   In fuzzy-trace theory, response competition in the form of scheduling effects and feedback effects, produced by the act of making responses. (Chapter 5)

overextensions   In the study of language development, the stretching of a familiar word beyond its correct meaning; for example, calling all four-legged mammals "doggie." (Chapter 11)

overregularization   In the study of language development, the tendency to apply rules to words when they are not appropriate, for example, runned, foots, mices. (Chapter 11)

passive rehearsal   Style of rehearsing in which a person includes few (usually one) unique items per rehearsal set; contrast with *cumulative rehearsal*. (Chapter 6)

perceptual centration   See *centration*.

perceptual classification   In classification tasks, the grouping together of items on the basis of perceptual characteristics; contrast with *idiosyncratic*, *complementary*, and *conceptual classification*. (Chapter 9)

perceptual decentration   See *decentration*.

personal fable   A belief in one's uniqueness and invulnerability, which is an expression of adolescent egocentrism. (Chapter 4)

phonemes   Individual sounds that are used to make up words. (Chapter 7)

phonemic awareness   The knowledge that words consist of separable sounds; contrast with *phonological recoding*. (Chapter 14)

phonics   Reading instruction method based on learning letter-sound correspondence; see also *phonological recoding*. (Chapter 14)

phonological recoding   Reading skills used to translate written symbols into sounds and words; contrast with *phonemic awareness*. (Chapter 14)

phonology   In language acquisition, the knowledge of how words are pronounced. (Chapter 11)

phylogenetic development   Development over evolutionary time. (Chapter 3)

pidgins   Structurally simple communication systems that arise when people who share no common language come into constant contact. (Chapter 11)

plasticity (of cognition and behavior)   The extent to which behavior can be changed. (Chapter 1)

positive manifold   In psychometric approaches to intelligence, the high correlations among scores on sets of cognitive tests that have little in common with one another in terms of content or types of strategies used. (Chapter 15)

pragmatics   In the study of language development, knowledge about how language can be adjusted to fit different circumstances. (Chapter 11)

preference-for-novelty paradigms   Tasks in which an infant's preference, usually measured in looking time, for a novel as opposed to a familiar stimulus is used as an indication of memory for the familiar stimulus. (Chapter 10)

preoperations   In Piaget's theory, the second major stage of cognitive development (approximately ages 2 to 7 years), characterized by prelogical, intuitive thought. (Chapter 4)

primary circular reactions   In Piaget's theory, the second substage of sensorimotor development, in which infants extend their reflexes to acquire new patterns of behavior that were not present at birth. (Chapter 4)

primary visual system   The phylogenetically more recent visual system, functioning poorly in newborns; processing of visual information is done by the fovea, permitting careful analysis of stimulus properties; contrast with *secondary visual system*. (Chapter 7)

private (egocentric) speech   Children's speech apparently for self and not directed to others. (Chapter 11)

problem solving   Process in which someone has a specific goal in mind that cannot be attained immediately because of the presence of one or more obstacles; problem solving involves a goal, obstacles to that goal, strategies for overcoming the obstacles, and an evaluation of the results. (Chapter 12)

procedural memory   See *nondeclarative memory*.

procedural metacognition   The knowledge about when strategies are necessary as well as monitoring how well one is performing on a task. (Chapter 6)

production deficiency   Children's tendency not to use spontaneously a strategy that they are capable of using when instructed; contrast with *mediational deficiency* and *utilization deficiency*. (Chapter 6)

productive language   The language a child can actually produce, or speak; contrast with *receptive language*. (Chapter 11)

productivity   The fact that speakers can combine a finite set of words to produce an infinite set of sentences. (Chapter 11)

proliferation (of neurons)   The process of nerve-cell division by mitosis. (Chapter 2)

propositional logic   A form of symbolic logic that involves two or more factors (conventionally, P and Q), with each factor having two possible values (for instance, true or false), used by Piaget and Inhelder to describe formal operational thought. (Chapter 12)

prosody   The intonational and stress pattern and the tempo of an utterance. (Chapter 11)

psychometric (differential) approach   The theory that intelligence can be described in terms of mental factors and that tests can be constructed that reveal individual differences in the factors underlying mental performance. (Chapter 15)

qualitative versus quantitative differences   The degree to which cognitive development reflects changes in type or kind (qualitative) versus amount or rate (quantitative). (Chapter 1)

reading comprehension   The ability to relate the meaning of individual words and sentences to abstract the broader meaning of a written text. (Chapter 14)

reasoning   A particular type of problem solving that involves making inferences. (Chapter 12)

receptive language   The language that a child can understand; contrast with *productive language*. (Chapter 11)

reciprocal determinism   In Bandura's theory, the belief that children have as much of an effect on their environment as their environment has on them. (Chapter 13)

reciprocity   See *compensation*.

recognition   Process in which a person remembers a familiar stimulus upon being presented with it again; contrast with *free recall*. (Chapter 10)

reduction to essence rule   In fuzzy-trace theory, the assumption that people of all ages are biased to extract the gist from a message. (Chapter 5)

reflective abstraction   In Piaget's theory, the ability to reflect upon knowledge one already possesses, and without the need of additional information from the external environment, to arrive at new knowledge; characteristic of adolescent thought. (Chapter 4)

rehearsal   A memory strategy in which target information is repeated; see also *passive rehearsal, cumulative rehearsal*. (Chapter 6)

relational mapping   The application of what one knows about one set of elements (the relation of A to B) to relations about different elements (the relation of C to D). (Chapter 12)

relational primacy hypothesis   The hypothesis that analogical reasoning is available early in infancy. (Chapter 12)

relational shift   In analogical reasoning, the proposal that there is in development a shift from focusing on perceptual similarity to relational similarity to solve problems. (Chapter 12)

representation   The mental encoding of information. (Chapters 1, 9)

representational change   In false-belief tasks, children's false memory for their initial belief. (Chapter 9)

representational constraints (or representational innateness)   Representations that are hard-wired into the brain so that some types of "knowledge" are innate. (Chapter 1)

representational insight   The knowledge that an entity can stand for something other than itself. (Chapter 9)

representational redescription   In Karmiloff-Smith's theory, processes whereby the mind redescribes (re-represents) its own representations. (Chapter 4)

resistance to interference   The ability to ignore irrelevant information so that it does not impede task performance; its inverse is interference sensitivity. (Chapter 5)

reversibility   In Piaget's theory, the knowledge that an operation can be reversed, characteristic of the concrete operational period; see also *compensation, negation*. (Chapter 4)

rule-assessment approach   An approach that explains cognitive development in terms of the acquisition of increasingly powerful rules for solving problems. (Chapter 12)

scaffolding   An expert, when instructing a novice, responding contingently to the novice's responses in a learning situation, so that the novice gradually increases his or her understanding of a problem. (Chapter 3)

schema   An abstract representation of an object or event. (Chapter 7)

schematic representation   The representation of objects in terms of real or potential interactions with other objects. (Chapter 9)

schemes   See *structures*.

scientific reasoning   A type of reasoning that involves the generation of hypotheses and the systematic testing of those hypotheses. (Chapter 12)

scripts   A form of schematic organization, with real-world events organized in terms of temporal and causal relations between component acts. (Chapters 10, 11)

secondary circular reactions   In Piaget's theory, the third substage of sensorimotor development, in which infants first learn to control events in the external world. (Chapter 4)

secondary visual system   The phylogenetically older visual system, functioning relatively well in the newborn; processing is done primarily in the visual periphery (that is, nonfoveally), and orients the infant toward a stimulus, providing information concerning where a stimulus is; contrast with *primary visual system*. (Chapter 7)

selectionist theories   Any theory that proposes that a large number of brain cells/cognitive operations/behaviors are generated and only those "successful" ones are selected by the immediate environment and survive; whereas, nonselected cells/cognitive operations/behaviors decrease infrequency or die. (Chapter 2)

selective attention   Concentration on chosen stimuli without distraction by nontarget stimuli. (Chapter 6)

selective cell death   Early developmental process in which neurons that are not activated by sensory or motor experience die. (Chapter 2)

self-concept   The way a person defines himself or herself. (Chapter 13)

self-efficacy   The belief that one can influence one's own thoughts and behavior. (Chapter 13)

self-organization   In dynamic systems theories, the process whereby patterns emerge from interactions of the components of a complex system without explicit instructions either in the organism itself or from the environment. (Chapter 1)

self-reflection   In Bandura's social cognitive theory, the ability to analyze one's thoughts and actions. (Chapter 13)

self-regulation   The process of adopting standards of acceptable behavior, including aspirational standards (hoped-for levels of accomplishment) as well as social and moral standards. (Chapter 13)

semanticity   The fact that language can represent events, ideas, actions, and objects symbolically. (Chapter 11)

semantic memory   Long-term memory representation of definitions and relations among language terms; contrast with *episodic memory*. (Chapter 5)

semantics   In language acquisition, knowledge of the meaning of words and sentences. (Chapter 11)

semiotic function   See *symbolic function*.

sensorimotor stage   In Piaget's (and Fischer's) theory, the first major stage of cognitive development (birth to approximately 2 years), in which children understand their world through sensory and motor experiences. (Chapter 4)

sensory registers   Memory stores for each sensory modality (touch, vision, hearing) that presumably can hold large quantities of information but only for very brief periods (milliseconds). (Chapter 5)

shared environment   An environment shared by different family members. (Chapter 16)

short-term store (primary memory, contents of consciousness)   Memory store that can hold a limited amount of information for a matter of seconds; cognitive operations are executed in the short-term store and information can be maintained indefinitely in the short-term store through operations such as rehearsal; see also *working memory*. (Chapter 5)

slot-filler categories   Groups of items that could successfully complete a script (for example, juice and cocoa for a breakfast script). (Chapter 11)

social cognition   Cognition about social relationships and social phenomena. (Chapter 13)

social cognitive theory   Bandura's theory of how individuals operate cognitively on their social experiences and how these cognitive operations influence behavior and development. (Chapter 13)

social information processing   As exemplified by Dodge's theory, the view that social information must be encoded, compared with other pertinent information, and retrieved so that social interactions run smoothly. (Chapter 13)

social learning   The acquisition of social information and behavior; situations in which one individual comes to behave similarly to others. (Chapter 13)

social learning theory   An earlier version of Bandura's social cognitive theory. (Chapter 13)

sociocultural perspective   A perspective of cognitive development that emphasizes that development is guided by adults interacting with children, with the cultural context determining to a large extent how, where, and when these interactions take place; see also *guided participation*; *zone of proximal development*. (Chapter 3)

sociohistorical development   Changes that have occurred in one's culture and the values, norms, and technologies such a history has generated. (Chapter 3)

source monitoring   The awareness of the origins of one's memories, knowledge, or beliefs. (Chapters 9, 10)

span of apprehension The number of items that people can keep in mind at any one time, or the amount of information that people can attend to at a single time. (Chapter 5)

spatial cognition The type of cognition that involves processing visual information in terms of spatial relationships, including spatial orientation, spatial visualization, and object and location memory. (Chapter 8)

spatial orientation How people understand the placement of objects in space with themselves as the reference point. (Chapter 8)

spatial visualization An aspect of spatial cognition that involves the mental manipulations of visual stimuli, such as performing mental rotation or solving embedded-figures problems. (Chapter 8)

Spearman's g See *g* (general intelligence).

speech register A distinct style of speaking, which is used only in specific contexts (for example, when talking to children; when talking in school). (Chapter 11)

speed of processing How quickly any cognitive operation can be executed; hypothesized to be a measure of limited capacity and related to performance on many cognitive tasks. (Chapter 5)

stability In developmental psychology, the degree to which a person maintains the same rank order over time in comparison with peers for a particular characteristic. (Chapters 1, 16)

stages Relatively discrete periods of time in which functioning is qualitatively different from functioning at other periods. (Chapter 1)

Stanford-Binet An individually administered IQ test. (Chapter 15)

Sternberg's triarchic theory See *triarchic theory*.

storage space In Case's theory of working memory, the mental space that an individual has available for storing information. (Chapter 5)

strategies Goal-directed and deliberately implemented mental operations used to facilitate task performance; see also *mnemonics*. (Chapters 1, 6)

strategy change The number of trial-by-trial changes people make in the strategies they use. (Chapter 6)

strategy diversity The number of different strategies a person uses on a task. (Chapter 6)

structural constraint theory See *neonativism*.

structure In developmental psychology, a substrate of the organism that develops, such as muscle, nervous tissue, or mental knowledge; contrast with *function*; see *bidirectionality of structure and function*. (Chapter 1)

structure-of-the-intellect model A theory of intelligence derived from factor analysis, postulating 180 factors. (Chapter 15)

structures (schemes) In Piaget's theory, the enduring knowledge base by which children interpret their world. (Chapter 4)

structures of the whole (structures d'ensemble) In Piaget's theory, the proposal that operations exist in an organized system, with all operations being integrated with all others. (Chapter 4)

subitizing Quantifying small numbers of items without conscious counting. (Chapter 9)

sum strategy A simple addition strategy used by young children that involves counting together the two addends of a problem. (Chapters 6, 14)

surface structure In Chomsky's theory, the actual words of a sentence, derived from the deep structure. (Chapter 11)

symbolic (semiotic) function In Piaget's theory, the underlying symbolic nature of cognition, occurring toward the end of the sensorimotor period and expressed via deferred imitation, language, symbolic play, and mental imagery. (Chapter 9)

symbolic play Pretending; in Piaget's theory, an expression of the symbolic function. (Chapters 3, 9)

symbolization In Bandura's social cognitive theory, the ability to think about one's social behavior in terms of words and images. (Chapter 13)

synapse The tiny space between the dendrite of one neuron and the axon of another through which chemical messages are passed. (Chapter 2)

synaptogenesis The process of synapse formation. (Chapter 2)

syntax In language acquisition, the knowledge of how words are put together to form grammatical sentences. (Chapter 11)

taxonomic assumption A type of lexical constraint in which children assume that words refer to things that are similar. (Chapter 11)

telegraphic speech Children's economical use of words, including only high-information words that are most important in conveying meaning. (Chapter 11)

tertiary circular reactions In Piaget's theory, the fifth substage of sensorimotor development, in which infants invent slightly new behaviors to achieve their goals. (Chapter 4)

theory of mind A person's concepts of mental activity; used to refer to how children conceptualize mental activity and how they attribute intention to and predict the behavior of others; see also *belief-desire reasoning*. (Chapter 9)

theory of multiple intelligences Gardner's theory postulating eight components, or modules, of intelligence (1) linguistic, (2) logical-mathematical, (3) musical,

(4) spatial, (5) bodily-kinesthetic, (6) interpersonal, (7) intrapersonal, and (8) naturalistic. (Chapter 15)

theory theories   Theories of cognitive development that combine neo-nativism and constructivism, proposing that cognitive development progresses by children generating, testing, and changing theories about the physical and social world. (Chapter 4)

tools of intellectual adaptation   Vygotsky's term for methods of thinking and problem-solving strategies that children internalize from their interactions with more competent members of society. (Chapter 3)

total processing space   In Case's theory of working memory, the sum of storage and operating space, or the total mental space in working memory a person has available for the execution of a task. (Chapter 5)

training studies   Experiments in which children's cognitive task performance is assessed after they are instructed in the use of a strategy. (Chapter 6)

transactional model   A framework that views development as the continuous and bidirectional interchange between an active organism with a unique biological constitution, and a changing environment. (Chapter 16)

triarchic theory   Sternberg's theory that describes intelligence in terms of three subtheories: contextual, experiential, and componential. (Chapter 15)

underextensions   Incorrectly restricting the use of a term (for example, believing that only one's pet, Fido, deserves the label "dog"). (Chapter 11)

universal grammar   In nativist theories of language acquisition, the innate grammar that characterizes all human languages. (Chapter 11)

utilization deficiency   The inability of children to benefit from strategies they are able to implement; contrast with *mediational deficiency* and *production deficiency*. (Chapter 6)

verbatim traces   In fuzzy-trace theory, precise, literal memory representations that are less easily accessed, generally require more effort to use, and are more susceptible to interference and forgetting than fuzzy traces. (Chapter 5)

vicarious learning   In Bandura's social cognitive theory, learning without the need to receive specific reinforcement for one's behavior; rather, learning is achieved by observing others. (Chapter 13)

violation-of-expectation method   Based on habituation/dishabituation procedures, techniques in which increases in infants' looking time are interpreted as reflecting a violation of an expected outcome. (Chapter 8)

visual preference paradigm   In research with infants, observing the amount of time infants spend looking at different visual stimuli to determine which one they prefer (that is, look at more often); such preferences indicate an ability to discriminate between stimuli. (Chapter 7)

Wechsler scales   Individually administered IQ tests, including the WPPSI-R, the WISC-R, the WISC-III, and the WAIS-R. (Chapter 15)

whole-language approach   A top-down approach to teaching reading that emphasizes the readers' active construction of meaning; often excludes the use of phonics. (Chapter 14)

whole-object assumption   A type of lexical constraint in which children assume when hearing a word that it refers to the whole object and not to some part of that object. (Chapter 11)

wishful thinking   A characteristic of preschool thought such that children often do not differentiate between their wishes and their expectations. (Chapter 13)

word spurt   The rapid increase in word (mostly noun) learning, occurring at about 18 months of age. (Chapter 11)

working memory   The capacity to store and transform information being held in the short-term system. See *short-term store*. (Chapter 5)

zone of proximal development   In Vygotsky's theory, the difference between a child's actual level of ability and the level of ability that he or she can achieve when working under the guidance of an instructor; contrast with *guided participation*; see *sociocultural perspective*. (Chapter 3)

ABRAVANEL, E., & GINGOLD, H. (1985). Learning via observation during the second year of life. *Developmental Psychology, 21*, 614–623.

ABRAVANEL, E., & SIGAFOOS, A. D. (1984). Explaining the presence of imitation during early infancy. *Child Development, 55*, 381–392.

ACKERMAN, B. P. (1986). Retrieval search for category and thematic information in memory by children and adults. *Journal of Experimental Child Psychology, 42*, 355–377.

ACKERMAN, B. P. (1996). Induction of a memory retrieval strategy by young children. *Journal of Experimental Child Psychology, 62*, 243–271.

ACKIL, J. K., & ZARAGOZA, M. S. (1995). Developmental differences in eyewitness suggestibility and memory for source. *Journal of Experimental Child Psychology, 60*, 57–83.

ADAMS, J. W., & HITCH, G. J. (1997). Working memory and children's mental addition. *Journal of Experimental Child Psychology, 67*, 21–38.

ADAMS, M. J., TREIMAN, R., & PRESSLEY, M. (1998). Reading, writing, and literacy. In I. E. Sigel & K. A. Renninger (Vol. Eds.), *Child psychology in practice*, Vol. 4. In W. Damon (Gen. Ed.), *Handbook of child psychology*. New York: Wiley.

ADAMS, R. J., & COURAGE, M. L. (1998). Human newborn color vision: Measurement with chromatic stimuli varying in excitation purity. *Journal of Experimental Child Psychology, 68*, 22–34.

ADAMS, R. J., COURAGE, M. L., & MERCER, M. E. (1994). Systematic measurement of human neonatal color vision. *Vision Research, 34*, 1691–1701.

ADEY, P. S., & SHAYER, M. (1992). Accelerating the development of formal thinking in middle and high school students: II. Postproject effects on science achievement. *Journal of Research in Science Teaching, 29*, 81–92.

ADLER, S. (1990). Multicultural clients: Implications for the SLP. *Language, Speech, and Hearing in the Schools, 21*, 135–139.

AGUIAR, A., & BAILLARGEON, R. (1998). Eight-and-a-half-month-old infants' reasoning about containment events. *Child Development, 69*, 636–653.

AHMED, A., & RUFFMAN, T. (1998). Why do infants make A not B errors in a search task, yet show memory for the location of hidden objects in a nonsearch task? *Developmental Psychology, 34*, 441–453.

AINSWORTH, M. D. S., BLEHAR, M. C., WATERS, E., & WALL, S. (1978). *Patterns of attachment: A psychological study of the strange situation*. Hillsdale, NJ: Erlbaum.

ALDRIDGE, M. A., STILLMAN, R. D., & BOWER, T. G. R. (2001). Newborn categorization of vowel-like sounds. *Developmental Science, 4*, 220–232.

ALEXANDER, J. M., & SCHWANENFLUGEL, P. J. (1996). Development of metacognitive concepts about thinking in gifted and nongifted children: Recent research. *Learning and Individual Differences, 8*, 305–325.

ALEXANDER, J. M., SCHWANENFLUGEL, P. J., & CARR, M. (1995). Development of metacognition in gifted children: Directions for future research. *Developmental Review, 15*, 1–37.

ALEXANDER, R. D. (1989). Evolution of the human psyche. In P. Mellers & C. Stringer (Eds.), *The human revolution: Behavioural and biological perspectives on the origins of modern humans*. Princeton, NJ: Princeton University Press.

ALIBALI, M. W. (1999). How children change their minds: Strategy change can be gradual or abrupt. *Developmental Psychology, 35*, 127–145.

ALIBALI, M. W., & GOLDIN-MEADOW, S. (1993). Gesture-speech mismatch and mechanisms of learning: What the hands reveal about a child's state of mind. *Cognitive Psychology, 25*, 468–573.

ALLEN, D., BANKS, M. S., & SCHEFRIN, B. (1988). Chromatic discrimination in human infants. *Investigative Ophthalmology and Visual Science, 29* (Suppl.), 25.

ALLEN, G. L., KIRASIC, K. C., & BEARD, R. L. (1989). Children's expression of spatial knowledge. *Journal of Experimental Child Psychology, 48,* 114–130.

ALS, H. (1995). The preterm infant: A model for the study of fetal brain expectation. In J-P. Lecanuet, W. Fifer, N. Krasnegor, & W. Smotherman (Eds.), *Fetal development: A psychobiological perspective.* Hillsdale, NJ: Erlbaum.

AMSEL, E., GOODMAN, G., SAVOIE, D., & CLARK, M. (1996). The development of reasoning about causal and noncausal influence on levers. *Child Development, 67,* 1624–1646.

ANDERSON, D. R., & LORCH, E. P. (1983). Looking at television: Action or reaction? In J. Bryant & D. R. Anderson (Eds.), *Children's understanding of television: Research on attention and comprehension.* New York: Academic.

ANDERSON, R. C., HIEBERT, E. H., SCOTT, J. A., & WILKINSON, I. A. G. (1984). *Becoming a nation of readers: The report of the Commission on Reading.* Washington, DC: U.S. Department of Education.

ANGLIN, J. M. (1970). *The growth of word meaning.* Cambridge, MA: MIT Press.

ANGLIN, J. M. (1977). *Word, object, and conceptual development.* New York: Norton.

ANISFELD, M. (1991). Neonatal imitation: A review. *Developmental Review, 11,* 60–97.

ANISFELD, M., TURKEWITZ, G., ROSE, S. A., ROSENBERG, F. R., SHEIBER, F. J., COUTURIER-FAGAN, D. A., GER, J. S., & SOMMER, I. (2001). No compelling evidence that newborns imitate oral gestures. *Infancy, 2,* 111–122.

ANNETT, M. (1973). Laterality of childhood hemiplegia and the growth of speech and intelligence. *Cortex, 9,* 4–33.

ANNETT, M. (1985). *Left, right, hand, and brain: The right shift theory.* London: Erlbaum.

ANOOSHIAN, L. J., & YOUNG, D. (1981). Developmental changes in cognitive maps of a familiar neighborhood. *Child Development, 52,* 341–348.

ANTELL, S. E., & KEATING, D. P. (1983). Perception of numerical invariance in neonates. *Child Development, 54,* 695–701.

ARNETT, J. (1992). Reckless behavior in adolescence: A developmental perspective. *Developmental Review, 12,* 339–373.

ARTERBERRY, M. E., & BORNSTEIN, M. H. (2001). Three-month-old infants' categorization of animals and vehicles based on static and dynamic attributes. *Journal of Experimental Child Psychology, 80,* 333–346.

ARTERBERRY, M., YONAS, A., & BENSEN, A. S. (1989). Self-produced locomotion and the development of responsiveness to linear perspective and texture gradients. *Developmental Psychology, 25,* 976–982.

ASHCRAFT, M. H. (1990). Strategic processing in children's mental arithmetic: A review and proposal. In D. F. Bjorklund (Ed.), *Children's strategies: Contemporary views of cognitive development.* Hillsdale, NJ: Erlbaum.

ASHER, S. R., & MARKEL, R. A. (1974). Sex differences in comprehension of high- and low-interest reading material. *Journal of Educational Psychology, 66,* 680–687.

ASLIN, R. N. (1977). Development of binocular fixation in human infants. *Journal of Experimental Child Psychology, 23,* 133–156.

ASLIN, R. N., & JACKSON, R. W. (1979). Accommodative-convergence in young infants: Development of a synergistic sensory-motor system. *Canadian Journal of Psychology, 33,* 222–231.

ASLIN, R. N., JUSCZYK, P. W., & PISONI, D. B. (1998). Speech and auditory processing during infancy. In D. Kuhn & R. S. Siegler (Eds.), *Cognitive, language, and perceptual development,* Vol. 2. In W. Damon (Gen. Ed.), *Handbook of child psychology.* New York: Wiley.

ASLIN, R. N., SAFFRAN, J. R., & NEWPORT, E. L. (1998). Computation of conditional probability statistics by 8-month-old infants. *Psychological Science, 9,* 321–324.

ASTINGTON, J. W., & JENKINS, J. M. (1995). Theory of mind development and social understanding. *Cognition and Emotion, 9,* 151–165.

ATKINSON, R. C., & SHIFFRIN, R. M. (1968). Human memory: A proposed system and its control processes. In K. W. Spence & J. T. Spence (Eds.), *The psychology of learning and motivation: Advances in research and theory,* Vol. 2. New York: Academic.

AUGUST, G. J. (1987). Production deficiencies in free recall: A comparison of hyperactive, learning-disabled, and normal children. *Journal of Abnormal Child Psychology, 15,* 429–440.

AUSLEY, J. A., & GUTTENTAG, R. E. (1993). Direct and indirect assessments of memory: Implications for the study of memory development. In M. L. Howe & R. Pasnak (Eds.), *Emerging themes in cognitive development: Vol. 1. Foundations.* New York: Springer-Verlag.

AVIS, J., & HARRIS, P. L. (1991). Belief-desire reasoning among Baka children: Evidence for a universal conception of mind. *Child Development, 62,* 460–467.

AZMITIA, M. (1992). Expertise, private speech, and the development of self-regulation. In R. M. Diaz & L. E. Berk (Eds.), *Private speech: From social interaction to self-regulation.* Hillsdale, NJ: Erlbaum.

BADDELEY, A. D. (1983). Working memory. *Philosophical Transactions of the Royal Society, B302,* 311–324.

BADDELEY, A. D. (1986). *Working memory*. Oxford, England: Clarendon.

BADDELEY, A. D., & HITCH, G. J. (1974). Working memory. In G. Bower (Ed.), *The psychology of learning and motivation: Advances in research and theory*, Vol. 8. New York: Academic.

BADIAN, N. A. (1983). Dyscalculia and nonverbal disorders of learning. In H. R. Myklebust (Ed.), *Progress in learning disabilities*. New York: Stratton.

BAENNINGER, M., & NEWCOMBE, N. (1995). Environmental input to the development of sex-related differences in spatial and mathematical ability. *Learning and Individual Differences, 7*, 363–379.

BAGHURST, P. A., McMICHAEL, A. J., WIGG, N. R., VIMPANI, G. V., ROBERTSON, E. F., ROBERTS, R. J., & TONG, S-L. (1992). Environmental exposure to lead and children's intelligence at the age of seven years. *New England Journal of Medicine, 327*, 1279–1284.

BAHRICK, L. E. (1995). Intermodal origins of self-perception. In P. Rochat (Ed.), *The self in infancy: Theory and research*. New York: Elsevier Science.

BAHRICK, L. E. (2002). Generalization of learning in three-and-a-half-month-old infants on the basis of amodal relations. *Child Development, 73*, 667–681.

BAHRICK, L. E., HERNANDEZ-REIF, M., & PICKENS, J. N. (1997). The effect of retrieval cues on visual preferences and memory in infancy: Evidence for a four-phase attention function. *Journal of Experimental Child Psychology, 67*, 1–20.

BAHRICK, L. E., MOSS, L., & FADIL, C. (1996). The development of self-recognition in infancy. *Ecological Psychology, 8*, 189–208.

BAHRICK, L. E., PARKER, J. F., FIVUSH, R., & LEVITT, M. (1998). The effects of stress on young children's memory for a natural disaster. *Journal of Experimental Psychology: Applied, 4*, 308–331.

BAHRICK, L. E., & PICKENS, J. N. (1995). Infant memory for object motion across a period of three months: Implications for a four-phase attention function. *Journal of Experimental Child Psychology, 59*, 343–371.

BAHRICK, L. E., & WATSON, J. S. (1985). Detection of intermodal proprioceptive-visual contingency as a potential basis of self-perception in infancy. *Developmental Psychology, 21*, 963–973.

BAI, D. L., & BERTENTHAL, B. I. (1992). Locomotor status and the development of spatial skills. *Child Development, 63*, 215–226.

BAILLARGEON, R. (1987). Object permanence in 3½- and 4½-month-old infants. *Developmental Psychology, 23*, 655–664.

BAILLARGEON, R. (1994). How do infants learn about the physical world? *Current Directions in Psychological Science, 3*, 133–140.

BAILLARGEON, R., & DE VOS, J. (1991). Object permanence in young infants: Further evidence. *Child Development, 62*, 1227–1246.

BAILLARGEON, R., KOTOVSKY, L., & NEEDHAM, A. (1995). The acquisition of physical knowledge in infancy. In G. Lewis, D. Premack, & D. Sperber (Eds.), *Casual understandings in cognition and culture*. Oxford: Oxford University Press.

BAKER, D. P. (1992). Compared to Japan the U. S. is a low achiever—really. *Educational Research, 22*, 18–20.

BAKER, L. (1985). How do we know when we don't understand? Standards for evaluating text comprehension. In D. L. Forrest-Pressley, G. E. MacKinnon, & T. G. Waller (Eds.), *Metacognition, cognition, and human performance*, Vol. 1. Orlando, FL: Academic.

BAKER-WARD, L., GORDON, B. N., ORNSTEIN, P. A., LARUS, D. M., & CLUBB, P. A. (1993). Young children's long-term retention of a pediatric visit. *Child Development, 64*, 1519–1533.

BAKER-WARD, L., HESS, T. M., & FLANNAGAN, D. A. (1990). The effect of involvement on children's memory for events. *Cognitive Development, 5*, 55–69.

BAKER-WARD, L., & ORNSTEIN, P. A. (1988). Age differences in visual-spatial memory performance: Do children really out-perform adults when playing Concentration? *Bulletin of the Psychonomic Society, 26*, 331–332.

BALDWIN, D. A. (1993). Infant's ability to consult the speaker for clues to word reference. *Journal of Child Language, 20*, 395–418.

BALDWIN, J. M. (1895). *Mental development in the child and the race*. New York: Macmillan.

BAND, G. P. H., VAN DER MOLEN, M. W., OVERTOOM, C. C. E., & VERBATEN, M. N. (2000). The ability to activate and inhibit speeded responses: Separate developmental trends. *Journal of Experimental Child Psychology, 75*, 263–290.

BANDURA, A. (1986). *Social foundations of thought and action: A social cognitive theory*. Englewood Cliffs, NJ: Prentice-Hall.

BANDURA, A. (1989). Social cognitive theory. In R. Vasta (Ed.), *Annals of child development*. Greenwich, CT: JAI.

BANDURA, A. (1997). *Self-efficacy: The exercise of control*. New York: Freeman.

BANDURA, A., BARBARANELLI, C., CAPRARA, G. V., & PASTORELLI, C. (1996). Multifaceted impact of self-efficacy beliefs on academic functioning. *Child Development, 67*, 1206–1222.

BANDURA, A., & WALTERS, R. H. (1963). *Social learning theory and personality development*. New York: Holt, Rinehart & Winston.

BANKS, M. S. (1980). The development of visual accommodation during early infancy. *Child Development, 51,* 646–666.

BARKLEY, R. A. (1990). Attention deficit disorders: History, definition, and diagnosis. In M. Lewis & S. M. Miller (Eds.), *Handbook of developmental psychopathology. Perspectives in developmental psychology*. New York: Plenum.

BARKLEY, R. A. (1997). Behavioral inhibition, sustained attention, and executive functions. Constructing a unifying theory of ADHD. *Psychological Bulletin, 121,* 65–94.

BARKLEY, R. A. (1998). *Attention deficit hyperactivity disorder: A handbook for diagnosis and treatment*. New York: Guilford Press.

BARKLEY, R. A., KOPLOWITZ, S., ANDERSON, T., & McMURRAY, M. B. (1997). Sense of time in children with ADHD: Effects of duration, distraction, and stimulant medication. *Journal of the International Neuropsychological Society, 3,* 359–369.

BARKOW, J. H., COSMIDES, L., & TOOBY, J. (EDS.). (1992). *The adapted mind: Evolutionary psychology and the generation of culture*. New York: Oxford University Press.

BARNES, M. A., DENNIS, M., & HAEFELE-KALVAITIS, J. (1996). The effects of knowledge availability and knowledge accessibility on coherence and elaborative inferencing in children six to fifteen years of age. *Journal of Experimental Child Psychology, 61,* 216–241.

BARNETT, W. S. (1995). Long-term effects of early childhood programs on cognitive and school outcomes. *The Future of Children, 5* (No. 3, Winter).

BARON-COHEN, S. (1995). *Mindblindness: An essay on autism and theory of mind*. Cambridge, MA: MIT Press.

BARON-COHEN, S., WHEELWRIGHT, S., STONE, V., & RUTHERFORD, M. (1999). A mathematician, a physicist and a computer scientist with Asperger syndrome: Performance on folk psychology and folk physics tests. *Neurocase, 5,* 475–483.

BARTLETT, F. C. (1932). *Remembering: A study in experimental and social psychology*. Cambridge: Cambridge University Press.

BATES, E. (1999). On the nature of language. In R. Levi-Montalcini, D. Baltimore, R. Dulbecco, & F. Jacob (Series Eds.) & E. Bizzi, P. Calissano, & V. Volterra (Vol. Eds.), *Frontiere della biologia [Frontiers of biology], The brain of Homo sapiens*. Rome: Giovanni Trecanni.

BATES, E., BRETHERTON, I. M., & SNYDER, L. (1988). *From first words to grammar: Individual differences and dissociable mechanisms*. New York: Cambridge University Press.

BATES, E., CARLSON-LUDEN, V., & BRETHERTON, I. (1980). Perceptual aspects of tool use in infancy. *Infant Behavior & Development, 3,* 127–140.

BATES, E., & GOODMAN, J. C. (1997). On the inseparability of grammar and the lexicon: Evidence from acquisition, aphasia and real-time processing. In G. Altman (Ed.), Special issue on the lexicon. *Language and Cognitive Processes, 12,* 507–586.

BATKI, A., BARON-COHEN, S., WHEELWRIGHT, S., CONNELLAN, J., & AHLUWALIA, J. (2000). Is there an innate gaze module? Evidence from human neonates? *Infant Behavior & Development, 23,* 223–229.

BAUER, P. J. (1993). Memory for gender-consistent and gender-inconsistent event sequences by twenty-five-month-old children. *Child Development, 64,* 285–297.

BAUER, P. J. (1997). Development of memory in early childhood. In N. Cowan (Ed.), *The development of memory in childhood*. Hove East Essex, UK: Psychology Press.

BAUER, P. J. (2002). Long-term recall memory: Behavioral and neuro-developmental changes in the first 2 years of life. *Current Directions in Psychological Science, 11,* 137–141.

BAUER, P. J., DOW, G. A., & HERTSGAARD, L. A. (1995). Effects of prototypicality on categorization in 1- to 2-year-olds: Getting down to basics. *Cognitive Development, 10,* 43–68.

BAUER, P. J., & MANDLER, J. M. (1989). One thing follows another: Effects of temporal structure on 1- to 2-year-olds' recall of events. *Developmental Psychology, 25,* 197–206.

BAUER, P. J., & MANDLER, J. M. (1992). Putting the horse before the cart: The use of temporal order in recall of events by one-year-old children. *Developmental Psychology, 28,* 441–452.

BAUER, P. J., WENNER, J. A., DROPIK, P. L., & WEWERKA, S. S. (2000). Parameters of remembering and forgetting in the transition from infancy to early childhood. *Monographs of the Society for Research in Child Development, 65* (Serial No. 263).

BAUER, P. J., WENNER, J. A., & KROUPINA, M. G. (2002). Making the past present: Later verbal accessibility of early memories. *Journal of Cognition and Development, 3,* 21–47.

BAUER, P. J., WIEBE, S. A., WATERS, J. M., & BANGSTON, S. K. (2001). Reexposure breeds recall: Effects of experience on 9-month-olds' ordered recall. *Journal of Experimental Child Psychology, 80,* 174–200.

BAUER, R. H. (1979). Memory, acquisition, and category clustering in learning-disabled children. *Journal of Experimental Child Psychology, 27,* 365–383.

BAUMRIND, D. (1993). The average expectable environment is not good enough: A response to Scarr. *Child Development, 64,* 1299–1317.

BAYLEY, N. (1949). Consistency and variability in the growth of intelligence from birth to eighteen years. *Journal of Genetic Psychology, 75,* 165–196.

BAYLEY, N. (1969). *Manual of the Bayley Scales of Infant Development.* New York: Psychological Corporation.

BAYLEY, N. (1993). *The Bayley Scales of Infant Development.* (2nd ed.) (BSID-II). New York: Psychological Corporation.

BEAL, C. R., & FLAVELL, J. H. (1982). Effects of increasing salience of message ambiguities on kindergarteners' evaluations of communicative success and message adequacy. *Developmental Psychology, 10,* 43–48.

BECKER, W. C., & GERSTEN, R. (1982). A follow-up of Follow Through: The later effects of the direct instruction model for children in fifth and sixth grades. *American Educational Research Journal, 19,* 75–92.

BEHREND, D. A., ROSENGREN, K., & PERLMUTTER, M. (1989). A new look at children's private speech: The effects of age, task difficulty, and parent presence. *International Journal of Behavioral Development, 12,* 305–320.

BEILIN, H. (1992). Piaget's enduring contribution to developmental psychology. *Developmental Psychology, 28,* 191–204.

BELL, M. A., & FOX, N. A. (1992). The relations between frontal brain electrical activity and cognitive development during infancy. *Child Development, 63,* 1142–1163.

BELL, R. Q. (1968). A reinterpretation of the direction of effects in studies of socialization. *Psychological Review, 75,* 81–95.

BEM, S. (1981). Gender schema theory: A cognitive account of sex-typing. *Psychological Review, 88,* 354–364.

BENBOW, C. P., LUBINSKI, D., SHEA, D. L., & EFTEKHARI-SANJANI, H. (2000). Sex differences in mathematical reasoning ability at age 13: Their status 20 years later. *Psychological Science, 11,* 474–480.

BENBOW, C. P., & STANLEY, J. C. (1980). Sex differences in mathematical ability: Fact or artifact? *Science, 210,* 1262–1264.

BENBOW, C. P., & STANLEY, J. C. (1983). Sex differences in mathematical reasoning: More facts. *Science, 222,* 1029–1031.

BENEDICT, H. (1979). Early lexical development: Comprehension and production. *Journal of Child Language, 6,* 183–200.

BERENBAUM, S. A., & HINES, M. (1992). Early androgens are related to childhood sex-typed toy preferences. *Psychological Science, 3,* 203–206.

BERENBAUM, S. A., & SNYDER, E. (1995). Early hormonal influences on childhood sex-types activity and playmate preferences: Implications for the development of sexual orientation. *Developmental Psychology, 31,* 31–42.

BERING, J. M., BJORKLUND, D. F., & RAGAN, P. (2000). Deferred imitation of object-related actions in human-reared juvenile chimpanzees and orangutans. *Developmental Psychobiology, 36,* 218–232.

BERK, L. E. (1986). Relationship of elementary school children's private speech to behavioral accompaniment to task, attention, and task performance. *Developmental Psychology, 22,* 671–680.

BERK, L. E. (1992). Children's private speech: An overview of theory and the status of research. In R. M. Diaz & L. E. Berk (Eds.), *Private speech: From social interaction to self-regulation.* Hillsdale, NJ: Erlbaum.

BERK, L. E., & LANDAU, S. (1993). Private speech of learning disabled and normally achieving children in classroom academic and laboratory contexts. *Child Development, 64,* 556–571.

BERK, L. E., & SPUHL, S. T. (1995). Maternal intervention, private speech, and task performance in preschool children. *Early Childhood Research Quarterly, 10,* 145–169.

BERKO, J. (1958). The child's learning of English morphology. *Word, 14,* 150–177.

BERKO GLEASON, J. (ED.). (1997). *The development of language* (4th ed.). Boston: Allyn & Bacon.

BERMEJO, V. (1996). Cardinality development and counting. *Developmental Psychology, 32,* 263–268.

BERNSTEIN, B. (1971). *Class codes and control,* Vol. 1. London: Routledge & Kegan Paul.

BERTENTHAL, B. I., & CAMPOS, J. J. (1987). New directions in the study of early experience. *Child Development, 58,* 560–567.

BERTENTHAL, B. I., CAMPOS, J., & BARRETT, L. (1984). Self-produced locomotion: An organizer of emotional, cognitive, and social development in infancy. In R. Emde & R. Harmon (Eds.), *Continuities and discontinuities in development.* New York: Plenum.

BERTENTHAL, B. I., CAMPOS, J. J., & KERMOIAN, R. (1994). An epigenetic perspective on the development of self-produced locomotion and its consequences. *Current Directions in Psychological Science, 3,* 140–145.

BERTHIER, N. E., DEBOIS, S., POIRIER, C. R., NOVAK, M. A., & CLIFTON, R. K. (2000). Where's the ball? Two- and three-year-olds reason about unseen events. *Developmental Psychology, 36,* 384–401.

BEST, D. L. (1993). Inducing children to generate mnemonic organizational strategies: An examination of long-term retention and materials. *Developmental Psychology, 29,* 324–336.

BEST, D. L., & ORNSTEIN, P. A. (1986). Children's generation and communication of mnemonic organizational strategies. *Developmental Psychology, 22,* 845–853.

BHATT, R. S., ROVEE-COLLIER, C., & SHYI, C.-W. G. (1994). Perception and 24-hour retention of feature relations in infancy. *Developmental Psychology, 30,* 142–150.

BIALYSTOK, E. (1996). Preparing to read: The foundations of literacy. In H. W. Reese (Ed.), *Advances in child development and behavior,* Vol. 26. San Diego: Academic.

BICKERTON, D. (1990). *Language and species.* Chicago: University of Chicago Press.

BILLINGSLEY, R. L., SMITH, M. L., & MCANDREWS, M. P. (2002). Developmental patterns in priming and familiarity in explicit recollection. *Journal of Experimental Child Psychology, 82,* 251–277.

BISANZ, J., MORRISON, F. J., & DUNN, M. (1995). The effects of age and schooling on the acquisition of elementary quantitative skills. *Developmental Psychology, 31,* 221–236.

BIVENS, J. A., & BERK, L. E. (1990). A longitudinal study of the development of elementary school children's private speech. *Merrill-Palmer Quarterly, 36,* 443–463.

BJORKLUND, D. F. (1985). The role of conceptual knowledge in the development of organization in children's memory. In C. J. Brainerd & M. Pressley (Eds.), *Basic processes in memory development: Progress in cognitive development research.* New York: Springer-Verlag.

BJORKLUND, D. F. (1987A). How age changes in knowledge base contribute to the development of children's memory: An interpretive review. *Developmental Review, 7,* 93–130.

BJORKLUND, D. F. (1987B). A note on neonatal imitation. *Developmental Review, 7,* 86–92.

BJORKLUND, D. F. (1997A). The role of immaturity in human development. *Psychological Bulletin, 122,* 153–169.

BJORKLUND, D. F. (1997B). In search of a metatheory for cognitive development (or, Piaget's dead and I don't feel so good myself). *Child Development, 68,* 142–146.

BJORKLUND, D. F. (1999). What individual differences can teach us about developmental function and vice versa. In F. E. Weinert & W. Schneider (Eds.), *The Munich Longitudinal Study on the Genesis of Individual Competencies (LOGIC).* Cambridge: Cambridge University Press.

BJORKLUND, D. F., & BERING, J. M. (2003). Big brains, slow development, and social complexity: The developmental and evolutionary origins of social cognition. In M. Brüne, H. Ribbert, & W. Schiefenhoevel (Eds.), *The social brain: Evolutionary aspects of development and pathology.* New York: Wiley.

BJORKLUND, D. F., & BERNHOLTZ, J. F. (1986). The role of knowledge base in the memory performance of good and poor readers. *Journal of Experimental Child Psychology, 41,* 367–373.

BJORKLUND, D. F., & BJORKLUND, B. R. (1992). *Looking at Children: An Introduction to Child Development.* Belmont, CA: Wadsworth.

BJORKLUND, D. F., BJORKLUND, B. R., DOUGLAS, R. B., & CASSEL, W. S. (1998). Children's susceptibility to repeated questions: How misinformation changes children's answers and their minds. *Applied Developmental Science, 2,* 101–113.

BJORKLUND, D. F., BROWN, R. D., & BJORKLUND, B. R. (2002). Children's eyewitness memory: Changing reports and changing representations. In P. Graf & N. Ohta (Eds.), *Lifespan memory development.* Cambridge, MA: MIT Press.

BJORKLUND, D. F., CORMIER, C., & ROSENBERG, J. S. (IN PRESS). The evolution of theory of mind: Big brains, social complexity, and inhibition. In W. Schneider, R. Schumann-Hengsteler, & B. Sodian (Eds.), *Young children's cognitive development: Interrelationships among executive functioning, working memory, verbal ability and theory of mind.* Mahwah, NJ: Erlbaum.

BJORKLUND, D. F., COYLE, T. R., & GAULTNEY, J. F. (1992). Developmental differences in the acquisition of an organizational strategy: Evidence for the utilization deficiency hypothesis. *Journal of Experimental Child Psychology, 54,* 434–448.

BJORKLUND, D. F., GAULTNEY, J. F., & GREEN, B. L. (1993). "I watch, therefore I can do": The development of meta-imitation during the preschool years and the advantage of optimism about one's imitative skills. In M. L. Howe & R. Pasnak (Eds.), *Emerging themes in cognitive development: Vol. 2. Competencies.* New York: Springer-Verlag.

BJORKLUND, D. F., & GREEN, B. L. (1992). The adaptive nature of cognitive immaturity. *American Psychologist, 47,* 46–54.

BJORKLUND, D. F., & HARNISHFEGER, K. K. (1987). Developmental differences in the mental effort requirements for the use of an organizational strategy in free recall. *Journal of Experimental Child Psychology, 44,* 109–125.

BJORKLUND, D. F., & HARNISHFEGER, K. K. (1990). Children's strategies: Their definition and origins. In D. F. Bjorklund (Ed.), *Children's strategies: Contemporary views of cognitive development.* Hillsdale, NJ: Erlbaum.

BJORKLUND, D. F., & HARNISHFEGER, K. K. (1995). The role of inhibition mechanisms in the evolution of human cognition. In F. Dempster & C. Brainerd (Eds.), *New perspectives on interference and inhibition in cognition.* New York: Academic.

BJORKLUND, D. F., & HERNÁNDZ BLASI, C. (IN PRESS). Evolutionary developmental psychology. In D. Buss (Ed.), *Evolutionary psychology handbook.* New York: Wiley.

BJORKLUND, D. F., HUBERTZ, M. J., & REUBENS, A. C. (2004). Young children's arithmetic strategies in social context: How parents contribute to children's strategy development while playing games. *International Journal of Behavioral Development*.

BJORKLUND, D. F., & KIPP, K. (1996). Parental investment theory and gender differences in the evolution of inhibition mechanisms. *Psychological Bulletin, 120*, 163–188.

BJORKLUND, D. F., & KIPP, K. (2002). Social cognition, inhibition, and theory of mind: The evolution of human intelligence. In R. J. Sternberg & J. C. Kaufman (Eds.), *The evolution of intelligence*. Mahwah, NJ: Erlbaum.

BJORKLUND, D. F., & MILLER, P. H. (EDS.). (1997). New themes in strategy development. Special Issue of *Developmental Review, 17*, December issue.

BJORKLUND, D. F., MILLER, P. H., COYLE, T. R., & SLAWINSKI, J. L. (1997). Instructing children to use memory strategies: Evidence of utilization deficiencies in memory training studies. *Developmental Review, 17*, 411–442.

BJORKLUND, D. F., MUIR-BROADDUS, J. E., & SCHNEIDER, W. (1990). The role of knowledge in the development of strategies. In D. F. Bjorklund (Ed.), *Children's strategies: Contemporary views of cognitive development*. Hillsdale, NJ: Erlbaum.

BJORKLUND, D. F., & PELLEGRINI, A. D. (2002). *The origins of human nature: Evolutionary developmental psychology*. Washington, DC: American Psychological Association.

BJORKLUND, D. F., & ROSENBLUM, K. E. (2002). Context effects in children's selection and use of simple arithmetic strategies. *Journal of Cognition and Development, 3*, 225–242.

BJORKLUND, D. F., & SCHNEIDER, W. (1996). The interaction of knowledge, aptitudes, and strategies in children's memory performance. In H. W. Reese (Ed.), *Advances in child development and behavior*, Vol. 26. San Diego: Academic.

BJORKLUND, D. F., SCHNEIDER, W., CASSEL, W. S., & ASHLEY, E. (1994). Training and extension of a memory strategy: Evidence for utilization deficiencies in the acquisition of an organizational strategy in high- and low-IQ children. *Child Development, 65*, 951–965.

BJORKLUND, D. F., & SCHWARTZ, R. (1996). The adaptive nature of developmental immaturity: Implications for language acquisition and language disabilities. In M. Smith & J. Damico (Eds.), *Childhood language disorders*. New York: Thieme Medical.

BJORKLUND, D. F., THOMPSON, B. E., & ORNSTEIN, P. A. (1983). Developmental trends in children's typicality judgments. *Behavior Research Methods and Instrumentation, 15*, 350–356.

BJORKLUND, D. F., YUNGER, J. L., BERING, J. M., & RAGAN, P. (2002). The generalization of deferred imitation in enculturated chimpanzees (*Pan troglodytes*). *Animal Cognition, 5*, 49–58.

BJORKLUND, D. F., & ZEMAN, B. R. (1982). Children's organization and metamemory awareness in their recall of familiar information. *Child Development, 53*, 799–810.

BLACK, J. E., JONES, T. A., NELSON, C. A., & GREENOUGH, W. T. (1998). Neuronal plasticity and the developing brain. In N. E. Alessi, J. T. Coyle, S. I. Harrison, & S. Eth (Eds.), *Handbook of child and adolescent psychiatry: Vol. 6. Basic psychiatric science and treatment*. New York: Wiley.

BLACK, M. M., & ROLLINS, H. A. (1982). The effects of instructional variables on young children's organization and free recall. *Journal of Experimental Child Psychology, 31*, 1–19.

BLAKEMORE, C., & VAN SLUYTERS, R. C. (1975). Innate and environmental factors in the development of the kitten's visual cortex. *Journal of Physiology, 248*, 663–716.

BLANCHET, N., DUNHAM, P. J., & DUNHAM, F. (2001). Differences in preschool children's conceptual strategies when thinking about animate entities and artifacts. *Developmental Psychology, 37*, 791–800.

BLEWITT, P., & KRACKOW, E. (1992). Acquiring taxonomic relations in lexical memory: The role of superordinate category labels. *Journal of Experimental Child Psychology, 54*, 37–56.

BLEWITT, P., & TOPPINO, T. C. (1991). The development of taxonomic structure in lexical memory. *Journal of Experimental Child Psychology, 51*, 296–319.

BLOM, G. E., WAITE, R. R., & ZIMET, S. (1968). Content of first-grade reading books. *The Reading Teacher, 21*, 317–323.

BLOOM, L. (1998). Language acquisition in developmental contexts. In D. Kuhn & R. S. Siegler (Eds.), *Cognitive, language, and perceptual development*, Vol. 2. In W. Damon (Gen. Ed.), *Handbook of child psychology*. New York: Wiley.

BLOOM, L., HOOD, L., & LIGHTBOWN, P. (1974). Imitation in language development: If, when and why. *Cognitive Psychology, 6*, 380–420.

BLOOM, L., LIGHTBOWN, P., & HOOD, L. (1975). Structure and variation in child language. *Monographs of the Society for Research in Child Development, 40* (Serial No. 160).

BLOOM, P. (2000). *How children learn the meaning of words*. Cambridge, MA: MIT Press.

BOESCH, C. (1993). Toward a new image of culture in wild chimpanzees? *Behavioral and Brain Sciences, 16*, 514–515.

BOESCH, C., & TOMASELLO, M. (1998). Chimpanzee and human cultures. *Current Anthropology, 39*, 591–604.

BOGARTZ, R. S., & SHINSKEY, J. L. (1998). On perception of a partially occluded object in 6-months olds. *Cognitive Development, 13*, 141–163.

BOGARTZ, R. S., SHINSKEY, J. L., & SPEAKER, C. (1997). Interpreting infant looking: The event set x event set design. *Developmental Psychology, 33*, 408–422.

BORKE, H. (1975). Piaget's mountains revisited: Changes in the egocentric landscape. *Developmental Psychology, 11*, 240–243.

BORKOWSKI, J. G., & PECK, V. A. (1986). Causes and consequences of metamemory in gifted children. In R. J. Sternberg & J. C. Davidson (Eds.), *Conceptions of giftedness*. Cambridge: Cambridge University Press.

BORKOWSKI, J. G., PECK, V., REID, M. K., & KURTZ, B. (1983). Impulsivity and strategy transfer: Metamemory as mediator. *Child Development, 54*, 459–473.

BORKOWSKI, J. G., REID, M. K., & KURTZ, B. E. (1984). Metacognition and retardation: Pragmatic, theoretical and applied perspectives. In P. H. Brooks, R. Sperber, & C. McCauley (Eds.), *Learning and cognition in the mentally retarded*. Hillsdale, NJ: Erlbaum.

BORKOWSKI, J. G., & TURNER, L. A. (1988). Transituational characteristics of metacognition. In W. Schneider & F. E. Weinert (Eds.), *Interactions among aptitudes, strategies, and knowledge in cognitive performance*. Hillsdale, NJ: Erlbaum.

BORNSTEIN, M. H. (1989). Stability in early mental development: From attention and information processing in infancy to language and cognition in childhood. In M. H. Bornstein & N. A. Krasnegor (Eds.), *Stability and continuity in mental development: Behavioral and biological perspectives*. Hillsdale, NJ: Erlbaum.

BORNSTEIN, M. H., FERDINANDSEN, K., & GROSS, C. G. (1981). Perception of symmetry in infancy. *Developmental Psychology, 17*, 82–86.

BORNSTEIN, M. H., & HAYNES, O. M. (1998). Vocabulary competence in early childhood: Measurement, latent construct, and predictive validity. *Child Development, 69*, 654–671.

BORNSTEIN, M. H., HAYNES, O. M., O'REILLY, A. W., & PAINTER, K. M. (1996). Solitary and collaborative pretense play in early childhood: Sources of individual variation in the development of representational competence. *Child Development, 67*, 2910–2929.

BORNSTEIN, M. H., KESSEN, W., & WEISKOPF, S. (1976). Color vision and hue categorization in young infants. *Journal of Experimental Psychology: Human Perception and Performance, 2*, 115–129.

BORNSTEIN, M. H., & SIGMAN, M. D. (1986). Continuity in mental development from infancy. *Child Development, 57*, 251–274.

BOSTON, M. B., & LEVY, G. D. (1991). Changes and differences in preschoolers' understanding of gender scripts. *Cognitive Development, 6*, 417–432.

BOUCHARD, T. J., JR., LYKKEN, D. T., MCGUE, M., SEGAL, N. L., & TELLEGEN, A. (1990). Sources of human psychological differences: The Minnesota study of twins reared apart. *Science, 250*, 223–228.

BOUCHARD, T. J., JR., & MCGUE, M. (1981). Familial studies of intelligence: A review. *Science, 212*, 1055–1059.

BOUCHARD, T. J., JR., & SEGAL, N. (1985). Environment and IQ. In B. Wolman (Ed.), *Handbook of intelligence*. New York: Wiley.

BOYSEN, S. T. (1993). Counting in chimpanzees: Nonhuman principles and emergent properties of number. In S. T. Boysen & E. J. Capaldi (Eds.), *The development of numerical competence: Animal and human models*. Hillsdale, NJ: Erlbaum.

BOYSEN, S. T., & BERNTSON, G. G. (1989). Numerical competence in a chimpanzee (*Pan troglodytes*). *Journal of Comparative Psychology, 103*, 23–31.

BRADLEY, R. H. (1989). The use of the HOME inventory in longitudinal studies of child development. In M. H. Bornstein & N. A. Krasnegor (Eds.), *Stability and continuity in mental development: Behavioral and biological perspectives*. Hillsdale, NJ: Erlbaum.

BRADLEY, R. H., BURCHINAL, M. R., & CASEY, P. H. (2001). Early intervention: The moderating role of the home environment. *Applied Developmental Science, 5*, 2–8.

BRADLEY, R. H., & CALDWELL, B. M. (1976). The relation of infants' home environment to mental test performance at fifty-four months: A follow-up study. *Child Development, 47*, 1172–1174.

BRADLEY, R. H., CALDWELL, B. M., & ELARDO, R. (1977). Home environment, social status, and mental test performance. *Journal of Educational Psychology, 69*, 697–701.

BRADLEY, R. H., CALDWELL, B. M., ROCK, S. L., RAMEY, C. T., BARNARD, K. E., GRAY, C., HAMMOND, M. A., MITCHELL, S., GOTTFRIED, A. W., SIEGEL, L., & JOHNSON, D. L. (1989). Home environments and cognitive development in the first 3 years of life: A collaborative study including six sites and three ethnic groups in North America. *Developmental Psychology, 25*, 217–235.

BRAINERD, C. J. (1978A). *Piaget's theory of intelligence*. Englewood Cliffs, NJ: Prentice-Hall.

BRAINERD, C. J. (1978B). The stage question in cognitive-developmental theory. *The Behavioral and Brain Sciences, 2*, 173–213.

BRAINERD, C. J. (1996). Piaget: A centennial celebration. *Psychological Science, 7*, 191–195.

BRAINERD, C. J. (1997). Children's forgetting, with implications for memory suggestibility. In N. L. Stein, P. A. Ornstein, B. Tversky, & C. J. Brainerd (Eds.), *Memory for everyday and emotional events*. Hillsdale, NJ: Erlbaum.

BRAINERD, C. J., & ALLEN, T. W. (1971). Training and generalization of density conservation: Effects of feedback and consecutive similar stimuli. *Child Development, 42*, 693–704.

BRAINERD, C. J., & BRAINERD, S. H. (1972). Order of acquisition of number and liquid quantity conservation. *Child Development, 43*, 1401–1405.

BRAINERD, C. J., & GORDON, L. L. (1994). Development of verbatim and gist memory for numbers. *Developmental Psychology, 30*, 163–177.

BRAINERD, C. J., & KASZOR, P. (1974). An analysis of two proposed sources of children's class inclusion errors. *Developmental Psychology, 10*, 633–643.

BRAINERD, C. J., & MOJARDIN, A. H. (1999). Children's and adults' spontaneous false memories for sentences: Long-term persistence and mere-testing effects. *Child Development*.

BRAINERD, C. J., & ORNSTEIN, P. A. (1991). Children's memory for witnessed events: The developmental backdrop. In J. Doris (Ed.), *The suggestibility of children's memory*. Washington, DC: American Psychological Association.

BRAINERD, C. J., & POOLE, D. A. (1997). Long-term survival of children's false memories: A review. *Learning and Individual Differences, 9*, 125–152.

BRAINERD, C. J., & REYNA, V. F. (1990). Gist is the grist: Fuzzy-trace theory and the new intuitionism. *Developmental Review, 10*, 3–47.

BRAINERD, C. J., & REYNA, V. F. (1993). Domains of fuzzy trace theory. In M. L. Howe & R. Pasnak (Eds.), *Emerging themes in cognitive development: Vol. 1. Foundations*. New York: Springer-Verlag.

BRAINERD, C. J., & REYNA, V. F. (1996). Mere memory testing creates false memories in children. *Developmental Psychology, 32*, 467–478.

BRAINERD, C. J., & REYNA, V. F. (2002). Fuzzy-trace theory and false memory. *Current Directions on Psychological Science, 11*, 164–169.

BRAINERD, C. J., REYNA, V. F., & BRANDSE, E. (1995). Are children's false memories more persistent than their true memories? *Psychological Science, 6*, 359–364.

BRAY, N. W., FLETCHER, K. L., & TURNER, L. A. (1996). Cognitive competencies and strategy use in individuals with mild retardation. In W. E. MacLean Jr. (Ed.), *Handbook of mental deficiency, psychological theory and research* (3rd ed.). Hillsdale, NJ: Lawrence Erlbaum.

BRAZELTON, T. B. (1973). *Neonatal Behavioral Assessment Scale*. Clinics in Developmental Medicine, No. 50. Philadelphia, PA: Lippincott.

BREDEKAMP, S., & COPPLE, C. (EDS.). (1997). *Developmentally appropriate practice in early childhood programs* (rev. ed.). Washington, DC: National Association for the Education of Young Children.

BRIARS, D., & SIEGLER, R. S. (1984). A featural analysis of preschoolers' counting knowledge. *Developmental Psychology, 20*, 607–618.

BROBERG, A. G., WESSELS, H., LAMB, M. E., & HWANG, C. P. (1997). Effects of day care on the development of cognitive abilities in 8-year-olds: A longitudinal study. *Developmental Psychology, 33*, 62–69.

BRODY, N. (1997). Intelligence, schooling, and society. *American Psychologist, 52*, 1046–1050.

BRONFENBRENNER, U., & CECI, S. J. (1994). Nature-nurture reconceptualized in developmental perspective: A bioecological model. *Psychological Review, 101*, 568–586.

BRONSON, G. (1974). The postnatal growth of visual capacity. *Child Development, 45*, 873–890.

BRONSON, G. W. (1990). Changes in infants' visual scanning across the 2–14-week age period. *Journal of Experimental Child Psychology, 49*, 101–125.

BROOKS-GUNN, J., & LEWIS, M. (1984). The development of early self-recognition. *Developmental Review, 4*, 215–239.

BROWN, A. L., & KANE, M. J. (1988). Preschool children can learn to transfer: Learning to learn and learning by example. *Cognitive Psychology, 20*, 493–523.

BROWN, A. L., KANE, M. J., & LONG, C. (1989). Analogical transfer in young children: Analogies as tools for communication and exposition. *Applied Cognitive Psychology, 3*, 275–293.

BROWN, A. L., & SMILEY, S. S. (1978). The development of strategies for studying texts. *Child Development, 49*, 1076–1088.

BROWN, R. (1973). *A first language: The early stages*. Cambridge, MA: Harvard University Press.

BROWN, R., & HANLON, C. (1970). Derivational complexity and the order of acquisition in child speech. In R. Brown (Ed.), *Psycholinguistics*. New York: Free Press.

BRUCK, M., CECI, S. K., FRANCOEUR, E., & BARR, R. (1995). "I hardly cried when I got my shot!" Influencing children's reports about a visit to their pediatrician. *Child Development, 66*, 193–208.

BRUNER, J. S. (1966). On cognitive growth. In J. S. Bruner, R. R. Olver, & P. M. Greenfield (Eds.), *Studies in cognitive growth*. New York: Wiley.

BRUNER, J. S. (1972). The nature and uses of immaturity. *American Psychologist, 27*, 687–708.

BRUNER, J. S. (1983). *Child's talk: Learning to use language*. New York: Norton.

BRYANT, P. E., MacLEAN, M., BRADLEY, L. L., & CROSSLAND, J. (1990). Rhyme and alliteration, phoneme detection, and learning to read. *Developmental Psychology, 26*, 429–438.

BUGENTAL, D. B. (2000). Acquisition of the algorithms of social life: A domain-based approach. *Psychological Bulletin, 126*, 187–219.

BULL, R., & JOHNSTON, R. S. (1997). Children's arithmetical difficulties: Contributions from processing speed, item identification, and short-term memory. *Journal of Experimental Child Psychology, 65*, 1–24.

BULLOCK, M., & LÜTKENHAUS, P. (1988). The development of volitional behavior in the toddler years. *Child Development, 59*, 664–674.

BURGESS, S. R., & LONIGAN, C. J. (1998). Bidirectional relations of phonological sensitivity and prereading abilities: Evidence from a preschool sample. *Journal of Experimental Child Psychology, 70*, 114–141.

BUSHNELL, I. W. R., SAI, F., & MULLIN, J. T. (1989). Neonatal recognition of the mother's face. *British Journal of Developmental Psychology, 7*, 3–15.

BUSS, D. M. (1995). Evolutionary psychology. *Psychological Inquiry, 6*, 1–30.

BUSSEY, K., & BANDURA A. (1999). Social-cognitive theory of gender development and differentiation. *Psychological Review, 106*, 676–713.

BYRD, D. M., & GHOLSON, B. (1985). Reading, memory, and metacognition. *Journal of Educational Psychology, 77*, 428–436.

BYRNE, R., & WHITEN, A. (EDS.). (1988). *Machiavellian intelligence: Social expertise and the evolution of intellect in monkeys, apes, and humans*. Oxford: Clarendon.

BYRNES, J. P., & FOX, N. A. (1998). The educational relevance of research in cognitive neuroscience. *Educational Psychology Review, 10*, 297–342.

BYRNES, J. P., & TAKAHIRA, S. (1993). Explaining gender differences on SAT-Math items. *Developmental Psychology, 29*, 805–810.

CAHAN, S., & COHEN, N. (1989). Age versus schooling effects on intelligence development. *Child Development, 60*, 1239–1249.

CAIRNS, R. B. (1979). *Social development: The origins and plasticity of interchanges*. San Francisco: W. H. Freeman.

CALDERA, Y. M., O'BRIEN, M., TRUGLIO, R. T., ALVAREZ, M., & HUSTON, A. C. (1999). Children's play preferences, construction play with blocks, and visual-spatial skills: Are they related? *International Journal of Behavioral Development, 23*, 855–872.

CALDWELL, B. M., & BRADLEY, R. H. (1978). *Home Observation for Measurement of the Environment*. Little Rock: University of Arkansas at Little Rock.

CAMPBELL, F. A., PUNGELLO, E. P., MILLER-JOHNSON, S., BURCHINAL, M., & RAMEY, C. T. (2001). The development of cognitive and academic abilities: Growth curves from an early childhood educational experiment. *Developmental Psychology, 37*, 231–242.

CAMPBELL, F. A., & RAMEY, C. T. (1994). Effects of early intervention on intellectual and academic achievement: A follow-up study of children from low-income families. *Child Development, 65*, 684–698.

CAMPBELL, F. A., RAMEY, C. T., PUNGELLO, E., SPARLING, J., & MILLER-JOHNSON, S. (2002). Early childhood education: Young adult outcomes from the Abecedarian project. *Applied Developmental Science, 6*, 42–57.

CAMPOS, J., LANGER, A., & KROWITZ, A. (1970). Cardiac responses on the visual cliff in pre-motor human infants. *Science, 170*, 195–196.

CANFIELD, R. L., SMITH, E. G., BREZSNYAK, M. P., & SNOW, K. L. (1997). Information processing through the first year of life. *Monographs of the Society for Research in Child Development, 62* (Serial No. 250).

CANTOR, D. S., ANDREASSEN, C., & WATERS, H. S. (1985). Organization in visual episodic memory: Relationships between verbalized knowledge, strategy use, and performance. *Journal of Experimental Child Psychology, 40*, 218–232.

CAPON, N., & KUHN, D. (1979). Logical reasoning in the supermarket: Adult females' use of a proportional reasoning strategy in an everyday context. *Developmental Psychology, 15*, 450–452.

CAREW, J. V. (1980). Experience and the development of intelligence in young children at home and in day care. *Monographs of the Society for Research in Child Development, 45* (Serial No. 187).

CAREY, S. (1978). The child as a word learner. In M. Halle, J. Bresnan, & G. A. Miller (Eds.), *Linguistic theory and psychological reality*. Cambridge, MA: MIT Press.

CAREY, S. (1985). Are children fundamentally different kinds of thinkers and learners than adults? In S. F. Chapman, J. W. Segal, & R. Glaser (Eds.), *Thinking and learning skills*, Vol. 2. Hillsdale, NJ: Erlbaum.

CARLSON, S. M., & MOSES, L. J. (2001). Individual differences in inhibitory control and children's theory of mind. *Child Development, 72*, 1032–1053.

CARLSON, S. M., MOSES, L. J., & HIX, H. R. (1998). The role of inhibitory processes in young children's difficulties with deception and false belief. *Child Development, 69*, 672–691.

CARPENTER, M., AKHTAR, N., & TOMASELLO, M. (1998). 14- through 18-month-old infants differentially imitate intentional and accidental actions. *Infant Behavior & Development, 21,* 315–330.

CARPENTER, M., CALL, J., & TOMASELLO, M. (2002). Understanding "prior intentions" enables two-year-olds to imitatively learn a complex task. *Child Development, 73,* 1431–1441.

CARPENTER, M., NAGELL, K., & TOMASELLO, M. (1998). Social cognition, joint attention, and communicative competence from 9 to 15 months of age. *Monographs of the Society for Research in Child Development 63* (Serial No. 255).

CARPENTER, T. P., & MOSER, J. M. (1982). The development of addition and subtraction problem-solving skills. In T. P. Carpenter, J. M. Moser, & T. A. Romberg (Eds.), *Addition and subtraction: A cognitive perspective.* Hillsdale, NJ: Erlbaum.

CARR, M., BORKOWSKI, J. G., & MAXWELL, S. E. (1991). Motivational components of underachievement. *Developmental Psychology, 27,* 108–118.

CARR, M., & JESSUP, D. L. (1995). Cognitive and metacognitive predictors of mathematics strategy use. *Learning and Individual Differences, 7,* 235–247.

CARR, M., KURTZ, B. E., SCHNEIDER, W., TURNER, L. A., & BORKOWSKI, J. G. (1989). Strategy acquisition and transfer among American and German children: Environmental influences on metacognitive development. *Developmental Psychology, 25,* 765–771.

CARRAHER, T. N., CARRAHER, D., & SCHLIEMANN, A. D. (1985). Mathematics in the streets and in the schools. *British Journal of Developmental Psychology, 3,* 21–29.

CARROL, J. B. (1993). *Human cognitive abilities.* New York: Cambridge University Press.

CARSON, M. T., & ABRAHAMSON, A. (1976). Some members are more equal than others: The effect of semantic typicality on class-inclusion performance. *Child Development, 47,* 1186–1190.

CARVER, L. J., & BAUER, P. J. (1999). When the event is more than the sum of its parts: Individual differences in 9-month-olds long-term ordered recall. *Memory, 2,* 147–174.

CASE, R. (1974). Mental strategies, mental capacity and instruction: A neo-Piagetian investigation. *Journal of Experimental Child Psychology, 18,* 382–397.

CASE, R. (1985). *Intellectual development: Birth to adulthood.* New York: Academic.

CASE, R. (1991). Stages in the development of the young child's first sense of self. *Developmental Review, 11,* 210–230.

CASE, R. (1992). *The mind's staircase: Exploring the conceptual underpinnings of children's thought and knowledge.* Hillsdale, NJ: Erlbaum.

CASE, R. (1998). The development of conceptual structures. In D. Kuhn & R. S. Siegler (Vol. Eds.), *Cognition, perception, and language,* Vol. 2. In W. Damon (Gen. Ed.), *Handbook of child psychology.* New York: Wiley.

CASE, R., KURLAND, M., & GOLDBERG, J. (1982). Operational efficiency and the growth of short-term memory span. *Journal of Experimental Child Psychology, 33,* 386–404.

CASELLI, M. C., BATES, E., CASADIO, P., FENSON, J., FENSON, L., SANDERL, L., & WEIR, J. (1995). A cross-linguistic study of early lexical development. *Cognitive Development, 10,* 159–199.

CASEY, B. J., & DE HAAN, M. (2002). Introduction: New methods in developmental science. *Developmental Science, 5,* 265–267.

CASEY, M. B. (1996). Understanding individual differences in spatial ability within females: A nature/nurture interactionist framework. *Developmental Review, 16,* 241–260.

CASEY, M. B., & BRABECK, M. M. (1989). Exceptions to male advantage on a spatial task: Family handedness and college major as a factor identifying women who excel. *Neuropsychologia, 27,* 689–696.

CASEY, M. B., NUTTALL, R. L., & PEZARIS, E. (1999). Evidence in support of a model that predicts how biological and environmental factors interact to influence spatial skills. *Developmental Psychology, 35,* 1237–1247.

CASEY, M. B., NUTTALL, R., PEZARIS, E., & BENBOW, C. P. (1995). The influence of spatial ability on gender differences in mathematics college entrance test scores across diverse samples. *Developmental Psychology, 31,* 697–705.

CASPI, A., MCCLAY, J., MOFFITT, T. E., MILL, J., MARTIN, J., CRAIG, I. W., TAYLOR, A., & POULTON, R. (2002). Role of genotype in the cycle of violence in maltreated children. *Science, 297* (2 August), 851–854.

CASSEL, W. S., & BJORKLUND, D. F. (1995). Developmental patterns of eyewitness memory and suggestibility: An ecologically based short-term longitudinal study. *Law & Human Behavior, 19,* 507–532.

CASSEL, W. S., ROEBERS, C. E. M., & BJORKLUND, D. F. (1996). Developmental patterns of eyewitness responses to increasingly suggestive questions. *Journal of Experimental Child Psychology, 61,* 116–133.

CATTELL, R. B. (1971). *Abilities: Their structure, growth and action.* Boston: Houghton Mifflin.

CAUGHY, M. O. (1996). Health and environmental effects on the academic readiness of school-age children. *Developmental Psychology, 32,* 515–522.

CAVANAUGH, J. C., & BORKOWSKI, J. G. (1980). Searching for metamemory-memory connections: A developmental study. *Developmental Psychology, 16,* 441–453.

CECI, S. J. (1983). Automatic and purposive semantic processing characteristics of normal and language/learning disabled (L/LD) children. *Developmental Psychology, 19,* 427–439.

CECI, S. J. (1991). How much does schooling influence general intelligence and its cognitive components? A reassessment of the evidence. *Developmental Psychology, 27,* 703–722.

CECI, S. J. (1993). Contextual trends in intellectual development. *Developmental Review, 13,* 403–435.

CECI, S. J. (1996). *On intelligence: A bio-ecological treatise on intellectual development* (2nd ed.). Cambridge, MA: Harvard University Press.

CECI, S. J., & BRUCK, M. (1993). Suggestibility of the child witness: A historical review and synthesis. *Psychological Bulletin, 113,* 403–439.

CECI, S. J., & BRUCK, M. (1995). *Jeopardy in the courtroom: A scientific analysis of children's testimony.* Washington, DC: American Psychological Association.

CECI, S. J., & BRUCK, M. (1998). Children's testimony: Applied and basic issues. In I. E. Sigel & K. A. Renninger (Vol. Eds.), *Child psychology in practice,* Vol. 4. In W. Damon (Gen. Ed.), *Handbook of child psychology.* New York: Wiley.

CECI, S. J., BRUCK, M., & BATTIN, D. (2000). The suggestibility of children's testimony. In D. F. Bjorklund (Ed.), *False-memory creation in children and adults: Theory, research, and implications.* Mahwah, NJ: Erlbaum

CECI, S. J., & LIKER, J. (1986). A day at the races: A study of IQ, expertise, and cognitive complexity. *Journal of Experimental Psychology: General, 115,* 255–266.

CECI, S. J., & LIKER, J. (1988). Stalking the IQ-expertise relation: When the critics go fishing. *Journal of Experimental Psychology: General, 117,* 96–100.

CECI, S. J., LOFTUS, E. F., LEICHTMAN, M., & BRUCK, M. (1994). The role of source misattributions in the creation of false beliefs among preschoolers. *International Journal of Clinical and Experimental Hypnosis, 62,* 304–320.

CECI, S. J., ROSS, D. F., & TOGLIA, M. P. (1987). Age differences in suggestibility: Psycholegal implications. *Journal of Experimental Psychology: General, 117,* 38–49.

CECI, S. J., & WILLIAMS, W. M. (1997). Schooling, intelligence, and income. *American Psychologist, 52,* 1051–158.

CERVANTES, C. A., & CALLANAN, M. A. (1998). Labels and explanations in mother-child emotion talk: Age and gender differentiation. *Developmental Psychology, 34,* 88–98.

CHALL, J. S. (1979). The great debate: Ten years later, with a modest proposal for reading stages. In L. B. Resnick & P. A. Weaver (Eds.), *Theory and practice of early reading.* Hillsdale, NJ: Erlbaum.

CHALMERS, D., & LAWRENCE, J. A. (1993). Investigating the effects of planning aids on adults' and adolescents' organization of a complex task. *International Journal of Behavioral Development, 16,* 191–214.

CHAN, C. K. K., & SIEGEL, L. S. (2001). Phonological processing in reading Chinese among normally achieving and poor readers. *Journal of Experimental Child Psychology, 80,* 23–43.

CHANDLER, M., FRITZ, A. S., & HALA, S. (1989). Small-scale deceit: Deception as a marker of two-, three-, and four-year-olds' early theories of mind. *Child Development, 60,* 1263–1277.

CHANGEUX, J. P., & DEHAENE, S. (1989). Neural models of cognitive function. *Cognition, 33,* 63–109.

CHASE, W. G., & SIMON, H. A. (1973). Perception in chess. *Cognitive Psychology, 4,* 55–81.

CHECHILE, R. A., & RICHMAN, C. L. (1982). The interaction of semantic memory with storage and retrieval processes. *Developmental Review, 2,* 237–250.

CHELUNE, G. J., & BAER, R. A. (1986). Developmental norms for the Wisconsin Card Sorting Test. *Journal of Clinical and Experimental Neuropsychology, 8,* 219–228.

CHEN, C., & STEVENSON, H. W. (1988). Cross-linguistic differences in digit span of preschool children. *Journal of Experimental Child Psychology, 46,* 150–158.

CHEN, C., & STEVENSON, H. W. (1995). Motivation and mathematics achievement: A comparative study of Asian-American, Caucasian-American, and East Asian high school students. *Child Development, 66,* 1215–1234.

CHEN, Z., & KLAHR, D. (1999). All other things being equal: Acquisition and transfer of the control of variables strategy. *Child Development, 70,* 1098–1120.

CHEN, Z., SANCHEZ, R. P., & CAMPBELL, T. (1997). From beyond to within their grasp: The rudiments of analogical problem solving in 10- and 13-month-olds. *Developmental Psychology, 33,* 790–801.

CHEN, Z., & SIEGLER, R. S. (2000). Across the great divide: Bridging the gap between understanding of toddlers' and older children's thinking. *Monographs of the Society for Research in Child Development 65* (Serial No. 261).

CHERNEY, I. D., & RYALLS, B. O. (1998, MARCH). *Incidental memory as a function of gender and development.* Paper presented at Conference on Human Development, Mobile, AL.

CHEYNE, J. A., & RUBIN, K. H. (1983). Playful precursors of problem solving in preschoolers. *Developmental Psychology, 19,* 577–584.

CHI, M. T. H. (1977). Age differences in memory span. *Journal of Experimental Child Psychology, 23*, 266–281.

CHI, M. T. H. (1978). Knowledge structure and memory development. In R. S. Siegler (Ed.), *Children's thinking: What develops?* Hillsdale, NJ: Erlbaum.

CHI, M. T. H., FELTOVICH, P. J., & GLASER, R. (1981). Categorization and representation of physics problems by experts and novices. *Cognitive Science, 5*, 121–152.

CHOMSKY, N. (1957). *Syntactic structures.* The Hague: Mouton.

CHOMSKY, N. (1959). A review of Skinner's *Verbal Behavior. Language, 35*, 26–58.

CHRISTIAN, K., MORRISON, F. J., FRAZIER, J. A., & MASSETTI, G. (2000). Specificity in the nature and timing of cognitive growth in kindergarten and first grade. *Journal of Cognition and Development, 1*, 429–448.

CHUAH, Y. M. L., & MAYBERY, M. T. (1999). Verbal and spatial short-term memory: Common sources of developmental change? *Journal of Experimental Child Psychology, 73*, 7–44.

CHUGANI, H. T., PHELPS, M. E., & MAZZIOTTA, J. C. (1987). Positron emission tomography study of human brain functional development. *Annals of Neurology, 22*, 487–497.

CHURCH, R. B., & GOLDIN-MEADOW, S. (1986). The mismatch between gesture and speech as an index of transitional knowledge. *Cognition, 23*, 43–71.

CICCHETTI, D. (1989). How research on child maltreatment has informed the study of child development: Perspectives from developmental psychopathology. In D. Cicchetti & V. Carlson (Eds.), *Child maltreatment: Theory and research on causes and consequences of child abuse and neglect.* New York: Cambridge University Press.

CLARK, E. A., & HANISEE, J. (1982). Intellectual and adaptive performance of Asian children in adoptive American settings. *Developmental Psychology, 18*, 595–599.

CLARKE, A. D. B., & CLARKE, A. M. (1976). Formerly isolated children. In A. M. Clarke & A. D. B. Clarke (Eds.), *Early experience: Myth and evidence.* London: Open Books.

CLEMENTS, W. A., & PERNER, J. (1994). Implicit understanding of belief. *Cognitive Development, 9*, 377–395.

CLEMENTS, W. A., RUSTIN, C. L., & McCALLUM, S. (2000). Promoting the transition from implicit to explicit understanding: A training study of false belief. *Developmental Science, 3*, 81–92.

CLUBB, P. A., NIDA, R. E., MERRITT, K., & ORNSTEIN, P. A. (1993). Visiting the doctor: Children's knowledge and memory. *Cognitive Development, 8*, 361–372.

COHEN, L. B., & STRAUSS, M. S. (1979). Concept acquisition in the human infant. *Child Development, 50*, 419–424.

COHEN, L. B., & YOUNGER, B. A. (1983). Perceptual categorization in the infant. In E. K. Scholnick (Ed.), *New trends in conceptual representations: Challenges to Piaget's theory?* Hillsdale, NJ: Erlbaum.

COHEN, M. (1996). Preschooler's practical thinking and problem solving: The acquisition of an optimal solution. *Cognitive Development, 11*, 357–373.

COIE, J. D., & DODGE, K. A. (1998). Aggression and antisocial behavior. In N. Eisenberg (Vol. Ed), *Social, emotional, and personality development,* Vol. 3. In W. Damon (Gen. Ed.), *Handbook of child psychology.* New York: Wiley.

COLE, M. (1990). Cognitive development and formal schooling: The evidence from cross-cultural research. In L. C. Moll (Ed.), *Vygotsky and education.* New York: Cambridge University Press.

COLE, M., & SCRIBNER, S. (1977). Cross-cultural studies of memory and cognition. In R. V. Kail, Jr., & J. W. Hagen (Eds.), *Perspectives on the development of memory and cognition.* Hillsdale, NJ: Erlbaum.

COLLIE, R., & HAYNE, R. (1999). Deferred imitation by 6- and 9-month-old infants: More evidence for declarative memory. *Developmental Psychobiology, 35*, 83–90.

COLOMBO, J. (1986). Recent studies in early auditory development. In G. J. Whitehurst (Ed.), *Annals of child development,* Vol. 3. Greenwich, CT: JAI.

CONNOR, J. M., & SERBIN, L. A. (1977). Behaviorally based masculine and feminine-activity-preference scales for preschoolers: Correlates with other classroom behaviors and cognitive tests. *Child Development, 48*, 1411–1416.

COOPER R. P., & ASLIN, R. N. (1990). Preference for infant-directed speech in the first month after birth. *Child Development, 61*, 1584–1595.

COOPER, R. P., & ASLIN, R. N. (1994). Developmental differences in infant attention to the spectral properties of infant-directed speech. *Child Development, 65*, 1663–1677.

COSMIDES, L., & TOOBY, J. (1987). From evolution to behavior: Evolutionary psychology as the missing link. In J. Dupre (Ed.), *The latest and the best essays on evolution and optimality.* Cambridge, MA: MIT Press.

COSMIDES, L., TOOBY, J., & BARKOW, J. H. (1992). Introduction: Evolutionary psychology and conceptual integration. In J. H. Barkow, L. Cosmides, & J. Tooby (Eds.), *The adapted mind: Evolutionary psychology and the generation of culture.* New York: Oxford University Press.

COURAGE, M. L., & HOWE, M. L. (1998). The ebb and flow of infant attentional preferences: Evidence for long-term recognition memory in 3-month-olds. *Journal of Experimental Child Psychology, 70*, 26–53.

COURAGE, M. L., & HOWE, M. L. (2001). Long-term retention in 3.5-month-olds: Familiarization time and individual differences in attentional style. *Journal of Experimental Child Psychology, 79,* 271–293.

COURAGE, M. L., & HOWE, M. L. (2002). From infant to child: The dynamics of cognitive change in the second year of life. *Psychological Bulletin, 128,* 250–277.

COWAN, N. (1997). The development of working memory. In N. Cowan (Ed.), *The development of memory in childhood.* Hove East Sussex, UK: Psychology Press.

COWAN, N., NUGENT, L. D., ELLIOTT, E. M., PONOMAREV, I., & SAULTS, J. S. (1999). The role of attention in the development of short-term memory: Age differences in the verbal span of apprehension. *Child Development, 70,* 1082–1097.

COX, B. C., ORNSTEIN, P. A., NAUS, M. J., MAXFIELD, D., & ZIMLER, J. (1989). Children's concurrent use of rehearsal and organizational strategies. *Developmental Psychology, 25,* 619–627.

COX, D., & WATERS, H. S. (1986). Sex differences in the use of organization strategies: A developmental analysis. *Journal of Experimental Child Psychology, 41,* 18–37.

COYLE, T. R. (2001). Factor analysis of variability measures in eight independent samples of children and adults. *Journal of Experimental Child Psychology, 78,* 330–358.

COYLE, T. R., & BJORKLUND, D. F. (1996). The development of strategic memory: A modified microgenetic assessment of utilization deficiencies. *Cognitive Development, 11,* 295–314.

COYLE, T. R., & BJORKLUND, D. F. (1997). Age differences in, and consequences of, multiple- and variable strategy use on a multitrial sort-recall task. *Developmental Psychology, 33,* 372–380.

COYLE, T. R., READ, L. E., GAULTNEY, J. F., & BJORKLUND, D. F. (1998). Giftedness and variability in strategic processing on a multitrial memory task: Evidence for stability in gifted cognition. *Learning and Individual Differences, 10,* 273–290.

CRABTREE, J. W., & RIESEN, A. H. (1979). Effects of the duration of dark rearing on visually guided behavior in the kitten. *Developmental Psychobiology, 12,* 291–303.

CRAIN-THORESON, C., & DALE, P. S. (1992). Do early talkers become early readers? Linguistic precocity, preschool language, and emergent literacy. *Developmental Psychology, 28,* 421–429.

CRICK, N. R., & DODGE, K. A. (1994). A review and reformulation of social information-processing mechanisms in children's social adjustment. *Psychological Bulletin, 115,* 74–101.

CRICK, N. R., & DODGE, K. A. (1996). Social information-processing mechanisms in reactive and proactive aggression. *Child Development, 67,* 993–1002.

CRONBACH, L. J. (1957). The two disciplines of scientific psychology. *American Psychologist, 12,* 671–684.

CROWLEY, K., CALLANAN, M. A., TENNENBAUM, H. R., & ALLEN, E. (2001). Parents explain more often to boys than to girls during shared scientific thinking. *Psychological Science, 12,* 258–261.

CUMMINS, D. D. (1998). Social norms and other minds: The evolutionary roots of higher cognition. In D. D. Cummins & C. Allen (Eds.), *The evolution of mind.* New York: Oxford University Press.

CUNNINGHAM, A. E. (1990). Explicit versus implicit instruction in phonemic awareness. *Journal of Experimental Child Psychology, 50,* 429–444.

CURTISS, S. (1977). *Genie: A psycholinguistic study of a modern day "wild child."* New York: Academic.

CYNADER, M., BERMAN, N. M., & HEIN, A. (1976). Recovery of function in cat visual cortex following prolonged deprivation. *Experimental Brain Research, 25,* 139–156.

CZIKO, G. (1995). *Without miracles: Universal selection theory and the second Darwinian revolution.* Cambridge, MA: MIT Press.

DABBS, J. M., JR., CHANG, E-L., STRONG, R. A., & MILUN, R. (1998). Spatial ability, navigation strategy, and geographic knowledge among men and women. *Evolution and Human Behavior, 19,* 89–98.

DAEHLER, M., & CHEN, Z. (1993). Protagonist, theme and goal objects: Effects of surface features on analogical transfer. *Cognitive Development, 8,* 211–229.

DAEHLER, M. W., LONARDO, R., & BUKATKO, D. (1979). Matching and equivalence judgments in very young children. *Child Development, 50,* 170–179.

DALLAGO, M. L. P., & MOELY, B. E. (1980). Free recall in boys of normal and poor reading levels as a function of task manipulations. *Journal of Experimental Child Psychology, 30,* 62–78.

DAMAST, A. M., TAMIS-LEMONDA, C. S., & BORNSTEIN, M. H. (1996). Mother-child play: Sequential interactions and the relation between maternal beliefs and behaviors. *Child Development, 67,* 1752–1766.

DANEMAN, M., & BLENNERHASSETT, A. (1984). How to assess the listening comprehension skills of prereaders. *Journal of Educational Psychology, 76,* 1372–1381.

DANEMAN, M., & GREEN, I. (1986). Individual differences in comprehending and producing words in context. *Journal of Memory and Language, 25,* 1–18.

DANIEL, M. H. (1997). Intelligence testing: Status and trends. *American Psychologist, 52,* 1038–1045.

DANNER, F. W., & DAY, M. C. (1977). Eliciting formal operations. *Child Development, 48,* 1600–1606.

DARWIN, C. (1859). *The origin of species.* New York: Modern Library.

DAS, J. P. (1984). Cognitive deficits in mental retardation. A process approach. In P. H. Brooks, R. Sperber, & C. McCauley (Eds.), *Learning and cognition in the mentally retarded.* Hillsdale, NJ: Erlbaum.

DASEN, P. R. (ED.). (1977). *Piagetian psychology: Cross-cultural contributions.* New York: Gardner.

DAVIS, H., & PÉRUSSE, R. (1988). Numerical competence in animals: Definitional issues, current evidence, and a new research agenda. *Behavioral and Brain Sciences, 11,* 561–615.

DE HAAN, M., OLIVER, A., & JOHNSON, M. H. (1998). Electro physiological correlates of face processing by adults and 6-month-old infants. *Journal of Cognitive Neural Science* (Annual Meeting Supplement), *36.*

DE RIBAUPIERRE, A., & BAILLEUX, C. (1995). Development of attentional capacity in childhood: A longitudinal study. In F. E. Weinert & W. Schneider (Eds.), *Memory performance and competencies: Issues in growth and development.* Mahwah, NJ: Erlbaum.

DE VILLIERS, J. G., & DE VILLIERS, P. A. (1973). A cross-sectional study of the acquisition of grammatical morphemes in child speech. *Journal of Psycholinguistic Research, 2,* 267–278.

DE VILLIERS, J. G., & DE VILLIERS, P. A. (1978). *Language acquisition.* Cambridge, MA: Harvard University Press.

DE VILLIERS, P. A., & DE VILLIERS, J. G. (1979). *Early language.* Cambridge, MA: Harvard University Press.

DE VRIES, R. (1969). Constancy of generic identity in the years three to six. *Monographs of the Society for Research in Child Development, 34* (Serial No. 127).

DECASPER, A. J., & FIFER, W. P. (1980). Of human bonding: Newborns prefer their mother's voice. *Science, 208,* 1174–1176.

DECASPER, A. J., LECANUET, J.-P., BUSNEL, M.-C., GRANIER-DEFERRE, C., & MAUGEAIS, R. (1994). Fetal reactions to recurrent maternal speech. *Infant Behavior & Development, 17,* 159–164.

DECASPER, A. J., & SPENCE, M. J. (1986). Prenatal maternal speech influences newborns' perception of speech sounds. *Infant Behavior & Development, 9,* 133–150.

DELEVATI, N. M., & BERGAMASCO, N. H. P. (1999). Pain in the neonate: An analysis of facial movements and crying in response to nociceptive stimuli. *Infant Behavior & Development, 22,* 137–143.

DELOACHE, J. S. (1987). Rapid change in the symbolic functioning of very young children. *Science, 238,* 1556–1557.

DELOACHE, J. S. (1991). Symbolic functioning in very young children: Understanding of pictures and models. *Child Development, 62,* 736–752.

DELOACHE, J. S. (1995). Early understanding and use of symbols: The model model. *Current Directions in Psychological Science, 4,* 109–113.

DELOACHE, J. S. (2000). Dual representation and young children's use of scale models. *Child Development, 71,* 329–338.

DELOACHE, J. S., & BROWN, A. L. (1983). Very young children's memory for the location of objects in a large scale environment. *Child Development, 54,* 888–897.

DELOACHE, J. S., CASSIDY, D. J., & BROWN, A. L. (1985). Precursors of mnemonic strategies in very young children's memory for the location of hidden objects. *Child Development, 56,* 125–137.

DELOACHE, J. S., & MARZOLF, D. P. (1992). When a picture is not worth a thousand words: Young children's understanding of pictures and models. *Cognitive Development, 7,* 317–329.

DELOACHE, J. S., MILLER, K. F., & PIERROUTSAKOS, S. L. (1998). Reasoning and problem solving. In D. Kuhn & R. S. Siegler (Vol. Eds.), *Cognitive, language, and perceptual development,* Vol. 2. In W. Damon (Gen. Ed.), *Handbook of child psychology.* New York: Wiley.

DELOACHE, J. S., MILLER, K. F., & ROSENGREN, K. S. (1997). The credible shrinking room: Very young children's performance with symbolic and nonsymbolic relations. *Psychological Science, 8,* 308–313.

DELOACHE, J. S., PIERROUTSAKOS, S. L., UTTAL, D. H., ROSENGREN, K. S., & GOTTLIEB, A. (1998). Grasping the nature of pictures. *Psychological Science, 9,* 205–210.

DELPIT, L. D. (1990). Language diversity and learning. In S. Hynds & D. L. Rubin (Eds.), *Perspectives on talk and learning.* Urbana, IL: National Council of Teachers of English.

DEMARIE-DREBLOW, D. (1991). Relation between knowledge and memory: A reminder that correlation does not imply causality. *Child Development, 62,* 484–498.

DEMARIE-DREBLOW, D., & MILLER, P. H. (1988). The development of children's strategies for selective attention: Evidence for a transitional period. *Child Development, 59,* 1504–1513.

DEMPSTER, F. N. (1981). Memory span: Sources of individual and developmental differences. *Psychological Bulletin, 89,* 63–100.

DEMPSTER, F. N. (1985). Short-term memory development in childhood and adolescence. In C. J. Brainerd & M. Pressley (Eds.), *Basic processes in memory development: Progress in cognitive development research.* New York: Springer-Verlag.

DEMPSTER, F. N. (1992). The rise and fall of the inhibitory mechanism: Toward a unified theory of cognitive development and aging. *Developmental Review, 12*, 45–75.

DEMPSTER, F. N. (1993). Resistance to interference: Developmental changes in basic processing mechanisms. In M. L. Howe & R. Pasnak (Eds.), *Emerging themes in cognitive development*, Vol. 1, *Foundations*. New York: Springer-Verlag.

DENNEY, N. (1974). Evidence for developmental changes in categorization criteria for children and adults. *Human Development, 17*, 41–53.

DENNIS, W. (1973). *Children of the Crèche*. New York: Appleton-Century-Crofts.

DESTEFANO, J. (1972). Social variation in language: Implications for teaching reading to Black ghetto children. In J. A. Figurel (Ed.), *Better reading in urban schools*. Newark, DE: International Reading Association.

DETTERMAN, D. K. (1987). What does reaction time tell us about intelligence? In P. E. Vernon (Ed.), *Speed of information processing and intelligence*. Norwood, NJ: Ablex.

DETTERMAN, D. K., & DANIEL, M. H. (1989). Correlations of mental tests with each other and with cognitive variables are highest for low IQ groups. *Intelligence, 13*, 340–359.

DETTERMAN, D. K., & THOMPSON, L. A. (1997). What is so special about special education? *American Psychologist, 52*, 1082–1090.

DEVLIN, B., DANIELS, M., & ROEDER, K. (1997). The heritability of IQ. *Nature, 388*, 468–471.

DIAMOND, A. (1985). Development of the ability to use recall to guide action as indicated by infants' performance on AB. *Child Development, 56*, 868–883.

DIAMOND, A. (1991). Frontal lobe involvement in cognitive changes during the first year of life. In K. R. Gibson & A. C. Petersen (Eds.), *Brain maturation and cognitive development: Comparative and cross-cultural perspectives*. New York: Aldine de Gruyter.

DIAMOND, A., CRUTTENDEN, L., & NEIDERMAN, D. (1994). AB with multiple wells: 1. Why are multiple wells sometimes easier than two wells? 2. Memory or memory + inhibition? *Developmental Psychology, 30*, 192–205.

DIAMOND, A., KIRKHAM, N., & AMSO, D. (2002). Conditions under which young children can hold two rules in mind and inhibit a prepotent response. *Developmental Psychology, 38*, 352–362.

DIAMOND, A., & TAYLOR, C. (1996). Development of an aspect of executive control: Development of the abilities to remember what I said and to "Do as I say, not as I do." *Developmental Psychobiology, 29*, 315–324.

DIAZ, R. M., NEAL, C. J., & VACHIO, A. (1991). Maternal teaching in the zone of proximal development: A comparison of low- and high-risk dyads. *Merrill-Palmer Quarterly, 37*, 83–108.

DIESENDRUCK, G., & MARKSON, L. (2001). Children's avoidance of lexical overlap: A pragmatic account. *Developmental Psychology, 37*, 630–641.

DIRKS, J., & NEISSER, U. (1977). Memory for objects in real scenes: The development of recognition and recall. *Journal of Experimental Child Psychology, 23*, 315–328.

DODGE, K. A. (1986). A social information processing model of social competence in children. In M. Perlmutter (Ed.), *Minnesota symposium on child psychology*, Vol. 18. Hillsdale, NJ: Erlbaum.

DODGE, K. A., PETIT, G. S., BATES, J. E., & VALENTE, E. (1995). Social information processing patterns partially mediate the effect of early physical abuse on later conduct problems. *Journal of Abnormal Psychology, 104*, 632–643.

DODGE, K. A., PETTIT, G. S., MCCLASKEY, C. L., & BROWN, M. M. (1986). Social competence in children. *Monographs of the Society for Research in Child Development, 51* (Serial No. 213).

DODGE, K. A., & PRICE, J. M. (1994). On the relation between social information processing and socially competent behavior in early school-age children. *Child Development, 65*, 1385–1397.

DOMAN, G. (1984). *How to multiply your baby's intelligence*. Garden City, NY: Doubleday.

DOUGHERTY, T. M., & HAITH, M. M. (1997). Infant expectations and reaction time as predictors of childhood speed of processing and IQ. *Developmental Psychology, 33*, 146–155.

DRACHMAN, D. B., & COULOMBRE, A. J. (1962). Experimental clubfoot and arthrogryposis multiplex congenita. *Lancet*, 523–526.

DRUMMEY, A. B., & NEWCOMBE, N. (1995). Remembering versus knowing the past: Children's explicit and implicit memory. *Journal of Experimental Child Psychology, 59*, 549–565.

DUNCAN, J., SEITZ, R. J., KOLODNY, J., BOR, D., HERZOG, H., AHMED, A., NEWELL, F. N., & EMSLIE, H. (2000). A neural basis for general intelligence. *Science, 289* (21 July), 457–460.

DWECK, C. S., & LEGGETT, E. L. (1988). A social-cognitive approach to motivation and personality. *Psychological Review, 95*, 256–273.

EAGAN, S. K., & PERRY, D. G. (2001). Gender identity: A multidimensional analysis with implications for psychological adjustment. *Developmental Psychology, 37*, 451–463.

EASTERBROOK, M. A., KISILEVSKY, B. S., HAINS, S. M. J., & MUIR, D. W. (1999). Faceness or complexity: Evidence from newborn visual tracking of facelike stimuli. *Infant Behavior & Development, 22,* 17–35.

EATON, W. O., & VON BARGEN, D. (1981). Asynchronous development of gender understanding in preschool children. *Child Development, 52,* 1020–1027.

EDELMAN, G. M. (1987). *Neural Darwinism: The theory of neuronal group selection.* New York: Basic Books.

EILERS, R. E., GAVIN, W. J., & WILSON, W. R. (1979). Linguistic experience and phonemic perception in infancy: A cross-linguistic study. *Child Development, 50,* 14–18.

EIMAS, P. D., & QUINN, P. C. (1994). Studies on the formation of perceptually based basic-level categories in young infants. *Child Development, 65,* 903–917.

EIMAS, P. D., SIQUELAND, E. R., JUSCZYK, P., & VIGORITO, J. (1971). Speech perception in infants. *Science, 71,* 303–306.

EIZENMAN, D. R., & BERTENTHAL, B. I. (1998). Infants' perception of object unity in translating and rotating displays. *Developmental Psychology, 34,* 426–434.

ELKIND, D. (1967). Egocentrism in adolescence. *Child Development, 38,* 1025–1033.

ELKIND, D. (1987). *Miseducation: Preschoolers at risk.* New York: Knopf.

ELKIND, D. (1996). Inhelder and Piaget on adolescence and adulthood: A postmodern appraisal. *Psychological Science, 7,* 216–220.

ELKIND, D., & BOWEN, R. (1979). Imaginary audience behavior in children and adolescents. *Developmental Psychology, 15,* 38–44.

ELLIS, H. (1894). *Man and woman: A study of human secondary sexual characters.* London: Walter Scott.

ELLIS, N. C., & HENNELLEY, R. A. (1980). A bilingual word-length effect: Implications for intelligence testing and the relative ease of mental calculation in Welsh and English. *British Journal of Psychology, 71,* 43–52.

ELLIS, N. R., KATZ, E., & WILLIAMS, J. E. (1987). Developmental aspects of memory for spatial location. *Journal of Experimental Child Psychology, 44,* 401–412.

ELLIS, S., & ROGOFF, B. (1986). Problem solving in children's management of instruction. In E. Mueller & C. Cooper (Eds.), *Process and outcome in peer relationships.* Orlando, FL: Academic.

ELLIS, S., & SIEGLER, R. S. (1997). Planning and strategy choice, or why don't children plan when they should? In S. L. Friedman & E. K. Scholnick (Eds.), *Why, how, and when do we plan: The developmental psychology of planning.* Hillsdale, NJ: Erlbaum.

ELMAN, J. (1994). Implicit learning in neural networks: The importance of starting small. In C. Umilta & M. Moscovitch (Eds.), *Attention and performance XV: Conscious and nonconscious information processing.* Cambridge, MA: MIT Press.

ELMAN, J. L., BATES, E. A., JOHNSON, M. H., KARMILOFF-SMITH, A., PARISI, D., & PLUNKET, K. (1996). *Rethinking innateness: A connectionist perspective on development.* Cambridge, MA: MIT Press.

EMERSON, H. F., & GEKOWSKI, W. L. (1976). Interactive and categorical grouping strategies and the syntagmatic-paradigmatic shift. *Child Development, 47,* 1116–1121.

ERDELYI, M. (1994). Hypnotic hypermnesia: The empty set of hypermnesia. *International Journal of Clinical and Experimental Hypnosis, 42,* 379–390.

ERIKSSON, P. S., PERFILIEVA, E., BJOERK-ERIKSSON, T., ALBORN, A-M., NORDBORG, C., PETERSON, D. A., & GAGE, F. H. (1998). Neurogenesis in the adult human hippocampus. *Nature Medicine, 4,* 1313–1317.

ESPY, K. A., MOLFESE, V. J., & DILALLA, L. F. (2001). Effects of environmental measures on intelligence in young children: Growth curve modeling of longitudinal data. *Merrill-Palmer Quarterly, 47,* 42–73.

EVANS, M. A. (1985). Self-initiated speech repairs: A reflection of communicative monitoring in young children. *Developmental Psychology, 21,* 365–371.

EYSENCK, H. J. (1987). Speed of information processing, reaction time, and the theory of intelligence. In P. E. Vernon (Ed.), *Speed of information processing and intelligence.* Norwood, NJ: Ablex.

FABRICIUS, W. V. (1988). The development of forward search planning in preschoolers. *Child Development, 59,* 1473–1488.

FAGAN, J. F., III. (1973). Infants' delayed recognition memory and forgetting. *Journal of Experimental Child Psychology, 16,* 424–450.

FAGAN, J. F., III. (1974). Infant recognition memory: The effects of length of familiarization and type of discrimination task. *Child Development, 45,* 351–356.

FAGAN, J. F., III. (1984). The relationship of novelty preferences during infancy to later intelligence and recognition memory. *Intelligence, 8,* 339–346.

FAGAN, J. F., III. (1992). Intelligence: A theoretical viewpoint. *Current Directions in Psychological Science, 1,* 82–86.

FAGEN, J., PRIGOT, J., CARROLL, M., PIOLI, L., STEIN, A., & FRANCO, A. (1997). Auditory context and memory retrieval in young infants. *Developmental Psychology, 68,* 1057–1066.

FAGAN, J. F., III, & SINGER, L. T. (1983). Infant recognition memory as a measure of intelligence. In L. P. Lipsitt & C. K. Rovee-Collier (Eds.), *Advances in infancy research,* Vol. 2. Norwood, NJ: Ablex.

FAGOT, B. I., LEINBACH, M. D., & HAGAN, R. (1986). Gender labeling and the adoption of sex-typed behaviors. *Developmental Psychology, 22,* 440–443.

FANTZ, R. L. (1958). Pattern vision in young infants. *Psychological Record, 8,* 43–47.

FANTZ, R. L. (1961). The origin of form perception. *Scientific American, 204,* 66–72.

FANTZ, R. L., & MIRANDA, S. B. (1975). Newborn attention to form of contour. *Child Development, 46,* 224–228.

FARRONI, T., CSIBRA, G., SIMION, F., & JOHNSON, M. H. (2002). Eye contact detection in humans from birth. *Proceedings of the National Academy of Science, 99,* 9602–9605.

FEINGOLD, A. (1988). Cognitive gender differences are disappearing. *American Psychologist, 43,* 95–103.

FEINGOLD, A. (1992). Sex differences in variability in intellectual abilities: A new look at an old controversy. *Review of Educational Research, 62,* 61–84.

FERNALD, A. (1992). Human maternal vocalizations to infants as biologically relevant signals: An evolutionary perspective. In J. H. Barkow, L. Cosmides, & J. Tooby (Eds.), *The adaptive mind: Evolutionary psychology and the generation of culture.* New York: Oxford University Press.

FERNALD, A., & MAZZIE, C. (1991). Prosody and focus in speech to infants and adults. *Developmental Psychology, 27,* 209–221.

FERNALD, A., PINTO, J. P., SWINGLEY, D., WEINBERG, A., & MCROBERTS, G. W. (1998). Rapid gains in speed of verbal processing by infants in the 2nd year. *Psychological Science, 9,* 228–231.

FERNALD, A., TAESCHNER, T., DUNN, J., PAPOUSEK, M., & FUKUI, I. (1989). A cross-language study of prosodic modifications in mothers' and fathers' speech to infants. *Journal of Child Language, 16,* 477–501.

FERREIRA, F., & MORRISON, F. J. (1994). Children's knowledge of syntactic constituents: Effects of age and schooling. *Developmental Psychology, 30,* 663–678.

FIELD, D. (1987). A review of preschool conservation training: An analysis of analyses. *Developmental Review, 7,* 210–251.

FIELD, T. M., WOODSON, R., GREENBERG, R., & COHEN, D. (1982). Discrimination and imitation of facial expression by neonates. *Science, 218,* 179–181.

FINKELSTEIN, N. W., & RAMEY, C. T. (1977). Learning to control the environment in infancy. *Child Development, 48,* 806–819.

FIREMAN, G. (1996). Developing a plan for solving a problem: A representational shift. *Cognitive Development, 11,* 107–122.

FISCHER, K. W. (1980). A theory of cognitive development: The control and construction of hierarchies of skills. *Psychological Review, 87,* 477–531.

FISCHER, K. W., & BIDELL, T. (1991). Constraining nativist inferences about cognitive capacities. In S. Carey & R. Gelman (Eds.), *The epigenesis of mind: Essays on biology and cognition.* Hillsdale, NJ: Erlbaum.

FISCHER, K. W., & BIDELL, T. (1998). Dynamic development of psychological structures in action and thought. In R. M. Lerner (Vol. Ed.), *Theoretical models of human development,* Vol. 1. In W. Damon (Gen. Ed.), *Handbook of child psychology* (5th ed.). New York: Wiley.

FISCHER, K. W., & HENCKE, R. W. (1996). Infants' construction of actions in context: Piaget's contribution to research on early development. *Psychological Science, 7,* 204–211.

FISCHER, K. W., & ROSE, S. P. (1996). Dynamic growth cycles of brain and cognitive development. In R. W. Thatcher, G. R. Lyon, J. Rumsey, & N. Krasnegor (Eds.), *Developmental neuroimaging: Mapping the development of brain and behavior.* San Diego: Academic.

FISHBEIN, H. D. (1976). *Evolution, development, and children's learning.* Pacific Palisades, CA: Goodyear.

FISHER, C., & TOKURA, H. (1996). Acoustic cues to grammatical structure in infant-directed speech: Cross-linguistic evidence. *Child Development, 67,* 3192–3218.

FIVUSH, R. (1988). The functions of event memory: Some comments on Nelson and Barsalou. In U. Neisser & E. Winograd (Eds.), *Remembering reconsidered: Ecological and traditional approaches to the study of memory.* New York: Cambridge University Press.

FIVUSH, R. (1997). Event memory in early childhood. In N. Cowan (Ed.), *The development of memory in childhood.* Hove East Sussex, UK: Psychology Press.

FIVUSH, R., & HAMOND, N. R. (1989). Time and again: Effects of repetition and retention interval on 2-year-olds' event recal. *Journal of Experimental Child Psychology, 47,* 259–273.

FIVUSH, R., & HAMOND, N. R. (1990). Autobiographical memory across the preschool years: Toward reconceptualizing childhood amnesia. In R. Fivush & J. A. Hudson (Eds.), *Knowing and remembering in young children.* Cambridge: Cambridge University Press.

FIVUSH, R., & HUDSON, J. A. (EDS.). (1990). *Knowing and remembering in young children.* Cambridge: Cambridge University Press.

FIVUSH, R., KUEBLI, J., & CLUBB, P. A. (1992). The structure of events and event representations: A developmental analysis. *Child Development, 63,* 188–201.

FLANNAGAN, D., BAKER-WARD, L., & GRAHAM, L. (1995). Talk about preschool: Patterns of topic discussion and elaboration related to gender and ethnicity. *Sex Roles, 32,* 1–15.

FLAVELL, J. H. (1970). Developmental studies of mediated memory. In H. W. Reese & L. P. Lipsitt (Eds.), *Advances in child development and child behavior,* Vol. 5. New York: Academic.

FLAVELL, J. H. (1971). Stage-related properties of cognitive development. *Cognitive Psychology, 2,* 421–453.

FLAVELL, J. H. (1978). Developmental stage: Explanans or explanandum? *Behavioral and Brain Sciences, 2,* 187.

FLAVELL, J. H. (1982). On cognitive development. *Child Development, 53,* 1–10.

FLAVELL, J. H. (1992). Cognitive development: Past, present, and future. *Developmental Psychology, 28,* 988–1005.

FLAVELL, J. H. (1996). Piaget's legacy. *Psychological Science, 7,* 200–203.

FLAVELL, J. H., BEACH, D. R., & CHINSKY, J. H. (1966). Spontaneous verbal rehearsal in a memory task as a function of age. *Child Development, 37,* 283–299.

FLAVELL, J. H., EVERETT, B. A., CROFT, K., & FLAVELL, E. (1981). Young children's knowledge about visual perception: Further evidence for level 1-level 2 distinction. *Developmental Psychology, 17,* 99–107.

FLAVELL, J. H., & GREEN, F. L. (1999). Development of intuitions about the controllability of different mental states. *Cognitive Development, 14,* 133–146.

FLAVELL, J. H., GREEN, F. L., & FLAVELL, E. R. (1986). Development of knowledge about the appearance-reality distinction. *Monographs of the Society for Research in Child Development, 51* (Serial No. 212).

FLAVELL, J. H., GREEN, F. L., & FLAVELL, E. R. (1995). The development of children's knowledge about attentional focus. *Developmental Psychology, 31,* 706–712.

FLAVELL, J. H., GREEN, F. L., & FLAVELL, E. R. (1998). The mind has a mind of its own: Developing knowledge about mental uncontrollability. *Cognitive Development, 13,* 127–138.

FLAVELL, J. H., GREEN, F. L., FLAVELL, E. R., & GROSSMAN, J. B. (1997). The development of children's knowledge about inner speech. *Developmental Psychology, 68,* 39–47.

FLAVELL, J. H., & MILLER, P. H. (1998). Social cognition. In D. Kuhn & R. S. Siegler (Vol. Eds.), *Cognition, perception, and language,* Vol. 2. In W. Damon (Gen. Ed.), *Handbook of child psychology.* New York: Wiley.

FLAVELL, J. H., SPEER, J. R., GREEN, F. L., & AUGUST, D. L. (1981). The development of comprehension monitoring and knowledge about communication. *Monographs of the Society for Research in Child Development, 46* (Serial No. 192).

FLAVELL, J. H., & WOHLWILL, J. F. (1969). Formal and functional aspects of cognitive development. In D. Elkind & J. H. Flavell (Eds.), *Studies in cognitive development.* London: Oxford University Press.

FLEMING, V. M., & ALEXANDER, J. M. (2001). The benefits of peer collaboration: A replication with a delayed posttest. *Contemporary Educational Psychology, 26,* 588–601.

FLETCHER, K. L., & BRAY, N. W. (1997). Instructional and contextual effects on external memory strategy use in young children. *Journal of Experimental Child Psychology, 67,* 204–222.

FLIELLER, A. (1999). Comparison of the development of formal thought in adolescent cohorts aged 10 to 15 years (1967–1996 and 1972–1993). *Developmental Psychology, 35,* 1048–1058.

FLIN, R., BOON, J., KNOX, A., & BULL, R. (1992). The effect of a five-month delay on children's and adult's eyewitness memory. *British Journal of Psychology, 83,* 323–336.

FLYNN, J. R. (1987). Massive IQ gains in 14 nations: What IQ tests really measure. *Psychological Bulletin, 101,* 171–191.

FODOR, J. A. (1983). *The modularity of mind.* Cambridge, MA: MIT Press.

FODOR, J. A. (2000). *The mind doesn't work that way: The scope and limits of computational psychology.* Cambridge, MA: MIT Press.

FOLDS, T. H., FOOTO, M., GUTTENTAG, R. E., & ORNSTEIN, P. A. (1990). When children mean to remember: Issues of context specificity, strategy effectiveness, and intentionality in the development of memory. In D. F. Bjorklund (Ed.), *Children's strategies: Contemporary views of cognitive development.* Hillsdale, NJ: Erlbaum.

FOLEY, M. A., & RATNER, H. H. (1998). Distinguishing between memories for thoughts and deeds: The role of prospective processing in children's source monitoring. *British Journal of Developmental Psychology, 16,* 465–484.

FOLEY, M. A., RATNER, H. H., & PASSALACQUA, C. (1993). Appropriating the actions of another: Implications for children's memory and learning. *Cognitive Development, 8,* 373–401.

FOLEY, M. A., SANTINI, C., & SOPASAKIS, M. (1989). Discriminating between memories: Evidence for children's spontaneous elaborations. *Journal of Experimental Child Psychology, 48,* 146–169.

FOX, L. H. (1976). Sex differences in mathematical precocity: Bridging the gap. In D. P. Keating (Ed.), *Intellectual talent: Research and development.* Baltimore: Johns Hopkins University Press.

FRANKEL, M. T., & ROLLINS, H. S. (1985). Associative and categorical hypotheses of organization in the free recall of adults and children. *Journal of Experimental Child Psychology, 40,* 304–318.

FRAZIER, J. A. (1993, MARCH). *Influences of extended-year of schooling on academic achievement and cognitive development.* Paper presented at meeting of the Society for Research in Child Development, New Orleans, LA.

FRAZIER, J. A., & MORRISON, F. J. (1998). The influence of extended-year schooling on growth of achievement and perceived competence in early elementary school. *Child Development, 69*, 495–517.

FREUD, S. (1963). Three essays on the theory of sexuality. In J. Strachey (Ed. and Trans.), *The standard edition of the complete psychological works of Sigmund Freud* (Vol. 7). London: Hogarth.

FREUND, L. S. (1990). Maternal regulation of children's problem-solving behavior and its impact on children's performance. *Child Development, 61*, 113–126.

FRIEDMAN, S. (1972). Habituation and recovery of visual response in the alert human newborn. *Journal of Experimental Child Psychology, 13*, 339–349.

FRY, A., & HALE, S. (1996). Processing speed, working memory, and fluid intelligence: Evidence for a developmental cascade. *Psychological Science, 7*, 237–241.

FRY, A., & HALE, S. (2000). Relationships among processing speed, working memory and fluid intelligence in children. *Biological Psychology, 54*, 1–34.

FRYE, D., ZELAZO, P. D., & PALFAI, T. (1995). Theory of mind and rule-based reasoning. *Cognitive Development, 10*, 483–527.

FULIGNI, A. J., & STEVENSON, H. W. (1995). Time use and mathematics achievement among American, Chinese, and Japanese high school students. *Child Development, 66*, 830–842.

FURLOW, F. B., ARMIJO-PREWITT, T., GANGSTEAD, S. W., & THORNHILL, R. (1997). Fluctuating asymmetry and psychometric intelligence. *Proceedings of the Royal Society of London, Series B, 264*, 823–829.

FURMAN, L. N., & WALDEN, T. A. (1990). Effects of script knowledge on preschool children's communicative interactions. *Developmental Psychology, 26*, 227–233.

FURTH, H. G. (1969). *Piaget and knowledge: Theoretical foundations.* Englewood Cliffs, NJ: Prentice-Hall.

FUSON, K. C. (1988). *Children's counting and concepts of number.* New York: Springer-Verlag.

FUSON, K. C., PERGAMENT, G. G., LYONS, B. G., & HALL, J. W. (1985). Children's conformity to the cardinality rule as a function of set size and counting accuracy. *Child Development, 56*, 1429–1436.

FUSON, K. C., SECADA, W. G., & HALL, J. T. (1983). Matching, counting, and conservation of numerical equivalence. *Child Development, 54*, 91–97.

FUSTER, J. M. (1989). *The prefrontal cortex: Anatomy, physiology, and neuropsychology of the frontal lobe.* New York: Raven.

GALLAGHER, A. M., DE LISI, R., HOLST, P. C., MCGILLICUDDY-DE LISI, A. V., MORELY, M., & CAHALAN, C. (2000). Gender differences in advanced mathematical problem solving. *Journal of Experimental Child Psychology, 75*, 165–190.

GALLUP, G. G., JR. (1979). Self-recognition in chimpanzees and man: A developmental and comparative perspective. In M. Lewis & L. A. Rosenblum (Eds.), *Genesis of behavior: Vol. 2. The child and its family.* New York: Plenum.

GALSWORTHY, M. J., DIONNE, G., DALE, P. S., & PLOMIN, R. (2000). Sex differences in early verbal and nonverbal cognitive development. *Developmental Science, 3*, 206–215.

GANGESTAD, S. W., & THORNHILL, R. (1997). Human sexual selection and developmental stability. In J. A. Simpson & D. T. Kenrick (Eds.), *Evolutionary social psychology.* Mahwah, NJ: Erlbaum.

GARBER, H. L. (1988). *The Milwaukee Project: Preventing mental retardation in children at risk.* Washington, DC: American Association on Mental Retardation.

GARDNER, H. (1983). *Frames of mind: The theory of multiple intelligences.* New York: Basic.

GARDNER, H. (1984). Assessing intelligence: A comment on "Testing intelligence without IQ tests." *Phi Delta Kappan, 65*, 699–700.

GARDNER, H. (ED.). (1993). *Multiple intelligences: The theory in practice.* New York: Basic.

GARDNER, H. (1999). Are there additional intelligences? The case for naturalist, spiritual, and existential intelligences. In J. Kane (Ed.), *Education, information and transformation.* Englewood Cliffs, NJ: Prentice-Hall.

GARDNER H., & HATCH, T. (1989). Multiple intelligences go to school: Educational implications of the theory of multiple intelligences. *Educational Researcher, 18* (8), 4–10.

GARNER, R. (1990). Children's use of strategies in reading. In D. F. Bjorklund (Ed.), *Children's strategies: Contemporary views of cognitive development.* Hillsdale, NJ: Erlbaum.

GARNHAM, W. A., & RUFFMAN, T. (2001). Doesn't see, doesn't know: Is anticipatory looking really related to understanding belief? *Developmental Science, 4*, 94–100.

GAULTNEY, J. F. (1995). The effect of prior knowledge and metacognition on the acquisition of a reading comprehension strategy. *Journal of Experimental Child Psychology, 59*, 142–163.

GAULTNEY, J. F. (1998). Utilization deficiencies among children with learning disabilities. *Learning and Individual Differences, 10*, 13–28.

GAULTNEY, J. F., BJORKLUND, D. F., & GOLDSTEIN, D. (1996). To be young, gifted, and strategic: Advantages for memory performance. *Journal of Experimental Child Psychology, 61*, 43–66.

GAUVAIN, M. (2001). *The social context of cognitive development.* New York: Guilford.

GAUVAIN, M., & ROGOFF, B. (1989). Collaborative problem solving and children's planning skills. *Developmental Psychology, 25,* 139–151.

GEARY, D. C. (1993). Mathematical disabilities: Cognitive, neuropsychological, and genetic components. *Psychological Bulletin, 114,* 345–362.

GEARY, D. C. (1995). Reflections of evolution and culture in children's cognition: Implications for mathematical development and instruction. *American Psychologist, 50,* 24–37.

GEARY, D. C. (1996). Sexual selection and sex differences in mathematical abilities. *Behavioral and Brain Sciences, 19,* 229–284.

GEARY, D. C. (1998). *Male, female: The evolution of human sex differences.* Washington, DC: American Psychological Association.

GEARY, D. C. (2001). Sexual selection and sex differences in social cognition. In A. V. McGillicuddy-DeLisi & R. DeLisi (Eds.), *Biology, society, and behavior: The development of sex differences in cognition.* Greenwich, CT: Ablex.

GEARY, D. C., & BJORKLUND, D. F. (2000). Evolutionary developmental psychology. *Child Development, 71,* 57–65.

GEARY, D. C., BOW-THOMAS, C. C., FAN, L., & SIEGLER, R. S. (1993). Even before formal instructions. Chinese children outperform American children in mental arithmetic. *Cognitive Development, 8,* 517–529.

GEARY, D. C., BOW-THOMAS, C. C., LIU, F., & SIEGLER, R. S. (1996). Development of arithmetic competencies in Chinese and American children: Influence of age, language, and schooling. *Child Development, 67,* 2022–2044.

GEARY, D. C., & BROWN, S. C. (1991). Cognitive addition: Strategy choice and speed-of-processing differences in gifted, normal and mathematically disabled children. *Developmental Psychology, 27,* 398–406.

GEARY, D. C., BROWN, S. C., & SAMARANAYAKE, V. A. (1991). Cognitive addition: A short longitudinal study of strategy choice and speed of processing differences in normal and mathematically disabled children. *Developmental Psychology, 27,* 787–797.

GEARY, D. C., FAN, L., & BOW-THOMAS, C. C. (1992). Numerical cognition: Loci of ability differences comparing children from China and the United States. *Psychological Science, 3,* 180–185.

GEARY, D. C., & HUFFMAN, K. (2002). Brain and cognitive evolution: Forms of modularity and functions of mind. *Psychological Bulletin, 128,* 667–698.

GEARY, D. C., SALTHOUSE, T. A., CHEN, G-P., & FAN, L. (1996). Are East Asian versus American differences in arithmetical ability a recent phenomenon? *Developmental Psychology, 32,* 254–262.

GELMAN, R. (1969). Conservation acquisition: A problem of learning to attend to relevant attributes. *Journal of Experimental Child Psychology, 7,* 167–187.

GELMAN, R., & GALLISTEL, C. R. (1978). *The child's understanding of number.* Cambridge, MA: Harvard University Press.

GELMAN, R., MECK, E., & MERKIN, S. (1986). Young children's numerical competence. *Cognitive Development, 1,* 1–30.

GELMAN, R., & WILLIAMS, E. M. (1998). Enabling constraints for cognitive development and learning: Domain-specificity and epigenesis. In D. Kuhn & R. S. Siegler (Vol. Eds.), *Cognition, perception, and language,* Vol. 2. In W. Damon (Gen. Ed.), *Handbook of child psychology.* New York: Wiley.

GENTNER, D. (1989). The mechanisms of analogical learning. In S. Vosniadou & A. Ortony (Eds.). *Similarity and analogical reasoning.* London: Cambridge University Press.

GESELL, A., & AMATRUDA, C. (1954). *Developmental diagnosis.* New York: Paul B. Holber.

GHATALA, E. S. (1984). Developmental changes in incidental memory as a function of meaningfulness and encoding condition. *Developmental Psychology, 20,* 208–211.

GHATALA, E. S., LEVIN, J. R., PRESSLEY, M., & GOODWIN, D. (1986). A componential analysis of the effects of derived and supplied strategy-utility information on children's strategy selections. *Journal of Experimental Child Psychology, 41,* 76–92.

GIBBS, A. C., & WILSON, J. F. (1999). Sex differences in route learning by children. *Perceptual & Motor Skills, 88,* 590–594.

GIBSON, E. J., & SPELKE, E. S. (1983). The development of perception. In J. H. Flavell, & E. M. Markman (Eds.), *Cognitive development,* Vol. 3. In P. H. Mussen (Gen. Ed.), *Handbook of child psychology.* New York: Wiley.

GIBSON, E. J., & WALKER, A. S. (1984). Development of knowledge of visual-tactual affordances of substance. *Child Development, 55,* 453–460.

GIBSON, K. R. (1991). Myelination and behavioral development: A comparative perspective on questions of neoteny, altriciality and intelligence. In K. R Gibson & A. C. Petersen (Eds.), *Brain maturation and cognitive development: Comparative and cross-cultural perspectives.* New York: Aldine de Gruyter.

GINSBURG, H. P., KLEIN, A., & STARKEY, P. (1998). The development of children's mathematical thinking: Connecting research with practice. In I. E. Sigel & K. A. Renninger (Vol. Eds.), *Child psychology in practice,* Vol. 4. In W. Damon (Gen. Ed.), *Handbook of child psychology.* New York: Wiley.

GLICK, J. (1975). Cognitive development in cross-cultural perspective. In F. Horowitz (Ed.), *Review of child development research,* Vol. 4. Chicago: University of Chicago Press.

GOLDFIELD, B. A., & REZNICK, J. S. (1990). Early lexical acquisition: Rate, content, and the vocabulary spurt. *Journal of Child Language, 17,* 171–184.

GOLDSTEIN, D., HASHER, L., & STEIN, D. K. (1983). Processing of occurrence-rate and item information by children of different ages and abilities. *American Journal of Psychology, 96,* 220–241.

GOLDSTEIN, S., & BARKLEY, R. A. (1998). ADHD, hunting, and evolution: "Just so stories." *ADHD Report,* Vol. 6, No. 5.

GOLOMB, C., & GALASSO, L. (1995). Make believe and reality: Explorations of the imaginary realm. *Developmental Psychology, 31,* 800–810.

GOODMAN, G. S., AMAN, C. J., & HIRSCHMAN, J. (1987). Child sexual and physical abuse: Children's testimony. In C. J. Ceci, M. P. Toglia, & D. F. Ross (Eds.), *Children's eyewitness memory.* New York: Springer-Verlag.

GOODMAN, G. S., & CLARKE-STEWART, A. (1991). Suggestibility in children's testimony: Implications for sexual abuse investigations. In J. Doris (Ed.), *The suggestibility of children's recollections: Implications for eyewitness testimony.* Washington, DC: American Psychological Association.

GOODMAN, G. S., QUAS, J. A., BATTERMAN-FAUNCE, J. M., RIDDLESBERGER, M. M., & KUHN, J. (1994). Predictors of accurate and inaccurate memories of traumatic events experienced in childhood. *Consciousness and Cognition, 3,* 269–294.

GOODMAN, G. S., QUAS, J. A., BATTERMAN-FAUNCE, J. M., RIDDLESBERGER, M. M., & KUHN, J. (1997). Children's reactions to and memory for a stressful event: Influences of age, anatomical dolls, knowledge, and parental attachment. *Applied Developmental Science, 1,* 54–75.

GOODMAN, J. F. (1992). *When slow is fast enough: Educating the delayed preschool child.* New York: Guilford.

GOODZ, N. S. (1982). Is before really easier to understand than after? *Child Development, 53,* 822–825.

GOPNIK, A. (1996). The post-Piaget era. *Psychological Science, 7,* 221–225.

GOPNIK, A., & ASTINGTON, J. W. (1988). Children's understanding of representational change and its relation to the understanding of false belief and the appearance-reality distinction. *Child Development, 59,* 26–37.

GOPNIK, A., & CRAGO, M. D. (1991). Familial aggregation of a developmental language disorder. *Cognition, 39,* 1–50.

GOPNIK, A., & MELTZOFF, A. N. (1992). Categorization and naming: Basic-level sorting in eighteen-month-olds and its relation to language. *Child Development, 63,* 1091–1103.

GOPNIK, A., & MELTZOFF, A. N. (1997). *Words, thoughts, and theories.* Cambridge, MA: MIT Press.

GOPNIK, A., & SLAUGHTER, V. (1991). Young children's understanding of changes in their mental states. *Child Development, 62,* 98–110.

GORDON, B. N., ORNSTEIN, P. A., NIDA, R. E., FOLLMER, A., CRENSHAW, M. C., & ALBERT, G. F. (1993). Does the use of dolls facilitate children's memory of visits to the doctor? *Applied Cognitive Psychology, 7,* 459–474.

GOSWAMI, U. (1995). Transitive relational mapping in three- and four-year-olds: The analogy of Goldilocks and the Three Bears. *Child Development, 66,* 877–892.

GOSWAMI, U. (1996). Analogical reasoning and cognitive development. In H. W. Reese (Ed.), *Advances in child development and behavior,* Vol. 26. San Diego: Academic.

GOSWAMI, U. (2002). Phonology, reading development and dyslexia: A cross-linguistic perspective. *Annals of Dyslexia, 52,* 1–23.

GOSWAMI, U., & BROWN, A. L. (1990). Higher-order structure and relational reasoning: Contrasting analogical and thematic relations. *Cognition, 36,* 207–226.

GOTTARDO, A., STANOVICH, K. E., & SIEGEL, L. S. (1996). The relationships between phonological sensitivity, syntactic processing, and verbal working memory in the reading performance of third-grade children. *Journal of Experimental Child Psychology, 63,* 563–582.

GOTTLIEB, G. (1971). Ontogenesis of sensory functioning in birds and mammals. In E. Tobach, L. R. Aronson, & E. Shaw (Eds.), *The biopsychology of development.* New York: Academic.

GOTTLIEB, G. (1991A). Experiential canalization of behavioral development: Theory. *Developmental Psychology, 27,* 4–13.

GOTTLIEB, G. (1991B). Experiential canalization of behavioral development: Results. *Developmental Psychology, 27,* 35–39.

GOTTLIEB, G. (1992). *Individual development and evolution: The genesis of novel behavior.* New York: Oxford University Press.

GOTTLIEB, G. (1995). Some conceptual deficiencies in "developmental" behavior genetics. *Human Development, 38,* 131–141.

GOTTLIEB, G. (1997). *Synthesizing nature-nurture: Prenatal roots of instinctive behavior.* Mahwah, NJ: Erlbaum.

GOTTLIEB, G. (2000). Environmental and behavioral influences on gene activity. *Current Directions in Psychological Science, 9,* 93–102.

GOTTLIEB, G., WAHLSTEN, D., & LICKLITER, R. (1998). The significance of biology for human development: A developmental psychobiological systems view. In R. M. Lerner (Vol. Ed.), *Theoretical models of human development*, Vol. 1. In W. Damon (Gen. Ed.), *Handbook of child psychology*. New York: Wiley.

GOULD, E., BEYLIN, A., TANAPAT, P., REEVES, A., & SHORS, T. J. (1999). Learning enhances adult neurogenesis in the hippocampal formation. *Nature Neuroscience, 2*, 260–265.

GOULD, S. J. (1981). *The mismeasure of man*. New York: Norton.

GOULD, S. J. (1992, FEBRUARY). Mozart and modularity. *Natural History, 101*, 8–14.

GOULD, S. J. (2002). *The structure of evolutionary theory*. Cambridge, MA: Harvard University Press.

GOUZE, K. R. (1987). Attention and social problem solving as correlates of aggression in preschool males. *Journal of Abnormal Child Psychology, 15*, 181–197.

GRAHAM, S., & HUDLEY, C. (1994). Attributions of aggressive and nonaggressive African-American male early adolescents: A study of construct accessibility. *Developmental Psychology, 30*, 365–373.

GRAY, W. M., & HUDSON, L. M. (1984). Formal operations and the imaginary audience. *Developmental Psychology, 20*, 619–627.

GREDLEIN, J., BJORKLUND, D. F., & HICKLING, A. (2003, APRIL). *Play styles and problem-solving in preschool children*. Paper presented at meeting of the Society for Research in Child Development, Tampa, FL.

GREENE, T. R. (1991). Text manipulations influence children's understandings of class inclusion hierarchies. *Journal of Experimental Child Psychology, 52*, 354–374.

GREENFIELD, D. B., & SCOTT, M. S. (1986). Young children's preferences for complementary pairs: Evidence against a shift to a taxonomic preference. *Developmental Psychology, 22*, 19–21.

GREENOUGH, W. T., BLACK, J. E., & WALLACE, C. S. (1987). Experience and brain development. *Child Development, 58*, 539–559.

GREENOUGH, W. T., MCDONALD, J., PARNISARI, R., & CAMEL, J. E. (1986). Environmental conditions modulate degeneration and new dendrite growth in cerebellum of senescent rats. *Brain Research, 380*, 136–143.

GRICE, H. P. (1975). Logic and conversation. In P. Cole & J. Morgan (Eds.), *Speech acts: Syntax and semantics*, Vol. 3. New York: Academic.

GRIESER, D., & KUHL, P. K. (1989). Categorization of speech by infants: Support for speech-sound prototypes. *Developmental Psychology, 25*, 577–588.

GROEN, G. J., & RESNICK, L. B. (1977). Can preschool children invent addition algorithms? *Journal of Educational Psychology, 69*, 645–652.

GRUNAU, R. E., OBERLANDER, T. F., WHITFIELD, M. F., FITZGERALD, C., MORISON, S. J., & SAUL, J. P. (2001). Pain reactivity in former extremely low birth weight infants at corrected age 8 months compared with term born controls. *Infant Behavior & Development, 24*, 41–55.

GUBERMAN, S. R. (1996). The development of everyday mathematics in Brazilian children with limited formal education. *Child Development, 67*, 1609–1623.

GUERRA, N. G., HUESMANN, L. R., & HANISH, L. (1995). The role of normative beliefs in children's social behavior. In N. Eisenberg (Ed.), *Review of personality and social psychology, development, and social psychology: The interface*. Thousand Oaks, CA: Sage.

GUILFORD, J. P. (1988). Some changes in the structure-of-the-intellect model. *Educational and Psychological Measurement, 48*, 1–4.

GULYA, M., ROVEE-COLLIER, C., GALLUCCIO, L., & WILK, A. (1998). Memory processing of a serial list by young infants. *Psychological Science, 9*, 303–307.

GUTTENTAG, R. E. (1984). The mental effort requirement of cumulative rehearsal: A developmental study. *Journal of Experimental Child Psychology, 37*, 92–106.

GUTTENTAG, R. E., ORNSTEIN, P. A., & SIEMANS, L. (1987). Children's spontaneous rehearsal: Transitions in strategy acquisition. *Cognitive Development, 2*, 307–326.

HADEN, C. A., HAINE, R. A., & FIVUSH, R. (1997). Developing narrative structure in parent-child reminiscing across the preschool years. *Developmental Psychology, 33*, 295–307.

HADEN, C. A., ORNSTEIN, P. A., ECKERMAN, C. O., & DIDOW, S. M. (2001). Mother-child conversational interactions as event unfold: Linkages to subsequent remembering. *Child Development, 72*, 1016–1031.

HADEN, C. A., & REESE, E. (1994, APRIL). *Gender differences in development of autobiographical memory*. Paper presented at the Conference on Human Development, Pittsburgh, PA.

HAGEN, J. W. (1972). Strategies for remembering. In S. Farnham-Diggory (Ed.), *Information processing in children*. New York: Academic.

HAGEN, J. W., & STANOVICH, K. G. (1977). Memory: Strategies of acquisition. In R. V. Kail, Jr., & H. W. Hagen (Eds.), *Perspectives on the development of memory and cognition*. Hillsdale, NJ: Erlbaum.

HAIER, R. J., SIEGEL, B. V., NUECHTERLEIN, K. H., HAZLETT, E., WU, J. C., PAEK, J., BROWNING, H. L., & BUCHSBAUM, M. S. (1988). Cortical glucose metabolic rate correlates of abstract reasoning and attention studies with positron emission tomography. *Intelligence, 12*, 199–217.

HAIER, R. J., SIEGEL, B. V., TANG, C., ABEL, L., & BUCHS-BAUM, M. S. (1992). Intelligence and changes in regional cerebral glucose metabolic rate following learning. *Intelligence, 16,* 415–426.

HAITH, M. M. (1966). The response of the human newborn to visual movement. *Journal of Experimental Child Psychology, 3,* 235–243.

HAITH, M. M. (1993). Preparing for the 21st century: Some goals and challenges for studies of infant sensory and perceptual development. *Developmental Review, 13,* 354–371.

HAITH, M. M., & BENSON, J. B. (1998). Infant cognition. In D. Kuhn & R. S. Siegler (Eds.), *Cognition, perception, and language,* Vol. 2. In W. Damon (Gen. Ed.), *Handbook of child psychology.* New York: Wiley.

HALA, S., & CHANDLER, M. (1996). The role of strategic planning in accessing false-belief understanding. *Child Development, 67,* 2948–2966.

HALA, S., CHANDLER, M., & FRITZ, A. S. (1991). Fledgling theories of mind: Deception as a marker of three-year-olds' understanding of false belief. *Child Development, 62,* 83–97.

HALBERSTADT, J., & RHODES, G. (2000). The attractiveness of nonface averages: Implications for an evolutionary explanation of the attractiveness of average faces. *Psychological Science, 11,* 285–289.

HALE, S., FRY, A. F., & JESSIE, K. A. (1993). Effects of practice on speed of information processing in children and adults: Age sensitivity and age invariants. *Developmental Psychology, 29,* 880–892.

HALFORD, G. S. (1982). *The development of thought.* Hillsdale, NJ: Erlbaum.

HALFORD, G. S. (1993). *Children's understanding: The development of mental models.* Hillsdale, NJ: Erlbaum.

HALPERN, D. F. (1992). *Sex difference in cognitive abilities* (2nd ed.). Hillsdale, NJ: Erlbaum.

HALPERN, D. F. (ED.). (1995). Special issue: Psychological and psychobiological perspectives on sex differences in cognition. I. Theory and research. *Learning and Individual Differences, 7.*

HALPERN, D. F. (1996). Sex, brains, and spatial cognition. *Developmental Review, 16,* 261–270.

HALPERN, D. F. (1997). Sex differences in intelligence. *American Psychologist, 52,* 1091–1102.

HALVERSON, C. F., & WALDROP, M. F. (1973). The relations of mechanically recorded activity level to varieties of preschool play behavior. *Child Development, 44,* 678–681.

HAMM, V. P., & HASHER, L. (1992). Age and the availability of inferences. *Psychology and Aging, 7,* 56–64.

HAMOND, N. R., & FIVUSH, R. (1991). Memories of Mickey Mouse: Young children recount their trip to Disneyworld. *Cognitive Development, 6,* 433–448.

HAN, J. J., LEICHTMAN, M. D., & WANG, Q. (1998). Autobiographical memory in Korean, Chinese, and American children. *Developmental Psychology, 34,* 701–713.

HANNA, E., & MELTZOFF, A. N. (1993). Peer imitation by toddlers in laboratory, home, and day care contexts: Implications for social learning and memory. *Developmental Psychology, 29,* 701–710.

HANSEN, J., & PEARSON, P. D. (1983). An instructional study: Improving the inferential comprehension of good and poor readers. *Journal of Educational Psychology, 75,* 821–829.

HARLOW, H. (1959, DECEMBER). The development of learning in the Rhesus monkey. *American Scientist,* 459–479.

HARLOW, H. F., DODSWORTH, R. O., & HARLOW, M. K. (1965). Total isolation in monkeys. *Proceedings of the National Academy of Science, 54,* 90–97.

HARNISHFEGER, K. K. (1995). The development of cognitive inhibition: Theories, definitions, and research evidence. In F. Dempster & C. Brainerd (Eds.), *New perspectives on interference and inhibition in cognition.* New York: Academic.

HARNISHFEGER, K. K., & BJORKLUND, D. F. (1990A) Children's strategies: A brief history. In D. F. Bjorklund (Ed.), *Children's strategies: Contemporary views of cognitive development.* Hillsdale, NJ: Erlbaum.

HARNISHFEGER, K. K., & BJORKLUND, D. F. (1990B). Memory functioning of gifted and nongifted middle school children. *Contemporary Educational Psychology, 15,* 346–363.

HARNISHFEGER, K. K., & BJORKLUND, D. F. (1993). The ontogeny of inhibition mechanisms: A renewed approach to cognitive development. In M. L. Howe & R. Pasnak (Eds.), *Emerging themes in cognitive development:* Vol. 1. *Foundations.* New York: Springer-Verlag.

HARNISHFEGER, K. K., & BJORKLUND, D. F. (1994). Individual differences in inhibition: Implications for children's cognitive development. *Learning and Individual Differences, 6,* 331–355.

HARNISHFEGER, K. K., & BRAINERD, C. J. (1994). Nonstrategic facilitation of children's recall: Evidence of triage with semantically related information. *Journal of Experimental Child Psychology, 57,* 259–280.

HARNISHFEGER, K. K., & POPE, R. S. (1996). Intending to forget: The development of cognitive inhibition in directed forgetting. *Journal of Experimental Child Psychology, 62,* 292–315.

HARNQUIST, K. (1968). Relative changes in intelligence from 13 to 18. *Scandinavian Journal of Psychology, 9,* 50–64.

HARRIS, J. R. (1995). Where is the child's environment? A group socialization theory of development. *Psychological Review, 102,* 458–489.

HARRIS, L. J. (1978). Sex differences in spatial ability: Possible environmental, genetic and neurological factors. In M. Kinsborne (Ed.), *Asymmetrical function of the brain.* New York: Cambridge University Press.

HARRIS, P. L., BROWN, E., MARRIOTT, C., WHITTALL, S., & HARMER, S. (1991). Monsters, ghosts and witches: Testing the limits of fantasy-reality distinction in young children. *British Journal of Developmental Psychology, 9,* 105–123.

HARTER, S. (1998). The development of self-representation. In N. Eisenberg (Vol. Ed), *Social, emotional, and personality development,* Vol. 3. In W. Damon (Gen. Ed.), *Handbook of child psychology.* New York: Wiley.

HARTER, S., WATERS, P., & WHITESELL, N. R. (1998). Relational self-worth: Differences in perceived worth as a person across interpersonal contexts among adolescents. *Child Development, 69,* 756–766.

HASHER, L., & ZACKS, R. T. (1979). Automatic and effortful processes in memory. *Journal of Experimental Psychology: General, 108,* 356–388.

HASHER, L., & ZACKS, R. T. (1988). Working memory, comprehension, and aging: A review and a new view. In G. H. Bower (Ed.), *The psychology of learning and motivation: Advances in research and theory,* Vol. 22. San Diego: Academic.

HASSELHORN, M. (1992). Task dependency and the role of category typicality and metamemory in the development of an organizational strategy. *Child Development, 63,* 202–214.

HAUSER, M. D. (2000). *Wild minds: What animals really think.* New York: Holt.

HAUSER, M. D., CAREY, S., & HAUSER, L. B. (2000). Spontaneous number representation in semi-free-ranging rhesus monkeys. *Proceeding of the Royal Society of London B, 267,* 829–833.

HAWKINS, J., PEA, R. D., GLICK, J., & SCRIBNER, S. (1984). "Merds that laugh don't like mushrooms": Evidence for deductive reasoning by preschoolers. *Developmental Psychology, 20,* 584–594.

HAYES, B. K., & HENNESSY, R. (1996). The nature and development of nonverbal implicit memory. *Journal of Experimental Child Psychology, 63,* 22–43.

HAZEN, N. L. (1982). Spatial exploration and spatial knowledge: Individual and developmental differences in very young children. *Child Development, 53,* 826–833.

HEATH, S. B. (1989). Oral and literate traditions among Black Americans living in poverty. *American Psychologist, 44,* 367–373.

HEBB, D. O. (1949). *The organization of behavior.* New York: Wiley.

HECHT, S. A., TORGESEN, J. K., WAGNER, R. K., & RASHOTTE, C. A. (2001). The relationship between phonological processing abilities and emerging individual differences in mathematical computation skills: A longitudinal study from second to fifth grades. *Journal of Experimental Child Psychology, 79,* 192–227.

HEDGES, L. V., & NOWELL, A. (1995). Sex differences in mental test scores, variability, and numbers of high-scoring individuals. *Science, 269* (July 7), 41–45.

HEIDER, E. R. (1972). Universals in color naming and memory. *Journal of Experimental Psychology, 93,* 10–20.

HEIMANN, M. (1989). Neonatal imitation gaze aversion and mother-infant interaction. *Infant Behavior & Development, 12,* 495–505.

HELD, R., & HEIN, A. (1963). Movement-produced stimulation in the development of visually guided behavior. *Journal of Comparative and Physiological Psychology, 56,* 872–876.

HENDLER, M., & WEISBERG, P. (1992). Conservation acquisition, maintenance, and generalization by mentally retarded children using equality-rule training. *Journal of Experimental Child Psychology, 54,* 258–276.

HENRY, L. A., & MILLAR, S. (1991). Memory span increases with age: A test of two hypotheses. *Journal of Experimental Child Psychology, 51,* 459–484.

HERMAN, J. F., SHIRAKI, J. H., & MILLER, B. S. (1985). Young children's ability to infer spatial relationships: Evidence from a large, familiar environment. *Child Development, 36,* 1195–1203.

HERMAN, J. F., & SIEGEL, A. W. (1978). The development of cognitive mapping of the large-scale environment. *Journal of Experimental Child Psychology, 26,* 389–406.

HERNÁNDEZ BLASI, C. (1996). Vygotsky y la escuela socio-histórica. In R. A. Clemente & C. Hernández Blasi (Eds.), *Contextos de desarrollo psicológico y educación.* Mâlaga, Spain: Aljibe.

HERRNSTEIN, R. J., & MURRAY, C. (1994). *The bell curve: Intelligence and class structure in American life.* New York: Simon & Schuster.

HINES, M., GOLOMBOK, S., RUST, J., JOHNSTON, K. J., GOLDING, J., AND THE AVON LONGITUDINAL STUDY OF PARENTS AND CHILDREN STUDY TEAM. (2002). Testosterone during pregnancy and gender role behavior of preschool children: A longitudinal, population study. *Child Development, 73,* 1678–1687.

HIRSH-PASEK, K., & GOLINKOFF, R. M. (1991). Language comprehension: A new look at some old themes. In N. A. Krasnegor, D. R. Rumbaugh, R. L. Schiefelbusch, & M. Studdert-Kennedy (Eds.), *Biological and behavioral determinants of language development*. Hillsdale, NJ: Erlbaum.

HIRSH-PASEK, K., GOLINKOFF, R. M., & NAIGLES, L. (1996). Young children's use of syntactic frames to derive meaning. In K. Hirsh-Pasek & R. M. Golinkoff (Eds.), *The origins of grammar: Evidence from early language comprehension*. Cambridge, MA: MIT Press.

HITCH, G. J., & TOWSE, J. (1995). Working memory: What develops? In F. E. Weinert & W. Schneider (Eds.), *Memory performance and competencies: Issues in growth and development*. Hillsdale, NJ: Erlbaum.

HOFF, E. (2000). Soziale umwelt und sprachlernen. (The social environment and language learning.) In H. Grimm (Hrsg) *Enzyklopadie der Psychologie*, Vol. C3/3 Sprachentwicklung (*Encyclopedia, Vol 3: Language Development*). Gottingen: Hogrefe.

HOFF, E. (2001). *Language development* (2nd ed.). Belmont, CA: Wadsworth.

HOFF-GINSBURG, E. (1985). Some contributions of mothers' speech to their children's syntactic growth. *Journal of Child Language, 12*, 367–385.

HOFFMAN, M. L. (1975). Developmental synthesis of affect and cognition and its implications for altruistic motivation. *Developmental Psychology, 11*, 607–622.

HOGREFE, G.-J., WIMMER, H., & PERNER, J. (1986). Ignorance versus false belief: A developmental lag in attribution of epistemic states. *Child Development, 57*, 567–582.

HOLLICH, G., HIRSH-PASEK, K., & GOLINKOFF, R. M. (2000). Breaking the language barrier: An emergentist coalition model of word learning. *Monographs of the Society for Research in Child Development, 65* (Serial No. 262).

HOLOWKA, S., & PETITTO, L. A. (2002). Left hemisphere cerebral specialization for babies while babbling. *Science, 297* (30 August), 1515.

HOLYOAK, K. J., JUNN, E. N., & BILLMAN, D. O. (1984). Development of analogical problem-solving skills. *Child Development, 55*, 2042–2055.

HONZIK, M. P., MACFARLANE, J. W., & ALLEN, L. (1948). Stability of mental test performance between 2 and 18 years. *Journal of Experimental Education, 17*, 309–324.

HOOD, B., CAREY, S., & PRASADA, S. (2000). Predicting the outcomes of physical events: Two-year-olds fail to reveal knowledge of solidity and support. *Child Development, 71*, 1540–1554.

HOPKINS, S. L., & LAWSON, M. J. (2001). Explaining the acquisition of a complex skill: Methodological and theoretical considerations uncovered in the study of simple addition and the moving-on process. *Educational Psychology Review, 14*, 121–154.

HOUDÉ, O., & GUICHART, E. (2001). Negative priming effect after inhibition of number/length interference in a Piaget-like task. *Developmental Science, 4*, 119–123.

HOWE, M. L. (1991). Misleading children's story recall: Forgetting and reminiscence of the facts. *Developmental Psychology, 27*, 746–762.

HOWE, M. L. (2000). *The fate of early memories: Developmental science and the retention of childhood experiences*. Washington, DC: American Psychological Press.

HOWE, M. L., & BRAINERD, C. J. (1989). Development of long-term retention. *Developmental Review, 9*, 302–340.

HOWE, M. L., & COURAGE, M. L. (1993). On resolving the enigma of infantile amnesia. *Psychological Bulletin, 113*, 305–326.

HOWE, M. L., & COURAGE, M. L. (1997). Independent paths in the development of infant learning and forgetting. *Journal of Experimental Child Psychology, 67*, 131–163.

HOWE, M. L., & O'SULLIVAN, J. T. (1997). What children's memories tell us about recalling our childhoods: A review of storage and retrieval processes in the development of long-term retention. *Developmental Review, 17*, 148–204.

HUDSON, J. A. (1990). The emergence of autobiographical memory in mother-child conversation. In R. Fivush & J. A. Hudson (Eds.), *Knowing and remembering in young children*. Cambridge: Cambridge University Press.

HUDSON, J. A., SHAPIRO, L. R., & SOSA, B. B. (1995). Planning in the real world: Preschool children's scripts and plans for familiar events. *Child Development, 66*, 984–998.

HUGHES, C., & CUTTING, A. L. (1999). Nature, nurture, and individual differences in early understanding of mind. *Psychological Science, 10*, 429–432.

HULME, C., HATCHER, P. J., NATION, K., BROWN, A., ADAMS, J., & STUART, G. (2002). Phoneme awareness is a better predictor of early reading skill than onset-rime awareness. *Journal of Experimental Child Psychology, 82*, 2–28.

HULME, C., THOMSON, N., MUIR, C., & LAWRENCE, A. (1984). Speech rate and the development of spoken words: The role of rehearsal and item identification processes. *Journal of Experimental Child Psychology, 38*, 241–253.

HUMPHREY, N. K. (1976). The social function of intellect. In P. P. G. Bateson & R. A. Hinde (Eds.), *Growing points in ethology*. Cambridge: Cambridge University Press.

HUMPHREYS, L. G. (1980). Me thinks they do protest too much. *Intelligence, 4*, 179–183.

HUMPHREYS, L. G., & PARSONS, C. K. (1979). Piagetian tasks measure intelligence and intelligence tests assess cognitive development. *Intelligence, 3,* 369–382.

HUMPHREYS, L. G., RICH, S. A., & DAVEY, T. C. (1985). A Piagetian test of general intelligence. *Developmental Psychology, 21,* 872–877.

HUNT, E., DAVIDSON, J., & LANSMAN, M. (1981). Individual difference in long-term memory access. *Memory and Cognition, 9,* 599–608.

HUNTSINGER, C. S., JOSE, P. E., & LARSON, S. L. (1998). Do parent practices to encourage academic competence influence the social adjustment of young European American and Chinese American children? *Developmental Psychology, 34,* 747–756.

HUTTENLOCHER, J., LEVINE, S., & VEVEA, J. (1998). Environmental input and cognitive growth: A study using time-period comparisons. *Child Development, 69,* 1012–1029.

HUTTENLOCHER, P. R. (1994). Synaptogenesis, synapse elimination, and neural plasticity in human cerebral cortex. In C. A. Nelson (Ed.), Threats to optimal development. *The Minnesota symposium on child psychology,* Vol. 27. Hillsdale, NJ: Erlbaum.

HYDE, J. S. (1981). How large are cognitive gender differences? A meta-analysis using ω^2 and d. *American Psychologist, 36,* 892–901.

HYDE, J. S., FENNEMA, E., & LAMON, S. J. (1990). Gender differences in mathematics performance: A meta-analysis. *Psychological Bulletin, 107,* 139–155.

HYDE, J. S., & LINN, M. C. (1988). Gender differences in verbal ability: A meta-analysis. *Psychological Bulletin, 194,* 53–69.

HYMES, D. (1972). On communicative competence. In J. B. Pride & J. Holmes (Eds.), *Sociolinguistics.* Harmondsworth, England: Penguin.

HYMOVITCH, B. (1952). The effects of experimental variations on problem solving in the rat. *Journal of Comparative and Physiological Psychology, 45,* 313–321.

HYSON, M. C., HIRSH-PASEK, K., & RESCORLA, L. (1990). Academic environments in preschool: Challenge or pressure? *Early Education and Development, 1,* 401–423.

INGRAM, D. (1989). *First language acquisition: Method, description, and explanation.* London: Cambridge University Press.

INHELDER, B., & PIAGET, J. (1958). *The growth of logical thinking from childhood to adolescence.* New York: Basic.

INHELDER, B., & PIAGET, J. (1964). *The early growth of logic in the child.* New York: Norton.

ISTOMINA, Z. M. (1975). The development of voluntary memory in preschool-age children. *Soviet Psychology, 13,* 5–64.

JACKSON, J. F. (1993). Human behavioral genetics: Scarr's theory, and her views on intervention: A critical review and commentary on their implications for African American children. *Child Development, 64,* 1318–1332.

JACOBSON, S. W. (1979). Matching behavior in the young infant. *Child Development, 50,* 425–430.

JACOBY, L. L. (1991). A process dissociation framework: Separating automatic from intentional uses of memory. *Journal of Memory and Language, 30,* 513–541.

JACOBY, R., & GLAUBERMAN, N. (EDS.) (1995). *The Bell Curve debate: History, documents, opinions.* New York: Times.

JAKOBSON, R. (1968). *Child language, aphasia, and phonological universals.* The Hague: Mouton.

JANSEN, B. R. J., & VAN DER MAAS, H. L. J. (2002). The development of children's rule use on the balance scale task. *Journal of Experimental Child Psychology, 81,* 383–416.

JENKINS, J. M., & ASTINGTON, J. W. (1996). Cognitive factors and family structure associated with theory of mind development in young children. *Developmental Psychology, 32,* 70–78.

JENSEN, A. R. (1993). Why is reaction time correlated with psychometric g? *Current Directions in Psychological Science, 2,* 53–56.

JENSEN, A. R. (1998). *The g factor: The science of mental ability.* Westport, CT: Praeger

JENSEN, P. S., MRAZEK, D., KNAPP, P. K., STEINBERG, L., PFEFFER, C., SCHWALTER, J., & SHAPIRO, T. (1997). Evolution and revolution in child psychiatry: ADHD as a disorder of adaptation. *Journal of the American Academy of Child & Adolescent Psychiatry, 36,* 1672–1681.

JOHNSON, D. W., & JOHNSON, R. T. (1987). *Learning together and alone: Cooperative, competitive, and individualistic learning* (2nd ed.). Englewood Cliffs, NJ: Prentice-Hall.

JOHNSON, D. W., & JOHNSON, R. T. (1989). *Cooperation and competition: Theory and research.* Edina, MN: Interaction.

JOHNSON, J. S., & NEWPORT, E. L. (1989). Critical period effects in second language learning: The influence of maturational state on the acquisition of English as a second language. *Cognitive Psychology, 21,* 60–99.

JOHNSON, K. E., & MERVIS, C. B. (1994). A microgenetic analysis of first steps in children's acquisition of expertise on shorebirds. *Developmental Psychology, 30,* 418–435.

JOHNSON, K. E., & MERVIS, C. B. (1998). Impact of intuitive theories on feature recruitment throughout the continuum of expertise. *Memory & Cognition, 26,* 383–401.

JOHNSON, M. H. (1998). The neural basis of cognitive development. In D. Kuhn & R. S. Siegler (Vol. Eds.), *Cognition, perception, and language*, Vol. 2. In W. Damon (Gen. Ed.), *Handbook of child psychology* (5th ed.). New York: Wiley.

JOHNSON, M. H. (2000). Functional brain development in infants: Elements of an interactive specialization framework. *Child Development, 71*, 75–81.

JOHNSON, M. H. (2001). Functional brain development in humans. *Nature Reviews, 2*, 475–483.

JOHNSON, M. H., & DE HAAN, M. (2001). Developing cortical specialization for visual-cognitive function: The case of face recognition. In J. L. McClelland, & R. S. Siegler (Eds.), *Mechanisms of cognitive development: Behavioral and neural perspectives*. Mahwah, NJ: Erlbaum.

JOHNSON, M. H., DZIURAWIEC, S., ELLIS, H. D., & MORTON, J. (1991). Newborns' preferential tracking of faces and its subsequent decline. *Cognition, 40*, 1–19.

JOHNSON, S. P., & ASLIN, R. N. (1995). Perception of object unity in 2-month-old infants. *Developmental Psychology, 31*, 739–745.

JOHNSON, S. P., & ASLIN, R. N. (1996). Perception of object unity in young infants: The roles of motion, depth, and orientation. *Cognitive Development, 11*, 161–180.

JUSTICE, E. M., BAKER-WARD, L., GUPTA, S., & JANNINGS, L. R. (1997). Means to the goal of remembering: Developmental changes in awareness of strategy use-performance relations. *Journal of Experimental Child Psychology, 65*, 293–314.

KAGAN, J. (1971). *Change and continuity in infancy*. New York: Wiley.

KAGAN, J. (1976). New views on cognitive development. *Journal of Youth and Adolescence, 5*, 113–129.

KAIL, R. (1991). Development of processing speed in childhood and adolescence. In H. W. Reese (Ed.), *Advances in child development and behavior*, Vol. 23. San Diego: Academic.

KAIL, R. (1993). The role of a global mechanism in developmental change in speed of processing. In M. L. Howe & R. Pasnak (Eds.), *Emerging themes in cognitive development: Vol. 1. Foundations*. New York: Springer-Verlag.

KAIL, R. (1997). Processing time, imagery, and spatial memory. *Journal of Experimental Child Psychology, 64*, 67–78.

KAIL, R. V., & LEVINE, L. E. (1976). Encoding processes and sex-role preferences. *Journal of Experimental Child Psychology, 21*, 256–263.

KAIL, R. V., & SALTHOUSE, T. A. (1994). Processing speed as a mental capacity. *Acta Psychologica, 86*, 199–225.

KAIL, R. V., JR. (1979). Use of strategies and individual differences in children's memory. *Developmental Psychology, 15*, 251–255.

KAIL, R. V., JR., & SIEGEL, A. W. (1977). Sex differences in retention of verbal and spatial characteristics of stimuli. *Journal of Experimental Child Psychology, 23*, 341–347.

KAITZ, M., MESCHULACH-SARFATY, O., AUERBACH, J., & EIDELMAN, A. (1988). A reexamination of newborns' ability to imitate facial expressions. *Developmental Psychology, 24*, 3–7.

KALER, S. R., & FREEDMAN, B. J. (1994). Analysis of environmental deprivation: Cognitive and social development in Romanian orphans. *Journal of Child Psychology and Psychiatry, 35*, 769–781.

KALICHMAN, S. C. (1988). Individual differences in water-level task performance: A component-skill analysis. *Developmental Review, 8*, 273–295.

KAPLAN, H., HILL, K., LANCASTER, J., & HURTADO, A. M. (2000). A theory of human life history evolution: Diet intelligence, and longevity. *Evolutionary Anthropology, 9*, 156–185.

KARMILOFF-SMITH, A. (1979). *A functional approach to language*. Cambridge: Cambridge University Press.

KARMILOFF-SMITH, A. (1991). Beyond modularity: Innate constraints and developmental change. In S. Carey & R. Gelman (Eds.), *The epigenesis of mind: Essays on biology and cognition*. Hillsdale, NJ: Erlbaum.

KARMILOFF-SMITH, A. (1992). *Beyond modularity: A developmental perspective on cognitive science*. Cambridge, MA: MIT Press.

KAROLY, L. A., GREENWOOD, P. W., EVERINGHAM, S. S., HOUBÉ, J., KILBURN, M. R., RYDELL, C. P., SANDERS, M., & CHIESA, J. (1998). *Investing in our children: What we know and don't know about the costs and benefits of early childhood interventions*. Santa Monica, CA: RAND Distribution Services.

KARP, S. A., & KONSTADT, N. (1971). *Children's Embedded Figures Test*. Palo Alto, CA: Consulting Psychologists.

KARZON, R. G. (1985). Discrimination of polysyllabic sequences by one- to four-month-old infants. *Journal of Experimental Child Psychology, 39*, 326–342.

KATZ, S., & LAUTENSCHLAGER, G. J. (1994). Answering reading comprehension items without passages on the SAT-I, the ACT, and the GRE. *Educational Assessment, 2*, 295–308.

KATZ, S., LAUTENSCHLAGER, G. J., BLACKBURN, A. B., & HARRIS, F. (1990). Answering reading comprehension items without passages on the SAT. *Psychological Science, 1*, 122–127.

KAYE, K., & MARCUS, J. (1981). Infant imitation: The sensory-motor agenda. *Developmental Psychology, 17,* 258–265.

KEE, D. W. (1994). Developmental differences in associative memory: Strategy use, mental effort, and knowledge-access interactions. In H. W. Reese (Ed.), *Advances in child development and behavior,* Vol. 25. New York: Academic.

KEE, D. W., & DAVIES, L. (1990). Mental effort and elaboration: Effects of accessibility and instruction. *Journal of Experimental Child Psychology, 49,* 264–274.

KEEN, R. (2003). Representation of objects and events: Why do infants look so smart and toddlers look so dumb? *Current Directions in Psychological Science, 12,* 79–83.

KEIL, F. C. (1998). Cognitive science and the origins of thought and knowledge. In R. M. Lerner (Vol. Ed.), *Theoretical models of human development,* Vol. 1. In W. Damon (Gen. Ed.), *Handbook of child psychology.* New York: Wiley.

KEIL, F. C., & BATTERMAN, N. (1984). A characteristic-to-defining shift in the development of word meaning. *Journal of Verbal Learning and Verbal Behavior, 23,* 221–236.

KELLER, A., FORD, L. H., JR., & MEACHUM, J. A. (1978). Dimensions of self-concept in preschool children. *Developmental Psychology, 14,* 483–489.

KELLER, D., & KELLAS, G. (1978). Typicality as a dimension of encoding. *Journal of Experimental Psychology: Human Learning and Memory, 4,* 78–85.

KELLMAN, P. H., & BANKS, M. S. (1998). Infant visual perception. In D. Kuhn & R. S. Siegler (Vol. Eds.), *Cognitive, language, and perceptual development,* Vol. 2. In W. Damon (Gen. Ed.), *Handbook of child psychology.* New York: Wiley.

KELLMAN, P. J., & SPELKE, E. S. (1983). Perception of partly occluded objects in infancy. *Cognitive Development, 15,* 483–524.

KELSO, J. A. S. (1995). *Dynamic patterns: The self-organization of brain and behavior.* Cambridge, MA: MIT Press.

KERMOIAN, R., & CAMPOS, J. J. (1988). Locomotor experience: A facilitator of spatial cognitive development. *Child Development, 59,* 908–917.

KERSTEN, A.W., & EARLES, J. L. (2001). Less really is more for adults learning a miniature artificial language. *Journal of Memory and Language, 44,* 250–273.

KESSEN, W. (1996). American psychology just before Piaget. *Psychological Science, 7,* 196–199.

KIM, K. H. S., RELKIN, N. R., LEE, K-M., & HIRSCH, J., ET AL. (1997). Distinct cortical areas associated with native and second languages. *Nature, 388* (July 12), 171–174.

KINGMA, J. (1984). Traditional intelligence, Piagetian tasks, and initial arithmetic in kindergarten and primary school grade one. *Journal of Genetic Psychology, 145,* 49–60.

KIPP, K., & POPE, S. (1997). The development of cognitive inhibition in stream-of-consciousness and directed speech. *Cognitive Development, 12,* 239–260.

KITAMURA, C., THANAVISHUTH, C., BURNHAM, D., & LUKSANEEYANAWIN, S. (2002). Universality and specificity in infant-directed speech: Pitch modifications as a function of infant age and sex in a tonal and nontonal language. *Infant Behavior & Development, 24,* 372–392.

KLACZYNSKI, P. A. (1997). Bias in adolescents' everyday reasoning and its relationship with intellectual ability, personal theories, and self-serving motivation. *Developmental Psychology, 33,* 273–283.

KLACZYNSKI, P. A., & NARASIMHAM, G. (1998). Development of scientific reasoning biases: Cognitive versus ego-protective explanations. *Developmental Psychology, 34,* 175–187.

KLAHR, D., & MACWHINNEY, B. (1998). Information processing. In D. Kuhn & R. S. Siegler (Vol. Eds.), *Cognitive, language, and perceptual development,* Vol. 2. In W. Damon (Gen. Ed.), *Handbook of child psychology.* New York: Wiley.

KLAHR, D., & ROBINSON, M. (1981). Formal assessment of problem solving and planning processes in preschool children. *Cognitive Psychology, 13,* 113–148.

KLAUS, R. A., & GRAY S. (1968). The early training project for disadvantaged children: A report after five years. *Monographs of the Society for Research in Child Development, 33* (Serial No. 120).

KOCHANSKA, G., MURRAY, K., JACQUES, T. Y., KOENIG, A. L., & VANDEGEEST, K. A. (1996). Inhibitory control in young children and its role in emerging internalization. *Child Development, 67,* 490–507.

KOHLBERG, L. (1966). A cognitive-developmental analysis of children's sex-role concepts and attitudes. In E. E. Maccoby (Ed.), *The development of sex differences.* Stanford, CA: Stanford University Press.

KOHLBERG, L., YAEGER, J., & HJERTHOLM, E. (1968). Private speech: Four studies and a review of theories. *Child Development, 39,* 691–736.

KÖHLER, W. (1925). *The mentality of apes.* London: Kegan Paul.

KOLB, B., & WHISHAW, I. Q. (1981). Neonatal frontal lesions in the rat: Sparing of learned but not species-typical behavior in the presence of reduced brain weight and critical thickness. *Journal of Comparative and Physiological Psychology, 95,* 235–276.

KOLB, B., & WHISHAW, I. Q. (1990). *Fundamentals of human neuropsychology* (3rd ed.). San Francisco: W. H. Freeman.

KOLUCHOVA, J. (1976). A report on the further development of twins after severe and prolonged deprivation. In A. M. Clarke and A. D. B. Clarke (Eds.), *Early experience: Myth and evidence*. London: Open Books.

KOPP, C. B., & McCALL, R. B. (1982). Predicting later mental performance for normal, at-risk, and handicapped infants. In P. B. Baltes & O. G. Brim (Eds.), *Life-span development and behavior*, Vol. 4. New York: Academic.

KOPP, C. B., SIGMAN, M., & PARMELEE, A. H. (1974). Longitudinal study of sensorimotor development. *Developmental Psychology, 10*, 687–695.

KORNER, M. (1991). Universals of behavioral development in relation to brain myelination. In K. R. Gibson & A. C. Petersen (Eds.), *Brain maturation and cognitive development: Comparative and cross-cultural perspectives*. New York: Aldine de Gruyter.

KORNHUBER, H. H., BECHINGER, D., JUNG, H., & SAUER, E. (1985). A quantitative relationship between the extent of localized cerebral lesions and the intellectual and behavioral deficiency in children. *European Archives of Psychiatry and Neurological Science, 235*, 125–133.

KOSHMIDER, J. W., & ASHCRAFT, M. H. (1991). The development of children's mental multiplication skills. *Journal of Experimental Child Psychology, 51*, 53–89.

KRACKOW, E., & GORDON, P. (1998). Are lions and tigers substitutes or associates? Evidence against slot filler accounts of children's early categorization. *Child Development, 69*, 347–354.

KRATOCHWILL, T. R., & GOLDMAN, J. A. (1973). Developmental changes in children's judgments of age. *Developmental Psychology, 9*, 358–362.

KREUTZER, M. A., LEONARD, C., & FLAVELL, J. H. (1975). An interview study of children's knowledge about memory. *Monographs of the Society for Research in Child Development, 40* (Serial No. 159).

KRUMHANSL, C. L., & JUSCZYK, P. W. (1990). Infants' perception of phrase structure in music. *Psychological Science, 1*, 70–73.

KUHL, P. K. (1987). Perception of speech and sound in early infancy. In P. Salapatek & L. Cohen (Eds.), *Handbook of infant perception*. New York: Academic.

KUHL, P. K., ANDRUSKI, J. E., CHRISTOVICH, I. A., CHRISTOVICH, L. A., KOZHEVNIKOVA, E. V., RYSKINA, V. L., STOLYAROVA, E. I., SUNDBERG, U., & LACERDA, F. (1997). Cross-language analysis of phonetic units in language addressed to infants. *Science, 277* (1 August), 684–686.

KUHN, D. (1976). Relation of two Piagetian stage transitions to IQ. *Developmental Psychology, 12*, 157–161.

KUHN, D. (1989). Children and adults as intuitive scientists. *Psychological Review, 96*, 674–689.

KUHN, D. (2000). Does memory development belong on an endangered topic list? *Child Development, 71*, 21–25.

KUHN, D., AMSEL, E., & O'LOUGHLIN, M. (1988). *The development of scientific thinking skills*. San Diego: Academic.

KUHN, D., & BRANNOCK, J. (1977). Development of the isolation of variable scheme in experimental and "natural experiment" contexts. *Developmental Psychology, 13*, 9–14.

KUHN, D., GARCIA-MILA, M., ZOHAR, A., & ANDERSEN, C. (1995). Strategies of knowledge acquisition. *Monographs of the Society for Research in Child Development, 60* (Serial No. 245).

KUHN, D., LANGER, J., KOHLBERG, L., & HAAN, N. S. (1977). The development of formal operations in logical and moral judgment. *Genetic Psychology Monographs, 95*, 97–188.

KURTZ, B. E. (1990). Cultural differences in children's cognitive and metacognitive development. In W. Schneider & F. E. Weinert (Eds.), *Interactions among aptitudes, strategies, and knowledge in cognitive performance*. New York: Springer-Verlag.

KURTZ, B. E., SCHNEIDER, W., CARR, M., BORKOWSKI, J. G., & RELLINGER, E. (1990). Strategy instruction and attributional beliefs in West Germany and the United States: Do teachers foster metacognitive development? *Contemporary Educational Psychology, 15*, 268–283.

KURTZ, B. E., & WEINERT, F. E. (1989). Metamemory, memory performance, and causal attributions in gifted and average children. *Journal of Experimental Child Psychology, 48*, 45–61.

KURTZ-COSTES, B., SCHNEIDER, W., & RUPP, S. (1995). Is there evidence for intraindividual consistency in performance across memory tasks? New evidence on an old question. In F. E. Weinert & W. Schneider (Eds.), *Memory performance and competencies: Issues in growth and development*. Hillsdale, NJ: Erlbaum.

LABORATORY OF COMPARATIVE HUMAN COGNITION. (1983). Culture and cognitive development. In W. Kessen (Ed.), *History, theory, and methods*, Vol. 1. In P. H. Mussen (Gen. Ed.), *Handbook of child psychology*. New York: Wiley.

LAMB, M. E., STERNBERG, K. J., & ESPLIN, P. W. (1998). Conducting investigative interviews of alleged sexual abuse victims. *Child Abuse & Neglect, 22*, 813–823.

LAMB, M. E., & THIERRY, K. L. (IN PRESS). Understanding children's testimony regarding their alleged abuse: Contributions of field and laboratory analog research. In D. M. Teti (Ed.), *Handbook of research methods in developmental psychology*. Malden, MA: Blackwell.

LANDRY, S. H., SMITH, K. E., MILLER-LONCAR, C. L., & SWANK, P. R. (1997). Predicting cognitive-language and social growth curves from early maternal behaviors in children at varying degrees of biological risk. *Developmental Psychology, 33,* 1040–1053.

LANE, D. M., & PEARSON, D. A. (1982). The development of selective attention. *Merrill-Palmer Quarterly, 28,* 317–337.

LANE, M. K., & HODKIN, B. (1985). Role of atypical exemplars of social and nonsocial superordinate categories within the class inclusion paradigm. *Developmental Psychology, 21,* 909–915.

LANGE, G., GUTTENTAG, R. E., & NIDA, R. E. (1990). Relationships between study organization, retrieval organization, and general strategy-specific memory knowledge in young children. *Journal of Experimental Child Psychology, 49,* 126–146.

LANGE, G., & JACKSON, P. (1974). Personal organization in children's free recall. *Child Development, 45,* 1060–1067.

LANGE, G., & PIERCE, S. H. (1992). Memory-strategy learning and maintenance in preschool children. *Developmental Psychology, 28,* 453–462.

LANGLOIS, J. H., RITTER, J. M., ROGGMAN, L. A., & VAUGHN, L. S. (1991). Facial diversity and infant preferences for attractive faces. *Developmental Psychology, 27,* 79–84.

LANGLOIS, J. H., & ROGGMAN, L. A. (1990). Attractive faces are only average. *Psychological Science, 1,* 115–121.

LANGLOIS, J. H., ROGGMAN, L. A., CASEY, R. J., RITTER, J. M., RIESER-DANNER, L. A., & JENKINS, V. Y. (1987). Infant preferences for attractive faces: Rudiments of a stereotype? *Developmental Psychology, 23,* 363–369.

LARSON, G. E., HAIER, R. J., LACASSE, L., & HAZEN, K. (1995). Evaluation of a "mental effort" hypothesis for correlations between cortical metabolism and intelligence. *Intelligence, 21,* 267–278.

LASKY, R. E., SYRDAL-LASKY, A., & KLEIN, R. E. (1975). VOT discrimination by four- to six-and-a-half-month-old infants from Spanish environments. *Journal of Experimental Child Psychology, 20,* 215–225.

LAVE, J., & WENGER, E. (1991). *Situated learning: Legitimate peripheral participation.* Cambridge, UK: Cambridge University Press.

LAVOIE, J. C., ANDERSON, K., FRAZE, B., & JOHNSON, K. (1981). Modeling, tuition, and sanction effects on self-control at different ages. *Journal of Experimental Child Psychology, 31,* 446–455.

LAZAR, I., DARLINGTON, R., MURRAY, H., ROYCE, J., & SNIPPER, A. (1982). Lasting effects of early education: A report from the Consortium for Longitudinal Studies. *Monographs of the Society for Research in Child Development, 47* (Serial No. 195).

LEAPER, C., ANDERSON, K. J., & SANDERS, P. (1998). Moderators of gender effects on parents' talk to their children: A meta-analysis. *Developmental Psychology, 34,* 3–27.

LECOURS, A. R. (1975). Myelogenetic correlates of the development of speech and language. In E. H. Lenneberg & E. Lenneberg (Eds.), *Foundations of language development: A multidisciplinary approach.* New York: Academic.

LEE, E. S. (1951). Migration: A Philadelphia test of the Klineberg hypothesis. *American Journal of Sociology, 16,* 227–232.

LEGERSTEE, M. (1991). The role of person and object in eliciting early imitation. *Journal of Experimental Child Psychology, 51,* 423–433.

LEGERSTEE, M., ANDERSON, D., & SCHAFFER, A. (1998). Five- and eight-month-old infants recognize their faces and voices as familiar social stimuli. *Child Development, 69,* 37–50.

LEHMAN, E. B., MCKINLEY-PACE, M. J., WILSON, J. A., SAVSKY, M. D., & WOODSON, M. E. (1997). Direct and indirect measures of intentional forgetting in children and adults: Evidence for retrieval inhibition and reinstatement. *Journal of Experimental Child Psychology, 64,* 295–316.

LEICHTMAN, M. D., & CECI, S. J. (1993). The problem of infantile amnesia: Lessons from fuzzy-trace theory. In M. L. Howe & R. Pasnak (Eds.), *Emerging themes in cognitive development: Vol. 1. Foundations.* New York: Springer-Verlag.

LEICHTMAN, M. D., & CECI, S. J. (1995). The effect of stereotypes and suggestion on preschoolers reports. *Developmental Psychology, 31,* 568–578.

LEINBACH, M. D., HORT, B. E., & FAGOT, B. I. (1997). Bears are for boys: Metaphorical associations in young children's gender stereotypes. *Cognitive Development, 12,* 107–130.

LENNEBERG, E. H. (1967). *Biological foundations of language.* New York: Wiley.

LERNER, R. M. (1991). Changing organism-context relations as the basic process of development: A developmental contextual perspective. *Developmental Psychology, 27,* 27–32.

LESLIE, A. (1994). ToMM, ToBy, and agency: Core architecture and domain specificity. In L. Hirschfeld & S. Gelman (Eds.), *Mapping the mind: Domain specificity in cognition and culture.* Cambridge: Cambridge University Press.

LEVINE, S. C. (1993). Effects of early unilateral lesions: Changes over the course of development. In G. Turkewitz & D. A. Devenny (Eds.), *Developmental time and timing.* Hillsdale, NJ: Erlbaum.

LEVINE, S. C., HUTTENLOCHER, J., TAYLOR, A., & LANGROCK, A. (1999). Early sex differences in spatial skills. *Developmental Psychology, 35,* 940–949.

LEWIS, C., FREEMAN, N. H., KYRIAKIDOU, C., MARIDAKI-KASSOTAKI, K., & BERRIDGE, D. M. (1996). Social influence on false belief access: Specific sibling influences or general apprenticeship? *Child Development, 67,* 2930–2947.

LEWIS, K. D. (1999). Maternal style in reminiscing: Relations to child individual differences. *Cognitive Development, 14,* 381–399.

LEWIS, M. (1969). Infants' responses to facial stimuli during the first year of life. *Developmental Psychology, 1,* 75–86.

LEWIS, M. (1991). Ways of knowing: Objective self-awareness of consciousness? *Developmental Review, 11,* 231–243.

LEWIS, M., ALESSANDRI, S. M., & SULLIVAN, M. W. (1990). Violation of expectancy, loss of control and anger expression in young infants. *Developmental Psychology, 63,* 630–638.

LEWIS, M., & BROOKS-GUNN, J. (1979). *Social cognition and the acquisition of self.* New York: Plenum.

LEWIS, M., & FREEDLE, R. O. (1973). Mother-infant dyad: The cradle of meaning. In P. Pilner, L. Krames, & T. Alloway (Eds.), *Communication and affect: Language and thought.* New York: Academic.

LEWIS, M., SULLIVAN, M. W., STANGER, C., & WEISS, M. (1989). Self-development and self-conscious emotions. *Child Development, 60,* 146–156.

LEWIS, M. D. (2000). The promise of dynamic systems approaches for an integrated account of human development. *Child Development, 71,* 36–43.

LEWKOWICZ, D. J. (1992). Infants' response to temporally based intersensory equivalence: The effect of synchronous sounds on visual preferences for moving stimuli. *Infant Behavior & Development, 15,* 297–324.

LEWKOWICZ, D. J. (2000). The development of intersensory temporal perception: An epigenetic systems/limitations view. *Psychological Bulletin, 126,* 281–308.

LEWKOWICZ, D. J., & TURKEWITZ, G. (1980). Cross-modal equivalence in early infancy: Auditory-visual intensity matching. *Developmental Psychology, 16,* 597–607.

LI, S-C. (2003). Biocultural orchestration of developmental plasticity across levels: The interplay of biology and culture in shaping the mind throughout the lifespan. *Psychological Bulletin, 129,* 171–194.

LIBEN, L. S., & GOLBECK, S. L. (1980). Sex differences in performance on Piagetian spatial tasks: Differences in competence or performance? *Child Development, 51,* 594–597.

LIBEN, L. S., & GOLBECK, S. L. (1984). Performance on Piagetian horizontality and verticality tasks: Sex-related differences in knowledge of relevant physical phenomena. *Developmental Psychology, 20,* 595–606.

LIBEN, L. S., & SIGNORELLA, M. L. (1993). Gender-schematic processing in children: The role of initial interpretations of stimuli. *Developmental Psychology, 29,* 141–149.

LIBEN, L. S., & YEKEL, C. A. (1996). Preschoolers understanding of plan and oblique maps: The role of geometric and representational correspondence. *Child Development, 67,* 2780–2796.

LIBERMAN, I. Y., & SHANKWEILER, D. (1977). Speech, the alphabet, and teaching to read. In L. B. Resnick & P. A. Weaver (Eds.), *Theory and practice of early reading.* Hillsdale, NJ: Erlbaum.

LIBERMAN, I. Y., SHANKWEILER, D., FISCHER, R. N., & CARTER, B. (1974). Explicit syllable and phoneme segmentation in the young child. *Journal of Experimental Child Psychology, 18,* 201–212.

LICKLITER, R. (1990). Premature visual stimulation accelerates intersensory functioning in bobwhite quail neonates. *Developmental Psychobiology, 23,* 15–27.

LICKLITER, R. (1996). Structured organisms and structured environments: Development systems and the construction of learning capacities. In J. Valsiner & H. Voss (Eds.), *The structure of learning processes.* Ablex: Norwood, NJ.

LICKLITER, R. (2000). The role of sensory stimulation in perinatal development: Insights from comparative research for care of the high-risk infant. *Developmental and Behavioral Pediatrics, 21,* 437–447.

LICKLITER, R., & BAHRICK, L. E. (2000). The development of infant intersensory perception: Advantages of a comparative convergent-operations approach. *Psychological Bulletin, 126,* 260–280.

LIE, E., & NEWCOMBE, N. S. (1999). Elementary school children's explicit and implicit memory for faces of preschool classmates. *Developmental Psychology, 35,* 102–112.

LIEBERMAN P. (1967). *Intonations, perception, and language.* Cambridge, MA: MIT Press.

LILLARD, A. (1998). Ethnopsychologies: Cultural variations in theories of mind. *Psychological Bulletin, 123,* 3–32.

LIN, C.-Y. C., & FU, V. R. (1990). A comparison of child-rearing practices among Chinese, immigrant Chinese, and Caucasian-American parents. *Child Development, 61,* 429–433.

LINDBERG, M. (1980). The role of knowledge structures in the ontogeny of learning. *Journal of Experimental Child Psychology, 30,* 401–410.

LINDBERG, M. A. (1991). An interactive approach to assessing the suggestibility and testimony of eyewitnesses. In J. Doris (Ed.), *The suggestibility of children's recollections: Implications for eyewitness testimony*. Washington, DC: American Psychological Association.

LINDBERG, M. A., KEIFFER, J., & THOMAS, S. W. (2000). Eyewitness testimony for physical abuse as a function of personal experience, development, and focus of study. *Journal of Applied Developmental Psychology, 21*, 555–591.

LINN, M. C., & PETERSEN, A. C. (1985). Emergence and characterization of sex differences in spatial ability: A meta-analysis. *Child Development, 56*, 1479–1498.

LISTON, C., & KAGAN, J. (2002). Brain development: Memory enhancement in early childhood. *Nature, 419* (31 October), 896.

LIVESEY, D. J., & INTILI, D. (1996). A gender difference in visual-spatial ability in 4-year-old children: Effects on performance of a kinesthetic acuity task. *Journal of Experimental Child Psychology, 63*, 436–446.

LIVESLEY, W., & BROMLEY, D. (1973). *Person perception in childhood and adolescence*. New York: Wiley.

LOCKE, J. L. (1983). *Phonological acquisition and change*. New York: Academic.

LOCKE, J. L. (1993). *The child's path to spoken language*. Cambridge, MA: Harvard University Press.

LOCKE, J. L. (1994). Phases in the child's development of language. *American Scientist, 82*, 436–445.

LOCKE, J. L. (1997). A theory of neurolinguistic development. *Brain and Language, 58*, 265–326.

LOCKMAN, J. J. (2000). A perception-action perspective on tool use development. *Child Development, 71*, 137–144.

LOFTUS, E. F. (1992). When a lie becomes memory's truth: Memory distortion after exposure to misinformation. *Current Directions in Psychological Science, 1*, 121–123.

LOFTUS, E. F., & PICKRELL, J. E. (1995). The formation of false memories. *Psychiatric Annals, 25*, 720–725.

LONGSTRETH, L. E. (1981). Revisiting Skeels' final study: A critique. *Developmental Psychology, 17*, 620–625.

LONIGAN, C. J., BURGESS, S. R., & ANTHONY, J. L. (2000). Development of emergent literacy and early reading skills in preschool children: Evidence from a latent-variable longitudinal study. *Developmental Psychology, 36*, 596–613.

LOPEZ, D. F., LITTLE, T. D., OETTINGEN, G., & BALTES, P. B. (1998). Self-regulation and school performance: Is there optimal level of action-control? *Journal of Experimental Child Psychology, 70*, 54–74.

LORCH, E. P., & CASTLE, V. J. (1997). Preschool children's attention to television: Visual attention and probed response times. *Journal of Experimental Child Psychology, 66*, 111–127.

LORSBACH, T. C., KATZ, G. A., & CUPAK, A. J. (1998). Developmental differences in the ability to inhibit the initial misinterpretation of garden path passages. *Journal of Experimental Child Psychology, 71*, 275–296.

LORSBACH, T. C., & REIMER, J. F. (1997). Developmental changes in the inhibition of previously relevant information. *Journal of Experimental Child Psychology, 64*, 317–342.

LOVELL, K. (1961). A follow-up study of Inhelder and Piaget's "The growth of logical thinking." *British Journal of Psychology, 52*, 143–153.

LUBINSKI, D., & BENBOW, C. P. (1992). Gender differences in abilities and preferences among the gifted: Implications for the math-science pipeline. *Current Directions in Psychological Science, 1*, 61–66.

LUBINSKI, D., BENBOW, C. P., & SANDER, C. (1993). Reconceptualizing gender differences in achievement among the gifted. In K. A. Keller, F. J. Monks, & A. H. Passow (Eds.), *International handbook of research on and development of giftedness and talent*. New York: Pergamon.

LUCARIELLO, J. (1998). Together wherever we go: The ethnographic child and the developmentalists. *Child Development, 69*, 355–358.

LUCARIELLO, J., KYRATZIS, A., & NELSON, K. (1992). Taxonomic knowledge: What kind and when? *Child Development, 63*, 978–998.

LUCARIELLO, J., & NELSON, K. (1985). Slot-filler categories as memory organizers for young children. *Developmental Psychology, 21*, 272–282.

LUECKE-ALESKA, D., ANDERSON, D. R., COLLINS, P. A., & SCHMITT, K. L. (1995). Gender constancy and television viewing. *Developmental Psychology, 31*, 773–780.

LUKAS, W. D., & CAMPBELL, B. C. (2000). Evolutionary and ecological aspects of early brain malnutrition in humans. *Human Nature, 11*, 1–26.

LUNA, B., THULBORN, K. R., MONOZ, D. P., MERRIAM, E. P., GARVER, K. E., MINSHEW, N. J., KESHAVAN, M. S., GENOVESE, C. R., EDDY, W. F., & SWEENEY, J. A. (2001). Maturation of widely distributed brain function subserves cognitive development. *NeuroImage, 13*, 786–793.

LUNDBERG, I., FROST, J., & PETERSON, O.-P. (1988). Effects of an extensive programme for stimulating phonological awareness in pre-school children. *Reading Research Quarterly, 23*, 264–284.

LUNZAR, F. A., DOLAN, T., & WILKINSON, J. E. (1976). The effectiveness of measures of operativity, language, and short-term memory in the prediction of reading and mathematical understanding. *British Journal of Educational Psychology, 46*, 295–305.

LURIA, A. R. (1961). *The role of speech in the regulation of normal and abnormal behavior.* New York: Liveright.

LURIA, A. R. (1973). *The working brain.* New York: Basic Books.

LURIA, A. R. (1976). *Cognitive development: Its cultural and social foundations.* Cambridge, MA: Harvard University Press.

LUTCHMAYA, S., BARON-COHEN, S., & RAGGATT, P. (2002). Foetal testosterone and vocabulary size in 18- and 24-month-old infants. *Infant Behavior & Development, 24,* 418–424.

LYNCH, M. P., EILERS, R. E., OLLER, K., & URBANO, R. C. (1990). Innateness, experience, and music perception. *Psychological Science, 1,* 272–276.

LYNN, S. J., LOCK, T. G., MYERS, B., & PAYNE, D. G. (1997). Recalling the unrecallable: Should hypnosis be used to recover memories in psychotherapy? *Current Directions in Psychological Science, 6,* 79–83.

LYONS, J. (1978). *Semantics,* Vol. 1. New York: Cambridge University Press.

MACCOBY, E. E., & JACKLIN, C. N. (1974). *The psychology of sex differences.* Stanford, CA: Stanford University Press.

MACFARLANE, A. (1975). Olfaction in the development of social preferences in the human neonate. *CIBA Foundation Symposium 33: Parent-infant interaction.* Amsterdam, The Netherlands: Elsevier.

MACLEAN, P. D. (1990). *The triune brain in evolution: Role in paleocerebral functions.* New York: Plenum.

MAKIN, J. W., & PORTER, R. H. (1989). Attractiveness of lactating females' breast odors to neonates. *Child Development, 60,* 803–810.

MALLOY, P. (1987). Frontal lobe dysfunction in obsessive-compulsive disorder. In E. Perecman (Ed.), *The frontal lobes revisited.* New York: IRBN.

MANDEL, D. R., JUSCZYK, P. W., & PISONI, D. B. (1995). Infants' recognition of sound patterns of their own names. *Psychological Science, 5,* 314–317.

MANDLER, J. M. (1992). How to build a baby: II. Conceptual primitives. *Psychological Review, 99,* 587–604.

MANDLER, J. (1998). Representation. In D. Kuhn & R. S. Siegler (Eds.), *Cognition, perception, and language,* Vol. 2. In W. Damon (Gen. Ed.), *Handbook of child psychology.* New York: Wiley.

MANDLER, J. M. (2000). Perceptual and conceptual processes in infancy. *Journal of Cognition and Development, 1,* 3–36.

MANDLER, J. M., & McDONOUGH, L. (1993). Concept formation in infancy. *Cognitive Development, 8,* 291–318.

MANION, V., & ALEXANDER, J. M. (1997). The benefits of peer collaboration on strategy use, metacognitive causal attribution, and recall. *Journal of Experimental Child Psychology, 67,* 268–289.

MARATSOS, M. (1998). The acquisition of grammar. In D. Kuhn & R. S. Siegler (Eds.), *Cognitive, language, and perceptual development,* Vol. 2. In W. Damon (Gen. Ed.), *Handbook of child psychology.* New York: Wiley.

MARCHE, T. A., & HOWE, M. L. (1995). Preschoolers report misinformation despite accurate memory. *Developmental Psychology, 31,* 554–567.

MARCUS, G. F. (1995). Children's overregularization of English plurals: A quantitative analysis. *Journal of Child Language, 22,* 447–460.

MARCUS, G. F., PINKER, S., ULLMAN, M., HOLLANDER, M., ROSEN, T. J., & XU, F. (1992). Overregularization in language acquisition. *Monographs of the Society for Research in Child Development, 57* (Serial No. 228).

MAREAN, G. C., WERNER, L. A., & KUHL, P. K. (1992). Vowel categorization by very young infants. *Developmental Psychology, 28,* 396–405.

MARIANI, M. A., & BARKLEY, R. A. (1997). Neuropsychological and academic functioning in preschool boys with attention deficit hyperactivity disorder. *Developmental Neuropsychology, 13,* 111–129.

MARKMAN, E. M. (1994). Constraints on word meaning in early language acquisition. In L. Gleitman & B. Landau (Eds.), *The acquisition of the lexicon.* Cambridge, MA: MIT Press.

MARKMAN, E. M., & WACHTEL, G. A. (1988). Children's use of mutual exclusivity to constrain the meaning of words. *Cognitive Psychology, 20,* 121–157.

MARKOVITS, H., & BARROUILLET, P. (2002). The development of conditional reasoning: A mental model account. *Developmental Review, 22,* 5–36.

MARKOVITS, H., & VACHON, R. (1989). Reasoning with contrary-to-fact propositions. *Journal of Experimental Child Psychology, 47,* 398–412.

MARLIER, L., SCHAAL, B., & SOUSSIGNAN, R. (1998). Neonatal responsiveness to the odor of amniotic and lacteal fluids: A test of perinatal chemosensory continuity. *Child Development, 69,* 611–623.

MARSH, H. W. (1989). Sex differences in the development of verbal and mathematics constructs: The High School and Beyond Study. *American Educational Research Journal, 26,* 191–225.

MARTIN, C. L., & HALVERSON, C. F. (1981). A schematic processing model of sex-typing and stereotyping in children. *Child Development, 49,* 1119–1134.

MARTIN, C. L., RUBLE, D. N., & SZKRYBALO, J. (2002). Cognitive theories of early gender development. *Psychological Bulletin, 128,* 903–933.

MARTIN, C. L., WOOD, C. H., & LITTLE, J. K. (1990). The development of gender stereotype components. *Child Development, 61,* 1891–1904.

MARX, M. H., & HENDERSON, B. (1996). A fuzzy trace analysis of categorical inferences and instantial associations as a function of retention interval. *Cognitive Development, 11,* 551–569.

MASANGKAY, Z. S., McCLUSKEY, K. A., McINTYRE, C. W., SIMS-KNIGHT, J., VAUGHN, B. E., & FLAVELL, J. H. (1974). The early development of inferences about the visual precepts of others. *Child Development, 45,* 357–366.

MASATAKA, N. (1996). Perception of motherese in a signed language by 6-month-old deaf infants. *Developmental Psychology, 32,* 874–879.

MASATAKA, N. (1998). Perception of motherese in Japanese sign language by 6-month-old hearing infants. *Developmental Psychology, 34,* 241–246.

MASON, J. M. (1992). Reading stories to preliterate children: A proposed connection to reading. In P. B. Gough, L. C. Ehri, & R. Treiman (Eds.), *Reading acquisition.* Hillsdale, NJ: Erlbaum.

MASTEN, A. S., & COATSWORTH, J. D. (1998). The development of competence in favorable and unfavorable environments. *American Psychologist, 53,* 205–220.

MASTERS, S., & SOARES, M. (1993). Is the gender difference in mental rotation disappearing? *Behavioral Genetics, 23,* 337–341.

MASTROPIERI, M. A., & SCRUGGS, T. E. (1991). *Teaching students ways to remember: Strategies for learning mnemonically.* Cambridge, MA: Brookline Books.

MATHENY, A. P., JR., WILSON, R. S., DOLAN, A. B., & KRANTZ, J. Z. (1981). Behavioral contrasts in twinships: Stability and patterns of differences in childhood. *Child Development, 52,* 579–598.

MATTHEWS, M. H. (1987). Sex differences in spatial competence: The ability of young children to map "primed" unfamiliar environments. *Educational Psychology, 7,* 77–90.

MATTHEWS, M. H. (1992). *Making sense of place: Children's understanding of large-scale environments.* Savage, MD: Barnes & Noble Books.

MAURER, D., & SALAPATEK, P. (1976). Developmental changes in the scanning of faces by young infants. *Child Development, 47,* 523–527.

MAURER, D., STAGER, C. L., & MONDLACH, C. J. (1999). Cross-modal transfer of shape is difficult to demonstrate in one-month-olds. *Child Development, 70,* 1047–1057.

MAZZONI, G. (1998). Memory suggestibility and metacognition in child eyewitness testimony: The roles of source monitoring and self-efficacy. *European Journal of Psychology of Education, 13,* 43–60.

McCABE, A. E., SIEGEL, L. S., SPENCE, I., & WILKINSON, A. (1982). Class-inclusion reasoning: Patterns of performance from three to eight years. *Child Development, 53,* 780–785.

McCALL, R. B. (1981). Nature-nurture and the two realms of development: A proposed integration with respect to mental development. *Child Development, 52,* 1–12.

McCALL, R. B., APPELBAUM, M. I., & HOGARTY, P. S. (1973). Developmental changes in mental performance. *Monographs of the Society for Research in Child Development, 38* (Serial No. 150).

McCALL, R. B., & CARRIGER, M. S. (1993). A meta-analysis of infant habituation and recognition memory performance as predictors of later IQ. *Child Development, 64,* 57–79.

McCALL, R. B., EICHORN, D. H., & HOGARTY, P. S. (1977). Transitions in early mental development. *Monographs of the Society for Research in Child Development, 42* (Serial No. 171).

McCALL, R. B., HOGARTY, P. S., & HURLBURT, N. (1972). Transitions in infant sensori-motor development and the prediction of childhood IQ. *American Psychologist, 27,* 728–748.

McCALL, R. B., KENNEDY, C. B., & APPELBAUM, M. I. (1977). Magnitude of discrepancy and the distribution of attention in infants. *Child Development, 48,* 772–785.

McCALL, R. B., PARKE, R. D., & KAVANAUGH, R. D. (1977). Imitation of live and televised models by children one to three years of age. *Monographs of the Society for Research in Child Development, 42* (Serial No. 173).

McCARTHY, D. (1954). Language development in children. In L. Carmichael (Ed.), *A manual of child psychology* (2nd ed.). New York: Wiley.

McCARTNEY, K., HARRIS, M. J., & BERNIERI, F. (1990). Growing up and growing apart: A development meta-analysis of twin studies. *Psychological Bulletin, 107,* 226–237.

McCAULEY, C., WEIL, C. M., & SPERBER, R. D. (1976). The development of memory structure as reflected by semantic-priming effects. *Journal of Experimental Child Psychology, 22,* 511–518.

McDONOUGH, L., MANDLER, J. M., McKEE, R. D., & SQUIRE, L. R. (1995). The deferred imitation task as a nonverbal measure of declarative memory. *Proceedings of the National Academy of Sciences, 92,* 7580–7584.

McGILLY, K., & SIEGLER, R. S. (1990). The influence of encoding strategic knowledge on children's choices among serial recall strategies. *Developmental Psychology, 26,* 931–941.

McGUE, M., BOUCHARD, T. J., JR., LYKKEN, D. T., & FEUER, D. (1984). Information processing abilities in twins reared apart. *Intelligence, 8,* 239–258.

MCPHERSON, S. L., & THOMAS, J. R. (1989). Relation of knowledge and performance in boys' tennis: Age and expertise. *Journal of Experimental Child Psychology, 48,* 190–211.

MEHLER, J., JUSCZYK, P., LAMBERTZ, G., HALSTED, N., BERTONCINI, J., & AMIEL-TISON, C. (1988). A precursor of language acquisition in young infants. *Cognition 29,* 143–178.

MEINTS, K., PLUNKET, K., & HARRIS, P. (1999). When does an ostrich become a bird? The role of typicality in early word comprehension. *Developmental Psychology, 35,* 1072–1078.

MELOT, A-M. (1998). The relationship between metacognitive knowledge and metacognitive experiences: Acquisition and re-elaboration. *European Journal of Psychology of Education, 13,* 75–89.

MELTZOFF, A. N. (1985). Immediate and deferred imitation in fourteen- and twenty-four-month-old infants. *Child Development, 56,* 62–72.

MELTZOFF, A. N. (1988A). Infant imitation after a 1-week delay: Long-term memory for novel acts and multiple stimuli. *Developmental Psychology, 24,* 470–476.

MELTZOFF, A. N. (1988B). Imitation of televised models by infants. *Child Development, 59,* 1221–1229.

MELTZOFF, A. N. (1990). Towards a developmental cognitive science: The implications of cross-modal matching and imitation for the development of memory in infancy. In A. Diamond (Ed.), *The development and neural bases of higher cognitive functions,* Vol. 608, *Annals of the New York Academy of Sciences.*

MELTZOFF, A. N. (1995). What infant memory tells us about infantile amnesia: Long-term recall and deferred imitation. *Journal of Experimental Child Psychology, 59,* 497–515.

MELTZOFF, A. N., & BORTON, R. W. (1979). Intermodal matching by human neonates. *Nature, 282,* 403–404.

MELTZOFF, A. N., & MOORE, M. K. (1977). Imitation of facial and manual gestures by human neonates. *Science, 198,* 75–78.

MELTZOFF, A. N., & MOORE, M. K. (1985). Cognitive foundations and social functions of imitation and intermodal representation in infancy. In J. Mehler & R. Fox (Eds.), *Neonate cognition: Beyond the booming buzzing confusion.* Hillsdale, NJ: Erlbaum.

MELTZOFF, A. N., & MOORE, M. K. (1992). Early imitation within a functional framework: The importance of person identity, movement, and development. *Infant Behavior & Development, 15,* 479–505.

MENDELSON, M. J., & HAITH, M. M. (1976). The relation between audition and vision in the human newborn. *Monographs of the Society for Research in Child Development, 41* (Serial No. 167).

MERVIS, C. B., & BERTRAND, J. (1994). Acquisition of the novel name-nameless category (N3C) principle. *Child Development, 65,* 1646–1662.

MERVIS, C. B., & ROSCH, E. (1981). Categorization of natural objects. *Annual Review of Psychology, 32,* 89–115.

MEULEMANS, T., VAN DER LINDEN, M., & PERRUCHET, P. (1998). Implicit sequence learning in children. *Journal of Experimental Child Psychology, 69,* 199–221.

MILLER, K. F., SMITH, C. M., ZHU, J., & ZHANG, H. (1995). Preschool origins of cross-national differences in mathematical competence. *Psychological Science, 6,* 56–60.

MILLER, L. C., LECHNER, R. E., & RUGS, D. (1985). Development of conversational responsiveness: Preschoolers' use of responsive listener cues and relevant comments. *Developmental Psychology, 21,* 473–480.

MILLER, L. T., & VERNON, P. A. (1996). Intelligence, reaction time, and working memory in 4- to 6-year-old children. *Intelligence, 22,* 155–190.

MILLER, L. T., & VERNON, P. A. (1997). Developmental changes in speed of information processing in young children. *Developmental Psychology, 33,* 549–554.

MILLER, P. H. (1990). The development of strategies of selective attention. In D. F. Bjorklund (Ed.), *Children's strategies: Contemporary views of cognitive development.* Hillsdale, NJ: Erlbaum.

MILLER, P. H., & COYLE, T. R. (1999). Developmental changes: Lessons from microgenesis. In E. K. Scholnick, K. Nelson, S. A. Gelman, & P. H. Miller (Eds.), *Conceptual development: Piaget's legacy.* Mahwah, NJ: Erlbaum.

MILLER, P. H., HAYNES, V. F., DEMARIE-DREBLOW, D., & WOODY-RAMSEY, J. (1986). Children's strategies for gathering information in three tasks. *Child Development, 57,* 1429–1439.

MILLER, P. H., & SEIER, W. L. (1994). Strategy utilization deficiencies in children: When, where, and why. In H. W. Reese (Ed.), *Advances in child development and behavior,* Vol. 25. New York: Academic.

MILLER, P. H., SEIER, W. L., PROBERT, J. S., & ALOISE, P. A. (1991). Age differences in the capacity demands of a strategy among spontaneously strategic children. *Journal of Experimental Child Psychology, 52,* 149–165.

MILLER, P. H., & WEISS, M. G. (1982). Children's and adults knowledge about what variables affect selective attention. *Child Development, 53,* 543–549.

MILLER-JONES, D. (1989). Culture and testing. *American Psychologist, 44,* 360–366.

MILNER, B. (1964). Some effects of frontal lobectomy in man. In J. M. Warren & K. Akert (Eds.), *The frontal granular cortex and behavior.* New York: McGraw-Hill.

MISTRY, J. (1997). The development of remembering in cultural context. In N. Cowan (Ed.), *The development of memory in childhood*. Hove East Sussex, UK: Psychology Press.

MIX, K., HUTTENLOCHER, J., & LEVINE, S. C. (1996). Do preschool children recognize auditory-visual numerical correspondence? *Child Development, 67*, 1592–1608.

MIX, K. S., HUTTENLOCHER, J., & LEVINE, S. C. (2002). Multiple cues for quantification in infancy: Is number one of them? *Psychological Bulletin, 128*, 278–294.

MOELY, B. E., HART, S. S., LEAL, L., SANTULLI, K. A., RAO, N., JOHNSON, T., & HAMILTON, L. B. (1992). The teacher's role in facilitating memory and study strategy development in the elementary school classroom. *Child Development, 63*, 653–672.

MOELY, B. E., SANTULLI, K. A., & OBACH, M. S. (1995). Strategy instruction, metacognition, and motivation in the elementary school classroom. In F. Weinert & W. Schneider (Eds.), *Memory performance and competencies: Issues in growth and development*. Hillsdale, NJ: Erlbaum.

MOFFAT, S. D., HAMPSON, E., & HATZIPANTELIS, M. (1998). Navigation in a "virtual" maze: Sex differences and correlation with psychometric measures of spatial ability in humans. *Evolution and Human Behavior, 19*, 73–87.

MOLENAAR, P. C. M., BOOMSMA, D. I., & DOLAN, C. V. (1993). A third source of developmental differences. *Behavior Genetics, 23*, 519–524.

MONDLOCH, C. J., LEWIS, T. L., BUDREAU, D. R., MAURER, D., DANNEMILLER, J. L., STEPHENS, B. R., & KLEINER-GATHERCOAL, K. A. (1999). Face perception during early infancy. *Psychological Science, 10*, 419–422.

MONEY, J. (1988). *Gay, straight, and in-between: The sexology of erotic orientation*. New York: Oxford University Press.

MONTEMAYOR, R., & EISEN, M. (1977). The development of self-conceptions from childhood to adolescence. *Developmental Psychology, 13*, 314–319.

MONTEPARE, J. M., & MCARTHUR, L. B. (1986). The influence of facial characteristics on children's age perceptions. *Journal of Experimental Child Psychology, 42*, 303–314.

MOOD, D. W. (1979). Sentence comprehension in preschool children: Testing an adaptive egocentrism hypothesis. *Child Development, 50*, 247–250.

MOORE, D. S. (2001). *The dependent gene: The fallacy of "nature vs. nurture."* New York: Freeman Books.

MOORE, D. S., SPENCE, M. J., & KATZ, G. S. (1997). Six-month-olds' categorization of natural infant-directed utterances. *Developmental Psychology, 33*, 980–989.

MOORE, T. (1967). Language and intelligence: A longitudinal study of the first eight years. Part I. Patterns of development in boys and girls. *Human Development, 10*, 88–106.

MORISSET, C. E., BARNARD, K. E., & BOOTH, C. L. (1995). Toddlers' language development: Sex differences within social risk. *Developmental Psychology, 31*, 851–865.

MORRISON, F. J., GRIFFITH, E. M., & ALBERTS, D. M. (1997). Nature-nurture in the classroom: Entrance age, school readiness, and learning in children. *Developmental Psychology, 33*, 254–262.

MORRISON, F. J., GRIFFITH, E. M., & FRAZIER, J. A. (1996). Schooling and the 5–7 shift: A natural experiment. In A. Sameroff & M. M. Haith (Eds.), *Reason and responsibility: The passage through childhood*. Chicago: University of Chicago Press.

MORRISON, F. J., SMITH, L., & DOW-EHRENSBERGER, M. (1995). Education and cognitive development: A natural experiment. *Developmental Psychology, 31*, 789–799.

MORTON, J., & JOHNSON, M. H. (1991). CONSPEC and CONLERN: A two-process theory of infant face recognition. *Psychological Review, 98*, 164–181.

MOSHMAN, D. (1998). Cognitive development beyond childhood. In D. Kuhn & R. S. Siegler (Vol. Eds.), *Cognitive, language, and perceptual development*, Vol. 2. In W. Damon (Gen. Ed.), *Handbook of child psychology*. New York: Wiley.

MOSKOWITZ, B. A. (1978, NOVEMBER). The acquisition of language. *Scientific American*, 92–108.

MUIR-BROADDUS, J. E. (1995). Gifted underachievers: Insights from the characteristics of strategic functioning associated with giftedness and achievement. *Learning and Individual Differences, 7*, 189–206.

MULLEN, M. K. (1994). Earliest recollections of childhood: A demographic analysis. *Cognition, 52*, 55–79.

MULLEN, M. K., & YI, S. (1995). The cultural context of talk about the past: Implications for the development of autobiographical memory. *Cognitive Development, 10*, 407–419.

MÜLLER, U., OVERTON, W. F., & REENE, K. (2001). Development of conditional reasoning: A longitudinal study. *Journal of Cognition and Development, 2*, 27–49.

MUNROE, R. H., SHIMMIN, H. S., & MUNROE, R. L. (1984). Gender understanding and sex role preference in four cultures. *Developmental Psychology, 20*, 673–682.

MUTER, V., HULME, C., SNOWLING, M., & TAYLOR, S. (1998). Segmentation, not rhyming, predicts early progress in learning to read. *Journal of Experimental Child Psychology, 71*, 3–27.

MYOWA-YAMAKOSHI, M., & TOMONAGA, M. (2001). Development of face recognition in an infant gibbon (*Hylobates agilis*). *Infant Behavior & Development, 24,* 215–227.

NADIG, A. S., & SEDIVY, J. C. (2002). Evidence of perspective-taking constraints in children's on-line reference resolution. *Psychological Science, 13,* 329–336.

NAGELL, K., OLGUIN, K., & TOMASELLO, M. (1993). Processes of social learning in the tool use of chimpanzees (*Pan troglodytes*) and human children (*Homo sapiens*). *Journal of Comparative Psychology, 107,* 174–186.

NAITO, M., & MIURA, H. (2001). Japanese children's numerical competencies: Age- and schooling-related influences in the development of number concepts and addition skills. *Developmental Psychology, 37,* 217–230.

NASH, M. R. (1987). What, if anything, is age regressed about hypnotic age regression? A review of the empirical literature. *Psychological Bulletin, 102,* 42–52.

NASH, M. R., DRAKE, M., WILEY, R., KHALSA, S., & LYNN, S. J. (1986). The accuracy of recall of hypnotically age regressed subjects. *Journal of Abnormal Psychology, 95,* 298–300.

NEISSER, U. (ED.). (1998). *The rising curve: Long-term gains in IQ and related measures.* Washington, DC: American Psychological Association.

NEISSER, U., BOODOO, G., BOUCHARD, T. J., BOYKIN, A. W., BRODY, N., CECI, S. J., HALPERN, D. F., LOEHLIN, J. C., PERLOFF, R., STERNBERG, R. J., & URBINA, S. (1996). Intelligence: Knowns and unknowns. *American Psychologist, 51,* 77–101.

NELSON, C. A. (1997). The neurobiological basis of early memory development. In N. Cowan (Ed.), *The development of memory in childhood.* Hove East Sussex, UK: Psychology Press.

NELSON, C. A. (2001). Neural plasticity and human development: The role of experience in sculpting memory systems. *Developmental Science, 3,* 115–130.

NELSON, C. A., & BLOOM, F. E. (1997). Child development and neuroscience. *Child Development, 68,* 970–987.

NELSON, K. (1974). Variations in children's concepts by age and category. *Child Development, 45,* 577–584.

NELSON, K. (1983). The derivation of concepts and categories from event representatives. In E. K. Skolnick (Ed.), *New trends in conceptual representation: Challenges to Piaget's theory?* Hillsdale, NJ: Erlbaum.

NELSON, K. (1993). The psychological and social origins of autobiographical memory. *Psychological Science, 4,* 7–14.

NELSON, K. (1996). *Language in cognitive development: The emergence of the mediated mind.* New York: Cambridge University Press.

NELSON, K. (IN PRESS). Evolution and development of human memory systems. In B. J. Ellis & D. F. Bjorklund (Eds.), *Origins of the social mind: Evolutionary psychology and child development.* New York: Guilford.

NESSE, R. M., & WILLIAMS, G. C. (1994). *Why we get sick: The new science of Darwinian medicine.* New York: Times Books.

NEWCOMBE, N. S. (2002). The nativist-empiricist controversy in the context of recent research on spatial and quantitative development. *Psychological Science, 13,* 395–401.

NEWCOMBE, N., BANDURA, M. M., & TAYLOR, D. C. (1983). Sex differences in spatial ability and spatial activities. *Sex Roles, 9,* 377–386.

NEWCOMBE, N. S., DRUMMEY, A. B., FOX, N. A., LIE, E., & OTTINGER-ALBERTS, W. (2000). Remembering early childhood: How much, how, and why (or why not). *Current Directions in Psychological Science, 9,* 55–58.

NEWCOMBE, N., & DUBAS, J. S. (1992). A longitudinal study of predictors of spatial ability in adolescent females. *Child Development, 63,* 37–46.

NEWCOMBE, N., & FOX, N. A. (1994). Infantile amnesia: Through a glass darkly. *Child Development, 65,* 31–40.

NEWCOMBE, N., & HUTTENLOCHER, J. (1992). Children's early ability to solve perspective-taking problems. *Developmental Psychology, 28,* 635–643.

NEWCOMBE, N., HUTTENLOCHER, J., DRUMMEY, A. B., & WILEY, J. (1998). The development of spatial location coding: Use of external frames of reference and dead reckoning. *Cognitive Development, 13,* 185–200.

NEWCOMBE, N., HUTTENLOCHER, J., & LEARMONTH, A. (1999). Infants' coding of location in continuous space. *Infant Behavior & Development, 22,* 483–510.

NEWPORT, E. L. (1990). Maturational constraints on language learning. *Cognitive Science, 14,* 11–28.

NEWPORT, E. L. (1991). Contrasting concepts of the critical period for language. In S. Carey & R. Gelman (Eds.), *Epigenesis of mind: Essays in biology and knowledge.* Hillsdale, NJ: Erlbaum

NICHD EARLY CHILD CARE RESEARCH NETWORK (2002). Child-care structure → process → outcome: Direct and indirect effects of child-care quality on young children's development. *Psychological Science, 13,* 199–206.

NOWAKOWSKI, R. S. (1987). Basic concepts of CNS development. *Child Development, 58,* 568–595.

NYITI, R. M. (1982). The validity of "cultural differences explanation" in the rate of Piagetian cognitive development. In D. A. Wagner & H. W. Stevenson (Eds.), *Cultural perspectives on child development.* San Francisco: W. H. Freeman.

O'BRIEN, M., & HUSTON, A. C. (1985). Development of sex-typed play behavior in toddlers. *Developmental Psychology, 21,* 866–871.

O'CONNOR, J. J., COHEN, S., & PARMELEE, A. H. (1984). Infant auditory discrimination in preterm and full-term infants as a predictor of 5 year intelligence. The effects of global severe privation on cognitive competence: Extension and longitudinal follow-up. *Developmental Psychology, 20,* 159–165.

O'CONNOR, T. G., RUTTER, M., BECKETT, C., KEAVENEY, L., KREPPNER, J. M., AND THE ENGLISH AND ROMANIAN ADOPTEES STUDY TEAM. (2000). The effects of global severe privation on cognitive competence: Extension and longitudinal follow-up. *Child Development, 71,* 376–390.

O'SULLIVAN, J. T., HOWE, M. L., & MARCHE, T. A. (1996). Children's beliefs about long-term retention. *Child Development, 67,* 2989–3009.

OAKES, L. M., & MADOLE, K. L. (2000). The future of infant categorization research: A process-oriented approach. *Child Development, 71,* 119–126.

OAKES, M. A., & HYMAN, I. E., JR. (2000). The changing face of memory and self. In D. F. Bjorklund (Ed.), *False-memory creation in children and adults: Theory, research, and implications.* Mahwah, NJ: Erlbaum.

OLDS, D. L., HENDERSON, C. R., & TATELBAUM, R. (1994). Intellectual impairment in children of women who smoke cigarettes during pregnancy. *Pediatrics, 93,* 221–227.

OLLER, D. K. (1980). The emergence of the sounds of speech in infancy. In G. Yeni-Komshian, J. F. Kavanaugh, & C. A. Ferguson (Eds.), *Child phonology:* Vol. 1. *Productions.* New York: Academic.

OMANSON, R. C., BECK, I. L., VOSS, J. F., & McKEOWN, M. G. (1984). The effects of reading lessons on comprehension: A processing description. *Cognition and Instruction, 1,* 45–67.

OPPENHEIM, R. W. (1981). Ontogenetic adaptations and retrogressive processes in the development of the nervous system and behavior. In K. J. Connolly & H. F. R. Prechtl (Eds.), *Maturation and development: Biological and psychological perspectives.* Philadelphia: International Medical Publications.

ORNSTEIN, P. A., BAKER-WARD, L., GORDON, B. N., & MERRITT, K. A. (1997). Children's memory for medical experiences: Implications for testimony. *Applied Cognitive Psychology, 11,* 87–104.

ORNSTEIN, P. A., BAKER-WARD, L., & NAUS, M. J. (1988). The development of mnemonic skill. In M. Weinert & M. Perlmutter (Eds.), *Memory development.* Hillsdale, NJ: Erlbaum.

ORNSTEIN, P. A., GORDON, B. N., & LARUS, D. M. (1992). Children's memory for a personally experienced event: Implications for testimony. *Applied Developmental Psychology, 6,* 49–60.

ORNSTEIN, P. A., & GREENHOOT, A. F. (2000). Remembering the distant past: Implications of research on children's memory for the recovered memory debate. In D. F. Bjorklund (Ed.), *False-memory creation in children and adults: Theory, research, and implications.* Mahwah, NJ: Erlbaum.

ORNSTEIN, P. A., & HADEN, C. A. (2001). Memory development or the *development* of memory? *Current Directions in Psychological Science, 10,* 202–209.

ORNSTEIN, P. A., HALE, G. A., & MORGAN, J. S. (1977). Developmental differences in recall and output organization. *Bulletin of the Psychonomic Society, 9,* 29–32.

ORNSTEIN, P. A., MERRITT, K. A., BAKER-WARD, L., FURTADO, E., GORDON, B. N., & PRINCIPE, G. F. (1998). Children's knowledge, expectation, and long-term retention. *Applied Cognitive Psychology, 12,* 387–405.

ORNSTEIN, P. A., & NAUS, M. J. (1978). Rehearsal processes in children's memory. In P. A. Ornstein (Ed.), *Memory development in children.* Hillsdale, NJ: Erlbaum.

ORNSTEIN, P. A., NAUS, M. J., & LIBERTY, C. (1975). Rehearsal and organizational processes in children's memory. *Child Development, 46,* 818–830.

ORNSTEIN, P. A., NAUS, M. J., & STONE, B. P. (1977). Rehearsal training and developmental differences in memory. *Development Psychology, 13,* 15–24.

OSBORNE, J. G., & CALHOUN, D. O. (1998). Themes, taxons, and trial types in children's matching to sample: Methodological considerations. *Journal of Experimental Child Psychology, 68,* 35–50.

OVERMAN, W., BACHEVALIER, J., MILLER, M., & MOORE, K. (1996). Children's performance on "animal tests" of oddity: Implications for cognitive processes required for tests of oddity and delayed nonmatch to sample. *Journal of Experimental Child Psychology, 62,* 223–242.

OYAMA, S. (2000). *The ontogeny of information: Developmental systems and evolution* (2nd ed.). Durham, NC: Duke University Press.

PALINCSAR, A. S., & BROWN, A. L. (1984). Reciprocal teaching of comprehension-monitoring activities. *Cognition and Instruction, 1,* 117–175.

PALINCSAR, A. S., BROWN, A. L., & CAMPIONE, J. C. (1993). First-grade dialogues for knowledge acquisition and use. In E. A. Forman, N. Minilk, & C. A. Stone (Eds.), *Contexts for learning.* New York: Oxford University Press.

PANKSEPP, J. (1998). Attention deficit hyperactivity disorders, psychostimulants, and intolerance of childhood playfulness: A tragedy in the making? *Current Directions in Psychological Science, 7,* 91–98.

PAPOUSEK, H. (1977). The development of learning ability in infancy (Entwicklung der Lernfähigkeit im Säuglingsalter). In G. Nissen (Ed.), *Intelligence, learning, and learning disabilities (Intelligenz, Lernen und Lernstörungen)*. Berlin: Springer-Verlag.

PARIS, S. G. (1973). Comprehension of language connectives and propositional logical relationships. *Journal of Experimental Child Psychology, 16*, 278–291.

PARIS, S. G., & OKA, E. R. (1986). Children's reading strategies, metacognition, and motivation. *Developmental Review, 6*, 25–56.

PARK, D., & JAMES, Q. J. (1983). Effects of encoding instructions on children's spatial and color memory: Is there evidence for automaticity? *Child Development, 54*, 61–68.

PARKER, J. F. (1995). Age differences in source monitoring of performed and imagined actions on immediate and delayed tests. *Journal of Experimental Child Psychology, 60*, 84–101.

PASCALIS, O., DE HAAN, M., & NELSON, C. A. (2002). Is face processing species-specific during the first year of life? *Science, 296* (17 May), 1321–1323.

PASCUAL-LEONE, J. (1970). A mathematical model for the transition rule in Piaget's developmental stages. *Acta Psychologia, 32*, 301–345.

PASCUAL-LEONE, J. (2000). Is the French connection neo-Piagetian? Not nearly enough! *Child Development, 71*, 843–845.

PASCUAL-LEONE, J., & JOHNSON, J. (1999). A dialectical constructivist view of representation: Role of mental attention, executives, and symbols. In I. Sigel (Ed.), *Development of mental representation: Theories and applications*. Mahwah, NJ: Erlbaum.

PASSOLUNGHI, M. C., & SIEGEL, L. S. (2001). Short-term memory, working memory, and inhibitory control in children with difficulties in arithmetic problem solving. *Journal of Experimental Child Psychology, 80*, 44–57.

PAUEN, S. (2000). Early differentiation within the animate domain: Are humans something special? *Journal of Experimental Child Psychology, 75*, 134–151.

PAULESU, E., DÉMONET, J.-F., FAZIO, F., McCRORY, E., CHANOINE, V., BRUNSWICK, N., CAPPA, S. F., COSSU, G., HABIB, M., FRITH, C. D., & FRITH. U. (2001). Dyslexia: Cultural diversity and biological unity. *Science, 291* (16 March), 2165–2167.

PEARSON, P. D., HANSEN, J., & GORDON, C. (1979). The effect of background knowledge on young children's comprehension of explicit and implicit information. *Journal of Reading Behavior, 11*, 201–209.

PENNISI, E. (2001). Behind the scenes of gene expression. *Science, 293* (10 August), 1064–1067.

PERLMUTTER, M., & LANGE, G. (1978). A developmental analysis of recall-recognition distinctions. In P. A. Ornstein (Ed.), *Memory development in children*. Hillsdale, NJ: Erlbaum.

PERNER, J. (1991). *Understanding the representational mind*. Cambridge, MA: MIT Press.

PERNER, J., & LANG, B. (2000). Theory of mind and executive function: Is there a developmental relationship? In S. Baron-Cohen, H. Tager-Flusberg, & D. Cohen (Eds.), *Understanding other minds: Perspectives from autism and developmental cognitive neuroscience* (2nd ed.). Oxford: Oxford University Press.

PERNER, J., RUFFMAN, T., & LEEKAM, S. R. (1994). Theory of mind is contagious: You catch it from your sibs. *Child Development, 67*, 1228–1238.

PERRY, D. G., PERRY, L. C., & RASMUSSEN, P. (1986). Cognitive social learning mediators of aggression. *Child Development, 57*, 700–711.

PERRY, D. G., WHITE, A. J., & PERRY, L. C. (1984). Does early sex typing result from children's attempts to match their behavior to sex role stereotypes? *Child Development, 55*, 2114–2121.

PESKIN, J. (1992). Ruse and representations: On children's ability to conceal information. *Developmental Psychology, 28*, 84–89.

PETRILL, S. A. (1997). Molarity versus modularity of cognitive functioning? A behavioral genetic perspective. *Current Directions in Psychological Science, 6*, 96–99.

PETRILL, S. A., SAUDINO, K., CHERNY, S. S., EMDE, R. N., FULKER, D. W., HEWITT, J. K., & PLOMIN, R. (1997). Exploring the genetic etiology of low general cognitive ability from 14 to 36 months. *Developmental Psychology, 33*, 544–548.

PETRILL, S. A., SAUDINO, K., CHERNY, S. S., EMDE, R. N., FULKER, D. W., HEWITT, J. K., & PLOMIN, R. (1998). Exploring the genetic and environmental etiology of high general cognitive ability in fourteen- to thirty-six-month-old twins. *Child Development, 69*, 68–74.

PETRILL, S. A., THOMPSON, L. A., & DETTERMAN, D. K. (1995). The genetic and environmental variance underlying elementary cognitive tasks. *Behavioral Genetics, 25*, 199–209.

PEZDEK, K., & HODGE, D. (1999). Planting false childhood memories in children. The role of event plausibility. *Child Development, 70*, 887–895.

PHILLIPS, S., KING, S., & DuBOIS, L. C. (1978). Spontaneous activity of female versus male newborns. *Child Development, 49*, 590–597.

PIAGET, J. (1930). *The child's conception of physical causality*. London: Routledge & Kegan Paul.

PIAGET, J. (1952). *The origins of intelligence in children*. New York: Norton.

PIAGET, J. (1954). *The construction of reality in the child.* New York: Basic.

PIAGET, J. (1955). *The language and thought of the child.* New York: World.

PIAGET, J. (1962). *Play, dreams, and imitation in childhood.* New York: Norton.

PIAGET, J. (1965). *The child's conception of number.* New York: Norton.

PIAGET, J. (1967). Genesis and structure in the psychology of intelligence. In J. Piaget, *Six psychological studies.* New York: Vintage.

PIAGET, J. (1968). *On the development of memory and identity.* Worcester, MA: Clark University Press.

PIAGET, J. (1969A). *The child's conception of the world.* Totowa, NJ: Littlefield & Adams.

PIAGET, J. (1969B). *Judgment and reasoning in the child.* London: Routledge.

PIAGET, J. (1971). *Biology and knowledge.* Chicago: University of Chicago Press.

PIAGET, J. (1972). *Play and development* (Maria W. Piers, Ed.). New York: Norton.

PIAGET, J. (1980). *Language and learning* (M. Piatelli-Palmarini, Trans.). Cambridge, MA: Harvard University Press.

PIAGET, J., & INHELDER, B. (1967). *The child's conception of space.* New York: Norton.

PIAGET, J., & INHELDER, B. (1969). *The psychology of the child.* New York: Basic.

PIAGET, J., & INHELDER, B. (1973). *Memory and intelligence.* New York: Basic.

PIERCE, K. A., & GHOLSON, B. (1994). Surface similarity and relational similarity in the development of analogical problem solving: Isomorphic and nonisomorphic transfer. *Developmental Psychology, 30,* 724–737.

PILLEMER, D. B., & WHITE, S. H. (1989). Childhood events recalled by children and adults. In H. W. Reese (Ed.), *Advances in child development and behavior,* Vol. 21. New York: Academic.

PILLOW, B. H. (1988). Young children's understanding of attentional limits. *Child Development, 59,* 31–46.

PINE, K. J., & MESSER, D. J. (1998). Group collaboration effects and the explicitness of children's knowledge. *Cognitive Development, 13,* 109–126.

PINKER, S. (1994). *The language instinct: How the mind creates language.* New York: Morrow.

PINKER, S. (1997). *How the mind works.* New York: Norton.

PLOMIN, R., DeFRIES, J. C., McCLEARN, G. E., & RUTTER, M. (1997). *Behavioral genetics* (3rd ed.). New York: Freeman.

PLOMIN, R., FULKER, D. W., CORLEY, R., & DeFRIES, J. C. (1997). Nature, nurture, and cognitive development from 1 to 6 years: A parent-offspring adoption study. *Psychological Science, 8,* 442–447.

PLOMIN, R., & PETRILL, S. A. (1997). Genetics and intelligence: What's new? *Intelligence, 24,* 53–77.

PLUMERT, J. M. (1995). Relation between children's overestimation of their physical abilities and accident proneness. *Developmental Psychology, 31,* 866–876.

PLUMERT, J. M., & NICHOLS-WHITEHEAD, P. (1996). Parental scaffolding of young children's spatial communication. *Developmental Psychology, 32,* 523–532.

PLUNKET, K., KARMILOFF-SMITH, A., BATES, E., ELMAN, J. L., & JOHNSON, M. H. (1997). Connectionism and developmental psychology. *Journal of Child Psychology and Psychiatry, 38,* 53–80.

POIRIER, F. E., & SMITH, E. O. (1974). Socializing functions of primate play. *American Zoologist, 14,* 275–287.

POOLE, D. A. (1995). Strolling fuzzy-trace theory through eyewitness testimony (or vice versa). *Learning and Individual Differences, 7,* 87–93.

POOLE, D. A., & LAMB, M. E. (1998). *Investigative interviews of children: A guide of helping professionals.* Washington, DC: American Psychological Association.

POOLE, D. A., & LINDSAY, D. S. (2002). Reducing child witnesses' false reports of misinformation from parents. *Journal of Experimental Child Psychology, 81,* 117–140.

POOLE, D. A., & WHITE, L. T. (1991). Effects of question repetition on the eyewitness testimony of children and adults. *Developmental Psychology, 27,* 975–986.

POOLE, D. A., & WHITE, L. T. (1993). Two years later. Effects of question repetition and retention interval on the eyewitness testimony of children and adults. *Developmental Psychology, 29,* 844–853.

POOLE, D., & WHITE, L. T. (1995). Tell me again and again: Stability and change in the repeated testimonies of children and adults. In M. S. Zaragoza, J. R. Graham, C. N. Gordon, R. Hirschman, & Y. S. Ben Porath (Eds.), *Memory and testimony in the child witness.* Newbury Park, CA: Sage.

POSNER, M. I., ROTHBART, M. K., FARAH, M., & BRUER, J. (EDS.). (2001). The developing human brain. *Developmental Science, 4,* 253–387.

POVINELLI, D. J., LANDAU, K. R., & PERILLOUX, H. K. (1996). Self-recognition in young children using delayed versus live feedback: Evidence of a developmental asynchrony. *Child Development, 67,* 1540–1554.

POVINELLI, D. J., & SIMON, B. B. (1998). Young children's understanding of briefly versus extremely delayed images of the self: Emergence of the autobiographical stance. *Developmental Psychology, 34,* 188–194.

POWELL, M. B., ROBERTS, K. P., CECI, S. J., & HEMBROOKE, H. (1999). The effects of repeated experience on children's suggestibility. *Developmental Psychology, 35,* 1462–1477.

PREMACK, D., & WOODRUFF, G. (1978). Does the chimpanzee have a theory of mind? *Behavioral and Brain Sciences, 1,* 515–526.

PRESSLEY, M. (1982). Elaboration and memory development. *Child Development, 53,* 296–309.

PRESSLEY, M., BORKOWSKI, J. G., & SCHNEIDER, W. (1989). Good information processing: What is it and what education can do to promote it. *International Journal of Educational Research, 13,* 857–867.

PRESSLEY, M., & WOLOSHYN, V. (1995). *Cognitive strategy instruction that really improves children's academic performance* (2nd ed.). Cambridge, MA: Brookline Books.

PRICE, T. S., ELEU, T. C., DALE, P. S., STEVENSON, J., SAUDINO, K., & PLOMIN, R. (2000). Genetic and environmental covariation between verbal and nonverbal cognitive development in infancy. *Child Development, 71,* 948–959.

PROVENCE, S., & LIPTON, R. C. (1962). *Infants in institutions: A comparison of their development with family-reared infants during the first year of life.* New York: International Universities Press.

QIN, J. M., QUAS, J. A., REDLICH, A. D., & GOODMAN, G. S. (1997). Children's eyewitness testimony: Memory development in the legal context. In N. Cowan (Ed.), *The development of memory in childhood.* Hove East Sussex, UK: Psychology Press.

QUARTZ, S. R., & SEJNOWSKI, T. J. (1997). The neural basis of cognitive development: A constructivist manifesto. *Behavioral and Brain Sciences, 20,* 537–596.

QUINE, W. V. (1972). *Methods of logic.* New York: Holt, Rinehart & Winston.

QUINN, P. C. (1994). The categorization of above and below spatial relations by young infants. *Child Development, 65,* 58–69.

QUINN, P. C. (2002). Category representation in young infants. *Current Directions in Psychological Science, 11,* 66–70.

QUINN, P. C., & EIMAS, P. D. (1996). Perceptual cues that permit categorical differentiation of animal species by infants. *Journal of Experimental Child Psychology, 63,* 189–211.

QUINN, P. C., & EIMAS, P. D. (1998). Evidence for a global categorical representation of humans by young infants. *Journal of Experimental Child Psychology, 69,* 151–174.

RABINOWITZ, M., FREEMAN, K., & COHEN, S. (1992). Use and maintenance of strategies: The influence of accessibility to knowledge. *Journal of Educational Psychology, 84,* 211–218.

RABINOWITZ, M., & KEE, D. (1994). A framework for understanding individual differences in memory: Strategy-knowledge interactions. In P. A. Vernon (Ed.), *Handbook of the neuropsychology of individual differences.* New York: Academic.

RADZISZEWSKA, B., & ROGOFF, B. (1988). Influence of adult and peer collaborators on children's planning skills. *Developmental Psychology, 24,* 840–848.

RAMEY, C. T., CAMPBELL, F. A., BURCHINAL, M., SKINNER, M. L., GARDNER, D. M., & RAMEY, S. L. (2000). Persistent effects of early childhood education on high-risk children and their mothers. *Applied Developmental Science, 4,* 2–14.

RAMEY, C. T., CAMPBELL, F. A., & FINKELSTEIN, N. W. (1984). Course and structure of intellectual development in children at risk for developmental retardation. In P. H. Brooks, R. Sperber, & C. McCauley (Eds.), *Learning and cognition in the mentally retarded.* Hillsdale, NJ: Erlbaum.

RATNER, H. H. (1984). Memory demands and the development of young children's memory. *Child Development, 55,* 2173–2191.

RATNER, H. H., FOLEY, M. A., & GIMPERT, N. (2002). The role of collaborative planning in children's source-monitoring errors and learning. *Journal of Experimental Child Psychology, 81,* 44–73.

RAVEN, J. C., COURT, J. H., & RAVEN, J. (1975). *Manual for Raven's Progressive Matrices and Vocabulary Scales.* London: Lewis.

RAYMOND, C. L., & BENBOW, C. P. (1986). Gender differences in mathematics: A function of parental support and student sex typing? *Development Psychology, 22,* 808–819.

RECHT, D. R., & LESLIE, L. (1988). Effect of prior knowledge on good and poor readers' memory of text. *Journal of Educational Psychology, 80,* 16–20.

REED, M. A., PIEN, D. L., & ROTHBART, M. K. (1984). Inhibitory self-control in preschool children. *Merrill-Palmer Quarterly, 30,* 131–147.

REEDER, K. (1981). How young children learn to do things with words. In P. S. Dale & D. Ingram (Eds.), *Child language—An international perspective.* Baltimore: University Park.

REESE, E. (1995). Predicting children's literacy from mother-child conversations. *Cognitive Development, 10,* 381–405.

REESE, E., HADEN, C., & FIVUSH, R. (1993). Mother-child conversations about the past: Relationships of style and memory over time. *Cognitive Development, 8,* 403–430.

REESE, E., HADEN, C. A., & FIVUSH, R. (1996). Mothers, fathers, daughters, sons: Gender differences in autobiographical reminiscing. *Research on Language and Social Interaction, 29,* 27–56.

REESE, H. W. (1962). Verbal mediation as a function of age level. *Psychological Bulletin, 59,* 502–509.

REINISCH, J. M., SANDERS, S. A., MORTENSEN, E. L., & RUBIN, D. B. (1995). In utero exposure to phenobarbital and intelligence deficits in adult men. *Journal of the American Medical Association, 274,* 1518–1525.

REISS, D., & MARINO, L. (2001). Mirror self-recognition in the bottlenose dolphin: A case of cognitive convergence. *Proceedings of the National Academy of Sciences, 98,* 5937–5942.

RENNINGER, K. A. (1992). Individual interest and development: Implications for theory and practice. In K. A. Renninger, S. Hidi, & A. Krapp (Eds.), *The role of interest in learning and development.* Hillsdale, NJ: Erlbaum.

RENNINGER, K. A., HIDI, S., & KRAPP, A. (Eds.) (1992). *The role of interest in learning and development.* Hillsdale, NJ: Erlbaum.

REPACHOLI, B. M., & GOPNIK, A. (1997). Early reasoning about desires: Evidence from 14- and 18-month-olds. *Developmental Psychology, 33,* 12–21.

RESCORLA, L., HYSON, M. C., & HIRSH-PASEK, K. (EDS.). (1991). *Academic instruction in early childhood: Challenge or pressure?* San Francisco: Jossey-Bass.

REYNA, V. F., & BRAINERD, C. J. (1995). Fuzzy-trace theory: An interim synthesis. *Learning and Individual Differences, 3,* 27–59.

REYNOLDS, A. J., MAVROGENES, N. A., BEZUCZKO, N., & HAGEMANN, M. (1996). Cognitive and family-support mediators of preschool effectiveness: A confirmatory analysis. *Child Development, 67,* 1119–1140.

REZNICK, J. S., FUESER, J. J., & BOSQUET, M. (1998). Self-corrected reaching in a three-location delayed-response search task. *Psychological Science, 9,* 66–70.

REZNICK, J. S., & KAGAN, J. (1983). Category detection in infancy. In L. P. Lipsitt & C. K. Rovee-Collier (Eds.), *Advances in infancy research,* Vol. 2. Norwood, NJ: Ablex.

RHEINGOLD, H. L. (1985). Development as the acquisition of familiarity. *Annual Review of Psychology, 36,* 1–17.

RHEINGOLD, H. L., HAY, D. F., & WEST, M. J. (1976). Sharing in the second year of life. *Child Development, 47,* 1148–1158.

RICE, C., KOINIS, D., SULLIVAN, K., TAGER-FLUSBERG, & WINNER, E. (1997). When 3-year olds pass the appearance-reality test. *Developmental Psychology, 33,* 54–61.

RIDDERINKHOF, K. R., & VAN DER MOLEN, M. (1995). A psychophysiological analysis of developmental differences in the ability to resist interference. *Child Development, 66,* 1040–1056.

RIDDERINKHOF, K. R., & VAN DER MOLEN, M., & BAND, G. P. H. (1997). Sources of interference from irrelevant information: A developmental study. *Journal of Experimental Child Psychology, 65,* 315–341.

RINGEL, B. A., & SPRINGER, C. J. (1980). On knowing how well one is remembering: The persistence of strategy use during transfer. *Journal of Experimental Child Psychology, 29,* 322–333.

RITTLE-JOHNSON, B., & SIEGLER, R. S. (1999). Learning to spell: Variability, choice, and change in children's strategy use. *Child Development, 70,* 304–316.

RIVA, D., & CAZZANIGA, L. (1986). Late effects of unilateral brain lesions sustained before and after age one. *Neuropsychology, 24,* 423–428.

ROBERTS, K. (1988). Retrieval of a basic-level category in prelinguistic children. *Developmental Psychology, 24,* 21–27.

ROBERTS, K., & HOROWITZ, F. D. (1986). Basic level categorization in seven- and nine-month-old infants. *Journal of Child Language, 13,* 191–206.

ROBERTSON, I. H., & MURRE, J. M. J. (1999). Rehabilitation of brain damage: Brain plasticity and principles of guide recovery. *Psychological Bulletin, 125,* 544–575.

ROBINSON, B. F., & MERVIS, C. B. (1998). Disentangling early language development: Modeling lexical and grammatical acquisition using an extension of case-study methodology. *Developmental Psychology, 34,* 363–375.

ROCHAT, P., & MORGAN, R. (1995). Spatial determinants in the perception of self-produced leg movements by 3- to 5-month-old infants. *Developmental Psychology, 31,* 626–636.

ROCHAT, P., & STRIANO, T. (2002). Who's in the mirror? Self-other discrimination in specular images by four- and nine-month-old infants. *Child Development, 73,* 35–46.

ROE, K. V., DRIVAS, A., KARAGELLIS, A., & ROE, A. (1985). Sex differences in vocal interaction with mother and stranger in Greek infants: Some cognitive implications. *Developmental Psychology, 21,* 372–377.

ROEBERS, C. M. (2002). Confidence judgments in children's and adults' event recall and suggestibility. *Developmental Psychology, 38,* 1052–1967.

ROEBERS, C. M., MOGA, N., & SCHNEIDER, W. (2001). The role of accuracy motivation on children's and adults' event recall. *Journal of Experimental Child Psychology, 78,* 313–329.

ROEBERS, C. M., & SCHNEIDER, W. (2001). Individual differences in children's eyewitness recall: The influence of intelligence and shyness. *Applied Developmental Science, 5,* 9–20.

ROGOFF, B. (1990). *Apprenticeship in thinking: Cognitive development in social context.* New York: Oxford University Press.

ROGOFF, B. (1998). Cognition as a collaborative process. In D. Kuhn & R. S. Siegler (Vol. Eds.), *Cognition language, and perceptual development,* Vol. 2. In W. Damon (Gen. Ed.), *Handbook of child psychology.* New York: Wiley.

ROGOFF, B., MISTRY, J., GÖNCÜ, A., & MOSIER, C. (1993). Guided participation in cultural activity by toddlers and caregivers. *Monographs of the Society for Research in Child Development, 58* (Serial No. 236).

ROGOFF, B., & WADDELL, K. J. (1982). Memory for information organized in a scene by children from two cultures. *Child Development, 53,* 1224–1228.

ROHWER, W. D., JR., & LITROWNIK, J. (1983). Age and individual differences in the learning of a memorization procedure. *Journal of Educational Psychology, 75,* 799–810.

ROSCH, E. (1975). Cognitive representations of semantic categories. *Journal of Experimental Psychology: General, 7,* 192–233.

ROSCH, E., & MERVIS, C. B. (1975). Family resemblances: Studies in the internal structure of categories. *Cognitive Psychology, 7,* 573–605.

ROSCH, E., MERVIS, C. B., GRAY, W. D., JOHNSON, D. M., & BOYES-BRAEM, P. (1976). Basic objects in natural categories. *Cognitive Psychology, 8,* 382–439.

ROSE, S. A., & FELDMAN, J. F. (1995). Prediction of IQ and specific cognitive abilities at 11 years from infancy measures. *Developmental Psychology, 31,* 685–696.

ROSE, S. A., FELDMAN, J. F., JANKOWSKI, J. J., & CARO, D. M. (2002). A longitudinal study of visual expectation and reaction time in the first year of life. *Child Development, 73,* 47–61.

ROSE, S. A., FELDMAN, J. F., & WALLACE, I. F. (1992). Infant information processing in relation to six-year cognitive outcomes. *Child Development, 63,* 1126–1141.

ROSE, S. A., FELDMAN, J. F., WALLACE, I. F., & MCCARTON, C. (1989). Infant visual attention: Relation to birth status and developmental outcome during the first 5 years. *Developmental Psychology, 25,* 560–576.

ROSE, S. A., FELDMAN, J. F., WALLACE, I. F., & MCCARTON, C. (1991). Information processing at 1 year: Relation to birth status and developmental outcome during the first 5 years. *Developmental Psychology, 27,* 723–737.

ROSE, S. A., GOTTFRIED, A. W., & BRIDGER, W. H. (1981). Cross-modal transfer in 6-month-old infants. *Developmental Psychology, 17,* 661–669.

ROSE, S., GOTTFRIED, A. W., MELLOY-CARMINAR, P., & BRIDGER, W. H. (1982). Familiarity and novelty preferences in infant recognition memory: Implications for information processing. *Developmental Psychology, 18,* 704–713.

ROSENGREN, K. S., & HICKLING, A. K. (1994). Seeing is believing: Children's explanations of commonplace, magical, and extraordinary transformations. *Child Development, 65,* 1605–1626.

ROSENTHAL, R., & RUBIN, D. B. (1982). Further meta-analytic procedures for assessing cognitive gender differences. *Journal of Educational Psychology, 74,* 708–712.

ROVEE-COLLIER, C. (1999). The development of infant memory. *Current Directions in Psychological Science, 8,* 80–85.

ROVEE-COLLIER, C., & GERHARDSTEIN, P. (1997). The development of infant memory. In N. Cowan (Ed.), *The development of memory in childhood.* Hove East Sussex, UK: Psychology Press.

ROVEE-COLLIER, C., SCHECHTER, A., SHYI, C.-W. G., & SHIELDS, P. (1992). Perceptual identification of contextual attributes and infant memory retrieval. *Developmental Psychology, 28,* 307–318.

ROVEE-COLLIER, C., & SHYI, C.-W. G. (1992). A functional and cognitive analysis of infant long-term retention. In M. L. Howe, C. J. Brainerd, & V. F. Reyna (Eds.), *Development of long-term retention.* New York: Springer-Verlag.

ROWE, D. C., JACOBSON, K. C., & VAN DER OORD, E. J. C. G. (1999). Genetic and environmental influences on vocabulary IQ: Parental education level as a moderator. *Child Development, 70,* 1151–1162.

RUBIN, K. H., & KRASNOR, L. R. (1986). Social cognitive and social behavior perspectives on problem solving. In M. Perlmutter (Ed.), *Minnesota Symposium on Child Psychology,* Vol. 18. Hillsdale, NJ: Erlbaum.

RUBLE, D. N., BALABAN, T., & COOPER, J. (1981). Gender constancy and the effects of sex-typed televised toy commercials. *Child Development, 52,* 667–673.

RUBLE, D. N., & MARTIN, C. L. (1998). Gender development. In N. Eisenberg (Vol. Ed.), *Social, emotional, and personality development,* Vol. 3. In W. Damon (Gen. Ed.), *Handbook of child psychology.* New York: Wiley.

RUDA, M. A., LING, Q-D., HOHMANN, A. G., BO PENG, Y., & TACHIBANA, T. (2000). Altered nociceptive neuronal circuits after neonatal peripheral inflammation. *Science, 289* (28 July), 628–630.

RUFF, H. A., & BIRCH, H. G. (1974). Infant visual fixation: The effect of concentricity, curvilinearity, and number of directions. *Journal of Experimental Child Psychology, 17,* 460–473.

RUFF, H. A., CAPOZZOLI, M., & WEISBERG, R. (1998). Age, individuality, and context as factors in sustained visual attention during the preschool years. *Developmental Psychology, 34,* 454–464.

RUFF, H. A., & LAWSON, K. R. (1990). Development of sustained, focused attention in young children during free play. *Developmental Psychology, 26,* 85–93.

RUFF, H. A., LAWSON, K. R., PARRINELLO, R., & WEISSBERG, R. (1990). Long-term stability of individual differences in sustained attention in the early years. *Child Development, 61,* 60–75.

RUFFMAN, T., PERNER, J., NAITO, M., PARKIN, L., & CLEMENTS, W. A. (1998). Older (but not younger) siblings facilitate false belief understanding. *Developmental Psychology, 34,* 161–174.

RUFFMAN, T., RUSTIN, C., GARNHAM, W., & PARKIN, A. (2001). Source monitoring and false memories in children: Relation to certainty and executive functioning. *Journal of Experimental Child Psychology, 80,* 95–111.

RUSSELL, J., MAUTHNER, N., SHARPE, S., & TIDSWELL, T. (1991). The "windows tasks" as a measure of strategic deception in preschoolers and autistic subjects. *British Journal of Developmental Psychology, 9,* 331–349.

RUTTER, M., & THE ENGLISH AND ROMANIAN ADOPTEES STUDY TEAM. (1998). Developmental catch-up, and delay, following adoption after severe global early privation. *Journal of Child Psychology and Psychiatry, 39,* 465–476.

SABBAGH, M. A., & TAYLOR, M. (2000). Neural correlates of theory-of-mind reasoning: An event-related potential study. *Psychological Science, 11,* 46–50.

SABIN, E. J., CLEMMER, E. J., O'CONNELL, D. C., & KOWAL, S. (1979). A pausological approach to speech development. In A. W. Siegman & S. Feldstein (Eds.), *Of speech and time: Temporal speech patterns in interpersonal contexts.* Hillsdale, NJ: Erlbaum.

SACCUZZO, D. P., JOHNSON, N. E., & GUERTIN, T. L. (1994). Information processing in gifted versus nongifted African American, Latino, Filipino, and white children: Speeded versus nonspeeded paradigms. *Intelligence, 19,* 219–243.

SACHS, J. (1977). The adaptive significance of linguistic input to prelinguistic infants. In C. E. Snow & C. A. Ferguson (Eds.), *Talking to children: Language input and acquisition.* Cambridge: Cambridge University Press.

SACKS, O. (1989). *Seeing voices: A journey into the world of the deaf.* New York: Harper Perennial.

SALAPATEK, P. (1975). Pattern perception in early infancy. In L. B. Cohen & P. Salapatek (Eds.), *Infant perception: From sensation to cognition,* Vol. 1. New York: Academic.

SALAPATEK, P., & KESSEN, W. (1966). Visual scanning of triangles by the human newborn. *Journal of Experimental Child Psychology, 3,* 155–167.

SALATAS, H., & FLAVELL, J. H. (1976). Behavioral and metamnemonic indicators of strategic behavior under remember instructions in first grade. *Child Development, 47,* 81–89.

SALMON, K., & PIPE, M-E. (1997). Props and children's event reports: The impact of a 1-year delay. *Journal of Experimental Child Psychology, 65,* 261–292.

SAMEROFF, A. J., & CHANDLER, M. J. (1975). Reproductive risk and the continuum of caretaking causality. In F. D. Horowitz (Ed.), *Review of child development research,* Vol. 4. Chicago: University of Chicago Press.

SAMEROFF, A. J., SEIFER, R., BALDWIN, A., & BALDWIN, C. (1993). Stability of intelligence from preschool to adolescence: The influence of social risk factors. *Child Development, 64,* 80–97.

SAMEROFF, A. J., & SUOMI, S. J. (1996). Primates and persons: A comparative developmental understanding of social organization. In R. B. Cairns, G. H. Elder, Jr., & E. J. Costello (Eds.), *Developmental Science.* New York: Cambridge University Press.

SANDBERG, E. H., & HUTTENLOCHER, J. (2001). Advanced spatial skills, and advanced planning: Components of 6-year-olds navigational map use. *Journal of Cognition and Development, 2,* 51–70.

SANDMAN, C. A., WASHWA, P., HETRICK, W., PORTO, M., & PEEKE, H. V. S. (1997). Human fetal heart rate dishabituation between thirty and thirty-two weeks gestation. *Developmental Psychology, 68,* 1031–1040.

SAPP, F., LEE, K., & MUIR, D. (2000). Three-year-olds' difficulty with appearance-reality distinction: Is it real or is it apparent? *Developmental Psychology, 36,* 547–560.

SAVAGE-RUMBAUGH, E. S., MURPHY, J., SEVCIK, R. A., BRAKKE, K. E., WILLIAMS, S. L., & RUMBAUGH, D. M. (1993). Language comprehension in ape and child. *Monographs of the Society for Research in Child Development, 58* (Serial No. 233).

SAXE, G. B. (1979). Developmental relations between notational counting and number conservation. *Child Development, 50,* 180–187.

SAXE, G. B., GUBERMAN, S. R., & GEARHART, M. (1987). Social processes in early number development. *Monographs of the Society for Research in Child Development, 52* (Serial No. 216).

SCAMMON, R. E. (1930). The measurement of the body in childhood. In J. A. Harris, C. M. Jackson, D. G. Paterson, & R. E. Scammon (Eds.), *The measurement of man*. Minneapolis: University of Minnesota Press.

SCARR, S. (1992). Developmental theories for the 1990s: Development and individual differences. *Child Development, 63*, 1–19.

SCARR, S. (1993). Biological and cultural diversity: The legacy of Darwin for development. *Child Development, 64*, 1333–1353.

SCARR, S. (1995). Psychology will be truly evolutionary when behavior genetics is included. *Psychological Inquiry, 6*, 68–71.

SCARR, S., & MCCARTNEY, K. (1983). How people make their own environments: A theory of genotype-environment effects. *Child Development, 54*, 424–435.

SCARR, S., & WEINBERG, R. A. (1976). IQ test performance of black children adopted by white families. *American Psychologist, 31*, 726–739.

SCARR, S., & WEINBERG, R. A. (1978). The influence of "family background" on intellectual attainment. *American Sociological Review, 43*, 674–692.

SCHACTER, D. L. (1992). Understanding implicit memory. *American Psychologist, 47*, 559–569.

SCHACTER, D. L., NORMAN, K. A., & KOUTSTAAL, W. (2000). The cognitive neuroscience of constructive memory. In D. F. Bjorklund (Ed.), *False-memory creation in children and adults: Theory, research, and implications*. Mahwah, NJ: Erlbaum.

SCHADE, J. P., & VAN GROENIGEN, W. B. (1961). Structural organization of the human cerebral cortex. I. Maturation of the middle frontal gyrus. *Acta Anatomica, 47*, 72–111.

SCHAFER, G., & PLUNKET, K. (1998). Rapid word learning by fifteen-month-olds under tightly controlled conditions. *Child Development, 69*, 309–320.

SCHANBERG, S. M., & FIELD, T. M. (1987). Sensory deprivation stress and supplemental stimulation in the rat pup and preterm human. *Child Development, 58*, 1431–1447.

SCHANK, R. C., & ABELSON, R. P. (1977). *Scripts, plans, goals and understanding*. Hillsdale, NJ: Erlbaum.

SCHAUBLE, L. (1990). Belief revision in children: The role of prior knowledge and strategies for generating evidence. *Journal of Experimental Child Psychology, 49*, 31–57.

SCHAUBLE. L. (1996). The development of scientific reasoning in knowledge-rich context. *Developmental Psychology, 32*, 102–119.

SCHELLENBERG, E. G., & TREHUB, S. E. (1996). Natural musical intervals: Evidence from infant listeners. *Psychological Science, 5*, 272–277.

SCHELLENBERG, E. G., & TREHUB, S. E. (1999). Culture-general and culture-specific factors in the discrimination of melodies. *Journal of Experimental Child Psychology, 74*, 107–127.

SCHIEFELE, U., KRAPP, A., & WINTELER, A. (1992). Interest as a predictor of academic achievement: A meta-analysis of research. In K. A. Renninger, S. Hidi, & A. Krapp (Eds.), *The role of interest in learning and development*. Hillsdale, NJ: Erlbaum.

SCHIFF, A. R., & KNOPF, I. J. (1985). The effect of task demands on attention allocation in children of different ages. *Child Development, 56*, 621–630.

SCHLAGMÜLLER, M., & SCHNEIDER, W. (2002). The development of organizational strategies in children: Evidence from a microgenetic longitudinal study. *Journal of Experimental Child Psychology, 81*, 298–319.

SCHLIEMANN, A. D. (1992). Mathematical concepts in and out of school in Brazil: From developmental psychology to better teaching. *Newsletter of the International Society for the Study of Behavioural Development* (Serial No. 22, No. 2), 1–3.

SCHNEIDER, W. (1986). The role of conceptual knowledge and metamemory in the development of organizational processes in memory. *Journal of Experimental Child Psychology, 42*, 218–236.

SCHNEIDER, W. (1993). Domain-specific knowledge and memory performance in children. *Educational Psychology Review, 5*, 257–273.

SCHNEIDER, W., & BJORKLUND, D. F. (1992). Expertise, aptitude, and strategic remembering. *Child Development, 63*, 461–473.

SCHNEIDER, W., & BJORKLUND, D. F. (1998). Memory. In D. Kuhn & R. S. Siegler (Vol. Eds.), *Cognitive, language, and perceptual development*, Vol. 2. In W. Damon (Gen. Ed.), *Handbook of child psychology*. New York: Wiley.

SCHNEIDER, W., & BJORKLUND, D. F. (2003). Memory and knowledge development. In J. Valsiner & K. Connolly (Eds.), *Handbook of developmental psychology*. London: Sage.

SCHNEIDER, W., BJORKLUND, D. F., & MAIER-BRÜCKNER, W. (1996). The effects of expertise and IQ on children's memory: When knowledge is, and when it is not enough. *International Journal of Behavioral Development, 19*, 773–796.

SCHNEIDER, W., GRUBER, H., GOLD, A., & OPWIS, K. (1993). Chess expertise and memory for chess positions in children and adults. *Journal of Experimental Child Psychology, 56*, 328–349.

SCHNEIDER, W., KNOPF, M., & STEFANEK, J. (2003). The development of verbal memory in childhood and adolescence: Findings from the Munich Longitudinal Study. *Journal of Educational Psychology, 94*.

SCHNEIDER, W., KÖRKEL, J., & WEINERT, F. E. (1989). Domain-specific knowledge and memory performance: A comparison of high- and low-aptitude children. *Journal of Educational Psychology, 81,* 306–312.

SCHNEIDER, W., KÜSPERT, P., ROTH, E., & VISÉ, M. (1997). Short- and long-term effects of training phonological awareness in kindergarten: Evidence from two German studies. *Journal of Experimental Child Psychology, 66,* 311–340.

SCHNEIDER, W., & LOCKL, K. (2002). The development of metacognitive knowledge in children and adolescents. In T. Perfect & B. Schwartz (Eds.), *Applied metacognition.* Cambridge: Cambridge University Press.

SCHNEIDER, W., & NÄSLUND, J. C. (1999). The impact of early phonological processing skills on reading and spelling in school: Evidence from the Munich Longitudinal Study. In F. E. Weinert & W. Schneider (Eds.), *The Munich Longitudinal Study on the Genesis of Individual Competencies (LOGIC).* Cambridge: Cambridge University Press.

SCHNEIDER, W., PERNER, J., BULLOCK, M., STEFANEK, J., & ZIEGLER, A. (1999). The development of intelligence and thinking. In F. E. Weinert & W. Schneider (Eds.), *The Munich Longitudinal Study on the Genesis of Individual Competencies (LOGIC).* Cambridge: Cambridge University Press.

SCHNEIDER, W., & PRESSLEY, M. (1997). *Memory development between 2 and 20* (2nd ed.). Mahwah, NJ: Erlbaum.

SCHNEIDER, W., SCHLAGMÜLLER, M., & VISÉ, M. (1998). The impact of metamemory and domain-specific knowledge on memory performance. *European Journal of Psychology of Education, 13,* 91–103.

SCHNEIDER, W., & SODIAN, B. (1988). Metamemory-memory behavior relationship in young children: Evidence from a memory-for-location task. *Journal of Experimental Child Psychology, 45,* 209–233.

SCHNEIDER, W., & WEINERT, F. E. (1995). Memory development during early and middle childhood: Findings from the Munich Longitudinal Study (LOGIC). In F. E. Weinert & W. Schneider (Eds.), *Memory performance and competencies: Issues in growth and development.* Hillsdale, NJ: Erlbaum.

SCHULMAN, A. H., & KAPLOWITZ, C. (1977). Mirror-image response during the first two years of life. *Developmental Psychobiology, 10,* 133–142.

SCHUMANN-HENGSTELER, R. (1989, JULY). *Memory development: The analysis of a popular picture game.* Paper presented at the Tenth Biennial Meeting of the International Society for the Study of Behavioral Development, Jyvaskyla, Finland.

SCHUMANN-HENGSTELER, R. (1992). The development of visuo-spatial memory: How to remember location.

International Journal of Behavioral Development, 15, 445–471.

SCHWANENFLUGEL, P. J. (1991). An introduction to the psychology of word meaning. In P. J. Schwanenflugel (Ed.), *The psychology of word meanings.* Hillsdale, NJ: Erlbaum.

SCHWANENFLUGEL, P. J., GUTH, M. E., & BJORKLUND, D. F. (1986). A developmental trend in the understanding of concept attribute importance. *Child Development, 57,* 421–430.

SCHWANENFLUGEL, P. J., HENDERSON, R. L., & FABRICIUS, W. V. (1998). Developing organization of mental verbs and theory of mind in middle childhood: Evidence from extension. *Developmental Psychology, 34,* 512–524.

SCHWANENFLUGEL, P. J., & NOYES, C. R. (1996). Context availability and the development of word reading skills. *Journal of Literary Research, 28,* 35–54.

SCOTT, M. S., GREENFIELD, D. B., & STERENTAL, E. (1986). Abstract categorization ability as a predictor of learning disability classification. *Intelligence, 10,* 377–387.

SCOTT, M. S., SERCHUK, R., & MUNDY, P. (1982). Taxonomic and complementary picture pairs: Ability in two- to five-year olds. *International Journal of Behavioral Development, 5,* 243–256.

SEARLE, J. R. (1992). *The rediscovery of the mind.* Cambridge, MA: MIT Press.

SEGAL, N. (2000). Virtual twins: New findings on within-family environmental influences on intelligence. *Journal of Educational Psychology, 92,* 442–448.

SENDEN, M. VON (1960). *Space and sight: The perception of space and shape in the congenitally blind before and after operation.* Glencoe, IL: Free Press.

SENGHAS, A., & COPPOLA, M. (2001). Children creating language: How Nicaraguan Sign Language acquired a spatial grammar. *Psychological Science, 12,* 323–326.

SERBIN, L. A., & SPRAFKIN, C. (1986). The saliency of gender and the process of sex typing in three- to seven-year-old children. *Child Development, 57,* 1188–1199.

SEYMOUR, P. H. K., ARO, M., & ERSKINE, J. M. (2003). Foundations of literacy acquisition in European orthographies. *British Journal of Psychology, 94,* 143–174.

SHACKELFORD, T. K., & LARSEN, R. J. (1997). Facial asymmetry as an indicator of psychological, emotional, and physiological distress. *Journal of Personality and Social Psychology, 72,* 456–466.

SHAFFER, D. R. (1993). *Social and personality development* (3rd ed.). Pacific Grove, CA: Brooks/Cole.

SHAFFER, D. R. (1996). *Developmental psychology: Childhood and adolescence* (4th ed.) Pacific Grove, CA: Brooks/Cole.

SHATZ, M. (1983). Communication. In J. H. Flavell & E. M. Markman (Eds.), *Cognitive development*, Vol. 3. In P. H. Mussen (Gen. Ed.), *Handbook of child psychology*. New York: Wiley.

SHATZ, M., & GELMAN, R. (1973). The development of communication skills. *Monographs of the Society for Research in Child Development, 38* (Serial No. 152).

SHAYWITZ, S. E., SHAYWITZ, B. A., PUGH, K. R., FULBRIGHT, R. K., CONSTABLE, R. T., MENCL, W. E., SHANKWEILER, D. P., LIBERMAN, A. M., SKUDLARSKI, P., FLETCHER, J. M., KATZ, L., MARCHIONE, K. E., LACADIE, C., GATENBY, C., & GORE, J. C. (1998). Functional disruption in the organization of the brain for reading in dyslexia. *Proceedings of the National Academy of Science USA, 95,* 2636–2641.

SHERMAN, J. A. (1978). *Sex-related cognitive differences: An essay on theory and evidence.* Springfield, IL: Charles C. Thomas.

SHOLL, M. J., & LIBEN, L. S. (1995). Illusory tilt and Euclidean schemes as factors in performance on the water-level task. *Journal of Experimental Psychology: Learning, Memory, and Cognition, 15,* 110–125.

SHWE, H. I., & MARKMAN, E. M. (1997). Young children's appreciation of the mental impact of their communicative signals. *Developmental Psychology, 33,* 630–636.

SIEGEL, L. S. (1988). Evidence that IQ scores are irrelevant to the definition and analysis of reading disabilities. *Canadian Journal of Psychology, 42,* 201–215.

SIEGEL, L. S. (1993). The cognitive basis of dyslexia. In R. Pasnak & M. L. Howe (Eds.), *Emerging themes in cognitive development: Vol. II. Competencies.* New York: Springer-Verlag.

SIEGEL, L. S., MCCABE, A. E., BRAND, A. E., & MATHEWS, J. (1978). Evidence for the understanding of class inclusion in preschool children: Linguistic factors and training effects. *Child Development, 49,* 688–693.

SIEGEL, L. S., & RYAN, E. B. (1988). Development of grammatical-sensitivity, phonological, and short-term memory skills in normally achieving and learning disabled children. *Developmental Psychology, 24,* 28–37.

SIEGEL, L. S., & RYAN, E. B. (1989). The development of working memory in normally achieving and subtypes of learning disabled children. *Child Development, 60,* 973–980.

SIEGLER, R. S. (1976). Three aspects of cognitive development. *Cognitive Psychology, 8,* 481–520.

SIEGLER, R. S. (1981). Developmental sequences within and between concepts. *Monographs of the Society for Research in Child Development, 46* (Serial No. 189).

SIEGLER, R. S. (1987). The perils of averaging data over strategies: An example from children's addition. *Journal of Experimental Psychology: General, 116,* 250–264.

SIEGLER, R. S. (1996). *Emerging minds: The process of change in children's thinking.* New York: Oxford University Press.

SIEGLER, R. S. (2000). The rebirth of learning. *Child Development, 71,* 26–35.

SIEGLER, R. S., & CHEN, Z. (2002). Development of rules and strategies: Balancing the old and new. *Journal of Experimental Child Psychology, 81,* 446–457.

SIEGLER, R. S., & ELLIS, S. (1996). Piaget on childhood. *Psychological Science, 7,* 211–215.

SIEGLER, R. S., & JENKINS, E. (1989). *How children discover new strategies.* Hillsdale, NJ: Erlbaum.

SIEGLER, R. S., & SHRAGER, J. (1984). Strategy choices in addition and subtraction: How do children know what to do? In C. Sophian (Ed.), *Origins of cognitive skills.* Hillsdale, NJ: Erlbaum.

SIEGLER, R. S., & STERN, E. (1998). Conscious and unconscious strategy discoveries: A microgenetic analysis. *Journal of Experimental Psychology: General, 127,* 377–397.

SIEGLER, R. S., & SVETINA, M. (2002). A microgenetic/cross-sectional study of matrix completion: Comparing short-term and long-term change. *Child Development, 73,* 793–809.

SIGEL, I. E. (1987). Does hothousing rob children of their childhood? *Early Childhood Research Quarterly, 2,* 211–225.

SIGMAN, M., COHEN, S. E., BECKWITH, L., & PARMELEE, A. H. (1986). Infant attention in relation to intellectual abilities in childhood. *Developmental Psychology, 22,* 788–792.

SIGNORELLA, M. L., BIGLER, R. S., & LIBEN, L. S. (1993). Developmental differences in children's gender schemata about others: A meta-analytic review. *Developmental Review, 13,* 147–183.

SIGNORELLA, M. L., JAMISON, W., & KRUPA, M. H. (1989). Predicting spatial performance from gender stereotyping in activity preferences and in self-concept. *Developmental Psychology, 25,* 89–95.

SILVERMAN, I., CHOI, J., MACKEWN, A., FISHER, M., MORO, J., & OLSHANSKY, E. (2000). Evolved mechanisms underlying wayfinding: Further studies on the hunter-gather theory of spatial sex differences. *Evolution and Human Behavior, 21,* 201–213.

SILVERMAN, I., & EALS, M. (1992). Sex differences in spatial abilities: Evolutionary theory and data. In J. H. Barkow, L. Cosmides, & J. Tooby (Eds.), *The adapted mind: Evolutionary psychology and the generation of culture.* New York: Oxford University Press.

SIMCOCK, G., & HAYNE, H. (2002). Breaking the barrier? Children fail to translate their preverbal memories into language. *Psychological Science, 13,* 225–231.

SIMON, T., & SMITH, P. K. (1983). The study of play and problem solving in preschool children: Have experimenter effects been responsible for previous results? *British Journal of Developmental Psychology, 1,* 289–297.

SIMON, T. J., HESPOS, S. J., & ROCHAT, P. (1995). Do infants understand simple arithmetic? A replication of Wynn (1992). *Cognitive Development, 10,* 253–269.

SINGER, J. L. (1980). The power and limitations of television: A cognitive affective analysis. In P. H. Tannenbaum & R. Abeles (Eds.), *The entertainment functions of television.* London: Academic.

SKEELS, H. M. (1966). Adult status of children with contrasting early life experiences. *Monographs of the Society for Research in Child Development, 31* (Serial No. 105).

SKINNER, B. F. (1957). *Verbal behavior.* New York: Appleton-Century-Crofts.

SLABY, R. G., & FREY, K. S. (1975). Development of gender constancy and selective attention to same-sex models. *Child Development, 46,* 849–856.

SLABY, R. G., & GUERRA, N. G. (1988). Cognitive mediators of aggression in adolescent offenders: 1. Assessment. *Developmental Psychology, 24,* 580–588.

SLATER, A. (1995). Visual perception and memory at birth. In C. Rovee-Collier & L. P. Lipsitt (Eds.), *Advances in infancy research,* Vol. 9. Norwood, NJ: Ablex.

SLATER, A., COOPER, R., ROSE, D., & MORISON, V. (1989). Prediction of cognitive performance from infancy to early childhood. *Human Development, 32,* 137–147.

SLATER, A. M., & KINGSTON, D. J. (1981). Competence and performance variables in the assessment of formal operational skills. *British Journal of Educational Psychology, 51,* 163–169.

SLATER, A., MATTOCK, A., & BROWN, E. (1990). Size constancy at birth: Newborn infants' responses to retinal and real size. *Journal of Experimental Child Psychology, 49,* 314–322.

SLATER, A., MATTOCK, A., BROWN, E., & BREMNER, G. J. (1991). Form perception at birth: Cohen and Younger (1984) revisited. *Journal of Experimental Child Psychology, 51,* 395–406.

SLATER, A. M., MORISON, V., SOMERS, M., MATTOCK, A., BROWN, E., & TAYLOR, D. (1990). Newborn and older infants' perception of partly occluded objects. *Infant Behavior & Development, 13,* 33–49.

SLATER, A. M., QUINN, P. C., HAYES, R., & BROWN, E. (2000). The role of facial orientation in newborn infants' preference for attractive faces. *Developmental Science, 3,* 181–185.

SLATER, A., VON DER SCHULENBURG, C., BROWN, E., BADENOCH, M., BUTTERWORTH, G., PARSONS, S., & SAMUEL, C. (1998). Newborn infants prefer attractive faces. *Infant Behavior & Development, 21,* 345–354.

SLOBIN, D. I. (1970). Universals of grammatical development in children. In G. B. Flores, J. Arcais, & W. J. M. Levelt (Eds.), *Advances in psycholinguistics.* Amsterdam, The Netherlands: North-Holland.

SMILEY, S. S., & BROWN, A. L. (1979). Conceptual preference for thematic or taxonomic relations: A nonmonotonic age trend from preschool to old age. *Journal of Experimental Child Psychology, 28,* 249–257.

SMITH, E., SHOBEN, E., & RIPS, L. (1974). Structure and process in semantic memory: A featural model for semantic decisions. *Psychological Review, 81,* 214–241.

SMITH, P. K. (1982). Does play matter? Functional and evolutionary aspects of animal and human play. *Behavioral and Brain Sciences, 5,* 139–184.

SNOW, C. (1972). Mother's speech to children learning language. *Child Development, 43,* 549–565.

SNOW, C. E., ARLMAN-RUPP, A., HASSING, Y., JOBSE, J., JOOSTEN, J., & VORSTER, J. (1976). Mothers' speech in three social classes. *Journal of Psycholinguistic Research, 5,* 1–20.

SNOW, C. E., & FERGUSON C. A. (EDS.). (1977). *Talking to children: Language input and acquisition.* Cambridge: Cambridge University Press.

SOCHA, T. J., & SOCHA, D. M. (1994). Children's task-group communication. In L. R. Frey (Ed.), *Group communication in context: Studies of natural groups.* Hillsdale, NJ: Erlbaum.

SODIAN, B., & SCHNEIDER, W. (1999). Memory strategy development: Gradual increase, sudden insight, or roller coaster? In F. E. Weinert & W. Schneider (Eds.), *The Munich Longitudinal Study on the Genesis of Individual Competencies (LOGIC).* Cambridge: Cambridge University Press.

SODIAN, B., SCHNEIDER, W., & PERLMUTTER, M. (1986). Recall, clustering, and metamemory in young children. *Journal of Experimental Child Psychology, 41,* 395–410.

SODIAN, B., TAYLOR, C., HARRIS, P. L., & PERNER, J. (1991). Early deception and the child's theory of mind: False trails and genuine markers. *Child Development, 62,* 468–483.

SONGUA-BARKE, E. J. S., TAYLOR, E., SEMBI, S., & SMITH, J. (1992). Hyperactivity and delay aversion—I. The effect of delay on choice. *Journal of Child Psychology and Psychiatry, 33,* 399–409.

SOPHIAN, C. (1995). Representation and reasoning in early numerical development: Counting, conservation, and comparison between sets. *Child Development, 66,* 559–577.

SOPHIAN, C. (1997). Beyond competence: The significance of performance for conceptual development. *Cognitive Development, 12,* 281–303.

SPEAR, L. P. (2000). Neurobehavioral changes in adolescence. *Current Directions in Psychological Science, 9,* 111–114.

SPEARMAN, C. (1927). *The abilities of man.* New York: Macmillan.

SPELKE, E. S. (1976). Infants' intermodal perception of events. *Cognitive Psychology, 5,* 553–560.

SPELKE, E. S. (1985). Perception of unity, persistence and identity: Thoughts on infants' conceptions of objects. In J. Mehler & R. Fox (Eds.), *Neonate cognition.* Hillsdale, NJ: Erlbaum.

SPELKE, E. S. (1991). Physical knowledge in infancy: Reflections on Piaget's theory. In S. Carey & R. Gelman (Eds.), *Epigenesis of mind: Essays in biology and knowledge.* Hillsdale, NJ: Erlbaum.

SPELKE, E. S. (1994). Initial knowledge: Six suggestions. *Cognition, 50,* 431–455.

SPELKE, E. S., BREINLINGER, K., MACOMBER, J., & JACOBSON, K. (1992). Origins of knowledge. *Psychological Review, 99,* 605–632.

SPELKE, E. S., & NEWPORT, E. L. (1998). Nativism, empiricism, and the development of knowledge. In R. Learner (Vol. Ed.), *Theoretical models of human development,* Vol. 1. In W. Damon (Gen. Ed.), *Handbook of child psychology.* New York: Wiley.

SPENCE, M. J. (1996). Young infants' long-term auditory memory: Evidence for changes in preference as a function of delay. *Developmental Psychobiology, 29,* 685–695.

SPENCE, M. J., & FREEMAN, M. S. (1996). Newborn infants prefer the maternal low-pass filtered voice, but not the maternal whispered voice. *Infant Behavior & Development, 19,* 199–212.

SPERLING, G. (1960). The information available in brief visual presentations. *Psychological Monographs, 74* (No. 11).

SPITZ, R. (1945). Hospitalism: An inquiry into the genesis of psychiatric conditions in early childhood. *Psychoanalytic Study of the Child, 1,* 53–74.

SPREEN, O., RISSER, A., & EDGELL, D. (1995). *Developmental neuropsychiatry.* New York: Oxford University Press.

STANKOV, L. (2000). The theory of fluid and crystallized intelligence: New findings and recent developments. Introduction to special issue of *Learning and Individual Differences, 12,* 1–3.

STANLEY, J. C., BENBOW, C. P., BRODY, L. E., DAUBER, S., & LUPKOWSKI, A. E. (1992). Gender differences on eighty-six nationally standardized aptitude and achievement tests. In N. Coangelo, S. G. Assouline, & D. L. Ambroson (Eds.), *Talent development.* Unionville, NY: Trillium.

STANOVICH, K. E. (1988). Explaining the differences between the dyslexic and garden variety poor reader: The phonological-core variance-difference model. *Journal of Learning Disabilities, 21,* 590–604.

STARK, R. (1978). Features of infant sounds: The emergence of cooing. *Journal of Child Language, 5,* 1–12.

STARKEY, P., SPELKE, E. S., & GELMAN, R. (1990). Numerical abstraction by human infants. *Cognition, 36,* 97–127.

STEIN, N. L., WADE, E., & LIWAG, M. D. (1997). A theoretical approach to understanding and remembering emotional events. In N. L. Stein, P. A. Ornstein, B. Tversky, & C. J. Brainerd (Eds.), *Memory for everyday and emotional events.* Hillsdale, NJ: Erlbaum.

STEINER, J. E. (1979). Human facial expressions in response to taste and smell stimulation. In H. W. Reese & L. P. Lipsitt (Eds.), *Advances in child development and behavior,* Vol. 13. New York: Academic.

STERN, D. N., SPIEKER, S., BARNETT, R. K., & MACKAIN, K. (1983). The prosody of maternal speech: Infant age and context related changes. *Journal of Child Language, 10,* 1–15.

STERN, D. N., SPIEKER, S., & MACKAIN, K. (1982). Intonation contours as signals in maternal speech to prelinguistic infants. *Developmental Psychology, 18,* 727–735.

STERNBERG, K. J., LAMB, M. E., ORBACH, Y., ESPLIN, P. W., & MITCHELL, S. (2001). Use of a structured investigative protocol enhances young children's responses to free recall prompts in the course of forensic interviews. *Journal of Applied Psychology, 86,* 997–1005.

STERNBERG, R. J. (1984). Fighting butter battles: A reply. *Phi Delta Kappan, 65,* 700.

STERNBERG, R. J. (1985). *Beyond IQ: A triarchic theory of human intelligence.* Cambridge: Cambridge University Press.

STERNBERG, R. J. (1988). *The triarchic mind: A new theory of human intelligence.* New York: Viking.

STERNBERG, R. J. (1997). The concept of intelligence and its role in lifelong learning and success. *American Psychologist, 52,* 1030–1037.

STERNBERG, R. J., FERRARI, M., & CLINKENBEARD, P. (1996). Identification, instruction, and assessment of gifted children: A construct validation of a triarchic model. *Gifted Child Quarterly, 40,* 129–137.

STERNBERG, R. J., GRIGORENKO, E. L., & BUNDY, D. A. (2001). The predictive value of IQ. *Merrill-Palmer Quarterly, 47,* 1–41.

STERNBERG, R. J., TORFF, B., & GRIGORENKO, E. L. (1999). Teaching triachically improves school achievement. *Journal of Educational Psychology, 90,* 374–384.

STEVENSON, H. W., & LEE, S. Y. (1990). Context of achievement. *Monographs of the Society for Research in Child Development, 55* (Serial No. 221).

STIPEK, D. (1984). Young children's performance expectations: Logical analysis or wishful thinking? In J. G. Nicholls (Ed.), *Advances in motivation and achievement: Vol 3. The development of achievement motivation.* Greenwich, CT: JAI.

STIPEK, D., & DANIELS, D. (1988). Declining perceptions of competence: A consequence of changes in the child or the educational environment? *Journal of Educational Psychology, 80,* 352–356.

STODDART, T., & TURIEL, E. (1985). Children's concepts of cross-gender activities. *Child Development, 56,* 1241–1252.

STOEL-GAMMON, C., & MENN, L. (1997). Phonological development: Learning sounds and sound patterns. In J. Berko Gleason (Ed.), *The development of language* (4th ed.). Boston: Allyn & Bacon.

STONE, C. A., & DAY, M. C. (1978). Levels of availability of a formal operational strategy. *Child Development, 49,* 1054–1065.

STONE, L. J., & CHURCH, J. (1973). *Childhood and adolescence: A psychology of the growing person.* New York: Random House.

STOOLMILLER, M. (1999). Implications of the restricted range of family environments for estimates of heritability and nonshared environment in behavior genetic adoption studies. *Psychological Bulletin, 125,* 393–407.

STORCH, S. A., & WHITEHURST, G. J. (2002). Oral language and code-related precursors to reading: Evidence from a longitudinal structural model. *Developmental Psychology, 38,* 934–947.

STRAUSS, M. S., & CURTIS, L. E. (1981). Infant perception of numerosity. *Child Development, 52,* 1146–1152.

STRERI, A., LHOTE, M., & DUTILLEUL, S. (2000). Haptic perception in newborns. *Developmental Science, 3,* 319–327.

STRERI, A., & SPELKE, E. S. (1989). Effects of motion and figural goodness on haptic object perception in infancy. *Child Development, 60,* 1111–1125.

STRIANO, T., TOMASELLO, M., & ROCHAT, P. (2001). Social and object support for early symbolic play. *Developmental Science, 4,* 442–455.

SUGARMAN, S. (1983). *Children's early thought: Development in classification.* Cambridge: Cambridge University Press.

SULKOWSKI, G. M., & HAUSER, M. D. (2001). Can rhesus monkeys spontaneously subtract? *Cognition, 79,* 239–262.

SULLIVAN, K., & WINNER, E. (1991). When 3-year-olds understand ignorance, false belief and representational change. *British Journal of Developmental Psychology, 9,* 159–171.

SULLIVAN, K., & WINNER, E. (1993). Three-year-olds' understanding of mental states: The influence of trickery. *Journal of Experimental Child Psychology, 56,* 135–148.

SULLIVAN, M. W., ROVEE-COLLIER, C. K., & TYNES, D. M. (1979). A conditioning analysis of infant long-term memory. *Child Development, 50,* 152–162.

SUOMI, S., & HARLOW, H. (1972). Social rehabilitation of isolate-reared monkeys. *Developmental Psychology, 6,* 487–496.

SUSSMAN, A. L. (2001). Reality monitoring of performed and imagined interactive events: Developmental and contextual effects. *Journal of Experimental Child Psychology, 79,* 115–138.

SWANSON, H. L., & BERNINGER, V. W. (1996). Individual differences in children's working memory and writing skills. *Journal of Experimental Child Psychology, 63,* 358–385.

SWANSON, H. L., & SACHSE-LEE, C. (2001). Mathematical problem solving and working memory in children with learning disabilities: Both executive and phonological processes are important. *Journal of Experimental Child Psychology, 79,* 294–321.

SWANSON, H. L., ASHBAKER, M. H., & LEE, C. (1996). Learning-disabled readers' working memory as a function of processing demands. *Journal of Experimental Child Psychology, 61,* 242–275.

SZKRYBALO, J., & RUBLE, D. N. (1999). "God made me a girl": Sex-category constancy judgments and explanations revisited. *Developmental Psychology, 35,* 393–402.

TAMIS-LEMONDA, C. S., & BORNSTEIN, M. H. (1989). Habituation and maternal encouragement of attention in infancy as predictors of toddler language, play, and representational competence. *Child Development, 60,* 738–751.

TANNER, J. M. (1978). *Fetus into man: Physical growth from conception to maturity.* Cambridge, MA: Harvard University Press.

TARDIF, T., & WELLMAN, H. M. (2000). Acquisition of mental state language in Mandarin- and Cantonese-speaking children. *Developmental Psychology, 36,* 25–43.

TAYLOR, M., & FLAVELL, J. H. (1984). Seeing and believing: Children's understanding of the distinction between appearance and reality. *Child Development, 55,* 1710–1720.

TAYLOR, M., & HORT, B. (1990). Can children be trained in making the distinction between appearance and reality? *Cognitive Development, 5,* 89–99.

TEASLEY, S. D. (1995). The role of talk in children's peer collaborations. *Developmental Psychology, 31,* 207–220.

TERMAN, L. M., & MERRILL, M. A. (1937). *Measuring intelligence.* Boston: Houghton Mifflin.

THATCHER, R. W. (1996). Neuroimaging of cyclic cortical reorganization during human development. In R. W. Thatcher, G. R. Lyon, J. Rumsey, & N. Krasnegor (Eds.), *Developmental neuroimaging: Mapping the development of brain and behavior.* San Diego: Academic.

THELEN, E., & SMITH, L. B. (1994). *A dynamic systems approach to the development of cognition and action.* Cambridge, MA: MIT Press.

THELEN, E., & SMITH, L. B. (1998). Dynamic systems theories. In R. M. Lerner (Vol. Ed.), *Theoretical models of human development,* Vol. 1. In W. Damon (Gen. Ed.), *Handbook of child psychology.* New York: Wiley.

THIERRY, K. L., & SPENCE, M. J. (2002). Source-monitoring training facilitates preschoolers' eyewitness memory performance. *Developmental Psychology, 38,* 428–437.

THOMAS, H., JAMISON, W., & HUMMEL, D. D. (1973). Observation is insufficient for discovering that the surface of still water is invariantly horizontal. *Science, 101,* 173–174.

THOMAS, H., & LOHAUS, A. (1993). Modeling growth and individual differences in spatial tasks. *Monographs of the Society for Research in Child Development, 58* (Serial No. 237).

THOMAS, H., & TURNER, G. F. (1991). Individual difference and development in water-level task performance. *Journal of Experimental Child Psychology, 51,* 171–194.

THOMPSON, J. R., & CHAPMAN, R. S. (1977). Who is "Daddy" revisited? The status of two-year-olds' overextended words in use and comprehension. *Journal of Child Language, 4,* 359–375.

THOMPSON, L. A., FAGAN, J. F., & FULKER, D. W. (1991). Longitudinal prediction of specific cognitive abilities from infant novelty preference. *Child Development, 62,* 530–538.

THORNDIKE, R. L., HAGEN, E. P., & SATTLER, J. M. (1986). *The Stanford-Binet Intelligence Scale* (4th edition): *Guide for administering and scoring.* Chicago: Riverside.

THURSTONE, L. L. (1938). *Primary mental abilities.* Chicago: University of Chicago Press.

TIMNEY, B., MITCHELL, D. E., & CYNADER, M. (1980). Behavioral evidence for prolonged sensitivity to effects of monocular deprivation in dark-reared cats. *Journal of Neurophysiology, 43,* 1041–1054.

TINBERGEN, N. (1951). *The study of instinct.* New York: Oxford University Press.

TOMASELLO, M. (2000). Culture and cognitive development. *Current Directions in Psychological Science, 9,* 37–40.

TOMASELLO, M., & CALL, J. (1997). *Primate cognition.* New York: Oxford University Press.

TOMASELLO, M., DAVIS-DASILVA, M., CAMAK, L., & BARD, K. A. (1987). Observational learning of tool use by young chimpanzees. *Journal of Human Evolution, 2,* 175–183.

TOMASELLO, M., KRUGER, A. C., & RATNER, H. H. (1993). Cultural learning. *Behavioral and Brain Sciences, 16,* 495–511.

TOMASELLO, M., SAVAGE-RUMBAUGH, S., & KRUGER, A. C. (1993). Imitative learning of actions and objects by children, chimpanzees, and enculturated chimpanzees. *Child Development, 64,* 1688–1705.

TONKOVA-YOMPOL'SKAYA, R. V. (1969). Development of speech intonation in infants during the first two years of life. *Soviet Psychology, 7,* 48–54.

TOOBY, J., & COSMIDES, L. (1992). The psychological foundations of culture. In J. H. Barkow, L. Cosmides, & J. Tooby (Eds.), *The adapted mind: Evolutionary psychology and the generation of culture.* New York: Oxford University Press.

TRAINOR, L. J., AUSTIN, C. M., & DESJARDINS, R. N. (2000). Is infant-directed speech prosody a result of the vocal expression of emotion? *Psychological Science, 11,* 188–195.

TRAINOR, L. J., & HEINMILLER, B. M. (1998). The development of evaluative responses to music: Infants prefer to listen to consonance over disconsonance. *Infant Behavior & Development, 21,* 77–88.

TREHUB, S. E. (1976). The discrimination of foreign speech contrasts by infants and adults. *Child Development, 47,* 466–472.

TREHUB, S. E., SCHNEIDER, B. A., & ENDMAN, M. (1980). Developmental changes in infants' sensitivity to octave-band noises. *Journal of Experimental Child Psychology, 29,* 282–293.

TREHUB, S. E., TRAINOR, L. J., & UNYK, A. M. (1993). Music and speech processing in the first year of life. In H. W. Reese (Ed.), *Advances in child development and behavior,* Vol. 24. San Diego: Academic.

TUDGE, J. R. H. (1992). Processes and consequences of peer collaboration: A Vygotskian analysis. *Child Development, 63,* 1364–1379.

TUDGE, J., PUTNAM, S., & VALSINER, J. (1996). Culture and cognition in developmental perspective. In R. B. Cairns, G. H. Elder, Jr., & E. J. Costello (Eds.), *Developmental science.* New York: Cambridge University Press.

TULKIN, S. R., & KONNER, M. J. (1973). Alternative conceptions of intellectual functioning. *Human Development, 16,* 33–52.

TULVING, E. (1985). Memory and consciousness. *Canadian Psychology, 26,* 1–12.

TULVING, E. (1987). Multiple memory systems and consciousness. *Human Neurobiology, 6,* 67–80.

TURKEWITZ, G. (1993). The influence of timing on the nature of cognition. In G. Turkewitz & D. A. Devenny (Eds.), *Developmental time and timing.* Hillsdale, NJ: Erlbaum.

TURKEWITZ, G., & DEVENNY, D. A. (EDS.). (1993). *Developmental time and timing.* Hillsdale, NJ: Erlbaum.

TURKEWITZ, G., & KENNY, P. (1982). Limitations on input as a basis for neural organization and perceptual development: A preliminary theoretical statement. *Developmental Psychobiology, 15,* 357–368.

TURKHEIMER, E. (2000). Three laws of behavior genetics and what they mean. *Current Directions in Psychological Science, 9,* 160–164.

TURKHEIMER, E., & WALDRON, M. (2000). Nonshared environment: A theoretical, methodological, and quantitative review. *Psychological Bulletin, 126,* 78–108.

TURNBULL, C. M. (1961). *The forest people.* New York: Simon & Schuster.

TURNER, A. M., & GREENOUGH, W. T. (1985). Differential rearing effects on rat visual cortex synapses. I. Synaptic and neuronal density and synapses per neuron. *Brain Research, 329,* 195–203.

ULLER, C., CAREY, S., HUNTLEY-FENNER, G., & KLATT, L. (1999). What representations might underlie infant numerical knowledge? *Cognitive Development, 14,* 1–36.

USHER, J. A., & NEISSER, U. (1993). Childhood amnesia and the beginnings of memory for four early life events. *Journal of Experimental Psychology: General, 122,*155–165.

UTTAL, D. H. (2000). Seeing the big picture: Map use and the development of spatial cognition. *Developmental Science, 3,* 247–286.

UTTAL, D. H., GREGG, V. H., TAN, L. S., CHAMBERLIN, M. H., & SINES, A. (2001). Connecting the dots: Children's use of a systematic figure to facilitate mapping and search. *Developmental Psychology, 37,* 338–350.

UTTAL, D. H., & WELLMAN, H. M. (1989). Young children's representation of spatial information acquired from maps. *Developmental Psychology, 25,* 128–138.

UZGIRIS, I. C. (1964). Situational generality of conservation. *Child Development, 35,* 831–841.

UZGIRIS, I. C. (1983). Organization of sensorimotor intelligence. In M. Lewis (Ed.), *Origins of intelligence: Infancy and early childhood* (2nd ed.). New York: Plenum.

UZGIRIS, I. C., & HUNT, J. McV. (1975). *Assessment in infancy: Ordinal scales of psychological development.* Urbana: University of Illinois Press.

VALDEZ-MENCHACA, M. C., & WHITEHURST, G. J. (1992). Accelerating language development through picture book reading: A systematic extension to Mexican day care. *Developmental Psychology, 28,* 1106–1114.

VALLACHER, R. R., READ, S. J., & NOWAK, A. (2002). The dynamical perspective in personality and social psychology. *Personality and Social Psychology Review, 6,* 265–273.

VAN DER MAAS, H. L. J., & MOLENAAR, P. C. M. (1992). Stage-wise cognitive development: An application of catastrophe theory. *Psychological Review, 99,* 395–417.

VAN GEERTZ, P. (1994). *Dynamic systems of development: Change between complexity and chaos.* New York: Prentice-Hall.

VAN LOOSBROEK, E., & SMITSMAN, A. W. (1990). Visual perception of numerosity in infancy. *Developmental Psychology, 26,* 916–922.

VANDENBERG, S. G., & KUSE, A. R. (1978). Mental rotations, a group test of three-dimensional spatial visualization. *Perceptual and Motor Skills, 47,* 599–604.

VANDER LINDE, E., MORRONGIELLO, B. A., & ROVEE-COLLIER, C. (1985). Determinants of retention in 8-week-old infants. *Developmental Psychology, 21,* 601–613.

VARNHAGEN, C. K., MORRISON, F. J., & EVERALL, R. (1994). Age and schooling effects in story recall and story production. *Developmental Psychology, 30,* 969–979.

VASTA, R., & LIBEN, L. S. (1996). The water-level task: An intriguing puzzle. *Current Directions in Psychological Science, 5,* 171–177.

VELLUTINO, F. R., & SCANLON, D. M. (1985). Free recall of concrete and abstract words in poor and normal readers. *Journal of Experimental Child Psychology, 39,* 363–380.

VENTER, J. C., ET AL. (2001). The sequence of the human genome. *Science, 291* (16 February), 1304–1351.

VERNON, P. E., & KANTOR, L. (1986). Reaction time correlations with intelligence test scores obtained under either timed or untimed conditions. *Intelligence, 10,* 315–330.

VINTER, A. (1986). The role of movement in eliciting early imitations. *Child Development, 57,* 66–71.

VINTER, A., & PERRUCHET, P. (2000). Implicit learning in children is not related to age: Evidence from drawing. *Child Development, 71,* 1223–1240.

VURPILLOT, E. (1968). The development of scanning strategies and their relation to visual differentiation. *Journal of Experimental Child Psychology, 6,* 632–650.

VURPILLOT, E., & BALL, W. A. (1979). The concept of identity and children's selective attention. In G. Hale and M. Lewis (Eds.), *Attention and cognitive development.* New York: Plenum.

VYGOTSKY, L. S. (1962). *Thought and language.* Cambridge, MA: MIT Press.

VYGOTSKY, L. S. (1978). *The mind in society: The development of higher psychological processes.* Cambridge, MA: Harvard University Press.

VYGOTSKY, L. S. (1981). The genesis of higher mental functions. In J. V. Wertsch (Ed.), *The concept of activity in Soviet psychology.* Armonk, NY: Sharpe.

WAGNER, R. K., TORGESEN, J. K., RASHOTTE, C. A., HECHT, S. A., BARKER, T. A., BURGESS, S. R., DONAHUE, J., & GARON, T. (1997). Changing relations between phonological processing abilities and word-level reading as children develop from beginning to skilled readers: A 5-year longitudinal study. *Developmental Psychology, 33,* 468–479.

WAKELEY, A., RIVERA, S., & LANGER, J. (2000). Can young infants add and subtract? *Child Development, 71,* 1525–1534.

WALK, R. D., & GIBSON, E. J. (1961). A comparative and analytical study of visual depth perception. *Psychological Monographs, 75* (No. 519).

WALKER, C. H. (1987). Relative importance of domain knowledge and overall aptitude on acquisition of domain-related information. *Cognition and Instruction, 2,* 25–42.

WALTON, G. E., BOWER, N. J. A., & BOWER, T. G. R. (1992). Recognition of familiar faces by newborns. *Infant Behavior & Development, 15,* 265–269.

WANT, S. C., & HARRIS, P. L. (2001). Learning from other peoples' mistakes: Causal understanding in learning to use a tool. *Child Development, 72,* 431–443.

WANT, S. C., & HARRIS, P. L. (2002). How do children ape? Applying concepts from the study of non-human primates to the developmental study of "imitation" in children. *Developmental Science, 5,* 1–13.

WARREN, A., HULSE-TROTTER, K., & TUBBS, E. C. (1991). Inducting resistance to suggestibility in children. *Law and Human Behavior, 15,* 273–285.

WARREN, A. R., & MCCLOSKEY, L. A. (1997). Language in social contexts. In J. Berko Gleason (Ed.), *The development of language* (4th ed.). Boston, MA: Allyn & Bacon.

WARREN, A. R., & TATE, C. S. (1992). Egocentrism in children's telephone conversations: Recent evidence regarding Piaget's position. In R. Diaz & L. Berk (Eds.), *From social interaction to self-regulation.* Hillsdale, NJ: Erlbaum.

WARREN-LEUBECKER, A., & BOHANNON, J. N. (1989). Pragmatics: Language in social context. In J. B. Berko Gleason (Ed.), *The development of language* (2nd ed.). Columbus, OH: Charles E. Merrill.

WATERS, H. S. (2000). Memory strategy development: Do we really need another deficiency? *Child Development, 71,* 1001–1012.

WAXMAN, S., & GELMAN, R. (1986). Preschoolers' use of superordinate relations in classification and language. *Cognitive Development, 1,* 139–156.

WEBER, A., & STRUBE, G. (1999). Memory for events experienced and events observed. In F. E. Weinert & W. Schneider (Eds.), *The Munich Longitudinal Study on the Genesis of Individual Competencies (LOGIC).* Cambridge: Cambridge University Press.

WECHSLER, D. (1974). *Manual for the Wechsler Intelligence Scale for Children–Revised.* New York: Psychological Corporation.

WECHSLER, D. (1991). *Wechsler Intelligence Scale for Children* (3rd ed.). San Antonio, TX: Psychological Corporation.

WEINBERG, R. A., SCARR, S., & WALDMAN, I. D. (1992). The Minnesota Transracial Adoption Study: A follow-up of IQ test performance at adolescence. *Intelligence, 16,* 117–135.

WEINERT, F. E., & SCHNEIDER, W. (1992). *The Munich Longitudinal Study on the Genesis of Individual Competencies (LOGIC).* Munich, Germany: Max Planck Institute for Psychological Research.

WEISFELD, G. (1999). *Evolutionary principles of human adolescence.* New York: Basic Books.

WELCH, M. K. (1999). Preschoolers' understanding of mind: Implications for suggestibility. *Cognitive Development, 14,* 101–131.

WELCH-ROSS, M. K. (1995). An integrative model of the development of autobiographical memory. *Developmental Review, 15,* 338–365.

WELLMAN, H. M. (1988). The early development of memory strategies. In F. Weinert & M. Perlmutter (Eds.), *Memory development: Universal changes and individual differences.* Hillsdale, NJ: Erlbaum.

WELLMAN, H. M. (1990). *The child's theory of mind.* Cambridge, MA: MIT Press.

WELLMAN, H. M., CROSS, D., & WATSON, J. (2001). Meta-analysis of theory-of-mind development: The truth about false belief. *Child Development, 72,* 655–684.

WELLMAN, H. M., & GELMAN, S. A. (1998). Knowledge acquisition in foundational domains. In D. Kuhn & R. S. Siegler (Vol. Eds.), *Cognition, perception, and language*, Vol. 2. In W. Damon (Gen. Ed.), *Handbook of child psychology*. New York: Wiley.

WELLMAN, H. M., & LEMPERS, J. D. (1977). The naturalistic communicative and organismic points of view. In D. B. Harris (Ed.), *The concept of development*. Minneapolis: University of Minnesota Press.

WERKER, J. F., GILBERT, J. H. V., HUMPHREY, K., & TEES, R. C. (1981). Developmental aspects of cross-language speech perception. *Child Development, 52*, 349–355.

WERTSCH, J. V., & TULVISTE, P. (1992). L. S. Vygotsky and contemporary developmental psychology. *Developmental Psychology, 28*, 548–557.

WEXLER-SHERMAN, C., GARDNER, H., & FELDMAN, D. H. (1988). A pluralistic view of early assessment: The Project Spectrum approach. *Theory Into Practice, 27*, 77–83.

WHELDALL, K., & JOSEPH, R. (1986). Young black children's sentence comprehension skills: A comparison of performance in standard English and Jamaican Creole. *First Language, 6*, 149–154.

WHITE, S. H., & PILLEMER, D. B. (1979). Childhood amnesia and the development of a socially accessible memory system. In J. F. Kihlstrom & F. J. Evans (Eds.), *Functional disorders of memory*. Hillsdale, NJ: Erlbaum.

WHITEHURST, G. J., FALCO, F., LONIGAN, C. J., FISCHAL, J. E., DEBARYSHE, B. D., VALDEZ-MANCHACA, M. C., & CAUFIELD, M. (1988). Accelerating language development through picture book reading. *Developmental Psychology, 24*, 552–559.

WHITEHURST, G. J., & LONIGAN, C. J. (1998). Child development and emergent literacy. *Child Development, 69*, 848–872.

WHITEHURST, G. J., & SONNENSCHEIN, S. (1985). The development of communication: A functional analysis. In G. J. Whitehurst (Ed.), *Annals of child development*, Vol. 2. Greenwich, CT: JAI.

WHITEN, A., CUSTANCE, D. M., GÓMEZ, J. C., TEIXIDOR, P., & BARD, K. A. (1996). Imitative learning of artificial fruit processing in children (*Homo sapiens*) and chimpanzees (*Pan troglodytes*). *Journal of Comparative Psychology, 110*, 3–14.

WHITEN, A., GOODALL, J., MCGREW, W. C., NISHIDA, T., REYNOLDS, V., SUGIYAMA, Y., TUTIN, C. E. G., WRANGHAM, R. W., & BOESCH, C. (1999). Cultures in chimpanzees. *Nature 399* (June), 682–685.

WHITEN, A., & HAM, R. (1992). On the nature and evolution of imitation in the animal kingdom: Reappraisal of a century of research. In P. Slater, J. Rosenblatt, C. Beer, & M. Milinski (Eds.), *Advances in the study of behavior*, Vol. 21. New York: Academic.

WHITNEY, P., & KUNEN, S. (1983). Development of hierarchical conceptual relationships in children's semantic memories. *Journal of Experimental Child Psychology, 35*, 278–293.

WICKELGREN, L. (1967). Convergence in the human newborn. *Journal of Experimental Child Psychology, 5*, 74–85.

WILCOX, J., & WEBSTER, E. (1980). Early discourse behavior: An analysis of children's responses to listener feedback. *Child Development, 51*, 1120–1125.

WILKINSON, A. (1976). Counting strategies and semantic analysis as applied to class inclusion. *Cognitive Psychology, 8*, 64–85.

WILLATTS, P. (1990). Development of problem-solving strategies in infancy. In D. F. Bjorklund (Ed.), *Children's strategies: Contemporary views of cognitive development*. Hillsdale, NJ: Erlbaum.

WILSON, R. S. (1983). The Louisville Twin Study: Developmental synchronies in behavior. *Child Development, 54*, 298–316.

WILSON, S. P., & KIPP, K. (1998). The development of efficient inhibition: Evidence from directed-forgetting tasks. *Developmental Review, 18*, 86–123.

WIMMER, H., & PERNER, J. (1983). Beliefs about beliefs: Representation and constraining function of wrong beliefs in young children's understanding of deception. *Cognition, 13*, 103–128.

WINER, G. A. (1980). Class-inclusion reasoning in children: A review of the empirical literature. *Child Development, 51*, 309–328.

WINICK, M., MEYER, K. K., & HARRIS, R. C. (1975). Malnutrition and environmental enrichment by early adoption. *Science, 190*, 1173–1175.

WINSLER, A. (2003). Overt and covert verbal problem-solving strategies: Developmental trends in use, awareness, and relations with task performance in children age 5 to 17. *Child Development, 74*, 659–678.

WITELSON, S. F. (1985). On hemisphere specialization and cerebral plasticity from birth; Mark II. In C. Best (Ed.), *Hemispheric function and collaboration in the child*. New York: Academic.

WITELSON, S. F. (1987). Neurobiological aspects of language in children. *Child Development, 58*, 653–688.

WITKIN, H. A., DYK, R. B., FATERSON, H. F., GOODENOUGH, D. R., & KARP, S. A. (1962). *Psychological differentiation*. New York: Wiley.

WITKIN, H. A., GOODENOUGH, D. R., & KARP, S. A. (1967). Stability of cognitive style from childhood to young adulthood. *Journal of Personality and Social Psychology, 7*, 291–300.

WITKIN, H. A., LEWIS, H. B., HERTZMAN, M., MACHOVER, K., MEISSNER, P., & WAPNER, S. (1954). *Personality through perception*. New York: Harper.

WOOD, D., BRUNER, J. S., & ROSS, G. (1976). The role of tutoring in problem-solving. *Journal of Child Psychology and Psychiatry, 17*, 89–100.

WOODS, B. T., & CAREY, S. (1979). Language deficits after apparent clinical recovery from childhood aphasia. *Annals of Neurology, 6*, 405–409.

WOOLLEY, J. D. (1997). Thinking about fantasy: Are children fundamentally different thinkers and believers from adults? *Child Development, 68*, 991–1011.

WOOLLEY, J. D., & BOERGER, E. A. (2002). Development of beliefs about the origins of controllability of dreams. *Developmental Psychology, 38*, 24–41.

WOOLLEY, J. D., & BRUELL, M. J. (1996). Young children's awareness of the origins of their mental representations. *Developmental Psychology, 32*, 335–346.

WOOLLEY, J. D., & WELLMAN, H. M. (1992). Children's conceptions of dreams. *Cognitive Development, 7*, 365–380.

WOOLLEY, J. D., & WELLMAN, H. M. (1993). Origin and truth: Young children's understanding of imaginary mental representations. *Child Development, 64*, 1–17.

WYNN, K. (1992). Addition and subtraction by human infants. *Nature, 358*, 749–750.

YAKOVLEV, P. I., & LECOURS, A. R. (1967). The myelenogenetic cycles of regional maturation of the brain. In A. Minkowski (Ed.), *Regional development of the brain in early life*. Oxford, England: Blackwell.

YAN, J. H., THOMAS, J. R., & DOWNING, J. H. (1998). Locomotion improves children's spatial search: A meta-analytic review. *Perceptual and Motor Skills, 87*, 67–82.

YOUNGBLOOD, L. M., & DUNN, J. (1995). Individual differences in young children's pretend play with mother and sibling: Links to relationships and understanding of other people's feelings and beliefs. *Child Development, 66*, 1472–1492.

YOUNGER, B., & GOTLIEB, S. (1988). Development of categorization skills: Changes in the nature or structure of infant form categories? *Developmental Psychology, 24*, 611–619.

ZELAZO, P. D. (2000). Self-reflection and the development of consciously controlled processing. In P. Mitchell & K. Rigg (Eds.), *Children's reasoning and the mind*. New York: Psychology Press.

ZELAZO, P. D., & BOSEOVSKI, J. J. (2001). Video reminders in a representational change task: Memory for cues but not beliefs or statements. *Journal of Experimental Child Psychology, 78*, 107–129.

ZELAZO, P. D., CARTER, A., REZNICK, J. S., & FRYE, D. (1997). Early development of executive function: A problem-solving framework. *Review of General Psychology, 1*, 198–226.

ZELAZO, P. D., & FRYE, D. (1997). Cognitive complexity and control: A theory of the development of deliberate reasoning and intentional action. In M. Stamenov (Ed.), *Language Structure, Discourse, and the access to consciousness*. Amsterdam & Philadelphia: John Benjamins.

ZELAZO, P. D., FRYE, D., & RAPUS, T. (1996). An age-related dissociation between knowing rules and using them. *Cognitive Development, 11*, 37–63.

ZELAZO, P. D., & JACQUES, S. (1997). Children's rule use: Representation, reflection and cognitive control. *Annals of Child Development, 12*. London: Jessica Kingsley Press.

ZELAZO, P. D., KEARSLEY, R. B., & STACK, D. M. (1995). Mental representation for visual sequences: Increased speed of central processing from 22 to 32 months. *Intelligence, 20*, 41–63.

ZELAZO, P. D., & REZNICK, J. S. (1991). Age-related asynchrony of knowledge and action. *Child Development, 62*, 719–735.

ZELAZO, P. D., REZNICK, J. S., & PIÑON, D. E. (1995). Response control and the execution of rules. *Developmental Psychology, 31*, 508–517.

ZELAZO, P. D., SOMMERVILLE, J. A., NICHOLS, S. (1999). Age-related changes in children's use of external representation. *Developmental Psychology, 35*, 1059–1071.

ZESKIND, P. S. (1996, APRIL). *Infant crying: A biobehavioral synchrony between infants and caregivers*. Paper presented at the Conference on Human Development, Birmingham, AL.

ZESKIND, P. S., & RAMEY, C. T. (1978). Fetal malnutrition: An experimental study of its consequences on infant development in two caregiver environments. *Child Development, 49*, 1155–1162.

ZESKIND, P. S., & RAMEY, C. T. (1981). Sequelae of fetal malnutrition: A longitudinal, transactional, and synergistic approach. *Child Development, 52*, 213–218.

Chapter 1. 10: Changing organism-context relations as the basic process of development: A developmental contextual perspective, by R. M. Lerner, 1991, *Developmental Psychology, 27,* 27–32. Copyright © 1991 American Psychological Association. Reprinted with permission. **16, 17:** From Siegler, R. S. & Svetina, M. (2002). A microgenetic/cross-sectional study of matrix completion: Comparing short-term and long-term change. *Child Development, 73,* 793–809. Reprinted with permission of the Society for Research in Child Development.

Chapter 2. 31: From *Male, females: The evolution of human sex differences* (p. 180) by D. C. Geary (1998), Washington, DC: American Psychological Association. Copyright © 1998 American Psychological Association. Reprinted with permission. **34:** From *Individual development and evolution: The genesis of novel behavior* by Gilbert Gottlieb, copyright © 1991 by Oxford University Press, Inc. Used by permission of Oxford University Press, Inc. **35:** Adapted from Caspi, A., McClay, J., Moffitt, T. E., Mill, J., Martin, J., Craig, I. W., Taylor, A., & Poulton, R. (2002). Role of genotype in the cycle of violence in maltreated children. *Science, 297* (2 August), 851–854. Copyright © 2002 American Association for the Advancement of Science. Reprinted with permission. **39:** H. Harlow (1959 December). The development of learning in the Rhesus monkey. *American Scientists,* 459–479. Reprinted with permission. **41:** Adapted from How people make their own environments: A theory of genotype-environment effects, by S. Scarr and K. McCartney, *Child Development, 54,* 424–435. Copyright © 1983 The Society for Research in Child Development, Inc. Adapted with permission. **46:** Schade, J. P., & van Groenigen, W. B. (1961). Structural organization of the human cerebral cortex. I. Maturation of the middle frontal gyrus. *Acta Anatomica, 47,* 72–111. Reprinted with permis-

sion. **47:** The myelenogenetic cycles of regional maturation of the brain, by P. I. Yakovlev and A. R. Lecours. In A. Minkowski (ed.), *Regional development of the brain in early life.* Copyright © 1967 Blackwell Scientific Publications, Ltd. Reprinted with permission. **55:** Adapted from Neurobiological aspects of language in children, by S. F. Witelson, 1987, *Child Development, 58,* 653–688. Copyright © 1987 The Society for Research in Child Development, Inc. Adapted with permission.

Chapter 3. 64: Miller, K. F., Smith, C. M., Zhu, J., & Zhang, H. (1995). Preschool origins of cross-national differences in mathematical competence. *Psychological Science, 6,* 56–60. Reprinted with permission. **70:** From Guided participation in cultural activity by toddlers and caregivers, by B. Rogoff, J. Mistry, A. Goncu, C. Moiser, 1993, *Monographs of the Society for Research in Child Development, 58* (Serial No. 236, No. 8). Copyright © 1993 The Society for Research in Child Development, Inc., reprinted with permission.

Chapter 4. 101: The pendulum problem, from *The growth of logical thinking from childhood to adolescence,* by B. Inhelder and Jean Piaget. Copyright © 1985 Basic Books. Reprinted with permission. **108:** Adapted from Processes of cognitive development: Optimal level and skill acquisition, by K. W. Fischer and S. L. Pipp. In R. J. Sternberg (Ed.), *Mechanisms of cognitive development.* Copyright © 1994 W. H. Freeman and Company. Adapted with permission of the author. **109:** Fischer, K. W., & Rose, S. P. (1996). Dynamic growth cycles of brain and cognitive development. In R. W. Thatcher, G. R. Lyon, J. Rumsey, & N. Krasnegor (Eds.) *Developmental neuroimaging: Mapping the development of brain and behavior* (p. 263–279). Reprinted with permission from Elsevier.

Chapter 5. 121: Based on Shaffer, D. R. (1996). *Developmental psychology: Childhood and adolescence* (4th ed.) Pacific Grove, CA: Brooks/Cole, as adapted from Human memory: A proposed system and its control processes, by R. C. Atkinson & R. M. Shiffrin, 1968, in K. Spence and J. T. Spence (Eds.), *The psychology of learning and motivation: Advances in research and theory* (Vol. 2), copyright 1968 by Academic Press, Inc. **124:** Memory span: Sources of individual and developmental

permission. **223:** From *Children's Embedded Figures Test,* by S. A. Karp and N. Konstadt. Copyright © 1971 by Consulting Psychologists Press, Inc. Reproduced with permission from the author. **224:** Vandenberg, S. G., & Kuse, A. R. Mental rotations, a group test of three-dimensional spatial visualization. *Perceptual and Motor Skills,* 1978, 47, 599–604. © Perceptual and Motor Skills 1978. **226, 227:** Sex differences in spatial abilities: Evolutionary theory and data, by I. Silverman and M. Eals. In J. H. Barkow, L. Cosmides, and J. Tooby (Eds.), *The adapted mind: Evolutionary psychology and the generation of culture,* p. 537. Copyright 1992 by Oxford University Press. Used by permission of Oxford University Press, Inc. **229:** Casey, M. B. (1996). Understanding individual differences in spatial ability within females: A nature/nurture interactionist framework. *Developmental Review,* 16, 241–260. Used by permission from Elsevier.

Chapter 9. 240: Addition and subtraction by human infants, by K. Wynn, 1992, *Nature,* 358, 749–750. Copyright © 1992 Macmillan Magazine Ltd. Reprinted with permission from Nature. **243:** Rapid changes in the symbolic functioning of very young children, by J. S. DeLoache, 1987, *Science,* 238, 1556–1557. Copyright © 1987 American Association for the Advancement of Science. Reprinted with permission. **249:** Dennis the Menace® used by permission of Hank Ketcham and © 1990 by North American Syndicate. **249:** *The child's theory of mind,* by H. M. Wellman. Copyright © 1990 Massachusetts Institute of Technology Press. Reprinted with permission. **251:** Children's understanding of the representational changes and its relation to the understanding of false belief and the appearance-reality distinction, by A. Gopnik & J. W. Astington, 1988, *Child Development,* 59, 26–37. Copyright © 1988 The Society for Research in Child Development. Reprinted with permission. **253:** Clements, W. A., & Perner, J. (1994). Implicit understanding of belief. *Cognitive Development,* 9, 377–395. **254, 255:** Small-scale deceit: Deception as a marker of two-, three-, and four-year-olds' early theories of mind, by M. Chandler, A. S. Fritz, and S. Hala, 1989, *Child Development,* 60, 1263–1277. Copyright © 1989 The Society for Research in Child Development. Reprinted with permission. **261:** Adapted from Blancher, N., Dunham, P. J., & Dunham, F. (2001). Differences in preschool children's conceptual strategies when thinking about animate entities and artifacts. *Developmental Psychology,* 37, 791–800. Copyright © 2001 by the American Psychological Association. Adapted with permission.

Chapter 10. 268: Courage, M. L., & Howe, M. L. (2001). Long-term retention in 3.5-month-olds: Familiarization time and individual differences in attentional style. *Journal of Experimental Child Psychology,* 79, 271–293. Copyright © 2001 Elsevier. Reprinted with permission. **271:** Rovee-Collier, C. (1999). The development of infant memory. *Current Directions in Psychological Science,* 8, 80–85. © 1999 Blackwell Publishers. Reprinted with permission. **272:** Data from Bauer, P. J., Wenner, J. A., Dropik, P. L., & Wewerka, S. S. (2000). Parameters of remembering and forgetting in the transition from infancy to early childhood. *Monographs of the Society for Research in Child Development,* 65 (Issue no. 4, Serial No. 263). Figure from Bauer, P. J. (2002). Long-term recall memory: Be-

havioral and neuro-developmental changes in the first 2 years of life. *Current Directions in Psychological Science,* 11, 137–141. © 2002 Blackwell Publishers. Reprinted with permission. **273:** Calvin and Hobbes © Watterson. Reprinted with permission of Universal Press Syndicate. All rights reserved. **283:** Lindberg, M. A. (1991), An interactive approach to assessing the suggestibility and testimony of eyewitnesses. In J. Doris (Ed.), *The suggestibility of children's recollections: Implications for eyewitness testimony* (p. 47–55). Copyright © 1991 by the American Psychological Association. Reprinted with permission. **286, 287:** P. A. Ornstein & A. F. Greenhoot, Remembering distant past, in D. F. Bjorklund (Ed.), *False-memory creation in children and adults.* © 2000 Lawrence Erlbaum Associates, Inc. Reprinted with permission. **292:** Ceci, S. J., Loftus, E. F., Leichtman, M., & Bruck, M. (1994). The role of source misattributions in the creation of false beliefs among preschoolers. *International Journal of Clinical and Experimental Hypnosis,* 62, 304–320. © 1994 by Sage Publications, Inc. Reprinted by permission. **295:** Schneider, W. & Weinert, F. E. (1995). Memory development during early and middle childhood: Findings from the Munich longitudinal study (LOGIC). In F. E. Weinert & W. Schneider (Eds.), *Memory performance and competencies: Issues in growth and development.* Hillsdale, NJ: Erlbaum. Reprinted with permission from the author.

Chapter 11. 304: Brown, R. (1973). *A first language: The early stages,* p. 271, 274. Cambridge, MA: Harvard University Press. Copyright © 1973 by the President and Fellows of Harvard College. Reprinted by permission. **315:** Warren A. R., & McCloskey, L. A. Language in social contexts. In J. Berko Gleason (Ed.), *The development of language* (4th ed.). Published by Allyn and Bacon. Copyright © 1997 by Pearson Education. Reprinted by permission. **321:** Berko, J. (1958). The child's learning of English Morphology. *Word,* 14, 50–177. **322:** Critical period effects in second language learning: The influence of maturational state on the acquisition of English as a second language, by J. S. Johnson and E. L. Newport, 1989. *Cognitive Psychology,* 21, 60–99. Copyright © 1989 Academic Press. Reprinted with permission. **328, 329, 330:** Locke, J. L. (1997). A theory of neurolinguistic development. *Brain and Language,* 58, p. 268. Copyright © 1997, reprinted with permission from Elsevier and the author. **331:** Bates, E. (1999). On the nature of language. In R. Levi-Montalcini, D. Baltimore, R. Dulbecco, & F. Jacob (Series Eds.) & E. Bizzi, P. Calissano, & V. Volterra (Vol. Eds.), *Frontiere della biolgia [Frontiers of biology], The brain of Homo sapiens.* Rome: Giovanni Trecanni. **333:** Dennis the Menace®, used by permission of Hank Ketcham and © 1986 by North American Syndicate.

Chapter 12. 341: From Stephen J. Ceci, *On intelligence . . . more or less: A bioecological treatise on intellectual development,* © 1990, p. 39. Reprinted by permission of Prentice-Hall, Englewood Cliffs, New Jersey. **344:** Zelazo, P. D., Frye, D., & Rapus, T. (1996). An age-related disassociation between knowing rules and using them. *Cognitive Development,* 11, 37–63. Copyright © 1996, reprinted with permission from Elsevier. **346, 347:** Chen, Z., & Siegler, R. S. (2000). Across the great divide: Bridging the gap between understanding of toddlers' and older children's thinking. *Monographs of the Society for Research in Child Development* 65 (Issue no. 2, Serial

No. 261). Reprinted with permission of the Society for Research in Child Development. **350:** Fireman, G. (1996). Developing a plan for solving problems: A representational shift. *Cognitive Development, 11,* 107–122. Copyright © 1996, reprinted with permission from Elsevier. **352, 353:** Chen, Z., Sanchez, R. P., & Campbell, T. (1997). From beyond to within their grasp: The rudiments of analogical problem solving in 10- and 13-month-olds. *Developmental Psychology, 33,* 790–801. Copyright © 1997 by the American Psychological Association. Reprinted with permission. **354:** Goswami, U., & Brown, A. L. (1990). Higher-order structure and relational reasoning: Contrasting analogical and thematic relations. *Cognition, 36,* 207–226. Reprinted with permission of Elsevier Science. **360:** Chen, Z., & Klahr, D. (1999). All other things being equal: Acquisition and transfer of the control of variables strategy. *Child Developmental, 70,* 1098–1120. Reprinted with permission of the Society for Research in Child Development.

Chapter 13. 368: Tomasello, M., Savage-Rumbaugh, S., & Kruger, A. C. (1993). Imitative learning of actions and objects by children, chimpanzees, and enculturated chimpanzees. *Child Development, 64,* 1688–1705. Reprinted with permission of the Society for Research in Child Development. **373:** Tomasello, M., Kruger, A. C., & Ratner, H. H. (1993). Cultural learning. *Behavioral and Brain Sciences, 16,* 495–511. Copyright © 1993 Cambridge University Press. Reprinted with permission of Cambridge University Press. **375:** From Social competence in children, by Dodge, et al., 1986, *Monographs of the Society for Research in Child Development, 51* (Serial No. 213). Copyright © 1986 The Society for Research in Child Development, Inc. Reprinted with permission. **381:** Adapted from Gender constancy and the effects of sex-typed television toy commercials, by Ruble, D. N., Balaban, T., & Cooper, J., 1981, *Child Development, 52,* 667–673. Copyright © 1981 The Society for Research in Child Development, Inc. Adapted with permission. **386:** Adapted from Early androgens are related to childhood sex-typed toy preferences, by S. A. Berenbaum & M. Hines, 1992, *Psychological Science, 3,* p. 205. Copyright © 1992 Blackwell Publishers. Reprinted with permission.

Chapter 14. 397, 399: The cognitive basis of dyslexia, by L. S. Siegel. In R. Pasnak and M. L. Howe (Eds.), *Emerging themes in cognitive development, Vol. II: Competencies.* Copyright © 1993 Springer-Verlag. Reprinted with permission. **402:** Adapted from Asher, S. R., & Markel, R. A. (1974). Sex differences in comprehension of high- and low-interest reading material. *Journal of Educational Psychology, 66,* 680–687. Copyright © 1974 by the American Psychological Association. Adapted with permission. **403:** How large are cognitive gender differences? A meta-analysis using w^2 and d, by J. S. Hyde, 1981, *American Psychologist, 36,* 892–901. Copyright © 1981 by the American Psychological Association. Reprinted with permission. **408:** Adapted from Developmental relations between notational counting and number conservation, by G. Saxe, 1979, *Child Development, 50,* 189–197. Copyright © 1979 The Society for Research in Child Development, Inc. Adapted with permission. **416:** Context of achievement, by H. W. Stevenson & S. Y. Lee, 1990, *Monographs of the Society for Research in Child Development, 55,* (Se-

rial No. 221). Copyright © 1990 The Society for Research in Child Development, Inc. Reprinted with permission. **419:** Explaining gender differences on SAT-Math items," by J. P. Byrnes and S. Takahira, 1993, *Developmental Psychology, 29,* 805–810. Copyright ©1993 American Psychological Association. Adapted with permission. (Original problem from November 1987 SAT exam, Educational Testing Service.)

Chapter 15. 434: Adapted from *The Stanford-Binet Intelligence Scale (4th Edition). Guide for administering and scoring,* by R. L. Thorndike, E. P. Hagan, and J. M. Sattler. Copyright © 1986 The Riverside Publishing Company. Reprinted with permission. **436:** Adapted from *Manual of the Bayley Scales of infant development,* by N. Bayley, 1969 The Psychological Corporation. Adapted with permission. **444:** Gaultney, J. F., Bjorklund, D. F., & Goldstein, D. (1996). To be young, gifted, and strategic: Advantage for memory performance. *Journal of Experimental Child Psychology, 61,* p. 51. Reprinted with permission. **452:** Sternberg, R. J. (1988). *The triarchic mind: A new theory of human intelligence.* New York: Viking. Reprinted by permission of the author. **457:** Adapted with permission from Wexler-Sherman, C., Gardner, H., & Feldman, D. H. (1988). A pluralistic view of early assessment: The Project Spectrum approach. *Theory Into Practice, 27,* 77–83. Copyright © 1988 Ohio State University.

Chapter 16. 463: Sameroff, A. J., & Suomi, S. J. (1996). Primates and persons: A comparative developmental understanding of social organization (p. 97–120). In R. B. Cairns, G. H. Elder, Jr., & E. J. Castello (Eds.), *Developmental Science.* New York: Cambridge University Press. Reprinted with permission of Cambridge University Press. **465:** Adapted from Zeskind, P. S., & Ramey, C. T. (1981). Sequelae of fetal malnutrition: A longitudinal, transactional, and synergistic approach. *Child Development, 52,* 213–218. Copyright © 1981 The Society for Research in Child Development, Inc. Adapted with permission. **471:** Plomin, R., Fulker, D. W., Corley, R., & De Fries, J. C. (1997). Nature, nurture, and cognitive development from 1 to 6 years: A parent-offspring adoption study. *Psychological Science, 8,* 442–447. Reprinted with permission. **477:** Adapted from The relation of infants' home environment to mental test performance at fifty-four months: A follow-up study, by R. H. Bradley and B. M. Caldwell, 1976, *Child Development, 47,* 1172–1174. Copyright © 1976 The Society for Research in Child Development. Adapted with permission. **486:** Adapted with permission from A follow-up of follow-through: The later effect of the direct instruction model on children in fifth and sixth grades, by W. C. Becker and R. Gersten, 1982, *American Educational Research Journal, 19,* 75–92. Copyright © 1982 American Educational Research Association. **489:** Fagan, J. F., III, & Singer, J. T. (1983). Infant recognition memory as a measure of intelligence. In L. P. Lipsitt & K. Rovee-Collier (Eds.), *Advances in infancy research* (Vol. 2). Norwood, NJ: Ablex. Reprinted with permission. **493:** Developmental changes in mental performance, by R. B. McCall, M. I. Appelbaum, and P. S. Hogarty, 1973, *Monographs of the Society for Research in Child Development, 38* (Series No. 150). Copyright © 1973 The Society for Research in Child Development, Inc. Reprinted with permission.